DATE DUE

DEMCO 38-296

INTERNATIONAL
ENCYCLOPEDIA
OF PUBLIC
POLICY AND
ADMINISTRATION

INTERNATIONAL
ENCYCLOPEDIA
OF PUBLIC
POLICY AND
ADMINISTRATION

Jay M. Shafritz

EDITOR IN CHIEF

Volume 2: D-K

Westview Press
A Member of the Perseus Books Group

Copyright © 1998 by Westview Press, A Member of the Perseus Books Group

Published in 1998 in the United States of America by Westview Press, 5500 Central Avenue, Boulder, Colorado 80301-2877, and in the United Kingdom by Westview Press, 12 Hid's Copse Road, Cumnor Hill, Oxford OX2 9JJ

Library of Congress Cataloging-in-Publication Data

The international encyclopedia of public policy and administration /
    Jay M. Shafritz, editor in chief.
        p.   cm.
    Includes bibliographical references (p.   ) and index.
    Contents: v. 1. A-C – v. 2. D-K – v. 3. L-Q – v. 4. R-Z, index.
    ISBN 0-8133-9973-4 (vol. 1 : hardcover : alk. paper). – ISBN
0-8133-9974-2 (vol. 2 : hardcover : alk. paper). – ISBN
0-8133-9975-0 (vol. 3 : hardcover : alk. paper). – ISBN
0-8133-9976-9 (vol. 4 : hardcover : alk. paper)
    1. Public policy–Encyclopedias.   2. Public administration–
Encyclopedias.   I. Shafritz, Jay M.
H97.I574   1998
351'.03–dc21   97-34169
                                                                                CIP

The paper used in this publication meets the requirements of the American National Standard for Permanence of Paper for Printed Library Materials Z39.48-1984.

10   9   8   7   6   5   4   3

D

DAMAGES. The amount of money awarded in a lawsuit to compensate for losses or injuries sustained to the person, property, or legal rights through the unlawful actions of another. The primary goal of damages is to compensate a person for such injury, using monetary terms. Under the theory of the law of damages, a victim is entitled to a damage award that equates with the loss incurred, that is, to restore the victim to the position he or she would have had prior to sustaining the injury.

The major classifications include compensatory damages, exemplary damages, liquidated damages, and nominal damages.

Compensatory damages are awarded in accordance with the principles and limitations of just compensation. As such, compensatory damages are intended to equate with and to offset the amount of damage the injured person has suffered. The largest category of compensatory damages is general damages. These are also known as actual, direct, or necessary damages, which are those that flow as a direct and necessary consequence from the unlawful conduct of the party being sued. Another category is special damages. Special damages are actual, but not necessarily the result of the unlawful conduct. Special damages include such items as medical expenses or lost wages.

To illustrate the difference between general and special damages, take as an example a person injured in an automobile accident. The person who is injured, and making a claim for his injuries, necessarily has suffered at least some general damages, which would include pain and suffering. The injured person would not necessarily, however, have sustained medical expenses or loss of wages. Hence the latter damages are classified as "special," and the person making a claim for injuries must set forth specifically the kinds and amounts of special damages he claims.

Taken together, these damages—general and special—are intended to compensate the victim for losses or injuries.

Another category of damages is exemplary or punitive damages. Such damages are intended to punish the wrongdoer and to deter similar conduct by others in the future. Such damages may be awarded in cases that involve intentional wrongdoing, such as fraud, willful and wanton negligence, or malice.

Actions for punitive damages have public policy implications. For example, where officials abuse their power outrageously—as in police brutality cases—punitive damages may be sought as a means of enforcing public policy against police misconduct. (See, for example, *Allen, Helms, and King v. City of Los Angeles,* 1995, Westlaw 433720, C. D. CA, the "Rodney King case.")

The law of contracts has the concept of liquidated damages. Liquidated damages are those amounts specified by the parties to the contract prior to the occurrence of a breach. By including a liquidated damage figure as a term of the contract, the parties agree that this figure approximates the injury that would be expected to occur should a breach ensue. In general, liquidated damage agreements are enforced, provided that the amount is not disproportionate to the damage that would actually result from the breach and provided that the agreement does not contradict other principles of law or public policy.

In contrast to monetary awards that provide compensation, nominal damage awards are available to establish a legal right. Nominal damages are utilized to substantiate the legal right and to remedy technical infringements of this right where actual damages have not occurred or cannot be proved. Nominal damages, where awarded, are often used in conjunction with punitive or exemplary damages.

Michael A. Wolff

BIBLIOGRAPHY

25 *Corpus Juris Secundum,* Damages §§ 1–18, 37, 71, 101, 117–120.
Black's Law Dictionary, 6th ed., p. 392.

DATA PROTECTION. Concerns the public policy-making and governance of access to information. The issues of privacy addressed involve individuals in various domains—worklife, the home, the Internet, and other venues. It is also known as "privacy protection" and "information privacy."

Data protection concerns the governance of access to information about identifiable persons in many domains. These include workplaces, the home, public service institutions, law enforcement, commercial establishments, and on the "information superhighway." Data protection, also known as privacy protection or information privacy, is of interest to public administration and public policy in two broad senses. First, because an indispensable part of the infrastructure of the modern state is the ability to make extensive and sophisticated use of information about individuals, but this is challenged by rights or claims to personal privacy that have implications for the operations of government. Second, because the perceived need for regulation of information practices and systems to which this conflict gives rise has spawned a search for administrative, social, and judicial controls and policies at several levels. However, the development of these controls flies in the face of dramatic increases in the capability of information technology to process personal data in the state as well as in commercial and other endeavors. Public policy-making for protecting personal privacy therefore is highly conflictual. It encounters powerful interests, rests on unclear premises and objectives, and must contend with rapid and global technological change.

The Problem

Administrative systems require detailed knowledge of individuals in order to implement policies and programs, deliver services, and meet the requirements of a host of rights and obligations. Public bureaucracies increasingly gather, process, match, store, and communicate large quantities of personal data about their clients, including patients, students, taxpayers, motorists, employees, claimants, and others. New ways of organizing the public sector typically involve management and financial information systems that are built up from personal data that may then be aggregated without necessarily losing their ability to identify individuals. Modern technologies vastly extend the range and flexibility of such uses of personal data, thus playing a major part in improving the efficiency and effectiveness of public administration, but they also give added impetus to administrative and political desires to gather and use information about individuals. For example, the collection and processing of personal information through surveillance technologies, such as closed-circuit television in public places and DNA "fingerprinting," are playing an increasing part in combating crime and maintaining law and order.

Public policymakers and business organizations frequently find new and potentially beneficial, albeit controversial, uses for data in which individuals can be identified. These developments include, for example, road-use charging schemes, personal identification cards, electronic service delivery and payments systems, telephone caller ID facilities, workplace surveillance, international police cooperation (e.g., the Schengen and Europol Conventions), direct marketing of goods and services, epidemiological research, and the reduction of welfare benefits fraud. Many of these innovations and programs rest on the matching of diverse databases and on identifying or profiling individuals by bringing together details of personal characteristics from a variety of sources, including digitized images and biometric information such as retina scans and hand geometry. Some practices are often covert, and the inaccuracy of data often results in mistaken suspicion of individuals or broad categories of persons. The right to be left alone—a conventional, though debatable, interpretation of privacy—appears to be threatened by certain techniques and programs, giving rise to demands for rules and limits to be placed on intrusive information practices.

One side of the coin is the mutual benefit of states and citizens from the "informatization" of government and the state, in which advanced technologies are put to use in public administration. Citizens have a legitimate interest in the efficient delivery of services, and in the elimination of waste and fraud. The other side of the coin, however, is the real or perceived invasion of privacy that accompanies data-gathering and surveillance, jeopardizing the trust in which institutions are held by the public, and thus even the functioning of beneficial information-dependent systems themselves. Without reassurance that their personal and often highly sensitive details will not be used in ways that are unknown, unconsented to, and uncontrolled, individuals have sometimes been reluctant to give information even where they are required by law to do so. West German population censuses during the 1980s, for example, aroused considerable controversy as well as noncompliance because of mistrust over the use to which the information would be put.

Developments in Regulation

Data protection or privacy laws and regulatory mechanisms aim at establishing the rules for the handling of personal information and thus increasing public confidence that privacy will be protected. They have grown in importance in the industrialized world as states and international organizations have sought ways of regulating the increasing governmental and business use of personal data, especially those that are held on computers. In a number of countries this is seen explicitly in terms of privacy protection, drawing attention to the conceptual and legal roots of data protection in the notion of privacy—however unclear that term is—and thus to the realm of human rights. Although the main purpose of data protection is usually taken to be the safeguarding of privacy in the information age of computerization and advanced communications technology, privacy considerations have not necessarily been the sole or even the dominant motive in the establishment of data protection laws and regulatory systems. The interests of public administration and of private industry as data users have made themselves felt powerfully in the policymaking process through which groundrules have been established for the flow of personal data within and among countries, firms, state agencies, and other organizations.

These rules, and their interpretation in practice, often lean in the direction of safeguarding the use of personal data rather than towards the requirements of personal privacy, protecting the latter only to the extent that is thought necessary for the maintenance of public confidence and trust in the administrative or commercial exploitation of personal information. Thus has arisen the doctrine of balance: the regulatory objective is seen as the balancing of privacy against the use of data. But whether this objective is conceptually sound or empirically possible depends upon several conditions. These include the commensurability of the values involved, the development of agreed conventions for balancing, and the ability of decisionmaking processes to reflect changes in the social, economic, technological, and other factors that challenge the existing balancing point. These conditions cannot easily be assumed.

Beginning in 1970 in the German *Land* of Hessen, many national and subnational governments in Western Europe, North America, the Pacific Rim, and elsewhere have devised general data protection or privacy laws. The laws are broadly similar, converging on general principles but diverging in practice as their implementation reflects the different economic, public administration, political, and juridical contexts of different countries or areas. In the United States and Canada (with the exception, so far, of Quebec), privacy protection in the private sector is not covered by a general law, and in other countries, such as the United Kingdom, data held in nonautomatically processed systems falls outside the scope of the law as originally enacted. Some countries also have privacy or data protection laws for specific sectors or activities: for example, computer matching in the United States, and the police sector in the Netherlands. A more recent development in the European Union has been the adoption of a directive in 1995 by the European Union, forming an international regulatory system. This initiative was a response to the inadequacy, and to the varying levels, of data protection afforded by national systems in face of increasingly large flows of personal data across national boundaries, both among the member states of the European Union and with third countries.

The "fair information" principles that are held in common seek to ensure that personal data are: collected and used fairly and lawfully; held and used for specified purposes; adequate, relevant, and not excessive for these purposes; accurate and up to date; not held indefinitely; and held securely. Individuals (considered as "data subjects") should be able to learn what is held on them, to have errors deleted or corrected, and to seek remedies. Special safeguards might be required for sensitive data about racial origin, political and religious beliefs, health and sexual life, and criminal convictions, though it can be argued that sensitivity is a matter of the context and circumstances in which information is used and does not necessarily define types of data.

Data protection principles evolved in the 1970s and were enshrined in documents such as the Organization for Economic Cooperation and Development's 1981 Guidelines and the Council of Europe's 1981 Convention. Translating these principles into regulatory practice has involved experimentation with institutions and strategies of governance, and the development of jurisprudence concerning informatics. It has also led to a greater appreciation of the effects of information systems upon privacy, and to attempts to raise the level of awareness of rights and obligations among data subjects and data users. The establishment of an independent regulatory agency or commission is seen as a crucial step, and has been a feature of most privacy protection systems; the absence of central machinery of this kind in the United States has received much adverse comment. In implementing the law, these bodies are involved in a range of activities. Depending upon the legislative approach that is adopted, these include registering data users, monitoring and auditing their compliance with legal requirements, interpreting the letter of often vague principles and rules in specific instances, investigating complaints, and applying sanctions. In addition, they promote better data protection through public education and publicity, including the framing of guidelines and advice for data users. Another prominent role of regulatory agencies is the exertion of influence where possible in the decision-making process when public policy or industry proposes or entails new uses of personal data.

State Control, Self-Regulation, and Technological Solutions

The efficacy of statutory protection of privacy through the mechanism of regulatory bodies rests, however, upon the style and strategy adopted by the agency and its staff, within the available scope that is determined by its formal powers and financing, and thus ultimately by the political system in which it exists. This means that the level and quality of data protection is likely to vary across countries, and to be uneven within countries as official data protectors meet different degrees of resistance among the sectors of data users whom they try to regulate. An interesting aspect of the work of these officials has been the development and increasing institutionalization of contact amongst them at an international or multicountry level. This network or policy community has provided the means for sharing experience, lessons learned, and views that have been inserted into policymaking processes transcending national boundaries. For example, data protection officials of the European Union were important participants in the processes leading to the establishment of the 1995 European Union Data Protection Directive, and also collectively expressed their views on the data protection aspects of the 1995 Europol Convention that established a European Police Office with an information system and an intelligence analysis capability.

The policy community has increasingly recognized that the complexity and diversity of information practices, coupled with revolutionary technological and economic developments towards a global networked environment, outpace the ability of laws, regulatory bodies, and official sanctions to protect individual privacy without the active assistance of data users themselves. Self-regulation has therefore become an attractive avenue for the further development of data protection policy, although it is not regarded as a sufficient response to problems. National data protection laws, as well as the European Union Directive, provide scope for self-regulation by data users as a complement to state control. In Germany, companies must appoint officials charged with implementing compliance with data protection regulations within the firm.

In many countries, sectors of data users, such as the direct marketing industry, the police, or health care providers, have formulated codes of practice in order to tailor the regulation of information practices to the specific characteristics of the sector. In The Netherlands, such codes can receive official approval by the Registration Chamber—the statutory regulatory body—as conforming to the legal regime, whereas in the United Kingdom they play a less formal, but still important role in the data protection system. There have been developments in Canada toward the creation of a model code that could serve as a formal, publicized standard with specifications to which users of personal data should adhere if they wish such accreditation. Self-regulation is still in a developmental state, and its effects—perhaps especially its articulation with statutory requirements and state regulation—remain to be evaluated. However, it is likely to become a prominent mode of data protection, insofar as it also accords with trends in management and public administration away from top-down controls and towards decentralized forms of governance and steering. By fixing responsibility and accountability at lower levels, self-regulation might promote learning, awareness, and monitoring of the impact of information systems on privacy among a variety of data users. It might also improve the application of general rules to the specific and diverse requirements of different industries or public agencies where personal data are used.

In addition to state regulation and data users' self-regulatory adherence to codes, it is considered that data protection might also be assisted by technology itself as used directly by individuals. "Smart cards" and certain kinds of encryption can provide ways of protecting privacy in a wide range of transactions in which goods, services, and state benefits are obtained, by increasing the individual's control of the flow of personal information, by making transactions anonymous, or by helping to confine the data to the purpose for which it was gathered. Given the many advantages accruing to organizations through their ability to use advanced information and communications technologies in providing public services or goods, such privacy technologies, when incorporated in the design of equipment and information systems at an early stage, are likely to play an important part in data protection. The widespread adoption of partial solutions of this kind are likely to alter the configuration of data protection strategies, roles, and institutions as a whole, as well as to throw a new light on the underlying philosophy that has long motivated the policy and implementation of privacy protection.

CHARLES D. RAAB

BIBLIOGRAPHY

Beniger, James R., 1986. *The Control Revolution: Technological and Economic Origins of the Information Society.* Cambridge, MA: Harvard University Press.

Bennett, Colin J., 1992. *Regulating Privacy: Data Protection and Public Policy in Europe and the United States.* Ithaca and London: Cornell University Press.

Burkert, Herbert, 1981. "Institutions of Data Protection—An Attempt at a Functional Explanation of European National Data Protection Laws." *Computer/Law Journal*, 3:167–188.

Flaherty, David H., 1989. *Protecting Privacy in Surveillance Societies: The Federal Republic of Germany, Sweden, France, Canada, and the United States.* Chapel Hill, NC: University of North Carolina Press.

Raab, Charles, D., 1993. "The Governance of Data Protection." In Jan Kooiman, ed., *Modern Governance: New Government-Society Interactions.* London, Newbury Park and New Delhi: Sage Publications, pp. 89–103.

Simitis, Spiros, 1987. "Reviewing Privacy in an Information Society." *University of Pennsylvania Law Review,* 135:707–746.

Simmel, Arnold, 1968. "Privacy." In David L. Sills, ed., *International Encyclopedia of the Social Sciences.* London: Collier-Macmillan Publishers, vol. 11, pp. 480–487.

Taylor, John A. and Howard Williams, 1991. "Public Administration and the Information Polity." *Public Administration,* vol. 69 (Summer) 171–190.

U.S. Congress, Office of Technology Assessment, 1986. *Federal Government Information Technology: Electronic Record Systems and Individual Privacy,* OTA-CIT-296. Washington, D.C.: U.S. Government Printing Office.

Warren, Samuel D. and Louis D. Brandeis, 1890. "The Right to Privacy." *Harvard Law Review,* vol. 4:193–220.

Westin, Alan F., 1967. *Privacy and Freedom.* New York: Atheneum.

DE FACTO (AND DE JURE).

In reality or in fact, as in actual authority, but not necessarily "a matter of law" or legal authority. *De facto* is an accidental result which ensues from individual or governmental decisions made without any purpose or intent to cause the result. *De jure* (by legitimate, legal right, or authority; as a matter of law) is an intentional result ensuing from individual or governmental action or inaction.

The most often cited example of a *de jure* result is school segregation in many areas of the United States. During the nineteenth century, many U.S. states adopted "separate but equal facilities" legislation. This legislation dictated that separate, but equal, facilities would be established so that blacks and whites would be separated in public accommodations, restaurants, restroom facilities, hospitals, public housing, and so forth. Many states enacted statutes or state constitutional amendments that required that blacks and whites would be educated in separate facilities so as to avoid a mixing of the races in educational institutions. For decades, separate institutions were operated and no mixing of the races occurred. This is a classic example of an intentional result ensuing from governmental action.

An example of a *de facto* result would be the legal exercise of governmental authority in zoning matters. A real estate developer applies for a zoning permit to develop a subdivision in a municipality. The governmental authority requires a minimum lot size and a minimum square footage of house size such that the final cost of the homes built is very expensive. The result of this legal exercise of the governmental authority results in homes which are only within the price range of the wealthy, thereby excluding availability to entire classes of the population who are poor or needy. Although the result of the governmental action is to exclude ownership of these homes by disadvantaged classes of individuals, it cannot be said that the action creates an intentional result to discriminate against those excluded classes.

While the distinction between *de facto* and *de jure* turns on intentional conduct, actions which are not intentional are subject to later analysis to prove a *de jure* result. Actions may be reviewed under a standard of "foreseeability." The fact that an imbalance exists is not the same as a showing that the imbalance was foreseeable. Therefore, actions which at first blush appear to be the end result of intentional action can be classified as such if the end result was foreseeable at the time the action was engaged in. The foreseeability measure is said to arise from governmental action or inaction that does not serve the avowed governmental policies and purposes or that overlooks less offensive options that were available at the time the policies evolved.

The fact that policies are *de facto* does not mean that they are free from future scrutiny. Policies which create a *de facto* result are allowed, but only for so long as that policy is applied in a consistent and neutral fashion and is not changed when the composition of the groups change. An example of a *de facto* policy that became *de jure* is found in police and fire departments. Police and fire departments historically excluded women from participation based upon a notion that women were somehow physically inferior to men and thus unable to perform the tasks of police or firemen. Although this policy of inferiority was universally accepted at one time, attitudes and knowledge eventually eroded that notion. Thus, a discriminatory intent could be shown even though the discrimination resulted from historically neutral policies.

The exercise of authority must be thoroughly reviewed and analyzed at the time of the implementation of policy to ensure that discrimination will not occur. This analysis should weigh alternative options to determine if a less discriminatory result would ensue. Finally, after implementation, the policy should be systematically reviewed to ensure that its original purpose is still valid.

THOMAS A. CONNELLY

BIBLIOGRAPHY

Rabkin, Jeremy, 1989. *Judicial Compulsions: How Public Law Distorts Public Policy.* New York: Basic Books.
Rossum, Ralph A. and G. Alan Tarr, 1991. *American Constitutional Law: Cases and Interpretation.* 3d ed. New York: St. Martin's Press.

DEBT, NATIONAL. Divided into two categories in the United States: debt held by the public, and debt the government owes itself. Debt held by the public is the total of all federal deficits, minus surpluses, over the years. This is the cumulative amount of money the federal government has borrowed from the public, through the sale of notes and bonds of various sizes and for differing time periods. Debt the government owes itself is the total of all trust fund surpluses over the years, such as the Social Security surpluses, which the law says must be invested in federal securities. There is also a legal limit on the amount of federal debt. This is roughly the same as gross federal debt (debt held by the public and debt owed to trust funds such as Social Security) and is the maximum amount of federal securities that may be legally outstanding at any time. When the limit is reached, the president and Congress must enact a law to increase the debt limit or take other extraordinary measures to ensure that interest is paid to those holding public debt instruments in order to maintain faith in U.S. government obligations.

At the end of 1995, the government owed $3603 billion (*Analytical Perspectives* 1996, p. 187) of principal to the people who had loaned it money to pay for past deficits (see **deficit**). This amounted to approximately 50.2 percent of gross domestic product. The gross federal debt, which also includes the securities held by trust funds and other government accounts, was $4.921 trillion. In the 1990s surpluses in the Social Security trust funds helped reduce the size of annual operating deficits. However, in terms of what the government is obligated to pay back at some point in the future, the number for gross federal debt is probably the more correct measure ($4.921 trillion). This came to 70.3 percent of GDP in 1995 and has doubled since 1980 as a percentage of GDP, when it was 34.4 percent (Budget FY 1997, Table 7.2). At some point the Social Security surpluses invested in public debt will have to be paid back or Social Security taxes raised again to keep the system solvent. The stock of debt held by the public will probably never be paid back so long as investors are assured their principal is safe and the rate of interest return is competitive.

One of the striking trends in debt held by the public is the growth of debt held by foreign investors. In 1965, debt held by foreign investors amounted to 4.7 percent of debt held by the public; by 1995 this had increased to 23.5 percent and the change from 1994 to 1995 almost tripled, from $64.3 billion to $192.5 billion. This was said to be due to rising U.S. bond prices (*Analytical Perspectives* 1996, 196–197). While this was a beneficial event in 1995, this change could be somewhat ominous. For example, if U.S. credit instruments become less desirable to foreign investors, they could flee U.S. credit markets, thereby increasing the interest rates the Treasury would have to offer to get domestic investors to invest or foreign investors to return. This would, in turn, increase the amount paid for interest in that fiscal year, which amounted to approximately 15 percent of the federal budget in 1995. A seemingly small interest rate adjustment could have a dramatic affect on the deficit, on the amount of interest paid on the national debt, and on reduced spending for other public programs. Conversely, some argue that at a certain point defaulting on debt is a viable option if most of it is owned by foreigners. The 1994 default in Orange Country, California, was perceived by some in Orange County as being acceptable because most of those who were hurt in the default were not in Orange County. Default on U.S. debt is not a serious option.

The debt numbers do not adequately describe the total obligation of the national government, considering the implicit commitments to provide social benefit programs including medical care, particularly for the aged. For example, based on current government pension and health programs, net public debt as a percent of GDP would more than triple from the year 2000 to the year 2030 in the United States. The United States is not alone with this problem. In Germany the ratio would double; in Japan the ratio would rise tenfold. (Weiner 1995, p. xxii; see also Masson and Mussa 1995; Shigehara 1995).

Most industrialized countries have run persistent deficits since the mid-1970s, leading to rising debt to GDP ratios. This deterioration in fiscal balance sheets has been due to a large extent to rapidly expanding expenditures on public pension and health care programs (Weiner 1995, p. xxi; see also Masson and Mussa 1995). As industrialized countries have become wealthier, the demands to help the less fortunate with more governmental services have increased and beneficiaries of such services have come to see the services and payments as a right or entitlement; they have also come to consider a full inflation adjustment or COLA (see **cost of living adjustment**) as a right, making it doubly difficult to reverse this trend, especially in pension and health care programs. Moreover, miscalculations have caused deficit and debt levels to be higher than originally anticipated; reasons for these miscalculations include rising health care costs, increased structural unemployment, larger than expected increases in life span, and a general slowdown in productivity growth (Weiner 1995, p. xxi). While several countries have taken steps to curtail deficits, the long run prognosis is not good, since most countries face unfunded liabilities relating to care of the elderly.

Even the consequences of relatively small deficits (less than 3 percent of GDP) need to be carefully considered. Ball and Mankiw (1995) argue that running deficits reduces national savings and reduced savings lead to reduced investment and reduced net exports. Over the long run, the decline in investment lowers capital stock, reducing productive capacity and output. The crowding out of investment capital (by the flow of savings into purchase of Treasury offerings to finance the debt) lowers productivity growth and hence real wages (see **crowding out**). This leads to a lower standard of living and deficits generate an ever-growing national debt, whose interest payments keep tax rates restrictively high (Weiner 1995, p. xxxv; Feldstein 1995, pp. 403–412). A continued flow of assets abroad leaves residents with less and foreigners with more of any interest, rents, and profits earned. Ball and Mankiw (1995) calculate that output in the U.S. is 3 to 6 percent lower than it would otherwise due to the fiscal imbalances of recent years (pp. 95–120). Feldstein has calculated that if the government had run a balanced budget since 1980 the national debt would only be 10 percent of GDP and tax rates could be 30 percent lower. (Feldstein 1995, p. 407; Weiner 1995, p. xxxv).

The United States is not alone in being unable to avoid continuous deficits and an increase in debt. In Table I, only Norway and the UK have decreased debt as a percentage of GDP form 1980 to 1994.

TABLE I. INDUSTRIALIZED COUNTRIES: GENERAL GOVERNMENT GROSS DEBT AS A PERCENT OF GDP

Country	1980	1994
Austria	37.2	59
Belgium	81.6	136.0
Canada	44.3	95.6
Denmark	33.5	68.7
Finland	11.8	60.1
France	20.8	48.4
Germany*	31.8	49.8
Greece	24.2	114.1
Italy	57.8	129.0
Japan	52.0	83.3
Netherlands	46.6	79.4
New Zealand	44.8	55.2
Norway	52.2	50.1
Spain	17.5	62.8
Sweden	44.3	92.2
United Kingdom	49.6	46
United States	43.6	68.9

*Data refer to W. Germany in 1980 and united Germany thereafter.

SOURCE: Extracted from Masson and Mussa 1995, p. 30. The source for their table was the IMF *World Economic Outlook* database.

Lessons learned from deficit reduction from both Sweden and Canada in the mid-1990s would seem to indicate that deficits and debt as a percentage of GDP can be brought under control, but that success rests on making sure that all see that the pain is being shared equitably; that the program is comprehensive rather than a series of ad hoc measures so that interest groups see that all are sacrificing; and that the reform process and budgeting procedures be as transparent as possible to ensure that credibility is established and kept with the public and with capital markets and those who buy the country's debt instruments. (Person 1995, pp. 413–418; Martin 1995, pp. 203–227).

Without program change, further fiscal stress is assured; for example, for the United States the net liability of public pension plans (Social Security *et al.*) amounted to 31 percent of 1994 GDP in present value terms, subtracting the value of future Social Security taxes and present surpluses from the future payment liability. This leaves a pension liability amount equal to 31 percent of the 1994 GDP that will have to be met, either with increased taxes or decreased programs (Masson and Mussa 1995, p. 31). This is a long-term problem because the public has expectations that these commitments will be met, and changing those expectations while presenting alternative plans that people will have time to shift into will take time and persistent policy care. If that does not happen, the debt burden will continue to increase and the lives of citizens now and in the future will be slowly impoverished as productivity decreases, tax burdens increase, and the quality of life decreases. Moreover, without change, current intergenerational inequities will continue as present retirees receive significant net benefits while current and future workers make large net payments. This profile is probably not sustainable and without policy change, those who contribute a lot in the present risk getting back a little in the future. While political delay in fixing this painful problem is often expedient, the longer the delay, the more difficult it will be to design, get agreement on, and implement a solution.

JERRY MCCAFFERY

BIBLIOGRAPHY

Ball, Laurence and N. Gregory Mankiw, 1995. "What Do Budget Deficits Do?" In *Budget Deficits and Debt: Issues and Options,* Stuart Weiner, ed. Proceedings of symposium sponsored by the Federal Reserve Bank of Kansas City (September), pp. 95–120.
Budget of the U.S. Government, FY 1997. Washington, D.C.: U.S. Government Printing Office.
"Federal Borrowing and Debt," 1996. In *Analytical Perspectives: Budget of the U.S. Government, Fiscal Year 1997.* Washington, D.C.: U.S. Government Printing Office.
Feldstein, Martin, 1995. "Information on Crowding Out." In *Budget Deficits and Debt: Issues and Options,* Stuart Weiner, ed. Proceedings of symposium sponsored by the Federal Reserve Bank of Kansas City (September), pp. 403–412.
Martin, Paul, 1995. "Information on Canada." In *Budget Deficits and Debt: Issues and Options.* Proceedings of symposium sponsored by the Federal Reserve Bank of Kansas City (September), pp. 203–227.
Masson, Paul and Michael Mussa, 1995. "Long-term Tendencies in Budget Deficits and Debt." In *Budget Deficits and Debt: Issues and Options,* Stuart Weiner, ed. Proceedings of symposium sponsored by the Federal Reserve Bank of Kansas City (September), pp. 5–56.
Person, Goran, 1995. "Information on Sweden." In *Budget Deficits and Debt: Issues and Options,* Stuart Weiner, ed. Proceedings of symposium sponsored by the Federal Reserve Bank of Kansas City (September), pp. 413–418.
Shigehara, Kumiharu, 1995. "Commentary." In *Budget Deficits and Debt: Issues and Options,* Stuart Weiner, ed. Proceedings of symposium sponsored by the Federal Reserve Bank of Kansas City (September), pp. 55–88.
Weiner, Stuart, 1995. *Budget Deficits and Debt: Issues and Options.* Proceedings of symposium sponsored by the Federal Reserve Bank of Kansas City (September), pp. 57–88.

DECENTRALIZATION. A shift of power from a center whose jurisdiction is relatively large to a center or set of centers of smaller jurisdiction.

The term, like its antonym, centralization, was first used in the first half of the nineteenth century, no doubt as a response to the emergence of the modern nation state. In the century that followed, the bulk of relevant writings was concerned with local governments and their relations with national governments. It was during this period that the convention emerged that defined the size of a center primarily in terms of the numbers of people under its jurisdiction. More recently, the scope of discussion has widened, with the transformations of state systems that have accompanied the passing of major empires. There has, however, been a paucity of theoretical work on processes of decentralization: in the English language, B. C. Smith (1985) has produced the sole substantial and widely read book-length treatment.

Although terminologies have inevitably varied, most writers distinguish two main forms of decentralization: (largely political) devolution and (largely administrative) deconcentration. Political devolution inevitably is expressed in statutory terms, which are often entrenched constitutionally, as in federal systems. However, those federations which were brought into existence by a centralizing agreement between previously independent entities—the majority—are most accurately described as being noncentralized. The principal subnational governmental entities—provinces—enjoy constitutional protections from at least some of the arbitrary policymaking of the national government, and, because they are so protected, they are often endowed with significant political resources as well.

Devolution entails a clear transfer of political responsibility. Henceforth, the smaller center will enjoy a measure of autonomy in policymaking that will not be easily be reclaimed by the devolver. There is, however, a striking irony in all devolutions, for the greater the amount of policymaking power being decentralized, the greater the accretion of centralized regulatory power is likely to be.

Bodies receiving devolved powers may be either territorially based (and in the most significant instances multifunctional, as with municipalities) or functionally specialized, as with most statutory corporations. In recent years, the most important recipients of devolved powers have been nongovernment corporations benefiting from privatization programs. Such programs may validly be classified as cases of devolution because the functions affected have predominantly been public ones which will require close governmental regulation and which may at some future time be subjected to centralizing movements, such as those of renationalization.

Devolution to elective public bodies is often claimed to strengthen democracy by bringing government closer to the people. Such a claim is best put in terms of potentialities: the fewer the voters in a constituency, the greater the potential influence of the individual voter over the elected representative. However, in the realm of practical politics, the ability of the individual to translate potential into actual influence depends in large part on the local structures of power. If the local structures are more closed and their elites more privileged than they are at the national level, as has been the case in many societies (especially those undergoing modernization), devolution to local bodies may weaken rather than strengthen democracy.

The process of administrative deconcentration may be similarly analyzed. There are two principal types of deconcentration: intraorganizational (as with delegations of authority to field officers) and interorganization (as when the central government, without relinquishing political responsibility, contracts local authorities and nongovernment organizations to act as its agents). It is often claimed that deconcentration enhances organizational effectiveness. Increasing the discretionary powers of the field officers of a central bureaucracy is likely to increase responsiveness to local interests, as will the negotiation of agency agreements with local authorities. However, this will lead to more effective service delivery only if the individual recipients, and not the local elites, are most salient for the field officers. Even if they are so salient, the capacity of the field officer to deliver will depend critically on the internal politics of the organization. Whatever happens politically in the field is most likely to be mirroring the political dynamics at the center. This phenemenon has always rendered problematic the position of an official such as the prefect, who in such formally centralized systems as the French has been the principal mechanism for the coordination of local service providers, including those of national government agencies.

These analyses suggest that there are two competing values underlying processes of decentralization—those of equality of status, and of individual liberty. Centralized bureaucracies are typically the most certain vehicles for the delivery of equality of status, and often of associated entitlements as well. Decentralization of any form will increase the freedom of action of at least some actors located at or near the smaller center, and if the ranks of these increasingly empowered people are not restricted to local elites and their bureaucratic allies, the overall outcome is likely to be an enhancement of individual liberty overall. Observing these tendencies, Kochen and Deutsch (1980) produced the bold generalization (to which many exceptions may be found but which nevertheless represents a rare advance in the theorizing of such processes): "Decentralization is in the interest of both the very weak and the locally very strong. Centralization, on the other hand, favors those in between or those in transition."

The political left, especially that segment of it which holds the freedom of the individual to be severely constrained by class-based structures of power, is in most political systems likely to be guarded in its approach to decentralization, for it will be reluctant to place in jeopardy the value of equality of status in the problematic pursuit of enhanced individual liberty. On occasions, however, populist elements may seek to reform local power structures themselves through decentralizing programs, such as those of the U.S. government's 1960s War on Poverty.

The political right, especially those segments of it under the influence of such U.S. schools of thought as that of public choice, is in most modernized political systems prepared to define the extent of equality very narrowly, so that processes of decentralization may not be constrained in their maximization of liberty. Some elements on the right, such as those based in traditionally conservative social movements, may of course be guarded in their approach to decentralization for precisely that reason.

Irrespective of the political complexion of the national government, there is a tendency for devolution to be most strongly pursued by national governments in times of fiscal constraint. In this way, the national government will seek to avoid the electoral consequences for increased taxes and reductions in services. The right is more likely than the left to seek a further political objective in pursuing devolutionary policies—that of reducing the overall size of the public sector. This objective was a central one for both the U.S. Reagan and UK Thatcher administrations, however different their approaches to devolution may have been.

Major decentralizing initiatives are thus highly political, for they must be implemented in the context of intergovernmental relations. Whether these relations are more effectively handled through federal or unitary systems remains an open question. On the one hand, actors in federal systems are likely to have developed skills in negotiations with other governments. On the other, federal systems are more likely to encounter policy gridlock, because of the political resources at the disposal of provincial governments. However, assessment of instances where the government of a unitary state has imposed its will on its subnational bodies, as in the Thatcher government's treatment of local government, does not inspire confidence in centrally imposed decentralizing initiatives. The most effective decentralizing policies are usually those which have been successfully negotiated through intergovernmental relations.

In the second half of the twentieth century, one of the most important structural movements in and between most governments has been that of regionalization, which on occasion has led to the achievement of regionalism (the establishment at the regional level of general purpose and usually elective government). A region was once wittily defined as an area safely larger or smaller than the last one to whose problems no solution could be found. Regional bodies may be supranational, such as the European Community, or, within a nation state, either supra- or sub-provincial. In North America, the former type of subnational regionalization has been most salient; in Australia, the latter. Regionalization has thus been closely associated with both centralizing and decentralizing processes, for they are all manifestations of structural change in governmental systems.

When it takes a regionalist form, decentralization may unleash forces that threaten the constitutional order of the nation state. If national integration remains fragile, as in many developing countries and some developed ones such as Canada, ethnicity and regionalism can prove an explosive mix.

In this entry, the government of the nation state has been treated as the primary center. Until now, the United Nations and its agencies have not been mentioned, as it would be premature to identify one overriding political center for the world, and yet it does not seem appropriate to treat the globe as just another region. However, the author of the corresponding entry in the encyclopedia of the next generation may well be able to take a global center of governance as her starting point, if current movements towards the globalization of the political economy continue.

JOHN POWER

BIBLIOGRAPHY

Adamolekun, Ladipo, 1991. "Decentralization Policies: Problems and Perspectives." *Asian Journal of Public Administration*, vol. 13, no. 1 (June) 67–92.
Bennett, Robert J., ed., 1990. *Decentralization, Local Governments, and Markets: Towards a Post-Welfare Agenda.* Oxford: Clarendon Press.
Cheema, G. S. and D. A. Rondinelli, 1983. *Implementing Decentralizing Programmes in Asia: Local Capacity for Rural Development.* Nagoya, Japan: United Nations Centre for Regional Development.
Fesler, James W., 1949. *Area and Administration.* Montgomery: University of Alabama Press.
———, 1965. "Approaches to the Study of Decentralization." *Journal of Politics*, vol. 27, no 4. (August) 536–566.
———, 1968. "Centralization and Decentralization." *International Encyclopedia of the Social Sciences*, vol. 2:370–379.
Kochen, Manfred and Karl W. Deutsch, 1980. *Decentralization: Toward a Rational Theory.* Cambridge, MA: Oelgeschlager, Gunn and Hain.
Maddick, Henry, 1963. *Democracy, Decentralisation and Development.* Bombay: Asia Publishing House.
Rhodes, R. A. W., 1988. *Beyond Westminster and Whitehall: The Sub-central Governments of Britain.* London: Unwin Hyman.
Sharpe, L. J., ed., 1979. *Decentralist Trends in Western Democracies.* London: Sage Publications.
Smith, B. C., 1985. *Decentralization: The Territorial Dimension of the State.* London: George Allen and Unwin.

DECISION. A form of secondary legislation in the European Union. According to article 189 of the treaty establishing the European Economic Community signed in Rome in 1957, "a decision shall be binding in its entirety upon those to whom it is addressed." A decision tends to be specific to the member state or states, undertaking, or person to whom it is addressed. It takes effect upon notification of those concerned. For the most part decisions are administrative rather than legislative in nature. Examples of decisions include the Council Decision of March 6, 1995, on the conclusion of the agreement in the form of an exchange of letters amending the Cooperation Agreement between the European Economic Community and the Yemen Arab Republic; the Commission Decision of March 6, 1995, on a special financial contribution from the Community for the eradication of swine vesicular disease in Belgium; and the Commission Decision of March 6, 1995, approving the program for the eradication of infectious bovine rhinotracheitis in Austria.

Decisions are known as individual decisions under the Paris Treaty signed in 1951, which established the European Coal and Steel Community in 1952.

MARGARET MARY MALONE

BIBLIOGRAPHY

Hartley, T. C., 1989. *The Foundations of European Community Law.* 2d ed. London: Clarendon Press.
Lasok, D. and J. W. Bridge, 1987. *Law and Institutions of the European Communities.* 4th ed. London: Butterworths.
Nugent, Neill, 1991. *The Government and Politics of the European Community.* 2d ed. London: Macmillan.
Parry, Anthony and James Dinnage, 1981. *EEC Law.* 2d ed. London: Sweet and Maxwell.
Wyatt, D. and A. Dashwood, 1987. *The Substantive Law of the EC.* 2d ed. London: Sweet and Maxwell.

DECISIONMAKING IN THE EUROPEAN UNION.

A complex system of variable procedures, variable voting systems, and a variable involvement of the different institutions.

The considerable complexity and lack of transparency of the Union's decisionmaking process can be explained by two factors. First, it is the result of treaties and treaty amendments (such as the Single Act of 1986 and the Treaty on European Union of 1992) that added new procedures without replacing the previously existing procedures or rationalizing the existing system of decisionmaking. Second, it is the result of a whole range of compromises between different views of the member states and the institutions about the prefered mix of intergovernmental and supranational features that should characterize the decisionmaking process of the European Union.

Institutions

The Council of Ministers (the Council) is the main legislative institution in the European Union, involved in nearly all decisions. The Council consists of a representative of each member state at ministerial level, authorized to commit the government of that member state. In the Common Foreign and Security Policy, the Council decides on the basis of general guidelines adopted by the European Council, which consists of the heads of state or of government of the member states and the president of the European Commission. In other politically important policy fields, the European Council outlines the major policy options, which are then formalized and further elaborated by the Council.

For most policy areas, the work of the Council is prepared by the Committee of Permanent Representatives (COREPER), which consists of the Permanent Representatives (or "Ambassadors") of the member states to the European Union. A Coordinating Committee prepares the decisions in the fields of justice and home affairs. In the Common Foreign and Security policy, the Council's decisions are prepared by the Political Committee.

The second legislative institution is the European Parliament, which consists of directly elected representatives of the peoples of the member states of the European Union. The European Parliament is involved to varying degrees in the decisionmaking process, with its position ranging from being completely neglected in some policy areas to having a right of veto in other areas.

The European Commission (the Commission) is the third institution that plays a major role in the European Union's decisionmaking. It consists of two members of the larger member states and one member of the other states, which are chosen on the grounds of their general competence and whose independence is beyond doubt. The members of the Commission are expected to act in the general interests of the Community. In practice, most members of the Commission previously played an important political role in their own country and hold often ministerial positions. This implies that the requested independence is not always easy to sustain in reality.

The Commission plays an important role in decisionmaking as it initiates Community policy: Council and Parliament can only decide on the basis of a proposal from the Commission. The Council and Parliament can, however, request that the Commission submit a proposal on matters on which it considers that a Community act is required. The power of initiative of the Commission is aimed at guaranteeing that the common interest of the European Union is at the basis of any decision. Besides taking the initiative, the Commission is also involved in the subsequent stages of the decisionmaking (and in the implementation of decisions). It can mediate between Council and European Parliament and influence the final decision.

Voting Systems

The European Parliament takes decisions either by a majority of the votes cast or by an absolute majority of its members.

The Council can take decisions in three different ways. First, some decisions have to be taken by unanimity. Whereas this was the normal requirement in the past, the Single Act and the Treaty of Maastricht greatly reduced the cases in which this unanimity requirement applies. Unanimity is still the rule, however, for nearly all decisions in the field of justice and home affairs and in the Common Foreign and Security Policy. Unanimity is also required when the Council wants to amend a proposal against the wish of the Commission.

Second, the Council can decide by a simple majority vote. This voting system, in which all states have one vote each, is used mainly for procedural purposes. The third voting system, qualified majority voting, applies for most decisions in most policy areas. Under this voting system, the member states have a different number of votes depending on the size of the states, ranging from two votes for Luxembourg to ten votes for the United Kingdom, France, Germany, and Italy. The number of votes required for a qualified majority is defined such that the largest countries cannot outvote the smaller countries and two large member states cannot by themselves constitute a blocking minority. A variant on the normal qualified majority vote provided in a limited number of cases includes the supplementary requirement that a minimum number of member states must have supported the decision.

The Consultation Procedure

Under this procedure, which includes only one reading, the European Parliament gives its opinion on the proposal of the Commission. The Council takes the final decision and is not obliged to take this opinion into account. Under the original Treaties of Rome, Parliament's involvement in the legislative process was restricted to this procedure.

The Cooperation Procedure

The cooperation procedure, which involves two readings, was introduced by the Single Act of 1986 and is described in Article 189c of the Treaty on European Union of 1992.

It strengthens the position of the European Parliament because the Parliament gains the possibility to influence the voting requirements within the Council and to make it more difficult for the Council to neglect the opinion of Parliament. The Council retains the final say. The cooperation procedure leaves the Commission with a substantial role to play because the Parliament's influence depends on the support of the Commission for its views.

If the European Parliament rejects the decision (or "common position") of the Council, the Council can only adopt this common position by unanimity. This implies that the European Parliament can block the decision if at least one member state in the Council votes against the common position. If the European Parliament amends the common position and the Commission supports this amendment, only a qualified majority is needed in the Council to accept this amended common position. This implies that the common position as amended by the European Parliament can also be accepted by the Council if a limited number of member states vote against this amended common position. A member state in this case no longer has the ability to block the decision in the Council, as the unanimity rule does not apply.

Stages in the Cooperation Procedure

The Council, acting by a qualified majority on a proposal from the Commission and after obtaining the opinion of Parliament, adopts a "common position." This is referred to Parliament, which is informed of the reasons that led the Council to adopt its common position. The European Parliament has three months in which to endorse it (expressly or implicitly), reject it, or amend it.

If the European Parliament approves this common position or has not taken a decision within three months, the Council adopts definitively the act in question in accordance with the common position.

If the European Parliament, by an absolute majority of its component members, rejects the Council's common position, unanimity is required for the Council to adopt the act in second reading.

If the European Parliament, by an absolute majority of its component members, proposes amendments to the Council's common position, the Commission has one month in which to decide whether or not to accept any amendments proposed by Parliament. The Commission reexamines the proposal on the basis of which the Council adopted its common position, by taking into account the amendments proposed by the European Parliament. The Council then proceeds to a second reading.

The Council votes by qualified majority where the Commission has endorsed the amendments of the Parliament and unanimously where the Commission has not accepted the Parliament's amendments. Unanimity is also required when the Council amends the proposal as reexamined by the Commission. If the Council takes no decision within a period of three months, the proposal is deemed not to have been adopted (the periods of three months mentioned in this procedure can be extended by one month by common accord between the Council and the European Parliament).

Acts adopted by the Council are published in the Official Journal and enter into force on the date specified in them or, in the absence thereof, on the twentieth day following that of their publication.

The Codecision Procedure

The codecision procedure was introduced by Article 198b of the Treaty on European Union of 1992. It contains three readings, with the first two resembling to some extent those of the cooperation procedure, except for the involvement of the new Conciliation Committee. The codecision procedure increases the European Parliament's legislative powers through the introduction of a right of veto in the third reading and through the establishment of a Conciliation Committee, both of which making the European Parliament a genuine partner of the Council in the process of decisionmaking.

The first characteristic of the codecision procedure is the involvement of a Conciliation Committee, composed of the members of the Council or their representatives and an equal number of representatives of the European Parliament. This Committee has the task of reaching agreement on a joint text, which is then laid before the full Council and Parliament for adoption. The Commission takes part in the Conciliation Committee's proceedings and takes all necessary initiatives with a view to reconciling the positions of Parliament and Council. However, the Commission does not have the same decisive role as in the cooperation procedure. One of the important features of the Conciliation Committee is that it allows the European Parliament to negotiate directly with the Council and to reach an agreement on the proposal with the Council. The Parliament is thus not dependent on the support of the Commission to the same degree as in the cooperation procedure.

The second characteristic of the codecision procedure is the introduction of a third reading and the possibility it includes for the European Parliament to reject the text accepted by the Council. The possibility to see its text rejected by the European Parliament forces the Council to take the Parliamentary views more seriously. This right of veto is, however, of a negative nature: the Parliament can reject a text but does not have the power to force the Council to accept the text proposed by the European Parliament.

Stages in the Codecision Procedure

The Council, acting by a qualified majority on a proposal from the Commission and after obtaining the opinion of

Parliament, adopts a common position. This is referred to Parliament, that is informed of the Commission's position and of the reasons that led the Council to adopt its common position. The European Parliament has three months in which to endorse it (expressly or implicitly), reject it, or amend it.

If the European Parliament approves this common position or has not taken a decision within three months, the Council adopts definitively the act in question in accordance with the common position.

If the European parliament indicates, by an absolute majority of its component members, that it intends to reject the common position, it immediately informs the Council. The Council may convene a meeting of the Conciliation Committee to explain its position. The European Parliament thereafter either confirms, by an absolute majority of its members, its rejection of the common position—in which event the proposed act shall be deemed not to have been adopted—or proposes amendments.

If the European Parliament, by an absolute majority of its component members, proposes amendments to the Council's common position, the amended text is forwarded to the Council and to the Commission, which deliver an opinion on those amendments.

In the second reading, within three months, the Council can approve all the amendments of the European Parliament and amend its common position accordingly and adopt the act in question. It acts by a qualified majority on the amendments on which the Commission has delivered a positive opinion, by unanimity on the amendments on which it delivered a negative opinion. If the Council does not approve the act in question, the president of the Council, in agreement with the president of the European Parliament, convenes a meeting of the Conciliation Committee.

If within six weeks the Conciliation Committee approves a joint text, by a qualified majority of the members of the Council or their representatives and by a majority of the representatives of the European Parliament, this text is laid before the full Council and Parliament for adoption. The European Parliament, acting by an absolute majority of the votes cast, and the Council, acting by a qualified majority, have a period of six weeks in which to adopt the act in question in accordance with the joint text. If one of the two institutions fails to approve the proposed act, it is deemed not to have been adopted.

If the Conciliation Committee is not able to approve a joint text, the proposed act is deemed not to have been adopted unless the Council, acting by a qualified majority within six weeks, confirms its common position, incorporating some of Parliament's amendments if it wishes. In this case, the act in question is adopted unless the European Parliament, within six weeks, rejects the text by an absolute majority of its members, in which case the act is deemed not to have been adopted (the periods of three months and six weeks mentioned in this procedure can be extended by one month and two weeks respectively by common accord between the Council and the European Parliament).

Acts adopted under the codecision procedure are signed by the presidents of Parliament and the Council and published in the *Official Journal of the European Communities*. They enter into force on the date specified in them or, in the absence thereof, on the twentieth day following that of their publication.

The Assent Procedure

The assent procedure was established by the Single Act of 1986 for decisions on association agreements with third countries or groups of third countries and on agreements covering the enlargement of the European Community. The assent procedure was extended in the Treaty on European Union of 1992 to a wider range of international agreements as well as to a limited number of legislative decisions (with regard to the right of citizens to move and reside freely within the territory of the member states, the objectives of the Structural Funds, the powers of the European Central Bank, and the proposals relating to the establishment of a uniform electoral procedure for the elections for the European Parliament). This procedure strengthens the power of the European Parliament, as it gives the Parliament veto powers. However, it has the disadvantage for the European Parliament that it can only decide on the final decision and not on the preceding negotiations.

In the assent procedure, the European Parliament must give its approval, at a single reading and with no provision for amendments, to proposals. In most cases, a majority of the votes cast is needed for the Parliament to give its assent. In a limited number of cases, an absolute majority of its component members is required, making it more difficult for the Council to get the assent of Parliament (i.e., for decisions with regard to the application of new member states).

Intergovernmental Decisionmaking Procedures

Decisionmaking in the second pillar (Common Foreign and Security Policy) and the third pillar (cooperation in the field of justice and home affairs) of the European Union is characterized by its intergovernmental features: the unanimity requirement, the preponderance of the (European) Council, and the marginal role of the European Parliament and the Commission.

Both in the Common Foreign and Security Policy and in the cooperation in the fields of justice and home affairs, the Council is the only institution with power of decision. The Commission is "fully associated," the European Parliament is consulted and can make recommendations, but neither has a real influence on the decision-making of the Council. In some policy areas in the third pillar, the Commission is allowed to submit proposals. In the Common Foreign and Security Policy, a special role is played by the European Council, which defines the principles of and general guidelines for this policy. The Council takes the decisions necessary for defining and implementing the Common Foreign and Security Policy on the basis of the general guidelines adopted by the European Council.

In both pillars, the Council in general acts unanimously, except for procedural questions and in a very limited number of cases provided for in the Treaty. In both pillars, when adopting a joint action, the Council can define by unanimity those matters on which decisions are to be taken by a qualified majority (with this qualified majority having as supplementary requirement that at least eight member states vote in favor). This implies that decisions by majority votes are possible, but that any member state can block this possibility of departing from the unanimity rule, which relativizes the possibility of use of majority votes. Majority voting is also possible in the field of justice and home affairs for measures implementing conventions. In this case, these measures have to be adopted in the Council by a majority of two-thirds.

STEPHAN KEUKELEIRE

BIBLIOGRAPHY

Bulmer, Simon and Wolfgang Wessels, 1987. *The European Council: Decisionmaking in European Politics.* London: Macmillan.

Engel, Christian and Wolfgang Wessels, eds., 1992. *From Luxembourg to Maastricht: Institutional Change in the European Community after the Single European Act.* Bonn: European Union Verlag.

Jacobs, Francis, Richard Corbett and Michael Shackleton, 1992. *The European Parliament.* Essex: Longman.

Keohane, Robert O. and Stanley Hoffmann, eds., 1991. *The New European Community: Decisionmaking and Institutional Change.* Oxford: Westview.

Kirchner, Emil J., 1992. *Decisionmaking in the European Community: The Council Presidency and European Integration.* Manchester: Manchester University Press.

Nugent, Neill, 1994. *The Government and Politics of the European Union.* London: Macmillan.

Sbagria, Alberta M., ed., 1992. *Euro-Politics: Institutions and Policymaking in the European Community.* Washington, D.C.: Brookings Institution.

Weslake, Martin, 1994. *The Commission and the Parliament: Partners and Rivals in the European Policymaking Process.* London: Butterworths.

DECISION THEORY. The science of problem solving and the methods used by managers to make successful choices under conditions of uncertainty and risk. It provides both a description of human behavior in problem solving and the science of methods to optimize decisions.

Decision theory developed in the twentieth century as an outgrowth of scientific management and the work of Frederick Taylor and Frank and Lillian Gilbreth (see **scientific management**). Its roots are found in business, economics, and mathematics. The evolution of decision theory expanded geometrically after World War II with the development of cybernetics and the science of operations research.

Public administration has traditionally incorporated the function of decisionmaking as scholars have searched for the best ways to manage public organizations. Early scholars such as Woodrow Wilson (1887) and Leonard White (1926) urged the development of a science of administration to make government management more businesslike. Luther Gulick (1937) included decisionmaking in the D (directing) of his mnemonic POSDCORB.

The incorporation of decision theory into public administration began with Herbert Simon's 1946 article in *Public Administration Review*, "The Proverbs of Administration." Simon argued that the essence of management activity is decisionmaking and that organizations should seek ways to improve managers' decisionmaking capabilities rather than trying to find the ideal organizational structure. Simon later published a number of influential books outlining an administrative theory for decisionmaking.

Decision theory gained prominence in the 1960s with the development of management science, operations research, computer modeling, and systems analysis. Because decision theory can be used to design mathematical representations of reality, it is essential for the development of computer models that attempt to replicate conditions in the real world.

Decision theory is used by managers and policy analysts to structure problems and identify options for solutions. Game theory, a branch of decision theory, is used by the military and the U.S. State Department to structure decisions with international players. Another application of decision theory, risk assessment, is increasingly used by regulatory agencies, such as the U.S. Environmental Protection Agency, to set priorities for the implementation of regulatory strategies.

Underlying Theoretical Framework

Decision theory begins with the rational choice model of decisionmaking. Drawn from microeconomics theory of human behavior, the model outlines the scientific steps of a decision:

1. *Define the problem to be solved.* Limit it to its essential parts and describe the relationships of these parts to each other.

2. *Gather all the facts.* Facts should be obtained in an objective (scientific) manner. Values should be excluded from the decision framework as they cannot be quantified or measured scientifically.
3. *Construct alternative solutions.* Using the facts, alternative methods for solving the problem are designed.
4. *Scientifically analyze alternatives.* Using a scientific process, usually incorporating a mathematical tool, analyze the alternatives to measure their worth for solving the problem.
5. *Select the best alternative.* The analysis provides a ranking of alternatives according to scientific measures and permits the decisionmaker to make the best rational choice.

A decision is rational when it maximizes the welfare of the decisionmaker, whether an individual or organization. Welfare can mean anything of value, such as satisfaction, goal achievement, and so forth, but most commonly is measured in terms of dollars or profits.

Decisions are made under conditions of either certainty or uncertainty. Conditions of certainty enable decisionmakers to pick the right alternative since the outcome of the decision is known. Conditions of uncertainty, on the other hand, are characterized by outcomes that are affected by various factors, and the decision outcome cannot be projected for sure. Therefore, decisionmakers must incorporate measures of probability and risk evaluation into their analysis.

Probability is a mathematical estimate of the chance of a given event occurring. It is expressed as a percentage from 0 to 100. Probability is the ratio of an outcome to all possible outcomes. Probability may be known to the decisionmaker—for example, the probability of getting a head when flipping a coin is one out of two or 0.5—or it may be estimated based on a sample of the possible outcomes. Often the experience of the decisionmaker or other experts is used to judge the probability of an event in a given circumstance.

Risk refers to the probability of an undesired outcome occurring. The higher the probability, the greater is the chance that the decision will result in a negative outcome. High-risk situations often have highly desirable payoffs as well.

Choosing the best alternative depends on the decisionmaker's risk averseness and subjective utility for the decision outcome. Risk averseness refers to the decisionmaker's personal tolerance for a negative outcome. Decisionmakers with low risk averseness may be willing to choose a lower probability for success, that is, a higher risk. Managers with high risk averseness, on the other hand, will likely make more conservative decisions with a low risk of failure.

Subjective utility is a measure of the decisionmaker's utility or preference for a certain outcome. It is used in de-

cisions where there are a number of choices, each with various strengths and weaknesses. Examples would include hiring a new employee, buying a car, or renting an apartment, where each alternative has different levels of the same attributes. Using a device called the Multiattribute Utility Model, a numerical value is attached to the decisionmaker's preference for each individual attribute, based on a scale of one to ten. Attributes are weighted according to the decisionmaker's utility and a score is calculated for each choice based on these utilities. Decisionmakers may choose the alternative with the highest score (for more information on the model, see Huber, 1980).

Risk assessment is a form of decisionmaking based on these same concepts. In policy areas such as pollution control or human exposures to health risks, decisionmakers estimate the probability/risk of damage to human health or environmental attributes. These risks are then organized as priorities for implementing policy and administrative decisions to balance environmental contamination against other social values such as economic development.

The mathematical representation of the probable payoff of all alternatives is called the expected value. It is calculated by multiplying the value of an outcome by its probability and adding the results. The sum is the average value for a given alternative considering all possible outcomes. By comparing the expected values of various decision strategies, decisionmakers can choose the one that will most likely produce the most favorable outcome, either the highest payoff or the lowest cost.

Practice: The Science of Decisionmaking

Decision theory describes a science of decisionmaking through processes that structure problems so that they can be solved systematically. The object of the exercise is to reach that decision which will maximize the decisionmaker's welfare or utility.

Graphic representations are used to identify the choices and possible outcomes given different future conditions and probabilities of their occurence. Two common representations are decision trees and the payoff matrix.

Decision trees are used to picture a decision process and show the possible outcomes of an alternative as branches on a tree. Figure I shows a simple decision tree.

The tree is constructed by first identifying the alternative decision choices (A or B), the possible outcomes for each alternative (A1, A2 and B1, B2) and the payoff for the alternative given each outcome (C1, C2, C3, C4). Payoff can be either a positive or negative number. It is usually expressed in dollars as a benefit or a cost, but can also be expressed as a utility or preference. The probability or risk of each outcome is estimated and placed on the appropriate branch. Working back from the payoff, the expected value of each outcomes node is calculated. The decisionmaker

FIGURE I. Decision Tree

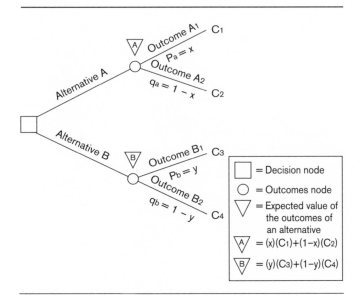

can then identify the branch of the tree that offers the greatest payoff, whether highest profit or lowest cost. In the private sector, generally profits are maximized; in the public sector, however, the best decision is often one that minimizes costs.

Decision trees are useful for multistage decisions where succeeding decisions are dependent on earlier choices and the overall outcome for each decision set is difficult to visualize. Use of a decision tree enables a decisionmaker (or a computer) to calculate the expected value of complex multiyear decisions so that the initial decision may be optimal (for more information on decision trees, see Huber, 1980; White *et al.*, 1985).

A payoff matrix is a graphic representation of a problem situation that enables the decisionmaker to identify the payoffs for decision choices given possible future conditions. Figure II shows a payoff matrix for a simple decision.

This matrix illustrates a farmer's choices of what crop to plant and his or her potential profit for possible future weather conditions. To utilize the information on a payoff matrix, a decisionmaker must adopt a decision rule.

Decision rules have been developed by mathematicians and economists to guide decisionmakers in accordance with their own risk averseness and experience. The criteria generally used as bases for decisions are pessimism, optimism, or regret. Figures III-IV illustrate each of these criteria.

The criterion of pessimism or maximin is used when the decisionmaker assumes the worst will happen. The payoff matrix shows the lowest payoff for each strategy; the decisionmaker chooses that strategy which will give him or her the highest payoff given the worst future condition. In

this case, the decision-maker decides to plant beans because the worst payoff for beans, which occurs in dry weather, is $10,000 higher than the worst payoff for corn, which occurs in wet weather. This way the farmer cannot be disappointed no matter what the summer weather brings.

The criterion of optimism or maximax is used when the decisionmaker is optimistic that the best will happen and chooses that strategy that provides the maximum payoff given optimum conditions. In this case, the farmer decides to plant corn, betting that the summer will be dry.

The criterion of regret allows the decisionmaker to ask the question: If I knew the future condition (i.e., rainy or dry), how much would I lose if I don't choose the best strategy for that condition? That is, how much will I regret not choosing the other strategy? Figure V is a regret matrix in which the highest payoff for each future condition is shown as zero. The other cell in the column shows the difference between the maximum payoff and the payoff for that strategy given that future condition. Thus, in the example, the maximum payoff for the condition "Rainy Weather" is $35,000 for planting beans. If the farmer plants corn and the weather is wet, the regret matrix shows that the value of this regret will be $25,000 since profit will be only $10,000. The decisionmaker chooses that strategy which will lead to the least regret. In this case, the farmer decides to plant beans.

In this example, the probability for rainy or dry is assumed to be equal (i.e. 0.5 each). Decisionmakers often use sensitivity testing to examine how sensitive the decision is

FIGURE II. Payoff Matrix for a Planting Decision

Strategies	Future Conditions	
	Rainy Weather (N1)	Dry Weather (N2)
Plant Corn (S1)	$10,000	$40,000
Plant Beans (S2)	$35,000	$20,000

The dollar figures in the cells represent the estimated payoff or profit for each strategy given each future condition occurring.

FIGURE III. Payoff Matrix for Criterion of Pessimism

Strategy	Worst Payoff
Plant Corn	$10,000 (N1)
Plant Beans	$20,000 (N2)

FIGURE IV. PAYOFF MATRIX FOR
CRITERION OF OPTIMISM

Strategy	Best Payoff
Plant Corn	$40,000 (N2)
Plant Beans	$35,000 (N3)

FIGURE V. REGRET MATRIX FOR CRITERION OF REGRET

Strategy	Rainy Weather	Dry Weather
Plant Corn	$25,000	0
Plant Beans	0	$20,000

to different probabilities. Using different probabilities for future conditions, decisionmakers calculate the expected value for each strategy. Expected values for the farmer's decision are shown below:

Case I: Assume that the probability of rain is 0.4 and of dry weather is 0.6:

EV(corn) = (0.4)($10,000) + (0.6)($40,000) = $28,000
EV(beans) = (0.4)($35,000) + (0.6)($20,000)
= $26,000

Case II: Assume the probability of rain is 0.6 and of dry weather is 0.4:

EV(corn) = (0.6)($10,000) + (0.4)($40,000) = $22,000
EV(beans) = (0.6)($35,000) + (0.4)($20,000)
= $29,000

The farmer would choose corn in Case I and beans in Case II. He makes the decision based on his or her confidence in his or her own estimates of the weather.

From this example, we see that decision theory can provide information but cannot make the decision. The decisionmaker must examine all the evidence in relationship to his or her own preferences and hunches and choose that decision which will achieve his or her personal goals. Since none of the rules leads to the same answer, decision theory must be seen only as a tool for decisionmakers, not a scientific method to make the "right" decision. A decision is right when the decisionmaker is comfortable with it.

The most valuable information in any decision exercise—knowledge of the future—cannot be obtained; thus, decisionmakers will always make decisions that are less than optimal. In practice, decisionmaking is as much an art as it is a science.

Decisionmaking in Organizations

In organizations, decisionmaking is generally a group exercise; rarely are decisions made by individuals working to maximize their own interests. Group decisionmaking is more complex than the model of rational choice for individuals.

First, individual differences among group members make defining rational outcomes difficult. Each individual may have a different preference for given outcomes and different perceptions of the level of risk the organization should be exposed to. Organizational culture also impairs the development of pure rationality in organizations; the individual most knowledgable in a given area may be a subordinate in the hierarchy and therefore not an equal participant in the decisionmaking process. The needs of the organization may be complex, which again limits pure rationality for decisionmaking. Once beyond the individual decisionmaker, rational choice quickly becomes less effective as a decision model (see Hult and Walcott, 1990 for an analysis to the decision to launch the space shuttle *Challenger*).

In public organizations, decisionmakers must also consider political factors. The most rational decisions, from a benefit to cost perspective or from the standpoint of equity, are usually subject to extensive political bargaining and compromise. An example is the Tax Reform Act of 1986. One original proposal for tax reform was to eliminate the tax deductibility of interest payments on home mortgages. From a rational perspective this proposal made good sense: the deduction represents a significant loss of revenue from the federal income tax and is, in essence, a progressive housing subsidy for middle- and upper-income taxpayers. It is also the primary tax shelter for millions of taxpayers. The mortgage interest deduction was retained in the final bill for not one but two residences, most helpful for members of Congress who have homes in Washington as well as their home districts.

Public administrators must include the interests of citizens and significant stakeholders in making decisions to implement the policy directives of Congress. An agency attempting to make purely rational decisions without regard to subsidiary interests would quickly lose political and budget support.

Models of Organizational Decisionmaking

Scholars have attempted to address the weaknesses of the rational choice model by identifying the dynamics of how decisions are actually made. Prominent in this area are Herbert Simon, Charles Lindblom, Amitai Etzioni, and James G. March.

Herbert Simon (1946, 1957a, 1957b) argued that achieving pure rationality is impossible for many reasons: limits of time and resources in organizations to collect all data, limited ability of decisionmakers to identify all facets of a problem and all alternatives to solve it, and the limits of the human brain to deal simultaneously with all factors of a problem. Furthermore, all decisions are influenced by the future, which cannot be known ahead. Simon called this condition "bounded rationality" and proposed that decisionmakers should make the decisionmaking process as efficient as possible by choosing any alternative which satisfies the decisionmaker's goals sufficiently, even if not perfectly. This process is called "satisficing."

Charles Lindblom (1959) argued that organizations, particularly public organizations, are basically conservative decisionmakers and generally "muddle through" a problem rather than adopt a purely rational solution that might create organizational instability. Lindblom called the decision process "disjointed incrementalism" by which problems are solved in piecemeal fashion over time. Rationality may ultimately be achieved, but the slow process allows the organization to adjust to change and avoid making big mistakes which could be costly, both financially and politically. Lindblom and others have defended disjointed incrementalism as a decision model that works well with the principles of U.S. democracy.

Amitai Etzioni (1967) called his decision model "mixed scanning," which is a hybrid of rational choice and incrementalism. He pointed out that not all problems are equally significant and not all require the full analysis of the rational choice model. Rather, he argued, decisionmakers should reserve rational analysis for major or fundamental decisions, which require a full consideration of alternatives and result in significant policy decisions. Another level of decisions, bit decisions, can be made incrementally in relation to fundamental decisions. Once the major policy decisions have been established, smaller decisions aimed at achieving policy goals can be made through incremental analysis.

James G. March (1994) has outlined what he calls the "garbage can process" of decisionmaking in organizations. Based on the principle that timing is everything, the garbage can process assumes that decisions are dependent on the chance interactions of choice opportunities, decisionmakers, and resource availability. Thus, a decision will vary according to the presence of these factors at any given time. Because bigger or more significant problems tend to have a greater number of choice opportunities, a natural system of prioritization can develop in the garbage can process. The process can be seen as either detrimental to organizations because of its lack of systematic rationality, or as an opportunistic method for ensuring that the most important problems get addressed.

Use of Decision Theory in Public Administration

All these decision models are used extensively by public administrators at all levels of government. The rational choice model, incorporating operations research, was used significantly by NASA in implementing the space program. Incrementalism is used by budgeteers, especially for essential programs that change little from year to year. Mixed scanning is used by political leaders and high level administrators in determining which policies will be enacted and how quickly their goals will be achieved. All organizations, to some extent, use the garbage can process simply because of the interaction of people within organizations.

Decision theory, in the final analysis, provides a means of analyzing problem situations and identifying different ways to solve them. It is a tool for decisionmakers, not a method of finding the "right" answer. The problems of public policy and public administration are complex and defy simple solutions. Having a variety of tools for decisionmaking can help decision makers identify the weaknesses in each one and better choose the appropriate process or method for individual problem situations.

MARY M. TIMNEY

BIBLIOGRAPHY

Allison, Graham T., 1971. *Essence of Decision: Explaining the Cuban Missile Crisis.* Glenview, IL: Scott, Foresman & Co.
Etzioni, Amitai, 1967. "Mixed Scanning: A 'Third' Approach to Decisionmaking." *Public Administration Review,* vol. 27: 385–92.
Gulick, Luther, 1937. "Notes on the Theory of Organization." *Papers on the Science of Administration,* eds. Luther Gulick and Lyndall Urwick. New York: Institute of Public Administration: 3-13.
Huber, George P., 1980. *Managerial Decisionmaking.* Glenview, IL: Scott, Foresman & Co.
Hult, Karen M. and Charles Walcott, 1990. *Governing Public Organizations: Politics, Structures and Institutional Design.* Pacific Grove, CA: Brooks/Cole.
Lindblom, Charles E., 1959. "The Science of Muddling Through." *Public Administration Review,* vol. 19: 79–88.
March, James G., 1994. *A Primer on Decisionmaking: How Decisions Happen.* New York: The Free Press.
Miller, David W. and Martin K. Starr, 1967. *The Structure of Human Decisions.* Englewood Cliffs, NJ: Prentice-Hall.
Simon, Herbert A., 1946. "The Proverbs of Administration." *Public Administration Review,* vol. 6: 53–67.
———, 1957a. *Administrative Behavior.* New York: The Free Press.
———, 1957b. *Models of Man.* New York: John Wiley & Sons.
White, Michael J., Ross Clayton, Robert Myrtle, Gilbert Siegel, and Aaron Rose, 1985. *Managing Public Systems: Analytic Techniques for Public Administration.* Lanham, MD: University Press of America.
White, Leonard D., 1926. *Introduction to the Study of Public Administration.* New York, Macmillan.
Wilson, Woodrow, 1887. "The Study of Administration." *Political Science Quarterly,* Vol. 2 (June).
Wright, George, 1984. *Behavioral Decision Theory.* Beverly Hills, CA: Sage Publications.
Zagare, Frank C., 1984. *Game Theory: Concepts and Applications.* Beverly Hills, CA: Sage Publications.
Zey, Mary, ed., 1992. *Decisionmaking: Alternatives to Rational Choice Models.* Newbury Park, CA: Sage Publications.

DEFAULTS, MUNICIPAL.

Failure to repay debt. Borrowing money carries an obligation to repay the funds, often with interest during the interim. A default occurs when any debt repayment condition fails to be honored. Individuals and organizations usually find it best to avoid defaulting on a debt obligation. There is a point where the benefits of default outweigh the costs, and bankruptcy laws deal with this situation. In the United States, federal law lets individuals, corporations, and municipalities seek court protection from creditors, under certain conditions. Given that default is always a possibility, investors must exercise caution in entering into loans. Furthermore, investors must maintain vigilance throughout the duration of the loan. At their peril, investors can rely too much upon credit ratings to provide a summary assessment as to the probability of nonpayment of a debt. Borrowers with sterling reputations and credit ratings have defaulted.

Generally, default is the failure to repay the principal amount borrowed and/or the scheduled interest payments, by the stated due date. A delay of only a day is a default under most loan agreements, although the delay may impose a negligible economic impact on bondholders. A different burden arises when nonpayment of principal or interest extends over weeks, months, or years.

Failure to follow agreed-upon procedures, not just economic nonpayment, also is a default. In return for capital, borrowers agree to detailed legal obligations, duties, and responsibilities. Default, then, means an omission or failure to keep a promise or meet an obligation. Structural provisions of municipal bonds provide illustrative examples. General obligation bonds, backed by the full faith and credit of the issuing political jurisdiction, typically do not require additional legal covenants. Revenue bonds, however, do need legal specifications since the pledge is so precise. An indenture is the document that contains specific covenants binding the debtor to particular practices and policies. Typical covenants include pledges to: transfer and retain a specified stock of funds in certain restricted accounts; maintain levels of property and casualty insurance; revise rates to levels sufficient to cover yearly operation and maintenance expenses and over a year of debt service; restrict additional debt that dilutes security interests; and many other features designed to protect the assets covering the bondholders' claims. A violation of any single covenant is an event of default allowing "the bondholders or their representative (indenture trustee) to take appropriate action, including the institution of the remedies set forth in the indenture" (Spiotto 1993, sec.13.42).

Indenture agreements provide trustees with several remedies to apply as needed. Trustees can gain legal control over the project to protect bondholders' interests. The ultimate remedy, however, is to accelerate as due and payable all outstanding bonds. Yet, investors prefer to use the threat of remedies, instead of their actual imposition.

Few investors, if any, want to assume operational responsibility for a project. They prefer to have their principal and interest paid as agreed. Indentures help anticipate repayment problems by forcing problems to the forefront before the bondholders incur economic loss.

A technical default is an inexact term referring to a noneconomic default. These defaults represent a violation of procedural covenants, not a loss of timely principal and interest payments. There is a linkage, however. A technical default "ripens into an Event of Default after notice has been given to the issuer for the commencement of the grace period and, after a lapse of time, the default remains uncured" (Spiotto 1993, sec. 13.42).

Spiotto (1993) isolates three default phases. The first phase involves gathering information on the reasons for the default. Also, it helps to take steps to correct any defected security for the debt. For example, in 1983 the Washington Public Power Supply System (WPPSS) defaulted on $2.25 billion of municipal bonds used to finance two nuclear power plants. The precipitating factor in the largest municipal default in history was state court action. The court invalidated power sales agreements requiring several public utilities to take electricity from WPPSS nuclear plants, at WPPSS prices, or pay even without taking power (termed "take or pay" contracts). These agreements offered the security upon which WPPSS borrowed money to build the electric generation power facilities. As a direct result of the court's action, the WPPSS financial plan collapsed, leading to a default on the associated bonds. As the WPPSS case shows, actions that impair the security of bonds increase the probability of default. In contrast, action taken to correct the defective security improves the odds of avoiding a default. However, correcting defective features at this late stage of a project's financial history may not be easy.

The second phase involves attempts to work out of the default. The goal is for bondholders and the debt issuer to resolve their differences. A workout occurs "when the parties agree that their financial interests are best served by restructuring the borrower's debt and reorganizing its operation" (General Accounting Office 1984, p. 39). An example is the mayor who kept all the parties to a troubled waste-to-energy enterprise talking, instead of litigating, while restructuring the project's finances (Hildreth 1994).

The third stage occurs when there is a workout failure. In this last phase, bondholders' assert their rights to obtain payment. This includes calling the bonds due and payable immediately (acceleration of payments using the full force of litigation to uphold their interests). Litigation often follows, with suboptimal resolution for all parties. In the WPPSS example, years of litigation and settlements yielded bondholders less than the desired returns.

Municipal securities default, but at a lower dollar amount than corporate bonds, despite the much larger size of the municipal market. Defaults in the municipal securities market, however, raise questions well beyond the local community. A municipal bond default tests the interests of bondholders and the state and federal governments. Bondholders are many and often scattered (in an economically random process) around the country. This makes bondholders the constituents of many public officials, who try to respond to public pressure. In addition, a municipal bond issuer is either a state government or a state-created political entity (for example, a municipality, county, or statutory agency), thus justifying state monitoring and fiscal control (see **financial emergency**).

The legal status of the municipal market rests with the federal government. Congress has the power to eliminate the tax-exempt securities market (*South Carolina v. Baker,* 1988). As the search intensifies for more U.S. income tax receipts to aid in the federal deficit reduction effort, the tax expenditures associated with the tax-exempt market are enticing targets (Carter and Hildreth 1992). Therefore, financial emergencies and defaults give Congress and the president ammunition for imposing tighter federal supervision over municipal securities.

Disclosure is central to federal securities law and the functioning of efficient capital markets. Yet, federal securities regulation is weaker for the municipal market than for corporate bonds. In a theme reminiscent of its earlier report on New York City's debt problems, the U.S. Securities and Exchange Commission's report on circumstances surrounding the WPPSS default noted systematic disclosure problems in the municipal securities industry and deficient disclosures to WPPSS investors (U.S. Securities and Exchange Commission 1977 and 1988). The WPPSS report questioned whether the bond disclosure documents adequately revealed significant facts regarding the projects. Without adequate disclosure, investors are unable to make an intelligent decision regarding the probability of repayment. Thus, defaults have encouraged federal securities regulators to assert tighter regulation over the municipal securities market (U.S. Securities and Exchange Commission 1993).

Municipal debt defaults are the culmination of legal, economic, political, managerial, and financial problems (see generally Hillhouse 1936; Hemple 1971; Advisory Commission on Intergovernmental Relations 1973 and 1985). Although the court's invalidation of the power sales agreements was the legal event that precipitated the WPPSS default, the original energy demand estimates were unrealistic, the political pressures to keep low power rates were high and growing, project schedules were too hard to maintain, and the escalating project costs occurred in a high interest rate environment (see Jones 1984; Myhra 1984). In Cleveland, the city defaulted on the repayment of short-term notes (not bonds). While the Cleveland default occurred during a highly charged political debate between the mayor and the local banks holding the notes, the city faced significant underlying managerial and financial

problems (see Swanstron 1985). Municipal defaults, therefore, reflect underlying problems that, left unresolved, can impose a burdern on investors.

W. BARTLEY HILDRETH

BIBLIOGRAPHY

Advisory Commission on Intergovernmental Relations, 1973. *City Financial Emergencies: The Intergovernmental Dimension.* Washington, D.C.: U.S. Government Printing Office.
———, 1985. *Bankruptcies. Defaults, and Other Local Government Financial Emergencies.* Washington, D.C.: U.S. Government Printing Office.
Carter, Rosalyn Y. and W. Bartley Hildreth, 1992. "The Evolving Regulatory Environment of State and Local Tax-Exempt Securities." *Public Budgeting and Financial Management,* vol. 4:491–527.
General Accounting Office, 1984. *Guidelines for Rescuing Large Failing Firms and Municipalities.* Washington, D.C.: U.S. Government Printing Office.
Hempel, George H., 1971. *The Postwar Quality of State and Local Debt.* New York: National Bureau of Economic Research.
Hildreth, W. Bartley, 1994. "The Gordian Knot of a Project Revenue Bond Default." In Aman Khan and W. Bartley Hildreth, eds., *Case Studies in Public Budgeting and Financial Management.* Dubuque, IA: Kendall/Hunt Publishing Company, pp. 403–421.
Hillhouse, A. M., 1936. *Municipal Bonds.* New York: Prentice-Hall, Inc.
Jones, Larry R., 1984. "The WPPSS Default: Trouble in the Municipal Market." *Public Budgeting and Finance,* vol. 4 (Winter) 60–77.
Myhra, David, 1984. *Whoops! WPPSS: Washington Public Power Supply System Nuclear Plants.* Jefferson, NC: McFarland & Company, Inc.
South Carolina v. Baker (1988). U.S. Supreme Court, April 20.
Spiotto, James E., 1993. "Municipal Insolvency: Bankruptcy, Receivership, Workouts and Alternative Remedies." In M. David Gelfand, ed., *State and Local Government Debt Financing.*Vol. 3. Deerfield IL: Clark Boardman Callaghan, Sections 13:01–13:56.
Swanstrom, Todd, 1985. *The Crisis of Growth Politics: Cleveland, Kucinich and the Challenge of Urban Populism.* Philadelphia: Temple University Press.
United States Securities and Exchange Commission, 1977. *Staff Report on the Transactions in Securities of the City of New York.* Washington, D.C.: Securities and Exchange Commission.
———, 1988. *Staff Report on the Investigation in the Matters of Transactions inWashington Public Power Supply System Securities.* Washington, D.C.: Securities and Exchange Commission (September).
———, 1993. *Staff Report on the Municipal Securities Market.* Washington, D.C.: Securities and Exchange Commission.

DEFERENCE PRINCIPLE. A court doctrine used by judges to yield or defer to the judgment of agency administrators (experts). The deference principle is a basic doctrine in administrative law. It is rooted in the separation of powers doctrine and in plain common sense. In honor of the constitutional separation of powers doctrine and out of respect for the expertise of administrators, judges have relied upon the deference doctrine to guide their interpretations and applications of Section 706, "Scope of Review," dictates. Despite the tendency towards judicial activism, which has brought a general broadening of the courts' scope of review, deference to administrative authority and expertise by the courts is still the rule rather than the exception. As the 1980s began, Bernard Schwartz exclaimed: "Of course, the scope of review is normally dominated by the doctrine of deference to the agency. This has not yet been altered by the changed atmosphere that is starting to prevail in the regulatory area" (1986, p. 434). In the context of the Airline Deregulation Act of 1978 (92 Stat. 1075), which called for the gradual dissolution of the Civil Aeronautics Board, the D.C. Circuit Court in *Frontier Airlines v. CAB*, 602 F. 2d 375, 378–379 (1979) nevertheless acknowledged the applicability of the deference principle by stating: "New era or old, so long as the Board continues to be entrusted by Congress with the primary responsibility for the health of air transportation, it remains true that . . . courts have no special qualifications in this area for second-guessing the Board as to the merits of its determinations, once they have been arrived at within a framework of procedural fair play."

In this assertion the court paid recognition again to the solidly established principle that the courts should normally defer problems involving questions of fact, as contrasted to questions of law, to the judgment of administrators. Questions of fact basically pertain to the factual "what was" or "what is" evidence administrators need to evaluate in order to reach rational decisions. In contrast, questions of law essentially relate to the ways in which laws affect the "what was" and "what is" evidence, focusing on how laws apply to the evidentiary facts. Typical administrative law questions pertain to administrative jurisdictional and procedural due process considerations, particularly in regard to the use of administrative discretion, and in the specific context of constitutional, statutory, and common law mandates. Thus, the Frontier Airlines case conveys the message that the deference principle is applied to limit the court's scope of review over administrative decisionmaking, just as it was in the precedential case *Gray v. Powell*, 314, U.S. 402 (1941), where Justice Stanley F. Reed, speaking for the Court, wrote: "Where, as here, a determination has been left to an administrative body, this delegation will be respected and the administrative conclusion left untouched. . . . Although we have here no dispute as to the evidentiary facts, that does not permit a court to substitute its judgment for that of the Director" (at 412). Justice Reed concluded that "it is the Court's duty to leave the Commission's judgment undisturbed" (at 413).

The courts in the 1980s, as contrasted to the 1960s and 1970s, expressed a greater willingness to defer to agency discretionary authority and expertise. This was especially true for the Supreme Court, as a few cases should make clear. In *United States v. Erika, Inc.,* 102 S.Ct. 1650 (1982), the Supreme Court held that it was the clear intention of Congress to have the courts limit their scope of review by deferring to agency expertise in regard to the determination of benefits under Part B of the Medicare program. In *Capital Cities Cable, Inc. v. Crisp*, 104 S. Ct. 2694 (1984), the high court stressed that courts should defer to agency discretion when Congress has sanctioned such discretion. Quoting from *Fidelity Federal Savings and Loan Assn. v. de la Cuesta*, 458 U.S. 141 (1982), the Court exclaimed: "Where Congress has directed an administrator to exercise his discretion, his judgments are subject to judicial review only to determine whether he has exceeded his statutory authority or acted arbitrarily" (at 2700). In the famous precedential case *Chevron, U.S.A., Inc. v. Natural Resources Defense Council*, 104 S.Ct. 2778 (1984), the Supreme Court deferred to the expertise of the Environmental Protection Agency, contending that "considerable weight should be accorded to an executive department's construction of a statutory scheme it is entrusted to administer, and the principle of deference to administrative interpretations" (at 2782). In *Regents of the University of Michigan v. Ewing*, 106 S.Ct. 507 (1985), the Supreme Court emphasized that utmost deference should be accorded academic institutions to protect their academic freedom. "When judges are asked to review the substance of a genuinely academic decision . . . they should show great respect for the faculty's professional judgment. Plainly, they may not override it unless it is such a substantial departure from accepted academic norms as to demonstrate that the person or committee responsible did not actually exercise professional judgment" (at 13). And in *FTC v. Indiana Federation of Dentists*, 106 S. Ct. 2009 (1986), the Court asserted that although the courts are entrusted with reviewing legal issues in agency disputes, they "are to give some deference to the Commission's informed judgment that a particular commercial practice is to be condemned as "unfair"" (at 2016). However, in *Bowen v. American Hospital Assn.*, 106 S.Ct. 2101 (1986), the Supreme Court acknowledged that although considerable use has been made of this deference principle, "agency deference has not come so far that we will uphold regulations whenever it is possible to 'conceive a basis' for administrative action" (at 2112).

The actual impact of *Chevron* on the courts' willingness or unwillingness to defer to agency discretion and expertise is open to question. However, evidence does suggest that despite so much judicial and academic rhetoric supporting the deference principle, many courts seem to ignore the Chevron doctrine and insist on playing an active public policymaking role. And, of course, this is the chief question raised by *Chevron*. Should courts readily defer to agency expertise when statutes seem to be ambiguous, allowing agency administrators to exercise broad discretion in interpreting statutes or the intent of Congress, or should the courts take the responsibility of interpreting vague statutes?

Despite considerable noncompliance with the Chevron doctrine by the lower courts, at least the Supreme Court in the 1990s has continued to uphold the wisdom of *Chevron*. In *Pauley v. Bethenergy Miner, Inc.*, 111 S. Ct. 2524 (1991) the Supreme Court argued that *Chevron* should be followed because the judiciary should play a very limited role in making public policies and interpreting statutes is very much a part of the public policymaking process that Congress reserved for public agencies, not the courts. Specifically citing *Chevron*, the Court summarized its position on deference: "Judicial deference to an agency's interpretation of ambiguous provisions of the statutes it is authorized to implement reflects a sensitivity to the proper roles of the political and judicial branches . . . '[F]ederal judges–who have no constituency–have a duty to respect legitimate policy choices made by those who do'). . . . As *Chevron* itself illustrates, the resolution of ambiguity in a statutory text is often more a question of policy than of law. . . . When Congress, through express delegation or the introduction of an administrative gap in the statutory structure, has delegated policymaking authority to an administrative agency, the extent of judicial review of the agency's policy determination is limited" (at 253).

But what perplexes so many about the reasoning in *Chevron* is that it is also true that "the resolution of ambiguity in a statutory text" is often more a question of law than of policy. This makes applying *Chevron* difficult for some judges, especially those who are predisposed to thinking that it is more up to the courts to interpret ambiguous statutes because, after all, what are the courts for?

KENNETH F. WARREN

BIBLIOGRAPHY

Schwartz, Bernard, 1980. "Administrative Law Cases During 1979," *Administrative Law Review*, vol. 32 (Summer).
Warren, Kenneth F., 1996. *Administrative Law in the American System*, 3d ed. Upper Saddle River, NJ: Prentice Hall.

DEFERRED GIVING.

A binding legal arrangement whereby a charity receives a contribution after a period of time, usually after a fixed number of years or upon the death of an individual. It is also referred to as a "planned gift."

Overview

Wealthy donors in the United States often make deferred gifts, partly because they are granted very favorable tax benefits. Deferred gifts are much less common in the rest of the world, possibly because they do not qualify for such tax benefits (see **charitable contributions**).

Most deferred gifts pay income to a donor over the donor's life and then distribute the remaining assets to a charity upon the donor's death. Since a portion of the property is used for noncharitable purposes, there is only a partial charitable tax deduction: the present value of the remainder interest that will pass to charity. For example, a donor can deposit $100,000 into an eligible charitable deferred giving arrangement and may be able to claim an immediate income tax deduction for $40,000, assuming that is the present value of the remainder interest that will pass to charity.

Eligible Deferred Giving Arrangements

A deferred giving arrangement must be carefully structured because the tax laws generally prohibit a tax deduction for a gift of a "partial interest in property" to a charity. For example, no deduction is allowed for a contribution to an ordinary trust that will pay income to an individual and then will distribute the remainder interest to a charity. Congress concluded in 1969 that the trustees of such trusts had too much discretion to favor the noncharitable beneficiaries over the charitable ones. It therefore limited the range of tax-deductible deferred giving arrangements to a few situations that give trustees much less discretion.

The principal deferred giving arrangements that qualify for an immediate income, gift or estate tax charitable deduction under current law are:

Charitable Remainder Annuity Trust. A tax-exempt trust that pays a fixed dollar amount (at least 5 percent of the value of the property contributed to the trust) each year to one or more income beneficiaries for life (or for a fixed term of years–maximum 20), after which the remaining proceeds are distributed to one or more charitable organizations.

Charitable Remainder Unitrust. A tax-exempt trust that pays a fixed percentage (at least 5 percent) of the value of the trust's assets each year (as valued at the beginning of each year) to one or more income beneficiaries for life (or for a fixed term of years–maximum 20), after which the remaining proceeds are distributed to one or more charitable organizations.

Charitable Remainder Net-Income Unitrust. A tax-exempt trust that pays the lesser of that year's net income or a fixed percentage (at least 5 percent) of the value of the trust's assets each year (as valued at the beginning of each year) to one or more income beneficiaries for life (or for a fixed term of years–maximum 20), after which the remaining proceeds are distributed to one or more charitable organizations. The trust instrument may contain a "make-up" provision for years when net income is less than the stated percentage, although this is not required. These trusts are well suited for gifts of hard-to-sell assets, such as real estate or closely held stock, that may produce very little investment income until they are sold.

Pooled Income Fund. A trust maintained by a public charity that operates like a mutual fund. Income beneficiaries receive their proportionate share of the actual net income generated by the entire fund over their lives. Upon the death of an income beneficiary, the assets allocated to that person's account are separated from the fund and transferred to the charity.

Charitable Gift Annuity. A contract between a person and a charity under which the charity pays a fixed dollar amount each year over the life of one person (or two). Whereas payments usually begin shortly after a contribution is received, it is possible to have a "deferred gift annuity" with larger payments beginning at a later date (e.g., age 65).

Other Deferred Gifts. There are a few other deferred gifts hat qualify for tax deductions despite the general prohibition against gifts of partial interests in property.

- A person can claim an immediate tax deduction for a gift of a remainder interest in a personal residence or a farm. With such a gift, the person can continue to live in the residence of farm until his or her death, at which time the charity owns the property. Charities rarely accept such gifts since there can frequently be disputes over maintenance and repair costs, such as whether a new roof should be put on the property and who will pay for it.
- A donor can deduct a contribution of a partial interest in property if it constitutes the donor's only rights to that property. For example, if all that a donor owns is a remainder interest in property, the donor can claim a tax deduction for a contribution of the entire remainder interest.

Charitable Lead Trust. This is the inverse of a charitable remainder trust: the trust pays income to a charity for a period of years and then the remainder interest is distributed to non-charitable beneficiaries. It is used almost exclusively for estate and gift tax savings; it is only rarely used for income tax purposes.

The most popular form of deferred gifts are charitable remainder trusts, followed by charitable gift annuities and pooled income funds. A 1993 National Committee on Planned Giving study (reported in the *Chronicle of Philanthropy*) reports that the percentages of types of deferred gifts made by donors are:

- Charitable remainder annuity trusts   30.6 percent
- Charitable remainder unitrusts   27.8 percent
- (42 percent of which are net-income unitrusts)
- Charitable gift annuities   22.9 percent
- Pooled income funds   9.7 percent

- Other (installment sales, charitable lead trusts)   9.0 percent

There are currently over 36,000 charitable remainder trust that hold over $8 billion of assets (*Tax Notes Today 1991*).

Amount of Tax Deduction

Since a portion of a donor's gift to a deferred giving arrangement is used for noncharitable purposes, there is only a partial charitable deduction: the present value of the remainder interest that will pass to charity. The amount of the deduction can change dramatically from one month to the next, because the present value is computed based on the market interest rate that is in effect in the month that the property is contributed.

Generally a contribution to a unitrust will produce a smaller tax deduction than a comparable gift to a similar charitable remainder annuity trust or a charitable gift annuity. The amount of the tax deduction for a contribution to a pooled income fund depends upon the investment performance of that fund over the preceding three years.

How Charities and Estate Planners Promote Tax Advantages of Deferred Giving Arrangements to Donors

Deferred giving arrangements provide donors with many benefits in addition to a charitable tax deduction. Attention is principally paid to charitable remainder trusts since they are tax-exempt and the donor can have a greater voice on how the trust's assets will be invested.

Some of the benefits that estate and financial planners have cited to promote deferred charitable gifts include the following:

- A donor can claim an immediate tax deduction for a gift that a charity will not receive for many years. If a donor was going to make a bequest to a charity, the donor could instead contribute the property to a deferred giving arrangement and claim a current income tax deduction even though the donor will retain much of the income generated by the property over the rest of the donor's life.
- A deferred giving arrangement permits the tax-free conversion of appreciated low-yield growth assets into high-yield income-producing assets, which can be beneficial either at retirement or shortly before a major asset is about to be sold. For example, a donor may have purchased growth stock for $50,000 twenty years ago that is currently worth $1,000,000, but which pays no dividends. If the donor sells the stock, there will be a large capital gains tax and only a portion of the sales proceeds will be available to invest in income-

producing assets. Instead the donor could contribute the stock to a tax-exempt charitable remainder trust with instructions to make sizable annual distributions. The tax-exempt trust could sell the stock free from tax, so that the donor would have more investment income each year. In addition, the donor could claim a partial income tax charitable tax deduction for a portion of the value of the property.

■ A "wealth replacement" plan permits the tax-free conversion of the donor's investments and permits both the heirs and the charity to inherit substantial amounts. The heirs might complain that a gift to a deferred giving arrangement will mean that they will inherit less. One solution is a wealth replacement plan. This is where the donor gives appreciated property to the deferred giving arrangement, just as was done in the preceding example. The donor then uses the tax refund produced by the income tax charitable deduction to purchase a life insurance policy that names the heirs as the beneficiaries.

Charitable Remainder Trusts

The donor usually selects the trustee of a charitable remainder trust. The trustee can be the donor under some circumstances. Charities currently act as trustees of 32 percent of charitable remainder trusts and donors are trustees of 25 percent (*Chronicle of Philanthropy* 1993). Individuals other than donors are the trustees of 31 percent of the trusts; banks are trustees of only 11 percent. A donor can also retain the power to replace a trustee with a new trustee and to replace the remainder recipient charity with a new charity. Such rights must be mentioned in the trust instrument, since it is virtually impossible to amend the trust after it is established.

The maximum term of the trust is either (1) the lives of the individuals who are income beneficiaries or (2) a term not to exceed 20 years. If multiple individuals are named as income beneficiaries, it is possible to name each person as a successor beneficiary, provided that each person is alive when the trust is established. For example, the trust could make payments to the donor's spouse for life, then to the donor's child for life. Alternatively, payments can be distributed concurrently among named beneficiaries or among a class of beneficiaries, such as the donor's children.

A charitable remainder trust is exempt from income tax. Consequently, if the investment income exceeds the amount distributed to the beneficiary, the excess may be accumulated in the trust free from income tax. Accumulated income will generally be distributed to the charity upon the termination of the trust, unless it is needed for a distribution to an income beneficiary in a year when the current income is insufficient to meet the required payout.

A charitable remainder trust is subject to some, but not all, of the excise taxes that apply to private founda-

tions. It is subject to the excise tax on self-dealing and taxable expenditures but is usually exempt from the excise tax on excess business holdings, jeopardy investments, and minimum annual charitable distributions (see **private foundations**).

The IRS takes the position that in order to have a valid charitable remainder annuity trust, there must be more than a 5 percent probability that the charitable remainder recipient will actually receive something. In other words, a donor cannot set the payout to income beneficiaries so high that the trust assets will likely be exhausted before the income beneficiary dies. For example, a donor cannot require a 13 percent annual payout at a time when interest rates are only 8 percent. By comparison, charitable remainder unitrusts are not subject to this restriction because they distribute a percentage of their existing assets, so that, at least in theory, there will always be some assets in the trust. However, the IRS has publicly stated that it will intervene if it determines that a charitable remainder unitrust is abusive.

A donor can only make one contribution to an annuity trust. By comparison, it is possible to make additional contributions to a unitrust.

Taxation of Income Beneficiaries

There is a special four-tier rule for distributions from charitable remainder trusts. The net effect of the four-tier rule is to have as much of the distribution as possible be taxable before the income beneficiary receives anything that is tax-exempt (e.g., corpus).

The four-tier distribution rule provides that amounts distributed by a charitable remainder trust shall have the following characteristics to the income beneficiary:

1. First, as amounts of income (e.g., interest, dividends, and other income, but not capital gains) received in the current year as well as undistributed income that has been accumulated in prior years.
2. Second, as a capital gain to the extent of the capital gain for the year and the undistributed capital gain of the trust for prior years:
3. Third, as other income (such as tax-exempt municipal bond interest) to the extent of such income for the year and undistributed income of the trust for prior years; and
4. Fourth, as a distribution of trust corpus.

Pooled Income Funds

A pooled income fund is a trust maintained by a specific type of public charity that commingles deferred gifts made by donors to that charity. It is similar to a mutual fund. Contributions from various donors are pooled into the fund and an account is established for each income beneficiary. The beneficiary then receives a proportionate share of the income generated by the entire fund over that person's life. Upon the death of the income beneficiary, the balance in the account is removed from the fund and is transferred to the charity that maintains the fund. By accepting contributions from numerous donors, a pooled income fund can accept smaller contributions from each donor than a charitable remainder trust, which usually receives contributions from only one donor.

Whereas a charitable remainder trust is established by a donor with a trustee selected by the donor, a pooled income fund must be established and maintained by the public charity that will receive the remainder interest. This rule is satisfied if the charity selects, and has the power to replace, the trustee. Congress's logic was that the charity's self-interest will prevent any abuse by a trustee to favor a noncharitable income beneficiary over the charitable remainder beneficiary. Consequently, pooled income funds are the only sanctioned deferred gifts that distribute actual net investment income. The other deferred giving arrangements only distribute relatively rigid amounts to the income beneficiaries.

A pooled income fund is a trust that consists entirely of contributions of property, where each donor (1) transfers an irrevocable remainder interest in the contributed property to a public charity; and (2) retains an income interest for the life of one or more beneficiaries (usually the donor and the donor's spouse) who are alive at the time of the transfer. As with a charitable remainder trust, payments may be made over concurrent or successive lives to income beneficiaries. However, unlike a charitable remainder trust, payments may not be made over a fixed term of years.

The property transferred by each donor must be commingled with property transferred by other donors. The pooled income fund can sell and reinvest the sales proceeds from contributed property. Although a pooled income fund can hold most forms of property, it is prohibited from ever holding tax-exempt securities. It must also establish a depreciation reserve if it holds, or is willing to accept, contributions of depreciable assets. Many charities simply refuse to accept contributions of depreciable property as a way to deal with this requirement.

Despite being controlled by a public charity, a pooled income fund is subject to the same private foundation excise taxes as a charitable remainder trust. It is subject to the excise tax on self-dealing and taxable expenditures but it is usually exempt from the excise tax on excess business holdings and jeopardy investments.

Unlike a charitable remainder trust, a pooled income fund is not a tax-exempt trust. A pooled income fund avoids paying income tax by distributing all of its net income. Since its income distribution deduction is usually equal to its net income, no tax is due.

There is, however, special treatment for long-term capital gains of a pooled income fund. If the trust instrument provides that long-term capital gains will be added to the corpus (so that it will eventually be distributed to the remainder beneficiary: the public charity), then the trust may claim a charitable income tax deduction for this amount. The trust instruments of most pooled income funds contain such a provision. However, the charitable income tax deduction does not extend to short-term capital gains and the trust may be liable for tax. A common solution is to provide that short-term capital gains will be distributed to income beneficiaries so that the trust may claim an income.

Taxation of Beneficiaries

Distributions from pooled income funds are treated the same as distributions from conventional trusts. The income beneficiaries receive a Schedule K-1 that indicates the portion of their income that was derived from interest, dividends, rents, etc.

Charitable Gift Annuities

A charitable gift annuity is a contract that obligates a charity to pay fixed annual payments to a donor for the rest of the donor's life. Charities have been paying annuities to donors for over a century. Religious organizations and universities have traditionally issued the largest number of gift annuities but recently other charities have begun to issue them. A 1994 survey found that religious organizations had 8.369 annuities outstanding with average annual payments of $12,854. Public and private colleges had 3,359 annuities outstanding with average annual payments of $33,019 (*Chronicle of Philanthropy*, 1995).

Probably the most controversial legal issue during the 1990s is whether a charitable gift annuity constitutes an investment security that is subject to regulation by state and federal authorities. A charity should examine its state law before it begins a charitable gift annuity program.

Charities generally find charitable gift annuities much easier to administer than other forms of deferred gifts, such as charitable remainder trusts and pooled income funds. For example, there is no need to file a separate tax return or to establish a separate trust. In some states, however, the laws that regulate these annuities make the administration more complicated.

Some charities take part of a donor's contribution and immediately purchase a commercial annuity that will satisfy the charity's obligation to make payments to the donor. This reduces the charity's financial risk and also allows it to spend or invest the difference as a charitable contribution immediately. However, many charities have found that they will accumulate a greater amount by administering the gift annuity program by themselves.

Because the value of a charitable gift annuity is significantly less than the value of a commercial annuity, donors may claim a partial charitable tax deduction for the pur-

chase of the annuity. As is the case with charitable remainder trusts and pooled income funds, the amount of the deduction is the present value of the amount that is projected to be paid to the charity, in light of market interest rates at the time of the contribution.

Determining the Amount of Annuity Payments

Nearly 90 percent of the charities that issue gift annuities follow the guidelines that are recommended by the American Council on Gift Annuities (formerly the Committee on Gift Annuities). That organization meets every three years to reexamine annuity tables in light of changing mortality rates and interest rates. Its general practice has been to compute annuity payouts so that a charity can expect to receive half of the original contribution upon a donor's death.

Although a charity can choose to either accept or reject the guidelines of the American Council on Gift Annuities, it must follow certain tax laws or there could be complications. First, an annuity should qualify as a charitable gift annuity in order to protect the charity from an argument that it is selling taxable commercial insurance. Of greater significance to most charities, a contribution in exchange for an annuity could produce unrelated debt-financed income that could cause a charity to be liable for income tax. Consequently most charities follow the requirements of Section 514(c)(5) to avoid paying that tax.

The statute requires that:

■ The value of the annuity must be less than 90 percent of the value of the property contributed by the donor;

■ The annuity must be paid over one life or a maximum of two lives;

■ The contract cannot guarantee a minimum or maximum amount of payments; and

■ The contract cannot change the amount of payments based on the income produced by the property contributed by the donor, or based on any other variable.

Taxation of Beneficiaries

Distributions from a charitable gift annuity are taxed in the same manner as a commercial annuity. Thus, most payments are treated as ordinary income except for the portion that is a return of the donor's contribution. If a donor contributed cash, then the portion of each payment that represents a return of the contribution is tax-free. If the annuity was acquired with a lifetime gift of appreciated capital gain property (such as stock), then each annuity installment will have three tax consequences: part ordinary income, part capital gain, and part tax-fee return of capital.

Example of a cash contribution: Ms. Donor is 60 years old and has a remaining life expectancy of 24 years. she contributed $100,000 cash to acquire a charitable gift annuity that will pay her $7,000 each year for the rest of her life.

If the value of the annuity is $60,000, based on the interest rates in effect in the month of the contribution, then she can claim an immediate charitable income tax deduction for the charitable component of $40,000. As she receives her payment of $7,000, she will have taxable annuity income of $4,500 (64.4 percent of each payment) and the remaining $2,500 (35.6 percent) of each payment is a tax-free return of her original $60,000 contribution.

CHRISTOPHER HOYT

BIBLIOGRAPHY

The Chronicle of Philanthropy, 1993. "Many Donors Make Bequests Without Telling Charities, Study Finds." (August 10) 32.
———, 1995. "Battling a Lawsuit, National Organization Won't Recommend Annuity Payout Rates." Report on the 1994 Survey of Charitable Gift Annuities, 1995, by the American Council on Gift Annuities (May 18).
Tax Notes Today, 1991. "Transcript for July 24 Ways and Means Committee Hearing on Tax Simplification." (July 29) 141–158.

DEFICIT. Results when spending is greater than what is received in revenues for a fiscal year; a surplus results when revenues exceed spending. When spending and revenues are equal, the budget is said to be in balance or balanced.

In government, a deficit results when revenues do not equal expenditures at the end of the fiscal year. This is called an operating budget deficit. This deficit must be financed somehow; otherwise suppliers, employees, and others who depend on the commitment of government resources could not be cared for or paid. Usually governments issue debt instruments to pay for the deficit (see **debt, national**). Some jurisdiction have rainy day funds to provide for emergencies where more revenue is needed than provided by the current year's taxes (see **rainy day fund**). States and local governments are often prohibited by law from going into debt for operating budget expenses, but for the U.S. federal government operating budget deficits have been a fact of life since the Great Depression of the 1930s and World War II; the U.S. federal budget has been in a deficit position since 1969, and has been in a surplus position only eight times since 1930. For their part, even though guided by statutes forbidding deficits on operating budgets, state and local governments do not find it easy to come out even at the end of the fiscal year; often they must take draconian actions to cut down expenditures and sometimes they still run short-term deficits which are paid for out of the next year's funds; when their resources are not up to the burdens that political choices have imposed on them they may face various conditions of fiscal stress (see **financial emergency**, **municipal bonds**) and their ability to finance capital improvements by selling bonds may be impaired as their credit rating falls (see **credit rating, municipal bonds, policy** and **strategy**).

Using a separate capital budget for planning and financing capital purchases such as parks, highways, and buildings helps state and local governments keep their operating budgets in balance (see **capital budgeting**). The federal government does not maintain separate capital and operating budgets.

Until recently, a modest annual deficit was tolerated at the national level, but the growth of the national debt and the prospect that caring for an aging population will be even more expensive as the baby boom generation born after World War II begins to retire have stimulated efforts to enact a balanced budget amendment or register a path to a balanced budget in law. While these concepts have accumulated bipartisan support (see **balanced budget requirement**), the road to a balanced budget is very complex, and competing ideologies about the role of government, its size, and its cost are matters of great disagreement.

Furthermore, while annual operating deficits may be banished, no one envisions a substantial paydown of the national debt.

For the first 150 years, U.S. federal budgets were small and deficits were created by emergencies such as wars and depressions. When the emergency had passed, the debt it had caused was generally paid down. Except for periods of war (when spending for defense increased sharply), depressions, or other economic downturns (when receipts fell precipitously), the federal budget was generally in surplus until the Great Depression of the 1930s and World War II. While still stabilizing the currency and paying down Revolutionary War debt, the U.S. generated its first deficit in 1792 and there ware deficits during the war of 1812, the recession of 1838, the Civil War, the depression of the 1890s, and World War I (OMB 1995, p. 8). For its first 60 years as a nation (through 1849), cumulative budget surpluses and deficits yielded a net surplus of $70 million in the U.S. The Civil War, along with the Spanish-American War and the depression of the 1890s, resulted in a cumulative deficit totaling just under $1 billion during the 1850–1900 period.

Between 1901 and 1916, the budget hovered very close to balance every year. World War I brought large deficits that totaled $23 billion over the 1917–1919 period. The budget was then in surplus throughout the 1920s. However, the combination of the Great Depression followed by World War II resulted in a long, unbroken string of deficits that were historically unprecedented in magnitude. As a result, federal debt held by the public mushroomed from less than $3 billion in 1917 to $15.4 billion in 1930 and then to $242 billion by 1946. In relation to the size of the economy, debt held by the public grew from 16 percent of GDP in 1930 to 114 percent in 1946 (Budget FY 1997).

Aaron Wildavsky (1988) has argued that one of the legacies of the revolutionary war period was the creation of a balanced budget ideology in the United States that has basically been honored except in times of emergency

(Chap. 2). The history of the deficit seems to support his argument, at least through World War II. While there still may be a balanced budget culture, in point of fact deficits have been a constant since 1969.

During much of the nineteenth century, revenues could be raised from customs fees and import duties. This allowed policymakers to raise revenues from external sources while protecting the nation's infant industrial base and to pay out benefits internally. This was a relatively easy political choice. This system worked because the federal government's functions were few and favorable geography separated it from foreign entanglements not of its own choosing. As a result, in 1930, federal government outlays totaled $3.3 billion; the budget was in a surplus position (receipts were $4.1 billion); and the total debt held by the public was $15.4 billion New Deal programs led to a doubling of federal expenditures by 1934 ($6.5 billion) and a near tripling by 1940 ($9.5 billion). The shock of World War II almost quadrupled federal outlays by the end of 1942 ($35.1 billion) and that figure more than doubled by the end of 1943 to $78.6 billion. By the end of 1945 federal outlays were $92.7 billion and the deficit for that year was $47.6 billion. In this year alone, the operating deficit was larger than all the stock of debt prior to the beginning of World War II and the total national debt had reached $235.2 billion. From 1930 through 1996, surpluses occurred in only eight years; in 58 of these 66 years the budget was in a deficit position.

These trends are documented in Table I. The first column is the year, the second is outlays for that year, and the third is the deficit for that year. The fourth column shows the growth of total debt. Column five shows the deficit as a percent of GDP and the last column shows the growth of total debt as a percent of GDP. The chart illustrates the growth of deficits and debt. While total debt was small in 1940, its percentage of GDP was high (44.8 percent), illustrating the cumulative strain of the Great Depression. In 1945 and 1946 the cumulative debt was actually greater than the total GDP for those years; this is some indication of the cost to the United States of becoming the arsenal for democracy during World War II. The year 1943 represents the worst operating deficit year, where the deficit amounted to 31.1 percent of GDP. This level of effort would never be approached again in this century.

What the years 1980 through 1994 illustrate is the impact of relatively modest annual deficits; at the end of this period debt as a percentage of GDP had grown to just over 50 percent. When operating deficits are built into the budget year after year, they are referred to as structural deficits. Deficits that occur as a result of emergencies or underperformance in the economy so that revenues are less than predicted and unemployment and/or welfare expenditures are more may be called frictional deficits. Despite efforts to contain annual deficits, the last two decades of this century must be seen as a period of structural deficits.

As the responsibility of the federal government grew, the size and complexity of the budget increased, and deficits became an annual event, attention changed from the dollar amount of the deficit to measurement of the deficit as a percentage of gross domestic product. The theory was that the size of the deficit only mattered in relation to the ability of the country to carry the debt load. Steven Mufson (1991) argues that from 1947 through 1980, both Democrats and Republicans tacitly agreed that the deficit should not exceed 1 percent of GDP in time of prosperity; in fact, the average for the entire period was less than 1 percent of GDP (.86 percent). Thus while the ideology of a balanced budget continued, actual outcomes resulted in a marginal deficit.

This profile changed in the 1980s with the election of President Ronald Reagan and the combination of the defense buildup, an income tax cut and a recession. Deficits in the early 1980s reached sizes basically unknown since World War II and the accumulation of annual deficits caused the national debt to quintuple in a decade. The size of the annual deficit and the growth of the debt became powerful political issues that were almost always at center stage from 1981 through 1996. Some observers believe that these issues preempted other policy issues and that efforts to contain the annual deficits prevented policymakers from considering other national issues. Some analysts believe this was an intended outcome of the Reagan revolution; if government could not be shrunk directly, then diminishing its revenue capacity would ultimately force the national government to do less. Others suggest that the real villains in this picture were entitlements (see **entitlement**), growth in the number of people who qualified for entitlements, the rising costs of medical care and its reflection in Medicare and Medicaid costs, and the perceived ownership of a full annual cost of living increase (see cost of living adjustment) for people in entitlement programs and on public pensions, such as Social Security.

For the period from 1980 through 1994, the deficit as a percentage of GDP averaged 4.1 percent. In 1995, interest on the national debt resulting from past deficits

TABLE I. DEFICITS AND THE GROWTH OF DEBT

Year	Outlay $ in Billions	Surplus or Deficit $ in Billions	Total Debt in Billions	Surplus or Deficit as % GDP	Total Debt as % of GDP
1930	3.3	+0.7	15.4	.8	15.9
1940	9.5	−2.9	42.8	−3.1	44.8
THE IMPACT OF WWII					
1941	13.7	−4.9	48.2	−4.4	42.9
1942	35.1	−20.5	67.8	−14.5	47.8
1943	78.6	−54.6	127.8	−31.1	72.8
1944	91.3	−47.6	184.8	−23.6	91.6
1945	92.7	−47.6	235.2	−22.4	110.9
1946	55.2	−15.9	241.9	−7.5	113.8
THE DEFICIT YEARS 1980–1994					
1980	590.9	−73.8	709.8	−2.8	26.8
1981	678.2	−79	785.3	−2.7	26.5
1982	745.8	−128	919.8	−4.1	29.5
1983	808.4	−207.8	1131.6	−6.3	34.1
1984	851.8	−185.4	1300.5	−5.0	35.2
1985	946.4	−212.3	1499.9	−5.4	37.8
1986	990.3	−221.2	1736.7	−5.2	41.2
1987	1003.9	−149.8	1888.7	−3.4	42.4
1988	1064.1	−155.2	2050.8	−3.2	42.7
1989	1143.2	−152.5	2189.9	−2.9	42.3
1990	1252.7	−221.4	2410.7	−4.0	44.0
1991	1323.4	−269.2	2688.1	−4.7	47.4
1992	1380.9	−290.4	2998.8	−4.9	50.6
1993	1408.7	−255.1	3247.5	−4.1	51.9
1994	1460.9	−203.2	3432.2	−3.1	51.7

SOURCE: Extracted from *A Citizen's Guide,* FY 1996. Historical Summary, pp. 12–14

amounted to 15 percent of federal expenditures, the third largest single category in the federal budget, trailing only Social Security (22 percent) and defense (18 percent) (OMB 1996, p. 7). In the 1960s and 1970s net interest payments consumed about 7 percent of federal spending, less than half of current levels. While the federal government can afford this level of deficit, some observers worry that this level of interest payment has shifted money away from programs and frozen the will of government and its ability to come up with progressive policies and carry them out; they suggest that the U.S. is beginning to resemble developing countries where citizens labor to pay for past consumption and serve their creditors rather than invest in their future and the futures of their children. Others argue that the deficit debate has led to a much needed reexamination of the appropriate role and size of government in society.

JERRY McCAFFERY

BIBLIOGRAPHY

Budget of the U.S. Government, FY 1997: Historical Trends. Washington, D.C.: U.S. Government Printing Office.
Mufson, Steven, 1991. "The Thing That Wouldn't Die." *The Washington Post National Weekly Edition* (February 11–17) 6.
Office of Management and Budget (OMB), 1995. *A Citizen's Guide to the Federal Budget.* FY 1996. Washington, D.C.: U.S. Government Printing Office.
Wildavsky Aaron, 1988. *The New Politics of the Budgetary Process.* Boston: Scott, Foresman and Co.

DEINSTITUTIONALIZATION. The policy and practice of transferring incarcerated people from large, dense, homogeneous, restrictive environments to less restrictive, less crowded, heterogeneous environments. Outpatient mental health care and intermediate sentencing represent deinstitutionalization in the fields of mental health and criminal justice.

Institutionalization by the state was a nineteenth-century reform to care for society's outcasts, who had previously been cared for at home, by local governments, or not at all. The nineteenth-century vision of progress motivated reformers to assemble into a modern facility those people who exhibited behaviors that were unwanted of feared. Juveniles and adults who break the law, the mentally ill, the mentally retarded, and the aged are the categories of people usually institutionalized. Institutionalization was justified as a humane practice in caring for people who are unable or unwilling to conduct themselves in a societally approved manner, and whose roaming freely constitutes a risk to themselves or others. "Penitents" (hence the term "penitentiary") were to be given time alone, to reflect on and to improve their behavior.

Institutionalization is currently being described as an ineffective and/or inefficient way to deal with people who have difficulty caring for themselves or who exhibit socially inappropriate behavior. Issues of institutionalization versus deinstitutionalization face citizens and governments of all Western nations. Since criminal and statutory offenders differ from the mentally disabled and aged, these two categories will be discussed separately.

The Mentally Ill, the Mentally Retarded, and the Aged

According to the supporters of institutionalization, an isolated, supportive environment protects the mentally ill, mentally retarded, and the aged from abuse or neglect, and provides these people with caring, professional treatment. Perhaps some can be cured. Mental health and retardation institutions grew to meet societal demand, and as a result, people who were unruly, obstinate, or addicted to drugs and alcohol found themselves committed to these institutions, thereby turning these intended havens for rest and rehabilitation into the dumping ground for society's unwanted.

A large client population, coupled with deteriorating budgets to support caring and treatment, meant that harried mental health workers could do little more than act as warehouse custodians. By the 1960s cries for change came from across the ideological spectrum. Critics such as psychiatrist R. D. Laing (1969) and sociologist Erving Goffman (1961) considered incarceration inhumane. Institutionalization labeled the individual with a stigma, which the individual internalized into a self-concept, thereby inhibiting intellectual and emotional growth, and causing the client to become psychologically trapped in a dependency relationship with powerful caregivers. Incarcerated clients, kept in a restrained and dependent condition, were coerced to display acquiescent behavior to ease the task of the custodians. For critics such as Goffman and Laing, the institution was the problem, and the first step for improving mental health care was to close these places of confinement and to substitute an environment where the patient could gain self-respect and be challenged to grow.

Cost-conscious legislators attacked from a different direction, criticizing institutions as inefficient, a waste of taxpayers' money. The discovery (or rediscovery) of psychotropic drugs in the 1950s demonstrated that mood shifts and violent outbursts could be minimized by medication, so patients were less likely to be a danger to themselves or others, which undercut one argument for long-term incarceration. After undergoing crisis intervention and becoming stabilized on medication, the client could live with family, in a group home, or alone, without the need of highly trained professionals in attendance 24 hours daily. A professional case manager could serve as liaison and advocate for the client, connecting the client with the appropriate medical or social service. With emotional outbursts controlled through drug therapy, the mentally ill could not be readily distinguished from "normal" people. Community care would eliminate the labeling stigma, provide a challenging environment to stimulate growth and development, and reduce substantially the financial burden on the state.

Deinstitutionalized (outpatient) care aims to achieve the following three goals:

- treatment in the least restrictive setting possible;
- treatment at the lowest possible cost;
- supportive services available to clients.

Since mid-century institutionalization has been on the decline. Outpatient services have been established, including programs for families to learn to deal effectively with their disabled member. In some locations outpatient services are available 24 hours each day, and some studies have shown that after clients become accustomed to a de-institutionalized arrangement, they are satisfied and would not wish to return to the previous institutional arrangement.

A British study of the deinstitutionalized mentally ill found that patients' confidence in their medication to improve their condition had declined. The ability of the client to adopt a critical attitude toward medication indicates enhanced client self-esteem, a positive sign. The same study also argued that when patients have their own apartments and supportive staff available in a residential complex, they are more likely to behave according to societal expectations. Quality community care costs no more than institutional care (Murphy 1991).

Deinstitutionalization is currently the dominant policy for dependent populations throughout Europe and North America. Properly implemented, the aged and mentally ill are provided choice in living arrangements and access to short-term crisis care in a residential facility.

Criticisms of Deinstitutionalization

Critics of deinstitutionalization in the United States charge that although the goal of deinstitutionalizing the mentally disabled and aged is worthy, implementation has resulted in "transinstitutionalization"–moving dependent populations from a bad system of state institutions to a worse system of for-profit and not-for-profit facilities where only low cost is guaranteed, and services are minimal. Their rationale for why this occurs can be explained as follows.

The state contracts with the low cost bidder to serve the clients, so the decision frame is market-based. Markets operate efficiently to provide a variety of goods and services pleasing to customers under three conditions:

1. There are multiple sources of the goods and services demanded;
2. The purchaser has sufficient resources so that there is a real choice; and
3. The purchaser has the mental functioning to make a reasoned choice.

If (1) and (2) do not hold true, then (3) is irrelevant. Without meaningful choices, "freedom" rings hollow. In fact, because of changed workplace demographics and increased regulation, purchasers have limited choice. Outpatient residential care has changed from small-scale to large-scale. Until the recent past in the United States, to supplement their income, a family would take in as boarders one or two elderly or mentally disabled people. Typically, the host wife would not work outside the home. Now, women increasingly work outside the home, which has reduced the supply of home environments available for placement. Requirements for building codes, personnel qualifications, and attendant documentation that must be met by providers of residential services have driven the small-scale provider from the market. To cope with the wholesale discharge of patients from institutions, the typical provider of residential care now operates on a grand scale. The effect has been to substitute a private sector warehouse for a public sector warehouse.

Philosophically, critics charge that the deinstitutionalization model, which in the United States depends on for-profit or not-for-profit providers of residential services, rests upon self-interest rather than the public interest. Self-interest motivation in the absence of a meaningful market drives the level of services provided down to the minimum level required to maintain licensing. The more cheaply that services can be provided, the greater the profit. Without carefully written laws and public scrutiny, side payments may be made by entrepreneurs to patients, professionals, or political campaigns to enhance the likelihood of government contracts or to maintain a high occupancy rate in residential facilities for the dependent population.

In addition to the problem of inadequate residential care, concern has arisen over providing medical or psychological services on an outpatient basis. In the controlled environment of an institution, staff administers medication regularly to patients. With deinstitutionalization comes the freedom to escape, ignore, or forget needed medicine. If clients neglect their medications, they can revert to behaviors that harm themselves or others. One aspect of the homeless problem is former institutionalized psychiatric patients who are deinstitutionalized, fail to take their medications, and end up on the streets as perpetraters or victims of crime. Police officers called upon to deal with such mentally ill persons may have no place to take these vagrants other than to jail. A national study indicates that 7 percent of the jailed population in the United States suffers serious mental illness (Torrey et al. 1992).

What is the likely outcome of this debate over institutionalization? While the academic press is divided in its support, the popular press is dominated by calls for further deinstitutionalization. The pressure on political leaders at the federal and state levels to lower taxes and to increase expenditures for defense, education, or prisons drowns out the voice of the helpless. Advocacy groups are divided—some support community-based care (deinstitutionalization), while others support an inpatient system of institutional care to supplement deinstitutionalization, arguing that, in the absence of careful individual monitoring, deinstitutionalization is but a justification for abrogating the state's responsibility to its needy citizens.

In England the community care concept dominates. However, privatization has not been a part of the English system. Local governments have assumed responsibility, and quality of care varies randomly across the country. Costs are maintained by restricting access to the service, which means that some needy people are not well-served. the government is committed to the deinstitutionalization model, and large institutions are likely to close over the next decade.

Corrections

To title the administrative agency that handles adults and juveniles who ignore society's rules "correction(s)" implies a rehabilitative model. However, rather than rehabilitate, society's primary concern is to keep potential criminals off the street at the lowest possible cost. Although the public desires inmate rehabilitation, public opinion holds that attempts at rehabilitation have not been effective. Deinstitutionalization in corrections is driven not by rehabilitative values, but by the high cost of incarceration.

The commonly used term to reflect deinstitutionalization in corrections is "intermediate sentencing." Criminal justice scholars and practitioners are exploring various ways to protect society that avoid incarceration and probation, the two traditional means of disposing of criminal cases. Incarceration is expensive and does little to rehabilitate; probation is inexpensive but places the public at risk. Intermediate sentencing includes ideas such as home confinement, community service sentences, electronic monitoring, intensive supervision, and boot camps. Home confinement (sometimes called house arrest or community sentencing) is usually coupled with electronic monitoring and intensive supervision. Supervision varies by specific program, and ranges from a few contracts each month up to 50 contacts per week by an officer, either in person or by telephone. As a condition for intermediate sentencing, prisoners agree to community service work, electronic monitoring, curfew, and intensive supervision. The cost is about $15 per day per person, compared to halfway house costs of $35 per day per person. As long as prison populations continue to increase, confinement-monitoring-supervision will likely be used to minimize prison crowding. Drug testing is a part of most intermediate sentencing programs, and drug use, more often than commission of crime, causes revocation of the intermediate sentence.

Boot camps, a more recent alternative, are modeled on military basic training. Young first offenders spend three to six months under a strict regime of closely supervised physical activity and education. Convicts who cannot maintain

this disciplined schedule are returned to prison for longer sentences; those who complete the program are paroled. Although popular with the public, the effectiveness of these programs in reducing the recidivism rate has not yet been established.

Deinstitutionalization in corrections has two prime concerns—low cost and public safety—and these work against each other. Effective, low-cost means of protecting the public is an ongoing challenge which at present has no clear direction. The public must decide on the desired level of sentencing and incarceration. In the field of corrections, deinstitutionalization options at present cannot provide citizen protection to the extent available through incarceration.

Conclusion

Western nations are moving to deinstitutionalize dependent populations. Community care for the mentally ill and aged is rationalized as showing greater responsibility to and respect for the client, while at the same time slowing the rapid budget increases that accompany institutionalization. Prime questions about deinstitutionalization deal not with the goals and intentions of the movement, but with whether implementation of the goals results in clients being treated with greater respect (and thereby being satisfied with the service), whether citizens generally feel comfortable with the emotionally needy possibly missing their medications, and whether costs can be contained. In Europe, where service rationing occurs, can a larger proportion of the needy be extended the service without degrading the quality of the program?

In the criminal justice system, cost and citizen protection are the dominant considerations. Alternatives to institutionalization that do not compromise security are welcomed, and will likely be adopted quickly, perhaps with little prior testing.

It is not presently clear whether deinstitutionalization is the direction of the future, a passing fad, or one component of a strategy to deal with people who cannot or will not conform to the will of society. Perhaps of greater concern than the institutionalization versus deinstitutionalization debate is that cost factors appear to dominate quality of care factors in dealing with these clients. If a civilization is evaluated by the way it treats its least favored, how will we be judged?

ROBERT B. CUNNINGHAM

BIBLIOGRAPHY

American Behavioral Scientist, 1981. 24(6):721–842.
Byrne, James, Arthur Lurigio and Joan Petersilia, eds., 1992. *Smart Sentencing*. Newbury Park, CA: Sage.
Challis, David, Bleddyn Davies and Karen Traske, eds., 1994. *Community Care: New Agendas and Challenges from the UK and Overseas*. Aldershot, GB: Ashgate.

DeLeonardis, Ota and Diana Mauri, 1992. "From Deinstitutionalization to the Social Enterprise." *Social Policy* 23(2):50–54.

Goffman, Erving, 1961. *Asylums.* Garden City, NY: Anchor Books.

Halpern, Joseph, Karen Sackett, Paul Binner and Cynthia Mohr, 1980. *The Myths of Deinstitutionalization: Policies for the Mentally Disabled.* Boulder, CO: Westview Press.

Laing, R. D., 1969. *The Divided Self.* New York: Pantheon Books.

Lewis, Dan, Stephanie Riger, Helen Rosenberg, Hendrik Wagenaar, Arthur Lurigio and Susan Reed, 1991. *Worlds of the Mentally Ill.* Carbondale, IL: Southern Illinois Press.

McKnight, John, 1992. "Redefining Community." *Social Policy* 23(2):56–62.

Murphy, Elaine, 1991. *After the Asylums.* London: Faber and Faber.

Torrey, E. Fuller, Joan Stieber, Jonathan Ezekiel, Sidney Wolfe, Joshua Sharfstein, John H. Noble, and Laurie Flynn, 1992. "Criminalizing the Seriously Mentally Ill: The Abuse of Jails as Mental Hospitals." *Innovations and Research in Clinical Services, Community Support, and Rehabilitation* 2 (1) (Winter) 11–14.

DELEGATION DOCTRINE.

The doctrine applied by the courts that permits the legislature to transfer (delegate) some of its powers, especially its lawmaking power, to administrative agencies (see **agency**).

Background

The colonists in the future United States fought against what they considered an abuse of power by British governors in the colonies. As a result, the founding fathers made sure after the Revolutionary War that the powers granted to the executive branch were limited and controllable. This pattern was also established in the states. In some cases, state governors were not even given enough power to govern properly, a fact of political life which still plagues some governors today. But despite the fact that most state governors and even city mayors are still relatively weak, most governmental administrators today enjoy tremendous power—power that would almost certainly make the constitutional writers gasp with alarm.

The demand for public services caused government to increase, especially after President Franklin D. Roosevelt was elected and given a mandate by the people to employ administrative machinery to end the suffering caused by the Great Depression. As government expanded its operations and agency tasks became more specialized, legislators lost the ability and enthusiasm to scrutinize administrative activities as closely as they had done when governmental bureaucracy was smaller and simpler. To allow the president to lead and the government's bureaucracy to administer public programs expeditiously, U.S. legislators increasingly began to delegate and subdelegate their legislative powers to agency heads and their subordinates. But could legislative power be so delegated? Did this transfer of power from one branch to another violate the separation of powers doctrine, which seemed to be such a vital part of the U.S. Constitution?

Glen O. Robinson (1991) asserts that delegating legislative power to administrators has always presented a problem to liberal constitutionalists because concepts of trusteeship, rooted in English common law and Lockean theory, strictly prohibit the entrusted lawmaking power to be delegated away to undemocratically accountable administrators. Robinson notes that such "is a simple notion that requires no elaborate legal or political theory to defend, at least in principle. If the legislature is truly a trustee, any general transfer of entrusted power would seem a plain evasion of responsibility. The irresponsibility is heightened by the transfer of powers to a politically unresponsible bureaucracy" (p. 70). Of course, delegation is also restricted in theory by the separation of powers doctrine, which the founders regarded as fundamental to the U.S. Constitution.

A literalist look at the Constitution seems to indicate that the constitutional framers did not intend for the legislative branch to weaken itself by giving away its policy-making powers. The framers clearly made the legislative branch the strongest of the three branches, at least rhetorically. Article 1, Section 1 of the U.S. Constitution states clearly that "all legislative powers herein granted shall be vested in a Congress of the United States, which shall consist of a Senate and House of Representatives." Section 8 of the same article also makes clear that "the Congress shall have power . . . to make all laws which shall be necessary and proper for carrying into execution" all the enumerated powers listed in the section.

Article 1, Section 8 specifically grants to Congress the powers to collect taxes, borrow money, regulate commerce, coin money, establish post offices and post roads, declare war, raise and support armies, provide and maintain a navy, and so on. Could these specific powers be legally delegated to an administrative branch, thus encouraging the growth of vast bureaucratic power? Why did constitutional framers spell out what powers Congress should have if they did not really care who, for example, regulated commerce or maintained a navy? These questions are difficult to answer comfortably, especially since what was said in the Constitution and what was practiced by the constitutional framers clashed so sharply in the early years of the Republic, when many who developed the Constitution served as congressmen. Despite what was written in the Constitution, as soon as the framers became congressmen, they enacted legislation that had the effect of giving away some of their legislative powers. For example, they allowed the courts to make all the rules necessary for carrying out the business of the courts as long as their rules were not offensive or inconsistent with United States law. They authorized the president to regulate the provision of military pensions and establish pay scales for injured or disabled soldiers as he saw fit. The first Congress also delegated to the Secretary of the Treasury the power to handle fines and forfeitures under certain circumstances, and it permitted superintendents to license at their will persons deemed proper to carry out commercial intercourse with the Indians.

Before Curtiss-Wright: Court Ambivalence Toward Delegation

Ironically, especially in light of the rocky history of the delegation doctrine until well into the twentieth century, the first real challenge to the legitimacy of Congress to delegate legislative powers to administrators was overruled. In *The Cargo of the Brig Aurora, Brunside, claimant v. United States*, 11 U.S. (7 Cranch) 382 (1813), it was charged that the president should not be able, even under statutory authority, to determine when the Non-Intercourse Act of 1809 should come into force because this task is legislative in nature and not purely executive in function. Justice William Johnson held, however, that it would be improper for such discretion not to be granted to a president: "We can see no reason, why the legislature should not exercise its discretion in reviewing the act . . . either expressedly or conditionally, as their judgment should direct." In an extremely perceptive decision that even today sounds contemporary, Chief Justice John Marshall gave more support to the delegation doctrine in 1825, although his insightful decision was later overruled but then restored to some extent during the 1930s. In reflecting on the ability of Congress to handle all legislative tasks itself, Marshall commented: "It will not be contended that Congress can delegate to the courts, or to any other tribunal, powers which are strictly and exclusively legislative. But Congress may certainly delegate to others, powers which the legislature may rightfully exercise itself; the line has not been exactly drawn which separate those important subjects, which must be entirely regulated by the legislature itself, from those of less interest, in which a general provision may be made, and power given to those who are to act under such general provisions to fill up the details" (*Wayman v. Southward*, 23 U.S. (10 Wheat) 1, 15–16). When Marshall talked about distinguishing between "important subjects" and those which amount to only "provisions to fill up the details," he put his finger on the basic delegation doctrine controversy which is still argued heatedly among some scholars today. That is, what constitutes significant legislative activity by administrators? What types of legislative functions by administrators seem truly minor or quasi-legislative in character? This is an important distinction, especially for those persons who are interested in preserving the democratic operating procedures in government, because different answers to the question make meaningful differences in the way the U.S. system approaches the making of public policies.

The key to settling the dispute really centers around what the framers meant by "law" and what they felt con-

stituted the lawmaking function. In 1852 a judicial attempt was made to distinguish between laws that should only be made by legislators, and those "laws" (actually rules) that could be made by administrators. The position was taken that only legislators have the authority to make basic laws or determine what laws U.S. citizens should live under. It was argued that the power to decide on what "shall be" out laws should not be delegated: "The true distinction is between the delegation of power to make the law, which necessarily involves a discretion as to what it shall be, and conferring authority to discretion as to its execution to be exercised under and in pursuance of the law" (*Cincinnati, W. & Z. P. Co. v. Commissioner*, 1 Ohio St. 77, 88).

The Cincinnati case had the effect of helping to develop a nondelegation doctrine because it was held that legislators should not be allowed to permit those outside the legislative branch to engage in meaningful rulemaking that might infringe, even slightly, upon their policymaking powers. The opinion that significant legislative power should not be delegated was developed further in *Field v. Clark*, 143 U.S. 649 (1892), and *United States v. Shreveport Grain and Elevator Co.*, 287 U.S. 77 (1932). In these two cases the principle of nondelegation was upheld, although specific delegations were allowed. In Field the Court permitted the president to alter import duties at his discretion, yet acknowledged: "That Congress cannot delegate legislative power to the president is a principle universally recognized as vital to the integrity and maintenance of the system of government ordained by the Constitution" (at 1692). In Shreveport Grain and Elevator, a relatively recent case in terms of the long court history of delegation disputes, the Court paid lip service to the virtues of nondelegation, yet allowed "reasonable variations" so that the specific delegation could be upheld: "That the legislative power of Congress cannot be delegated is, of course, clear" (at 85). But Kenneth C. Davis (1977) argues that such court decisions have befuddled the status of delegation before the courts, "It is statements of this kind that have caused much of the difficulty in law development. Congress persisted in delegating, and the Court perceived that delegation was often necessary if the tasks of government were to be performed" (p. 34). Nevertheless, there exists a long list of cases, even since 1930, in which the courts have allowed the specific delegation and yet opposed delegation in principle.

But for practical reasons, and the courts admitted this by their actions, the nondelegation doctrine could not survive in a climate which demands that administrative agencies must occasionally act alone and devise rules and regulations so that the administrative process will not break down when implementing public programs. Administrators simply must make "shall be" policies themselves if their agencies are to be effective. It is difficult to imagine a practical administrative situation where all details, procedures, and so on, were anticipated and accounted for by Congress so that an administrator's sole task was to follow the prescribed course of action.

Since Schechter: Toward Broad Delegation

Today, various applications of doctrines limiting delegation are yielding to doctrines permitting broad delegation; the latter take into account the limited capabilities of legislators in watching over administrative activities and the problems of administering public programs if the administrator's hands are tied. Only twice in U.S. legal history did the courts find it appropriate to absolutely invalidate the delegation of power to public officials by Congress. And in both cases unusual circumstances prevailed because power was not delegated to a normal administrative agency that functioned according to established procedures. In *Panama Refining Co. v. Ryan,* 293 U.S. 388 (1935), unusual administrative chaos prevailed, while in *Schechter Poultry Corp. v. United States,* 295 U.S. 495 (1935), an unreasonable, excessive amount of delegated authority was involved. Nevertheless, in these cases the Supreme Court did declare the National Industrial Recovery Act of 1933 unconstitutional, arguing that it authorized the unconstitutional delegation of legislative powers to the president and an executive agency. At this point there was significant confusion over how far Congress could go in delegating its powers to the administrative branch.

But starting with *United States v. Curtiss-Wright Export Co.,* 299 U.S. 304 (1936), the courts have ruled consistently in favor of Congress's right to delegate authority, as long as Congress sets forth some meaningful standards to guide administrators in their efforts to implement governmental policies. For example, in *Sunshine Anthracite Coal Co. v. Atkins,* 310 U.S. 381 (1940) the Court noted that Congress must delegate some of its legislative powers to escape legislative futility. In *SEC v. Chenery Corp.,* 332 U.S. 194 (1947), the Court took the position that the delegation of legislative power is acceptable if administrators "strive to do as much as they reasonably can to develop and to make known the needed confinements of discretionary power through standards, principles, and rules." In *United States v. Southwestern Cable Co.,* 392 U.S. 157 (1968), the Court vaguely interpreted "standards" in terms of administering in a manner which is consistent with law as "public convenience, intent, or necessity requires."

It is interesting to acknowledge that frequently the courts bend to allow the inevitable to happen with legal sanctioning. During the New Deal days governmental bureaucracy was expanding rapidly to respond to public demands caused by the Great Depression. While the courts initially fought the trend, which involved a major transfer of public policymaking power from the legislative to the executive branch and the creation of an enormous, powerful public service system, they eventually yielded.

On the question of delegation, the reasoning behind the Chenery and Southwestern Cable Co. decisions has by now been widely accepted by the courts. These decisions, without doubt, have allowed administrative power to reach new heights in American society because although judges paid lip service to proper standards, their holdings did not define standards in a way that could effectively control abuses of administrative discretion. This has caused many legal scholars to worry over the possible emergence of uncontrollable, irresponsible, and oppressive administrative power, especially in light of a federal district court's upholding of the constitutionality of the Economic Stabilization Act of 1970. This act gave the president sweeping powers to "issue such orders and regulations as he may deem appropriate to stabilize prices, wages and salaries at levels not less than those prevailing on May 25, 1970." On August 17, 1971, President Richard Nixon did freeze all prices in the absence of any significant standards laid down by Congress. Believing that Nixon's actions were without precedent and clearly unconstitutional, the Amalgamated Meat Cutters Union brought suit, but the suit was flatly rejected by the court on the grounds that Congress had provided sufficient standards (*Amalgamated Meat Cutters v. Connally,* 337 F. Supp. 737, D.D.C., (1971).

In 1974, in *National Cable Assn. v. United States,* 415 U.S. 336, the Court felt that delegation of legislative power to administrative agencies was acceptable as long as "an intelligible principle" was attached. In this case Justice Thurgood Marshall seemed to even want to bury the nondelegation idea forever when he commented that nondelegation "was briefly in vogue in the 1930s, has been virtually abandoned by the Court for all practical purposes," and today "is surely as moribund as the substantive due process approach of the same era" (at 352–53). The spirit of Marshall's position was reiterated in *Algonquin SNG, Inc. v. Federal Energy Administration,* 518 F2d 1051, 1063 (1975): "Here the delegated power is broad, and Congress has had repeated opportunities to limit it or withdraw it altogether. It has not done so, and I think this court should not do so." Although this was said by Judge Robb in dissent, the United States Supreme Court later upheld the wisdom of this opinion in overturning the appeals court's majority (426 U.S. 548, 1976).

Justice Marshall is unquestionably right. The nondelegation doctrine is and has been dead since 1935. In fact, 15 years after Marshall pronounced the nondelegation definitely "very dead," the Supreme Court reaffirmed Marshall's pronouncement by noting: "After invalidating in 1935 two statutes as excessive delegations . . . we have upheld, again without deviation, Congress's ability to delegate power under broad standards" in *Mistretta v. United States,* 109 S.Ct. 647, 655 (1989).

Ironically, however, despite the "deadness" of the nondelegation doctrine, the Supreme Court agreed to hear several cases that focused upon the basic constitutional issues pertaining to delegation and the directly related issue of separation of powers. Presumably, the high court heard such cases because the conservative political climate during these years encouraged such old, basic constitutional questions pertaining to the very legitimacy of administrative power to be asked once again. The Supreme Court responded, but even this quite conservative court could not bring itself to reversing a well-established legal trend in complete support of broad delegation.

In *Mistretta,* for example, the Supreme Court upheld a broad delegation of discretionary legislative power to a Sentencing Commission, consisting of three federal judges, three academics, and one prison warden, all appointed by the president subject to Senate confirmation. Prisoners (Mistretta and others) argued that the Sentencing Reform Act (18 U.S.C.A., Sec. 3551 et req.) allowed Congress to delegate excessive legislative or policymaking discretion to the Commission in violation of Article 1, Section 1 of the U.S. Constitution, which prohibits Congress from delegating such basic lawmaking powers to another branch. But the Supreme Court disagreed, arguing "that the separation-of-powers principle, and the non-delegation doctrine in particular, do not prevent Congress from obtaining the assistance of its coordinate branches" (at 654). As long as an "intelligible principle" is attached to congressional delegations, the Court asserted, the delegation, however broad, is constitutional (at 654). The Court concluded "that in creating the Sentencing Commission . . . Congress neither delegated excessive legislative power nor upset the constitutionally mandated balance of powers among the coordinate Branches" (at 675).

In 1991 in *Touby v. United States,* 111 S.Ct. 1752, the Supreme Court upheld another broad delegation which allowed the Attorney General, under the provisions of the Comprehensive Drug Abuse Prevention and Control Act of 1970 [21 U.S.C.A., Sections 811(h), 812(b)], the discretionary authority to temporarily designate new controlled substances or "designer drugs" in order to avoid an "imminent hazard to the public safety." Petitioners argued that ". . . more than an 'intelligible principle' is required when Congress authorizes another branch to promulgate regulations that contemplate criminal sanctions." However, the Supreme Court concluded that the "intelligible principle" "passes muster even if greater congressional specificity is required in the criminal context" (at 1756). Reiterating what it said in *Mistretta,* the Court argued that "the nondelegation doctrine does not prevent Congress from seeking assistance, within proper limits, from its coordinate branches. Thus, Congress does not violate the Constitution merely because it legislates in broad terms, leaving a certain degree of discretion to executive or judicial actors" (at 1756).

Systems analysis can help us understand what happened to the nondelegation doctrine. In 1831 Justice Story exclaimed in *Shankland v. Washington,* 5 Pet. 390, 395 (U.S. 1831), that "[T]he general rule of law is, that a delegated

authority cannot be delegated." In 1892, Justice Harlan noted similarly "[T]hat Congress cannot delegate legislative power . . . is a principle universally recognized as vital to the integrity and maintenance of the system of government ordained by the Constitution." (*Field v. Clark,* 143 U.S. 649, 692). And in 1989 Justice Scalia, dissenting in *Mistretta,* stressed that the Courts "must be particularly rigorous in preserving the Constitution's structural restrictions that deter excessive delegation. The major one . . . is that the power to make law cannot be exercised by anyone other than Congress" (at 678).

Bernard Schwartz (1991) points out that "[T]he law on delegation has moved from the theoretical prohibition against any delegation of legislative power . . . to a rule against unrestricted delegations (i.e., those that are not limited by standards)" (p. 44). But the question remains, how could such a basic constitutional principle of nondelegation reach a point where it plays virtually no role in the constitutional system? Actually, the reasons are quite clear and, from a system's perspective, very understandable. One reason is that the judiciary really cannot practically develop meaningful tests to distinguish permissible delegations from nonpermissible ones. But second, and much more important, is that the U.S. governmental system simply could not and cannot function efficiently and effectively unless broad delegations of legislative powers are permitted. In other words, broad delegations are upheld by the courts, not because they are technically constitutional, but because practicality or sound government requires such broad delegations to administrators. Possibly Justice Blackmun, writing for the majority in *Mistretta,* said it best when he wrote that "our jurisprudence has been driven by a parctical understanding that in our increasigly complex society, replete with ever changing and more technical problems, Congresss simply cannot do its job absent an ability to delegate power under broad general directives" (at 654). Or, as Talcott Parsons, a noted systems theorist espousing action theory, claimed long ago, the action taken (for example, the judiciary's actions in support of broad delegation) must be understood in the context of what the system demands (Parsons 1951).

Delegation of Judicial Powers

Most delegation cases deal with the issue of whether Congress can delegate legislative power to administrative agencies, but agency power has increased through Congress's delegation of adjudicative powers as well. Article 3, Section 1 of the Constitution clearly states that "the judicial power of the United states shall be vested in one Supreme Court and in such inferior Courts as the Congress shall from time to time ordain." In this light, can Congress legally bestow judicial powers on nonjudicial bodies or administrative agencies? The answer is yes. Actually, the delegation of judicial power to administrative agencies has never caused the same intense concern as when legislative powers have been delegated, despite the similar encroachment upon the separation of powers doctrine. This is probably largely due to the fact that legislative acts, whether by Congress or public agencies, have normally and traditionally had a much greater impact on society than judicial acts. It is true that although federal appellate and United States Supreme Court holdings have had profound social consequences (for example, in the areas of education, housing, criminal procedure, and civil rights), agency-adjudicated decisions in general have had comparatively minor impact. This is not to suggest that agency adjudications have not significantly affected some industries. But agency rulemaking is macro-oriented, while order-making is more micro-oriented. Thus, as methods for promulgating public policies, the former would, likely cause more public concern than the latter (see **adjudication** and **rulemaking**).

However, it is also important to emphasize that agency rules are generally less reviewable than agency orders (see reviewability). This makes the delegation of judicial power much less threatening to those concerned about the undermining of the separation of powers principle. As long as judicial review is not precluded, the Court argued in the precedential case *Cromwell v. Benson*, 285 U.S. 22 (1932), the delegation of judicial power to administrative agencies seems both reasonable and necessary. In judging the constitutionality of delegated judicial power to public agencies, the Court held that "Congress did not attempt to define questions of law, and the generality of the description leaves no doubt of the intention to reserve to the federal court full authority to pass upon all matters which this Court has held to fall within that category. There is thus no attempt to interfere with, but rather provision is made to facilitate, the exercise by the court of its jurisdiction to deny effect to any administrative finding which is without evidence, of 'contrary to the indisputable character of the evidence,' or where the hearing is 'inadequate,' or 'unfair,' or arbitrary in any respect" (at 49–50). In *City of Waukegan v. Pollution Control Board*, 57 Ill. 2d 170 (1974), Justice Ward argued that the U.S. Supreme Court has never found it appropriate to rule that judicial power had been vested improperly in a public agency. In addition, he contended, citing several administrative law experts, any delegation of authority, whether legislative or judicial, does not violate the separation of powers doctrine as long as effective legislative or judicial checks exist. He maintained "it may be irrelevant if an agency has legislative or judicial characteristics so long as the legislature or the judiciary can effectively correct errors of the agency" (at 175).

However, in *Northern Pipeline Construction Co. v. Marathon Pipe Line Co.*, 458 U.S. 50 (1982), the Court handed down a decision that created some confusion regarding the delegation of adjudicative powers to administrative agencies. In *Northern Pipeline* the Court's plurality applied the old public rights/private rights test to agency adjudicative authority vaguely, apparently arguing that questions of public rights can be heard in agency adjudications, but those involving private rights must be heard before a regular court established under Article 3 of the U.S. Constitution. Parenthetically, although not always easy to distinguish, an issue involving a public right involves the government and another party (for example, the Federal Communications Commission and a TV station), while a private right involves a question between only private parties (for example, TWA and a mechanic's union). Bernard Schwartz (1986), as well as many others, severely criticized this decision, arguing that the employment of the public rights/private rights test to determine adjudicative authority was rejected nearly a century ago. "It is too late in the development of our administrative law for there to be any question of the legislative power to delegate adjudicatory power to agencies. Adjudications of both public and private rights may be committed to administrative agencies, as long as their decisions are subject to judicial review. To indicate otherwise, as *Northern Pipeline* did, is to go back almost a century in administrative law development" (p. 295). Fortunately, three years later in *Thomas v. Union Carbide Agricultural Products Co.*, 105 S.Ct. 3325 (1985), the Supreme Court rectified its apparent error in judgment by flatly rejecting the public rights/private rights test and reaffirming the long-established judicial opinion that the legislature has the authority to delegate adjudicative powers to administrative agencies, regardless of whether public or private rights are involved, as long as agency adjudicative decisions are subject to judicial review.

A year later the high court reaffirmed its position in *Union Carbide in Commodity Futures Trading Commission v. Schor*, 478 U.S. 835 (1986).

However, in 1989 the Supreme Court in *Granfinanciera S.A. v. Nordberg*, 109 S.Ct. 2782, relied again on the public right/private right distinction, causing more confusion regarding when agency adjudications are unconstitutional because a party is entitled to a jury trial in an Article 3 court and when agency adjudications are constitutional because no jury trial is required. In *Granfinanciera* the Court held that the Seventh Amendment's jury trial requirement applies because the disputes pertaining to a bankruptcy involves only private parties. Thus, as a result of inconsistent reliance on the public right/private right test by the Supreme Court when reviewing the constitutionality of agency adjudicative authority, it is not clear today exactly what delegations of judicial powers to agencies are constitutional. Nonetheless, as a general rule, as developed in *Cromwell*, it can be said that most agency adjudications are constitutional, under the separation of powers doctrine, as long as the delegation of judicial power to administrative agencies in the statutory scheme permits judicial review (*Glenborough New Mexico Assoc. v. Resolution Trust*, 802 F.Supp. 387, 391, D.N.M. (1992).

In concluding, it should be noted that the courts will continue to permit agencies to adjudicate a variety of disputes, even when involving only private parties, because our courts simply don't have the time or expertise to settle such disputes. The fact is that the Social Security Administration alone adjudicates more than 280,000 cases each year, or over ten times the total caseload of all federal judges.

Delegation at the State Level

As suggested, the judiciary has in general significantly contributed to the growth of administrative power by upholding broad delegations of power from legislatures to administrators. Although for a few decades after *Curtiss-Wright* (1936) the courts timidly espoused that broad delegation was only acceptable if meaningful standards were attached, by the 1970s the federal courts seemed to have abandoned any serious efforts to make legislators comply with the meaningful standard requirement. Even though the prevalent judicial mood appears to indicate that the nondelegation doctrine is dead, there are definite signs at the state level that some questions pertaining to the legitimate limits of delegated authority still exist.

State courts, following the trend set by the federal courts, have normally upheld broad delegations, but occasionally they have refused to uphold the constitutionality of broad delegations when the legislative body failed to attach any meaningful standards to guide administrative actions. The fact is that state judges are more likely than federal judges to question the competence of state and local administrators and less likely to trust them. Consequently, according to Bernard Schwartz (1991), "[S]tate judges may be less willing to allow administrators of inferior caliber to exercise power unrestrained by standards in delegating statutes" (p. 65). Of course, most states, particularly the more rural states, have simpler regulatory problems and can afford to insist that state legislatures attach more meaningful standards. Also, state courts have invoked a fundamental administrative law principle that agencies, including municipalities, are mere creatures of state statute powers delegated to them by the legislative branch since they have to inherently independent or common law powers. To cite some examples: In *Biomedical Laboratories, Inc. v. Trainor*, 370 N.E. 2d 223 (1977), the Illinois Supreme Court made it clear that it would not uphold administrative authority in the total absence of standards set by the legislature because standards are necessary to indicate the scope of authorized administrative power. In *Subcontractors Trade v. Koch*, 62 N.Y. 2d 422 (1984), a New York court held that Mayor Ed Koch was not delegated the legislative power to mandate that "locally based enterprises" must get at least 10 percent of all construction contracts awarded by New York City. "In order for the executive to lawfully mandate the award of construction contracts to a particular group or category of business enterprise, the legislature must specifically delegate the power to him and must provide adequate guidelines and standards for the implementation of that policy" (at 429). And in another case, *Louisiana v. Broom*, 439 So. 2d 357 (1983), a Louisiana court held that the secretary of public safety could not promulgate standards for transporting explosives that carried criminal penalties when violated. The court invalidated the penalty provision, reasoning that the delegation to create standards to the secretary of public safety essentially authorizes the official to determine what constitutes felonies. Such delegation violates the separation of powers doctrine, the court maintained, because only the state legislature can define serious offenses or felonies. In *State Dept. of Env. Reg. v. Puckett Oil*, 577 So. 2d 988 (Fla. App. 1 Dist. 1991), A Florida court struck a blow against broad delegation by overruling a state agency's actions which were "in excess of any express or reasonably implied delegated legislative authority" (at 991). The court noted that "[I]t is well recognized that the powers of administrative agencies are measured and limited by statutes or acts in which such powers are expressly granted or implicitly conferred" (at 991).

KENNETH F. WARREN

BIBLIOGRAPHY

Davis, Kenneth C., 1977. *Administrative Law: Cases–Text–Problems*. 6th ed. St. Paul, MN: West Publishing Company.
Parsons, Talcott, 1951. *The Social System*. New York: The Free Press.
Robinson, Glenn O., 1991. *American Bureaucracy: Public Choice and Public Law*. Ann Arbor, MI: University of Michigan Press.
Schwartz, Bernard, 1986. "Administrative Law Cases During 1985." *Administrative Law Review*, vol. 38 (Summer).
———, 1991. *Administrative Law*. 3d ed. Boston: Little, Brown and Company.
Warren, Kenneth F., 1996. *Administrative Law in the American System*. 3d ed. Upper Saddle River, NJ: Prentice-Hall.

DELPHI TECHNIQUE. An approach using a series of questionnaires to elicit responses from experts, frequently to attempt to achieve a consensus of opinion—often used to produce forecasts of future events or conditions, but also to identify critical issues, to evaluate the desirability of certain outcomes or problem solutions, and to explore and refine expert opinion on a subject.

The delphi technique, or delphi method, is a set of procedures for eliciting and refining the opinions of a group of people (Dalkey 1972a). It uses a panel of key informants to seek consensus among experts without face-to-face interaction. Agreement is attempted by having the participants complete a series of questionnaires, or event statements, in surveys interspersed with controlled opinion feedback provided by the moderator of the process (Parker and Taylor 1980). Even when agreement is not reached after successive rounds of survey responses, the results can be extremely informative. With quantitative subjects, results may be presented in terms of averages (means), medians, and interquartile ranges, accompanied by a narrative.

Because the principles of the delphi technique are simple, it is easily adapted to many applications ranging from extremely elementary to very complex. Elaborate theory or methodology is not necessary to provide rules of standard practice. The literature is rich in the variety of examples. Participants may be asked to sketch simple graphs showing personal estimates of future sales trends, or to respond to a series of sophisticated surveys. Panel participants may range from two or three to several hundred.

Sometimes panelists help to develop questions for the initial questionnaire. Only the questionnaire items or event statements on which consensus was not reached are presented in subsequent rounds, resulting in fewer and fewer items. Some questions may inquire into the reasons for previously expressed opinions. The moderator may provide supplemental information to panelists. The experts sometimes are asked to rate their confidence in their own responses. Respondents are sometimes informed of the identities of other participants after the exercise is completed.

An Example Applied to Forecasting

The application of the delphi technique to forecasting illustrates how the use of questionnaires is intended to lead gradually to agreement on a forecast (Martino 1972). A panel of experts works toward consensus by filling out a series of questionnaires instead of meeting face-to-face as a committee. In completing the first questionnaire, the participants make their individual forecasts. The completed questionnaires are compiled by a moderator as a composite forecast that shows the differences of opinion among the members of the panel without disclosing identities. In a second questionnaire, the members are asked to comment on the composite forecast and give reasons why they disagree with the synthesized result, if they do disagree. In a third, and possible subsequent questionnaires, the participants review the most recent composite forecast as well as a summary of the reasons the panelists gave for changing it (i.e., arguments as to why an event would take place earlier or later than the majority of the panelists thinks it will).

In each succeeding round of questionnaire completion, the members are expected to consider the arguments of the other panelists and either defend their positions with counterarguments, or change their positions to agree with the majority. Anonymity makes it easy for them to consider arguments on their merits, without being influenced by their personal judgments about the reputations of the individuals who originated the arguments. Partici-

pants find it easy to abandon their earlier positions without "losing face" (public credibility) if they become convinced that their earlier positions were incorrect. In practice, four or five rounds of questionnaires are usually sufficient to converge on a common position, if that is the purpose of the forecast.

Origin and Development

The delphi technique was developed in 1953 by Olaf Helmer and Norman Dalkey at the Rand Corporation. Studies at Rand focused on ways to improve the statistical treatment of combining individual opinions. Delphi was invented as a means of resolving differences among experts. Because it was first applied to a classified military project, the first published account of that effort did not appear until 1963, although the first published reference to the technique appeared in 1959 (Helmer and Rascher 1959).

The delphi technique received a large boost in general interest, and worldwide attention, with the publication in 1964 of Gordon and Helmer's study of forecasting technological events, *Report on a Long-Range Forecasting Study.* Their research examined long-range trends in science and technology, and their probable effects on U.S. society and the world. Its publication coincided with a surge of interest in long-range forecasting using expert opinions.

Applications of the Delphi Technique

The great utility and merit of the delphi technique are demonstrated by its extremely diverse uses. Since 1964, a tremendous variety of applications has been completed. Initial responses to the 1964 study were industrial forecasts of technological developments. In addition, a variety of organizations used the procedure for exploring policy decisions in education, public transportation, and public health, resulting in hundreds of studies. The delphi methodology soon became standard practice in the "futures field" concerned with predicting key future trends.

The variety of applied fields and academic disciplines that has used the delphi technique is almost unlimited. It is known to have been applied in planning, decisionmaking, structured conferences, cross-impact analysis, technology assessment, model building, and gaming. Academic disciplines include education, marketing, economics, medicine, health care, food science, human resources, transportation, communication, economics, criminal justice, international relations, organizational behavior, library science, information science, management information systems, operations research, management, product development, nutrition, housing, energy, population, pollution, social policy, social studies, and labor forecasting. Applied areas include the military, steel, plastics, chemicals, automobiles, technology, and drug abuse. It has been used to explore alternative futures of municipal, county, state, and federal agencies; industries; firms; governments at all levels worldwide; criminal justice; and military systems and strategies. Other subjects include the quality of life, epistemology of science, values and the future, institutional goals, technology in education, retirement policy, the future of associations, and project management.

Recent examples of practical applications include: production economics, agriforestry in developing countries, location planning in engineering, bank employee management, nursing care, occupational medicine, dietetics, campus alcohol abuse, scientific and industrial research location, energy research, executive development, tourism and environmental impacts, employee benefits, recreation management, emergency care, elk habitat, organizational politics, electronic data exchange, insecticide use in cotton production, recreational fisheries, physical education, air pollution, casualty insurance, financial planning, telecommunications, curriculum planning, econometrics, inventory control, tax reform, licensure of public accountants, emergency care, wetland conservation, retail banking, contract administration, and regional economics.

The technique has been applied in countries all over the world. Examples include: economic planning and agriforestry research in developing nations; the textile industry, and occupational and environmental medicine in Britain; libraries in Sweden; Australian banking; Singapore tourism; productivity management in India; fire safety, health care, and the automobile industry in Western Europe; real estate and health services planning in Canada; information technology in Taiwan; marketing business services in Eastern Europe; technology in Japan; Dutch technology; and retail banking in New Zealand.

Advantages and Disadvantages

An examination of the advantages and disadvantages of the delphi technique, compared with typical face-to-face committee processes, provides insights into its nature and mechanics. The effectiveness of the technique depends upon the care devoted to its design and administration. Issues of validity, reliability, and social scientific rigor are examined by Tafoya (1986).

Advantages

- Individual, anonymous answers reduce the effects of the opinions of "socially" dominant individuals, the "supersalespersons" with overpowering personalities, or individuals with superior rank or expert reputation—statements are judged strictly on their merits.
- It avoids false consensus, results watered down to the least common denominator, and the bandwagon effect, often found in committees.

- Controlled feedback reduces the redundant or irrelevant "noise" often found in direct confrontations.
- Conformity to majority opinions typical of committee meetings is avoided through the presentation of a statistical group (quartile) response in relation to the feedback of previous estimates—at the end of the exercise there may still be a significant spread in individual opinions.
- Statistical group response assures that the opinion of every member of the group is represented in the final response.
- It permits a spread of opinion so that the uncertainties surrounding a situation can be reflected.
- It is possible to narrow the range among opinions without pressuring the panelists to the extent that deviant opinion would no longer be allowed—this can be done in part by asking deviants to justify their positions.
- It can use a wide variety of experts from both within and outside of an organization—each expert need not be well qualified in exactly the same portion of the area of interest, but can be qualified in subparts, as long as at least one expert is qualified in every subpart of the subject.
- The technique permits progressive focusing and narrowing; in product development, for example, an initial questionnaire could establish general products or production processes, and final phases could seek detail on specifics and identify the most likely alternatives to be developed first.
- It is a means of anticipating events that would not be expected from conventional extrapolation.
- It overcomes the limited perspectives of experts with extensive knowledge of constraints that limit their appreciation of future possibilities.
- It expands the awareness of experts of knowledge in different, but related, sectors of their profession or in different disciplines.
- The anonymity of the technique enables experts to share their candid opinions without being subject to the ridicule of their peers that forecasting developments that appear to be beyond the bounds of reasonable credibility—individuals may give free rein to their imaginations without risking their reputations.
- It assures proper attention to all significant aspects of the subject, and minimizes the likelihood of overlooking important information, at least in the fields represented by the panel.
- The "chain effect" of new ideas being generated from the ideas of others can result in synergism—the whole becomes greater than the sum of its parts.
- It overcomes the reluctance of junior experts to oppose the views of senior experts.
- It eliminates the costs and logistical problems of bringing experts together in one place.

- Much less effort is needed to respond to a questionnaire than to participate in a conference or write a paper.
- It can be a highly motivating experience for respondents.
- Feedback can be novel and interesting to all.
- The use of a systematic procedure lends an aura of objectivity to the outcome.
- The anonymity and group response allow a sharing of responsibility that is refereshing and that releases the respondents from social inhibitions.
- It is good in the context of policy formulation where group acceptance is important.
- The value of the method is not merely in its ability to induce consensus, but also in its ability to highlight a diversity of underlying assumptions. Uncovering the basis for divergence of opinion by experts may be more important than identifying the basis for convergence.

Disadvantages

- The reliability of results depends upon the care devoted to design and administration.
- Ambiguity in the questions may weaken the value of the results.
- It produces different results when different sets of experts are used.
- It is sometimes difficult to assess the degree of expertise of the panelists.
- It will rarely predict the unexpected.
- There may be pressure toward consensus as the rounds progress.
- Opinions will not necessarily converge toward an agreed-upon forecast or result.
- Convergence of results does not guarantee accuracy.
- It is not necessarily an improvement over a more straightforward committee process.
- Participants may be selected more on the basis of their willingness to participate and their accessibility than on their real knowledge or representativeness of opinion in a field.
- It can take a great deal of time to arrive at consensus.
- The process may suffer because of a high dropout rate of participants.
- Many business people are not familiar with the method and may be reluctant to participate.

J. WALTON BLACKBURN

BIBLIOGRAPHY

Armstrong, J. Scott, 1985. *Long-Range Forecasting: From Crystal Ball to Computer.* New York: John Wiley.

Dalkey, Norman C., 1972a. "Delphi." In Joseph T. Martino, ed., *An Introduction to Technological Forecasting.* London: Gordon and Breach Science Publishers, pp. 25–30.

———, 1972b. "The Delphi Method: An Experimental Study of Group Opinion." In Norman C. Dalkey, ed., *Studies in the Quality of Life–Delphi and Decision-Making.* Lexington, MA: Lexington Books, pp. 13–54.

Gordon, Theodore J., and Olaf Helmer, 1964. *Report on a Long-Range Forecasting Study.* Santa Monica, CA: The Rand Corporation.

Helmer, Olaf and Nicholas Rascher, 1959. "On the Epistemology of the Inexact Sciences." *Management Science,* vol. 6, no. 1 (October) 25–52.

Hudson, Ivan, 1974. *A Bibliography on the "Delphi Technique."* Monticello, IL: Council of Planning Librarians.

Kennington, Don and Gordon Pratt, 1976. *Public Libraries and Long Range Planning: An Exercise in Delphi Forecasting Carried Out in Behalf of the Public Libraries Research Group in 1973–74.* Brighton, England: Public Libraries Research Group.

Kress, George, 1985. *Practical Techniques of Business Forecasting–Fundamentals and Applications for Marketing, Production, and Financial Managers.* Westport, CT: Quorum Books.

Linstone, H. A. and M. Turoff, 1975. *The Delphi Method: Techniques and Applications.* Reading, MA: Addison-Wesley.

Makridakis, Spyros and Steven C. Wheelwright, 1989. *Forecasting Methods for Management.* 5th ed. New York: John Wiley.

Makridakis, Spyros, Steven C. Wheelwright and Victor E. McGee, 1983. *Forecasting: Methods and Applications.* 2d ed. New York: John Wiley.

Martino, Joseph T., 1972. "Forecasting the Progress of Technology." In Joseph T. Martino, ed., *An Introduction to Technological Forecasting.* London: Gordon and Breach Science Publishers, pp. 13–23.

———, 1983. *Technological Forecasting for Decision Making.* New York: Elsevier North-Holland.

Parker, James T. and Paul G. Taylor. 1980. *The Delphi Survey–CBAE through the Eyes of Leading Educators.* Belmont, CA: Fearon Pitman Publishers, Inc.

Sackman, Harold, 1975. *Delphi Critique: Expert Opinion, Forecasting and Group Process.* Lexington, MA: Lexington Books.

Tafoya, William L., 1986. A *Delphi Forecast of the Future of Law Enforcement.* College Park, MD: University of Maryland. Unpublished Ph.D. dissertation.

Worsham, John P., 1980. *Application of the Delphi Method: A Selected Bibliography.* Monticello, IL: Vance Bibliographies.

DEREGULATION. The process by which the public sector divests itself of controls on a variety of areas of economic activity, thereby handing more responsibility to the private sector. Deregulation became part of the New Right agenda in the 1980s in a number of Western countries, perceived as the most direct means by which the state was rolled back and the felicitous invisible hand of Adam Smith orthodoxy was ungloved (Hutton 1995, p. 11).

Deregulation is the opposite of everything that intervention, subsidy, and nationalization were held to stand for. In the United States, deregulation can be seen as part of the attempt to return to Jeffersonian rectitude. In many parts of the European Union, deregulation is what governments claim to want from the European Commission. In the United Kingdom, it is synonymous with Thatcherism. There, financial markets were deregulated in order to ensure the continuing status of London as one of the three financial centers of global finance; nationalized industries were freed from public ownership; trade union powers in national wage determination were emasculated. In each case, the British government did not dismantle all controls, sometimes replacing one set with another, suitably packaged to conform to the doctrine of deregulation. For example, the government-appointed watchdogs of the newly privatized monopolies act in ways very similar to the old, decried interference by ministers in the running of the nationalized monopolies.

For its devotees, deregulation is the means by which capitalism can be freed, following the alleged distortions of demand management regimes, and the operation of market forces ensured. It is the badge of those who, in government, seek to facilitate economic growth through an unfettered private sector. A slightly more balanced approach might be that deregulation has moved a number of mixed economy countries away from a half-public, half-private system to one that marginally emphasizes the private sector over the public. Governments, after all, of whatever ideological hue, find the giving away of power something best left to rhetorical celebration.

PETER FOOT

BIBLIOGRAPHY

Hutton, Will, 1995. *The State We're In*. London: Jonathan Cape.
Jenkins, Simon, 1995. *Accountable to None: The Tory Nationalization of Britain*. London: Hamish Hamilton.
Riddell, Peter, 1991. *The Thatcher Era and Its Legacy*. London: Blackwell.
Young, Hugo, 1991. *One of Us*. London: Macmillan.

DETERRENCE.   A feature of some elements of public policy used by governments to dissuade either individuals or other states from doing something that might damage the interests of the state. At the heart of any deterrent policy is a threat of such a nature that those exposed to it conclude that the possible benefit to be gained from pursuing a particular course of action is not worth the risk associated with the possible or probable consequences. The term deterrence is today most frequently associated with strategic theory and the use of military power, especially but by no means exclusively with those aspects concerned with the utility of nuclear weapons; in relation to military affairs in general, it has only appeared in print since World War II. It has its origins, however, in nineteenth-century jurisprudence dealing with punishment in criminal justice systems. Deterrence in the broadest sense, therefore, has applications in the domestic as well as in the international sphere and is by no means restricted to the military dimension of public policy.

The core of any deterrent policy is a threat. No matter how or in what context deterrent threats are employed, to be consistently and fully effective four essential ingredients

must be in place. In theory, if all of those ingredients are in place the policy will be sound and invariably effective. If any of those ingredients are missing the policy will be unsound or flawed (although it will not necessarily fail to deter).

First and foremost, the core threat must be credible. The target of the threat (be it an individual or another state) must believe that there is a realistic chance of it being carried out if the action it is designed to deter is taken. An important element of credibility is proportionality. If the threat is out of all proportion to the action it is intended to deter, the target may not take it seriously. This could be the case whether threat is too great or too small. Even if the threat is proportional the target still needs to be convinced that there is a sufficiently high risk that the threat will be carried out. There is, therefore, an important psychological dimension to deterrence, arising from both the determination of a government to activate the threat and a calculation by the target of the strength of that determination. Neither side can know for sure what the other will do; each has to live with a degree of uncertainty. In the case of a sound deterrent policy, the degree of that uncertainty will be minimized, but it cannot be erased altogether. Where uncertainty does exist it is important that it is minimized to the point at which a rational target would not be prepared to take the risk of the threat being activated.

The second ingredient of sound deterrence is capability: a government must be able to deliver its threat if the action it is meant to deter is carried out. There is an important distinction to be made here between sound deterrence (which will invariably work) and flawed deterrence (which might also appear to do so). The threat might appear credible despite the government being quite incapable of turning it into action. If the target of the threat does not realize that the capability is lacking, the threat might be just as effective as if it were backed up by the ability to deliver. Such a flawed deterrent policy might go on working provided the government is able to hide from view the fact that it is incapable of carrying out its threat. It goes without saying that if the lack of capability is ever exposed, the deterrent policy will surely fail.

The third essential ingredient is rationality. If either the government or the target act irrationally the policy will be flawed. Rationality is extremely difficult to define; one could say that it is largely in the eyes of the beholder. For that reason, governments need to base their deterrent policies, in particular their core threats, on careful analyses of the likely reaction of those against whom they are targeted. There will be occasions when it will prove quite impossible to deter—when an individual or a state is determined on a course of action based on emotional conviction or insanity rather more than careful calculation. In truth there is more likelihood of irrationality in individuals than there is in states, although neither can be ruled out entirely. A state might appear to be charting an irrational course when in reality its leaders are calculating every move. They may even justify their actions using emotional rhetoric, but that will not necessarily mean that the actions themselves are irrational. The important thing for governments to analyze when fashioning an appropriate deterrent threat is the underlying rather than the openly declared motive of those they are attempting to deter.

The final ingredient is communications. The target of a deterrent threat must be aware of it and must appreciate the likely consequences should that threat be ignored. It will often not be enough merely to imply a threat. Similarly, a clearly and openly expressed threat may serve only to exacerbate an already tense situation. It might, for example, force the target to challenge the threat in order to save face, thereby having the opposite effect from that intended. The target must be able to back down without looking foolish, which means that the deterrent threat might need to be expressed in confidence, albeit clearly and precisely. It may be rather vague to put it in such terms but what is required is an appropriate level of communication or promulgation; what is appropriate will vary depending on the situation.

Each of the four ingredients of deterrence is inextricably bound up with the other three and it will often be impossible to draw strict lines of distinction between them. Credibility goes with capability, which must be communicated in a manner that will provoke a rational response.

Ultimately, sound deterrence will always work. If deterrence fails it will do so because one of the four essential ingredients is not in place. Only flawed deterrence fails. Failure will be obvious to all. Regrettably one can never be sure that deterrence has been successful. The fact that the action being deterred does not happen does not necessarily mean that it would have done if the policy had not been in place. There can never be conclusive proof to the utility of deterrence but the weight of evidence is sufficient to ensure that it remains an important form of public policy deployed in both the domestic and international spheres.

By its very nature, deterrence is concerned with the maintenance of security and good order and the protection of national interest. A government threatens to impose a sanction unless another state or individual refrains from a course of action that itself threatens the security or interests of state.

With both domestic and external applications, deterrence could be dealt with under two headings only. The term has particularly strong military connotations, however, and because it has become especially associated with nuclear strategy the discussion which follows is conducted under three headings.

Domestic Applications

Deterrence is one rationale for punishment in most criminal justice systems. Jurisprudentially, punishment serves a number of objectives. It can be retribution providing satis-

faction to both society as a whole and, more specifically, the individual victims of illegal acts. It may have a reforming element; indeed, this is increasingly regarded by penal reformers as perhaps its most, if not its only, important function. Punishment also has a role to play in preventing crime. This may be as crude as depriving a criminal of his or her liberty, thereby physically restraining him or her from reoffending. But there may also be a deterrent element in punishments, indicating to all members of society what the consequences may be if they offend. These consequences are communicated by formal promulgation, typically in enacted laws, but also by usage, with the treatment meted out to convicted criminals serving as a warning to others. Deterrence operates at all levels. The likely loss of a driving license as punishment for serious or persistent breaches of traffic regulations may serve to deter a great many drivers from speeding or driving under the influence of alcohol. At the other end of the criminal spectrum, the death sentence may be employed to deter murder. However, the important word in this context is "may." The evidence supporting or challenging the efficacy of deterrent punishment is by no means convincing either way. Take, for example, the case of capital punishment in relation to the crime of murder. In the United States there is a growing murder rate despite the reintroduction of capital punishment in a great many states. In contrast, the United Kingdom and other European countries have a relatively low murder rate, despite the abolition of capital punishment. It may well not be the case, therefore, that a death sentence deters the determined murderer, especially as the alternative punishment (a lengthy custodial sentence, often life) is itself severe in its consequences.

Assessing the effectiveness of punishment as a deterrent is difficult. The target of deterrence in criminal justice systems is the individual, not society as a whole. Inevitably, some will be deterred by the promulgated consequences of crime, others will not. The range of sanctions available to judges is usually sufficiently wide to allow them to fit the punishment to the individual as well as to the crime but, as punishment is imposed after the crime is committed, the precise scale and nature of the deterrent threat to the individual contemplating a criminal act cannot be certain. In addition, while there will be a range of punishments promulgated for each crime, there is no certainty that these will follow the criminal act. First the offense must be detected, then the suspect must be caught, and, finally, he or she must be tried and convicted. The extent of the uncertainty as to the consequence of crime makes it extremely difficult to create a sound deterrent. It is possible for a rational individual to assess the chances of detection and conviction and conclude that the rewards outweigh the risk. There are shortcomings in both the credibility of the deterrent threat of punishment and in the capability to carry out that threat. In the majority of cases, therefore, the deterrent element of punishment is likely to be flawed.

Punishment as a deterrent is potentially controversial, therefore. It is difficult to establish its effectiveness beyond doubt and, even if it does appear to work, it is based on the fear of consequences rather than on a responsible approach to community. Nevertheless, it is very likely indeed that deterrence will continue to be an important element of punishment. Politically, retribution and deterrence can have more appeal to the majority than the need for reform and rehabilitation. While penal reformers may regard the deterrent element of punishment as both flawed and an inappropriate way of dealing with crime, many people and many of their political representatives will continue to demand that deterrence remains a feature of criminal justice systems.

General External Applications

The threat of sanctions is one of the central components of the international system. Governments have traditionally protected their interests by threatening sanctions against any other states likely to challenge them. While customary usage of the term deterrence tends to refer to the imposition of military sanctions, in reality it can refer to both diplomatic and economic sanctions as well. The sanctions available to a government are related to the elements of national power: military power, economic power, and the power of persuasion (or diplomatic power). It is no coincidence that this same categorization appears in Chapter VII (Articles 41 and 42) of the UN Charter, which deals with the imposition of sanctions in response to threats to international peace and security. The UN Charter is itself, therefore, an attempt at universal deterrence.

There is often assumed to be a hierarchy of power related to the seriousness of its application and its effectiveness, with diplomatic power at the bottom and military power at the top. This simplistic assumption ignores the need to choose the most appropriate instrument for the prevailing circumstances. The threat of diplomatic or economic sanctions could deter military action. A classic example was the U.S. threat to undermine British sterling currency as a means of deterring further British incursion into Egypt during the Suez Crisis of 1956. The threat was credible, the United States certainly had the capability, it would have been irrational for the Eden Government to ignore the threat (which was potentially profound in its consequences), and the threat as a whole was very effectively communicated by Washington to London.

The threat of sanctions is ever present in the international system. All states have the power to respond to attacks on their national interest. Of course, a great deal of that inherent deterrence is flawed because it is not the result of deliberate government attempts to deter specific actions by specific states. It is only when the general foreign and security policy objectives of governments result in a detectable posture that deterrence begins to focus on particular states that might undermine national interest. A general posture implies a degree of threat to other states but this implicit deterrence is still likely to remain flawed in relation to specific threats. It is not focused enough to be targeted on specific states in order to deter specific actions. It is only with explicit deterrence that governments promulgate a specific threat in order to deter a specific action and it is at this level of deterrence that the presence of all four ingredients becomes vital.

Communications are important in all these levels of deterrence; by definition, they become an especially vital ingredient when deterrence becomes explicit.

There is no question that the term deterrence usually implies a military threat. To apply it to military threats alone, however, is to imply, even unintentionally, that a government's chosen security posture does not have either a diplomatic or economic dimension. This is absurd.

In the modern interdependent world it is inconceivable that an advanced state would threaten military action in isolation. The threats to impose both diplomatic and economic sanctions are as much a part of a deterrent posture as the threat to deploy military forces.

Nuclear Deterrence

The post–World War II development of atomic and nuclear weapons introduced a scale of destructive military potential well in excess of anything envisaged before. In particular, once the thermonuclear bomb in the megaton range was both available and deliverable, the whole question of deterrence took on a different meaning. Nuclear deterrence became a distinct form of policy in the context of the Cold War between the two superpowers and their allies.

The superpowers' nuclear relationship developed through various phases, but there were two fundamentally different strategies employed at different times. Initially, the tripwire notion that a single attack of any sort by the Soviet Union on any noncommunist state would be met by a massive nuclear retaliation from the United States might have appeared credible; in the very early days the United States had a monopoly or near monopoly capability. As the destructive potential of nuclear weapons increased, and once the Soviet Union itself achieved the ability to respond in kind, the credibility of the United States declared policy of massive retaliation was increasingly questioned. The British idea of graduated deterrence, incorporating both nuclear and conventional military threats in a process of escalation, evolved into the NATO doctrine of flexible response, which placed the use of nuclear weapons at the far end of a range of options. Ultimately, a nuclear exchange would lead to mutual assured destruction (MAD) because a first strike would fail to destroy all an opponent's retaliatory capability. The result was a stalemate.

Whether nuclear deterrence was sound or flawed is difficult to determine. Arguably, there is something fundamentally irrational about a decision to launch a nuclear strike in the face of a certain fatal retaliation. The irrationality of the launch of a nuclear attack in the context of MAD is undeniable. And yet, it is possible that the only certain means of deterring a nuclear attack on oneself or one's allies is to threaten certain nuclear destruction in response. If looked at in that way, nuclear deterrence is the only defense against nuclear attack and must, on that basis be regarded as rational. If the fear of nuclear war also prevented conventional war, perhaps the rationality of nuclear deterrence is even more marked.

Does it work? It is impossible to say. Those who argue that the fear of escalation to nuclear exchange also had the effect of deterring conventional military aggression can be accused of forgetting the suicidal nature of the nuclear deterrent. It is by no means certain that a Soviet conventional assault on West Germany, for example, would have led to a U.S. nuclear attack on the Soviet Union. At the heart of NATO strategy was the notion of extended deterrence, by which the nuclear members of the alliance would retaliate with nuclear weapons in the event of a Soviet attack (and not necessarily a nuclear attack) on the nonnuclear members. This was and is, given MAD, tantamount to threatening to commit suicide if someone harms one's friend. Is this credible? Is this rational? As stated above, rationality is in the eye of the beholder.

Nuclear deterrence, by virtue of the profound destructive consequences of its failure, is in a class of its own. Its existence has resulted in nonnuclear deterrent threats being described as conventional deterrence. While nuclear deterrence cannot be regarded entirely separately from other military forms of deterrence, the nuclear threshold represents a distinct psychological barrier. It is to be hoped that the barrier remains in place, particularly in the event of further nuclear proliferation.

STEVEN HAINES

BIBLIOGRAPHY

Aron, Raymond, 1966. *Peace and War: A Theory of International Relations.* London: Wiedenfeld and Nicolson.

Baylis, J. *et al.,* 1987. *Contemporary Strategy Vol I: Theories and Concepts.* 2d ed. London: Croom Helm.

Beaufre, Andre, 1965. *Deterrence and Strategy.* London: Faber and Faber.

Dougherty J. E. and R. L. Pfaltzgraff, 1981. *Contending Theories of International Relations: A Comprehensive Survey.* 2d ed., Cambridge, MA: Harper and Row.

Freedman, Lawrence, 1987. *The Evolution of Nuclear Strategy.* London: Macmillan.

Mearsheimer, J. J., 1983. *Conventional Deterrence.* Ithaca, NY: Cornell University Press.

Paton, Sir G. W., 1967. *A Textbook of Jurisprudence.* 3d ed., ed. by D. P. Derham. Oxford: Clarendon Press.

Schelling, Thomas, 1960. *The Strategy of Conflict.* New York: Oxford University Press.

Smith J. C. and B. Hogan, 1988. *Criminal Law.* 6th ed. London: Butterworths.

Wortley, B. A., 1967. *Jurisprudence.* Manchester: Manchester University Press.

DEVELOPMENT. The all-inclusive process of institutional or organizational fund-raising.

For many years fund-raising activities in nonprofits were seen as a separate and distinct activity. While it was generally believed that public relations had a positive affect on fund-raising results, the usual structure kept the interaction between the functions to a minimum.

In the past two decades, however, a holistic view of "resource development" has taken hold and promoted a more inclusive perspective that includes most activities of the nonprofit as having something to do with fund-raising results. That broader function is now known as "development."

The term "development" is used to describe the entire process of resource acquisition for organizations and institutions. The development office, while primarily responsible for active solicitation of gifts, may also direct the ancillary processes that are conducive to success in fund-raising. This is especially true in higher education.

The following activities have an impact upon fund-raising and are often under the direction of the chief development executive:

Public relations. This field may also be found under titles such as community relations, public affairs, or external relations. The work of this unit may entail directing communications and interactions between the organization and its external stakeholders.

Publications. The production of publications in an organization may reside solely in the development office, be under the direction of the public relations office, or be from a communications or publications department. It is generally understood by nonprofits that all communications representing policies, practices, and general information about activities and the current status of the organization can have positive and negative effects on fund-raising results.

Constituent relations. The relationship with ancillary support groups is generally under the direction of development departments, but they may function quite independently, even to the extent of having their own exempt status. It is not unusual to see an alumni office operating as a standalone entity within higher education institutions, or a hospital auxiliary keeping separate accounts and staff assignments.

Grants administration. Many larger nonprofits have offices responsible for the identification of grant opportunities, the processing of grant applications (proactively or in response to requests for proposals), the follow-up to the proposals, and the management and reporting of grants once acquired. These offices usually concentrate on governmental sources, although they may pursue other avenues, such as corporate and foundation funders. Staff is knowledgeable about research and innovative program activities of other staff and faculty and the wide range of sources that can match such endeavors.

Corporation and foundation relations. This operation usually functions in much the same way as that described under grants administration, with a concentration on grants and gifts from corporations and foundations. In today's philanthropic culture, however, much is being made of opportunities for nonprofits to gain support from corporations by partnering the marketing of the products of the company. This was first pioneered as "cause-related marketing" by American Express and the Statue of Liberty–Ellis Island Foundation in the late 1980s.

Other organizational interactions. To a lesser extent, the cooperation garnered from other departments relative to relationship building, information distribution, customer satisfaction, and donor acknowledgment and recognition has an impact on fund-raising results. The availability of key leadership, both staff and volunteer, to participate in the cultivation and solicitation of prospective donors is an integral part of the development process. The attention of the business office in handling and reporting on the accounts of clients, patients, students, and donors of endowment funds has a bearing on future gifts and grants. The responses of receptionists and groundskeepers who encounter the various publics leave an impression on people that can be negative or positive.

In summary, "development" encompasses a process in which resources—human, monetary, social, and political—are brought to the nonprofit. Development occurs by design when specific activities and programs are instituted to culminate in solicitations for resources. Development can also occur in the day-to-day processes of doing the nonprofit's business and providing its services. In the final analysis, anyone involved with a nonprofit can encounter potential resources that would further the mission of the nonprofit. Successful development programs are those that have instilled a corporate culture that enables volunteers and staff to recognize these opportunities and react in a manner that offers access to the proper channels for acquisition.

Robert W. Buchanan and
William Bergosh

DEVELOPMENT ADMINISTRATION.

According to the standard definition by Riggs (1971, p. 73): "refers to organized efforts to carry out programs or projects thought by those involved to serve developmental objectives. The phrase (development administration) arises by simple analogy, with such expressions as agricultural administration, educational administration, and social welfare administration, each of which involves organized efforts to implement agricultural, educational, and social welfare programs, respectively."

The terms development administration, development management, and development planning are broadly synonymous, although practitioners trained in the different subfields often draw substantive and historical distinctions among them. Riggs's definition above, however, identifies the essence of all three: organizations, programs and projects, and developmental objectives. Development administration in the contemporary sense—since the early 1950s—was initiated in Europe with implementation of the Marshall Plan (Rondinelli 1983). Its objectives were set at the political levels as rebuilding the continent's basic infrastructure and industrial capacity in order to promote economic development and renewed political stability. Administrators were to carry out these policies through a growing number of national and international institutions, programs, and projects. Lead organizations in these efforts were the United Nations-related International Bank for Reconstruction and Development (World Bank) and the Economic Commission for Europe. Their institutional forms, activities, and methods were transferred directly to the problems of newly independent developing countries during the latter 1950s and early 1960s (Hope 1984; Rondinelli 1984, 1987; Siffin 1976). The objectives of physical infrastructure building and urban industrialization were endorsed by economists and planners (Lewis 1966; Waterson 1965) and put into practice through development administration, whether or not such goals and objectives met the actual needs of the emerging nations.

The experiences of development practice, as well as changing fashions in the broader world of public administration, planning, and policymaking, called into question first the division between development policymaking and administration, by the second half of the 1960s, and then the very purposes of development itself by the mid-1970s (Hope 1984; Rondinelli 1984, 1987). Once again, a decade later, questions arose challenging the validity of bureaucratic and rational-scientific approaches to development. By the mid-1980s calls were heard for a more market-oriented, hands-off development strategy, stressing liberal economics, enterpreneurship, and public-private collaboration (Mitchell-Weaver and Manning 1991). Institutions such as the World Bank and later the U.S. Agency for International Development (USAID) adapted to and helped to elaborate each of these development models or paradigms. Perhaps significantly, such paradigms have followed almost precisely the changing ideas in good currency put forward by administration and planning theorists in the United States, who focused their work primarily on domestic issues (see the outline of paradigm change suggested by Stokes 1994).

Combining the historical analyses of both developmental and U.S. domestic theorists, a sequence of four dominant development administration paradigms can be posited: (1) the Development Administration Movement (early 1950s to mid-1960s), (2) Planning and Policy Analysis (mid-1960s to mid-1970s), (3) Development Management and Decentralization (mid-to late 1970s to mid-1980s), and (4) Liberalization and Partnerships (early to mid-1980s to mid-1990s). The basic components of each of these models of development administration are discussed below.

The Development Administration Movement

During the Progressive Era in the United States, the 1910s and 1920s, one of the major goals of reformers such as Theodore Roosevelt and Robert M. LaFollette was to remove control of government from the hands of corrupt big city political bosses and their city hall machines. Reformers felt the best way to do this was to create a separate government civil service, staffed on the basis of merit—not political patronage—and trained in the most advanced rational-scientific methods of public administration. These ideas created both the city planning movement (Friedmann and Weaver 1979) and the public administration movement (Stokes 1994). Both were centered at first at the local level of government, and later moved up to the federal level during Franklin D. Roosevelt's New Deal in the 1930s. Policy was to be made at the political level by Progressive reformers, and administration and planning were to be entrusted to Max Weber's rational-scientific bureaucracy. This was the birth of modern public administration, and soon university programs were founded to train the new administrators, at places such as the Maxwell School of Citizenship at Syracuse University.

Such public administrative thinking was carried onto the international scene by the Marshall Plan and the orientation of the United Nations and early Bretton Woods institutions. Donald Stone was a U.S. citizen first interested in the local reform ideas of the Progressives. Working in the Truman Administration, he helped organize the first plenary session of the UN in San Francisco and was involved in implementation of the Marshall Plan. Stone believed in the public administration movement, and brought its creed to the organization of international institutions and international development. As the focus of UN activity turned from rebuilding Europe toward new nation building, Stone applied these same concepts to development in former colonial areas, contributing to the birth of a new Development Administration Movement.

In 1957 Stone was appointed founding Dean of the Graduate School of Public and International Affairs (GSPIA) at the University of Pittsburgh. GSPIA soon became an important training ground for development administrators from all over the world. In 1960 it created a special program dedicated to development administration and planning, borrowing the United Nations name, Economic and Social Development. By the mid-1960s, the GSPIA model provided recognized guidelines for training development administrators (Stone 1966) and improving government capacity for administering and planning development (Stone 1971, 1973; Stone and Stone 1976). Oth-

ers, including Edward Weidner (1962, 1964) Victor A. Thompson (1964), and Moshe Weiss (1966), made similar arguments.

By the time Stone began writing from the prospective of the development administration movement, the model he had created at GSPIA was under widespread attack from other quarters, however, and Stone's school at Pittsburgh did little to respond to the new thinking. In fact, the public administration ideas of the Progressives had already come under fire in the United States during the 1950s because of the artificial separation of policymaking and implementation, which had opened the way for the public affairs model partially embodied in Stone's own school (Stokes 1994). Critics of mere administration argued that the policy content of development activities was key to their success and could not be separated from implementation. The development administrator would have to be a policy analyst and planner as well.

Planning and Policy Analysis

Comprehensive national planning had been a part of both U.S. and European thinking about development since the Great Depression of the 1930s (Friedmann and Weaver 1979). In the context of development administration, it got its real impetus from World Bank Economic Missions to developing countries in the 1950s (Rondinelli 1983) and U.S. President John Kennedy's Alliance for Progress in Latin America. Most countries, to qualify for multilateral and bilateral foreign aid, created institutes or ministries of development and planning. The two terms became all but indistinguishable. These new organizations were dedicated to the use of mathematical economic models to promote long-range, centralized planning for development (Friedmann and Weaver 1979; Lewis 1966; Rondinelli 1983, 1987; Waterston 1965). Their operations coincided with some of the highest rates of economic growth ever experienced in Latin America and Africa, although the global macroeconomic context must take much of the credit for this expansion.

For development administration there was also another, exogenous force pushing for the introduction of top-down mathematical decisionmaking. The use of rigorous analytical techniques had been pioneered by the U.S. Department of Defense during World War II, and emerged as the planning, programming, budgeting system (PPBS) adopted by the Rand Corporation in Los Angeles and U.S. President Johnson's Great Society programs in the mid-1960s. A public policy movement swept through U.S. academia in the late 1960s and early 1970s, marked by the creation of Harvard's Kennedy School and the Graduate School of Public Policy at the University of California at Berkeley (Stokes 1994). Aaron Wildavsky, at Berkeley, was probably more responsible than any other individual for forcefully and eloquently spreading belief in the virtues of policy analysis for solving public problems in the United States. Because of the role of the United States on the international scene at the turn of the 1970s, policy analysis soon became a requisite ally of rational-comprehensive planning in developing countries.

What this meant for development administration was an almost complete break with the earliest principles of modern public administration. Center stage was taken by the need to analyze policy choices rigorously. Professionalized, disinterested implementation became quite unfashionable. Policy analysis of goals and objectives, followed by long-range rational planning, were the tokens of progressive development thinking and progressive development administration.

In fact, for developing countries outside the emerging East Asian NIEs (newly industrializing economies), the 1970s was to prove a difficult decade. The 1960s—the First UN Development Decade—had already been evaluated as a failure (Friedmann and Weaver 1979), and the 1970s held in store a radical neo-Marxist rethinking of all manner of development questions (Hope 1984), and, more importantly, two oil shocks and an ever-deepening world recession. Developing countries were hit the worst by global economic conditions, and the verities of development planning and administration were once again open to challenge. It seemed that the "right" policy wasn't enough. Implementing it on the ground, in the local environment was the real test.

Development Management and Decentralization

The reaction of development administration to the critique of the early 1970s created development management, a two-headed hydra with odd and sometimes conflicting characteristics. Change was first forecast by members of the comparative administration group like Milton J. Esman (1971) and those interested in "administrative reform," meaning primarily decentralization and devolution of authority toward the local community (Caiden 1973). USAID became interested (Gable 1975), and top-down rational planners began proposing bottom-up participatory development strategies (Friedmann and Douglass 1975; Friedmann and Weaver 1979). New emphasis was placed on project management and implementation (Rondinelli and Radosevich 1974; Rondinelli 1976), especially by USAID and the U.S. Department of Agriculture (Ingle 1979; Ingle et al. 1981).

The other side of the coin was a lingering concern for strategic management and planning—not entirely divorced from the ideals of policy analysis and rational-comprehensive planning, but this time stressing project management and bureaucratic decentralization (Rondinelli 1982; Paul 1983a, 1983b). The need for strategic intervention points and project monitoring and evaluation methods is obvious for a decentralized, local approach to development, such as

USAID's "Integrated Rural Development" (IRD) strategy (late 1970s to mid-1980s). It should also be clear, however, that conceiving development as a communal-based learning process (Korten 1980), and calling for the participatory reorientation of bureaucracy to serve the grassroots (Korten 1982; Korten and Uphoff 1981; Korten and Carner 1984) may have very different dynamics and parameters than integrated project management (Kettering 1980; Rondinelli 1986). Management for social transformation (Korten 1981) and management for successful project implementation (Rondinelli 1986)—direct democracy and bureaucratic efficiency—may indeed frequently work at cross-purposes.

This potential conflict is best represented by contrasting the arguments for decentralization presented on one hand by John Friedmann (Friedmann and Douglass 1975; Friedmann and Weaver 1979) and David C. Korten (1980), and on the other by Dennis A. Rondinelli (Rondinelli 1981; Rondinelli, Nellis and Cheema 1983). Friedmann and Korten both construct a model of grassroots basic needs development that depends for its dynamism on local political mobilization, small-scale social learning, local control of economic resources, and local authority over the structures of civil society and the powers of the state. On the other hand, Rondinelli's decentralism is founded on the necessarily local nature of rural development, the bottlenecks inherent in top-down centralized planning, the need for projects to be adapted to their immediate environment, the hands-on monitoring system required for integrated rural development, and the necessity of gaining local knowledge and support for project identification and implementation. The purpose and rationale of the two models are fundamentally different. And despite some shared vocabulary (e.g., learning-based management) and structural similarities in practice, the first model represents a modernized anarcho-syndicalism, while the second is a functionally decentralized form of national development administration.

By the second half of the 1980s USAID decided that the problems inherent in Integrated Rural Development—basically Rondinelli's functional decentralization with some bottom-up participatory components—were impossible to reconcile. IRD was pronounced ineffective and scrapped as the agency's flagship program. Rondinelli's two wide-ranging reviews of development administration written toward the end of the IRD period (1983, 1987) provide an interesting insider's perspective on the perplexities and decline of development management and decentralization. But decentralization and local action were to remain at the heart of development administration for another decade, albeit in a very different guise.

Liberalization and Partnerships

Development management and planning were both in disarray by the late 1980s. Centralized models of development administration had been rejected, and now decentralized approaches to public-led development were out of favor. What next? The answer once again came from domestic policies of developed countries, including Britain and the United States. At the turn of the 1980s both countries had elected ideologically conservative governments that pursued "neo-orthodox" economic strategies, that is policies based on the original free market doctrines of classic British political economy (Mitchell-Weaver and Manning 1991). This meant an emphasis on macroeconomics and getting government out of the way of the everyday working of market forces. Liberalization supposedly implied careful monetary, fiscal, and interest policies, as well as further moves toward free trade within the GATT framework. In practice, two of its hallmarks were deregulation of economic pursuits by the private sector and privatization of publicly controlled economic activities. All planning and management below the macroeconomic level—namely, sectoral and spatial development—were declared taboo, because they would interfere with efficient resource allocation by the marketplace.

The global economic recession of the 1970s had sent developing countries shopping for loans, not only through multilateral and bilateral public channels, but also from private commercial banks fat with the deposits of petrodollars generated by OPEC through the two oil shocks (1973 and 1978). Development failures and escalating energy costs pushed many countries over the edge: they borrowed and borrowed, and then were unable to pay back their loans. Beginning with Mexico's default, the integrity of the international banking and monetary system seemed at risk. In Washington, London, and New York drastic action was felt necessary. A new development paradigm gradually emerged during the first half of the 1980s, meant to restore stability in developing countries through a program of economic reform and structural adjustment (World Bank 1991). This was a macroeconomic strategy that soon came to be identified as "World Bank Conditionality."

In the worst cases, the first step was stabilization through strict monetary, interest rate, and income policies, and special International Monetary Fund (IMF) loans to deal with current account balances. Then would come ERSAP (Economic Reform and Structural Adjustment Program) proper. Decoded, economic reform meant tight fiscal policies, especially in the areas of price supports, income transfers, and the social safety net, and structural adjustment meant privatization of government holdings in both the production and service sectors. These policies were accompanied by a gradual opening of trade to free competition in the global market. Such actions were in such contrast to everything that had been done for over three decades that they have thrown developing countries into a state of trauma, as the World Bank, IMF, USAID, and the UN Development Program (UNDP) made continued development assistance contingent on conditionality—following ERSAP.

In response to ERSAP, development administration has attempted to become involved through a model of liberalization and partnerships. Liberalization has involved participation in the process of privatizing public holdings and parastatals (Dinavo 1995; Lehman 1993; Mutahaba and Balogun 1992; Nkya 1995). Alongside this has been a necessary emphasis on trying to promote private sector organization and especially economic enterpreneurship, through training, capacity-building, and the operation of business incubators (Rasheed and Fashole 1995). As in developed countries (Stokes 1994), administration has become involved with more specialized tasks as well, such as development finance institution building (Krahnen and Schmidt 1994). While the disciplinary side of ERSAP tends to take place at the macro level, training and capacity building are often decentralized small-scale activities. They build in an odd way on the local initiative traditions of development management and decentralization, but this time within the context of small- and mid-sized enterprises in the capitalist marketplace. The decentralist thrust of sustainable development advocates also adds to an administrative interest in capacity-building at the local level (Holmberg 1992).

Capacity-building is key to filling the void left by the retreat of government, as Stokes (1994) explained for the United States. In the partnership element of the current model, development administrators move back and forth from public to quasi-public and private institutions, such as NGOs (nongovernmental organizations), PVOs (private voluntary organizations), and profit-making businesses operating in the public realm. Public-private partnerships are being formed to create an innovative environment in civil society: a network of actors who can help meet development needs, both economic and social (Mitchell-Weaver and Manning 1991). This stress on institution and capacity-building harks back to some of the values of the first public administration movement, but much of it takes place outside the sphere of government proper.

In the mid-1990s ERSAP and the minimalist state are beginning to be put into question by mainstream international institutions (World Bank 1995). Reform and adjustment have demonstrated their ability to stabilize macroeconomic accounts and, perhaps, kick-start development, but the short- and interim-term social costs are very high. Despite the U.N.'s special Fund for Social Development included in each UNDP Country Agreement, much more needs to be done in terms of societal guidance and social protection. This means more activist institutions, in the partnership area and in government itself. While it is impossible to predict the political course of the next several years, development administration at the beginning of the twenty-first century will probably manifest many more of the familiar aspects of public administration, planning, and management than has been the case in recent years. The main difference may be the degree of specialization and technical skills required. Professionals will very possibly be financial specialists, accountants, labor specialists, economic development analysts, and the like, rather than generalists in development administration. This is also the apparent trend in the industrialized world (Stokes 1994).

CLYDE MITCHELL-WEAVER

BIBLIOGRAPHY

Caiden, Gerald E., 1973. "Development, Administrative Capacity and Administrative Reform." *International Review of Administrative Sciences,* 39(4): 327–344.
Dinavo, Jacques V., 1995. *Privatization in Developing Countries: Its Impact on Economic Development and Democracy.* Westport, CT: Praeger Publishers.
Esman, Milton J., 1971. "CAG and the Study of Public Administration." In Fred W. Riggs, ed., *Frontiers of Development Administration.* Durham, NC: Duke University Press.
Friedmann, John and Mike Douglass, 1975. "Agropolitan Development: Towards a New Strategy for Regional Development in Asia." In UNCRD, *Growth Pole Strategy and Regional Development in Asia.* Nagoya, Japan: U.N. Center for Regional Development.
Friedmann, John and Clyde Weaver, 1979. *Territory and Function: The Evolution of Regional Planning.* Berkeley, CA: University of California Press.
Gable, Richard W., 1975. "Development Administration: Background, Terms, Concepts, Theories and a New Approach." Washington, D.C.: U.S. Agency for International Development.
Holmberg, Johan, ed., 1992. *Making Development Sustainable: Redefining Institutions, Policy, and Economics.* Washington, D.C.: Island Press. See especially Chapter 2 by Robin Sharp, "Organizing for Change: People-Power and the Role of Institutions," 39–64.
Hope, Kempe R., 1984. *The Dynamics of Development and Development Administration.* Westport, CT: Greenwood Press.
Ingle, Marcus D., 1979. "Implementing Development Programs: A state of the Art Review." Washington, D.C.: U.S. Agency for International Development.
Ingle, Marcus D., Morris J. Soloman, Pierrette J. Countryman, and Merlyn H. Kettering, 1981. Promising Approaches to Project Management Improvement." Washington, D.C.: Development Project Management Center, U.S. Department of Agriculture.
Kettering, Merlyn H., 1980. "Action Training in Project Planning and Management: A Review of the Experience of the National Planning Project of USAID-Government of Jamaica, 1976-1979." Working paper. Washington, D.C.: Development Project Management Center, U.S. Department of Agriculture.
Kettering, Merlyn H. and Terry D. Schmidt, 1981. "Improving Project Monitoring and Implementation Systems: A Strategy and Implementation Plan for a Project Management Information System for USAID/Thailand." Washington, D.C.: Development Project Management Center, U.S. Department of Agriculture.
Korten, David C., 1980. "Community Organization and Rural Development: A Learning Process Approach." *Public Administration Review,* 40(5): 480–511.
———, 1981. "Management of Social Transformation." *Public Administration Review,* 41(6): 609–618.
———, 1982. "The Working Group as a Mechanism for Managing Bureaucratic Reorientation: Experience from the Philippines." *NASPAA Working Paper, No. 4.* Washington, D.C.: National Association of Schools of Public Affairs and Administration.
Korten, David C. and Norman T. Uphoff, 1981. "Bureaucratic Reorientation for Participatory Rural Development." *NASPAA Working Paper, No. 1.* Washington, D.C.: National Association of Schools of Public Affairs and Administration.
Korten, David C. and George Carner, 1984. "Reorienting Bureaucracies to Serve People: Two Experiences in the Philippines." *Canadian Journal of Development Studies,* 5(1):7–24.
Krahnen, Jan Pieter and Reinhard H. Schmidt, 1994. *Development Finance as Institution Building: A New Approach to Poverty-Oriented Banking.* Boulder, CO: Westview Press.
Lehman, Howard P., 1993. *Indebted Development: Strategic Bargaining and Economic Adjustment in the Third World.* New York: St. Martin's Press.
Lewis, W. Arthur, 1966. *Development Planning.* London: Allen and Unwin.
Mitchell-Weaver, Clyde and Brenda Manning, 1991. "Public-Private Partnerships in Third World Development: A Conceptual Overview." *Studies in Comparative International Development,* vol. 7: 45–67.
Mutahaba, Gelase and M. Jide Balogun, eds., 1992. *Enhancing Policy Management Capacity in Africa.* West Hartford, CT: Kumarian Press.
Nkya, Estomih J., 1995. "From Divestment to Public Sector Reform in Tanzania: Explaining Forms of Privatization as Policy Choice Options." Unpublished Ph.D. dissertation. Graduate School of Public and International Affairs, University of Pittsburgh.
Paul, Samuel, 1983a. *Strategic Management of Development Programmes.* Geneva: ILO.
———, 1983b. "Training for Public Administration and Management in Developing Countries: A Review." *World Bank Staff Working Paper, 584.* Washington, D.C.: World Bank.
Rasheed, Sadig and David Fashole Luke, eds., 1995. *Development Management in Africa.* Boulder, CO: Westview Press.
Riggs, Fred W., 1971. "The Context of Development Administration." In Fred W. Riggs, ed., *Frontiers of Development Administration.* Durham, NC: Duke University Press.
Rondinelli, Dennis A., 1976. "Why Development Projects Fail: Some Problems of Project Management in Developing Countries." *Project Management Quarterly,* 7(1):10–15.
———, 1981. "Government Decentralization in Comparative Perspective: Theory and Practice in Developing Countries." *International Review of Administrative Sciences,* 47(2): 133–45.
———, 1982. "The Dilemma of Development Administration: Uncertainty and Complexity in Control-Oriented Bureaucracies." *World Politics,* 35(1): 43–72.
———, 1983. *Development Projects as Policy Experiments: An Adaptive Approach to Development Administration.* London: Routledge.
———, 1984. "Development Administration." In Adam Kuper and Jessica Kuper, eds., *The Social Science Encyclopaedia.* London: Routledge.
———, 1986. "Practical Lessons for Development Management: Experience with Implementing Agricultural Development Projects in Africa." *AID Evaluation Special Study.* Washington, D.C.: U.S. Agency for International Development.
———, 1987. *Development Administration and U.S. Foreign Aid Policy.* Boulder, CO: Lynne Rienner Publishers.
Rondinelli, Dennis A. and H. Raymond Radosevich, 1974. "An Integrated Approach to Development Project Management." Report to the U.S. Agency for International Development for Modernizing Management for Development. Washington, D.C.: U.S. Agency for International Development.

Rondinelli, Dennis A., John R. Nellis and G. Shabbir Cheema, 1983. "Decentralization in Developing Countries: A Review of Recent Experience." *World Bank Staff Working Paper, No. 581*. Washington, D.C.: World Bank.

Siffin, William J., 1976. "Two Decades of Public Administration in Developing Countries." *Public Administration Review*, 36(1): 61–71.

Stokes, Donald E., 1994. "The Changing World of the Public Executive." Paper presented to the Conference on Public Affairs and Management in the 21st Century, School of Public Affairs, Baruch College, City University of New York, 2 December.

Stone, Donald., 1966. "Guidelines for Training Development Administrators." *Journal of Administration Overseas*, 5(4): 229–242.

———, 1971. "Government Machinery Necessary for Development." In Martin Kriesberg, ed., *Public Administration in Developing Countries*. Washington, D.C.: Brookings Institution.

———, 1973. "Removing Administrative and Planning Constraints to Development." *Journal of Administration Overseas*, 12(1): 4–10.

Stone, Donald and Alice B. Stone, 1976. "Creation of Administrative Capability: The Missing Ingredient of Development Strategy." In John Baratt, David S. Collier, Kurt Glaser, and Herman Monning, eds. *Strategy for Development*. London: Macmillan Press.

Thompson, Victor A. 1964, "Administrative Objectives for Development Administration." *Administrative Science Quarterly*, 9: 91–108.

Waterston, Albert, 1965. *Development Planning: Lessons of Experience*. Baltimore, MD: Johns Hopkins University Press.

Weidner, Edward W., 1962. "Development Administration: A New Focus of Research." In F. Heady and S. L. Stokes, eds., *Papers in Comparative Public Administration*. Ann Arbor, MI: Institute of Public Administration, University of Michigan.

———, 1964. *Technical Assistance in Public Administration Overseas: The Case of Development Administration*. Chicago, IL: Public Administration Service.

Weiss, Moshe, 1966. "Some Suggestions for Improving Development Administration." *International Review of Administrative Sciences*, 32(3): 193–196.

World Bank, 1991. *World Development Report, 1991*. New York: Oxford University Press.

———, *World Development Report, 1995*. New York: Oxford University Press.

DEVELOPMENT GOVERNANCE.

Governance as envisioned by international development agencies; the power and influence relationship between government and citizens in developing countries (DC) that is utilized to implement social and economic programs. Development governance does not seek to redo the DC regime type since effective projects and programs have emerged out of different political systems. The main concern is that development governance breed successful projects.

Origin and Subsequent History

Reforming the governmental machinery of DC to achieve planned economic and social development activities effectively is not a new undertaking for public policy and administration. Under colonial rule, the indigenous administrative systems of DC were reorganized to pursue their colonizer's development agenda. After independence, DC turned to public administration specialists from Western countries to assist them in restructuring their postcolonial state bureaucracies for the effective implementation of their bilaterally and multilaterally funded economic and social projects and programs. Some of the early development governance strategies prescribed by these public administration experts were basically structural and functional reforms that dealt with the civil service, personnel pay and promotion, tax administration, budget, and finance. However, interest in development governance declined after funding agencies shifted their emphasis to the technical efficiency and economic soundness of development projects and programs.

A resurgence of interest in development governance resurfaced in the 1990s after a series of studies performed by the World Bank emphasized that a country's capacity to implement planned projects was a critical determining component to project effectiveness and sustainability. These World Bank findings, based on their 50-year experience of funding development projects, were also reinforced by a 1994 Asian Development Bank study, "Report of the Task Force on Improving Project Quality," which similarly pointed out that the quality of a recipient country's local administrative agencies was a strong determinant of project success or failure. Other bilateral and multilateral development institutions also confirmed their conclusions—thus the global concern to enhance development governance in the 1990s.

Current Practice

Development governance is currently being promoted by individual countries and international organizations through bilateral and multilateral means. Bilateral aid agencies such as the United Kingdom's Overseas Development Agency (ODA) and the United States' Agency for International Development (AID), nongovernmental organizations such as the Canada-based Institute on Governance (IOG) and the Ford Foundation in the United States, and multilateral development organizations such as the World Bank and the United Nations Development Programme (UNDP) prescribe development governance to DC as part of the overall institutional reform needed by their public sector to increase the rates of success in their project implementation especially at the local level.

There are essentially three facets of governance that need to be examined, namely: (1) political regime type (e.g., communist, democratic, authoritarian, monarchy, dictatorship); (2) organizational process by which authority and control is exercised; and (3) institutional capacity to plan and implement policies and carry out functions. However, international organizations concentrate their reform efforts and operational advice to deal with only the last two facets of governance since the first dimension is considered a domestic political issue that is not within their mandate of social and economic development. Moreover, many public management specialists argue that the political regime type is not a critical factor to project success. But they are aware that in certain instances, the inter related nature of these three dimensions often causes crossover issues that make it difficult for change to be limited to just the latter two aspects of development governance.

In their development governance (often simply called governance) work at the World Bank and the Development Assistance Committee (DAC) of the Organization for Economic Cooperation and Development (OECD), seven specific areas of the DC public sector are targeted for improvement as embodied in their business operations: (1) public sector management, (2) accountability, (3) legal and regulatory framework, (4) transparency and information, (5) human rights, (6) participatory approaches, and (7) military expenditure. The Asian Development Bank (ADB) and European Bank for Reconstruction and Development (EBRD) subscribe to the first four areas in much the same way. Some variations in interpretation, however, are evident in their operations and prescribed applications. Moreover, the United Nations Development Programme (UNDP), Inter-American Development Bank (IADB), African Development Bank (AFDB), the United Kingdom's Overseas Development Agency (ODA), and Canadian International Development Agency (CIDA) all concur with this renewed concern in development governance but place a greater emphasis on basic public sector management in personnel pay and promotion, tax administration, budget, and finance.

At the United Kingdom's ODA, serious DC attempts at improving the quality of public administration (or in their terms "good government") are a key determining factor for development assistance, and certain cases of noncompliance with the ODA's good government guidelines have resulted in the suspension or reduction of a recipient country's aid (Central Office of Information 1993).

Variations of Practice in the United States

In the United States, implementing governance changes is interpreted to mean simply the restructuring and reorganization of government, but new ways to manage the peoples' business have expanded beyond the context of government or the U.S. public sector. Mounting domestic pressure and a changing global environment have persuaded the Reagan, Bush, and Clinton administrations to implement policies that encourage: (1) privatization of public services, (2) use of nongovernmental organizations, and (3) development of more public-private partnerships. Thus, a new era of governance concern was born in the United States.

The Clinton administration's "reinvention exercise" is one clear manifestation of the U.S. commitment to a new

type of development governance even in a developed country setting. At the federal government level, it is envisioned that reinventing governance would eliminate overlapping and duplication to increase the speed by which central agencies respond to fast-changing public needs.

Popular usage of the generic term governance spans across a number of other disciplines and subfields—business, political science, economics, sociology, and law—aside from it being one of the core themes of international aid administration in the 1990s. Within the United States, private sector governance, more specifically known as corporate governance, refers to the framework of laws, regulatory institutions, and reporting requirements that condition the way the corporate sector is managed.

Development governance became a formal scholarly issue of concern within the academic community with the publication in 1991 of the International Political Science Association's Structure and Organization of Government (SOG) Research Committee journal, entitled *Governance: An International Journal of Policy and Administration*. In terms of substantive content, policy, administration, and the organization of the state vis-à-vis society are covered from an intercultural perspective that goes beyond appropriate administration and management in the United States. Numerous other public administration journals such as *Public Administration Review* also have articles covering the various subthemes of governance.

JOAQUIN L. GONZALEZ III

BIBLIOGRAPHY

Asian Development Bank, 1994. *Report of the Task Force on Improving Project Quality*. Manila, Philippines.
Brautigam, Deborah, 1991. *Governance and Economy: A Review*. Washington, D.C.: World Bank Working Paper (WPS 815).
Central Office of Information, 1993. *Britain 1994: An Official Handbook*. London: HMSO.
John, DeWitt, 1994. "What Will New Governance Mean for the Federal Government?" *Public Administration Review*, vol. 54, no. 2:170–175.
World Bank, 1991. "Managing Development: The Governance Dimension." Discussion paper. Washington, D.C.: World Bank.
———, *Governance: The World Bank's Experience*. Washington, D.C.: IBRD.

DEVELOPMENT OFFICER. A nonitinerant, goal-oriented, professional fund-raising expert who works as a staff member within a nonprofit organization and has primary responsibility for strategically planning, focusing, and coordinating the organization's fund-raising techniques with competence and ethical discipline. The officer may work alone or be part of a development team.

Fund-raising and development are irrevocably linked to each other. Development implies more than the process of solicitation. It includes the process of researching potential donors, cultivating, and soliciting them, often with formal presentations developed to appeal to the specific interests of the potential philanthropist or wealthy social activist. Integral to this, particularly with donors who are capable of and interested in making substantial contributions to the organization, the development officer must be prepared to provide tax information on laws and options for giving. Processing and acknowledging gifts large and small, and developing mechanisms for the formal recognition of donors, as well as exercising discretion when the donor seeks anonymity are the development officers' responsibilities. Strategic planning designed to further the institution's mission, and administering the office of development, are often additional functions of the development officer and his or her staff. (See **fund-raising**.)

ERNA GELLES

BIBLIOGRAPHY

Bloland, Harland G. and Rita Bornstein, 1991. "Fund-raising in Transition: Strategies for Professionalism." In Dwight F. Burlingame and Lamont J. Hulse, eds., *Taking Fund Raising Seriously: Advancing the Profession and Practice of Raising Money*. San Francisco: Jossey Bass Nonprofit Sector, pp. 103–123.

Burlingame, Dwight F. and Lamont J. Hulse, eds., 1991. *Taking Fund Raising Seriously: Advancing the Profession and Practice of Raising Money*. San Francisco: Jossey Bass Nonprofit Sector Series.

DEVOLUTION. The transfer of powers from a central to a local, regional, or peripheral authority. In the twentieth century, the most obvious example of the devolution of power is contained in the process of decolonization. With the winning of independence from the British Crown by India and Pakistan in 1947, there began an unprecedented concession of political and (to a degree) economic control to the successor regimes nurtured during the latter stages of empire. Between the late 1940s and the late 1980s, only the Soviet Union—itself the last of the nineteenth-century European empires—failed to devolve power from the political core to the periphery. Decolonization is, however, as extreme example of devolution. For the most part, devolutionists argue about tax-raising rights, regional autonomy, educational integrity, linguistic purity, and cultural safeguards.

The call for devolution has three main manifestations. The first is from the peripheral area. This has been variously evident from the 1960s onwards in such diverse areas as Quebec and Scotland; in both, the demand was for the proper recognition of national identity. The claim was, and remains, that ethnic, religious, linguistic, and cultural differences have not been sufficiently protected by the dominant political culture, respectively in these examples of Canada and the United Kingdom. In its most extreme form, the demand for devolution takes the form of a terrorist-based campaign for independence, as in the Basque areas of France and Spain.

The second push is from the center itself, usually by political parties that have invested heavily in the virtues of local government; the Liberal Democratic Party in the United Kingdom is typical of this, a political institution that places a relatively low value on the unitary state. Throughout Western Europe, such political parties or groups are predisposed to federal solutions to national or regional government. This view holds that democracy is best served where local concerns are given to those with local responsibilities. The third view is an essentially economic one; the People's Republic of China from the mid-1980s showed this to an unusual extent. There, in seeking a transition from Maoist, centralist dogmas, the policy was to create regional hegemony, albeit within an overall national design, to facilitate that economic takeoff into sustained growth so long forecast for China. Reflected in the 1984 agreement on the formal handback to China of Hong Kong by the British, this version of devolution was characterized by the phrase "One Nation, Two Systems;" since then, China has allowed the development of a considerable degree of regional diversity, autonomy, development, and authority.

Another way of looking at devolution in the last decade of the twentieth century is to see it as a challenge to the primacy of the nation state. Since the rise of the modern international system, popularly dated from the Treaty of Westphalia (1648), the presumption has been that no rival to the national state was available for the provision of those most basic services to the people—freedom from want and freedom from fear. Devolution accepts this to be true in the limited sense that the existing state system contains within it artificial "states," encompassing more than one nation. These, it is argued, could better serve their peoples if they were broken up. To that extent, the call for devolution by national groups within existing states, while domestically disruptive, is not essentially revolutionary.

There is no perfect balance between the needs of centralism and the demands of the periphery. Power is something that tends to be taken rather than given: even where a central authority concedes power, the implication is that it can withdraw its concession. Within that assumption, devolutionists will always argue that more is better than less, centralists will argue the contrary, and the outcome will be determined by the price that the political traffic can bear.

PETER FOOT

DIMOCK, MARSHALL EDWARD (1903–1991). Political science educator, public administration theorist, public servant, mentor, and distinguished author best known for his insistence that humanity and balance pervade the profession of public administration.

In many ways, Marshall Dimock was a scholar unto himself. As his contemporaries honed the science of public administration, he championed essential values of its art. After tucking himself into a Vermont mountain in mid-career, he chopped the wood that fueled the stove that warmed the chair where he wrote the books for which he is well-known. For a co-author and collaborator, he frequently looked no further than across the dinner table at his second wife, Gladys Ogden Dimock.

Yet this is too simple a description of a man whose intellectual hand touched generations of public administrators. His intellectual discontent with the increasing pervasiveness of bureaucracy never tainted his personal relationships with established and budding bureaucrats. Equally at home with heads of state and beginning students of public administration, he gently encouraged each to take the next step to improve the quality of public service. Even while teaching the historical lessons of crisis in the public sector, he never lost faith that the status quo could be improved.

The portrait of a public administrator that emerges from Dimock's works is that of the broadly educated person who has taken time to develop sensitivity for the full range of constituents affected by contemporary social problems. He believed that public administrators should be lifetime learners, committed to professionalism and willing to lead when called upon to do so. The development of good instincts when faced with complex problems was, to Dimock, as important as the development of good analytical skills. Time and time again he urged public administrators never to lose their humanity and their commitment to the good of the community.

The quality of graciousness that pervaded Dimock's professional life was likewise promoted by him as an essential element of organizational behavior in the academic and practical spheres of public administration. The theoretical door to public administration was propped open by Dimock, who believed that scholars from other disciplines should be welcomed to participate in the growth of public administration, and even encouraged to defect from their own discipline when such a defection was mutually beneficial to the scholar and the field. Good leaders could come to public administration from any discipline; Dimock was a prime scout and promoter of any such talent. Similarly, Dimock taught lessons from the histories of many countries from a belief that good ideas could come from governments other than that of the United States. While examining the private sector, Dimock likewise urged cooperation and adoption of many business principles for the smooth running of government. His unpretentiousness in this regard made him a role model for his contemporaries as well as for generations of public administrators that followed him.

The picture of public organization drawn by Marshall Dimock is a wedding of the best qualities of bureaucracy with the essential elements of successful enterprise. While acknowledging the efficiencies of technological innovation, delegation of authority and division of labor, in *Administrative Vitality* (1959) he nonetheless called for an openness to organizational change, which he felt has impeded by bureaucratic structure (p. 102). The cultivation of human potential was likewise deemed essential by Dimock, along with the development of appropriate, personalized rewards for administrative genius. In *A Philosophy of Administration* (1958), he joined Max Weber and others in bemoaning the unchecked growth of bureaucracy, especially as it dehumanizes the practice of public administration (p. 161).

Dimock believed that policy should govern administration, and conversely, in *Business and Government* (4th ed., 1961) he cautioned public administrators to pay close attention to the means by which policies are enacted (pp. 482–483). He characterized the policy formulator as scientist (someone facile with empirical methods) and the policy implementer as artist—someone whose best qualities included inventiveness and flexibility. In *A Philosophy of Administration* (1958), Dimock stated his belief that the motivation of both scientists and artists in administration should be grounded in the ethical imperative of doing one's best for the good of society (p. 145).

Dimock's career was as broad as his academic interests. Beginning in 1928, he was on the faculty of colleges and universities in several countries, including the United States, England, Japan, and Turkey. Bridging the gap between theory and practice, he lent his administrative skills to the United States Department of Labor, where he was Assistant Secretary (1938–1940); the United States Department of Justice, where he was Associate Commissioner in the Immigration and Naturalization Service (1940–1942); and the War Shipping Administration of the United States, where he was a Director and Assistant Deputy (1942–1944). He provided technical assistance to the United Nations in Turkey (1953–1954) and consulted with several public organizations in the United States, including the Natural Resources Commission (1935–1939), the War Department (1933–1935, 1944), the General Accounting Office (1946–1948), the office of the Secretary of Defense (1948–1949), and the President's Advisory Council Executive Organization (1969–1971). In addition, he was a member of the Vermont state legislature (1949–1950). During his lifetime he contributed to more than 40 books about administration, economics, and political science. In 1968, he was elected to the National Academy of Public Administration.

Dimock balanced his brilliant public administration career with such activities as writing children's stories, moderating the Unitarian Universalist Association (1961–1964) near his home in Bethel, Vermont, growing much of his own food, and raising his children to appreciate the amenities of country life. His second wife was his soulmate

and sounding board for over 40 years (1940–1989). According to Marlene Provost of the Public Administration Program at the University of Vermont, those who knew Dimock intimately attribute his success to the Dimocks' unique personal and professional relationship.

SARA ANN CONKLING

BIBLIOGRAPHY

The following represent some of the best of Dimock's timeless work in public administration:

Dimock, Marshall E., 1958. *A Philosophy of Administration*. New York: Harper and Brothers.
———, 1959. *Administrative Vitality*. New York: Harper and Brothers.
———, 1961. *Business and Government*. 4th ed. New York: Holt, Rinehart and Winston.
———, 1991. "Crisis Management: Shoring Up America's Economy and Government." *International Journal of Public Administration*, vol. 14, no. 4: 499–762.

DIPLOMACY. The conduct of international relations by negotiation and other peaceful means (such as clarifying intentions and gathering information) that are either directly or indirectly, immediately or in due course, designed to promote negotiation. Diplomacy develops where power is dispersed and a shared culture facilitates communication. The foreign policy which diplomacy serves may, of course, be belligerent rather than peaceful, as when alliances are negotiated in preparation for war or cemented by diplomacy for its duration.

Diplomacy with recognizably modern features (most critically the immunity of the envoy) existed in the ancient world, the best early evidence of this being the archive of diplomatic correspondence of the Egyptian court in El-Amarna generated in the fourteenth century B.C.E. Records from Greece, India, and China dated roughly a thousand years later provide more copious evidence of familiar diplomatic forms, as do those from Europe in the Middle Ages. By this time, diplomacy had been placed principally in the hands of a *nuncius* or, with growing frequency after the late twelfth century, a plenipotentiary. The former was simply a "living letter" whereas the latter had full powers—*plena potestas*—to negotiate on behalf of and bind his principal, but both remained temporary envoys who were required to return home when their narrowly focused tasks were completed. It was not until the middle of the fifteenth century, in the relations between the city-states of Italy, that we find the origins of the most characteristic of all modern diplomatic practices: the resident embassy. (Though it should be noted that in ancient Greece a city-state might employ as a diplomatic representative and grant citizenship to a resident of a city with which it had to deal; such a person was known as a *proxenos*.)

The Origins and Development of the Resident Embassy

The resident ambassador, who did not of course altogether replace the temporary envoy, was a response to the intensification of diplomatic activity in Italy in the fifteenth century. This made the financial costs of using ad hoc missions increasingly hard to bear and, while travel remained slow and hazardous, their practical drawbacks increasingly obvious. However, the appearance of the permanent mission also signalled a new awareness, clearly expressed in the political testament of Cardinal Richelieu (1585–1642), first minister of the French king, Louis XIII, that diplomacy functions best when it is a continuous rather than episodic process: maximum familiarity with local conditions is achieved, openings to develop a policy are more readily grasped, and diplomatic initiatives can be launched without attracting the attention characteristically accompanying the arrival of a special envoy.

Developing in Italy, the resident embassy spread northwards over the Alps and became the key mode of diplomatic activity until the early twentieth century. Despite its origins, it was described as the "French system of diplomacy" in *The Evolution of Diplomatic Method* (1954) by Harold Nicolson, probably the most well-known writer on diplomacy in the English language. This description was legitimate because it was the French who cleaned up and professionalized the Italian inheritance during the seventeenth and eighteenth centuries; French writers, notably François de Callières (1645–1717), who were the most important theorists of this diplomatic system; and the French language which replaced Latin as its *lingua franca*.

In the first half of the twentieth century the French system came to be known more commonly as the "old diplomacy." In addition to major reliance on permanent embassies with special immunities from local jurisdiction, its characteristic features were secrecy, elaborate ceremonial, careful protocol, honesty, and—at least by this time—professionalism. Secret negotiation prevented the making of concessions from being sabotaged by foreign friends and domestic constituences before they could be presented alongside any gains. Ceremonial was used to burnish the prestige of a prince, flatter allies, and solemnize any agreements which might be reached. Protocol brought order to diplomatic encounters. Honesty made it more likely that agreements would be negotiated on the basis of a true estimate of interests and that states would be regarded as worthy negotiating partners in the future. For its part, the professionalization of diplomacy, which was not seriously under way, even in France, until well into the nineteenth century, eventually broadened the recruitment of diplomats and improved their training. Their classic manual, which in revised form is still in print, was published in 1917 as *A Guide to Diplomatic Practice* by the distinguished British diplomat, Sir Ernest Satow (1843–1929).

The Diplomatic Corps

The professionalization of diplomacy also contributed to the growth of the diplomatic corps. Not to be confused with the diplomatic service (the diplomats who serve a particular state), the *corps diplomatique* is the multinational community of diplomats accredited to a particular government. With its own rules of procedure, for example that the longest serving ambassador should be *doyen* or *doyenne* (two-way channel of communication on matters of common interest between the corps and the host government), this institution reached an extraordinary apogée in China at the turn of the twentieth century. Here the diplomatic corps was restricted by the Manchu court to an enclave in Peking, which was not in itself unusual for any suspicious government wanting to keep a watchful eye on the doings of foreigners. However, under the International Protocol of 1901, which was imposed by the powers following relief of the siege of the legations by the Boxers in 1900, the Legation Quarter, as it had come to be known, was removed altogether from the control of the Chinese authorities. Protected by substantial detachments of their own armed forces, new fortifications and a perimeter "glacis" of razed ground, the foreign diplomats themselves administered life within the quarter: it was a city within a city. This situation endured until the Communist seizure of power in 1949, after which the missions of those states that remained in China were gradually moved to the eastern part of the city.

The Vienna Convention on Diplomatic Relations, 1961

Until 1961 the international regulation of diplomacy conducted by permanent embassies was based chiefly on custom and courtesy. However, in this year a Conference on Diplomatic Intercourse and Immunities was held in Vienna to codify the existing law, not least in order to enthuse the new states with its support. The upshot was the Vienna Convention on Diplomatic Relations, the hallmark of which was a rigorously functional approach to diplomatic privileges and immunities. These were justified, in other words, not by such archaic fictions as extraterritoriality but only by the need to secure the efficient functioning of the permanent mission. Accordingly, those privileges which were essential (such as the inviolability of mission premises) were generally strengthened, while those which were less so were reduced—as were the numbers of those by whom they could be invoked. The Convention was signed on April 18, 1961, and, adequately ratified, came into force on April 24, 1964. With 165 states having ratified by 1992, the Vienna Convention on Diplomatic Relations is one of the most secure and broadly based multilateral regimes in the entire field of international relations.

Multilateral Diplomacy

The old diplomacy, now usually referred to as bilateral diplomacy, is still important today, not least because of its underpinning by the Vienna Convention. Nevertheless, even Nicolson (1954) was aware of its drawbacks: gratuitous secretiveness, the tendency of the resident ambassador to "go native," overrepresentation of the traditional aristocracy, and—as the feverish twentieth century multiplied the participants and stretched out the international agenda—an excessively leisurely pace. These drawbacks, together with the growing popularity of the liberal democratic notion that power should rest on consent expressed via public assemblies, stimulated the explosion in the twentieth century of multilateral diplomacy, that is, diplomacy conducted in conferences of three or more states.

The origins of multilateral diplomacy are as ancient as diplomacy itself, and it was important, at least in Europe, in the nineteenth century. But the interwar League of Nations and the post war United Nations, with their crowded assemblies and (in the latter case) majority voting procedures, are eloquent testimonies to the peculiar faith of the twentieth century in this mode of diplomacy. Over recent decades, however, against a background in which bilateral diplomacy via the resident embassy has displayed remarkable tenacity, this faith has been severely tested. Third World states have expressed disillusionment with its results; the United States, finally reacting to years of financing programs to which it was opposed, began to withhold funds from the UN system; and the number of international organizations began to drop. Nevertheless, multilateral diplomacy, which is valuable when urgent attention must be given by many parties to a particular question and it is important to advertise the fact that this is being done, is here to stay. What has helped to guarantee this is the now widespread acceptance that important decisions must be based on consensus.

Summitry

Summitry—diplomacy conducted (bilaterally or multilaterally) with the personal involvement of heads of state or government—also has ancient antecedents. However, television, democracy, and jet planes gave it unprecedented diplomatic importance in the second half of the twentieth century. Professional diplomats have traditionally loathed summitry, and not without reason. The involvement of political leaders in diplomacy tends too often to inject sloppiness where there should be precision, publicity where there should be discretion, ignorance where there should be intimate acquaintance with detail, and personal considerations where there should only be objective consideration of the requirements of the national interest. Nevertheless, summits—especially those which are held as part of a regular series—can make a broad contribution to diplo-

macy as well, not least because of their ability to revive the momentum of a flagging negotiation. Among other examples, the European Council—a serial summit—and the Camp David summit on the Middle East in September 1978—an ad hoc summit—provide evidence of just how useful this mode of diplomacy can be if properly prepared and carefully managed.

Negotiation

Negotiation is not by any means the only function of diplomacy but it is without doubt the most important. It is regulated argument designed to give expression to a harmony or, more often, to reconcile a conflict of interests. It commands most attention in contemporary theorizing about diplomacy, as it did in the work of Callières at the beginning of the eighteenth century. Negotiations generally proceed through three states: prenegotiations, where it is necessary to agree on the need to negotiate at all, on the agenda, and on such procedural matters as venue; the formula stage, where the broad principles of a settlement are established; and the details stage, where they are fleshed out. Which stage is the most difficult tends to vary with kind of negotiation and kind of party involved. The last stage, which is the moment of truth, is generally the most difficult, though the first is a strong challenger for this dubious honour when the negotiation involves recently or still warring parties. If the momentum of a negotiation falters, deadlines and other techniques may be employed with reasonable hope of reviving it. If agreement is reached it remains to be "packaged." Saving face is often an important consideration here; as a result, since someone's face saved is someone else's put out, presentation itself provides ample scope for negotiation.

Mediation

A special but important case of negotiation occurs when the main parties to a dispute invoke the assistance of an intermediary, as when Algeria assisted the United States and Iran in the diplomacy that brought to an end the Tehran embassy hostages crisis in January 1981. Mediation, employed when at least one of the main parties cannot bring itself to deal directly with the other, may entail a more or less active role for the intermediary: at one end merely providing "good offices," at the other trailing inducements or arm-twisting the parties towards a settlement. The role adopted clearly bears on the question of the ideal attributes of the mediator, power being largely irrelevant at the good offices end but indispensable at the other. Or is it? Controversy surrounds this question. Power may produce a formal settlement but if it is not just will it last? There is also argument about the importance of impartiality. Long a staple of the conventional wisdom on the grounds that in the absence of impartiality trust will be impossible, in his book *The Peace Brokers* (1982) Saadia Touval not only dis-

misses impartiality as useless to a mediator but as a positive handicap; for Touval, power and acceptability are all that matter, while partiality will induce the antagonists to curry favor with the mediator, either to win or retain that party's favor.

Mediation is ubiquitous in international relations but those at odds are often anxious to cut out the middle party at the first available opportunity, as the Nixon administration and Communist China did at the beginning of the 1970s. (France, Romania and—above all—Pakistan had assisted at the beginning of this rapprochement.) This is partly to avoid unwanted pressure and the risk of distorted communications; but in some circumstances it is also to avoid payment, for, as Touval notes rather sweepingly in *The Peace Brokers*, "mediators, like brokers, are in it for profit" (p. 321). (There are those in the UN Secretariat, the Vatican, and a host of nongovernmental organizations promoting "multitrack diplomacy" who would no doubt take issue with this view.)

Diplomacy Without "Diplomatic Relations"

When states are "in diplomatic relations" they are willing to engage in direct communication via official representatives. This does not necessarily entail an exchange of embassies and often does not, especially if one or the other is poor or simply has little interest in developing the relationship. However, if states lack representation in each other's capitals this may also be because they are not in diplomatic relations, a condition that may come about as a result either of nonrecognition of a state or its government or formal severance of relations where recognition is unimpaired. (When the United States severed diplomatic relations with Cuba several years after Fidel Castro came to power, it did not withdraw recognition either from his government or the state over which he presided.)

Whereas hitherto severing relations had generally been a prelude to war and thus limited in extent, during the 1960s this became popular as a weapon of propaganda. Nevertheless, many of the states resorting to this expedient were anxious for the substance of resident diplomacy to continue, and it was against this background that "disguised embassies"—though hardly unknown in earlier periods—began to flourish.

The most significant of the disguised embassies is the interests section, which appeared only in 1965 but is now an almost reflexive response to a breach in diplomatic relations. It represents an elaboration of the old diplomatic institution of the protecting power, a state appointed to employ its own mission to protect the interests of a second in the country of a third, a role most frequently played by Switzerland. An interests section exists when the protecting power permits the work of protection to be undertaken, under the flag of its embassy, by nationals of the state which has theoretically been expelled. The United States first employed interests sections in the Middle East following the Six-Day War, when various Arab states, alleging U.S. complicity in the Israeli offensive, severed relations with it.

Other disguised embassies include offices with nondiplomatic covers, such as trade missions and travel agencies; representative offices (sometimes known as liaison offices), which are useful where recognition is a problem, as in Sino-American relations between 1973 and 1979; and consulates or the consular sections of embassies; which are usually employed to deal with the problems of individual citizens abroad. Consulates are sometimes exploited for purposes of political communication as well because they operate under their own legal regime, the Vienna Convention on Consular Relations, 1963. As a result, consulates may survive a breach in diplomatic relations or be created—as in Soviet-Israeli relations in 1990–91—as a first step towards their full restoration.

Variations in Practice

Since diplomacy is by definition an international activity and is substantially regulated by an international regime ratified by almost every state, it is hardly surprising that variations in practice are not considerable. Nevertheless, some may be noted.

In *Negotiating Across Cultures* (1991), Raymond Cohen has argued that there are significant differences between the negotiating styles of states such as the United States and Israel with a predominantly individualistic and rationalistic ethos ("low context" cultures), and those such as China, Egypt, and Japan with a more collectivist character attaching importance to form and hierarchy ("high context" cultures). Among other things, the former tend to adopt a no-nonsense problem-solving approach emphasizing the importance of detail, while the latter—disliking explicit confrontation—are more inclined to indirectness and to stress the importance of agreement on broad principle. Against this is the view advanced by I. W. Zartman and M. R. Berman in *The Practical Negotiator* (1982) that diplomats, irrespective of their country of origin, are members of an international community with its own distinctive subculture.

As for the channels through which negotiations are conducted, these appear to vary (other than by character of relationship and diplomatic ends sought) chiefly with levels of wealth and only marginally with character of political regime. Poor states tend to employ an ambassador based in a major capital such as Paris to handle relations with any number of neighboring states (multiple accreditation); they also rely more for the conduct of bilateral relations on their permanent missions to international organizations such as the UN. Political regimes with executives who chafe under the influence of strong legislatures and

the drag of sprawling bureaucracies, as in the United States, have a strong incentive to resort to informal modes of diplomacy: personal rather than official envoys, and back channels rather than regular ones. In the end, in other words, diplomacy always finds a way.

GEOFFREY R. BERRIDGE

BIBLIOGRAPHY

Berridge, Geoffrey R., 1995. *Diplomacy: Theory and Practice.* Hemel Hempstead: Prentice Hall/Harvester.
Callières, François de, 1983. *The Art of Diplomacy,* ed. by H. M. A. Keens-Soper and K. Schweizer. Leicester: Leicester University Press. *First published* Paris 1716 *Translated* AF Whyte, London, 1919.
Cohen, Raymond, 1991. *Negotiating Across Cultures: Communication Obstacles in International Diplomacy.* Washington, D.C.: U.S. Institute of Peace Press.
Gore-Booth, Lord, ed., 1979. *Satow's Guide to Diplomatic Practice,* 5th edition. London: Longman.
Hamilton, Keith and Richard Langhorne, 1995. *The Practice of Diplomacy: Its Evolution, Theory and Administration.* London and New York: Routledge.
James, Alan M., 1980. "Diplomacy and International Society." *International Relations,* vol. 6 (November) 931–948.
Mattingly, Garrett, 1965. *Renaissance Diplomacy.* Harmondsworth: Penguin.
Nicolson, Harold, 1954. *The Evolution of Diplomatic Method.* London: Constable.
Peyrefitte, Alain, trans. by J. Rothschild, 1993. *The Collision of Two Civilizations: The British Expedition to China in 1792–94.* London: Harvill.
Queller, Donald E., 1967. *The Office of Ambassador in the Middle Ages.* Princeton, NJ: Princeton University Press.
Touval, Saadia, 1982. *The Peace Brokers.* Princeton, NJ: Princeton University Press.
Zartman, I. William and Maureen Berman, 1982. *The Practical Negotiator.* New Haven and London: Yale University Press.

DIPLOMATIC PRIVILEGES AND IMMUNITIES.

The special rights given to formally accredited diplomatic officials that make them immune from the civil and criminal laws of the state to which they are assigned. These rights are a means for maintaining order in the international system. They facilitate the practice of diplomacy, the system of official communication between and among states. States recognize each other formally through the exchange of ambassadors and other diplomatic personnel. Diplomatic immunities assure sending states that their diplomats will be able to discharge their duties in receiving states without fear of harm or legal reprisal.

Interstate relations are steadily expanding beyond the traditional realm of military and political issues. More and more, economic and quality of life issue areas (e.g., trade, environmental degradation, immigration, etc.) are areas where the majority of diplomatic maneuvering by states is taking place. The existence of diplomatic immunities clearly puts members of the international community on notice that receiving states have no right under international law to "kill the messenger" when they dislike the contents of a message. Put another way, diplomats cannot be used as pawns upon whom to wreak vengeance when tensions rise between states over policy stances and/or issues. Until recently, states in the international system have routinely and rigorously recognized and respected diplomatic immunities. The Iranian hostage crisis, the most notorious violation of diplomatic immunities by a receiving state in recent decades, has called into question the continued recognition of these special rights.

Historical Overview

The Westphalian System

The current structure and functioning of the international state system has a Western orientation. It came into being as a result of the signing of the Treaty of Westphalia in 1648. Based upon the concept of state sovereignty, it incorporated the practice of the Italian city-states in the fifteenth century of maintaining permanent diplomatic missions on foreign soil. Aside from carrying out representational, reporting, and negotiating duties, diplomats serving in such missions often were actively engaged in espionage. If caught in the act, they were subject to punishment by the government in the state where they were serving.

The Congress of Vienna Reforms

In 1815 the Congress of Vienna standardized diplomatic practices. This effort was an integral part of the body's attempt to codify a set of rules to guide state behavior in interstate relations. One of the major breakthroughs in terms of the practice of diplomacy has proved to be the institution of diplomatic immunities. Protocols established rankings for diplomatic personnel. They also created real and substantive protections for ambassadors and other diplomatic personnel attached to a permanent mission. For example, a sending state's diplomat cannot be arrested or tried by a receiving state no matter the crime charged. Only if the sending state revokes a diplomat's immunity can the receiving state then arrest and try the diplomat. Otherwise, its only recourse is to declare the diplomat to be *persona non grata* and expel him or her from its territory.

The 1961 Vienna Convention

This convention refined the Congress of Vienna reforms, creating a well-developed framework for the practice of diplomacy in the jet age. It identified three major classes of diplomats, indicated how diplomatic personnel (and their families and possessions) were to be treated while on site in receiving states, and clearly established specific privileges and immunities with respect to civil and criminal matters to be granted to diplomatic personnel while in service in receiving states. Additionally, the agreement reaffirmed the limitation on diplomats' activities as concerns interference in the internal affairs of receiving states. The norms and procedures created by this convention remain in effect to the present day.

Cold War Practices

Throughout the years of the Cold War, the principal antagonists—the United States and the Soviet Union—steadfastly adhered to prevailing diplomatic customs and practices. This included recognition of immunities for diplomatic personnel serving in each other's state. A closer examination of their behavior during this period indicated that each (together with their respective allies) used diplomatic missions to do battle in the nonshooting Cold War. More specifically, staff positions in embassies and other diplomatic missions were often occupied by individuals whose primary purpose was espionage, not diplomacy. If such individuals were discovered, the receiving state tended immediately to declare them *persona non grata* and expelled them. As a result, there were constant turnovers of diplomatic personnel in the Soviet embassy in Washington, D.C., and in other major Western European capitals. Such turnovers were also commonplace in the U.S. embassy in Moscow. Members of the East and West blocs would retaliate against each other in a tit-for-tat fashion in having diplomats recalled from a receiving state. Despite the widespread abuse of the spirit of diplomatic norms, the letter of written agreements was scrupulously recognized. Keeping the channels of communication open was a top priority for both the United States and the Soviet Union.

Current Dilemmas

As noted earlier, until very recently states had uniformly adhered to the protocols developed by the Congress of Vienna and modified by the 1961 Vienna Convention. This practice included recognition by receiving states of the premises of permanent diplomatic missions as being foreign soil. No law enforcement official could at will enter the grounds of such a mission and/or carry out search or seizure procedures. In November 1979 the Iranians alarmed the international community by overrunning the U.S. embassy compound and taking U.S. diplomatic personnel hostage. Their act constituted a willful violation of generally accepted norms of diplomatic behavior. The crisis inadvertently presented the international community with another motivation to assess the purpose, scope, and suitability of diplomatic immunities in today's world. An upward trend in abuses of immunities by diplomatic personnel covering a wide range of activities (ranging from not paying parking tickets to smuggling drugs across state boundaries) has also set off alarms. In cities where an appreciable number of diplomatic personnel reside (New York City or Washington, D.C.) municipal governments are hard pressed to cope with the effects of higher levels of abuse. Loss of revenues from unpaid parking tickets are a drain on city budgets. Broken rental and lease agreements with landlords adversely affect local housing stocks. The breakdown of the international system today (in terms of diplomatic practices) can be attributed to growing diversity in the international system. States in the international system which have a non-Western legal system and whose populations hold non-Western ethical and belief systems may tend to disregard the Westphalian legacy as they become more active on the global scene.

In order for diplomacy to succeed, all interested parties must speak the same language and agree on fundamental principles. A worrisome problem facing the international community today is the seeming unwillingness of some members of the international community to adopt the prevailing terminology and norms of diplomacy as set forth in the 1961 Vienna Convention. This stance renders it more difficult to achieve harmonization of policies among states in wide-ranging issue areas. One of the key distinguishing characteristics of the quality of life issue areas in which much diplomatic activity is currently occurring is that problems cannot be solved by states unilaterally. Joint efforts are required to reduce environmental degradation, improve trading patterns, and cope with the dislocation of immigrants, for example. The willful disregard by renegade states of the safeguards built into current practices to protect diplomatic personnel has explosive potential. If not defused, it can lead to a staggering breakdown in international diplomacy.

PERNILLA M. NEAL

BIBLIOGRAPHY

Callières, François de, 1983. *The Art of Diplomacy*. New York: Holmes & Meier Publishers.
Gore-Booth, Lord, ed., 1979. *Satow's Guide to Diplomatic Practice*. 5th ed. London: Longman.
Nicolson, Harold G., 1964. *Diplomacy*. 3rd ed. London: Oxford University Press.

DIRECTIVE. A form of secondary legislation in the European Union. According to Article 189 of the treaty establishing the European Economic Community signed in Rome in 1957, "a directive shall be binding, as to the result to be achieved, upon each Member State to which it is addressed, but shall leave to the national authorities the choice of form and methods."

Unlike regulations, directives are not binding in their entirety but only as to the result to be achieved. A directive, which is normally though not necessarily addressed to all member states, requires national measures to bring it into effect at national level. Thus directives are general in nature and lay down policy guidelines and principles. The choice of means of achieving the end set out in the directive is left to the discretion of national authorities, which introduce measures as appropriate given their different

legislative and constitutional systems. Directives usually specify a deadline by which the objective is to be achieved. The European Commission is notified by national authorities of the national implementing measures put in place.

Where member states fail to comply with directives by the specified dates, proceedings may be initiated against them and they may ultimately be arraigned in front of the Court of Justice. Moreover, the Court has ruled that, in certain cases, directives may be directly applicable—for example, where there has been an undue delay in complying with directives, or where national implementing measures fail to meet adequately the objective as set out in the directive. Since the European Union treaty, which was signed in Maastricht in February 1992 and came into effect in November 1993, the Court is entitled to impose fines on those authorities that come before it for the same offense twice. For the most part directives are adopted by the Council of Ministers; however, the European Union Treaty of 1992 amended article 189 to involve the European Parliament more closely in the adoption of legislation in particular policy areas. Examples of directives include Council Directive 95/5/EC of February 27, 1995, amending Directive 92/120/EEC on the conditions for granting temporary and limited derogation's from specific European Community health rules on the production and marketing of certain products of animal origin; Directive 95/1/EC of the European Parliament and of the Council of February 2, 1995, on the maximum design speed, maximum torque and maximum net engine power of two- or three-wheel motor vehicles; and European Parliament and Council Directive No 95/2/EC of February 20, 1995, on food additives other than colors and sweeteners.

Directives are known as recommendations under the Paris Treaty signed in 1951, which established the European Coal and Steel Community in 1952.

MARGARET MARY MALONE

BIBLIOGRAPHY

Hartley, T. C., 1989. *The Foundations of European Community Law*. 2d ed. London: Clarendon Press.
Lasok, D. and J. W. Bridge, 1987. *Law and Institutions of the European Communities*. 4th ed. London: Butterworths.
Nugent, Neill, 1991. *The Government and Politics of the European Community*. 2d ed. London: MacMillan.
Parry, Anthony and James Dinnage, 1981. *EEC Law*. 2d ed. London: Sweet and Maxwell.
Wyatt, D. and A. Dashwood, 1987. *The Substantive Law of the EC*, 2d ed. London: Sweet and Maxwell.

DISCIPLINE. Any action on the part of management that is intended to encourage compliance with organizational rules and performance standards. Two broad types of discipline are present in almost all organizations, preventive and corrective. Preventive discipline is the more obscure form, and relates to management's efforts to deter unacceptable behavior through training, indoctrination, slogans, and other measures that reinforce organizational norms. Most organizations, for example, will attempt to avoid future performance problems by emphasizing significant rules in a proactive program of employee awareness (e.g., "No Smoking!" and "Safety First!"). Military organizations generally operate the most highly articulated programs to promote discipline; they combine extensive training efforts, numerous symbolic and emotional appeals, and the threat of severe sanctions for noncompliance.

In its more common usage, discipline refers to the ways that organizations deal with any employee who fails to honor important requirements. Corrective discipline is aimed at punishing employees for rule violations or for otherwise deviating from accepted standards of behavior. Its focus is more reactive than proactive, yet the fundamental purpose of all disciplinary activity is to ensure that disfunctional behavior is minimized. Thus, even when their primary focus is punitive, systems of worker discipline also encompass certain developmental objectives. They focus not only on punishing workers for their misdeeds, but on correcting behavioral problems so that they will not recur.

Discipline constitutes one of the organization's most important control systems. Without some means of detecting and correcting misbehavior, managers would be vulnerable to many potential problems posed by corrupt, incompetent, or poorly trained subordinates. For this reason, systems of employee discipline have almost certainly existed since human civilization first emerged.

Historical Background

Legend, folklore, and recorded history all indicate that early forms of discipline were exceedingly harsh and unforgiving. Individuals who strayed too far from the conventional way of doing things were routinely relieved of their duties, and were sometimes even subjected to such punishments as banishment, imprisonment, and execution. In many societies, relatively brutal treatment of rule-breakers persisted into more modern times. Some of the great works of literature, such as the social commentaries in the novels of Charles Dickens (1812–1870), are based in part on the ruthless punishments that were routinely meted out to workers for relatively minor transgressions in nineteenth-century England.

During the past one hundred years, society's attitudes toward employee discipline have experienced a gradual transformation. Whereas discipline previously focused almost exclusively on punishment, developments in the twentieth century altered the orientation toward more positive ends. Disciplinary proceedings came to be seen by some managers as an opportunity to engage in employee development and as a means by which workers could (in some settings) participate in policing themselves. Among

the factors contributing to this changing view of discipline were the post–World War II behavioral revolution within management thought (industrial humanism) and the spread of labor organizations throughout much of the industrialized world. These movements tended to soften management's treatment of workers. Industrial humanism provided the theoretical justification for this development (i.e., "workers are valued resources that should be treated with respect"), while unionism added an element of necessity ("treat workers better, or else!").

The behavioral movement sensitized managers to the perceived relationships among worker morale, workplace justice, and productivity. Simply stated, managers began to believe that workers who are treated fairly and compassionately will produce more than those who are abused. These sentiments, in turn, were reinforced by the union movement's strong opposition to the harsh treatment of workers. Cruel and arbitrary disciplinary actions on the part of many employers were a major catalyst for union activism early in this century, especially during the Great Depression. A primary objective of organized labor during this formative period was the control and routinization of employee disciplinary proceedings. Unions lobbied for worker rights and the restriction of supervisory discretion over disciplinary decisions. Contemporary disciplinary actions often reflect this dual heritage in two interrelated ways: concern for employee rights, and procedural formality.

The Role of Worker Rights

Once they have successfully passed a probationary period, employees in most public organizations accrue certain rights in their employment that protect them from arbitrary or capricious disciplinary actions. These rights stem from many sources, including legislation (some of which grants public employees "permanent" status), judicial decisions (which extend constitutional protections to some forms of government employment), and personnel system rules (which guarantee certain rights in employment, and which the courts often treat as binding contracts between management and labor). In the United States, for instance, many state and federal laws restrict the ability of public employers to punish their workers without showing cause. Thus, any disciplinary action against a civil servant must be based on a job-related reason such as misfeasance (incompetence) or malfeasance (unethical or illegal conduct). Causes that are not job-related, or that stem from a person's socioeconomic condition (including race, religion, ethnicity, and the like), are not acceptable grounds on which to base disciplinary decisions.

Although a significant majority of public employees in the United States is protected from arbitrary discipline, this is not necessarily the case with private sector workers. In their international treatment of workplace justice, Wheeler and Rojot (1992) conclude that only about 20 percent of the

U.S. labor force is thus formally protected. This is the lowest rate among all industrialized countries, most of which extend job protections to 100 percent of their labor forces.

The conservatism of the U.S. workplace is largely based on the predominance of the at-will legal doctrine. This doctrine, which arose during the nation's flirtation with laissez-faire economic policy, maintains that workers may be hired and fired "at will," without cause and without recourse. At-will workers include all those in private sector nonunion settings whose organizations have not voluntarily expanded the rights of their labor forces. Additionally, civil servants who work within small and/or poorly developed public personnel systems (such as those that exist in many county governments) are essentially treated as at-will workers. It should also be noted that, even if employees are technically protected under a legal umbrella, the complexities and costs associated with litigation may discourage many from seeking redress if they are wronged in the workplace; instead of suing, they simply "cut their losses" and look for alternative employment.

The practical effect of this situation is that workers in at-will settings can be disciplined for any reason or for no reason. The only exceptions are those that have recently been carved out by statutes and court decisions. Among the most noteworthy are: the public policy exception (workers can't be penalized for complying with a statutory duty, such as when a police officer arrests the mayor's son for shoplifting); the implied contract exception (disciplinary actions that violate the terms of an employment agreement, such as those contained in an employee handbook, are invalid); and those disciplinary actions that result in tortious invasions, including "outrageous" managerial actions that produce severe emotional distress and/or unfairly defame the employee.

Thanks to both the expansion of employee rights and the growing number of exceptions to the at-will doctrine, managers are left with some clear obligations concerning the treatment of their subordinates in disciplinary situations. In order to comply with "for cause" requirements, discipline must be based on specific and job-related grounds. It cannot be initiated on personal considerations, nor can prejudice or malice be permitted to color a supervisor's judgment. Employees are also entitled to a measure of respect and dignity; they cannot be subjected to unnecessary mental abuse, threats, or intimidation. Finally, employers are bound by the principle of "fair dealing," meaning that they should treat workers equitably and consistently.

Procedural Formality

In order to comply with the above obligations, numerous procedural protections have been devised to ensure that worker rights are not trampled in disciplinary actions. These procedures roughly parallel what in the United States is known as due process. That is, employees threatened with a disciplinary action are provided with a statement of charges against them (notice) and an opportunity to defend themselves (confrontation and rebuttal). In order to impose discipline, supervisors are expected to have sufficient evidence of the alleged shortcoming to justify the punishment that is recommended. If, for example, a manager wishes to discipline a subordinate for poor performance, appropriate evidence might include one or more negative performance evaluations, tangible records of inadequate output, or other specific examples of unacceptable behavior. Within unionized settings, this evidence may be reviewed by a third party (such as a union steward or hearing officer) who serves either as a mediator or as an employee representative. Under such circumstances, the disciplinary action may stop at this level with the imposition of a penalty or alternative recommendation (e.g., the employee may be required to undergo special training).

Often, however, the employee does not believe that the supervisor's action is justified. When this occurs, most organizations permit their workers to appeal supervisory decisions up the chain of command. Some of these matters are ultimately decided by the agency director; in other organizations they may be referred to a special worker committee for final resolution.

Depending upon a number of factors—such as the severity of the allegations and the organization's size and formality—disciplinary disputes may be settled in a hearing that resembles a trial. The most formal of these include legal representation by both parties, along with relatively strict rules of evidence. Moreover, many public organizations permit employees to file grievances against their supervisors if they believe that their rights have been bruised during a disciplinary proceeding. These grievances are often adjudicated by special committees composed of other employees, but may also be forwarded to external bodies such as civil service commissions or merit system review boards for final resolution.

In effect, then, a supervisor attempting to discipline a subordinate may be required to attend a considerable number of informal and formal hearings as the case progresses through the appeals process (within the federal government, for instance, employees who have exhausted all internal agency avenues may then avail themselves of six external levels of appeal). During each encounter, the supervisor must potentially justify his or her actions in a potentially stressful setting. There is wide agreement within the public management profession that worker rights are thoroughly protected by this formalistic process. The down side, however, is the fear among most commentators that the complexity and formality of the process discourages public sector supervisors from initiating disciplinary actions against their subordinates. As such, cumbersome disciplinary procedures are commonly cited as one of the major contributors to what is often perceived as excessive job security within the public service.

Progressive Discipline

Given this (probably valid) criticism, it is especially ironic to note that public sector disciplinary procedures are often superior to those employed in the private sector. Perhaps because of the difficulties that they have encountered, public agencies both in the United States and abroad have developed relatively sophisticated systems of employee discipline. The prevalent approach in most public personnel systems is termed "progressive discipline." Research indicates that such procedures are present in about 80 percent of all public jurisdictions in the United States, and in most public bureaucracies of the industrialized world. Third World nations, in contrast, rarely operate anything more than the most rudimentary and informal schemes of worker discipline.

The typical progressive discipline procedure consists of an extensive list of punishable offenses, including tardiness, absenteeism, insubordination, rule violations, drug or alcohol impairment, misuse of equipment, and the like. A specific punishment is prescribed for each offense, as well as for any recurrences of the original infraction. Thus, for example, an employee who falls asleep on the job may receive a written reprimand for the first offense, a five-day suspension for the second offense, and termination for any subsequent violation. Thus, the term "progressive" connotes that fact that an ascending hierarchy of penalties exists, depending upon the seriousness of the offense and the number of occurrences.

To moderate the procedure's punitive thrust, modern personnel offices emphasize the developmental side of the disciplinary mechanism. This is accomplished through a multiphased process designed to involve the worker in corrective action and to emphasize improvement of future performance rather than punishment of past conduct. Upon identifying a work deficiency, the supervisor's first obligation is to confront the employee and discuss the problem openly. Then, the manager and worker set improvement goals and agree upon an action plan. Elements of this plan include a specific (preferably quantifiable) statement of the expected improvement in performance, designation of a timeframe in which the improvement should take place, and the creation of a written record on which to build any further action should the poor performance continue. Remedial steps, such as specialized training or reassignment to different duties, may also be specified at this stage. The manager's responsibility is then to monitor performance and, if necessary, implement an appropriate sanction if the performance problem continues. With some variation among jurisdictions, most progressive discipline procedures contain the following forms of discipline in ascending order of severity: verbal warning, formal (written) reprimand, suspension with pay, suspension without pay, reduction of pay within the same job class, demotion to a lower classification, and dismissal.

In summary, progressive discipline procedures provide a framework in which the rights and obligation of both management and labor can be nurtured. If followed carefully, they permit supervisors to correct dysfunctional behavior without invading the rights of their subordinates. By specifying the punishment that is appropriate for each offense, consistency and impartiality are (theoretically) ensured. Similarly, the procedures' emphasis on employee counseling and correction conforms with modern attitudes concerning the development—rather than the punishment—of workers. Problem employees are given prior notice of inadequate performance, as well as one or more opportunities to correct their deficiencies.

Although progressive discipline procedures currently represent the state of the art in public personnel management, they are by no means universally advocated. Detractors complain, for example, that this form of discipline "proceeds from the premise that the worse and worse an employer treats an employee in the name of discipline, the better and better the employee will become" (Redeker, 1985, p. 7). A few strident proponents of the industrial humanism tradition maintain that corrective disciplinary systems are obsolete, and that public organizations ought to refine nonpunitive means of dealing with problem employees. The vast majority of authorities, however, embrace the fundamental assumptions of progressive discipline. There is nothing wrong with these procedures, provided that they are faithfully followed. By this reasoning, if public organizations are not doing an adequate job of disciplining workers, the blame may lie more with government's supervisors than with its personnel procedures.

STEVEN W. HAYS

BIBLIOGRAPHY

Brake, Charles, 1982. "Limiting the Right to Terminate at Will—Have the Courts Forgotten the Employer?" *Vanderbilt Law Review*, vol. 35:201–234.

Bryant, Alan, 1984, "Replacing Punitive Discipline with a Positive Approach." *Personnel Administrator*, vol. 29 (February) 79–87.

Daley, Dennis, 1993, "Formal Disciplinary Procedures and Conflict Resolution Remedies," *Public Personnel Management*, vol. 22 (Spring) 153–166.

Deitsch, Clarence and David Dilts, 1990. *The Arbitration of Rights Disputes in the Public Sector*. New York: Quorum Books.

Hays, Steven W., 1995, "Employee Discipline and Removal: Coping with Job Security." In Steven Hays and Richard Kearney, *Public Personnel Administration: Problems and Prospects*. eds., Englewood Cliffs, NJ: Prentice Hall, pp. 145–161.

O'Reilly, Charles and Barton Weitz, 1980, "Managing Marginal Employees: The Use of Warnings and Dismissals." *Administrative Science Quarterly*, vol. 25 (September) 467–484.

Redeker, James, 1985, "Discipline, Part 2: The Nonpunitive Approach Works by Design." *Personnel*, vol. 62 (November) 7–14.

Reeves, T. Zane, 1989, "Handling Employee Grievances Without Grief." In *Public Personnel Administration: Policies and Practices.* Paramus, NJ: Prentice Hall Information Services.

Tidwell, Gary, 1983. "Employment at Will: Limitations in the Public Sector," *Public Personnel Management,* vol. 12 (June) 293–304.

Wheeler, Hoyt and Jaques Rojot, 1992. *Workplace Justice.* Columbia, SC: University of South Carolina Press.

Williams, Thomas, 1985. "Fire at Will." *Personnel Journal,* vol. 64 (June) 72–77.

DISCOURSE.

As used in public policy/administration theory, any domination-free social formation wherein the promotion of the public interest is the goal of public conversation. The world discourse is commonly joined with theory as in discourse theory. That is because it connotes a normative ideal, something toward which to strive, more than any particular empirical practice. Concomitantly, in the context of public policy and administration, discourse theory is a specific solution to the crisis of representative or so called "overhead" democracy; that is, doubts about the ability of current institutions to express the sovereign will of the people. It visualizes public servants not as interchangeable links in an hierarchical chain of command, but as potential actors in discursive public will formation.

There are two primary philosophical sources of contemporary discourse theory as it is meant here: Hannah Arendt and Jurgen Habermas. Both are twentieth-century figures. Habermas, now in his sixties, has been the most influential so we begin with his thought as a base.

Habermas's Discourse Theory

Habermas has been associated with the Frankfurt School of critical theory. This school counts among its members such well known and important theorists as Max Horkheimer, Theodore Adorno, Walter Benjamin, Herbert Marcuse, and Eric Fromm. The Frankfurt School is known for its critique of modern capitalist societies. The combined position of this school can, at a high level of generalization, be typified as a critique of capitalist ideology. That is to say, they make questionable or problematic the self-justification of capitalist societies. In particular, domination is decried. Capitalism, they believed, produced gross inequalities. These, in turn, were justified by a dominating ideology that produced false consciousness. False consciousness led to an otherwise inexplicable acceptance of a fundamentally unequal and exploitative capitalist status quo.

The Frankfurt School, however, had this problem to overcome: From what standpoint could their critique be validated? If what had become normal life for the masses was false consciousness, and the result was a self-justifying capitalist ideology, where could true consciousness be found? On what grounds could the Frankfurt School philosophers justify their own vision as nonideological? By

what fundamental principle could ideology be differentiated from the nonideological? It is to these questions that Habermas, a younger member of the Frankfurt School, formed a response.

Habermas found a solution to what can be called the standpoint or foundational problem in language. Language presupposes communication between humans. For authentic communication to work there must be a rough equality between speakers. There is built into linguistic communication itself an egalitarian standard. This standard is not merely a subjective preference nor is it relative to time, place, or situation. Taking up a language entails also taking up the intention to communicate. Communication, if it is to be true and authentic, requires an absence of domination. The prospect of emancipation from domination is entailed by linguistic communication. Because the use of language is universal, it follows that there is a kind of universal standard against which social conditions of domination may be judged as just or unjust. Indeed, nondominated speech is a telos (utopian goal) toward which human progress is drawn. Moreover any system of thought that is an apology for domination may then be seen as ideological. Here is where discourse comes in.

Any authentic discussion between competent human actors implies consensus on four backdrop validity claims; as backdrop they need not be continuously invoked. These are: understandability, truth of propositional content, sincerity of speaker, and appropriateness of the speech performance. In an authentic discourse, any or all of these backdrop validity claims may at any time be questioned. When that happens the conversation turns back into itself to what Habermas calls discursive redemption. Validity claims are redeemed or not, before the discourse moves back to substantive matters. The point is that these discourse protocols are immanent and potentially realizable anywhere people discuss honestly and openly. When they are totally absent, dominated speech is extant. If one cannot, or especially if one is afraid to, ask "what are you saying?" (understandability); "really?" (truth); "are you kidding?" (sincerity); "you are interrupting!" (appropriateness); the goal of communication and the purpose of language is thwarted. This, by Habermasian lights, is a fundamental fettering of the human spirit and ultimately, he optimistically holds, the human spirit will break loose. This is Habermas's version of the engine of emancipatory historical progress. Communication requires autonomous others. It is a damning critique of any status quo when such autonomy and authenticity cannot be found.

Arendt's Discourse Theory

Hannah Arendt's contribution to contemporary discourse theory occurs in the context of her elucidation of a public sphere. This is distinguished from the private sphere that

Arendt paints as the realm of necessity: fulfilling the requirements of life or mere existence not unlike those activities required of other species for base mundane survival. Politics, meaning discourse, occurs in the public sphere. Politics within the public sphere provides challenges whereby humans can achieve, nay become, something other than passive acquiescent beings. By this rendering, politics/discourse is heroic, agonistic (oppositional), and performative. As performative, discourse is not about some consensual process of discovering some preexisting harmonious truth, as Habermasian discourse theory might be interpreted to imply. From the viewpoint of the individual, it is a launching of oneself onto a public stage whereupon the individual will not so much find a self, but develop one in agonistic tension with similarly developing agonistic others. Consensus within a discourse, it follows, will never be complete; points of view will not swallow each other up.

The Place of Discourse Theory in Public Policy/ Administration Theory

Discourse theory is one of several alternative conceptualizations available to those attempting to develop a normative theory for public administration. One task incumbent on any such theory is to valorize the undeniable and irreducible exercise of discretion by nonelected public officials. Discourse theory is a strategy similar to Mary Parker Follett's "circular response" of individuals to each other and as parts of the group, for will formation. It is also close to the communitarian strategy to promote community/administrator interface as exemplified, for instance, by Terry L. Cooper in his *An Ethic of Citizenship for Public Administration* (1991). All such moves presuppose, often quite specifically, the incapacity of the current electoral representative practices to express the sovereign will of the people.

Perhaps the most fully developed use of discourse theory occurs in Charles J. Fox's and Hugh T. Miller's *Postmodern Public Administration: Toward Discourse* (1995). They hold out authentic discourse as both an alternative lens by which current practices might be more positively interpreted and as an in principle feasible ideal toward which those practices can be encouraged to strive. Those practices include interagency task forces, ad-hocracies, intergovernmental cooperative arrangements, policy networks, and so called "reg-neg" (regulation by negotiation). This favorable assessment is in stark opposition to mainstream political science interpretive schemes. The literature on iron triangles and sub-governments casts potentially discursive practices in a negative light. The iron triangle literature assumes the legitimacy and viability of the formal electoral representative system and regards informal policy-relevant discourse as a potential theft of sovereignty from the electorate. So from this overhead democracy point of view, the

practices that Fox and Miller promote as benign appear to be malignant. Conversely, Fox and Miller use discourse to affirm a more interagency bottom-up concept of democracy. Such an interpretation is consistent with ethical exercise of discretion by nonelected public servants.

Discourse as an in principle feasible normative ideal is articulated by Fox and Miller through the concept of "warrants for discourse." These are specific extensions of Habermas's discursive validity claims. Specifically, authentic discourse about public policy and its implementation requires sincerity, situation-regarding intentionality, willing attention, and substantive contribution. The extent that these warrants are violated is the extent to which authentic discourse is not achieved. The warrants alert participants in public conversations to violations of commission and omission. Egoists and dissemblers are foiled by the requirement to be sincere. The merely self-aggrandizing are trumped by the standard of a higher public interest entailed in situation-regarding intentionality. The apathetic and inattentive are encouraged to become engaged lest the willing attention warrant be violated. Free riders will ultimately be shunned for violating the substantive contribution warrant. Warrants for discourse are presented as tough-minded normative standards, but they are self-enforcing, not rules enforced by some sort of discourse police. They are proffered as a corrective to the many instances of unauthentic manipulation that often pass for public policy will formation in these postmodern times.

CHARLES J. FOX AND HUGH T. MILLER

BIBLIOGRAPHY

Arendt, Hannah, 1963. *On Revolution.* New York: Penguin.
Fox, Charles J. and Hugh T. Miller, 1995. *Postmodern Public Administration: Toward Discourse.* Newbury Park, CA: Sage.
Habermas, Jurgen, 1983. *The Theory of Communicative Action.* Boston: Beacon Press.
——, 1989. *The Structural Transformation of the Public Sphere,* trans. by Thomas Burger and Frederick G. Lawrence. Cambridge, MA: MIT Press.
Villa, Dana R., 1992. "Postmodernism and the Public Sphere." *American Political Science Review,* vol. 86, no. 3 (September) 712–721.

DISCRIMINATION, AGE.

DISCRIMINATION, AGE. Disparate, unfavorable, or inconsistent treatment of a individual in the United States over the age of forty with respect to compensation, terms or conditions of employment, or privileges of employment.

Origin and Subsequent History

A broad network of programs addresses the special needs of the employed, unemployed, and unemployable aged population in American society, including the problem of age-based discrimination at work. President John F. Kennedy proposed legislation authorizing federal funds for training personnel to deal with the elderly, developing services, and building recreational centers. His proposals became the Older Americans Act of 1965.

Neither Title VII of the Civil Rights Act of 1964 nor Executive Order 11246, which regulates federal contractors, prohibited discrimination based on age. In 1967, the Age Discrimination in Employment Act (ADEA-67) was passed and it became law on June 12, 1968. It prohibits discrimination against persons over forty who are job applicants or employees in private sector firms with 20 or more workers or in labor organizations with 25 or more members, unless a bona fide occupational qualification (BFOQ) intervenes. The 1967 act protected employees between 40 and 65 years old; a 1978 amendment extended the limit to age 70. Federal, state, and local government employers became subject to ADEA-67 by a 1974 amendment.

Current Practice in the United States

ADEA-67 and its amendments are enforced by the United States Department of Labor's Wage and Hour Division. When complaints arise, compliance officers first try to get a voluntary agreement between the employee and the employer. If negotiation is unsuccessful, the Department of Labor may go to court to seek a judgment requiring an employer to reinstate or promote an employee and to pay lost compensation if the employer is liable. Unlike many other civil rights cases that are decided by judges, age discrimination cases are typically decided by jury trials.

A large proportion of age discrimination cases focus on involuntary dismissals. According to ADEA-67, an employer is empowered to set a maximum age when the normal operation of a business creates a reasonable necessity for the age limit. The upper limit on age is an important restriction often linked to an alleged involuntary dismissal because of mandatory retirement.

Since 1978, mandatory retirement for federal employees has been disallowed, except in certain instances such as employees of the Federal Bureau of Investigation. A 1986 amendment eliminated mandatory retirement for all covered employees with the exception of firefighters, law enforcement officers, and employees of colleges and universities. They were denied protection by a seven-year exemption. The exemption expired December 31, 1993, and has not yet been extended by Congress. State and local bodies now do not have grounds to force the early retirement of public safety officers, typically at age 55.

Pension systems in America are subject to the provisions of the Employment Retirement Income Security Act of 1978 (ERISA). Retirement systems may define a minimum age requirement that has to be met before benefits are payable. A minimum age requirement may be imposed regardless of a person's years of service to an organization. Such employment anniversaries are not mandatory retirement ages, but merely criteria for pension payouts. The Tax Reform Act of 1986 requires that pension plan payout begin at age 70.5 regardless of whether the individual has retired from the workforce.

Future Context

The Age Discrimination in Employment Act is one part of a constellation of developing policies for older persons in America that deal with such problems as adequate pensions or needed social services. A reauthorization of the 1965 Older Americans Act in 1992 provided for elder abuse prevention, expanded outreach services and benefits including pension counseling, and authorized a new White House Conference on Aging. A hotly contested component of the general debate that did not become a part of the 1992 legislation was an increase in the Social Security earnings test, that is, the amount of money an older worker might earn from current employment before losing Social Security benefits.

The population of the United States 65 years of age and older is expected to reach 20 percent by the year 2030. This population will be expected to take care of itself with the help of in-home medical care and social services. Increasingly, balancing work and family concerns will involve a growing group of workers in caring for elderly parents, relatives, or friends who cannot manage alone. Elder care responsibilities will fall disproportionately on employees in middle age and on women employees. The future context of aging will impact the potential course of equitable treatment of employees who are aging or who have responsibility for care of an elderly family member.

COLE BLEASE GRAHAM, JR.

BIBLIOGRAPHY

Eglit, H. C., 1994. *Age Discrimination.* 2d ed. Colorado Springs, CO: Shepard's/McGraw-Hill.
Handa, J., 1994. *Discrimination, Retirement and Pensions.* Brookfield, VT: Avebury.

DISCRIMINATION, DISABILITIES.

With regard to people who have mental and/or physical disabilities, denying civil rights in the workplace as well as in the delivery of, or provision of access to, services provided by public and private organizations. In the United States, nearly 20 percent of the population—over 45 million people—suffer from one form of disability or another. It is important to note that nearly two-thirds of U.S. citizens of working age who have disabilities have trouble securing employment as a result of their disabilities.

Legislative and Judicial Protection

The two primary pieces of national legislation that protect the civil rights of disabled individuals are the 1973 Vocational Rehabilitation Act and the 1990 Americans with Disabilities Act (ADA). The contents of these two policies are similar, especially in terms of who is covered and what activities are protected (see Acquired Immune Deficiency Syndrome policy). Individuals with disabilities are protected in terms of (1) employment and workplace practices, (2) access to public accommodations and services provided by public entities, (3) access to public accommodations and services provided by private entities, and (4) access to telephone services.

The two laws differ, however, in three important ways. First, coverage under the Vocational Rehabilitation Act extends only to entities that "do business" with the federal government. Most commonly these entities consist of private contractors and state and local government units that receive federal funding. Coverage under the ADA extends to most organizations, regardless of their association with the federal government, that have 15 or more full-time employees. (It should be noted, however, that as of this writing the federal government is not required to comply with either piece of legislation. Workers with disabilities in the executive branch are protected through executive orders. Workers with disabilities employed by Congress are unprotected.)

Second, the affirmative action component in the Vocational Rehabilitation Act is absent in the ADA. Hence, organizations covered solely by the ADA are not required to report annually to the Equal Employment Opportunity Commission (EEOC) about their practices and record in the hiring and retention of disabled individuals.

Third, the term "handicap" is used in the Vocational Rehabilitation Act while the term "disability" is used in the ADA. This difference represents more than semantics, especially given the other two distinctions between the acts. If a legislatively qualified individual believes he has been the victim of discriminatory personnel practices or the denial of services by an organization that receives federal funding, he can request remedy of the EEOC and may do so on the basis of the affirmative action component of the Vocational Rehabilitation Act. In doing so, he must use the term "handicapped." If a legislatively qualified individual believes she has been the victim of discriminatory personnel practice or the denial of services by an organization without direct financial ties with the federal government, she must contest the decision under the ADA and use the term "disabled."

It is also possible for an individual to contest a variety of actions through both pieces of legislation. Hence, it is imperative for both the employer/manager and the employee or customer with a handicap/disability to be aware of the differences between these two pieces of legislation,

to realize that the organization might be covered by both, and to use the appropriate terminology. While the substance of definitions is similar under both pieces of legislation, the remainder of this entry will refer to the language used in the ADA.

Who Is Disabled?

Both pieces of legislation answer this question in three identical ways. An individual can claim to be disabled if he or she:

1. has a physical or mental impairment that substantially limits one or more of the major life activities of the individual; or
2. has a record of having such an impairment; or
3. is regarded as having such an impairment.

It is important to note that, between the passage of the two laws, the courts further refined the definition of disability to protect people with contagious diseases. Four court cases represent mile posts in this effort. In *School Board of Nassau County, Fla. v. Airline* (1987) the Supreme Court affirmed that a school teacher with tuberculosis was protected from workplace discrimination. In *Chalk v. U.S. District Court* (1988), a California federal district court ruled that a teacher with AIDS (see **Acquired Immune Deficiency Syndrome (AIDS) policy**) was also protected from workplace discrimination. In *Thomas v. Atascadero Unified School District* (1987), a California federal district court ruled that a child with Human Immunodeficiency Virus (see **Acquired Immune Deficiency Syndrome (AIDS) policy**), who also had a habit of biting other children, could not be denied access to a kindergarten class in a public school district. In *Miller v. Spicer* (1993), a Delaware federal district court ruled that publicly funded hospitals could not deny services to someone with a contagious disease, in this case a man seeking emergency room services who was suspected of have HIV/AIDS (see **Acquired Immune Deficiency Syndrome (AIDS) policy**). The findings of these cases were incorporated into the language of the ADA.

What Is a Disability?

Most long-term, if not permanent, disabilities qualify under both acts. Physical impairments include: anatomical losses, cancer, deformities, HIV/AIDS, impairments that affect sight, hearing, and speech, and heart disease, to name a few. Mental impairments include: mental retardation, emotional or mental illness, and learning disorders, to name a few. The key is a disability that "substantially limits" the person from pursuing life's activities, such as working and accessing public services. Hence, short-term conditions—those that do not have a substantially limiting affect—are excluded: physical impairments, such as pulled muscles and broken bones; mental impairments, such as compulsive gambling, kleptomania, and pyromania.

Obligations of Americans with Disabilities

In order to receive protection and assistance under the ADA, a person with a disability must: (1) provide notification and documentation of the disability to the service provider or employer, (2) offer documentation stating that he or she does not represent a direct health threat to self or others, and (3) demonstrate that he or she is "otherwise qualified" for the particular service. In the case of job applicancy or other employment/career opportunities, the worker must demonstrate that he or she is otherwise qualified to perform the essential functions of a job with or without "reasonable accommodations."

Obligations of Service Providers and Employers

Service providers and employers must be prepared to handle all information pertaining to disabilities with the utmost confidentiality. Much of the current and projected litigation against organizations covered by the ADA concerns the issues of confidentiality and rumor control.

In order to determine whether or not an individual is "otherwise qualified," employers must recast individual job descriptions to delineate essential functions from those tasks which are marginal to successful job performance. Service providers must be prepared to determine which clients or customers are otherwise qualified by developing detailed standards and decision rules.

Employers must be prepared to provide reasonable accommodations for disabled individuals, which will be aided by recasting job descriptions. Both the legislative intent and the courts assess the "reasonableness" of accommodations on a case-by-case basis, noting that each organization is different and disabilities have a unique effect on each individual.

However, the ADA and EEOC offer some guidelines. In terms of access to public accommodations and services, examples of reasonable accommodations might include wheelchair ramps at entrances, wider aisles in restaurants, and hydraulic lifts on buses. Examples of reasonable accommodations at the workplace might include flextime, special assistants, and modification of workplace equipment.

Finally, it is the responsibility of service providers and employers to determine initially the balance between providing accommodations to those with disabilities and the potential adverse impact that such accommodations might have on the organization itself. Neither the laws nor the courts expect private businesses to fail because of the costly nature of specific accommodations rendered to workers or customers. The same is true for service providers and the

public sector. They are not expected to have to reduce service delivery or to enter into reductions-in-force strategies as a result of providing accommodations to disabled employees or clients. These organizations are expected to demonstrate a clear level of "undue hardship" and, as with the issue of reasonable accommodation, this must be done on a case-by-case basis. Courts will take into consideration (1) the size and economic well-being of the organization, (2) the nature and cost of the requested accommodation, and (3) the potential impact that such accommodation will have on the well-being of the organization, its employees, and clients or customers.

Effective governmental responses to the needs of disabled individuals can be costly and, therefore, are not usually found in developing countries. The cost is not typically as substantial as feared initially by most organization managers. Indeed, the cost of compliance with the Vocational Rehabilitation Act and the ADA is typically outweighed by the benefits gained from incorporating members of this growing segment of society into organizational activities.

JAMES D. SLACK

BIBLIOGRAPHY

Bishop, Peter C. and Augustus J. Jones, Jr., 1993. "Implementing the Americans with Disabilities Act of 1990: Assessing the Variables of Success." *Public Administration Review,* vol. 53 (March-April), 121–128.

Chalk v. United States District Court, Central District of California, 840 F2d. 701 (9th Cir. 1988).

Desario, Jack P. and James D. Slack,. 1994. "The Americans with Disabilities Act and Refusals to Provide Medical Care to Persons with HIV/AIDS." *The John Marshall Law Review,* vol. 27 (Winter).

Miller v. Spicer, 822 F. Supp. 158 (D. Del. 1993).

Sarch, Anne Covey, 1994. "Solutions to an Employment Nightmare." *New Jersey Law Journal* (December 19).

School Board of Nassau County, Fla. v. Airline, 480 U.S. 273 (1987).

Slack, James D. 1995. "The Americans with Disabilities Act and the Workplace: Observations About Management's Responsibilities in AIDS-Related Situations." *Public Administration Review* (July-August).

Strama, Brenda T., ed. 1993. *AIDS and Governmental Liability: State and Local Government Guide to Legislation, Legal Issues, and Liability.* Chicago, IL: The American Bar Association.

Thomas v. Atascadero Unified School District, 662 F. Supp. 376 (C. D. Cal. 1987).

DISCRIMINATION, GENDER.

Employment practices whether deliberate or unintentional which fail to treat men and women equally. Gender discrimination most usually has the effect of limiting employment and advancement opportunities for females.

Origin and Subsequent History

In the United States, state protective laws were an early obstacle to the federal Equal Employment Opportunity Commission (EEOC) when it began to implement Title

VII of the Civil Rights Act of 1964 with respect to the interests of women. In the mid-1960s, the majority of the states still had laws restricting female employment, for example, the number of work hours for women or the amount of weight a woman could be allowed to lift at work. Employers avoided state protective law violations by not requiring regular overtime for women or assigning them more effortless work. They also paid women less.

The early twentieth-century protective laws were passed by states as reforms. Despite their interference with a "free" marketplace, they were generally held constitutional, especially under the influence of the "Brandeis Brief." This widely circulated essay by the famous American jurist Louis D. Brandeis (1856–1941) described the horrors, inequities, and long hours suffered by women at work, but it also incorporated the opinion that women were the "weaker sex." The Brandeis Brief was acknowledged by the United States Supreme Court in *Muller v. Oregon,* 208 US 412 (1908) as it upheld a state law restricting the work day to ten hours for a female after taking "judicial cognizance" of factors such as "woman's physical structure, and the functions she performs in consequence thereof" in order to place women in a special category.

Other typical employment practices embodying gender-based discrimination included widespread use of "help wanted" advertisements that separately identified "men's" and "women's" jobs, dismissal of women employees who became pregnant, and higher paying retirement benefit plans for males. These practices began to be dealt with by the EEOC after 1964, but not with the same speed and intensity generated by problems of racial discrimination.

Current Practice in the United States

Equal Pay

Legal rejection of disparate treatment of male and female employees in the United States is perhaps first seen in the Equal Pay Act of 1963, an Amendment to the 1938 Fair Labor Standards Act (EPA-63). Under EPA-63, businesses with two or more employees and $250,000 gross income from interstate commerce, as well as all federal, state, and local employers must provide equal pay for men and women who do equal work. There are some exceptions, such as seniority, a merit system, wages determined by a production system, or wage differentials based on a factor other than gender. The Wage and Hour Division in the Department of Labor enforces EPA-63.

Affirmative Action

After passage of the 1964 Civil Rights Act, which includes sex as one of the categories of illegal discrimination, state and local government employers receiving federal funds had to have an affirmative action program, under Executive Order 11246, issued by President Lyndon Johnson in 1965. In a 1967 revision, Executive Order 11375 specifically added sex as a protected category to be applied under the earlier presidential action.

In regulations promulgated by the Department of Labor to implement Order 11246 in 1971, the Secretary of Labor defined the obligations for federal contractors or subcontractors with 50 or more employees of a $50,000-plus contract regarding job groups in which females or minority groups may be underutilized. These regulations are administered by the Office of Federal Contract Compliance Programs (OFCCP). Affected businesses must identify jobs in which there is female representation below availability benchmarks and adopt a written affirmative action plan to correct that underutilization (see **affirmative action plan**).

Measure of the utilization of females below availability results from the application of eight factors in plans prepared for the OFCCP:

- The size of the female unemployment force in the labor area surrounding the facility;
- The percentage of the female work force as compared with the total work force in the immediate labor area;
- The general availability of women having requisite skills in the immediate labor area;
- The availability of women having requisite skills in an area in which the contractor can reasonably recruit;
- The availability of women seeking employment in the labor or recruitment area of the contractor;
- The availability of promotable and transferable women within the contractor's organization;
- The existence of training institutions capable of training persons in the requisite skills; and
- The degree of training which the contractor is reasonably able to undertake as a means of making all job classes available to women.

These factors differ marginally from the assessment factors for minority groups required by the OFCCP.

The Equal Employment Opportunity Act of 1972 (EEOA-72) applied Title VII to federal, state, and local governments as well as most public and private educational institutions. EEOA-72 strengthened the regulatory powers of the Equal Employment Opportunity Commission (EEOC) to process job discrimination complaints. When negotiated solutions to discrimination charges are not possible, the EEOC enforces Title VII through the courts. Under EEOA-72, charges may be filed by employees, job applicants, and external organizations on behalf of complainants. Allowing an organization to file assists an employee who may feel intimidated by an employer or who is without individual resources to file a complaint.

The EEOC moved slowly to address gender discrimination problems. Different help wanted ads were used until the late 1960s; women were denied pregnancy disability benefits and differential pension benefit deductions continued until 1978; and differential pension payouts continued until 1983.

The Supreme Court in *Dothard v. Rawlinson,* 433 U.S. 321 (1977) established that the bona fide occupational qualification (BFOQ) exception must be narrowly construed with regard to female employment opportunities. The 1980s saw the Court advance gender discrimination to a level more commensurate with its decisions regarding race. With respect to affirmative action plans to remedy gender discrepancies, the Supreme Court in *Johnson v. Transportation Agency,* 480 U.S. 616 (1980) upheld appointment of a female supervisor through an agency's voluntary affirmative action plan to remedy underrepresentation or nonpromotion of women.

Civil Rights Act of 1991

The Civil Rights Act of 1991 established a "Glass Ceiling" Commission to study how business fills management and executive positions, how women and minorities gain qualifications for management or executive jobs, and how pay and reward structures affect women and minorities (see **glass ceiling**).

COLE BLEASE GRAHAM, JR.

BIBLIOGRAPHY

Guy, M. E., 1993. "Three Steps Forward, Two Steps Backward: The Status of Women's Integration into Public Management." *Public Administration Review* (July-August) 285–292.

Kelly, R. M., and J. Bayes, eds. 1988. *Comparable Worth, Pay Equity, and Public Policy.* Westport, CT: Greenwood Press.

Rhode, D., 1989. *Justice and Gender.* Cambridge, MA: Harvard University Press.

DISCRIMINATION, PREGNANCY.

Practices by which employers arbitrarily treat or avoid obligations to pregnant employees. Unequal treatment of an employee on the basis of pregnancy, childbirth, or associated medical conditions is unlawful sex discrimination.

Origin and Subsequent History

Unlawful sex discrimination in the form of arbitrary treatment of pregnant employees or disregard of an employer's obligations to an employee who becomes pregnant was first defined in Equal Employment Opportunity Commission (EEOC) guidelines in 1972. Before 1972, the EEOC's position was that disability insurance programs excluding pregnancy were not gender discrimination. The 1972 guidelines held that a plan excluding pregnancy from a comprehensive disability benefits program was discriminatory.

In *Cleveland Board of Education v. Lafleur,* 414 U.S. 632 (1974), the United States Supreme Court found that arbitrarily required maternity leave for an employed female worker violated the Fourteenth Amendment to the United States Constitution. Unpaid maternity leave required for pregnant teachers five months before expected childbirth was unconstitutional. Although the case looked to the U.S. Constitution in this instance, the case did not address treatment that may be based on statutes.

Subsequently, the Supreme Court did not agree with the EEOC's 1972 guidelines. In *General Electric v. Gilbert,* 429 U.S. 125 (1976), the Court ruled that Title VII was not violated if an employer excluded pregnancy-related disabilities from its comprehensive disability plan. Despite difficulty in explaining how denial of pregnancy benefits does not relate to gender, the Court did not find an intent to discriminate through denial of pregnancy benefits and it did not apply an adverse impact standard. Also, the fact that women annually collect more in benefits program payments than men seemed important in the decision.

As a result, women were largely denied disability benefits due to pregnancy until 1978 when, in response to *Gilbert,* the U.S. Congress passed an amendment to Title VII of the Civil Rights Act of 1964, called the Pregnancy Discrimination Act of 1978 (PDA-78).

Current Practice in the United States

The pregnancy discrimination amendment to the Civil Rights Act has some specific features which establish that:

1. Title VII is directly, *prima facie,* violated if an employer has a written employment policy or unwritten employment practice through which applicants are excluded or employees separated from a job because of pregnancy, childbirth, or related medical conditions;

2. A disability which results from or is contributed to by pregnancy, childbirth, or related medical conditions must be treated the same for all job purposes as any other disability caused or contributed to by any medical condition with regard to insurance for health or disability and with regard to any sick leave plan. A pregnancy-related disability has to be treated the same as other disabilities. This applies to written employment policies or unwritten employment practices involving such decisions as: (1) when leave begins and ends; (2) whether extensions to leave are available; (3) how seniority and other benefits or privileges accrue during disabilities; or (4) formal or informal payment or reinstatement under any health insurance, disability insurance, or sick leave plan. Although abortion benefits may be granted by an employer, the PDA-78 does not require an employer to pay for health insurance benefits for an abortion. However, in health benefits programs for which employers pay, abortion benefits may not be denied for a mother who would be endangered by a full-term pregnancy or for an individual for whom medical complications have resulted from an abortion; and

3. Title VII is violated by an employment policy which results in the firing of a temporarily disabled employee, if the policy allows insufficient leave or no leave, if that policy has a disparate impact on employees of one gender, if it is not justified by business necessity.

PDA-78 does not require an employer to treat pregnant employees differently from other employees in hiring, promoting, or establishing new medical leave or benefit programs where none existed before. A specific amount of maternity leave time is not required. The law establishes the practice that women experiencing pregnancy, childbirth, or related medical conditions must be treated similarly for their ability or inability to work for all employment-related purposes as any employee not affected. This includes the receipt of benefits under fringe benefits programs.

After 1978, pregnant workers were recognized for benefits in a variety of ways, including fair employment or labor codes, state temporary disability insurance laws, and regulations and court decisions regarding employment discrimination based on gender.

PDA-78 led to reinterpretation of *Gilbert* by the Supreme Court. In *Newport News Shipbuilding and Drydock Co. v. EEOC*, 462 U.S. 669 (1983), the Court found that PDA-78 applied to spouses of employees. The employer's program allowed benefits for pregnant employees only, not their spouses who may become pregnant. Under the broader civil rights standard of sex discrimination, the case concluded spouses were eligible. Male employees of Newport News Shipbuilding could be paid health insurance benefits for their pregnant spouses, since a male spouse would benefit were the employee a female who became eligible for employer-paid pregnancy benefits. The Court reversed *Gilbert* and also rejected the reasoning that sex discrimination required proof of intent.

In *California Savings and Loan Association v. Guerra*, 479 U.S. 272 (1987), the court upheld a California statute requiring employers to give leave, although without pay, to pregnant female employees. The employer argued that the statute violated the "equal treatment" provision in PDA-78 since similar leave was not given to males. The required leave was a "floor" guarantee that women would be treated the same as men with respect to disability, since employers could give equal leave to males.

In *UAW v. Johnson Controls, Inc.*, 111 S.Ct. 1196 (1991), the Court interpreted PDA-78 to prohibit substitution of an employer's judgment for that of a female employee of childbearing age with regard for the health of future children as a result of a job in which there is exposure to lead. The Court found that the decision was for the female employee, not the employer, to make. The case is a rejection of the paternalistic view of women in employment enshrined in *Muller v. Oregon*, 208 US 412 (1908).

A more uniform, basic approach to leave is provided in the Family and Medical Leave Act of 1993 (FMLA-93).

It requires covered employers to grant eligible employees up to 12 weeks of unpaid leave during any 12-month period for the birth and first-year care of a child; adoption or foster placement of a child in the employee's home; the care of a spouse, child, or parent with serious health condition; or the serious health condition of the employee.

Cole Blease Graham, Jr.

BIBLIOGRAPHY

Guy, M. E., 1992. *Women and Men of the States: Public Administrators at the State Level*. Armonk, NY: M. E. Sharpe, Inc.
Levit, K. R., G. L. Olin and S. W. Letsch, 1992. "Americans' Health Insurance Coverage, 1980–91." *Health Care Financing Review* (Fall) 31–57.
Maschke, K. J., 1989. *Litigation, Courts, and Women Workers*. New York: Praeger.

DISCRIMINATION, RACIAL.

Political, social, or employment practices, whether intentional or unintentional, that result in limited employment and individual advancement opportunities because of one's race.

Origin and Subsequent History

In the United States, racial and ethnic discriminations has historical origins in legalized systems of slavery in the Southern states. Many early state constitutions and the 1789 U.S. Constitution did little to address slavery and equity for native populations. Slavery was formally abolished in 1870 by the Fifteenth Amendment. It was not until 1964 in the Civil Rights Act that Congress acted forcefully to ensure the civil liberties of African Americans and other racial/ethnic minority groups.

Delays and difficulties in meaningful legislation against racial discrimination illustrate the political intensity underlying equal employment opportunity (EEO) and affirmative action (AA) programs in a democratic society. Equal employment opportunity aims to prevent racial discrimination in the future and affirmative action serves as a remedy for discrimination from the past.

Title VII of the Civil Rights Act of 1964 (CRA-64) makes it illegal for a private sector employer to treat an employee or prospective employee differently because of race. Title VII covers all aspects of employment practice from recruitment through promotion, discipline, wages and benefits, and discharge.

Under Executive Order 11246, issued by President Lyndon Johnson on September 24, 1965, to support implementation of CRA-64, businesses with government contracts had to have an affirmative action program. Executive Order 11246 also applied to state and local government employees receiving federal funds. As a result, virtually all government contractors and subcontractors with 50 or more employees who receive more than $50,000 of federal government money per year, and all state and local governments, must take positive steps against racial discrimination.

The executive order is administered by the Office of Federal Contract Compliance Programs (OFCCP) in the United States Department of Labor. OFCCP insures that the employer must identify jobs in which there is apparent underutilization of minorities or women and adopt a written plan to correct that underutilization. The plan must show the number of minorities and women in each job grouping.

In Revised Order No. 4 (December, 1971) the Secretary of Labor defined components of affirmative action more specifically by differentiating between goals and quotas. Goals are reasonable targets for affirmative action that are attainable by good faith effort. Quotas, by contrast, are selection or promotion requirements that must be met to avoid legal penalties. Roots of the "reverse discrimination" argument lie in the contrast, since quotas imply the exclusion of qualified white males. Majorities often argue that AA programs unfairly limit their employment or advancement, but minorities require firm targets for significant results. AA programs are implemented most frequently by goals rather than quotas. Quotas are most often ordered by courts where past discriminatory practices have successfully been proven in a legal proceeding.

Underlying Theoretical Framework

Adam Smith, in *The Wealth of Nations,* argued that equal opportunity decisions should reflect natural liberty. People own their skills, talents, and labor and no barriers should impede the ability to sell or bargain them. EEO/AA opponents support natural liberty. EEO/AA advocates support liberal equality. They suggest that government needs to compensate for the natural inequalities among individuals if opportunity is to be truly equal. Thus, government provides free education to enable individuals to acquire the knowledge and skills necessary for competitive economic performance. Government may also abolish barriers to entry and promotion, such as racial discrimination, that exclude otherwise qualified individuals.

Illegal racial discrimination may result from discriminatory or disparate treatment of an employee or as a result of a discriminatory or disparate impact. Discriminatory treatment is employer intent. An example of a discriminatory treatment is when an employer refuses to consider an individual for employment just because that person is African American. The race of an applicant or employee may never be a bona fide occupational qualification (BFOQ). Discriminatory impact results when an employer's practices, even unintentionally, negatively affect the hiring or promotion of African Americans. Word of mouth or targeted recruitment methods are policies that have a discriminatory impact.

Current Practice in the United States

The Equal Employment Opportunity Act of 1972 (EEOA-72) formally expanded Title VII to include federal, state, and local governments as well as public and private educational institutions, except for religious educational institutions such as seminaries. Today, private business, quasi-public, and governmental employers with 15 or more people working for them, private and public employment agencies, labor unions with 15 or more members, and apprenticeship and training committee jointly run by labor and management must treat all employees without regard to race.

Under Title VII, complaint or class action legal proceedings may be brought by protected individuals or by the United States Equal Opportunity Commission (EEOC) against private employers, labor unions, and employment agencies. Individuals or the United States Department of Justice may seek remedies from state or local governments and an individual may bring a suit against an agency of the United States government.

Administrative Practice

EEOA-72 significantly extended the powers of the Equal Employment Opportunity Commission (EEOC). The EEOC is a regulatory body. It receives and investigates job discrimination complaints. When charges seem justified, it tries to negotiate an agreement that eliminates all the aspects of discrimination revealed through the investigation. If conciliation fails, then EEOC has the power to go to court directly to enforce Title VII. EEAO-72 allows discrimination charges to be filed by employees, job applicants, and external organizations on behalf of complainants. The provision for filing by an organization enhances the possibilities for a remedy for an employee who feels intimidated by an employer or who does not have the resources to file a complaint individually.

Supreme Court Decisions

Decisions of the United States Supreme Court often define major aspects of appropriate employment practice to remedy possible racial discrimination. Some examples are:

Goals and Quotas. Goals, quotas, and "reverse discrimination" have concerned the Court. In *Regents of the University of California v. Bakke,* 428 US 265 (1978), the Court struck down a system of medical school admission quotas in an affirmative action plan at the UC-Davis medical school and ordered a white male admitted. Employers may voluntarily adopt race-conscious affirmative action plans to encourage minority employment, according to *United Steelworkers of America v. Weber,* 443 U.S. 193 (1979). *Fullilove v. Klutznick,* 448 U.S. 448 (1980) upheld the constitutionality of an act of Congress that used racial quotas as a remedy for past discrimination by establishing a 10 percent set-aside for minority-owned business in federally funded public works projects. But later, the Court narrowed the scope of antidiscrimination laws for colleges assisted by federal funds in *Grove City College v. Bell,* 465 U.S. 555 (1984).

Seniority Plans. CRA-64, Title VII expressly protects seniority plans enacted in good faith from challenges that such plans discriminate. The Supreme Court in *Firefighters Local Union #1794 v. Stotts,* 467 U.S. 561 (1984) upheld this protection. In necessary layoffs, the Court ordered federal judges to maintain the seniority rights of white workers, even if it means laying off minority workers who typically are most recently hired. The Supreme Court upheld minority quotas in other situations, including in union admissions (*Local #28 of the Sheet Metal Workers' International v. Equal Employment Opportunity Commission,* 478 U.S. 421 [1986] and *Local #93, International Association of Firefighters v. City of Cleveland Vanguards,* 478 U.S. 501 [1986]); promotion in public employment (*United States v. Paradise,* 480. U.S. 149 [1987]); and to remedy past gender-based discrimination (*Johnson v. Transportation Agency of Santa Clara County,* 480 U.S. 616 [1987]).

Protection of Employee Property Interests. Constitutional protections for merit system employees generally require that personnel practices in government conform to the Constitution's due process clauses in the Fifth and Fourteenth Amendments. For example, firing a tenured public employee causes that employee to lose salary payments. A salary for a tenured public employee is a property interest that is protected by the Constitution from unpredictable or unreasonable action by government as an employer (*Perry et al. v. Sinderman,* 408 U.S. 493 [1972]).

Procedural due process means that merit system employee have an overriding constitutional guarantee to an adjudicatory-type hearing for relief when questionable or adverse actions are taken against them by their employer. A hearing gives the employee a chance to tell his or her side of the story to an impartial hearing officer or panel who makes a final decision based on the evidence and legal reasoning rather than on emotion. The employee can still lose the fight, but overall, the governmental agency must take procedurally fair, fact-based, and constitutionally acceptable actions, in addition to adhering to statutes, regulations, and agency policies, in order to prevail.

Supreme Court Challenges to EEO/AA

In *Wards Cove Packing Co. v. Antonio,* 490 U.S. 642 (1989), the Court reversed its decision in *Griggs v. Duke Power Company,* 401 U.S. 424 (1971). Under *Griggs,* an employer had to be prepared to provide evidence to a reviewing court that job requirements were job-related. *Wards Cove* made it more difficult for a worker to prove racial discrimination solely by presenting statistics showing underrepresentation of minorities in a work group. A worker had to prove that there was no business necessity for a challenged employment practice. The decision also lowered standards for businesses to comply with civil right requirements, making it easier for businesses to justify discriminatory practices.

In addition to *Wards Cove,* other 1989 decisions also seemed to challenge achievements in EEO/AA. The Supreme Court struck down a minority set-aside program requiring that prime contractors on municipal construction projects award 30 percent of the dollar amount of the prime contract to minority-owned firms (*City of Richmond v. J. A. Croson Co,* 488 U.S. 428 [1989]). In *Price Waterhouse v. Hopkins,* 490 U.S. 228 (1989) the Supreme Court said that Title VII is not violated if an employer makes an employment decision motivated in part by prejudice, if the employer can show that the same decision would be made for nondiscriminatory reasons. *Lorance v. AT&T Technologies,* 490 U.S. 900 (1989) held that the time limits within which to challenge a seniority plan in a discrimination action began when the plan was adopted, not when a worker was first hurt by it. This gave workers less time to bring legal action against a seniority plan. *Martin v. Wilks,* 490 U.S. 755 (1989) allowed white firefighters to challenge a consent judgment that gave preference to minorities or women as a remedy to past discrimination by their employer after the judgment was complete, even though they were silent during the negotiation. *Patterson v. McLean Credit Union,* 491 U.S. 164 (1989) held that U.S. Code, Title 42, Section 1981, dealing with making and enforcement of contracts, applied only to hiring decisions when considering a remedy for racial discrimination.

In response, Senator Edward M. Kennedy (D-MA) and Rep. Augustus Hawkins (D-CA) introduced the Civil Rights Act of 1990, expressly to overturn the Court's finding in *Wards Cove* and related cases that narrowed the application of laws to job discrimination claims. The bill passed both houses, but President George Bush vetoed it and the Senate override fell one vote short. National attention was focused on the issue when incumbent Senator Jesse Helms (R-NC) ran an attack television commercial against his African American Democratic challenger, Harvey B. Gantt, mayor of Charlotte, in the 1990 general election. The ad pictured a pair of white hands crushing a rejection notice for a job application and suggested that the white applicant lost the job to a lesser qualified minority applicant.

Civil Rights Act of 1991 (CRA-91)

In January 1991, House Democrats introduced a civil rights bill that reversed many of the 1989 Supreme Court decisions. The political effects of the court decisions and the political fallout from the Clarence Thomas–Anita F. Hill hearing stimulated final passage of CRA-91. President George Bush signed the bill on November 21, 1991.

CRA-91 includes far-reaching provisions that expand statutory remedies for intentional workplace discrimination and that discourage unlawful harassment. It specifically reverses many 1989 court decisions. CRA-91 establishes that: (1) an employment practice is unlawful when a worker demonstrates that the practice has a disparate impact on the basis of race, color, religion, sex, or national origin and the employer cannot show that the practice is job-related, changing *Wards Cove;* (2) an employment practice related to race, color, religion, sex, or national origin is unlawful even if motivated by other factors, changing *Price Waterhouse;* (3) a judgment consenting to an affirmative action plan may not be challenged after the judgment takes effect by a worker who had notice of the judgment or who could have challenged it during negotiations, changing *Martin;* (4) deadlines for challenges to seniority systems were revised, changing *Lorance.*

CRA-91 defines "business necessity" and "job related," terms first used by the Supreme Court in *Griggs.* CRA-91 also expands the scope of other civil rights statutes to enhance protections available to discrimination victims. For example, U.S. Code, Title 42, Section 1981 is amended to prohibit all racial discrimination in the making and enforcement of contracts. Antidiscrimination rights are specifically protected for government and private employees and racial minorities can win unlimited money damages under Section 1981. In addition to Title VII's guarantees of attorneys' fees and back pay, workers covered by Title VII, the Americans with Disabilities Act of 1990, and the 1973 Rehabilitation Act may, for the first time, recover compensatory and punitive damages if intentional bias can be proven. Alleged harassment requires the worker to demonstrate that the employer was malicious or recklessly indifferent with respect to federal protections. There are caps in the statute that limit money damages according to the size of a business for victims of harassment, or intentional discrimination based on sex, religion, or disability.

Among other provisions, CRA-91 extends Title VII protections to persons who work abroad for U.S. companies; allows winning parties for the first time to recover fees charged by experts; and bars adjusting scores of employment-related tests on the basis of race, color, religion, sex, or national origin.

In spite of CRA-91, a new round of Supreme Court-Congressional controversy may be in the making. In *St. Mary's Honor Center v. Hicks,* 61 LW 4782 (1993) the Court increased a plaintiff's burden under Title VII. Even when an employee, as plaintiff, is able to discredit every reason an employer states for demoting, then discharging him, a judgment for the employee under Title VII is not automatic.

Managing Future Employment Decisions

EEO/AA statutes, executive orders, and court decisions have profound impacts on the policies that business and governments use to recruit, hire, and promote employees under conditions of racial fairness. They also reflect deep social values through emphasizing business employment and public jobs as ways to achieve more equitable public policy outcomes. Affirmative action, particularly, challenges a strict construction of the merit system, the convention of promotion by seniority, and the disproportionate representation of minority groups at various levels in the public work force with respect to their percentage of the overall population.

Background of an Affirmative Action Plan

The statutes and executive orders outlined above prohibit job discrimination and typically imply an affirmative action plan. As is true with most policies, the first formal requirement for successful EEO/AA compliance is awareness and commitment by executive management. The phrase, "This is an EEO/AA employer," in its various forms on memos, letters, and job announcements reflects an official endorsement of equal employment requirements and affirmative action principles. As a result, EEO/AA policies become more easily embodied in the organization's operations and not just automatically dealt with as more bureaucratic "red tape."

Requirements Relating to Employment Inquiries and Applications

Employment applications should not contain direct or indirect questions about an applicant's race, sex, color, religion, national origin, age, or handicap. Neither should an interviewer ask a job applicant direct questions about these matters. Information about race and sex may be collected at the time of application for affirmative action programs. But that information must be kept separate from regular employment files to ensure that it is not used to discriminate in making a personnel decision.

Application procedures also involve other kinds of data that may trigger a CRA-64, Title VII violation. After CRA-91, employers once again generally have the obligation to prove that all information used in hiring decisions is job-related. Specific evidence may be required in a formal legal proceeding if the hiring decisions are contested. For example, members of some minority groups are more likely to be touched by crime than are whites. Any application information should be limited to conviction records. The need for information about conviction records should be job-related so that, for example, a convicted embezzler is not hired for a job handling large sums of money. Religious beliefs must be accommodated and should not be asked about. However, if the job legitimately requires work on holidays or weekends, the availability of the applicant for work at these times can be determined; an employer does not have to hire an applicant who will not reasonably be available for work. Marital status, pregnancy, number of children, child-care arrangements, or future childbearing plans are not job-related questions. Employers typically get this information for tax, insurance, or Social Security reporting purposes after a person is hired.

Written and other tests are appropriate only when they are clearly job-related. If the results of testing adversely affect minorities, the employer should ensure that the test is job-related before using it. Usually, validation by a professional source is necessary to support any testing procedure.

The Affirmative Action Plan

An affirmative action plan is a series of goals and defined actions designed to eliminate the effects of past employment inequities. There is no specific format for an AA plan, but the major elements include: (1) a policy statement; (2) a utilization analysis of current employment practices to identify problem areas; (3) a statement of hiring and promotion goals for future employment practices; and (4) provisions for a monitoring system to measure and assess goal achievements so that the original statement of goals can be revised and kept current.

Policy Statement A strong policy statement demonstrates commitment to affirmative action as the employment policy of the agency. In addition, the statement should identify and assign responsibility for developing and implementing the program to an affirmative action manager.

The status, authority, time, and staff available to the affirmative action manager are important factors that indicate the seriousness and extent of the agency's commitment. A passive affirmative action manager develops and publicizes the program and prepares reports for agency executives and for supervising governmental agencies, but actual agency changes may come slowly. An active affirmative action manager is more assertive in identifying organizational problems, goals, and timetables and will be more demanding that executive and line managers implement AA findings and recommendations. The "cutting edge" of affirmative action is at the levels of the line manager and supervisor. Managers and supervisors deal with employees daily and make regular decisions about hires, performance appraisals, promotions, discipline, and discharges. If they are receptive to EEO/AA practices, goals, and objectives, the affirmative action plan will have a much greater chance of successful implementation.

Analysis of Current Practices. The first step in a utilization analysis is for an employer to classify all positions in its existing workforce according to occupational or job categories. Some smaller jurisdictions may have to develop a personnel classification system in order to classify and analyze jobs, while large agencies are concerned with maintaining an up-to-date system. All employers need explicit, job-related requirements for each position. The utilization analysis compares both males and females by number and percentage in each job category to their availability in the local geographic job market. Specific groups must also be treated, including African Americans, those with Spanish surnames, American Indians, and Asians.

Hiring and Promotion Goals. The next step is to identify new positions and positions for which openings have occurred through attrition during the past year. On this basis, the number of vacancies by category may be projected for future hiring periods and related to hiring needs for each affected applicant group. The same planning, analytic, and implementation techniques apply to EEO/AA problems whether in work force cutbacks or expansions.

Monitoring. Based on prior analysis and plans, the affirmative action manager will be able to identify by race and sex the number of applicants for each position and salary level. At this stage, executives, line managers, and the affirmative action officer can pinpoint specific position vacancies in underrepresented categories that might be filled by a minority group member or female and monitor agency success in achieving AA hiring and promotion goals.

The discussion in this section has emphasized prescriptive techniques and approaches to EEO/AA management. Most of these techniques grow out of steps that are necessary to comply with statutes and regulations of enforcing agencies. Some of them reflect managerial judgments about what is or is not a desirable action. Yet, compliance with the letter of the law does not always achieve results. Actual policy results may vary considerably by level of government and may be influenced significantly by the perceptions of managers who implement the policy.

Most of the responsibility for AA/EEO falls on front-line managers and supervisors who, at a minimum, must formally comply with changing laws and regulations and accommodate the outcomes of detailed court battles between an worker and an employer. Managerial perceptions and attitudes about EEO/AA critically influence successful implementation. Successful supervisors achieve more positive EEO/AA policy results by reducing their negative attitudes and by relating to workers' perceptions and fears of potential discrimination.

Reduced impetus for future improvements began in the 1980s as a result of deregulated federal and state EEO enforcement authority and diminished executive and political support for AA. It is premature to conclude that employment discrimination has vanished so that EEO enforcement is not needed. Despite EEO legislation and AA policies for government and business, ongoing decisions depend on interchanges between advocates of natural liberty and liberal equality and on managerial attitudes and worker expectations.

COLE BLEASE GRAHAM, JR.

BIBLIOGRAPHY

Barry, Brian, 1988. "Equal Opportunity and Moral Arbitrariness." In Norman E. Bowie, ed., *Equal Opportunity*. Boulder, CO: Westview Press.

Biskupic, Joan, 1991. "Civil Rights Act of 1991." *Congressional Quarterly Weekly Report*, vol. 49, no. 49 (December 7) 3620–3622.

Bloch, Farrell, 1994. *Antidiscrimination Law and Minority Employment*. Chicago: University of Chicago Press.

Civil Rights Act of 1964, Public Law 88-352, 78 Stat. 241 (1964), 42 U.S.C. Sec. 2000e *et seq.*

Civil Rights Act of 1991, Public Law 102-166, 105 Stat. 1071 (1991), 42 U.S.C. Sec. 1981 *et seq.*

Coil III, James H. and Charles M. Rice, 1993. "Managing Work-Force Diversity in the Nineties: The Impact of The Civil Rights Act of 1991." *Employee Relations Law Journal*, vol. 18, no. 4 (Spring) 547–565.

Donohue, John J. and Peter Siegelman, 1991. "The Changing Nature of Employment Discrimination Litigation." *Stanford Law Review*, vol. 43, no. 5 (May): 983–1033.

Equal Employment Opportunity Act of 1972, Public Law 92-261, 86 Stat. 104 (1972), 42 U.S.C. Sec. 2000e-4 *et seq.*

Equal Pay Act of 1963, Public Law 88-38., 77 Stat. 56 (1963), 29 U.S.C. Secs. 203 and 206 (d).

Kellough, J. Edward, 1990. "Integration in the Public Workplace: Determinants of Minority and Female Employment in Federal Agencies." *Public Administration Review*, vol. 50, no. 5 (September-October) 557–566.

Turner, Margery A., Michael Fix and Raymond J. Struyk, 1991. *Opportunities Denied, Opportunities Diminished: Racial Discrimination in Hiring*. Washington, D.C.: Urban Institute Press.

DISCRIMINATION, SEXUAL ORIENTATION.

Differential treatment of job applicants and employees based on their status as homosexual (lesbian or gay male), bisexual, or heterosexual (straight).

Unlike employment discrimination based on race, gender, national origin, color, religion, or disability, discrimination on the basis of an employee or job applicant's sexual orientation is not prohibited by federal statute. (See **discrimination, disability; discrimination, gender; discrimination, racial.**) A serious, though unsuccessful, effort was made in the U.S. Congress to pass such legislation 1994 and similar legislation is likely to be introduced in future sessions of Congress. A number of federal agencies, including most of the Cabinet departments, have adopted agency or departmental orders that prohibit discrimination on the basis of sexual orientation. Fifteen states and an estimated 140 local government jurisdictions in the United States have passed laws or issued executive orders prohibiting employment discrimination on the basis of sexual orientation (sometimes called sexual preference or affectional preference) to protect workers in the public sector and, in many instances, in the private sector, too. The passage of such laws, however, has frequently been controversial and, in several cases such as Dade County, Florida, and Cincinnati, Ohio, and the state of Colorado, voter initiatives have been relied upon as an effort to repeal laws that protected workers from discrimination on the basis of sexual orientation.

Debate over Homosexuality

The different legal treatment, and controversial nature, of employment discrimination on the basis of sexual orientation is the result of several factors. First, there is continuing scientific, legal, and moral debate over the nature of human sexuality. Is a person's sexual orientation a neutral biological characteristic that should be classified in a manner similar to race and gender, or a behavioral choice a person makes similar to the way a choice about religion is made or whether one chooses to use drugs or commit a crime? No universally agreed upon answer has emerged. Although the position was essentially rejected by the scientific community in the 1970s, nonheterosexual orientations are considered by some medical professionals and laypersons as an illness or disability that should be legitimately considered in determining a person's suitability for employment.

Legal Debate

Whether one's sexuality constitutes a "status"—that is, a state of being biologically (or in some other immutable manner) attracted to a specific sex or sexes—or a "behavior"—that is, a sexual act one performs—has been the focus of much legal argument. As of 1994, there were 20 states that made engaging in consensual sodomy a crime, although states differ on the exact definition of sodomy and whether or not it applies only to sexual contact between people of the same sex or includes people of the opposite sex. In those states, the basis for discriminating against lesbians and gay men in employment decisions is that they either have engaged in or are likely to engage in behavior that violates the law (*England v. Dallas Police Department*, 1993; *Shahar v. Bowers*, 1993). If one's sexual orientation is a status, rather than a behavior, legal justification for discrimination is weak. Debates in the United States over whether or not homosexual military personnel should be allowed to remain in service have highlighted this problem. A number of military personnel have publicly stated that they are homosexuals, but have not admitted, nor been discovered, engaging in any sexual activities with persons of the same sex. The military has sought to discharge them arguing at various times that the statement indicated a propensity to engage in behavior in violation of military regulations or that the statement itself was disruptive enough to justify dismissal.

Moral Debate

The moral debate covers ground similar to the scientific and legal fields. Some persons believe that homosexuality is a sinful behavior, violative of the teachings of many religious faiths, rightfully prohibited by civil law, and a legitimate criterion on which to base an employment decision. Others believe that one's sexual orientation is not a behavioral choice but a biological (or otherwise relatively fixed) characteristic which has no more relevance to employment decisions than one's race or sex and should be treated as such. There are others who may believe that homosexuality constitutes morally unacceptable behavior, but regardless of that belief feel that civil law should not be used to enforce this particular moral preference. And still others argue that it is unnecessary to determine whether or not sexual orientation is a biological or behavioral attribute because consensual sexual choices made by an individual are essentially a private matter over which the state should exercise no control other than to protect the right of persons to make such choices. Even the fundamental question of whether or not discrimination on the basis of sexual orientation should be prohibited is still strongly debated.

Nondiscrimination Laws

Where employment discrimination on the basis of sexual orientation has been prohibited, refinement of its exact meaning continues to evolve. In passing such laws, most jurisdictions were concerned with basic hiring and firing decisions that might be made by an employer who knew, or learned, that an applicant or employee was a lesbian or a gay man. Using such knowledge to make a hiring or firing decision was clearly meant to be prohibited. However, protection against employment discrimination usually includes protection against all aspects of the employment situation including working conditions, promotion, training, salaries, and benefits.

Some of these areas have been handled in a relatively simple and direct manner; for example, promotion decisions are treated like hiring decisions and, hence, subject to the same prohibition on discrimination. In addition, sexual harassment regulations have been modified to cover same sex as well as opposite sex harassment. Employee benefits, however, have proven to be a much more difficult issue to address. Many employers provide benefits not only to the employee, but to the spouse and minor children of the employee as well (see **fringe benefits**). Health benefits and retirement survivor benefits are the most important. Lesbian and gay male employees argue that they have family members equivalent to spouses who are not granted the same benefit opportunities only because state laws prohibit them from marrying. This argument contends that to design a benefit program that only recognizes civil marriages performed by state agents simply perpetuates discrimination in employment conditions on the basis of sexual orientation. A number of private and public sector employers have responded to this by creating a new category of relationship called "domestic partnership" (see **domestic partnership benefits**), through which lesbian and gay male couples (and sometimes unmarried heterosexual couples) are eligible for at least some of the same benefits as employees who are in civil marriages.

Conclusion

Whether or not employment discrimination on the basis of sexual orientation should be prohibited by government action is still a matter of heated debate in large part because there is no agreement on the nature of sexual orientation itself. At the present time a number of state and local governments have taken steps to prohibit such discrimination, but in other governments the issue has not even risen to the level of public discussion, or antidiscrimination laws have been defeated or repealed. The federal government has used agency executive orders to prohibit sexual orientation discrimination against civilian employees in many departments, but has refused to apply such protections to uniformed military personnel. And even when laws prohibiting discrimination are adopted, just how such laws are to be interpreted, the extent of their coverage, and the remedies that are appropriate remain to be determined.

CHARLES W. GOSSETT

BIBLIOGRAPHY

Arriola, Elvia Rosales, 1988. "Sexual Identity and the Constitution: Homosexual Persons as a Discrete and Insular Minority." *Women's Rights Law Reporter,* 10:143–176.
Case Barbara, 1989. "Repealable Rights: Municipal Civil Rights Protections for Lesbians and Gays." *Law & Inequality,* 7:441–457.
Cooper, Melinda, 1993. "Equal Protection and Sexual Orientation in Military and Security Contexts: An Analysis of Recent Federal Decisions." *Law & Sexuality,* 3:201–243.
Dyer, Kate, ed., 1990. *Gays in Uniform: The Pentagon's Secret Reports.* Boston: Alyson Publications, Inc.
Rubenstin, William B., ed., 1993. *Lesbians, Gay Men, and the Law.* New York: The New Press.

DISMISSAL.   The act of discharging a worker from employment. This term—along with such synomyms as termination, discharge, and the colloquial "to fire"—is almost always used when the action is taken for cause. In other words, the worker has committed some offense for which dismissal is the appropriate managerial response. The term layoff, in contrast, applies to situations in which the individual's employment is ended due to financial difficulties, reorganization, or other reasons not related to the worker's behavior or performance.

Although the effects of both dismissals and layoffs are the same—the workers no longer have jobs—termination for cause usually carries a stigma that may impede the individual's future employability. Relatedly, it exerts a predictably negative impact on their immediate financial status; this often contributes to both short- and long-term hardship for the workers and their families. For these obvious reasons, dismissal is the harshest action that an organization can legally take against its members. It can therefor be a traumatic event both for the individual facing dismissal and the manager who must make the ultimate termination decision.

Perhaps because it is such an unpleasant topic, dismissal is rarely discussed in the public personnel management literature. If the subject is mentioned at all, it is usually given only a laconic comment in the context of a broader discussion of employee discipline. The inattention may also be attributable to the conventional wisdom of employee development. Most authors seem to believe that managers have an obligation to "save" their subordinates by showing them the way to improved behavior and/or performance. According to this modern (human resources) view of the workplace, dismissal should occur only as a last resort. Implicitly, a dismissal is perceived as a failure on the part of both the worker and the manager. Although this perspective is currently under widespread attack, its influence is evident in the theory—if not the practice—of contemporary public management.

Historical Background

Up until modern times, dismissals occurred frequently and with little fanfare. In all but the most progressive organizations, employees who failed to meet performance expectations or whose behavior was in any way inappropriate could be terminated on the spot without any procedural impediments. The legal principle that permitted this situation to persist was the at-will doctrine, which is premised on the assumption that both labor and management are free actors. Management is free to terminate workers' employment, just as workers are free to take their skills elsewhere. Within this legal framework, workers had no right to, nor expectation of, continued employment. They could be fired without cause and without recourse.

Although remnants of the at-will doctrine continue to dominate is some employment settings (especially the non unionized private sector), the doctrine's significance has gradually waned in most public agencies. As it eroded, public employees were provided with an expanding array of protections against arbitrary or capricious dismissals.

Civil servants first began to accrue protections against unjustified removal from office during the early years of the merit reform period in the late nineteenth century. In the process of supplanting the spoils (patronage) system, civil service reformers initially believed that the government workforce could be insulated from political manipulation merely by "guarding the front door" (Van Riper 1958). The assumption was that, if politicians could not dictate who was hired thanks to competitive selection procedures, then they would have no incentive to terminate public workers for political (or other) reasons. The reformers were quickly disabused of that notion. Questionable terminations soon became commonplace; minor offenses that might go unnoticed if committed by employees of the "correct" political party would be severely punished if committed by workers of the opposite political persuasion. Even worse, the practice of removing civil servants on the basis of secret charges (so-called "star chamber" proceedings) became disturbingly widespread (Shafritz 1975).

Abuses such as these soon prompted reformers at every level to begin closing the merit system's back door. In the federal government, for example, the Lloyd LaFollette Act of 1912 introduced the requirement that employees can be removed "only for such cause as will promote the efficiency of the service." The need to demonstrate a job-related reason for dismissal was thus established. Later legislation, such as the Veterans' Preference Act of 1944 and Executive Orders 10987 and 10988, created elaborate appeals mechanisms through which public employees could vindicate their rights in disputes with their superiors. Meanwhile, the central government promoted the spread of such provisions by requiring that the employees administering federal funds be part of formal merit systems. This goal was initially advanced through the Social Security Act of 1935, and then through an avalanche of legislation in the succeeding decades. One indirect byproduct was the proliferation of civil service commissions that were established in many jurisdictions to monitor employee dismissals; the vast majority were empowered to reinstate any worker whose removal was deemed to be either unjustified or contrary to procedure.

By the late 1970s, a complex web of procedural and statutory protections insulated most public workers from dismissal. Not only was the government required to show cause in any termination action (or, for that matter, in any other type of adverse action), but the employer was also required to bear the burden of proof in such proceedings. As a consequence, most public managers were very reluctant to initiate dismissal actions against their subordinates, and the actual number of involuntary separations from government employment was extraordinarily low. These factors contributed to the widespread view that civil servants enjoy excessive job security, and to the public's impatience with workers they often perceived to be pampered and unresponsive.

In recent years, governments throughout much of the industrialized world have taken steps to expedite the dismissal of incompetent or corrupt civil servants. For the most part, efforts of this type are based on management practices in the private sector, where worker protections are far less generous. As part of the "reinventing government" movement, public managers are reportedly being provided with enhanced flexibility in making a wide range of staffing decisions. Reforms aimed at making public employees more accountable for their performance have been especially popular. To that end, governments are aggressively attempting to establish performance standards by which worker output can be objectively evaluated. One of the goals of this movement is, of course, to give public managers a weapon to use against underperforming subordinates. Related reforms include the

loosening of restrictions on worker reassignments and transfers, the virtual disappearance of civil service commissions (which once served as the "police" that protected public workers), and a reduction in the number of appeals that dismissed employees can file. As of this writing, public decisionmakers have a clear preference for more rather than fewer dismissals of civil servants.

The Reality of Public Sector Dismissals

Despite the contemporary desire to give public managers the requisite tools to dismiss deserving employees, there is little evidence that a significant increase in terminations has occurred in recent years. When public sector discharge rates are compared with those in the private sector, it becomes apparent that far fewer civil servants are dismissed for cause that are their counterparts in business and industry. The reported discharge rates for various categories of employees in the private sector range from 10.5 percent (among service workers) to 1.8 percent (a composite figure for industrial employees as derived from a Bureau of National Affairs study). Among unionized private sector employees—the labor sector that enjoys job protections that are most similar to those in government—the discharge rate hovers around .9 percent. Public jurisdictions, in contrast, generally report annual discharge rates of about .3 percent or below. These figures seem to hold true even after specific steps are taken to expand the discharge powers of public managers (General Accounting Office 1993).

The only major exceptions to these general trends apply to public employees in three broad categories: unclassified workers, probationary workers, and those who are employed in jurisdictions that do not provide extensive career protections.

The unclassified designation includes confidential and political appointees, and workers who are engaged on a temporary, part-time, or seasonal basis. Unless they are covered by explicit statutes or procedural guarantees, these groups are ordinarily deprived of the career protections that are granted to the classified service. Probationary workers, in contrast, are those who have been newly hired into the classified ("protected") career system. Most jurisdictions enforce a six-month to one-year probationary period, during which the employee can be fired for any reason. Because of the difficulties that attend the termination of nonprobationary workers, there is a pronounced trend toward lengthening probationary periods.

The final group consists of workers in poorly articulated public personnel systems. Thousands of very small public entities (towns, villages, rural counties, special purpose districts, councils of governments) often operate very informal personnel systems that do not expressly provide for employee appeals of supervisory actions. In these settings, the legal rights of public employees are comparable to those of private sector workers. Thus, they are essentially at-will employees who serve at the pleasure of the appointing authority.

Dismissal Procedures

Dismissal is the culminating event of the organization's disciplinary process, which is thoroughly discussed in this volume under discipline. Suffice it to say here that progressive discipline procedures in most merit systems dictate a multistage process that is intended to detect and correct dysfunctional behavior. Except for the most serious offenses, the procedures call for intermediary steps that are intended to give the worker one or more opportunities to improve before the ultimate penalty–dismissal–is invoked.

As is apparent from the preceding discussion, however, the decision to terminate an employee does not end the matter. In fact, it simply begins the review process that may progress through four or more appellate levels. Most public agencies contain at least two internal stages of review (the manager's immediate superior and the agency director). Others operate formal grievance committees consisting of agency employees. In most settings, the decision of the agency grievance panel is reviewed externally by one or more additional appellate bodies. Thus, the manager's decision to dismiss a worker is essentially reviewed *de novo* many times before it is finalized.

If the worker commits a particularly grievous act, the manager may be justified in recommending immediate dismissal. The violation of a critical rule (leaving the jailhouse door unlocked), illegal activity (filing fraudulent travel vouchers), violent behavior toward a coworker or client (as has happened at the U.S. Postal Service), or blatant insubordination (shouting expletives at one's superior) are typical examples. Provided that there is plentiful evidence, these are the "easy" cases, in that the behavior is sufficiently outrageous that the dismissal has a decent chance of surviving legal challenge. However, it is important to note that some grievance bodies have reinstated workers whose guilt in the most egregious of circumstances was unquestioned.

Slightly less obvious are the cases involving chronic tardiness, absenteeism, and minor rule violations. In these instances, managers are advised to counsel, warn, and otherwise notify their subordinates that improvement is necessary. Dismissal should occur only after the worker has been given a fair chance to improve and has failed to do so. A critical consideration in this regard is the amount of documentation that can be mustered to support management's allegations. Given the worker-friendly orientation of many appellate bodies, a manager can never have too much evidence to substantiate his or her claims. Moreover, the consistent treatment of workers is essential. A manager cannot afford to appear as if he or she is singling out a worker for especially harsh treatment. If, for example, a dismissal is based on "unauthorized use of the telephone," then the manager must be able to demonstrate that others who have engaged in similar activity have also been terminated. Otherwise, the action is clearly discriminatory.

The most difficult cases to prosecute are those involving incompetence or poor performance. These are relatively subjective concepts for which adequate documentation may be lacking (and inherently problematic to generate). Because poor performance is a difficult charge to prove (at least to the satisfaction of many appellate bodies), public managers are often reluctant to dismiss workers who are incompetent. Studies by the U.S. General Accounting Office, for example, have shown that public managers use a variety of informal strategies to deal with poor performers. If they are not simply ignored, many are assigned to units that are known dumping grounds for incompetents (the GAO refers to these agencies as "turkey farms"). Problems of this type demonstrate why public agencies today are so anxious to develop objective performance standards for all positions.

Before proceeding with a dismissal, the manager must be satisfied that the offending behavior is well-documented, that the employee is not being treated in a discriminatory manner, and that the relevant procedures are being followed. Once these questions have been answered, a few simple guidelines are usually recommended. First, the dismissal interview should be conducted in private both to preserve the employee's dignity and to avoid charges of "outrageous termination." In a few celebrated cases, workers who were fired in public settings successfully pressed claims that their constitutional right to privacy had been violated. Second, managers are strongly encouraged to have one witness present during the discussion. Should a dispute arise about the content of the dismissal interview, the witness provides a reliability check. Finally, the agency should provide a consistent reason for the dismissal in all subsequent actions. That is, it should not tell the employee one thing, the coworkers another, and the unemployment compensation office something else. A certain level of discretion is also essential, since spreading uncomplimentary information about a former employee might prompt a defamation lawsuit.

In summary, dismissal is probably the most unpleasant task that any manager will face in a career. It is frought with both personal and professional peril. In addition to the interpersonal tension that inevitably arises, any dismissal can trigger a legal challenge that requires the manager to defend his or her actions before both internal and external review bodies. This problem is especially prevalent in the public sector, where dismissals have been exceedingly rare due to the rigidities of the public personnel system. But, as pressures build for a more efficient and responsive public service, so too will demands for more effective dismissal procedures. Whether or not public managers will be willing to use the procedures, once they have been simplified, remains to be seen.

STEVEN W. HAYS

BIBLIOGRAPHY

Belker, Loren. B., 1993. *The First-Time Manager.* New York: AMACOM.
Bureau of National Affairs, 1991. *Employee Termination by Employment Sector.* Washington, D.C.: Bureau of National Affairs.
Hays, Steven, 1995. "Employee Discipline and Removal: Coping with Job Security." In Steven Hays and Richard Kearney, eds., *Public Personnel Administration: Problems and Prospects.* Englewood Cliffs: Prentice Hall, pp. 145–161.
Kleeman, R., 1979. "How to Deal with Nonproductive Federal Employees," *Civil Service Journal* (April-June) 44–48.
Newman, G., 1991. "The Model Employment Termination Act in the United States: Lessons from the British Experience." *Stanford Journal of International Law,* vol. 27 (Spring) 393–435.
O'Reilly, Charles and Barton Weitz, 1980. "Managing Marginal Employees: The Use of Warnings and Dismissals." *Administrative Science Quarterly,* vol. 25 (September) 467–484.
Shafritz, Jay, 1975. *Public Personnel Management: The Heritage of Civil Service Reform.* New York: Praeger.
U.S. General Accounting Office, 1979. *A Management Concern: How to Deal with the Nonproductive Federal Employee.* Washington, D.C.: Comptroller General.
———, 1993. *Employee Discipline Since the Civil Service Reform Act of 1978.* Washington, D.C.: Comptroller General.
Van Riper, Paul, 1958. *History of the United States Civil Service.* Evanston, IL: Row, Peterson.

DIVISION OF LABOR. "The separation of labor into its various distinct processes and their apportionment among different individuals, groups, or machines for the purpose of increasing productive efficiency" (Webster's *Third International Dictionary*). This concept undergirds all societal activities conducted by complex organizations, such as industries, schools, and governmental agencies. Division of labor is pervasive in all human activities without regard to culture, ethnicity, or geographic location. It is probable that what we know as division of labor—the focusing of skills development to accomplish a single or related tasks in cooperation with other participants—occurred intuitively beginning with the formation of a family unit. In primitive societies the males became hunters while the females tended to the young and were probably the first agronomists. Each family unit joined with others to form a larger unit, such as a tribe, to improve its ability to survive. This cooperation among members of a group of individuals contributed to efficiency; as the group's activities expanded it became necessary for individuals to specialize in areas in which they had talents and abilities to perform certain tasks better than others.

As societies became more and more complex, clusters of individuals formalized rules to govern themselves. Beyond this, the groups soon noted that they could trade and barter with neighboring villages to obtain products that they could not make or grow. Modern societies are made up of numerous production units, each specializing in certain functions. When taken as a whole, these units fit, some better than others, to form a large complex entity that serves the interests of the individual units as well as those of the larger coordinating entity. For the large entities to function well, all of the individual components need to fulfill their roles.

Division of labor reciprocally promotes and is promoted by specialization of functions and skills. When translated to organizational structure, this truism promotes bigger central staffs. According to Henri Fayol, specialization promotes organizational growth, which promotes growth of central staffs. While Luther Gulick was a pioneer in enunciating the proposition that division of labor was the "foundation for organization," he was by no means alone. Frederick Taylor (1911) is, perhaps, best known for influencing the study of public administration. Taylor is the developer of "time-and-motion" studies to measure efficiency, defined as the shortest time required to perform a specific activity.

Although Taylor was able to eliminate wasted motion and decrease time spend on doing the job, he ultimately failed in instituting his system because workers rebelled. While in theory, central planning and control by experts appears to be the most efficient way of managing an enterprise, what is not factored into the equation is the human dimension. And, indeed, Taylor's failure was the lack of motivation of the workers to perform as well-trained mindless beings.

Much of Taylor's and Luther Gulick's notions of administration as a science was undermined by Herbert Simon and Dwight Waldo. Simon attacked the basic principle of administration as a science. He was also critical of the notion that experts would reduce confusion. He found that experts ignored formal organizational channels and "unity of command," and created confusion by bypassing the formal organization and communicating directly with other experts. Simon noted that experts form a second informal origination that bypasses the formal organization.

Waldo was in sharp disagreement with Gulick's concept of efficiency as the fundamental value that undergirds the science of administration. Waldo felt that efficiency was not a measure that could be universally applied to various purposes and that what was efficient for one purpose may be inefficient in another. He contended that efficiency was neither scientific nor impartial as assumed by Gulick.

Specialization, coupled with hierarchical organization, leads to communication dysfunction, as in the now famous Cuban missile crisis. Rival agencies will not voluntarily share information even though there are communication channels that link them. Harold Wilensky credits such information glitches to the contest rivalry that exists among specialists. Upward flow of information through the hierarchy could also be sabotaged to protect the self-interests of individuals at the lower levels.

Specialized focus honed both skill and unity of direction, according to Taylor and Fayol. This principle is best illustrated by assembly line production, such as the Ford Motor Company's assembly line, hailed as arguably the greatest innovation in industrial productivity. However, the monotony of repetitive activity had a negative effect on productivity over time. Much of the period after World War II has been devoted to the reexamination of assembly line work. As a result, today's assembly line has been changed from a single task to a multitask activity, in recognition that, the worker has the capacity to make decisions about job-related matters. Worker-directed actions were further enhanced by such feedback mechanisms as quality circles, which opened vertical communications channels to top-level management and horizontal communication channels among coworkers.

In the context of public administration, as is suggested by Lindblom, division of labor, in theory, occurs when various agencies each address a value not addressed by the others and become the advocate of that value. Under this scheme, no agency would have tasks beyond its capacities. The problem here is that Lindblom does not explain how the activities of the components achieve cohesiveness to promote the productivity of the integrating entity. How would loosely connected organizations react to change? His theory of incrementalism suggests an answer. Incremental decisionmaking allows the organization to adapt to changes slowly over a long period of time. Rapid change, which could adversely affect the organization, is not possible under incremental decisionmaking.

The decade of the 1990s will be the watershed years for the computerization of nearly all functions of private and public entities. Changes on how work is being performed are already reshaping existing organizational structures. The most dramatic is communication. With a computer in every office, executives are able to communicate nearly anywhere in the world by accessing the Internet, or they can draft letters with a voice-activated computer and send the file to the secretary to be processed for mailing. Even more dramatic changes have occurred in the way accounts are recorded and handled because of the ease with which spreadsheets can be generated and manipulated by a computer.

The impact of technology on public administration will undoubtedly be significant. This ability to facilitate the transfer of information could well result in information overload, which could then jam communication channels so that little useful and needed information is received. Despite the availability of the tools of communication technology, unless they are used properly, their capacity for information dissemination will not be realized. For example, one of the applications for communication technology is the building of organizational cohesiveness by socializing members of an organization to adopt its norms and values. Additionally, the technology will crosscut rigidly separated functions.

Division of labor, as we know it today, will remain, but computers and communication technology will enable interchange of information that will reduce the rigidity of the divisions. No matter what an individual's function is, computers and technology have the capacity to cross arbitraily defined boundaries.

ROSE T. PFUND

BIBLIOGRAPHY

Fayol, Henri, 1949. *General and Industrial Management.* New York: Pittman Publishing Corp.

Gulick, Luther, and Lyndall Urwick, eds., 1937. *Papers on the Science of Administration.* New York: Augustus M. Kelley Publishers.

La Porte, Todd R., ed., 1975. *Organized Social Complexity: Challenge to Politics and Policy.* Princeton, NJ: Princeton University Press.

Lindblom, Charles, 1959. "The Science of 'Muddling Through,'" *Public Administration Review* (Spring) 19:79–88.

——, 1965. *The Intelligence of Democracy: Decision Making through Mutual Adjustment.* New York: The Free Press.

McCurdy, Howard E., 1977. *Public Administration: A Synthesis.* Menlo Park, CA: Benjamin/Cummings.

Simon, Herbert, 1947. *Administrative Behavior.* New York: Macmillan Co.

Taylor, Frederick, 1911. *Principles of Scientific Management.* New York: W. W. Norton & Co.

Waldo, Dwight, 1948. *The Administrative State.* New York: Ronald Press.

Wildavsky, Aaron, 1974. *The Politics of the Budgetary Process*, 2nd Ed. Boston: Little Brown & Co.

DOCTRINE OF EXHAUSTION.

A doctrine that is well established in the jurisprudence of administrative law. The doctrine essentially provides that no one person is entitled to seek judicial relief for a supposed or threatened injury until certain prescribed administrative remedies have been exhausted. Until administrative appeals are completed, the doctrine holds that a lawsuit in a court of law is premature and must be dismissed.

Exhaustion has old common law roots and came about for two basic reasons. First, it protects administrative agency authority in that it recognizes the notion that governmental agencies, not the courts, ought to have primary responsibility for the programs that Congress has charged them to administer. This idea is grounded in deference to Congress's delegation of authority to coordinate the various branches of government. Exhaustion applies particularly when an action under review involves the exercise of an agency's discretionary power or when the agency proceedings in question allow the agency to apply its special area of expertise. In addition, the doctrine embraces the concept that an agency ought to have an opportunity to correct its own mistakes before it is drawn into federal court.

Second, the doctrine of exhaustion promotes judicial efficiency. When an agency has the opportunity to correct its own errors, a judicial controversy that could be long and drawn out may be avoided. At the very least, piecemeal or repeated appeals can be avoided. Also, even when a controversy cannot be resolved by administrative review, exhaustion of administrative procedures may produce a useful record for subsequent judicial review, especially in a complex case. Exhaustion thus provides a way in which an agency can compile an efficient record for review by the courts.

The exhaustion doctrine has never been a particularly controversial one. It has been consistently applied by the courts since the early 1900s. Sometimes the results seem harsh, but the doctrine is almost universally perceived as an essential legal tool. It is designed to prevent unnecessary disruption of the administrative process by according agencies their due autonomy, and it is therefore very difficult to circumvent.

Nevertheless, it is important to note that there are situations in which the courts elect not to use exhaustion, feeling instead that judicial intervention is justified. First, exhaustion may produce undue prejudice to subsequent assertion of a court action. For example, an unreasonable or indefinite time frame may unnecessarily delay a plaintiff's remedies. Similarly, a plaintiff may suffer irreparable harm if not granted immediate judicial relief. Second, an administrative remedy may not be adequate because of some doubt as to whether the agency itself has the power to grant effective relief. Similarly, exhaustion has not been required or the challenge is to the agency procedure itself. Third, administrative relief may be inappropriate when the administrative body may be biased or has otherwise predetermined the question before it. Finally, exhaustion has not been mandated in cases in which an agency has violated or will in the future violate constitutional rights.

In sum, the exhaustion doctrine is alive and well and will almost always be applied unless certain administrative actions or inactions clearly deprive parties of adequate and reasonable appeal procedures.

CARL CANNON POHLE

BIBLIOGRAPHY

Darby v. Cisneros, 113 Sup. Ct. 2539 (1993).

McCarthy v. Madigan, 112 Sup. Ct. 1081 (1992).

McKart v. U.S., 395 U.S. 185 (1969).

Warren, Kenneth F, 1997. *Administrative Law in the Political System.* Abridged 3rd ed., Upper Saddle River, New Jersey: Prentice Hall.

DOMESTIC PARTNERSHIP BENEFITS.

Employee benefits such as health insurance and sick leave that may be made available with respect to a person designated as a "domestic partner" of an employee.

Employee benefits are becoming an increasingly important part of employee compensation. The value of health benefits, life insurance, retirement benefits, leave, and mandated government programs (e.g., Social Security, unemployment compensation, workers compensation) can reach as high as 40 percent of total payroll (see **retirement, fringe benefits,** and **family leave**). Many of the benefits provided by employers include provisions that not only cover the employee, but recognize that employees are parts of families and offer coverage for other family members as well. Family members, for employee benefits purposes, usually include only the spouse and minor children of the employee. Benefits provided include family coverage under health plans, life insurance coverage on family members, survivor pension benefits for spouses and minor children, and higher disability benefits for married employees. Beginning in the mid-1980s, some employers, both public and private, began to expand the definition of family used in their employee benefit programs to cover a new category of persons known as "domestic partners."

There is no universal definition of the term "domestic partners;" each employer that has decided to offer such benefits has established its own definition. There are, however, strong similarities between definitions of domestic partnerships and of marriage. For example, most, though not all, definitions of domestic partnerships are limited to two people only and include requirements with respect to age, mental competency, blood relationship, and emotional commitment much like those required of two people seeking to marry. The major difference is that, unlike marriage laws, two persons of the same sex are allowed to be domestic partners and, in a few jurisdictions (e.g., Washington, D.C., and Madison, WI), two persons who are closely related by blood (e.g., two sisters or a mother and adult child) may also be considered domestic partners. Most employers require that persons wishing to be considered domestic partners register their status in some form, similar to the way in which civil marriages are registered. Terminating a domestic partnership, however, is usually much less onerous than securing a divorce.

Currently, only a few European countries (e.g., Denmark, Norway, and France), two states in the U.S. (Vermont and New York), the province of Ontario in Canada, and approximately 30 U.S. county, municipal, and special district governments offer domestic partnership benefits to their employees. In the private sector in the United States, the number of employers offering benefits of their type is closer to 100, although the number is increasing rapidly in certain fields, such as computer-related industries and the entertainment industry. The adoption of such policies is often defended as necessary to provide private sector employers with a competitive advantage in recruiting employees who are homosexuals. Universities, both public and private, have been adopting domestic partnership benefits polices in recent years, as well, although their policies are more often justified as being consistent with their policies prohibiting employment discrimination on the basis of sexual orientation (see **discrimination, sexual orientation**).

Opposition to domestic partnership registration and benefit programs is often expressed in both moral and economic terms. Some opponents feel that recognition, particularly by a governmental body, of a family relationship between lesbians, gay men, or heterosexual partners who are not legally married undermines the cultural importance of marriage as a social institution or that it violates specific religious teachings in which they believe. Others oppose such benefits because of the potential financial costs of covering additional persons with unknown medical risks. Supporters of domestic partnership benefit programs argue that it is the responsibility of employers to treat all employees equally regardless of how they choose to construct their private family lives and that the enforcement of particular religious values, especially by government employers, is wrong. Also, costs may legitimately be considered in deciding whether or not to offer a particular benefit to any employee, but not in deciding to limit the benefit to a class of employees based on marital status. In any event, the evidence from employers who have adopted domestic partnership benefits does not indicate disproportionate costs to provide benefits to domestic partners when compared to the cost of providing benefits to marriage partners.

A debate also arises over whether domestic partnerships should be limited to partners of the same sex or should include partners of opposite sexes, as well. One finds that public sector employers are much more likely to provide benefits to both same sex and opposite sex partners than private sector employers, which tend to limit these benefits programs to same sex partners only. The argument in favor of limiting domestic partnership benefits to same sex partners is that opposite sex partners have the option of marrying while same sex partners do not. A more inclusive definition of partnerships is based on the idea that once an employer has decided to recognize family relationships other than that of a legally married man and woman, excluding opposite sex partners is illogical and, possibly, discriminatory.

The question of domestic partnership benefits is being raised more frequently in both the public and private sectors. Expansion in the private sector is based on considerations of cost, competitive advantage in recruiting, and, to a lesser extent, the values of corporate leaders. In the public sector, the question of domestic partnerships generates heated debates as it is a stark illustration of differing values among different parts of the community and expansion is likely to occur more slowly, if at all.

CHARLES W. GOSSETT

BIBLIOGRAPHY

Gossett, Charles W., 1994. "Domestic Partnership Benefits: Public Sector Patterns." *Review of Public Personnel Administration* (Winter) 64–84.
Laabs, J. L., 1991. "Unmarried . . . With Benefits." *Personnel Journal,* vol. 70, no. 12 (December) 62–70.
National Gay and Lesbian Task Force, 1992. *Domestic Partnership Organizing Manual.* Washington, D.C.: NGLTF Policy Institute.

DONATIONS. Contributions of Money or Other Property Having Value. Donations usually come in the form of cash contributions to charitable organizations through one or more of the organization's fund-raising activities. However, donations need not be monetary. For example, contributions may take the form of anything from old clothes to the family farm.

For tax purposes, it is important to determine that a gift has occurred (control having passed from the donor to the donee) and that whatever was given has deductible value—that is, it represents a decrease in the value to the donor, and an increase in the resources available to the donee organization to carry out its charitable purposes.

Complicating such determinations are quid pro quo arrangements in which the donor received something of value from the nonprofit in exchange for the contribution—a ticket to a play, or commemorative coffee mug, for example. So long as the value of that which was received by the donor is less that the value of that which was transferred to the nonprofit, a donation will have occurred. However, the deductible amount is the difference between the value received by the donor and the full value of the donation.

For many years, the Internal Revenue Service has recognized that the area of "in-kind" donations (nonmonetary gifts of tangible personal property) has been most abused by taxpayers. This concern has extended to Congress, and it has become incumbent upon nonprofits to follow regulations strictly in reporting these gifts and the values exchanged.

Many nonprofits are taking great pains to educate their donors about deductibility issues as a service to the donor and to avoid disputes with either the donor or the Internal Revenue Service. For example, many donors are unaware that the time they spend performing the professional services for a nonprofit that they employ to earn a living are not deductible. On the other hand, the out-of-pocket expenses they incur while performing services for nonprofits are deductible.

In the colloquial, donation often refers to small or below-average contributions and those gifts acquired by nonprofits through special events and broad fund-raising efforts such as donor acquisition mailings, charity golf tournaments, and collection cans. (See also **gifts; cause-related marketing**).

ROBERT BUCHANAN AND
WILLIAM BERGOSH

DONOR. One who gives or donates cash, materials, or other items having monetary value to a nonprofit.

A donor may be an individual; foundation; corporation; local, state, or national governmental agency; association; church; club; or other group of people with common interest in supporting a nonprofit. A donation may include money, tangible personal property items, securities, real estate, or other items of value.

According to Webster's Dictionary, the word gift means "something that is voluntarily transferred by one person to another without compensation." This would seem simple and straightforward when applied to gifts to nonprofits. However, through the years, the courts have applied several tests to determine whether or not a true gift to charity has been made. This has complicated the definition of whether or not there has been a donation.

In the eleventh edition of *Tax Economics of Charitable Giving,* a publication of Arthur Andersen & Co., S.C. (1991), the subjective tests examined donative intent, "detached and disinterested generosity," or "affection, respect, admiration, charity or like impulses" in the heart and mind of the donor. The courts have more recently rejected such tests with one court explaining that "if the policy of the income tax laws favoring charitable contributions is to be effectively carried out, there is good reason to avoid unnecessary intrusions of subjective judgments as to what prompts the financial support of the organized but nongovernmental good works of society."

The more valid measurement of whether or not a deductible gift was made lies in determining that the donor transferred money or property without adequate consideration in return. In a sense, the courts have returned to the dictionary in identifying deductible gifts.

In the real world in which nonprofits must pursue gifts or expire, they must cope with the myriad motivations of donors of all stripes. Donors who have given anything, even nondeductible contributions such as those of their time, still consider themselves to be donors of equal importance to the most generous of the wealthy relative to their abilities to give. Recognizing this, most nonprofts define donors liberally.

Increasingly, research is under way to define the term donor and why they support not for profit organizations. For example, *The Seven Faces of Philanthropy* attempts to provide a "detailed understanding of the concerns, interests, needs, and motivations of affluent individual donors as ... by categorizing wealthy donors into seven motivational types" (Prince and File 1994).

ROBERT W. BUCHANAN AND
WILLIAM BERGOSH

BIBLIOGRAPHY

Arthur Andersen & Company, 1991. *Tax Economics of Charitable Giving.* 11th ed. New York: Arthur Andersen & Company.
Prince, Russ Alan and Karen Maru File, 1994. *The Seven Faces of Philanthropy: A New Approach to Cultivating Major Donors.* San Francisco: Jossey-Bass Publishers.

DOWNSIZING. Decreasing, cutting back, retrenching, or streamlining the size and scope of activities of a government or individual agencies and programs within it.

Downsizing involves a decrease in expended resources, namely budget and staffing (see **reduction in force**). In difficult economic times, downsizing becomes a prevalent factor for many agencies at the federal, state, and local levels of government. Downsizing can lead to innovations in the planning, implementation, and evaluation of cutbacks, an area of administration known as cutback management (see **cutback management**). It is important to understand that downsizing relates to possible cuts in a wide variety of government programs in such areas as social benefits, regulation of business, economic development, science and technology, the arts, foreign aid, and others.

Recent History of Downsizing

Over the last few decades, downsizing in government has occurred in conjunction with events such as the New York City fiscal crisis of the mid-1970s, California's taxpayer revolt, the more conservative, laissez-faire ideology of the Reagan and Bush administrations between 1980 and 1992, the fall of the Soviet Union and the subsequent U.S. military cutbacks, and the takeover of both branches of Congress by a conservative Republican Party majority after the 1994 elections. In addition to ideological pressures favoring less reliance on federal social/redistributive programs and less government regulation of business, the pressing needs to provide middle class tax relief, to balance governmental budgets, and to reduce the national deficit have all emerged to spearhead the downsizing movement in the U.S. during the 1990s. It should also be noted that many large U.S. companies have been forced to downsize in order to survive and remain competitive. The list includes such giants as IBM, General Electric, Apple Computer, Xerox, and General Dynamics. Most of these companies had become dependent on large government contracts, which have been severely curtailed in recent years. Finally, the necessity to downsize has also been felt in the public sectors of countries such as Germany, Great Britain, Finland, France, and even Japan.

Managing Downsizing

The management of downsizing, cutback management, or the rightsizing of government presents a special challenge. First and foremost is the rethinking and rejustification of each affected agency's mission and objectives in relation to current and expected resource levels. From a political, as opposed to a management, context this can prove to be a difficult process given the external stakeholders that are usually closely linked to an agency's programs and activities. In addition, the employees themselves comprise the internal stockholders and are bound to feel threatened and insecure in a downsizing or cutback environment.

For a strictly management perspective, there are a number of downsizing or cutback management concepts and techniques that have received a great deal of attention beginning with the economic recession of the mid-1980s. One approach for managing cutbacks that has been implemented with varying success is the use of one or another of the participatory management strategies such as Total Quality Management (TQM), Management by Objectives (MBO), Theory Z (techniques borrowed from the Japanese), and strategic planning (see participation management). These have all been used to assist in redefining an agency's mission, the basis for its restructuring, and ultimately to justify the cutting back of individual positions.

During a period of downsizing, strategic planning in particular has been used extensively by public agencies. This is because strategic planning not only assists in the downsizing process, but frequently provides an aggressive, proactive plan to help the organization cope with future threats and realize whatever vision it has of itself after the downsizing process is completed. Unfortunately, as revealed during a special 1994 Cutback Management Conference sponsored by the American Society for Public Administration (ASPA), the University of Hawaii, and several other organizations, the strategic planning process has to be carefully designed to elicit genuine and honest participation by all those involved.

A list of some of the more prevalent management and/or organizational approaches that have been used by government agencies in attempting to deal with the challenge of downsizing includes:

- Using the strategic planning process to provide an overall framework for downsizing or as a downsizing model.
- Overcoming cutbacks with more efficient technology and better use of information processing systems. This has included the expanded and improved application of microcomputers in government and experiments in substitution of technological investment for labor investment.
- Redesigning work processes and procedures. This has involved the streamlining of work procedures, work simplification applications, paperwork reduction efforts, and the like.
- Attempting to accomplish more effective employee-management negotiation in times of fiscal stress. This has been achieved by the use of productivity bargaining, better conflict resolution techniques, and efforts to improve employee-management relations when resources are scarce.
- The extensive use of continuous program evaluation in order to assess the costs and benefits and the overall effectiveness of government programs when hard choices have to be made.
- Using program budgeting, zero-based budgeting, and performance budgeting to rejustify expenditures on an annual basis. In the early 1990s, Eric Herzik presented a budgeting system known as expenditure control

budgeting. This technique was used to control expenditures in the city of Indianapolis by encouraging department heads to find ways of performing tasks more cost effectively by offering retained savings. In the Spring 1991 issue of the *Public Productivity and Management Review,* Herezik summarizes this approach by explaining that department directors are responsible for the costs of future increases in programming and service levels. Each year's savings are carried over into the subsequent year's budget, where the agency can make use of the funds. It is quite logical to assume that the incentive to develop and experiment with innovative public budgeting systems will increase during a period of downsizing.

- Developing innovative Human Resource Management (HRM) techniques to cope with downsizing. These include more effective training, cross-training and retraining, methods and techniques to maintain motivation and cope with declining morale, stress management programs, the empowerment of workers who survive the downsizing process, as well as concerted efforts to prepare laid-off employees for the outside job market.

- Exploring ways to reorganize government so as to streamline or reconfigure agencies while looking for increased efficiency and reduced cost of providing services. According to Keon Chi (1992), the state of Iowa underwent a successful reorganization in 1992 with the help of outside consultants that realized considerable cost savings. The reorganization approach to accomplishing downsizing objectives is frequently attempted during difficult fiscal times.

- Searching for "win-win" cost-cutting strategies. These would include such things as waste reduction programs, early retirement schemes, the use of volunteers and/or interns placed in various agencies, creative cost accounting techniques, more frugal and efficient leasing, purchasing, and contracting operations, and more cost-conscious facilities management.

- Devising policies and programs to promote economic development and strengthen a government's economic base. Downsizing notwithstanding, this may actually result in additional spending in certain areas. Examples might include tax collection enforcement, tourism promotion, the creation or expansion of a state lottery system, tax credits and other devices to encourage private sector investment, and the revitalization of designated commercial urban centers.

- Increasing public-private sector collaboration. During the downsizing era of the 1980s and 1990s public-private joint ventures and contracting for services have occurred with varying degrees of success in such areas as prison and hospital management, mass transit, infrastructure renewal, wastewater management, sanitation pickup and disposal, substance abuse and community correctional programs, upgrading of information processing systems, housing project management, and others. Most research has indicated that private sector involvement usually results in decreased costs, but with mixed results regarding quality of service.

- Examining the potential impact of regulatory reform in cutting back red tape, shrinking the size of bureaucracy and freeing up the private sector to do business more flexibly and expeditiously. This is a controversial area of downsizing since deregulation has to be balanced with concerns for public safety. In *The Uncertain Balance* (1985), Helfand and Davis point to the inherent difficulty in determining exactly how much and what kind of regulation is needed to protect the consumer without doing irreparable harm to business. They concluded that each area of regulation has to be examined separately since no arbitrary or ideological predetermined approach seems to work well across the board. Consequently, even within a downsizing environment, the extent of regulatory reform should vary in such areas as environmental protection, occupational safety, the manufacturing and sale of food and drugs, the stock market, the electronic communication media, corporate mergers, and banking. As an illustration of the difficulty in carrying out effective regulatory reform, we have only to look at three major events of the 1980s: (1) the disastrous deregulation of the savings and loan industry, (2) the mixed success of airline deregulation, and (3) the reasonably successful, although only partial, deregulation of the electronic media and especially cable television.

- More extensive sharing of services among state and local governments. This has been undertaken successfully in many instances to cope with cutbacks and realize cost savings. For example, as a form of interlocal cooperation the sharing of services has been used with some success in Los Angeles County. It has also taken place in several states where savings have been realized through economics of scale and cost sharing of purchases and services.

Conclusion

The downsizing of government is a complex issue that presents may challenges for public administrators and legislators alike. When it becomes necessary to downsize, a wide variety of organizations and their external stakeholders will be potentially affected. As a result, downsizing is fraught with political as well as management problems which have to be carefully examined and dealt with. It is critical that an agency that is about to downsize have a clear vision of how to optimize its mission and resources once the downsizing process is completed. It should also be noted that, although downsizing can foster fear and insecurity, it can also be a time for fresh approaches and new ways of doing things. As the prominent New York educator Dr. John Theobald remarked during New York City's fiscal crisis of the 1970s: "If necessity is the mother of invention, downsizing can be the mother of innovation."

GARY D. HELFAND

BIBLIOGRAPHY

Applebaum Steven H., 1991. "How to Slim Successfully and Ethically: Two Case Studies of Downsizing." *Leadership and Organizational Development Journal*, vol. 12, no. 2: 11–16.

Bahl, Roy and William Duncome, 1992. "Economic Change and Fiscal Planning. The Origins of the Fiscal Crisis in New York State." *Public Administration Review*, vol. 52 (November-December) 547–558.

Chi, Keon, 1992. "Trends in Executive Reorganization." *Journal of State Government*, vol. 65 (April-June) 183–190.

Davis, Glenn and Gary Helfand, 1985. *The Uncertain Balance.* New York: Avery Publishing Group.

Herzik, Eric B., 1991. "Improving Budgetary Management and Fostering Innovation: Expenditure Control Budgeting." *Public Productivity and Management Review*, vol. 14 (Spring) 237–248.

Markusen, Ann and Joel Yudken, 1992. *Dismantling the Cold War Economy.* New York: Basic Books.

Mercer, James L., 1992. *Public Management in Lean Years: Operating in a Cutback Management Environment.* Westport, CT: Quorum Books.

Moravec, Milan, 1994. "Mistakes to Avoid During Downsizing." *Human Resources Focus*, vol. 71 (September) 7–8.

West, Jonathon P. and Charles Davis, 1988. "Administrative Values and Cutback Politics in American Local Government." *Public Personnel Management*, vol. 17 (Summer) 207–222.

DROR, YEHEZKEL (b. 1928).

The Israeli policy scientist, strategic planner and government expert, well-known for his ideas on improving policymaking and upgrading capacities to govern. By 1995 Dror had written 15 books, eight of them in English, and nearly 80 articles for journals dealing with public administration, policy studies, and governance.

Yehezkel Dror was born in Vienna, Austria, and moved with his family to Palestine in 1928. He studied political science, sociology, and law at the Hebrew University of Jerusalem, and received a lawyer's license, but preferred to continue his studies at Harvard University in philosophy of law, legislation, and planning, receiving the coveted doctorate in judicial studies (SJD).

He is married to Rachel Elboim-Dror, a professor at the Hebrew University and a well-known scholar in the history of education, policy and management, and culture and the history of ideas. They have three sons.

Dror's Multiple Careers

To understand Dror's work, the interaction between five main careers of his must be understood.

He is an academician who served as professor of political science and Wolfson Chair professor of public administration at the Hebrew University of Jerusalem for 40 years, from 1953 to 1992, when he retired from active university teaching. As an academician he was a distinguished guest professor and academic visitor at many universities abroad, such as the University of California at Berkeley, the London School of Economics and Political Science, and Edinburgh University. He also spent years at various academic centers and institutes of advanced studies, including the Center for Advanced Study in the Behavioral Sciences, Palo Alto; the Woodrow Wilson Center, Washington, D.C.; the Center for Advanced Study, Berlin; and the Russell Sage Foundation, New York.

However, this "standard" academic part of his life program is accompanied by four other main lines of activity: close involvement in Israeli policymaking and politics; policy advisory tasks in more than 30 countries; mentoring of top decisionmakers and their advisors in more than 25 countries; and work on global issues.

Already as a high school student, Dror was active in Israeli politics. While serving as a young officer at the Israeli General Staff during the War of Independence (1947–1949), he started his experiences as a policy planner. As a university student, he headed the Israeli Student Association. Highlights of his involvement in Israeli policymaking and politics include: two years as full-time senior policy analysis and policy planning adviser of the Israel Ministry of Defense; one year as Chief Scientist of the Israeli Labor Party; chairperson and member of many public government commissions that addressed subjects including civil service reforms, health services, and government corporations; candidate for the Knesset (the Israeli Parliament); adviser to the Prime Minister's Office and the Cabinet Secretariat; and more.

These "hands-on" involvements were accompanied by extensive writings on Israeli policy issues, including a six-volume corpus of books of which four were published by 1995, dealing with the dynamics of Israel, state-building, grand strategic issues, and refounding of Zionism.

Another main stand of Dror's work involves policy advisory activities in other countries. This included extensive work at major think tanks, such as two years at the RAND Corporation in California (as the first non-American serving as a senior RAND staff member); two years with the European Institute of Public Administration in Maastricht, working on European Union issues; and shorter periods at the Science Center, Berlin, and the Washington Institute for Near East Policy. Another main part of his policy advisory activities included advising multinational and international organizations, including the United Nations, the United Nations Development Program, the Organization for Economic Cooperation and Development, the World Bank, and more. The third component of his advisory activities included missions to more than 30 countries all around the world, to advise them on policymaking and governance redesign. Some work with multinational corporations provided an additional "laboratory" for Dror's ideas.

Another main "career" includes one of the most original of Dror's endeavor, namely "Workshops in Policy Planning" for top decisionmakers and their advisers. These workshops, which last from three to ten days, present an integrated set of approaches to coping with complex issues, which are applied in exercises to concrete problems facing participants. These workshops have been given in more than 25 countries on all continents, with participants including politicians and policy planners.

In 1982 at one of his workshops in Rome Dror met Aurelio Peccei, the founder and first president of the Club of Rome. In 1983 Dror proposed to Peccei a project on "upgrading governnance," claiming that substantive proposals by the Club of Rome, such as in *The Limits to Growth*, cannot achieve adequate impact without "central minds of governments" being radically upgraded. This initiative resulted in Dror becoming a member of the Club of Rome and finishing in 1994 his book *The Capacity to Govern: A Report to the Club of Rome*. With the publication of the report, Dror became more involved in global policy issues, which are now rapidly becoming a main additional "career" of his.

It is the interactions between these careers which serve as drivers for most of the innovations in Dror's work. Thus, his experiences with Israeli defense planning produced the major insight that critical choices are in essence fuzzy gambles with history. His work at the RAND Corporation stimulated his designs for public policy teaching, which served as a main input into the first public policy programs at Harvard University, at the University of California at Berkeley, and at the RAND Graduate Policy Analysis School. His interface with senior policymakers at the workshops serves as the basis for his current work on a "text for rulers." And his advisory positions provided the "laboratory" for developing and pilot testing his applied ideas, such as his designs for advisory staffs for top decisionmakers.

To complete the background for considering Dror's main ideas, one should add that he is a voracious reader. From his school days on, he regards a week in which he reads less than two books as "lost time." His reading menu is both very broad and limited. Dror freely admits his ignorance is music, drama, and literature, unless they deal with governance. But his readings cover all fields of human knowledge, from cognitive sciences to history and philosophy, and of course the literature dealing with policy issues, governance, and management, in a number of languages.

Substantive Policy Work

Because of the confidential nature of much of Dror's work in Israel and his consultative missions to governments, not much is known on his work on substantive policy issues, other than in his Hebrew books. One major exception in English is his book *Crazy States: A Counterconventional*

Strategic Issue (1971), written at the RAND Corporation. Its proposals include holding leaders of "fanatic" countries personally responsible, inhibiting such countries from gaining advanced weapons and, as a last resort, "decapacitating" them with surgical strikes. This book is widely recognized as a pioneering treatment of fanaticism armed with modern weapons long before this danger became clear to others.

Dror regards his extensive work on substantive policy issues as an essential basis for his suggestions on policymaking improvement, and also as evidence for the utility of his policy analysis approaches. It is therefore a pity that not more is known on this work, which could throw light on his writings dealing with structures and processes.

Policymaking Improvement

Dror's main contribution to knowledge and practice is in policymaking. His self-image as "doctor to governments" and "mentor to rulers" well expresses three main characteristics of this work. It is prescriptive, focusing on methodological and structural recommendations to upgrade policymaking. It is elitist, oriented at high level political and governance staffs. And it is ambitious, presuming to render advice to make "central minds of governments" and top decisionmakers perform significantly better.

Five ideas as presented in his two best-known books, *Public Policymaking Reexamined* (1968) and *Policymaking Under Adversity* (1986) serve as a sample of Dror's more original contributions:

- Critical choices should be viewed as " fuzzy gambles with history." Because of ontological and epistemological reasons, the future cannot be reduced to probabilistic maps. Instead, uncertainty and inconceivability should be frankly recognized, with decisionmakers needing tolerance for ambiguity, intelligence inputs being reconceptualized as "helping gambling, but not providing certainty," and dynamic sets of protocols being proposed to upgrade "policygambling."
- Dror emphasized the crucial importance of "extrarational" elements in policymaking (he knew Michael Polanyi well and absorbed tacit knowledge concepts into his thinking). Therefore Dror rejects most "rationality" models as inadequate. Instead, Dror emphasizes the "nonrational" nature of value judgments as crucial for choice, while proposing methods to improve them, such as by Socratic dialogue approaches, consistency, and sensitivity testing.
- Because of the shifting nature of problems, creativity—as another "extrarational" component of policymaking—is crucial. Therefore, governmental structures and staffing should be changed to encourage creativity and attract creative persons. Much wider use of think tanks illustrates another proposal in this direction.

- Dror views present governance staffs as grossly outdated. Having evaluated civil service in many countries, he proposed a new type of senior civil service elite focusing on rendering policy advice to politicians, while public management functions are moved to semi-autonomous bodies subject to policy directives. Thus, Dror demands from senior civil servants both numeracy and the capacity to "think in history," deep understanding of their country together with good understanding of global processes, and science and technology literacy, together with politics sophistication.

- Perhaps most radical of all is his recommendation to provide "training" for politicians, in addition to being democratically elected. In his view, there is no hope to improve governnance unless politicians know more. Therefore, he proposes leaves of absence to engage in studies; special learning occasions, as illustrated by his own workshops; and preparation of "study books" designed for politicians.

Upgrading Capacities to Govern

Dror's work has moved into another phase with his report to the Club of Rome. Six additional elements characterize this most recent work of his:

First, a reemphasis on the importance of governance and politics, as against tendencies to overrely on markets and civil societies. In Dror's opinion, governments have unavoidable and essential higher order tasks of influencing the trajectory of their societies and humanity as a whole into the future, whether we like it or not, for better or for worse. Unemployment, global tensions and disparities, biotechnology, mass media, climate issues—these are some illustrations of such "trajectory influencing" tasks of governance.

Second, to cope with such tasks requires governance capacities going far beyond traditional efficiency and effectiveness. Therefore, Dror requires radical governance redesigns. Thus, he moves even more in an elitist direction, proposing careful selection and long professional training for governance professionals, and improved democratic electoral regimes for politicians followed by "schooling."

Third, to maintain democracy while coping with new types of problems, "publics must be policy enlightened." Secondary schools and universities should include courses on "policy thinking," public television should present pluralistic "deep analysis" of main policy issues, and independent think tanks should propose alternatives for public consideration.

Four, as future generations have no vote but present decisions may influence them a lot, special "Councils of State," composed of "the best thinkers available," should be charged with considering main policy issues within a multigenerational perspective, with a constitutional right to present their opinion to governments and parliaments and the power to delay decisions for a limited time unless overruled by a special majority.

Five, strengthened global governance is a must, with the United Nations to be made more decisive and better equipped.

Six, a new political philosophy is proposed, focusing on the concept of *raison d'humanie,* to be advanced as a part-substitute for *raison d'etat,* together with codes of ethics for politicians, to be strictly enforced.

Improving Rulers

A new phase in Dror's work is hinted at in *The Capacity to Govern: A Report to the Club of Rome* and in some articles, especially "Visionary Political Leadership: On Improving a Risky Requisite" (1988).

It is based on two main findings presented by Dror: A very small number of "rulers" in fact make decisions of pivotal importance, however constrained they may be, and this will continue to be the case in the foreseeable future. And, such rulers are selected and elected by criteria having little to do with their decisionmaking qualifications, moral as well as cognitive. From this rather depressive diagnosis, Dror draws a main conclusion, namely that upgrading of top decisionmakers is a main imperative.

However, another main finding of his is that the importance of rulers, while well recognized on a practical level, constitutes "repressed" knowledge. Therefore, very few proposals concerning what to do to improve the performance of rulers are available; this subject is avoided by most of management, public administration, and political science. He quotes the scarcity of writings for politicians as compared with the classical genre of "Mirrors for Princes" and the proliferation of literature for business CEOs as a manifest symptom of this situation. Hence, his conclusion that the democratic taboo on considering the improvement of politicians—as if being elected is enough—must be broken, and his demand to put the necessity to upgrade rulers into the center of attention of political philosophy, political science, statecraft studies, and management interests.

Dror's announced books in progress, *The Superior Ruler* and *Remaking the World: Memorials to a Global Potentate,* are sure to elaborate this controversial view of his and to present his prescriptions for improving rulers and rulership.

Critique and Controversy

Dror's work has been widely recognized as pathbreaking, as testified by him being elected a Fellow of the World Academy of Art and Science, having received the First Annual Harold Lasswell Award of the Policy Studies Association, serving as a Fulbright Fortieth Anniversary Distinguished Lecturer, being elected as the President of the Policy Studies Association, giving the Ludwig Von Bertalanffy memorial lecture at an International Society for the Systems Sciences Annual Meeting, and being invited for fellowships, lectures, workshops, and consultation around the world.

Still, his work is controversial. Dror does not accept any disciplinary or cultural limits to his writings, he insists on providing prescriptions not always based on empiric evidence, he rejects widely accepted concepts such as "subjective probability," and he specializes in "thinking on the unthinkable" (Herman Kahn was a good friend of his) and proposing what is anathema to most. His books are not easy to read. And, by dispersing his energy between multiple careers, he may fail to reach a critical mass in any one of them.

It remains to be seen if future writings of his will redress these weaknesses and make him a major founder of "governance and management of the future," or whether it will remain for others to take up the leads provided by him.

AHARON KFIR

BIBLIOGRAPHY

Books in English by Yehezkel Dror

Israel: High Pressure Planning (with Benjamin Akzin). Syracuse: Syracuse University Press, 1966.
Public Policymaking Reexamined. San Francisco: Chandler, 1968 (reissued with new introduction by Transaction Books, 1983).
Ventures in Policy Sciences. New York: Elsevier, 1971.
Design for Policy Sciences. New York: Elsevier, 1971.
Crazy States: A Counterconventional Strategic Issue. Lexington, MA: Heath, 1971 (reissued with new introduction by Kraus Reprints, 1980).
Improvement of Policy Making in Israel. Haifa: Neaman Institute, 1982.
Policymaking under Adversity. New Brunswick: Transaction Books, 1986 (paperback 1988).
The Capacity to Govern: A Report to the Club of Rome, in publication in main languages.

In Progress

The Superior Ruler (a mentoring book for top level governmental and corporate decisionmakers).
Remaking the World: Memorials to a Global Potentate (analysis of critical global issues and policy recommendations).
Policy Gambling (a theoretical treatment of policymaking as fuzzy gambling with history).

DRUG TESTING.

Those formal organizational programs for determining whether job applicants and/or employees are users of either legalized or illegal drugs. Testing employees for possible drug use is a common practice by many private and public sector employers, as well as one that remains frustrating and emotionally charged for all concerned. Drugs include both the legalized variety, such as alcohol and prescription medicines and illegal controlled substances: marijuana, cocaine, heroin, amphetamines, hallucinogens, and countless other addictive substances. Testing commonly involves securing a sample of an individual's body fluids, such as blood, saliva, or urine, for purposes of determining through chemical analysis whether the drug itself (in the case of alcohol) or a metabolite (residue) is present at a level unacceptable to the employer.

The controversy surrounding drug testing arises when an individual's right to privacy regarding personal drug use comes in conflict with an employer's need to ensure an efficiently and safely run organization. Potential drug testing for either legalized or illegal drugs requires that an employer respond to four primary questions when developing a drug testing program:

- What drugs are the targets in testing?
- Why is drug testing important to do?
- How can one be certain the test is valid?
- What are the options once drugs are found?

The aforementioned issues must be addressed whenever an employer intends to require drug testing for job applicants and/or current employees. In addition, employers may implement drug testing for employees in cases of suspected impairment in the workplace or randomly for all or designated groups of employees.

Drug Testing in the Governmental Workplace

Private sector employers are relatively unrestricted in their ability to develop intrusive drug testing policies and procedures for employees. However, such is not the case with public sector or governmental employers. In fact, government as a regulator of drug use among the citizenry may be in sharp divergence with government in its role as employer.

In the United States, substance abuse testing in the governmental workplace has been a deep concern since President Reagan's Executive order 12564 (1986) drew national attention to the issue. The executive order allowed drug testing of federal employees even though no substantiated proof of widespread drug abuse had been found among federal workers. In 1988, the Drug-Free Workplace Act required federal contractors to establish drug-free workplace awareness programs as well as notify the government of any employee convicted of drug use in the workplace. Subsequently, federal agencies issued a variety of regulations mandating the random testing of contract workers in positions related to public safety or national security. State and local governments, although not required by the Drug-Free Workplace Act, promulgated regulations and policies establishing not only an awareness program, but substance abuse testing of employees, which included random drug testing.

Government as policymaker further intruded into the arena of employee drug testing with passage of the Omnibus Transportation Employee Testing Act of 1991, which required alcohol and drug testing of safety-sensitive transportation employees, that is, employees who are required to possess a commercial driver's license (CDL). This law also directed the Department of Transportation (DOT) to promulgate regulations establishing a program to compel employers to conduct preemployment, reasonable suspicion, random, and post-accident testing of operators of commercial motor vehicles regarding alcohol or a controlled substance (U.S. Department of Transportation 1994). Final rules to implement the act went into effect on February 15, 1994, and became effective for employers of 50 or more safety-sensitive employees on January 1, 1995; for employers with fewer than 50 such employees the implementation date was January 1, 1996.

Thus, the United States Congress created a regulatory policy that includes random drug and alcohol testing for the nearly 7 million CDL holders, most of whom are public sector employees. The reaction to the federal government's "carrot and stick" coercion of local governments into random drug testing continues to be vociferous on the part of numerous unions, civil rights advocates, labor law attorneys, and private citizens who joined forces in protesting these policies as an unjust invasion of worker privacy rights.

Although a variety of arguments pro and con exist regarding such testing (Redeker and Segal 1989), most seem to focus on one specific question: Is random drug testing an unconstitutional invasion of an employee's "zone of privacy" as defined by the Supreme Court and thus, a possible tool for employee oppression (*Griswold v. Connecticut*, 381 U.S. 479, 1965)? Random drug testing for public employees continues to make it one of the most controversial issues faced by employers and employees.

While endorsing preemployment testing and suspicion-based testing, these groups vigorously oppose random testing of public employees as an unjust invasion of worker privacy and have taken their cases to the courts and to the bargaining table. However, public sector employees are confronted with intense societal pressures to implement and expand drug testing on a massive scale in the work place. Employee representatives oppose unlimited testing by demanding that governmental agencies adopt rules and procedures to guarantee protection of the constitutional rights of employees, establish a bona fide need to seize an employee's body fluids, provide treatment, rehabilitation and counseling, as well as meet the standard of probable cause that an employee is impaired in the performance of his or her duties by the use of alcohol or controlled substances.

How Drug Testing Works

Under provisions of the Omnibus Act, all urine specimens are analyzed for the following drugs:

- Marijuana (THC metabolite);
- Cocaine;
- Amphetamines;
- Opiates (including heroin);
- Phencyclidine(PCP).

The testing is a two-stage process. First, a screening test is performed and if it is positive for one or more of the drugs, then a confirmation test is performed for each identified drug using state-of-the-art gas chromatography/mass spectrometry (GC/MS) analysis. GC/MC confirmation ensures that over-the-counter medications or preparations are not reported as positive results.

All drug test results are reviewed and interpreted by a physician medical review officer (MRO) before they are reported to the employer. If the laboratory reports a positive result to the MRO, the MRO contacts the employee, in person or by telephone, and conducts an interview to determine if there is an alternative medical explanation for the drugs found in the employee's urine specimen. For all the drugs except PCP, there are some limited, legitimate medical uses that may explain the positive test result. If the employee provides appropriate documentation and the MRO determines that it is legitimate medical use of the prohibited drug, the drug test result is reported as negative to the employer.

The DOT drug and alcohol testing procedures rule (49 CFR Part 40) sets forth the procedures for drug testing; analysis is performed at laboratories certified and monitored by the National Institutes of Drug Abuse (NIDA). The employee provides a urine specimen in a location that affords privacy and the "collector" seals and labels the specimen, completes a chain of custody document, and prepares the specimen and accompanying paperwork for shipment to a drug testing laboratory. the specimen collection procedures and chain of custody are intended to ensure that the specimen's security, proper identification, and integrity are not compromised.

Furthermore, the Omnibus Act requires that drug testing procedures for commercial motor vehicle drivers include split specimen procedures. Each urine specimen is subdivided into two bottles labeled as a "primary" and a "split" specimen, with both bottles sent to a laboratory. Only the primary specimen is opened and used for the urinalysis, while the split specimen bottle remains sealed and is stored at the laboratory. If the analysis of the primary specimen confirms the presence of illegal, controlled substances, the employee has 72 hours to request that the split specimen be sent to another certified laboratory for analysis. This split specimen procedure essentially provides the driver with an opportunity for a second opinion.

The drug rules prohibit any unauthorized use of the controlled substances. Illicit use of drugs by safety-sensitive employees is prohibited on or off duty. Additional rules prohibit the use of legally prescribed controlled substances (such as barbiturates, amphetamines, morphine, etc.) by safety-sensitive drivers involved in interstate commerce. Other regulations require drivers involved in interstate commerce to report any medical use of controlled substances.

As with an alcohol misuse violation, an employee must be removed from safety-sensitive duty if he or she has a positive drug test result. The removal cannot take place until the MRO has interviewed the employee and determined that the positive drug test resulted from the unauthorized use of a controlled substance. An employee cannot be returned to safety-sensitive duties until he or she has been evaluated by a substance abuse professional or MRO, has complied with recommended rehabilitation, and has a negative result on a return-to-duty drug test. Follow-up testing to monitor the driver's continued abstinence from drug use may be required.

Employers are responsible for conducting random, unannounced drug tests. The total number conducted each year must equal at least 50 percent of the safety-sensitive drivers. Some employees may be tested more than once each year, some may not be tested at all, depending on the random selection. Random testing for drugs does not have to be conducted in immediate time proximity to performing safety-sensitive functions. Once notified of selection for testing, however, a driver must proceed to a collection site to accomplish the urine specimen collection.

The comprehensive drug testing rules also mandate other requirements that pertain to public employers, including the following:

- Employers must provide safety-sensitive employees with information on drug and alcohol use and treatment resources;
- All supervisors and administrators with responsibilities over safety-sensitive employees must attend at least one hour of training each on both the signs and symptoms of drug use and alcohol misuse and indicators in order to assist them in making appropriate determinations for reasonable suspicion testing;
- Employers must keep detailed records of their alcohol and drug testing programs, which may be inspected or audited by DOT to determine compliance with its rules.

Labor Opposition

The mandatory requirement to establish a drug and alcohol testing program for safety-sensitive employees is required by federal law and may not be blocked or impeded by provisions contained in collective bargaining agreements covering safety-sensitive employees. Moreover, there may be aspects of an employer's program which may

require bargaining. In the DOT preamble to the final rules, the following is noted:

> The rules contemplate that many aspects of the employer/employee relationship with respect to these programs will be subject to collective bargaining. For example, who pays for assessment and evaluation is one area we explicitly do not regulate. However, employers and employees are not free to bargain away any of the requirements of these rules. Whatever rights they may have to bargain collectively or otherwise agree on employer-employee relations, they cannot change or ignore federal safety standards (59 Fed. Reg. 7317, 1994.)

Whether a given public employer will be required to negotiate over aspects of its alcohol and drug testing program for safety-sensitive employees depends on state law and whether the employer has retained the right to take such action during the term of an existing agreement. For example, if an employer has retained the contractual right to take unilateral action in this area during the term of the agreement, there would normally be no further legal obligation to negotiate over the issue. Some public employers have even encouraged local union representatives to attend technical assistance programs sponsored by the Department of Transportation so that they better understand what their employers are obligated by law to do in this important area.

Most public employee unions oppose random drug testing as unconstitutional intrusion into employee privacy. For example, the American Federation of State, County and Municipal Employees (AFSCME) feels so strongly concerning the issue of random drug testing in the public sector that it emphasizes the issue at conferences and repeatedly states its opposition to random drug testing. AFSCME also demands collective bargaining on drug testing, probable cause requirements, due process, and the right of privacy. Other unions are also challenging drug testing in the courts, through administrative grievance procedures, and through contract negotiations.

The determination of unions to protect employee rights is equally matched by the tenacity of government agencies to hold the line regarding managerial rights. Advocates of random drug testing argue its necessity because of the debilitating effects of drugs on workers. A number of researchers have conducted studies to determine the economic affects of substance abuse on businesses and government agencies, and the documented effects of widespread substance abuse in the workplace are uncontested (Redeker and Segal 1989a; Muczyk and Heshizer 1988). Whether applied in the public or private sectors, the literature suggests that drug testing results in:

- absenteeism and accidents declining (Ogborn 1987);

- workers' compensation claims being dramatically lowered (U.S. Office of Personnel Management 1986);
- insurance costs being reduced (Hamilton 1985);
- much lower voluntary turnover rate (Normand, Salyards and Mahoney 1990).

Employers point to these studies and claim that substance abuse threatens the economic growth of the United States as a whole and individual businesses separately. It is estimated that it costs the United States in excess of $100 billion each year through decreased productivity and tax revenue, as well as increased insurance rates and inflated prices for goods and services (Redeker and Segal 1989b). Other observers contend that drug testing reduces productivity by its negative effect on worker morale (Gordon 1987). Researchers have also substantiated that there is a greater acceptance of drug testing programs when there is greater potential danger to the public associated with impaired performance on the job (Murphy, Thornton and Prue 1990).

Consequently, any government entity charged with the duty to safeguard the health and welfare of the public might decide to implement substance abuse testing even though it risks the clamor of protest from employee advocates. An employer might typically defend its decision as a trade-off between the public interest and individual liberties. Other employers believe that drug addiction is due to weak moral character and drug users should be treated as criminals or deprived of their property right to a job (Bennett, Blum and Roman 1994).

In less than a decade, testing bodily fluids for evidence of past drug use has become part of the American way of life. It has become the American way for employees to provide urine on demand for government bureaucrats or low level supervisors. How did we get to this point? Are these new policies justified? How should drug testing be controlled? What is the future direction of this "Great Experiment" in individual liberty? (Zeese 1990, p. 545)

Finally, it is important to note a decline in the number of workers who have tested positive for drugs even though the number of tests given continues to rise. In the years 1987 to 1990 positive tests decreased by 23 percent, from 18 to 14 tests per 100 administered (Sante and Shaw 1990). Certain employers, such as Sandia National Laboratories, have completely eliminated positive drug tests in its random drug screening program for armed security personnel.

Judicial Framework

United States Code 42, section 1983, also known as the Civil Rights Act, is the premise upon which all of the precedent drug testing court challenges were originally filed. These and related federal lawsuits allege that drug testing policies and procedures implemented by public employers violate constitutional search and seizure provisions of the Fourth Amendment to the United States Constitution. Under 42 U.S. 1983, the right of citizens to bring suit against anyone, including the government, for deprivation of their rights under statue, rule, or constitutional law, is set forth.

In the case of a successful drug testing court challenge, the courts can issue declaratory judgment and find the drug testing policy unconstitutional, or issue injunctive relief, which would direct the public employer to cease and desist. The courts can also issue monetary damages which would, in essence, put a price on the worth of the right to privacy.

Interestingly, the U.S. Supreme Court has addressed the constitutionality of drug tests for public employees in only two cases. In *Skinner v. Railway Labor Executives Association*, 489 U.S. 602 (1989) and *National Treasury Employees Union, et al. v. Von Raab*, 489 U.S. 656, 109 S. Ct. (1989) the United States Supreme Court interpreted the constitutionality of public employee testing programs. These cases hold that a government employer's taking of a random sample from an employee to conduct a test for illegal drugs constitutes a search and seizure under the Fourth Amendment to the United States Constitution. The Fourth Amendment guards against unreasonable searches and seizures by government officials and their agents. To comply with the requirements of the Fourth Amendment, drug testing must be reasonable under the circumstances.

Case law cites that governmental employers in the United States may only conduct such intrusive drug testing procedures without reasonable suspicion when there is a special and compelling governmental need to protect the public safety, a need which outweighs the employee's privacy interest (Mazaroff and Ayers 1989). The Supreme Court in *Von Raab* distinguishes most government employees in general from the much narrower class of government employees subject to suspicionless or random drug testing because of the magnitude of the risk that their use of drugs in the workplace imposes on public safety.

In *Skinner* (1989), which concerned post-accident testing of railroad workers, the Court defined the much narrower class that can be tested without individualized suspicion as including those who "discharge duties fraught with such risks of injury to others that even a momentary lapse of attention can have disastrous consequences."

In *Von Raab*, where the government sought to test certain customs officials and agents, the narrow class of those who could be tested without suspicion was limited to those whose drug use might "irreparably damage" the national interest and those who might be impaired in the use of the firearms they carried.

In circuit court cases, *Harmon v. Thornburgh,* 878 F2d 484, D.C. Cir. (1989), *Bell v. Thornburgh,* 493 U.S. 1056 (1990), and *Taylor v. O'Grady,* 888 F2d 1189, 1196, 7th Cir. (1989), a nexus between the nature of the employment and the potential risk to the public safety was required to sustain a random drug testing policy. However, neither the desirability of a drug-free workplace nor the integrity of the workforce provide the necessary connection. The determination that a particular employment position is of such a nature that the public good might be irreparably damaged, or the national security threatened, or that disaster or great tragedy could result from momentary inattention, is only the first step in the constitutional qualification of a governmental drug testing program. The permissibility of a particular program is judged by "balancing its intrusion on the individual's Fourth Amendment interests against its promotion of legitimate governmental interests" (Skinner). Thus, once it is determined that the governmental interest in drug testing is distinct and goes beyond the interest in law enforcement, courts must balance the governmental and privacy interests to assess the practicality of the warrant and probable cause requirements in the particular context.

Some courts have taken a cautious approach to permitting urinalysis of public employees, preferring interests predicated on concrete issues, such as protecting classified information and vehicle passengers, over more subjective interests, such as preserving the integrity of the workplace or alleged cost savings (*American Federation of Government Employees v. Sullivan,* 787 F. Supp. 255, D.D.C., [1992]).

Urinalysis testing which reveals marijuana use is particularly intrusive because of the lack of demonstrable relationship between the test and actual impairment or performance in the workplace. Because metabolites of some drugs such as marijuana are stored in the fatty tissues of the body, they remain detectable for extended periods of time after the last use. (*Railway Labor Executives Association v. Burnley,* 839 F2d 575, 583, 9th Cir. [1988]). As indicated in Figure I, random testing that yields positive tests for a drug such as marijuana may actually be indicative of stored metabolites and may have no bearing on impairment at the time of the test (Montagne, Pugh and Fink 1988).

Drug Testing Methods

Although many employers institute drug testing programs, they do not often accurately reflect the intent of their drug testing policy in actual practice. One key issue to be decided when selecting a drug testing program is whether the employer is simply interested in identifying a metabolite of a potentially impairing substance in an employee's body, or if the employee is actually suffering from an impairment that would adversely affect job performance and safety. Urinalysis drug testing does not test for the presence of an

FIGURE I. AVERAGE LENGTH OF TIME DRUGS DETECTABLE IN URINE

Drug	*Detection Period	
	Naive User	Long-term User
Alcohol	3–10 hours	3–10 hours
Amphetamines	24–48 hours	7–10 days
Barbiturates		
Socobarbital	24 hours	2–3 days
Phenobarbital	2–6 weeks	2–6 weeks
Benzodiazepines	3–5 days	2 weeks
Cocaine	5 hours	5 hours
Benzoylecgonine (Metabolite)	2–4 days	2–4 days
Codeine	1–2 days	1–2 days
Heroin (as Morphine)	1–2 days	1–2 days
Hydromorphone (Dilaudid)	1–2 days	1–2 days
Methaqualone (Quaalude)	2 weeks	2 weeks
Methadone (Dolophine)	2–3 weeks	2–3 weeks
Morphine	1–2 days	1–2 days
PCP	2–8 days	2–4 weeks
Propoxyphene (Darvon)	6 hours	1–2 days
Propoxyphene Metabolite	6–48 hours	1–2 days
THC (Marijuana Metabolite)	1–5 days	2 weeks

*The peak result in THC in blood is reached 30 minutes after ingestion, the peak in urine is reached in 5 hours.

The detection period is relative to the total body burden of parent drug and/or its metabolite. The body burden is dependent on drug dose, frequency of dose, and efficiency of drug absorption into the tissues.

SOURCE: S.E.D. Medical Laboratories.

active drug. It tests for the presence of a metabolite, or what's left after the drug has been metabolized. In other words, does an employer want to detect impairment or simply detect whether an employee has used a controlled substance sometime in the past? (Fine 1992)

If the employer chooses to test for past drug use or potential impairment, such as for active drug use on or off duty, then the testing processes by their very nature are intrusive, and, except for reasonable suspicion testing, fall into the categories not protected by the Court's decisions. They often include testing procedures such as blood, hair, urine, or saliva analyses. Reasonable suspicion testing for impairment using a nonintrusive testing procedure is somewhat different, less intrusive, and more frequently supported by civil rights advocates. Additionally, there does not appear to be any case law infringing on the public employer's right to test for impairment using nonintrusive measures.

Non-intrusive Tests

Less intrusive tests measure employee performance impairment through such techniques as hand-eye coordination,

voice analysis, papillary-reaction, and hair analysis (Segal 1992).

One such performance-based testing program involves a computerized impairment test called Factor One, which operates on an IBM PC or compatible computer coupled with a control panel and software furnished by the manufacturer. Each employee who operates the system has an independent password which, when entered, calls up from the computer's memory that employee's past performance level. The entire test takes about 30 seconds, and upon completion, provides a printed readout of an employee's test results.

Another impairment test purports to determine impairment based on voice analysis. Impairment Measures Incorporated offers the "Vocalyzer," which they contend provides 99.9 percent accurate results. According to promotional materials for the "Vocalyzer," a typical operation would involve a supervisor calling the Vocalyzer system on a toll-free line using a four-digit company code and three-digit employee number. The employee would respond and recite four digits into the phone. The supervisor then receives the impairment level over the phone or facsimile machine.

Just as performance testing will not expose the type of drug being used by a drug user, intrusive drug testing won't test for impairment caused by drug use. However, civil rights advocates, attorneys, unions, and the American Civil Liberties Union support the use of nonintrusive impairment tests over the more intrusive urinalysis, blood, saliva, or hair follicle tests because performance testing not only detects whether an employee is impaired as a result of drugs and alcohol, but it also detects impairment caused by other influences such as illness, fatigue and stress.

Summary and Future Issues

By 1994, there were only two U.S. Supreme court cases relating directly to the constitutional issue of public employee drug testing; however, as societal values change so does law. Although there is not a large volume of precedent-setting litigation, one could speculate that the litigation that does exist may in fact, be taking its course through the courts. With this in mind, it should be noted that case law indicates that the lower courts "have consistently invalidated drug-testing programs when they have determined that public agencies have not compelling reasons for using them" (Nigro and Nigro 1994, p. 251). As a result, the courts generally support the constitutionality of public employee drug testing as long as protection for individual privacy rights is guaranteed, whereas Congress and regulatory bureaucracies are generally much less concerned with employee privacy rights in the area of off-duty drug use. Thus it is also true that it is quite difficult to speculate as to the future course of drug testing in the public

sector. This sphere of controversy is in a state of continuous change at the local, state, and federal levels. Drug testing programs currently relate to the balancing tests of "intrusion of privacy versus legitimate government interest;" other balancing tests are likely to develop from statute and case law. For example, the Department of Transportation, under the Omnibus Transportation Act, labels Commercial Driver License (CDL) recipients and select others as safety-sensitive employees requiring random urinalysis testing for alcohol and controlled substances (U.S. Department of Transportation 1994).

Conceivably, the new balancing test in this case will not question who should be tested, but rather who should be required to obtain a CDL. Is there a legitimate government interest supporting drug testing if a public employer requires a nondriver employee to obtain a CDL? As a logical next step, a future Congress might mandate random drug tests for all state and local employees who are required to possess noncommercial driver's licenses, even though such an action would clearly be an unconstitutional invasion of privacy. Why have so many jurisdictions chosen to follow the path of noncompliance with judicial decisions? One cannot assume mass ignorance of the Court's decisions on the part of Congress or state and local governments that require random drug testing for safety-sensitive employees. Rather one must and should assume that Congress and others are simply choosing to ignore U.S. Supreme Court decisions and substitute their own interpretations of a "legitimate government interest." Thus, the U.S. Supreme Court is following the "constrained court view" wherein it simply lacks powers to implement and enforce compliance with its decisions (Rosenberg 1991).

Critics of "government as employer" argue that to respect the rights of public sector employees, subjective interpretation of intergovernmental mandates and of legislated policies should be somewhat less rigid. They contend that this practice would also benefit the public entity. It can also be surmised that erring on the side of discretion when implementing drug testing policies, and toward rehabilitation and leniency when doling out discipline for positive tests, would lead to fewer civil rights challenges, wrongful termination suits, experienced staff turnover, and generally, increased overall costs. Furthermore, employee rights advocates stress that drug testing does not reduce overall costs, that testing acts as a double-edged sword and actually increases liability and costs. This creates the necessity for balancing the need to reduce personnel liability brought on by drug use versus the need to reduce personnel liability brought on by employee civil rights litigation. With this in mind, it can be further hypothesized that due to the continuously changing nature of drug testing mandates and legislated policies, governmental employers who continue on the same path of strict enforcement of drug testing combined with stern penalties will likely see an increase in litigation. This conclusion is drawn from the idea that with the greater number of testing policy restrictions on civil liberties that exist, or may come to exist, come greater opportunities for challenge by employees and civil liberty activists.

Further research needs to explore the influence of collective bargaining upon drug testing policies and processes by which drug testing policies are formulated as well as comparison with alcohol testing. Finally, although a hotly debated issue, it is concluded that the evolution of drug testing policies and programs is more frequently determined by the political and moral perceptions of congressional and bureaucratic policymakers rather than directives from the judicial system.

T. ZANE REEVES

BIBLIOGRAPHY

American Federation of Government Employees v. Sullivan, 787 F.Supp. 255 D.D.C. (1992).
Bell v. Thornburgh, 493 U.S. 1056 (1990).
Bennett, Nathan, Terry C. Blum, and Paul M. Roman, 1994. "Employee Attitudes Toward Drug Testing." *Employee Rights and Responsibilities Journal,* vol. 7, no. 2.
Civil Rights Act, 42 USC § 1983.
Executive Order 12564, Drug-Free Federal Workplace, 1986.
Fine, Cory R., 1992. "Video Tests Are the New Frontier in Drug Detection." *Personnel Journal,* 71(6): 148–161.
Green, A., 1991. "Unions Seek Alternatives to Random Drug Testing." *AFL-CIO News* (July 22) 9.
Gordon, J., 1987. "Drug Testing as a Productivity Booster?" *Training,* vol. 3: 22–33.
Griswold v. Connecticut, 381 U.S. 479 (1965).
Hamilton, William A., 1985. "Drug Testing of Florida's Public Employees: When May a Public Employer Require Urinalysis?" *Florida State University Review,* vol. 15: 101–121.
Harmon v. Thornburgh, 878 F.2d 484, D.C. Cir. 1 (1989).
Mazaroff, Stanley and Jeffrey Ayers, 1989. *Controlling Drug Abuse in the Workplace: The Legal Groundrules.* Legal report. American Society for Personnel Administration.
Montagne, Michael, Carol B. Pugh and Joseph L. Fink III, 1988. "Testing for Drug Use, Part 2: Legal, Social and Ethical Concerns." *American Journal of Hospital Pharmacy,* 45 (7): 1509–1522.
Muczyk, J. P., and B. P. Heshizer, 1988. "Mandatory Drug-Testing: Managing the Latest Pandora's Box." *Business Horizons* (March-April) 14–22.
Murphy, K., G. Thornton III, and K. Prue, 1990. "Influence of Joab Characteristics on the Acceptability of Employee Drug Testing." *Journal of Applied Psychology,* vol. 76:447–453.
National Treasury Employees Union, et al. v. Von Raab, 489 U.S. 656, 109 S. Ct. (1989).
Nigro, Lloyd G. and Felix A. Nigro, 1994. The New Public Personnel Administration. 4th ed. Itasca, IL: F.E. Peacock Publishers, Inc.
Normand, J., S. Salyards, and J. Mahoney, 1990. "An Evaluation of Preemployment Drug Testing." *Journal of Applied Psychology,* vol. 75:625–639.
Ogborn, Michael J., 1987. "Substance Abuse Testing in the Public Sector." *South Dakota Law Review,* 32(2):252–263.
P.A. Times, 1994. "Local Governments for Drug Testing." (May 1) 3.
Railway Labor Executives Association v. Burnley, 839 F2d 575, 583, 9th Cir. (1988).
Redeker, James R. and Jonathan A. Segal, 1980. "Labor Personnel Issue, Trends and Management Techniques." *American Management Association,* vol. 72.
Redeker, James R. and Jonathan A. Segal, 1989b. "Profits Low? Your Employees May Be High!" *Personnel,* vol. 66:72–78.
Sandia National Laboratories, 1993. "Labor Relations Conference for Managers." (April 1).
Sante, Mike and Donna Shaw, 1990. "Lab Reports Big Decline in Workers Failing Drug Tests." *Business Outlook* (July 16) 3.
Segal, Jonathan A., 1992. "To Test or Not to Test." *HR Magazine,* vol. 4:40–43.
Skinner v. Railway Labor Executives Association, 489 U.S. 602 (1989).
Taylor v. O'Grady, 888 F.2d 1189, 1196, 7th Cir. (1989)
Thompson, Frank J., Norma M. Riccucci, and Carolyn Ban, 1991. Drug Testing in the Federal Workplace: An Instrumental and Symbolic Assessment. *Public Administration Review,* 51(6):(November-December) 507–516.
United States Department of Transportation, Federal Highway Administration, 1994. *Alcohol and Drug Rules: An Overview.* Washington, D.C.: U.S. Government Printing Office.
United States Office of Personnel Management, 1986. *Establishing a Drug-Free Workplace. Federal Personnel Manual.* Washington, D.C.: U.S. Government Printing Office.
Walters, J., 1989. *Presenting an Arbitration Case Involving Allegation of Drug Abuse.* Paper and Drug Testing Policy Statement of the American Federation of State, County and Municipal Employees (AFSCME), AFL-CIO, presented at the AFSCME Lawyers Conference, Phoenix, AZ (October).
Zeese, K., 1990. "Drug Testing Here to Stay." *George Mason University Law Review,* vol. 12:545.

DUAL-CAREER COUPLES.

A situation in which two adults both pursue a career and maintain a family life. These arrangements include unmarried, as well as the more traditional married, partnerships, and they encompass both heterosexual and homosexual relationships. They are distinguished from a variety of other types of situations—single wage earner, single parent, and dual-earner arrangements—in that the two individuals who are involved in a family relationship simultaneously pursue their own professional careers.

Origins and History

Dual-career couples are a fairly recent phenomenon in contemporary society; however, their size and importance have grown steadily throughout the second half of the twentieth century. There are three main reasons for the rise of dual-career couples in the modern workforce. First, there is the obvious economic stimulant. Two adults can earn more money and attain a higher total family income than can families with one wage earner. This is particularly important when the costs of goods and services in society increase faster than a family's ability to pay for them. Second, changes in the composition of the labor force have also prompted the rise of dual career couples. The shift from a manufacturing economy to a service-oriented one accelerated the demand for certain types of jobs, many of which were traditionally held by women—teaching positions, administrative support personnel, service-industry workers, data processing posts, and so on. Third, broader social and cultural changes have made it acceptable, and in some cases even preferable, for women to pursue their own professional careers. The civil rights and feminist movements of the 1960s and 1970s altered popular attitudes about the role of women in society, encouraging females to achieve higher levels of education and more prestigious occupational positions. All three of these factors have played a major role in encouraging the rise of two-career families.

Consider the labor force statistics from the United States. In the late 1960s, the typical U.S. family had one wage earner—usually the husband. This situation changed dramatically over the next 20–25 years: by 1990, both the husband and wife were employed in 60 percent of all married couple families. And, recent estimates suggest that over 20 percent of all married, working couples in the United States fit the definition of dual-career—with both members being committed to, and working towards, their own respective professional goals (U.S. Bureau of Labor Statistics 1989, 1991).

Today, dual-career couples are an important segment of the workforce in all contemporary societies. They also represent a prominent subgroup within the public sector. Although their exact numbers are unknown, they are believed to account for somewhere between 16 percent to 60 percent of all married public employees. One reason for the imprecise figures is that "dual career," as it pertains to public sector employment, can actually be defined in several different ways. The term can be used quite generally to encompass any relationship involving two individuals who have professional careers, so long as one is working in a public organization even if the other holds a position in the private sector. Or, it can be restricted more precisely to include only those couples where both individuals are pursuing public-sector careers. Even here, however, there are several possible types of arrangements, depending upon where both individuals work (i.e., the branch of government, departmental unit, level of government, etc.) and the nature of their positions (i.e., political appointees versus career civil servants, supervisory versus subordinate posts, etc.). In any event, the dual-career phenomenon is a prominent and growing characteristic of government employment and public-sector life (Bruce and Reed 1991).

Current Issues and Challenges

Dual-career couples present a unique set of concerns and challenges for government agencies. The challenges are most profound in government agencies that adhere to traditional notions about the roles, motivations, and behaviors of individual workers. More specifically, if the individuals holding supervisory positions in a public organization believe that there should be a clear separation between their employees' work and family situations, then dual-career couples may be viewed as problems. It may be difficult, and in some cases even impossible, to differentiate between the personal linkages and the professional, job-related commitments of the individuals who are involved in dual career relationships. After all, the personal linkage between two individuals is one of the distinguishing features of a dual-career couple. However, these personal linkages may also appear to be incompatible with the norms and expectations of organizational life.

The apparent conflict between individual relationships and organizational commitments for dual-career couples in government can manifest itself in several ways. Public personnel systems find that normal hiring decisions take on an added dimension when they involve dual-career couples. For example, a public agency may want to recruit and hire an individual who is the most meritorious for a given position. If that particular individual, however, has a spouse or a significant other who is also pursuing a professional career, the hiring process becomes more complicated. The recruited individual may refuse to take a position unless some concessions or steps are taken to find suitable employment possibilities for the other individual. This situation becomes even more difficult if the spose or significant other is also in the public sector, and it is particularly problematic if that person already occupies a position within the same government agency. The latter situations give rise to potential conflict of interest problems, even nepotism charges. As a result, some public organizations have developed policies and procedures to prevent dual-career couples from working within the same department and/or to regulate their contact with one another.

Similarly, transfer and promotion actions regarding dual-career couples can also be more difficult. Many of the same sets of problems that emerge with hiring practices for dual-career couples can arise here as well—the unwillingness of one member of a couple to transfer to a new position without some consideration of the other family member's career options, or an agency's reluctance to have two individuals who are personally tied to one another working within the same area or unit. Promotion decisions regarding dual-career couples are often viewed as particularly troublesome. For example, should both members of a dual-career couple be able to compete for the same position?

And, if one member of a dual-career couple receives a promotion, should that individual be prohibited from supervising the spouse or significant other? Such issues present a special set of problems for public personnel systems, disrupting the division between supervisory/subordinate relationships within an organization.

Dual-career couples also put a strain on traditional forms of organizational support and assistance. When both of the adult members of a family work outside of the home, this increases the need for certain types of employment services. For example, the availability of reliable child care is a major concern of dual-career couples with families, as is the ability for both adults to be able to take time off from work in order to care for sick or injured children. Moreover, dual-career couples may not be able to work a normal "8 to 5" day job. Instead, they may require more flexible work schedules—each one working slightly different shifts or times—so that each adult family member can accommodate the professional obligations of the other. Such requests may not be compatible within the traditional employment practices of an organization.

Finally, the retention of employees in dual-career relationships can also become an issue for public organizations. What happens if one member of a dual-career couple is reprimanded or even fired? What are the repercussions for the other individual? Basically, the question is: Are the two individuals treated independently, or is consideration given to the fact that the two individuals are involved in a personal relationship? Questions and issues also develop in terms of retirement policies. If one member of a dual-career couple is eligible to retire, but the other is not, the organization may not have a standard policy for handling this kind of situation. Some personnel systems treat the individuals separately, while others try to take into consideration the personal family relationships that exist between the employees.

Despite these concerns, there are significant reasons why the public sector must learn to accommodate and manage dual-career couples more effectively. First, dual career couples are now a prominent segment of the government's workforce. There is every indication that their numbers will continue to increase in the coming years. So, on a purely practical level, government agencies will be forced to address the needs and demands of dual-career couples. Second, the problems encountered by dual-career couples are indicative of other management and organizational problems often found in government agencies. Public agencies have been criticized for adhering to rigid merit system principles and practices that do not fit the changing demographics of modern, public sector workforces—more women, more minorities, and so on. So, the problems faced by dual-career couples are representative of more general public sector management dilemmas. Third, there is also a growing concern that the public sector cannot recruit or retain qualified employees. This is partially due to the lower pay scales and salary levels used in government, compared to the private sector. But, it is also a manifestation of personnel systems that have not been flexible enough to accommodate the needs of working women, single-parent families, and dual-career couples. Finally, there is the broader argument that the entire public sector needs to be revitalized, reenergized, and reinvented. Public organizations are said to be unable (or unwilling) to respond to societal problems in a quick or efficient manner, and public sector employees are often pictured as unqualified, uncaring, and lackadaisical.

Dual-career couples are a source of high-quality talent. Public agencies could use this talent to help overcome many of the criticisms that have been leveled against them, such as governmental incompetence and nonresponsiveness. Thus there are a number of reasons why public agencies should develop management practices and personnel systems that more appropriately address the dual-career couple phenomenon.

Current Practices

Organizations can develop policies and procedures more attuned to the need of dual-career couples. Such policies often include the following practices:

Establishing Special Employment Provisions for Dual-Career Couples

Here, efforts can be made to help the spouse of a prospective employee find suitable employment in the same geographic area. This can involve a variety of different kinds of services and assistance, ranging from housing assistance packages to career management counseling programs. It can also include more direct actions to find and secure a suitable job in another agency or to actually create a position for the spouse or significant other within an organization.

Modifying Antinepotism Policies

Many public agencies have rules prohibiting two married individuals from working in the same agency, unit, or jurisdiction; others have regulations that prevent one individual from supervising his or her own spouse. Personnel policies can be modified to accommodate dual-career couples, without uprooting entire personnel systems. Such modifications can include provisions to hire dual-career couples as members of a team, or they can involve more direct changes requiring that each individual's qualifications be evaluated independently, regardless of any personal relationships that exist with other employees.

Creating Flexible Work Arrangements

Government organizations have at their disposal a variety of family-oriented services that can better accommodate the needs of dual-career couples. These include the use of flextime (altering the starting and ending times for an employee's work day or changing the number of days per week that an employee will work) and "flexiplace" (adjusting the places or locations where employees actually perform their work). Both provisions can make it easier and more feasible fore employees involved in dual-career relationships to balance their work and family obligations.

Promoting Family-Oriented Employee Benefits

Members of dual-career couples often have pressing family responsibilities, such as caring for young children or taking care of an elderly relative. Agencies can alleviate the burdens imposed by these responsibilities by establishing child care assistance programs (on-site day care centers) and more flexible leave policies (e.g., allotting additional time off to employees so that they may stay home with a sick child or an elderly relative).

Establishing Clear Organizational Guidelines to Deal with Dual-Career Personnel Matters

Although some agencies still explicitly prohibit their employees from engaging in personal relationships with one another, most have established more realistic personnel guidelines for dual-career couples. Such guidelines might prohibit one member of a dual career couple from serving as a supervisor of the other member, or they might specify the situations where potential conflicts of interest may arise. Often times these provisions are established as much to prevent the mere appearance of "wrongdoing" as they are in actual response to instances of impropriety or collusion among dual career employees.

All of these provisions have one thing in common. They are designed to accommodate the special needs of dual-career couples, while simultaneously maintaining a general set of personnel practices that treat all employees fairly and equally.

SAUNDRA K. SCHNEIDER

BIBLIOGRAPHY

Bruce, Willa M., and Christine M. Reed, 1991. *Dual-Career Couples in the Public Sector: A Management Guide for Human Service Professionals.* New York: Quorum Books.
Reed, Christine M., and Willa M. Bruce. 1993, "Dual-Career Couples in the Public Sector: A Survey of Personnel Policies and Practices." *Public Personnel Management,* vol. 22, no. 2 (Summer):187–197.
U.S. Bureau of Labor Statistics, 1989. *Handbook of Labor Statistics.* Washington, D.C.: U.S. Government Printing Office.
———, 1991. *Labor Force Statistics Derived from the Current Population Survey: A Databook.* Washington, D.C.: U.S. Government Printing Office.
U.S. Bureau of Labor Statistics, Women's Bureau, 1991. *Facts on Working Women.* Washington, D.C.: U.S. Government Printing Office.

DUE PROCESS.

Fundamental fairness in legal procedures. The word "due" is used in several different contexts such as due care, due and deliberate speed, and due process, and has several distinct meanings. When used in the phrase due process or due process of the law, it refers to certain fundamental rights which our system of jurisprudence generally recognizes as legitimate, as right and proper. It refers to law in its regular course of administration through courts of justice.

The discussion of due process that follows is cast within the framework of an examination of how to insure that the laws of our nation are executed in a fair and equitable manner. What steps must be taken by judges and public administrators to secure due process or fair treatment? Answering this question has proven to be a formidable, ongoing and, at times, frustrating challenge for the question arises, due process for whom? The obvious response is for the individual involved in a particular case. Yet this response is problematic, for what may appear to be fair and just for an individual may well prove to be unjust for society. This suggests that any consideration of due process will necessarily involve attempting to balance the needs and interests of the individual with the needs and interests of society.

Judges and public administrators are continually faced with difficult decisions and choices as they attempt to balance the interests of society with the interests of the individual. As tyrannical and abusive governments can suppress and deny fundamental individual rights and freedoms, so individuals can abuse their constitutional rights, causing an undue threat to the public interest. When courts attempt to employ a balanced doctrine, they are faced with protecting the constitutional rights of individuals while simultaneously preserving the interests of society. As society grows in size and complexity, and the social problems we face grow more acute and intractable, government involvement in everyday life expands, underscoring both the herculean task as well as the significance of defining and implementing due process. A brief historical note prefaces a continuation of this discussion of the meaning and significance of the phrase due process.

Historical Background

Tracing the historical roots of due process reveals that the phrase suggests conformity with the ancient and traditional laws of the English people or laws as indicated by Parliament (*Davidson v. New Orleans,* 96 U.S. 97, 24 L.Ed. 616 [1819]). The history of Anglo-Saxon jurisprudence displays an incipient notion of due process within the Magna Carta. When King John of England signed this "great charter" in 1215, certain basic civil and political rights were extended to the English people. For instance, the principle that no one should be denied justice because of financial considerations was established, thereby recognizing that not only the wealthy, but the poor as well, deserve their day in court. Due process is therefore regularly associated with the phrase the "law of the land" as used in the Magna Carta.

A review of the history and evolution of the phrase "due process of the law" clearly indicates that the constitutional meaning of the phrase has not been given the precise definition associated with almost all other guarantees of personal rights included in the constitutions of the states and the United States. Although much has been written, the phrase has never been fully and precisely defined. On first glance, a precise yet comprehensive definition of due process that could readily be applied to each and every case would appear to be highly desirable. However, there is wisdom in allowing judicial decisions to define due process on a case-by-case basis by including and excluding rights and obligations as appropriate to the circumstances and demands of the particular case.

The essence of due process of the law is providing notice and opportunity to be heard and to defend at an orderly proceeding, but no fixed procedure is demanded. The exact procedures adopted to insure due process must be adapted to the nature and requirements of the particular case. Proceedings in court, for instance, are not always necessary (*Ballard v. Hunter*, 204 U.S. 241, 27 Sup. Ct. 261, 51 L.Ed. 461 [1933]. Nevertheless, statutes which would deprive a citizen of the basic rights of person or property in absence of a trial, consistent with the body of common law, are a violation of the constitutional guarantee of due process. An oft-cited explanation of due process or the law of the land was articulated by Daniel Webster (1782–1852) in the *Dartmouth College Case* (4 Wheat; U.S. 518, 4 L.Ed 629 [1819]): "By the law of the land is more clearly intended the general law, a law which hears before it condemns; which proceeds upon inquiry, and renders judgment only after trial. The meaning is that every citizen shall hold his life, liberty, property, and immunities, under the protection of the general rules which govern society. Everything which may pass under the form of an enactment is not, therefore, to be considered the law of the land."

As a constitutional guarantee, due process means the law shall not be arbitrary, capricious, or unreasonable and that the means selected shall have a substantial relation to the object (*Nebbia v. People of the State of New York*, NY 54 S.Ct. 505, 291 U.S. 502, 78 L.Ed. 940, 89 A.L.R. 1469 [1933]). Clearly, due process refers to certain fundamental rights which have been established in all systems of jurisprudence for protecting and enforcing private rights against the interference of government.

The first ten amendments of the Constitution of the United States comprise the Bill of Rights. State constitutions also have bills of rights. The enactment of the Bill of Rights reflected the fact that the founders of our country were especially concerned about a federal government that

was too powerful. Specific provisions of the Bill of Rights provide individual citizens various protections against arbitrary intrusions by the government into their personal lives. Unless the government can demonstrate adequate legal cause as to why it should be otherwise, individuals should be left alone. Important protections provided by the Bill of Rights include: Fourth Amendment protection against unreasonable search and seizure, Fifth Amendment protection against self-incrimination, Sixth Amendment protection against arbitrary convictions, and protections against cruel and unusual punishment as provided by the Eighth Amendment.

Initially limited to the federal level, various provisions of the Bill of Rights have been extended to the states by a number of court decisions through the years. The passage of the Fourteenth Amendment after the Civil War set the stage for extending significant due process protections to the states: "no State shall make or enforce any law which shall abridge the privileges or immunities of citizens of the United States, nor shall any State deprive any person of life, liberty, or property without due process of law; nor deny to any person within its jurisdiction the equal protection of the laws." Although the Supreme Court of the United States did not use the Fourteenth Amendment to review state court proceedings for some time, by the 1920s it had begun to apply federal due process safeguards to the states. A decisive shift was signaled in 1961 when the Supreme Court declared that the Bill of Rights in its entirety applied to the states through the Fourteenth Amendment (*Mapp v. Ohio*, 367 U.S. 643 [1961]).

Several trends can be discerned in the ongoing attempt by the courts and public administrators to define and interpret due process through balancing individual rights with the rights of society. In sum, although the Bill of rights and other legal safeguards have placed restrictions upon the government, the courts have never declared due process rights to be absolute. For instance, Justice Oliver Wendell Holmes concluded that the misuse of due process rights can create a "clear and present danger" for others or for society in general. In a famous decision (*Schenck v. United States*, 249 U.S. 47 [1919]) he noted, for example, that no one ought to have the right to yell "Fire!" in a crowded theater, claiming a constitutional right to do so. Justice Holmes stated, "The question in every case is whether the words used are in such circumstances and are of such a nature as to create a clear and present danger that they will bring about the substantive evils that Congress has a right to prevent. It is a question of proximity and danger."

Expansion of Due Process

Although the courts have never interpreted due process rights to be absolute, two general tendencies are apparent.

The right to have a hearing has been extended to situations previously not deemed sufficiently significant to warrant procedural protections, and the procedural safeguards afforded individuals at the hearing stage have been strengthened.

The expansion of due process rights can be seen with clarity in a series of procedural ruling issued by the Warren Court in the 1960s and early 1970s. Within the area of criminal law, for example, the following procedural safeguards developed. The exclusionary rule, which prohibits the use of illegally obtained evidence in a trial, was established in the aforementioned *Mapp v. Ohio* case when the United States Supreme Court overruled the Ohio Supreme Court and overturned the conviction of Dolly Mapp. The right to an attorney when police activity changes from investigation to accusation was established in *Escobedo v. Illinois,* 364 U.S. 478 (1964). The right to be informed of the protection against self-incrimination and the right to counsel was established in *Miranda v. Arizona,* 384 U.S. 436 (1966).

It is important to recall that these and other Supreme Court rulings were in response to numerous and flagrant abuses on the part of law enforcement agents. What has been referred to as the due process model of criminal justice emerged. This approach emphasized that individuals need protection from government interference in their lives and that in criminal cases the government must prove a person guilty of a crime according to certain procedural rules. In the *Escobedo v. Illinois* case Danny Escobedo was moved from precinct to precinct by the Chicago Police Department every time his lawyer appeared to meet with him. His interrogation could then proceed without "interference" from his lawyer. Prior to these court rulings, abuses of individual rights were common at the state and local level. The emergence of a due process model of criminal justice reflected the belief that the defendant can become a victim of the state in the absence of procedural protections.

Since the 1970s, growing opposition to the due process model of criminal justice has surfaced. With the increased fear of crime in the United States, what can be called a crime control model has emerged in response to the due process model. Proponents of this approach contend the primary responsibility of the criminal justice system is the enforcement of substantive criminal law. Many of the procedural protections that have been enacted such as Miranda warnings and search and seizure protections were seen as interfering with the arrest, prosecution, and incapacitation of criminals. Efforts at overturning and eroding procedural safeguards increased. Charges of favoring the rights of the defendant at the expense of society, generally, and the crime victim, specifically, were voiced. Critics demanded that the rule of law must involve a greater recognition of social provisions, not simply of individual rights.

The difficulties in balancing the rights and interests of the individual with the rights and interests of society are once more apparent. The fact that this balance has continually shifted throughout U.S. history reminds us that due process, specifically, and the law, generally, are matters of interpretation, continually being defined anew. Law is simultaneously a social force and a social product. Once enacted and applied, the law impacts society through influencing the thoughts and actions of individuals in everyday life. Simultaneously, the law is also a social product, continually being influenced by the beliefs, values, and attitudes prevalent in society. As the political, economic, and social forces at work in society impact our notions of due process, so the prevailing standards of due process rights influence the expression of those political, economic and social forces in society.

Procedural and Substantive Due Process

The concept of due process raises a number of questions regarding the types of rights and interests protected from government interference. Additional questions arise concerning the exact nature of the rules and forms that have been established and that must be followed for the protection of these individual rights. The former involves substantive due process while the latter is referred to as procedural due process.

In comparing and contrasting the concepts of substantive and procedural due process, it is necessary to distinguish common law from statutory or substantive law. Common law is law that is the result of judicial decisions. Judges, through the years, have rendered decisions on a case-by-case basis, thereby creating a body of "judge-made law." Substantive or statutory law is law that has been made by elected representatives of the people. Statutory law is law passed by a legislative body and spelled out in a formal document. Ideally, laws made by elected representatives of the people are the very essence of democracy. However, due to the increasing size and complexity of society and the concomitant increase in the number, size, and complexity of both public agencies and the issues they grapple with, many areas of the law including administrative law are overwhelmingly derived from common rather than statutory law. In practical terms, public administrators in a variety of government agencies provide the everyday meaning of due process through their interpretations of statutes and court decisions.

As indicated, although due process is mentioned in the Constitution, it is never fully defined. Legislative enactments, such as the Administrative Procedure Act, have offered some meaning to due process, but the most authoritative statements on due process have come from major policy-setting court decisions that form the body of common law.

Focusing on the substantive statements in the Bill of Rights that consider what protections should be granted to individuals is the starting point for distinguishing substantive and procedural due process. Substantive due process deals with the substance or content of the written law. What is the subject matter of the law? Given its content, are the laws appropriate, reasonable, legal? When a court holds that an executive or legislative act is unreasonable, capricious, or arbitrary and strikes it down, the act is said to be lacking substantive due process. The substance or content of the act is not consistent with substantive due process requirements concerning basic legal rights, duties, and obligations. Substantive due process is the formal legal requirement that government or its instrumentalities comply with the provisions of due process through enacting laws whose content or substance is reasonable or appropriate and whose legality can, therefore, be upheld on that basis. As such, due process has emerged as *the* substantive safeguard of property rights. Bernard Schwartz (1974), and other legal historians, have gone as far as suggesting that there has been "a virtual takeover of American public law by the due process clause of the Fourteenth Amendment."

Procedural due process, in contrast, involves the legal means and mechanisms that seek to ensure due process. It entails the legal system following required procedures and rules in the application of substantive law. Daniel Webster conveys a sense of procedural due process in his portrayal of procedure "which hears before it condemns, which proceeds upon inquiry, and renders judgment only after trial." When an appellate court, for example, overturns a lower court ruling on the ground that proper procedural steps were not followed, it is doing so on the basis of violation of procedural due process.

To a considerable degree, procedural due process and substantive due process are intertwined. The more basic the right or interest, the more considerable the procedural protections. This again suggests that due process cannot be defined in general or comprehensive terms, but must be defined appropriate to the demands of the case. Where an extremely fundamental right or property interest is involved, the procedural safeguards might involve a wide range or protections including the right to a hearing involving the right to counsel, confrontation, and cross-examination of witnesses in an impartial setting, the right to a jury trial, and appellate processes. In other instances, where the private rights or interests involved are less significant, an administrative hearing may suffice with the citizen having little or no opportunity to be heard. This does not necessarily mean, however, that courts are always more likely to reflect the principles of basic fairness than hearings conducted by agency administrators.

The distinction between administrative due process and constitutional due process is also instructive. Recent court decisions have reinforced the expanding power of both federal and state administrative agencies. In *Vermont Yankee Nuclear Power Corp. v. Natural Resources Defense Council*, 435 U.S. 519 (1978), the U.S. Supreme Court rejected the public interest intervenor's argument that the courts should require administrative agencies to utilize more stringent rulemaking procedures with regard to complicated scientific issues that might result in the formulation of potentially dangerous rules or public policies. The Court upheld the notion that agency administrators have the discretion to follow only rulemaking procedures required specifically by the Administrative Procedure Act or other relevant statutes. To compel agency officials to require more elaborate procedures for all rulemaking activities almost forces the agency to adopt the full range of procedural safeguards usually associated with judicial hearings.

Extending this line of reasoning, the Court did not require the University of Missouri Medical School to follow Fourteenth Amendment guarantees in daily administrative business, such as expelling a student, as long as the university followed its own established administrative procedures (*Board of Curators of University of Missouri v. Horowitz*, 435 U.S. 78 [1978]). In deciding that state public agencies need follow only fair nonconstitutional administrative procedures, not constitutional due process procedures, the Court effectively distinguished between administrative due process and constitutional due process. The Court felt, in certain instances, the need for elaborate hearings would be unnecessarily burdensome. In *Davidson v. Cannon*, 106 S. Ct. [1986] the Supreme Court made it more difficult to sue state administrators for tortious acts by a state official when it ruled that mere negligence which causes deprivations of constitutionally protected property rights does not make due process protections applicable.

Substantive due process and procedural due process are inseparable in a second sense. What we study is always related to how we proceed. The content of rules is always influenced by the procedures or steps applied or undertaken in the process of creating the rules. That is, how we proceed in fashioning rules or laws will influence what is eventually created. Reciprocally, the procedural steps themselves are influenced and constrained by the content of the rules or law enacted. That is, the content or subject matter of a rule of law certainly impacts the procedural steps employed in the creation, interpretation, and application of the rule or law.

In the area of administrative law, for example, agency administrators in the process of rulemaking can shape public policies by using their considerable discretionary power to help determine who participates in the rulemaking process as well as the relative importance given to the inputs of different participants. What procedures are employed in the process helps to determine the content of the rules and public policies. Reciprocally, once the content of these rules and public policies is established, it helps to further define the nature of the procedural protections that ought to be implemented to ensure that the policies and rules are fairly applied.

Although procedural and substantive due process are in many respects inseparable, many students of the law believe procedural due process may be more significant in preserving democratic life than substantive due process. Political theorists have long suggested that the constitution of the former Soviet Union was substantively more democratic than the Constitution of the United States. But a democratic constitution is of little value if it is not upheld by fair and impartial procedures regularly applied. Such procedures are the very essence of the democratic life, providing real meaning to the words of constitutions and other formal legal documents in the daily lives of ordinary citizens.

Key Court Decisions Defining Due Process

The evolution of "due process" reveals a phrase whose meaning and application is continually being shaped, incrementally, by an ongoing process of legislation, adjudication, and administration. A brief summary of key decisions can help to frame the major issues facing legislatures, judges, and administrators as they attempt to formulate, interpret, and execute the law of the land in a fair manner. Sketching the essence and limits of due process reveals a number of longstanding political-legal issues including state rights, the legal foundation and limits of public agencies, as well as the fundamental relationship of the individual and the state.

French v. Paving Co., (181 U.S. 324, 329, 21 Sup. Ct. 625, 45, L.Ed. 879 [1900]) held that it was not intended by the Fourteenth Amendment to impose on the states, when exercising their power of taxation, any more rigid or stricter curb than that imposed on the federal government in the exercise of a similar power by the Fifth Amendment. In *Bartemeyer v. Iowa*, U.S. 129, 21 L.Ed. 929 (1873) J. Field noted, "No one has ever pretended, that I am aware of, that the Fourteenth Amendment interferes in any respect with the police power of the state." In this case it was held that the right to sell liquor, as far as it exists, is not a right growing out of citizenship of the United States.

The historical dimension of due process or the law of the land is captured in the ebb and flow of court decisions attempting to give meaning to this phrase. A central concern of this effort is the necessity of and difficulty in balancing the rights and interests of the individual with those of society.

Although the Fourteenth Amendment protects the right to engage in any lawful business, this does not mean legislation cannot regulate useful occupations which, because of their nature and location, may prove injurious or offensive to the public. Nor does it prevent a state from regulating or prohibiting a non-useful occupation which may become harmful to the public, and the regulation or prohibition need not be postponed until the evil is flagrant (*Murphy v. California*, 225 U.S. 623, 32 Sup. Ct. 697, 56 L.Ed. 1229 L.R.A. (N.S.) 153 [1911]). Certain statutes or ordinances that have been held as valid, as not being deprivations of liberty or property without due process of law, include the prohibition of carrying dangerous weapons (*Miller v. Texas*, 153 U.S. 535, 14 Sup. Ct. 874, 38 L.Ed. 812 [1893]) and the creation of a registration board for physicians where it was stated that due process of law is not necessarily judicial process and that the right of appeal is not essential to it (*Reetz v. Michigan*, 188 U.S. 505, 23 Sup. Ct. 390, 47 L.Ed. 563 [1902]).

In *Matthews v. Eldridge*, (424 U.S. 319 (1976]) the Court noted that although financial considerations alone could not determine whether due process requires a particular procedural safeguard prior to some administrative decision, the government's interest, and hence the public's, in conserving financial and administrative resources must be considered. In this precedential case, the Court indeed noted that at some point the benefit of added due process safeguards to the individual is outweighed by the cost to society.

In contrast to the aforementioned decisions, which have generally broadened the rights and interests of the state at the expense of the individual, other court decisions have denounced, criticized, and in some cases overturned a number of discretionary court and agency actions, in the process strengthening due process rights. In gauging the importance of written standards and rules in ensuring due process rights, the court argued that such standards were required in administering a township assistance program (*White v. Roughton*, 530, F. 2d 750, 753-754, 7th Cir., [1976]). Because administrator Roughton had established no written guidelines to limit his discretion, the court held he could not apply eligibility requirements for the assistance program in a consistent and equitable manner. By not limiting his own discretion, the administrator possessed "unfettered discretion," a clear violation of procedural due process according to the court.

In several rulings, the courts have restricted the use of discretion by limiting an agency's implied power. Two Supreme Court decisions, *FCC v. Midwest Video Corp.*, 99 S. Ct. 824 (1979) and *NLRB v. Catholic Bishop of Chicago*, 99 S. Ct. 1313 (1978), have reduced agency discretion by refusing to allow administrators to extend the scope of their delegated powers by freely interpreting legislation to include powers not specifically conferred. Unless the implied powers can be justified as necessary and proper, administrative agencies cannot exercise powers that are not specifically delegated to them. Beyond these specific cases, numerous actions and proceedings on the part of the state have been held to infringe on the guarantee of due process of the law including such diverse issues as: taking property by the state for public use without compensation, forbidding the manufacturing of cigars in tenement houses, requiring every member of a firm of plumbers to be a registered plumber, and limiting hours of labor for employees of bakers, for example.

Reviewing the body of applications, interpretations, and evaluations of due process reminds us that each generation must grapple anew with determining the meaning of this seemingly simple yet deceptively complex phrase. Although a core set of meanings can be associated with due process, a measure of vagueness and uncertainty remains. The wisdom of this inexactness is that within the shadows of doubt each new generation is allowed some measure of flexibility in defining and applying due process relative to the changing circumstances, situations, and contexts which define their era, collectively, and their lives personally.

CHARLES E. MARSKE

BIBLIOGRAPHY

Schwartz, Bernard, 1974. *The Law in America: A History.* New York: McGraw-Hill.
Warren, Kenneth, 1996. *Administrative Law in the Political System.* 3d ed. Englewood Cliffs, N.J.: Prentice Hall.

DUTY OF FAIR REPRESENTATION.

The responsibility of a union, as exclusive representative and bargaining agent for members of a bargaining unit, to represent each member fairly, honestly, and in good faith, even if the individual is not a dues-paying member of the union. The duty of fair representation is provided for in collective bargaining contracts or in state labor law. Its origins may be traced to problems with discrimination against African Americans by labor unions in the private sector.

Standards for determining the duty of fair representation were developed in the federal courts in the private sector and applied directly to public employment with few modifications. It was first affirmed by the U.S. Supreme Court in the 1944 case of *Steele v. Louisville and N.R.R,* in an interpretation of the Railway Labor Act. This decision was later extended to all unions having exclusive representation under the Labor Management Relations Act. In one of the most frequently cited cases, *Vaca v. Sipes* (1967), the Supreme Court ruled that a union violates its duty of fair representation when it decides not to arbitrate a grievance only if it acts in an arbitrary or discriminatory fashion or in bad faith. A subsequent case, however (*Hines v. Anchor Motor Freight,* 1976), resulted in a decision that the "perfunctory" processing of a grievance may violate the duty of fair representation. The union is legally responsible for exercising a minimal level of care in meeting time limits and investigating the evidence submitted by the grievant, and should not act in a superficial or disinterested manner. Grievances are dropped by the union when, after a thorough investigation, it is determined that the case has no merit. If the union does not properly exercise its duty, it may be charged with an unfair labor practice or a civil suit for breach of contract.

The U.S. Supreme Court ruling in *Bowen v. United States Postal Service* (1983) that a federal postal workers union failed to fulfill its duty of fair representation nearly bankrupted the American Postal Workers Union. The employee-grievant, who was fired illegally from his job over an alleged altercation with a fellow worker, was awarded financial damages from both his employer and the union. The union's liability began when final resolution of the grievance would have been obtained if the union had fairly represented him. This liability included back wages. An important result of the *Bowen* case is that unions now tend to err on the side of caution, often carrying meritless grievances all the way to final arbitration, at substantial cost to the union and employer in terms of time and money. Ironically, however, a 1989 Supreme Court ruling excluded other (nonpostal) federal employee unions from damages for breach of the duty of fair representation, because an administrative remedy is available to them (the Federal Labor Relations Authority).

In sum, the duty of fair representation constitutes a significant burden on the labor organization. The union must determine the merits of a grievance, based on language of the contract and the apparent facts of the case, and adequately represent the grievant in carrying forward the case. If it fails in exercising its obligation, the union may be liable for actual (but not punitive) damages.

RICHARD C. KEARNEY

BIBLIOGRAPHY

Clyde W. Summers, 1985. "Measuring the Union's Duty to the Individual: An Analytical Framework." In Jean T. McKelvey, ed., *The Changing Law of Fair Representation.* Ithaca, NY: ILR Press, Cornell University.

E

EARMARKED REVENUE. Revenues from a particular public revenue source, a tax or a user charge, which have been legally dedicated on a continuing basis in whole or in part to the finance of a specified public purpose. The dedication, known as hypothecation in the United Kingdom, may be constitutional or statutory, but the commitment extends beyond the life of a single annual appropriation process and normally is permanent.

Many governments specifically dedicate the proceeds of a particular revenue stream to a particular public purpose. For instance, 46 states earmark the proceeds from their motor fuel tax to the finance of their highways (Gold et al. 1987, p. 11). By that earmarking of a benefit-based tax, the states are trying to divide the cost of providing those highways in rough proportion to use of those facilities, inasmuch as to use those highways normally involves the purchase of taxed motor fuel. In some sense, applying the tax to a complementary private good amounts to a synthetic price that must be paid for use of the public facility, but without the need to erect the special barriers that would allow direct charging for those public facilities. Other earmarking may involve prices directly charged for use, for example, park admission revenue dedicated to operation and maintenance of the recreation facility. The earmarked link between payment and use, where such a connection is feasible, would appear to be a logical extension of market principles to government action.

Much of the U.S. social insurance system, including Social Security, Medicare, and unemployment compensation, is financed by dedicated taxes, mostly on payrolls. This longstanding dedication is entrenched in the fiscal system and emerges from decisions to employ insurance-like logic to defend the early development of the system. Dedications outside social insurance—in other words, earmarks in the general budget system—involve much less money but, in practical terms, are more consistent with ideas of using earmarks as a tool in applying user pay principles to government finance.

Across the nation, states earmark less than one-quarter of their revenue, with motor fuel tax dedication to highway finance constituting a major portion of the total, but at least one state earmarks each of the major state taxes (Gold et al. 1987). At the federal level, around 20 percent of revenue outside Social Security and Medicare is earmarked (U.S. General Accounting Office 1990). Some earmarks reflect an effort to accommodate the quasi-price logic, like that of the motor fuel tax linked to highway finance. Other earmarks reflect the exercise of political power in which an interest uses its clout to assure a revenue flow to a particular purpose for many fiscal cycles, as with a California ref-

erendum which guaranteed a particular portion of state spending for education. And other dedications may result from a desire to make a politically difficult activity more acceptable. For instance, there is no clear link between state lottery profits and the earmarked programs they often support—primary and secondary education or economic development; because the revenues are used in an attractive way, ethical dilemmas about state support for gambling are overcome.

The Argument for Earmarking

There is considerable dispute about the political and economic advisability of earmarking. Proponents make three major points in support of earmarking. First, earmarking can make part of government operate more like a business in regard to responding to public demands for service. A benefit-related tax or charge levied on users of a service with those revenues dedicated to provision of that service makes agencies react to market forces. When the agency provides what the public wants, it will have the resources for its operations. If the agency gets out of touch with its clients, its revenue base will decline. The agency thus has a real interest in serving the public, regardless of what the independent ideas of the bureaucracy might be. Rather than convince agency heads and legislatures of what the citizenry ought to want, a standard bureaucratic practice, the operation has to respond to what the citizenry actually wants and, more importantly, will pay for through the dedicated revenue base. Revenue flows show the nature of public preferences and the government need not speculate about or try to interpret what the public really wants; the quasi-market data from earmarked revenue provide the signals for supply of government services. In order for this system to provide meaningful signals, however, there must be close complementarity between what is being taxed and the public service being provided. Otherwise, dedicated revenue flows provide no information about demand for service. In other words, dedicating motor fuel taxes for highways may give demand information; dedicating a portion of individual income tax revenue to a similar use would not.

Second, earmarking may thaw political resistance to higher taxes by showing the citizenry exactly how the proposed new revenue will be used. If the voters are skeptical about government in general, possibly believing that services are provided inefficiently or that government is simply too big, they will not be sympathetic to additional taxes. If, however, the new revenue source is tied to a particular service to be delivered to the public and the service will be delivered only if the new revenue source is approved, the new revenue may be approved. This linkage is consistent with ideas about the contractual nature of democratic government (Wagner 1991).

Third, earmarking may assure continuity of funding for particular projects. This dedication accommodates long-range planning and provides some confidence that plans will receive some resources in the future. For instance, several states have dedicated a legally defined portion of a particular tax to the support of local education: thus, that program can be assured of the revenue generated by this source, so the earmark assures a minimum funding even if difficult fiscal conditions exist.

The Argument Against Earmarking

There are important arguments against earmarking, however. First, earmarking reduces flexibility and control in the budget process. The government (or a population, if the law comes from a referendum) in place when the earmark occurs effectively limits the ability of new governments or populations to move resources in response to new or changing public demands. This rigidity may cause the public sector to be artificially inflated; because available resources are tied by the existing earmark, any new compelling problem that might arise can be accommodated only by enacting new or higher taxes, rather than through the reallocation of existing funds to the now more pressing needs. Earmarking without an expiration date, whether originating by referendum or by statute, presumes that the problems at the time of the earmark will continue, forever, to be the most critical that the government will have to deal with. As Burkhead (1956) observed: "earmarking . . . represent an attempt, not to introduce an improved pattern of fiscal management, but to protect and isolate the beneficiaries of specific governmental programs" (p. 228).

Second, earmarking breaks the comprehensiveness of the budget. It means that there will not be an even competition for fiscal resources, that there will be no level playing field in the process. This often creates a feast-famine situation in the budget because growth in revenue seldom matches growth in demand for the function. Earmarking sets the rate of the tax. As taxpayer preferences change, collections will be related to taxpayer demand only by coincidence.

Finally, earmarking can delude the public into false security about service provision. Earmarking provides no fundamental protection for a function against the basic fiscal problems of the government and no guarantee that earmarked receipts will not simply replace funds that would have been provided from other sources. Nothing about earmarking can change the fact that revenues are fungible and legislatures are independent. They are likely to regard government revenue as government revenue, to be distributed according to public needs as seen by the legislature at the time that funds are being appropriated.

Conclusion

Nothing protects a government service better than a political consensus on the need for that service. If a consensus exists, earmarking is not necessary to fund a service. And earmarking will not insulate a service from cuts during a fiscal crisis. If the public bureaucracy is wasteful, earmarking simply assures a revenue flow for one section of government to waste. During normal times, earmarking complicates bookkeeping, impedes fiscal flexibility, but makes little fiscal difference. Except for use in some circumstances involving true benefit taxation, in which a tax is on a private good, the consumption of which is complementary to use of a public good—rare conditions in the real world—earmarking is largely a gimmick that at worst represents a trick on the public and at best achieves what general fund budgeting and a responsible legislative leadership would achieve. Earmarking cannot establish credibility in an irresponsible government.

JOHN L. MIKESELL

BIBLIOGRAPHY

Burkhead, Jesse, 1956. *Government Budgeting.* New York: John Wiley.
Gold, Steven D., Brenda Erickson and Michelle Kissell, 1987. *Earmarking State Taxes.* Denver: National Conference of State Legislatures.
U.S. General Accounting Office, 1990. *Budget Issues: Earmarking in the Federal Government.* Washington, D.C.: U.S. Government Printing Office.
U.S. Congressional Budget Office, 1993. *The Growth of Federal User Charges.* Washington, D.C.: U.S. Government Printing Office.
Wagner, Richard E., 1991. "Tax Norms, Fiscal Reality, and the Democratic State: User Charges and Earmarked Taxes in Principle and Practice." In R. E. Wagner, ed., *Charging for Government: User Charges and Earmarked Taxes in Principle and Practice.* London: Routledge.

ECOLE NATIONAL d'ADMINISTRATION (ENA).

The National School of Adminstration created by an ordinance of October 9, 1945, as one component of a broader reform of the French civil service. It is through the ENA that top-level government officials are recruited and trained. Thus, the school is intermediate between advanced university studies and entry into the public service.

It was created in response to both moral and technical objectives. The former relates to the need to democratize the system of recruitment for top-level administrators. Previous systems of specialized competitive examinations led to a form of cooptation and limited recruitment mainly to the Parisian upper classes. One goal was therefore to open up access to the higher ranks of the public service to the entire range of social classes. The second objective was to enhance the skills and competence of these officials. The creation of the ENA is just one in a series of measures put into effect in 1945 to improve the functioning of the French state's central administrations. Other reforms complemented the creation of the ENA, concerning both the preceding phase of university studies and the structures of the public service itself.

At the university level, the aim of the reforms was to develop "the teaching of political, economic, administrative, and social sciences," and the immediate result was the creation of the National Foundation of Political Science (Fondation nationale des sciences politiques, FNSP) and of a new type of school, the institutes for political studies. The presence of these sciences in the traditional university programs was extremely limited, although they were considered necessary to the training of the public service corps. In addition, students at the institutes who were preparing for the ENA entrance examinations could receive scholarships from the state to pay for their studies. Thus, the goals of diversifying the social and geographic origins of the future top public officials, and of improving their basic education, were already pursued in the phase preceding entry to the ENA.

The 1945 ordinances also reorganized the upper echelons of the administration itself. A Center for Advanced Administrative Studies (Centre des hautes études administratives, CHEA) ensures the training of top-level public servants, as well as providing individuals from the private sector with administrative training and, subsequently, the possibility to enter the public service (Kessler 1978). Before 1945, the differing standings of the *grands corps*, or major public service bodies, and central administrations were reflected in extreme variations of employment conditions and statuses. Unifying the recruitment and training of top public officials thus necessitated the unification of these conditions between the corps and the central administrations, as well as between the various central administrations themselves. This quest for unity was consecrated with the creation of a general authority for public service and a permanent council for public administration. An instrument of the government's personnel policy (through the coordination of statutory rules, the development of principles guiding personnel remuneration, documentation, and statistics), the general authority lays the groundwork for an overall public service policy, and particularly that of the upper-level administration. It was seconded by the permanent council for public administration, which was especially concerned with questions of status, recruitment, and discipline. This unification of public service administration was accompanied by the homogenization of statuses among upper-level adminstration officials. Homogenization was sought through the creation of a corps of civil administrators common to all the central administrations, assisted by a new corps of administrative secretaries. The civil administrators corps was to constitute a fourth *grand corps,* along with the Tax Inspectorate (Inspection des finances),

the Council of State, and the State Audit Office (Cour des comptes).

An additional principle laid down in the 1945 texts was that all the corps recruited by the ENA be subject to the same statutory regulations, excepting particular provisions allowable due to the character of a given assignment. This principle was the precursor to the future general public service status (October 19, 1946).

Organization and Methods

The defining characteristics of the ENA's organization and methods were set down from the outset. Three points are to be considered: entry to the school, the course of study, and graduation.

Entry to the ENA is open to university graduates through an "external" or "student" competitive examination. A second, "internal" or "public servant" competitive examination is limited to public officials of 26 to 30 years of age, with the condition that they have five years of experience in the public service. This latter examination is a system of internal advancement for individuals who were unable to attend university. The programs and tests for the public officials therefore differ from those in the external examination. As part of the policy to open up the recruitment process, women are permitted to compete (French women gained the right to vote during the same period). As a broad education was judged better suited than narrow specializations to ensuring qualified personnel, the examination was largely designed to test candidates' general culture, their personalities, and even their characters.

From the beginning, the ENA's program seeks to combine theory and practice. An internship in France or abroad provides students with concrete knowledge of the public service sector. Within the school, the curriculum is practical in outlook: preparing decisions, working in teams or commissions, learning languages. The desire to strengthen the character of future public officials led in 1945 to an emphasis on physical education and military training. The ENA has changed since its creation, altering the length of study as well as admissions conditions to the entrance exams, but the major reforms (1958, 1965, 1971) have not altered the original organizing principles. The most important reform is the creation, in 1991, of a third competitive examination open to individuals under 40 years of age from all sectors of activity except public administration. This measure reflects the school's constant quest for democratization and openness. The recent (partial) transfer of the ENA to Strasbourg, near the European institutions of this city, is the result of a twofold objective: to demonstrate a European outlook and to carry out, as an example to other administrations, the territorial development policy of transferring Parisian services to other regions.

Currently, teaching is postgraduate and professional and takes place over a period of 26 months. The first year is given over to internships, one in a company and one in a government service. The second year is one of study, in which three basic aims are pursued:

- Improving knowledge in the core subjects (law, economics, international relations, etc.), taking into account the diverse educational and professional backgrounds of the students;
- Helping students to master the administrative tools they will need in their future careers (drafting of legal texts, management skills, and foreign languages, for example);
- Developing both students' pragmatism and their innovative skills through research projects carried out in groups and destined to contribute to the elaboration of actual policies within the administration.

Since 1986, the internship year has been split in two. It is composed of a six-month internship in a public or private sector company, including an obligatory factory experience, followed by a six-month internship within a government service in France (prefecture, town hall, department, or regional council) or abroad (embassy or international organization). In theory, at least, this range of internships is an important aspect of the education dispensed by the ENA.

The entrance examination puts particular emphasis on legal and judicial subjects, thus ensuring students' knowledge of fundamental concepts in these areas. The basics of law are considered to be mastered; the task is then to learn to apply this legal knowledge. An important aspect of the curriculum is training in analysis and drafting techniques for legal, administrative, and financial texts. Many students will be expected to be able to draft such documents rapidly, as the preparation of legislative and regulatory texts will be an essential facet of their work.

The first stage of preparation for these tasks at the ENA is orientation courses concerning legal and administrative issues, which aim to furnish concrete reference points and to update students' knowledge, rather than to review the entire body of administrative law. Small group seminars working with a packet distributed three weeks previously present the documents necessary to the analysis of an administrative problem and to the drafting of texts to remedy it. The study of budgetary and fiscal issues completes these seminars.

After one year of internships (or even two for those who complete their military service), it can be necessary to review certain fundamental concepts and to point out evolutions in jurisprudence and other influencing factors. A refresher course in taxation and preparatory seminars for working with budgetary documents are also required. This area of study also includes simulations of the preparation

of a text through the two successive steps of an interministerial meeting at the governmental general secretariat, and examination by the Council of State, where each student plays an assigned role. The aim in the future is progressively to extend these sessions towards earlier stages in the decisionmaking process. Each group of students would be linked to an official in a certain administration, who would give them the task of elaborating a draft of a legal or regulatory text. Currently, however, this exercise is limited to the final stages of interministerial harmonization and the Council of State's evaluation, and the difficulty involved in extending it is evident.

Students are familiarized with the concepts and methods of analysis used in diplomacy, mastering particularly the diplomatic memo, habitual method of communication between diplomats, and European Community law, the importance of which in the entry examination has grown. It is in the subject of economics that the disparities in knowledge between students are doubtless the greatest. Many lack the mathematical tools necessary for this largely quantitative subject, rendering its teaching difficult. Two pitfalls are to be avoided: that of a too mathematical form of economics, which many would have trouble understanding and which would later be useful to only a tiny minority, and that of unoriginal and repetitive analyses of economic policy. The aim is to familiarize students with methods of economic reasoning, through decisionmaking exercises based on briefs covering concrete issues.

Finally, in the area of management, students are to be acquainted with possibilities for improving public services, in terms of both cost and quality. The course seeks to familiarize students with the principal concepts used in management disciplines, to provide them with the tools for carrying out financial analyses, and to help them to develop certain basic skills and methods (in management control, finance, human resources management, strategic management). Given their diverse university backgrounds, this is the area in which the greatest differences in initial knowledge between students are apparent.

The public servant is not a lone official. The ENA thus ensures, through seminar projects, an initiation in teamwork skills. These seminars, lasting three months each, put each student in the position of a member of a study group which must analyze an administrative issue or problem in depth and formulate operational proposals in response. The end result is an administrative report providing precise responses to the problem in question. Seminars are also the method of study for the major sectors of social policy, such as employment, health, and social aid. Each seminar leads to the drafting of two reports, individual and group. Due to the diversity in the courses of study previously pursued by students, personalized classes are also offered for those who need them, in the areas of quantitative analysis techniques, foreign languages (12 in all), reading skills development, negotiation techniques, and the use of audio-visual materials. Physical education is a required course in which all students are graded.

The ENA trains just over 100 administration officials each year (around 50 each from the student and public servant examinations, and another 10 from the third competitive examination). At the end of the program, students are ranked by order of merit determined by the grades obtained in the internships, seminars, and final examinations (known as exit exams). The peculiarity of the system is that each student chooses the administration or corps which he or she will enter according to the rank obtained. Graduates may enter the Council of State, the Tax Inspectorate, the State Audit Office, the diplomatic corps, the prefectoral corps, regional audit offices, administrative courts, various inspectorate corps (general inspectorate for the administration, general inspectorate for social affairs), as well as the civil administrator corps common to the various ministries. Administrations publish lists of available positions and students make their selection, beginning with the top-ranking graduate. Each administration or corps tries to be chosen by the best-ranked students for reasons of prestige. In general, graduates select the first three administrative corps in order, the Economics and Finance ministry often coming after the diplomatic and prefectoral corps. The lowest-ranking graduates have very little choice and are required to accept positions in the services remaining.

The ENA curriculum, constantly evolving, is defined by two major parameters; the most important is the forced strategy of polyvalence for students, who are kept ignorant of their position in the ranking system until graduation; the second is that of time, the total length of the course of study as well as the examination times being limited, hardly allowing for more than the reconstitution of formulaic responses. In other words, it could be argued that the lack of time stifles students' creative capacities. In addition, a perception that innovations in management, negotiation skills, and meeting and human resources management courses are costly and useless gimmicks has made their implementation difficult (Bodiguel and Rouban 1991).

The ENA's Functions

The ENA's official purpose is to be a vocational school providing first-rate education and training to future public service officials, whose careers will generally lead them to positions in the upper echelons of the administration. Currently, graduates of the ENA occupy a number of the central administration directorships, prefectural, and ambassadorial posts. Many also preside over companies in both the public and private sectors.

However, parallel to the explicit function of rigorously selecting the best students for service to the State, the administrative *grandes écoles,* and particularly the ENA, perform a latent, but far more important function of desig-

nating the elite of French society. The costs of the ranking system as opposed to its advantages, and the tendency systematically to prefer breadth of knowledge and skills to specialization, support this hypothesis. To be admitted to the ENA, a candidate must have an excellent knowledge of law, economics, and, currently, management techniques, in addition to the necessary foreign languages. Recruiting specialists for public administration is a secondary goal, after the more important one of constituting the elite, the ruling class, and ensuring its recognition as such by French society as well as by its members themselves. It is an established fact that, at the present time, the "general culture" orientation of the entrance examinations favors a certain category of candidate, those whose social milieu has already acquainted them with the various cultural demands of the exam. The system favors the privileged. The fact that the *Ecole polytechnique* (the top graduate school for engineers) has remained largely unchanged in its two centuries of existence, and that the many reforms aimed at widening the ENA's recruitment base have systematically failed, tend to support the conclusion that these schools do not have for their sole purpose the training of public officials (Bodiguel and Quermonne 1983).

It is true that the majority of the some 5,000 students who have graduated from the ENA since its creation are public officials who have pursued a typical career in public service (Bodiguel 1978). However, this group, tiny in relation to the whole of French society, contains an impressive number of politicians (one French president, several prime ministers, numerous government ministers, around 10 percent of National Assembly members on average, a great many mayors of large cities, etc.), as well as heads of companies in every sector (energy, transportation, industry and trade, banking and insurance firms, information, press, advertising, etc.). Others are found in teaching, in the arts, in entertainment. The Compagnie Saint-Gobain, the Peugeot group, and Elf-Aquitaine all have or have had graduates of the ENA (or *"énarques"*) at their head, to give just a few examples. What can explain such a phenomenal success rate?

Two major factors contribute to the ENA's success. The first is of a technical nature. Teaching at the school is multifaceted and cannot be otherwise, given the ranking system that only allows students to learn their position at the end of the program. This education can lead to a wide variety of professions: the jobs of a diplomat, a judge, an inspector, a tax auditor, and an administrator do not have much in common. Thus, the ENA trains generalists, men and women able to cope with the management of large organizations and large companies, as well as with the complexity of public policy issues, who can therefore achieve success in most areas. The second factor relates to the fact that every society needs a system for attributing influence and power at any given level. In France, this system is strongly linked to service to the state. Ever since the Ancien Régime, public service has been a source of prestige and wealth. Social advancement depends upon it. Public service is the area through which upward social mobility is achieved. There is thus strong social pressure to attend the top public *grandes écoles*, and in a system where each selection process reinforces another, those with the greatest success rates are children from families who already belong to the social elite. The ENA not only selects the top performers within a given age group and trains them for service to the state, through its intellectual but also social selection process, it also designates the members of the ruling political, economic, administrative, social, and cultural class (Bodiguel 1992).

JEAN-LUC BODIGUEL
TRANS. BY JOY BUFFET

BIBLIOGRAPHY

Bodiguel, Jean-Luc, 1978. *Les anciens élèves de l'ENA*. Paris: Presses de la Fondation nationale des sciences politiques.
———, 1992. "Une voie de la promotion sociale: la fonction publique?" In S. Berstein and O. Rudelle, eds., *Le modèle républicain*. Paris: Presses de la Fondation nationale des sciences politiques.
Bodiguel, Jean-Luc and Jean-Louis Quermonne, 1983. *La haute fonction publique sous la Ve République*. Paris: Presses universitaires de France.
Bodiguel, Jean-Luc and Luc Rouban, 1991. *Le fonctionnaire détrôné?* Paris: Presses de la Fondation nationale des sciences politiques.
Kesler, Jean-François, 1985. *L'ENA, la société, l'Etat*. Paris: Berger-Levrault.
Kessler, Marie-Christine, 1978. *La politique de la haute fonction publique*. Paris: Presses de la Fondation nationale des sciences politiques.

ECONOMIC RATIONALISM.

A public policy position which assumes that markets and money are the only reliable means of setting values on anything, or, alternatively, that economies, markets, and money can always, at least in principle, deliver better outcomes than states, bureaucracies, and the law.

Theoretical Framework

These are the normal assumptions of contemporary economics and of its offshoots in public choice and rational choice theories. Accordingly, economic rationalism is generally associated with the New Right in the political spectrum, with laissez-faire, economic liberalism, and mainstream U.S. and British public policy in the post-Keynesian period from the mid-1970s to the 1990s. These positions all contain, with varying degrees of intensity, negative evaluations of the role of the state in society. This has given rise

to ideological comparisons with the former command economies of the communist world; inasmuch as these regimes do, conversely, assign primacy to coordination by states, bureaucracy, and the law, they do stand in polar opposition to economic rationalism. However, for most comparative purposes, the more useful contrast is with the Western European social democracies (especially the Netherlands, Denmark, Sweden, Belgium, and France), which reject economic rationalism in favor of public policies premised on a greater complementarity and balance between the two coordinating structures. Indeed the Social Charter of the European Economic Community may be construed as bulwark against a British and U.S. economic rationalism.

The case for economic rationalism takes its criteria of reason and rationality from modern economics. The individual is assumed to be an egoistic, self-interested *homo economicus* for whom rational action means the maximization of utilities, wealth, and advantage (Brennan and Lomasky 1993). The implicit behaviorist psychology has its roots in classical utilitarianism and assumes that all significant motivations reduce to the maximization of pleasure and the minimization of pain. Accordingly, economic rationalists equate rationality with the strategic, instrumental, or rational purposive action of individuals. From this perspective other actors are normally defined principally as competitors for scarce resources.

For these same reasons economic rationalists place little or no faith at all in cooperative action and still less in any form of collective action. As utilitarian welfare economics has come under fire in recent times (Sen 1987, 1988) economic rationalists and like-minded public policy specialists have found other philosophical defences for their neoconservative and anticollectivist orientations. These have come in the main from the neo-libertarian rights-based liberalism of Hayek (1960), Rawls (1971), Nozick (1974), and Dworkin (1978) that has given normative force to the right of the individual to freedom of choice. Such theories explicitly treat virtue, merit, and needs as morally arbitrary constructs that may not be used, under any circumstances, to legitimate redistributive policies, or any other structures or actions of governments that could trespass on individual freedom of exchange in the marketplace. This involves a more or less complete rejection, a priori, of modern notions of citizenship, participative democracy, community, and social justice.

Goals of Economic Rationalism

Not surprisingly we find that this view contains its own criteria for institutional design and reform. Here there is always a preference for what are called, after Adam Smith, invisible hand mechanisms, or, in other words, for a coordination of individual actions that is achieved through markets, prices, and incentives and which, accordingly, places minimum reliance on civic virtue, negotiation, organization, and trust. At the global level, and through the agency of mainly U.S. dominated international economic organizations such as the World Bank, the International Monetary Fund, the General Agreement on Tariffs and Trade, and the Organization for Economic Cooperation and Development, economic rationalists have strenuously opposed attempts by national governments to intervene in the operation of markets with legislation or policies that seek to protect labor, to impose tariffs, to fix price floors and ceilings, to moderate the distribution of income, or otherwise to interfere with the "free" play of market forces (Buchanan 1977). The underlying standard for good institutional design requires that economies, markets, and prices should, as far as possible, be removed from the political domain and allowed to function autonomously and as a self-referential system.

Consequently economic rationalists have a built-in preference for small, virtual, and even token government and a bias against the public sector and public administration generally. They will normally assume that efficiency is best served by moving as many functions as possible from the public sector to the business or private sector. Strategies for bringing this about normally begin with a process of corporatization that seeks to restructure public, welfare, and social service organizations along private sector lines as business corporations. This involves the internal monetization of allocations as well as structural innovations such as the separation of funders from providers, together with many other accounting practices that are all designed to force compliance with markets and prices in the external money economy. This frequently leads to the privatization, sale, and transfer of public utilities and social service organizations to the private sector. Privatization is one of several budgetary policies favored by economic rationalists. Since government is seen as a restriction on the efficiency of markets, a priority is set on the deregulation of the business or private sector. By the same token the preference for less government always leads to pressure to reduce taxes, cut public spending, and reduce welfare and transfer payments. For the sake of efficiency, economic rationalists press, wherever possible, for a transfer of the remaining burden of taxation away from business corporations to wage and salary earners and consumers. At the national level and in the developed English-speaking nations, these neoconservative economic rationalist agendas have been driven by U.S.-trained economists and business school graduates, by U.S.-based international consulting houses and credit rating agencies, by financial journalists in the privately owned media, and by neoconservative business-funded think tanks and foundations such as the Centre for Independent Studies in Britain and Australia and the Heritage and Atlas Foundations in the United States.

The Case Against Economic Rationalism

One set of arguments comes mainly from within economics itself. Here the accusation is that economic rationalism fails in its own terms and, that it is, in any case, intellectually misconceived "bad" economics. International comparisons of economic performance in the developed member nations of the Organization for Economic Cooperation and Development have largely disproved the claims of economic rationalists that strong and generously funded public sectors are inimical to economic growth and productive investment. The evidence (Wilenski et al. 1985) points in the contrary direction and shows that, in the post-Keynesian period, it is the smaller corporatist social democratic economies of Western Europe with "interventionist" governments, redistributive policies, large public sectors, and strong trade unions that have, for the most part, performed better than the United States and Great Britain.

Among the several recent criticisms that have come from economists perhaps the most influential are perhaps those of Amartya Sen (1987, 1989), who has argued that valuation is a complex reflective and social activity that does not reduce to the typical constructions of choice, utility, or desire fulfillment found in utilitarian and contemporary welfare economics. Other economists such as Harcourt (1982), McCloskey (1983), and Heilbronner (1988) have added to older criticisms of the inherently ideological character of modern "positive" economics. Although these new challenges have not yet had any significant impact on economic rationalist policies they have produced some limited soul-searching within academic economic circles (COGEE report 1991). They have also drawn some acknowledgement among economists that their increasingly abstracted and idealized mathematical models of economic relations have little or no practical relevance to policy in the real world.

The second principal criticism of economic rationalist policies is that they fly in the face of evidence concerning the factors that make for quality of life and, still more fundamentally, that they are socially harmful and detrimental to the reproduction of society. With respect to this first line of arguments the work of Robert Lane has found broad confirmation from longitudinal and comparative psychological studies of quality of life showing that most people in developed Western nations overwhelmingly value health, family relationships, friendship, tension-free leisure, and social peace ahead of personal wealth, income, and consumption. There is little real evidence for the core economic rationalist assumption that selfishness, competitiveness, or aggressive individualism is either natural, admired, or even broadly accepted.

The most common criticism of the social effects of economic rationalism is that it has, demonstrably, produced an upward redistribution of income from the poor to the rich and, *inter alia*, that it is "destroying," or "dispersing," the middle classes. Contractarian and liberal apologists for economic rationalism may argue that social equality is a contestable policy norm, but such defenses have tended to lose momentum in the face of increasing evidence that these public policies have also caused increasing unemployment, a decline in the dignity and security of work, environmental degradation, and, rather more indirectly, urban decay, rising crime, alienation, and drug dependency, and new forms of patriarchy. Communitarian critics of economic rationalism (Sandel 1984, Etzioni 1994) in North America now have much in common with Continental social-theoretical arguments (Habermas 1975, 1984, 1987) that economic rationalist policies are inimical to identity, reciprocal obligation, social cohesion, and good government and, further, that they also undermine the social constructions of both time and trust necessary for the reproduction of society and for continuing productive economic development.

MICHAEL PUSEY

BIBLIOGRAPHY

Buchanan, J., 1977. *Freedom in Constitutional Contract.* College Station: Texas A & M University Press.

Commission on Graduate Education in Economics (COGEE) Report, 1991. *Journal of Economic Literature,* vol. 29:1035–1053.

Dworkin, R., 1978. "Liberalism." In Stuart Hampshire, ed., *Public and Private Morality,* Cambridge, England: Cambridge University Press.

Etzioni, Amitai., 1994. *The Spirit of Community.*

Habermas, J., 1984, 1987. *The Theory of Communicative Action,* trans. Thomas McCarthy, 2 vols. Boston: Beacon Press.

———, 1975. *Legitimation Crisis,* trans. Thomas McCarthy. Boston: Beacon Press.

Harcourt, G., 1982. *Social Science Imperialists.* London: Routledge & Kegan Paul.

Hayek, Friedrich A., 1960. *The Constitution of Liberty.* Chicago: Chicago University Press.

Heilbroner, R., 1988. *Behind the Veil of Economics.* New York: W.W. Norton & Co.

Klamer A., D. McCloskey and R. Solow, eds., 1988. *The Consequences of Economic Rhetoric.* Cambridge, England: Cambridge University Press.

McCloskey, D., 1983. "The Rhetoric of Economics." *Journal of Economic Literature,* vol 22 (June) 481–517.

Nozic, R., 1974. *Anarchy, State and Utopia.* New York: Basic Books.

Ormerod, P., 1994. *The Death of Economics.* London: Faber & Faber.

Pusey, M.; 1991 *Economic Rationalism in Canberra.* Cambridge, England: Cambridge University Press.

Rawls, J., 1971. *A Theory of Justice.* Cambridge, MA: The Belknap Press of Harvard University.

Rosenblum, N., ed., 1989. *Liberalism and the Moral Life.* Cambridge, MA: Harvard University Press.

Sandel, M., ed., 1984, *Liberalism and Its Critics.* New York: University Press.

Sen, A., 1987. *The Standard of Living.* Cambridge, England: Cambridge University Press.

———, 1989. *On Ethics and Economics.* Oxford: Basil Blackwell.

Wilenski, H., G. Luebbert, S. Hann, and A. Jamieson, 1985. *Comparative Social Policy: Theories, Methods, Findings,* Research Monograph Series #62. Berkeley: Institute of International Studies, University of California–Berkeley.

ECONOMIC WARFARE.

The imposition by a nation or alliance in a conflict of a range of economic and military activities designed either to reduce the opponent's capacity to wage and sustain war, or to preserve a capacity to prevail in the conflict, or both. More narrowly, it is the aggressive use of the means of production and trade to achieve national objectives. It is an odd phrase in that war is itself an economic activity. When Norman Angell published his *The War of Illusions* (1910) just before the onslaught of World War I, he was doing no more than pointing out that the economic consequences of a European general war would be so catastrophic as to render it an irrational act for any leader to contemplate. The only mistake in his analysis was the assumption that leaders behave rationally and would therefore avoid such a conflict at all costs. More generally, economic warfare has a variety of levels of intensity, ranging from freezing an enemy's assets and confiscating its property during a formally declared war to using secret methods to destabilize an opponent's economy during a cold war.

Economic warfare is a term of relatively recent coinage; the establishment during World War II of the British Ministry of Economic Warfare helped to legitimize the term. In reality, all wars have an economic component. This is evident in the earliest theories of air power. The whole point of delivering munitions from the air on enemy territory was to deplete the war-making potential of the opposing ground and naval forces. When the British Prime Minister, Stanley Baldwin, said, "The bomber will always get through," he was demonstrating the vulnerability to attack of armaments factories, supply lines, and other elements of military capability and its supporting structures as decisive factors in a major war. For much of World War II, the rationale for bombing German cities was that large concentrations of people coincided with economic activity. Damage that, it was argued, and the war effort of the adversary must suffer. Conversely, not attacking such economic centers—perhaps out of respect for the Thomist Just War tradition that holds that civilians must be left free from military dangers—was self-defeating in modern warfare.

Much of the economic result of aerial bombing was disappointing, from the perspective of all belligerents in World War II. Machine tools for such vital components as ball bearings, for example, were found to be almost indestructible. All that was necessary after an air raid was to create temporary shelter and rig a generator, and production could begin again with relatively little delay. German production levels were either sustained or actually increased, despite the weight of Anglo-American bombing. In such circumstances, it is not surprising that the rationale for bombing should shift from its economic effects to an interest in destroying the morale of a population. Again, there is very little evidence to suggest that this was effective. Indeed, but for the advent of the atomic bomb, and the dramatic evidence provided by the bombing of Hiroshima and Nagasaki, strategic bombing as an weapon of economic warfare would have lost all credibility. As the Cold War doctrines of deterrence evolved, the economic element of the collateral damage that could be caused by a strategic exchange became part of the calculation as to what was deemed to be unacceptable damage and, therefore, of deterrent value.

The 1939–1945 war saw a range of economic warfare methods other than aerial bombing. Navies were used to blockage belligerents. (Hitler's policy of *lebensraum* was, in part, a strategic recognition of what maritime power might otherwise be able to do to the German economy, if the population and economic resources of Slavic lands to the east were not exploited.) The strategy of convoy was adopted early on in World War II by the Allies precisely to avoid the economic consequences of merchant ship losses of the kind that brought Britain to within a few weeks of economic collapse, and therefore military defeat, in 1916. Strategic primary products, such as wolfram and chrome ore, were bought in huge quantities from neutral suppliers in order to deprive the Axis powers. However, even considering the whole range of economic warfare methods, the prevailing judgment is that enthusiasm for them is historically unsupportable. As Alan S. Milward (1977) has argued, success from such relatively slow-working methods will come only from the most detailed knowledge of the opponent's economic system (pp. 294–328). Such knowledge was certainly not available about Germany and Japan in World War II. Equally, little understanding exists today about what warfare might entail economically. Had the long-feared, if always unlikely, war between the Soviet Union and NATO ever happened, the first probable global consequence would have been the collapse of the international banking system; what that would have done to the efforts of either side the world is fortunate not to know. It would certainly have meant that the economic preconditions of waging global war for a third time in the twentieth century—access to foreign sources of finance in a relatively stable set of conditions—would not have existed.

Discussion about economic warfare since the end of the Cold War has centered on the issue of sanctions. Can the international community use the experience of economic warfare to put decisive pressure on regional belligerents? The track record is held not to be encouraging. Frequently cited is the case of Rhodesia after 1967, when it illegally declared itself to be independent of the British Crown and Parliamentary authority. Against that country,

the full range of economic constraints were imposed. The results were minimal and even counter-productive. The Rhodesian economy, far from collapsing, was rendered more robust and self-reliant; and, as is often the case, public opinion developed a level of unity not seen hitherto. Its allies, either the Republic of South Africa or individual smugglers operating through neighboring countries, regularly broke through the cordon of international monitoring set up under UN auspices. If this blockade was in any way part of the reason why the white supremacist regime opened discussions on the handover of power in the early 1980s, it was only a small part.

In sum, as with sanctions against the Soviet Union following the invasion of Afghanistan in 1979, or the economic blockage of Iraq after its invasion of Kuwait in 1991, and for long after the liberation of Kuwait, the net effect is either too slow in having an effect or insufficiently decisive to persuade decisionmakers to develop enthusiasm for the methods of economic warfare. Additionally, the international isolation of Iraq for over five years after the liberation of Kuwait showed the extent to which a domestic population can swing behind a leader against the "unfairness" imposed by the rest of the world, despite the manifold ruthlessness of his regime.

Ironically, the reluctance of most major countries' populations to endure casualties in battle might provide incentive for the international community to reexamine economic warfare: its implicit promise is a politically sustainable outcome at the minimal loss of blood and treasure. What is needed is a better understanding of the relationship between political and economic power if economic warfare is to overcome its reputation for being marginal in the management of international relations, and if economic methods are to substitute for the tragically age-old habit of war as the means of resolving differences.

PETER FOOT

BIBLIOGRAPHY

Angell, Norman, 1910. *The War of Illusions: A Study of the Relationship of Military Power in Nations to Their Economic and Social Advantage.* London: Heinemann.
Milward, Alan S., 1977. *War, Economy and Society, 1939–1945.* London: Allen Lane.

ECONOMIES OF SCALE.

Defined by economists as increasing returns or profits to size when the long-run average cost is decreasing. Hence, the term "returns to scale" refers to the effect of increased output or productivity upon average costs when all inputs increase in the same proportion.

Returns to scale is also related directly to output. Initial economies result from spreading fixed costs over a larger amount of output and fully utilizing resources, such as labor, equipment, and other inputs, to reduce unit cost. Further discounts could result from increasing the unit size of equipment and buildings or the volume of production and the volume purchasing of inputs, such as raw materials. Establishing specialized management procedures to increase worker productivity also increases return to size. Returns to scale, therefore, is a measure of the change in output resulting from a proportionate change in all inputs.

However, there are diseconomies when the long-run average cost increases. At this point, further increase in scale or size will not contribute to productivity and is discouraged. Causes of rising costs include poor managerial skill, difficulty in coordinating a large workforce dispersed over a large geographic area, and increasing need to travel. The first problem, poor management, would adversely affect any operation but would be magnified in large systems that are dispersed over a large area. The difficulty in effecting cohesiveness among geographically dispersed operations is a significant challenge for managers. Site visits are a remedy, but their effectiveness in achieving operational cohesiveness is not a guaranteed outcome. The cost of travel to distant sites adds to long-run average costs. Thus, diseconomies of scale result when the proportionate change in output is less than the proportionate change in inputs.

External economies and diseconomies occur when the industry as a whole expands. The positive results of industry expansion could lie, for example, in improvements in the labor market, in the establishment of new industries that produce byproducts from wastes produced by the first operation, or in investment in research. A growing industrial sector encourages new recruits to obtain the required training to enter the labor market and create a pool of trained workers to sustain the human resources needs of the enterprises. Under conditions of growth, the quality of worker skills will improve as training programs and institutions scale up and improve their curricula to meet labor demands.

External diseconomies include increase in the cost of inputs unless there is proportional decrease in demand for the inputs or an increase in the supply of the inputs. The long-term effect of decrease in demand of the inputs could be a severely diminished supply and increase in price as producers scale down. The better option for stabilizing or decreasing cost of inputs would be to increase supply to levels that meet existing demand or exceed demand to dampen any tendency to raise the price of the inputs. Studies of agricultural enterprises have found that the mix of inputs will change as the size of the enterprises change.

The notion of economies of scale can also be applied to organizational structures, and indeed, bureaucracies and large corporate structures are by nature complex systems that are predicated on centralizing functions to effect

economies on human resources and fixed overhead costs. However, there has been a change in the perception of large organizations. "Big" is no longer seen as contributing positively to the purpose and productivity of an organization. The result has been downsizing, or terminating not only the line workers but top management as well by government agencies and blue chip corporations. In addition to downsizing, changes have been made in the structure of large corporate organizations to decentralize such functions as accounting and marketing, which were traditionally centralized, and assign them to specific product lines. A third organizational change has been the establishing of subsidiaries that form conglomerates under a holding company. These restructuring efforts by corporate organizations are predicated on size reduction to promote efficiency and worker productivity.

Public organizations are not as results oriented. The attempts to reorganize or "reinvent" government by both the executive and legislative branches of government have been almost solely motivated by a desire to downsize "big government" in the interest of cutting budgets and are not predicated on making government operations more efficient. Hence, although the size of public organizations and the quality of their operation have not been evaluated, a "lean" government appears to be equated with efficient delivery of government services to the public.

The ultimate centralization of public services will be possible in the future with the use of computers programmed to interact with the public. The use of electronic equipment to handle and respond to routine public requests, such as license and permit purchases, through a system totally devoid of human interaction, offers a potential for government personnel to be reduced to a handful of technicians. The requirement in this scenario shifts input requirements from human resources to information.

ROSE T. PFUND

BIBLIOGRAPHY

Kay, Ronald, 1981. *Farm Management: Planning, Control, and Implementation.* New York: McGraw-Hill Book Company.
Doll, John P. and Frank Orazem, 1978. *Productions Economics: Theory with Applications.* Columbus, OH: Grid Inc.

EDUCATION POLICY. The process by which governments formulate strategic directions and initiatives in respect of education and schooling.

Recent History

No other single issue in education has been so uniformly, profoundly, and readily grasped by governments around the world in the last decade, as the place of education policy in the broader field of public policy and administration. The emergence of education policy as a major policy field has its origins in the perceived nexus between education (what goes on in schools, colleges, universities, curriculum, pedagogy, and instruction) and their presumed capacity to deliver enhanced economic productivity via skills enhancement, a connection that has yet to be empirically validated. The reasons for the focus on this relationship is that in the context of wider global economic restructuring, there is a need to more readily identify an explanatory source (in this case, declining economic performance and competitiveness in postcolonial centers of power), while providing a solution in terms of what needs to be done. It is this combination of "cause" and "solution" that has brought education (and in particular education policy) to center stage. Schools and institutions of teaching and learning are a convenient quarter in which to locate part of the need for economic restructuring.

Current Interest

Education policy has, therefore, given major expression to a dramatically changed set of relationships in respect of the nature and purpose of education. It is no longer a provision made by government on the grounds of a need to improve the life chances and social mobility of sizeable sections of society. Rather, education has become squarely nested within a set of policy options and levers that are increasingly used by government to produce what it sees as changes in economic direction. The emphasis is upon setting measurable educational targets and disbursing resources to providers to achieve targets in ways that ensure continued resourcing.

In large measure, the policy tendencies evident in education around the world are not really options but rather policies that are driven by wider processes of "structural adjustment"; national economies are adjusting to a global market in which no "country can afford to veer too far from an equilibrium established by global capital and trade markets" that involves trade forces centered around structural shifts towards "liberalization, deregulation, privatization and stabilization" (Ilon 1994, p. 96).

Education has very clearly and demonstrably become a big budget item, as all countries have come to embrace mass education systems, and in this context it is not hard to make the economic connection, even if only as an expenditure and as an opportunity cost. Education as a form of social policy has become a decidedly unfashionable one, as Western countries seek to reposition themselves in the race to regain economic ascendancy while global restructuring moves the economic epicenter to parts of Asia, the Pacific Rim, and South America. Australia is not at all untypical of most other countries in that it has been swept up in a virtual frenzy of activity designed to convert its

public education system into an annex of business and industry; indeed the catch cry of politicians there has been that Australia must convert itself into the "clever country" (a counter-reference to Australia's earlier self-perception as the "lucky" country by virtue of its climate, agricultural, extractive, and mineral resources).

Leo Maglen (1990) has questioned the orthodoxy of the education-productivity linkage, that is, the view that education makes a direct economic contribution via the labor force to the increased productivity of workers. In his view, this is an orthodoxy which is not only beginning to be reexamined in the light of evidence, but one in respect of which the "links between education and productivity . . . are . . . inconclusive" (p. 281). The linkage has, he says, been much more presumed than proven. In his words: "It is . . . a measure of the strength of the orthodoxy that even amongst economists who are aware of the paucity of the evidence supporting it, there is a reluctance to question its veracity. This [has] . . . allowed the policy makers to proceed unabashed" (p. 282). He concludes: "If the basic tenet that education enhances worker productivity remains unproven, then the whole role of education in the economic growth and development process is cast in doubt" (p. 292).

If true, this leaves education policy in a difficult situation in most countries. Clearly, it is the largest single budgetary item (other than defense, health, and transport infrastructure) in many countries, and there is a compulsion to show value for money. But the effects of education in purely economic terms are proving much more illusive than first thought—the nexus has yet to be clearly demonstrated. To make matters worse, public policymakers have decidedly nailed themselves to the economic policy mast in ways that have completely obliterated the social policy effects of education (in terms of, for example, a concern for matters of democratic citizenship and values of humanity and social justice).

The United States as an Exemplar

That publicly funded schools, colleges, and universities are under an obligation to do their economic work is a notion that is hardly even contested these days. The orthodoxy of human capital theory, originally conceived in the 1950s, then largely discredited, and now resurrected to the status of mainstream economic thinking, has been given expression and prominence in U.S. education policy. The impetus came from the 1983 U.S. document *A Nation at Risk*, with its now infamous line that: "if an unfriendly foreign power had attempted to impose on America the mediocre educational performance that exists today, we might well have viewed it as an act of war" (National Commission on Excellence in Education 1983, p. 5).

This document produced a decade of "educational reform," most of which encapsulated policies designed to reintroduce a sense of lost rigor to schools and other educational institutions. Not dissimilar processes occurred in Thatcher's England, Hawke's Australia, and Lange's New Zealand. These reforms were implemented through education policies that were designed to "recentralize" education in the sense that schools, teachers, students, and parents had been allowed to assume too much control, and that a measure of strategic control had to be reasserted by politicians; the way to do that was to spot-weld education onto economic policy. That way, the professionals in education (those who were soft on "the basics") could be brought back into line (or extirpated), and a measure of control reasserted by having policymakers, at the level of central government (usually in economics, business, and industry departments), exercise "steering at a distance"; that is to say, setting the broad policy parameters, with parents and other stakeholders being led to believe they were participating at a local level through the exercise of "consumer capture" via the exercising of processes of school choice. In the process, schools, while still funded and finally controlled by government, increasingly moved in the direction of thinking and acting like private enterprises, increasingly prepared to actually become so, as governments shifted responsibility from themselves to private providers, maintaining strategic policy setting.

Educational policy in the United States and elsewhere, through the decade of the 1980s, has thus become inextricably linked to industry's concern for international economic competitiveness. We can point to a range of documents in the United States (but they had their equivalents in other countries, too) that pushed that set of connections into the area of teacher quality. For example:

- *A Nation Prepared: Teachers for the 21st Century;*
- *Investing in Our Children: Business and the Public Schools;*
- *Technical Excellence in America: Incentives for Investment in Human Capital.*

As Garman (1995) put it, less than a decade after *A Nation at Risk,* it was as if "we were awash in education with commission reports. In less than a year following *A Nation at Risk* more than 260 'blue ribbon commissions' had been created across the nation, established to supposedly attack the problem of poor and mediocre educational institutions" (p. 24). Interestingly, these policy moves operated largely at arm's length from the very groups they were supposed to be reforming—teachers and educators. By the late 1980s it was clear that U.S. educational policies that so vigorously excluded teachers would not work, so there was a reversal, and what had been previously called "educational reform" became renamed "educational restructuring," with the twist that this time educators were to be included, but only within a context whereby their real powers were to be heavily circumscribed by centrally devised policy.

The Difficulties with Education Policy

It is not hard to make the case, at least rhetorically, that a large measure of the economic slippage is due to declining literacy and numeracy, inadequate processes of skills formation, lax curricula, a failure of traditional forms of school discipline, and the need for more rigorous forms of testing and teacher evaluation. Generally, the case can be made that the reasons protracted problems have emerged in Western countries is that they have allowed their education systems to atrophy and deviate too much from traditional values and processes, and that what needs to be done is a process of restoring these in areas such as education. Answers are portrayed as lying in a removal of progressive approaches and the restoration of education systems that value such goals as: children holding greater respect for the ideas of their teachers; demonstration of whether learning is occurring or not through standardized testing; and, when schools, teachers, and students are deviating too radically, quick identification and appropriate remedies. This is the thesis, and it is proving difficult to discredit or even dislodge (despite the lack of any compelling evidence substantiating the basic thesis).

Processes of educational restructuring work through an apparently contradictory set of arrangements. Central policymaking occurs in areas such as curriculum formation (frameworks and profiles), outcomes measurement, testing, and teacher evaluation/appraisal. At the same time, there is extensive emphasis upon shifting responsibility for the achievement of outcomes closer to the point of delivery of learning—schools, classrooms, and local communities—and away from distant bureaucracies. This has a good deal of popular appeal, especially when couched in the language of "site-based management," "local school management," and the "self-managing school." It is predicated on a set of views that those closest to teaching and learning should be involved in decisionmaking. However, the reality is that decisions over the real educational ends, purposes, and overall strategic direction are being set by educational policymakers, and school practitioners and parents are left to decide which of the range of options might be most feasible in achieving the prespecified policy objectives. Resources are, therefore, increasingly divested to schools, but in a context in which funding is tied to the delivery of specified policy outcomes (particular levels of attainment, standards, competencies, completion rates, and rates of attrition), and these are measured by centrally set performance indicators.

Hartley (1994) concurs with this analysis in his commentary on educational policy in the UK. According to him we are in an era of "mixed messages in educational policy," and this is something of a sign of the times as we move more broadly from forms of capitalist organization less characterized by modernist and Fordist modes, to ones that are more "disorganized" and post-Fordist in orientation. He claims that what may appear to be a contradiction on the surface, of recentralizing while appearing to be decentralizing, is not so much a contradiction—it only appears that way. Rather, it is indicative of a new regulative mode—one that is characterized by a quest by governments to reduce expenditure and wind back the welfare state, in a context where the placatory rhetoric is one of "choice," "ownership," and "partnership" (p. 231). In Britain this has taken fullest expression in the Educational Reform Act (1988), where the education system has been restructured "along the lines of a market, free and unfettered by state intervention" (p. 234). This tendency can take various forms: "free-standing" educational institutions (held in place by national curriculum and testing); "charter schools" (that enter into formal agreements with central agencies and obtain funding conditional upon achieving targets); "local support models" (with tight central control and devolution of resources); and "recentralization models" (the retention of some semblance of a national system, tightly regulated at various levels).

In sum, the planning and implementation of education policy worldwide is coming to be characterized by modes of regulation that represent sharp breaks with the recent past. As Fraser (1989) expressed it, we have "pseudo-autonomy in the conditions of pseudo-symmetry" (p. 49) in the contexts which are represented in Hartley's (1994) terms as "choice, diversity and ownership" (p. 242), except that they fall far short of the authentic meaning attaching to those terms.

JOHN SMYTH

BIBLIOGRAPHY

Fraser, Nancy, 1989. *Unruly Practices*. Minneapolis: University of Minnesota Press.
Garman, Noreen, 1995. "The Schizophrenic Rhetoric of School Reform and the Effects on Teacher Development." In John Smyth, ed., *Critical Discourses on Teacher Development*. London: Cassell, 21–36.
Hartley, David, 1994. "Mixed Messages in Education Policy: Sign of the Times?" *British Journal of Educational Studies*, vol. 42, no. 3 (September) 230–244.
Ilon, Lyn, 1994. "Structural Adjustment and Education: Adapting to a Growing Global Market." *International Journal of Educational Development*, vol. 14, no. 2:95–108.
Maglen, Leo, 1990. "Challenging the Human Capital Orthodoxy: The Education-Productivity Link Reexamined." *Economic Record*, vol. 66:281–294.
National Commission on Excellence in Education, 1983. *A Nation at Risk: The Imperative for Educational Reform*. Washington, D.C.

EDUCATION AID.

Financial assistance, generally in the form of an intergovernmental grant, provided by state governments to local school districts in the United States, often to alleviate inequities between school districts.

Educational aid provided by state governments to local school districts represents one of the major sources for funding of public education in the United States. In 1991, state governments raised over $100 billion in revenue for education, close to 50 percent of national spending on education. State education assistance has been growing steadily in importance during the last century (see Table I). Besides its importance, state education aid has been the center of a continuing controversy over the reform of school finance in the United States. In the last two decades, scores of lawsuits have been filed against state governments challenging the equity of state school finance systems. Changes in school aid distribution are often the outcomes of this litigation.

History of State Education Aid

The role of state governments in the financing of public education has evolved over the history of the United States. Until the middle of the nineteenth century, schools were primarily private and religious institutions. Due in part to efforts of education reformers, such as Horace Mann and Henry Barnard, publicly supported common schools became the educational norm by the beginning of the twentieth century. However, financial and curriculum decisions remained principally in the hands of local school boards. In 1920, over 80 percent of education revenue came from local governments (Table I). What state assistance was provided to local school districts was in the form of a flat grant per pupil. The role of the federal government in financing schools was practically nonexistent until the 1930s.

TABLE I. GROWTH IN EDUCATIONAL EXPENDITURES AND CHANGES IN SOURCES OF EDUCATION REVENUES

Year	Real expenditures per pupil (1992–93 dollars)	PERCENT DISTRIBUTION OF EDUCATION REVENUE BY LEVEL OF GOVERNMENT		
		Federal	State	Local
1919–20	478	0.3	16.5	83.2
1929–30	903	0.4	16.9	82.7
1939–40	1,078	1.8	30.3	68.0
1949–50	1,567	2.9	39.8	57.3
1959–60	2,285	4.4	39.1	56.5
1969–70	3,603	8.0	39.9	52.1
1979–80	4,573	9.8	46.8	43.4
1990–91	6,249	6.2	47.3	46.5

SOURCE: U.S. Department of Education, National Center for Education Statistics, *Digest of Education Statistics, 1993*, Tables 156 and 165.

Growth of state involvement in financing and regulating education had its roots in the Progressive reform movements of the early twentieth century. Growing concern over inequalities of educational opportunity among local school districts prompted a generation of education scholars, including Ellwood Cubberley, George Strayer, Sr., and Paul Mort, to explore various mechanisms for state financing of local schools. The most popular of the concepts developed during this period was by George Strayer and Robert Haig (1923). The "Foundation Plan," as their concept became known, proposed that state governments support a minimum level or foundation of expenditures per pupil. A number of state governments adopted some form of foundation state aid plan from 1930 to 1970 and it remains the most common form of state aid system today. Changes in state aid systems were accompanied by rapid growth in education spending and state education assistance. Education expenditures increased tenfold from 1920 to 1980 even adjusting for inflation, and the state government share of the education budget grew from 17 percent to 47 percent.

Evidence began to mount during the 1960s of the persistence, under foundation plans, of vast inequalities in per pupil spending. John Coons, William Clune, and Stephan Sugarman (1970) published a scathing criticism of present school finance systems and provided the legal basis for challenging them in federal and state courts. The first successful legal challenge of an existing school finance system came in the *Serrano v. Priest* (1971) decision by the California Supreme Court. As eloquently stated in the opening paragraph of the decision.

> We are called upon to determine whether the California public school financing system, with its substantial dependence on local property taxes and resultant wide disparities in school revenue, violates the equal protection clause of the Fourteenth Amendment. We have determined that this funding scheme invidiously discriminates against the poor because it makes the quality of the child's education a function of the wealth of his parents and neighbors.

Advocates of school aid reform hoped the Serrano decision would serve as the basis for a successful challenge of the constitutionality of state school finance systems in federal courts. However, shortly after the Serrano decision, the U.S. Supreme Court in *Rodriquez v. San Antonio School District* (1973) rejected the argument that the school finance system in Texas violated the U.S. Constitution. While the Rodriquez decision removed school finance equity from jurisdiction of the federal courts, there has been a rash of court challenges to state school finance systems in state courts. Since 1968, school finance cases have been decided in close to 30 states, with approximately half of these

decisions overturning the existing system. (For an excellent review of school finance litigation, see Odden and Picus 1992.) Although court challenges slowed during the 1980s, by the late 1980s a new round of court cases has emerged in more than 20 states. Particularly significant were reforms in Kentucky, where the whole educational system was declared unconstitutional in 1989. In response to this decision, Kentucky implemented a far-reaching reform of school finances, school operations and accountability systems.

Educational Equity and Grand Design

Since the early research on school aid, equity has been one of the principal stated objectives of the distribution of state school aid. Recent court challenges of state education finance systems have put even more emphasis on the equalizing impact of aid. The proper design of an educational aid system first requires defining the educational equity standard which the aid system is trying to achieve.

Equity Concepts

Robert Berne and Leanna Stiefel (1984) have provided a comprehensive review of education equity definitions and measures. They find that equity standards can vary depending on (1) for whom equity is going to be achieved, (2) what is going to be equalized, and (3) how much discretion should be given to local school districts in their use of aid. Most educational equity principles use children as the targeted group; however, some standards focus on achieving equity for local taxpayers. Concerning the second question, equity definitions focus on equalizing either per pupil expenditures, the tax base—usually property wealth—of local school districts, or the expenditure needs of a district. Expenditure needs are defined as the expenditures required to provide a given quality of service (e.g., achieve some level of test scores) and will vary between school districts depending on cost-of-living differences and variation in the relative number of high needs students within a district (e.g., students with special needs, limited English proficiency, and those from disadvantaged households). Finally, equity standards depend on whether their objective is to provide the opportunity for school districts to equalize resources or to assure that school districts achieve certain results.

Minimum Foundation. One widely used equity standard requires that all students have access to a minimum level of educational resources. The minimum standard is usually expressed in terms of a minimum level of expenditures per pupil. This standard implies that school districts with low capacity should be provided with sufficient resources to achieve the minimum. However, once districts achieve the minimum foundation, they should be free to spend above this level. Districts could either be forced to achieve the minimum or could be allowed discretion in setting the budget below the foundation.

Providing a Standard Level of Service. A more ambitious standard would be one where resources are distributed to school districts so that all districts can achieve the same level of educational resources. This standard can vary depending on whether educational resources are defined as per pupil expenditures or some combination of a district's tax capacity or expenditure needs. In implementation, this approach involves redistribution of resources from high capacity to low capacity districts. Districts could either be forced to spend the same amount of resources or provided discretion in setting their budgets.

Fiscal Neutrality. This concept is based on a negative definition of equality of opportunity–children's educational opportunity should not depend on factors outside their control. Fiscal neutrality is typically defined as a distribution of educational resources among school districts such that differences in school spending are not correlated with district wealth or income. Variation in expenditures across districts is permitted as long as it does not reflect differences in school district wealth.

Equality of Outcomes. The most stringent equity standard which could be adopted by a state would be one where the ultimate objective would be to achieve some measure of equality of educational outcomes across districts. Such an approach would require first defining and measuring educational outcomes. While scores on standardized achievement tests are typically used as outcome measures, they are controversial and not necessarily linked very closely with a student's success in the job market (see the excellent review by Hanushek 1986). Whether outcomes are defined as average test scores or some minimum standard of achievement, for example, will affect measures of equity. This standard would imply significant redistribution of resources among school districts and limited discretion in how school districts used these resources.

Grant Design

Since the pioneering work in the early twentieth century, research continues on the design of educational aid systems. Grant design can vary depend on the equity standard selected, the educational resources equalized, the level of discretion provided local school districts, and how grant funds are distributed to districts. In the latter case, grants are usually of two general forms; lump-sum or matching. A lump-sum grant is a set amount of financial aid provided to a government regardless of local expenditure decisions. Matching grants, on the other hand, involve a state subsidy of a certain percentage (the matching rate) of local expen-

ditures. Under an open-ended matching grant, the more the local government spends, the more aid they receive. School finance scholars generally classify grants into several broad categories. (For excellent reviews of education grant types see Monk 1990, and Cohn and Geske 1990.)

Flat Grants. While not in common use today, most states originally provided aid with some form of flat grant. A flat grant is a fixed amount of aid provided per pupil. Total aid to a school district equals the flat grant times the number of pupils. Flat grants can be adjusted to provide more funds for pupils with special educational needs.

Foundation Grants. The objective of the foundation grant is to achieve a minimum level of educational resources in a school district. The foundation level of resources is typically defined as a minimum level of expenditures per pupil. A foundation grant formula attempts to distribute funds among districts so that every district can achieve this foundation level with the same property tax rate. Before grants are distributed, a foundation expenditure level and a common tax rate must be selected. Districts are provided a lump-sum grant equivalent to the difference between the minimum expenditure level and what the district could have raised at the common tax rate.

Lump-Sum Grant to Equalize Fiscal Condition. While the foundation grant equalizes the tax base up to the minimum expenditure level, expenditures beyond the minimum are not capped. States can raise the equity standard by providing resources to school districts so that they all can achieve an average level of service. Helen Ladd and John Yinger (1991) have provided a detailed methodology for developing lump-sum grants to achieve this objective by equalizing the fiscal condition among governments. The fiscal condition of a school district depends on both the tax base of the district and its expenditure needs. A fiscal condition index measures the gap between a district's fiscal capacity and its expenditure needs, and would be used to distribute aid across districts.

Matching Grants to Achieve Fiscal Neutrality. Several forms of matching grants have been developed to achieve the standard of fiscal neutrality. Generally, these grants try to reduce the relationship between a school district's wealth and education spending per pupil. The rate at which a state government will match local spending varies inversely with the property tax base of a district. Poorer districts would receive a greater state match than wealthier districts. The most common form of matching aid, the percentage equalizing grant, adjusts state matching rates so that to reach any particular spending level per pupil, all districts are able to impose the same property tax rate. Thus, this grant achieves a form of fiscal neutrality by decoupling educational spending from property tax rates.

Other Issues in Grant Design. The actual implementation of these types of educational grants can vary depending on several other factors. The first issue is the level of redistribution from wealthy to poor school district that actually occurs under the grant system. Theoretically, it is possible under each of these grants for some districts to receive negative state aid, implying that they pay additional taxes to the state to support poor districts (typically called a "recapture" provision). In actual practice, recapture provisions are not used in state aid systems; however, there are significant differences among states in the amount of redistribution achieved by their educational aid systems.

Another issue that is receiving increasing attention in aid design is how to incorporate expenditure needs or cost differences into education aid. Presently, most aid formulas distribute grants based on differences in the tax capacity of school districts. What adjustments are made for differences in expenditure needs are based on measures of "weighted pupils," which reflect the higher costs of educating certain types of students. For example, a student with limited English proficiency would receive a higher weight, leading to more aid than the average student. Recent research has focused on developing comprehensive cost of education indices that reflect both differences in cost of living and composition of the student body among school districts.

Current Educational Aid Systems in the United States

The education finance system in the United States is very decentralized. While the role of the federal government has increased over the last century, still over 90 percent of education expenditures is funded out of state and local revenues. This financial decentralization contrasts with most other industrial countries where their central governments play a much more prominent role in funding education. Out of 19 industrial countries, the United States ranked next to last in the percent of its central government budget spent on education (Table II). The federal government spent less than 2 percent of its budget on education, one-fifth of the average budget share in other industrial countries. The low federal budget share cannot be accounted for by below average total spending on education in this country. The United States ranks fifth in per pupil spending on K-12 education and tenth when education spending is taken as a percent of the total output of the economy (gross domestic product). The decentralization of the U.S. education system has lead to significant variation in how states fund public education. The following is a brief comparison of actual state education aid systems for basic operating aid and other forms of education aid.

TABLE II. COMPARISON OF EDUCATION SPENDING IN U.S. AND OTHER INDUSTRIAL COUNTRIES*

	United States	Rank of U.S. (out of 19)	Highest Ranking Country	U.S. as Percent of Country of Highest Rank
Central government education spending as percent of budget (1988)	1.7	18	14.4 (Finland)	11.8
Per pupil education expenditures (dollars in 1989)	$3,917	5	$4,911 (Luxembourg)	79.8
Education expenditures as percent of GDP (1989)	3.4	10	4.5 (Denmark)	75.6

*Includes all countries in the Organization for Economic Cooperation and Development (OECD) except Belgium, Greece, Iceland, New Zealand, and Turkey. Central government expenditures are for 1987 in the Netherlands and data are not available for Japan. Education expenditures per pupil and as percent of GDP apply to expenditures for the first through the twelfth grades.

SOURCE: U.S. Department of Education, National Center on Education Statistics, *Condition of Education, 1993,* Table 53-1, and International Monetary Fund, *Government Finance Statistics Yearbook, 1993,* Volume XVII, p. 64.

Basic Operating Aid

Almost all states provide some form of general education aid to school districts to cover their basic operating expenses. Formulas for the distribution of operating aid are usually designed to address inequities in the fiscal capacities or expenditure needs of districts. However, important differences exist among states in the form that this aid takes and what factors are considered in aid formulas. Using a recent review of state education aid systems for the American Education Finance Association (Gold, et al. 1992), Table III summarizes some of variation in operating aid systems among regions in the United States. One of the important areas where states differ is the percent of school district budgets funded by state governments. State involvement ranges from close to full funding of education in Hawaii and Washington to almost no state funding in New Hampshire. Some regional differences in state funding exist with state governments in the Northeast and Midwest providing a significantly lower percent of the education budget, on average, than the states of the South and West.

Turning to the types of state aid systems used for operating aid, over three-quarters of states continue to use some form of foundation grant. Foundation grants particularly dominate aid systems in the South and the West. Eight states, all located in the Northeast or Midwest, use some form of a matching (percent equalizing) grant to fund general operations. However, all of these states have

TABLE III. DIFFERENCES IN STATE EDUCATION OPERATING AID SYSTEMS ACROSS REGIONS IN THE UNITED STATES

Category	Northeast	Midwest	South	West
Percent of revenue provided by state*	37.7	36.4	54.1	52.9
State Aid Systems:		Number of States		
Flat grant	0	0	2	0
Foundation grant	4	9	14	11
Percent equalizing grant	5	3	0	0
Full state funding	0	0	0	2
Fiscal capacity measure:				
Property wealth only	2	7	9	6
Property wealth and other tax bases	7	5	6	5
Cost adjustment:				
Weighted pupils	8	10	13	12
Other cost adjustment**	2	3	5	8

*Unweighted average of state percentages. The average for West does not include Hawaii.
**Other cost adjustments are typically for small or sparse districts or those with high cost of living.
SOURCE: S. Gold, D. Smith, S. Lawton, and A Hyary, *Public School Finance Programs of the United States and Canada, 1990–91*, vol. Albany, NY: The Nelson A. Rockefeller Institute of Government, and U.S. Department of Education, National Center for Education Statistics, *Digest of Education Statistics, 1993*, Table 158.

imposed ceilings on the amount of aid that any particular school district can receive. At the extremes of state aid distribution are several states which either use full state funding of basic education or some form of flat grant.

While most U.S. states tend to rely on some form of foundation grant to distribute operating aid; there remains important variation between these foundation systems. Differences exist in the foundation level set, the measures of expenditures and pupils used, and adjustments for costs and fiscal capacity. Almost all states include estimates of the property wealth of a school district as a measure of fiscal capacity. Some states have broadened their tax capacity estimates to include measures of income and retail sales. To adjust for differences in the needs of particular students, all but seven states include some form of "weighted pupil" measure in the aid formula. Pupils who are handicapped, have limited English proficiency, or have other special needs are given a heavier weight than other students in the distribution of aid. It is much less common for states to take into account other factors affecting expenditure needs, such as higher costs of living, low population density, or declining enrollment. Eighteen states include some form of cost adjustment but it is usually in the form of some simple adjustment factor rather than the use of a more comprehensive cost of education index.

Categorical Aid
Besides funding for basic operating expenditures of a school district, state governments often provide support for a number of separate categories, such as special education, transportation, capital acquisition, education for disadvantaged students, and vocational education. These grant programs are called categorical aid because the funds are to be used for specific functions. Most of these state categorical grants are tied directly to areas of federal aid. Frequently, such programs are accompanied by an administrative apparatus to assure that funds are being targeted to the right students and spent for appropriate programs.

State distribution of categorical aid usually does not take into account local fiscal capacity. Special education aid or transportation aid are commonly distributed as a flat dollar grant per student in a district classified with special needs or requiring bus transportation. A number of states either subsidize capital construction or debt service or help school districts obtain favorable financing. Other types of categorical aid often provided by states include funding for disadvantaged students, commonly called compensatory education (29 states), gifted and talented programs (41 states), bilingual education (28 states), and pre-kindergarten education (24 states).

WILLIAM D. DUNCOMBE

BIBLIOGRAPHY
Berne, Robert and Leanna Stiefel, 1984. *The Measurement of Equity in School Finance.* Baltimore: Johns Hopkins University Press.
Cohn, Elchanan and Terry Geske, 1990. *The Economics of Education.* 3d ed. New York: Pergamon Press.

Coons, John, William Clune III, and Stephen Sugarman, 1970. *Private Wealth and Public Education.* Cambridge, MA: Harvard University Press.
Gold, Steven, David Smith, Stephen Lawton, and Andrea C. Hyary, 1992. *Public School Finance Programs of the United States and Canada, 1990–91.* Albany, NY: The Nelson A. Rockefeller Institute of Government.
Hanushek, Eric, 1986. "The Economics of Schooling: Production and Efficiency in Public Schools." *Journal of Economic Literature* 24 (September) 1141–1177.
Ladd, Helen and John Yinger, 1991. *America's Ailing Cities: Fiscal Health and the Design of Urban Policy.* Baltimore: Johns Hopkins University Press.
Monk, David, 1990. *Educational Finance: An Economic Approach.* New York: McGraw-Hill Publishing Company.
Odden, Allan and Lawrence Picus, 1992. *School Finance: A Policy Perspective.* New York: McGraw-Hill.
San Antonio Independent School System v. Rodriquez, 1973. 411 U.S. 1.
Serrano v. Priest, 1971. 487 P2d 1241.
Strayer, George and Robert Haig, 1923. *The Financing of Education in the State of New York.* New York: McMillan.

EFFECTIVENESS.

The assessment of policy or program outcomes against stated goals or objectives.

Effectiveness, either singly or in association mainly with efficiency, has long been a goal of public management. Under the traditional model of public administration, effectiveness was understood to refer to the achievement of formal goals, in the sense getting "the right things done" (Drucker 1967). As public management has undergone a major reform process, or as some would have it a reinvention, in the U.S., the UK, Canada, New Zealand, Australia, and elsewhere in the 1980s and 1990s, effectiveness has become increasingly associated with a focus upon the quality of outcomes (Pollitt 1993).

In this regard, effectiveness is one of a number of performance criteria–which include efficiency and economy–applied to public management. Of these, effectiveness–with its emphasis on the quality of outcomes and links to performance measurement and performance monitoring–is now the preeminent yardstick by which public management is judged. However, it is far more difficult to assess the effectiveness of an agency or one of its programs than it is its economy or efficiency. The chief reason is that effectiveness is essentially a qualitative judgment, whereas efficiency and economy involve quantitative assessments.

Because qualitative judgements are seen as subjective, necessarily imprecise, and thus not always defensible in a political context, the trend within public management has been for effectiveness to be assessed on the basis of tangible or measurable outcomes against clearly articulated goals and performance indicators. As with other aspects of the new public management, this trend has its critics.

For example, it is argued that attempting to "measure" effectiveness is incompatible with the intangible nature of much of the work of government, such as human services (which are the predominant domain of government) and the provision of policy advice. To rely upon a statistics or data-based methodology in fields such as these may lead to misleading or even incorrect conclusions regarding effectiveness and to a decline in the overall quality of public management itself. This latter concern arises from the view that what is measured is what is inevitably valued and rewarded. What is not measured may be devalued and left to deteriorate or cease altogether, with potentially serious consequences for the effectiveness of a service.

Critics also claim that the pressure to use measurement-based techniques in public management has tended to blur in practice the distinction between efficiency and effectiveness. This is because performance indicators are focused in the main on measuring efficiency, which is the easier of the two to measure. The result, it is said, is that efficiency is measured at the expense of effectiveness and that fundamental issues relating to effectiveness have been marginalized (Pollitt 1993).

Thus, although efficiency and effectiveness are by no means mutually exclusive, they are not always compatible. As Drucker (1988) has observed, "even the most efficient business cannot survive, let alone succeed, if it is efficient at doing the wrong things, that is, if it lacks effectiveness" (p. 44).

DEIRDRE O'NEILL

BIBLIOGRAPHY

Drucker, Peter, 1967. *The Effective Executive.* London, UK: Heinemann.
———, 1988. *Management.* Rev. ed. Oxford, UK: Butterworth-Heinemann.
Pollitt, Christopher, 1993. *Managerialism and the Public Services.* 2d ed. Oxford, UK: Blackwell.

EFFICIENCY.

The measurement of the inputs, or resources, required to produce, or achieve, a unit of output.

Under the traditional model of public management–which melded the key recommendations of the British Northcote-Trevelyan Report (1854) with the principles of bureaucratic organization espoused by the German sociologist and economist Max Weber and the U.S. political scientist Woodrow Wilson's theory of the dichotomy of policy and administration in government–efficiency was viewed narrowly in terms of an acceptable level of administrative performance. A public agency that in a technical sense operated smoothly, made few if any errors (thus minimizing political flak or fallout), and kept within its budgetary limits was considered to be a model of efficiency.

However, in the second half of the twentieth century the traditional model of public management has been consistently criticized on the grounds of unacceptably low levels of efficiency. According to these critiques, spending by public agencies has been dominated by the influence of interest groups, public sector managers have been unrestrained empire builders, and the public sector itself has been allowed to become flabby and wasteful in the absence of market discipline.

Such has been the force of these claims that the traditional model has been progressively replaced in the U.S., Great Britain, Canada, New Zealand, Australia, and elsewhere with new models of public management. In the process, the introduction of corporate planning techniques, including the establishment of clear, measurable, output-based objectives for public sector agencies and their staff, has led to a much more precise measurement of both the agency's and the individual's performance.

This contemporary focus on efficiency has tended to overshadow other performance criteria—such as economy, effectiveness, and equity—with which efficiency is now sometimes erroneously confused. For example, an organization may be economical in its use of resources but not efficient if the sole emphasis is upon reducing costs; it may be efficient, according to the ratio of inputs to outputs, but if the outcome of its activity is a failure to realize its goals then it is not effective; and what may be deemed efficient for an agency's operation may not necessarily lead to equitable, or fair, outcomes for those the agency exists to serve.

These distinctions are at the heart of much of the debate about the new models of public management. It is claimed by some that there is now too much emphasis on monitoring and measurement of quantifiable and/or tangible outputs and too little emphasis on qualitative and/or intangible outcomes—that is to say, too much concern for efficiency at the expense of effectiveness. In the process, efficiency has in a practical sense become almost indistinguishable from economy. Efficiency is thus associated with such trends as cost-cutting, downsizing, productivity savings, benchmarking, outsourcing, privatization and, by its critics, with the marginalizing of less easily measured social costs that are defined as "externalities" (Mintzberg 1989).

Critics of these trends argue that efficiency alone is essentially a limited value, a view acknowledged even by the proponents of new forms of public management. As Vice President Al Gore stated in his *Report of the National Performance Review* (1993), "Our goal is . . . not simply to produce a more efficient government, but to create a more effective government. After all, Americans don't want a government that fails more efficiently. They want a government that works" (p. 8).

DEIRDRE O'NEILL

BIBLIOGRAPHY

Gore, Al, 1993. *From Red Tape to Results: Report of the National Performance Review*. Washington, D.C.: Government Printing Office.

Hughes, Owen E., 1994. *Public Management and Administration: An Introduction*. London, UK: Macmillan.
Mintzberg, Henry, 1989. *Mintzberg on Management: Inside Our Strange World of Organization*. New York: The Free Press.
Pollitt, Christopher, 1993. *Managerialism and the Public Services*. 2d ed. Oxford, UK: Blackwell.
Report on the Organisation of the Permanent Civil Service, 1854 (The Northcote-Trevelyan Report). London: HMSO.

EMERGENCY MANAGEMENT. The processes of preparing for, preventing, or lessening the effects of, responding to, and recovering from natural and human disasters.

Emergency management is a relatively new professional specialization and a field of study which is receiving increased attention from government officials, policy analysts, and public administration educators. The growing interest in emergency management is easy to understand. Devastating earthquakes, typhoons, volcanic eruptions, epidemics, wars, and other disasters present government leaders with important challenges and opportunities. Failure to respond effectively can have serious political repercussions, while success can enhance prestige and power and lend legitimacy to the government.

While the modern media have drawn attention to the function of emergency management, the role of emergency managers in preparing for and responding to disasters and in assisting communities during recovery efforts in the aftermath of disaster is as old as the institution of government itself. Procedures for responding to disaster have been common in most societies, although they were most often ad hoc or reliant upon social organizations such as churches and civic groups. Emergency management was initially focused on disaster response. The recognition that catastrophic disasters might be averted or at least lessened through broader government programs and that environmental hazards can be managed has been a recent development. For example, government regulation of building standards, most notably requirements that city structures be built of stone or brick rather than flammable wood and be situated away from flood-prone areas, is only a few centuries old.

In the United States, with a few exceptions such as firefighting in urban areas and forests, programs to address hazards and respond to disasters were almost unknown prior to World War II. Disaster relief or recovery in the U.S. was largely the province of charitable and religious institutions. Just as communities relied on church and nonprofit organizations to provide social services for the poor, infirm, and homeless, they relied on those same organizations to respond to minor and major disasters and to assist disaster victims. In many respects, as a matter of public policy. American communities still rely very heavily on organizations such as the American Red Cross and the Salvation Army. The Red Cross remains the principal source of aid to families left homeless by fires sand floods in most communities. Responses to larger scale disasters, however, have increasingly required concerted regional and national government action. As society has become more knowledgeable about and vulnerable to catastrophic disasters, the day-to-day activities to reduce the potential for massive losses of human lives and property have increasingly been assumed by local, state, and federal governments.

The broadening of the scope of emergency management and the development of emergency management capabilities have generally followed the same pattern in other nations. Much depends upon the resources that can be invested in planning and training programs and the abilities of the governments to regulate activities such as building and land use that might increase risk, and to manage environmental hazards themselves.

Prior to World War II, public awareness of and government programs to reduce environmental hazards were very limited. Regulation of construction through enforcement of building standards, land use regulation, and other environmentally oriented programs to reduce hazards were rare in rural areas and only sporadically enforced in most urban areas. The exceptions to this generalization were the floodplain management programs designed and managed by the U.S. Army Corps of Engineers along the nation's major waterways to address severe flooding problems, and civil defense programs designed and managed by the U.S. Department of Defense. Communities still maintained fire departments, often using volunteers rather than full-time professional firefighters, but the role of the fire service was limited to responding to fires, rather than assisting in prevention efforts.

In large measure U.S. emergency management programs have improved since World War II. But, in some parts of the U.S. building standards are still inadequate and regulations, when in force, are often ineffectively applied. Fire departments have professionalized in some communities and not in others. Emergency management capabilities are still very uneven.

The Evolution of Emergency Management

The management of disasters likely began with efforts to address growing threats of fire and disease in the major cities of the world. Highly flammable wooden structures and increasingly crowded urban areas offered hazards that were potentially devastating. Effective disaster response was beyond the capacities of public and private organizations. During the 1800s, for example, hundreds died in major fires in New York City; Canton, China; Chicago; St. John, New Brunswick, Canada; Vienna, Austria; Paris, France; and Exeter, England. The Great Chicago Fire and the firestorm that destroyed San Francisco following the

Great Earthquake of 1906 are legendary disasters in the United States. Growing populations in crowded cities created new and catastrophic threats to life and property. Theaters, hospitals, hotels, factories, stores, and other large facilities were particularly vulnerable to fire and city fire services were often inadequate protection under the best of circumstances. Similarly, when crowded urban populations were beset by epidemics, concern for public health services grew accordingly.

History reinforced concerns for potential health disasters, from the devastation of Europe by the bubonic plague in the Middle Ages to much more recent epidemics of smallpox, yellow fever, cholera, and other diseases. In recent years the spread of AIDS worldwide had heightened sensitivity to the potential for more public health disasters. Wars, famines, and other assaults on civilian populations and the environment, too, have increased concern for the prevention, mitigation, and management of disasters. Risk and hazard reduction are the focal points in current emergency management efforts. Those goals are highlighted by the International Decade for Natural Disaster Reduction. Government action to reduce potential losses of human life and property has been slow in coming, however.

Emergency Management in the United States

In the United States, while local governments focused on fire hazards, the first national emergency management programs dealt with floods and civil defense. The National Flood Program was set up under the Flood Control Act of 1936 and the Disaster Relief Act of 1950. During World War II, civil defense programs were established in the Department of Defense to make the nation less vulnerable to attack. By the early 1950s, protection from nuclear attack became the principal focus of the U.S. civil defense programs, with offices established in hundreds of towns and cities.

Gradually, concerns grew about the potential for other kinds of catastrophic natural and technological disasters. By the late 1960s and early 1970s, opposition to military programs in many communities, concerns about the inadequacy or inappropriateness of civil defense programs as preparation for nonnuclear disasters, and conflicts over funding of emergency management-related programs in particular prompted questions about the relationships among defense and nondefense agencies and their priorities. In 1978, President Jimmy Carter initiated a reorganization of federal programs in response to criticism of federal handling of the Three Mile Island nuclear accident. The reorganization created the Federal Emergency Management Agency (FEMA), drawing civil preparedness programs from the Department of Defense, the National Flood Insurance Program from the Department of Housing and Urban Development, the National Fire Prevention and Control Administration and the National Fire Academy from the U.S. Department of Commerce, the Community Preparedness Program from the National Weather Service and the U.S. Department of Commerce, and programs in dam safety, earthquake hazard reduction, and terrorism and the national emergency warning systems from the Office of the President.

While FEMA was responsible for a variety of programs, the first directors were drawn from the military and the agency gave greatest priority to civil defense related programs. In response to the criticism of its civil defense orientation, FEMA officials developed the Integrated Emergency Management System (IEMS) in the early 1980s. IEMS was predicated on the belief that generic emergency management functions could be adapted as needed in response to both national security and other disasters. It was also a logical extension of the comprehensive role expected of FEMA. State and local officials, however, generally felt that federal priorities were different from their own and some communities refused to participate in programs that might have a national security purpose. The fear was that an effective, or presumed effective, national civil defense program might encourage risk taking by nuclear strategists.

The comprehensive emergency management model, developed under the auspices of the National Governors Association, provided the basic framework for FEMA's IEMS model and became the basis for most state and local emergency management systems. The comprehensive emergency management model has four phases: mitigation, preparedness, response, and recovery. Mitigation is a predisaster activity that involves assessing risk and lessening the potential effects of disasters. Mitigation programs include land use regulation, building codes, structural barriers (such as dams and levees), and insurance programs to lessen the economic impact of disaster. Preparedness is the predisaster activity of readying for expected threats, including such actions as planning for contingencies, positioning of resources, developing cooperative agreements with other jurisdictions and response agencies, clarifying jurisdictional responsibilities, and training response personnel.

Response is the activity that occurs during the disaster and includes search and rescue, emergency medical services, and firefighting. Response also includes acting to reduce the likelihood of secondary damage, such as putting plastic over damaged roofs to limit damage to furniture and appliances within buildings, and preparing for recovery. Recovery is the postdisaster phase, largely dealing with the restoration of lifelines. Recovery includes the provision of temporary housing, food and clothing, psychological services, job services, restoration of electrical power, and small business loans. The recovery phase stops short of full

reconstruction of the community. The conceptual framework of the comprehensive model has become the language of contemporary emergency management in the United States and, increasingly, in other nations.

The National Emergency Management System

In general terms, the national emergency management system is designed to assure state assistance to communities when catastrophic events outstrip local capabilities and resources and federal assistance to states and localities when state capabilities and resources are outstripped. To receive federal aid, a formal request must be communicated by the state's governor. That request must document the need for federal assistance, therefore it must include a reasonable initial damage assessment and must indicate the kinds of aid that are requested. To formulate the request, the governor's office must collect data from the distressed communities, determine needs, and assure that state resources have been effectively applied. The process requires considerable administrative capability and technical expertise, but more importantly it requires an effective communications link between state and local emergency management officials. The application for and the award of disaster aid are also political processes that are facilitated when governor and president are of the same political party. If the need for federal assistance is adequately documented, the president may issue a Presidential Disaster Declaration. Such a declaration makes states, communities, businesses, and individuals eligible for a wide variety of federal programs. FEMA is the coordinating agency for federal aid and is responsible for establishing disaster assistance centers in the affected area to provide "one-stop shopping" for those seeking assistance from federal, state, and local agencies.

A smaller disaster that does not warrant a President Disaster Declaration is handled by state and local agencies and nonprofit organizations. Local agencies have generally been the lead agencies in lesser disasters, since few state governments have well-developed response capabilities beyond the National Guard. States do, however, have emergency management agencies that assist in coordinating state assistance.

Evident failures in the national emergency management system during and following Hurricane Hugo in 1989, Hurricanes Andrew and Iniki in 1992, the Loma Prieta earthquake in 1992, and the Northridge earthquake in 1994 prompted the U.S. Congress to commission reviews of the national emergency management system by the U.S. Government Accounting Office and the National Academy of Public Administration. Hearings were also held by the U.S. Senate's Committee on Governmental Affairs. The perception expressed by the news media, and evident in the organizational changes recommended in the studies and hearings, was that there were fundamental problems in the organization of FEMA. The studies focused on conflicts between civil defense-related programs and natural disaster-related programs; the relatively large number of political appointees in the agency; the lack of emergency management experience among many (if not most) of the appointees; conflicts among and between federal officials and their state and local counterparts; and the lack of a proactive orientation among FEMA officials. Reorganizations of FEMA under Director James Lee Witt, who was appointed by President Bill Clinton, and reforms suggested in the agency's National Performance Review studies acted to correct some of the identified weaknesses, particularly in terms of reorienting the agency from its previous civil defense focus to one more responsive to state and local needs and interests, integrating many of the program functions, and focusing the agency's mission on mitigation programs. Other suggested reforms, such as reducing the large number of political appointees in FEMA, have not been implemented, however.

Regional and Local Emergency Management

State emergency management agencies take many forms, although there is a decided tendency to mimic FEMA. The major disasters of the last decade have increased interest in the structure and effectiveness of state offices and, in particular, their relationships with the state governor. Local agencies range from single, part-time coordinators with few resources and little authority to large, highly professional organizations with state-of-art information technology. Due to the potential legal liability of local officials for failures to prepare for and respond to disasters effectively, there has been increased interest in the organization of local offices. But reform has been slow. The common wisdom is that local emergency management offices should be directly responsible to the local government executive, either as part of the office of the mayor or city/county manager or tied very closely to that office. Close proximity to the local government executive facilitates communication and can serve to give the emergency manager greater visibility and, possibly, greater access to the resources of the government.

The structure of the national emergency management system is of paramount importance. The history of disaster preparedness and recovery legislation in the United States has been characterized by sporadic interest. The tendency has been to create programs in the aftermath of disaster that offer little utility in preparing for future disasters. FEMA's programs were funded individually, involving dozens of congressional committees and a variety of interest groups, with little provision for shifting resources where they are most needed or coordinating activities among the programs. Reforms during the Clinton administration have attempted to provide more coordinated action, but

the nature of the programs and the large number of involved authorization committees make coordination difficult at best.

At the federal and state levels, the costs of disasters encourage greater attention to the need for risk reduction. It is also argued that the availability of state and federal assistance may discourage individual home and business owners from adequately insuring their property. The National Flood Insurance Program, for example, requires that property owners purchase flood insurance if their property is located in a floodplain. It also requires local governments to regulate building within that floodplain. Studies indicate that property owners would not purchase insurance, particularly those in lower risk areas, if not required by the federal government in order to qualify for FHA and VA mortgage loans and, in the event of a flood, disaster assistance. That issue has been central to the debate over requiring earthquake insurance in higher risk areas. While floodplains are managed under federal law, earthquake zones are not as effectively managed under state and local law. States such as California have stringent building codes and land use plans to reduce earthquake hazards, but many other states have few regulations regarding land use and building standards. The billions of dollars paid out in the aftermaths of Hurricanes Hugo and Andrew, however, are encouraging the insurance industry to examine the problem of inadequate regulation of building. Even when building codes are in place, some local governments lack the resources to enforce them effectively. Following Hurricane Hugo, for example, it was found that some county governments in South Carolina had building codes but no inspectors and others had no building standards at all. Faulty construction was judged responsible for much of the property damage in south Florida during Hurricane Andrew, as well. From the perspective of the insurance companies, the problems are how to encourage communities to adopt appropriate building codes and how to help them enforce the codes effectively. State mandated codes are an alternative, but adjustments would necessarily have to be made to accommodate local hazard and state monies would be necessary to assure adequate funding. For local officials the problems are twofold, funding and politics. Effective code enforcement costs money that local governments may not have. Land use and building regulation are intensely political issues at the local level and are issues that local officials may not be equipped to resolve.

The Professionalization of Emergency Management

In large measure, national, regional, and local emergency management offices tend to be staffed by individuals experienced in national security programs, but inexperienced in many natural and technological hazards programs. That is, as with most other government hiring, the recruitment of emergency management personnel is characterized by a preference for military veterans rather than those experienced in managing environmental programs. An early stereotype of the emergency manager has been the circa 1950 air raid warden or civil defense coordinator with whistle and armband and little professional expertise. That is an image difficult to overcome as positions in emergency management agencies professionalize.

Emergency management professionals find some commonality of interest with other public sector professionals. Many are affiliated with the Section on Emergency and Crisis Management of the American Society for Public Administration, the Council on Emergency Management of the American Public Works Association, the American Planning Association, and/or the International City/County Management Association. Increasingly, however, emergency managers are finding support in organizations specifically focused on emergency management, such as the National Coordinating Committee on Emergency Management (NCCEM), the National Emergency Management Association, and the International Emergency Management and Engineering Society.

With the assistance of FEMA, a professional certification program was developed by representatives of the several professional associations. Administered by the NCCEM, the Certified Emergency Manager program permits individuals to earn professional certification by demonstrating a minimum level of education, specific training in emergency management, and experience in the field. To maintain certification, individuals must continue their training and education. As in most professional certification programs, the process permits the certification of those currently professionally experienced in the field, but lacking the requisite formal education or training.

Emergency Management as a Field of Study

The study of emergency management has expanded tremendously with the increased public and government interest in the field. The literature is diverse, ranging from technical reports in architecture, engineering, construction sciences, and floodplain management to studies in community psychology, sociology, and, increasingly, political science. The earliest literature focused on technical issues, mostly dealing with building construction with increasing emphasis on seismic safety concerns. The current literature is a mixture of technical reports and social science analyses.

Social science research, particularly on the sociology of disasters, was centered in the Disaster Research Center at Ohio State University and then the University of Delaware. To improve communication within the fragmented scientific community and between researchers and practitioners in the field, the Natural Hazards Information and Applications Center was created at the University of Colorado in Boulder in 1975. The center grew out of a social science project funded by the National Science Foundation. The initial concern was with disseminating information from a variety of public and private sources. Now the center is funded by the National Science Foundation, Federal Emergency Management Agency, National Oceanic and Atmospheric Administration, U.S. Geological Survey, Tennessee Valley Authority, U.S. Army Corps of Engineers, U.S. Environmental Protection Agency, and National Institute of Mental Health (Myers 1993). In recent years, similar centers have been created in England, Australia, Canada, the Netherlands, the Caribbean, and other nations and regions. In the United States, research and education expanded through the development of educational programs specifically designed for emergency managers, such as the degree and/or certificate programs at the University of North Texas, University of Wisconsin, University of Louisville, New York University, George Washington University, University of California-Berkeley, as well as FEMA's Emergency Management Institute.

FEMA itself encouraged greater attention to emergency management issues among policy analysts and public administrators in 1984 when the agency and the National Association of Schools of Public Affairs and Administration (NASPAA) cosponsored a two-week workshop at the National Emergency Training Center's Emergency Management Institute and Senior Executive Center in Emmitsburg, Maryland, for approximately 20 public administration faculty. Many of the participants in that workshop were founders of the American Society for Public Administration's Section on Emergency Management (now the Section on Emergency and Crisis Management) and have been active researchers in the field.

A major problem in defining emergency management today is finding the boundaries of the field. In addition to dealing with natural and technological disasters, there are compelling reasons to include public health threats that may affect millions of people (such as AIDS), environmental issues that may result in tremendous economic loss such as acid rain and global warming and deforestation, and even astronomical issues as seemingly farfetched as the possibility of large meteor strikes on the Earth. It is a challenge to find common ground for discussions of sinkholes in Florida, avalanches in the Alps, killer bees in Mexico, and tsunami on Pacific shores, as well as to accommodate professional interests in everything from structural engineering to psychological counseling for disaster workers and victims.

The Future of Emergency Management

The field of emergency management is undergoing great change in the 1990s. As an issue, emergency management is finding greater public support. The principal reason for the increased public and government interest is the unusual number of recent catastrophes. Major earthquakes, volcanic eruptions, hurricanes, droughts, nuclear accidents, wars, floods, and other disasters are frequent occurrences and television coverage is compelling. The international media provided graphic accounts of the devastating hundred-year floods in northern Europe and the Kobe earthquake in Japan. Less dramatic, but no less devastating, disasters such as the persistent droughts in Africa and Australia may be less familiar to people outside of the regions, but their effects are broadly felt. The wars that have caused famine, displacement and homelessness, disease, and devastation of populations have become all too familiar to the international community. Millions have died and many more have been physically and psychologically injured. The economic impact of the disasters has been staggering and some impacts have yet to be fully realized. The health costs of the nuclear disaster at Chernobyl, for example, will likely be paid by generations of Ukrainians. While the negative effects of the 1989 *Exxon Valdez* oil spill on Prince William Sound are touted as resolved, the long-term impact on that fragile environment remains. The human and economic costs of disaster are addressed internationally through the activities of the International Decade for Natural Disaster Reduction, but concerns have been raised about the slow adoption of adequate mitigation programs (National Research Council 1994).

While scientists improve their capabilities to predict earthquakes, the frequency and intensities of cyclones (hurricanes and typhoons), and the development of droughts and floods, other natural phenomena increase the risks to society. Terrorist attacks, including bombing of aircraft in flight and the World Trade Center in New York City, have the potential to be as destructive as natural and technological disasters. Bombings of oil and gas pipelines, mines, oil rigs, gas storage facilities, dams, and transportation facilities can be catastrophic in terms of property damage and the loss of human life. Natural hazards, too, are becoming more dangerous as people build homes and businesses along flood-prone rivers and on storm-prone coastlines, with too little regard for seismic, fire, and wind hazards. Society continues to create new hazards, from super-toxic biological materials to high speed trains.

The challenge may be to develop a flexible strategy for managing a variety of environmental hazards and preparing for a variety of potential disasters. That would require a commitment to address known hazards, to identify potential hazards, and to cultivate public awareness of hazards to assure appropriate responses by individuals, families, communities, and states. Increased professionalization of emergency management personnel and agencies and increased scientific expertise that can be brought to bear in the assessment of environmental risks and the prediction of disasters are positive developments in that regard. At issue, however, is how to reduce the levels of risk to minimize costs without seeming to overregulate individual behaviors. For example, it is often suggested that private insurance can take the place of government programs. But, it is also argued, can government officials refuse to provide aid to those who chose not to purchase insurance when those victims of disaster may number in the thousands? More stringent construction standards and land use regulations, too, may keep people out of harm's way if officials and voters can be persuaded to support the regulations. The fundamental questions are: how much risk is there and how much are citizens willing to spend to reduce the risk?

WILLIAM L. WAUGH, JR.

BIBLIOGRAPHY

Comfort, Louise K., ed., 1988. *Managing Disaster: Strategies and Policy Perspectives*. Durham, NC: Duke University Press.

Drabek, Thomas E., 1987. *The Professional Emergency Manager*. Boulder: University of Colorado, Institute of Behavioral Science, Monograph #44.

May, Peter J., and Walter Williams, 1986. *Disaster Policy Implementation: Managing Program Under Shared Goverance*. New York: Plenum Press.

McLoughlin, David, 1985. "A Framework for Integrated Emergency Management." *Public Administration Review*, vol. 45, special issue (January) 165–172.

Myers, Mary Fran, 1993. "Bridging the Gap Between Research and Practice: The Natural Hazards Research and Applications Information Center." *International Journal of Mass Emergencies and Disasters*, vol. 11, no. 1 (March) 41–54.

National Academy of Public Administration, 1993. *Coping with Catastrophe: Building an Emergency Management System to Meet People's Needs in Natural and Manmade Disasters*. Washington, D.C.: National Academy of Public Administration.

National Research Council, 1994. *Facing the Challenge: The U.S. National Report to the IDNDR World Conference on Natural Disaster Reduction, Yokohama, Japan, May 23–27, 1994*. Washington, D.C.: National Academy Press.

Sylves, Richard T. and William L. Waugh, Jr., eds., 1995. *Cities and Disaster: North American Studies in Emergency Management*. 2d ed. Springfield, IL: Charles C. Thomas Publishers.

Waugh, Jr., William L., 1990. *Terrorism and Emergency Management: Policy and Administration*. New York: Marcel Dekker.

———, and Ronald John Hy, ed., 1990. *Handbook of Emergency Management: Policies and Programs Dealing with Major Hazards and Disasters*. Westport, CT: Greenwood Press.

EMINENT DOMAIN. The right of government to acquire private property for "public use" in exchange for "just compensation"; also known as condemnation. This government action can take place at any level of government, whether municipal, county, state, or federal, as long as it is within the territorial limits of its jurisdiction. The taking of private land must be in accordance with the due process of law spelled out in the Fourth and Fifth Amendments of the Constitution.

The Fifth Amendment recognizes this privilege by stating: "No person shall be deprived of . . . property . . . without due process of law; nor shall private property be taken for public use, without just compensation." Most state constitutions have similar wording. Precisely what the interpretation of these words mean has been subject to debate and much litigation for over two hundred years.

Eminent domain is a politically unpopular procedure used generally as a last resort when negotiations between the government and the private property owner break down. The chances that the private party can stop the seizure of private land by the government for public purposes is very remote. The only recourse for a private party is in the area of "just compensation," which is based on fair market value. Fair market value is ascertained by the price of the property at the time it is taken. It is determined from what a willing buyer would pay in cash to a willing seller based on the highest and best use of the property taken, even though the owner may not have been using the property to its fullest potential when it was taken. Ninety-eight percent of the cases involve only the expansion of the amount of compensation awarded to the owner and not the question of whether the taking is legal.

The use of eminent domain has increased substantially over the past 50 years. The reasons are twofold. First of all, because of the increased involvement of the government, courts have expanded the meaning of "public use." The Supreme Court ruled in *Berman v. Parker,* 75 S.Ct.98. that public use can include giving the land for private use in cases of urban renewal because this form of taking is viewed as benefiting the public good.

Second, eminent domain usually arises because of growth. As the population expands, the intensity of land use increases and the boundaries expand. This creates a steadily increasing demand for public services such as pipelines for gas and water, fire stations, schools, highways, streets, bridges, airports, landfills and dumps, sewage treatment systems and the like. With expansion, there has become a growing tendency for the courts to defer to state and local government interpretations of the Fifth Amendment's "public use" requirement.

It should also be noted that property does not have to be physically taken by the government in order for someone to be compensated. The Supreme Court has ruled that if government action leads to a lower property value, a taking has occurred and the landowner is entitled to receive compensation equal to his or her loss.

SUZANNE LELAND

BIBLIOGRAPHY

Durham, James, 1985. "Efficient Just Compensation as a Limit on Eminent Domain." *Minnesota Law Review,* vol. 69 (June).

Hagman, Donald G., 1975. *Urban Planning and Land Development Control Law.* St. Paul, MN: West Publishing Company.

Platt, Rutherford H. 1991. *Land Use Control: Geography, Law, and Public Policy.* Englewood Cliffs, NJ: Prentice Hall.

Wilder, Margaret and Joyce E. Stigler, 1989. "Rethinking the Role of Judicial Scrutiny in Eminent Domain." *Journal of the American Planning Association,* vol. 55 (Winter) 57–66.

EMPLOYEE ASSISTANCE PROGRAM (EAP).

A plan implemented by an employer to help employees with alcohol and drug abuse, family, financial, medical, gambling and other problems that can affect job performance.

Troubled employees are employees whose job performance has been affected by one or more problems in their lives. The most common of these problems are alcoholism and alcohol abuse, drug dependency, mental and emotional disorders, compulsive gambling, financial difficulties, marital discord, family problems, and legal problems. Public and private organizations are responding to the needs of these employees by establishing employee assistance programs.

History of EAPs: Alcohol Rehabilitation and Broad Brush Programs

Mental health programs were present in industry as early as 1917. R. H. Macy and Company and Northern State Power Company in Minneapolis provided employee assistance services in 1917 and Metropolitan Life Insurance began a program in 1919. In 1929 the first book on the subject was published, *Psychiatry in Industry,* by V. V. Anderson, Director of Medical Research for R. H. Macy & Co., Inc. Dr. Anderson believed that the most important element in labor difficulties is the mental condition of the worker. He found that "physical, mental, and social factors produce unacceptable reactions, create faulty attitudes, and develop mental patterns and habits that mold the worker's character and personality, and that determine his career." So he suggested the use of psychological tests to prevent or alleviate some personnel problems. Today EAPs seek to prevent work failures by studying whole personalities, assisting employees in dealing with their problems, and enabling them to perform acceptably for the business. Dr. Anderson's work was very early and directly related to contemporary EAP objectives (Anderson 1977).

In the 1940s the DuPont Corporation developed the first systematic program to assist employees with alcohol problems. Much of what has been written about EAPs attribute DuPont with having given birth to the programs.

The reason for this is that the earliest EAPs were implemented primarily to assist employees with alcohol-related problems, and thus to help employers to deal with productivity problems.

DuPont's research showed that the number of disability days per year for the alcoholic employee was 13, compared to 5.8 disability days per year for a control group. The 7.2 days difference, excess disability due to alcoholism, was a cost that could be quantified. The company saw the alcoholism treatment program as a means to reduce that cost.

The cost benefit was not the only concern for DuPont; human need was also evident. DuPont recognized that some costs were difficult to quantify and the company believed that the alcoholism treatment program could also reduce these costs. Some of these costs were low morale among employees who worked with the sick alcoholic, product mishandling, damaged to customer relationships, lost sales, product liability suits, and poor executive judgment due to alcoholism (see **morale**). Other costs that were difficult to quantify were the time that medical personnel and supervisors spent dealing with alcoholic employees, premature death and disability, and the costs of terminations where management and the legal staff of the company were tied up in arbitration. The motives that DuPont had to reduce these affects of alcoholism correspond to the motives of companies that institute EAPs today.

There was little growth in the number of companies implementing alcoholism treatment programs in the 1940s and 1950s. In 1959 there were approximately 50 companies with some type of program. Some increase in the number of programs was effected by the American Medical Association's 1956 declaration that alcoholism is a disease and a medical responsibility. Private organizations such as the National Council on Alcoholism (NCA) and the Christopher D. Smithers Foundation promoted the early growth of the programs. In 1960 the NCA encouraged a new approach, a combined community organization and management consultation approach. By 1965 this approach facilitated the increase in the number of new companies developing the programs by 357 percent.

A catalyst on the federal government level was the formation of the National Institute of Alcoholism and Alcohol Abuse (NIAAA) in 1971. Through NIAAA, federal funds were distributed for occupational alcoholism programs. Grants were given to states and territories to employ consultants and to develop programs for public and private employers.

The same national legislation which created NIAAA, the Hughes Act (Public Law 91-616), required that federal government agencies establish EAPs. Other acts also encouraged agencies to establish programs to assist alcoholic employees. Office of Personnel Management (OPM) regulations and Public Law 93-282 encourage agencies to establish EAPs and assure that information about employees'

referral and treatment will be kept confidential. Merit System Protection Board decisions require agencies to provide employees with alcoholism "reasonable accommodation," that is, an offer of rehabilitation assistance and the opportunity to take sick leave, if necessary.

On the local government level there was no consistent, formal policy requiring EAPs as there was on the federal level, so the majority remained without formal policies or employee assistance programs. Some local governments have established programs for cost-effectiveness and humanitarian reasons, and in response to court decisions in favor of terminated alcoholic employees.

In 1972 the NIAAA recommended an expanded approach, to help all employees with poor work performance rather than limiting assistance to alcoholics. From 1973 to 1974 the EAP model changed to one that covered a wide range of employee problems beyond alcoholism, a model called the broad brush approach. The words alcohol or alcoholism were dropped from program titles. Employee counseling or employee assistance services were new program titles. By 1976 this EAP model was dominant in government, business, and industry.

Concurrent with this maturing of program structure was a great increase in the number of EAPs in the public and the private sectors. In 1950 there were about 50 such programs. There were 230 in 1965, 2500 in 1977, and 5,000 in 1981. In 1994 there are approximately 10,000 such programs (anonymous 1994).

Costs of Troubled Employees

One important motive for employers to establish EAPs is economic. When the productivity of a troubled employee declines so do the profits in a profit-making business, and so does the budget performance in a public organization. The estimated economic cost of alcohol abuse, drug abuse, and mental illness in the United States in 1988 is $273.3 billion. Most of this, $129.3 billion, is attributable to mental illness, another $85.8 is attributable to alcohol abuse, and $58.3 billion is attributable to drug abuse. Several factors contribute to these costs. One factor is lost output because the impaired employee is less productive, misses work, and may die prematurely. Another factor is health care, including hospital care, physician and other professional services, and prescription drugs. Other related costs include crime, motor vehicle accidents, social welfare program costs, and costs associated with property destruction and fire (HHS 1990).

Aware of these costs, employers implement EAPs after cost-effectiveness and cost-benefit analyses. The cost of an employee assistance program varies depending upon the type of service provided and the number of employees in an organization, generally ranging from $12 to $20 per employee (NCADD 1992). The objectives, strategies, and methods are negotiated for each program. In addition to counseling services, some EAPs also facilitate career development, training, and team-building. In some cases full-time counselors are employed within organizations and employees receive assistance from them. In other cases employers enter contracts with counseling service providers outside the organizations who assess problems and refer employees to other sources of treatment for specific problems. Many smaller organizations find that it is most cost-effective for them to enter a consortium, a contract that public and private organizations enter with employee assistance service providers.

Employers who implement EAPs realize a $5 to $16 return on each dollar invested in programs (NCADD 1992) by reducing the costs of troubled employees. How many employees are troubled? How much do their problems cost? Bergmark (1991) summarizes estimates given in various studies: 15 to 18 percent suffer from emotional or mental health problems which affect their ability to function; an estimated 13.3 million Americans have a disabled elderly parent or spouse; over 1 million Americans are infected with HIV and an estimated one-half million have AIDS; drug abuse costs employers nearly $60 billion per year in productivity losses, accidents, medical claims, absenteeism, and employee theft. Alcohol is a factor in 47 percent of industrial accidents and 40 percent of fatal industrial accidents and the average cost of one on-the-job injury is $16,800. Compared to other employees the absentee rate of employees with emotional problems is five times higher, of employees with family problems 5.7 times higher, of alcohol abusers four times higher, and of drug abusers five times higher.

In the United States, public and private sector employers were encouraged to implement EAPs to assist alcoholic employees as a result of legislation and their need to reduce costs. Broad brush programs evolved from these alcohol rehabilitation programs. In recent years similar programs began to appear in the former Soviet states where the economy suffered greater losses than the United States as a result of alcohol abuse. Computed as a percentage of gross national product (GNP), Soviet economic losses in the 1970s were 11.8 times U.S. losses. In the 1980s Soviet losses were 10 to 15.4 times the U.S. rate. The Soviet system for treating alcoholism was in two parts: mental health centers and hospitals that provided service in specific districts without charge. By 1990 the system was enhanced, and semi-voluntary treatment was introduced in workplaces, much like U.S. employee assistance programs (Segal 1990).

Reducing the Costs of Troubled Employees

To what extent have EAPs reduced the costs of troubled employees in public agencies? A review of the EAP implemented in the Commonwealth of Virginia revealed that the number of employees referred to the program who

were transferred to another job or terminated employment with Virginia, their rate of accidents, and the number of coworkers' complaints all declined while job performance ratings improved. Approximately one-half of the supervisors surveyed indicated improved performance, decreased work absences, and decreased tardiness of referred clients. This study also indicated that there was a 22.3 percent lower accident rate after clients were referred to the program.

A study of Hennepin County, Pennsylvania, employees showed decreases in absenteeism, use of workers' compensation and health insurance, and the number of sick and medical days used. A study of the Philadelphia fire and police departments showed that the costs of counseling and sick leave for employees rehabilitation were exceeded by projected annual savings (Spicer, Owen, and Levine 1983). Employees of the Philadelphia Police Department reduced their sick days by an average of 38 percent and their injured days for 62 percent (NCADD 1992).

Qualitative Benefits of EAPs

In addition to these economic incentives a major motive for organizations to establish EAPs is humanitarian. Humanitarian concerns rest on the assumption that an employee who can work through his or her problems and improve the overall quality of life will be more productive in the work environment.

EAPs also provide benefits difficult to quantity. For example, program implementation reflects organizations' motives to improve employees' well-being, to improve morale and the organizations' public image, and to facilitate employees' future development. In addition, some organizations institute the programs with no motives other than the perceived need to provide EAP services as a benefit to employees and as a cost of doing business.

The EAP Process

The Internal Revenue Service (IRS) provides one example of a federal agency with an EAP. Employees learn that the program exists and is available in orientations and through brochures that are distributed periodically. Many employees in the agency have no contact with the program. A troubled employee may access the program one of two ways. First, an employee with a problem may voluntarily call a telephone number, providing assistance 24 hours a day, and describe the problem. Second, an employee with a problem that has affected job performance may be referred to the employee assistance program by a supervisor. In either case, the EAP will choose an appropriate provider in the area and refer the employee. The employee visits the counselor and describes the situation. This counselor assesses the problem and chooses an appropriate course of action. It is possible that the problem will be resolved in a short time with this therapist. In some cases it is necessary to refer employees to other health care providers, for example, an alcoholic may be referred to an alcohol rehabilitation program.

In many cases employees make the initial telephone call to the EAP but never visit the therapist when they are referred. Some employees visit the therapist but do not comply with treatment recommendations. For example, an alcoholic in denial may not enter a recommended 28-day inpatient treatment program. Therefore follow-up systems are important components of employee assistance programs. Through these systems EAP program staff and administrators determine the number of clients who comply with treatment recommendations, assess treatment outcomes, and discover ways to improve programs.

Employee assistance programs develop evaluation systems to help managers and program administrators make decisions about the appropriateness of EAP services, identify ways to improve the delivery of intervention, and may be a requirement of the funding groups who have responsibility for allocation of program funding. Evaluations of EAPs also meet ethical needs by assessing the extent to which programs deliver services that meet promises to reduce the costs of troubled employees and ameliorate problems that impact employees' lives and job performance. Standards of the Employee Assistance Professionals Association and the Employee Assistance Society of North America may provide some criteria for these program evaluations.

BONNIE G. MANI

BIBLIOGRAPHY

Anderson, V. V., 1977. *Psychiatry in Industry*. New York: Arno Press.

Anonymous, 1994. "EAPs: Cost-Effective." *Chief Executive*, issue 91 (January-February) 35.

Bergmark, R. Edward, Marcie Parker, Philip H. Dell, and Cynthia L. Polich, 1991. "EA Programs: The Challenge, The Opportunity." *Employee Assistance*. vol. 3, no. 12 (July) 7–14.

U.S. Department of Health and Human Services, 1990. *The Economic Costs of Alcohol and Drug Abuse and Mental Illness: 1985* (DHHS) Publication No. ADM 90-1694). San Francisco: Institute for Health & Aging, University of California.

National Council on Alcoholism and Drug Dependence, Inc., 1992. *NCADD Fact Sheet: Alcohol and Other Drugs in the Workplace*. New York: National Council on Alcoholism and Drug Dependence, Inc.

Segal, Boris, 1990. *The Drunken Society: Alcohol Abuse and Alcoholism in the Soviet Union A Comparative Study*. New York: Hippocrene Books.

Spicer, Jerry, with Patricia Owen and David Levine, 1983. *Evaluating Employee Assistance Programs: A Sourcebook for the Administrator and Counselor*. Center City, MN.

EMPLOYMENT AT WILL.

When an employee's continued employment depends entirely upon the willingness of the employer to retain him or her. In other words, the employee has no contractual or other right to the job and, strictly speaking, can be dismissed for any reason or at the whim of the employer. However, because employment in the United States is now regulated by myriad labor relations, civil rights, wage, hour, health, and safety laws, the term "employment at will" is often used more loosely to mean that the employee can be dismissed at the will of the employer without significant procedural safeguards. In the public-sector, employment at will, which typically pertains to high-level or confidential political appointees, stands in distinction to civil service employees who can be fired only for just cause and have constitutional due process protection against arbitrary, capricious, or unlawful dismissals.

Employment at will was the dominant condition in the public sector in the United States prior to development of civil service systems. It was first sanctioned by the U.S. Supreme Court in *Ex parte Hennen* (1839). A federal judge fired a judicial clerk, stating explicitly that "unreservedly, . . . the business of the office for the last two years had been conducted promptly, skillfully and uprightly, and that in appointing [a successor], he had been actuated purely by a sense of duty and feelings of kindness towards one whom he had long known, and between whom and himself the closest friendship had ever subsisted" (p. 256). The Court was unwilling to provide the clerk with any constitutional protection against the dismissal because it feared that the alternative to at-will employment would be lifetime tenure. In the Court's words, "it cannot, for a moment be admitted that is was the intention of the Constitution that those offices which are denominated inferior offices should be held during life" (p. 259). Coming a decade after President Andrew Jackson called for widespread reliance on patronage appointment and dismissal in the federal service, the ruling assured that the Constitution afforded no barrier to entrenchment of the spoils system.

At-will employment remained the norm even after enactment of the federal Civil Service Act (Pendleton Act) of 1883. In principle, it was eliminated for federal employees in the competitive (or classified) civil service by the Lloyd–La Follette Act of 1912, which allowed dismissal only for such cause as would promote the efficiency of the service. In more recent decades, court decisions have afforded public employees throughout the nation protection against adverse actions that encroach on their constitutional rights. In the late 1990s, even rank-and-file public employees who lack civil service protection enjoy a constitutional right not to be dismissed or otherwise adversely treated on the basis of their political affiliation (*Elrod v. Burns*, 1976; *Rutan v. Republican Party of Illinois*, 1990). They also have constitutional protection against adverse actions that infringe on their right to nonpartisan free speech (*Rankin v. McPherson*, 1987; *Waters v. Churchill*, 1994), freedom of association (*Shelton v. Tucker*, 1960; *Chicago Teachers Union v. Hudson*,

1986), Fourth Amendment and substantive due process privacy (*O'Connor v. Ortega*, 1987; *Cleveland Board of Education v. LaFleur*, 1974), procedural due process (*Cleveland Board of Education v. Loudermill*, 1985), and equal protection (*Baker v. City of St. Petersburg*, 1968; *Wygant v. Jackson*, 1986). Furthermore, public employees have a fledgling constitutional right to disobey unconstitutional directives (*Harley v. Schuylkill County*, 1979).

These constitutional protections have so severely eroded the scope of at-will employment that nowadays it applies in pure form only to political executives, if at all. Even probationary employees who can be discharged without cause cannot be dismissed for reasons that infringe upon their constitutional rights (*Rankin v. McPherson*, 1987). High-level political appointees who serve at the pleasure of elected executives such as mayors, governors, and the President are basically at-will employees. However, in theory they cannot be dismissed for just any reason at all, such as their race or gender.

Dismissal of public employees who are otherwise serving at will but allege that they are being fired in retaliation for exercising constitutional rights is subject to a standard legal formula. In *Mt. Healthy City School District Board of Education v. Doyle* (1977) the Supreme Court held that if the employee can show that the public employer was motivated by a constitutionally impermissible factor, then the employer must demonstrate "by a preponderance of the evidence that it would have reached the same decision . . . even in the absence of the protected conduct" (p. 287).

As indicated previously, in addition to the constitutional limitations on at-will employment, both public and private employees enjoy a wide range of statutory rights in the context of the employment relationship. At-will employment may also be modified by state common law. Although enforcement is imperfect, many employees enjoy legal rights to engage in labor organizing and whistleblowing, to name just two activities employers often find particularly odious. Consequently, although employers typically can dismiss employees for a wide range of reasons, today the principle of at-will employment is broadly constrained.

DEBORAH D. GOLDMAN

BIBLIOGRAPHY

Baker v. City of Petersburg, 400 F. 2d 294 (1968).
Chicago Teachers Union v. Hudson, 475 U.S. 292 (1986).
Cleveland Board of Education v. LaFleur, 414 U.S. 632 (1974).
Cleveland Board of Education v. Loudermill, 470 U.S. 532 (1985).
Elrod v. Burns, 427, U.S. 347 (1976).
Ex parte Hennen, 13 Peters 230 (1839).
Harley v. Schuylkill County, 476 F. Supp. 191 (1979).
Mt. Healthy City School District Board of Education v. Doyle, 429 U.S. 274 (1977).
O'Connor v. Ortega, 480 U.S. 709 (1987).
Rankin v. McPherson, 483 U.S. 378 (1987).
Rutan v. Republican Party of Illinois,110 S. Ct. 2729 (1990).
Shelton v. Tucker, 364 U.S. 479 (1960).
Waters v. Churchill, 114 S. Ct. 1878 (1994).
Wygant v. Jackson, 478 U.S. 267 (1986).

EMPLOYMENT POLICY.

Consists of government programs, expenditures, and fiscal and monetary actions whose stated purpose is to maintain employment, reduce unemployment, and sustain wages. Critics charge that the United States has never had a coherent employment policy. Although sometimes relevant in some political campaigns, the issue of jobs is often an afterthought in public policy development. Commitment to full employment has rarely been articulated, and indeed, the desirability of such a state has even been questioned. Various types of unemployment require different solutions, but when and how those solutions should be implemented lacks consensus among policymakers and the general public. Tension between management, labor, and the government in the United States has made the development of a national employment policy difficult. Current efforts to create a national employment policy are complicated by several factors, including the absence of a national pension system and globalization of the economy.

The Role of Employment in Free Enterprise Theory

The United States was founded on a deep belief in individualism and unfettered markets. Massive pools of new immigrant labor allowed management to ignore workers' demands for greater rights and job security. Justifying this absence of attention to, and concern for, workers and jobs was the free enterprise theory of classical economy, a theory first published by Adam Smith in 1776.

Later quantified and mathematicized by neoclassist Alfred Marshall, free enterprise theory was essentially a theory of production. In his neoclassical theory of relative wages, Marshall concluded that workers are paid the relative value of their marginal products and are employed in the job in which their marginal value product—that is, their wage—is the highest. One worker earning more than another, according to Marshall, was the consequence of a proportionately greater contribution to total output. This type of analysis ignored the impact of race, sex, and class discrimination on whether workers got jobs, the type of jobs, and their earnings. The total demand for labor, and therefore the level of employment and the wages paid to those employed, was seen as determined by the marginal productivity in the production of national output. (There were two ways to increase labor's marginal productivity—that is, the contribution of the last worker to total output. The first was to provide workers more or better capital goods to use in production, and the second was to improve the level of "human capital" through education and training.) Wage and differential employment rates for various groups reflected differences in either capital per worker or skill level of workers. Critics of this theoretical perspective noted that the differences in employment rates for groups are too great to be explained by relative marginal productivities; rather, they reflect discrimination. Unemployment rates have been particularly high for African Americans, inner-city residents, and teenagers.

Ironically, an improvement in labor productivity leads to a reduction in the demand for it, as fewer workers are able to produce the same or more and as unemployment rises. Employment, and its counterpart, unemployment, then are seen as being regulated by the market and, in particular, by the demand for labor, which is partly determined by its relative efficiency (marginal productivity). Attempts to intervene in wages and employment levels that do not fundamentally change labor productivity are viewed as impediments to efficient market functioning that artificially cause wages and employments to rise to a level above their natural equilibrium. Free enterprise theory views union-negotiated job security and wage increases, as well as government employment programs, as market interference that are among factors that may artificially set employment and wages too high.

Employment and the Labor Supply

The total supply of labor refers to the number of hours the population wants to work. If the total supply of labor increases significantly relative to the labor supply, free enterprise theory holds that not only will unemployment likely increase but also wages will drop. Unemployment, then, holds down average wage rates and results in lower wage costs, something businesses and stockholders desire but something full employment policy makers and workers do not.

Labor supply is determined by three factors: the hours worked, labor force participation, and immigration. Workers may vary in the number of hours they work per week; the average in the United States falls between 35 and 45 hours per week. The labor supply increases if a large number of workers desire overtime work or second jobs. It decreases if workers choose leisure over work by rejecting overtime work and eschewing full-time jobs in favor of part-time work.

Labor force participation also effects the total labor supply. The total labor force participation rate is the labor force divided by the population over 16 years old. Historically, due to different gender roles, the participation rate of women in the paid labor market has been lower than that for men. Since the mid-1960s, the participation rate of women (percentage of all women looking for jobs or working in the labor force) has increased from about 40 percent

to over 60 percent. Higher participation rates by women increase the total supply of labor and may increase unemployment for certain groups. In 1992, when 128 million people were in the labor force, the total labor force participation rate was 67 percent, higher than the rate of approximately 60 percent that prevailed in the 1980s. During the post–World War II period, but especially during the decades of the 1980s and 1990s, participation rates for women increased dramatically, from 34 percent in 1950 to 58 percent in 1992, and those for men decreased, from 87 percent in 1950 to 76 percent in 1992.

Immigration is a third factor impacting the supply of labor. Immigrants composed a rising share of the U.S. labor force in the 1980s and 1990s; and immigration constituted about 40 percent of U.S. population growth in the 1980s. Estimates of the number of immigrants to the United States each year are about one million, including about 200,000 illegal immigrants. An intricate quota system, which now favors skilled workers and their families and close relatives of U.S. citizens and permanent residents, controls the flow of immigrants. In addition to these groups, special quotas regulate immigration of political refugees, although economic refugees are not given special consideration. Unlike in earlier decades in which the largest number of refugees came from Europe, in recent years the largest numbers of legal immigrants have come from Mexico and other Central American countries, China, the former Soviet Union, Korea, Philippines, Vietnam, and the Caribbean. In recent years the educational level of U.S. immigrants has been high. About 25 percent of recent male immigrants have college degrees, for example, a proportion equal to that of native-born American males.

Employment and Unemployment Rates

An examination of employment and unemployment rates provides an overall picture of labor markets. The employment rate is the total number employed, divided by the number in the labor force. The unemployment rate is the ratio of those in the labor force.

Data collection for measuring the unemployment rate is done through a random sample of the population. Each month, the Department of Labor (DOL) interviews about 60,000 households about their recent work history. The survey divides those age 16 and older into four groups: employed, unemployed, not in the labor force, and in the labor force. The DOL findings, in turn, are used to calculate employment and unemployment rates and to determine changes in the status of each group that underlie macrolevel changes. Employed workers may become unemployed either by voluntarily quitting or by involuntarily being laid off. Unemployed workers may obtain employment by being newly hired or by being recalled to a job from which they were temporarily laid off. Those in the labor force, both employed and unemployed, may leave the labor force either by retiring or by dropping out, deciding to no longer seek work for pay. Those who have never worked may decide to enter the labor force, and those who previously dropped out may decide to reenter it. Each of these changes affects the employment and unemployment rates.

A relatively stable overall employment rate may camouflage dramatic shifts within sectors. Throughout the 1900s, agricultural employment declined and industrial employment increased. In 1900, 38 percent of the labor force was employed in agriculture, 38 percent in manufacturing, 20 percent in nongovernment services, and 4 percent in government services. More recently, industrial employment has declined or stabilized and employment in the service sector has increased dramatically. Until 1970, goods-producing jobs increased at about the same rate as total employment. After 1970, the relative share of goods-producing industrial jobs declined. While manufacturing jobs were decreasing, service sector jobs, including government, were increasing. By 1991, only 3 percent of the labor force was employed in agriculture and 28 percent was employed in manufacturing, but over half of the labor force was now employed in services (52% in nongovernment services and 17% in government services).

The Impact of Employment on Wages

Employment growth and policies overlap with income policies and have a significant impact on the growth and distribution of income. The shift to a service rather than an agricultural or industrial economy has been accompanied by declining real wages, in part because many nongovernment service jobs are low skilled and lower paying than are many skilled manufacturing jobs. A drop in the annual percentage change in real hourly wages measured in purchasing power over the previous ten years reflects this decline. In 1925, real wages averaged a 3.1 annual increase over the past ten years. The figures through the 1950s also showed healthy increases: 2.3 percent in 1935; 3.7 percent in 1945; 2.1 percent in 1955. In the 1960s, however, for the first time the average annual increases for the past ten years in real wages dropped below 2 percent. This marked the beginning of a long-term decline. The average annual increase in real wages in 1965 was 1.7 percent, and in 1975, 0.8 percent. In the 1980s and 1990s the United States actually saw negative growth in real wages: −0.1 percent in 1985, and −0.6 percent in 1992.

Types of Unemployment

Economists have distinguished several types of unemployment, each with a different source and potential policy solution.

Frictional Unemployment

This kind of unemployment occurs because labor markets are dynamic and information flows are imperfect. Frictional unemployment reflects the time it takes for unemployed workers and employers with job vacancies to connect. Even when the economy is thriving and the size of the labor force is constant, some frictional unemployment will occur. In the 1960s, policymakers considered 3 percent unemployed to be a "full employment" economy, implying that 3 percent was frictional and not due to systemic difficulties. By the 1980s, however, 5 percent and even 6 percent was considered to be frictional. The policy solution to frictional unemployment is to increase the efficiency of the labor market by improving information flows and the abilities of employers and potential employees to find each other quickly. Job banks and clearing houses do this. Most efforts to create job clearing houses have been in the private sector.

Structural Unemployment

This kind of unemployment results from changes in the demand for labor that create either occupational or geographic imbalances, or both. Occupational imbalances occur when there is a mismatch between the skills workers have and the demand for skills. With the decline of employment in the manufacturing sector, workers in skilled manufacturing jobs have sometimes found that their skills were no longer needed. Equivalently paying or better-paying jobs in high-tech industries, such as computer engineering, repair, and development, required different skills. Structural unemployment may also be the result of geographical imbalances, in which plant closings and industry declines leave workers but few jobs remaining.

Policy solutions to structural unemployment include providing subsidized job training to allow workers to acquire new skills, providing information about job market conditions in other geographic regions, and minimizing the impact of plant closings when possible. A federal program that includes these components is the Trade Adjustment Assistance Program, which was created by the Trade Expansion Act of 1962 (and amended several times in the 1970s and 1980s). The program was developed to provide assistance to individuals who became unemployed because of changes in product demand resulting from foreign competition. It provides expanded unemployment compensation benefits, but due to restrictive eligibility rules, it seems to have had limited impact on increasing the probability that structurally unemployed workers will find jobs.

Other policy solutions the federal government has used to reduce structural unemployment include providing relocation allowances to unemployed workers residing in economically depressed areas through the Area Redevelopment Act of 1961, providing classroom and on-the-job training to both disadvantaged and unemployed workers through the Manpower Development and Training Act of 1962, and providing both training and public sector employment opportunities through the Comprehensive Employment and Training Act of 1973. With the Job Training Partnership Act of 1982, the federal government began to emphasize public and private cooperation in providing training.

Demand-Deficient, or Cyclical, Unemployment

Demand-deficit unemployment results from fluctuations in the business cycle. It occurs when the aggregate demand for goods and services declines, causing the demand for labor to decrease. As wages are typically downwardly inflexible, unemployment results. Macroeconomic policies to increase aggregate demand are appropriate in this situation. Such policies include increasing government spending, reducing taxes, and increasing the rate of growth in the money supply. Policies that focus more specifically on labor market conditions include temporary tax credits for firms that increase employment and public sector employment programs. The federal government typically has greater capacity than state and local governments to address demand-deficient unemployment because it has the capacity to spend counter-cyclically including using deficit spending.

Seasonal Unemployment

Like demand-deficient unemployment, seasonal unemployment is caused by fluctuations in the demand for labor. With seasonal unemployment, cyclical fluctuations occur within a year, as those for agricultural and construction workers. There is also some retooling for annual changes and production for seasonal products. Most types of seasonal unemployment are also covered by unemployment insurance, which critics contend has induced even greater unemployment in seasonal industries. Others note that, typically, unemployment benefit levels are less than half of the wages workers earn, thus questioning that unemployment insurance induces even voluntary unemployment.

Unemployment Compensation

Unemployment compensation is paid to eligible unemployed workers in the United States. The unemployment insurance system is a system of separate state systems, the details of which can vary across states, although all operate similarly. Most private sector employees are covered by a state unemployment insurance (UI) system. Eligibility for benefits for unemployed workers is based on their previous labor market experience and the reason for unemployment. States require individuals to demonstrate "permanent" attachment to the labor force by meeting rules about minimum earnings and weeks worked during some base

period before they can become eligible. In all states, worker who are laid off and meet these tests can receive benefits. In some states, workers who voluntarily quit their jobs and meet the tests can also receive benefits in some circumstances. New workers and reentrants into the labor force who do not meet the tests, and workers who are fired for cause, are not eligible for benefits.

States require a waiting period of usually one week before the unemployed can receive benefits. Within a band bracketed by minimum and maximum allowable benefit levels, individual benefits are related to the individual's previous earnings. Some states also have dependents' allowances for unemployed workers, although in a number of these states the additional dependents' allowance cannot increase the worker's total payment above the maximum benefit level. Once benefits begin, the unemployed worker must demonstrate "suitable efforts" to find a job to continue receiving payments. States also impose a limit on the time period benefits will be awarded. Some states used a set fixed length. In other states the period may vary with a worker's prior labor market experience, so that workers with a "more permanent attachment" to the labor force receive benefits longer.

Unemployment benefits are financed by a payroll tax. Unlike the Social Security payroll tax, which is split between the employer and employee, in all but four states the UI tax is paid solely by employers. UI tax rates may vary across employers within a state. The employer's tax rate is determined by general economic conditions in the state, the industry in which the employer is operating, and the employer's layoff experience. Using the employer's own layoff history as a factor in assessing the UI rate for that company is called experience rating.

Employment and Job-Training Programs

Despite the lack of a coherent employment policy, the role of the federal government in employment and training programs expanded greatly in the twentieth century, peaking in the 1960s and 1970s. Before 1960, federal intervention in labor markets to provide education and training had been limited to establishing and maintaining a network of land-grant colleges, providing loans for postsecondary education, and developing temporary employment programs during the Great Depression.

New Deal legislation in response to the Great Depression included the Federal Emergency Relief Act of 1933 and the Emergency Relief Appropriations Act of 1935. New Deal agencies designed to increase employment (often by direct federal hiring of workers to build public projects) included the Civil Works Administration (CWA), the Civilian Conservation Corps (CCC), and the Works Projects Administration (WPA). During an eight-year period the WPA built 651,087 miles of highways, worked on

124,087 bridges, and constructed 125,110 public structures, 8,192 parks, and 853 airports. It also operated community centers and carried out numerous surveys of federal, state, and local archives. The WPA hired unemployed artists, and through various theater, dance, art, music, and writing projects, supplied jobs to thousands. When it ended in 1943, more than 8.5 million people had been employed by WPA to work nearly 1.5 million projects, at a cost of about $11 billion, thus leaving a permanent imprint on the American infrastructure and life.

In 1935, the Wagner Act established the Federal-State Employment Security System, which included unemployment compensation as well as state employment agencies. In 1937, the Bureau of Apprenticeship and Training was created within the Department of Labor. The Fair Labor Standards Act of 1938 established a wage rate below which hourly wages could not be reduced, as well as overtime pay for workers who worked more hours than the normal work week and restrictions on the use of child labor. The minimum-wage provisions were constructed to guarantee workers a reasonable wage and were designed to protect workers and reduce the incidence of poverty. When the minimum wage was established at $0.25 per hour, its provisions covered about 43 percent of all nonsupervisory personnel. By 1991, it covered 88 percent of nonsupervisory personnel and was set at $4.25 per hour. Critics contended that increases had not kept up with the cost of living. The minimum wage typically vacillated between 45 percent and 50 percent of the average hourly earnings in manufacturing until the 1990s, when it fell to as low as 32 percent of manufacturing wages.

In 1946, amid concerns that returning veterans from World War II would glut labor markets and create a depression, Congress passed the 1946 Full Employment Act. This legislation expressed support for fiscal policy directed toward the generation of full employment and created the Council of Economic Advisors (CEA) to advise the President on economic affairs.

Federal efforts to reduce unemployment through employment and training programs were greatly increased during the Kennedy and Johnson administrations. The 1961 Area Redevelopment Act, which introduced federally financed skill-training for unemployed workers in distressed areas, was short-lived. The 1962 Manpower Development and Training Act and the 1964 Economic Opportunity Act expanded the concepts of direct federal employment and training for the unemployed. Within the Office of Economic Opportunity (OEO) a major operating division was the Job Corps. This program trained up to 100,000 participants, but fell into disfavor.

The largest federal employment programs occurred during the 1970s, a decade plagued with "stagflation," the oil embargo, and double-digit unemployment and inflation. In 1971 the Emergency Employment Act authorized the first large-scale direct federal employment initiative

since the 1930s; it cost $2.25 billion across two years. Bipartisan support pushed through the Comprehensive Employment and Training Act (CETA) in 1973. The purpose of CETA was to consolidate more than a dozen separate employment and training programs that had been developed in the 1960s and to turn administrative control over to elected state and local officials. The primary goal of CETA was to provide skill-training and other employment-related services to unemployed, low-income persons.

When demand-deficient cyclical unemployment continued, two additional public service employment programs (PSEs) were folded into CETA, causing its expenditures to triple. CETA received considerable criticism and was replaced in 1982 during the Reagan administration by the Job-Training Partnership Act (JTPA). The philosophy of the Reagan administration was to assign both elected officials and Private Industry Councils (PICs) administrative responsibilities. Despite these efforts, unemployment remained stubbornly stuck at about 6 percent throughout most of the 1980s.

Pensions

Pensions are an important aspect of employment policy. The structure of pensions and the level of benefits affects individual employment decisions and mobility, as well as overall labor market efficiency. By the year 2030, experts estimate that over one-fifth of the population will be age 65 or older, increasing the ratio of retirees to labor force participants. The 1935 Social Security Act established the Old Age, Survivors, and Disability Insurance program in the United States. By the 1990s about 90 percent of all employees were covered under the Social Security Act. Although it was originally sold to the public as an annuity-based pension program, today Social Security meets both pension and welfare functions. Periodic reforms have been adopted to retain system solvency. Current workers pay the benefits of current retirees, and the ratio of retired beneficiaries to working contributors has been increasing. In contrast, a funded liability pension plan would have accrued assets that exist to cover the incurred retirement commitments to working as well as retired workers. Some policy analysts fear that the Social Security system may have funding difficulties when the baby boom generation retires. Though never intended to become the primary retirement income for citizens, Social Security has come to fill that role for large segments of the currently retired, partially because they lacked an adequate private pension plan and partially because U.S. savings for all functions, including retirement, are so low.

The current private pension system is a patchwork that some critics contend impedes labor mobility and contributes to labor market inefficiencies. Workers with pensions become reluctant to move to other jobs when pension benefits will be lost if they do so. Nor is the current patchwork system adequate to guarantee income security to the retired. Pension fraud and abuse led to the 1974 Employment Retirement Income Security Act (ERISA). ERISA attempted to regulate and protect private pensions by establishing new requirements in pension administration and funding for private plans. The act created the Pension Benefit Guaranty Corporation within the Labor Department to protect plan participants through insurance in the event a covered pension plan is terminated. In termination cases, however, ERISA requires full vesting of accrued benefits, and many critics contend that it is underfunded itself.

Tension between Management and Labor

In the United States, management and labor have typically regarded each other as adversaries and have taken different views on the development of employment policy. Each has attempted to shape government legislation to its own purposes. Management has stressed the use of tax incentives as tools in employment policy and has opposed unions and collective bargaining. Labor has typically supported government programs and direct government expenditures to achieve employment goals, and it has supported legislation that strengthened unions.

In comparison to other nations, the growth of the U.S. labor movement has been slow. Not until the 1930s was labor strong enough to gain legislation that supported its purposes, and then only after the Great Depression coalesced public opinion behind government intervention. The 1935 National Labor Relations Act, also called the Wagner Act, gave workers the right to call for a secret vote to determine whether they would be represented by a union, and if so, which one. If a union received a majority vote of support from workers, it had exclusive rights to bargain on behalf of that group of workers. The employer was required to bargain in good faith with the union to arrive at a written agreement. Even though employers were given the right to present their views to employees, they were prohibited from interfering with union organization. The Wagner Act protected workers against unfair employer labor practices and guaranteed them the right to organize and bargain. The National Labor Relations Board (NLRB) was created to supervise and administer the act. It was empowered to prevent management's attempts to interfere with the right to unionize and bargain, to dominate a union, to discriminate because of union membership, or to impose reprisals on an employee for testifying before the NLRB.

The legislative pendulum swung back toward the interests of management with the Taft-Hartley Act, passed as amendments to the Wagner Act. This act targeted unfair union practices as illegal and created legal protection for workers not wanting union membership. It established

penalties for unions forcing employers to engage in unfair hiring practices and for violence while picketing. It outlawed a "closed shop" in which workers were required to belong to a union prior to being employed by a firm but allowed a "union shop" in which workers may be required to join a union 30 days after being hired.

In 1959, the Labor-Management Reporting and Disclosure Act strengthened reporting requirements for both labor and management. This act also created a bill of rights for union members, regulated internal union election procedures, established limits on the control of national officers over local unions, and began reporting and disclosure requirements. Numerous issues dealing with the union contract were regulated.

Today in the late 1990s, unions are in decline in terms of membership and political power. In past decades, they have been charged with corruption on occasion and with resisting technological improvements that firms need to adopt in order to remain economically competitive. The loss of power of unions parallels the decline of the manufacturing sector, the sector of greatest union strength. Public employee unions have made some gains in acquiring membership. But recent trends, including employee leasing by firms that contract-out workers on a temporary basis, continued influx of both legal and illegal immigrants, and pressure from globalization of the economy are not encouraging to the growth of unions.

Employment and Globalization of the Economy

Economic globalization at the close of the century has significantly affected employment in the United States. Robert Reich, secretary of labor in the Clinton administration, identified three jobs of the future: routine production services, in-person services, and symbolic-analytic services. Employment policy of the future must take account of this new configuration of jobs and the economy. Routine production services involve repetitive tasks done sequentially and include not only traditional blue collar jobs but also routine supervisory jobs performed by low- and mid-level managers. The product produced can be information-oriented as well as manufacturing-oriented. Routine producers work in the company of many other people who do the same thing, guided by standard procedures and codified rules. Their cardinal values are reliability, loyalty, and the capacity to take directions. In 1990, about 25 percent of all U.S. workers were performing routine production services. Global competition, both for the products produced by these types of jobs and for the jobs themselves, holds down wages.

In-person services also involve simple repetitive tasks that must be provided person-to-person and cannot be sold worldwide. These jobs include retail sales workers, waiters and waitresses, hotel workers, janitors, cashiers, hospital attendants and orderlies, nursing-home aides, taxi drivers, secretaries, hairdressers, auto mechanics, sellers of residential real estate, flight attendants, physical therapists, and security guards. In addition to being reliable, these workers are expected to have a pleasant demeanor. About 30 percent of the U.S. labor force worked in in-person services in 1990. These jobs are not exportable, and they are not typically well paid.

Symbolic-analytic services include all problem-solving, problem-identifying, and strategic-brokering activities and involve manipulation of data, words, and oral and visual images. These activities can be traded and sold worldwide, so U.S. providers must compete with foreign providers, even in the U.S. market. Jobs in this category include research scientists, design engineers, software engineers, public relations executives, investment bankers, lawyers, real estate developers, accountants, management consultants, financial consultants, tax consultants, energy consultants, management information specialists, organization development specialists, strategic planners, corporate headhunters, and system analysts. Other symbolic jobs are advertising executives, marketing strategists, art directors, architects, cinematographers, film editors, production designers, publishers, writers and editors, journalists, musicians, television and film producers, and university professors. Symbolic analysts are typically well educated, work in flat organizations and teams, and have incomes that vary, depending on the quality of their problem solutions. Those who are globally competitive have gained an increasing share of income and wealth. With education, a greater proportion of the labor force can move into the symbolic analytic category, so that in the future, employment policy and education policy may become one and the same.

MARCIA LYNN WHICKER

BIBLIOGRAPHY

Ehrenberg, Ronald G., and Robert S. Smith, 1994. *Modern Labor Economics: Theory and Public Policy.* 5th ed. New York: HarperCollins College Publishers.
Louchheim, Katie, ed., 1983. *The Making of the New Deal: The Insiders Speak.* Cambridge: Harvard University Press.
Reich, Robert B., 1991. *The Work of Nations.* New York: Alfred A. Knopf.
Samuelson, Paul A., and William D. Nordhaus, 1995. *Economics.* 5th ed. New York: McGraw-Hill.
Whicker, Marcia Lynn, and Raymond A. Moore; 1988. *Making America Competitive: Policies for a Global Future.* New York: Praeger.

ENABLING ACT. A statute empowering an entity such as a corporation or governmental unit to peform a function. Enabling legislation, through delegation, also has

enabled or authorized administrative agencies to exercise vast regulatory powers contributing to the rise of the administrative state. In the governmental context of the United States, enabling acts usually refer to state legislatures empowering units of local government to act. The relationship of local government to state government is one in which the state governments hold all the power. They, through their constitutions or state statutes, delegate some of that power to other units within the state. Thus, local governments traditionally have been dependent upon the states for any of their authority to deal with local problems. The dependency was articulated by Iowa Supreme Court Justice John F. Dillon in an 1868 court case. The doctrine that municipal governments are creations of the state legislatures and thus derive all their powers and existence from the legislatures has become known as Dillon's Rule.

As a result of Dillon's Rule and its acceptance by courts across the country, local governments were very carefully controlled by state statute. Many court decisions took a very rigid view, thus limiting local governments to only those powers explicitly extended to them by state legislatures. Some courts, however, were a little more flexible in examining the needs for local governments to conduct their business. Nonetheless, restrictions on what types of taxes a municipality may impose, whether or not municipalities may enter into contracts with one another, and even what personnel policies they could adopt were types of controls imposed by state legislation.

In most states, the realities of these restrictions hampered local governments from dealing with their problems, especially as society became more complex and problems became more difficult to deal with. As a result, the concept of home rule emerged and is granted in all states, although not to all local governments. Most state statutes or constitutional provisions governing home rule limit it to the larger local governments, mostly municipalities. Some states also extend it to county governments, but many do not. Home rule permits the local government to govern itself and exercise whatever powers are necessary to do so. There are general limits, such as the local government's policies cannot conflict with state law; and restrictions applied to all local governments by state statute still exist. The effect, however, has been to grant much more flexibility to local governments. Local control over what revenue sources are available, however, has still been limited in most states. Thus, for example, municipalities are prohibited from levying income taxes in almost all the states.

Home rule is a general enabling act that provides greater autonomy to the local government to resolve its own problems. It has the advantage of allowing more targeted and probably quicker solutions to problems. Home rule also frees the state legislature so that it can spend its time on statewide issues rather than having to be bogged down in dealing with multiple local government problems. Home rule applies only to municipalities or, in a few instances, counties. Other units of local government, such as special districts, still are governed under enabling acts whose restrictions are very specific.

N. Joseph Cayer

BIBLIOGRAPHY

Advisory Commission on Intergovernmental Relations, 1981. *Measuring Local Discretionary Authority*. Washington, DC: Advisory Commission on Intergovernmental Relations.

Dillon, John F., 1911. *Commentaries on the Law of Municipal Corporations*. 5th ed. Boston: Little Brown.

ENDOWMENT.   A permanent fund that distributes investment income to a beneficiary but does not distribute principal.

General Practice

Many charitable organizations seek to establish endowment funds to provide a permanent source of support to the organization. Endowments permit an organization to operate with a more stable budget than if it had to depend solely upon revenue sources that vary from year to year, such as contributions and sales revenue. As a practical matter, well-established organizations that demonstrate financial stability are in the best position to attract contributions to endowment funds. Organizations that are newly established or are in a financial crisis rarely succeed.

An endowment is sometimes confused with an operating reserve. An operating reserve provides investment income, but the charity can also withdraw principal if there is an emergency. With a true endowment the charity cannot withdraw principal even if there is an emergency.

Some charities own and invest their own endowment funds, but many others have the funds invested in a separate trust or corporation or by a local community foundation. A separate entity can increase contributions to the endowment fund because donors often want assurance that the charity will be unable to invade the principal of the fund. For example, when several symphonies became insolvent, the symphonies that controlled their own endowment funds either spent their principal or were forced to pay the amounts to creditors. Endowment funds that were invested separately, such as in a community foundation, continued to exist to support classical music after the symphony went out of existence. The funds endowed a new symphony or distributed income each year to other classical music organizations.

Legal Issues

Whether the principal of an endowment fund can be invaded depends upon the legal documents that govern the endowment fund. An important document is the "instrument of transfer" that a donor uses to make a gift to the endowment fund. Other important documents, particularly if the fund is held by a separate entity, are the fund's organizational documents: articles of incorporation (for a corporation) or the trust instrument (for a trust). These documents may contain numerous restrictions, including restrictions on the distribution of principal.

An instrument of transfer can be as complicated as a trust instrument or as simple as a letter. The donor may have imposed restrictions on the use of the assets in the endowment fund and the charity must honor them. In addition to specifying whether distributions can be made from principal, the instrument of transfer may contain specific restrictions about how the income is to be used. For example, a donor can require an endowment to be used to fund certain types of scholarships for a designated class of students (for example, graduates of a specific high school). If the instrument of transfer fails to specify what should happen if a requirement is not met or if circumstances change (for example, if the endowed charity goes out of existence), the affected parties may have to petition a court to resolve the problem. Courts often apply the legal doctrines of "cy-pres" or "equitable deviation" to modify the donor's restrictions in a manner that is consistent with the donor's intent. In extreme cases a court can order a trust to be terminated and the proceeds distributed to the donor's heirs rather than to a charity if it is impossible to carry out a donor's intentions.

The amount of the net income that should be distributed depends upon the terms of the governing document of the endowment fund and whether it is held by a trust or a corporation. In addition to administrative restrictions that may have been imposed by a charity on its endowment funds and specific restrictions that may have been imposed by a donor, there could be provisions in the organization's governing instrument (the articles of incorporation or the trust instrument) that govern the administration of the fund. For example, such documents might contain definitions of income and principal.

In the absence of specific provisions in the governing instrument, most states have laws that determine what is income and what is principal. Most trusts are governed by the Uniform Principal and Income Act. It defines income to include interest, dividends, rents, and royalties, but generally excludes capitals gains. For example, if a trust had $20,000 of interest, $10,000 of dividends, and $40,000 of gain from the sale of stock, the trust would have income of $30,000. The $40,000 of gain would be classified as principal and would be reinvested. If, however, the trust instrument has a provision that conflicts with the act (e.g., it defines a capital gain as income rather than principal), then generally the trust instrument takes priority over the act.

Many states have adopted the Uniform Management of Institutional Funds Act, which applies to many endowment funds held or administered by corporations and certain trusts. It is possible under this law that capital gains will be classified as income that can be distributed, unless a donor specifically, requires such gains to be retained as principal.

CHRISTOPHER HOYT

ENERGY POLICY.

The means by which governments respond to concerns over the supply, utilization, and consequences of energy use.

Energy policy is of particular importance to modern industrial societies because of their fundamental dependence upon the transformation of energy for their continued well-being and for their very existence. Some characteristics of energy resources and the technology of their transformation into useful forms add to the complexity of energy policy.

Industrialization was marked historically by the substitution of fossil fuels for renewable energy sources such as wood, wind, water, and human and other animal motive power. Initially, this involved the use of coal, and, later, reliance upon oil, natural gas, and nuclear energy.

Consumption of energy on a global basis has increased about eightfold since 1900, with half of this being consumed in Western Europe, North America, Australia, and Japan.

In addition to direct applications of heat produced by burning fossil fuels, modern societies have become increasingly reliant upon electricity, necessary for many industrial processes and domestic appliances as well as for the information and communications technology which is at the core of modern society.

For these reasons, energy policy is an important concern for most governments, in a way in which policy relating to many other resources or commodities is not. Most countries are dependent to a greater or lesser extent upon imported energy, rather than that coming from domestic production, and are thus vulnerable to exogenous shocks in supply or price. Hence, energy policy is an area of government activity that is international in orientation, but comprises many domestic issues.

Dependency on energy is primarily a reliance on fossil fuels (oils, gas, and coal), which provide 90 percent of global consumption. One of the greatest issues for energy policy concerns the problems of resource depletion, since oil supplies almost 40 percent of energy demand and current reserves can only provide for about 40 years' consumption at this level. Coal is less scarce, with adequate reserves for 250 years, but it cannot technically be substituted for many uses of oil products.

Petroleum Industry and Policies

At the international level, oil is the most important focus of energy policy. Though oil deposits are located predominantly in the Middle East (63 percent of reserves), in North Africa, and in other non-Western nations, the demand for oil products developed more quickly in the industrial economies of Western Europe, North America, Australasia, and Japan (55 percent of consumption). This dependency upon imported energy elevated oil to strategic significance for these Western nations. Access to oil supplies became a vital consideration for all nations during World War II and the Cold War. Because many oil-producing nations were Islamic, oil became embroiled in the conflict surrounding the state of Israel in Middle East politics.

Ownership in the petroleum products industry exhibits substantial vertical integration, with large transnational conglomerates—such as Shell, British Petroleum, Exxon, and Texaco—owning tankers, refineries, and wholesale and retail distribution plants. This dominant market position, coupled with the strategic importance of oil, has made the industry the subject of much government regulation to control prices and ensure security of supply.

A vital political actor since its formation in 1960 has been the Organization of Petroleum Exporting Countries (OPEC), an organization that, especially between 1973 and 1986, exercised domination over world oil markets by acting as a cartel and limiting production to drive up prices. (The members of OPEC during this period were Algeria, Ecuador, Gabon, Indonesia, Iran, Iraq, Kuwait, Libya, Nigeria, Qatar, Saudi Arabia, the United Arab Emirates, and Venezuela.)

OPEC's tactics succeeded in driving up the price of oil from $3 to $10 per barrel in 1973, thus taking advantage of uncertainty over supplies during war in the Middle East. Again, after the Iranian Revolution in 1979, OPEC drove the price to $30 per barrel by 1980. Both of these events caused considerable disruption to national economies dependent upon oil, but, this exposure of the countries' vulnerability stimulated policy responses aimed at reducing their dependence on oil.

During the 1980s, OPEC's market dominance was undermined by increasing production from non-OPEC sources, as well as by the substitution of fuels, such as coal for oil, and the conservation of energy, both of which were actively encouraged by government policies. These factors led to the collapse of oil prices in the first half of 1986, when they fell from $28 per barrel to $10 per barrel.

One policy problem for the governments has been how to set prices for oil produced from domestic sources when prevailing world prices had escalated rapidly. The economically preferable prescription was to set prices at world parity, since this price would encourage conservation, fuel substitution, and further exploration for new sources, all of which would decrease reliance on oil imported from OPEC countries. This path was followed in many countries, sometimes with additional government taxes encouraging demand reduction still further.

In the United States, however, attempts by the Carter administration to develop a comprehensive national energy policy were undermined in Congress by oil and consumer interests, and so prices in the United States have not reflected prevailing world prices. Though the impact of this failure has been lessened by the softening of world prices from 1986, it has done little to encourage substitution and conservation. Meanwhile the United States is becoming increasingly reliant on imports as domestic reserves become depleted.

Electricity Industry and Policies

In most countries, including the United States, electricity has been more effectively regulated. This is largely because this energy source has long been regarded to be of special importance in modern societies, since there are many uses for which there is no substitution. It cannot be stored economically, and it must be produced and delivered on demand through large complex transmission and distribution systems. Because electrical energy has long been regarded as a natural monopoly, it has either been placed in government ownership or subjected to regulation. Increasingly, technological change has undermined its natural monopoly status, and many governments (such as that of the United Kingdom) have sold electricity industry assets into private ownership, subject to regulation.

Regulation has traditionally been undertaken primarily to protect consumers from producers exploiting their market domination to extract, however, excess profits. Increasingly, however, utility regulation has also been used in the United States to encourage conservation, by allowing utilities to benefit from expenditure on demand management. On the supply side, there have been policies adopted to break down monopolies and require utilities to buy the output from independent producers at fair prices—usually the cost of the generating unit, which, consequently, can be unloaded.

These measures have been important in ensuring that greater economies are achieved in the utilization of energy, since electricity can often be generated as a byproduct of many industrial processes ("co-generation"). Formerly this was not done because there was no market for it, and utilities often preferred instead to build their own large-scale plants. Supply from independent producers and demand management have also been useful for utilities in dealing

with the costs of uncertainty in their planning activities, when they must make decisions about whether to make large capital investments a decade or so ahead. Both purchases from other producers and conservation have provided a means of dealing with this uncertainty, and they have been incorporated in new planning approaches known as least-cost utility planning or integrated resource planning.

The lead time for new electricity generation plants and other energy projects has been extended by the imposition of environmental regulations, which have required much more careful site selection and environmental modeling. The long lead-time problem in nuclear power station planning and construction caused severe financial difficulties for utilities in the United States when recession following the 1979 OPEC oil price rise suppressed demand.

Environmental Aspects of Energy Policy

Environmental issues have also surrounded the oil industry, particularly the impact on the marine environment of oil spills from tankers, the most notorious of which were those involving the Torrey Canyon (1967), Amoco Cadiz (1978), and Exxon Valdez (1989). Such issues are becoming more significant as much oil exploration and production shifts offshore.

Aside from resource depletion and localized pollution, concern has also developed over the effect of energy use on the global environment, with the production of massive amounts of carbon dioxide from fossil fuel combustion likely to produce climate change. This has resulted in proposals in the United States and elsewhere for the introduction of a carbon tax. California has addressed these issues particularly aggressively, mandating progressive reductions in the use of vehicles with internal combustion engines.

Although many governments have encouraged research in an effort to develop renewable energy resources, the most likely alternative to fossil fuel consumption, nuclear energy, has failed to fulfill its early promise, and it has met with considerable public apprehension, particularly after accidents at Three Mile Island in 1979 and Chernobyl in 1986. Large-scale reliance upon nuclear electricity generation (as in France) has also been seen as increasing the reliance of society upon technical specialists to a degree that poses risks for democracy.

These factors combine to make energy policy a difficult policy field for most governments, and will continue to do so for the foreseeable future.

AYNSLEY KELLOW

ENTERPRISE ZONES. Geographically defined areas in which tax incentives, preferential tax treatment, and in some cases, special governmental services are offered to retain existing businesses or to entice new businesses into economically distressed areas.

Enterprise zones are an important economic development and revitalization tool used in some U.S. states and in localities throughout the world to promote the redevelopment of blighted areas (Berman 1991). Although the enterprise zone concept has generated much excitement as a policy tool for helping urban areas and inner cities suffering from economic distress, the central thrust of such programs today is nonurban (Wolf 1991).

The History of Enterprise Zone Programs in the United States

Enterprise zone programs are a policy option borrowed from the British Conservative Party and vigorously supported by the Reagan, Bush, and Clinton administrations, and by both liberal and conservative American politicians. The idea was initially proposed by Peter Hall, a British urban planner, professor of geography, and Labour Party activist. In England, the enterprise zone program was an economic development tool targeted to help alleviate some of the chronic long-term social and economic problems of older industrial areas. The British Conservative Party recognized the appeal of the concept as a quick-fix policy to address structural unemployment and urban decay.

In 1979, Stuart Butler, a Heritage Foundation economist, introduced the enterprise zone concept to the United States as a way to revitalize economically distressed areas. The concept was raised to national prominence during Ronald Reagan's 1980 presidential campaign as a way to revitalize urban economies. The Reagan administration was receptive to the enterprise zone concept because it differed from established urban programs by reducing intergovernmental aid and called for a reduced federal presence in cities. The enterprise zone design is based on the assumption that a free-market environment will be created by reducing government taxes and regulations. These factors contribute to the revitalization of specially designated and geographically defined depressed areas. The assumption behind the enterprise zone concept is that economic opportunities will expand within designated areas when taxes are reduced, business loans and financing are made easier to obtain, and regulations are reduced or eliminated. Many believe that this pro-business environment encourages private sector firms and entrepreneurs to remain or to go into the nation's forgotten regions (Wolf 1991).

The enterprise zone program was popular with the Reagan administration because both the responsibility and administration of these programs were concentrated at the state and local level, reserving only a small role for the national government. The program was also appealing as an economic development tool because the private sector, not the national government, would create jobs in America's distressed areas (Gunn 1993).

The enterprise zone bill was first introduced in March 1982 by former U.S. Representatives Jack Kemp (Republican) and Robert Garcia (Democrat). The bill proposed the creation of 75 enterprise zones over a three-year period, with state and local governments nominating areas to the program. Once an area became an enterprise zone, businesses were eligible for tax incentives and regulatory relief. However, partisan politics and estimates of lost tax revenue played a significant role in slowing the passage of the enterprise zone legislation. The first piece of legislation to pass Congress was Title VII of the Housing and Community Development Act of 1987 (Public Law 100–242). Title VII authorized the Secretary of Housing and Urban Development (HUD) to designate 100 severely distressed enterprise zones across the nation. The legislation was weakened because it did not provide tax incentives to areas receiving zone designation. Instead, enterprise zone designees were eligible for HUD regulatory relief and received priority consideration for other HUD programs (Erickson and Friedman 1991).

When President George H. W. Bush came into office in 1989, he appointed Jack Kemp, one of the original proponents of the enterprise zone program, to become the new secretary of HUD. Kemp suspended implementation of the legislation by refusing to designate any federal enterprise zones until the program included tax breaks and other financial incentives.

President William Jefferson Clinton designated the first national enterprise zones in December 1994. At the time, six urban and three rural empowerment zones and 95 enterprise communities were selected to receive federal grants, tax breaks, and other forms of federal assistance. Urban designations were made by Henry Cisneros (Secretary of HUD), based upon a community's potential to satisfy five key principles: economic opportunity, sustainable community development, community-based partnerships with grassroots support, a strategic vision for change, and innovation and creativity. The program provides about US $2.5 billion in tax incentives and approximately US $1.3 billion in cash awards to cities and communities over a ten-year period (Simendinger and Saenz 1994).

Differences in and Criticisms of Enterprise Zone Programs

During the 1980s, states across the nation did not wait for the national government to make the enterprise zone designations. Instead, the states created their own versions of enterprise zones and a variety of different and unique enterprise zone programs emerged from their efforts (Erickson and Friedman 1991).

State enterprise zone programs differ in their size, structure, and complexity and in the criteria used to create them. Zones also vary according to their administration and in their relationship to other government programs. The variations among enterprise zone programs are even greater considering the different incentives offered to entice businesses into an area. Some of the most common incentive packages include tax breaks (i.e., sales, property, personal, corporate, income, and franchise taxes), loan guarantees, subsidies, and permitting or rezoning options (Wolf 1991, pp. 58–74). These incentives are often buttressed with government expenditures for infrastructure improvements, public works projects, job-training programs, and increased police protection. Without enterprise zones in place, it is likely that cities, states, and the national government would neglect such programs (Gunn 1993, pp. 432–449).

Enterprise zones have been successful in states where tax incentives and other strategies for eliminating poverty are combined (e.g., Indiana and New Jersey). In contrast, zone programs have failed in states where government officials offer tax incentives, but have turned away from the area's larger socioeconomic problems (e.g., Connecticut and Louisiana). Since enterprise zone programs strive to be unique, it has been difficult to measure their achievements or to evaluate the costs and benefits that they entail (James 1991, pp. 225–240).

Although enterprise zone programs are popular, critics have raised questions regarding the fairness of a program that singles out a limited number of geographic areas for special treatment. This is a serious concern because gains in employment and investment within zones may contribute to employment and investment declines outside the zones (James 1991, pp. 225–240). Critics also point out instances in which localities have clashed with their neighbors, with other political actors, and with state bureaucrats over the location, value, and operation of enterprise zones (Wolf 1991, pp. 58–74). However, the latter criticism may diminish over time due to the Clinton Administration's program, which emphasizes building multicommunity collaborative partnerships. Despite these criticisms, the attractiveness of the enterprise zone program is evidenced by the selection of over 3,000 zones in 38 states and the District of Columbia (Gunn 1993, pp. 432–449).

BERNADETTE T. MUSCAT

BIBLIOGRAPHY

Berman, David R., 1991. "The Politics of Planning and Development." In David R. Berman, *State and Local Politics*. 6th ed. Dubuque, IA: Wm. C. Brown, 356.
Erickson, Rodney A., and Susan W. Friedman, 1991. "Comparative Dimensions of State Enterprise Zone Policies." In Roy E. Green, ed., *Enterprise Zones, New Directions in Economic Development*. Newbury Park, CA: Sage, 155–176.
Gunn, Elizabeth M., 1993. "The Growth of Enterprise Zones: A Policy Transformation," *Policy Studies Journal*, vol. 21 (3): 432–449.
James, Franklin, 1991. "The Evaluation of Enterprise Zone Programs." In Green, *Enterprise Zones, New Directions in Economic Development*. Newbury Park, CA: Sage, 225–240.
Simendinger, Alexis, and Julian Saenz, 1994. "Tax Policy: Clinton Names Nine Empowerment Zones Eligible for Grants, Aid, Tax Breaks." *The Bureau of National Affairs (BNA), Washington Insider*, December 22.
Wolf, Michael Allan, 1991. "Enterprise Zones through the Legal Looking-Glass." In Green, *Enterprise Zones, New Directions in Economic Development*. Newbury Park, CA: Sage, 58–74.

ENTITLEMENT. A benefit, either financial or in kind, provided by the federal government to individuals, subordinate units of government, or businesses. Entitlements are established by legislation, or statutory law, which spells out the size or nature of the benefit and the criteria that recipients must meet to qualify for the benefit. The fact that entitlement benefits derive from statutory law implies that they are inviolate and, like traditional property rights, protected by the courts. If the government failed to provide the benefits established by entitlement legislation, those eligible to receive benefits could sue to enforce payment. Thus recipients are said to be entitled to these benefits.

The largest, best known, and most popular entitlement programs in the United States are Social Security, Medicare, and Medicaid. These three programs, combined with the retirement programs for federal government workers and members of the United States military, made up more than 80 percent of all federal entitlement spending in 1995 (Congressional Budget Office [CBO] 1995a, p. 26).

Depending upon the degree of specificity used to characterize them within the federal budget, there may be as many as 232 entitlements or as few as 17. The larger number represents all entitlement accounts paid from either the general fund of the United States Treasury or a trust fund. These 232 entitlement accounts composed 97 percent of entitlement spending in 1992 (Cahill 1992, p. 17). At a greater level of aggregation, Congress has stipulated 78 accounts as "appropriated entitlements and mandatories" (U.S. Congress. House. 1990, p. 1176). At the highest level of aggregation, entitlements are reflected by the 17 programs (plus "other") listed by the Congressional Budget Office in its annual reports to the Congress (CBO 1995c, p. 41).

The Establishment of Contemporary Entitlements

Entitlement programs have been in existence since the beginning of the American governmental experience. Military retirement was provided in 1776 and civilian federal

retirement in 1920. (Hagar 1993, pp. 24, 25) However, the structure of the modern entitlement system was put in place in two waves of legislation later in the twentieth century. The first wave occurred during the 1930s, the period of the Great Depression. The Social Security Act of 1935 was the centerpiece of a set of programs that used public resources to provide economic security for large numbers of private citizens and to stabilize the economy. Other entitlements established during this period were unemployment compensation, railroad retirement, Aid to Families with Dependent Children, and deposit insurance (Schick 1984, p. 36).

The second wave came in the 1960s when Medicare and Medicaid, the two largest federal health care entitlement programs, were added. These programs were the most significant achievements of the "Great Society," the policy agenda of President Lydon Johnson. The food stamp program, which has been treated as an entitlement by Congress even though, technically, it is not in that category, was also established during the Great Society period (Hagar 1993, p. 24).

Evolution of the Term Entitlement

The use of the term "entitlement" dates to the middle part of the twentieth century. Until the 1990s, entitlement programs such as Social Security and Medicare were usually referred to by their particular programmatic names rather than as entitlements. Popular usage of entitlement to describe these programs was the result of three phenomena. The first of these began in the 1960s, roughly coincident with the Great Society wave of entitlement creation. This phenomenon primarily concerned the policy and legal characteristics of entitlement programs. During this period, supporters of new and more broadly defined entitlement programs defended them by arguing that beneficiaries were "entitled" to such benefits under the law, much as holders of property enjoyed legal protection. The "new property" theory of public law, which emerged during this period, asserted that beneficiaries had rights of due process in the distribution of program benefits. (Weaver 1985, p. 308)

The second source of the popularization of entitlement originated in the 1980s and 1990s and is linked to the fiscal stress characteristic of U.S. politics during this period. The fiscal impact of spending for entitlement programs, particularly its contribution to the budget deficit, and the treatment of entitlement programs within the budget process became an important part of the annual budget debate in Congress. The federal budget deficit became a significant and persistent political problem in the 1980s. The deficit and the debt hit unprecedented peacetime levels during the Reagan administration (1981–1989), when the deficit exceeded $200 billion and 6 per-

cent of the gross domestic product (GDP) and the debt grew to more than $1.1 trillion and 42 percent of the GDP (CBO 1995c, pp. 92, 93).

As the deficit grew, attention was drawn to those portions of federal spending that were experiencing significant growth. Entitlement spending was contrasted with discretionary spending, the other major category of federal spending, as well as interest on the federal debt. The most dramatic surge in entitlement spending took place between 1966 and 1976, during which it grew from 30 percent of the budget to 51 percent (CBO 1995, p. 96). This growth was attributed to spending for the newly established health care programs (Medicare and Medicaid), food stamps, and Supplemental Security Income, and expansions in Social Security benefits (Hagar 1993, p. 27).

By the mid-1990s, entitlement spending had increased slightly to 55 percent of total federal spending, and its rate of growth continued to outpace other federal spending. In 1995, the CBO estimated that entitlement spending would grow by an average of 6.8 percent annually for the rest of the decade, while the remaining components of the budget would grow half as fast, at an average of 3.4 percent annually. At this pace entitlement spending would account for nearly two-thirds of total federal spending by 2004, absent changes in fiscal policy (CBO 1995b, pp. 3, 219).

Although the entitlement component of the federal budget grew faster than other components, certain large entitlements have experienced extraordinary growth, and others have grown moderately or declined. The health care entitlements, that is, Medicare and Medicaid, have seen the most rapid growth and are expected to continue such growth unless effective reforms are put in place. The CBO estimated that spending for these two entitlements will increase 8 percent annually, after inflation, between 1993 and 1999. Aid to Families with Dependent Children, by contrast, is projected to increase by less than 1 percent annually, after inflation, over this same period (CBO 1994, p. 3). Because spending for the health care programs makes up such a large percentage of total entitlement spending, the growth in health care spending explains much of the overall entitlement growth pattern.

The status of the health care entitlements is important for two other reasons. When Congress and the President attempt to restrain entitlement spending as part of deficit reduction, they have usually attempted to restrain these large and rapidly growing programs. But controlling their growth is difficult, not only because Medicare in particular enjoys broad voter support but also because Medicare and Medicaid are part of a larger health care economy where growth is typically greater than overall economic growth. Moreover, the number of U.S. citizens who receive health care through Medicare and Medicaid has grown significantly since they were established. By 1992, 21 percent of the population was receiving health care through these programs, and estimates indicated that this number will continue to rise through the end of the century (CBO 1992, p. 38).

It became increasingly difficult for Congress and the President to reduce the deficit without combining entitlement cuts with reductions in spending for discretionary programs, such as defense. Cutting the large entitlements, particularly Social Security, was politically risky, however, because of the high levels of support they enjoyed among voters. The more an entitlement is considered a "right," the more difficult it is for elected officials to propose cuts. Social Security, it was said, was the "third rail" for U.S. politicians—"touch it and you die."

The third source of the growth in the popularization of the term "entitlement" stems from the means of financing the largest of these programs. Recipients of Social Security and Medicare are thought to be "entitled" to benefits by virtue of the contributions they and their employers made. These contributions are in the form of taxes paid into trust funds established to receive them and make benefit payments. The payroll tax used for its purpose is referred to as the FICA tax, for Federal Insurance Contributions Act.

Entitlements and Trust Funds

Social Security, Medicare, federal civilian and military retirement benefits are paid out of trust funds. With the exception of military retirement, which is entirely funded by the government, beneficiaries of these other major entitlements contribute to the trust fund through taxes on wages paid by employers and employees during their working years. When they become eligible to receive benefits, beneficiaries receive payments from the trust funds. The trust funds for Social Security and the portion of Medicare that pays hospital bills are provided by the FICA tax.

Benefits, are not determined solely on the basis of the amount paid through these taxes, however. Consequently, the amount received by a beneficiary during his or her life may be greater or lesser than the amount paid in by employee and employer. The difference between these amounts is determined by such factors as the length of time during which the payroll tax was paid as compared with the length of time during which benefits are received and the extent to which benefits were increased during a beneficiary's retirement period. From the beginning, the Social Security program—the largest entitlement—has paid beneficiaries more than was contributed, including interest on those contributions (Steuerle and Bakija 1994, p. 108).

Social Security and Medicare, best exemplify the "self financing" dimension of entitlements associated with trust funds, as well as the intergenerational equity issues that

sometimes arise from it. Combined, these programs ran surpluses of more than $70 billion in 1995, in other words, payroll taxes earmarked for these programs (plus the interest earned on existing surpluses) exceeded payments to beneficiaries by this amount (CBO 1995, p. 30). Because there was a surplus, and because beneficiaries and their employers contributed to the trust fund during their working years, the beneficiaries assert entitlement to their benefits. The benefits are considered to be earned, much as those from a conventional insurance policy. The fact that beneficiaries contributed to these programs is sometimes used to distinguish Social Security and Medicare from "welfare," that is, programs such as food stamps, which require no contributions.

But due to disparities between the amounts paid in and the formula for making payments, older Americans in 1995 were receiving two to five times as much in Social Security benefits and more than ten times as much in Medicare benefits as they and their employers contributed in taxes, including interest on those contributions (Peterson 1994, p. 44). This issue, referred to as the individual equity or actuarial fairness issue, was particularly relevant for Social Security during that program's early years. During that period, no recipients of Social Security made contributions that approximated the benefits they received (Steuerle and Bakija 1994, p. 19).

In general, the benefit formula for Social Security combines some redistribution of wealth with the notion of universal participation in a retirement plan funded by contributions. Social Security has been regressive within generations for most of its history. Within a cohort of beneficiaries, those with the highest incomes have received the largest increment of benefits above their contributions. It is becoming less regressive within generations, as higher income recipients will no longer receive more in benefits than they paid in contributions plus interest. (Steuerle and Bakija 1994, p. 111).

The Budget Process and Entitlements

Within the context of the federal budget, spending for entitlement programs is frequently referred to as "direct," "backdoor," "relatively uncontrolled," or "mandatory" spending. These terms indicate that budgeting for entitlements is different from the process used to fund nonentitlement programs; specifically, there is less flexibility involved in the budget procedures affecting entitlements. Unless Congress changes the statutes underlying entitlements, it must make the appropriate levels of funds available each year (see **Reconciliation**). The amount to be made available is determined by the number of people eligible for benefits, the size of the benefits and the state of the economy (because many benefits are linked to infla-

tion). Once established by statute, most entitlements are permanently appropriated. The funds for some entitlements, for example, veterans' pensions and food stamps, are also included in annual appropriations bills. However, spending for these "appropriated entitlements" is still considered mandatory because Congress must make the funds available unless it changes the underlying statutes.

Programs that are not established by statute, spending for which is referred to as discretionary, are funded by Congress on an annual basis. Defense, criminal justice, environmental protection, and road construction are examples of discretionary programs. Each year, decisions are made regarding the proper level of funding for these programs, which is then included in one of the appropriations bills passed by Congress and sent to the President for approval. These decisions take place within the framework of classical budgeting—resources are compared to requirements and adjustments are made, usually at the margin, on an annual basis.

To adjust spending for entitlement programs, however, the underlying legislation that established the program and set criteria for receipt of benefits, as well as the level of those benefits must be changed. This is a more demanding task, both procedurally and politically, and it departs from the decision mode characteristic of classical budgeting. Allen Schick, one of the foremost experts on U.S. public budgeting, observes that entitlement budgeting "merges the legislative and the spending decisions (and in the trust funds, such as Social Security, the revenue decision) in a single measure, thereby separating these decisions from discretionary annual appropriations" (1987, p. 18). Another authority on public budgeting, Aaron Wildavsky, asserted that combining legislation and appropriation in a single measure in an environment hostile to increased taxation to support increased spending "broke the back of classical budgeting" (1988, p. 292).

Means-Testing and Entitlements

An important distinction is made between entitlements that are means-tested and those that are not. Means-testing an entitlement limits it to those whose "means" are insufficient, that is, those who need assistance of some kind. Levels of need, most frequently determined by income, are set by Congress in the statutes establishing entitlement programs. In 1995, 23 percent of entitlement spending was means-tested. Medicaid, easily the largest means-tested entitlement, made up nearly half of this amount. The remaining 77 percent of entitlement spending goes for non-means-tested programs. Social Security, Medicare, and federal retirement benefits dominate the non-means-tested programs, composing more than 90 percent of 1995 spending in this category (CBO 1995c, p. 26).

The Distribution of Entitlement Spending

The fact that most federal spending is now targeted for entitlements and most entitlements are not means-tested underscores the significance of entitlements as social welfare policy in the United States. It explains some of the difficulty Congress faces when it considers reducing entitlement spending. The distribution of entitlement benefits across income categories indicates that income redistribution is only part of this policy. It favors the elderly to a greater extent than the social welfare policies of most other industrialized states (Taylor 1991).

By 1990, nearly half of all U.S. families received at least one federal benefit, with average benefits per family totaling $10,320. Even though low-income families were more likely to receive entitlement benefits of some kind, families with high incomes had higher average benefits. Almost all families (98 percent) with one member at least 65 years or older and no children received some entitlement benefits, and their average benefits were twice those for families without an elder member. Nearly three-fifths of all entitlement benefits were paid to such elderly families. (CBO 1994, p. 29).

U.S. Entitlements and Global "Social Security"

The 80 percent of entitlements within the U.S. federal budget comprising Social Security, Medicare, Medicaid, and retirement for government workers and the military are the rough equivalent of the "social security" practices that have taken root in most societies in this century. As many as 150 countries have social security programs of some kind. These programs derive from such traditions as the Poor Law tradition, the master-servant tradition, the insurance tradition, the occupational provident fund tradition, and the Marxist-Leninist-Stalinist tradition (Dixon and Scheurell 1993, pp. 86, 85).

The major U.S. entitlements considered broadly as Social Security are most similar to the social insurance strategy, which has dominated global social security policy. Like Social insurance practices in other countries, these U.S. social insurance benefits are employment based. Their purpose is to minimize poverty among mostly middle-class citizens, rather than to effect significant income redistribution.

The small portion of U.S. entitlements (roughly one-fifth) that is means-tested resembles the social assistance strategy. Standards of need determine who will receive such benefits, and income from tax payers is transferred to those in need through the general fund.

Two other Social Security traditions evident outside the United States are absent here. The social allowance approach provides benefits universally, without regard to income, employment, or means. National provident funds, which reflect still another approach to Social Security, are mandatory savings plans that are publicly administered. Employees and, frequently, employers contribute to these plans, which then provide lump sum benefits. These approaches to social security have no meaningful counterparts within the U.S. system of entitlement benefits.

RICHARD DOYLE

BIBLIOGRAPHY

Cahill, Kenneth, 1992. "Entitlements and other Mandatory Spending." Washington, DC: Congressional Research Service.

Congressional Budget Office (CBO), 1992. *Projections of National Health Expenditures.* Washington, DC: GPO.

———, 1994. *Reducing Entitlement Spending.* Washington, DC: GPO.

———, 1995a. *The Economic and Budget Outlook: Fiscal Years 1996–2000.* Washington, DC: GPO.

———, 1995b. *The Economic and Budget Outlook: An Update.* Washington, DC: GPO.

———, 1995c. *Reducing the Deficit: Spending and Revenue Options.* Washington, DC: GPO.

Dixon, John, and Robert Scheurell, 1993. "Social Security: A Cross-cultural Perspective." *Policy Studies Review* 12: 85–91.

Executive Office of the President, Office of Management and Budget, 1995. *Budget System and Concepts of the United States Government.* Washington, DC: GPO.

Hagar, George, 1993. "Entitlements: The Untouchable May Become Unavoidable." *Congressional Quarterly,* Jan. 2: 22–30.

Ornstein, Norman, 1993. "Roots of 'Entitlements,' and Budget Woes." *Wall Street Journal,* Dec. 14.

Peterson, Peter, 1994. "Entitlement Reform: The Way to Eliminate the Deficit." *New York Review of Books,* Apr. 7:39–47.

Rubin, Irene, 1990. *The Politics of Public Budgeting.* Chatham, NJ: Chatham House Publications.

Safire, William, 1993. *Safire's New Political Dictionary.* New York: Random House.

Schick, Allen, 1984. *Legislation, Appropriations, and Budgets: The Development of Spending Decision-Making in Congress.* Washington, DC: Congressional Research Service.

——— (U.S. Congress. House Committee on the Budget), 1987. *The Whole and the Parts: Piecemeal and Integrated Approaches to Congressional Budgeting.* Washington, DC: GPO.

Schick, Allen, Robert Keith, and Ed Davis, 1991. *Manual on the Federal Budget Process.* Washington, DC: Congressional Research Service.

Steuerle, Eugene, and Jon Bakija, 1994. *Retooling Social Security for the 21st Century.* Washington, DC: Urban Institute Press.

Taylor, Paul, 1991. "Like Taking Money From a Baby." *Washington Post National Weekly Edition* Mar. 4–10:31.

U.S. Congress. House. 1990. *Omnibus Budget Reconciliation Act of 1990,* H. Rpt. 101–964. Washington, DC: GPO.

Weaver, R. Kent, 1985. "Controlling Entitlements." In John Chubb and Paul Peterson, eds., *The New Directions in American Politics.* Washington, DC: Brookings Institution, pp. 307–41.

Wildavsky, Aaron, 1988. *The New Politics of the Budgetary Process.* Glenview, IL: Scott, Foresman.

ENTREPRENEURIAL PUBLIC ADMINISTRATION.

A philosophical position and a managerial style that stresses innovation, the search for new opportunities, calculated risk taking, an emphasis on results and performance (such as outcome measurement, revenue generation, and profit making), rewards for merit, managerial autonomy, competitive market forces, and a future orientation. It is often contrasted with bureaucratic public administration, which is characterized by stability, standard operating procedures, monopolies, close limitations on authority, lack of measurable outputs, and a short-term orientation.

French economist J. B. Say (1767–1832) is credited with coining the term "entrepreneur" in about 1800 to refer to industrialists who shifted resources from areas of low yield to areas of higher yield. Early uses of entrepreneurial management referred to the expeditions of French military leaders and French businessmen who undertook major public works. The economist Joseph Schumpeter (1883–1950) described businessmen who took calculated risks with capital, increased profits and productivity, and opened new markets as entrepreneurs.

Entrepreneurship has been most associated with start-up ventures, innovation, risk taking, and profit making in the private sector. Although some of the elements of public entrepreneurship—such as municipal airports run as revenue-generating public enterprises—have been around for many years, it was not until the 1980s that a few public administrators began to refer to themselves as public entrepreneurs. The most notable of them, Ted Gaebler, former city manager of Visalia, California, went on to help establish the reinventing government movement with the publication of *Reinventing Government* (with David Osborne) in 1992. This book expanded the notion of entrepreneurial public administration to include a focus on the customer, decentralized government structures, empowerment of employees and communities, a catalyst role for government, and mission-driven organizations.

Types of Entrepreneurial Public Administration

Entrepreneurial public administration can be viewed as either economic entrepreneurship or political or policy entrepreneurship. The most widely referred to type is economic entrepreneurship, where public managers, under pressure to limit or reduce taxes, have developed clever means to increase nontax revenues. In 1983, the International City Management Association published a collection of readings entitled *The Entrepreneur in Local Government,* which detailed the activities of several public managers who practiced this economic entrepreneurial style of management. An example of an economic entrepreneurial project is a city using its powers to acquire and prepare land for a private developer's shopping mall and in turn receiving a share of the developer's profits. This is an instance of a public-private partnership. Another example is building a municipal facility with additional space that can be leased out to private sector businesses (a municipal leasing scheme) creating nontax income that can be used to pay off the original cost of the municipal facility. Other examples of public economic entrepreneurship include the following: user fees (charging individual users for the cost of the public service consumed), developer fees (charging developers for the public costs associated with housing or business development such as roads and schools), privatization (letting the private sector take over a previously publicly provided service such as garbage collection), load shedding (ceasing to provide a service such as a city library), creation of public enterprises (such as a city harbor), and selling a public service to another entity (such as providing fire protection services to another city for a fee). These activities are supported by budgetary processes that give project managers greater control and reward saving. Public entrepreneurship outside of the United States most often refers to public enterprise development.

A second type of entrepreneurial public administration described in the literature is political or policy entrepreneurship. Eugene Lewis and Jameson Doig have used the term "public entrepreneurship" to refer to leaders in the political arena who have developed new agencies or created new policy directions, such as J. Edgar Hoover's creation of the Federal Bureau of Investigation (FBI) and Gifford Pinchot's formation of the U.S. Forest Service. Political entrepreneurs are skillful at setting public agendas, creating new agencies, and implementing new policy directions.

Democratic Concerns

Some democratic theorists have argued that the philosophy of entrepreneurial public administration as well as some of the techniques of the entrepreneurial management style conflict with democratic values such as public accountability and citizen input. Autonomy and risk taking (even calculated risk taking) with public funds by public managers are causes for serious concern. Indeed, not all public entrepreneurial activities have been successful. In the 1980s, the City of San Jose, California lost millions of dollars through failed arbitrage investments. The City of St. Petersburg, Florida, built a baseball stadium that as of yet has failed to attract a major league team. The plans that public entrepreneurs have and their strong determination to carry them out, sometimes in secrecy for competitive reasons, is also of concern to democratic theorists. The tenets of democratic theory require that public managers be held readily accountable and that the public has a right to meaningful input into the plans and actions of its public leaders and managers.

Entrepreneurial public administration's emphasis on economic rationality and market mechanisms—as well as problems with public accountability and citizen input—has resulted in criticism of entrepreneurship as an inappropriate model for a democratic public administration. Supporters, however, argue that the failures of traditional bureaucratic public administration and the public's desire for high service levels, coupled with their reluctance to pay for these services, makes entrepreneurial public administration attractive even if there are democratic concerns (which they propose can be mitigated) and a less than 100 percent success rate.

CARL J. BELLONE

BIBLIOGRAPHY

Bellone, Carl, and George Frederick Goerl, 1992. "Reconciling Public Entrepreneurship and Democracy." *Public Administration Review,* vol. 52 (March-April): 130–134.
Doig, Jameson W., and Erwin C. Hargrove, eds., 1990. *Leadership and Innovation Entrepreneurs in Government.* Abridged ed. Baltimore: Johns Hopkins University Press.
Lewis, Eugene, 1984. *Public Entrepreneurship.* Bloomington, IN: Indiana University Press.
Moore, Barbara H., ed., 1983. *The Entrepreneur in Local Government.* Washington, DC: International City Management Association.
Osborne, David, and Ted Gaebler, 1992. *Reinventing Government.* Reading, MA: Addison-Wesley.

ENVIRONMENTAL JUSTICE.

Concerns over the harmful effects of environmental hazards; in particular, attempts to address disparities in the distribution of these harmful effects and possible benefits.

Environmental justice has implications for both domestic and international environmental policies. It is germane to administrative and policy issues in an array of policy areas, including health and health care, economic development, food production and distribution, and international trade. Addressing disparities in the distribution of environmental hazards requires the creation of numerous new public policies and international agreements and changes in many others. New administrative practices, procedures, and structures may also be required.

The focus of environmental justice is not, however, just on the distribution of environmental hazards. Also of concern is the process for decisionmaking in the environmental arena. One of the principal assertions made by advocates of environmental justice is that decisionmaking involving the location of environmental hazards has been exclusive. The result has led to a disproportionately negative impact on low-income and minority communities.

These communities are said to experience few of the benefits that accrue as a result of these hazards. Thus at the heart of environmental justice is the premise that equity has not been a principal component in environmental decisionmaking, which has led to social injustice.

Justice or Equity: Does It Matter?

Although equity is a principal concern of environmental justice, it should not be confused with the more theoretical concept of "environmental equity." Although they are similar, these concepts have different historical foundations. Their differences reflect the antiquity of the dispute between philosophers and practitioners concerning the consideration of justice. Consequently, these concepts have different constituencies.

The historical development of environmental equity involved a search for the nature of justice and for acceptable principles of justice for the use of the earth's resources. Environmental justice has been more concerned with the realities of injustice and with assuring individuals that they get a just share of scarce resources. Thus at the center of the difference between these concepts is concern about the "practicality of justice." That is, can justice become a practical reality or is it merely a theoretical ideal? Environmental equity is generally an expression of the latter.

For instance, environmental equity is rooted in the moral, social, and economic philosophy of the eighteenth century. It relies heavily upon the utilitarianism that applies economic theory to moral philosophy. It is this application that gives rise to the issue of the "practicality of justice." Under this utilitarian application of economics, the just distribution of environmental benefits and costs is primarily a matter of consequences produced by a set of normative economic behaviors. Similarly, humans' behavior toward the environment is said to be determined by the moral value they assign to nature. Hence, the moral and economic philosophy that gives rise to these behaviors is the focus of environmental equity.

Two groups of scholars are the major contributors to the concept of environmental equity. Economists developed the distributive focus of the concept and ethicists provided the focus on the moral nature of human beings' interaction with the environment. Normative and empirical bodies of literature have emerged in this area replete with discussions of one's ethical responsibility toward nature and prescriptions for the optimal distributive uses of the earth's resources. The concept of environmental equity was thus spawned by philosophers and economists and is the term commonly used by academics and environmentalists. In contrast, "environmental justice" is the term used most often by social activities.

The concept of environmental justice is a product of the social justice movement. Environmental justice advocates argue that equity is more than the distribution of environmental benefits and costs that may be the consequences of normative economic behavior and the moral value humans assign to nature. Justice involves both processes and results. As Bunyan Bryant (1995) pointed out, environmental justice concerns those rules, regulations, policies, and decisions, as well as the norms, values, and behaviors needed to support sustainable communities, where people can interact with confidence that their environment is safe, nurturing, and productive. Thus, the lack of control over one's destiny, the frustration and the anger generated by both the results and the processes through which the results were derived are said to be important considerations in the "practicality of environmental justice."

These considerations are important aspects of the origins of environmental justice and can be traced back to the late 1970s when the linkage between social justice and environmental protection began to emerge. Out of this linkage developed what is commonly referred to as the environmental justice movement. Hence, in contrast to the abstract reasoning that characterizes environmental equity, environmental justice emanates from the same social realities that stimulated the civil rights movement and social activism prevalent in communities where people of color and low-income individuals live.

As Deeohn Ferris and David Hahn-Baker (1995) pointed out, the connection between environmental justice and civil rights became evident in the late 1970s when a group of civil rights activists, which included Vernon Jordan, Coretta Scott King, and Bayard Rustin, commented on the importance of environmental issues in a brochure explaining the impact of pollution on people of color. This was followed by a short-lived National Urban League initiative with the Sierra Club to broaden the definition of environment beyond wilderness and wildlife issues.

Environmental justice's linkage to social activism was further revealed in the early 1980s through a series of protest movements by people of color against the location of environmental hazards in their communities. The most famous of these involved the arrest of activists in Warren County, North Carolina, who were protesting the siting of a polychlorinated biphenyl (PCB) disposal facility in a predominantly African-American community. Also of notice were the activities of African-American children in Chicago, Illinois, who chained themselves to the axles of waste-filled dump trucks, and the multiracial coalition organized by people of color in South-Central Los Angeles that blocked the placement of an incinerator in that section of the city. The linkage between environmental justice and social activism was also evidenced by Native Americans in their resistance to the siting of waste facilities on their lands.

A stimulus for the linkage between environmental justice and social activism is the arguments, assertions, and inferences that serve as prima facie evidence of "environmental injustice" against people of color and low-income individuals—many of which were addressed in the "Principles of Environmental Justice," adopted 27 October 1991, in Washington, D.C., at the first Peoples of Color Environmental Leadership Summit. These principles affirm the right of all individuals to a healthy environment, which includes universal protection from environmental hazards that threaten the fundamental right to clean air, land, waste, and food. They call for full compensation for those who are victims of environmental injustice and demand participation as equal partners for people of color and low-income individuals at every level of environmental decisionmaking.

The Principles of Environmental Justice are buttressed by an emerging body of empirical research. Findings from this research contain persuasive data on the exposure of people of color and low-income individuals to environmental hazards. They suggest that individuals in these groups experience disproportionate exposure in every aspect of their lives; including places where they work, live, play and learn; and in the foods they eat.

Two assessments of this research are particularly noteworthy. One was undertaken by Vicki Been (1993), and the other was provided by Benjamin Goldman (1993). Both scholars conclude that there is significant empirical evidence of disproportionate siting of environmental hazard in communities where people of color and low-income individuals live.

Been's work, published in the *Cornell Law Review*, cites more than 50 studies that examine the differential location of what is termed "locally unwanted land uses" (LULUs), many of which were environmental hazards. She found that the most significant determinant for the location of these LULUs were race and income. As Been pointed out, the evidence from these studies is more than sufficient to require action to address the unfairness of the distribution of LULUs. Goldman's analysis led him to a similar conclusion.

Goldman's work contains extensive reviews of empirical research in the environmental justice field. Particularly relevant is his analysis of findings on environmental disparities in the 64 studies he examined.

From his review of these studies Goldman concluded that there are significant racial and income disparities in the distribution of environmental hazards. All of the studies, except one, reported environmental disparities either by race or income. Racial disparities were found in 87 percent of the studies and income disparities were found in 74 percent. Disparities were found to exist in a variety of areas (i.e., exposure to toxins, siting of hazardous facilities, solid waste and occupational health). These disparities were observed in all regions of the county and in both urban and rural communities.

Scholars who conducted the studies reviewed by Been and Goldman are from various professional fields and disciplines. They used a variety of research methods to complete their work. Their findings not only constitute a persuasive body of evidence but also illustrate the increasing attention given to environmental justice in the academic community. Their findings are also receiving considerable attention in policy and administrative arenas as well.

Environmental Justice as a Policy and Management Issue

Environmental justice received official recognition as a policy and management concern in the United States from the federal government in 1993, when the Clinton administration established by executive order the President's Council of Sustainable Development. This concern was further addressed in 1994 with the creation of the National Environmental Justice Advisory Council in the U.S. Environmental Protection Agency and the signing of Executive Order 12898, which spelled out federal actions to address environmental justice in minority and low-income populations.

Executive Order 12898 has had the most impact on public administration and policy. As Bryant (1995) accurately pointed out, it calls for the development of environmental justice strategies throughout a number of organizations. For instance, it mandates (1) the coordination of government agencies in addressing environmental justice problems, and (2) the support of grassroots community participation in human health research, including data collection and analysis where practical and appropriate.

Although significant, the President's administrative initiatives constitute only one portion of the effort that has made environmental justice a policy concern. Legislative initiatives at the state and federal levels have also helped to focus attention on the strong body of evidence supporting charges that people of color and low-income individuals suffer disproportionately from environmental hazards. According to Goldman, legislation has been initiated in ten states, and at least five bills have been introduced in Congress that address environmental justice concerns. These initiatives are, at least in part, a response to the mounting body of evidence on the disproportionate impact of environmental hazards. They are also the result of grassroots organizing efforts by people of color.

Several environmental justice initiatives undertaken in Congress have been the focus of significant media attention and are often referenced in the literature. Mentioned most frequently is Georgia Representative (D.) John Lewis's Environmental Justice Act, which had a companion version introduced in the Senate by Montana Senator Max Baucus (D.). This act would require the Environmental Protection Agency to assure nondiscriminatory compliance with all environmental health and safety laws and equal protection of the public health from toxic releases of chemicals.

Other federal legislative initiatives in this area include bills introduced by Illinois Representative Cardiss Collins (D.) and by Ohio Senator John Glenn (D.). Representative Collins's legislation allows for the disapproval of the construction of various types of waste facilities in environmentally disadvantaged communities. Senator Glenn's bill calls for the preparation of a demographic community information statement as a part of the waste facility permit-granting process.

Environmental justice legislative initiatives have not been limited to the federal level. Similar efforts have been undertaken in state legislatures in Arkansas, California, Georgia, Kentucky, Louisiana, New York, North Carolina, South Dakota, South Carolina, and Tennessee. Several initiatives have already become state law. These federal, state, and local initiatives have major implications for public administration in the United States that could result in a rethinking of many administrative paradigms.

This rethinking, at a minimum, will require an expansion of the regulatory science base for environmental management. For example, Executive Order 12898 instructs federal officials to collect, maintain, and analyze more information on race, national origin, and income level for individuals near planned federal facilities that are expected to have a substantial environmental, human health, or economic effect on the surrounding population. Similarly, this executive order requires that federal officials give appropriate attention to populations who principally rely on fish or wildlife for subsistence when establishing consumption standards. (This requirement is in contrast to the current practice of relying on consumption patterns in the general population.) Each agency is also required to develop an agencywide environmental justice strategy that identifies and addresses disproportionately high and adverse human health or environmental effects of its programs, policies, and activities on minority and low-income populations. Many other administrative practices and processes in the environmental arena may have to be reconsidered if a significant portion of proposed policies in pending legislation become law.

Environmental Justice as an International Policy Issue

The globalization of the environmental justice movement also has major public policy and management implications. Of major concern is how to identify, monitor, control, and prevent the transfer of environmental haz-

ards across international borders, including intentional and unintentional transfer of these hazards. In the latter category is the significant quantities of radiation released because of the 1986 Chernobyl nuclear power plant disaster in Ukraine. More then twenty nations were in the path of radiation from this accident. The disaster triggered an unprecedented wave of information gathering and information sharing between Eastern- and Western-bloc countries.

A more common transfer of environmental hazards across international borders involves the use of chemicals on fruits and vegetables, and the injection of foreign substances into animals. These have become issues of much negotiation in trade relations between the United States, Western Europe, and Japan. This negotiation has not, however, become an environmental justice issue for these countries. This situation changes, however, when products are exported to developing countries.

Environmental justice is becoming a major policy issue in international trade primarily because developing countries are not in a position to enter into negotiation over the quality of products they import. In most instances, their dependence on foreign aid is forcing them to accept trade constraints placed upon them, which usually include opening their markets to products from donor nations. This practice is believed to constitute an environmental injustice because developing countries are likely to be infused with Western products that are potential environmental health hazards. The main concern is that individuals in developing countries will be provided Western products without being provided the accompanying knowledge and technology for understanding environmental and health risks, appropriate usage, and health care that may be required.

Although the unintentional export of environmental hazards is a concern, it is the intentional export of banned or restricted products to developing countries that is commanding the most attention. This attention has been focused on two types of exports: agrochemicals and hazardous waste. Of most concern in the agrochemical area is the export of pesticides to developing countries. As bans have been imposed on dangerous chemicals in industrial nations, manufacturers have marketed them in developing countries instead. The poor regulation and control of agrochemicals in these countries has resulted in populations with the world's highest concentrations of pesticides. That this is an environmental injustice is quite clear. D. Weir (1981) and Weir and Shapiro (1987) described the dual nature of this environmental injustice issue more than a decade ago. R. Norris (1982) has also studied the international trade of these chemicals.

The hypocrisy, the duplicity of saying that what we have found out in this country is too dangerous for us but it's okay to dump it on Third World people, is startling. And furthermore, it seems to me that it is hypocritical to say that we can export our advanced technological products on unsuspecting people, but not export our knowledge and our environmental concerns to those people. (p. 102)

As Gareth Porter and Janet Welsh Brown (1991) have made clear, the expanding trade in hazardous waste is causing a similar concern. For instance, although developing countries generate less than 10 percent of the world's hazardous waste, they have become depositories for more than 20 percent of it. Most of these countries lack the technology or administrative capacity to dispose hazardous waste safely. Nevertheless, many poor countries have been tempted to become depositories for this waste by substantial offers of revenue. Estimates suggest that as much as US$3 billion is paid to developing countries annually for accepting hazardous waste. In a number of cases waste has been exported to developing without approval or as a result of bribery.

The export of hazardous waste has been the focus of many policy and administrative discussions. It continues to be a crucial issue in regional development meetings and negotiations. The Organization of African Unity (OAU) expressed its concern about the trade in hazardous waste by passing a resolution declaring the dumping of toxic waste in Africa a crime against Africa and African people. African nations in the OAU called for a ban on the trade in hazardous waste as early as 1988. They characterized this trade as a form of economic blackmail and an environmental injustice.

These countries were not without allies in industrialized nations. For instance, this trade in hazardous waste was referred to by a Dutch minister of the environment as "waste colonialism." Also in 1988, parliamentarians from the European Community (EC) joined with representative from 68 African, Caribbean, and Pacific (ACP) states to demand the banning of international trade in toxic wastes.

Trade in hazardous waste has been the focus of several United Nations sponsored meetings, including that of the United Nations Environment Program Working Group, which produced the Cairo Guidelines. It was also the focus of intense debate at the 1989 Basel Convention. The Conference of Parties, which evolved out of the convention, resulted in a protocol between the EC and 30 ACP states for a voluntary ban on trade in hazardous waste. This protocol was later expanded to include 68 ACP states. Members of the 1989 Basel Convention approved a global treaty in 1995 banning rich countries from dumping toxic waste in the Third World. Trade in hazardous waste was also given considerable attention at the 1992 UN-sponsored Conference on the Environment held in Rio de Janeiro, Brazil, and is expected to continue to be a major subject for discussion within the World Trade Organization.

Summary

President William Jefferson Clinton's executive order, as well as Congress's legislation, and international meetings, conventions, and agreements on hazardous waste represent a clear indication that environmental justice is a public administration and policy issue. This is also evidenced by the intensity with which individuals from minority communities, low-income groups, and developing countries have sought to address the disproportionate impact they experience from hazardous waste. The result is policy outputs that prescribe definitive administrative procedures for preventing future disparities. The challenge for public administration, however, is developing the technological tools and human resource capacity necessary for identifying, monitoring, controlling, preventing, and remediating hazards that are the focus of environmental justice.

HARVEY L. WHITE

BIBLIOGRAPHY

Been, Vicki, 1993. "What's Fairness Got to Do with It? Environmental Justice and the Siting of Locally Undesirable Land Uses." *Cornell Law Review*, vol. 78 (September): 1001–1085.

Bryant, Bunyan, ed., 1995. *Environmental Justice: Issues, Policies, and Solutions*. Washington, DC: Island Press.

Ferris, Deeohn, and David Hahn-Baker, 1995, "Environmentalists and Environmental Justice Policy, pp. 66–75. In Bunyan Bryant, ed. *Environmental Justice: Issues, Policies, and Solutions*. Washington, DC: Island Press.

Goldman, Benjamin A., 1993. *Not Just Prosperity: Achieving Sustainability with Environment Justice*. Washington, DC: National Wildlife Federation.

Norris, R., 1982. *Pills, Pesticides and Profits: International Trade in Toxic Substances*. With contributions by A. K. Ahmed, S. J. Sherr, and R. Richter. New York: North River Press.

Porter, Gareth, and Janet Welsh Brown, 1991. *Global Environmental Politics*. Boulder: Westview Press.

Weir, D., 1987. *The Bhopal Syndrome*. Center for Investigative Reporting. San Francisco: Sierra Club Books.

Weir D., and M. Shapiro, 1981. *The Circle of Poison*. San Francisco: Institute for Food and Development.

ENVIRONMENTAL POLICY, DOMESTIC.

The study of the interactions of natural phenomena and human society. It is distinct from ecology, environmental science, and environmental studies in that it is concerned with the choices made by individuals and groups in society as they relate to the natural environment. The purpose of environmental policy as a field is to inform choices made concerning the human-environment relationship. To do so, the field of environmental policy draws upon and synthesizes information derived from numerous other disciplines.

Environmental policy as a subfield within the study of public policy is thought to have emerged formally less than 35 years ago when Lynton Keith Caldwell published an article entitled "Environment: A New Focus for Public Policy?" in *Public Administration Review* (1963). The study of the relationship between human society and natural phenomena, however, has a rich legacy that may be traced back throughout the course of human history. In order to understand the formation of modern environmental policy as we know it, it is useful to examine the historical context in which it arose by reviewing the conservationist movement that took place in the United States at the turn of the century.

History: Domestic Environmental Policy

Since the onset of the modern environmental movement in the 1960s, primarily two types of theories concerning the scope and size of environmental problems have been set forth: The first is based upon limits to the earth's resources and the second is based upon a no-limits-to-growth perspective. The limits-to-growth ideology stems in part from conservationist and preservationist beliefs. Conservationist and preservationist theories have a rich and deeply rooted history that may be traced back to Ralph Waldo Emerson and Henry David Thoreau in the United States, and even earlier in Europe to Thomas Malthus and others. During the mid-1800s conservationist theory began to develop in the United States, but it was not until the turn of the century that environmental concerns entered the national political arena.

The conservation movement was based upon the controlled use of resources or multiple-use resource management (essentially an economic concern), and the preservationist movement was concerned primarily with the preservation of the natural environment, as the name implies (essentially an ecological concern). Underlying conservationist notions is the assumption that resources exist for the benefit of society. However, conservationists recognize resource limits, and therefore believe that resources should be used wisely (e.g., efficiently), not wastefully. Preservationists adhere to a biocentric perspective, believing that the human species is one among equals and that nature should be valued for its intrinsic worth.

Under the Theodore Roosevelt administration the conservationist movement dominated, popularizing the ideas of multiple-use and sustained yield. The conservation movement was led by Gifford Pinchot, who was chief of the U.S. Forest Service under Roosevelt. John Muir, the founder of Sierra Club in 1892, led the preservationists in their battles against the conservationist movement, but was unable to stand up against the politically powerful conservationists in most cases. The conservationist movement of the early 1900s and the environmental movement

of the 1960s both stressed a common goal—the achievement and maintenance of a sustainable long-term relationship between humankind and the environment. One aspect of the environmental movement that separated it from the conservationist movement, however, was its concern with a selective set of issues. Where the conservationists were primarily concerned with the efficient consumption of resources, the environmentalists asserted the need for protection of quality of life and long-term sustainability. In addition, the environmental movement of the 1960s was rooted in a blend of conservationist and preservationist ideology.

The introduction of the term "environment" into the vocabulary of public policy scholars took place at approximately the same time that a number of valuable contributions were made to environmentalism more generally by Aldo Leopold, Rachel Carson, and Stewart Udall. Throughout the 1960s dozens of bills were introduced in Congress regarding the protection of the environment, and by 1970 the environmental movement had enough momentum to pass several laws, including, most notably, the National Environmental Policy Act (1970), the Clean Air Act (1970), the Clean Water Act (1972), the Endangered Species Act (1973), the Safe Drinking Water Act (1974), and the Resource Conservation and Recovery Act (1976). This first generation of environmental laws was based on a medium-by-medium approach to the control of pollution and included provisions to eliminate pollution regardless of cost through a statutory framework that created a national policy for the environment. The federal government demanded results by promulgating command-and-control regulations that often called for solutions that were unattainable, given current technology, in order to force the development of the needed technology.

The one notable exception to this trend was the National Environmental Policy Act (NEPA). The substantive purpose of NEPA was to call for a national policy for the environment. In implementation, however, the procedural component of NEPA overshadowed its substantive goals. Section 102 (2)(C) required all federal agencies to formulate an Environmental Impact Statement (EIS) for any project that would have a significant impact upon the environment. NEPA also created the Council on Environmental Quality (CEQ), which is not a regulatory agency but a multimember council set up to provide the administration with timely information about human-environment relations. In addition, the CEQ was given the task of developing guidelines for formulating EISs.

To implement environmental policy the Nixon administration created the Environmental Protection Agency (EPA). The creation of the EPA was initially supported by many industry officials who wanted to one federal regulator, not several, establishing pollution control standards.

The new agency also was supported by conservationists who believed that no organization charged with promoting the development of a natural resource (such as minerals, oils, or forests) should be charged with protecting the environment against the potentially negative effects of this development. Throughout the years, the EPA has been caught between the White House, which generally has expressed concerns about the potential negative impact on the economy that pollution control laws may have, and Congress, which generally has sought to push the EPA toward rapid pollution cleanup. Other major actors in the EPA's environment include the public, environmental interest groups, industry, and state and local governments.

The EPA was given the task of working with states and localities to implement every one of the environmental statutes mentioned above, with the exception of the Endangered Species Act and NEPA. As a young agency the EPA lacked the money, personnel, and experience necessary to implement properly such a vast array of laws. As a result, states and localities were asked to play a sizable role in implementation efforts. In some areas—such as municipal sewage treatment and lead air pollution—the EPA, along with the states and localities, was able to make major strides to protect human health and the environment. However, in many other areas, problems seemed to be getting worse, and new problems continually arose.

By 1980 it had become apparent that the lofty environmental goals set during the first half of the 1970s would be difficult to achieve. The situation was exacerbated by the election of Ronald Reagan as president, who ran on a platform of providing the private sector with regulatory relief from environmental laws. Throughout the 1980s the complexity of human-environment relations became ever more apparent as policy faltered. This complexity was fueled by more sophisticated scientific understanding of the natural world and the effects humans are having upon it.

One area where this complexity seemed to overwhelm the ability of government to provide an efficient and effective solution was the area of hazardous waste site remediation. Through a number of well-publicized events during the late 1970s—including, most notably, Love Canal, which involved a hazardous waste site that was subsequently developed as a residential area and an elementary school—abandoned hazardous waste sites entered onto the national agenda. In 1980 the Comprehensive Environmental Response, Compensation, and Liability Act (CERCLA or Superfund) was passed, directing the EPA to identify and clean up old and abandoned hazardous waste sites. Though Superfund was intended to provide the EPA with the ability to take decisive action to clean up sites and recover costs from responsible parties, since its inception enforcement of the law has been riddled with problems. Relatively few sites have been fully remediated, and

Superfund critics contend that a large proportion of the money being spent is supporting private consultants and lawyers and only a small fraction actually is allocated to the cleanup of sites.

In order to move beyond past failures, the new generation of environmental laws includes a variety of attempts to improve upon environmental policies, increasing their efficiency and effectiveness. Using new regulatory approaches, such as market incentives, and proactive methods, such as pollution prevention, policymakers are attempting to increase the cost-effectiveness of regulations while at the same time improving the quality of the environment.

History: International Environmental Policy

The first efforts to coordinate conservation across borders took place in Europe in the mid-eighteenth century in order to protect migratory birds. Other efforts to coordinate the actions of two or more nation-states were pursued through the first half of the twentieth century. Virtually all of these actions were aimed at the conservation of migratory wildlife. One exception is the Boundary Waters Treaty of 1909, signed by the United States and Canada, which included a provision to limit cross-border pollution that would damage human health or property.

Even though efforts to protect the environment at the domestic level began to achieve tangible results in the early 1970s with the creation of the EPA and the passage of NEPA and other major federal environmental legislation, international environmental policy was still in its infancy. A number of works written throughout the 1970s by scholars such as Kenneth Boulding, Lynton K. Caldwell, Donella Meadows, William Ophuls, Dennis Pirages, Marvin Soroos, and Harold Sprout and Margaret Sprout provided the cornerstone upon which other work in the field now rests. In addition, the United Nations Conference on the Human Environment that took place in Stockholm in 1972 provided a starting point for many efforts to improve international cooperation to protect the environment.

A large number of the international environmental problems that have served as catalysts for action have been placed on the policy agenda only in the past 20 years. These include acid rain, the protection of wetlands, ozone depletion, the trade in endangered species, global warming, and deforestation. At least three forces coalesced in order to increase awareness of these issues and the impetus for action. First, at the domestic level many nation-states were being lobbied by citizens to promote environmental protection. Second, our scientific understanding of the complexity of ecological interactions was increasing, providing policymakers with more detailed and accurate knowledge about given phenomena. Third, at the international level there was a tendency toward increasing acceptance of multilateralism. The doctrine of sovereignty—while still dominant—was being limited voluntarily in order to establish cooperative efforts to protect the environment.

At the end of the 1980s the World Commission on Environment and Development produced an influential report on human relations with the global environment entitled *Our Common Future* (1987). This report popularized the term "sustainable development," defining it as the ability to meet "the needs of the present without compromising the ability of future generations to meet their own needs." Five years later in 1992 the Earth Summit held in Rio de Janeiro, Brazil, brought the world a step closer to realizing the concept of sustainable development. Out of the summit came a document entitled *Agenda 21,* which is a blueprint for the implementation of sustainable development on a global scale.

One tool increasingly used at the international level to secure cooperation and implement sustainable development is the international regime. International regimes (a form of international institutions) are sets of rules, norms, and decisionmaking procedures agreed upon by two or more nation-states that regulate actions that may be taken by those nation-states. Scholars of regime theory study the nature of these agreements, their causes, and their impacts upon international environmental problems.

Theory

At the most general level, the purpose of environmental policy literature is to inform. More specifically, at least three goals of the literature can be identified: to build theory in order to explain and predict, to solve problems, and to alter beliefs. At times these goals may overlap; however, they are useful as distinct categories. When the field of environmental policy is evaluated, it may be helpful to keep in mind the fact that theory-building is only one of multiple goals that scholars of environmental policy pursue. Problems solving is a more common goal.

Theory-building in environmental policy has developed slowly, primarily because contributions to theory more often than not are rooted within one of the traditional academic disciplines. Environmental policy research, however, has contributed to regime theory in international relations, bureaucratic politics theory in American politics, and a greater understanding of organizational change within the organizational theory literature, to mention a few examples. Environmental policy theory also often blends the normative and the objective.

Another challenge involved in attempting to build theory within the field of environmental policy is the fact that the concept of environment is pervasive, broad, and all-encompassing. Environment signifies relations and encompasses both the natural and the social sciences. As a result, classifications, conceptual frameworks, and theoretical systems are very difficult to develop. In addition, environment is a phenomenon that refuses to be governed by humans and human conceptions of reality. Finally, that which is political, economic, sociocultural, scientific, ethical, and historical often complicates theory-building in environmental policy.

If theory-building in environmental policy means to integrate and to synthesize on a grand scale, then little theory exists in the field. J. E. Lovelock's (1979) Gaia hypothesis, which states that "the biosphere is a self-regulating entity with the capacity to keep our planet healthy by controlling the chemical and physical environment" is one of the only "grand theories" in environmental policy. However, this is not a theory that may be easily applied by environmental policy scholars.

It is more likely that theory-building in environmental policy will take place on a lesser scale than the Gaia hypothesis. As suggested previously, environmental policy theory has developed at the margins and it will probably continue to do so. In order to increase the pace of theory-building, scholars must continue to generate and test hypotheses through use of empirical observation and analysis. The number of works in environmental policy that are based upon empirical observation and analysis of human-environment relations has grown but continues to be relatively small. In order to increase the quality of theory-building in environmental policy, scholars must take care to produce research that portrays reality in an accurate manner and must avoid the injection of bias into studies whenever possible. Further improvements will continue to lend credibility to those who study environmental policy and will yield a base of understanding from which to explain and predict.

Current Trends

As people's understanding of environmental problems continues to improve, and as policy analysts continue to search for ways to improve upon the current situation, new issues continuously emerge in environmental policy. A number of the most important issues that have emerged in the 1990s are explored next.

Pollution Prevention

Proactive approaches to environmental protection (i.e., pollution prevention) have been recognized as more efficient and effective than the reactive approaches that have been dominant up to this point. Those who advocate this aspect of environmental protection adhere to the view that an ounce of prevention is worth a pound of cure. Total Quality Environmental Management (TQEM) is centered around the notion of reducing inefficiency, which is often the cause of pollution. Pollution prevention techniques vary widely, from simple steps to reduce paper consumption by double-siding copies to complex evaluation and reformulation of manufacturing processes to reduce waste products.

Gene Blake (1994) outlined five key principles of pollution prevention, pointing out that TQEM can positively affect corporate profitability.

1. Make environment a commitment that each employee understands.
2. Put a total price on pollution, not [on] the cost of control.
3. Support the U.S. technological advantage for pollution control [which will give U.S. companies an edge in the international market].
4. Fairly value sources of pollution beyond smokestacks and outfalls.
5. Be sure products are "green" before investing in them.

Pollution prevention is not without its critics. Some fear that such a philosophy may encourage the channeling of resources to prevent problems that we are not certain exist. An example is changing manufacturing processes to address concerns about global warming.

Market Incentives for Pollution Prevention

The command-and-control regulations as administered in the 1970s proved, at times, to be inefficient from an economic perspective. This inefficiency arose in part from the application of "one size fits all" standards in a uniform manner across sources of pollution. Different sources may incur widely different costs in reducing their emissions. Pollution represents a failure of markets since those causing the pollution do not necessarily bear its costs.

To address this concern, market incentives, which have been proposed on regional, national, and international levels, offer increased flexibility to government and industry. They are intended to "internalize" the externalities of pollution. Since the amount of external costs will differ depending on such factors as location and type of pollution, the market incentive approach is intended to be more flexible than the heavier-handed approach of pure regulation.

Market incentives encourage the development of innovative technologies to reduce pollution, and they work with the market instead of opposing it. Market incentives may tend to decentralize the locus of decisionmaking, resulting in greater discretion and increased flexibility. For example, user fees are charged based on the number of units consumed of a given commodity. Such fees may be implemented for water usage or solid waste removal. The locus of decisionmaking in a flat-fee system is usually at the level of local or state government. If a user fee is im-

plemented, individuals are given some discretion to decide how much they would like to pay for what quality of benefits. If certain segments of the population are not able to pay due to income constraints, a progressive user fee system is possible.

Market incentives are also integrated into Title IV of the U.S. Clean Air Act Amendments of 1990. Title IV regulates nitrogen oxides and sulfur oxides, which are the precursors of acid deposition (commonly referred to as acid rain), by establishing an emission allowance and trading program for these pollutants. Sources regulated under Title IV are allocated allowances that permit them to pollute. Those sources that are able to attain emission rates below the allotted level may sell excess allowances at an auction held by the EPA each year. This method of pollution control gives incentives to companies to establish emissions at the lowest possible rate, in order that they may sell their excess shares. By doing so, an emissions allowance and trading program encourages efficiency and innovation.

Another example of a market incentive is the subsidy. Subsidies may provide incentives to individuals and groups to meet environmental standards by making these standards economically feasible. For example, subsidies may be provided to land owners to reconvert land use from crop land to wetlands where the overall environment will be aided by decreased erosion and protection of wildlife stemming from the wetlands.

The issue of subsidies is a double-edged sword. Whereas subsidies may be used to protect human health and the environment, they also may result in the degradation of the environment. The provision of subsidies in a variety of forms to those who harvest timber from government-owned lands provides perhaps the most prominent example of the environmental degradation subsidies may cause. As market incentives are implemented more widely, a similar ethical issue of granting individuals and organizations a "right to pollute" is likely to become increasingly prominent.

Unfunded Environmental Mandates

In 1995, one of Congress's first priorities was to address the issue of unfunded mandates. Public Law (PL) 104-4 was signed into law on March 22, 1995. The law is designed to curb the ability of Congress to impose expensive mandates on states and localities. In 1993, President Clinton signed Executive Order 12875 calling for a reduction in unfunded mandates. October 27, 1993, was declared National Unfunded Mandates Day by the U.S. Conference of Mayors and the National Association of Counties.

One purpose of all of these actions was to call attention to the growing number of environmental mandates handed down from federal and state governments to local governments. Increasingly, the duty to implement environmental laws is falling on local governments in what some call "the shift and the shaft": environmental responsibility is shifted downward but without the needed funds to implement the programs mandated by the laws. Unfunded environmental mandates affect most of our nation's governments.

The costs of federally mandated environmental programs has been estimated by the EPA to exceed US$100 billion annually. In one of the few studies undertaken, the city of Columbus, Ohio, estimated its portion of these costs to be US$1 billion from 1992 to the year 2000. In another study, the city of Anchorage, Alaska, estimated the overall impact of environmental mandates on that city to be US$430 million from 1992 to the year 2000. The 1995 federal law would make it more difficult for Congress to impose expensive mandates on states and localities by forcing Congress to take a separate majority vote to impose such a mandate. Analysis done by the Advisory Commission on Intergovernmental Relations suggests that PL 104-4 will have its greatest impact on environmental legislation. However, a provision of the law exempts all mandates that are a condition of federal aid. Therefore, in the future, if Congress has difficulty passing environmental mandates, it is possible that these mandates will be written as conditions for federal assistance. As a result, it is not clear that PL 104-4 will accomplish its intended goal.

Risk Assessment

Because environmental mandates have become more and more costly to implement over time, a number of experts have called for the use of a risk-based planning process to assist the EPA and state and local regulatory agencies in setting priorities among competing environmental regulations. The purpose of such a process would be twofold: to prioritize among various risks and to identify methods that may be used to minimize risk in the most cost-effective manner. Although risk-based planning may include a number of scientific and technical criteria, individual perceptions also affect such planning. As a result, risk assessment must be recognized as having technical, political, and emotional components.

In the early 1990s, the EPA initiated a comparative risk project that funded discussions among community leaders, environmentalists, and scientists to study local environmental conditions, rank priorities, and to attempt to forge a consensus concerning how government should address these problems. Acknowledging that state and local governments already prioritize environmental problems, the real task was to encourage such a prioritization consciously and with full deliberation. Implementing such agreements also will pose formidable challenges for public managers, as will merging risk assessment with current environmental laws. Risk assessment, like cost-benefit analysis, depends greatly on criteria that often are subjective and amenable to manipulation. Environmental impacts, though often moderately understood, are easier to verify.

Sustainable Development

Sustainable development has become an important concept at the international, national, state, and local levels of government, even though its critics view it as abstract and impossible to apply. A useful comparison is the national debt. The point of sustainable development is that because the earth and its natural resources are finite (as is the U.S. national budget), it makes sense to not live off our "capital." The idea provides us with a nontraditional perspective that unifies economy and ecology. Furthermore, sustainable development has forced scholars to consider intergenerational equity. The idea that degradation of the natural environment imposes costs and should therefore be viewed as an inefficiency that must be eliminated if at all possible draws support from business and economics as well as the natural sciences and ethics.

For example, mining towns that allow the unrestricted depletion of their natural resources eventually will be in bankruptcy. Agricultural economies that allow excessive removal of nutrients from the soil without allowing them to be replaced will go out of business. Tourist communities that allow themselves to grow to such an extent that they are polluted and congested will soon be unattractive to the very individuals upon whom they depend for their livelihood. Sustainable development requires an examination of the "ecological threshold" or "carrying capacity" of particular areas, and in the long run, the entire earth.

Environmental Justice

One of the growing environmental concerns of the 1990s is that risks associated with environmental degradation are disproportionately borne by lower-income groups. As a result, at the domestic level in the United States many groups have formed to fight for "environmental justice." In addition, a number of agencies, including the EPA and the Department of the Interior, have created offices to address this issue of environmental justice systematically. Within the environmental justice movement there is a group of people who believe race to be the determining factor, not income. This has become an emotional area of study for many, pointing to the need for further empirical evidence.

Critics of our current environmental programs point out that environmental policy in the United States generally is controlled by the "elite" of the population, usually white, male, upper and middle class. Many call for environmental policy decisions to be made with the public, not for the public. Ethnic integration of our environmental institutions—both public and private—is essential to ensure that a diversity of interests, values, and perspectives permeate our environmental policy decisionmaking processes.

Impact of Courts

Among the most significant trends in environmental policy is the increasing intervention of courts in the administration of environmental agencies and programs. This phenomenon, often called the "new partnership" between courts and administrative agencies, has its roots in citizen suit provisions of most major federal environmental statutes that encourage and reward lawsuits against polluters, as well as regulatory agencies that are not adequately enforcing the law.

Rosemary O'Leary's study (1993) of 20 years of lawsuits against and by the EPA found that federal court decisions have prompted a redistribution of budgetary and staff resources within the EPA, reducing the discretion and autonomy of EPA administrators, increasing the power of the EPA legal staff, decreasing the power and authority of EPA scientists, and selectively empowering certain organizational units within the EPA. In addition, court decisions have yielded an increase in external power and authority for the EPA as a whole.

From a macro, or agencywide, perspective, compliance with court orders has become one of the agency's top priorities, at times overtaking congressional mandates. The courts have dictated which issues get attention at the EPA. In an atmosphere of limited resources, coupled with unrealistic and numerous statutory mandates, the EPA has been forced to make decisions among competing priorities. With few exceptions, court orders have been the "winners" in this competition.

From a micro, or individual organizational unit, perspective, compliance with court orders also has become the top priority of many EPA divisions. For example, EPA staff members reported concentrating the majority of their efforts on implementing court decrees. Other programs and priorities became secondary or were dropped. Moreover, members of the EPA staff developed specific programmatic policies and changed regulations in response to court decisions.

Such judicial dominance over the formulation of environmental policy, both at the EPA and at other environmental agencies, has grave ramifications. First, the most pressing U.S. environmental issues are not necessarily being addressed by the nation's environmental agencies. Huge amounts of resources have been dedicated to meeting court decisions, when the environmental and health benefits, at times, have been marginal. Second, from the perspective of representative democracy, court decisions can differ, and have differed, from the mandates of our elected officials. Also, judicial dominance of environmental policy makes it difficult for those not a party to a lawsuit to participate in the development of environmental policies.

Regulatory Takings

A significant area that has been opened by the Supreme Court that represents a shift of authority from state and local administrative agencies—as well as state legislatures and state courts—to the federal courts is that of regulatory takings. This doctrine has not been developed pursuant to a federal environmental statute but according to the courts' prerogatives of judicial review and constitutional interpretation. The regulatory takings doctrine has been developed by the courts based on the Fifth Amendment's prohibition that property not be taken for public use without just compensation. The recent invigoration of the regulatory takings doctrine and its increased application to state and local government regulation comes at a time when states and localities have been statutorily mandated by the federal government to take responsibility for several major environmental regulatory programs, including clean air regulation, hazardous waste, wetlands protection, and coastal zone management. Many of these programs require regulation of private use of land, which has been a traditional area of state and local responsibility.

With the increased regulatory activity has come escalating conflicts over land use that have now made their way to the U.S. Supreme Court. Although the Court has consistently maintained the doctrine of regulatory takings that it devised in 1922 in the case of *Pennsylvania Coal v. Mahon* (260 U.S. 393), the courts had also almost always applied that doctrine in favor of state and local regulators, until the mid-1980s. In addition, since the 1922 opinion, the Supreme Court had largely left the application of the Fifth Amendment's just compensation requirement up to the state courts. Since the late 1980s, major shifts have occurred as a result of federal court decisions, which opened up many new uncertainties for state regulators, legislators, and, to some extent, state jurists, while also shifting more of the decisionmaking power to the federal courts. Following remand from the Supreme Court in *Lucas v. South Carolina Coastal Council* (112 Sup. Ct. 2886 [1992]), for example, South Carolina had to pay US$1,575,000 for the application of a coastal zone regulation to two lots a landowner possessed.

In *Dolan v. Tigard* (114 Sup. Ct. 1395 [1994]), the owner of a plumbing and electrical supply store applied to the city of Tigard for a permit to redevelop the site to expand the size of the store and to pave the parking lot. The city, pursuant to a state-required land-use program, had adopted a comprehensive plan, a plan for pedestrian-bicycle pathways, and a master drainage plan. The city planning commission conditioned the granting of the permit with the requirements that Dolan dedicate (convey title to) the portion of her property lying within the 100-year floodplain for improvement of a storm drainage system and that she dedicate an additional 15-foot strip of land adjacent to the floodplain as a pedestrian-bicycle pathway. The planning commission declared that the required floodplain dedication would be reasonably related to the owner's request to intensify use of the site, given the increase in impervious surface, and that creation of the pedestrian-bicycle pathway system as an alternative means of transportation could offset some of the traffic demand on nearby streets and lessen the increase in traffic congestion.

The Court sought in its analysis to determine whether the degree of the exactions demanded by the city's permit conditions bore the required relationship to the projected impact of the store owner's proposed development. After reviewing various doctrines that state courts had used to guide such analyses, the Court enunciated its own test of "rough proportionality," and stated that "no precise mathematical calculation is required, but the city must make some sort of individualized determination that the required dedication is related both in nature and extent to the impact of the proposed development." The Supreme Court decided that the city had not made any individualized determination to support its requirement that the land be transferred to the city (rather than set aside as green space while Dolan retained ownership) and concluded that the findings the city had made did not show the required reasonable relationship between the floodplain easement and the owner's proposed new building. The Court also decided that the city had not met its burden of demonstrating that the additional number of vehicle and bicycle trips generated by the store expansion reasonably related to the city's requirement for a dedication of the pedestrian-bicycle pathway easement. The Court said that the city must make some effort to quantify its findings in support of the dedication for the pedestrian-bicycle beyond the conclusionary statement that it could offset some of the traffic demand generated.

Examples of current regulatory takings issues in environmental policy include the following: When a state water pollution control agency digs a test well to monitor the flow of groundwater pollution, must it condemn the site and pay an uncooperative landowner full market value for the use of the site? Will a zoning change that reduces the development value of the land by 50 percent end up being litigated in federal court? Will exaction fees demanded of a developer by a municipality be judged insufficiently related to a legitimate regulatory purpose by a federal court? These and other questions await state and local regulators as they attempt to deal with the imperatives of environmental regulation under the watchful eyes of the federal courts.

Out-of-State Waste

Prior to the passage of the Resources Conservation and Recovery Act (RCRA) of 1976 little attention was paid to waste management in the United States. In many parts of the country open dumps and junkyards were commonplace into the 1960s and 1970s. As environmental activism increased, however, attention was focused upon the negative impacts that haphazard disposal of waste could have, including land degradation, groundwater contamination, and air pollution. Because waste disposal was not recognized as an environmental problem until after air and water quality problems were recognized (the Clean Air Act and Clean Water Act were passed in 1970 and 1972, respectively), waste management has not received the same attention as air and water pollution control.

Three factors have contributed to increasing disposal costs: the decrease in the availability of landfill space, the national regulation of disposal facilities, and the opposition to incineration as a waste disposal option. At the same time, production of waste has grown steadily since the end of World War II, and many have labeled the United States "the disposable society." The resulting waste crisis has driven landfill prices up across the nation. The East Coast has been hardest hit, with large price increases in some areas in the past 15 years. Disposal costs average from $30 to $150 per ton across the United States.

In response to waste management problems and heightened public awareness of the environment, Congress passed the Hazardous and Solid Waste Amendments (to RCRA) of 1984. The purpose of these amendments was to promote the protection of public health and the environment and conserve material and energy resources through improved waste management techniques, including the separation and recovery of waste and the disposal of nonrecoverable residues. Among other things, the amendments required the states to increase their regulation of waste. In addition to these mandated efforts at the national level, in the late 1980s a number of state governments promulgated waste management acts of their own, mandating the control and reduction of wastes. The burden of implementing such mandates, however, typically was placed upon local governments. Therefore, both states and localities were given responsibility for the reduction of waste and the proper disposal of nonrecoverable waste, promoting tensions both among levels of government and between law and policy.

Although states and localities have been expected to develop and implement policies aimed at the reduction of resources entering into the waste stream and the proper disposal of waste, current policy regarding the interstate transport of waste limits their ability to do so. Policy in this area has been shaped by the courts and their interpretation of the Commerce Clause of the Constitution. The Commerce Clause states that "the Congress shall have the power to regulate Commerce among foreign Nations, and among the several states, and with the Indian Tribes."

In a series of cases, the Supreme Court has tied the hands of state and local governments, severely limiting their options in regulating waste. Using a strict legalistic

Commerce Clause analysis, the Court has called waste "interstate commerce" and has refused to allow state and local governments to keep waste either in (see *C & A Carbone, Inc.* et al. *v. Clarkstown*, New York, 114 Sup. Ct. 1677 [1994]) or out (see, for example, *Fort Gratiot Sanitary Landfill, Inc. v. Michigan Department of Natural Resources*, 112 Sup. Ct. 2019 [1992]) of its jurisdictions.

Conclusion

Environmental policy is a young, growing, and challenging field. In 1990 the EPA concluded that the United States devoted 2 percent of its gross national product to controlling pollution and to cleaning up the environment. As new sources of pollution are discovered and the full impact of old and new sources of pollution becomes more fully understood, the delayed effects on our ecosystem become increasingly apparent and the percentage of the gross national product that is devoted to pollution cleanup is expected to rise. The policy questions and administrative challenges inherent in environmental issues are of interest to academics and nonacademics, public managers, policy analysts, environmentalists, conservationists, preservationists, and members of the general public alike. Environmental policy is here to stay.

ROSEMARY O'LEARY AND PAUL WEILAND

NOTE

The authors thank Lynton K. Caldwell and Larry Schroeder for helpful comments on a previous draft.

BIBLIOGRAPHY

Blake, Gene, 1994. "TQM and Strategic Environmental Management," in John T. Willig, ed., *Environmental TQM*. New York: McGraw-Hill.
Caldwell, Lynton K., 1991. *International Environmental Policy: Emergence and Dimensions*. 2d ed. Durham, NC: Duke University Press.
Caldwell, Lynton K., 1963. "Environment: A New Focus for Public Policy." *Public Administration Policy*, vol. 23: 132-139.
Haas, Peter, Robert Keohane, and Marc Levy, eds., 1993. *Institutions for the Earth: Sources of Effective International Environmental Protection*. Cambridge: MIT Press.
Kamieniecki, Sheldon, ed., 1993. *Environmental Politics in the International Arena: Parties, Organizations, and Policy*. Albany, NY: State of New York Press.
Lester, James, ed., 1995. *Environmental Politics and Policy: Theories and Evidence*. 2d ed. Durham, NC: Duke University Press.
Lovelock, J. E., 1979. *Gaia, a New Look at Life on Earth*. Oxford and New York: Oxford University Press.
Marcus, Alfred, 1991. "EPA's Organizational Structure." 54 *Law and Contemporary Problems* 4.
Nash, Roderick, 1990. *American Environmentalism: Readings in Conservation History*. 3d ed. New York: McGraw-Hill.
O'Leary, Rosemary, 1993. *Environmental Change: Federal Courts and the EPA*. Philadelphia: Temple University Press.
Rosenbaum, Walter, 1995. *Environmental Politics and Policy*. 3d ed. Washington, DC: CQ Press.
World Commission on Environment and Development, 1987. *Our Common Future*. New York: Oxford University Press.

COURT DECISIONS

C & A Carbone Inc., et al. v. Clarkstown, New York, 114 Sup. Ct. 1677 (1994).
Dolan v. Tigard, 114 Sup. Ct. 1395 (1994).
Fort Gratiot Sanitary Landfill, Inc., v. Michigan Department of Natural Resources, 112 Sup. Ct. 2019 (1992).
Lucas v. South Carolina Coastal Council, 112 Sup. Ct. 2886 (1992).
Pennsylvania Coal v. Mahon, 260 U.S. 393 (1922).

ENVIRONMENTAL POLICY, INTERNATIONAL.

Multinational plans to protect and preserve the environment in the best interest of humankind. The word "environment" refers to both natural and artificial surroundings. Humans have altered the environment by their actions, both willfully and inadvertently. Years of industrial abuse, misguided use of technology, and lack of governmental concern have been responsible for the rapid deterioration in the quality of the environment (Jackson 1973). The realization of the harmful consequences of environmental degradation have fostered an urgency to formulate environmental policies. Environmental policies are not single-purpose policies to preserve and protect the natural and other aspects of the environment in its unaltered state (Jackson 1973); instead, they are comprehensive policies aimed at preservation and protection of the environment, in harmony with the social and economic welfare of the country.

Science and technology had once aided humans in their intensive exploitation of the natural world, and it is now helping to determine the extent and nature of the damages and crises in it. This action has brought about a consequent change in attitude toward the environment (McCormick 1989). In fact, it has created a dramatic shift in paradigm. In the past, it was generally believed that the earth was bountiful, with inexhaustible resources for exploitation, but over-exploitation of natural resources has brought about a disequilibrium in our natural environment. It has posed serious threats to survival of various forms of life on this planet and has further helped to confirm the new findings of the limitations of the ecological system (Caldwell 1990). This situation has led to the recognition of the fragility of the ecosystem of "spaceship earth," with limited resources (Boulding 1993, p. 303). This realization has also been beneficial in creating a greater need for protection, maintenance, and restoration of the quality of the environment.

At the beginning of the twentieth century, environmental problems were local and were considered mainly to be national issues. The rapid industrialization of nations, and often the misguided application of science and technology in every aspect of our lives, has aggravated environmental deterioration. As a result, environmental problems are no longer localized; they have crossed national boundaries and have become global concerns, with an increasing need for restrictive policies to halt environmental abuses. In view of the environmental issues confronting U.S. society in the late 1990s, there exists the need for promotion of scientific and technological advancements that do not have any deleterious environmental impact. Over the past few decades, increasing reliance has been placed upon global and national environmental policies to save the planet. These policies, regardless of their scale of application, help to address a diverse range of issues—from deforestation of mountains and rainforests to depletion of the ozone layer in the stratosphere.

The need for management of natural resources has helped the various conservation movements of the past to develop into an environmental movement with reemphasis on the values of preservation. As early as 1863, the world's first environmental law was passed in Britain to control smog and air pollution. In 1865, the first environmental movement was formally started in Britain, with the formation of private environmental groups such as the Commons, the Footpaths, and the Open Spaces Preservation Society (McCormick 1989). In the United States, the beginning of the twentieth century saw the growth of protectionist movements to preserve wilderness and conserve resources.

The environmental movement was a global social phenomenon, however. In other countries, different types of soil and forest conservation measures were already being practiced during the same period. As the environmental movement gathered momentum in various countries of the world, it spread across continents and created revolutionary changes in attitudes toward protection of the global environment.

The global concern for the protection of the environment led to the United Nations Conference on the Human Environment at Stockholm in 1972. This conference helped to reach a consensus in the prioritization of environmental issues in international and national agendas and paved the way for international cooperation in environmental matters (Caldwell 1995). The international concern for environmental protection has also led to the formation of diverse non governmental organizations (NGOs). These organizations range from scientific and professional associations to religious and philanthropic coalitions with the common objective of defending Earth.

The global and local organizations had a profound impact upon the environmental policies of nations. The environmental movement across the world has helped to make private issues of interference with the environment a public concern. Since the beginning of the movement, the public has protested over the indiscriminate exploitation of both renewable and nonrenewable natural resources. The high transaction costs and the problem of free ridership have made private negotiation of environmental problems inefficient (Goodstein 1995).

The negative externalities, which are the negative impacts inflicted upon a community from the production process of private goods, can be partly controlled by internalizing the external costs, that is, by the imposition of fines and penalties on misuse of such public goods as air, land, and water. It is believed that these measures will cause people to value and conserve the natural resources. Such assumptions, along with the high costs of private negotiations with polluters, have led to public pressure on government to implement environmental policies to protect and preserve the environment for public use and benefit.

Public demand for environmental protection and preservation of open spaces dates from as early as the nineteenth century. In England, the need to offset the demands of industrialization and to preserve open spaces led to the creation of a National Trust in 1893. Its goal was to protect the national culture and heritage from the destruction caused by industrial development.

At present in Europe, the environmental polices of the member countries of the European Community (EC) (mainly those of Germany, France, United Kingdom, Northern Ireland, Greece, Italy, the Netherlands, Belgium, Denmark, Ireland, Luxembourg, Portugal, and Spain) have been formulated in accordance with the environmental objectives of the EC Commission. In its realization of the interconnectedness between economic development and the environment, the commission has formulated environmental polices for qualitative improvement of the environment. The policies are aimed at reducing pollution and protecting the biosphere, protecting and preserving natural resources, and reducing environmental risks at work and in various other settings. The EC Commission also seeks to integrate environmental concerns with urban planning, especially development of land-use patterns to minimize the impacts of environmental disturbances to the ecosystem. Other environmental concerns of the EC include the safe disposal of polychlorinated biphenyls (PCBs) and the protection of water quality and of migratory birds and their habitats (Caldwell 1990).

The Baltic Sea states of Sweden, Finland, Denmark, Germany, Poland, and Russia, as well as the newly formed republics of Estonia, Latvia, and Lithuania, have formed the Interim Baltic Marine Environmental Protection Commission (IC). The IC tries to protect the marine environment by monitoring the levels of DDT discharged from intensively farmed agricultural lands, and of other harmful substances and oil residues discharged from the shipping vessels. Denmark and Sweden have also joined together to protect the natural bays and to prevent their pollution from sewage discharges and industrial wastes (Caldwell 1990).

In the United States and Canada, the problems of air pollution and deterioration in water quality in lakes and rivers, along with the disposal problem of both hazardous and nonhazardous wastes, have created a serious concern among public and government officials. This concern has led to the formulation of elaborate environmental policies. Also, the regional characteristics of air and water pollution have led to joint efforts in pollution control. Strict government regulations and the use of economic incentives have helped to establish cooperative ties between the industry and the government in addressing the environmental problems that affect the fragile ecosystem and the social fabric of life in both of these countries.

As early as 1872 in the United States, policies of conservation and preservation of wilderness led to the designation of 2 million acres of land in Wyoming as the world's first national park, Yellowstone National Park (McCormick 1989). In 1892, the Sierra Club was founded by the American naturalist John Muir. In 1905, the Audubon Society was started, with a federation of local and state chapters. Also in 1905, Gifford Pinchot further popularized the conservation movement (McConnell 1973). In the years to follow, there was a lapse of public interest in the environment, but in 1962, the publication of *Silent Spring* by Rachel Carson brought about an environmental revolution. This book aroused public consciousness about the adverse effects of the use of chemical pesticides and insecticides (McCormick 1989) and created the urgency to protect the environment from the ravages of harmful industrial products.

In 1969, the National Environmental Protection Act (NEPA), a thorough and comprehensive piece of federal legislation, was passed to support, manage, and preserve the historic, cultural, and natural aspects of the national heritage (Rosenbaum 1977). The act also paved the way for international cooperation in environmental matters (Caldwell 1990). As public awareness grew, the environmental coalition groups doubled their membership. Also in 1969, traditional conservation groups, such as the National Wildlife Federation, joined with newer groups, such as Friends of the Earth, and the League of Women Voters and governmental associations, in their commitment to support public interest policies in protect and preserve the environment. In fact, public support for the environment reached its peak when the first Earth Day was celebrated on April 22, 1970, and since then it has become a national tradition (Rosenbaum 1977). Over the years, the federal government has formulated environmental policies that help to address the problems of ecology, commerce, human health, and welfare.

In Australia, environmental policies were adopted to halt environmental deterioration caused by soil erosion and flooding. This action led to the introduction of conservation policies, with an emphasis upon reforestation. In addition to the local environmental problems of soil erosion, in Australia and New Zealand there exists the problem of pollution of the marine environment and destruction of coral reefs from thermal pollution. Another problem that poses a serious threat to the population of these countries is the exposure to radioactive material from the French atmospheric nuclear tests, conducted mainly in the South Pacific territory of New Caledonia (Caldwell 1990).

In Africa, the disappearance of wildlife had created the need for control over professional hunting and for preservation of game reserves. In 1857, the dedication of the Knysna and Tsitsikama forest as the first game reserve of Africa led to the emphasis on wildlife and forest preservation with a reserve status (McCormick 1989). In 1968, the scope of environmental policy in Africa was further broadened with the signing of an agreement by 38 member countries of the Organization of African Unity (OAU) at the African Convention for Conservation of Nature and Natural Resources, at Algiers. This agreement was aimed at conservation, utilization, and development of natural resources in accordance with scientific principles for a sustainable pattern of growth in these countries (Caldwell 1990).

The OAU Lagos Plan of Action 1980–2000, has tried to link socioeconomic planning in the African nations with policies in the following environmental area: environmental sanitation and health, and safe water supply; desertification and drought; deforestation and drought; marine pollution and conservation of marine resources; human settlements; mining; air pollution; and environmental education and training and legislation and information (Caldwell 1990). Further, to offset the imbalance in the ecological equilibrium brought about by agricultural expansion in the African nations, the Food and Agricultural Organization (FAO) has helped the Joint Anti-Locust and Anti-Avarian Organization of Central and West Africa to save the crops from destruction by swarms of locusts and grain-devouring birds that pose a serious threat to agriculture. The FAO also provides technical assistance in the application of fertilizers and pesticides in agricultural practices so as to minimize their impacts upon the natural ecosystems.

In South America, the need for conservation of the tropical rainforests and promotion of economic development in the Latin American nations has created a dilemma. The unrestrained exploitation of natural resources in these countries has led to the clearing of vast stretches of forested land for mining, timber, agriculture, and industrialization. The global impact of the *deforestation* of tropical rain forests has been responsible for international protests over their merciless destruction. Such protests have been ignored because they seem to be a threat to the goals of economic development in the South American nations.

The developed countries of the world have offered economic incentives to countries in South America to halt the destruction of valuable tropical rainforests. These *economic incentives* range from reduction of financial debts in lieu of conservation of forested land to provision of ready markets in developed nations for natural products of the forest. Further, assistance in adoption of a *sustainable policy* of economic growth and management has created a greater willingness among the South American nations to accept a policy of conservation and preservation of its forest wealth and wildlife (Caldwell 1990).

The Persian Gulf–with its warm and salty waters bordering the Middle Eastern countries of Kuwait, Bahrain, Qatar, United Arab Emirates, Iran, and Iraq–is considered to be a fragile and endangered sea and is highly susceptible to environmental abuses. The intense navigational activities of oil tankers and shipping vessels in the region, along with offshore exploration for oil and industrial development along the shore, poses a serious threat to the marine environment. *Regional cooperation* in abatement of pollution and scientific research and monitoring in this region suffers serious setbacks from time to time. Hostilities between neighboring countries has proved to be not always conducive for the implementation of environmental programs to protect and preserve the Persian Gulf's marine environment.

In Asia, the environmental problems range from deforestation of forested land for fuel and commercial purposes to indiscriminate disposal of waste, both hazardous and nonhazardous, into the air and water. In the southeast Asian countries of Indonesia, Malaysia, Philippines, Singapore, and Thailand, environmental problems have been created by oil spills from offshore exploration of oil, runoff from agricultural lands, and toxic discharges of industrial effluent into the rivers. Industrial development and urbanization in these countries has been responsible for deterioration in their air and water quality. The threats thus posed to the natural ecosystem and to public health have led to environmental cooperation among these countries. Their adoption of an action plan has provided guidelines for the formulation of environmental policies to protect and scientifically manage the environment in this region (Caldwell 1990).

The South Asian countries of India, Pakistan, Bangladesh, Sri Lanka, and Myanmar (formerly Burma), suffer from varied environmental problems, the most important being the destruction of forested land for agricultural expansion. This deforestation has aggravated the problems of flooding and soil erosion in these countries, creating serious imbalances in the ecosystem. The rapid pace of industrialization and urbanization there has also led to unrestricted discharge of toxic and hazardous substances into the air and water, which has been responsible for the rapid deterioration in the quality of the environment. In recent years, greater consciousness about the environment and pressure from environmental organizations has had a profound influence toward the adoption of environmental policies that seek to redress the problems as efficiently as possible, with the optimum utilization of the available, but limited, resources in these countries.

Many countries throughout the world have adopted some kind of environmental policies, with variations in the severity of the regulations embraced to protect and preserve the environment. These environmental policies, like other policies, are subject to *substantive assessment* of outcomes. In such assessments the question that arises is: Are environmental policies effective in achieving their desired objectives? The answer is that these policies have both intended and unintended outcomes, excluding their impact on environmental quality (Ringquist 1995).

There are three types of outcomes of environmental policy: political, economic, and environmental. First, the *political outcomes* can be discussed in terms of effects (a) on public participation, (b) on political powers of various groups, and (c) on interagency and intergovernmental reactions. In a democratic process of decisionmaking, the public participates in environmental policymaking by appearing at public hearings, by demanding policy relevant information, and (as empowered by statues) by keeping a strict vigilance over enforcement of regulations. Regarding political power, environmental policy does effect the political power of economic interest groups. Often, the interests of these groups are protected, along with public interests, in environmental legislation. Finally, the sharing of power between the state and the federal government in implementation of environmental policy determines the strength of intergovernmental regulatory agencies (Ringquist 1995).

Most economists try to evaluate environmental polices in terms of cost-benefit studies. The *economic outcomes* of environmental policy are studied mainly in terms of its impact on efficiency and productivity. According to economists, the command-and-control system of regulation is less effective than the market-oriented approach to regulation, with incentives. But the disadvantages of the market-oriented system are that uncertainly and information costs impede the ability of market transactions to yield desirable results (Schultze 1977). The imposition of fines on violators for externalities of the firm as dictated by the latter approach can cause resentment toward voluntary compliance. This not only threatens the political future of the program but also enhances the legal cost, as all violations must be proven and the accused given the opportunity to appeal rulings (Kelman 1981). But command-and-control regulations, in certain instances, may have costs exceeding benefits, as in control of toxic and hazardous substances. The opposite is not uncommon either, with benefits exceeding costs, as in water pollution control regulation. Often, the implementation of environmental policy is expensive. No regulations can be blamed solely for significant reduction in productivity of industries nor for producing any competitive disadvantages in the global economy (Ringquist 1995).

In assessment of *environmental outcomes* of policy, there exists evidences of improvement in environmental quality over time even though substantive assessment is a difficult process. It is the limitations in measurement that pose obstacles to social scientists in determining the extent of improvement in environmental quality. Often, the data required to evaluate the impact of environmental regulations are unavailable. Limitations in modeling also fail to determine whether improvements in environmental quality have been achieved through regulations or through other natural changes in the environment. In addition, the unfamiliarity of social scientists with the technical aspects of measurement have been responsible for negligence in assessment of true substantive outcomes of environmental policy (Ringquist 1995).

In conclusion, it can be stated that the multidimensional aspects of environmental policy cannot be blamed for its incompetency. Environmental policies are essential to address the various complex problems arising from the industrial, and agricultural structure of our society. The regulations that are now responsible for the multitudinous laws that restrict agricultural, industrial and commercial activities all over the world in the name of protection of the environment are all based upon human needs and demands for preservation of the environment. It is the existence of environmental policy that assures citizens of all countries the protection and preservation of the environment for us and for our future generations.

SARMISTHA R. MAJUMDAR

BIBLIOGRAPHY

Boulding, Kenneth, 1993. "The Economics of the Coming Spaceship Earth." In Herman E. Daly, and Kenneth N. Townsend, eds., *Valuing the Earth.* Cambridge: MIT Press.
Caldwell, Lynton K., 1990. *International Environmental Policy.* Durham, NC: Duke University Press.
———, 1995. *Environment as a Focus for Public Policy.* College Station, TX: Texas A & M University Press.
Goodstein, Eban, 1995. *Economics and the Environment.* Englewood Cliffs, NJ: Prentice-Hall.
Jackson, Henry M., 1973. "Environmental Policy and the Congress." In Albert E. Utton, and Daniel H. Henning, eds., *Environmental Policy.* New York: Praeger.
Kelman, Steven, 1981. *Regulating America, Regulating Sweden.* Cambridge: MIT Press.
McConnell, Grant, 1973. "The Environmental Movement: Ambiguities and Meanings." In Utton and Henning, *Environmental Policy.* New York: Praeger.
McCormick, John, 1989. *Reclaiming Paradise.* Bloomington, IN: Indiana University Press.
Owen, Oliver S., 1985. *Natural Resource Conservation.* New York: Macmillan.
Ringquist, Evan J., 1995. "Evaluating Environmental Policy Outcomes." In James P. Lester, ed., *Environmental Politics and Policy.* Durham, NC: Duke University Press.
Rosenbaum, Walter A., 1977. *The Politics of Environmental Concern.*" New York: Praeger.
———, 1985. *Environmental Politics and Policy.* Washington, DC: Congressional Quarterly Press.
Schultze, Charles L. 1977. *The Public Use of Private Interest.* Washington, DC: Brookings Institution.

EQUAL EMPLOYMENT OPPORTUNITY.

The concept that all persons, regardless of race, ethnicity, gender, religion, age, disability status, or other non-job related criteria should be given an equal chance to compete for employment on the basis of merit. Efforts to ensure equal employment opportunity (EEO) are designed to prevent and overcome intentional and nonintentional discrimination against minorities, women, and other groups who have historically borne the burden of discrimination (see **discrimination, disability; discrimination, gender; discrimination, racial;** and **affirmative action**). In the United States and many other nations, the principle of equal opportunity is widely shared, but programs designed to ensure equal opportunity in employment did not begin to operate before the 1940s, and early efforts were extremely limited in scope and effectiveness. It is only in the past few decades that these efforts have received considerable attention.

EEO programs usually begin with policy statements prohibiting discrimination on the basis of race, ethnicity, gender, age, or other factors. In the United States, such statements have been articulated in presidential executive orders and in statutes such as the Civil Rights Act of 1964, the Age Discrimination in Employment Act of 1967, the Equal Employment Opportunity Act of 1972, the Americans with Disabilities Act of 1990, and the Civil Rights Act of 1991, among others. Individual employers also usually include antidiscrimination statements in personnel policy manuals or similar documents. Statements forbidding discrimination are, however, unlikely by themselves to be effective. For that reason, statutes, orders, or other directives containing such statements commonly provide for additional programmatic efforts to overcome the effects of discrimination.

Most equal employment opportunity programs, for example, include procedures through which individual complaints of discrimination are investigated and, hopefully, resolved. Typically, the first step in this process involves efforts by a supervisor or other representative of the employer to informally resolve the dispute. If that proves impossible, most programs provide opportunity for the employee to file a formal complaint with the employer alleging discrimination, and an investigation by the employer will take place. On the basis of that investigation, the employer may take action to settle the case. In the

United States, if employees remain dissatisfied, they have the option of taking the complaint to the federal government's Equal Employment Opportunity Commission (EEOC) or a similar state government agency charged with responsibility for implementing EEO law. Ultimately, these disputes may find their way into the court system.

Another aspect of EEO programs is affirmative action. This term refers to positive recruitment, hiring, promotion, and training programs to further the employment of minorities and women, as well as the use of numerical goals and timetables that actually set targets for the employment of women and minorities (see **goals and quotas**). Goals and timetables, because they are established on the basis of race, ethnicity, and gender, have proved to be a controversial approach to affirmative action. In principle, the establishment of goals and timetables helps the organization to focus recruitment and other efforts to enhance employment prospects for targeted groups.

Some people argue that goals and timetables, although they are frequently an important part of organizational EEO efforts, actually are inconsistent with the concept of equal employment opportunity because they result in preferential treatment for minorities and women. Others counter that such preferences are necessary to effectively overcome the effects of past and current discrimination against various racial and ethnic groups and women.

J. Edward Kellough

BIBLIOGRAPHY

Kellough, J. Edward, 1989. *Federal Equal Employment Opportunity Policy and Numerical Goals and Timetables: An Impact Assessment.* New York: Praeger.
Livingston, John C., 1979. *Fair Game? Inequality and Affirmative Action.* San Francisco: W.H. Freeman.
Ratner, Ronnie Steinberg, 1980. *Equal Employment Policy for Women: Strategies for Implementation in the United States, Canada, and Western Europe.* Philadelphia: Temple University Press.
Rosenbloom, David H., 1977. *Federal Equal Employment Opportunity: Politics and Public Personnel Administration.* New York: Praeger.

EQUAL PROTECTION. A legal doctrine that prohibits the government from discriminating against certain persons or groups. The source of the doctrine is the Equal Protection Clause of the U.S. Constitution's Fourteenth Amendment, which became effective in 1868, after the Civil War. (The Thirteenth Amendment, prohibiting slavery, was ratified in 1865; the Fifteenth Amendment, prohibiting racial discrimination in voting, was ratified in 1870).

The purpose of the Equal Protection Clause was to prohibit the states from enacting laws that discriminated against blacks, who had just been freed from slavery. The Equal Protection Clause reads: "No State shall . . . deny to any person within its jurisdiction the equal protection of the laws." No similar language prohibiting discrimination by the federal government appears in the Bill of Rights—the first 10 amendments to the Constitution—but the antidiscrimination concept has been applied to the United States by Supreme Court case law interpreting the due process clause of the Fifth Amendment (*Bolling v. Sharpe* [1954]), which held that due process prevented the federal government from segregating public schools in the District of Columbia. In general, whatever the Equal Protection Clause of the Fourteenth Amendment prohibits a state from doing, the Due Process Clause of the Fifth Amendment prohibits the United States from doing. State constitutions may contain the same, or similar, language prohibiting discriminatory laws.

Equal protection requires that a state treat similarly situated persons similarly (Tussman and tenBroek [1949]). Discriminatory laws usually fall into one of the two categories: They are either overinclusive, that is, they regulate a problem more broadly than necessary, or they are underinclusive, that is, they do not regulate far enough (Tussman and tenBroek [1949]). But because no laws can ever reach perfection, the courts have been willing to tolerate a great deal of discriminatory laws. In fact, very few discriminatory laws will he held to be a denial of equal protection.

Laws that are likely to be struck down are those that discriminate against certain groups or certain protected activities. Immediately after the ratification of the Fourteenth Amendment, the Supreme Court said that equal protection was meant to prohibit only those laws that discriminated against blacks on account of their race or class, and that "a strong case would be necessary for its application to any other" race or class (Slaughter-House Cases [1873]). But as time went on, the Court extended the clause's protection to other races, as well as to such classifications as religion, national origin, alien status, illegitimacy, and gender. These classifications had in common one or more of the following characteristics: The traits were immutable, that is, a person cannot change his or her race; they often had nothing to do with one's ability; there was often past discrimination against members of these groups; and it was not the fault of the individual that he or she was a member of the group. Further, laws that adversely affect certain interests—such as the right to travel, the right to vote, or the rights of persons accused of crime—also are likely to be looked at closely by the Court.

The first type of legislation struck down as a violation of equal protection was that which was directed against blacks, for example, a law prohibiting blacks from serving on juries (*Strauder v. West Virginia* [1880]). Laws that merely segregated the races were upheld as consistent with equal protection since, said the Court, they treated the races equally. For example, in *Plessy v. Ferguson*, 1896, the Court upheld a Louisiana law that required railroads to provide separate but equal accommodations for blacks and whites. It was not until the famous case of *Brown v. Board of Education,* 1954, involving laws requiring separate but equal schools, that the Court held that equal protection was violated by segregation as well as by discrimination. In 1967, the Supreme Court held that equal protection was violated by state laws banning interracial marriages (*Loving v. Virginia* [1967]).

The Equal Protection Clause prohibits governmental, not private, discrimination. Governmental discrimination includes state laws and city ordinances, as well as action by public officials, such as school boards, police chiefs, mayors, and so on. For example, in the case of *Yick Wo v. Hopkins,* 1886, a city ordinance required all laundries to be operated in a brick or stone building, unless a local board gave a permit. Permits were denied to all Chinese applicants but were given to all but one non-Chinese applicant. The Court stated: "Though the law itself be fair on its face and impartial in appearance, yet, if it is applied and administrated by public authority with an evil eye and an unequal hand," equal protection is denied.

In the 1960s, the Supreme Court began to use the Equal Protection Clause in a new way—to strike down laws that discriminated against certain activities rather than the traditional focus on the class of persons affected. Thus laws that affected interstate travel, the right to vote, and protections for persons accused of crime were invalidated under an equal protection analysis. For example, a state law that denied welfare benefits to persons who had not been residents of the state for one year was invalidated by the Court because it penalized the recipient's constitutional right to travel (*Shapiro v. Thompson* [1969]). In another case, equal protection was violated by a state law that required a prospective voter to pay a poll tax, in violation of the right to vote (*Harper v. Virginia Board of Elections* [1966]). In the 1956 case of *Griffin v. Illinois,* the Court held that requiring an indigent person to pay for a court transcript in order to appeal violated equal protection.

Depending on whether the law affected one of the protected classes—race or gender—or one of the protected activities—interstate travel—the Court developed different tests to determine the law's validity. A law challenged as violative of equal protection that did not involve one of the protected categories would be subject to the "rational basis test." As long as the Court could conceive of a reason the classification was adopted by the legislature, the law would survive an equal protection challenge.

Since courts can almost always conceive of reasons for a legislative classification, use of the rational basis test results in upholding the laws as consistent with equal protection. The few exceptions to this rule have occurred when the classification is arguably a suspect class but the Court is unwilling explicitly to state that the class is suspect; instead it uses the rational basis test but strikes down the law anyway. This has occurred when the Court used ra-

tional basis to strike down legislation affecting illegitimate children (*Jimenez v. Weinberger* [1974]), hippies, (U.S. *Dept. of Agriculture v. Moreno* [1973]), and mentally retarded persons (*Cleburne v. Cleburne Living Center, Inc.* [1985]). Supreme Court Justice Thurgood Marshall criticized the rigid categories of review and advocated a flexible approach that would more accurately reflect what the Court was actually doing in cases like Cleburne, but the Court has never explicitly adopted his suggestion.

At the other extreme from the rational basis test is the strict scrutiny approach used for so-called suspect classifications, such as race, national origin, or religion. A law that uses racial classifications can only withstand an equal protection attack if the state has a compelling reason for the law and the classification is necessary to carry out that reason. Rarely can a law survive this "strict scrutiny," although occasionally it can; for example, in the first case in which the Court used strict scrutiny, it upheld the removal of Japanese Americans from their homes during World War II on the grounds that it was a military necessity to do so (*Korematsu v. United States* [1944]). Forty years later, Congress passed a reparations law that awarded $20,000 to each person affected by the military orders.

The third test, called the "intermediate" standard of review, has been used when laws classify on such bases as gender or illegitimacy. Such laws can withstand attack only if the state can justify its action on the basis of an "important" state interest and the classification has a "significant" relationship to that state interest.

The first time the Supreme Court held that discrimination on the basis of gender triggered the intermediate test was the 1976 case of *Craig v. Boren,* involving a law that discriminated against men—Oklahoma permitted women to drink 3.2 (percent alcohol) beer at age 18, but men could not do so until they were 21. The Court found that the law was based on impermissible stereotypes about males.

Occasionally, laws that are subject to the intermediate standard of review have been upheld by the courts; for example, in *Rostker v. Goldberg,* 1981, a federal law that required men, but not women, to register for the draft, was upheld by the Supreme Court. More often, however, such laws are held unconstitutional.

Occasionally, the Court will apply a hybrid approach of a semi-suspect class and a quasi-fundamental right. The best example is the case of *Phyler v. Doe,* 1982, in which Texas denied free public education to children of illegal aliens. The Supreme Court held that intermediate scrutiny should apply since there was a semi-suspect class—children of illegal aliens—and a semi-fundamental right, education. The Court invalidated the law, noting that the law punished the children through no fault of their own.

The U.S. Supreme Court has held that only laws that intentionally discriminate are subject to strict intermediate scrutiny; if the resulting discrimination occurs merely because of the impact of the law rather than its intent, the law is subject to the low-level rational basis review. For example, a state law that reserved high-level state jobs to persons who had served in the armed forces had the effect, but not the intent, of keeping women out of the best jobs, but the Supreme Court rejected an equal protection attack because the law was passed in spite of, not because of, the effect it would have on women (*Personnel Administrator of Massachusetts v. Feeney* [1979]).

Quite controversial is the treatment of affirmative action programs under equal protection–that is, laws meant to make up for past discrimination against minorities and designed to help members of that minority. Typically, affirmative action programs are used to achieve a diverse student body on college campuses and to ensure that minorities and women have access to better-paying jobs. However, these programs are often attacked in "reverse discrimination" suits by persons who allege, for example, that they are being denied admission to medical school (*Regents of the University of California v. Bakke*, 1978), or are being denied the opportunity to get a government contract. An example of the latter is the case of *Richmond v. J. A. Croson Company*, 1989, in which the U.S. Supreme Court held that where a state's affirmative action law is being challenged, the law is subject to strict scrutiny. When the affirmative action program is that of Congress, enacted pursuant to its power under Section 5 of the Fourteenth Amendment to enforce the provisions of the amendment, the Court held that intermediate scrutiny had been the appropriate standard in *Metro Broadcasting, Inc. v. the Federal Communications Commission (FCC)*, 1990. However, the Court overruled Metro Broadcasting in the 1995 case of *Adarand Constructors, Inc., v. Peña*, so all affirmative action programs, state and federal, are now subject to strict scrutiny. Whether affirmative action plans can withstand a strict scrutiny challenge is the major question still to be addressed by the Supreme Court.

The framers of the Equal Protection Clause assumed that Congress would be the primary branch of the federal government to enforce the clause through Section 5 of the Fourteenth Amendment, called the "enforcement clause." However, in the Civil Rights Cases decided in 1883, the Supreme Court struck down the federal Civil Rights Act of 1875 that banned racial discrimination in inns, theaters, and public transportation since the Fourteenth Amendment was only concerned about state action. The Court held that Congress had no power under Section 5 beyond what was already a violation of equal protection in the absence of congressional legislation. Thereafter, until the 1950s, Congress did not attempt to enforce the Equal Protection Clause.

Starting in the 1950s, Congress did pass legislation banning discrimination, pursuant to the enforcement clauses of the Civil Rights amendments (the Thirteenth, Fourteenth, and Fifteenth Amendments), and relying also

on its power over interstate commerce and the power to tax and spend for the general welfare. Laws were passed banning discrimination in public accommodations, employment, voting, and housing, and by institutions that received federal funds.

In some cases, administrative agencies were created to enforce the ban, including the Equal Employment Opportunity Commission and the United States Civil Rights Commission, whose job was to hold hearings and recommend new legislation. In other cases, existing agencies were given enforcement power to ensure that programs within the agency were operated in a nondiscriminatory fashion, such as the Office of Civil Rights in the Department of Health, Education, and Welfare. The Civil Rights Division of the Department of Justice represented the United States in court in civil rights matters of a civil nature; the Civil Rights Section of the Justice Department's Criminal Division enforced the criminal law, for example, prosecuting police officers who violated the civil rights of suspects.

Ever since the case of *Marbury v. Madison* in 1803, it has been the rule of the Supreme Court, in most instances, to have the final say on the meaning of the Constitution through cases it decides. However, Congress has occasionally passed legislation pursuant to the enforcement clauses of the Civil Rights amendments that can be viewed as giving a different meaning to those amendments, in particular, to the Equal Protection Clause. For example, the Supreme Court has held that states may, without violating equal protection, require that its citizens pass literacy tests before they are allowed to vote (*Lassiter v. Northampton Election Board* [1959]). Congress, however, passed legislation pursuant to Section 5 striking down such tests, and the Court upheld Congress's action in *Katzenbach v. Morgan*, 1966, even though, in effect, Congress was disagreeing with the Supreme Court by finding that such tests violate equal protection. The Court in the Morgan case limited Congress's enforcement power to actions that expand, rather than restrict or dilute, individual rights. In this case the Court effectively overruled that part of the Civil Rights cases that held that Congress could not use its Section 5 power to give more protection to individuals than the Court.

Constitutions of many other countries have the equivalent of an equal protection clause, and often, in addition, they prohibit specific types of discrimination. For example, Article 3 of the Basic Law for the Federal Republic of Germany (the German Constitution) first provides that "all persons shall be equal before the law," and then goes on to state that "men and women shall have equal rights," followed by a longer provision: "No one may be disadvantaged or favored because of his sex, his parentage, his race, his language, his homeland and origin, his faith, or his religious or political opinions." The constitution of the Russian Federation, adopted in 1993, has antidiscrimination provisions similar to the German Constitution and, in addition, provides for nondiscrimination because of a person's membership in social associations.

ROGER L. GOLDMAN

BIBLIOGRAPHY

Adarand Constructors, Inc. v. Peña, 115 Sup. Ct. 2097 (1995).
Basic Law for the Federal Republic of Germany, Art. 3.
Bolling v. Sharpe, 347 U.S. 497 (1954).
Brown v. Board of Education, 347 U.S. 483 (1954).
Civil Rights Cases, 109 U.S. 3 (1883).
Cleburne v. Cleburne Living Center, Inc., 473 U.S. 432 (1985).
Constitution of the Russian Federation, Art. 19.
Craig v. Boren, 429 U.S. 190 (1976).
Griffin v. Illinois, 351 U.S. 12 (1956).
Harper v. Virginia Board of Elections, 383 U.S. 663 (1966).
Jimenez v. Weinberger, 417 U.S. 628 (1974).
Katzenbach v. Morgan, 384 U.S. 641, (1966).
Korematsu v. United States, 323 U.S. 214 (1944).
Lassiter v. Northampton Election Board, 360 U.S. 45 (1959).
Loving v. Virginia, 388 U.S. 1 (1967).
Marbury v. Madison, 5 U.S. 137 (1803).
Metro Broadcasting, Inc. v. FCC, 497 U.S. 547 (1990).
Personnel Administrator of Massachusetts v. Feeney, 442 U.S. 256 (1979).
Plessy v. Ferguson, 163 U.S. 537 (1896).
Plyler v. Doe, 457 U.S. 202 (1982).
Regents of University of California v. Bakke, 438 U.S. 265 (1978).
Richmond v. J. A. Croson Company, 488 U.S. 469 (1989).
Rostker v. Goldberg, 453 U.S. 57 (1981).
Shapiro v. Thompson, 394 U.S. 618 (1969).
Slaughter-House Cases, 83 U.S. 36 (1873).
Strauder v. West Virginia, 100 U.S. 303 (1880).
Tussman and tenBroek, "The Equal Protection of the Laws," 37 *Calif. L. Rev.* 341 (1949).
U.S Constitution Amendment XIV, Secs. 1 and 2.
U.S. Department of Agriculture v. Moreno, 413 U.S. 528 (1973).
Yick Wo v. Hopkins, 118 U.S. 356 (1886).

EQUITABLE DELIVERY OF SERVICES.

A fair allocation and distribution of resources, services, and their outcomes. Concerns for equitable service delivery arose in the United States in the late 1960s and early 1970s. Social equity, as it was termed, was suggested as a third criteria by which to evaluate government action. In addition to delivering services efficiently and economically, public officials were expected to achieve social equity.

The intent behind the goal of social equity is to reduce harm done to disadvantaged populations as a result of social programs, or due to the lack of programs, opportunities, and so on. Led by George Frederickson and colleagues, the early discussions acknowledged economic, political, and social differences in populations and urged the government to adjust for these disparities. This meant that government, at all levels—local, state, and federal—was expected to develop programs and plans to alleviate hardships. Particular attention was focused on the delivery of services from education, public health, and garbage collection to street maintenance and recreation.

The concept of equitable service delivery is linked to theoretical and practical developments in moral philosophy dating back to the Ancient Greeks. Aristotle postulated about the ideal form of government and coexistence among people in society. He argued against extremes in wealth, but suggested that any attempt to achieve pure equality would also be unsettling. Instead, he called for proportionate equality, or the distribution of resources according to a citizen's contribution to society. This stance was tempered, however, by his belief in a substantial middle class. Therefore, to the extent that there are disparities in society, action should be taken to bring low-income people to a higher standard of living. The ultimate goal is to ensure a certain quality of life for all residents. These themes continue to run through debates about equitable service delivery.

In the seventeenth and eighteenth centuries, such British and French theorists as Thomas Hobbes, John Locke, and Jean Jacques Rousseau offered a series of social contract theories that also inform discussions of social equity. Hobbes and Locke described relationships between people, and asserted the primacy of human liberties and rights. They argued that people govern themselves and make determinations about what is just based on a mutual agreement to uphold some preestablished social contract. Although they did not explicitly address equity, their theories suggested that notions of fairness and equity may vary across populations and cultures.

Rousseau argued that civil society, property, and all that it entails results in inequalities among people. Further, where these inequities exist, they have been created by institutions. While speculating about the best form of government, Rousseau suggested that equality among individuals be held up as a chief objective of laws and civil associations. These ideas taken collectively suggest that equitable service delivery is context-bound and might only be achieved through purposeful government action.

Expanding on social contract theories, John Rawls (1971) outlined a theory of distributive justice that recognized differences in individuals and communities. He argued that social and economic inequalities should be arranged so that no group is disadvantaged more often, or to a greater extent, than another. To achieve this, government and society have an obligation to devote more resources to those people in less-privileged positions. The underlying theme of all these theories is fourfold: (1) civil society results in political, social, and economic inequalities; (2) society as a whole, but government in particular, should work to address these disparities; (3) there is some minimum standard of living that is due all citizens; and (4) to the extent that inequalities exist in service delivery, they should be in favor of the less-fortunate members of society.

These theoretical frameworks form the backdrop for much of the debate about equity. However, in the abstract, they do not fully explain what equitable service delivery is and how it can be achieved. Instead, terms like "equal results," "equal opportunity," and "market equity" indicate how public officials attempt to address this issue on a daily basis; they represent the practical side of equity and service delivery. It is difficult, if not impossible, to satisfy these goals simultaneously. Therefore, public officials have to make conscious choices about which standard to use in a given situation. These choices are linked to specific resource allocation and service distribution patterns.

One distribution pattern involves delivering equal services to all. It is comparable to creating an equal chance for everyone to benefit from services. In this context, equity (input equity) is achieved by allocating resources equally across all service areas. This approach does little to lessen the gap between the haves and the have-nots; however, it does ensure that no one group is denied services. It is often the most politically viable and expedient of all equity goals. A related definition of equitable service delivery has to do with ensuring that every area receives some basic level of service. In this case, the government may set a minimum standard that must be met. Then services are delivered to the various neighborhoods according to that standard.

These two perspectives, input equity, and universal minimum standards, arose in the United States largely in response to concerns raised in the 1960s and 1970s about who received what services. Linked to this were questions about whether some citizens systematically received inadequate levels of local services; and if this distribution pattern was sanctioned by the government. Concerns about inequities in service delivery led to court actions in various U.S. cities. One prominent case involved the town of Shaw, Mississippi, *Hawkins v. Town of Shaw* [Mississippi] 461 F. 2d 1171 [1972]), which was found to have engaged in racial discrimination in service delivery. The U.S. Fifth Circuit Court ruled that the town had violated the equal protection clause of the Fourteenth Amendment by not providing a number of services to its black residents. As a result, in that case and others, the U.S. federal courts have imposed standards of input equity, or equal opportunity as it is also referred to, in service delivery. Equal opportunity has often been used as a standard of fairness in education in the United States. It was behind much of the actions to integrate schools and residential neighborhoods.

A second service delivery pattern distributes unequal services to citizens depending on differences in social need, or willingness and ability to pay. In the context of social need, resources are allocated and distributed in a manner to improve the quality of life for disadvantaged groups after services have been delivered. It is a means of narrowing the gap between the more- and less-fortunate members of society. In order to achieve equal results, more resources are distributed to those neighborhoods or target populations most in need. Thus unequal service inputs are distributed across service areas in order to obtain somewhat equal outcomes.

The goal of distributions according to social need is to ensure that people will be in relatively equal positions once services are delivered. The Responsiveness Public Services Program in Savannah, Georgia, is an example of this view of equitable service delivery. It was developed in the early 1970s in an attempt to achieve equity in service delivery. The intent of the program was to (1) provide the city with a way to measure key differences in the quality of life across neighborhoods; and (2) close the gap in quality of life between neighborhoods by delivering more services to those areas with the highest needs.

Determinations of equitable service delivery can also be based on the viability of capitalism. This corresponds to resources according to consumer or market demand, measured by willingness and ability to pay for services. Thus, market equity can represent a fair and equitable distribution of services when people pay for services rendered. In this case, only those residents that receive a service pay for it. This allows municipalities, states, counties, and so forth, to demand payment from people using a service that may not actually live within its boundaries. Therefore, residents that are not using a service do not bear its costs simply as a matter of living in a certain area. Market equity can only be applied to services that easily identify users and that can assign prices. This is typically the case for public utilities, garbage collection, and recreational facilities such as tennis courts and golf courses.

Market equity is usually achieved through (1) user fees, or (2) consumer prices imposed under franchises, when residents make arrangements with private companies for the delivery of services. It is consistent with the move to shift service delivery responsibilities, especially financing, to the private sector. Support for this view of equitable service delivery grew in the 1980s and 1990s, particularly at the local level of U.S. government. Proponents of market equity argue that it saves governmental resources, since services will only be produced at a level at which there are people willing to use them. Furthermore, the costs of service delivery are assumed by the user and are not passed on to a second or third party through government spending.

This definition of equitable service delivery, market equity, is highly controversial. Opponents argue that market equity may place undue burdens on low-income individuals, given the unequal distribution of incomes, as well as the regressive nature of taxes and fee-for-service plans in the United States. The argument is that rich and poor people will not receive the same level or quality of services since they have unequal abilities to express demand and pay for services. One way to address these concerns is to issue vouchers, or direct payments, to low-income residents to help offset the costs of services.

A third distribution pattern, proportional equality, can be viewed as a variation of the first two. In this case, services are distributed based on some preestablished relationship. For instance, precincts with higher crime rates might be assigned more patrols than those with relatively less crime. Precincts with similar crime rates would receive equal services. This pattern of service distribution offers little additional insight to equitable service delivery as framed in the current discussion. Rather, most of the focus is on issues related to providing the same level of services across communities or differentiating services based on need or willingness to pay.

There is little consensus on the term "equity" or "equitable service delivery." Some discuss it in terms of quantity and level of service. Others regard equity to be a matter of service quality and responsiveness to citizen demands and needs. Still others argue that these two dimensions are intricately linked. In a broad sense, equitable service delivery can also be viewed from at least two additional perspectives that include all of the issues mentioned earlier. The first considers the actual allocation and distribution of services. The second focuses on the effects, outcomes, or results of service delivery. This approach distinguishes between the process of service delivery and the tangible products of service delivery.

Over the years, the various views of equitable service delivery have resulted in a series of judicial, legislative, and administrative decisions and actions. No one construct of equitable service delivery is right. Rather, one's perspective on it is shaped largely by social, political, moral, and economic values. Thus, equitable service delivery is value-laden and context-bound. It is a function of the rights and responsibilities that a society assigns to both itself and its government. Assessing fairness is a function of societal norms, the types of services being delivered, the level of government, and the country.

CYNTHIA Y. JACKSON

BIBLIOGRAPHY

Aristotle, 1985. *Politics.* J.A.K. Thompson, tr. Harmondsworth, UK: Penguin Books.
Chitwood, Steven R., 1974. "Social Equity and Social Service Productivity." *Public Administration Review* 34 (1):29–35.
Frederickson, H. George, 1990. "Public Administration and Social Equity." *Public Administration Review* 50 (2): 228–236.
Hawkins v. Town of Shaw, 1972. 461 F. 2nd 1171.
Lineberry, R. L., 1977. *Equality and Urban Policy: The Distribution of Municipal Services.* Beverly Hills, CA: Sage Publications.
Rae, Douglas, 1981. *Equalities.* Cambridge: Harvard University Press.
Rawls, John, 1971. *A Theory of Justice.* Cambridge: Harvard University Press.
Wise, Frank, Jr., 1976. "Toward Equity of Results Achieved: One Approach." *Public Management* (August): 9–12.
Young, H. Peyton, 1994. *Equity in Theory and Practice.* Princeton: Princeton University Press.

ESTOPPEL. The legal principle that basically operates to preclude a party from asserting a particular position, usually because the party has either taken a contrary position on the same question or taken some action that has caused another party to act, or refrain from taking an act, in reliance upon the estopped party's prior action or position.

Estoppel was originally not favored by courts in early cases, on the grounds that it is a technical doctrine that operates, in the words of the English jurist Edward Coke (1552-1634), "to shut a man's mouth from speaking the truth." Although the doctrine has over time gained acceptance as any other legal doctrine, it is still frequently stated that the doctrine may only be invoked to "prevent injustice." Estoppel is usually a defensive measure and may not be used to create new substantive rights.

There are three common types of estoppel. Estoppel *by record* prevents a party from denying the truth of any matter that is set forth in a judicial or legislative record. Estoppel *by deed* prevents a party to a deed from claiming any right to property that conflicts with the deed. Equitable estoppel, or estoppel *in pais,* is the subject of this article and refers to estoppels that are not estoppels *by record* or estoppels *by deed.*

State Government

As a general rule, the doctrine of estoppel is not applied against a state government acting in its governmental capacity. The United States Supreme Court has held that a state cannot estop itself from the exercise of its police power. For example, a state is not precluded from exercising its power to declare a truck and its cargo of liquor to be contraband, despite previous failures by authorities to stop the truck in enforcement of a liquor control law. Likewise, the failure of a state highway patrol officer to stop a speeding driver on several occasions does not operate to estop the officer from stopping the speeder on a subsequent occasion. A state is not estopped by acts of its officers made in excess of their authority, or by erroneous statements made by its officers.

There are instances in which the state *is* subject to estoppel. Estoppel may arise against the state to prevent fraud, provided the estoppel does not operate to impair the state's exercise of its sovereign power. A state may also be estopped when acting in a proprietary—as opposed to governmental—capacity. The distinction between proprietary and governmental functions is often blurred, however, and varies from jurisdiction to jurisdiction. A common definition provides that an act is deemed to be governmental if the act is carried out for the common good, whereas an act for the special benefit of the governmental entity—state, county, or municipal—is usually deemed to be a proprietary function. The collection of garbage, for example, is considered to be a governmental function, but the operation by a municipality of a municipal garage for the maintenance and repair of government-owned vehicles would usually be deemed a proprietary function.

A state may also be estopped by operation of contract, provided the estoppel does not impair the operation of a governmental function.

County Government

A county is considered to be an arm of state government and is therefore likewise generally not subject to estoppel in cases involving governmental functions. A county may be estopped in matters relating to proprietary functions, but not when the act giving rise to the estoppel is *ultra vires,* or beyond the authority of the officials or employees involved.

Municipal Corporations

Municipal governments, alternately, may be estopped even when acting within the scope of their designated powers, but not when the acts were beyond the officials' or employees' authority.

LEO V. GARVIN, JR.

ETHICS IN NONPROFIT ORGANIZA-TIONS.
A subset of ethical theory and practice that seeks to apply ethical philosophy to the particular characteristics and needs of nonprofit organizations.

Introduction

The nonprofit sector has developed without a firm grounding in economic, organizational, or legal theory. The lack of clarity about foundational issues leaves the sector open to attack and without much of a normative theory with which to defend itself. It is in this context that a theory of ethical behavior must be established. Indeed, it may be that such an ethical grounding would help theorists and practitioners in the nonprofit sector to better focus their efforts and clarify the principles upon which the sector is and should be based.

In the Western tradition the first activities that could be considered voluntary community service were founded by the early Christian Church. These included hospices for the sick and for lepers, homes for orphans and widows, and sanctuaries for criminals. The American colonial period saw a variety of similar enterprises, which later developed into organizations to assist fleeing slaves and to push for abolition of the slave trade, for ministries to immigrants, and for schools and hospitals. In the early nineteenth century, although Alexis de Tocqueville (1835) noted the propensity of Americans to form associations, many of these were based in churches and in religious movements.

In the late nineteenth century a number of foundations developed to support a variety of causes. Among the more notable were the efforts of Trinity Church, Wall Street, to use the great resources of that congregation for the alleviation of poverty in the growing tenements of New York City, and the support of libraries and other community projects funded by the bequests of Andrew Carnegie. Community service organizations flourished after World War II, and were spurred by the Great Society programs of the 1960s.

One consequence of this growth has been blurring of the line between government and nonprofit agencies, as the latter receive larger and larger proportions of their budgets from public coffers. Recent attempts by Republican lawmakers to slow the growth of government and diminish its reach have created some doubt about how the nonprofit sector will be able to function in the future.

On the other end of the spectrum has been the growing criticism of the sector by business groups who see many nonprofit organizations as competing unfairly because of their tax-exempt status (see Bennett and DiLorenzo 1989). For example, so-called "nonprofit" hospitals claim a certain charitable purpose, but studies have failed to show that nonprofit hospitals provide more charitable care than do for-profit hospitals. The tendency of large nonprofit organizations to have substantial real estate holdings that are exempt from property taxes and to enter into traditionally for-profit enterprises, such as publishing and manufacturing, create suspicion and antagonism. At the same time, for-profit enterprises have not been reluctant to form nonprofit entities when they have served their own purposes, such as trade associations and political action committees. These developments further obscure any ability to predict the future breadth and reach of the nonprofit sector.

It is this diverse history of the development of the sector that makes the ethical enterprise so difficult. The multiplicity of forms that nonprofit organizations take makes the creation of a simple ethical framework impossible. Therefore, for the purposes of this entry the focus will be on charitable organizations that have as their purpose work that changes the life of an individual or a community for the better (Drucker 1990). These eleemosynary organizations receive their name from the Greek root for charity, alms, pity, and mercy. They include social or community service organizations, medical clinics providing substantial charitable care, private schools, religious organizations, arts groups, and nongovernmental organizations that engage in international development. Excluded for the purposes of this discussion are trade associations, fellowships, fraternal groups, family trusts or other private enterprises, and other mutual benefit organizations. As will be seen, this distinction is important to the development of a clear ethic for organizational life in the nonprofit sector.

Values, Ethics, and Morals

Ethics are the principles by which one is guided in relations with other persons and groups, which become rules of interpersonal conduct. Thus, ethics is what we do once we have decided to live together in society. Morals, alternately, have to do with principles that guide the behavior of individuals in regard to their own integrity. The two form and inform one another, but the arenas of concern are different. The terms can be confusing because in everyday discussion they are often used interchangeably.

The notion of values was not applied to questions of ethics until relatively modern times. In fact, it was borrowed from economics, where the term refers to goods or services that have worth for a potential consumer. James Davison Hunter (1991) has pointed out that much of the inability of groups to reach a consensus on matters of great importance, such as abortion policy, civil rights, homosexuality, or school prayer, involves the unwillingness to compromise values.

Virtue refers to the character of individuals or groups in terms of their internal moral compasses and their relations with one another. Virtue more clearly connects the internal and external moral worlds of human existence. It is the overarching and complex sets of principles by which individuals and groups form their moral and ethical lives (Hauerwas 1981).

When the question of ethics is raised—that is, the moral relations of persons with one another in society—it is important to identify which ethical system one is using. Knowing how your own ethical system functions as well as knowing how another person or group's ethical system functions increases the likelihood of communication across potentially divisive issues. The major ethical systems include teleological (religious or "given" ethical principles, such as the ten commandments), deontological (duty-based ethics), utilitarian (balancing good in society), and virtue ethics (seeking the good). Additionally, liberal ethics are based on the notion that individuals have rights that override the needs of groups and societies. In each case the ethical system seeks to discover what is required to create a good society, what our obligation is to ourselves and to one another, and what is required of us as individuals and groups as we interact one with another. Indeed, it raises the question of what the "good" is in the first place.

Questions of community standards, moral absolutes, and policy issues revolving around identifiable moral concerns must be analyzed in terms of this sort of systematic understanding that is brought to the public discussion. It is not helpful to counter an argument based in religious conviction with liberal notions of individual rights. The two systems create incommensurate categories of understanding and definition. Thus, discussions of what can seem simple practicalities can very quickly change to involve deeply held convictions of what the "good" is for society. One does not have to look far for examples of "public discourse" that have degenerated into accusations of immorality by public officials who are not living up to the expectations of their constituencies. Language at public meetings can involve more accusations that bureaucrats are violating community standards than discussions of how diverse understandings of those standards can be reconciled.

Because nonprofit organizations are most often created in response to a perceived "wrong" that must be made "right," nonprofit managers often find themselves in the midst of discussions of ethics and the public good. Understanding the ethical implications of policy decisions becomes an important task of the nonprofit manager.

This discussion of ethics is far too brief to provide anything more than suggestions about complexities of ethical discourse. What becomes clear in the next sections is that ethics, morals, and virtue are at the very core of what the nonprofit organization is and does.

The Nature of Nonprofit Organizations

Nonprofit organizations in the United States arose in order to meet economic and social needs not addressed by the for-profit sector or government. Some economists believe that this is a defect in the economy, sometimes described as a theory of market failure. This failure can happen in three ways. First, the real costs of goods and services may be hidden or obscure so that the participants in the market have no way of measuring the real value of a good or service. Second, potential consumers may not be able to judge the quality of goods and services, perhaps because of lack of information or lack of comparisons, and so the cost to them is too high in order for them to participate in the market. That is, there is a lack of competition, which would in other circumstances help to regulate supply and demand. Third, certain important needs may not be met because there is no profit incentive for a firm to enter that market. In this case certain goods and services desired or necessary for the economy are not being produced; therefore, the economy must be repaired by organizations that fit neither into the for-profit nor government sectors. The tax advantages given to nonprofit organizations are a compensation for attempts to address these defects. Public

---

policy encourages the formation of nonprofit groups to produce goods and services that meet perceived needs.

Significantly, the consumers of nonprofit goods and services are rarely the payers for those services. Since the potential consumers cannot participate fully in the market, others step in and provide resources at a cost to themselves. Generally, these secondary payers are donors, contractors, or grantors to nonprofit organizations who want an agent to perform a task in their name; for example, a foundation or government agency that pays a nonprofit agency to provide food, shelter, or other services. Since the altruistic motives and the specific resources given are rarely sufficient to meet a perceived need in themselves, the resources are gathered together for more effective delivery. Thus many nonprofit organizations were created because of economic choices made by consumers who were willing to sacrifice some of their own resources for others in a defective market economy.

Peter Drucker (1990) maintains that business supplies, government controls, and nonprofits change the life of an individual or a community for the better. Different incentives drive organizations in each sector. For business it is the profit motive. For government it is power. For the nonprofit organization it is doing good or virtue. (Drucker uses the term "values" here.) The primary purpose for the nonprofit organization is to serve a constituency by providing a good or service that would not otherwise be supplied.

Lohman (1992) calls the nonprofit sector "the commons," a consensus grounded in voluntary participation, common purposes, shared resources, mutuality, and justice. The nonprofit organization functions on the basis of these shared virtues. Things are of value to the participants in a commons because they are of value to other persons whom the participants value. This again highlights the ethical nature of the nonprofit organization.

Another way of looking at this is to imagine that individuals and groups view the world through an ethical frame. That is, what is acceptable and what is not acceptable is framed by the principles and virtues of the individual or group. Understanding this ethical frame helps us to see how our language describes our experience in this regard: Certain things are "in bounds" or acceptable, but others are "out of bounds." Our ethical "comfort zone" is defined by this frame of reference. We become discomfited and disturbed when we are asked or forced to act outside the ethical and moral bounds we are used to or committed to.

The ethical frame can be shifted by the exigencies of organizational life in the government or private sectors. Government and business utilize ethical frames only as secondary mechanisms by which to measure performance. The rightness or wrongness of an act may be modified by whether it makes a profit for the firm or supports a government's appropriate need to control.

However, for a nonprofit organization the ethical frame is primary. Thus the very existence of a nonprofit organization depends on its moral standing, its integrity, and its virtue. The unique historical and societal dimensions of nonprofit organizations create a different expectation for organizational ethics, both within and outside of the organization (Jeavons 1994). The term Jeavons uses is "trustworthiness," which refers to the implicit social contract between nonprofits and organizations in the other two sectors. The special standing and the legal or tax advantages enjoyed by nonprofit organizations depends on their trustworthiness. Drucker (1990) defines this trust as integrity, openness, accountability, service, commitment, and caring. This trust creates an implicit social contract between the nonprofit organization and the larger society, in which the nonprofit organization is expected to act in a trustworthy manner, and for which the larger society grants the nonprofit organization legal and tax advantages. The nature of nonprofit organizations requires them to have clarity about the ethical and moral grounds on which they operate.

The Nature of Nonprofit Leadership

John Gardner (1990) has said that nonprofit organizations are designed to serve critically important social objectives, and that leaders of these organizations serve as symbols of the underlying virtues that have led to a commitment to those objectives. Leaders continually affirm the commitments of the organization so that those who work in and with the organization keep in mind its core virtues. In so doing, the leader brings together disparate individuals into a cohesive unit in which there is a shared commitment to virtue.

The literature on nonprofit leadership is consistent in its assertion about the importance of ethical leaders. Interestingly, the literature on for-profit management has begun to reflect a similar concern (for examples see Waitley 1995, Covey 1992, Smith 1995, Wheatley 1992, Schein 1992). A consensus is developing that authentic leaders should put principles first. Planning should include statements of vision, mission, and operating philosophy before goals and objectives are finalized. Perhaps if nonprofit organizations can learn efficiency from the private sector and service delivery from government, then perhaps the other sectors can learn leadership from nonprofit organizations.

Ethical Issues for Nonprofit Organizations

There can be no comprehensive listing of ethical issues facing nonprofit organizations. They are too varied and too numerous. Issues are grouped here as those involving management in general, human resource management, financial accountability, fund-raising, and competition with the private sector.

Management in General

Management in general involves both the day-to-day and strategic planning processes of the organization. Ethical issues can arise daily and may emerge most often at the place where decisionmaking power is mediated in the organization. The primary role of the executive is to set an ethical tone for the organization in its relationships within and outside itself. Edgar H. Schein (1992) has suggested that managers first must manage the culture of an organization. This is first and foremost an oversight role. It involves identifying, setting, and maintaining ethical (behavioral) boundaries.

There are obvious legal implications to this. John Carver (1990) recommends that boards also adopt a resolution that states that the director will neither cause nor allow any illegal or unethical behavior to take place in the organization. This may seem vague and overly general, but it sets an ethical tone, and the wise executives uses this to good advantage for the life of the organization and its members. The leadership by setting an ethical tone focuses the energy of the organization's members into productive directions. Internal conflict is minimized and decisions that in other organizations would be insoluble can be made with relative ease. The setting and maintaining of boundaries—openly arrived at, reinforced, and tested—can release an organization's power and vigor for tremendous good. The alternative is an organization that flounders, blunders its way through decisions, and wastes valuable resources on backtracking and miscalculations. Such an organization is contrary to the very nature of what we understand a nonprofit agency to be.

Schein (1992) has suggested that in order to be successful, managers must first manage the corporate culture of the organization. He suggests, as do Stephen Covey and others, that the first focus in planning is to create a culture of integrity in which moral principles are reflected in ethical behavior. Covey (1992) has reported on certain organizations that have taken work teams on three-and four-day retreats, which are focused on creating a common philosophy for the working of that team. Structures and processes need to arise from the agreed-upon ethics, and those need to include a system of rewards and incentives that reinforce the principles. The entire structure is maintained by consistent behavior by management, in which the principles are reiterated and lived into by example.

Gardner (1990) has said that a "group without shared values is virtually impossible to lead." Ethical management requires that organizational leaders put virtue and character at the front of the planning process in order to ensure a moral and humane performance. Putting off such concerns to later consideration leads only to confusion and conflict, which results in an ineffective and dissolute organization. Strategic planning, then, involves the entire membership of the organization in consideration of its core principles, its virtues. For the nonprofit organization, this concern is not peripheral but essential.

The director stands with one foot in each of the domains of board and staff. Thus a second role of the executive is to provide communication between the two groups, to serve as the "persona," or representative, of the organization to the larger community. In being the primary communication link between the board and the staff the executive has tremendous power to influence the perspective of both groups about the other, and to filter information flowing both directions. It may be objected that the executive should *control* the information flow. However, this can only lead to behaviors in which such control is circumvented. Margaret Wheatley (1992) has suggested that the organization that encourages information flow is a healthier, more active, and more energetic system. Attempting to defeat such information flow simply leads members of the organization to devote scarce resources—time, energy, emotional investment—in unethical and unproductive behaviors.

John Carver (1990) has a rule that can address the concern for monitoring rather than controlling information flow. He suggests that each organization adopt a policy that states that all persons working in the organization, whether paid or volunteer, are understood to be working under the authority of the executive director. When properly understood by staff such a policy keeps the director in the information loop, even without needing to know the details of every conversation or meeting. As long as the executive encourages staff and board to bring concerns directly to the people involved—a systemwide open-door policy—information can flow throughout the organization. The long-term effect is a positive one, in that energy is used for productive behaviors, and performance thereby increases. This means that, ethically, relationships are straightforward and that there is mutual accountability.

The third role of the executive is to serve as the representative of the organization to the community. This infers, to some extent, that the executive will also be representing the community to the board and staff, although both should be in constant contact with the public they are serving and representing. This role is more than public relations. It means giving the community a sense of what the organization *is* and not merely what it *does* in its mission of change. This is another aspect of the ethical center that nonprofit organizations must have in order to justify their existence. It is what gives the community a sense of the organization's trustworthiness and creates confidence in the organization's role in its midst. Thus, as boards go about recruiting and hiring directors, this particular role is one that they should keep prominently in mind.

Human Resource Management

Nonprofit organizations have an ethical responsibility not only to their clients and to their donors; they have an ethical responsibility to their employees and volunteers. If the suggestions about management in general are pursued, that sets the stage for an ethical approach to employee relations. Clarity of purpose, for example, can lead to clear contracts and job descriptions for workers. Volunteers are due the same respect and consideration as are paid staff. Clear contracts, evaluations, and job descriptions will enable the nonprofit organization to utilize its human resources not only more humanely but also more effectively.

Financial Accountability

Financial matters are a common ethical problem for nonprofit managers. It is very easy to slip into unethical fundraising activities because of the ongoing financial needs of the organization. A helpful guideline is the inverse rule of accountability: The more open the accountability the less likely anyone or any organization is to get into trouble. Two examples of the importance of openness in financial affairs will suffice to demonstrate the necessity of the rule.

In the early 1990s an expanding scandal circled around the United Way of the United States and its executive director Robert Aramony. He was accused and later convicted of misuse of funds. Giving to the national effort as well as to local United Ways dropped dramatically as the scandal unfolded. For donors the issue was whether any entity with United Way in its title could be trusted, as well as how much of donated funds were or had been used to underwrite the waste in the national offices. For other nonprofit managers, however, the issue was one of trust and oversight. Aramony had recruited one captain of business after another to sit on his board. These men (and a few women) were used to large salaries, discretionary funds, and high living. Hardly anyone raised any questions about the expenditures for Super Bowl tickets, limousine service, or flights on the Concorde. The problem was that what voices were raised in protest were simply ignored. (For a full treatment of the United Way scandal, see Glaser 1994). The national board had no members representing a larger group of key stakeholders, including local United Ways, member agencies, or recipients of services. As a result, oversight was abdicated and the entire United Way system suffered.

The second example involves the Reverend Jim Bakker and his PTL (which stands for "Praise The Lord") ministry. He and his then-wife Tammy Faye received millions of dollars in donations over a period of years, much of which they used for their own purposes. Included in their PTL ministry was a theme park and hotel complex, for which shares were sold, apparently several times each. The financial empire soon collapsed and Bakker went to jail. This scandal, and related scandals involving other television evangelists, led to a significant decrease in viewership and donations to the national organizations, but led also to skepticism and decreased giving to more traditional and well-operated religious groups. In light of this, the Reverend Billy Graham and several other evangelicals came together to form the Evangelical Council for Financial Accountability (ECFA). Membership requires an organization to follow certain financial practices, including open accounting of receipts and expenditures. Many of the evangelical fold now recommend that their supporters make donations only to member organizations of ECFA.

Fund-Raising

Much of what was said about financial accountability can be said about fund raising. Whereas the names of donors may appropriately be kept confidential, the amounts given should always be reported to the board and in the annual report of the organization. The key ethical issue involving fund-raising concerns the propensity for organizations to shift their mission in subtle ways in order to acquire funds or in response to influence by large donors.

The financial contributors to nonprofit organizations can include government, private-sector organizations, individuals, or other nonprofit groups. This support can be given in terms of grants, contracts, contributions, or payment for goods or services. Trouble comes in two ways.

First, nonprofit managers have a tendency to wander "off mission" in order to cast the widest fund-raising net. That is, they will adjust a grant proposal in order to make it appear that their organization is providing a service within the purposes of the grant, when in fact the core mission may be in a completely different direction. This can lead very quickly to misuse of funds. Michael O'Neill (1990) describes a case, "Robbing Peter to Pay Paul," that illustrates this well. Managers can and do begin to use funds designated for one purpose in order to pay for services in another area. Not only might this be illegal, it is clearly unethical. The answer to this dilemma may lie in having the board expand the mission of the organization into a new area, or simply divulging in the application that the project is outside the normal operations of the agency. Although that may risk losing the grant, it is far less a risk than subverting the organization's entire life.

A variation of this ethical dilemma is that posed by the devolution of government services into the nonprofit sector and the greater number of government-funded contracts. These situations can easily create dependence and a shift of mission toward collusion with government. This may not be a bad thing in and of itself, but it requires careful oversight by boards and executives.

Many nonprofit managers have found that focusing carefully on the core mission leads to more significant financial support. Even though this may seem counterintuitive, casting one's net more widely simply leads to greater ambiguity about the organization's core purposes. The answer is to create clarity about mission that invites participation.

The second ethical problem occurs when a potentially large donor comes to the organization with a proposal that is outside the core mission or that will be accomplished in unethical ways. In an organization that is dependent on such individually large donations there is great temptation to accept the donation with the strings attached. In some cases the manager may try later to adjust the implementation of the donation back in an ethical direction, but the damage to the organization's life has already been done. If, indeed, part of the purpose of the executive is to monitor the organization's ethical boundaries, and those boundaries have been violated by the very person who is supposed to be monitoring them, then there is no reason for anyone else in the organization to observe ethical bounds thereafter. One or more persons in such as organization might serve as a whistleblower, but there are too many examples where organizations simply continued to slip into more unethical behavior. The only appropriate response to an unethical advance is to decline the offer or require that the relationship be announced. As Justice Holmes once said, the best disinfectant is the light of day.

Competition with the Private Sector

A growing controversy is competition between nonprofit and for-profit organizations. As funds dwindle in response to government devolution and lower individual contributions, nonprofits are led to provide goods and services for sale on the open market. These can and often do overlap with private sector activities, and lead to cries of foul play by for-profit managers due to the obvious tax advantages possessed by nonprofit organizations. The controversy has led to proposals as far-reaching as withdrawal of an organization's tax-exempt status, when such claims are verified, to a complete overhaul of tax codes by the states and national government.

It seems that two actions can be taken by nonprofit managers to address the concerns. First, any activity that apparently or actually competes with a private sector activity ought to be done openly and, indeed, in conversation with representatives of the competitor vendors. Such conservation can lead very quickly to cooperation rather than conflict, which helps organizations in both sectors. The comments made previously about key stakeholders apply here as well. Second, the nonprofit manager should participate in larger conversations about private sector competition in such arenas as the Small Business Administration or in schools of management at local colleges and universities. This, too, can help diminish suspicion and resistance, as well as potentially recruiting stakeholders to one's side, and that can only work to the nonprofit organization's advantage.

Conclusion

This entry has pointed up a dilemma for those who work in and who support nonprofit organizations with their time and money. Criticism of nonprofit organizations is rising. Representative Clarence Ishtook (R–OK) has proposed an amendment to the federal budget that would prohibit any nonprofit organization receiving federal grants from advocating or lobbying in any form. Hearings have

been held on the power, influence, and resources of such large nonprofits as the American Association of Retired Persons and the United Way of the United States. The trustworthiness of nonprofit organizations is very much in question.

The dilemma is the legal status of very different sorts of nonprofit organizations with very different purposes and the resulting tax benefits of their common status. The Internal Revenue Service (IRS) code already recognizes some differences within the sector. A question for the field is whether a clearer distinction should be made between various types of nonprofits. For example, one can clearly delineate at least six subsectors: Mutual benefit organizations (for example, clubs and fellowships), private schools (including universities and academic foundations), foundations that primarily make grants, business-related associations (trade associations or unions), churches and other religious organizations, and charitable organizations (such as food banks and free clinics). A further distinction might be made for advocacy groups, although one might expect that any of the above-mentioned groups would be advocating for themselves or their constituencies as an integral part of their reason for being. This also gets into First Amendment free speech rights of persons and corporations. The public policy issues surrounding these questions are at best murky. However, it seems obvious that there is a basic difference between the purposes of a trade association that represents homebuilders and a nonprofit community service agency that feeds and houses the homeless.

The contention put forward here is that the single differentiating character of the charitable nonprofit organization is its primary focus on ethics. This can be expressed as trust, as mission, as virtue, or as something else. The level of trust has eroded: the implicit social contract between nonprofit organizations and the larger society has been broken. It is at this point that the work must be done. Academics and practitioners need to articulate a clearer understanding of how this social contract operates in the real world in order to recreate the sense of virtue required of nonprofit organizations.

The implications for public administration are equally complicated. Many public manages have found their work devolving from service delivery to contract management. Nonprofit organizations have been major players in this development as they have received larger grants and contracts and have had greater demands for services placed upon them. Public managers have a stake in how the field develops. Questions include whether nonprofit or for-profit organizations are better equipped to provide goods and services in the name of the government, or indeed whether government should be so closely tied to either sector. Should public managers encourage the growth of the nonprofit sector? Where will public entities draw the line on tax advantages to the sector while there is an increasing crunch between revenues and expenditures, and while calls for tax cuts grow louder? What are the public policy issues surrounding concerns about a defective or failed economy in which the underclass grows larger and middle-class incomes fall, and a smaller percentage of the population controls a greater percentage of the total wealth of the nation? Public managers who would be leaders need to familiarize themselves with these and the many other issues surrounding the nonprofit sector in their domain, in order to be responsive to the rapidly changing needs and demands of those organizations and the people that they serve.

PETER J. VAN HOOK

BIBLIOGRAPHY

Bennett, James T., and Thomas J. DiLorenzo, 1989. *Unfair Competition: The Profits of Nonprofits.* Lanham, MD: Hamilton.

Carver, John, 1990. *Boards That Make a Difference: A New Design for Leadership in Nonprofit and Public Organizations.* San Francisco: Jossey-Bass.

Connor, Tracy Daniel, ed., 1988. *The Nonprofit Organization Handbook.* New York: McGraw-Hill.

Cooper, Terry L., 1990. *The Responsible Administrator: An Approach to Ethics for the Administrative Role.* 3d ed. San Francisco: Jossey-Bass.

Covey, Stephen, 1992. *Principle-Centered Leadership.* New York: Simon & Schuster.

Drucker, Peter F., 1990. *Managing the Nonprofit Organization.* New York: HarperCollins.

Gardener, John W., 1990. "Leadership and the Nonprofit Sector." Working paper No. 10. Institute for Nonprofit Organization Management. San Francisco: University of San Francisco.

Glaser, John S., 1994. *The United Way Scandal.* New York: Wiley.

Hauerwas, Stanley M., 1981. *A Community of Character.* Notre Dame, IN: University of Notre Dame Press.

Hunter, James Davison, 1991. *Culture Wars: The Struggle to Define America.* New York: Basic Books.

Jeavons, Thomas H., 1994. "Ethics in Nonprofit Management: Creating a Culture of Integrity." In Robert D. Herman, ed., *The Jossey-Bass Handbook of Nonprofit Leadership and Management.* San Francisco: Jossey-Bass, pp. 184–207.

Lohman, Roger A., 1992. *The Commons: New Perspectives on Nonprofit Organization and Voluntary Action.* San Francisco: Jossey-Bass.

O'Neill, Michael, 1990. *Ethics in Nonprofit Management: A Collection of Cases.* San Francisco: University of San Francisco.

Schein, Edgar H., 1992. *Organizational Culture and Leadership.* 2d ed. San Francisco: Jossey-Bass.

Smith, David Horton, 1995. *Entrusted: The Moral Responsibilities of Trusteeship.* Bloomington: Indiana University Press.

Waitley, Denis, 1995. *Empires of the Mind.* New York: William Morrow.

Wheatley, Margaret, 1992. *Leadership and the New Science.* San Francisco: Barret-Koehler.

Wolf, Thomas A., 1990. *Managing A Nonprofit Organization.* New York: Prentice-Hall.

EURATOM.

EURATOM. The name by which the European Atomic Energy Community is commonly known. This supranational organization was established by the Treaty of Rome, which was signed in 1957 and came into operation in 1958, together with the European Economic Community (EEC). The new organization was created by the founding member states of the European Coal and Steel Community, namely, France, Germany, Italy, Belgium, the Netherlands, and Luxembourg. The Rome Treaties of 1957 were an effort to relaunch the process of European integration after the failure of the proposed European Defense Community in 1954.

For Jean Monnet, who drafted the Schuman Plan, which led to the European Coal and Steel Community, and who was also the spiritual father of the Rome Treaty, Euratom was the more important of the two new organizations. It presented an important economic sector in which integration was desirable and could lead to "spillover," that is, would prompt further integration into other policy areas. The emergence of Euratom can only be understood in the context of its time: the growing realization that fossil-based fuel was destined to run sooner or later led European states to seek alternative sources of energy, including atomic or nuclear energy. Moreover, Monnet believed that a collective European approach to research and development in nuclear energy could forestall the emergence in France of its own nuclear bomb. This aim was supported by the U.S. government, which was not only concerned with safeguarding export opportunities in Europe but also eager to stem the proliferation of nuclear weapons.

The proposal to establish Euratom was accepted by the French National Assembly on the basis that, first, France could expect to benefit from the technological expertise of the other member states; second, France could gain access to the high-quality uranium deposits of the Belgian Congo, now Zaire; third, France could expect to be a net beneficiary of the Euratom budget since the French nuclear research program amounted to two-thirds of research of all the member states combined; fourth, the creation of Euratom with its supranational institutional structure meant that West Germany would not develop a national nuclear industry; finally, the French won an important concession during the negotiations that led to the Rome Treaty, namely, that in cases in which national security was concerned, it would not be obligatory to exchange technological information and expertise. Alternately, West Germany was less in favor of Euratom than of the EEC, fearing the adverse effects on its coal-producing regions, such as the Rhineland, of which Konrad Adenauer was a native. The French, however, were prepared to accept the EEC and its proposed customs union and common market only in return for Euratom.

The objective of Euratom was to control and direct the development of a European nuclear energy industry and, ultimately, a common nuclear energy policy. The institutional structure of the new organization was based on that of the European Coal and Steel Community. A new commission and a new council of ministers was created. The member states decided to expand the terms of reference of the Parliamentary Assembly and the Court of Justice of the European Coal and Steel Community rather than to create new bodies. This was achieved through the Common Conventions Act.

However, Euratom was not destined to achieve its original aims because it suffered from a number of early setbacks. The independent commission charged with initiating legislation got off to a slow start. Though the Rome Treaty came into effect in 1958, its first president became ill and had to be replaced, with the result that it was not until late 1959 that the commission began to function properly. By then, both Germany and Italy had begun their own national nuclear programs to ensure that France would not dominate the sector as a result of the joint funding that Euratom facilitated.

During the 1960s France and Germany went further and each independently introduced fast breeder reactor programs. No longer in the position of providing political impetus and leadership in terms of directing a European nuclear energy policy per se, the commission assumed the reduced role of coordinating national nuclear programs instead. A further weakness suffered by Euratom was the lack of a coordinated approach among the three communities, each of which had its own commission and council of ministers: the European Coal and Steel Community actively sought a protected market for coal; the European Economic Community advocated the importation of cheap energy from third countries; and, meanwhile, Euratom took the position that nuclear energy should supplant coal and other sources of energy altogether. In April 1965 the treaty establishing a single council and a single commission of the European Communities was signed. The Merger Treaty came into effect in July 1967; only then did the European Communities begin to operate functionally as three, and organically as one, through common institutions.

Not only did Euratom not lead to a common energy policy, but also it arguably prevented such a policy from emerging. The Rome Treaty neglected the potential of oil—presenting a stark choice for Europe between high-priced coal and low-priced nuclear energy—with no reference at all being made to oil. This omission to some extent led to unilateral energy policies among the member states. This oversight may be partially explained by the fact that oil was expensive within Europe at the time, and the Suez Crisis of 1956 highlighted the risk attendant on a dependency on imported energy supplies.

Euratom never fulfilled the high expectations of it that were entertained by Jean Monnet, that of facilitating "spillover" into other economic policy areas. It was destined to play only a modest role in the process of European integration, confining its activities largely to the coordination of research and development programs. It was to be overshadowed by the European Economic Community,

which was to become the best known of the three communities. The EEC committed member states to a decidedly more ambitious and wide-ranging set of objectives, namely, to create a customs union and a common market among the member states.

MARGARET MARY MALONE

BIBLIOGRAPHY

Archer, Clive, 1990. *Organizing Western Europe*. London: Edward Arnold.
Urwin, Derek W., 1989. *Western Europe Since 1945: A Political History*. 4th ed. London: Longman.
———, 1991. *The Community of Europe: A History of European Integration Since 1945*. London: Longman.
Willis, F. R., 1968. *France, Germany, and the New Europe, 1945–1967*. Rev. and Expanded. Stanford, CA: Stanford University Press.

EUROPEAN BANK FOR RECONSTRUCTION AND DEVELOPMENT (EBRD).

The main financial institution, based in London, created to serve the post-cold war economic and entrepreneurial needs of former European communist countries transitioning from command economies to capitalism. The coincidence of a perceived lack of resources and an official skepticism about the merits of a public sector-led European version of the Marshall Plan left European governments with little choice but to opt for a mixed-market solution to the security problems posed by the countries that were formally members of the Warsaw Pact and the Council for Mutual Economic Assistance (COMECON).

Purpose and Role

The idea of the "European Bank" was put forward by President François Mitterand of France in Strasbourg on October 25, 1989. It came to fruition on May 29, 1990, with the signature of its agreement by 40 countries, together with the approval of the European Communities (EC) Commission and the European Investment Bank. The European Bank for Reconstruction and Development effectively opened for business on April 15, 1991. Its mission is to foster the move toward market-oriented economies and to promote private and entrepreneurial initiative in the Central and Eastern European countries committed to and applying the fundamental principles of multiparty democracy, pluralism, and market economics.

The EBRD aims to help member countries implement structural and sectoral economic reform, including demonopolization, decentralization, and the application of instruments of privatization, taking into account the particular needs of countries at different stages of transition. Its activities include the promotion of private sector activity, the strengthening of financial institutions and legal systems, and the development of the infrastructure needed to support the private sector.

The EBRD encourages cofinancing and foreign direct investment from the private and public sectors, helps to mobilize domestic capital, and provides some technical cooperation. It works in close cooperation with international financial institutions and, where appropriate, other international organizations. As might be expected of an institution created in the 1990s, the EBRD aims to promote environmentally sound and sustainable development in all of its activities.

Membership, Capital, and Organization

The EBRD has 59 members (57 countries, the European Community, and the European Investment Bank), including 25 countries in central and eastern Europe and in the former Soviet Union. The bank's initial subscribed capital is ECU $10 billion, of which 30 percent is paid in. The EBRD also borrows in various currencies on the world's capital markets. The powers of the EBRD are vested in a board of governors, to which each member appoints a governor. The board of governors has delegated powers to a board of directors with 23 members, who are elected by governors for a three-year term. The board of directors is responsible for the direction of the general operations of the bank, including establishing policies, taking decisions concerning projects, and approving the budget. The president is elected by the board of governors for a four-year term.

Financing

The EBRD, as befits its economic, political, and theoretical parentage, can operate in both the private and public sectors. To this extent, it mirrors European confidence in continuing cooperation between the two sectors, whatever declaratory policy may require to be said publicly in favor of the private sector. It merges, in short, the principles and practices of merchant *and* development banking, providing both confidence and funding for private or privatizable enterprises and providing for physical and financial infrastructure projects to support the private sector. To that end, the EBRD uses a broad range of financing instruments, tailored to specific projects. Its offers include loans, equity investments, and guarantees. In all of its operations the bank aims to apply sound banking and investment principles. The terms of the EBRD's funding are designed to enable it to cooperate both with other international financial institutions, such as the World Bank and the International

Monetary Fund, and with public and private financial institutions through cofinancing arrangements.

From the beginning, confidence in the success of the enterprise has always depended on political developments in the former Warsaw Pact countries. The main critique of the bank and its founding economic ideology has been that it institutionalizes support for a particular region of the world that is, all things considered, less in need of such support than other regions of the globe. A cynic, or latter-day left-wing ideologue, might even suggest that, despite its good intentions to the contrary, the EBRD has less to do with Eastern European reconstruction and development than with maintaining Western Europe's position of relative economic importance. A fuller, less biased or short-term perspective will be available by the end of its first decade.

PETER FOOT

EUROPEAN CAPITAL BUDGETING. The financial procedure by which the European public sector separates capital outlays from current expenditure. A separate capital budget may serve as a policy instrument to help decisionmakers prioritize and select capital proposals among alternatives.

History

The idea of a capital budget is far from new. The Dutch constitution of 1815, for example, already required a division of the budget in a current and a capital budget. A persistent problem, however, is the distinction between current spending and capital outlays. This question has always been closely related to the "golden rule." According to this budgetary norm, the budget is allowed to borrow for capital outlays, but not for current expenditure. This makes the question of how to discriminate between current and capital outlays even more urgent.

In public budgeting the golden rule prevailed until World War II, at least in theory. After World War II, the Keynesian revolution led to the introduction of more flexible budget norms. They were anticyclical in nature, that is, they intended to level off business cycles. In the 1950s, however, it became obvious that functional finance or "fine-tuning" of the budget is a superb theoretical idea, but those who implement it face many problems in practice.

Pros

Two principal arguments have been put forward for implementing a capital budget. First, it is argued that a capital budget improves the balance of capital outlays against current expenditure and, thus, the efficiency of the use of scarce means. Cash outlays for productive uses are coordinated to consumptive expenditure in a unified budget, causing a budget bias against capital programs. A US $10 million outlay to construct a building in a given year contributes to the year's deficit the same as a US $10 million outlay for fuel costs or income transfers. The capital outlay may be undervalued, since its costs, but not its future benefit, are visible in the year. In a sense, it requires a capital asset to have a one-year payback to be able to compete equally with current operating programs. A capital budget corrects this budget bias by distributing outlays in budget reporting over the useful life of the capital investment. When one assigns the annual cost of capital to the current budget, one can visualize that the benefit of capital outlays is spread over a number of years. In addition, the record of interest payments and depreciation outlays over a range of years would permit one to have a better balance of capital outlays against each other, since the annual costs of different capital programs can be compared.

The second argument for a capital budget is that it provides a criterion for the means of revenue raising: Loans are proper instruments for funding capital outlays, whereas levies are appropriate instruments for funding current expenditure. The underlying idea is that the implementation of a capital budget, when coupled with the golden rule, improves expenditure control and budget discipline.

Cons

Four arguments have been put forward against the possible (re)implementation of a capital budget; essentially, they criticize the argument for a capital budget. First, it is argued that other means than a capital budget can be used to realize an efficient allocation of resources: Examples are cost-benefit analyses, the application of a full-accruals basis in the budget, and decentralization of budgetary management. In addition, one may take the view that the quality of political decisionmaking rather than the kind of bookkeeping determines the efficiency of the use of resources. In this view, there is nothing that prevents politicians and bureaucrats from judging current and capital outlays on their own merits. However, this does not harm the argument that a spread of the cost of capital over a range of years permits a better comparison of current expenditure and the annual cost of capital.

The second argument against a capital budget centers on the time dimension. An efficient allocation of resources would be hampered because the political benefits of expenditure are received in the present, whereas their costs are shifted to the future. A stronger tendency to spend capital outlays would be the result; and the growth of the capital budget could become uncontrollable. Essentially, this argument implies that political decisionmaking not necessarily corresponds to a rational balance of benefits and ex-

penditure from the social point of view. Politicians take all kinds of subjective considerations into account, such as a concern about the number of votes they may win at the next election. Thus this argument seems valid insofar as the underlying assumption holds, that is, that the politician's balance of expenditure differs from a rational balance to society as a whole.

A third argument against the capital budget centers on the golden rule. Effectively, this rule prevents the stabilization function of the budget from being exercised. According to the golden rule, the current budget has to be balanced, ruling out the possibility of functional finance. Consequently, the budget policy may bring about procyclical effects, since the current account has to be balanced at all times, even in the downswing. As a result, an increase of current public spending, which combats the downswing, is coupled with tax increases that reinforce the downswing. This objection could be met by applying the golden rule over the business cycle rather than on an annual basis, however. Consequently, temporary current budget deficits that merely result from cyclical causes are allowed during a downswing, whereas surpluses arise during the upswing. As a result, the current budget is balanced over the business cycle. Practice has shown, however, that if one pursues such a policy, he or she is then prone to a political bias in favor of a deficit, since the cyclical and structural components of economic growth are difficult to determine.

A fourth argument against a capital budget is that arbitrary decisions have to be made. Obviously, spending on physical investments would be recorded on the capital budget. But how does one deal with other expenditures that may also be considered investments, for example, spending on education (human capital), environment, and so on? Essentially, this type of spending bears the same characteristics as physical investments do in that they yield benefits over a longer period than a year and often over a very long term. Thus decisions on the distinction between current and capital outlays are almost by definition arbitrary. Arbitrary decisions have also to be made with regard to the distinction between current and capital outlays and with respect to the depreciation policy. Illustrative is that in the 1920s the Dutch government recorded guns on the capital budget and shells on the current budget, and it cut back its current expenditure by lengthening the depreciation period on guns.

European Practice

Empirical evidence suggests that in Europe a unified budget is the norm. Finland and Sweden used to have a capital budget, but abolished it in the 1980s. Though in Germany there is a distinction between a current and a capital budget, it is merely an administrative artifact. In practice, Germany uses a unified (federal) budget, which is related to the constitutional requirement that public borrowing does not exceed the amount of investments included in the budget. Only four European countries (Greece, Ireland, Luxembourg, and Portugal) somehow make an actual difference between a current and a capital budget. This classification of outlays appears to present a problem in all countries using a capital budget. Only after long-lasting debates did more or less general accepted definitions emerge, which were later adjusted under the pressure of the topical situation.

In Greece, outlays have to contribute to productive capacity and economic growth has to be recorded on the capital budget. In practice, spending on roads, buildings, infrastructure, and so on are recorded on the capital budget. Capital transfers from central government to lower-level governments are only recorded on the capital budget if they pertain to specific investment projects carried out by local governments. In addition, a small part of military investment expenditure pertaining to investments—such as radar stations—also used by the private sector is recorded on the capital budget. The Greek criterion for distinguishing between current and capital outlays resembles the principle of productivity (or indirect return).

Ireland has used a current and capital budget since the 1950s. The following expenditures are recorded on the capital budget: (1) investments by central and local governments, by the semi-public sector, and by health boards, insofar as their expected life exceeds one year; (2) capital transfers and loans of central and local governments and semi-public sector bodies to third parties; and (3) capital transfers related to international commitments. In addition, these expenditures should exceed a minimum amount. Military investments are recorded as current outlays, conforming to the national account system. The Irish definition of capital outlays concurs with the principle of durable benefit.

Since Luxembourg's constitution requires that the current budget be balanced, it is only permitted to borrow for those expenditures recorded on the capital budget. The criterion applied is that the investments' expected life must exceed one year. In practice, the capital budget contains special funds for investments in telecommunications, the environment, and roads.

Evaluation

The credibility of the main argument for a capital budget, being that it reinforces the allocation function of the budget, seems questionable. An important consideration is that, in principle, there is nothing that prevents politicians and bureaucrats from judging current and capital outlays on their own merits. It is difficult to accept the view that the kind of bookkeeping determines the balance of expenditure. And if it does, it seems to suggest that there is some-

thing wrong with the quality of political decisionmaking rather than the bookkeeping.

Admittedly, a sound argument for a capital budget seems that a spread of the cost of capital over a range of years permits a better comparison of current expenditure with the annual cost of capital. However, this may also be realized by other means, such as cost-benefit analyses. Thus a formal division of the budget in a current and a capital budget is not a prerequisite for a better comparison of current with capital outlays.

In addition, it is important to be conscious of the fact that a capital budget may not only reinforce the allocation function of the budget but also could hinder it, in particular if the capital budget is coupled with the golden rule. If current expenditures have to be financed by taxes, whereas outlays recorded on the capital budget may be funded by loans, politicians and bureaucrats may widen the concept of capital outlays.

All in all, the formal division of the budget seems less crucial to the allocation function than the politicians' willingness to accept a rational decisionmaking process and to take into account all relevant costs and benefits of public expenditure.

M. PETER VAN DER HOEK

BIBLIOGRAPHY

Boness, A. James, 1972. *Capital Budgeting.* London: Praeger.
Comiez, Maynard S., 1966. *A Capital Budget Statement for the U.S. Government.* Washington, DC: Brookings Institution.
General Accounting Office, 1988. *Budget Issues: Capital Budgeting for the Federal Government.* Washington, DC: General Accounting Office.
———, 1993. *Budget Issues: Incorporating an Investment Component in the Federal Budget.* Washington, DC: General Accounting Office.
Hagen, Jürgen von, 1992. "Budgeting Procedures and Fiscal Performance in the European Communities." *Economic Papers,* no. 96 (October). Brussels: European Commission.
Miller, Gerald J., 1991. *Government Financial Management Theory.* New York: Marcel Dekker.
Musgrave, Richard A., and Peggy B. Musgrave, 1989. *Public Finance in Theory and Practice.* New York: McGraw-Hill.
Rutherford, B. A., 1983. *Financial Reporting in the Public Sector.* London: Butterworths.

EUROPEAN COAL AND STEEL COMMUNITY.

The first supranational organization in Western Europe involving the delegation by national governments of decisionmaking power to a higher authority in respect to two key economic sectors, namely, coal and steel. It was the first of the three European Communities established in the post–World War II period. The European Economic Community (EEC) and the European Atomic Energy Community (EAEC) came into operation in 1958.

The European Coal and Steel Community was established on foot of the Paris Treaty, signed in 1951, that arose from the Schuman Plan announced by the French foreign minister, Robert Schuman, on May 9, 1950. The new organization was an effort to resolve a number of practical problems that had confronted European states in the postwar period. It arose essentially out of the so-called German problem. There was growing concern in the United States that a debilitated Germany could be susceptible to pressure from the East. Therefore the United States exerted pressure on France to find a means of strengthening Germany and aligning it clearly and unambiguously with Western Europe. An economically revitalized Germany was perceived to be necessary in order to forestall the further encroachment of Soviet communism in Western Europe.

The problem was how to facilitate German economic revival while allaying French fears that a resurgent Germany would not attempt again to dominate militarily the continent of Europe. The 1950 Schuman Plan provided a practical solution to a practical problem while laying the foundation for a future European federation. The plan, drafted by Jean Monnet, proposed that "Franco-German production of coal and steel as a whole be placed under a common High Authority, within the framework of an organization open to the participation of the other countries of Europe."

The Schuman Plan was underpinned by both economic and political motives. The benefits of economic integration in terms of increasing production and liberalizing trade, thus preparing the way for economic unification, was not the sole objective. The political motives of the plan were twofold: first, the basis of the new organization was a Franco-German rapprochement. The choice of coal and steel had a symbolic significance; they are traditionally known as the industries of war. The explicit purpose of the Schuman Plan was to make the possibility of any war between France and Germany not only unthinkable but also materially impossible. Second, the pooling of coal and steel production established the basis for economic development, which was envisaged to be the first step toward the evolution of a European federation.

The plan was greeted enthusiastically by Konrad Adenauer, the German chancellor, who was dissatisfied with the International Ruhr Authority established in April 1949 by Britain, France, the United States, the Benelux states, and Germany to control the distribution of the coal, coke, and steel of the Ruhr. The Benelux states and Italy agreed to participate in the new organization; the United Kingdom declined the invitation to join the new community. Britain's Labour government had just succeeded in nationalizing the coal industry and was just about to nationalize the steel industry; therefore the conditions were not propitious. Moreover, there was in general a degree of skepticism regarding the supranational nature of the new organization, which required participating states to surrender decisionmaking power in favor of supranational institutions in relation to the management of the coal and steel industries.

The treaty establishing the European Coal and Steel Community was signed in April 1951, ratified by the national parliaments of the participating states by June 1952, and came into force on July 25, 1952. The treaty, which is valid for 50 years, includes 100 articles, six protocols, as well as numerous annexes, including an exchange of letters between France and Germany on the Saar region. This region, with its coal and steel resources, was in 1947 a politically autonomous territory in an economic union with France. Following a referendum in the Saar region in 1955, the electorate of this overwhelmingly Germanic region voted to become a part of the Federal Republic of Germany.

Institutions

The objective of the European Coal and Steel Community was to create a common market in coal and steel in order to promote "economic expansion, growth of employment, and a rising standard of living."

Article 1 provided that the European Coal and Steel Community was to be "founded upon a common market, common objectives and common institutions." The new organization set out to ensure supply in coal and steel, to ensure reasonable prices, to increase production, to promote improved working conditions, as well as to promote orderly expansion and a modernization of production.

The nature of the organization was a departure from all other international organizations that had gone before. For the first time in their history, a number of European states agreed to accept a degree of supranationality, that is, the delegation of decisionmaking power from the national level to a higher level, that of the institutions of the European Coal and Steel Community. Thus the basic principle of the new organization was the abnegation of national sovereignty in a limited but decisive field.

Responsibility for carrying the objectives of the Paris Treaty into effect lay with the collective institutions of the European Coal and Steel Community. The community was served by four institutions, namely, the High Authority, the Special Council of Ministers, the Parliamentary Assembly, and the Court of Justice, as well as one organ, the Consultative Committee.

The innovative feature of the institutional structure established by the Paris Treaty was the High Authority, which was conceived of as a supranational body. The High Authority originally comprised nine members, appointed by common accord of member states for six years, on the grounds of their general competence. Each of the larger member states, Germany, France, and Italy, were entitled to appoint two members of the High Authority, and each of the smaller Benelux states were allowed to appointed one.

Article 9 provided that the members of the High Authority were to be "completely independent in the performance of their functions, in the general interest of the Community." In order to preserve the supranational character of their functions, the nine members were to neither seek nor take instructions from any government or other body, nor would member states seek to influence them in the performance of their duties. The powers of the High Authority were considerable: it could control prices and production levels; it could direct investment; it could also bring to task any national authority that failed to comply with its decisions. Jean Monnet was appointed the first president of the High Authority in 1952.

The Dutch and Belgians insisted on the creation of the Special Council of Ministers in order to safeguard the interests of the smaller member states vis-à-vis their larger partners. Articles 26 to 30 set out the powers and composition of the council. It was composed of representatives of member states' national governments and could make decisions by simple majority, qualified majority, or unanimity, as stipulated by the treaty.

The Common Assembly was the representative body of the European Coal and Steel Community, originally comprising 78 delegates appointed by national parliaments.

The Parliamentary Assembly was envisaged primarily as a supervisory body: It was empowered to debate the annual report of the High Authority and could dismiss the latter en bloc if it voted by two-thirds majority to do so. The formal powers of the assembly were therefore very limited: it possessed no budgetary powers, no legislative functions, and no power of appointment over the High Authority. Thus the assembly's power of dismissal was more apparent than real because the national governments could reappoint the members of the High Authority that the assembly had dismissed.

Article 31 of the Paris Treaty provided that the function of the Court of Justice was "to ensure that the law is observed in the interpretation and implementation of the Treaty and of the regulations made thereunder." The court was originally composed of seven judges and two advocates-general, who were appointed on the basis of their legal expertise and were expected to be independent in the performance of their duties.

The last body created by the Paris Treaty was the Consultative Committee, which was envisaged to be a purely advisory body to the High Authority. Article 18 of the Paris Treaty provided that the Consultative Committee be composed of an equal number of producers, workers, consumers, and dealers in the coal and steel industries, who would be appointed by the Council of Ministers for a two-year term.

The limitations to which the supranational High Authority and, by extension, the European Coal and Steel Community itself was subject was thrown into sharp relief in 1959. In that year, as a result of two mild winters and the increased use of oil as an energy source among European consumers, there was a surplus of coal in the European Coal and Steel Community. Given the substantial increase in coal stocks, the High Authority attempted to declare a "manifest crisis," provided for by the Paris Treaty. This would have granted the High Authority emergency powers to, for example, impose import controls and production quotas. Such a declaration required a qualified majority vote in favor by the Special Council of Ministers, however. This vote was not forthcoming because the individual states chose to adopt unilateral policies instead. The incident revealed the limits of the supranational authority when it was attempting to impose a general policy that the member states were resolved to resist.

The European Coal and Steel Community was hailed by Jean Monnet as the "first expression of the Europe that is being born." It differed from all other international organizations established in the post–World War II period in Europe in that its institutions were conferred with supranational authority; the decisions of the High Authority, now known as the commission, were legally binding on the participating states. The European Coal and Steel Community was envisaged as the "first concrete foundation of a European federation indispensable to the preservation of peace." It was followed in 1958 by the European Economic Community and the European Atomic Energy Community, or Euratom. Together the three became known collectively as the European Community.

MARGARET MARY MALONE

BIBLIOGRAPHY

Archer, Clive, 1990. *Organizing Western Europe.* London: Edward Arnold.

Diebold, W., 1959. *The Schuman Plan.* New York: Council on Foreign Relations.

Laqueur, Walter, 1992. *Europe in Our Time: A History, 1945–1992.* London: Penguin.

Lister, L., 1960. *Europe's Coal and Steel Community: An Experiment in Economic Union.* New York: Twentieth Century Fund.

Milward, A. S., 1984. *The Reconstruction of Western Europe, 1945–1951.* London: Methuen.

Pryce, Roy, 1987. *The Dynamics of European Union.* London: Croom Helm.

Urwin, Derek W., 1989. *Western Europe Since 1945: A Political History.* 4th ed. London: Longman.

———, 1991. *The Community of Europe: A History of European Integration Since 1945.* London: Longman.

Willis, F. R., 1968. *France, Germany, and the New Europe 1945–1967.* Rev. and expanded. Stanford, CA: Stanford University Press.

EUROPEAN ECONOMIC AREA (EEA).

An economic and trading area, comprising members of the European Union (EU) and the European Free Trade Association (EFTA), in which the free movement of goods, persons, services, and capital would be assured. In addition, certain other joint policies would be followed. This was established by an agreement signed at Oporto, Portugal, on May 2, 1992.

The EEA had a difficult gestation. Originally proposed by Jacques Delors when he was president of the European Communities (EC) Commission in 1988, negotiations finally resulted in an agreement in 1991. The European Court of Justice (ECJ), however, considered that the proposed court system (in which disputes with an EFTA element would be considered by the ECJ, with some EFTA judges added on) might threaten the ECJ's independence and refused to approve it. Urgent rethinking followed, and it was agreed that a separate EFTA Court should be established. This was acceptable to the ECJ. Then, on 6 December 1992, in a referendum, Switzerland voted against joining. Urgent adjustments were again made to the agreement, and it finally entered into force on January 1, 1994.

On January 1, 1995, Austria, Finland, and Sweden joined the EU. This left the EFTA side of the EEA consisting of only Iceland, Liechtenstein, and Norway; its institutions still function, however, even if in a reduced fashion. The centripetal forces of the European Union—institutional, legal, and economic—have overwhelmingly created what amounts to a West European economic condominium. The future of its relationship with the states of Central and Eastern Europe will be part of the European agenda well into the twenty-first century.

The highest legislative body of the European Economic Area is the EEA Council. This takes the serious political decisions. It consists of ministers from all of the countries concerned. The Joint Committee takes most of the day-to-day decisions and consists of high representatives (ministers or ambassadors) from the EU and from the EFTA states. The Joint Committee is also the main dispute-settling body for problems arising between the two sides. Each side has "one voice" and decisions can only be reached by consensus. Naturally, the EFTA side is conscious of its relatively small size and acts accordingly.

For the EU States, the EC Commission acts as watchdog, making sure that the free-trading rules in the agreement are observed by the EU states. The EFTA Surveillance Authority (ESA), based in Brussels, carries out the same tasks in relation to the EFTA states. The sharing-out of the jurisdiction of the two bodies in dealing with companies that have interests in both EFTA and EU states is complicated. Essentially, ESA will have jurisdiction if at least two-thirds of the EEA turnover of the company concerned occurs in the EFTA states.

Just as the EU has the European Court of Justice in Luxembourg to sort out the law, the EFTA States in the EEA have the EFTA Court. Currently based in Geneva, although shortly to move to Luxembourg as well, the EFTA Court hears disputes between ESA and the EFTA states about incorrect application of the agreement, and complaints (from companies, for example) about ESA's role. The court also gives "advisory opinions" to national (EFTA) courts on the interpretation of the agreement. Its powers mirror to a large extent those of the ECJ.

PETER RODNEY

EUROPEAN FREE TRADE ASSOCIATION (EFTA).

The economic institution established as the European rival to the European Communities (EC), now the European Union (EU). Western European countries that did not accept the loss of sovereignty involved in joining the EU nevertheless wanted to benefit from the free-trading rules the EU proposed and to liberalize trade between themselves and others. In order not to be excluded from EU and other markets, they set up EFTA as a rival organization to the EU, with the negotiating (and retaliatory) power not available to individual states.

The original member states were Austria, Denmark, Norway, Portugal, Sweden, Switzerland, and the United Kingdom. Finland, Iceland, and Liechtenstein joined later. Denmark and the UK joined the EU in 1973; Portugal in 1986; and Austria, Finland, and Sweden in 1995. Therefore the remaining members are Iceland, Liechtenstein, Norway, and Switzerland.

The decisionmaking body in EFTA is ultimately the EFTA Council. Ministers from each member state attend a ministerial meeting, which takes place every six months, or more often if required. The council, consisting of each state's ambassador to the organization's headquarters in Geneva, makes many important decisions, but most day-to-day business is done by "deputies," that is, the ambassador's deputy (who in fact specializes in EFTA affairs). Decisions are made only by consensus, and no one member can be forced to act against his or her country's will. The members take a realistic view of what is and is not possible, however, and many decisions that are unpalatable to one or another member may still get through.

Unlike the EU (but like most other international organizations), EFTA has only a small secretariat that organizes and assists in its work. The secretariat is headed by a secretary general and is based in Geneva, but with an office in Brussels. Indeed, most of the secretariat's work arises in Brussels since he or she works closely with the EC in many areas, but the ambassadors and deputies are based in Geneva.

The secretariat is organized to cover various wide subject fields, such as barriers to trade, technical standards, and the coordinating of trade agreements with other countries, although the latter are negotiated individually by the members. The situation is complicated by the fact that all of the member countries, except Switzerland, are members of the European Economic Area (EEA), and the secretariat also has a section dealing with that aspect of EFTA's work.

EFTA works entirely in English (including in its ministerial and council meetings). This makes, enormous savings, since there is no need for translation and interpretation. An English-speaking official makes sure that the texts produced are in correct English. Further, since no members official native language is English, no one member has an advantage over the others.

EFTA members achieved complete free trade among themselves by 1970–ahead of the EU. With its reduced membership, however, it is of reduced importance except as a useful bridge (with the European Economic Area) to the EU. There is some truth to the cruel jibe that the only matters its members now have left to discuss are fish and fondue.

PETER RODNEY

EUROPEAN INSTITUTE OF PUBLIC ADMINISTRATION (EIPA).

The Maastricht-based organization founded in 1981, which is the only independent institute of public policy and administration with a European mission of public service, linked to the European Union (EU), providing a variety of services to national administrations and institutions from the EU in support of their tasks and responsibilities related to European integration. The general aim of the institute is to make a practical contribution to the European unification process by way of applied research, training, consultancy, and publications on the institutions, decisionmaking processes, and policies of the EU, and public management and law.

Activities

EIPA is a nonprofit institution. It runs training activities and carries out research and consultancy on a contract basis. It also organizes multinational activities, which are open to all public servants from the member states, the future member states, and the institutions of the EU.

Its workshops, seminars, and colloquia are designed to improve and update the knowledge and skills of those responsible for policymaking and implementation in the member states and in the EU institutions.

The four units at the European Institute of Public Administration deal with very specific topics.

EU Institutions and Political Integration

Among the many challenges facing the European Union, the question of its institutional development and further political integration among the member states is high on the agenda. Issues such as the democratic deficit, the future role of the European Commission, and the application in concrete terms of the principle of subsidiarity have only been addressed in part by the Maastricht Treaty and continue to dominate the discussion on political union. The prospect of the EU's further enlargement only reinforces the need for institutional reforms.

The debate on institutional reforms also includes traditional forms of intergovernmental cooperation among the member states, such as the Common Foreign and Security Policy, as well as the policy on Cooperation in the Fields of Justice and Home Affairs. The Maastricht Treaty represents the start of these two pillars rather than the end of the debate on their future development.

Unit I develops training and research on these topical issues from both a legal as well as a political science point of view. It organizes activities explaining the functioning and decisionmaking process of the institutions of the EU and explores the possibilities for their adaptation to current challenges by means that include very topical simulation games. As regards intergovernmental cooperation among the member states of the EU, specific attention is paid to the problems related to the development of the Common Foreign and Security Policy as well as to the attempts to come to a common visa and coordinated asylum policy. The latter involves research and training on the problem of the free movements of persons in general.

Unit I also carries out comparative research on regional cooperation and integration, such as, for example, EU enlargement (widening versus deepening); the second and third pillar of the Maastricht Treaty; regional cooperation and integration; Schengen Agreements; institutions and decisionmaking process in the EU; external relations of the EU, including relations with Central and Eastern Europe and other states and regions of the world (such as the Association of Southeast Asian Nations [ASEAN] and Latin America).

European Public Management

The main objective of the European Public Management Unit (Unit II) is to undertake research, consultancy, and training activities designed to strengthen vertical cooperation between the European Commission and national administrations as well as horizontal cooperation among national administrations, with a view to increasing effectiveness and reaching uniformity in the implementation of common policies by the national administrations. The main activities of the unit focus on reform and development of public administration, public management in the European Community, and development of public managers and management systems in non-member states.

The unit conducts its own research programs into specialized aspects of public administration, and monitors the results of similar research in other organizations specialized in this field. Although this unit's most immediate contacts are with the administrations of the EU member states, it collects information from and maintains contacts with corresponding bodies on a worldwide basis.

Public management in the EU is a special application of the principles and practices of public administration and is the unit's particular field of specialization. This leads to detailed interest and involvement in the operations and development of the institutions of the EU, in the development of the practices and skills needed in the member states to work effectively, and in the development and management of the interfaces between them.

A wide range of consultancy and training activities is undertaken for senior civil servants of nonmember states. These exercises have generally involved the development of specialized knowledge and skills relating to the EU and the functioning of its institutions and policies.

Bearing in mind the common areas of interest between the institutions of the European Union and the administrations of the member states, the European Public Management Unit attempts to ensure that useful information and models are applied to its fields of activities.

In addition to the general field of public administration, this unit develops and delivers material on the specialized public management areas involved, such as budgetary and financial management, personnel management, and so forth.

Community Policies and the Internal Market

The operations and developments in Unit III are centered around the economics of integration and the political economy of European policymaking, with special emphasis on EU affairs. Issues of both theoretical and political relevance are covered, and analysis aims at policy design, implementation, and evaluation. The unit tries to develop a deep understanding of economic integration in order to explain European Community development.

Moreover, special expertise has been developed in individual EU policy areas, such as trade, competition, industry, taxation, budgets, social affairs, regional affairs, and environment. Area studies as well as detailed analyses of potential problems and possible solutions have been conducted and underline Unit III's ambitions as a think tank.

Particular emphasis is put on the future of the EU with regard to the economic and monetary union, the internal market, and the European Union's white paper to fight unemployment in Europe. The continual monitoring of Europe's standing in the global economy is a necessary prerequisite for fulfilling Unit III's mission.

Another most recent focus of interest is the role and significance of committees and other working groups at EU level. Unit III, in cooperation with the other units, investigates their structure and the interplay and influence they exert on political decisions.

It is the Unit III's philosophy to develop a high-quality knowledge base, describing the driving forces as well as the consequences of Europe's blueprints, plans and activities. To translate this applied research into political consultancy and political recommendation is its ultimate objective.

Community Legal Systems

As a result of the expertise EIPA accumulated in the field of legal training, in 1992 it set up the European Center for Judges and Lawyers, based in Luxembourg. Its aim is to focus on legal activities for judges and other members of the legal professions as well as for civil servants and officials from the EU institutions involved in legal issues. EIPA hopes to make this center the meeting point for all judges and lawyers from the member states and the applicant countries and thus contribute decisively to the uniform application of European Community law throughout the European judiciary and public service.

Staff

In addition to a wide network of visiting experts, EIPA has a multinational and multidisciplinary resident scientific staff. In view of its European character, the members of the scientific staff are drawn from all of the member states and from the countries preparing for eventual accession that have cooperation agreements with EIPA.

EIPA serves the entire public sector and is therefore in daily contact with and works in cooperation with the institutions of the European Union, national institutes of public administration, and ministries in the member states, as well as with the respective regional and local governments.

To support its scientific team, EIPA has a varied and multilingual administrative staff. Within the institute the working languages are English and French, which, according to its regulations, are its official languages. All staff are required to communicate in both those languages and to be fluent in at least one. Several activities are also organized with simultaneous translation in German, and some that are addressed to national audiences may be organized in one of the other official languages of the European Union.

EIPA in the World

EIPA's raison d'être is to be at the service of the EU and the member states, and its activities are designed in this light. However, it also operates on a more global level formed by the EU's international partners. Such activities may be concerned with relations between specific states, or groups of states, and the EU, or there may be training programs for such states on integration, on EC matters or on issues related to administrative reforms and public management.

ROBERTO PAPINI

BIBLIOGRAPHY

De Rosa, Gabriele, ed., 1990. *Luigi Sturzo e la Democrazia Europea.* Bari, Italy: Edition Laterza.

Durand, Jean-Dominique, 1995. *L'Europe de la Democratie Chretienne.* Brussels: Edition Complexe.

Hanley, Denis, ed., 1994. *Christian Democracy in Europe: A Comparative Perspective.* London & New York: Pinter.

Irving, Ronald, 1979. *The Christian Democratic Parties of Western Europe.* London: Allen and Unwin.

Letamendia, Pierre, 1977. *La Democratie Chretienne.* Paris: Presses Universitaires de France.

Maiier, Hans, 1988. *Revolution und Kirche. Studien Zur Fruhgeschichte der Christlichen Demokratie. 1789–1850.* Freiburg en Brisgau, Germany: Herder.

Mayeur, Jean-Marie, 1980. *Des Partis Catholiques a la Democratie Chretienne. XIX–XX Siecles.* Paris: Armand Colin.

Papini, Roberto, 1988. *L'Internationale Democratie Chretienne.* Paris: Editions du Cerf.

———, 1993. "Christianity and Democracy in Europe: The Christian Democratic Movement." In John Witte, Jr., *Christianty and Democracy in Global Context.* Boulder: Westview.

EUROPEAN PARLIAMENT.

The representative institution of the European Union and the only directly elected international assembly in Western Europe. The European Parliament was originally established as the Parliamentary Assembly of the European Coal and Steel Community, set up by France, Germany, Italy, Belgium, the Netherlands, and Luxembourg in 1952. The treaties that were signed on March 25, 1957 created the European Economic Community (EEC) and the European Atomic Energy Community, known as Euratom, in 1958. As a result of the Common Institutions Convention, the assembly served all three communities from 1967 onward. The Common Assembly, as it was then known, changed its name in 1962 to the "European Parliament," a title that was given formal treaty status in 1987 with the entry into force of the Single European Act.

Composition

Article 137 of the EEC treaty provides that the European Parliament "shall consist of representatives of the peoples of the States brought together in the Community." Originally, the assembly was an appointed body, with some 78 delegates appointed or elected by the national parliaments. Article 138 (3), however, empowered the European Parliament to "draw up proposals for elections by direct universal suffrage in accordance with a uniform procedure in all Member States." Thus the treaties confer on the Parliament a legal status as a representative institution and a political authority lacking in any other international assembly in Western Europe.

The assembly first introduced proposals for direct elections in 1960; however, it was not until 1976 that the Council of Ministers agreed on the form of direct elections adopting the enabling legislation on September 20, 1976, which provided for national electoral systems to be used pending the introduction of a uniform European electoral system. Once it was ratified by all member states the legislation came into effect (on July 1, 1978). The first direct elections were in 1979, from June 7 to June 10, and it holds elections every five years. To date an agreement on a uniform electoral system has proven to be elusive, so members continue to be elected according to national electoral systems.

Fourteen of the fifteen members states use different forms of proportional representation, with either party lists or the single transferable vote (in the case of Ireland); the majority system or the first-past-the-post system is used in all parts of the United Kingdom, with the exception of Northern Ireland, where proportional representation is used to ensure that the nationalist minority wins a seat. The European Union Treaty, more commonly known as the Maastricht Treaty, formally confers on European Union citizens the right to vote and stand as candidates in elections to the European Parliament, as well as in local elections.

The number of seats in the European Parliament that are allocated to member states varies roughly with population size. The total number of seats has increased over time as a result of internal developments within the EEC and successive enlargements. The original 78 delegates grew to 142 in 1958, with the creation of the two new communities. When the United Kingdom, Denmark, and Ireland joined the EEC in 1973, membership increased to 198. With the advent of direct elections, the number of representatives was increased to 400. Greece joined in 1981, bringing the total to 434. Spain and Portugal joined in 1986, increasing the number of seats to 518.

It was agreed among the member states prior to the European elections in June 1994 that the number of seats assigned to member states should be adjusted to take account in particular of the reunification of Germany and that other member states should be compensated for this. Thus with the June elections in 1994 the number of seats was increased to 567. Since January 1995, with the enlargement of the European Union to include Sweden, Austria, and Finland, the distribution of seats among member states has been as follows: Belgium 25; Denmark 16; Germany 99; Greece 25; Spain 64; France 87; Ireland 15; Italy 87; Luxembourg 6; the Netherlands 31; Austria 21; Portugal 25; Finland 16; Sweden 22; and the United Kingdom 87.

Powers and Functions

The European Parliament is unlike any national parliament in Western Europe to the extent that it is not an electoral chamber as such; elections to the Parliament do not result in any transfer of power from one government to another, nor do elections to the European Parliament necessarily result in any change in policy. The European Parliament does not legislate; it does not set the policy agenda of the executive, nor does it have any considerable impact on it. The European Parliament is part of a political organization that itself is still in the process of constitutional evolution: The European Union is more than an international organization and less than a federation, though it has federal aspirations. The powers and functions of the European Parliament have changed and will continue to change as the European Union itself changes.

The institutional structure created by the original treaties was innovative: a twin-headed executive, with the EC Commission on the one hand and the Council of Ministers on the other. In the decisionmaking process the Parliament is entitled to be consulted, though its opinions are not legally binding. In the case of the EEC the traditional executive-parliament dialogue was replaced by a dialogue between the EC Commission and the Council, and the position of the Parliament was not clearly defined. Article 137 of the EEC Treaty provides rather vaguely that the Parliament shall exercise "advisory and supervisory powers." Therefore, the Parliament not having been attributed a clear role, has from the outset been in search of one and has engaged in a virtually continual campaign to convert its advisory and supervisory powers into veritable powers of legislation and control. As such it has been a major source of pressure for constitutional and institutional reform in the EEC.

The powers of the European Parliament derive from the original treaties of Paris and, especially, Rome, as amended by the Single European Act (which came into effect in 1987) and the European Union Treaty (signed on February 7, 1992 in Maastricht, the Netherlands, which came into effect in November 1993). Both documents mark important stages in the constitutional development of the European Community. They have attempted to reduce the so-called "democratic deficit" in the EEC's decisionmaking process by increasing the powers of the European Parliament, the only directly elected institution in the EEC.

The European Parliament's organizational independence is guaranteed by Articles 139 to 142 of the EEC Treaty. It may determine the timing of its own annual session; it can be neither convened nor dismissed by the Council of Ministers. It elects its own president and bureau and determines its own quorum. The European Parliament is responsible for drawing up its rules of procedure and the publication of its proceedings. It also controls its own budget, which enables it to improve and enhance its services and facilities as it chooses. Therefore, the European Parliament enjoys greater independence vis-à-vis the executive authority than most parliaments at the national level in Europe.

The powers of the European Parliament fall into three distinct categories, namely, legislative powers, budgetary powers, and powers of political control over the executive authority. The legislative powers of Parliament have increased by means of procedures that have been introduced over time. Initially, the influence of the assembly on legislation and the policymaking process in general was slight, since its consultation procedure was restricted to 22 articles in the EEC Treaty and 11 articles in the Euratom Treaty. During the 1960s, however, the Council of Ministers, under pressure from the Parliament, broadened the scope of the procedure so that in time virtually all legislative proposals came to be sent to Parliament for an opinion (including: international agreements, negotiations with prospective associate member states, economic agreements under Articles 113 and 234 of the EEC Treaty, and international commercial agreements). Though Parliament's opinions are not legally binding, the council cannot adopt legislation until it receives the opinion of Parliament. In the so-called Isoglucous case of 1980, the Court of Justice struck down legislation adopted by the council before the latter received Parliament's opinion. Thus this procedure can amount to a de facto delaying power for Parliament, enabling it to gather more information.

In 1975 the Conciliation Procedure came into being, with respect to legislation having appreciable financial implications on foot of the Budget Treaties of 1970 and 1975. The procedure provides for the Conciliation Committee, comprising an equal number of Council ministers and representatives of the European Parliament to discuss matters such as the revision of the regional policy and the adoption of the financial regulation on the EEC's budget. This procedure was considered necessary since the enhanced budgetary powers of Parliament (as provided for under the Budget Treaties) were expected to lead to conflicts between it and the council. The aim of the procedure is essentially to enable both institutions to enter into direct dialogue with one another in order to reach an agreement or a compromise. In effect, this procedure enables Parliament to exercise a suspensive veto for as long as the conciliation negotiations continue.

The Single European Act introduced two new procedures that enhanced the European Parliament's role in the legislative process. The procedures have had the effect of causing the three institutions to interact in an unprecedented manner, encouraging informal contacts between them on a scale that was not necessary before.

The Cooperation Procedure (which applies to specific policy areas) provides for a second reading by Parliament of proposed legislation following Council's adoption of its common position. The Parliament has three courses of action open to it at this stage: (1) it may approve the common position expressly or tacitly by remaining silent for a period of three months; (2) it may reject the common position by means of an absolute majority (that is, 50% of its membership), but this rejection may be overridden by a unanimous Council, otherwise the legislation will fall; and (3) the Parliament may seek to amend the common position by means of an absolute majority (these amendments, where accepted by the EC Commission, may be rejected by the Council of Ministers, acting unanimously, or accepted by means of a qualified majority vote).

The Assent Procedure empowers Parliament to vote on accession treaties and association treaties negotiated by the EEC with third countries. Such treaties therefore only come into effect when or if Parliament votes by an absolute majority to accept them. This procedure, in effect, places the European Parliament on an equal footing with the Council in terms of adopting such agreements.

The European Union Treaty confers further legislative powers on the Parliament. Article 189 (b) of the treaty provides for the so-called "Codecision" Procedure. This procedure empowers Parliament in specific policy areas to exercise a veto on legislation adopted by the council, following an unsuccessful conciliation procedure. The Codecision Procedure applies to such policy areas as internal market rules; free circulation of workers; the right of establishment; incentive measures in the fields of education, public health, and culture; trans-European network guidelines; general environmental programs; and multiannual framework programs for research and technology.

The treaty also expanded the areas to which the assent procedure may apply to include: the future uniform electoral system for Parliament; citizenship rights; the reformed regional, social, and agricultural funds–known as the structural funds; and the role of the future European Central Bank. The European Union Treaty also gives Parliament a limited right of legislative initiative, a right jealously guarded by the EC Commission. The treaty formally recognizes the right of Parliament to submit a legislative proposal to the commission by way of what is called an own-initiative report.

The budgetary powers of the European Parliament derive from the original treaties, as amended by the Budget Treaties of 1970 and 1975. Since 1975 the Parliament, together with the Council of Ministers, has constituted the budgetary authority of the EEC. As a consequence, Parliament has four main budgetary powers. First, Article 203 (8) of the EEC Treaty, as amended in 1975, provides that Parliament "acting by a majority of its members and two-thirds of the votes cast may, if there are important reasons, reject the draft budget and ask for a new draft to be submitted to it." Parliament has, on two occasions, exercised this power: In 1979 with respect to the 1980 budget, and again in 1984 with respect to the 1985 budget. When Parliament rejects the budget, the one-twelfth rule comes into play, whereby the previous year's budget is divided by twelve and the institutions are given a monthly allowance until such time as Parliament is satisfied with the proposed budget.

The European Parliament's second budgetary power allows it to propose "amendments" with respect to noncompulsory expenditure, relating to, for example, social policy, regional policy, research policy, energy policy, and so on, up to a specified ceiling.

Third, Parliament may propose "modifications" to compulsory expenditures, which refers principally to the common agricultural policy. If the modifications involve increases in expenditures, a qualified majority vote in the Council of Ministers is required to accept them. If not, a "negative majority" or a qualified majority for rejection is required. Thus in the case of compulsory expenditure, the council has the final say.

Finally, the 1975 Budget Treaty also conferred on Parliament the sole responsibility to grant discharge with respect to each financial year. Parliament, acting on the recommendation of the council, is usually expected to give discharge to the EC Commission regarding its implementation of the budget by April 30 of each year. The right to grant discharge is regarded as being central to the budgetary control powers of Parliament, since it amounts to a political endorsement of the way in which the commission has implemented the budget. Conversely, refusal to grant discharge is tantamount to a grave reprimand and gives rise to the possibility of sanctions.

In 1984, in an unprecedented move, Parliament voted by more than two-thirds of a majority not to grant discharge to the commission. Though the conditions for passing a motion of censure on the commission were thus met, Parliament did not call on the College of Commissioners to resign because it was already close to the end of its term of office. However, the newly appointed commission introduced a number of reforms to address the shortcomings of the commission that had been identified by Parliament. The decision to refuse discharge was essentially seen to be a political device in 1984. Because it is the only budgetary power that Parliament may exercise exclusively, it has probably become the most effective instrument at the disposal of Parliament. It gives the European Parliament an important opportunity to hold an annual political debate on the performance of the commission.

As a result of a number of budgetary crises that plagued the EEC during the 1980s, the Interinstitutional Agreement on Budgetary Discipline and Improvement of the Budgetary Procedure was concluded in 1988. This agreement legally bound the commission, the Council of Ministers, and the Parliament to a four-year plan of expenditure. The first financial perspective (as this was called) covered the period from 1988 to 1992. The second financial perspective covered the period from 1993 to 1997.

Since 1988, conflicts between the institutions have become much less frequent. The European Union Treaty increased the budgetary powers of Parliament by making it unacceptable for the commission to withhold information from Parliament on its management of the budget when Parliament requests such information. The distinction between compulsory and noncompulsory expenditure remains, however.

In terms of political control, Article 144 of the EEC Treaty provides that if a "motion of censure is carried by a two-thirds majority of the votes cast, representing a majority of the members of the European Parliament, the members of the Commission shall resign as a body." If such a motion is passed, the College of Commissioners continues to fulfill its tasks until replaced. No such motion has ever been adopted, though four have been tabled. This power is regarded as a blunt instrument to the extent that there is nothing to prevent national governments from reappointing the same commissioners dismissed by Parliament. Parliament may also put both written and oral questions to members of the commission and the council, which may be followed by a debate. Furthermore, since 1973, when the United Kingdom joined the EEC, the Westminster practice of "question time" has become a feature of plenary sessions in Strasbourg, France. Article 143 of the EEC Treaty empowers Parliament to debate the annual *General Report of the Commission*. Parliament also developed the practice of holding a vote of confidence in the commission's program, which is announced each year.

The European Union Treaty provides the European Parliament with a formal role in the appointment of the College of Commissioners. In 1994 Parliament, for the first time, was formally consulted in the appointment of the commission president. Though this vote is not legally binding, it is difficult to imagine any president-designate taking up such a position without the explicit approbation of Parliament. Parliament is also entitled to give a vote of confidence to the College of Commissioners as a whole. The treaty also brings the term of office of the commission into line with that of the Parliament, increasing its term from four to five years from January 1, 1995. The treaty also provides for a number of smaller measures to increase parliamentary scrutiny and control in the Eu-

ropean Union. For example, it gives Parliament the right to appoint an ombudsman to deal with complaints of maladministration in the institutions. The treaty also confirms Parliament's right to establish temporary committees of enquiry, whose terms of reference are determined by an interinstitutional agreement. The treaty also recognizes the right of European citizens to petition Parliament. Finally, the treaty also gives Parliament the right to be consulted on the appointment of the future board of the European Central Bank.

Alternately, Parliament's powers of control vis-à-vis the Council of Ministers have always been somewhat vague and limited. In theory, ministers are accountable to national parliaments. In reality, however, this is difficult to implement. Over time a number of practices have grown up whereby, for example, members of the council have undertaken to respond to written and oral questions from Parliament. Furthermore, the president-in-office usually addresses Parliament at the beginning of the six-month term of office, outlining his or her program, and reports back to Parliament at the end of the six months. These practices have been gradually codified by the institutions in agreements.

Internal Structure and Modus Operandi

The internal leadership structure of the European Parliament comprises the president, the Bureau, the Enlarged Bureau and, to a lesser extent, the College of Quaestors. Parliament is assisted by a general secretariat. The president of the European Parliament is elected by the members themselves at the first meeting of a newly elected Parliament for a renewable two and one-half year term. The president fulfills a number of external and internal roles. Externally, the incumbent represents the Parliament in meetings with the other institutions and at international forums and conferences. Internally, the president is responsible for directing all the activities of Parliament and its organs, whether at part-sessions (as plenary sessions are known) or at committees. The president formally opens, presides over, and brings to a close part-sessions; he or she chairs meetings of the Bureau and the Enlarged Bureau; and, not least, he or she signs the budget of the European Union.

The president together with the 14 vice presidents constitutes the Bureau, which is responsible for the internal functioning of the Parliament. The responsibilities of the Bureau include determining where committees meet, referring documents to committees, organizing the secretariat, and establishing the initial draft of the Parliament's budget.

When it meets with the leaders of the political groups the Bureau becomes the Enlarged Bureau. (It has become more powerful than the Bureau, reflecting the preponderance of the political groups in Parliament). The Enlarged

Bureau determines the appointment of Parliament's leaders, including the president, the vice-presidents, the quaestors, the committee chairs and vice-chairs and the chairs of the interparliamentary delegations. The Enlarged Bureau also appoints committee rapporteurs, allocates speaking time during part-sessions, sets the agenda of part-sessions, allows oral questions with or without debate, organizes question time during part-sessions, decides the draft estimates of Parliament's budget, and interprets Parliament's rules of procedure.

As such the political groups that have their own secretariat play a decisive role in the functioning of the European Parliament. The preponderance of the political groups is thrown into sharp relief by the powerlessness of the nonaligned members, who are unlikely to hold an important position in the Parliament's internal leadership structure or chair a major committee.

The College of Quaestors, which always numbers five, performs an important internal function to the extent that it deals with administrative and financial matters concerning members, including travel allowances, secretarial and other allowances, social security arrangements, working conditions, and office facilities. The College of Quaestors was established in 1977, originally as part of the Bureau, but became separate from it after direct elections in 1979, though it continues to report to it.

In 1992 the General Secretariat of Parliament comprised some 3,344 posts. Permanent officials of Parliament are European civil servants who are recruited directly by the institution through open competitions that are held regularly. The policy is to keep a rough balance between the nationalities. Staff regulations require an official to carry out his or her duties and to conduct him- or herself solely with the interests of the EEC in mind and to neither seek nor take instructions from any government, authority, organization, or person outside his or her institution. Officials work in one or another of the Secretariat's Directorates-General (DG), which are listed below:

- DG I   Sessional Services
- DG II   Committees and Delegations
- DG III   Information and Public Relations
- DG IV   Research
- DG V   Personnel, Budget, and Finance
- DG VI   Administration
- DG VII   Translation and General Services

In addition, there are two services that report directly to the secretary general, namely, the Directorate for Data Processing and the Legal Service.

A recent development in DG IV for Research of the secretariat has been the 1987 emergence of the Scientific and Technological Options Assessment program (STOA). The establishment of STOA reflects a trend visible in a number of parliaments in Western Europe that originally began in the United States with the 1972 creation of the Office of Technology Assessment (abolished in 1995) as a support agency of the U.S. Congress. The stated aim of STOA is to provide "expert advice on scientific and technical matters to Members and Committees of the European Parliament in order to help them assess policy options; these may be options for science or technology policy, or they may be options in other areas, for example the environment or transport where scientific or technical factors are important."

Such a development reflects the view among reformist members of the role of the European Parliament as being that of a legislature exercising its formal legal powers independently of the executive authority. It is an incipient effort by Parliament to reduce its dependence on the EC Commission, the traditional repository of specialized information in the EEC, since this obliges members to rely on information emanating from the very body they purport to supervise and control.

Individual Members of the European Parliament (MEPs) are subject to great pressures on their time, in effect, having public duties at European, national, and even subnational levels. In marked contrast to congressional representatives in the United States, however, the average MEPs do not have a very large staff to assist them in the performance of their public duties. Each member is entitled to a secretarial allowance and has considerable freedom in the use of it in terms of deciding whether to hire full-time or part-time assistants and whether to base them in Brussels or in his or her home state. Such allowances are relatively recent, dating from the advent of direct elections in 1979, which brought to a virtual end the dual mandate that had enabled members of the appointed assembly to depend on national parties for secretarial and other support services.

Nowadays, the level of personal assistance varies widely: many members choose to have one full-time and one part-time assistant, one based in Brussels and the other in his or her home state; some members prefer to share assistants in Brussels; others, particularly some committee chairs have concentrated on building up a significant personal staff. The role of personal assistants varies greatly from routine office tasks to substantial political responsibilities, including drafting reports for their members. Assistants based in member states often act as constituency workers in place of the member, who spends much of his or her time in Brussels and Strasbourg each month. Assistants are employed on the basis of a personal contract with their member and are not staff of the Parliament as such. Thus their position is more precarious than permanent officials of the Parliament in terms of social security and other arrangements.

Members of the European Parliament associate in transnational political groups ranging from left to right of the political spectrum. Following the European elections in June 1994, there are now nine political groups in the fourth directly elected Parliament, as well as number of nonaligned members. The political groups are as follows:

- Party of the European Socialists
- European People's Party (Christian Democrats and Allies)
- European Liberal, Democratic, and Reformist Group
- Confederal European United Left
- Forza Europa
- European Democratic Alliance
- Green Group
- European Radical Alliance
- Nations of Europe

In June 1994 the minimum number of members required to form a political group was 13 from four or more member states, 16 from three member states, 12 from two member states, or 26 from just one member state.

The two largest groups are the Socialists and the European People's Party, which is also known as the Christian Democrats and Allies. They are the most representative of the groups having members from every state. Together with the European Liberal, Democratic, and Reformist Group, these three were the earliest political groups to emerge in Parliament. They represent the three political families of Europe, namely, socialism, Christian democracy, and liberalism. They are linked with transnational party federations at a European level.

The Confederal European United Left dates from 1979 and has representatives from Spain, France, Italy, Greece, and Portugal. The European Democratic Alliance comprises French Gaullists and members of an Irish political party, Fianna Fail. The Green Group, was formed after the first direct elections in 1979 and is dominated by a large German contingent. Three new groups appeared after the June 1994 elections, namely, Forza Europa, the European Radical Alliance, and Nations of Europe. Though Parliament's rules of procedure ostensibly protect the rights of nonaligned members, the latter are in practice disadvantaged, particularly in terms of the allocation of chairmanships and rapporteurships and of speaking time during part-sessions.

The European Parliament, like the U.S. House of Representatives, envisages itself as a working parliament as opposed to a discussive chamber on a par with the Westminster model of parliament. Members of the European Parliament, like members of the House, are expected to (and for the most part do) spend a great deal of time and energy dealing with legislative details. As the role of Parliament evolves the emphasis is being placed increasingly on legislative work.

There are three types of committees in the European Parliament: standing or permanent committees; temporary committees; and committees of inquiry. The function of standing committees is to draft opinions on proposed legislation. In principle, any standing committee may establish a subcommittee subject to the prior authorization of the Enlarged Bureau. In practice, their establishment is kept to a minimum. There are only three subcommittees in the 1994 to 1999 Parliament. There are now 20 standing committees in Parliament, and these are listed below:

- Committee on Foreign Affairs, Security, and Defense Policy
- Committee on Agriculture and Rural Development
- Committee on Budgets
- Committee on Economic and Monetary Affairs and Industrial Policy
- Committee on Research, Technological Development, and Energy
- Committee on External Economic Relations
- Committee on Legal Affairs and Citizen's Rights
- Committee on Social Affairs and Employment
- Committee on Regional Policy
- Committee on Transport and Tourism
- Committee on the Environment, Public Health, and Consumer Protection
- Committee on Culture, Youth, Education, and the Media
- Committee on Development and Cooperation
- Committee on Civil Liberties and Internal Affairs
- Committee on Budgetary Control
- Committee on Institutional Affairs
- Committee on Fisheries
- Committee on the Rules of Procedure, the Verification of Credentials, and Immunities
- Committee on Women's Rights
- Committee on Petitions

The allocation of chairmanships is determined by the d'Hondt system of proportional representation, which is based on the size of the political groups.

At the request of one-quarter of members, a committee on inquiry may be set up to investigate alleged contraventions of EEC law or incidents of maladministration in the institutions. Membership is restricted to a maximum of ten, and reports must be submitted within nine months.

Temporary committees are rarely established by the European Parliament and, if so, they are normally set up for a period of twelve months, in connection with matters of major topical concern, but this time period may be extended. Temporary committees are more powerful than committees of inquiry to the extent that they submit interim as well as final reports on which Parliament votes, and they may, therefore, submit a motion for a resolution to Parliament.

There are also 25 interparliamentary delegations in Parliament. In general, each member is a full member of one committee and a substitute on another, and also a full member on an interparliamentary delegation and a substitute on another.

The average member's monthly schedule is quite rigid. For two weeks each month he or she works in committee in Brussels; the following week he or she meets with his or her political group to decide on voting strategy in part-sessions, as plenary sessions are called; and for one week each month he or she meets in Strasbourg for a plenary session of Parliament to vote on opinions drawn up by the committees.

As the member states did not at the beginning decide where the Parliament should meet permanently, the institution has in fact three temporary seats. Its committees and political groups meet in Brussels; its General Secretariat is based in Luxembourg, and its part-sessions are held for one week each month in Strasbourg. The failure of the member states to fix a single seat for the Parliament has been heavily criticized.

In practice the activities of the Parliament have become increasingly concentrated in Brussels. For example, a newly created hemicycle has been in use since 1994 to facilitate extraordinary part-sessions, and large sections of the secretariat have been gradually transferred from Luxembourg to Brussels.

The European Union resembles a Heraclitean reality in that it seems to be perpetually in a state of becoming as opposed to being. As the role and functions of the European Union change, so too will the role and functions of the European Parliament. In terms of the future democratic development of the European Union, the model that enjoys the support of the majority of member states as well as that of the majority of members themselves is that of a parliamentary form of government as opposed to a presidential model. This model envisages the EC Commission becoming the government of the European Union and responsible to the European Parliament as the lower chamber in a bicameral legislature, with the Council of Ministers, representing the member states, being the upper chamber.

The Single European Act and the European Union Treaty have wrought significant changes in terms of increasing Parliament's legislative powers; however, such developments fall short of conferring Parliament with colegislature status, except in certain circumstances. The European Parliament, for the most part, is still in the position of persuading more than it decides. Its powers of control have also gradually increased, but it is its budgetary powers that are by far its strongest powers. The European Parliament in unlike any other existing parliament to the extent that it does not consider itself part of a finished institutional system, but as part of one requiring evolution or even transformation into something different (Jacobs, Corbett, Shackleton 1992). It will continue to play a promi-

nent role in promoting constitutional development in the European Union, the next phase of which occurred in 1996 when an intergovernmental conference was held to revise the European Union Treaty.

MARGARET MARY MALONE

BIBLIOGRAPHY

Bogdanor, Vernon, 1986. "The Future of the European Parliament, Separation and Interdependence of Powers," *Government and Opposition*, no. 2 (Spring): 161–176.
———, 1989. "Direct Elections, Representative Democracy and European Integration," *Electoral Studies*, no. 3, (December).
Coombes, David, 1979. "The Future of the European Parliament." *Studies in European Politics 1*. Policy Studies Institute, European Centre for Political Studies.
Corbett, Richard, 1989. "Testing the New Procedures: The European Parliament's First Experiences with Its New Single Act Powers." *Journal of Common Market Studies*, no. 4, (June).
———, 1992. "The Intergovernmental Conference on Political Union." *Journal of Common Market Studies*, vol. 30, no. 3 (September): 271–298.
Corbett, Richard, and D. Nickel, 1984. "The Draft Treaty Establishing the European Union." *The Yearbook of European Law*.
European Parliament, 1989. *Forging Ahead, the European Parliament 1952–1988, 36 Years*. Luxembourg: 3d ed. Directorate-General for Research, Office for Official Publications.
Fitzmaurice, John, 1975. *The Party Groups in the European Parliament*. London: Saxon House.
———, 1988. "An Analysis of the European Community's Cooperation Procedure." *Journal of Common Market Studies*, no. 4. (June).
Jacobs, Francis B., 1989. *Western Europe Political Parties: A Comprehensive Guide. London:* Longman.
Jacobs, Francis, Richard Corbett, and Michael Shackleton, 1992. *The European Parliament.* 2d ed. London: Longman.
Kirchner, Emil Joseph, 1984. *The European Parliament: Performance and Prospects.* Aldershot: Gower.
Lasok, D. and J. W. Bridge, 1991. *Law and Institutions of the European Communities.* London: Butterworths.
Nugent, Neill, 1991. *The Government and Politics of the European Community.* 2d ed. London: MacMillan.
Palmer, Michael, 1981. *The European Parliament, What It Is, What It Does, How It Works.* Oxford: Pergamon Press.
Reif, Karlheinz, and Oskar Niedermayer, 1987. "The European Parliament and the Political Parties." *Revue d'Integration Européen,* no. 2–3, Hiver, 1986-Printemps.
Wood, Alan, ed., 1989. *The Times Guide to the European Parliament.* London: Times Books.

EVALUATION. To judge the worth or value of a program or activity. (For the evaluation of individuals, see **performance evaluation.**) Evaluation determines the value or effectiveness of an activity for the purpose of decisionmaking.

The valuing or judging of people, processes, and things is a pervasive daily human activity. As such, most evaluation is informal. Formal evaluation makes the explicit judging process an integral part of program management. Evaluation determines value by weighing costs, both tangible and intangible, against benefits. It determines effectiveness by assessing whether a service or program has met identified needs or objectives, or has made a difference. In this process, evaluation provides information that aids decisionmakers in determining whether to continue, modify, or terminate a funded activity or which of several alternatives to support. Good evaluation improves the quality of those decisions.

In formal evaluation we make explicit (1) the object of our review, (2) the criteria with which value will be assigned and a judgment based, and (3) the behavior or outcomes necessary if the object of the evaluation is to be judged as having met standards or expectation. An evaluation that is not explicit about these three issues will generate fear or frustration among those affected by the evaluation and will mitigate its effect.

History of the Development of Program Evaluation

Formal evaluation is not new. We find formal evaluation as far back as 2000 B.C.E., when Chinese officials conducted civil service exams (DuBois 1970). Within Western tradition we find evaluation in a number of places, most notably in 1870 during the Age of Reform in England. There, the evaluation of educational achievement led to a call for what today we might term incentive pay or pay for performance (Madaus et al. 1983).

In the United States, the formal evaluation of organizations and their programs and services began in schools. In 1897–1898 Joseph Rice conducted a comparative study of the spelling performance of 33,000 students in a large city school system (DuBois 1970). Originally, formal evaluation in education was closely associated with the measurement tradition of psychology. Robert Thorndike, sometimes called the father of the educational testing movement, was an important influence in encouraging the application of measurement technology to the determination of human abilities (Thorndike and Hagen 1969). His prestige led to the introduction of standardized testing in the 1920s as a means to assess students. Evaluation approaches were next applied to pedagogy, in an effort to improve teaching (Smith and Tyler 1942). The evaluation practices developed for schools were applied to work relief and public housing programs of President F. D. Roosevelt's New Deal.

Evaluation gained in importance and visibility after World War II. In education, the Cold War threat of Soviet preeminence and the concern that American schools were second-class caused evaluators to increase their scrutiny of educational practices and outcomes. This work led to the development of a language, a research process, and a theoretical basis for the evaluation discipline (Cronbach and Suppes 1969; Scriven 1958). By the end of the 1960s the focus of educational evaluation included policy and political questions, especially related to equal education (Coleman et al. 1966; Jencks 1972).

Evaluation in public administration initially focused on programs of the federal government. There were two schools of development. One school focused on the management and allocation of resources for national defense programs. The Program Evaluation Review Technique (PERT), for example, was developed to correlate different contractor management systems in the development of complex weapon systems (Cook 1966). Planning, Programming, and Budgeting System (PPBS) also was developed primarily as a means of applying economic analysis to management systems (Wildavsky 1966). Systems analysis techniques were intended to improve decisionmaking about the development and implementation of military operations (Miser and Quade 1985). These were primarily planning or front-end analysis evaluation approaches.

The other school of public administration evaluation was linked to earlier efforts in education and focused on outputs or outcomes. Evaluation efforts with a foundation in experimental design, for example, were used to judge the relative merits of federally funded agricultural programs and products. The social welfare programs of the Great Society, which accounted for rapidly increasing federal expenditures, were accompanied by an increase in attention paid to evaluation (Rossi et al. 1979).

In the 1970s the U.S. Office of Management and Budget (OMB) created an Evaluation and Program Implementation Division, a reflection of the growing importance of evaluation. State governments also began to pay attention to evaluation in the mid-1970s, although there it was called productivity measurement rather than program evaluation, and often was linked to sunset legislation. The two schools of evaluation in public administration began to coalesce. Awareness and use of program evaluation grew with the publication of *The Handbook of Evaluation Research* (1975) and the initiation in 1977 of the journal *Evaluation Quarterly*.

In the past decade, evaluations of governmental programs have changed their focus from being dominated by the evaluation of achievement of great objectives, typical of the Great Society and War on Poverty programs, to using multifaceted approaches (Rossi and Freeman 1993). Evaluation continues to be an important part of most federally funded programs. As a result, the federal government plays a central role in the development of evaluation approaches, methodologies, and techniques.

Evaluation Purposes

Evaluation is a process to judge success, assure accountability, and determine more effective resource allocation. It does not simply measure; it also judges, or assigns value. It seeks to assess social utility. It is concerned with both program process and program product. Evaluation serves a variety of purposes. These purposes, and the name of the approach most frequently associated with each purpose, are (1) to inform planning decisions, particularly in the development of policy (front-end analysis); (2) to answer policy execution questions and determine if a full-scale evaluation of the program is useful and feasible (evaluability assessment); (3) to track program progress and identify actual or emerging problems (program and problem monitoring); (4) to determine whether a program has accomplished its goals or met its objectives (impact analysis or product evaluation); (5) to determine if a program has been implemented as planned, regardless of outcomes (process analysis or process evaluation); (6) to measure the effectiveness or efficiency of units or practices (management analysis or context evaluation); (7) to determine if there are unintended consequences from program implementation (goal-free analysis); (8) to assess the degree of public or stakeholder satisfaction with the program (service analysis); and (9) to compare various programs or approaches to determine which might be the best to implement in a new setting (policy analysis). In addition, a branch of evaluation research examines whether evaluation findings are used, or compares evaluation findings (utilization analysis, evaluation synthesis, or meta-evaluation). Program evaluation should result in a good explanation or generalization about why change did or did not take place.

Evaluation differs from the related practices of research and auditing. Research is a test of a theory and represents a more disinterested study, but results are intended to be generalizable to the greater population. Auditing is an attempt to measure the extent to which the procedures of a program are consistent with those intended in original legislation and to identify deficiencies or discrepancies.

Relation to Program Planning and Implementation

To be effective, program evaluation must be integral to the program cycle, from the initial needs assessment to the final formal evaluation stage. Failing to plan for program evaluation from the beginning of a program usually means the data or data sources necessary for making a judgment may not be available. An evaluation conducted under these circumstances can only answer questions for which data are available, which may not be the most important or most interesting questions.

Evaluation can occur in any phase of a program. During needs assessment evaluators ask, "What needs attention? What is the program trying to accomplish?" During planning, evaluators assess the outcomes to be achieved and the courses of action to be taken. During development, evaluators examine the extent to which program execution is taking place as planned. This is formative evaluation and can suggest changes to assure goal achievement or program improvement. Finally, during program delivery, evaluators judge the overall effectiveness of the project or program and recommend future courses of action. This is summative evaluation, which describes a program as a finished work.

Determination of Evaluation Feasibility

The temptation for most evaluators is to spend most of their time planning the design and technical elements of the study. However, it is at least as important to spend time thinking about the purpose of the evaluation and how its findings will be used, and to plan the evaluation with that in mind. Before undertaking any evaluation, three questions about the study's feasibility should be asked. First, can the results of the evaluation influence decisions about the program? If there are strong, preconceived ideas on the part of policymakers about the program, the effect of the evaluation will be limited or nonexistent. In addition, the evaluation schedule must be such as to assure that the study can be completed in time to inform decisions. Second, can the evaluation be carried out? There must be sufficient resources available to support the evaluation, and the program must be stable enough so that it can be studied. Finally, is the program consequential enough to merit evaluation? Programs most eligible for evaluation are those that require significant resources, those that are operating in a marginal or improvable manner, or those that are candidates for expansion or replication. A negative response to any of these questions will bring into question the likelihood that the study will be completed or that its results will be useful.

Audience and Constraints

It is important to identify the evaluation's audience. Evaluators should ask; Who needs the information to be provided by the study? What kind of information do they require? When will they need it? How will they use it? The early identification and involvement of potential users of evaluation results is critical to the study's success (Chelimsky 1985; Weiss 1982).

After having identified purpose, feasibility, and audience, the evaluator must determine what decisions must be informed by the evaluation and what constraints exist.

Constraints exist when there are insufficient materials and equipment, personnel, or funds, or when the political climate is adverse. Because evaluation takes place in a political environment, it is subject to political constraints and pressures. Understanding this political environment is important for the person who must manage the evaluation effort.

Approach or Design

The evaluator must determine the evaluation approach or design. At least twelve kinds of evaluation approaches or models have been identified, many of which can be used at any stage in a program's development or to inform any of the evaluation purposes identified earlier. These approaches are: (1) objectives-based or goal-oriented, in which the evaluation assesses the discrepancy between planned and achieved objectives (Smith and Tyler 1942); (2) consumer-oriented, or goal-free evaluation, which discovers what the program is by what it does, not by what is purports to do (Scriven 1972); (3) testing, or the comparison of performance against norms or preestablished criteria (Thorndike and Hagen 1969); (4) evaluation research, or the identification of causal relationships between variables (Campbell and Stanley 1966); (5) cost assessment or cost-benefit analysis, or the assessment of the costs and benefits of proposed or actual policies (Coleman et al. 1966; Jencks 1972); (6) accreditation or certification, or the determination if programs or people meet established standards; (7) management information systems, which provide information needed to fund, direct, and control programs, but which are not related to program outcomes directly; (8) accountability or performance contracting, which provides information to funding agencies on the extent to which program objectives have been met; (9) client-centered evaluation, which attempts to understand activities from the users' perspectives (Stake 1970; Guba and Lincoln 1989); (10) decision-oriented evaluation, used to provide information specifically to assist legislators or administrators in making or defending decisions (Stufflebeam et al. 1971); (11) adversary evaluation, which provides policymakers with opposing views in a kind of "judicial" framework (Wolf and Arnstein 1975); and (12) just-in-time evaluations, which are geared for smaller, more responsive evaluations of isolated elements of programs.

Although the tools, techniques, and methodologies used by each of these approaches may be the same, the perspective assumed by the evaluator influences the focus of the study, and thus the kind of information provided to decisionmakers.

Decisions about the procedures or methods to be used for gathering data are critical to a study's success. Data collection will be affected by costs associated with various methods, as well as by the availability and accessibility of records, documents, and informed sources, and the willingness of clients, program staff, or other stakeholders to provide accurate, reliable, and honest information. It is tempting to evaluate that which is easy to measure or for which data can be easily obtained. Evaluators should resist that temptation, since the most significant or interesting information may not be quantifiable or easy to access or report.

Data can be obtained from questionnaires (multiple-choice, checklist, ratings, rankings, or open-ended questions), surveys, tests, interviews, observations, performance records, data banks; or organizational documents (ordinances, laws, resolutions, and other public documents). Data should be both quantitative and qualitative (subjective). Information sources include legislators, citizen groups, individuals, program personnel, other executives in government, program clients, and evaluations by other governmental agencies. Multiple measures of the evaluation objects should be obtained whenever possible. Criteria must be valid, reliable, timely, and credible.

Data Analysis and Reporting

Analysis of data begins with the determination that data collected are useful. Data must be relevant, timely, accurate, and understandable. The evaluator, in analyzing data, also must be aware of the effects of attrition, the Hawthrone effect, evaluator bias, or any changes in organizational facilities, personnel, policies, or funding that may have affected the program or the analysis of program data.

The final role for the evaluator is the reporting of findings. The evaluator must decide how and to whom the evidence will be presented. The evaluation report should present information in a way that is useful to policymakers and aids in their decisionmaking. It should be structured so as to inform future decisions. Effective evaluation reports are free of jargon, focus directly and specifically on decisions or problems, provide the basis for setting priorities, and involve program administrators in the recommendations process.

Utilization of Evaluation Findings

Recently, critics have argued that the requirements of Total Quality Management (TQM) or of the "new public management" described by Osborne and Gaebler (1993) are antithetical to program evaluation (Behn 1991). These approaches require public managers to move decisionmaking to the lowest level possible, to eliminate unnecessary rules and regulations, and to innovate quickly. By contrast, traditional program evaluation requires time and a more-hierarchical decisionmaking process. "New" program evaluation must, therefore, be "just-in-time," providing smaller packages of evaluation findings for use in assessing innovations. TQM practices, such as statistical process control and the Plan-Do-Check-Act cycle, can be integrated into traditional evaluation practices.

Rapid change increases the requirement to demonstrate that an agency's program is accomplishing something (Behn 1991). Small-scale, timely evaluation can help others understand innovations and, if appropriate, replicate them (Levin and Sanger 1994). Formative evaluations, or evaluations that are process-oriented, that answer the questions of primary stakeholders, and that include qualitative methods that allow a "holistic assessment of relevant phenomena" (Thomas 1995), will be more useful to public managers and policymakers. The application of technological tools such as automated information systems, telephone surveys, and computer-assisted analysis and reporting can increase the possibility of evaluation being timely and useful to public managers. Benchmarking, or the establishing of standards or "best practices," leads not only to evaluation of current programs but also to goal-setting for program improvement.

The problems with evaluations fall into three categories: political, measurement, and usefulness. Political problems result from the tension between those being evaluated and the evaluators, especially when there is a probability of program termination or reduction. In public management, political problems also emerge when the priorities of a legislative of funding body are different from those of the agency. Measurement problems occur because many governmental programs or services are difficult to measure, and evaluators must develop measures for selected objectives. Stakeholders in the evaluation process may not agree as to the appropriateness or accuracy of those measurements. The usefulness of evaluations is compromised if the study is ad hoc or ex post facto rather than an integral and inherent part of the program from its inception. Then, necessary data may be incomplete or absent.

Usefulness is also limited when evaluators issue reports filled with technical terms and complex statistical analyses that confuse and mislead. Evaluation reports that are simple and easy to understand, however, may miss important, more complex elements of the program. Practitioners of the "new" evaluation must be more involved in the program planning and development process, building alliances with public managers so that these problems are avoided or minimized and evaluation findings have an impact on how social services are delivered.

The usefulness, and therefore the utilization of program evaluation, can be improved in a number of ways: (1) Be clear about premises underlying a program and conduct the evaluation in such a way that those premises are addressed; (2) identify objectives and evaluation criteria that

are people-oriented; (3) explicitly consider potential unintended consequences of programs, especially negative effects; (4) specify processes inherent in the program that the evaluation ought to investigate; (5) identify potential users of evaluation results early in the process; (6) analyze alternative approaches within the program; (7) consider more than one objective and multiple evaluation criteria; (8) do not reject evaluation criteria because they are difficult to measure; (9) err on the side of too many objectives or criteria, rather than two few; (10) specify client groups on which the analysis should attempt to estimate program impacts; (11) always include dollar costs as one criterion; (12) involve administrators and program practitioners at every step of the evaluation, from planning to the writing of the draft report; (13) involve potential users of the evaluation where possible; (14) complete the evaluation on time and release the results as soon as possible; and (15) use effective teaching and marketing approaches in presenting and disseminating findings. (Chelimsky 1985; Hatry 1987; Weiss 1982).

Evaluation is always a political process, since it involves identifying objectives, selecting measurement criteria, accessing a variety of information sources, analyzing data within a specified environment, and reporting those data in ways that are understandable and useful. The impact of politics on evaluation in the public management setting is even more profound. Evaluations can be used as a political tactic; evaluators who are aware of implicit or explicit politics can minimize this practice. Alternatively, evaluation can be used as a guide in shaping policy or program changes.

The very act of conducting an evaluation may be important, if it encourages members of the organization to examine their work and the structure that supports it (Weiss 1977). Evaluation may help agency administrators and staff, as well as legislators and other important parties, to review program goals and renew their commitment to program outcomes. This review may lead to behavioral and policy changes at a number of levels, regardless of the findings of the evaluation study. Thus effective evaluation may be even more important in today's environment of frequent and rapid changes and increasing fiscal constraints in assuring the success of public management programs and services.

SUSAN C PADDOCK

BIBLIOGRAPHY

Behn, Robert D., 1991. *Leadership Counts: Lessons for Public Managers from the Massachusetts Welfare, Training and Employment Program.* Cambridge: Harvard University Press.
Campbell, David T., and Julian C. Stanley, 1966. *Experimental and Quasi-experimental Designs for Research.* Chicago: Rand-McNally.

Chelimsky, Eleanor, (ed.), 1985. *Program Evaluation: Patterns and Directions.* Washington, DC: American Society for Public Administration.

Coleman, James S., et al., 1966. *Equality of Educational Opportunity.* Washington, DC: U.S. Government Printing Office (GPO).

Cook, Desmond L., 1966. *Program Evaluation and Review Technique.* Washington, DC: GPO.

Cronbach, Lee J., and P. Suppes, 1969. *Research for Tomorrow's Schools: Disciplined Inquiry for Education.* New York: Macmillan.

DuBois, P. H., 1970. *A History of Psychological Testing.* Boston: Allyn and Bacon.

Guba, Egon C., and Yvonne Lincoln, 1989. *Fourth Generation Evaluation.* Newbury Park, CA: Sage Publications.

Hatry, Harry, 1987. *Program Analysis for State and Local Government.* Washington, DC: Urban Institute.

Jencks, Christopher, 1972. *Inequality. A Reassessment of the Effect of Family and Schooling in America.* New York: Basic Books.

Levin, Martin A., and Mary Bryna Sanger, 1994. *Making Government Work: How Entrepreneurial Executives Turn Bright Ideas into Real Results.* San Francisco: Jossey-Bass.

Madaus, George F., Michael Scriven, and Daniel Stufflebeam, 1983. *Evaluation Models: Viewpoints on Educational and Human Services Evaluation.* Boston: Kluwer-Nijhoff.

Miser, Hugh J., and Edward S. Quade, eds., 1985. *Handbook of Systems Analysis.* New York: North-Holland.

Osborne, David, and Ted Gaebler, 1993. *Reinventing Government: How the Entrepreneurial Spirit Is Transforming the Pubic Sector.* New York: Penguin.

Rossi, Peter H., Howard E. Freeman, and Sonia R. Wright, 1979. *Evaluation: A Systematic Approach.* Beverly Hills, CA: Sage Publications.

Rossi, Peter H., and Howard E. Freeman, 1993. *Evaluation: A Systematic Approach.* 5th ed. Newbury Park, CA: Sage Publications.

Scriven, Michael, 1958. "Definitions, Explanations, and Theories." In H. Fiegl, M. Scriven, and G. Maxwell, eds., *Minnesota Studies in the Philosophy of Science,* Vol. 2. Minneapolis: University of Minnesota Press.

———, 1972. "Prose and Cons About Goal-Free Evaluation." *Evaluation Comment* 3:4.

Smith, E. R., and Ralph W. Tyler, 1942. *Appraising and Recording Student Progress.* New York: Harper & Row.

Stake, Robert E., 1970. "Objectives, Priorities, and Other Judgment Data." *Review of Educational Research* 40: 181–212.

Stufflebeam, Daniel L., et al., 1971. *Educational Evaluation and Decision Making.* Itaska, IL: F. E. Peacock.

Thomas, John Clayton, 1995. "Adapting Program Evaluation to New Realities: The Challenge of the New Public Management." Paper presented at Trinity Symposium, San Antonio, Texas, July 23.

Thorndike, Robert L., and E. Hagen, 1969. *Measurement and Evaluation in Psychology and Education.* New York: Wiley and Sons.

Weiss, Carol H. 1977. "Research for policy's sake: The enlightenment function of social research." *Policy Analysis.* 3: 532–545.

———, 1982. "Measuring the use of evaluation." *Evaluation Studies Review Annual.* 7: 129–145.

Wildavsky, Aaron, 1966. "The political economy of efficiency: Cost-benefit analysis, systems analysis and program budgeting." *Public Administration Review* (December) 293–302.

Wolf, R. L., and G. Arnstein, 1975. "Trial by jury: A new evaluation method." *Phi Delta Kappan,* 57:3 185–190.

EX POST FACTO LAWS.

Laws that apply to (i.e., make criminal) acts that were committed prior to the enactment of the law. The U.S. Constitution, in describing the legislative powers of Congress, states that "no Bill of Attainder or ex post facto Law shall be passed" (Article 1, Section 9, Clause 3). Article 1, Section 10 also forbids states from passing ex post facto laws. When the Constitution was written, it was widely held that ex post facto laws included all retrospective laws that applied to transactions or acts that predated the making of the law, regardless of whether the matter was criminal or civil.

In 1798 in the case of *Calder v. Bull* (3 Dall. 386, 393), however, the Supreme Court ruled that the constitutional prohibition applied only to criminal statutes. In 1878 the Supreme Court ruled further in *Burgess v. Salmon* (97 U.S. 381) that this prohibition cannot be circumvented by giving a civil form to a law that is criminal in nature. In three cases, the Calder decision, the Burgess decision, and Ex parte Garland (4 Wall. 333, 377 [1867]), the Supreme Court defined an ex post facto law forbidden by the Constitution to be, generally, any law that criminalizes a previously innocent act, or a law that provides for a greater punishment than that prescribed for a crime at the time it was committed.

In light of these early cases limiting the prohibition on ex post facto legislation to criminal and not civil matters, a key distinction (particularly for federal and state administrators and prosecutors) has been the question of what constituted a "punishment" that would trigger the prohibition. For example, an act of Congress in the Reconstruction Era that required attorneys to swear that they had not participated in the Southern Rebellion as a qualification for practicing law before federal courts was held to be unconstitutional as a retrospective punishment (Ex parte Garland [4 Wall. 333, 337][1867]). A law that denied polygamists the right to vote in a territorial election, however, was ruled a valid definition of a disqualification of a voter and not an increased punishment for the existing offense of polygamy (*Murphy v. Ramsey,* 114 U.S. 15 [1885]).

A decision with increasing importance in recent years regards the Supreme Court's 1924 ruling that the federal government could enforce deportation laws by expelling aliens who had committed criminal acts before the passage of the law, since deportation is not a punishment (*Mahler v. Eby,* 264 U.S. 32). According to this decision, a federal statute terminating Social Security benefits to an alien deported for Communist affiliation was held not to be an ex post facto punishment but a valid regulation aimed at relieving the Social Security Administration of the problems of administering Social Security benefits for beneficiaries living abroad (*Flemming v. Nestor,* 363 U.S. 603 [1960]).

Though a law is invalid as an ex post facto provision if it concerns acts committed prior to its enactment, it is valid when applied to subsequent offenses (*Jaehne v. New York,* 128 U.S. 189, 190 [1988]). Similarly, a law that criminalizes the continuation of conduct begun lawfully before the act's passage is not ex post facto. However, contrary to Ex parte Garland, the right to practice a profession may be withheld retrospectively for a person convicted of an offense who was innocent before the statute was enacted, if the offense may reasonably be considered as a basic disqualification for the profession (*Hawker v. New York,* 170 U.S., 189, 190 [1898]).

GEORGE DORIAN WENDEL

BIBLIOGRAPHY

Corwin, Edward S., ed., 1953. *The Constitution of the United States; Analysis and Interpretation.* Washington, DC: Legislative Reference Service, Library of Congress; Government Printing Office.
Pritchett, C. Herman, 1959. *The American Constitution.* 2d ed. New York: McGraw-Hill.

EXECUTIVE AGENCY POLICY.

A United Kingdom (UK) decentralization policy involving the transfer of executive functions previously conducted by a central government department to a semiautonomous agency, headed by a chief executive, operating within a policy and resource framework set by that government department. Executive agency creation represents a shift from hierarchical to quasi-contractual administrative arrangements.

Origins and Subsequent History

Since 1979, the UK government has implemented fundamental reforms of central government departments through the introduction of budgetary delegation and private sector management practices. An early attempt to inject individual managerial accountability was the 1982 Financial Management Initiative (FMI), which assumed scope for substantial efficiency improvements through devolution of financial and management responsibility in the Civil Service. Under FMI, decentralization was achieved in three ways: creation of a "top management" system to provide senior officials with information on the scope and scale of departmental operations and resource allocation; delegated budgetary control through a hierarchy of "cost centers"; and the introduction of performance indicators and appraisals to monitor departmental and individual performance. The success of this initiative was a precursor to more radical policy reform leading to executive agency creation.

The major driver for executive agency policy was the 1988 UK report entitled "Improving Management in Government: The Next Steps" (Efficiency Unit 1988). Although the report indicated that earlier reforms had increased cost consciousness and improved management systems in the Civil Service, it also pointed to residual obstacles to progress:

- insufficient focus on the delivery of government services (as opposed to policy and ministerial support), even though 95 percent of civil servants worked in service delivery or executive functions;
- a shortage of management skills and of experience of working in service delivery functions among senior civil servants;
- that short-term political priorities tended to squeeze out long-term planning;
- that there was too much emphasis on spending money, and not enough on getting results;
- that the Civil Service was too big and too diverse to manage as a single organization.

The major recommendation to address these deficiencies was for the establishment of semiautonomous agencies to carry out the executive functions of government. Agencies were to be given well-defined frameworks that set out the policy, budget, specific targets, and extent of the delegated authority of the agency's management. Strategic control was to remain with ministers, but once the policy and frameworks were set, the management of the agency would have as much independence as possible in deciding how those objectives were to be met. After accepting the principles of the report, the UK government began the process of executive agency creation throughout central government. Government targets are that some 450,000 civil servants from a total of 570,000 will be employed in agencies by the late 1990s.

Underlying Theoretical Framework

The anticipated benefits underpinning UK executive policy can be summarized as follows:

- Gains from separating public policy and service delivery functions. Executive agencies have been justified on the grounds of divorcing policy formulation and implementation. On one hand, agencies provide a mechanism to free senior civil servants and ministers from the mundane activities of routine administration. On the other hand, agency policy facilitates the release of managers in the new organizations to pursue their objectives, as stated in the framework document, using private sector management techniques (e.g., market testing, contracting-out, flexible pay-scales).

- Rationalizing central government. Executive agencies have been advocated as a means of subdividing the traditionally monolithic UK Civil Service into more manageable units. Moreover, it is argued that agencies are consequently more amenable to assessment by performance indicators set by sponsoring departments.

- Importing management skills. Agency policy, by creating semiautonomous business units within the public sector, provides a method of seconding private sector personnel from industry, and so augmenting commercial management expertise in public service delivery.

Prospects and Developments

On one hand, A. Massey described UK executive agency initiatives as "the most fundamental restructuring of the British Civil Service since the Northcote-Trevelyan reforms of the last century" (1993, p. 51). A host of UK government-sponsored assessments of policy have pointed to an increased commitment to improving value for money and quality of service as a consequence of agency policy (see, for example, Efficiency Unit 1991). Perceptions of success are reenforced by the UK government's longer-term objective of a residual "core" civil service and an extensive network of executive agencies concerned with public sector service delivery.

On the other hand, these fundamental reforms to UK public administration remain controversial. Some analysts argue that a limitation of agency policy had been its failure to exploit the full potential of private sector management techniques and competition. K. Hartley, for example, pointed out that efficiency incentives provided for managers in the new agencies are limited, and because agencies remain monopoly suppliers, policy has had little impact on market structure (1991, pp. 23–24). E. Mellon (1993) noted that, in practice, both private sector recruitment and delegation have been limited in executive agencies. Similarly, other commentators claim that, although policy has improved public sector service delivery, it has had limited impact in generating efficiency improvements and cost awareness in policy formulation at parent government departments (see, for example, Metcalfe and Richards 1987).

A second group of analysts insist that executive agency policy is flawed precisely because it attempts to import private sector management techniques to public service provision. L. Christie (1992), for example, argued that instead of improving efficiency, agency policy has been applied to "de-privilege" the career civil service, weaken public sector

trade unions, and prepare the ground for privatization. Finally, other commentators have raised and evaluated concerns over the implications of decentralization, and the policy and implementation divide that agencies imply, for traditional models of public accountability (see Dowling 1992).

Executive agency policy, therefore, remains an influential but contentious initiative in current UK public sector management.

MATTHEW R. H. UTTLEY

BIBLIOGRAPHY

Christie, L., 1992. "Viewpoint: Next Steps–A Union Critique." *Public Money and Management,* vol. 11, no. 4.
Dowling, K., 1992, "Managing the Civil Service." In R. Maidment, and G. Thompson, eds., *Managing the United Kingdom: An Introduction to Its Political Economy and Public Policy.* London: Sage.
Efficiency Unit, 1988, *Improving Management in Government: The Next Steps.* London: HMSO.
———, 1991, *Making the Most of Next Steps: The Management of Ministers' Departments and Their Executive Agencies.* London: HMSO.
Hartley, K., 1991, *The Economics of Defence Policy.* London: Brassey's.
Massey, A., 1993, *Managing the Public Sector: A Comparative Analysis of the United Kingdom and the United States.* Aldershot: Edward Elgar.
Mellon, E., 1993, "Executive Agencies: Leading Change from the Outside-In." *Public Money and Management,* vol. 13, no. 2.
Metcalfe, L., and S. Richards, 1987, *Improving Public Management.* London: Sage.

EXECUTIVE AGREEMENT.

A means for the United States President to conduct foreign relations and make international arrangements without United States Senate approval of a treaty.

Executive agreements give the President substantial latitude and broad authority in conducting foreign affairs. Executive agreements with other nations are valid international compacts (see Supreme Court cases as early as *Altman & Co. v. U.S.,* 224 U.S. 583 [1912]) and do not require Senate approval. These agreements can consider almost all interactions among nations, including economic, social, political, and defense issues–ranging from the routine and noncontroversial to the significant and controversial.

Controversial executive agreements include the Lend-Lease Destroyers-Bases Pact with Great Britain in 1940, the Yalta and Potsdam agreements of 1945, participation in the General Agreement on Tariffs and Trade (GATT) in 1947, the Vietnam Peace Agreement of 1973, and the Sinai Agreements of 1975.

The U.S. Constitution divides foreign policy responsibility between the President and Congress. Cooperation between these branches, as well as the Senate and House Foreign Relations Committees, can lead to a coherent foreign policy. In the absence of this cooperation, the President may use executive agreements to ensure a consistent approach to foreign policy issues. The executive agreement mechanism indicates that there may be conflicts between democratic decisionmaking and the consistency of a president's foreign policy.

Presidents increasingly rely upon executive agreements rather than treaties to conduct foreign relations. Howard Stanley and Richard Niemi (1992) reported that "between 1945 and 1990, the nation concluded 673 treaties and 12,107 executive agreements. President Ronald Reagan alone entered into 2,837 executive agreements but only 117 treaties" (p. 278).

Congress may pass legislation that negates executive agreements or negates the effects of such agreements by withholding funds for necessary programs. Congress rarely engages in either of these actions because it is reluctant to break with a prior commitment of U.S. policy. Presidents' increased use of executive agreements has raised policy concerns that the executive is bypassing congressional authority in international affairs.

Congress attempted to control presidential use of executive agreements by obtaining information about these agreements after their enactment. In 1972 it passed the Case Act and additional reporting requirements for U.S. departments and agencies. The Case Act requires the Secretary of State to transmit any international agreement text to Congress within 60 days. Agreements that require secrecy are to be submitted to the House and Senate Foreign Relations Committees. (These provisions exclude treaties.)

During the Richard Nixon and Gerald Ford administrations, an era of legislative-executive conflicts, these executives did not fully comply with the Case Act. George C. Edwards III (1980), found that, consequently, Congress reacted with further restrictions: "In 1977 Congress passed legislation requiring any department or agency of the U.S. Government that enters into any international agreement on behalf of the United States to transmit the text within twenty days of signing" (p. 17). Congressional actions do not limit presidents' constitutional authority or ability to enter into executive agreements, however.

Major controversies remain concerning the President's authority to engage in executive agreements and the legal relationships of executive agreements to treaties and state and federal law. Many agree that the President can negotiate executive agreements under constitutional authority as commander-in-chief and the power to conduct foreign relations, such as recognizing foreign governments. Louis Fisher (1978) contended that only the commander-in-chief rationale supports the President's ability to enter into executive agreements; but John Nowak and Ronald Rotunda (1991) found three additional sources of presidential authority regarding executive agreements: (1) authority found in a prior treaty; (2) authority from prior congressional authorization; and (3) congressional assent to an already negotiated agreement by the President, requiring a majority vote of both Houses.

Frequently, executive agreements and treaties consider the same subjects, and both are equally binding upon the U.S. government. A treaty is constitutionally authorized and requires a two-thirds vote of the Senate for approval. The U.S. Constitution does not provide any procedures or specific conditions for the enactment of executive agreements, however. Legal, administrative, and political questions determine to what extent an executive agreement is similar to a treaty and in what areas they differ. Executive agreements can have significant implications for the public policies and administrative practices stemming from such agreements.

In most ways, an executive agreement is similar to a treaty within federal law. Both treaties and executive agreements do not give additional powers to Congress or to any other branches of the U.S. government. Treaties and executive agreements must be consistent with the provisions of the Constitution and the Bill of Rights and other amendments. A treaty cannot override constitutional provisions concerning domestic matters (See *Reid v. Covert*, 354 U.S. 1 [1957]). By analogy, an executive agreement has a similar restriction. If treaties or executive agreements are inconsistent with the Constitution or Bill of Rights they are considered void.

The relationship between an executive agreement and a prior federal statute is a key distinction between the legal authority of an executive agreement and that of a treaty. The executive agreement, unlike a treaty, cannot override a previous congressional statute. Thus the President is not able to avoid or modify congressional actions. Another distinction is that Congress may nullify or alter executive agreements by passing a new statute, but amending or repealing a treaty would require a two-thirds vote.

Executive agreements have the binding force of U.S. law during the term of the President who negotiated them, but treaties remain in force until altered by Congress. Incoming presidents generally accept existing executive agreements. However, they have the authority to modify or reject executive agreements of past presidents. Executive agreements have the same relationship as treaties as concerns state law. Both treaties and executive agreements are superior to conflicting state laws.

The constitutional limits of executive agreements have been decided by the U.S. Supreme Court. The broad parameters of executive agreements led the Court to rule that such international compacts are a valid exercise of executive authority. The leading decision on the issue is *United States v. Pink*, 315 U.S. 203 (1942).

In 1933, President F. D. Roosevelt used an executive agreement to recognize the government of the Soviet Union, and the Soviet Union gave assets of a Russian insurance company to the United States. The Court ruled that the executive agreement was part of executive authority and that the agreement superseded state law concerning the insurance company's property.

Whether the President exceeded his constitutional authority under an executive agreement was decided in *Dames and Moore v. Ronald Reagan*, 453 U.S. 654 (1981). This case involved the application of both executive agreements and executive orders to domestic courts (see **executive order** entry). In 1980, when Iran took American hostages at the American embassy in Tehran, Iran, President Jimmy Carter froze all Iranian assets in the United States. His action was taken under the International Emergency Economic Powers Act (IEEPA). To obtain the release of the hostages, President Carter signed an executive agreement with Iran. This agreement included ending all legal proceedings against Iran in U.S. Courts. Presidents Carter and Reagan issued executive orders, which involved directives to federal government agencies to implement the executive agreement. One of the executive orders (no. 12294) "suspended all claims which may be presented to the United States Claims Tribunal." Dames and Moore Company claimed that President Reagan did not have the constitutional authority to impose claims settlement procedures by executive agreement. In *Dames and Moore v. Reagan*, the Supreme Court unanimously decided that the President had express congressional authority under IEEPA to take actions concerning a foreign country's property in the United States. If Congress authorizes presidential action or acquiesces in such behavior, then the President can enter into executive agreements without the advice and consent of Congress. Executive agreements assume that Congress cannot anticipate all possibilities concerning foreign events. According to Bernard Schwartz (1990), "The *Dames and Moore* case allows the U.S. President to take a broad delegation of Congressional power and act in similar and analogous situations. In the area of foreign relations, under the delegation doctrine, it is not necessary for Congress to specifically delegate authority" (p. 91). In this case, the Court supported the President's authority to enter into executive agreements that considered the claims of different nations.

Executive agreements give presidents substantial discretion and independence in foreign affairs. Presidential action under an executive agreement, which is based on congressional authorization or congressional acquiescence, places the President on firm constitutional grounds. Congress may disapprove an executive agreement, but this rarely occurs.

STEVEN PURO

BIBLIOGRAPHY

Dames and Moore v. Ronald Reagan, 453 U.S. 654 (1981).
Edwards III, George C., 1980. *Presidential Influence in Congress* San Francisco: W. H. Freeman.
Fisher, Louis, 1978. *The Constitution Between Friends: Congress, the President, and the Law*. New York: St. Martin's Press.
Henkin, Louis, 1972. *Foreign Affairs and the Constitution*. Mineola, NY: Foundation Press.
Margolis, Lawrence, 1986. *Executive Agreements and Presidential Power in Foreign Policy*. New York: Praeger.
Nowak, John E., and Ronald Rotunda, 1991. *Constitutional Law*. 4th ed. St. Paul: West.
Schwartz, Bernard, 1990. *The Ascent of Pragmatism: The Burger Court in Action*. Reading, MA: Addison-Wesley.
Stanley, Howard W., and Richard G. Niemi, 1992. *Vital Statistics on American Politics*. 3d ed. Washington, DC: Congressional Quarterly Press.
Symposium, 1982. "*Dames and Moore v. Reagan*." *UCLA Law Review*, Vol. 29: 977–1159.

EXECUTIVE BUDGET.   A budget proposal submitted to the legislature for resources prepared in the name of the chief executive of some governmental unit (town, county, state, or nation) that is designed to reflect that executive's policies, programs, and priorities. The budget request covers all resource requirements of executive branch agencies and activities. Budgeting requests of legislative and judicial branch organizations are usually appended to the executive budget without review or comment by the executive.

Politics and the Executive Budget

In the United States, the executive budget movement began at state and local government levels early in this century. An executive budget is currently used, in one variation or another, by 49 states (the exception is South Carolina) along with most county and local governments. The primary focus of this entry is at the (U.S.) national level, where the executive budget is generally referred to as "the President's Budget."

The federal government has utilized an executive budget since the passage of the Budget and Accounting Act of 1921. That law, in addition to mandating an annual executive budget submission, also established a central budget office called the Bureau of the Budget (BOB), which in 1970 was renamed the Office of Management and Budget (OMB) and the General Accounting Office (GAO). The BOB was created as an executive branch agency to assist the President in budget preparation, and the GAO was established as a legislative branch agency to perform auditing duties for the U.S. Congress.

Prior to the passage of the 1921 legislation (42 Stat 18, 1921), each federal agency developed its own budget request for submission to Congress. The budget requests were sent to Congress through the Treasury Department, but there is little evidence indicating that Treasury officials attempted to coordinate or consolidate the separate requests into a comprehensive financial or substantive program. For the first century and a quarter, the primary actors in the U.S. budget cycle were agencies that prepared budget requests, congressional committees that reviewed the budget requests, and individual members of Congress who approved budgetary expenditures by their votes.

From a late-twentieth century perspective, it is difficult to imagine how such an uncoordinated budgetary system could function effectively to finance a growing government. There are two reasons why it worked. First, there was usually an adequate amount of revenue collected in taxes to finance the limited activities of the federal government. From the beginning of the Republic until early in the twentieth century, the U.S. national budget usually had a surplus, except in periods of war (higher than normal spending) or periods of economic recession (lower than normal revenue). Once these unusual conditions passed, the budget tended to return to a surplus.

Budgeting as an instrument of financial management serves little purpose in the absence of scarcity and, until this century, there was normally adequate revenue to finance the real or perceived needs of the country—hence, no scarcity.

The second likely reason this system functioned effectively is that the norm of a balanced budget dominated the thinking of politicians and the interested citizenry for 150 years. The public expectation was that people and governments should "live within their means." A string of federal deficits from 1895 to 1899 seems to have suggested to many that something was wrong with federal policies and federal procedures. There appears to have been a widespread belief that in this era of "scientific management" there was little that could not be solved by being "more businesslike," and this included problems with the federal budget and deficit; enter budgetary reform to return the federal government to living within its means by making its procedures more systematic.

The early twentieth century brought together several disparate social movements that eventually culminated in the executive budget movement. One of these was the "Progressive Movement," with its emphasis on "good government" and holding politicians responsible to the electorate. The idea of budget reform (i.e., making somebody clearly responsible for the budget), soon turned to the chief executive—the mayor, the governor, or the president—as the focal point.

In U.S. politics "good government" movements, and reformers in general, usually are neither powerful nor influential enough to cause major legislative changes. Forces of reform are helped when the business community joins in to push for change. Although the reform groups and

business interests may have had different purposes in mind—the Progressives wanted budgetary reform and change in general, but business wanted what business always wants, lower taxes—they both focused on the executive budget as the means to achieve their objectives.

The major event that proved to be the catalyst for these two movements occurred when President William Howard Taft requested US$100,000 in 1909 to study ways for the government to improve how it conducted the "public business." When he was granted the appropriation, Taft appointed the Commission on Economy and Efficiency, which eventually recommended an executive budget. In 1912 he sent a report to Congress based on the commission findings ("The Need for a National Budget").

Any emphasis or political momentum there may have been from the recommendations of Taft's Commission on Economy and Efficiency was soon dissipated when Taft and the Republicans lost the election in 1912. The newly elected president, Woodrow Wilson, and a Democratic Congress had a domestic agenda that did not give the executive budget a very high priority. It focused instead on consolidating six appropriations committees into one. Wilson's program, called the "New Freedom," filled the legislative agenda with tariff reform, a proposal to create a federal reserve banking system, amendments to the Sherman Antitrust Act, and the creation of a regulatory commission to oversee trade and commerce. As Congress waded through these issues, events led to the U.S. involvement in World War I, which subsequently consumed virtually all of President Wilson's interest. The last years of the Wilson presidency revolved around the Treaty of Versailles and the League of Nations. However, budget reform, which had been a secondary issue, increased in importance when problems financing World War I arose. Financing problems and a national debt coupled with a desire to return to "normalcy" after the war rekindled congressional interest in budget reform.

Responding to this newfound interest, the House of Representatives established a Select Committee on the Budget, which, not surprisingly, ploughed much of the same ground that Taft's commission had a decade earlier. The same problems still existed and had actually been compounded by wartime financing. The Select Committee came up with the same major recommendation as the Taft Commission, an executive budget.

The House enacted a bill proposing an executive budget in October 1919, but the Treaty of Versailles kept the Senate from dealing with the issue in that session of Congress. In the next session of Congress, President Wilson endorsed the executive budget concept, and the House and Senate passed such a bill in May 1920—only to have President Wilson veto the bill in his final days in office because he disapproved of the provision regarding the removal of the head of the GAO. The election of 1920 soon subsumed interest in budget reform, but the victors, Warren Harding and the Republican Party, quickly endorsed the executive budget concept. The Budget and Accounting Act was passed and signed into law in June 1921, nearly a decade after it was proposed by President Taft.

The 1921 legislation represented a major shift in U.S. budgetary power from the Congress to the President. One of the most amazing aspects of the shift of power was that Congress apparently did not recognize that it was taking place. The report of the Select Committee (House Report 14, 67th Cong., 1st Sess. 1921) states, "The bill does not in the slightest degree give the Executive any greater power than he now has over the consideration of appropriations by Congress." This may be true, but it is hardly the central point. The shift of initiative for the budget to the President was praised for greatly reducing "the drudgery of committees in making inquiry into estimates." In perhaps its major step into unreality, the report concluded that "the budget under this plan will be an Executive budget only to the extent that the Executive initiates the budget. It is a congressional budget after it has been considered and acted upon by Congress."

The report, after maintaining that the bill was "no departure from the fundamental political principles of the present Government of the United States" ended with the Select Committee's observation that "the bill leaves intact present conditions in respect to the location and exercise of powers by the two branches of government but . . . provides the means for the more efficient exercise of these powers." In the end, just as the reformers and businesspeople had said, it was just a matter of efficiency.

Perhaps in the hands of a passive President like Warren Harding there was little or no increase in presidential power flowing from the Budget and Accounting Act, but that would have been because the President had few government initiatives in mind and chose not to use the new powers he had been given.

In the mid-1920s the newly developed executive budget, through its central budget office, focused on reducing agency requests for spending in order to reduce the overall size of the budget and thereby permit taxes to be cut from the high levels enacted during World War I. Both political parties appeared to favor low levels of spending and reduced taxes during the 1920s. The decade ended with federal spending at less than 3 percent of the gross national product (GNP) (compared to 23 percent in the late 1990s).

It is not the existence of an executive budget that "caused" this large increase in federal expenditures but that an executive budget facilitated the overall trends in the U.S. government over the past 70 years—an activist presidency that uses the executive budget to facilitate its domestic and foreign initiatives and a more passive Congress,

which until the mid-1970s was accustomed to deferring to executive judgments in times of crises—which seemed to be perpetual. U.S. presidents from the 1930s to the 1970s did not "steal" budgetary powers from Congress but accepted powers that Congress willingly gave up. What was true of Congress appears to be true of legislatures worldwide. The erosion of legislative powers from the 1930s to the 1970s was common and broadly recognized.

Most major executive programs cost a great deal of money, money that was framed in the context of executive budgets, which Congress usually approved after making marginal adjustments. Contrary to what Congress believed in 1921, beginning in the mid-1960s the budget had become the President's Budget from preparation to execution, with only a detour for legislative approval, which was almost always forthcoming.

In 1974, with the passage of the Budget and Impoundment Control Act, Congress attempted to reclaim its dissipated budgetary powers, at least to the extent that it now required itself to develop a budget resolution as the congressional answer to the executive budget (the 1974 law originally required two or more resolutions). The comprehensive plan of the President was to be answered by the comprehensive plan of Congress. Congress has thus reclaimed some, but not all, of the power it gave away. This reclaiming of some budgetary power occurred at the time of worldwide economic slowdown, so legislatures all over the world appeared to sense a need to reexamine spending levels and exert some financial control simply because revenues were declining.

The executive budget has evolved into a powerful tool in the expanding role of the president in U.S. politics. The same can be said of most governors and mayors. In measuring the "strength" of governors and mayors, control of an executive budget is usually first on a list of powers that is believed to enhance the chief executive's power to govern.

At the federal level, initiatives to alleviate the impact of the Great Depression or to force social reform with Great Society programs have had their fruition in presidential programs that Congress approved and then, most importantly, financed through the appropriation process. The executive budget lends itself to concerted presidential efforts to resolve complex, nationwide problems. Congress is too diversified and decentralized to put together a "War on Poverty" or an energy program, or, for that matter, any consolidated budget that represents a unified effort to achieve large-size national goals.

Within a decade of the initiation of the executive budget at the federal level the United States witnessed the birth of the activist presidency. World events and political perspectives probably did the most to create this activism in the White House, but the executive budget was quickly grasped as a tool to help bring it about where it matters most—in terms of money that enables presidents to "get things done." A clear shift in the momentum of initiative had occurred, thanks in large part to the executive budget.

Public Administration and the Executive Budget

From the perspective of the public administrator there are several important points to understand about the executive budget. First, in the U.S. system of a federal government of separated powers, the executive budget is a *request* by the chief executive to the legislature for action consistent with the constitutional distribution of power. Thus the legislature must act positively if it is to implement the proposals in the executive budget request.

The legislature is free to approve or disapprove all or some parts of the budget request. Congress can even disregard the budget request without provoking constitutional crisis. When the legislature enacts executive requests for resources it usually does so in the context of a single law or several laws that are in a different format than the executive budget request. Thus the executive proposes courses of action but the legislative branch disposes of the request in various ways.

Public administrators may be unsure at times of what specifically has been enacted. Budget execution is designed to resemble what has been proposed in the budget, but often what has been enacted must be restructured to fit approved ongoing activities and programs. In the end, the initiative rests with administrators to implement what they believe Congress enacted and the President wants. The two are not necessarily the same.

Another key point is that the existence of an executive budget usually requires some type of a central budget office that acts on behalf of the chief executive in reviewing, assembling, and consolidating the diverse requests submitted by the several executive agencies. Such central budget offices are likely to be organizationally part of the Treasury Department or in an independent office reporting directly to the chief executive. The central budget office is required to prepare and disseminate budget preparation instructions and procedural forms for agencies to use in budget preparation. As a starting point, the budgetary submission from agencies must look alike and be prepared using the same set of definitions and on the same timetable.

The central budget office also provides some type of programmatic and financial guidance to preparing agencies regarding what is to be included in their separate budget requests. The central budget office attempts to impose a degree of financial and programmatic discipline so that the final budget request reflects the priorities of the chief executive rather than the desires and wishes of each separate agency. After agency submissions are reviewed and approved for compliance with format instructions and programmatic guidance, the central budget office sends the prepared submission to the chief executive, who usually issues an accompanying budget message upon forwarding it to the legislature for its appropriate action.

A final element of considerable significance is that the executive budget is flexible enough to absorb a variety of budget preparation techniques that have found executive favor. In the United States, during the 1950s performance-budgeting techniques were applied in preparing executive budgets. Performance budgeting was designed to help executives manage the growing budgets by focusing on managing outcomes and thereby relate outputs of goods and services to budgetary inputs of dollars and people. In the 1960s, program budgeting—especially in the specific version adopted by the federal government called Planning, Programming, and Budgeting (PPB)—was adopted by the entire federal government at the direction of President Lyndon Johnson. President Jimmy Carter brought zero-based budgeting (ZBB) from Georgia to assist him in determining national budget priorities. President Ronald Reagan applied ideological perspectives to the executive budget, as if to demonstrate that ideological views, as well as rational analytical approaches to the executive budget, can serve presidents as they see fit to achieve their goals.

In the United States it has not only been chief executives who have found the executive budgets useful. The House of Representatives Appropriations Committee, still the most powerful voice in discretionary budgetary politics in Congress, traditionally uses the executive budget submission as the measuring rod against which to keep its score of how much it reduces and how it controls spending.

Baselines have been of increasing importance in congressional decisionmaking in recent years, but baselines lend themselves to varying interpretations. The President's Budget, however, is the number crunchers' document par excellence. In all the confusion of budgetary projections and baselines, the executive budget as submitted by the President remains the best starting point for discretionary budgetary calculations each year. It is at least the most easily understood starting point in an otherwise extremely complex process.

Over the years, the President's Budget has varied from one to seven separate documents. The Bush administration (1989–1993) consolidated the information into one very large document, which in fiscal year 1993–1994 consisted of over 1,700 pages. Currently, the Clinton administration utilizes five separate documents for this purpose, one of which is simply a pamphlet-sized explanation of the budget system and concepts.

Regardless of the number of volumes, the President's Budget now begins with a presidential budget message by which the chief executive submits the budget to Congress. Usually, the President then reviews the current budgeting and economic environment and describes what the current budget proposal will do to improve things. Sometimes in this message the President lays out the priorities for future spending. President George Bush's messages were more perfunctory, simply transmitting the document to Congress. The detailed explanation of the budget was left to President Bush's budget director.

The documents provide summary and detail of the various budgetary accounts, by agency and by function. Appropriation language proposed to Congress, along with current appropriation language, is included in the *Budget Appendix,* which is the most detailed document. Another volume called *Analytical Perspectives* discusses selected issues, such as capital investments, credit programs, and federal employment. These topics vary year to year. At one time, these items were in a *Special Analysis* volume.

Despite all this information being submitted to Congress and the general public, agencies will later submit more detailed justification material to congressional committees to support budget requests. This material generally appears at congressional hearings, when agency witnesses testify in support of their specific portion of the executive budget request.

Future Uses of Executive Budgets

As a device for executive presentation of a comprehensive program that reflects the chief executive's priorities, the executive budget appears to be in the process of losing its potency. This is not because of any deficiency on the part of the executive budget but because of the changing composition of U.S. federal expenditures. For fiscal year 1995–1996 it was expected that 62 percent of federal spending would be for interest payments and mandatory entitlement programs, which usually take the form of transfer payments from the government to individuals. (Mandatory spending is the current term for what was formerly referred to as "uncontrollable spending.") In fiscal year 1985–1986 the comparable number was 55 percent.

To the extent that interest and mandatory spending continue to rise—and there is no current indication of an abatement—the area of discretion remaining for presidential programs decreases. Entitlement and required spending for net interest are in many ways the antithesis of budgeting. If budgeting represents the rational allocation of scarce resources to competing claims, then mandatory spending represents a prior claim on resources that preempts weighing competing priorities. Under budgeting for

mandatory programs, the budget passes to a scorekeeping document, in which estimates of mandatory expenditures take first priority.

The executive budget was designed, in part, to provide a vehicle for the application of rational comprehensive techniques in a systematic manner to *all* federal expenditures. In 1921, other than interest payments, there were no mandatory programs. Mandatory spending or entitlements and interest payments reduce the area of discretion, since they must be financed before any discretionary programs can be supported. In addition, about half the budget classified as discretionary is for national defense. How discretionary this actually is becomes problematical and highly dependent on circumstances. Certainly, there will always be defense spending. Of the first budget of the United States, 21 percent was for defense. This is not much different from today's 18 percent.

The changing nature of expenditures also points out some further shortcomings of the executive budget. The extent of unfunded pension liabilities does not appear in executive budgets. Neither do assets of the federal government appear. When these issues are faced, it is usually in the context of supplemental information in a special analysis of the budget. It would appear that the executive budget was designed for simpler times, when government programs and commitments were annual. Now the United States has a multiyear budget for most expenditures, this is coupled with long-term obligations to continue funding into the future—some might say in perpetuity. This is not to infer that multiyear budgets have no drawbacks. It is likely that multiyear budgets increase rigidity in budgeting since long-term obligations are looked upon as a given. If a government budget is to be a document that reflects all spending and the financial condition of the government, the executive budget currently does an inadequate job.

As an organizing principle for articulation of executive priorities, the executive budget is a very useful document. In the United States, at the national level, however, this area is shrinking and being replaced by other factors and issues beyond the scope of current budgets.

If budget reform is designed to reflect the spirit of its times, then the executive budget is an instrument whose time may have passed. Concerns with multiyear spending commitments and generational impact of current policies have replaced discretionary executive judgments about national needs. The executive budget fits best into an era in which political discretion is high, revenues are growing, and deficits are small in relation to the gross national product (GNP) or to the gross domestic product (GDP). These conditions do not fit the current situation in the United States. In fact, they fit few, if any, of the situations in the industrialized democracies. The executive budget served the United States well for over half a century, but it now appears to be somewhat of an antiquated idea.

Variations of Executive Budgeting

The definition and concept of the executive budget used here fits the U.S. model of a government of separated, independently utilized powers. The chief administrator is an independent actor outside the legislative branch, and the legislators are independent actors who by legal authority and custom are free to change budget requests as they see fit. This, in most respects requires a unique presidential form of government.

A more expansive definition of an executive budget might conclude that any budget prepared by executive branch employees in administrative agencies, the Treasury or Finance Departments, has aspects of an executive budget. In a two-party parliamentary form of government in which the budget request is the result of negotiations among cabinet members (who are actually legislators as well as ministers) and then is presented to the Parliament (in which budget approval is assumed, as long as the majority party retains control), a different model of "executive" budgeting prevails. This is the case even more so in a multiparty parliamentary system in which cabinet ministers negotiate budgetary allocations among the parties before one budget is submitted for approval to Parliament. Whether this represents executive budgeting or not is a matter of opinion, but it does not fit the standard U.S. definition.

For the distinction to be made that something is or is not an executive budget there should be a clear distinction between the legislative branch and the executive. If not, then this simply constitutes a seamless budget without a descriptive adjective "executive." This would also appear to necessitate the ability of the legislature to change what has been submitted by the executive. Thus the submission of a budget by a king or a czar to a parliament that is powerless to make significant changes would in one sense be an executive budget par excellence, but it certainly is not what the current practice considers to be an executive budget.

If the defining characteristics of the executive budget are an independent chief executive and independent legislature, acting within the context of a clear separation of powers, then it is likely that only the United States truly functions under an executive budget concept. Models used in other countries should have different names to differentiate them, such as a Westminster executive budget to specify the parliamentary form of this model. Unique aspects, such as a bureaucracy-based budget or a parliamentary-based budget, are distinguishing features. Simply involving executive branch employees does not make a budget an executive budget in anything but the broadest sense, which has little, if any, analytical benefit.

Exactly what name is attached to the budget is not necessarily as important as how it fits into the structure and process of government in each nation or each supranational government. Fixed commitments for social spending have gained a growing portion of virtually all budgets. These commitments need to be accommodated in any new theory of budgeting, as must credit programs, government-sponsored enterprises, government assets and liabilities, and partially privatized or parastatal entities. In the end, the budget must fit into the structure of government and not vice versa.

BERNARD T. PITSVADA

BIBLIOGRAPHY

U.S. Congress. House. *National Budget System,* Report No. 4, 67th Cong., 1st sess., 25 April 1921.

EXECUTIVE DIRECTOR. A title that accompanies the management role for the highest-ranking staff position in a private nonprofit organization. In some states, the heads of public agencies are also referred to as executive directors.

A history of the position of executive director is difficult to reconstruct. Management and leadership have been evidenced by individuals throughout human history. The emergence of the executive director position may have been shaped by the historical and contextual forces that similarly influenced leadership needs in such settings as tribal, military, educational, religious, and political.

Early developments in commerce, followed by improved manufacturing technologies during the Industrial Revolution, led to stronger interests in management techniques during the late 1800s and into the twentieth century. During the same time period that scientific management principles were being advanced, Congress in 1894 created public policy that formally supported tax exemptions for charitable organizations. The development of management as a field of professional practice began to flourish during the first 20 years of the twentieth century. As attention to university programs developed and societies concerned with management practices formed, the importance of senior management positions became significant, not only in business but also in public administration and organizations of the private nonprofit sector.

The title and position of executive director is equivalent to chief executive officer (CEO) or president, both of which are executive management titles generally used in for-profit organizations to designate the foremost decisionmaker who is in charge of operations.

Among private nonprofit organizations, the title of president is often reserved for the highest-ranking volunteer (sometimes called the chief volunteer officer or otherwise known as chairperson of the board of directors). In some nonprofit organizations, however, the corporate title of president is substituted for the title of executive director. In such situations, the highest-ranking volunteer will be referred to as the chairperson of the board of directors.

The relationship between the chairperson, the board of directors, and the executive director position is initially forged through the process of hiring the executive director. In fact, the board of directors has ultimate responsibility for hiring and establishing the compensation of the executive director. The board is also responsible for evaluating the performance of the executive director and rewarding (or terminating, if required) him or her.

Once hired, the executive director may assume many governance and management roles and responsibilities. Though boards of directors can never truly delegate their legal obligations and fiduciary responsibilities, they are known to assign (or expect) their executive directors to help them fulfill their roles as effective board members. In some organizations, the role of the executive director is not shaped through the board's articulation of expectations, but rather the position is shaped by the executive director's experiences and know-how. In public sector organizations, the executive director has a responsibility to manage a department. Above all, the focus of the position is to support the policies and direction of the elected official who appointed the executive director.

How Does a Person Become an Executive Director?

In public sector organizations, the executive director position is generally the result of an appointment by an elected official in charge of a state or municipality. A person may be selected for the executive director position based primarily on his or her political connections rather than management skills.

Since politics help shape the nature and role of the executive director in public agencies, the remainder of this entry will focus on the intricacies of the executive director position in private sector nonprofit organizations.

How a person becomes an executive director of a private nonprofit organization may not always follow a clear and logical career path. There is much anecdotal evidence to suggest that many executive directors have been hired on the basis of their programmatic skills and not on their qualifications as executive managers. Laurence J. Peter coined the phrase "the Peter Principle," to identify this type of organizational ascendency into positions beyond one's competency. For example, competent social workers known for outstanding family counseling skills can find themselves hired into executive director positions on the basis of their proven clinical activities. In this example, the social worker may have no training or education in man-

agement, no experience with policy implementation, or no other competencies usually required of the executive director position. Consequently, the person is promoted into the highest of management level positions and removed from the one position in which he or she excelled. Thus promotion from a program specialist position to the executive director position may be the result of a board's uncertainty about the role of this management position. Furthermore, the managerial philosophy of executive director candidates may be overlooked because of the similar traits, values, and program philosophy they share with board members or agency personnel.

More recently, hiring pools of executive director applicants seem to comprise candidates with varied backgrounds. Some include individuals with program expertise along with a mix of individuals who have been trained or educated in nonprofit management. Many management oriented candidates seek management expertise through nonprofit management workshops, conferences, and continuing education opportunities, some of which lead to a certificate in nonprofit management from a host college or university. In more recent years, executive director position applicants may include individuals who have earned graduate degrees in nonprofit management or degrees from other disciplines that offer a concentration in nonprofit management, such as those degrees or areas of academic concentration available in the fields of human services, business, or public administration.

Whether individuals have backgrounds emphasizing program capabilities, management skills, or a combination of the two, there does not appear to be a shortage of candidates who willingly express their interest in vacant executive director positions, for a variety of reasons. The size of a nonprofit organization's budget and the complexity of the operations can be factors in attracting an executive director. Salary range and fringe benefits for the executive director position may influence both the size of an applicant pool and the characteristics and competencies of the candidates. For example, one would expect an executive director hired at US $20,000 a year to have competencies different from those of an individual who is paid US $100,000 a year. One might also expect that the larger, more-established nonprofit organization will be able to attract the most experienced and seasoned of executive directors, but the smaller-budgeted organization might be a valuable training ground for the newer and emerging executive manager.

Other important factors that have a bearing on the interest level of qualified applicants include the organization's mission, beliefs, and values; the geographical location of the organization; the reputation of the organization; the status of the board members in the community; the extent of (under-, over-, or balanced) involvement of board members in the organization; and the clarity of the board's expectations of the executive director.

When an organization is searching for a new executive director, it is important to identify clearly the skills and characteristics necessary for leading the organization toward the achievement of its mission and vision. When the board is clear about its organization's direction and purpose, the board has a higher probability of selecting the right person. The most critical factors are a candidate's knowledge about the role of executive director, proven management and human resource skills, and solid (and candid) references.

What Are Required Competencies for an Executive Director?

The executive director position comprises many multifaceted roles and responsibilities. The effective executive director possesses a range of qualifications that take into account personal characteristics, skills, knowledge, and abilities. Management expert Henry Mintzberg (1973) suggested that the position of an executive manager is organized around ten roles within three sets of behaviors: (1) four decisional roles (entrepreneur, disturbance handler, resource allocator, negotiator); (2) three informational roles (monitor, disseminator, spokesperson); and (3) three interpersonal roles (figurehead, leader, liaison). Mintzberg's concepts have also been applied to managing nonprofit organizations.

Daily work experiences of the nonprofit executive director illustrate the continuum of skills and abilities that are required of the position. Since executive directors tend to be involved in many activities simultaneously, their management focus must continually shift. This shifting can cause a blurring of the boundaries among the various roles categorized as either informational, decisional, or interpersonal, as illustrated in the following scenarios.

Informational

The executive director monitors the opinions of local stakeholders to determine if there will be any impact on the organization's reputation and its ability to raise private funds. This information is shared (as disseminator) in different formats with key staff and board members in order to plan appropriate responses and fund-raising activities. The executive director speaks (spokesperson) before civic groups and corporate funders to explain the mission and direction of the organization.

Interpersonal

The executive director represents the organization and its board of directors (as figurehead) at important community meetings. At a monthly meeting the executive director (as leader) encourages the staff to work on improving its skills and offers guidance for exploring individual beliefs in comparison with the organization's mission and purpose.

The executive director (as liaison) meets with the staff of the mayor's office to determine (as entrepreneur) if local community development funds exist to help finance a volunteer youth program.

Decisional

In response to a negative article in the local newspaper, the executive director (as disturbance handler) reacts to the external pressures to fend off a public relations crisis. In preparation for drafting the coming year's budget for the board's consideration, the executive director studies the agency's finances (as resource allocator) to shift the revenues among the key priorities and programs of the organization. The executive director also plays a negotiating role among department managers and board members with regard to establishing funding priorities and eliminating some favorite but underfunded projects.

Demands of the executive director position will vary among nonprofit organizations. Regardless of the organizational complexity of the position, the job generally requires some functional ability to shift attention back and forth between internal and external issues. Executive directors are expected to have the skill to assess their organizations' strengths and weaknesses and to analyze the results of the information. The results can be used to develop a purposeful and strategic course of action, such as designing activities to improve or maintain the capability of staff or to protect or enhance the quality of the organization's service delivery system.

The ability to project how current events or emerging trends in the community will positively or adversely impact the nonprofit organization is another critical management trait that is necessary for controlling or influencing outcomes and for planning thoughtful strategic reactions. The executive director is also expected to respond to the pressures of the external environment by developing a network of community supports and collaborative working relationships.

Paying attention to the organization's internal and external environments is just one of many important components of the executive director's job. In fact, there are several essential management tasks in which the results-oriented executive director will participate, lead, or carry out explicitly or implicitly.

The tasks are as follows: *mission development, visioning, goal setting.* The executive director will have an opportunity to assist the board, staff, and other community members in the creation of an organizational mission statement or to annually review and, if necessary, revise the organization's mission statement. The mission statement is a reflection of the needs of the community and represents a collective vision of what the community could strive to become as a result of the efforts of the organization. By exerting leadership, the executive director is in a position to interpret the significance of the mission statements for establishing operational goals and objectives, recommending policy changes, and for motivating staff, volunteers and others to believe in the importance of the mission.

Planning. The executive director plays an instrumental role in working with the board and staff to use the mission statement as a guide for establishing short-term and long-term goals and objectives of the organization and for developing action steps for implementation. The executive director is positioned to communicate to staff the purpose, time lines, and strategies of the plan. Managing the resources of money and people to accomplish the organization's plan and monitoring and developing strategies when obstacles impede progress are also major responsibilities of the executive director. The executive director assists the board of directors with its duties by assuring an evaluation of the plan's progress and reporting its results and, likewise, communicating the need to revise aspects of the plan on an ongoing basis.

Organizing. In practice, the executive director is responsible for determining what monetary resources and people are needed to accomplish an organization's plan, projects, and program services. Structuring the staffing patterns of the organization and establishing performance standards are other management responsibilities of the executive director.

Motivating. It is sometimes said that an effective manager is one who is able to get things accomplished through the work of the other people. The complexity of motivating individuals either through intrinsic or extrinsic rewards requires an understanding of basic human nature. The effective executive director is one who understands the varying needs of individuals and responds by providing enriching opportunities, which build a sense of spirit and belief in the organization. If the director stimulated an interest in the work of the organization, the staff, board members, and other volunteers will use their energies, knowledge, and skills to achieve accomplishments for the organization and to enhance its service capacity.

Decisionmaking. Herbert A. Simon once suggested that decisionmaking is synonymous with managing. Decisionmaking is a pervasive management task of the executive director and includes making a choice among varying alternatives and weighing the likely consequences and risks of choosing one alternative over another. The effective executive director is one who uses a model or framework for approaching complex and far-reaching organizational decisions. Of particular importance is the recurring task of seeking and analyzing information through informal and formal communication channels that are internal and external to the organization. Information is a necessary in-

gredient for recognizing the need to make a decision and for serving as a pertinent database for developing a decision. Savvy executive directors also monitor reactions to their decisions and use the feedback as additional critical bits of data for ongoing decisionmaking.

Delegating. The work of the executive director can be an enormous burden and overload one person. To be efficient and effective, the executive director must be able to recognize which aspects of his or her work can be scheduled or reorganized for attention during another time period. Also, it is important to identify which portions of the job can be accomplished by assigning responsibility to others within the organization or by making temporary assignments to outside consultants. Appropriate delegation of the executive director's work assignments to staff requires an understanding of staff's skills and abilities; a sensitivity to its workload demands; a level of trust in staff's ability and willingness to accomplish tasks at a level that will meet or exceed the executive director's own standards; and the capacity to thank staff for helping out, either on temporary or permanently assigned tasks. Even though executive directors can never truly delegate away their organizational management responsibilities, their uses of delegation can help to alleviate the stresses of work overload, which can adversely impact outcomes.

Coordinating. Executive directors of moderate to large organizations have a management challenge of coordinating the variety of tasks and activities that take place among different specialized departments within an organization. In addition, they need to assure the coordination of work activities that occur up and down the organizational hierarchy. Almost thirty years ago, the term "integration" was introduced, referring to the process of managing the linkages across the formal structures of the organization. Without attending to the function of coordination, departments and staff may work at cross purposes and thereby waste resources and adversely impact the opportunity for organizational success. The coordination of tasks and activities is also at play in smaller nonprofit organizations, due to smaller size and fewer staff, the executive director may have a greater level of participation in the different activities, thus minimizing the coordination challenges.

Reporting. The accountability concept of reporting is tied to the idea of lines of responsibilities and a chain of command. Different individuals in the organization are responsible for a variety of outcomes and are responsible to their supervisor for reporting on the progress of achieving assignments, goals, and objectives. The aggregate of all of this information is eventually reported by senior management staff to the executive director, who similarly must report on the organization's progress to the board of directors. The executive director's responsibility is to assure that there is no confusion in the lines of reporting, and that staff have available to them the proper supports and supervision that enable them to do their work and report their outcomes.

Supervising. The executive director must rely heavily on the capabilities of staff to accomplish the organization's plans; therefore, human resource management is central to an effective organization. In addition to the ability to motivate staff, coordinate activities, and delegate to other personnel, the executive director must have a mechanism of identifying performance outcomes and an acceptable process of supporting or promoting change among staff. The process of supervision is an interactive approach that is centered on developing the abilities of the employee by reflecting on work performance, jointly searching for solutions to work problems, clarifying expectations of the position, clarifying the direction of the organization, assessing the employee's progress in achieving performance objectives, and by modeling the values and beliefs of the organization. Supervisors will typically style their supervision of staff based on how executive directors comport themselves in supervisory conferences with senior management staff.

Managing Finances. All management decisions have some level of impact on an organization's allocation of resources, expenditure of funds, or the need for securing additional money. Technically, a board of directors has a fiduciary responsibility as representatives of the public to assure that there is an annual budget and a plan to acquire an adequate amount of financial resources for stabilizing the organization and implementing its services. Practically speaking, the management of the daily operations requires that the executive director be the one to provide the oversight for carefully monitoring the level of available cash, the organization's current debt, and its outstanding liabilities and receivables.

Complex or simple managerial decisions require that the executive director be fully aware of the organization's fiscal health. Most responsible executive directors rely on the use of financial management tools and the information they produce for making decisions. The tools include: financial statements, functional expense reports, and cash flow statements. An effective executive director knows how to interpret the financial reports and understands the implications of analysis on the stewardship of the organization's budget and resources. In addition, the executive director analyzes the organization's fiscal health by paying close attention to the effects of rising costs, increased or decreased activities, and the variable impacts from planned or unplanned changes in the organization's internal or external environment—including the organization's available working capital, current ratio, and debt-to-equity ratio.

The executive director also plays an important role in the organization's investment strategies. The executive director advises and supports the board after seeking expert advice on the development investment policy and its execution by locating reasonable investment risks. The executive director can also help the board to be prudent in its decisionmaking by watching the returns on investments and forecasting both the current and future needs of the organization.

Fund-Raising. Although many fund-raising experts claim that a primary leadership role of the board of directors is to raise sufficient capital for the operations and program, in reality, fund-raising becomes a management responsibility. The executive director should be as concerned, if not more so, for the organization to be financially sound and have the necessary funding to operate programs and pay staff wages and salary.

The executive director may take on a varying level of direct involvement for raising funds or see to it that the fund-raising activities are shared or carried out by specific staff, consultants, or volunteers. An executive director, for example, might secure appointments with community funders and solicit funding, but be accompanied by board members who bring credibility with their volunteer concerns and as examples for other volunteers like themselves who commit unpaid time and energy to the organization's cause.

Though the support and participation of board members is undeniably a critical factor to fund-raising success, the board's ability to be successful is often dependent on the management expertise and involvement of the executive director. The basis for successful fund-raising, for example, is to build off the needs, achievements and plans of the organization. The short-term or long-term capability of an organization's fund-raising program requires that the organization be in good working order, operating productively and efficiently, both of which are results of effective management. The executive director assures the soundness of the organization's operations and programs through the controls, processes, and systems that he or she manages, making certain they are supported by skillful and knowledgeable staff and, if applicable, a cadre of committed and dedicated volunteers, all of whom are knowledgeable about the organization's mission, vision, and direction.

The basic characteristics of volunteer support requires the involvement of the executive director, providing oversight and assurances that the tools of fund-raising are in place. Necessary fund-raising tools include a well-crafted "case statement," a donor or prospect list, an annual report or other significant brochures that illustrate the achievements of the organization, and a plan that has realistic goals with a time frame that is also reasonable. With regard to the implementation of a fund-raising plan, the executive director must also be up-to-date about the efforts of the staff, volunteers, or resource development committee members so that people are working together and not inadvertently at cross-purposes.

Volunteers are very important to fund-raising success; however, if volunteers do not follow through on important assignments or find that their personal lives and occupational demands are interfering with their volunteer commitment, the executive director must be ready to step in. More than one executive director has found him- or herself "jumping-in" to salvage a fund-raising project, while publicly giving the credit for the project's success to the volunteers, board, and staff.

Executive Director's Leadership Role in Relation to the Board's Governance Role

Clarifying the differences between the responsibilities of the board and those of the executive director, Kenneth Dayton stated simply that governance is governance, and not management. It is largely an indisputable custom that the executive director's role is to oversee the day-to-day operations of the organization, as well as to share jointly with the board in matters critical to the strategic direction and survival of the organization. Because the organizational stakes are high, there is good reason to have concern over the ambiguity that sometimes exists between what board members should actually do and what executive directors are expected to do on behalf of the board.

Some authors have suggested that the board–executive director relationship would be more productive if it were conceptualized as a partnership. Research investigations into what constitutes effective governance and executive leadership have led some researchers to suggest that an especially effective executive director is one who takes active responsibility for the accomplishment of the organizational mission and its stewardship by providing substantial "board-centered" leadership for steering the efforts of the board of directors.

This view also asserts that there are several flaws in the traditional governance model. In the traditional model, the executive director is ranked in a subordinate position to the board. The hierarchical relationship would suggest that the executive director's daily work activities are being directed and supervised by the board of directors. Robert Herman and Richard Heimovics (1991) affirm through their research findings what many executive directors have come to believe through practical experience: that the board may legally be in charge, but the work of the organization is accomplished by the leadership demonstrated by the executive director. In this alternative "board-centered" model of governance, the executive director's distinctive leadership skills, information base, and management expertise is used for leading the organization toward the accomplishment of its mission. Furthermore, this model acknowledges that board performance is reliant on the leadership and management skills of the executive director. In this way, the executive director works to promote board participation and to

facilitate decisionmaking. In addition, the executive director uses his or her interpersonal skills to craft respectful and productive interaction among the board members. With this approach, the executive director is (justifiably) credited with successful or unsuccessful organizational outcomes.

STEPHEN R. BLOCK

BIBLIOGRAPHY

Bennis, Warren, and Burt Nanus, 1985. *Leaders: The Strategies for Taking Charge*. New York: Harper & Row.
Block, Peter, 1989. *The Empowered Manager: Positive Political Skills at Work*. San Francisco: Jossey-Bass.
Boyatzis, Richard E., 1982. *The Competent Manager: A Model for Effective Performance*. New York: John Wiley & Sons.
Drucker, Peter F., 1990. *Managing the Non-Profit Organization*. Oxford, England: Butterworth-Heinemann.
Heimovics, Richard D., and Robert D. Herman, 1989. "The Salient Management Skills: A Conceptual Framework for a Curriculum for Managers in Nonprofit Organizations." *American Review of Public Administration*, vol. 18, no. 2: 119–132.
Herman, Robert Dean, and Richard D. Heimovics, 1991. *Executive Leadership in Nonprofit Organizations*. San Francisco: Jossey-Bass.
McCauley, Cynthia D., and Martha W. Hughes, 1993. In Dennis R. Young, Robert M. Hollister, and Virginia A. Hodgkinson, eds., *Governing, Leading, and Managing Nonprofit Organizations*. San Francisco: Jossey-Bass, 155–169.
Mintzberg, Henry, 1973. *The Nature of Managerial Work*. New York: Harper & Row.
Young, Dennis R., 1987. "Executive Leadership in Nonprofit Organizations." In Walter W. Powell, ed., *The Nonprofit Sector: A Research Handbook*. New Haven: Yale University Press, 167–179.

EXECUTIVE ORDER. Chief executive officers' ability to instruct government agencies, through rules or regulations, to enact government programs. Executive orders have the effect of law and are used during regular and emergency situations.

The chief executive of a government can modify government agency regulations or rules through executive orders. These orders are based upon executives' ability to execute the laws, and in the instance of the President of the United States to "take care that the laws be faithfully executed." Executive orders are based on previous practices or legislative authorization. These orders may give administrative agencies broader or narrower scope for their authority. If the order is not grounded in agency rules or legislative statutes, it may be overturned by courts.

Executive orders can be broad or specific tools for administrative enforcement of government policies. Executive orders raise two key questions: (1) To what extent can the President act for the public good based on his office's authority? And (2) Do executive orders indicate executive autonomy from the legislature or administrative agencies? John Locke's view of the executive implies that executives should have more authority than a limited doctrine of express and implied powers. Presidents of the United States have extensively used executive orders to enact broad-range policies and manage complex operations of the executive branch. For example, President John F. Kennedy and President Lyndon B. Johnson used executive orders to implement civil rights and liberties in federal programs (see, respectively, e.g., Executive Order 10925 [1961], which established affirmative action programs for federal government hiring, and Executive Order 11246 [1965], which instructed the Labor Department to require private contractors with the federal government to engage in affirmative-action hiring programs). President Harry S. Truman used Executive Order 9981 (1948) to integrate the armed forces. Thus, in a specific area, presidents may modify particular agency rules through an executive order.

Executive orders are direct instructions from the chief executive authority; and administrative agencies have a strong inclination to obey such instructions. Executives can use these orders to respond to current policy needs or to ensure consistency of administrative practices. Executive orders allow presidents to avoid legislative confrontations on controversial matters. For example, Executive Order 11246 (1965), concerning affirmative action, says that failure to comply with the nondiscriminatory employment practices could lead businesses or other institutions to lose their federal contracts. (Such a provision would have been nearly impossible to pass in Congress at this time.) Executive orders apply on the local level; for example, Mayor Kevin White of Boston issued an executive order that required one-half of all construction workers on city-funded projects to be residents of Boston. This executive order was sustained in *White, Mayor of Boston v. Massachusetts Council of Construction Employees*, 460 U.S. 206 (1983).

Executive orders have the binding force of U.S. law during the term of the president who issued the order. Incoming presidents generally accept existing executive orders. In this manner, past executive orders affect current executive decisions concerning administrative agencies. In contrast, presidents can issue new executive orders that modify or reject executive orders of past presidents. In addition, the current President can nullify or change allocations of federal funds through executive orders. In December 1994, President William Jefferson Clinton issued an executive order to the National Institutes of Health not to spend federal funds to create human embryos for medical research. Clinton's executive order concerning funding was far less sweeping than were the restrictions that the executive orders of Presidents Bush and Reagan imposed.

In January 1993, one of President Clinton's first actions was to issue an executive order negating regulations under Title X of the Public Health Services Act (1970). In 1988, the Secretary of the Department of Health and Human Services, William Sullivan, issued regulations that broadly prohibited recipients of departmental grants for

family planning services from engaging in activities that "encourage, promote or advocate abortion as a method of family planning." The United States Supreme Court upheld these regulations in *Rust v. Sullivan*, 111 Sup. Ct. 1759 (1991). Its decision was based upon an agency's permissible construction of the statute; in other words, the *Chevron* doctrine (see *Chevron v. Natural Resources Defense Council*, 467 U.S. 837 [1984]). The *Rust* decision prohibited indigent and low-income individuals from receiving information about abortion as a means of family planning through these clinics and medical facilities. Clinton's executive order overturned those regulations and made it possible for medical personnel in those facilities to convey the information.

Presidents have used executive orders to manage emergency situations, especially during World War I and World War II. For example, President Franklin D. Roosevelt's Executive Order 9066 permitted Japanese relocation from the West Coast of the United States during World War II, and those orders defined the relocation as a military problem and placed responsibility for implementation squarely upon the commanding general of the region. In this situation, Congress followed the executive order by passing a law that established criminal penalties for refusing to abide by provisions of the executive order. These activities led to the government's creation of relocation camps in the western United States.

Presidential executive orders may directly affect administrative agencies' authority in a variety of ways: First, the President may transfer authority of administrative agencies (e.g., Executive Order 6166, under the Merchant Marine Act [1936], transferred the powers of the former Shipping Board to the newly constituted United States Maritime Commission). Second, during the race riots in Detroit in 1967, a presidential executive order authorized the Secretary of Defense to federalize the state national guard, "to take all appropriate steps to restore law and order." Third, restrictions on agency authority may be enacted. In reaction to congressional hearings, President Gerald R. Ford, in February 1976, issued Executive Order 11905, which restricted domestic intelligence gathered by the Central Intelligence Agency. Fourth, the President may delegate his office's authority to another agency of government. For example, President Dwight D. Eisenhower delegated his authority to implement enforcement of arms control statutes to the Secretary of State (Executive Order 10575). If agencies should promulgate rules that violate a presidential executive order, the agency rules are invalid.

Executive orders are placed in difficult positions within the U.S. constitutional framework. If Presidents are authorized to do so by Congress, then they can execute the laws in a manner of their own choosing. However, there may be areas in which Congress does not grant or deny presidential authority. The latter is the major area of executive orders. U.S. Supreme Court Justice Robert Jackson's, concurring decision in *Youngstown Sheet and Tube v. Sawyer*, 343 U.S. 579 (1952) called the latter a "zone of twilight" of concurrent powers. This is an area in which both the President and Congress may claim independent authority. A central question is whether the ideas of Congress or of the President remain dominant in a given area; and, in terms of executive orders, how far can the President venture to deal with contemporary events? A related question is whether the President gains additional authority from the aggregation of separate parts of his powers under the Constitution. Conflicts between these legislative and executive definitions of authority are usually resolved by courts.

Youngstown Sheet and Tube v. Sawyer (1952) is a central Supreme Court case concerning the extent of presidential executive orders. A major question in this case regards whether the executive can use such orders to act independently from the legislature. In April 1952, President Harry Truman tried to prevent a nationwide steel strike during the Korean conflict. He believed such a strike would endanger the production of military equipment needed by U.S. troops. He issued Executive Order 10340 to U.S. Secretary of Commerce Charles Sawyer "to take possession of most of the steel mills and keep them running."

The Secretary of Commerce issued possessory orders to the presidents of the seized steel companies to operate the companies for the United States. The steel companies sued and claimed that the President had exceeded his constitutional authority with the executive order. The Supreme Court ruled that the President's actions were beyond his constitutional authority because they were not authorized by congressional statutes or constitutional provisions. In this case, the Court argued that the executive order expressly went against congressional statutes in the Labor-Management Relations Act (Taft-Hartley Act, 1947). The Court's majority opinion concluded that "Congress has exclusive authority to legislate, the President's executive order was an exercise of legislative power that impinged upon the authority of Congress, and was therefore unconstitutional."

Limits to presidential executive orders usually occur under two additional sets of circumstances. First, Congress may suspend or repeal the President's executive order by carefully defining purposes of legislation and passing new legislation. For example, the Tax Reform Act of 1976, (Public Law [PL] no. 94-455), repealed Presidential Executive Order 11766 (1974). The second situation in which the President may exceed his discretionary authority may occur when defining a class of activities. In *Joint Anti-Fascist Refugee Committee v. McGrath, Attorney General*, 341 U.S. 123 (1951), the Supreme Court struck down a president's executive order regarding agency dismissal of federal government employees concerned with "national security." The order failed to provide a due process hearing on charges against the government employees. Such hearings

were required for employees both by constitutional protection and congressional statutes. When individuals or groups challenge a president's executive order, plaintiffs sue the cabinet officer(s) who executed the presidential direction(s).

Executive orders apply to a broad range of administrative activities. These orders permit executives, ranging from presidents to local mayors, latitude in enacting and implementing governmental decisions. Administrative agencies carry out these orders consistently with underlying statutory or regulatory provisions. Courts or legislatures may overrule executive orders through new decisions, new laws, or new regulations. Executive orders provide substantial and significant tools for chief executives to create and implement government and administrative policies.

STEVEN PURO

BIBLIOGRAPHY

Smith, V. Kerry, ed., 1984. *Environmental Policy Under Reagan's Executive Order: The Role of Benefit-Cost Analysis*. Chapel Hill: University of North Carolina Press.
Chevron v. Natural Resources Defense Council, 467 U.S. 837 (1984).
Rust v. Sullivan, 111 Sup. Ct. 1759 (1991).
White, Mayor of Boston v. Massachusetts Council of Construction Employees, 460 U.S. 206 (1983).
Youngstown Sheet and Tube v. Sawyer, 343 U.S. 579 (1952).

EXECUTIVE PRIVILEGE. The United States President's ability to maintain the confidentiality and secrecy of his records, conversations, and documents. The legislature and judiciary cannot usually compel the U.S. President to provide such items, because such submissions would endanger vital executive processes. The presidential claim of executive privilege is used mainly in matters of national security and foreign affairs.

All governments require confidentiality for high-level communications. Confidentiality and secrecy permit frank expression of ideas without ramifications to individuals. Governments engage in plans that could be damaged if revealed to enemies or opponents, especially during periods of war or other international conflicts. Confidentiality of government communications is based on the public interest and the ability of government to pursue its goals and activities. In the U.S. political system, there is a competing demand "to know" about government activities. A key part of Congress's power is its ability to investigate executive, administrative, or judicial activities within the federal government and federally funded activities. If information is withheld based on the privilege of confidentiality, Congress could not engage in this key function. In a similar vein, the judiciary could not proceed if information was withheld in civil, criminal, or administrative cases.

In the United States, the major claim of the privilege of confidentiality has been made by the President. Presidents have claimed from early in U.S. history that revealing information to Congress or the judiciary would endanger vital executive processes. In 1796, President George Washington refused to give information and correspondence concerning the Jay Treaty to the House of Representatives. He refused because ratification of treaties is the Senate's responsibility.

Executive privilege is not specifically mentioned in the Constitution. The creation of this authority is a general part of governmental activity and may be considered within the broad powers of the Executive, such as the ability "to faithfully execute the laws." Some scholars have argued that executive privilege is part of certain powers that flow from executive enumerated powers.

Executive privilege allows confidentiality in the operation of the President's office. This confidentiality of conversations, records, and documents is connected to the President's ability to effectively discharge his duties. The President and presidential advisers must be able to explore freely alternatives to creating or administering policies.

The leading scholar on executive privilege, Raoul Berger (1974), claimed that executive privilege is a "constitutional myth." (For a critique of Berger's analysis, see Winter, 1974.) The U.S. Supreme Court did not address the implications of presidential authority stemming from executive privilege until 1974.

The first direct test of executive privilege in U.S. courts occurred in a major conflict between the powers of the executive and the powers of the judiciary. This struggle was a central part of the Watergate scandal, which led to the resignation of President Richard Nixon. The conflict was decided in *United States v. Richard M. Nixon, President of the United States,* 418. U.S. 683 (1974). The Watergate crisis raised fundamental questions of the extent of presidential power.

In the Watergate investigation, seven men were charged with breaking into or conspiring to break into the Democratic National Committee Headquarters in Washington, D.C.'s Watergate complex. President Nixon had installed an audio system to tape conversations in the Oval Office. Prosecutors believed these conversations could be a source of the planning of the Watergate affair and could contain information to what extent the President and presidential advisers were involved in a criminal conspiracy.

President Nixon claimed an absolute executive privilege to decide which Oval Office conversations would remain secret. He refused to give crucial tape recordings to Special Prosecutor Leon Jaworski. Subsequently, U.S. District Judge John Sirica issued a subpoena to the President, which called for his compliance with the prosecutor's request. This issue was expeditiously placed before the Supreme Court.

Two main issues emerged from Nixon's claim of absolute executive privilege: Could the President act on his own discretion and refuse to produce evidence in a pending criminal investigation, and was the President accountable to the rule of law and beyond the scope of judicial review?

In the Supreme Court hearing, President Nixon's representatives claimed an absolute executive privilege in order to prevent submission of the required documents. Additionally, they claimed that the "supremacy of each branch within its own assigned area of constitutional duties" barred executive privilege from the Supreme Court's jurisdiction. President Nixon attempted to connect arguments for executive autonomy with the scope of executive privilege. If the President was immune from investigation in claiming this privilege, neither the Court nor the Congress could question presidential actions.

The Supreme Court, in a unanimous decision on July 24, 1974, rejected this claim of absolute, unqualified, presidential privilege. Chief Justice Warren Burger said that the President's claim of executive privilege could not override obedience to a subpoena in the pending criminal trial. In this manner, the President is considered to be subject to judicial processes concerning pending criminal proceedings.

The Court permitted a qualified authority for executives' use of executive privilege in international or national security matters within the Constitution. Louis Henken (1974) provides an excellent analysis of the extent of executive privilege in that context and time period. President Nixon was forced to produce the requested material. The information found in the tapes eventually led to his resignation from the presidency on August 9, 1974.

In *U.S. v. Nixon*, the Supreme Court argued that executive privilege has a solid constitutional base. The Court saw that there was a qualified privilege of confidentiality for presidential conversations. These conversations are presumptively privileged based on two aspects: (1) the privilege resulting from the need "to protect military, diplomatic, or sensitive national security secrets"; and (2) the "claim of public interest in the confidentiality of presidential communications" (418 U.S. 706). If presidents constantly claim national security or similar interests in the first category, then it would be difficult for the Supreme Court to deny them the claim of executive privilege. This Court ruling rejects Raoul Berger's claim that executive privilege is a "constitutional myth."

The executive privilege claims in *U.S. v. Nixon* can be seen as a separation-of-powers issue within the federal government. Bernard Schwartz (1990) argued that if Nixon's views were supported, there would be an "unqualified presidential immunity from judicial process" (p. 81). This type of claim would conflict with the courts' functions in conducting criminal proceedings, which is a central part of the judiciary's functions under Article 3 of the U.S. Constitution. This case contained conflicts between a specific central part of judicial authority and general elements of executive authority. In this separation-of-powers issue between these branches, the Supreme Court rejected the presidential claim of an absolute privilege against a subpoena essential to the enforcement of criminal statutes.

The extent and applicability of executive privilege was examined in *Nixon v. Administrator of General Services,* 433 U.S. 425 (1977). The Supreme Court decided that executive privilege applies only to the current president. The privilege serves as a shield for executive officials against burdensome requests for information; these requests could interfere with the proper performance of their duties. The Court resolved the question of whether executive privilege applies to the presidency as an office. The Court adopted the latter view in this case and argued that executive privilege is a benefit to the nation at large.

There are regular confrontations between congressional committees' exercise of investigatory powers and presidential claims of executive privilege. Robert J. Spitzer (1993) found that the struggle for hegemony between executive and legislative branches is located in Congress's ability to investigate executive or administrative programs. Presidents have instructed executive officials to refuse to comply with congressional demands for information. The executive claims the requested information will interfere with the public good or confidential deliberations. William Lockhart et al. (1986) has argued that between 1952 and 1974 "executive privilege has been asserted more than fifty times to deny documents or testimony to Congress, at least twenty times in the Nixon Administration alone" (p. 179).

Questions of executive privilege concerning congressional investigations have usually been resolved through political negotiations among the parties. If these claims cannot be resolved, Congress may punish administrative agency representatives for contempt of its investigatory powers. The courts have not clearly resolved these conflicts concerning when the executive can withhold information from congressional investigatory committees.

An important element of Congress's investigatory powers is oversight of the administration and implementation of governmental programs. Louis Fisher (1990) argued that "in general Presidents agree to make papers and documents available for impeachment inquiries or congressional investigations of administrative corruption" (p. 233). However, Presidents may refuse to answer subpoenas from congressional committees by claiming executive privilege. The strongest confrontation on this issue occurred in 1974 when President Nixon repeatedly refused to honor subpoenas for information by the House Judiciary Committee. These subpoenas included information concerning the impeachment inquiry. The main question is, When does a congressional committee's need to know

outweigh the executive's general claims of confidentiality? *U.S. v. Nixon* specifically avoided this question. The Court's analysis in this case also avoided determining the application of executive privilege to civil litigation.

Executive privilege has been granted constitutional status in the latter part of the twentieth century. Executive privilege allows the President to retain confidentiality in communications concerning vital executive processes. Claims of executive privilege must be balanced against the demands of legislative and judicial branches.

STEVEN PURO

BIBLIOGRAPHY

Berger, Raoul, 1974. *Executive Privilege: A Constitutional Myth.* Cambridge: Harvard University Press.

Dorsen, Norman, and John H.F. Shattuck, 1974. "Executive Privilege, the Congress and the Courts." *Ohio State Law Journal,* vol. 35: 1–40.

Fisher, Louis, 1990. *American Constitutional Law.* New York: McGraw-Hill.

Friedman, Leon, and William F. Levantrosser, 1992. *Watergate and Afterward: The Legacy of Richard Nixon.* Westport, CT: Greenwood Press.

Hardin, Charles M., 1974. *Presidential Power and Accountability.* Chicago: University of Chicago Press.

Henkin, Louis, 1974. "Executive Privilege: Mr. Nixon Loses but the Presidency Largely Prevails." *University of California Los Angeles Law Review,* vol. 22: 40–46.

Lockhart, William et al., 1986. *The American Constitution: Cases, Comments, and Questions.* St. Paul: West.

Schwartz, Bernard, 1990. *The Ascent of Pragmatism: The Burger Court in Action.* Reading, MA: Addison-Wesley.

Shane, Peter M., 1992. "Negotiating for Knowledge: Administrative Responses to Congressional Demands for Information." *Administrative Law Review,* vol. 44 (Spring): 197–244.

Spitzer, Robert J., 1993. *President and Congress: Executive Hegemony at the Crossroads of American Government.* Philadelphia: Temple University Press.

United States v. *Richard M. Nixon, President of the United States,* 418 U.S. 683 (1974).

EXIT INTERVIEW.

An interview with any and all workers who are ending their employment with an organization. The term is usually applied to a routinized procedure that is intended to generate systematic feedback from workers who have quit or been terminated for cause. It is not customarily used to describe the more informal discussions that take place when workers are simply advised about benefits, unemployment compensation, or procedures for turning in keys and equipment.

A Very Brief History

Prior to recent times, departing workers were ordinarily sent off without much ceremony. One of the most persistent images from our recent past is that of the hapless employee finding an unanticipated "pink slip" (termination notice) in his or her pay envelope. This was a cheap and expedient means of trimming the workforce; the employee did not even receive the courtesy of a face-to-face meeting with a management representative.

As labor-management relations became more progressive, the act of terminating employment took on greater and greater significance. Workers were gaining additional rights and benefits that, at a minimum, required some form of explanation at the point of termination. Thus personnel departments began to initiate brief sessions with departing workers. Issues such as severance pay (which, in the public sector, often means that the worker is compensated for unused annual leave), unemployment compensation, and health insurance became common topics of discussion.

The most progressive organizations, meanwhile, recognized that the attitudes and opinions of their employees were sufficiently worthwhile to collect and consider. Workers on the threshold of leaving the organization represented an especially attractive target of opportunity. Because they had already committed to leaving, either voluntarily or involuntarily, it was often believed that they would provide candid feedback concerning both good and bad aspects of the organization's management. Thus, many of the largest and most modern organizations of the day, including AT&T and IBM, were administering fairly elaborate exit interviews by the mid-1960s.

In the public sector, formal exit interviews made a relatively late appearance. They were not widely used before the 1980s, and even now are common in only the most highly articulated public personnel systems. One indication of their rarity is the fact that exist interviews do not warrant a single mention in any of the current textbooks in public personnel administration.

In all likelihood, however, their popularity will soon increase. A major cause of this change is the growing recognition that exist interviews are an important means of *managing turnover*. The recruitment, selection, and training of replacement workers is an extraordinarily expensive and time-consuming enterprise. Organizations that can pinpoint the reasons why employees quit may be able to take corrective steps to slow the attrition rate. Interest in this topic is especially acute in portions of the public sector that are said to be experiencing a "brain drain" of talented professionals. Discovering the supervisory practices or terms of employment that are prompting the exodus might stimulate needed reforms. Similarly, during a prolonged period of downsizing (such as the one that now seems to be a permanent fixture in governments throughout the world), management has an increased incentive to keep the remaining workers as happy as possible, and to discover ways to improve productivity. Exit interviews represent an inexpensive way of addressing these goals.

Purposes of Exit Interviews

As is implicit above, exit interviews are used for two primary purposes: (1) to process departing employees in an orderly fashion, and (2) to collect information on the employees' reasons for leaving.

The topics that are covered while accomplishing the first function are in part dictated by the reason for employee's departure. If the worker is leaving voluntarily, then the discussion focuses on informing him or her about any applicable rights and benefits. In addition to covering such concerns as insurance and severance pay, the employee may wish to inquire about letters of reference or other personal issues (medical records, etc.). The same general conditions apply in departures stemming from *layoffs* (dismissals that arise from financial problems or reorganizations). In such instances, the interviewer will also devote considerable attention to unemployment compensation procedures and to *recall rights* (the process by which laid off workers are called back to work as the financial picture improves).

The exit interview provides a good opportunity to touch on two additional topics that are potentially relevant: *ethics* and *intellectual property* restrictions. Many government employees are forbidden from accepting certain jobs for a period of time—usually one to two years—after leaving public service. Workers who were formerly engaged in procurement or grant functions, for instance, are routinely banned from employment in companies with which they previously did business. Intellectual property considerations, in contrast, involve professional and technical workers who have created something (a written product, idea, or patent) while in the government's employ. The intellectual property that was generated may be viewed as belonging to the employing agency, since the worker was being paid a salary during the creative process. In such instances, a portion of the exit interview may be devoted to working out the conditions that will apply to the disputed property (Cundiff 1993).

When it involves a worker who is being terminated for cause, the exit interview follows a different path. At this point it essentially becomes a "dismissal interview." The session is used to inform the employee of the termination, to explain the reasons, and to delineate any procedural protections that may apply. One of management's concerns during this type of interview is to ensure that all of the employee's legal and procedural rights have been honored. If the employee later alleges that an important right was invaded (such as the supervisor's failure to follow stated termination procedures), then the organization may be subject to a *wrongful termination* lawsuit. The exit interview is thus an important precaution stage in the dismissal process.

The second major function of exit interviews—finding out about the employee's motives for leaving the organization—is probably more essential than the transfer of information about rights and benefits. As noted, the interview gives managers an excellent opportunity to elicit opinions about the job or related matters. This input often provides important insights concerning what is good or bad about the agency.

Conducting the Interview

To maximize the information-gathering advantages of the exit interview, experts agree on two major ground rules. First, because of the potentially sensitive nature of the discussions, they ought to be conducted by human resource professionals, *not* the employee's supervisors. Obviously, employees who are exiting an organization may be reluctant to "open up" in front of a supervisor who may well have been a prime contributor to their job dissatisfaction. Likewise, the supervisor's objectivity may be called into serious question.

The other important ground rule maintains that the interviews should follow a standardized format. Discussion begins with an analysis of administrative matters associated with the employee's departure, followed by a fact-finding session focusing on steps that can be taken to retain other employees. A typical interview protocol (termed a *patterned interview*) calls for coverage of the following specifics (Fisher, Schoenfeldt, and Shaw, 1993, p. 756):

1. resources and training: questions probe the adequacy of training and equipment, the clarity of instructions and job expectations, and the competence and attentiveness of supervision;
2. job challenge: questions examine the quality and quantity of work, the flexibility and discretion available to perform the work, and the difficulty in learning and updating skills;
3. salary and advancement: analysis of the employee's satisfaction with advancement opportunities, salary level, job security, and fringe benefits, emphasis on the perceived fairness of the evaluation and incentive systems, as well as the level of pay equity (i.e., is the compensation regarded as fair in the context of what others are being paid?);
4. relations with supervisors and co-workers: questions probe the internal dynamics of the organization, such as supervisor-subordinate interactions, the supervisor's handling of routine and exceptional situations, interdepartmental cooperation, and sources of friction;
5. working conditions: exploration of the employee's satisfaction with agency procedures, scheduling practices, physical surroundings, stress levels, and the like;
6. capstone questions: the interview concludes with open-ended explorations of the employee's opinions concerning the good and bad features of the organization, the reasons the employee is leaving, and recommendations concerning how the situation might be improved.

Although oral interviews are preferable, some public agencies conduct exit interviews by questionnaire. This practice is especially prevalent in very large organizations that experience high rates of turnover among workers performing similar jobs. For example, state departments of correction often experience turnover rates of 20 percent to 25 percent among correctional officers (guards), who usually number in the thousands. The costs of administering interviews to all of these workers would be prohibitive, so some states have instituted exit questionnaires. The quality of information obtained through these instruments in probably questionable. However, some personnel administrators prefer written questionnaires because they think that some workers are uncomfortable making criticisms face-to-face. The relative anonymity of a questionnaire is believed to improve candor.

Problem Areas

This raises the critical question, "Can we trust the results of exit interviews?" Are employees who have quit or been fired a reliable source of information about the organization? Intuitively, one can imagine many reasons why departing employees may intentionally obfuscate or distort reality. Some may have an axe to grind; they might use the opportunity to retaliate against their enemies, to defame those who were responsible for their departures, or to rail against organizational policies and practices with which they disagree. Other workers may refrain from criticisms simply because they do not want to cause trouble, or due to fear of future repercussions. Because former employers are always an important source of information in a job search, few of us are anxious to leave too many enemies behind as we move through our careers.

Unfortunately, not much research attention has focused on the reliability of exit interview data. The few studies that have been conducted suggest that managers need to exercise extreme caution in interpreting worker responses to exit questions. For example, one of the most systematic analyses concluded that the workers' "stories" change over time. At their times of departure, 38 percent of the workers in the study blamed salary and benefits for their dissatisfaction, and only 4 percent implicated supervisory practices as a contributing cause. Eighteen months later, when these same workers were reinterviewed, supervisors were blamed as the primary factor in 24 percent of the cases, and salary and fringe benefits were cited in only 12 percent of the departures (Zarandona and Camuso 1989). Among the possible explanations for this phenomenon are that the workers were reluctant to criticize their former supervisors until they had successfully obtained alternative employment (i.e., the compelling desire to receive a suitable reference).

Other research, in contrast, appears to support the conclusion that reliable clues about employee unhappiness can be obtained from exit interviews. The federal government, for instance, has spent a considerable amount of effort trying to understand the reasons behind attrition in the Senior Executive Service (SES). Interviews with SESers who have just quit consistently demonstrate that inadequate advancement opportunities are a major disincentive to remaining in the service (U.S. Merit Systems Protection Board 1989; U.S. General Accounting Office 1992). This finding has been applauded by both former and current executives, and is a major consideration in the Office of Personnel Management's efforts to revitalize the SES career system.

Perhaps the most important lesson that can be learned from these disparate experiences with exit interview data is the need for prudence. Information gleaned from departing workers must be thoughtfully assessed within the context in which it is offered. The reliability of worker reports should ordinarily be cross-checked and verified before any decisions are made on that basis alone. Identifying the "real" problems that contribute to a worker's decision to quit an organization will almost certainly require sensitivity and skill on the part of the interviewer.

These limitations notwithstanding, most managers would rather ask than not ask; they would at least like to give workers an opportunity to discuss their experiences and share their opinions. Where the workers' stories reiterate the same general themes, the organization has an obligation to investigate and follow up. Coupled with other sources of administrative intelligence, exit interview responses are, at an absolute minimum, a starting place for administrative action.

STEVEN W. HAYS

BIBLIOGRAPHY

Cundiff, Victoria, 1993. "How to Conduct an Exit Interview: An Intellectual Property Law Perspective." *Employee Relations*, vol. 19 (Summer): 159–168.

Fisher, Cynthia, Lyle Schoenfeldt, and James Shaw, 1993. *Human Resource Management*. Boston: Houghton Mifflin.

Grensing-Pophal, Lin, 1993. "Exit Interviews as a Tool for Examining Turnover." *Security Management* (June): 20–21.

U.S. General Accounting Office, 1992. *Senior Executive Service: Opinions About the Federal Work Environment*. Washington, DC: Comptroller General (May).

U.S. Merit Systems Protection Board, 1989. *The Senior Executive Service: Views of Former Federal Executives*. Washington, DC: Government Printing Office (October).

Zarandona, Joseph, and Michael Camuso, 1989. "A Study of Exit Interviews: Does the Last Word Count?" *Personnel*, vol. 62 (March): 36–38.

Zima, Joseph, 1983. *Interviewing: Key to Effective Management*. New York: Macmillan, and Science Research Associates.

EXPECTANCY THEORY. A theory of work motivation based on the proposition that behavior is regulated by choices influenced by goals (represented by the valence of possible outcomes) and beliefs about the consequences of choices (represented by expectancies).

The importance of human motivation in the workplace received relatively little attention until the 1930s when an Australian psychologist, Elton Mayo, then at the Harvard Business School, began a set of studies at the Hawthorne plant of the Western Electric Company. The results of this research were published in 1939 by Roethlisberger and Dickson in an influential book called *Management and the Worker*. The next two decades were characterized by a great amount of research on motivation by a number of psychologists, including Kurt Lewin, Abraham Maslow, and David McClelland, and a smaller number of psychoanalysts, such as Eric Trist. The implications of this research for management and administration were the focus of modified "theories" of management advanced by Rensis Likert and Douglas McGregor, published in the 1960s.

However, the research was fragmented and not grounded in any solid conception of underlying theoretical processes. As Mason Haire noted in a chapter written in 1954, "Unless there is a real advance here soon, the very richness of the empirical data threatens to be overwhelming in its systematic unintelligibility" (p. 1120).

Expectancy theory was first introduced by Victor Vroom (1964) in a book entitled *Work and Motivation*. The purpose of expectancy theory was to organize existing research into a systematic framework to "show us where we now stand in our efforts to find principles and generalizations, and to indicate promising avenues for new research" (p. 5).

Expectancy theory utilizes four concepts: force, valence, instrumentality, and expectancy. The last three concepts are responsible for the frequent reference to it as VIE theory. The theory is stated in formal mathematical terms, but I will not dwell on such formality here.

The theory holds that behavior is determined by the relative strength of forces acting on the person to move in different directions. Each force varies with the product of the valence of outcomes and the strength of the expectancy that the outcome will be obtained from that choice. It follows from this proposition that highly valent outcomes will have no effect on the generation of forces or on behavior unless there is some expectation that the probability of their attainment is affected by one's actions. The second proposition asserts that the valence of outcomes is dependent not only on its terminal or intrinsic properties but also on its instrumentality for the attainment of other outcomes. Specifically, the valence of an outcome increases with the product of its instrumentality for and the valence of other outcomes.

Expectancy theory is similar to and borrowed liberally from theories that had been advanced by other psychologists who had found such concepts useful in explaining other bodies of empirical evidence. Lewin (1938), Tolman

(1959), Peak (1955) and Atkinson (1958) had previously demonstrated the usefulness of such concepts in explaining human action. The originality of Vroom's contribution stemmed from its application to work behavior, thereby bringing the rather atheoretical discipline of industrial psychology closer to general psychology.

Expectancy theory is typically termed a "process theory" of motivation, to distinguish it from "content theories" such as those advanced by Maslow (1943) and by Alderfer (1972). Content theories assume the existence of classes of outcomes, the valence of which varies across persons and over time within persons (e.g., growth needs, need for achievement, etc.). Process theories deal with the relationship between behavior and needs (or more typically, specific manifestations of needs, such as goals, incentives, or valent outcomes). Since content and process theories address fundamentally different questions surrounding human motivation, they should not be thought of as incompatible but complementary.

Expectancy theory has arguably become the dominant process theory of work motivation. It was originally used by Vroom in an attempt to integrate and guide research on three primary questions: (1) Why do people choose the jobs and careers they do? (2) What factors cause people to be satisfied with their work? (3) What factors cause people to work effectively? There has been useful and informative work using the theory on each of these questions—but the greatest amount of empirical work has been directed toward the last of these questions—the sources of motivation for effective work performance.

Most researchers who have applied expectancy theory to the explanation of work performance, have followed Vroom's lead and focused on the determinants of amount of effort directed to work performance. People *choose* to work harder, and this choice must be systematically related to the person's goals (i.e., valence of outcomes) and two kinds of beliefs—a belief (expectancy) that effort will lead to higher performance, and a belief (instrumentality) that performance will lead to the attainment of one's goals.

The structure of expectancy theory provided a uniform basis for examining the impact of promotional incentives, payment systems, work groups, supervisory style, and even job content on motivation and on performance. Though not all of the research has supported the theory, it has frequently been noted that the more closely the research design has approximated the kinds of research methodology dictated by the theory, the greater the support found.

It should be emphasized that expectancy theory asserts that human choice is subjectively rational. People are not asserted to make optimal decisions, but decisions that they believe to be optimal at that time. Even this rather limited notion of rationality is inconsistent with other bodies of research, most of which have been developed since the original statement of expectancy theory. Herbert

Simon (1979), for example, has argued forcefully that there are serious cognitive limitations restricting people's ability to process information in the manner prescribed by expectancy theory. Such theories assume that the decision-maker will consider all alternatives and be capable of evaluating each on every relevant dimension. The demands that such behavior would place on cognitive processes are inconsistent with the current understanding of how humans process information. They process information slowly, and at a relatively slow speed. In many situations they cannot consider all alternatives or evaluate all possible consequences of each. To use Simon's language, they "satisfice" rather than optimize (i.e., search until a level of aspiration is exceeded).

The implications of "bounded rationality," as Simon's arguments have been called, depends on the complexity of the task confronting the decisionmaker. Expectancy theory would not be very appropriate to use in accounting for the behavioral processes in highly complex tasks such as a chess master's moves on a chess board or to an adolescent's contemplation of a future career. Its limitations are probably much less serious in somewhat simple choice problems in which the alternatives and their consequences are readily apparent. Such situations include, but are not restricted to, choices about how hard to work on a given day.

A further problem for expectancy theory is presented by recent research on persuasive communication. Several social psychological theories have distinguished two opposed levels of information processing, varying in the degree and care of consideration of alternatives. Systematic, or central, processing involves relatively detailed analysis and is more consistent with the tenets of expectancy theory. In contrast, heuristic, or peripheral, processing involves more casual and superficial evaluation. A situationally induced negative mood has been observed to produce more systematic information processing.

Expectancy theory also has a difficult time in dealing with a set of empirical findings that have been loosely organized under the term "prospect theory." There is a growing body of research showing that human choices can be led astray by heuristics, biases, and by the manner in which the alternatives have been framed. Prospect theory (Kahneman, Slovic, and Tversky 1982) is a set of organizing principles designed to account for systematic departures from optimality in human choice behavior.

Recently (1995), I have proposed a set of ideas for a reformulation of expectancy theory. These ideas fall far short of a well-developed theory. Instead, they are directions for constructing a "contemporary expectancy theory" that would be consistent with recent findings, including those mentioned previously. Among my suggestions are:

1. A contingency theory in which the level of processing of alternatives would not be fixed (as is the current ex-

pectancy theory) but would vary. At one extreme could be behavior under the control of strong habits or emotions, in which actions are largely independent of goals and of information. At the other extreme would be fairly simple choice problems, in which alternatives are clear and information is readily available. Here the level of processing could approximate that envisioned by expectancy theory, subject, of course, to the kinds of framing effects and biases identified by the prospect theorists.

2. Including mechanisms (some known and others yet to be understood) whereby motives are aroused. Valence does not have the same properties as utility. The attractiveness of outcomes is changed by the immediate situation. Adding to expectancy theory, mechanisms that would link valence to contextual factors could bring the theory closer to research on goal setting, (Latham and Locke 1979) and sequential attention to goals (Cyert and March 1963).

3. Reframing the theory to devote more explicit attention to intrinsic motivation. The valence of an outcome, such as successfully completing a task or job, is viewed in expectancy theory as dependent on beliefs about the consequences of performance for other outcomes (such as higher pay or self-esteem) and the value of these other outcomes. Buried in that formulation was a distinction that has become increasingly important in both research and practice. The distinction is between intrinsic motivation, in which the valence of performance is dependent on internally mediated processes (i.e., performance is its own reward), and extrinsic motivation, in which the valence of performance is reducible to anticipated actions of others and rewards or punishments that are under their control.

To elaborate on this last point, it is apparent that expectancy theory lent itself naturally to dealing with extrinsic motivation but was not so useful in tackling intrinsic motivation. Seminal research on the latter has been carried out by E. L. Deci and R. M. Ryan (1985), who have elaborated the concept to include not only what can be termed growth needs but also to include internalized norms and codes of conduct.

The importance of the intrinsic-extrinsic distinction lies not just in its usefulness in research but also in its relevance for practice. Participation, job design, self-managing work teams, and the like have fundamentally different characteristics than incentive compensation and promotional systems. Effectiveness of the former depends on systems of internal control or self-regulation, but effectiveness of the latter depends on mechanisms of organizational control. Evidence abounds that contemporary organizations are increasingly recognizing the superiority of intrinsic motivation in dealing both with the diverse labor force

and with the rapidly changing environments that are characteristic of today.

Victor H. Vroom

BIBLIOGRAPHY

Alderfer, C. P., 1972. *Existence, Relatedness, and Growth.* New York: Free Press.
Atkinson, J. W., 1958. "Towards Experimental Analysis of Human Motivation in Terms of Motives, Expectancies, and Incentives." In J. W. Atkinson, (ed.), *Motives in Fantasy, Action, and Society.* Princeton, NJ: Van Nostrand, pp. 288–305.
Cyert, R. M., and J. A. March, 1963. *A Behavioral Theory of the Firm.* Englewood Cliffs, NJ: Prentice-Hall.
Deci, E. L., and R. M. Ryan, 1985. *Intrinsic Motivation and Self-Determination in Human Behavior.* New York: Plenum.
Haire, M., 1954. "Industrial Social Psychology." In G. Lindzey ed., *Handbook of Social Psychology.* Reading, MA: Addison-Wesley, pp. 1104–1123.
Kahneman, D., P. Slovic, and A. Tversky, eds., 1982. *Judgment Under Uncertainty: Heuristics and Biases.* New York: Cambridge University Press.
Latham, G. P., and E. A. Locke, 1979. "Goal Setting: A Motivational Technique that Works." *Organizational Dynamics* 8: 68–80.
Lewin, K., 1938. "The Conceptual Representation and the Measurement of Psychological Forces." *Contributions of Psychological Theory.* vol. 1, no. 4. Durham, NC: Duke University Press.
Maslow, A. H., 1943. "A Theory of Human Motivation." *Psychological Review* 50: 370–396.
Peak, Helen., 1955. "Attitude and Motivation." In M. R. Jones, ed., *Nebraska Symposium on Motivation.* Lincoln: University of Nebraska Press, pp. 149–188.
Simon, H. A., 1979 "Rational Decision Making in Business Organizations." *American Economic Review.* vol. 69: 493–513.
Tolman, E. C., 1959. "Principles of Purposive Behavior." In S. Koch, ed., *Psychology: A Study of a Science.* vol. 2. New York: McGraw-Hill, pp. 92–157.
Vroom, V. H., 1964. *Work and Motivation.* New York: Wiley.
———, 1995. "Introduction to the Classic Edition." In V. H. Vroom, *Work and Motivation.* San Francisco, CA: Jossey-Bass.

EXPENDITURE FORECASTING. A process of estimating future budget authority, baseline service levels, outlays, and deficits.

Origin and Subsequent History of Expenditure Forecasting

The history and legacy of expenditure forecasting is rooted in drives to reform governmental budgeting. Perhaps the earliest twentieth-century foundations can be traced back to the Budget and Accounting Act (BAA) of 1921 and the Hoover Commissions of 1949 and 1955. Together, the BAA and the commissions recognized that governments need to collect and evaluate budgetary and program performance data, both of which are necessary inputs to successful forecasting. The BAA centralized responsibilities for executive budget preparation and skills in a new agency called the Bureau of the Budget (BOB), effectively institutionalizing presidential control over the budget. In turn, this opened the door for governments to use the budget for management and planning purposes, including forecasting.

Constructing a budget for the benefit of managers was an objective of the first Hoover Commission. The commission argued that federal budgeting should be arranged by programs and include data on costs, performance, and accomplishments (see U.S. Executive Office of the President 1950; U.S. Commission 1955). The Hoover Commission's ideas were implemented in the Department of Defense (DOD), with amendments to the National Security Act in 1949 (63 Stat. 578), and more broadly by the Budget and Accounting Procedures Act of 1950 (64 Stat. 832).

The first direct call for a multiyear federal forecast came in the 1961 executive budget, which included ten-year projections of aggregate numbers. Also at that time, the DOD began projecting the costs of defense systems with the Program Planning Budgeting System (PPBS). Shortly after, in 1965, the Rand Corporation published *Program Budgeting*, which recommended that long-term projections be made available to the Executive and Congress for review. The projections were intended to sharpen decisionmakers' "intuition and judgment" (Novick 1965). By October 1967, a report, published by the President's Commission on Budget Concepts, argued that the government needed more information on prospects for future budgets: "If major decisions of collective choice . . . are to be made wisely, the public and the Congress need to have forward estimates, not only of the benefits and costs of the particular programs in question, but of the total budget of which these proposals are intended to become a part."

Forecasting took a more serious turn in the 1970s and 1980s. In 1971, the executive budget included four-year projections of aggregate outlays and receipts. Shortly afterwards, the Legislative Reorganization Act (Public Law 91-510, § 221 [a]) required that five-year budget authority and outlay projections for major new or expanded programs be included in annual budgets. By 1979, the President asked agencies to prepare budget requests for three years beyond the request year. The Office of Management and Budget's (OMB) Circulars A-11 ("Preparation and Submission of Budget Estimates") and A-34 ("Instructions on Budget Execution") provided additional forecasting guidelines for the executive branch.

On the legislative side, guidelines identifying what was to be projected and the sources of data for making the projections were established by the Budget Reform Act of 1974 (the 1974 Budget Act), amended by Gramm-Rudman-Hollings (GRH) in 1985 and the Reaffirmation Act of 1987. Sections 301 and 308 required that concurrent reso-

lutions be accompanied by economic assumptions and objectives, five-year projections of estimated total budget outlays, total new budget authority, major revenues, surplus or deficit, and tax expenditures. These estimates, along with entitlement authority and credit authority, were to be presented in a five-year forecast after the beginning of each fiscal year. Section 403 called upon the Congressional Budget Office (CBO) director to estimate the costs over five fiscal years for "each bill or resolution of a public character reported by any committee" of the House or Senate. The projections were intended to direct budget priorities and to help guide assessments of the future budgetary impacts of current legislation. The House waited until fiscal year (FY) 1977–1978 and the Senate waited until FY1978–1979 to include projections in their budget resolutions. Together, executive and legislative budgetary reforms have laid the foundation for forecasting as it exists today.

Underlying Theoretical Framework

The theory underlying expenditure forecasting addresses two issues: concept and process. Conceptual arguments center around the need to forecast. Discussion about the process addresses how forecasting should be carried out. Both issues are fundamental to understanding the current practice of government expenditure forecasting.

The Concept of Forecasting

How forecasting is used depends in large part upon how it is valued. One view sees forecasting as having more in common with planning, which is oriented to the future, than budgeting, which is oriented more to the present. In this view, governments are not likely to tightly link planning (or forecasting) and budgeting, at least not in the short-term. This separatist view is promulgated most by "budgetary incrementalists."

According to budgetary incrementalism, budget requests are based on marginal adjustments to the prior year's budget base (see Davis et al. 1966). The requests are to be determined through political bargaining. In this bargaining process, prior years' agreements are rarely questioned, and to infuse the process with a means to debate such agreements would be dysfunctional. Expenditure forecasting, at least as it appears to be developing, is giving decisionmakers the technical and economic means for questioning historical decisions. To the incrementalist, such forecasting might unwisely elevate economic concerns above political realities, tantamount to turning over budgetary problems to technicians, where the computed solution (or budget) is technically sound but is politically unworkable. In short, they see little need for expenditure forecasting in a way that transcends incrementalism.

An alternative view, held by "budgetary rationalists," is that forecasting does not elevate economic over political values but postulates that both sets of values are critical to successful budgeting. The forecast should be future oriented, yet grounded in the immediate past and explicitly reflect on prior history. This broad informational base will help the forecast, and, in turn, the budget, to reflect a balance of political and economic values. There are no hard and fast rules, however, to indicate how historical the data need to be. To better appreciate the value of expenditure forecasting, the discussion will turn to the process of forecasting.

The Process of Forecasting

Forecasting is a technology people have devised to help them estimate the future. The techniques vary by methodology and complexity. Four common techniques are the expert, trend, deterministic, and econometric approaches. *Expert forecasting* is a means of estimating expenditures by a person who is very familiar with the expenditure being considered (e.g., a fire chief who estimates fire-fighting expenses based on 15 years of work experience). *Trend forecasting* is a way of estimating an expenditure based on prior changes in that expenditure (e.g., expenditures for a municipal pool's FY 1996–1997 budget could be a linear extrapolation of pool expenditures since 1986). With *deterministic forecasting,* future expenditures are estimated based upon a percentage change in social, economic, or other variables that directly affect the expenditure (e.g., if the state's cost is US$1,000 to inspect a small sewerage treatment facility, then the expected total cost would be US$1,000 multiplied by the number of small sewerage treatment facilities inspected). Finally, *econometrics* relies on statistically estimated coefficients of one or more economic predicator variables to estimate future expenditures. A combination of techniques may be used to generate the most reliable forecasts. The effectiveness of method(s) will be determined by several budgetary factors. Several of these are considered below.

First, the government must decide which expenditures to forecast. Forecasts may be generated for different types of expenditures, such as budget authority and baseline services. They may also be generated for different line-items, activities, programs, funds, or departments. Since nearly all governments rely in part on a line-item budget, they can be expected to forecast by line-item. Nevertheless, a government may forecast expenditures at a more aggregate level if data are available and trends are predictable. At the most aggregate level, forecasts may generated by fund, since government budgets, accounts, and audits are organized by funds.

Second, someone must be selected to generate the forecast. Expenditure forecasts can be generated in-house, externally, or as a combination of the two. Municipalities may rely on estimates provided by the state and federal governments, and by even economic "think tanks." At the federal level, the CBO, the OMB, and others generate the

forecasts. The federal forecasts are to be treated as an "analytical base from which various budget alternatives may be evaluated," not as budget recommendations or predictions (U.S. Congress 1976, p. 1). Governments should carefully consider who is to generate the forecast, since the forecaster will bring a degree of proficiency, assumptions, and bias to the estimates.

Third, the government must decide which information will be used to generate the forecast. Information may come from several possible sources. In addition to budget and finance departments, operating department personnel should be excellent sources of expenditure information because of their intimate knowledge of the services they provide. Prior year budgets and audits may provide reliable economy and efficiency data. Exactly how much data is needed to generate a reliable forecast, however, is not clear. Experts should reflect on at least five years worth of data along with years of experience. Trend-based models generally require 30 to 50 observations to account for seasonal economic trends. Using a deterministic method, the forecaster should have several years worth of data to estimate the trend coefficient (i.e., the m in $y = mx$ deterministic formula). The amount of data needed to generate a dependable econometric forecast is also unclear, but several observations will be needed to estimate the predictor variables' coefficients.

The fourth factor to reflect on is the government's experience with forecasting and computer technology. Experienced forecasters should have a better idea of what should be forecast and how to generate the forecast. With experience, budget participants, also may be able to better communicate their informational and expenditure needs (see Boswell and Carpenter 1986). Governments are also gaining experience with computer technology. Computers simply allow people to churn through countless numbers in little time. They will not, however, replace "judgments of which trends are worth analyzing and which are trivial, and which relationships merit most scrutiny" (p. 1982).

Finally, the forecast needs to be tailored to meet the consumer's needs. Managers like reports to reflect on activity economies and efficiencies. Legislatures are more likely to prefer reports that also include a more detailed assessment of program effectiveness. Depending upon the intended user, the forecast of expenditures could include statements on the future of the economy, the revenue structure, cost of services, service levels, the government's financial condition, assumptions, implications for public policy, and strategies to avoid undesirable predictions (Schroeder 1981, Boswell and Carpenter 1986).

Forecasting in the United States

Forecasting in the United States is a likely representative of applying forecasting in a generally wealthy setting, where aggregate levels of revenues and expenditures are fairly predictable. Societies suffering from more economic and political distress are likely to find expenditure forecasting increasingly problematic. Here, the frequency of governmental rebudgeting may effectively eliminate the reliability of nearly all expenditure forecasts.

At the federal level, expenditures are forecast for Congress by the Budget Analysis Division of the CBO, and the Executive by departments and the OMB. In carrying out their responsibilities, forecasters estimate many types of expenditures, the most common include budget authority, baselines, and bill-cost estimates. Budget authority may be one-year, multiyear, or no-year, and it gives agencies the right to obligate a maximum amount of resources. Forecasting budget authority is required by the 1974 Budget Act. Projecting estimates for bill costs and credit, also required by the 1974 Budget Act, is the responsibility of the CBO. Bill-cost estimates are prepared for public bills reported by committees to show how they are expected to affect federal, state, and local spending or revenues five years out (U.S. Congress 1988–1989, p. 3). Credit forecasts show the possible credit position of the government in the future.

Baseline estimates, computed by the OMB and the CBO "assume the continuation of taxing and spending policies in place at that time, including the carrying out of any future policy change (such as tax indexing) already enacted into law" (U.S. Congress 1984). Entitlement projections assume a continuation of current laws, and estimates of discretionary spending incorporate an inflationary factor; all baselines cover federal pay raises. The 1974 Budget Act requires that the CBO submit its baseline projections to the budget committees by February 15 (and are usually updated in mid-August). The projections are used by the committees to construct a budget resolution and reconciliation instructions, and to ascertain whether the annual deficit reduction target has been reached and, if not, "the amount and percentage by which defense and non-defense outlays must be cut to meet the annual deficit reduction level" (U.S. Congress 1988, p. 36)

To make their decisions, the budget committees may request two types of baselines, the most common of which is "current policy" or "current services": "A section of the President's budget, required by The 1974 Budget Act, that sets forth the level of spending or taxes that would occur if existing programs and policies were continued unchanged through the fiscal year and beyond, with all programs adjusted for inflation so that existing levels of activity are maintained" (U.S. Congress 1988, p. 37). Over time, the current service estimates of the OMB and the CBO tend to be very similar, and both tend to underestimate long-term outlays (Plesko 1987). The second type of baseline, used less frequently by Congress, is the "current law" baseline, which "adjusts programs for inflation only where required by law" (U.S. Congress 1988, p. 15). An example is the deficit forecast used since Gramm-Rudman-Hollings.

This baseline estimate is generated in the fall and reflects newly enacted legislation and expiring legislation.

Forecasting at the Local Level

Forecasting is also used at the local level. A 1989 survey of 170 municipal governments in cities with a population of 50,000 or more, conducted by the author, indicated that 60 percent of the cities forecast either revenues or expenditures. The remainder of this entry will examine findings of that survey, reflecting on the factors identified earlier.

First, consider the format of the budget. Budgeteers in forecasting cities tend to work with a budget format that accommodates a planning or a management focus, which is conducive to forecasting. Findings in Table I indicate that although all cities are more inclined to use line-item budgets than any other type of budget, forecasting cities are less likely to use the line-item format (based on a five-point scale from 0 to 4: mean of 2.27 versus mean of 2.75 of nonforecasting cities, significant at the 0.0087 level) and are more likely to use another approach, especially performance budgeting (mean of 1.25 versus a mean of 0.52 for nonforecasting cities, significant at the 0.0001 level). Also, annual operating budgets in forecasting cities are more likely to emphasize efficiency (mean of 3.20 versus a mean of 2.94 for nonforecasting cities), management decision-making (mean of 3.19 versus a mean of 2.84 for nonforecasting cities), and resource planning (a mean of 3.01 versus a mean of 2.48 for nonforecasting cities). Operating budgets in these cities are also a little more likely to use a variety of expenditure classification schemes and measurement tools that embrace management and planning values.

Of the cities that forecast, about half forecast by major items, 55.6 percent forecast by department or function, and between 68.5 percent and 56 percent report that they forecast by fund type (see Table II). On average, forecasts are computed for 3.3 out-years for major line items, 3.8 years for departments or functions, and 3.7 years for funds. And cities that forecast expenditures at the most aggregate level, by fund type, compute estimates for about 5.6 types of governmental funds, 4.6 types of enterprise funds, and 3.7 types of internal services funds. They frequently use expert, trend, or deterministic models in conjunction with expert and trend techniques. Small cities over the years have put more emphasis on expert and trend techniques, especially when forecasting expenditures. Large cities tend to have slightly more (but statistically insignificant) experience with increasingly sophisticated techniques. Overall, the widespread use of relatively simple techniques reflects the crude level of development of expenditure forecasting.

Who generally produces the forecasts? Reflecting the close tie between budgeting and expenditure forecasting,

TABLE I. COMPARING BUDGET PROCESSES AMONG FORECASTING AND NONFORECASTING CITIES

Elements of the budget process[a]	Non-forecasting cities (mean)	Forecasting cities (mean)	Probability[b]
How the budget officer classifies the city's budget[c]			
Performance budget	.52	1.25	0.0001
Line-item budget	2.75	2.27	0.0087
Program budget	12.9	1.73	0.0157
Program planning budget	0.35	0.72	0.0044
Zero-based budget	0.25	0.44	0.1776
Objective emphasized in the operating budget[d]			
Keep revenue needs low	2.18	2.09	0.6751
Efficiently use revenues	2.94	3.20	0.0768
Assist management decisionmaking	2.84	3.19	0.0148
Plan for optimal resource allocation	2.48	3.01	0.0031
Characteristics of the operating budget[e]			
Measurements of input-output ratios	0.18	0.36	0.0032
Expenditure classification by activity	0.94	0.97	0.2966
Expenditure classification by line-item	0.88	0.92	0.3339
A 5-year plan	0.13	0.36	0.0002
Packages of funding levels	0.11	0.33	0.0007
Measurement tools found in the operating budget[f]			
Benefit-cost analysis	0.19	0.36	0.0111
Dollar cost of purchases	0.81	0.85	0.4330
Dollar cost of services	0.32	0.59	0.0005
Quantity of a service provided	0.61	0.74	0.0765

[a]See Jerry McCaffery, *Budgetmaster, 2d ed.* Pacific Grove, CA: Author, p. 148.

[b]Probability that the means for Nonforecasting cities are different from the means for Forecasting cities.

[c]Based on a five-point scale (from 0 to 4): not = 0, minimally = 1, partly = 2, mostly = 3, only = 4; Nonforecasting $n = 62$, Forecasting $n = 108$.

[d]Based on a five-point scale: never = 0, a little = 1, some = 2, a lot = 3, always = 4; Nonforecasting $n = 61$, Forecasting $n = 107$.

[e,f]Based on a five-point scale: no = 0, yes = 1; Nonforecasting $n = 61$, Forecasting $n = 107$.

SOURCE: John P. Forrester, 1991. "Multi-Year Forecasting and Municipal Budgeting." *Public Budgeting and Finance.* vol. 11, no. 2 (Summer): 47–61.

63.9 percent of the respondents said that the budget officer is responsible for making the forecast, and 34.3 percent said that the responsibility lies with the finance officer. Just over 18 percent also said that the departments, which have responsibility for providing services, project their expenditures. Rarely are planners responsible for forecasting expenditures. One reason is the diversity of elements, accommodating to forecasting, that are found in many budgets. A second reason may be that, in comparing forecasting to nonforecasting cities, budget officers in forecasting cities are more likely to be formally educated in accountancy and public administration, two 'disciplines' that are sensitive to the need of budgeting in organizations. Nearly 41 percent of the budget officers in forecasting cities are educated in accountancy and 38 percent are educated in public administration, compared to about 32 percent in each in nonforecasting cities (see Table III). However, slightly more budget officers in nonforecasting cities are educated in management and economics.

The expenditure data municipal governments use to forecast expenditures primarily come from the finance departments (see Table IV). Prior year budgets and operating departments are also important sources of expenditure information, with slightly fewer cities relying much on audit data. Economic data used in forecasting are also most likely to come from finance departments. Others sources are more rarely used.

How much data do the sources provide? The findings indicate that multiyear forecasting is at least as historical as traditional budgeting, but is not as historical as recommended. Just over 40 percent of the cities use between five and ten years of prior data to project general fund revenues, and nearly 30 percent do so to forecast general fund expenditures (see Table V). Very few governments use more than ten years worth of data for either type of forecast. Also, perhaps because of the simplistic nature of expenditure forecasting, nearly two-thirds of the cities report that they do not use computers to make their estimates.

TABLE II. PERCENTAGE OF RESPONDENTS, HOW THEY GROUPED EXPENDITURES FOR FORECASTING, AND THE TECHNIQUES THEY USE TO PROJECT EXPENDITURES (*n* = 108)

FORECASTING TECHNIQUE	BY MAJOR LINE-ITEM					BY DEPARTMENT OR FUNCTION	BY FUND TYPE		
	Personal Services	Supplies	Services & Other Charges	Capital Outlays	Inter-Governmental Charges		Govern-mental	Enter-prise	Internal Service
None	50.0	50.0	50.9	50.0	59.3	44.4	31.5	37.0	44.0
Expert	0.9	4.6	5.6	8.3	5.6	2.8	5.6	4.6	3.7
Trend	10.2	13.9	12.0	6.5	7.4	12.0	8.3	7.4	8.3
Deterministic	1.9	0.9	0.9	2.8	2.8	1.9	1.9	1.9	0.9
Econometric	1.9	0.9	0.9	0.9	0.0	0.9	0.9	1.9	0.0
Expert and others	19.4	14.8	14.8	13.0	9.3	21.3	27.8	23.1	17.6
Trend and others	21.3	20.4	20.4	18.5	14.8	25.0	31.5	28.7	22.2
Deterministic and others	14.8	10.2	9.3	10.2	8.3	10.2	17.6	14.8	13.0
Econometric and others	6.5	5.6	8.3	3.7	5.6	7.4	13.0	13.0	11.1

SOURCE: John P. Forrester, 1991. "Multi-Year Forecasting and Municipal Budgeting." *Public Budgeting and Finance*, vol. 11, no. 2 (Summer): 47–61.

There are several possible reasons cities use such short data bases. One may be that simply relying on one or two years worth of data may be sufficient. Second, even though a lot of data may be available, no one may know how to model it. Or, since cities have had little experience with forecasting (Expert: 8.5 years, Trend: 8.6 years; Deterministic: 5.3 years; and Econometric 3.5 years), they have not needed to record expenditure prior data in a form required by forecasting models. Also, cities may not be willing to pay for expensive forecasting packages that require extensive amounts of data. Finally, use of more demanding methods may require that the government already use a management- or planning-oriented budget, and many cities still do not have such budgets.

Finally, consider the reporting and use of the forecast. Most forecasts are not only used by administrators, but in 85 percent of the respondent cities the forecast results are reported to the City Council. In 83 percent of the cities, costs of city services are included in the forecast report.

TABLE III. COMPARING EDUCATIONAL EXPERIENCE AMONG FORECASTING AND NONFORECASTING CITIES: PERCENTAGE OF BUDGET OFFICERS HOLDING A BACHELOR'S DEGREE OR HIGHER AND THEIR FIELD OF STUDY

Field of Study	Forecasting Cities (*n* = 108)	Non-forecasting Cities (*n* = 62)
Accountancy	40.9	32.0
Public administration	38.0	31.9
Management	12.1	19.4
Economics	12.0	12.5
Other[a]	20.4	12.5
None	0.9	1.4
Not specified	8.3	12.5

[a]Including urban, business, finance.

Note: some officers indicated multiple areas of specialty.

SOURCE: John P. Forrester, 1991. "Multi-Year Forecasting and Municipal Budgeting." *Public Budgeting and Finance*, vol. 11, no. 2 (Summer): 47–61.

TABLE IV. MEAN RESPONSES OF TYPES OF EXPENDITURE FORECASTING DATA GATHERED FROM VARIOUS SOURCES (*n* = 106, TWO MISSING OBSERVATIONS)

Type of Data	ORGANIZATIONAL UNITS			BUDGET DOCUMENTS		
	Operating Departments	Finance Departments	CEO	Prior Budgets	Prior Audits	Other
Expenditure	2.38	2.72	.98	2.42	1.28	0.24
Economic	1.62	2.49	.94	1.58	0.71	0.62

Note: Figures are based on a five-point scale, from 0 to 4: 0 = source is not used; 1 = source is used a little; 2 = source is used some; 3 = source is used a lot; 4 = source is always used.

SOURCE: John P. Forrester, 1991. "Budgetary Constraints and Municipal Revenue Forecasting." *Policy Sciences* 24: 333–356.

TABLE V. PERCENTAGE OF CITIES THAT USE PRIOR DATA IN MAKING MULTIYEAR PROJECTIONS OF THE GENERAL FUND

What Is Projected from the General Fund	HISTORICAL DATA				
	not used	< 5 years	5–10 years	> 10 years	not specified
Revenues	0.0	46.3	42.6	9.3	1.9
Expenditures	0.9	64.8	29.6	3.7	0.9

SOURCE: John P. Forrester, 1991. "Multi-Year Forecasting and Municipal Budgeting." *Public Budgeting and Finance*, vol. 11, no. 2 (Summer): 47–61.

Exactly which costs (indirect, opportunity, and so on) are included is not clear. Sixty-eight percent also include the forecast's implications for policy, while 62 percent reflect on the level of services produced by the city. Out-year expenditure forecasts tend to be "used some" by the Finance Department and the City Manager (see Table VI). Both need the expenditure information to budget—departments are responsible for providing specific services and the city manager is responsible for administering the services. Other actors also use the expenditure forecast, but they and the finance director are a little more likely to use revenue projections. For all users this may be partly a function of their responsibilities. Budget and finance directors, for example, are responsible for keeping a positive revenue flow so the city does not run a deficit. And the interest by councils and mayors in revenue estimates is likely in reaction to fiscal stress and cuts in federal grants-in-aid experienced by several local governments.

In conclusion, estimating future expenditures is becoming an increasingly important activity of all governments. The demand for expenditure forecasting arose out of the strides made in budgetary reform. How governments will view expenditure forecasting in the future will also be a product of how the budget process comes to be conceptualized, as incremental, rational, or otherwise. The forecasting methods available now and then will range from the most simple to the extremely complex and demanding. In the end, the measure of expenditure forecasting's value will be whether it is used to help governments budget for the future.

JOHN P. FORRESTER

BIBLIOGRAPHY

Boswell, Charles R., and J. Mark, Carpenter, 1986. "Long-Range Financial Forecasting in Fort Worth." *Government Finance Review* 2 (December): 7–10.

Davis, Otto A., M. A. H. Dempster, and Aaron Wildavsky, 1966. "A Theory of the Budgetary Process." *American Political Science Review* 60 (September): 529–547.

TABLE VI. BUDGET ACTORS AND HOW USEFUL THEY FIND FORECASTING IN MAKING DECISIONS (EXPENDITURES/REVENUES)

	FY	FY + 1	FY + 2	FY + 3
Departments	2.92/2.68	1.91/1.89	1.24/1.16	1.01/0.87
City Manager[a]	3.39/3.17	2.75/2.67	2.18/2.13	1.67/1.56
Budget/Finance Director	3.63/3.52	3.12/3.12	2.50/2.55	2.04/2.10
City Council	2.79/2.80	2.09/2.11	1.33/1.30	0.94/0.92
Mayor	2.77/2.81	2.07/2.23	1.40/1.52	1.14/1.18

[a]Number of respondent cities that are City Manager = 67.

Note: Figures are based on a five-point scale, from 0 to 4: 0 = projections for (the given fiscal year [FY]) are never used; 1 = projections for (the given FY) are used a little; 2 = projections for (the given FY) are used some; 3 = projections for (the given FY) are used a lot; and 4 = projections for (the given FY) are always used.

SOURCE: John P. Forrester, 1991. "Budgetary Constraints and Municipal Revenue Forecasting." *Policy Sciences* 24: 333–356.

Forrester, John P. 1991. "Multi-Year Forecasting and Municipal Budgeting." *Public Budgeting and Finance*, vol. 11, no. 2 (Summer): 47–61.

———, 1991. "Budgetary Constraints and Municipal Revenue Forecasting." *Policy Sciences* 24: 333–356.

Novick, David, ed., 1965. *Program Budgeting: Program Analysis and the Federal Budget,* a Rand Corporation–sponsored research study. Washington, DC: GPO.

Page, William, 1982. "Long-Term Forecasts and Why You Will Probably Get It Wrong." In Spyros Makridakis and Steven C. Wheelwright, eds., *The Handbook of Forecasting* New York: John Wiley & Sons, 449–456.

Plesko, George A.,1987. "Government Forecasts and Budget Projections: An Analysis of Recent History." U.S. Treasury Department, OTA Paper 58 (October).

Schroeder, Larry, 1981. "Forecasting Local Revenues and Expenditures." In J. Richard Aronson and Eli Schwartz, eds., *Management Policies in Local Government Finance*. Washington, DC: ICMA, 66–90.

U.S. Commission on Organization of the Executive Branch of the Government, 1955. *Budgeting and Accounting: A Report to Congress.* Washington, DC: GPO.

U.S. Congress. Congressional Budget Office, 1976. *Five-Year Budget Projections, Fiscal Years 1978–1982.* (December). Washington DC: GPO.

———, 1984. *Federal Debt and Interest Costs.* (September). Washington, DC: GPO.

———, 1988–1989. *Responsibilities and Organization.* Washington, DC: GPO.

U.S. Congress. Senate. Committee on the Budget. One Hundredth Congress, Second Sess., S. Prt. 100–189. 1988. *The Congressional Budget Process: An Explanation.* Washington DC: GPO.

U.S. Executive Office of the President, Bureau of the Budget, 1950. *Work Measurement in Performance Budgeting and Management Improvement.* Washington, DC: GPO.

F

THE FABIAN SOCIETY.

An organization formed in London in 1884, to combat widespread poverty and destitution and foster equality, through a reconstruction of the social order along socialist lines. Notable early Fabians included the sociologists Beatrice and Sidney Webb, the political scientist Graham Wallas, the Colonial Office civil servant and future colonial governor Sydney Olivier and the dramatist and polemicist George Bernard Shaw.

The name Fabian was derived from the Roman General, Quintus Fabius Cunctator, whose delaying tactics and guerilla warfare enabled him to turn back Hannibal's invasion of Italy in the third century B.C.E. The Fabian Society's motto reads: "For the right moment you must wait, as Fabius did patiently, when warring against Hannibal, though many censured his delays, but when the time comes you must strike hard, as Fabius did, or your waiting will be in vain and fruitless." Sidney Webb summarized the Fabian approach in succinct and memorable terms as "the inevitability of gradualness." The society's emblem is a tortoise with its right front foot raised, over the motto "When I strike, I strike hard."

The aims of the Fabian Society were socialist, but its methods were evolutionary and reformist. The strength of the Fabians stemmed from their insistence on painstaking research and reasoned argument. Beatrice and Sidney Webb saw clearly that social reform would not be brought about by "shouting." "What is needed," they wrote in *A Constitution for the Socialist Commonwealth of Great Britain* in 1920, "is hard thinking" (p. 174). "Above all," the historian Ben Pimlott pointed out in his preface to *Fabian Essays in Socialist Thought* in 1984, "the Fabians believed in the power of ideas" (p. vii). The society adopted the tradition of social investigation, which Charles Booth exemplified in 1892 with *Life and Labour of the People in London*. It was axiomatic for the Fabians that careful examination of social problems would provide the basis for their solutions. The solutions, in turn, could be counted on to be along socialist lines. In the view of the Webbs, it was from the actual facts and coldly impassive arguments that socialism drew its irresistible energy. A list of key Fabian achievements drawn up by Margaret Cole—chair of the Fabian Society in the years 1955-1956 and president from 1962 to 1980—includes "having insisted on laying a foundation of facts for all assertions" (p. 328).

Once facts had been accumulated and ideas and policies developed, the society had the further task of publicizing and disseminating them. The Fabian *Basis*—a statement of objectives adopted in 1887—in part commits the society to further its objectives "by the general dissemination of knowledge as to the relation between the individual and society in its economic, ethical and political aspects."

Fabian Essays in Socialism (Shaw 1889)—the society's first book—sold 46,000 copies prior to World War I and is still in print. Shaw's preface to the 1931 edition describes the collection as "inextinguishable." The establishment of the London School of Economics and Political Science in 1895 and the launching of the *New Statesman*, a weekly journal of fact and discussion, in 1912 were further Fabian initiatives, instigated by the Webbs in order to gain converts for socialism. An 1898 entry from Beatrice Webb's diary, in the edition prepared by Norman and Jeanne Mackenzie in 1982, reads in part: "No young man or woman who is anxious to study or to work in public affairs can fail to come under our influence" (p. 132).

Political Influence

In the absence of a Labour Party, which was not formed until 1900, the Fabians used their facts and arguments to induce the Liberal Party and the Tories to adopt socialist ideas without recognizing their socialist implications. The tactic was known to the Fabian Society as "permeation." As Shaw (1892) recalled: "We permeated the party organisations and pulled all the wires we could lay our hands on with our utmost adroitness and energy" (p. 19). G.D.H. Cole and Raymond Postgate in *The Common People 1746–1946* see the Fabians as having managed in this spirit "to express an essentially Socialist philosophy in terms of immediate proposals which made a strong appeal to many reformers who were by no means Socialists" (p. 423). Permeation gained the Fabian Society a number of notable successes, such as the adoption of Fabian policies by the Liberal-dominated Progressive Party in the London County Council in the 1890s and the 1902 and 1903 enactment by Arthur Balfour's Tory government of the Education Acts, which are seen by Margaret Cole (1961) as "very nearly the dream of Fabian 'permeators' come to life—proposals drafted by intelligent and hard-working Fabians, conveyed to puzzled or sympathetic administrators and carried into effect by a Conservative Government" (p. 107).

The Fabians also interested themselves extensively in improving public administration and the machinery of government. Fabian books and pamphlets routinely set out the administrative arrangements through which the society's proposals were to be given effect. Public administration was a key focus for the London School of Economics, where Sidney Webb was professor of Public Administration from 1912 until 1927. Official committees of inquiry into administrative issues—such as the Haldane committee on the machinery of government in 1919—included Fabians among their members and took evidence researched for them by specialist Fabian groups. The society's centenary historian, Patricia Pugh, writes in a letter that the Fabians "came to believe that they knew how to run things far better than other people, and that their role was both to teach others and take a practical part themselves by permeating all forms of local administration."

Campaign Against Poverty

Well before the turn of the century, the Fabian Society had acquired both within Britain and internationally a reputation for offering a philosophy, a process, and a capacity for getting results. Overseas Fabian Societies were formed, most notably in Australia. How the society worked in practice is illustrated by its enduring campaign against poverty. The commitment of the original Fabians to overcoming poverty was manifest in the choice of the title for the first Fabian tract *Why Are the Many Poor?* (1884). Tract five, *Facts for Socialists* (1887), followed shortly, devoted in part to a statistical comparison of the conditions of the "Two Nations" within British society. More Fabian publications, and more Fabian energy, have been devoted to poverty than to any other topic. The outcome of the society's concern was in part the proposals for a "National Minimum," which Beatrice and Sidney Webb put forward in 1897 in their book *Industrial Democracy.* The appointment of Beatrice Webb to the Royal Commission on the Poor Laws by Prime Minister Balfour in 1905 was a further Fabian milestone, enabling her to produce the *Minority Report,* which Cole (1961) describes as "one of the greatest State papers of the century." Cole concludes: "All that is implied in the later phrase 'Social Security,' including some things not yet put into effect, is to be found in essence in the *Minority Report* of fifty years ago" (p. 139).

Following the rejection of the *Minority Report* by the Liberal government in 1909, the Fabians launched a National Committee for the Breakup of the Poor Law—later the National Committee for the Prevention of Destitution—which rapidly attracted over 16,000 members. The *Minority Report* and the activities of the National Committee failed in their objective of securing an immediate implementation of Webb's recommendations, but contributed massively to a climate of opinion in which change was inevitable. Forty years later, the Poor Laws were finally abolished and the modern welfare state was finally put in place by Clement Attlee's predominantly Fabian Labour government, on the basis of the wartime *Beveridge Report.* William Beveridge, a Liberal, wrote in *Power and Influence* in 1958 that the report "stemmed from what all of us have imbibed from the Webbs" (p. 86).

Subsequent Fabian experts such as Richard Titmuss, Brian Abel-Smith. Peter Townsend, and David Donnison have written widely about ways of further strengthening the welfare state and harnessing it more closely to the core Fabian value of a more equal society.

World War I gave rise to a historic friendship between Sidney Webb and the secretary of the Labour Party, Arthur Henderson. Webb and Henderson were brought together in the War Emergency Workers' National Committee,

which Henderson chaired. Webb was the driving force behind the committee, and did most of its creative work. Joint action by Webb and Henderson gave the Labour Party a new constitution, which Cole (1961) describes as "a very 'Fabian' compromise" between the party's socialist and trade unionist adherents. Webb and Henderson were also the co-authors of a new party program, *Labour and the New Social Order* (1918), which represented in Cole's (1961) view "as nearly as possible the purest milk of the Fabian word" (p. 172). The upshot was an enduring partnership between the Fabian Society and the Labour Party, which outlived the vicissitudes of economic slump, party schism, and war to emerge triumphantly in Attlee's Labour government. The partnership remains in force, and had its most recent manifestation in the policy taken to the 1992 elections by the then-Labour leader, and sometime Fabian Society Executive member, Neil Kinnock.

An amendment to the Fabian Society rules in 1939—known widely as the society's "self-denying ordinance"—reads: "No resolution of a political character, expressing an opinion or calling for action, other than in relation to the running of the Society itself, shall be put forward in the name of the Society. Delegates to conferences of the Labour Party, or to any other conference, shall be appointed by the Executive Committee without any mandatory instructions." A further amendment requires that "all publications sponsored by the Society should bear a clear indication that they do not commit the Society, but only those responsible for preparing them." The changes marked the culmination of a process by which the Fabian Society had ceased increasingly to be a body advocating specific policies, as had been the case at its inception, and instead devoted itself to researching and publicizing ideas within a broad framework of democratic socialism and parliamentary democracy. In so doing, Fabianism was reinvented as being primarily about the method and process for social reform, and the Fabian Society reaffirmed its identity as the original political think tank.

RACE MATHEWS

BIBLIOGRAPHY

Beveridge, William H., 1944. *Full Employment in a Free Society.* London: Allen & Unwin.
———, 1955. *Power and Influence.* New York: Beechhurst Press.
Booth, Charles, 1892. *Life and Labor of the People in London.* London: Macmillan.
Britain, Ian, 1982. *Fabianism and Culture: A Study of British Socialism and the Arts 1884–1918.* Cambridge: Cambridge University Press.
Cole, Margaret, 1961. *The Story of Fabian Socialism.* London: Heinemann.
Fabian Society, 1884. *Why are the Many Poor?* London: Fabian Society, Fabian Tract No. 1.
———, 1887. *Facts for Socialists from the Political Economists and Statisticians.* London: Fabian Society, Fabian Tract No. 5.

Fremantle, Anne, 1960. *This Little Band of Prophets: The Story of the Gentle Fabians.* London: Allen & Unwin.

Labour Party, Great Britain, 1918. *Labour and the New Social Order.* London: Labour Party.

McBriar, Alan M., 1962. *Fabian Socialism and English Politics 1884–1918.* Cambridge: Cambridge University Press.

Mackenzie, Norman, and Jeanne Mackenzie, 1977. *The First Fabians.* London: Weidenfeld & Nicolson.

———, 1982. *The Diary of Beatrice Webb.* 4 Vol. London: Virago.

Mathews, Race, 1993. *Australia's First Fabians: Middle-Class Radicals, Labour Activists, and the Early Labour Movement.* Cambridge: Cambridge University Press.

Pimlott, Ben, ed., 1984. *Fabian Essays in Socialist Thought.* London: Heinemann.

Pugh, Patricia, 1984. *Educate, Agitate, Organise: 100 Years of Fabian Socialism.* London: Methuen.

Shaw, George Bernard, ed., 1889, *Fabian Essays in Socialism.* London: Fabian Society.

———, 1892. *The Fabian Society: Its Early History.* London: Fabian Society.

Webb, Sidney and Beatrice Webb, 1920. *A Constitution for the Socialist Commonwealth of Great Britain.* Cambridge: Cambridge University Press.

———, 1897. *Industrial Democracy.* London: Longman.

———, 1905. *Minority Report of the Poor Law Commission.* Clifton, NJ: A. M. Kelley.

FAMILY ALLOWANCES.

Payments made to assist parents in the task of raising children, often targeted specifically at low-income families as a poverty-alleviation measure.

Family allowances take a variety of forms worldwide, but their central aim is to transfer income to those who carry the burden of rearing the next generation of children, a form of compensation for the earnings forgone by parents, particularly women as the principal caregivers, whose income and quality of life are inevitably affected by the presence of children. They are rarely paid in the less-affluent developing countries where government priorities lie in improving public education or health systems rather than providing family income transfers.

Of central interest are the assumptions underlying different forms of family allowances. Some nations regard the level of family income as irrelevant, on the basis that a high-income family with children carries more costs than a high-income couple without children, just as does a low-income family with children compared with a childless low-income couple. The principle applied is one of "horizontal equity," aimed at the "equalization" of family burdens, usually with explicit support for those who choose to have children.

In contrast, the principle of "vertical equity," another form of "equalization," holds that low-income families deserve more support from the public purse than do high-income families, regardless of the presence or numbers of children; thus the "millionaire family" does not deserve or need government support in the form of family allowances. "Means-testing," "income-testing," and "targeting the needy" are the terms used here. Clearly, the latter view is more likely to hold sway in times of economic restraint because universal family allowances are costly and the justice of a horizontal equity approach is more difficult to explain to a public clamoring for cutbacks in taxation and government expenditures.

Questions also arise regarding the age of children for whom family payments may be made—infants only, school children, young people living away from home but still financially dependent on parents? Policies based on statistics of "family households" can often ignore across-household costs and dependencies, an issue most clearly recognized in relation to divorce and child support, but also affecting college-age students. Of importance, too, are policy decisions about paying more for subsequent children than for a first child (a pronatalist approach, but one not proven effective in increasing birth rates), and about paying the allowance to the mother or principal caregiver rather than to the assumed "head of the household." The latter usually happens when family income transfers are made via the taxation system, in the form of "rebates," rather than as direct payments—an inequitable approach in that it favors those on higher incomes and does not put money directly into the hands of the caregiver.

To illustrate, the family allowance system is very different in countries with an explicit family policy than that where family matters are seen as "private" and to be left alone by the state.

For example, the "Golden Age" of family policy in France began in 1938 with universal family allowances favoring those with three or more children. This practice continues with a specific Ministry of Solidarity, Health and Social Protection paying, through its National Allowance Fund, a nonmeans-tested family allowance and a nine-month young child's benefit, which is then means-tested up to age three. There is a single wage-earner's allowance for those who have a third child and targeted supplementary family allowances for low-income and sole-parent families. Such payments are complemented by a sliding tax scale based on the number of family members.

Germany, too, has an explicit family policy, with a Ministry of Family, Youth, Health, and Women caring for the needs of families. Tax rebates for children were replaced in the late 1970s by a universal and more generous family allowance, up to the third child, and more for subsequent children. By 1982, budget problems had led to means-testing, and there is now a dual-system of child allowances and child tax rebates, still a generous system aimed at supporting mothers at home in preference to paid employment.

In contrast, Great Britain has no explicit family policy, its long tradition of liberal individualism discouraging state intervention in the "private domain." However, child benefits are paid to all families with children, plus there is a means-tested Family Credit Scheme for those on lower incomes.

The United States has had a similar approach to that of Great Britain, since the 1935 Social Security Act first made matching federal grants to the states for financial assistance to "needy" dependent children. The Aid for Families with Dependent Children (AFDC) program is tightly means-tested on both family income and assets and applies only to children who meet a widely varying state definition of need. There is no family allowance to families not defined as being "in need."

The federal share is higher for states with lower per capita incomes. From 1990, the JOBS program requires recipients to undergo remedial education and training, with assistance in job skills and job placement, and payments are tied to the enforcement of child support payments by absent parents. By 1990, most states were using the more generous aid formula, which applies when Medicaid and AFDC grants are aggregated. Food stamps are also available to families whose gross income is below 130 percent of the poverty income guidelines. Current debate will lead to tighter restrictions on family payments.

Other countries around the world have varied family allowance systems that lie somewhere between these extremes. Belgium, like Germany, provides universal child allowances, not tied to family income, plus tax deductibility for the costs of child care. Denmark replaced means-testing in 1987 with a universal child allowance, prompted by fears of declining birthrates for Danes compared with immigrant families. Italy and the Netherlands, in contrast, have moved from a universal plan to payments targeted at lower-income families, because of the rising fiscal cost of such welfare measures. Singapore provides generous payments to encourage an increase in birthrates but also for those who support aging parents.

Australia changed from a system of child tax rebates and child endowment payments at birth to a universal Family Allowance system in 1975. Since that time, concerns about high costs in a declining economy have led to tightly targeted payments. A Basic Family Payment is available for those whose total family assets do not exceed about half a million (Australian) dollars, with the rate increasing with the number, but not the age, of children. An additional Family Payment is offered for families with a low combined annual income, in recognition of vertical equity needs, and more is paid for children aged between 13 and 15.

Clearly, the system adopted for family allowance payments has a varied rationale and differing outcomes for families in each nation. Nowhere do such payments cover the actual "cost" of children, but that is not the aim, nor would it be feasible in any economy. Family allowances are a method of recognizing the important work of parent-

hood and the opportunity costs that such a responsibility carries for parents.

DON EDGAR

FAMILY LEAVE. Time off from work for the purpose of caring for a newborn or adopted child or caring for a sick child, spouse, parent, or other family member.

The composition of the American workplace changed dramatically in the three decades between 1960 and 1990. The number of families in which both spouses were employed more than doubled, with the percentage increasing from 28 percent to 65 percent (BPWF 1993). In 1994 women were 46 percent of the working population, with the largest increase occurring in the category of women who had young children (Soloman 1994). In 1990, 69 percent of all children who lived in single-parent homes had a working parent. Almost 60 percent of all women with children under six years of age were in the workforce, a dramatic increase of 32 percentage points from 1970. Single fathers as a group have grown rapidly among American workers (BPWF 1993).

At the same time that women have entered the workplace in ever-growing numbers, the U.S. population as a whole has aged. By the year 2000 it is projected that there will be more Americans over the age of sixty than under the age of twenty. Most elderly dependents are not placed in nursing homes. The overwhelming majority, 90 percent, are cared for by their families. Two-thirds of these family caregivers are working women (BPWF 1993).

The consequence of these two trends has been to make the need to reconcile the conflicting needs of work responsibilities and dependent care both an important workforce and economic issue. Sinclair (1991) has described as a tenet of orthodox economics the belief that people make decisions about their work activities in the context of constraints, some of which may be of such great importance as to imply very little choice. Although the need for dependent care—defined as care for either children or the elderly—has always existed, the need has increased dramatically since 1980. As more and more women work and are thus unavailable for at-home dependent care, the workplace has had to make adjustments. This has not always been done willingly (Kizer 1987). Even though there has been an increase in the number of women working outside the home, there has not been a corresponding increase in the amount of male involvement in family responsibilities, in particular in the area of dependent care (Gilbert and Dancer 1992). One of the most difficult conflicts employees must face is when a child is born or adopted, a family member is seriously ill, or the employee him- or herself has a serious health condition. When vacation, sick, and personal leave is exhausted employees have often been torn between the need to work and the desire to care for their ill family members. The need to work has often triumphed because of the underlying fear that job loss would occur if the employee sought further time away from work. The result was a conflicted employee whose focus while at work was undermined by concerns for his or her family's health.

Some employers, notably larger corporations and family-owned businesses, have traditionally allowed some employees a limited system of family leave. In many cases this applied only to the salaried management staff and not to hourly or production employees. However, in general the provision of family leave, prior to 1993, was the exception rather than the rule. In roughly half of the states a version of family and medical, parenting, or pregnancy disability laws had been passed as part of an earlier wave of temporary disability legislation (Kamerman and Kahn 1991).

In February of 1993 President William Clinton signed the Family and Medical Leave Act (FMLA) into law. Prior to this time only the United States and South Africa, of the industrialized countries, did not have legislatively guaranteed family leave. In 1990 President George Bush had vetoed similar legislation, claiming that this issue was the prerogative of private industry (Kamerman and Kahn 1991). The law provides eligible employees with up to twelve weeks, per twelve month period, of unpaid leave for childbirth or adoption, to care for a child, parent, or spouse (including common-law partners) with a serious health condition or for a personal illness. The FMLA requires continuation of health care coverage during the leave and reinstatement of the employee into the same or equivalent position upon his or her return to work. Employees cannot lose any employee benefits such as vacation days, pensions, or disability benefits, that were accrued prior to the start of the leave. If an employee decides not to return to work he or she may be liable for repayment of the amount of insurance payments their employer paid for their health care benefits while they were on leave. All public and local education agencies, and all private-sector employers who employ 50 or more employees in 20 or more work weeks in the current or preceding year are subject to the provisions of the FMLA. As of 1993 only 5 percent of the nation's workplaces, encompassing approximately 45 million employees, or 40 percent of the workforce, were covered by the act. The FMLA is enforced by the United States Department of Labor's Employment Standards Administration, Wage and Hour Division. Employers are required to provide information to their employees regarding the provisions and protections afforded under the FMLA. Employees who feel that their rights under the FMLA may have been violated can file a complaint with the Department of Labor or file a civil lawsuit against their employer (Sayer 1993).

There are still concerns surrounding the issue of family leave. The majority of U.S. employees are not covered by the Family and Medical Leave Act. Some employers may be reluctant to hire employees that they perceive as being more likely to request family leave time. The FMLA does not cover leave for domestic partners, parents-in-law, or relatives who are not immediate family members. It is likely that many of these questions will be resolved piecemeal by the judicial system on a case-by-case basis.

PATRICE ALEXANDER

BIBLIOGRAPHY

Business and Professional Women's Foundation (BPWF), 1993. *Work and Family Policies: Options for the 90s and Beyond.* Washington, DC: BPWF.

Gilbert, Lucia Albino, and L. Suzanne Dancer, 1992. "Dual-Earner Families in the United States and Adolescent Development." In Suzan Lewis, Dafna N. Izraeli, and Helen Hootsmans, eds., *Dual-Earner Families: International Perspectives.* London: Sage Publications, pp. 151–171.

Hyde, Shibley, and Marilyn J. Essex, eds., 1991. *Parental Leave and Child Care: Setting a Research and Policy Agenda.* Philadelphia: Temple University Press.

Kamerman, Sheila B., and Alfred J. Kahn, eds., 1991. *Child Care, Parental Leave, and the Under 3s: Policy Innovation in Europe.* Westport, CT: Auburn House.

Kizer, William, 1987. *The Healthy Workplace.* New York: John Wiley & Sons.

Sayer, Liana, 1993. "Family and Medical Leave." *National Business Woman*, vol. 74, no. 3 (Fall): 21–24.

Sinclair, M. Thea, 1991. "Women, Work, and Skill: Economic Theories and Feminist Perspectives." In Nanneke Redclift, and M. Thea Sinclair, eds., *Working Women: International Perspectives on Labour and Gender Ideology.* London and New York: Routledge, pp. 1–24.

Solomon, Charlene, 1994. "Work/Family's Failing Grade: Why Today's Initiatives Aren't Enough." *Personnel Journal* (May): 72–87.

FAMILY POLICY.

Any government policy that affects the forms, functions, or well-being of families.

Family policy can be either explicit, as in some European countries that designate a government minister and department responsible for families, or it can be implicit, as it has been in the United States and Great Britain, where the state basically asserts that families are a "private" matter, not to be interfered with. But every policy has implications for the well-being of a nation's families, whether concerned with taxation, birthrates, health, housing, or welfare payments. Obviously, a family policy perspective is implicit in every political decision or legislative program, even though its varied impacts on families may not be specified in advance of implementation.

In countries such as the United States and Great Britain, a tradition of laissez-faire liberalism has kept the state away from explicit family policies, though the rhetoric merely serves to hide an implicit policy that families should be self-sufficient, despite the interdependency of modern industrialized society; and to hide the reality that programs such as Aid for Families With Dependent Children (AFDC) are clearly based on a set of assumptions about family policy.

The Carter White House Conferences on Families in the early 1980s broke up in disarray over attempts to define what "family" means, that is, which families should qualify for public support. The United States seems to have stayed away from the issue ever since, not taking national action even in 1994, the International Year of the Family. Many have argued that "child policy" should take precedence over the impossibly vague notion of family policy, and there have been numerous calls for a rejuvenation of the "mediating structures" in the community that might better support family life.

The main thrust, however, has been an antiwelfare view, which holds that it is the collapse of "family values," "caused" by overreliance on welfare handouts, that explains most of America's social problems, such as teenage pregnancy, the rise in one-parent families, divorce rates, poverty, drugs, and violence. Other structural "causes," such as lack of job opportunities, lack of an adequate safety net, lack of controls on guns or drugs, or an ailing education system, are ignored by some in favor of an argument that one preferred model of family life (the nuclear family of homemaker-breadwinner responsibly bringing up their own children) should be reimposed. Governments should not "interfere," but women who have children out of wedlock, or those who stay on welfare for too long should have all income support withdrawn and their children should be placed in orphanages, a clear case of severe state interference.

On one hand, the argument is based on a mixture of value judgments, economic costs, and hypotheses about likely behavior, none of which can be well supported. On the other hand, so too are the counterarguments, and one can only watch to assess the outcomes of an increasingly acrimonious family policy debate. The point here is that any family policy should spell out its value position clearly and should be subjected to systematic impact analysis.

The contrast between U.S. and European approaches points to a central issue of all family policies: the value placed on children and the roles best served by men and women. The coincidence of movements idealizing motherhood and theories of child psychology that stressed the importance of attachment in the early years was matched by a period of relative affluence in which one "family" wage was usually enough to support a family. For the first time in history, most people did marry and the nuclear family (which has always been the norm throughout history and in most societies) took on an ideological strength that is resistant to change. But change happens in response to demographic, economic and scientific shifts, regardless of current normative standards, and family policy is now much more complex.

Ironically, a cultural emphasis on the rights of the individual to pursue, if not to have, happiness has reinforced a more tolerant attitude toward separation and divorce when a marriage proves unsatisfactory to either partner, and to divorce laws that enshrine the principles of equality of the partners and their joint contributions to the marriage. At the same time, but less easily, the laws assert the "best interests of children" and the shared responsibility of partners for children after divorce. The difficulties of enforcing child support and a degree of access to both parents have been exacerbated by the rapid growth in numbers of single-mother families in which the father may or may not be known.

Critics of the welfare policies blamed for such social problems are often those most vocal about the virtues of free choice, family autonomy, the rights of the individual, and of keeping the state out of private family matters. The central dilemma is that modernity rests upon optionality and the flexibility for the individual to make choices within a free-market system, yet not everyone is able to make the "right" choices, as seen by others.

Social Change Affects Family Policy

Though families have always been subject to change, the decades since World War II have seen major shifts in the structure and processes of family life, and all of these affect the nature of the current family policy debate.

Availability of reliable contraception has finally separated sexuality from the institution of marriage and undermined its legitimacy as a controlling mechanism for social behavior. The emphasis on prolonged education and changes in labor market opportunities have altered the pathways into marriage and family formation, particularly for women, leading to delayed marriage and reduced fertility, a shift away from the breadwinner-homemaker model that became typical in the post–World War II years, and a greater acceptance of alternative family forms once regarded as deviant. Today, family policy faces a dilemma about preferred family forms and the targeting of public assistance for families.

With paid employment now a necessity for most women as well as men (and a preference for many women), the whole structure of caring in society has been transformed. Child care, flexible work practices, and principles of equal opportunity and nondiscrimination have become crucial family policy issues. The place of children, their healthy development and their care and education have become a heated topic of debate. So, too, have the issues of voluntary work, the quality of community life, and caring for the aged.

Technological restructuring, job displacement, and unemployment place pressures upon government taxation and social security systems, often threatening the "welfare safety net" established by most Western nations in the years of affluence. As well, reduced birthrates result in the ageing of societies and an intergenerational conflict for welfare funds between parents, children, and the elderly. The "welfare state," in its many forms, is under close scrutiny, and the responsibility of individuals and families for their own well-being is being reasserted.

These changes are common throughout the Western world, but are also gathering pace in the developing nations as modern technology transforms both markets and value systems. Singapore, for example, has very explicit family policies designed to shore up the institutions of marriage and filial family support in the face of Western influences seen as undermining them. The preference for the birth of boys has hampered population-control policies and attempts to improve the lot of women in countries such as China and India.

Such changes and the problems they create for traditional or conventional family forms indicate the difficulty both of defining what "family policy" is and of developing acceptable family policies in a pluralist and rapidly changing social context. Ironically, having no specific policy about family life or leaving families to their own devices are, in fact, decisions that affect family choices and lifestyles, often in unintended and undesirable ways.

Family Policy Is Not Limited to Population Policy

Family policy has frequently been seen as coterminous with population policy, the goal being to maintain or increase the birthrate. At times, immigration policy has served this end, as in Australia in the postwar years, where a shortage of labor led to government immigrant sponsorship, especially of males, and of family reunion programs to ensure stability and continuity. But it also gave family policy a bad name, as in Europe after Nazi Germany's pursuit of racist goals through discrimination and selective breeding programs. In China, the one-child policy to contain population growth has required draconian efforts to enforce birth control in a society in which family size has been important and boys have been more valued than girls. Many countries still practice infanticide for female offspring, males being seen as more economically valuable. Not all have the "choice" of effective birth control, and health issues affect family outcomes in ways the developed world can barely imagine.

Family Policy Always Reflects Gender Relations in Society

Most European countries after World War II encouraged marriage and childbirth through an adequate family wage, generous family allowances and tax concessions for children, and a network of community-based family organizations. The aim was to maintain the division of labor into paid work for men and child-rearing and household labor for women.

Such pronatalist policies succeeded for a time, until other forces at work led people to marry later, or not at all, and to have fewer children later in the life cycle. Even Catholic countries, such as France and Italy, have experienced declining birth rates, and inducements to have more children have had little effect.

As the Province of Quebec, Canada, discovered in the mid-1980s, people were more concerned with the level of support provided for rearing the few children they had than with having more children. Quebec's family policy, as a result, placed parents and the task of child-rearing at the center, with the schools and the workplace seen as partners in making this important social task as effective as possible. The same quality-of-life approach is taking hold in other countries, which have discarded attempts to impose one model of family life on all.

The Scandinavian countries, unlike France and Germany, combined pronatalist approaches with a deliberate policy of gender equity, building into their system high-quality public child care, generous maternity and parental leave provisions, and the encouragement of women to be educated and trained to take an equal place in the workforce, with men expected to share in household and child-caring tasks. The fact that women changed more readily than men was to be expected, but over time parental leave-taking by men has also increased, and the normative framework of joint partnership in marriage is now widely accepted.

Family Policy Can Be Given a More Systematic Framework

It is useful to group family policy issues into broader categories. This helps avoid the simple notion that there is only one thing that can be labeled "family policy." This grouping draws attention to the complex interaction between the family unit, as an active agent of its own volition and construction, and the role of the state and the economy in affecting family life and to the responsibility of other social institutions and organizations for the quality of family life in any society. This can be done in several ways.

One way is to place a clear policy goal at the center of a grid that asks questions about how well certain policies, legislation, programs, and procedures meet that goal. This is the approach followed in Quebec, for example, with *parents as the key persons in society* at the center and a set of questions asked about how well the schools, the workplace, and government or community programs support parents in their task of raising children. One could broaden this approach by placing "care" at the center, to include care of the aged, the disabled, the unemployed, and so on, as well as caring for children. Or, as in the Scandinavian case, *gender equity in carrying out the family's two main tasks of earning an income and of caring* could be the central goal, with all policies and programs then designed to achieve it. The Alberta, Canada, Premier's Council in Support of Families has developed a Family Policy Grid, which asks questions of every policy initiative regarding Equity, Family Roles, Family Diversity, Family Support, Family Ties, Family Commitment/Responsibility, Family Interest/Involvement, and Community Partnerships.

Another broad framework that lies behind most current writing about family policy implies that *family well-being* is the central goal. That, of course, can be variously interpreted, but its emphasis on the quality of life as lived inside family households and across family circles of extended kin focuses attention on the fact that economic policy or housing policy or technological innovations are not ends in themselves, particularly for elected governments, but are means by which to achieve the greatest good for the greatest number. Done well, they attract votes; done badly they lose votes. Certainly, from the perspective of individuals and family units, a sound economy is only a mechanism that ensures their quality of life. Equally, though work can have an intrinsic value, most people work in order to live, they do not live in order to work.

Thus one can group family policy into four main areas, all aimed at serving the goal of *family well-being*. This is a framework followed in various forms by the European Family Policy Forum, the Australian National Council for IYF94 and the International Family Policy Forum set up by Canada following the Montreal IYF Conference in November 1994.

Economic policies are not often seen as family policies, yet they are the crucial underpinning of everything families do. Decisions about employment, wage rates, competition in the market, taxation, housing interest rates, unemployment payments and other forms of income transfer in the welfare or social security system either help families to function as viable units or they do not. Thus in family policy terms, they can be seen as *economic enabling policies* and can be evaluated in terms of the extent to which they enhance or damage family well-being.

A second grouping can be labeled *family function and support services policies*. These include the vast array of services aimed at helping families cope, ranging from maternal and child health advice, marriage counseling or parenting courses to the availability of nonparental child care, crisis support, flexible work practices, and parental leave provisions in the workplace, and aged care assistance for families. Many of these services are provided by state governments or nongovernment agencies and local volunteer groups, but one can assess the relative degree of government financial support and encouragement across different

nations. The assumption here is that in a highly developed modern society, no family can survive alone; there must be schools, hospitals, public transport, and other forms of assistance from other social institutions. The question is the degree and nature of that assistance.

It is important also to note the distinction between "services" and "resources" for family support. Families may well be helped to function by ensuring access to a range of "resources," such as information about parenting, financial management, sources of expert advice, toy libraries, safe public parks and gardens, and so on, without the need for most families to use bureaucratic or professional welfare "services," which can be invasive and dependency-based. Every family needs support; not all need services being delivered by experts who "know what's best for them."

A third area, often overlooked in the literature on family policy, is that of *family law policies*. Obviously, the way a society handles marriage, divorce, and the disposition of property and children after separation is a central indicator of values about family life and the rights of family members. Family law as such is an important codification of changing social values as well as a framework for continuing change. But included here also are those laws and procedures that define the limits of parental and family autonomy, such as the treatment of child abuse and neglect, family violence, the rights of women, the treatment of street kids, the place of foster care and state institutions for the care of children without families or those taken away from families.

Such matters have clear moral as well as economic implications, and the current debate about the rights of single mothers on welfare support and the desirability of putting children into orphanages rather than being raised by their natural mothers, indicates how volatile the area is. The central question concerns the best interests of children and the right of the state to take over family functions, under what circumstances and with what outcomes.

There is a fourth area that affects family well-being that is also currently under close examination. The literature on family policy is thin in relation to what could be called *civil society and moral obligations*. Yet this is a key to emerging family policy debates.

Briefly, the quality of civil society is affected by the way in which the economic and political system encourages or discourages that sense of reciprocity and mutual care that underpins social action, our sense of shared responsibility for others, both within and beyond our family circle. If, as in authoritarian or Communist systems, the state dictates what can be done, provides all services, and takes total responsibility for community affairs, private autonomy and a sense of shared community responsibility is undermined and apathy results. If, on the other hand, a supposedly "free-market" philosophy prevails, the state provides little or nothing in the way of family or community support, and the individual is expected to survive alone in a fiercely competitive marketplace, there is little incentive for community sharing and caring for one's neighbors, so that distrust, jealousy, and atomization prevail.

Thus the calls for more "community," more private initiative, a greater sense of family and communal responsibility must be seen in the context of the system as a whole. A sense of community does not arise unless private individuals and families feel that other institutions in that locality are supportive of their needs, or that they share a "stake" in the quality of that location. Some families in new localities are active "makers" of community, seeking out those who can help, forming associations of like-minded people to lobby for better schools, recreational facilities, and so on, that will better serve their interests. But that depends upon their relative resources and know-how, and a "family-supportive community" is more likely to engender a sense of belonging and a willingness to help others than one that is uncaring and isolating. That sense of moral obligation, of responsibility for others, is developed not only within a family that teaches about mutual care and responsibility. It is reinforced, extended or reduced within a community context of shared responsibility versus indifference. Values do not exist in a vacuum; they are sustained in an ecology unique to each nation, state, and local community.

Family policy is thus not one "thing" that stands alone. Too often the term is used to support one model of family life only that does not match the reality of life as it is lived in the majority of families in the community. Rather, a "family policy perspective" leads us to identify the conditions under which the viability of all family forms and processes can be enhanced. Family policy is a value-laden area and one in which clear value positions should be stated if the actual impacts on families and society are to be assessed. One can take a pluralist view, or a more restricted view of desirable family forms. But in the end, the quality of life enjoyed by families of whatever shape determines the quality of that abstraction called "society" or "the nation."

DON EDGAR

BIBLIOGRAPHY

Alberta, 1994. *Family Policy Grid.* Edmonton, Alberta, Canada: The Premier's Council in Support of Alberta Families.

Australia, 1994. *Creating the Links: Families and Social Responsibility, Final Report by the National Council for International Year of the Family.* Canberra: Australian Government Printer.

Berger, Brigite, and Peter L. Berger, 1983. *The War Over the Family.* London: Hutchinson.

Blankenhorn, David, ed., 1990. *Rebuilding the Nest: A New Commitment to the American Family.* New York: Family Service America.

Commaille, Jacques, and Francois de Singly, eds., 1995. *The European Family: The Family Question in the European Community.* Paris: Kluwer & Nathan Press.

Dumon, Wilfried, ed., 1989. *Changing Family Policy in EEC Countries.* Leuven, Belgium: Katholieke Universiteit.

Edgar, Don, 1992. "Conceptualizing Family Life and Family Policies." *Family Matters,* No. 32, Australian Institute of Family Studies, Melbourne, pp. 28–37.

Moroney, Robert M., 1976. *The Family and the State: Considerations for Social Policy.* London: Longman.

Quah, Stella, ed., n.d. *The Family as an Asset: An International Perspective On Marriage, Parenthood, and Social Policy.* Singapore: Times Academic Press.

FAYOL, HENRI (1841–1925).

French industrialist and mining engineer who was the first person to write systematically on the subject of management. Fayol's *General and Industrial Management* remains a classic—a standard reading in introductory management courses in private and public administration. The classical management movement is generally understood to have begun with Fayol.

Henri Fayol was born into a lower-middle-class French family. His father was a construction foreman who desired that his sons improve their lot in life and thus sent them to engineering schools. Fayol attended the Lycée at Lyon for two years, preparing for his technical training. In 1858 he entered the School of Mines at St. Etienne, the youngest student in his class at age 17. Two years later he graduated as a fully qualified mining engineer and was immediately hired to work at the coal mines at Commentry in the center of France. He spent his entire working life with this firm.

Fayol was occupied in his early career with the issues on which one would expect a young coal mining engineer to focus: Fires in the mines, design of mine shafts, and concerns of production. In 1888 he was offered the position of managing director. The firm was nearly bankrupt, and Fayol had been asked to manage its closure. Instead of closing the operation, Fayol suggested a reorganization along the lines of the administrative principles he had been developing. The directors gave Fayol that opportunity, and by 1900 a newly organized and expanded firm was flourishing.

Fayol never purchased shares in the company for which he worked so many years, believing that his personal convictions should never be confused with the goals of the firm. This is an example of his subordinating his personal interests to those of the common good, one of the "principles of good character" he put forward in his writing.

One of the fragments of misinformation about Fayol is that he was opposed to the ideas of Frederick Taylor—his contemporary across the Atlantic—and the scientific management movement. He was, indeed, critical of certain elements of Taylor's work but wrote that his reservations did not prevent him from admiring the man who "meant the world to profit from his trials and experiments." He hoped that the example of "the great American engineer" would be followed in France. Fayol had come to see that Taylor was working from the shop floor upward, whereas he was working down from the level of the general manager.

In 1918, at the age of 77 and still in good health, Fayol retired, acclaimed by his industrial colleagues for his business success and praised for his writing by a growing international audience. He continued to speak and write about his management principles, frequently serving as a consultant to business and government. He was a vigorous proponent of teaching management generally, encouraging the formation of courses and schools on the subject.

Fayol was the first to realize that there are transferrable principles that apply to any administrative endeavor. His primary contribution to the literature on administration is to have articulated this basic truth, to have set out the first list of those principles, and to have pointed to the necessity for teaching them generally. "Administration . . . embraces not only the public service but enterprises of every size and description, of every form and every purpose. We are no longer confronted with several administrative sciences but with one alone, which can be applied equally well to public and to private affairs" (1937, p. 101).

Fayol was the first of the management theorists who differentiated what managers do from the activities of production. Industry, for him, consisted of six sets of activities: technical, commercial, financial, security, accounting, and managerial. Thus, his was a functional view of management ("Management is merely one of the six functions" [1949, p. 6]). He viewed managers chiefly as planners who organized, coordinated, and controlled organizational efforts. Such managerial skills, Fayol realized, were universal, if not universally needed. Thus, Fayol is equally important for his principles of management and for his conviction about the universality of management.

Fayol identified fourteen principles of the management role. He did not use the word "principle" to mean rule or law, but as an axiom or precept. Indeed, he used the term reluctantly, because he hoped that the principles would be signposts on the road to a complete theory of management. Fayol's fourteen principles are: Division of work; authority; discipline; unity of command; unity of direction; subordination of individual interests to the general interest; remuneration; centralization; the scalar chain (line of authority); order; equity; stability of tenure of personnel; initiative; and, esprit de corps. Fayol did not believe his list was exhaustive, but he did believe that a list of a dozen or so principles should be developed and discussed generally, from which theory could be developed.

Fayol popularized a number of management concepts. Along with the scalar chain—the idea that similar levels of administration in an organization carried similar weights of responsibility—was "Fayol's bridge." He stated strongly, almost sarcastically, that an organization could waste itself into failure by forcing employees to relate to peers in other parts of the firm only by way of the management ladder.

Instead, management should encourage "bridges" between people at similar levels, saving time and money, and encouraging responsibility and resourcefulness.

The first French edition of *Administration industrielle et générale* is found in the *Bulletin of the Société de l'Industrie Minérale*, 1916. Parts 3 and 4 of *General and Industrial Management* were never completed by the author. They were to cover his practical application of theory. The work was not well known outside of Europe until the second English translation was published in 1949 (reprinted several times through 1965). A later speech, "The Administrative Theory in the State," presented in 1923 to the Second International Congress of Administrative Science at Brussels and reproduced by Gulick and Urwick (1937), represented his definitive application of management principles to public administration.

Fayol's underlying purpose for delineating principles of management was to provide a basis for the teaching of managers. The entire first part of *General and Industrial Management* is a defense of the necessity of teaching management. In his view there were no schools of management because there was no management theory. He railed against courses of study that were exclusively technical. The second part of his book, in which he lays out his principles, exists to indicate what this teaching might be.

PETER J. VAN HOOK

BIBLIOGRAPHY

Fayol, Henri, 1930 [1916]. *General and Industrial Management.* Trans. J. A. Coubrough. Geneva: International Management Institute.
———,1937 [1923]. "The Administrative Theory in the State." In Gulick, Luther, and Lyndall Urwick, eds., *Papers on the Science of Administration*, Trans. Sarah Greer. New York: Institute of Public Administration, Columbia University.
———, 1965 [1916, 1949]. *General and Industrial Management.* Trans. Constance Storrs; foreword by Luther Gulick. London: Sir Isaac Pitman & Sons.

Works on Fayol

Bibliographical notes can be found in Breeze (1985) and Urwick (1956). In the latter there is a listing of articles and monographs by Fayol. Urwick's "Foreword" to the Storrs version contains a summary biography, an abstract of Fayol's administrative life, and a discussion of the difficulty of translating the French "administration" into the English "management" or "administration."
Breeze, John D., 1985. "Harvest from the Archives: The Search for Fayol and Carlioz." *Journal of Management* vol. 11 (1): 43–54.
Brodie, M. B., 1967. *Fayol on Administration.* London: Lyon, Grant, & Green.
Carter, Nancy M., 1986. "Review of General and Industrial Management." *The Academy of Management Review* vol. 11 (2): 454–456.
Urwick, Lyndall. 1937 [1934]. "The Function of Administration, with Special Reference to the Work of Henri Fayol." In Gulick, Luther, and Lyndall Urwick, eds., *Papers on the*

Science of Administration. New York: Institute of Public Administration, Columbia University.

———, 1956. *The Golden Book of Management: An Historical Record of the Life and Work of Seventy Pioneers.* London: Newman Neame.

FEDERAL RESERVE SYSTEM.

The central bank of the United States, which manages the nation's money supply, regulates the banking sector, and provides banking services to the federal government. To maintain the dollar's domestic and international value, the Federal Reserve System (Fed) controls the money supply by manipulating the currency in circulation, adjusting the interest rate it charges on loans to commercial banks, or changing the level of reserves commercial banks are required to hold.

Objectives and Policy Options

The Federal Reserve System was formed by the Federal Reserve Act, signed into law by President Woodrow Wilson on 23 December 1913. As a central bank, the Federal Reserve System maintains the value of the domestic money and credit, both internally and internationally; regulates and monitors individual banks; and acts as the federal government's banker.

The Fed's primary function is maintaining the domestic value of money and credit (i.e., combating inflation and deflation and international currency devaluation and appreciation). To accomplish this objective, the Fed has three policy options: open market operations (buying and selling U.S. government securities and securities from other federal agencies), setting the discount rate (the interest rate at which banks can borrow from the Fed to cover short-term reserve deficiencies), and setting the required reserve ratio (the percentage of bank deposits that must be held in the bank's vaults or as deposits with the Fed). These options all influence commercial banks' reserve positions. Commercial banks are only required to hold a fraction of their deposits as reserves. The remainder of the bank's reserves can be lent out or invested in interest-earning assets. As banks lend out their excess reserves, they "create money." Changes in the commercial banking sector's actual or required reserve position affects the money supply (see **monetary policy**).

The Fed also pursues other objectives. Due to its role as lender of last resort to commercial banks (through discounting), the Fed regulates the banking industry. Commercial banks adopt riskier lending policies when there is a lender of last resort. To compensate for this "moral hazard" problem, the Fed regulates and monitors individual commercial banks. In addition, the Fed influences the international value of the U.S. dollar. The Fed deals in international currency markets to support or deflate the dollar's international value, as appropriate. Finally, the Fed is the federal government's fiscal agent, holding the Treasury Department's checking account and processing the Treasury Department's security transactions. The Treasury reimburses the Fed for these activities.

Considering the scope of the Fed's objectives, and their limited set of policy tools, the Fed must frequently balance conflicting pressures. For example, in mid-1995, U.S. economic growth appeared to slow and the dollar's value fell dramatically relative to the German deutsch mark and the Japanese yen. To stimulate the domestic economy, the Fed could increase the currency in circulation, reduce the discount rate, or lower the required reserve ratio; to support the dollar's international value, the Fed could implement the opposite policies. Contractionary Fed policies would support the dollar's international value by increasing interest rates and attracting foreign investment into the United States (foreign investment in the United States increases the international demand for dollars). Identifying the appropriate course of action requires the Fed to balance conflicting pressures and determine the appropriate timing and level of response. These are difficult and often controversial decisions.

Organizational Structure

The Federal Reserve System's organizational structure is summarized in Figure I. The Board of Governors of the Federal Reserve System is the central decisionmaking body. The Board of Governors participates in open-market policy decisions, approves the discount rate, and sets the required reserve ratio. It also has broad supervisory and regulatory responsibilities over commercial and Federal Reserve Banks. The Board of Governors is located in Washington, D.C., and has seven members, appointed by the President and approved by the Senate. Members are appointed to overlapping 14-year terms. One new member is appointed every two years. Thus two members of the Board of Governors are appointed during a four-year presidency. In addition, the President designates one member of the Board of Governors to a four-year term as chair. The chair's and the President's terms are coincident.

The Federal Reserve System also includes 12 Federal Reserve District Banks (with 25 branches). The district banks and branch locations are summarized in Figure I. These banks hold the bulk of cash reserves for commercial banks, issue paper currency, clear checks, monitor commercial banks, provide checking accounts to the U.S. Treasury, and issue and redeem government securities. Each district bank is managed by a nine-member board of directors. The board includes three class-A directors (bankers elected by commercial banks in the district), three class-B directors (nonbanking representatives elected by commercial banks in the district), and three class-C directors (nonbanking representatives from the district appointed by the Board of Governors). The Board of Directors appoints the

FIGURE I. FEDERAL RESERVE SYSTEM

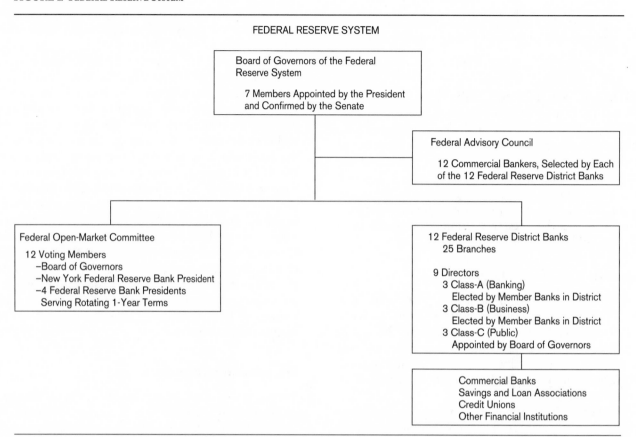

bank's president and first vice president, subject to approval by the Board of Governors. Branch banks have five- or seven-member boards of directors. A majority of the board members are appointed by their district bank's Board of Directors, the remainder by the Federal Reserve's Board of Governors.

Federal Reserve Banks are operated like profit-seeking commercial banks. They earn profits by making loans and purchasing interest-bearing securities with their excess reserves. However, there are two significant differences between commercial and Federal Reserve Banks. All stock in Federal Reserve Banks is owned by the member commercial banks in the district. Stock ownership is a condition of membership. However, the stockholders in Federal Reserve Banks do not have the normal voting rights. Furthermore, Federal Reserve Banks do not retain their profits. The banks use their earnings to defray their expenses and pay a mandatory return to stockholders. Any remaining profits are returned to the Federal Treasury. The Fed has returned more than 80 percent of its profits since it was established.

The Federal Open Market Committee (FOMC) establishes policy regarding open-market operations. The FOMC has 12 voting members, including the seven members of the Board of Governors, the president of the Federal Reserve Bank of New York, and presidents of four other Federal Re-

serve Banks. The president of the New York Fed is a permanent voting member because open-market operations are conducted through the New York Fed's trading desk. The presidents of the other Federal Reserve Banks serve one-year terms on a rotating basis. The FOMC meets every four-to-six weeks. All 12 Federal Reserve Bank presidents participate in the policy discussions. However, only five presidents are voting members at any one time.

The Federal Advisory Council is the final major policy related body. This council has 12 members, one from each of the 12 Federal Reserve districts. One member is appointed by the Board of Directors from each Federal Reserve District Bank. They are usually prominent bankers. The Federal Advisory Council meets with the Board of Governors at least four times a year. The council provides insight concerning general economic and banking conditions and makes recommendations regarding monetary policy. These recommendations are purely advisory, however.

To ensure that the Treasury Department does not manipulate the money supply to further its own objectives, Congress established the Fed as an independent institution. Its decisions do not have to be ratified by either the executive branch of the government or by Congress. However, members of the Board of Governors are appointed by the President and approved by the Senate. In addition, the

TABLE I. FEDERAL RESERVE DISTRICT BANKS AND BRANCHES

District	Federal Reserve District Bank	Branches
1	Boston, MA	
2	New York, NY	Buffalo, NY
3	Philadelphia, PA	
4	Cleveland, OH	Cincinnati, OH
		Pittsburgh, PA
5	Richmond, VA	Baltimore, MD
		Charlotte, NC
6	Atlanta, GA	Birmingham, AL
		Jacksonville, FL
		Miami, FL
		Nashville, TN
		New Orleans, LA
7	Chicago, IL	Detroit, MI
8	St. Louis, MO	Little Rock, AR
		Louisville, KY
		Memphis, TN
9	Minneapolis, MN	Helena, MT
10	Kansas City, MO	Denver, CO
		Oklahoma City, OK
		Omaha, NE
11	Dallas, TX	El Paso, TX
		Houston, TX
		San Antonio, TX
12	San Francisco, CA	Los Angeles, CA
		Portland, OR
		Salt Lake City, UT
		Seattle, WA

SOURCE: Compiled by author.

Board of Governors must report to Congress on its policies, and the minutes of FOMC meetings are published with a one-month lag. Finally, the chair of the Board of Governors meets regularly with the Secretary of the Treasury and the chair of the President's Council of Economic Advisers. Thus, the Fed is independent but not isolated from the executive and legislative branches.

WILLIAM R. GATES

BIBLIOGRAPHY

Board of Governors of the Federal Reserve System, 1974. *The Federal Reserve System: Purposes and Functions.* 6th ed. Washington D.C.: GPO.
Coit, Charles, 1941. *The Federal Reserve Bank of Richmond.* New York: Columbia University Press.

FEDERALISM. A genera of governmental forms that use a variety of legal, organizational, and political techniques to share governmental authority in such a way as to provide for the pursuit of national goals while maintaining the political integrity of diverse, locally situated populations.

Federalism has not been a common or popular form of government. Local jurisdictions, in most countries and for much of the world's history, have been subordinate to the authority and decisions of the central government. However, with the decline of monarchy and the rise of republics, federal forms of government have been adopted by more and more nations (Elazar 1987; Riker 1993). Much of the current appeal of federalism derives from the inflexibility of unitary forms of government to accommodate the complex population diversities in modern nation-states. Today, in the late 1990s, most nations are composed of many groups of people who differ by culture, ethnicity, language, race, religion, or tribe. This variation based on personal attributes is compounded by the spatial distribution of the different population groupings within a given country's territory. Because persons and places are intimately interrelated, many if not most political issues are fought across territories as well as across the more usual cleavages of economics and partisanship (Tarrow 1978). In contrast to the rigid pyramid model of the unitary nation-state, which presumes a single people and its culture, the federal model of government offers what Werlin (1970, pp. 185–209) termed an "elasticity of control." Federalism permits the citizens of a country to design (and alter over time) institutional forms so that authority and resources are shared in a manner that maintains the political integrity of groups or places (Friedrich 1925; Elazar 1968; Riker 1975). Simply put, federal forms of government make possible the achievement of national unity without the necessity of eliminating diversity.

Whether one examines the various definitions and the conditions that constitute a federal state, the origins and historical development of federalism, the number and types of federal arrangements and nations, or the theories of federalism, substantial disagreement and debate confronts the contemporary student of government. It is not possible in this entry to go into extensive detail on every point of disagreement. Readers out of necessity, some choices must be made about the topics covered and the issues reviewed. Readers are strongly encouraged to turn to this entry's Bibliography for more extensive elucidation of the many details and debates.

Origins and Historical Development

Scholars around the world generally mark the origin of modern federal government as the 1787 Constitution of the United States of America (e.g., Wheare 1953; Mello 1960; Dikshit 1975; Riker 1993). American federalism is a complex set of separated institutions and intertwined principles of government. Ronald Watts (1993, p. 11) has listed ten attributes of the U.S. federal form: (1) two orders (not levels) of government, (2) a national government that deals directly with individual citizens, (3) a formal distribution of legislative and executive authority, (4) revenue resources allocated between the two orders of government, (5) some autonomy for each order, (6) provision for the representation of regional views within the national policymaking institutions, (7) a written constitution, (8) a constitution not unilaterally amendable and requiring the consent of all or a majority of the constituent units, (9) an umpire (courts or referendums) to rule on disputes between governments, and (10) processes to facilitate intergovernmental relations.

To the question of what is novel or unprecedented about U.S. federalism, various scholars have answered by noting, among other features, (a) the placement of the nonnational governments on a coordinate plane with the center (Wheare 1953); (b) "contrary to earlier notions, . . . the federal system here is not composed merely of states, as in a league, but creates a new community, all-inclusive, of the citizens of all the states" (Friedrich 1968, p. 17); (c)"transformed and organized [already existing] principles of federalism into a practical system of government" (Elazar 1968, p. 363); and (d) the federation is "centralized," in that "the central government can force constituent governments to behave as the central government wishes with respect to those functions generally supposed to be vested in the center" (Riker 1975, p. 108).

Although the U.S. federal model is one of the most distinctive political inventions of the American experience, the authors of the 1787 Constitution relied on many different sources for their inspiration. Through their education they were familiar with the triumphs and defeats of the ancient leagues of Israel, Greece, and Rome, as well as the Swiss and Dutch confederacies of the medieval period. Recent scholarship also suggests that Benjamin Franklin and others at the U.S. Constitutional Convention were highly impressed with the confederal governance of the "five nations" of the Iroquois (Johansen 1982). Similarly, the arguments and theories of classical, medieval, and, especially, enlightenment philosophers shaped the ideas that went into the 1787 design. The list of putatively influential philosophers is quite lengthy; the most frequently acknowledged include Locke, Hobbes, Montesquieu, Rousseau, Althusius, Milton, Harrington, and Hume (Friedrich 1968; Ostrom 1991; Beer 1993; Walker 1995). According to S. Rufus Davis (1978), the authors of the U.S. federal document created their "constitutional alchemy" out of the "following ingredients . . . [of] alliance metal [which was transformed] into federal gold: the prevailing idea of the composite state, Hugo's notion of double rule, the division of 'the rights of Majesty,' the feudal obligation of princes to enact the will of the Empire in matters of common concern, the principle of majority rule in the af-

fairs of the common council, the commitment of all to an 'everlasting' treaty, and Althusius' catalyst of the sovereign people's will" (p. 70). The escalation of serious problems that could not be solved because of design flaws in the Articles of Confederation and Perpetual Union served as the immediate impetus to the creation of this highly original form of government.

Newer Forms of Federalism

Since its invention, the U.S. model of federalism has been copied with variable success by constitution drafters in other nations. For example, several Latin American countries (e.g., Argentina, Brazil, Mexico, and Venezuela), after gaining independence or later deposing strongman rulers, adopted almost wholesale the institutional features of the U.S. government. Of these efforts, only Brazil has functioned for any length of time as a federal government. The numerous and widespread British colonies, as they achieved independence, often experimented with federalism. Instead of adopting the American constitutional design in total, these new nations preferred parliamentary governments to presidential ones. Australia, Canada, and India offer examples of what many scholars label as "parliamentary federalism," or "executive-centered federalism."

Since the end of the two world wars, the central region of Europe has been home to the federal governments of Germany, Austria, and Switzerland, the prototype of European federalism. In contrast to the U.S. model of separated institutions, German federalism combines a legislatively elected chief executive (chancellor) with a powerful federal council (Bundesrat) representing the main constituent governments (Lander). All important legislation must garner a qualified majority from the Lander in the federal council, and then its implementation is the responsibility of the Lander's administrative agencies. Consequently, much federal policy depends heavily on action by the Lander governments (Hueglin 1995). Fritz Scharpf (1985) has claimed that the key feature of German federalism is its unique "institutionalized political interlocking" in which "important policy tasks have been transferred to the next higher institutional level, whereas policy formation and implementation remained tied to the unanimous consent of the member-governments" (pp. 324–350). Because of these unique attributes, Scharpf considers German federalism as one of two fundamental forms—the other being the U.S. model, based on institutional separation.

Other Western European nations such as Belgium, Spain, and Italy have adopted recent institutional reforms based on federal ideas. Over time, the European Common Market has increasingly manifested the attributes of federal governance (Padoa-Schioppa 1995; Pelkmans 1995). The spread of federalism into Eastern Europe and the post-Soviet Commonwealth of Independent States is anticipated by many observers of this region. In other parts of the world, a growing number of nations are either full-fledged federal governments or utilize one or more features commonly associated with federal institutions. It is curious that many standard textbooks on comparative government do not acknowledge the distinctions between unitary and federal governments or even discuss the existence of federal states (see, e.g., Mayer 1989; Andrain 1994).

Federalism as an Idea

For many authors, federalism represents more than a form of government. It embodies a compound set of ideas that undergird the institutional design and give rise to a distinctive form of political life. Richard Simeon and Katherine Swinton (1995) have noted that "as an idea, federalism points to issues such as shared and divided sovereignty, multiple loyalties and identities, and governance through multilevel institutions" (p. 3). Some authors have gone so far as to label federalism an ideology (King 1982) and have given it status with the other great "isms" of political philosophy (Elazar 1968). Carl Friedrich (1968) has traced the source of this ideological approach to the nineteenth-century writings of Proudhon, who sought "to promote federalism as comprehensive philosophy of 'diversity in unity.'"

The writings of Carl Friedrich (1968; 1974) and Karl Deutsch (1957) build from a developmental perspective that posits a "federalization process" within a political grouping that results in a "distinctive way of life." Friedrich (1974) described the movement toward a federal form as "the process by which a number of separate political organizations, be they states or any other kind of associations, enter into arrangements for working out solutions, adopting joint policies, and making joint decisions on joint problems. . . . The federalizing process accompanies, so to speak, the communal development as its organizational counterpart" (p. 53). For Friedrich (1968) and many others "federalism refers to this process, as it does to the structures and patterns which the process creates; it also encompasses the belief (ideas and ideologies) which it presupposes and generates." Thus, "federal behavior and federal belief are part and parcel of federalism" (p. 177).

Interestingly, this emergence and acceptance of federalism as an ideal political order parallels the spread of federalism as an institutional form of government. Similarly, the growing interest in the "distinctive way of life" associated with federalism is also a recent activity. Much of this current enthusiasm derives from the proposition (as yet not tested rigorously) that federalism offers a solution to the difficulties of building viable political entities out of unique sociocultural communities that find themselves trapped in a quandary of animosity and interdependence. Albert Breton (1991) explains this theory: "A federal structure is probably the most consistent with multiple identities and identifications, because it is designed to embrace entities that retain a certain degree of autonomy.

Federalism allows for a mixture of autonomy and integration into a larger system conducive to optimal conditions for the protection and enhancement of each level of collective organization" (p. 55). Thus federal "ideas" appeal to those seeking to build community and nation out of diverse and sometimes hostile peoples.

To elevate federalism to an "ism" akin to liberalism or socialism requires a consensus on just what ideas constitute the federal "ism" and an understanding of how those ideas get transformed into federal forms. Not all authorities on federalism are convinced of its "ideological" character. Arthur MacMahon (1955), for example, has argued that federal ideas are culture-bound. Davis (1978) has bluntly stated that one cannot make any statements about federal countries that can be attributed to their "federalness" or to "the special way they practice federalism, or in spite of their federalness" (p. 212). For John Kincaid (1995), federalism as an idea raises serious issues of how to transform ideas into workable formulas for power sharing. To argue that federalism in all its forms rests on a normative theory of political behavior requires that a clear connection be established between the ideal process of federalizing, the institutional forms characteristic of federal government, and the expected outcomes as expressed by a functional unity within a diversified nation.

Definitional Discord

Almost every important study of federalism offers its own unique definition of the term, thus there is at once a surfeit of definitions and a muddle. First, there are the legalistic definitions based on a constitutional "division of powers" among tiers of government, as exemplified by Wheare's (1953) statement, "By the federal principle I mean the method of dividing powers so that the general and regional governments are each, within a sphere, coordinate and independent" (p. 11). MacMahon (1972) has offered a similar definition: "Federalism in modern nations is a constitutional form that divides lawmaking powers between a central government for the whole area and a number of constituent governments" (p. 3). Perhaps the most influential version of this definitional approach is that of William Riker (1975): "Federalism is a political organization in which the activities of government are divided between regional governments and a central government in such a way that each kind of government has some activities on which it makes final decisions" (p. 101). Samuel Beer (1995) has provided the most elegant formulation of this "division-of-powers" approach when he said, "I start from the conventional definition of federalism as a political system in which a territorial division of authority between a general government and several regional governments is constitutionally established" (p. 225).

For many scholars, the narrow legalism of the division-of-powers definitions ignores the human realities of politics. A second definitional approach highlights the necessity of cooperation among public officials who represent different constituents. According to Friedrich (1963), a federation "is a union of group selves, united by one or more common objectives but retaining their distinctive group being for other purposes . . . it unites without destroying the selves that are uniting, and is meant to strengthen them in group relations. It organizes cooperation" (p. 585). Daniel Elazar (1968) has offered a similar "bargaining and cooperation" definition: "As a political device, federalism can be viewed more narrowly [compared to social contracts] as a kind of political order animated by political principles that emphasize the primacy of bargaining and negotiated coordination among several power centers as a prelude to the exercise of power within a single political system" (p. 354). More recent versions of these bargaining and cooperation definitions stress the contractual or conventual nature of the federal bargain among constituent units.

Building from the imperatives of geography and territory, most conventional definitions of federalism strive to lay the basis for a functional division of labor among the various tiers or levels of government within a federal state. The bargaining and cooperation definitions, rejecting the static institutionalism of the first definitional type, call attention to dynamic human processes, such as the development of trust and the establishment of compacts, that lead to the birth of a federation and are necessary to sustain a federation.

Other scholars reject both of these approaches. Livingston (1967) sees federalism as a device by which the "federal qualities of the society are articulated and protected" (p. 37). What makes for a federal state, according to this view, is neither division of powers nor an institutionalized process of bargaining, but a significant degree of diversity—cultural, economic, racial, or religious—in society, especially if the cultural diversity is also territorially based. Aaron Wildavsky (1979) accepted the necessity of cooperation, and he also pointed to the necessity of conflict in order to determine whether a federal state is "alive" (p. 142). Thomas Dye (1990), in his argument that federalism depends on competition, noted that federal governments create "opposite and rival interests" (p. 5). Vincent Ostrom (1991) has also relied on this "opposite and rival interest" formula. Some scholars go so far as to throw up their hands at the possibility of devising a widely accepted definition of federalism. Jean Blondel (1969) claims that "the analysis of federalism has remained encumbered with a series of obscurities" which prevent definitional consensus. Other authors, such as Preston King (1982), restrict the term federalism to the ideological or doctrinal usage, and prefer the term "federation" for the governmental form.

This lack of agreement on a definition of federalism is exacerbated by scholars who refine their ideas about what constitutes the essence of the concept. Compare the previously cited 1968 formulation to Elazar's (1987, p. 12) more recent one: "The simplest possible definition is *self*-rule *plus shared rule*" (italics in original). Or compare Riker's 1993 definition "federalism is a constitutionally determined tier-structure" (p. 508) with his earlier (1975) formulation.

Another important definitional distinction is that between federalism and the newer term intergovernmental relations (IGR). Dissatisfied with the overly constitutional-legal orientation of federalism as a concept, U.S. scholars in the 1930s began using the phrase IGR to highlight the interactions among officials representing various jurisdictions and levels of government (for a more detailed discussion, see the entry for **intergovernmental relations**). This terminological shift narrows the denotation of federalism to system-level or constitutional-division-of-powers issues, and assigns to IGR the nature, origin, and types of relationships among governments within a federal state. It is important to note the obvious interconnection between the bargaining and cooperation perspective to federalism and the development of the intergovernmental relations concept.

This definitional discord is further compounded by the sometimes humorous, sometimes maddening, use of metaphorical language used by federal scholars to communicate definitional nuances. In 1984 William H. Stewart published a list of nearly 500 modifications or variants of federalism, such as centralized federalism, competitive federalism, global federalism, judicial federalism, parliamentary federalism, and even upside-down cake federalism. The list grows longer daily. Thus, "the variety of meanings associated with federation," as King (1982) has noted with great understatement, "creates a genuine basis for misunderstanding" (p. 71). Simply put, after three millennia of experience, attempts to forge consensus on a definition of federalism are in a muddle.

Attributes of Federal States

The lack of definitional agreement is also reflected in the often sharp debates over which set of attributes are associated with a federal form of government. If one asks whether the government of a nation, say Mexico or post-Soviet Russia, is a federal government, one will get different answers from different scholars. Just as there are different and competing definitions of federalism, different lists of federal features also bedevil the study of federalism. Unfortunately, because multiple and somewhat contradictory lists exist, no agreement on which countries are federal has been achieved, nor can anyone specify the number of federal countries.

K. C. Wheare (1953), following his exclusive and stringent federal principle, found only four "genuine federal states"–Australia, Canada, Switzerland, and the United States. Ronald Watts (1993), using an expanded set of traits, identified four "classic" and six "new" federations. The most influential list of attributes used to distinguish federal from nonfederal governments was developed by Ivo Duchacek in 1970. His "ten yardsticks of federalism" (1987, pp. 207–275) include: (1) exclusive control over foreign relations rests with national/federal government; (2) immunity against or prohibition of secession; (3) independent sphere of central or national authority; (4) federal constitution may be amended and procedure is in the hands of *all* members of the federal union; (5) constituent units possess indestructible identity and autonomy; that is, these units cannot be abolished or modified without their own consent; (6) residual and significant powers exercised by constituent units; (7) bicameralism and equal representation of unequal units; (8) two sets of courts; (9) a highest or supreme court; and (10) clear division of power.

Duchacek noted that the first four attributes distinguish a federal state from an association or confederation of states, and the other six features distinguish federal governments from unitary ones. Based on his list of federal yardsticks, Duchacek (1987) counted 21 "existing nation-states considered or claimed to be federal." Recent empirical research suggests that an eleventh attribute–independent fiscal resources for constituent units–is also necessary to separate federal from unitary governments (Krane 1987).

A very different approach to classifying the features of federal states has been developed by Elazar (1987, pp. 38–64). Drawing on his "self-rule plus shared rule" formula, Elazar has created a nine-fold typology of "forms of federal arrangements": (1) union, (2) federation, (3) confederation, (4) federacy, (5) associated statehood, (6) condominium, (7) league, (8) foral system, or fueracy, and (9) interjurisdictional functional authority. Elazar has gone on to classify many countries as well as various bilateral and multilateral arrangements into the first seven categories. His scheme yields nineteen federations, including Argentina, Brazil, Malaysia, India, Nigeria, Pakistan, and the former USSR. He also proceeded to cross-classify 36 nations–first, by degree of unity and diversity versus homogeneity and diversity; second, by degree of federal structure and process; and third, by the degree to which federalism exists as a social phenomenon and a political phenomenon. Elazar's elaborate efforts demonstrate that different federal countries can be assigned to widely different locations on these various classification schema. Put another way, a federal form of government is not strongly associated with one specific set of conditions, such as cultural diversity or federal process. Riker's (1975) advice of "understanding of federalism as a range of phenomena rather than as a single constitutional thing" (p. 103) is the best stance to take at this stage in the conceptual development of federalism. The power of classification studies such as Elazar's is that

they expand the range of institutional forms included within the usual meaning of federalism as well as refine our understanding of the distinctions among federal forms, such as confederation and union, but also between federal and unitary forms.

Federalism as a Theoretically Useless Concept

Even though federalism is seen as one of the great "isms" by many political theorists, a small but significant group of scholars vigorously argue that the concept fails to distinguish a unique phenomenon and thus it contributes little or nothing to the study of government and politics. William Riker and Ronald Schaps (1957) found evidence that federal unions depended on a geographic dispersion of power within the political party system of a country. Federalism, according to Riker and Schaps, is an epiphenomenon of the party structure, and administrative differences between unitary and federal governments are not important. Riker (1964) continued this line of reasoning in his classic monograph, wherein he stated that "transfers of assignment (of administrative responsibilities), which appear to involve centralization, may reflect no more than a changing technology that has, for example, expanded markets to the point that local governments no longer can regulate them" (p. 128). Ten years later, Riker (1975) more bluntly stated that "federalism makes no difference for public policy.... One can never blame federalism for a political outcome, ... for outcomes are the consequences of the preferences of the population" (p. 155).

S. Rufus Davis, an Australian scholar, has developed a separate attack on federalism as an irrelevant, scientifically useless concept. Davis (1978, pp. 204–216) declared that the variation in federal institutional forms does not explain any of the differences found between federal countries nor do federal forms explain differences between federal and unitary nations. That is, there is no evidence that institutional differences are a better predictor of policy outcomes than are economic or social differences. Consequently, Davis has condemned federalism as "phylogenetically senile" and has recommended that the concept ought to be "retired from active duty." Preston King (1982) has concurred with Davis in his belief that the federal-unitary classification of nations "has never told us a great deal ... [And] there comes a time when an old dog should be eased out of its misery: so with the unitary/confederal/federal typology" (p. 134).

A third basis for discounting the importance of federalism derives from the systems theory approach to the comparative study of government and politics. Because systems analysis focuses on the relationships among and between a given system's components, it is the relationship and not the form that is critical. According to systems analysis, to focus solely on institutional forms ignores or misses the more important relationships among institutions. Gabriel

Almond and G. Bingham Powell, Jr. (1978) expressed this systems viewpoint: "One cannot draw a hard and fast distinction between unitary and federal systems, since even in the unitary ones there is some delegation of authority to local units" (p. 235). Work by Douglas Ashford (1976), by Jean-Claude Thoenig (1978), and by Henry Teune (1982) also support this "federalism makes no difference" thesis.

A fourth negative assessment of the explanatory utility of federalism can be found in the continual debates over the merits of centralization versus decentralization. The contradictory outcomes of adopting one or the other of these organizational strategies, in the minds of some scholars, undercuts the federal-unitary distinction. For example, Jean Blondel (1969) has associated federalism with decentralization. The now outmoded "convergence" hypothesis, which suggested that political structures in command and free market economies were becoming more alike, also held that the institutional and operational differences among public organizations were disappearing (Tinbergen 1961; Benjamin 1972).

To briefly summarize, no single or standard definition of federalism is widely accepted. At least three or four competing ways of conceptualizing federalism can be found in the professional literature. Even worse, no one list of attributes that mark a government as federal exists. Given this discordant state of affairs, one can quickly understand why some scholars go so far as to urge that federalism be abandoned as a theoretically useful concept. Ending this confusion over the definition of federalism will require, in part, research aimed at answering a question that goes to the heart of the argument for federalism: "What difference does it seem to make whether the distribution of power follows the federal or unitary formula?" (LaPalombara 1974, p. 102).

Research and Theory

There is no shortage of descriptive and behavioral analyses of institutions and politics in the states generally deemed to be federal. As might be expected, institutional analyses are common. Consequently, basic information is readily available on topics such as the workings of different levels of government (e.g., German Lander; Brazilian municipals), the significance of a specific institution (e.g., the "Triple-E senate" [elected, effective, equal] in Australia; the Council of States in India), and the degree of authority vested in a given type of jurisdiction (e.g., home rule exercised by U.S. municipalities; and the use of initiative and referendum in Switzerland). Also readily available are studies of the financial dimensions of federalism, which provide coverage of topics such as tax competition versus tax harmonization, the use of various forms of intergovernmental transfers, and the degree of fiscal autonomy possessed by local governments. A third and rather extensive area of institutional research is that exploring the implementation of public programs within a federal state. Fewer studies appear to be available on the "federal" behavior and motivations of public officials (elected or appointed); the relationship between political institutions, such as parties and interest groups, and federalism; and the impact that federal institutions have on policy formulation. The best source for research is *Publius: The Journal of Federalism*.

Empirical Research

While single-country studies of federal features are common, the existing body of comparative empirical research on federal nations is modest. The search to identify the conditions that lead to the formation of a federal state and the conditions that maintain the stability of a federal state is one of the few topics that has received extended comparative attention (Hicks 1978; Riker and Lemco 1987; Lemco 1991). Studies of fiscal federalism constitute a second important and highly practical area of comparative research into the operation of federal governments (Oates 1972; Pommerehne 1977; Hunter 1977; U.S. ACIR 1981; Bird 1986; Shah 1991; Bahl and Linn 1992). Third, only a few attempts have been made to determine whether federal states differ systematically from unitary states in policy outputs (Rose-Ackerman 1981; Krane 1987). Similarly, little comparative research has been conducted on variations in federal administrative systems and whether these variations have any consequences for public policy (Graham 1985).

Truly comparative analysis of federalism is seldom attempted. A review of the past ten years of research published in the two most prestigious journals of comparative politics did not find any research article with federalism in its title nor did any article use comparative analysis to study any aspect of federalism. To be sure, it is challenging and difficult; yet, unless comparative federal research is attempted, many of the most important questions raised about federal forms of government will go unanswered.

Theories of Federalism

Until recently, federal studies have been theoretically weak. Political scientists have devoted much energy to classifying the variations in federal countries or demarcating the phases of federal evolution in particular federal governments. Relatively few attempts have been made to apply more general social science theories to the study of federalism. Some examples of these theory-building efforts include the use of (a) power and exchange theory (Pressman 1975); (b) bargaining theory (Rosenthal 1980); (c) systems theory (Treadway 1985); (d) interorganizational networks (Hanf, Hjern, and Porter 1978; Rhodes 1980; Agranoff 1986); and (e) coalition theory (Anton 1989). Although

none of these particular conceptual approaches has become the primary paradigm for the study of federalism, the emergence of theorizing about federalism is a welcome new phase that will take federal studies beyond its long history of theoretical, descriptive analysis (Krane 1993).

Public finance economists and political scientists who have adopted an economic approach to politics have produced the most advanced theoretical work related to federalism. The fiscal aspects of federalism have long interested economists, and they have developed a substantial body of theory and research on such topics as intergovernmental fiscal transfers, tax harmonization, and equity in service distribution. Using what is labeled as "the theory of grants," economists use mathematical models to study questions about the efficiency of allocational formulas or distortions in performance among various jurisdictions (Hirsch 1970; Oates 1972; Breton and Scott 1978; Musgrave and Musgrave 1980).

Economists who assume that local governments behave as competitive economic markets have attracted the attention of an increasing number of political scientists. Charles Tiebout (1965) has suggested that local governments compete for citizens (and the taxes they pay) by manipulating the level and mix of public goods and services provided by the jurisdiction. This is so because citizens who are dissatisfied with local government policies will move to other jurisdictions in order to maximize the return they receive for their tax payments. From this initial beginning there has emerged what Breton (1991) labels the "new theory" of *competitive federalism*. This theory rejects the incrementalist bargaining among officials representing different jurisdictions found in *cooperative federalism* (Kenyon and Kincaid 1991). The competitive market model as applied to federalism has appeal not only because it offers the analyst a deductive and rigorous methodology but also because, according to the theory, its application would lead to more efficient and responsive government.

Other economic-based approaches to the theoretical analysis of federalism have sprung up in the past four decades. The *public choice* or *public goods* framework, developed primarily by James Buchanan (1960, 1968, 1987, 1991), is defined broadly by Mueller (1979) as the "economics of nonmarket decisionmaking" (p. 1). More specifically, the public choice approach begins with the different characteristics of public versus private goods—individual versus joint consumption, feasibility of excluding "free riders" (persons who do not pay for the good), and extent of externalities—and goes on to analyze the structure, organization, and outputs of public decisionmaking (Bish 1971; Peterson 1981; Ostrom, Bish, and Ostrom 1988). For students of federalism, public choice theorizing offers the advantages of the competitive framework without the necessity of rejecting the notion of cooperation. That is, competitive models of governmental behavior only focus on competition, whereas public choice models allow the analyst to accommodate both competition *and* cooperation among jurisdictions (Chubb 1991; Kincaid 1991).

Most recently, *agency theory* has also been applied to federalism. John Chubb (1985) explains, "The federal hierarchy is conceived as a two-tiered system of principal-agent relationships, the upper tier entailing the political control of a federal bureaucratic agency by elected officials and the lower tier the administrative control of state or local government grant recipients by a federal agency" (p. 1005). Agency theory sees social relations as a contract between a buyer, or "principal," and a provider of service, or "agent." Associated with this contract are a variety of costs, such as those of making the contract and enforcing it. The challenge to the principal is to insure that the agent does not shirk the contractual obligations, while at the same time keeping the cost of the contract to a minimum (Wood and Waterman 1994). As applied to federalism, agency theory combines economic and political behavior into one framework, which makes it possible to analyze deductively relationships between tiers of government (e.g., fiscal transfers) as well as to capture the dynamics inherent in federal governments.

Because the study of federalism remained atheoretical compared to other aspects of public policy and administration, it stagnated in terms of its development of concepts that possessed utility for explanation of what the descriptive studies had revealed about federal institutions. However, the recent emergence of several alternative theoretical frameworks, primarily grounded in economic-style analysis, augurs well for the future development of research strategies that may be able to answer some of the most critical questions about federal governments.

Federalism in the United States

The constitutional compromise that sought to balance the supremacy of a national government with an extensive set of already functioning state and local governments created two parallel and cosovereign tiers of government that constitute the U.S. federal arrangement. Some of the union's principal attributes (see the first section of this entry) emerged from the 150 years of colonial experience, and others were deliberately crafted as part of the 1787 Constitution. Since that time the federal experience in the United States has revolved around continuous struggles over the allocation of authority, functions, and finances among the two coordinate orders of government (Derthick 1987). It is important to note that "federalism" as a term in the United States refers generally to those system-level relationships between the national government (commonly, but mistakenly, referred to as the *federal government*) and the state governments (Wright 1990). Likewise, it is important to point out that U.S. local governments, whatever their authority or form, are the legal creatures of the individual state governments, and thus have no direct connection to the U.S. Constitution.

Continual political jockeying between the proponents of a nation-centered versus a state-centered interpretation of the 1787 Constitution characterized the first 70 years of the new republic. Advocates of a *nation-centered federalism* argued that the new nation's economic growth depended on a strong national government that could solve problems that were beyond the scope of any one state's abilities. They also argued that this was the reason the new constitution was written and that it was ratified by the people and not by the state governments, thus the national government was supreme. Conversely, advocates of a *state-centered federalism* held that the new constitution was written by delegates from the state governments and ratified by states at so-called conventions. While the new document created some important powers for the new national government, it also set clear limits on the extent of this new government's authority.

The inability to resolve these contradictory visions contributed in part to the American Civil War. Following the conflict, the U.S. Supreme Court laid down a series of court decisions, which produced a *dual federalism* built on the premise that the U.S. Constitution had created two "collateral political spheres," each having its own specific functions and each prohibited from entering into the realm of the other (from fear of dominance by the other). This convenient formula dominated political thought and most national policy making through the post–Civil War industrial revolution and the first three decades of the twentieth century. Dual federalism, because it sought to separate government into distinct national, state, and local levels, is often referred to metaphorically as "layer-cake federalism" (Leach 1970, pp. 10–15).

The economic disasters of the Great Depression led to an abandonment of the narrow scope of policy action accorded to the national government by dual federalism. In its place arose a new philosophy, one of cooperation between national and state governments in order to mobilize all available public resources in the campaign to restart the economic engine. Some national-state collaboration had occurred prior to the 1930s, but with the Depression and the soon-to-follow global war, on one hand, the American public called for a much wider scope of policy actions from the national government. On the other hand, U.S. citizens also did not want to establish a European-like central administrative state, so the solution entailed the avoidance of combative relationships between national and state governments, and the establishment of a cooperative federalism.

Monetary grants-in-aid from the national government to the states were used to spur economic growth. National government funds, matched with state dollars, covered anywhere from 50-to-90 percent of a program or project's cost (the percentage varied by program type, e.g., highways versus hospitals). Instead of increasing the number of national government bureaucrats, the U.S. Congress left the administration of most grant-in-aid programs in the hands of the states. For the first two decades after World War II, national dollars accounted for approximately 10 percent of state and local government expenditures. Much of the national aid was targeted to jurisdictions and designated primarily for physical infrastructure projects. *Cooperative federalism* came to be referred to by the metaphor of "marble-cake federalism" because the strategy of shared financing and administration of important public programs intertwined the actions of each governmental "layer."

Through this same period, serious economic and social pressures built up, which led to a deterioration of many large metropolitan areas. This crisis provoked strong demands for national action and prompted political leaders such as Nelson Rockefeller and Lyndon Johnson to expand the prevailing view of cooperative federalism to include local governments and private entities. *Creative federalism,* as this new approach was labeled, held that the urban crisis was so severe that its resolution could only be achieved through the combined actions of all levels of government as well as private organizations—for-profit and nonprofit. In other words, government alone could not solve the pressing problems of the day, rather it would require various public-private partnerships (Leach 1970).

Action taken by the national government during the 1960s and 1970s to end racial and gender discrimination, to improve the lot of the poor, and to protect the environment provoked sharp opposition, which initiated political campaigns to reduce the role of the national government in domestic public policy. President Richard Nixon called for a *New Federalism*, which would shift more program implementation responsibility to the states and localities and also transfer some functions back to the states. Nixon contended that the national government had become too big and too intrusive into local affairs. However, Nixon also insisted that if policy responsibility was to be returned to the states, then they would have to be provided with additional funds. Consequently, the Nixon era produced two new forms of aid—block grants and general revenue sharing—which increased the flow of funds to states and localities as well as their discretion in the use of the monies (Wright 1988).

Through the Richard Nixon and Gerald Ford years, national aid as a percentage of state and local government expenditures continued to increase as the national government moved to spend money on more and more activities that had previously been the traditional functions of states and localities. It is important to note that the newer grant programs targeted national funds toward individuals

rather than jurisdictions. Larger proportions of national funds were directed away from place-based projects, such as wastewater treatment plants; instead, funds paid for benefits to persons who were entitled by legislation for assistance with the costs of health care, disabilities, or lack of income (Anton 1989).

As the national government's aid grew, it imposed more controls over the use of the money. These regulations included not only planning and accounting requirements and anticorruption safeguards, but the national regulations covered a wide range of other actions by state and local officials–for example, discriminatory employment and compensation practices, historic preservation, animal welfare and environmental protection, and access for the handicapped. The regulations, especially those that impinged on traditional roles of subnational officials, fueled further demands for less intrusion by the national government (Walker 1981).

President Jimmy Carter and then President Ronald Reagan pushed for even more devolution. Under President Carter, the upward trend of national aid as a proportion of state and local expenditures was halted at about 26 percent. President Reagan, whose campaign promised less government, proposed an *even newer New Federalism,* which rejected both cooperative federalism and the Nixonian commitment to a national obligation to financially aid state and local governments as part of any effort to move program responsibility back to the states. President Reagan's first budget terminated 60 grant-in-aid programs, reduced funds for several entitlement programs, and consolidated 77 grant programs into 9 new block grants. These actions constituted "the first absolute reduction in federal aid outlays recorded in decades" (Beam 1984, p. 420). Much of the Reagan administration's cuts in grants fell hardest on programs that benefited the working poor and forced state governments to raise their own revenues in order to compensate for lost national dollars. John Shannon (1987, p. 34) noted that this devolutionist trend "halted the previous trend toward increased state dependence on the national government and has created a new condition that has been described best as 'fend-for-yourself federalism'" (Krane 1990 p. 122).

The Reagan presidency marked the low point in national aid as a percentage of state-local expenditures. Continued growth in income maintenance and health care costs reversed this ratio during the George Bush administration and, by the end of the first William Clinton administration, the ratio had returned to levels approaching its historical high point (nearly 25%). Unexpectedly, in 1994 the Republican Party captured control of both houses of Congress for the first time since the Dwight Eisenhower years. The Republicans campaigned for "smaller government, lower taxes, less power in Washington, and greater emphasis on individual responsibility and personal morality." It has not been clear from the legislative measures brought forward by this new majority, whether it favors placing more policy responsibility in the hands of the states or "load-shedding," where public programs are simply terminated rather than devolved (Walker 1996, pp. 275–279).

Although there was a temporary reversal in national funds going to states and localities during the 1980s, there was no similar trend in decisions by the U.S. Supreme Court to restrict the enlarging scope of national government action. The Court abandoned the dual federalism doctrine in 1937, but only gradually through the 1940s and 1950s moved to support an expanded role for the national government. With the battles over civil and political rights, environmental protection, fair labor, and treatment of the handicapped, the national courts in the 1960s and 1970s opened wide the door to extensive national government intervention in the activities of state and local governments (Kincaid 1993). A second parallel trend was the growing use of regulations to impose national policy objectives on state and local governments. In response to demands for uniformity in public policy, Congress adopted a strategy of preemption of state authority over the details of program implementation. That is, the national government dictated through congressional directives national standards with which state and local officials had to comply. As the national deficit ballooned, Congress increased its use of these regulations, not as conditions of aid, but as *unfunded mandates* (Zimmerman 1992).

Beginning in the middle-to-late 1960s, state governments, which earlier had been characterized by political inequities and administrative mismanagement, began to modernize their policies and practices. A number of states made significant constitutional changes, typically strengthening the governorship by reducing the number of elected statewide offices. Many states, in response to national regulations, acted to replace political patronage with civil service systems. Likewise, states overhauled their courts by creating merit procedures for the selection of judges, streamlining the number of courts, and establishing systems of judicial administration. Fourth, most states adopted additional forms of taxation, thus increasing their own fiscal capacity. All of these changes resulted in more state-level policy activity and an enhanced ability of state governments to implement effectively their own programs of service to their citizens (Reeves 1982).

One consequence of this enhanced state government capacity was a new argument for less national government activity. During the Great Depression, when the states were prostrate economically, it made sense for the national government to rescue the states. But today, with this newfound policy and administrative ability the argument goes, it is unnecessary for the national government to impose its objectives on states, especially if the national government also refuses to provide the necessary funds to implement its goals.

Most observers would agree with Joseph Zimmerman's (1992) summarization of the more than two centuries of U.S. federal history. "The gradual concentration of political powers in the national government had been a characterization of the evolution of the federal system in the United States until 1965 when the pace of centralization was accelerated as the Congress commenced to exercise its powers of preemption in new regulatory fields and in innovative ways" (p. 1). Certainly, the national government in the late 1990s plays a much larger role in the lives of U.S. citizens than it did in the 1920s; but this can also be said for state and local governments. If federalism is about questions of national versus state authority in the pursuit of various public purposes, then in the United States of the 1990s federalism may best be described as similar to the situation that prevailed during the nation's first 70 years—rancorous debates between advocates of a nation-centered federalism and advocates for a more state-centered federalism.

Federalism Around the World

At the end of the twentieth century, according to Daniel Elazar (1995), "We find more federations than ever before covering more people than ever before" (p. 15). Federal governments vary widely in their institutional arrangements. Some federal countries follow the American form, with its institutional power separation, other nations follow the German form of interlocking intergovernmental power. Some federal unions were born out of an effort to prevent the dissolution of the nation-state, while other countries adopted federal features in order to create governing institutions with sufficient power and resources to solve large-scale problems. It is possible to claim that each federal form of governance is sui generis (Simeon and Swinton 1995), and thus, no one single portrait of federalism can be painted. Fortunately, for the person who wishes to learn more about a particular country or federal arrangement, one can turn to several sources of detailed information. Some examples are *Federal Systems of The World* (Elazar 1991), the American Commission on Intergovernmental Relations (formerly the U.S. ACIR), the Center for the Study of Federalism at Temple University (Philadelphia, Pennsylvania), the Institute of Intergovernmental Relations at Queen's University (Kingston, Ontario), the Center for Research on Federal Financial Institutions at the Australian National University, and the publications of the Comparative Federalism Research Committee of the International Political Science Association.

The single most important fact about federalism today is the growing acceptance and rapid spread of federal arrangements around the world. Not only is the speed of adoption impressive, but also so is the global extent of this revolution. At the end of World War II, there were only four federal nations by Wheare's count—Australia, Canada, Switzerland, and the United States. Today, one can easily find several dozen federal governments of varying forms. Even more important than the numerical increase is the acceptance of federal forms by people of highly different cultures. Federalism is no longer an institution only for Anglo-Americans and the Swiss; it is used by Latins and Asians, Africans and Europeans. The best guess about federalism's popularity is that it offers officials and citizens a range of institutional choices and organizational options for sharing power in ways that balance local determination with the necessities of coordinated action to achieve national (and international) goals (Elazar 1995; Hueglin 1995).

The worldwide appeal of federalism raises several challenging questions about its future. Because its "shared rule, self-rule" features permit the establishment of local power centers, federalism has been prescribed as an organizational remedy for the ills of ethnic, religious, or social conflict. Federalism offers a middle way, it is suggested, between dominance by the political groups that control the central government and the resistance of other groups that could cause the dissolution of the nation. But this thesis fails to specify "what is the logical terminus" of local autonomy (Simeon and Swinton, 1995, p. 5)? How does one stop the domino effect or precedent of according self-rule to one group when almost all groups are "subject to divisive forces" that may well engender internal splits, leading to demands for self-rule by a subgroup of the original group previously granted self-rule (Meisel, 1995, p. 342)? Second, federal solutions to political problems generally focus on territorial distributions of power, but how do federal forms affect or help solve political conflicts that do not follow territorial lines (e.g., gender issues) (Jenson 1995)? Third, if federalism is as much a mindset as it is a tool kit of institutional forms, then what cultural or philosophical contexts are most conducive to its development? For example, what types of differences (economic versus religious) stand in the way of shared rule, and what answer to this question can we give by examining particular cases, such as the dissolution of Yugoslavia and Czechoslovakia (Meisel 1995)? And fourth, there is the already-mentioned question: Does federalism really make a difference in terms of modernization, political participation, and conflict reduction?

The rapidly occurring global changes at the end of the twentieth century—for example, the fall of communism, the continual splintering of groups into more and more subgroups, increasingly integrated economies, electronic access to information and ideas, rapid transportation—all contribute to a turbulent environment within which solutions to political conflicts will have to be devised.

Federalism as a genus of governmental forms offers citizens and officials alike a set of institutional tools by which to make an optimal choice of governing structure. The real advantage of federal forms derives from their inherent flexibility. Because this genera of governmental forms encompasses a range of institutional practices between the extremes of a centralized unitary state and completely autonomous units, the "elasticity" of federalism makes it possible to accommodate societal changes by readjusting the institutional design of the nation. The challenge to political leaders in the twenty-first century will be a federal one: How successful will they be in redesigning the organizational dimensions of the public sector in order to effectively pursue national goals, while maintaining the political integrity of locally situated populations?

DALE KRANE

REFERENCES

Agranoff, Robert, J., 1986. *Intergovernmental Management: Human Services Problem-Solving in Six Metropolitan Areas.* Albany: State University of New York Press.

Almond, Gabriel A., and G. Bingham Powell, Jr., 1978. *Comparative Politics: System, Process, and Policy.* 2d ed. Boston: Little, Brown.

Andrain, Charles F., 1994. *Comparative Political Systems: Policy, Performance, and Social Change.* Armonk, NY: M. E. Sharpe.

Anton, Thomas J., 1989. *American Federalism and Public Policy: How the System Works:* New York: Random House.

Ashford, Douglas E., 1976. "Democracy, Decentralization, and Decisions in Subnational Politics." Beverly Hills: Sage Professional Papers in Comparative Politics. No. 5: 1–59.

Bahl, Roy, and Johannes Linn, 1992. *Urban Public Finance in Developing Countries.* New York: Oxford University Press.

Baracho, José Alfredo de Oliveria, 1982. *Teoria Geral Do Federalismo.* Belo Horizonte, Brasil: Fundacao Mariana Resende Costa, Universidade Catolica de Minas Gerais.

Beam, David. R., 1984. "New Federalism, Old Realities: The Reagan Administration and Intergovernmental Reform." In Lester M. Salamon, and Michael S. Lund, eds., *The Reagan Presidency and the Governing of America.* Washington, DC: Urban Institute Press, pp. 415–442.

Beer, Samuel H., 1993. *To Make a Nation: The Rediscovery of American Federalism.* Cambridge: Belknap Press.

———, 1995. "Federalism and the Nation State: What Can Be Learned from the American Experience? In Karen Knop et al., eds., *Rethinking Federalism: Citizens, Markets, and Governments in a Changing World.* Vancouver: LIBC Press, pp. 224–249.

Benjamin, Roger W., 1972. *Patterns of Political Development: Japan, India, Israel.* New York: David McKay.

Bird, Richard, 1986. *Federal Finances in Comparative Perspective.* Toronto: Canadian Tax Foundation.

Bish, Robert L., 1971. *The Public Economy of Metropolitan Areas.* Chicago: Markham Publishing.

Blondel, Jean, 1969. *An Introduction to Comparative Government.* New York: Praeger.

Breton, Albert, 1991. "The Existence and Stability of Interjurisdictional Competition." In Daphne A. Kenyon, and John Kincaid, eds., *Competition Among States and Local Governments: Efficiency and Equity in American Federalism.* Washington, DC: Urban Institute Press, pp. 35–56.

Breton, Albert, and Anthony Scott, 1978. *The Economic Constitution of Federal States.* Toronto: University of Toronto Press.

Breton, Raymond, 1995. "Identification in Transnational Political Communities." In Karen Knop et al., eds., *Rethinking Federalism: Citizens, Markets, and Governments in a Changing World.* Vancouver: UBC Press, pp. 40–58.

Buchanan, James M., 1960. *Fiscal Theory and Political Economy.* Chapel Hill: University of North Carolina Press.

———, 1968. *Demand and Supply of Public Goods.* Chicago: Rand-McNally.

———, 1987. *The Constitution of Economic Policy.* Stockholm: Nobel Foundation.

———, 1991. *Constitutional Economics.* Oxford: Blackwell.

Chubb, John E., 1985. "The Political Economy of Federalism." *American Political Science Review,* vol. 79 (December): 994–1015.

———, 1991. "How Relevant Is Competition to Government Policymaking?" In Daphne A. Kenyon, and John Kincaid, eds., *Competition Among States and Local Governments: Efficiency and Equity in American Federalism.* Washington, DC: Urban Institute Press, pp. 57–63.

Davis, S. Rufus, 1978. *The Federal Principle: A Journey Through Time in Quest of a Meaning.* Berkeley: University of California Press.

Derthick, Martha, 1987. "American Federalism: Madison's 'Middle Ground' in the 1980s." *Public Administration Review,* vol. 47 (January-February): 66–74.

Deutsch, Karl W. et al., 1957. *Political Community in the North Atlantic Area.* Princeton: Princeton University Press.

Dikshit, Ramesh Dutta, 1975. *The Political Geography of Federalism: An Inquiry into Origins and Stability.* Delhi: The Macmillan Company of India.

Duchacek, Ivo D., 1987. *Comparative Federalism: The Territorial Dimension of Politics.* Lanham, MD: University Press of America.

Dye, Thomas R., 1990. *American Federalism: Competition Among Governments.* Lexington, MA: D. C. Heath.

Elazar, Daniel J., 1968. "Federalism." In David L. Sills, ed., *International Encyclopedia of the Social Sciences,* vol. 5: 353–367. New York: Macmillan and The Free Press.

———, 1987. *Exploring Federalism.* Tuscaloosa: The University of Alabama Press.

———, ed., 1991. *Federal Systems of the World: A Handbook of Federal, Confederal, and Autonomy Arrangements.* London: Longman Current Affairs.

———, 1995. "From Statism to Federalism: A Paradigm Shift." *Publius: The Journal of Federalism,* vol. 25 (Winter): 5–18.

Friedrich, Carl J., 1925. "Origin and Development of the Concept of Federalism in the United States." *Jahrbuch des Offentlichen Rechts der Gegenwert* Neue Fogle Band, 9:29.

———, 1963. *Man and His Government.* New York: McGraw-Hill.

———, 1968, *Trends of Federalism in Theory and Practice.* New York: Praeger.

———, 1974. *Limited Government: A Comparison.* Englewood Cliffs, NJ: Prentice-Hall.

Graham, Lawrence, 1985. "Public Policy and Administration in Comparative Perspective." In Howard J. Wiarda, ed., *New Directions in Comparative Politics.* Boulder, CO: Westview Press, chap. 9.

Hanf, Kenneth, Benny Hjern, and David O. Porter, 1978. "Local Networks of Manpower Training in the Federal Republic of Germany and Sweden." In Kenneth Hanf, and Fritz W. Scharpf, eds., *Interorganizational Policy Making: Limits to*

Coordination and Central Control. London: Sage Publications, pp. 303–341.

Hicks, Ursula K., 1978. *Federalism: Failure and Success: A Comparative Study.* New York: Oxford University Press.

Hirsch, Werner Z., 1970. *The Economics of State and Local Government.* New York: McGraw-Hill.

Hueglin, Thomas O., 1995. "New Wine in Old Bottles? Federalism and Nation States in the Twenty-First Century: A Conceptual Overview." In Knop et al., eds. *Rethinking Federalism: Citizens, Markets, and Governments in a Changing World.* Vancouver: UBC Press, pp. 203–223.

Hunter, J. S. H., 1977. *Federalism and Fiscal Balance.* Canberra: Australian National University.

Jenson, Jane, 1995. "Citizenship Claims: Routes to Representation in a Federal System." In Knop et al., eds., *Rethinking Federalism: Citizens, Markets, and Governments in a Changing World.* Vancouver: UBC Press, pp. 99–118.

Johansen, Bruce E., 1982. *Forgotten Founders: Benjamin Franklin, the Iroquois, and the Rationale for the American Revolution.* Ipswich: Gambit.

Kenyon, Daphne, and John Kincaid, 1991. "Introduction." In *Competition Among States and Local Governments: Efficiency and Equity in American Federalism,* Daphne A. Kenyon, and John Kincaid, eds. Washington, DC: Urban Institute Press, pp. 1–33.

Kincaid, John, 1991. "The Competitive Challenge to Cooperative Federalism: A Theory of Federal Democracy." In Daphne A. Kenyon, and John Kincaid, eds., *Competition Among States and Local Governments: Efficiency and Equity in American Federalism.* Washington, DC: Urban Institute Press, pp. 87–114.

———, 1993. "Constitutional Federalism: Labor's Role in Displacing Places to Benefit Persons." *PS: Political Science and Politics,* vol. 26 (June): 172–177.

———, 1995. "Value and Value Tradeoffs in Federalism." *Publius: The Journal of Federalism,* vol. 25, no. 2 (Winter): 29–44.

King, Preston, 1982. *Federalism and Federation.* Baltimore, MD: Johns Hopkins University Press.

Krane, Dale, 1987. "Does the Federal-Unitary Dichotomy Make a Difference?: One Answer Derived from Macrocomparative Research." In Louis Picard, and Raphael Zariski, eds., *Subnational Politics in the 1980s: Organization, Reorganization, and Economic Development.* New York: Praeger, pp. 35–54.

———, 1990. "Devolution as an Intergovernmental Reform Strategy." In Robert W. Gage, and Myrna P. Mandell, eds., *Strategies for Managing Intergovernmental Policies and Networks.* New York: Praeger, pp. 107–126.

———, 1993. "American Federalism, State Governments, and Public Policy: Weaving Together Loose Theoretical Threads." *PS: Political Science and Politics,* vol. 26 (June): 186–190.

LaPalombara, Joseph, 1974. *Politics Within Nations.* Englewood Cliffs, NJ: Prentice-Hall.

Leach, Richard H., 1970. *American Federalism.* New York: W. W. Norton.

Lemco, Jonathan, 1991. *Political Stability in Federal Governments.* New York: Praeger.

Livingston, Williams S., 1967. "A Note on the Nature of Federalism." In Aaron Wildvasky, ed., *American Federalism in Perspective.* Boston: Little, Brown.

MacMahon, Arthur W., ed., 1955. *Federalism: Mature and Emergent.* New York: Doubleday.

———, 1972. *Administering Federalism in a Democracy.* New York: Oxford University Press.

Mayer, Lawrence C., 1989. *Redefining Comparative Politics: Promises Versus Performance.* Newbury Park, CA: Sage.

Meisel, John, 1995. "Multinationalism and the Federal Idea: A Synopsis." In Knop et al., eds., *Rethinking Federalism: Citizens, Markets, and Governments in a Changing World.* Vancouver: UBC Press, pp. 341–346.

Mello, José Luiz de Anhaia, 1960. *O Estado Federal e as Novas Perspectivas.* Sao Paulo, Brasil.

Mueller, Dennis C., 1979. *Public Choice.* Cambridge: Cambridge University Press.

Musgrave, Richard A., and Peggy B. Musgrave, 1980. *Public Finance in Theory and Practice.* 3d ed. New York: McGraw-Hill.

Oates, Wallace, E., 1972. *Fiscal Federalism.* New York: Harcourt Brace Jovanovich.

Ostrom, Vincent, 1991. *The Meaning of American Federalism: Constituting a Self-Governing Society.* San Francisco: Institute for Contemporary Studies Press.

Ostrom, Vincent, Robert Bish, and Elinor Ostrom, 1988. *Local Government in the United States.* San Francisco: ICS Press.

Padoa-Schioppa, Tommaso, 1995. "Economic Federalism and the European Union." In Knop et al., eds., *Rethinking Federalism: Citizens, Markets, and Governments in a Changing World.* Vancouver: UBC Press, pp. 154–165.

Pelkmans, Jacques, 1995. "Governing European Union: From Pre-Federal to Federal Economic Integration?" In Knop et al., eds. *Rethinking Federalism: Citizens, Markets, and Governments in a Changing World.* Vancouver: UBC Press, pp. 166–182.

Peterson, Paul E., 1981. *City Limits.* Chicago: University of Chicago Press.

Pommerehne, Werner W., 1977. "Quantitative Aspects of Federalism: A Study of Six Countries." In Wallace E. Oates, ed., *The Political Economy of Fiscal Federalism.* Lexington: D. C. Heath, pp. 275–353.

Pressman, Jeffrey L., 1975. *Federal Programs and City Politics: The Dynamics of the Aid Process in Oakland.* Berkeley: University of California Press.

Reeves, Mavis Mann, 1982, "Look Again at State Capacity: The Old Gray Mare Ain't What She Used to Be." *American Review of Public Administration.* vol. 16 (Spring): 74–89.

Rhodes, R. A. W., 1980. "Analysing Intergovernmental Relations." *European Journal of Political Research,* vol. 8: 289–322.

Riker, William, H., 1964. *Federalism: Origin, Operation, Significance.* Boston: Little, Brown and Co.

———, 1975. "Federalism." Chap. 2 in Fred I. Greenstein, and Nelson W. Polsby, eds., *Handbook of Political Science.* Reading, MA: Addison-Wesley, vol. 5, pp. 93–172.

———, 1993. "Federalism." In Robert E. Goodin and Philip Pettit, eds. *A Companion to Contemporary Political Philosophy.* Oxford: Blackwell Reference, pp. 508–514.

Riker, William H., and Jonathan Lemco, 1987. "The Relation Between Structure and Stability in Federal Governments." In William Riker, *The Development of American Federalism.* Boston: Kluwer Publishers.

Riker, William H., and Ronald Schaps, 1957. "Disharmony in Federal Government." *Behavioral Science,* vol. 2: 276–290.

Rose-Ackerman, Susan, 1981. "Does Federalism Matter? Political Choice in a Federal Republic." *Journal of Political Economy,* vol. 89, no 1: 152–165.

Rosenthal, Donald B., 1980. "Bargaining Analysis in Intergovernmental Relations." *Publius: The Journal of Federalism,* vol. 10 (Summer): 5–44.

Scharpf, Fritz W., 1985. "Die Politikverflechtungs-falle: Europaische Integration und deutscher Foderalismus im

Vergleich." *Politische Vierteljahresschrift,* vol. 26, no. 4: 324–350, as quoted in Hueglin (1995).

Shah, Anwar, 1991. *The New Fiscal Federalism in Brazil.* Washington, DC: World Bank. World Bank Discussion Papers No. 124.

Shannon, John, 1987. "The Return to Fend-for-Yourself Federalism: The Reagan Mark." *Intergovernmental Perspective,* vol. 13 (Summer-Fall): 34–37.

Siemon, Richard, and Katherine Swinton, 1995. "Introduction: Rethinking Federalism in a Changing World." In Knop et al., eds. *Rethinking Federalism: Citizens, Markets, and Governments in a Changing World.* Vancouver: UBC Press. pp. 3–11.

Stewart, William H., 1984. *Concepts of Federalism.* Lanham, MD: University Press of America.

Tarrow, Sidney, 1978, "Introduction." In Sidney Tarrow, Peter Katzenstein, and L. Graziano, eds. *Territorial Politics in Industrial Nations.* New York: Praeger, pp. 1–23.

Teune, Henry, 1982, "Is Federalism Possible? Paper presented at the Twelfth World Congress of the International Political Science Association. Rio de Janeiro, Brazil (August).

Thoenig, Jean-Claude, 1978, "State Bureaucracies and Local Government in France." In Kenneth Hanf, and Fritz W. Scharpf, eds. *Interorganizational Policy Making: Limits to Coordination and Central Control.* London: Sage Publications, pp. 167–197.

Tiebout, Charles M., 1965. "A Pure Theory of Local Expenditures." *Journal of Political Economy,* vol. 64 (October): 416–424.

Tinbergen, Jan, 1961. "Do Command and Free Economies Show a Converging Pattern? *Soviet Studies,* vol. 12 (4).

Treadway, Jack M., 1985. *Public Policy-Making in the American States.* New York: Praeger.

U.S. Advisory Commission on Intergovernmental Relations, (U.S. ACIR), 1981. *Australia, Canada, the United States, and West Germany.* Washington, DC: Studies in Comparative Federalism, M–130.

Walker, David B., 1981. *Toward a Functioning Federalism.* Cambridge: Winthrop Publishers.

———, 1995. *The Rebirth of Federalism: Slouching Toward Washington.* Chatham: Chatham House.

———, 1996. "The Advent of an Ambiguous Federalism and the Emergence of New Federalism III." *Public Administration Review,* vol. 56 (May-June): 271–280.

Watts, Ronald, 1993. "Contemporary Views on Federalism." Paper presented at the Centre for Constitutional Analysis, Republic of South Africa (August 2–6), as quoted in Douglas V. Verney (1995), "Federalism, Federative Systems, and Federations: The United States, Canada, and India." *Publius: The Journal of Federalism* (Spring): 81–97.

Werlin, Herbert H., 1970. "Elasticity of Control: An Analysis of Decentralization," *Journal of Comparative Administration.* vol. 2 (August): 185–209.

Wheare, K. C., 1953. *Federal Government.* 3d ed. London: Oxford University Press.

Wildavsky, Aaron, 1979. "A Bias Toward Federalism." In A. Wildavsky, *Speaking Truth to Power: The Art and Craft of Policy Analysis.* Boston: Little, Brown, pp. 142–154.

Wood, B. Dan, and Richard W. Waterman, 1994. *Bureaucratic Dynamics: The Role of Bureaucracy in a Democracy.* Boulder, CO: Westview Press.

Wright, Deil S., 1988. *Understanding Intergovernmental Relations.* 3d ed. Pacific Grove, CA: Brooks-Cole Publishing.

———, 1990. "Federalism, Intergovernmental Relations, and Intergovernmental Management: Historical Reflections and Conceptual Comparisons." *Public Administration Review,* vol. 50 (March-April) 168–178.

Zimmerman, Joseph F., 1992. *Contemporary American Federalism: The Growth of National Power.* New York: Praeger.

FEDERATED FUND-RAISING.

The raising of money for numerous charities through one combined communitywide campaign, rather than through multiple solicitations by the various charities throughout the year. The federation then distributes the funds to its member charity organizations, in accordance with federation policies and procedures.

Origin and Subsequent History

American philanthropy has been strongly influenced by Judeo-Christian values. The Judaic culture emphasized responsibility not only to oneself but also to the community. Charity to the poor was encouraged through religious instruction and taxes. Christianity preached charity and relief of the poor. One's fate at the final judgment was based upon how one treated the needy. Those with excess worldly goods were encouraged to share with the underprivileged.

A tradition of private philanthropy developed quickly in colonial America due primarily to the Protestant ethic of charitable giving. Churches collected taxes for the relief of poor congregation members. Donations to charity were a way to alleviate guilt related to materialism and conspicuous wealth. Furthermore, donations were viewed as a means to personal salvation. Thus, charity was considered a relationship between giver and receiver that was good for both parties.

In colonial America, partnerships between the public and private sectors were a common arrangement for raising funds for human service programs such as orphanages, as well as for educational programs, libraries, and firefighting services. Later in the nineteenth century, the emerging captains of industry, men like Carnegie and Rockefeller, gave significant portions of their massive wealth to social welfare projects. These enormous charitable gifts from industrial philanthropists generated much public attention and goodwill for the donor.

Charity Organization Societies

Federated fund-raising resulted, in part, from the Charity Organization Society movement, which began in England in 1869. The first Charity Organization Society was established in the United States in Buffalo, New York, by an Episcopal clergyman, the Reverend Stephen Gurten. The year was 1877.

The idea spread, with charity organization societies established in several cities, including Boston (1879) and

New York (1882). A major objective of these societies was to organize in a systematic fashion the activities of the numerous charities in each community. They sought to develop a solidarity in the community regarding charitable efforts. This approach to philanthropy contrasted with indiscriminate and unorganized giving to the poor. The charity organization societies collected information on individuals in need and community service agencies in an effort to confirm individual need, make referrals to appropriate services, and document overall community needs. In so doing, the charity organization societies hoped to increase charitable giving in each community.

Community Chest Development

The origin of the community chest (today called United Way) is traced to the Charity Organization Society of Denver, Colorado, in 1887. Considered to be the first federated fund-raising organization in America, the Denver agency centrally organized fund-raising for several community charitable agencies. Although the community's religious leaders played the leading role in establishing the organization, the effort was supported by community business people. Similar organizations were developed in Boston (1895), and in Cincinnati (1896) and Cleveland (1913), Ohio.

The federated fund-raising organization in Cleveland, called the Cleveland Federation for Charity and Philanthropy, became a leader in organized charity in the United States. Far more than the Denver organization, the one in Cleveland was the result of the efforts of local business leaders. It further developed the Charity Organization Society model in that the federation required good management practice and cooperation from charitable agencies in return for admission to, and the support of, the federation.

The community chest movement built upon these earlier models of organized charity. Community chests gained momentum from the success of national campaigns to sell war bonds and to support agencies providing assistance to servicemen and their families. The first such agency was the Red Cross in 1917. A later campaign in 1918 created a "war chest" for seven other national voluntary organizations: the Young Men's and Young Women's Christian Associations (YMCA and YWCA respectively), Salvation Army, National Catholic War Council, Jewish Welfare Board, Playground and Recreation Association, and American Library Association. In that same year, the Rochester (New York) War Chest became the first organization to use the name "community chest."

Postwar community chests grew to total 363 in 1930. The chests were a vehicle for local merchant and manufacturing groups to mobilize funds for charity. The reasons for this were many. Business groups saw private charity as a preferred option to the higher taxes and political patronage associated with public agencies. Some recognized the public relations benefits of philanthropy. Others participated for religious reasons or for social status. Still others may have provided support in hope that philanthropy diffused social criticism and unrest.

Another reason for the popularity of community chests with American business was that community chests reflected the concept of scientific philanthropy. The chests provided a means to assess community needs and services systematically. Businesses as single entities lacked these social assessment and evaluation skills. Requests for support by local organizations could be investigated and evaluated for credibility in a manner similar to the charity organization society's investigation of individual need. The financial and other technical skills of the business community were utilized in doing so. The systemic perspective of the chests allowed business and professional leaders to identify duplication of effort and opportunities for service partnerships. Thus community chests were an instrument for community organization by American business.

The community chests provided business groups with a vehicle for community organization in another important way. The federated fund-raising drive proved to be an efficient, well-organized method of raising support for needed services. Instead of responding to multiple requests for donations throughout the year, the federated campaign solicited funds in a single communitywide drive.

In addition to the efficiency gained through a single campaign, business groups derived direct benefit to themselves through support of community chests. Businesses received a quid pro quo in that community chest services enhanced community living conditions, attracted skilled labor, reduced labor turnover, and relieved them of the responsibility of providing certain industrial welfare services directly. In this last case, company employees often utilized services provided by business donations to community chests.

During the 1930s, business executives began giving directly from corporate funds. In 1935, legislation was passed that recognized the right of corporations to make gifts. Corporations were allowed to deduct up to 5 percent of taxable income for charity. Expecting to benefit from the new law, the Association of Community Chests and Councils lobbied strenuously for its passage. With this legislative boost, the number of community chests expanded to 561 in 1940, and then to 1,318 in 1950. During the late 1940s, community chests began to be called "United Funds." This newest transformation included access by federated agencies to the workplace. In this way, business leaders in U.S. corporations encouraged their employees to give to the United Fund also.

Shifting Priorities in Federated Giving

Experiences of the Great Depression, New Deal, and World War II prompted American business to develop new priorities for charitable contributions during the 1950s. Corporations began directing philanthropic dollars to other community groups in addition to traditional health and human service recipients of the United Fund.

This transition was facilitated by the 1953 ruling of the Supreme Court of New Jersey, which legitimized corporate charitable giving, not only in the traditional terms of direct benefit to the corporation but also in terms of the broad social responsibility of corporations to the nation. Previous to this ruling, corporate charitable gifts could be legally justified to stockholders only if the donation was a direct worker benefit, such as YMCAs providing housing for railroad workers. The ruling interpreted direct benefit to mean a benefit to the free enterprise system and not solely to the corporation or its employees. Thus, a legal precedent was set for business giving to a wider range of causes including educational, cultural, and artistic organizations.

Corporate Social Responsibility

There were several underlying reasons for increased corporate giving to groups other than health and human services participating in the United Fund. First, there was an increasing awareness by corporate America of its responsibilities to a wide range of community groups. The Great Depression and resultant New Deal of President Franklin Roosevelt fundamentally challenged the trustee role of business management in American society. Throughout the 1930s, the business sector faced resentful, hostile public opinion as a result of the collapsed economy and widespread suffering. The New Deal legislation of Franklin Roosevelt, instituted to address the massive economic and social welfare crisis of the Great Depression, was perceived by business as an enormous threat to the free market system. In addition to the unprecedented increase in the federal government's responsibility for national social welfare, the business sector feared future increases in government regulation of its activity. Thus business was presented with the option of acknowledging its broader social welfare responsibilities on a voluntary basis or through increased government regulation.

The business sector responded to the prospect of further regulation with a renewed emphasis on management professionalism and corporate social responsibility. The idea of business management as the trustee for society at large was increasingly stressed. Business management was seen as a mediator between multiple groups in its environment, groups such as: stockholders, employees, customers, government, and communities. Furthermore, corporate management, to an ever greater extent, was held accountable by this broad range of stakeholders. Corporate stakeholders viewed American business as a quasi-public institution.

Business Management Professionalization

A second major reason for increased corporate contributions to groups other than health and human services agencies typically found in the United Fund was the growing dependence of the business sector in higher education. Higher education has been the most successful competitor to health and human services for corporate philanthropy since the end of World War II. Management of increasingly complex American industries demanded specialized training in a growing number of functions. As an emerging profession, business management required a quality system of higher education. This requirement was reinforced by the Allied victory in World War II, which was credited in part to American educational advances in science, engineering, and organizational development. Therefore, the importance of education to business was unquestionably established.

More Highly Educated Workforce

A third reason for changing priorities in corporate charitable contributions was related to the growing impact of higher education on American communities. A more educated American workforce created a growing demand for intellectual and cultural amenities, particularly in industrial centers. Corporate charity to health and human services had long been justified by the direct benefit doctrine. For example, employees needed the services provided through the community chest. In contrast, the services demanded by a more educated, increasingly white-collar workforce were libraries, museums, theaters and orchestras. As earlier, with health and human service giving, the justification for corporate giving to artistic and civic groups was that these community amenities benefited company employees directly. Corporations competing for the best and brightest minds in a mobile job market understood the importance of their community's cultural amenities in attracting professional talent to their business.

In addition, increased support of civic and cultural programs by corporations provided enormous public relations benefits. The opening of new performing arts centers, museums, and the like, produced much media coverage and community pride, which, in turn, enhanced the community image of sponsoring corporations. To the extent that public relations is the objective of corporate philanthropy, the corporation received more benefits for dollars expended.

Increased Philanthropic Competition

A final cause of increased corporate allocations to groups other than health and human services was the increased community competition for corporate support. Historically, donations from wealthy individuals and families had been a major source of support for higher education and civic and cultural groups. Corporations were replacing family-owned businesses as the primary generators of wealth in an increasingly advanced industrial economy. This fact, combined with higher taxes on private fortunes, made corporations and their employees an attractive new and, at times, the only fund-raising option for many community groups. The result has been that community groups rely increasingly on corporations, rather than wealthy philanthropists, for support.

Furthermore, competition for corporate philanthropy was fueled by a substantial increase in the number of nonprofit organizations in the 1960s and 1970s. Many were social action and advocacy oriented groups. During the 1970s and 1980s, these competing groups, organizations such as the Black United Fund, began to challenge United Way for employee giving in the workplace. Today, employees are increasingly requesting a choice in their donations to specific federations, member organizations, and causes.

Underlying Theoretical Framework

Federated fund-raising is an organized method for promoting private philanthropy—particularly in the workplace of business and other professional groups. Philanthropy can be understood on the basis of "social exchange theory." The theory provides a broad perspective through which philanthropic behavior can be examined. It stresses that no social exchange is ever purely altruistic, that seemingly one-way transfers of goods or services are, in fact, two-way exchanges based on a rational and self-interested decision-making.

P. M. Blau (1964) has defined "social exchange" as actions that are contingent on rewarding reactions from others and that cease when these expected reactions are not forthcoming. In other words, it is any behavior that is motivated by an expected return benefit from another. Blau elaborated several concepts that expand upon this definition of social exchange and that can be used to relate social exchange theory to philanthropy. The first is "reciprocity" (Blau 1964, p. 92). In a social exchange, one participant voluntarily provides a rewarding service to a second. The recipient is then obligated to provide a future benefit, in turn, to the first participant in the exchange. This future obligation is reinforced by a societal norm of reciprocity. That is, standard societal conduct creates an expectation that a benefit will be returned.

The exact nature of the return is further defined by the standard of "comparative expectation" (Blau 1964, p. 146). The term refers to the comparison of rewards and costs to each participant in a social exchange. Given unlimited needs and limited resources, the rational participant will choose those exchanges that maximize the difference between expected rewards and expected costs to the participant. When both parties believe this to be the case, an exchange takes place.

Social exchange, by definition, primarily involves extrinsic rewards, although intrinsic benefits may also be present (Blau 1964, p. 89). Intrinsic rewards are inherently gratifying. A donation given as a moral obligation with no expectation of a return is intrinsically rewarding. It is an end in itself. With extrinsic rewards, the relationship is a means to some further end. A return benefit is expected. Extrinsic rewards, like increased business sales, can be distinguished in concrete terms from the exchange relationship itself. As such, extrinsic rewards constitute objective criteria for comparing and choosing exchanges.

The preceding historical overview showed that business professionals have always expected an extrinsic return from contributions. During the direct benefit era, the extrinsic return was direct and specific. After the 1953 ruling, when companies were legally permitted to contribute to broader causes, the extrinsic return was often more general, for example, world peace. Thus a legal basis was established for business support of a wide array of federated fund-raising organizations.

Current Practice in Federated Fund-Raising

There are a great variety of national and international federations operating today in the late 1990s. Organizations and their employees have many choices for their donations. The major federations, including the various causes and services supported by each federation, are described as follows.

- *The American Red Cross* provides such services as disaster relief, emergency communications to the military and their families, veteran's programs, health and safety courses, blood services, and international aid.
- *Animal Funds of America* supports programs that protect pets, wildlife, and endangered species. The federation teaches people to treat animals with respect and promotes the humane training of animals as companions for needy people. Individual organizations that receive funds include the American Humane Association, the Guide Dog Foundation for the Blind, and People for the Ethical Treatment of Animals.
- *Children's Charities of America* provides services to feed, educate, protect, and care for children in the United States and internationally. Member agencies include the Adoption Exchange, the Children's Defense Fund, and Feed the Children.
- *Christian Service Organizations of America* funds Christian organizations providing services to the needy all over the world. Member organizations include the Christian Legal Society, Rescue Missions, International Union of Gospel Missions, and World Impact.
- *The Combined Federal Campaign* raises funds from federal employees in the United States for distribution to various other federations and individual charities. Potential recipients include United Way of America, the National Black United Federation of Charities, and Earth Share.

- *Earth Share* funds organizations working to protect the world's natural resources. Member organizations include the African Wildlife Foundation, the Clean Water Fund, and the National Audubon Society.
- *Human and Civil Rights Organizations of America* supports organizations that address the following issues: racial discrimination, religious bigotry, hate crimes, and unfair sex bias. Federation members include the American Civil Liberties Union Foundation, the Anti-Defamation League, and the Indian Law Resource Center.
- *Independent Charities of America* funds organizations providing food services to the hungry, shelter for the homeless, protection for children, and health care for the sick. Member charities include AIDS National Interfaith Network, American Public Radio, and the Family Violence Prevention Fund.
- *International Service Agencies* allocates funds to international organizations addressing issues such as refugee shelter, disaster relief, community development, blindness prevention, children services, and world peace. Organizations included in this federation include Children International, Helen Keller International, and the International Youth Foundation.
- *Medical Research Agencies of America* funds research on the prevention and cure of diseases like AIDS, arthritis, cancer, diabetes, heart disease, and herpes. Member organizations include the Diabetes Action Research and Education Foundation, the National Jewish Center for Immunology and Respiratory Medicine, and the Breast Cancer Foundation.
- *Military, Veterans, and Patriotic Public Service Organizations of America* funds organizations that provide services to veterans and their families. Organizations that receive support through this federation include the Air Force Memorial Foundation, the American Defense Institute, and the Marine Corps Scholarship Foundation, Inc.
- *The National Black United Federation of Charities* distributes funds to community agencies serving African Americans. Recipient organizations include the Black Women's Agenda, the Congress of National Black Churches, and the National Black Media Coalition.
- *National/United Service Agencies* funds organizations that address a variety of problems, including neighborhood development, human rights, medical research, and veteran's services. Member organizations include Amnesty International of the USA, the National Right to Life Educational Trust Fund, and the National Abortion and Reproductive Rights Action League Foundation.
- *National Voluntary Health Agencies* supports health organizations serving federal employees and their families through research, patient and community services, and public and professional education. Member

agencies include the Alzheimer's Association, the AMC Cancer Research Center, and the American Cancer Society.
- *The United Way of America,* in affiliation with its local chapters, allocates funds for health and human services such as child care, alcohol and drug abuse prevention, homeless shelters, and elder programs. Individual charities that receive United Way funds include Camp Fire, Inc., Goodwill Industries of America, Inc., and the YMCA of the USA.
- *The USO* provides the military community with such programs as foreign language classes, libraries, child care, educational workshops, and scholarship funds.
- *Women's Charities of America* funds agencies that empower women in dealing with issues such as discrimination, poverty, abuse, and injustice. Specific recipients include the YWCA of the USA, the National Organization for Women (Now) Legal Defense and Education Fund, and the National Coalition Against Domestic Violence.
- *World Service Organizations of America* addresses issues such as poverty, hunger, disease, economic opportunity, environmental protection, and world peace. Organizations receiving support include the American Friends Service Committee, the Food First-Institute for Food and Development Policy, and the International Voluntary Services, Inc.

JERRY D. MARX

BIBLIOGRAPHY

Blau, P. M., 1964. *Exchange and Power in Social Life.* New York: Wiley and Sons, Inc.
Brilliant, E. L., 1990. *The United Way: Dilemmas of Organized Charity.* New York: Columbia.
Combined Federal Campaign, 1995. *A World Of Difference.* Newark, NJ: Author.
Heald, M., 1988. *The Social Responsibilities of Business.* New Brunswick, NJ: Transaction, Inc.
Heath, A., 1976. *Rational Choice and Social Exchange.* New York: Cambridge University Press.
Homans, G. C., 1961. *Social Behaviour: Its Elementary Forms.* London: Routledge and Kegan Paul.
Leiby, J., 1978. *A History of Social Welfare and Social Work in the United States.* New York: Columbia.
Thibaut, J. W., and H. H. Kelley, 1959. *The Social Psychology of Groups.* New York: Wiley.

FEMINIST THEORY OF PUBLIC ADMINISTRATION.

The theory that interprets or explains public administration or its various aspects from a feminist perspective. Although feminism includes a wide range of viewpoints, most, if not all, feminists maintain a critical perspective on women's current economic and social status and prospects, employ gender as a central element in social analysis, and are committed to the idea that men and women should share equally "in the work, in the privileges, in the defining and the dreaming of the world" (Lerner 1984, p. 33). Feminist theories of public administration, then, use gender as a lens through which to analyze critically women's current status and role in public agencies, bring to light ways in which gender bias inhabits ideas and practices in the field, and formulate new theoretical approaches.

Two types of feminist theory can be observed in the literature of public administration. Descriptive theory, based on empirical study, reports on how gender influences current practice in public agencies, especially its effect on women's access to and status in public agency employment, and sometimes attempts to account for observed differences between men's and women's employment experiences. Conceptual theory aims to use gender to rethink the existing philosophy of public administration, focusing on such issues as the politics-administration dichotomy, public bureaucratic structure and practice, the bases for defending the legitimacy of the administrative state, professionalism, leadership, and citizenship in public administration. Initial feminist theorizing in public administration was largely descriptive; more recent literature includes both descriptive and conceptual theories.

Descriptive Theories

In comparison to closely related fields such as political science and business management, public administration was relatively slow to develop feminist perspectives, but beginning in the mid-1970s work began to appear that documented federal, state, and local government discrimination against women in public employment. This early work notably included a 1976 symposium in *Public Administration Review* edited by Nesta M. Gallas on "Women in Public Administration." Gallas was serving at the time as the first female president of the American Society for Public Administration (ASPA). In addition to two articles assessing the status of women in ASPA itself, the symposium included analyses of why so few women had by that time managed to land top jobs in federal agencies; the role of affirmative action in overcoming employment discrimination against women; strategies to help women administrators perform effectively; and the idea of women's rights as a basis for public policy.

Other examples of early feminist critiques of the status of women in public employment include Lorraine D. Eyde (1973), "The Status of Women in State and Local Government," in which she critically examined the segregation of women in low-level jobs, and Judith Mohr (1973), "Why Not More Women City Managers?" in which she found only seven women out of more than 2,300 city managers.

Debra Stewart (1990) reviewed a number of quantitative analyses of the proportions of women found at various grade levels in public agencies and found that in the 1980s there was a shift in quantitative analysis from a straightforward description of public executives' roles to an investigation and understanding of the important differences between male and female executives' attitudes about their work and how they achieve advancement; thus understanding the forces that drive them, in order to better predict alternative strategies for change.

An example of the type of comparative analysis referred to by Stewart is Mary E. Guy's edited collection (1992), which presents results of several studies finding consistent differences between the status of men and women managers in the governments of six states with widely varying political cultures, thus suggesting the persistence of factors that work against the equality of women in public employment. The articles in the collection, reflecting the focus on differences between men's and women's status characteristic of descriptive feminist theory, cover career patterns, personal characteristics, the impact of domestic responsibilities on individuals' ability to cope with work demands, mentoring, sexual harassment, and management style preferences and behaviors. Guy has concluded: "Only through a process of significant change and reform can we expect to see a more equitable balance between the numbers of female and male managers in state agencies" (p. 211). Her recommended strategies include job enrichment for women managers, mentoring, eliminating sexual harassment, job restructuring to facilitate family obligations, and promoting child care and family leave policies.

Conceptual Theories

Descriptive theories take for granted existing modes of thought in public administration and examine the extent to which women have gained access to the world of practice, but conceptual theories call into question the frameworks within which public administration is typically understood. The basic premise of conceptual feminist theories is that existing perspectives, for all their apparent objectivity, contain hidden gender biases. Taking gender into account, therefore, involves more than simply adding women to public agencies; instead it entails rethinking fundamental theoretical assumptions, approaches, and concepts.

An early example of this approach to the theory of public administration is that of Robert B. Denhardt and Jan Perkins (1976), who argued that mainstream organizational analysis works from within a paradigm in which the reigning means-ends model of rationality, though purportedly universal-neutral, is in actuality culturally masculine. Denhardt and Perkins suggested that feminist theory provides an alternative paradigm in which process replaces task as the primary orientation, and hierarchy is challenged by an egalitarian framework. They noted that simply adding women to public organizations will not be enough to dislodge the "administrative man" paradigm; instead, a change of consciousness is necessary, one that replaces traditional ideas of professional expertise with the feminist notion of the authority of personal experience as the ethical basis of administrative practice.

Kathy Ferguson (1984) expanded the idea that liberal reforms, such as increasing the number of women in management positions, is not enough to end gender bias in public administration; real change entails a new approach grounded in the historical-cultural experiences of women. Ferguson argued that to encounter bureaucracy on its own terms, such as by integrating women into public organizations, precludes a decisive attack on typical bureaucratic patterns of hierarchy. Only women's "marginal" perspective, which has emerged as a result of their historical exclusion from the public realm, offers the hope of real transformation, redefining notions of power, rationality, and leadership. As Ferguson has noted, "To challenge bureaucracy in the name of the values and goals of feminist discourse is to undermine the chain of command, equalize the participants, subvert the monopoly of information and secrecy of decision-making, and essentially seek to democratize the organization" (pp. 208–209).

Suzanne Franzway, Dianne Court, and R. W. Connell (1989) brought feminist theory to bear on the idea of the bureaucratic state, viewing it as an agent in sexual politics, maintaining and perpetuating through its policies gender bias in society at large and, in turn, being shaped by this bias. The bureaucratic state, in other words, is not "outside" society but enmeshed in it, including its patterns of gender relations. The authors maintained that no theory of the state can avoid issues of sex and gender; they are present, if not always visible, as grounding assumptions or limitations to argument. The bureaucratic state supports the interests of men over those of women not only directly through policies but also ideologically, through characterizing what are actually gender-biased state processes as being simply impersonal and neutral.

Camilla Stivers (1993) presented a feminist reading of the literature on the legitimacy of the administrative state, a central theme of current public administration scholarship. She argued that ideas of expertise, leadership, and virtue that mark defenses of administrative power have culturally masculine features that privilege masculinity over femininity. This characteristic masculinity of public administration, though ignored by most theorists, contributes to and is sustained by gender bias in society at large. In Stivers' (1993) view, "As long as we go on viewing the enterprise of administration as genderless, women will continue to face their present Hobson's choice, which is either to adopt a masculine administrative identity or accept marginalization in the bureaucratic hierarchy" (p. 10).

Even though scholars of public administration tend to praise its differences from private business, Stivers argued,

the publicness of public administration is problematic because of the historical and theoretical exclusion of women from the public sphere, which has barred issues such as the division of household labor from policy debate. The administrative state can only function as it does because women bear a lopsided share of the burden of domestic work, without which society would grind to a halt; thus public administrative structures and practices depend for their coherence and their effectiveness on the oppression of women.

Conceptual theorists agree that simply adding women to the bureaucracy will not be enough to end enduring patterns of gender bias; instead, new modes of thought are required, ones that call into question the neutrality of such central ideas as professionalism, leadership, and the public interest. The extent to which administrative agency policies and practices can change will also depend partly on such larger social transformations as the sexual division of labor in the household, a sphere that shapes and is shaped by the administrative state.

Future feminist theorizing in public administration is likely to continue to proceed on both descriptive and conceptual fronts; and indeed, careful empirical study of existing practices in government agencies and conceptual deconstruction and reconstruction reinforce one another. Empirical data on the status of women in public administration have the potential to reshape understanding of issues and justify the need for conceptual transformation, and new, gender-conscious modes of thought can revamp field research approaches in fruitful ways, opening researchers' eyes to new questions and new forms of evidence. Empirical and conceptual work in this area to date strongly suggests not only that gender is a cutting edge issue in public administration but also that there is a great deal of work still to be done.

CAMILLA STIVERS

BIBLIOGRAPHY

Denhardt, Robert B., and Jan Perkins, 1976. "The Coming Death of Administrative Man." *Public Administrative Review,* vol. 36, no. 4 (July-August): 379–384.

Eyde, Lorraine, D., 1973. "The Status of Women in State and Local Government." *Public Personnel Management* (May-June): 205–211.

Ferguson, Kathy E., 1984. *The Feminist Case Against Bureaucracy.* Philadelphia: Temple University Press.

Franzway, Suzanne, Dianne Court, and R. W. Connell, eds., 1989. *Staking a Claim: Feminism, Bureaucracy, and the State.* Sydney, Australia: Allen and Unwin.

Gallas, Nesta M., ed., 1976. "A Symposium: Women in Public Administration." *Public Administration Review,* vol. 36, no. 4 (July-August): 347–389.

Guy, Mary E., ed., 1992. *Women and Men of the States: Public Administrators at the State Level.* Armonk, NY: M. E. Sharpe.

Hall, Mary M., and Rita Mae Kelly, eds., 1989. *Gender, Bureaucracy, and Democracy: Careers and Equal Opportunity in the Public Sector.* Westport, CT: Greenwood Press.

Lerner, Gerda, 1984. "The Rise of Feminist Consciousness." In
E. M. Bender, B. Burk, and N. Walker, eds., *All of Us Are
Present.* Columbia, MO: James Madison Wood Research In-
stitute, Stephens College.
Mohr, Judith, 1973. "Why Not More Women City Managers?"
Public Management (February-March): 2–5.
Stewart, Debra, 1990. "Women in Public Administration." In
Naomi B. Lynn, and Aaron B. Wildavsky, eds., *Public Ad-
ministration: The State of the Discipline.* Chatham, NJ:
Chatham House.
Stivers, Camilla, 1993. *Gender Images in Public Administration: Le-
gitimacy and the Administrative State.* Newbury Park, CA:
Sage.

FIELD THEORY. A method for analyzing causal
relationships and building scientific constructs. Field theory is an approach to scientific tasks, not a theory about a
realm of data. The mathematical representation of a field is
the first derivative of x at time t.

Field theory in public administration and in the social
sciences owes its origins to the natural sciences. Originally used to conceptualize electromagnetic phenomena in
physics, social scientists in psychology adapted field theory
as an alternative method for measuring causal relationships. Kurt Lewin (1952) deserves much of the credit for
developing this theory for the social sciences. Field theory
was initially proposed as an approach for problematic concepts, including frustration and need, which eluded traditional methods of analysis. In the study of public policy
and management, the use of field theory has the potential
to provide insights into problematic, situation specific incidents that elude traditional time-based methods of examination.

Most psychological analyses use a teleological method
to examine behavior, inferring the future from historical information. One of the best examples of such psychological constructs commonly used for inference is the
stimulus-response pattern. The stimulus-response pattern
establishes a time-based (historical) link between the initiating element and its consequence. Field theory does not
rely on such measures of the past and present to make inferences; instead, it emphasizes the use of a concept
termed the "present field."

Since causation happens from the interaction of forces
within the present field, one can make no inferences about
future behavior outside the present field. The use of this
approach carries with it assumptions about the nature of
the field being examined. The present field captures relevant past information and exposes information that is
unfolding in the immediate future. Since this is the case,
those employing field theory use systematic rather than
historical causation to gain inferences. This theory also relies on the idea that living systems maintain equilibrium,
which is consistent with Gestalt psychology. The analysis
focuses on a single field, and yet encompasses an entire situation.

Since its adaptation into the social sciences, field theory has been used extensively to examine the relationships
between behavior and action. In order for a researcher to
accurately measure this relationship, he or she must first
create a geometric representation of the phenomena. Lewin
has argued that this can be accomplished through the
adoption of the geometric idea called "hodological space."
Through the use of hodological space, concepts including
aspiration, frustration, and conflict can be quantified and
measured empirically. The field is then constructed from
a geometric pattern in this hodological space, and the
pattern is used to operationalize the field for analysis,
thus enabling scholars to use empirical criteria to infer cau-
sality.

Later, scholars of organizational development adopted
field theory, incorporating it into the stream of literature
known as action research. Its use (though empirically not
as rigorous as Lewin's) was justified by field theory's association with systematic action experiments in the social sciences, originated by Lewin and Dewey. Scholars of action
research support this relaxed interpretation of field theory
and the related concepts that follow it, by arguing that the
methodological relaxation corrects the problem of experimental results being disconnected from reality or being un-
interpretable.

Public administration scholars and practitioners that
specialize in organizational development reap large rewards through the "force field analysis" technique drawn
directly from action research. Field theory, as Lewin conceptualized it, though mathematically more precise in its
conception, lacks the utility of the force field analysis that
public and private organizational development practitioners use for planned change. The empirically rigorous interpretation by Lewin enables practiced researchers in public
administration to measure empirically causation based on
a field that geometrically structures a difficult behavioral
phenomenon, such as conflict, desires, and aspirations.
This technique does not enable either the organizational
development practitioner or the practiced researcher to extrapolate into the future outside the present field. Field
theory can provide empirical understanding of the phenomenon of interest. In public administration, and particularly in public management, the techniques that grew out
of field theory are useful for difficult behavioral concepts
that escape traditional methods of empirical analysis. It
also, by conception, controls for many extraneous factors
that might limit the understanding of behavioral phenomena.

ARTHUR J. SEMENTELLI

BIBLIOGRAPHY

French, Wendell L., and Cecil H. Bell, 1995. *Organization Development: Behavioral Science Interventions for Organization Improvement.* Englewood Cliffs, NJ: Prentice-Hall.

Lewin, Kurt., 1952. *Field Theory in Social Science*. London, England: Tavistock.

FILER COMMISSION.

The short-lived but extremely influential ad hoc commission constituted in 1973 to produce the first comprehensive study of the third, voluntary, or nonprofit sector. The Filer Commission is known formally as the *Commission on Private Philanthropy and Public Needs* and was convened for less than two years, from late 1973 to 1975. The commission's common name, "Filer," refers to its chair, John H. Filer, of the Aetna Life and Casualty Company, and director, at the time, of the nonprofit Hartford Institute of Criminal and Social Justice.

As a private research endeavor, the Filer Commission was constituted to fill a research vacuum at an historical point when attitudes about the nonprofit philanthropic sector were negative and when questions about its legitimacy were being raised in public policy debates. John D. Rockefeller III was among the first to recognize that public ignorance about the nonprofit voluntary sector threatened its special place and privileged status in the U.S. economic system and tax structure. The Filer Commission was established to study the role of the third sector at a time when it was being attacked by hostile forces in the Richard Nixon administration and in the U.S. Congress, and when students, faculty, and staff at a large number of nonprofit educational institutions were engaged in publicly questioning the U.S. government's policy in Vietnam (Hall 1987). Following an August 1973 meeting of tax experts, economists, and sociologists at the Brookings Institution, at the behest of Rockefeller, the Filer Commission was convened to address potential policy incursions that were considered to be potential threats to the voluntary sector.

In the Preface to Volume 1 of the Filer Commission's *Research Papers* (Commission 1977) and in reference to congressional debate over the Tax Reform Acts of 1969 and 1977, according to Rockefeller, "Public opinion respecting nonprofit institutions and their donors is not, in tax terms (at least), universally benign." To save the sector from harmful public policy, information needed to be obtained and disseminated.

Academics and practitioners were authorized to conduct research, and although the work conducted by the Filer Commission was extensive, it was never claimed to be exhaustive. Studies addressed the impact of philanthropy, the role played by the nonprofit sector, and its role in relationship to government. Filer Commission members (or those authorized by the commission) wanted to compile a reliable empirical database and to replace intuitive, often hostile or unfriendly, judgments about the nonprofit sector.

The Commission was established as a partnership, with private sector funding. It enjoyed some strong administrative support, despite the era's political tensions, and was encouraged by Treasury Department officials George P. Schultz and William E. Simon. (The United States Department of the Treasury published the five volumes of the *Commission's Papers* in 1977.)

The Filer Commission reports (as the five-volume *Research Papers* are commonly called) comprise about 91 research articles, recommendations, and commentary. Before the reports were published by the Treasury Department, however, the (Filer) Commission on Private Philanthropy and Public Needs published *Giving in America* (1975). In this slim volume the Filer Commission made recommendations to Congress and the general public about ways in which the nonprofit philanthropic sector could become more effective. (Some of these suggestions have been instituted, but, a quarter century later, others are still being debated.)

According to the Foreword to the Filer Commission's first 1977 volume *History, Trends, and Current Magnitudes,* the scope of the research was largely determined by areas of Commission interest and covered activities such as health, education, welfare, religion, culture, social action, community action, and public policy. These areas were examined in terms of past and current financing and accomplishments and expectations for the future (pp. vii–viii).

The Preface to *Giving in America* summarizes the work of the Filer Commission, which included the commissioning of a study to glean information on taxpayer attitudes and giving practices, involving lengthy interviews with almost 3,000 individuals. Philanthropic contributors and noncontributors were included in the study's sample to reflect a cross section of the American public. Other studies the Filer Commission undertook included conducting a computerized econometric analysis of tax and income data to determine the effect of charitable deductions. In addition, the Commission's analysis provided information about the potential effects of alternative proposals to increase charitable giving. The Filer Commission's researchers conducted meetings across the nation to gather information from citizens, community leaders, and technical experts. They reviewed published documents and research articles (in addition to the authorized studies) from both the formal commission and from an academic-minority report compiled by a group seeking more focus on the "donee," or the recipient, instead of the "donor," or giver.

Giving in America provides a readable synthesis of the Filer Commission's work in one small edition, but it is the research, recommendations, and extensive commentary contained in the five volumes of reports that guided its writing; thus the 1977 *Research Papers* deserve a synoptic review. Volume 1, Part 1, contains a commentary on the Commission's recommendations. In the "Donee Report" (Commission 1977, vol. 1), influenced by an article in the January 1975 issue of *Grantsmanship Center News,*

Pablo Eisenberg postulated that "the emphasis of the Commission's work was at least partly the result [of its composition] and its advisory committee.... [thus it emphasized] very disproportionately the establishment side of both the voluntary sector and philanthropic organizations" (p. 50). The Donee Report suggested that questions such as "Who gets what?" and "Do current conditions meet society's changing needs?" were either played down or were totally ignored by the Filer Commission's initial work. According to the Donee Report, recipients need to see fewer organizations shut out of the philanthropic process; there needs to be a redefinition of the donor community (to include nonitemizers, for example); and some sort of nonpartisan oversight is required.

This minority report contained contributions from 26 signatory individuals, including David Horton Smith, who at the time served as the executive director of the organization now known as the Association for Research on Nonprofit Organizations and Voluntary Action (see **ARNOVA**). In all, the Donee Report (pp. 64–85) includes seven recommendations for improving the philanthropic process, six suggestions for redefining the donor community, seven proposals for improving government regulation of philanthropy, and four recommendations for addressing the status of exempt organizations and the public policy process. This volume also provides information on social action, for example, including data on patterns of class and ethnic discrimination in private philanthropy, as well as information pertinent to the funding limitations of the women's movement.

Part 2 of the first volume of the Filer Commission's *Research Papers* covers historical trends, the size and scope of the voluntary sector, financial data from the 1890s, the results of two national surveys, information on employment and earnings, and measures of economic input and output. In addition, Volume 1, Part 2, has a study by the Interfaith Research Committee of the Filer Commission, which summarized receipts and expenditures in this subsector of the nonprofit quarter, thus helping to identify its diversity, size, scope, procedures, and attitudes.

The Commission's report, Volume 2, Part 1, "Philanthropic Fields of Interest," cover areas of activity such as higher education; nonpublic schools; public support for science; health affairs; "evolving social policy," such as early childhood education and services for the aging; social welfare; numerous case studies; and information on the arts; environmental issues; and international affairs. Also contained in this part of Volume 2 are leadership surveys; "problems and challenges"; and research on the quality of volunteer activity.

Volume 2, Part 2, "Additional Perspectives" provides what the Filer Commission calls an "Agenda for the Future"; it includes various analyses of issues such as those addressing powerlessness, including advocacy, welfare rights, hunger, and community development. Also included is

"U.S. Foundations and Minority Group Interests," and some donee perspectives regarding activist groups, federated fund-raising, and ethnic and class discrimination in the corporate and philanthropic world.

Volume 3 of *Research Papers, Special Behavioral Studies, Foundations, and Corporations,* includes in Part 1 research articles on tax incentives and charitable deductions on contributions by high-income and low- and medium-income households, and articles on estate taxation and bequests and intergenerational wealth transfers. Part 2 addresses foundations and the 1969 Tax Reform Act and its effects, foundations and spending patterns, community foundations and their roles, and charitable foundations and their governance issues.

Volume 3, Part 3, *Corporations,* explores public service activities, rationales, tax considerations, measures of corporate giving, company foundations, and gifts in kind.

Volume 4, Part 1, *Taxes,* contains articles examining the exemption and deduction criteria for various types of organizations under the Internal Revenue Service (IRS) Code, Section 501(c) (3), as well as rules and policy regarding substantive areas of nonprofit activity—such as environmental and public interest work. Section 170 of the IRS code was reviewed to consider personal deductions, the original justifications for charitable deductions, and, for example, trusts. Parts 2 through 6 of Volume 4 cover areas addressing the appreciated property deduction, volunteer services (as distinct from property), estate and gift taxes, alternatives to tax incentives (federal matching grants, for example), and the property tax.

Volume 5 of the Filer Commission *Research Papers, Regulation,* addresses in Part 1 aspects of federal oversight, the status of state regulation (in Ohio), and self-regulation. Part 2 addresses foreign practices, with specific articles on Australia, Canada, England, France, the former West Germany, Italy, Japan, and Sweden.

The research of the (Filer) Commission on Private Philanthropy and Public Needs highlighted the voluntary philanthropic sector's importance as had never before been done. The Commission's work was premised on a belief in the sector's autonomy, and this guided the formulation of some of its questions.

Research since that of the Filer Commission has shown the public and private sectors to be integrally connected. Policy initiatives directed at the public sector, with the assumption that the private, nonprofit sector will rise to meet the new fiscal challenges, are likely to fail because of the connective tissue between them (see Hall 1987, p. 22); Salamon et al. 1982; Hodgkinson and Weitzman 1984). Despite this premise of sector autonomy, the Filer Commission provided groundbreaking work, which helped academics and policymakers to identify the extent to which people rely on the nonprofit sector to provide for domestic tranquility through art and health services, for example. Its research showed the need for extra governmental organizations that speak to the interests of various distinct minorities whose needs may not be adequately addressed through majoritarian political programs. In short, it emphasized the extent of the ignorance about this sector. The (Filer) Commission on Private Philanthropy and Public Needs was established to encourage ongoing research and to focus attention on the significance of the voluntary sector. Without question the Filer Commission fulfilled this mission. Its *Research Papers* continue to serve as a baseline for investigation decades later.

ERNA GELLES

BIBLIOGRAPHY

Commission on Private Philanthropy and Public Needs, 1975. *Giving in America: Toward a Stronger Voluntary Sector: Report of the Commission on Private Philanthropy and Public Needs.* Washington, D.C.: The Commission.
———, 1977. *Research Papers,* Vols. 1–5. Washington, D.C.: Department of the Treasury, GPO.
Hall, Peter Dobkin, 1987. "A Historical Overview of the Private Nonprofit Sector," in Walter W. Powell., ed., *The Nonprofit Sector.* New Haven: Yale University Press, pp. 3–21.
Hodgkinson, Virginia, and Murray Weitzman, 1984. *Dimensions of the Independent Sector.* Washington, D.C.: Independent Sector.
Salamon, Lester M., and Alan J. Abramson, 1982. *The Federal Budget and the Nonprofit Sector.* Washington, D.C.: Urban Institute Press.
Powell, Walter W., ed., 1987. *The Nonprofit Sector: A Research Handbook.* New Haven: Yale University Press.

FINANCIAL ADMINISTRATION.
The management of financial resources, including the analysis of the fiscal impacts of policy options.

Public financial management seeks to create and preserve value in society by helping public decisionmakers and mangers (1) to make choices about how large government should be within the capacity of the overall national economy and according to the preferences of the citizenry; (2) to raise resources from private hands so that they may be put to public use, but doing so in a fashion that minimizes social and economic damage; (3) to allocate and control resources carefully when they have been moved to government supervision so that they suffer neither waste nor misappropriation; and (4) to report periodically on the financial and program results to the public, and to legislative and executive bodies, and external observers.

The aggregate resources of society are mostly in the hands of private owners. They are used in the market economy but some resources are transferred to public use by the coercive power of taxation which democratic societies allow the sovereign only under limited circumstances. Public financial management helps to see that these resources are managed at the margin to achieve the maximum benefit to society. Financial administration choices include balancing the private and public use and the alternate use and timing of use of economic resources, the manner in which the revenue system allocates the cost of public operations among sectors of the private economy, the control of public resources to prevent waste and theft, and the creation and operation of systems to provide overall protection of assets in public control.

In many respects, these tasks closely follow those practiced in the financial management of a private business. Managers try to protect and to add to the value of the private firm by judicious allocation and control of that firm's resources. Differences emerge because the nature of goods and services provided in private markets–the domain of private financial management–is fundamentally different from that of the public sector, which causes the terms of the resource constraints faced, the ownership of goods and services, and the objectives of private and public managers to differ. Many tools and skills are, however, substantially transferrable between the sectors. To understand the role and functions of public financial management these differences need to be made explicit.

Public Versus Private

Governments provide services that, although valued by people, will not be provided in socially desirable amounts by private entities, either proprietary or charitable. Government services are not uniquely essential: most governments leave things necessary to life itself–food, clothing, and shelter–largely to the private sector. Indeed, private markets handle most production and consumption choices, but, as articulated in Richard Musgrave's (1959) concept of the multiple roles of the public household, markets cannot be expected (1) to yield optimal results when the actions of one party have external effect for good or evil on others, (2) to alter inequitable income distributions in socially desirable ways, or (3) to correct problems of inflation or general unemployment that contaminate the aggregate market economy. In these respects, a private entity–which can be expected to seek the best rewards for its owners, with casual attention at best to the interests of others–will not act optimally because that entity cannot recoup the external fruits of its actions. Governments legitimately act, even in an economy driven by strong free market principles, when these circumstances create failure in market provision; public financial management helps with the information and control tasks associated with a response to those failures.

Market failure means that true prices cannot be charged for government services, so services will be financed primarily by exercise of the sovereign coercive power of taxation, not voluntary market exchange. Services may reasonably be publicly provided if their value is greater than the full resource cost of their production; but what are public services worth? Values of services cannot be deduced from what people are willing to pay for them, because private payments reflect only private value, and market failure means that there is external value. People will not willingly pay for a service when those not paying receive the service as well. Therefore, there can be no easy test of profitability (returns minus cost) to measure success or determine viability.

Contingent valuation techniques offer some promise for estimation of values of some public goods, at least in certain circumstances (Hausman 1993), but most program choices will be judgmental and political. Choices will be made by some government process, hopefully a democratic one in which people get a fair chance to have their say. Public financial management can inform these choices, which, having been made, get implemented through other processes of financial management. Therefore, government fiscal choice differs from business finance: governments may tax to enlarge their resources; many entities share a legitimate stake in government decisions; and the return from government services is neither easy to measure nor conveniently collapsible in a single value.

Values of assets and services and rates of exchange between alternatives and across time must, in a market economy, reflect the preferences of the people living in that society, not those of philosopher-bureaucrats, let alone those of public dictators. This makes the task of policymakers and of those carrying out these kinds of policies more difficult, but capturing the interest of a diverse society is what sets democratic society and governments of democracies apart (Buchanan and Tullock 1965). The process of voting and representation adds complications to fiscal decisions. Some in society can gain without compensation given to those who lose; majorities can inflict considerable cost on minorities through transfers, subsidies, taxation, and expenditure programs driven by ballot victories. It is this problem of redistribution, along with major shortages of information, that prevents public financial management from becoming a computerized routine, even if some way to measure the direct value of public services were devised.

In practice, public financial management involves a mix and merger of skills from economics, finance, and accounting to provide information and options to public decisionmakers and managers, giving service to both executive and legislative roles and responsibilities. Over the years, financial administration has evolved from government recordkeeping, documentation and control, and theft prevention to an active role in analyzing policy options, tracking likely impacts of policies under consideration, and performing complex forecasting and fiscal impact estimation. This transformation has occurred as public financial management has integrated the analytical modeling of economics and finance with tasks of control and reporting and as data became both more readily available and subject to quick manipulation through computer information management systems.

Electronic information management systems help capture and organize information, regularly monitor operations, handle laborious calculations, and devise complicated "what if" scenarios to sort the implications from options available for choice. But the technology is a tool of financial management, not the skill itself, serving to speed the processes that could be done manually and with careful human logic.

Roles and Tasks

The roles of public financial management include the future (development of spending and revenue plans and forecasts for future fiscal years), the present (delivery of services and administering revenues in the present fiscal year), and the past (audit and evaluation of the record from prior fiscal years).

Several distinct elements of government operations involve financial management. One facet is the preparation of plans for service and of revenues to finance these services. Plans and priorities for both service delivery and revenues are the province of elected officials, not financial managers. Nevertheless, the analysis used to develop these proposals will be done by fiscal analysis units at the instruction of these officials. The work may involve estimation of the finances of maintaining the present fiscal baseline in the next year, estimation of longer-term implications of continuing the current policies, with best estimates of changing workloads and economic conditions, and preparation of fiscal impact statements for proposed policy changes.

Impact statements (or "scoring," in the terminology of the federal budget process) for either spending or revenue programs may encompass (1) static estimates, the effect assuming no public response from the policy change; (2) feedback estimates, the effect from public response to the microeconomics incentives inherent in the new policy, and (3) dynamic estimates, the effect of macroeconomic change produced by the new policy. The first two elements are regularly used in fiscal analysis; the latter is significantly more controversial. Estimation of baseline programs and revenues use the standard techniques of econometric time series analysis; impact statements employ microsimulations of varying degrees of complexity and sophistication.

Another financial management element of government operations is the control and accounting of expenditure programs that have been adopted. Financial management works to insure that adopted policies are carried out by controlling expenditure flows as they occur during the fiscal year. The concerns are that spending occurs according to the legislatively adopted plan, that spending does not exceed appropriated ceilings, and that reports prepared during the year reflect the actual financial activity during the year.

Control typically employs regular variance reports in which actual and planned activities are compared and corrections are taken on the basis of differences identified there. Much spending at the federal level occurs through the application of entitlement formulae, so control must focus on formula elements, rather than operations against a formal spending plan. The internal control system within spending agencies represents the first line of defense against fraud. These systems, following the principles of the International Organization of Supreme Audit Institutions, function to safeguard assets, check the accuracy and reliability of financial data, promote operating efficiency, and encourage operation according to the standard prescribed by the agency.

Administering revenue systems to obtain funds for government operations is also a financial management task. Governments collect some revenue from sales of goods or services; for instance, when admission is charged for a state recreation area. In these circumstances, collection procedures are no different than for a private business.

But much more revenue comes from taxes. Here, the government raises revenue through its sovereign authority to coerce payment. As Carl Shoup (1969) has pointed out, taxes are administered in several different formats, distinguishable "according to the degree of participation they require of the taxpayer or his agent, and the kind of response they elicit from the taxpayer" (p. 428). Much revenue in the United States comes from taxpayer active taxes, which require considerable taxpayer responsibility and are collected under the principle of voluntary compliance. Such taxes, the federal individual income tax being an example, require considerable effort on the part of the taxpayer to manage records, make progress payments through the year, and file returns on schedule.

The efforts of the government consist of efforts to induce that compliance. For people to make payments of roughly the correct amount of tax, without direct government action, seems to be the most reasonable course of action so that all honest taxpayers are protected. Most collections result without direct government activity, however.

A few taxes, that on real property being a good example, are taxpayer passive: A government agency maintains records, computes the tax base, applies appropriate rates to yield tax liability, and transmits bills, leaving the taxpayer only to protest or pay. Either taxpayer active or taxpayer passive systems can produce equitable collection of revenue; the former involves higher compliance costs relative to administrative costs. The latter involves higher administrative costs relative to compliance costs. Neither has an automatic advantage in terms of lower total collection cost.

Low total collection cost—the sum of administrative and compliance costs—is the desired goal, but only subject to an administration that gives adequate competitive protection to honest taxpayers and inflicts no arbitrary and capricious discrimination against certain types of taxpayers in the collection process.

A fourth facet of financial management is acquiring goods and services for use during the budget period and husbanding those acquired resources against theft, waste, or misuse. Financial managers seek to procure inputs to government production at the best price to taxpayers. They attempt to arrange for external acquisition (contracting) when others can produce the decided-upon level and quality of service on better terms than the government can produce the service itself, to monitor delivery of inputs and services as purchased, and to protect any assets while in public possession. A considerable share of government spending is for human resources, so the financial manager must monitor the arrangements of public pay most carefully so that taxpayer interests can be guarded.

Management of the treasury, including use of short-term idle cash and short-term credit, is another financial management element of government. Collections are regularly quickened by electronic transfer of collections, especially for large payments; disbursements are controlled to insure accuracy and that prompt payment discounts are taken if they are advantageous, and, while cash is in the treasury between collection and disbursement, something productive is done with it.

The need for treasury management arises because timing of revenue inflows seldom matches that of government outlays. Tax collections in particular lump around periodic due dates, and capital outlays are similarly irregular. During any fiscal year, a government will have periods of net cash inflows and outflows—including periods of high idle cash balance and, often, of negative cash position, even when the government is in surplus for the year as a whole.

Financial managers have to manage the cash position, because those funds are valuable, investable public assets that can earn interest in short-term cash pool investment. But their management must insure that payments can be made when due. Liquidity and security of principal are the guides for cash management, thus barring from the treasury idle-funds management portfolio long-term instruments, derivative investments, or other media that experience considerable fluctuation in value and, hence, risk to principal when market interest rates change.

A government operation that involves financial management is the management of benefits paid employees, especially investment management of long-term assets in pension systems. Public employee compensation includes a considerable array of fringe benefits. Among the most important are health insurance and retirement programs. In common with all employers, governments have experienced considerable increase in health costs in recent years. The costs have been particularly great because governments, as a rule, provide more generous coverage than do private employers. Public employee retirement programs generally are of the defined benefit type; that is, employees earn defined benefit payments based on employment history. The employer is responsible for financing the promised future benefits; logic of efficiency and equity suggests that the employer meet these payments in the future from funds set aside during the employee's work life (when the liability for the pension was incurred) so that the cohort of citizens receiving the benefits of that work bear the full cost, wage plus promised benefits, of that work. Any benefit payments not available from that accumulated fund will have to be met from taxpayers in the future. When sufficient assets have been set aside to meet those anticipated future liabilities, the pension system is fully funded. Unfortunately, few public employee pension funds are fully funded, but they do contain sizable asset balances.

Politicians often see these funds as "free money," usable as a slush fund for projects that are locally popular but unlikely to be undertaken by a prudent investor. Furthermore, to miss a scheduled pension fund payment is a frequent strategy when a government is experiencing fiscal stress. Failure to meet pension fund contributions is the equivalent of borrowing to support current expenditure and has the same impact on the long-term fiscal condition of the entity.

Management of debt issued for long-term asset acquisition is yet another management task. Governments regularly borrow to finance the purchase of high-price, long-life assets. When the service of the debt is managed across the years in rough match to the useful life of the project being financed, severe fluctuations in local tax rates during infrastructure development will be reduced. Government finances will not be unduly stretched in periods of such development, and taxpayers in the system at the time of project development do not bear excessive burdens in comparison to those receiving services when the project is in full service. Debt managers work to ensure that debt maturity is no longer than the useful life of the project being financed. They try to see to it that debt service guarantees (insurance, bank letters of credit, etc.) are acquired when their premiums are justified by resulting reductions in service costs that buying the guarantee brings, that agents (underwriters, paying agents, financial advisers, etc.) are retained on best terms for the issuer, that bond features (call provisions, serial structures, etc.) are tailored to reduce overall cost, and so on. Strong overall financial management reduces interest cost by improving the ratings on debt as evaluated by the private rating firms that report their estimates of credit worthiness to capital markets.

Government financial management entails the control of risks and use of insurance against potential liability, including the judicious use of self-insurance. Government operations offer abundant opportunities for hazard to people and property. Reducing loss potential can reduce the cost of providing public services. Tasks of risk management involve control of risk by avoiding, preventing, and reducing conditions that can produce loss and then insuring the risk of loss, which cannot be eliminated. The insurance may be either self-provided (with formal reserve funds, or informally by providing no coverage) or purchased from an outside provider. A number of governments have formed insurance pools, essentially establishing combined self-insurance programs as a risk-sharing alternative to private insurance. The risk-management program seeks to protect the citizenry and public resources against loss in a fashion that combines loss reduction with sufficient insurance to cover when loss occurs.

Government financial management operations entail the audit and evaluation of operations at the end of fiscal periods for compliance and accomplishment. Audits seek to establish whether governments have done what they promised when fiscal plans were enacted. Financial and compliance audits examine and verify financial transactions and reports, seeking to establish the fairness of those reports, whether transactions have been properly conducted, and whether the unit has complied with all applicable law. Economy and efficiency audits examine whether the unit has made wise use of resources under its control and seeks uneconomical practices. Program audits consider whether desired results are being accomplished and whether alternatives might achieve the result at lower cost.

Conclusion

Fiscal administration is the practice of balance and control within the guidance of elected representatives. Financial managers are responsible for analysis, control, and reporting, but the resources involved belong to the public. Public financial management, even when operating with broad discretion, advises and implements policies chosen by others. The choices that must be made involve the balancing of opportunity costs, that is, comparing the gain from one action against the gain that could result if that action were not taken. This is the essence of advising the movement of resources from private to public use, of choices between alternative public uses of resources, of deciding between purchasing insurance and using self-insurance, of opting for pay-as-you-use instead of pay-as-you-go finance of capital assets, and so on. The hard part is getting the trade-offs calibrated so that the choices made by elected officials are likely to be made in the public interest.

When a choice has been made, the problem becomes one of delivery and control. Decisions are irrelevant if attention is not paid to whether the decision is carried out according to the adopted plan. Financial administration works to assure accurate reports, timely comparisons of results against intentions, and implementation of corrections if there is variance. Financial administration, by identifying the trades and maintaining control, plays a critical role both in the process of making policy and in the implementation of those adopted policies.

JOHN L. MIKESELL

BIBLIOGRAPHY

Aronson, J. Richard, and Eli Schwartz, 1987. *Management Policies in Local Government Finance.* Washington, DC: International City Management Association.

Buchanan, James M., and Gordon Tullock, 1965. *The Calculus of Consent:* Ann Arbor, MI: Ann Arbor Paperbacks.

Coe, Charles K., 1989. *Public Financial Management.* Englewood Cliffs, NJ: Prentice-Hall.

Hausman, Jerry A., ed., 1993. *Contingent Valuation: A Critical Assessment.* New York: North Holland.

Internal Control Standards Committee, International Organization of Supreme Audit Institutions, 1992. *Guidelines for Internal Control Standards.* Washington, DC: International Organization of Supreme Audit Institutions.

Mikesell, John L., 1995. *Fiscal Administration, Analysis and Applications for the Public Sector.* Belmont, CA: Wadsworth.

Musgrave, Richard A., 1959. *The Theory of Public Finance.* New York: McGraw-Hill.

Petersen, John E., and Dennis R. Strachota, eds., 1991. *Local Government Finance, Concepts and Practices.* Chicago: Government Finance Officers Association.

Shoup, Carl S., 1969. *Public Finance.* Chicago: Aldine.

Steiss, Alan Walter, 1989. *Financial Management in Public Organizations.* Pacific Grove, CA: Brooks Cole.

FINANCIAL EMERGENCY. A legal condition more severe than fiscal stress, but not so severe as to cause municipalities to declare bankruptcy or default on contractual obligations to repay borrowed funds. A financial emergency assumes that a municipality will take appropriate corrective action to prevent bankruptcy or defaults.

A financial emergency is more serious than fiscal stress. A government under fiscal stress faces budget cuts, revenue increases, and changes in how it carries out its core responsibilities. Although many municipalities have dealt with bouts of fiscal stress, few have confronted a true financial emergency (Advisory Commission on Intergovernmental Relations 1973, 1985).

For our purposes, a financial emergency is a legal condition. In the United States, federal law provides a legal avenue for municipalities to use for declaring bankruptcy, if permitted by state law. An example is the wealthy area of Orange County, California. It filed for legal bankruptcy on 6 December 1994 because of poorly conceived investment practices. Federal law prescribes the resolution of a bankruptcy.

The second condition deals with a *default* of contractual provisions to repay borrowed funds (see entry for **defaults, municipal**). In 1979, Cleveland, Ohio, defaulted when it could not repay one-year loans backed by the full faith and credit taxing power of the city. For bonds backed by dedicated project revenues, indentures accompanying the bonds clarify the legal rights and responsibilities of bondholders.

Under the third condition, state laws specify the terms of a financial emergency. It is the third definition reviewed here. Specifically, this entry uses the state of Ohio's fiscal emergency law to illustrate how a state can respond to municipal fiscal inadequacy. Other state experiences provide useful comparisons.

In Ohio, there are six legal criteria, and failure of any single one requires the state to declare the municipality in a condition of fiscal emergency. The first two tests represent failures to meet obligations to other parties: a default in payment to debt holders, and the failure to issue a payroll to employees when due. Four others represent the lack of adequate fiscal controls, including insufficient cash to meet current obligations, excessive deficits, excessive past due accounts payable, and excessive unvoted debt. More specifically, Chapter 118 of the *Ohio Revised Code* specifies that any one of the following constitutes a fiscal emergency condition of a municipal corporation:

1. a default for more than 30 days;
2. failure for lack of funds to make all payroll payments to municipal employees within 30 days of when payment is due;
3. an increase in the municipality's minimum tax levy, affecting the levy of another political unit;
4. overdue accounts payable of the general fund from the preceding fiscal year exceeding one-twelfth of the general fund budget, or overdue accounts payable from all funds exceeding one-twelfth of the revenues for the general fund and special funds;
5. an aggregate deficit in all deficit accounts, less cash balances, which can be used to meet the deficits, exceeding one-twelfth of the year's general fund budget and receipts to the deficit funds for that year;
6. the amount in the unsegregated treasury is insufficient to meet the purposes of the general fund and special funds and the deficiency exceeds one-twelfth of the total amount received into the treasury during the year.

A municipality may fail certain tests at year-end, but correct its fiscal behavior in time to avoid entangling itself in the legal control. For example, existence of any year-end condition in tests four, five, or six is not a fiscal emergency if the condition no longer exists at the time of the fiscal emergency audit. It might appear that the best time to assess a city's fiscal emergency status is at the time of a regular year-end financial audit, but fiscal problems may emerge earlier in the year. Ohio law requires calculations at the prior year-end and at the time of the fiscal emergency audit. So, if the municipality had corrected its behavior by the later date, the fact that it had an earlier failure is not sufficient to justify invoking the law's remedial powers.

Although the state fiscal emergency conditions clarify unacceptable local fiscal behavior, the law is indifferent on the cause(s). The emergency could be due to long-term economic deterioration or to the inattention of local officials to make a debt payment on schedule. Regardless, the fiscal emergency law is a remedial action to restore a municipality's fiscal integrity.

State Response

Why does a state assume a special burden when one of its local governments runs into financial trouble? A state cannot afford a market perception that it allows its local governments to follow a callous approach to fiscal stewardship. The market associates the state with its local governments. For this and other reasons, some states have found it in their interest to take steps to deal with local fiscal problems. The states of New York, Ohio, and Pennsylvania created state control boards for particular municipalities. In calling for a control board for Yonkers, New York, the state legislature said:

> [I]t is hereby found and declared that a financial emergency and an emergency period exists in the city of Yonkers. . . . To end this disaster, to bring the emergency under control and to respond to the overriding state concern . . . , the state must undertake an extraordinary exercise of its police and emergency powers under the state constitution, and exercise controls and supervision over the financial affairs of the city . . . , but in a manner intended to preserve the ability of city officials to determine programs and expenditure priorities within available financial resources (see Mackey 1993).

The nature of the state's response can vary. State action can follow a continuum, from very formal to extremely informal responses. Examples from Ohio, New Jersey, New York, and Florida help illustrate possible responses.

In Ohio, the independently elected state auditor has the initial responsibility to certify that a particular municipality has a fiscal emergency. The state auditor may initiate a review based upon problems identified through its regular audit program and its ongoing monitoring of general events in municipal governance. There are provisions for others (e.g., the mayor, governor, or presiding officer of the city council) to request that the state auditor conduct a fiscal emergency analysis of a municipality. In seven out of the first fifteen fiscal emergencies in Ohio, local officials submitted a request. In the other cases, municipalities were reluctant recipients of a state initiative.

Upon the state auditor's determination that a fiscal emergency condition exists in Ohio, the governor has the responsibility to appoint a Financial Planning and Supervision Commission (FPSC) for the specified municipality. The FPSC consists of seven members, including the state

treasurer, the director of the state's Office of Budget and Management, the mayor, the presiding officer of the municipal council, and three "citizen" members. The governor selects the citizen members from a list submitted by the mayor and presiding officer of the municipality's legislative authority. These three members must have an understanding of financial matters and at least five years of experience in the private sector, must live or work in the municipality, and must not have held elective office within the past five years.

Each FPSC is an agency and instrumentality of the state, which pays the bills. A major decision of each FPSC is to appoint a firm of certified public accountants to serve as that municipality's "financial supervisor."

The duties and powers of the FPSC are expansive. The FPSC is a supervisory body in both name and purpose. All financial matters of the municipality require FPSC review and approval. The FPSC reviews the city's budgets, tax levy ordinances, and appropriation measures. It approves the purpose and amount of any debt obligation. It also serves as an adviser on the structure and terms of debt obligations, on methods to increase revenues, and ways to reduce costs.

The municipality has certain responsibilities under the terms of its fiscal emergency status. Each municipality must prepare a balanced budget and financial plan and then meet the stated timetable. Municipalities must contend with the FPSC monitoring its revenues and expenditures monthly to ensure that expenditures remain less than receipts. The financial plan must show that the municipality plans to deal with the areas of fiscal inadequacy that triggered the law's remedial provisions. Although armed with the power to approve or disapprove the financial plan, the FPSC cannot dictate action. Thus the municipality retains budgetary and financial priorities within approved fiscal parameters.

Florida has similar inadequacy tests to those found in Ohio, but the governor has broad discretion in designing a response to a local problem. The law allows the Florida governor's office to work out an informal solution to a community's financial hardship. This is instead of invoking gubernatorial power to establish a formal financial control commission.

New Jersey also has similar fiscal inadequacy tests, but the discretion resides in a board, not the governor. Similar to Florida, New Jersey deploys a technical assistance team to help a threatened community isolate its financial problems and set up minimal fiscal practices.

In Pennsylvania, the head of the Department of Community Affairs appoints a department employee, or a consultant, as the "coordinator" for the subject municipality. However, a special amendment passed in 1991 established Philadelphia's fiscal control board.

The state of New York has followed a different legal path by using a case-by-case approach. A specialized state law dictated the state response to each particular financial emergency. Yonkers and New York City had their fiscal oversight boards established in the 1970s. More recently, Troy faced similar treatment in 1994. For Yonkers, the cycle of creation and cancellation of a control board occurred twice. New York City operated under the strict pre-review conditions of a Financial Control Board until 1986, when the city's own success led to significant curtailment of the monitor's responsibilities as provided under its original enabling law (Gross 1986). New York City's control board (before 1987) had five primary responsibilities, namely,

1. to review and approve or disapprove the city's annual submission of a four-year financial plan;
2. to review and report on city operations and make recommendations for cost reduction and service improvement;
3. to review and approve or disapprove contracts or other obligations that require the payment of funds or the incurring of costs;
4. to review and approve or disapprove the terms of each proposed long-term and short-term borrowing by the city; and
5. to the extent it deems necessary or appropriate, to establish procedures for disbursement of moneys.

A state control board imposes financial discipline on the municipality. This can go as far as to include steps on what the city will do, how it will do it, and when it will be done. Since fiscal emergency laws typically limit elected city officials to a minority voting position, enhanced state control comes at the expense of local discretion.

Making a city live within its resources is attractive public policy. At a minimum, control boards can foster improved financial management capabilities. Independent control boards bolster the ability of local politicians to deflect various spending interests. In addition, a control board can help diffuse external voter and taxpayer opposition to revenue enhancements or severe service cuts.

As a buffer between the state and its local government, a control board can make life easier for both. This allows the state to avoid having to control local affairs from the state capitol. Local home rule is upset when the state supervises local affairs. The loss is not as great, however, if the state avoids assumption of responsibility for service levels, budget allocations, and local taxation decisions. Merely supervising local efforts to comply with state law and the local government's own financial plan gives the state leverage to remedy problems, but avoids the actual setting of allocation decisions. In this respect, a control board operates by holding local officials accountable for local decisions.

In Ohio, a control board's power to ensure compliance with state law emanates from the enabling legislation. Local officials who willfully violate a valid control board order are subject to legal penalties. Even if never invoked, the presence of such sanctions provides a threat to foster local compliance with the state's fiscal supervision.

Control Board Operations

A key element in a control board's work is the caliber of its daily relationship to the municipality. The municipality may acknowledge the legal role of the board, but the added layer of reporting and oversight confounds local decision-making channels.

A control board carries out its responsibilities through its staff. Three methods have evolved; namely, a separate professional staff, state agency management, and contractors. The two New York state experiences illustrate the professional staff method. New Jersey and Pennsylvania, however, rely on specialized state agencies to help smaller municipalities. In contrast, local control boards in Ohio typically engage the services of a certified public accounting (CPA) firm to serve as the city's "fiscal supervisor."

To do its work, a control board requires extensive access to reports, documents, and financial records. In response, the municipality has to devote staff time to gather and compile the requested information. This is compounded when the control board wants information on a given topic within a period that the city administration finds too difficult or confining. Meeting the deadlines avoids possible sanctions, however.

Municipalities subject to financial emergency oversight must do certain things. Ohio law, for example, requires that the municipality present to its FPSC an initial financial plan within 120 days of the state's certification of an emergency condition. Board action on approval of the financial plan, its modifications, and in the issuance of debt also represent formal roles of the board.

Just as critical to its formal role, the board and its staff (whether full-time public employees or an accounting firm under contract) develop an informal relationship with the municipality and its administration. In many Ohio municipalities, this translated into the fiscal supervisor, a CPA firm, helping the city improve its financial system so the city could ultimately comply with the control board's demands.

Influence on Taxing and Spending

If the state supervision is to ensure financial discipline, then the intervention should have an impact on budget balancing. In Ohio and New York, for example, financial emergency declarations require that municipalities prepare a multiyear financial plan for approval by the control board. These plans allow local decisionmakers to decide service allocations, but within revenue estimates and spending plans monitored by the control board.

On the matter of taxing (and revenue generation), the control board serves in several capacities. The board can require the city to begin more effective collective systems, especially in dealing with accounts receivables. Since several Ohio governments had difficulty determining expected receipts and revenues, basic improvements in the administration of existing fees and taxes resulted in more timely receipt of funds.

In neither Ohio nor New York, for example, were state supervision boards extended the power to begin a new tax on local citizens. State lawmakers are understandably reluctant to bear the burden for having a state-declared and administered fiscal emergency result in a mandated tax increase. Thus the laws make local officials propose those actions.

Control boards force troubled municipalities to live within existing resources. In one example, the Yonkers, New York, control board reduced the administration's estimate of estimated revenues, forcing the city to make service cuts instead (Volk and Grumet 1979). In Ohio, a subject municipality has to submit a three-year financial plan to its control board. The plan must include the city's proposals for eliminating all fiscal emergency conditions and deficits, paying all overdue bills, restoring misused fund moneys, balancing the budget, and regaining the ability to market long-term general obligation bonds. Also included is a timetable for realization of the plan elements, and steps to prevent any new fiscal emergency from arising in the future. In Ohio, failure to submit a timely financial plan results in automatic spending restrictions in the general fund. The spending ceiling is 85 percent of general fund expenditures for that month in the preceding year. New York City's board monitors threats to the board-approved city expenditure plan (Bailey 1984; New York State Financial Control Board 1992). Fiscal discipline, as imposed by control boards, usually means living within resource limits, not enlarging the taxing authority.

Control boards help local governments develop adequate financial practices. Such practices may prevent future fiscal problems from escalating into another emergency. This requires an improvement in the local jurisdiction's internal capacity to detect dangerous fiscal trends. The entity must have an accounting system and financial procedures that provide timely but adequate data for financial decisionmaking. Just by its presence, a control board shows that the governmental entity failed minimum standards in the past.

Under the Ohio law, covered municipalities must develop "an effective financial accounting and reporting system" to help it carry out and comply with the financial plan. This ensures that the entity will install minimal standards. To end state supervision, a municipality must have met the objectives of its financial plan, corrected and eliminated all fiscal emergency conditions, avoided any additional failures, and showed a reasonable expectation of finishing the conversion to an adequate financial accounting system within two years. Thus, before a municipality can emerge from under a state control board, it has to prove certain basic financial management abilities.

Special Financing

Since a financial emergency renders most governmental entities unable to enter the financial markets for funds, they often need special financing opportunities. In New York City, the Municipal Assistance Corporation (MAC) provided the city with long-term access to the financial markets well before the city could again issue debt. As an intermediary between the state and the city, MAC issued debt obligations. The collateral for these MAC bonds was a repayment stream of revenues due the city from the state, funneled instead through MAC. An intercept mechanism similar to this is a frequent design. For Troy, New York, the fiscal oversight law allowed the city to issue bonds to make up several years of budget deficits.

Unlike New York City, the Ohio municipal financial emergency law does not provide for new long-term financing options. Instead, the law allows short-term borrowing from the state treasurer, which, in turn, receives security for payment from anticipated property taxes or other revenue sources. The law also created an intermediate-term method of borrowing (up to eight years) to settle past due accounts, restore misspent restricted funds, and eliminate deficit balances. Short-term borrowing helped Cleveland, Ohio, deal with its liquidity problems.

Other states, such as Pennsylvania and New Jersey, provide special grants and loans to distressed local governments. These programs, combined with technical assistance, seek to remedy the fiscal problem.

Policy Choices

When a state establishes active supervision over a local government that has failed that state's fiscal adequacy standards, the state codifies both incentives and disincentives for local fiscal management. This section reviews five policy concerns.

A fiscal emergency law should give municipalities a strong economic incentive to avoid falling under its provisions. A state must strive to keep from making a bad situation even worse. Still, those municipalities that fail minimum fiscal standards should not be able to gain advantages over other municipalities that have struggled successfully for years to maintain their fiscal affairs in order. Unconditional grants of money do little to punish or change local behavior.

Municipalities should have an economic incentive to end quickly their coverage under the law. Prolongation of a fiscal emergency should not be in the state's interests. In Ohio, the state pays the bill for the control board. Thus municipalities have little fiscal incentive to end the control period.

Laws should allow the state to use a flexible response for municipal fiscal distress. Requiring the state to create costly control boards, with hired or contracted staff, may be overkill. Sometimes the municipality may need little more than strong state pressure to correct a problem, interim aid in drafting effective fiscal plans, or assistance in installing fiscal controls.

The law should allow a flexible definition for judging fiscal inadequacy. The tests for detecting a fiscal emergency incorporate some arbitrary hurdles. An Ohio municipality that does not pay its entire payroll on time is in trouble. If a municipality pays the payroll from the cash-rich enterprise fund and not from the cash-short general fund, it fails a fiscal test. In four additional tests the Ohio law specifies that 30 days (one-twelfth of a year) have to elapse before certain fiscal practices are considered to yield fiscal emergency. The rationale for a one-month window is unclear.

Fiscal emergency laws should encourage the state, and other municipalities, to learn from those municipalities that fail the fiscal tests. The state should have an interest in distributing the results of its remedial actions to discourage other municipalities from neglecting the norms of fiscal adequacy. States may find it cheaper to promote effective fiscal procedures than to "clean up" after a bankruptcy, default, or fiscal emergency.

W. BARTLEY HILDRETH

BIBLIOGRAPHY

Advisory Commission on Intergovernmental Relations, 1973. *City Financial Emergencies.* Washington, DC: Government Printing Office.
Advisory Commission on Intergovernmental Relations, 1985. *Bankruptcies, Defaults and Other Local Government Financial Emergencies.* Washington, DC: Government Printing Office.
Bailey, R. W., 1984. *The Crisis Regime: The MAC, the EFCB, and the Political Impact of the New York City Financial Crisis.* Albany: State University of New York Press.
Gross, George, 1986. *The Changing Role of the City's Fiscal Monitor.* New York: New York State Financial Control Board.
Mackey, S. R., 1993. *State Programs to Assist Distressed Local Governments.* Denver: National Conference of State Legislatures.
New York State Financial Control Board, 1992. *Structural Balance.* New York: New York State Financial Control Board.
Volk, Helen D., and Louis Grumet, 1979. "New York State's Action for Fiscal Survival: City of Yonkers." *New York State Bar Journal,* vol. 51 (August): 370–373, 402–405.

FINANCIAL INDICATORS.
Any financial measures that are used to evaluate the financial performance of government activities.

Origin and Subsequent History

When a governmental unit is established, it is generally the initial intent that the revenues be sufficient to cover the expenditures. Consequently, the key financial measure is a balanced budget. In other words, one dollar in estimated revenue equals one dollar in appropriations. However, the wants of any political body may exceed the desire of its constituents to pay. Through debates and public hearings, the elected or appointed officials reach consensus regarding the level of expenditures relative to the revenue to be generated.

Over time, as the governmental unit becomes larger and more sophisticated, debt is incurred to construct buildings, highways, and so on. Consequently, it becomes more difficult to determine the financial performance of the governmental unit. The level of debt incurred, and the subsequent repayment of principal and interest, are critical factors in determining the funds available to meet current operational needs.

To evaluate the extent to which units in the public sector can incur debt, bond rating agencies have been established. These agencies generally include four broad areas of concern covering established sectors of credit: economic, debt, administrative, and fiscal. Economic factors are used to ascertain the strength of the tax structure and the overall debt burden for repayment of debt. The stability of the administrative unit is evaluated along with an examination of fiscal performance versus the budget (Standard and Poor's 1989).

Underlying Theoretical Framework

The basic framework within which a governmental unit attempts to operate is referred to as intergenerational equity. Each generation is expected to pay for the services that it receives and the cost of these services should *not* be passed on to future generations.

The means by which financial measures are used to determine whether each generation is paying for services received is dependent upon the type of accounting method. The accounting methods are referred to as cash, modified accrual, or full accrual. The cash basis of accounting only recognizes the cash received and cash disbursed. Since this method is subject to manipulation and does not attempt to implement the concept of intergenerational equity, it is strongly discouraged.

The modified accrual basis of accounting is an attempt to move toward charging the costs of services to the persons who benefit from those services. Accounting principles associated with this method were established in the United States beginning in 1933 by national committees and councils under the auspices of the Municipal Government Finance Officers Association (later renamed the Government Finance Officers Association [GFOA]).

In 1984, the Government Accounting Standards Board (GASB) was established to assume responsibility for the government accounting principles of state and local governments in the United States. Since that time, GASB has worked diligently to move the United States toward a full accrual basis of accounting at the state and local levels. It would be inappropriate to compare a governmental unit that is using a cash basis of accounting to a governmental unit that has implemented a full accrual basis.

An example involving disposal of solid wastes through landfills might clarify the differences between the three methods of accounting. Prior to establishing accounting standards, many landfills were maintained on a cash basis, by which cash was received in sufficient amounts to pay the attendant for operating the landfill. In 1968, landfills were required to be maintained on the modified accrual basis of accounting, by which taxpayers were charged for the use of the landfill and liabilities were recorded for maintaining the landfill until its closure. As a result of actions by GASB, landfills are now required to be maintained on the full accrual basis of accounting for financial statements with periods beginning after 15 June 1993. Each user is required to pay for the *full* cost of the use of the landfill. These costs include assuring that the landfill is environmentally sound, for example, that there is no leakage from underground storage tanks or drums. Also, the costs to maintain the landfill for 30 years after its closure are estimated and charged to current users.

At the national level, U.S. legislation was passed to establish chief financial officers in each of the 23 federal agencies (Chief Financial Officers Act 1990). The principals charged with implementing the act are the United States treasurer, the director of the Office of Management and Budget, and the comptroller general. To assist the principals in assuring consistent application of accounting principles within U.S. federal agencies, the principals established the Federal Accounting Standards Advisory Board (FASAB). The advisory board deliberates the accounting issues and recommends the accounting procedures. The board currently is attempting to move the federal government from a cash basis toward a full accrual basis of accounting.

In any financial analysis, it is beneficial to understand the differences between financial *position* and *condition*. Financial position is taken from the balance sheet, which represents one point in time based on past transactions. Financial condition is forward-looking and attempts to assess a governmental unit's ability to pay its debts, based on financial projections, at a future date.

Current Practice in the United States

For business activities, accounting standards are based on the "capital maintenance" concept. That is, income is measured periodically to determine if the business activity is "as well off" after a period of operation as it was at the beginning of that period. Consequently, a full accrual basis of accounting is used.

This concept is not easily applied to governmental activities since the capital (i.e., owner's contribution) to be maintained is difficult to define. Therefore, a "standard of living maintenance" concept is used to develop governmental accounting standards. At the national level, a system of national income accounting has been developed for governments to determine if the national standard of living has been maintained. The per capita gross national product (GNP) is one measure that is used to identify the degree of change in this standard of living.

The financial measures used by bond rating agencies have generally served as the predominant measures of fiscal capacity used throughout the country. These measures are published annually to assist in the evaluation of a governmental unit (Moody's 1991).

Business Activities

The basis financial statements (income statement and balance sheet) are maintained on the full accrual basis of accounting. Ratios derived from the income statement provide measures of profitability (operating ratio percentages) and debt servicing capacity (interest coverage, debt service coverage, and debt service safety margin). Coverage levels demonstrate both current and prospective debt repayment ability, and safety margins denote additional levels of protection. The debt ratio percentage, which is calculated from the balance sheet, signifies the reliance of the enterprise on debt financing and its capacity to support additional debt.

Local Governmental Units

When comparisons are made between local governmental units it is critical to assure that the units being compared have a similar governmental structure, since differences in laws could create differences in results. Some cities are incorporated separately from counties, but other cities are a part of the county structure. Recognition of these differences is especially critical in the comparison of allocation ratios. Allocation ratios are those ratios that reflect the portion of total expenditures allocated to each functional area. The major functional areas are public safety, public health, education, social services, and miscellaneous.

The magnitude and the burden of debt are two measures crucial to an evaluation of debt position. As a starting approach, a method for calculating net debt has been developed that allows for comparability among local governments across the United States. This net debt figure is then applied to population and tax base data. When the government uses the population data and presents net debt on a per capita basis, a meaningful measure of the relative size of the debt is provided.

As a measure of the burden of debt on a government's tax base, a ratio is calculated between the overall net debt and the estimated full value of taxable property. The estimated full value serves as a measure of local government wealth and, therefore, is reflective of the capacity to service public debt. Taxable valuation is utilized as a wealth measure because it tends to be up to date and readily available for all municipal governments.

The International City Management Association (ICMA 1980) developed a system that permits a locality to track the financial health of its particular jurisdiction using the financial indicators. This financial trend monitoring system identifies 12 environmental, organizational, and financial factors. This management tool deals with 36 separate issues: such as cash liquidity, level of business activity, changes in fund balances, emergence of unfunded liabilities, and development of external revenue dependencies.

An illustrative Comprehensive Annual Financial Report (CAFR) has been published by the Government Finance Officers Association (GFOA 1988). The CAFR consists of three sections: introductory, financial, and statistical. The statistical section contains a number of suggested financial indicators, including ten fiscal year data for the following:

1. general governmental expenditures by function
2. general governmental revenue by source
3. property tax levies and collections
4. assessed and estimated actual value of taxable property
5. property tax rates
6. ratio of net bonded debt to assessed value and net bonded debt per capita
7. revenue bond coverage

A framework to identify the interrelationship of these financial indicators is available (Berne and Schramm 1986). Factors for analysis in the framework include revenues, expenditures, debt, pension, and internal resources.

State Governmental Units

The concept of tax-supported debt is used to account for all debt serviced by tax revenues of the state, whether or not the state itself was the issuer. Appropriate sinking funds and short-term debt, debt that is self-supporting from enterprise revenues, and debt that is serviced by another unit of government are deducted from gross debt to reach the net figure.

Per capita debt is computed by dividing the net tax-supported debt by the estimated population. The ratio of net debt to estimated full value of property is computed by adjusting assessed valuation to estimated market value; tax-supported net debt is then calculated as a percentage of the adjusted figure. To derive the ratio of net debt to personal income, tax-supported net debt is divided by the annual personal income reported by the U.S. Department of Commerce.

Many of the financial indicators used by local governments also apply to the state governments. As with local governmental units, it is best to compare financial indicators between those states that have similar characteristics. These characteristics include population density, wealth, crime rates, and so forth.

Federal Governmental Units

A national income accounting system was adopted globally in 1931 and is constantly under review. Most fiscal indicators at the national level are based on some measure of economic activity. Depending on the approach, it may be based on the value of all goods and services produced in one year (output), the expenditures that take place when the output is sold (expenditure), or the value of producers' incomes (income). Thus, output = expenditures = incomes.

The main concepts involved in measuring economic activity are gross domestic product (GDP), gross national product (GNP), and net national product (NNP). GDP is the total of all economic activity in one country, regardless of who owns the productive assets. GNP is the total of incomes earned by residents of a country, regardless of where the assets are located. NNP is GNP less depreciation. Depreciation is difficult to measure; thus, NNP is seldom used (Economist 1994).

It is difficult to look at national fiscal indicators without making comparisons with other nations. (For a comparison between the components of GNP between Japan and the United States, see Table I). It is difficult to make good comparisons without some knowledge of the sociodemographic factors, however (see Table II).

When making the comparisons to other countries, it is generally best to compare nations that have similar characteristics. In Tables III, IV, and V key fiscal indicators are used in comparing selected industrialized countries:

TABLE I. PERCENTAGE OF COMPONENTS OF GNP IN JAPAN AND THE UNITED STATES (1993)

Component	Japan	United States
Consumption	66	85
Investment	31	16
Exports	9	8
Imports	(6)	(9)
Total GNP	100	100

SOURCE: derived from *OECD Economic Outlook*, PARIS, OECD, selected years

TABLE II. COMPARATIVE SOCIODEMOGRAPHIC DATA OF JAPAN AND THE UNITED STATES (1993)

	Japan	United States
Land mass	1.0	25.0
Total population	1.0	2.0
Percentage 65 and over	13.1	12.6
GNP/population	1.3	1.0

SOURCE: derived from *OECD Economic Outlook,* PARIS, OECD, selected years

TABLE III. A COMPARISON OF SELECTED COUNTRIES' LONG-TERM GOVERNMENT DEBT VERSUS THEIR GROSS NATIONAL PRODUCT

Country	Year	Debt/GNP
France	1991	18.2
Germany	1992	21.0
Japan	1993	47.4
United Kingdom	1991	31.2
United States	1992	58.4

SOURCE: derived from *OECD Economic Outlook,* PARIS, OECD, selected years

TABLE IV. A COMPARISON OF SELECTED COUNTRIES' FISCAL DEFICITS VERSUS TOTAL EXPENDITURES

Country	Year	Fiscal Deficits/Total Expenditures
France	1994	19.6
Germany	1994	14.2
Japan	1993	13.9
United Kingdom	1992	16.9
United States	1994	17.4

SOURCE: derived from *OECD Economic Outlook,* PARIS, OECD, selected years

TABLE V. A COMPARISON OF SELECTED COUNTRIES' NATIONAL INCOME TO BURDEN RATIO

Country	Year	SOCIAL SECURITY TAX Contributions	Burden	Total
France	1988	28.0	34.1	62.1
Germany	1990	21.9	29.4	51.3
Japan	1992	12.3	25.2	37.5
United Kingdom	1990	10.3	39.9	50.2
United States	1992	10.4	26.1	36.5

SOURCE: derived from *OECD Economic Outlook,* PARIS, OECD, selected years

Variations of Practice in Other Countries

Before analyzing financial indicators in other countries, it is essential to understand the differences in the social culture and the organizational structure. For example, Japan has prefectures but Canada has provinces. These organizational structures could be considered similar to the 50 states in the United States, in some instances, yet in other instances, similar to counties within these states.

It is also beneficial to be aware of the different accounting methods among the countries. For example, Australia and New Zealand use a full accrual basis of accounting, but the United States and many of the other industrialized countries use variants of a modified accrual basis of accounting. Some countries that are centrally controlled, such as China, use a cash basis of accounting.

The Organization for Economic Cooperation and Development (OECD) uses the cyclically adjusted budget balance (CAB) as an indicator of fiscal policy (Blanchard 1990). The CAB was designed to reveal the impact of discretionary changes in fiscal policy on the overall actual budget balance, measure the sustainability of fiscal policy, and identify the effect of fiscal policy on aggregate demand and aggregate supply. Because of the difficulty in meeting design objectives, three indices have been suggested by the OECD to measure the impact of fiscal policy on the standard of living: (1) the index of discretionary change, (2) the medium tax gap, and (3) the adjusted deficit.

To determine if member countries meet the criteria for joining the European Economic Community (EEC), three convergence ratios are used: (1) government deficit to GDP (<3%), (2) government debt to GDP (<60%), and (3) inflation rate (which must not exceed the rate of the three best-performing member states by more than 1.5%).

Performance Measures

There is a movement toward the use of performance indicators with financial indicators. Performance indicators are those measures that assist in determining the level of effectiveness in accomplishing the organization's mission, but the financial indicator is a measure of its efficiency. For example, a student's score on a standardized test is a performance indicator, but the cost per student is a financial indicator.

In the United States, GASB has taken the lead to develop performance measures for governmental units at the state and local levels (GASB 1990). At the national level, the Federal Accounting Standards Advisory Board has initiated a project to develop performance measures for its agencies. Much work is being done throughout the international community, with varying degrees of success, to develop performance measures (IFAC, 1994; Buschor and Schedler, 1994).

JESSE W. HUGHES

BIBLIOGRAPHY

Berne, Robert, and Richard Schramm, 1986. *The Financial Analysis of Governments.* Englewood Cliffs, NJ: Prentice-Hall.

Blanchard, Olivier Jean, 1990. "Suggestions for a New Set of Fiscal Indicators." *OECD Working Papers*, no. 79 (April).

Buschor, Ernst, and Kuno Schedler, eds., 1994. *Perspectives on Performance Measurement and Public Sector Accounting.* Berne, Switzerland: Paul Haupt.

Chief Financial Officers Act of 1990. Public Law 101–576, 104 Stat. 2839. Dated 15 November 1990. 101st Cong.

Economist Series, 1994. *The Economist Guide to Global Economic Indicators.* New York: John Wiley and Sons.

Government Accounting Standards Board (GASB),1990. *Service Efforts and Accomplishments Reporting: Its Time Has Come—An Overview.* Stanford, CT: Government Accounting Standards Board.

Government Finance Officers Association (GFOA), 1988. *Governmental Accounting, Auditing, and Financial Reporting.* Chicago: Government Finance Officers Association.

International City Management Association, 1980. *Evaluating Local Government Financial Condition.* Washington, DC: International City Management Association.

International Federation of Accountants, Public Sector Committee (IFAC), June 1994. *Proposed Study of Performance Reporting by Government Business Enterprises.* New York: International Federation of Accountants.

Moody's Investors Service, Public Finance Department, Annual. (See esp. 1991.) *Medians for Selected Indicators of Municipal Performance.* New York: Moody's Investors Service.

Standard & Poor's Corporation, 1989. *S&P's Municipal Finance Criteria.* New York: Standard & Poor's Corporation.

FINANCIAL REGULATION.

The totality of measures and controls imposed by authorities to promote confidence in financial transactions and institutions and to achieve an efficient and fair operation of financial markets and the economy in general.

Objectives and Scope of Financial Regulation

Financial regulation covers a wide spectrum of measures employed by governments and authorities to ensure that financial markets operate in an open and fair manner, and that borrowers and lenders in financing transactions are given a reasonable degree of protection against illegal, unethical, or fraudulent behavior. Protection of the smaller, nonprofessional investors (the "mums and dads") is usually the focus for such regulation. The form of regulation can range from direct intervention by governments to indirect and persuasive measures. Direct regulatory techniques include product control (dictating the type of lending instruments institutions may provide); prudential requirements, which set financial ratios to maintain for banking and nonbank finance institutions; prescribing the format of public capital raisings (prospectuses) and the licensing of capital market operatives; mandating of financial disclosure standards and audit requirements; and ensuring that there is an adequate and consistent legal system governing the operation of corporations and contracts.

Indirect controls can include establishing government financial enterprises to compete with private banks, and "moral suasion" or "jawboning" by central banking authorities to obtain compliance with government policies.

Dimitri Vittas (1992) noted that the main rationale for financial regulation is the existence of market failure arising from externalities, market power, and information problems. Governments also look to financial regulation for assisting in achieving their economic and social goals of stability, efficiency, and equity (or fairness). The degree to which governments manage internal financial regulation is seen as a key part of the national infrastructure and is used as a measure of international competitiveness.

How far does financial regulation extend? A narrow view suggests only those visible measures that are applied to control the financial institutions, banking and nonbanking, which make up the finance intermediary sector. A broader view includes the reporting, auditing, and governance requirements of all finance market participants, both public and private, including all structures that borrow and lend money, ranging from listed joint stock corporations to private companies, not-for-profit organizations, unincorporated entities, and sole traders. A yet wider view also includes those macroeconomic tools of fiscal policy used by governments to influence interest rates, currency exchange rates, taxation policies, and so forth, as part of the overall framework within which the financial markets operate.

Viewed globally, financial regulation can cover the activities of various international financial institutions and bodies that facilitate the free movement of funds throughout the world, particularly between the developed and developing countries. The scope of financial regulation is therefore best summarized as being the totality of measures and controls imposed by authorities, both public and private, to promote confidence in financial and corporate institutions, financial markets, and the economy in general.

Types of Financial Regulation

Financial regulatory policy usually distinguishes between banking and nonbanking sectors. Traditionally, governments concentrated on regulating banking sectors with a series of direct quantitative controls, such as specifying the types of securities to be held, licensing entry of new banks, using "independent" central banking authorities to influence the banks through their "lender of last resort" guarantees, and occasionally legislating directly to make banks implement social and economic policies. In some countries governments operate state-owned banks and finance institutions in direct competition with private banks. This is usually initiated for promoting such social policies as providing house-purchase finance or helping disadvantaged borrowers. Because of the market failure of the private sector, it also provides effective market regulation by ensuring competition for private sector credit providers.

Nonbank institutions and corporations are mostly regulated through company and securities laws, enforced by a mixture of public agencies (securities commissions, central banks, and industry regulators, for example, the life insurance industry), and the scrutiny of private-sector or professional bodies (the accounting professions, stock exchange committees, and shareholder bodies).

The History of Financial Regulation

Financial regulation, together with manufacturing, trade, and shipping, has been a concern of governments since the sixteenth century, with the growth of the doctrine of mercantilism in Europe. The 1720 Bubble Act of the British Parliament was the initial legislative response to the speculative mania that surrounded the South Sea Bubble crisis. The act was an attempt at a companies act, although its actual effect was to prevent the growth of a corporate form that would have provided protection to shareholders and the public. One hundred twenty years later another series of financial failures and corruption led to William Gladstone's Joint Stock Companies Act, 1844, which introduced the three main principles of modern company law; that is, the distinction between private partnerships and joint stock companies (by requiring the registration of all new companies of more than 25 members), the formation of companies by registration rather than solely by charter, and, most important, the provision for capital raising by full publicity. It also created the role of registrar of companies. Soon after, limited liability was legislated, which allowed the true separation of capital and management in businesses for the first time, and therefore established the role of regulation through registration, auditing, reporting, and monitoring requirements for incorporated structures.

The repeated cycle of economic booms followed by financial failure and recriminations prompted governments to expand financial regulation and introduce quasi-judicial oversight agencies. The global economic chaos resulting from the Depression in the 1930s was widely blamed on banks and stock exchanges, leading to the creation of the Securities and Exchange Commission (SEC) in the United States in 1934. At the same time, many governments were adopting Keynesian principles of intervention in markets to engender growth, using central banks as direct tools for implementing monetary policy, setting stringent conditions on holdings of public securities and lending policies, prescribing interest rates and currency exchange rates, and using government guarantees and programs to underwrite investments and protect savings. Stock exchanges were given semiofficial status to vet capital raisings and regulate market transactions and behavior, typified by the regulations of the London Stock Exchange, sometimes known collectively as the "London Code."

During the 1960s and 1970s, the attitudes and practices of financial regulation remained reasonably static despite the adoption of post-Keynesian and monetarist economic theories with a laissez-faire approach to markets. Nonintervention, increased liberalization of trade, reliance on competition between institutions, and less direct controls over banks were international trends. Statutory reporting and auditing standards improved to ensure that markets were properly informed, and accounting bodies set tighter financial reporting standards. The process of harmonizing internationally generally accepted accounting practices commenced. Financial regulatory agencies were being strengthened and improved, although they often relied on a legalistic approach, which meant they were not always effective in dealing with rapidly changing finance market activities and attitudes.

Deregulation of Finance Markets and Controversy Over Market Failures

Economic reforms by many governments during the 1980s and 1990s included the privatization and liberalization of financial markets, summarized by the term "deregulation." Reform of the finance sector was inevitable because of the explosive growth of financing required for international trade and investment; the advances in technology enabling instantaneous global communications; the proliferation of financial instruments including "synthetics" or "derivatives"; the emergence of new financial intermediaries; and a breakdown of traditional state and national barriers to lending. Governments recognized that direct controls over finance markets were costly and ineffective and created an unfriendly climate for investment, which would eventually result in loss of investor confidence.

Measures in financial deregulation typically included reduced direct controls over banks and finance institution borrowing and lending policies, removal of restrictions over participants in the banking and securities markets, the sale or privatization of government-owned institutions, and reduced intervention by central banks in managing monetary policy. For example, in 1989, the New Zealand government removed direct Treasury control and influence over its Reserve Bank, replacing it with a contract between the governor of the bank and the finance minister to achieve price stability within specified percentage limits. Other examples of deregulation included the floating of exchange rates, opening of previously restricted official markets in government bond dealing, and the removal of barriers to persons allowed to trade in stocks and shares, such as the Big Bang reforms in the United Kingdom in the mid-1980s.

The role of deregulation and self-regulation by the finance industry received major criticism following a series of financial failures of the late 1980s, including the international stock market "correction" of October 1987, the insolvencies in the huge savings and loan industry of the United States, the failure of private and government-owned banks and nonbank institutions in many countries (Australia, Malaysia, and Indonesia, for example), the securities scams in India in 1993, and substantial losses resulting from derivatives speculation, leading to the collapse of the Barings Bank in 1995. Since failures are ultimately borne by smaller savers and taxpayers, calls for reregulation of the finance industry by governments resulted.

It is now generally accepted that regulation by quantitative controls is ineffective against capital movement and is expensive to implement. Emphasis is now being placed on prescribing disclosure and reporting requirements to keep markets continuously informed. A continuing tension in financial regulation is to strike the right balance between the freedom financial institutions require to compete in a global market with the need to maintain domestic and overseas confidence in the stability and consistency of an economy.

International Trends in Financial Regulation

Since the end of World War II, the massive transfers of capital from developed to developing countries through private, public (government to government), and international organizations, such as the World Bank and the International Monetary Fund, have created a need for international financial regulatory structures. The gradual removal of barriers to world trade through the General Agreement on Tariffs and Trade (GATT) and the World Trade Organization (WTO), combined with the use of instantaneous electronic communications for movement of funds, have made borderless economies a reality, but regulation has remained a national concern. Various organizations and groups have emerged out of the successive crises in order to deal with international regulation, including the Paris Club of major lending nations (or, Group of Ten), the international clearing houses, and the International Institute of Finance (IIF). Credit ratings have also been extended to sovereign nations and states.

Financial regulation measures can no longer be developed in sovereign isolation. On one hand, a financial climate caused by excessive regulation that is deemed unfavorable can lead to capital flight from one jurisdiction to another. On the other hand, insufficient or lax financial regulation can be a real deterrent to many potential lenders and investors, necessitating a substantial reregulation reform, such as that undertaken by Hong Kong in the late 1980s. Finding the balance between sufficient regulation of finance markets to engender confidence and protect national interests while not deterring foreign investment is a critical issue for governments of developing countries. It is made more difficult where domestic institutions and stock exchanges are new and small. A further constraint in developing countries is often the lack of resources or political resolve to implement an efficient regulatory framework.

Conclusion

The type and extent of financial regulation required will depend on the state of the development of the economy and the resources available to enforce regulations. The lessons learned from successive financial collapses are usually forgotten quickly by investors, and rapidly changing technology and techniques of financial markets plus the internationalization of transactions mean that the rules require constant updating and review for relevance. According to the World Bank (1990), "A main concern of financial regulation has been the achievement of stability without undermining efficiency. But finance remains a dynamic field, changing far too rapidly to achieve a perfect balance between the freedom needed to stimulate competition and growth and the control needed to prevent fraud and instability."

GRAEME MACMILLAN

BIBLIOGRAPHY

George, Susan, 1994. *A Fate Worse Than Debt*, London: Penguin.
Jackson, Peter, and Catherine Price, 1994. *Privatisation and Regulation: A Review of the Issues.* London: Longman.
Vittas, Dimitri, ed., 1992. *Financial Regulation: Changing the Rules of the Game.* Washington, DC: World Bank, EDI Development Studies.
World Bank, 1990. *Financial Systems and Development* (The 1989 World Development Report). Washington, DC: World Bank PRE, Policy and Research Series.

FISCAL EQUALIZATION, METROPOLITAN.

Programs designed to share tax base and revenues to create a more equal distribution of (1) the fiscal capacity of local governments, and (2) the tax obligations of citizens and businesses for the costs of local government within a region (a.k.a. Metropolitan Tax Base Sharing, Metropolitan Revenue Sharing).

Background

The need for metropolitan fiscal equalization is based on the economic problems of central cities. Often, cities with many lower-income people must increase taxes for all businesses and households to pay for public services (Ladd and Yinger 1989). This change can create incentives for businesses and affluent citizens to relocate to lower-taxed jurisdictions. For example, suppose central cities, in need of resources, raise taxes; this increase discourages new development and makes relocation an economic necessity for many businesses and residents. If central cities do not raise taxes, then necessary services might not be produced. These pressures force central cities to seek resources from federal and state governments or the surrounding region.

Two basic fiscal equalization concepts have been developed: revenue sharing from federal or state governments to counties, cities, and school districts, and a sharing of tax base among local governments. Revenue sharing and redistribution involving the federal government have decreased in the past, but state support for education and other services has actually increased (Lee and Johnson 1994). However, these increases have not materially reduced the tax differentials in metropolitan regions (Bowman, MacManus, and Mikesell 1992).

In response, some metropolitan areas have experimented with fiscal equalization. Fiscal equalization is designed to (1) reduce competition between cities within a region, (2) unify cities in their efforts to develop, (3) lower taxes on central city businesses to reduce the need to abandon downtown and other core areas, and (4) help central cities obtain more resources to address their needs (Wolman et al. 1992). But two challenges confront fiscal equalization experiments: the opposition from suburban areas that do not want to subsidize central cities, and the difficulty in designing programs that address the fiscal problems of central cities. These challenges account for the lack of experimentation with fiscal equalization programs in many metropolitan regions.

Examples of Metropolitan Fiscal Equalization

Traditionally, there have been two forms of fiscal equalization: tax base sharing and revenue sharing. Tax base sharing shares the basis on which taxes are collected (i.e., assessed value, retail sales, or income), and revenue sharing redistributes revenues generated through tax levies. Table I compares four fiscal equalization schemes in use in the United States.

Minneapolis–St. Paul Fiscal Disparities Program

The Minneapolis–St. Paul, Minnesota, program began in 1971, involving seven counties and 296 government units. This program has several characteristics (Baker, Hinze, and Manzi 1991): The variables used to define collection and distribution procedures are current city population, equalized market value (assessed valuation at 100% market value), fiscal capacity (equalized market value of all property per capita), certified levy (actual property tax revenue required), and net tax capacity (equalized assessed value of property). The base year for assessment of commercial and industrial (CI) property is 1971. Taxing jurisdictions contribute 40 percent of the growth (from the base year) in their CI property tax base to an areawide pool. Remaining CI growth and all residential tax base of each jurisdiction stays with the jurisdiction.

Distributions are based on the jurisdiction's fiscal capacity, a measure that compares each taxing unit to the metropolitan area as a whole. Fiscal capacity is defined as equalized market value per capita. Jurisdictions are ranked by the ratio of (1) the average fiscal capacity of all jurisdictions to (2) their own fiscal capacity. The city's population is weighted by this ratio to determine its share of the common pool. If its fiscal capacity is greater than the average, a smaller share (or no share) is awarded, and jurisdictions with capacity below the average receive more from the common pool.

Jefferson County and the City of Louisville, Kentucky

The city of Louisville, Kentucky, and Jefferson County, Kentucky, implemented a fiscal equalization plan based on sharing proceeds of an occupational license fee (OLF), an earned income tax amounting to 2.2 percent of earned wages and net business profits. Known as the Louisville–Jefferson County Compact, it was passed in 1985 for a 12-year term (City of Louisville 1985). Its objectives are to improve economic development, preserve Louisville's ability to prosper, increase the organizational effectiveness of the county and the city, and place more fiscal responsibility for governmental services in the hands of elected officials. The compact affects only the two jurisdictions.

It requires the city and the county to share OLF proceeds. Louisville and Jefferson County depend on the OLF for one-half of their revenues. The new OLF split between the two is based on three formulas that divide revenues according to a base-year calculation, an inflation-based distribution, and a new growth-based distribution. The contribution and distribution formulas are not based on public service need or demand criteria. The jurisdiction's contribution is the total amount of the OLF generated inside the jurisdiction, and distributions are based on fixed shares of total revenue, partitioned into the three amounts described previously.

Montgomery County and the City of Dayton, Ohio

Montgomery County, Ohio, initiated a fiscal equalization scheme in 1989 involving 30 jurisdictions in a single county with one central city, Dayton, Ohio (Pammer and Dustin 1993). The program, known as Economic Development/Government Equity, links economic development to fiscal equalization by creating two funds through sales, property, and income taxes. One fund is used for economic development projects, financed by a one-half-cent increase in the local sales tax. Another fund is created from a common pool consisting of a combination of shared tax base and property and income tax revenue; this fund is redistributed to the jurisdictions. To be part of one fund, a city must participate in the other.

The contribution rate for participants changes annually, based on changes in countywide property and income tax revenue, divided by total growth in the county-

TABLE I. COMPARISON OF BASIC FISCAL EQUALIZATION PARAMETERS IN MONTGOMERY COUNTY, OHIO, MINNEAPOLIS–ST. PAUL, MINNESOTA, THE MEADOWLANDS, NEW YORK, AND JEFFERSON COUNTY, KENTUCKY

Basic Parameter	Montgomery County	Minneapolis–St. Paul	Meadowlands	Jefferson County
Base Year	Rolling Three-Year Average	1971	1971	1985
Contribution rate used to determine amount contributed to common pool.	A ratio equal to 33% of growth (since the base year) in countywide property and sales tax revenue, as a percentage growth in countywide assessed value. Thus the contribution ratio changes each year based on relative changes in the numerator and denominator.	40%. This contribution rate is fixed and does not change from year to year.	40%. This contribution rate is fixed now, but it was phased-in gradually over a 10-year period from 10%.	100% of the occupational license fee (OLF) proceeds are contributed to the common pool.
The amount against which city's contribution rate is applied to calculate city's gross contribution to the common pool.	The sum of: (1) growth (since the base year) in the city's commercial and industrial assessed value (AV); (2) 25% of growth in residential AV; and (3) 50% of growth in total property and income taxes.	Growth (since the base year) in the equalized assessed value of commercial-industrial property.	Growth (since the base year) in the equalized assessed value of all property, reduced by county's share of the tax rate.	All OLF revenues are contributed. The city and county are guaranteed different pro rata shares of three "pots": (1) the base year pro rata, (2) the amount above the base but less than the base, adjusted upward for inflation, and (3) the amounts greater than the inflation (CPI) adjusted base.
Basis for redistribution of common pool to taxing units.	Pro rata share of countywide population.	Pro rata share of *weighted* population of all jurisdictions; city's weighted population is current population multiplied by the ratio of the areawide per capita assessed value to the city's per capita assessed value.	Pro rata share of total commission land area that is located within the municipality	If OLF proceeds equal or are less than the base year, city gets 58.735% and county gets 41.265%. For the amount above the base, up to consumer price index (CPI) adjusted amount (base proceeds x current year (CPI), city gets 59.7% and county gets 40.3%. For amounts above the CPI base, 10% remains in the jurisdiction and the remaining 90% is apportioned —57.2% to the city and 42.8 percent to the county.

SOURCE: Pammer and Dustin (1993); Baker et al. (1991); City of Louisville (1985); HMDC (1972).

wide assessed value (AV). One-third of countywide revenue growth is divided into countywide growth in AV, resulting in a new fractional contribution rate each year. The base year is established as a rolling three-year average of the variable involved. The contribution to the common pool, rather than being a share of AV, is a combination of tax base and tax revenues. The contribution is a pro rata share of the sum of growth in (1) the city's commercial and industrial AV, (2) 25 percent of residential AV growth, and (3) 50 percent of property and income tax growth. A city's contribution cannot exceed 13 percent of its property and income tax revenue for the current year. Cities with no tax growth do not contribute, but are eligible for a share of the distribution. Distribution is based on the share of county population in the city, so there is no measurement of fiscal need (e.g., fiscal capacity, age of infrastructure, or concentrations of poor or elderly population), except so far as need is reflected by population change.

Hackensack Meadowlands Development Commission

The Hackensack Meadowlands Development Commission (HMDC) introduced a municipal tax sharing program in 1970 among 14 municipalities in two counties located within the New York region (HMDC 1971). One municipality, Jersey City, New Jersey, is classified as a central city. The program involves a special district coterminous with the Meadowlands (New York) wetland area of the lower Hackensack River. The HMDC conducts land development and wetlands reclamation projects in the region. New development meant that the tax base of the involved cities would be differentially affected by HMDC land-use decisions. The purpose of the sharing arrangement was to distribute equitably the fiscal benefits of new development, regardless of where it occurs.

The arrangement divides up revenues from new development in the district. Beginning in 1993, the cities in the district kept 60 percent of revenue from new development. The HMDC formula requires contributions based on growth in total equalized assessed valuations of each city. Growth is defined as change in tax dollar levies. The sharing pool consists of a revenue base equal to the growth in all cities' total property tax revenue, adjusted downward by the amount owed to the county. The pool is reallocated to the cities based on each city keeping 40 percent of its revenue growth, along with a residual distribution of the remaining 60 percent to each city based upon how much of HMDC land is within the city.

Policy and Administrative Issues in Metropolitan Fiscal Equalization

Fiscal equalization will create a variety of legal problems. First, there is the question of the state legal environment.

Isolating Critical Legal Barriers to Equalization

This involves such issues as, first, whether all property classes (e.g., residential, commercial, industrial) must be taxed at a uniform rate and whether any tax caps in place exist. State legislation is a likely requirement, so how such legislation should evolve must be explored. Second, there are questions concerning the property value assessment system in the state. Suits have been filed against state tax boards concerning inequities in the appraisal process. Resolving the assessment practices issue may become an especially critical barrier.

Building Basic Fiscal Equalization Formulas

Formulas for common pool contributions and distributions should be linked to a measurement of fiscal and municipal service demand needs. Yet the fact is that no metropolitan region has devised a politically and operationally feasible method of creating a common revenue pool on the basis of need-based criteria. The age of the housing stock, proportions of indigent population, or public service cost weighting factors should be included in sharing formulas. If possible, the formula should take into account the impact of different expenditure demands on the taxing jurisdictions. This challenge is difficult. Suburban jurisdictions oppose need-based formulas because of fears that the declining central city would capture most of the distribution pool. Compromise may lead to a distribution formula that is based on a population pro rata that does not recognize municipal service demand factors. Although conflict is inevitable, it can perhaps be minimized through special efforts to formulate metropolitanwide objectives for regional fiscal equalization.

In addition, property taxes are not the only mode of fiscal equalization. The retail sales tax in most states is already a scheme in which local taxes are collected and redistributed to taxing units. Federal income taxes are similar redistributive mechanisms. From this perspective, city and county income tax systems may be appropriate vehicles for tax base sharing, as may be an employment "head tax" or commuter tax based on the location of jobs.

Tax Abatements, Exemptions, TIF Districts, and Other Governments

Existing claims to tax base and revenues present a barrier to fiscal equalization. Even though fiscal equalization should suspend the need for tax abatements, the existing roster of abatements must be accommodated in any equalization approach. In fact, one objective of fiscal equalization systems is to eliminate the motivation to use tax incentives to lure businesses to a city. Decisions must be made concerning the treatment of existing abatements and property tax exemptions. Care must be taken to craft an equalization arrangement that handles abatements, exemptions, and tax increment financing (TIF) districts. TIF bondholders have first lien on property tax revenue growth within the TIF district boundary. Given this legal claim on revenue growth, a conflict is created in the event a fiscal equalization scheme is developed that also claims growth in tax revenues. In addition, how will other nonmunicipal governments be treated under proposed fiscal equalization plans? What about schools and special districts? These questions illustrate the broader issue of what to do about the structure of overlapping taxing jurisdictions.

Organizational Means of Implementing Fiscal Equalization

How can fiscal equalization be implemented in a metropolitan region? What institutional channels should be the forum for designing and establishing fiscal equalization? Should existing organizations take the lead in promoting fiscal equalization? Should a new vehicle be created specifically to champion the most desirable programs? Once established, how should these organizations proceed? To answer these questions, various organizational means might be used, including nonpartisan public citizens groups, area elected officials, a special district format, working groups and task forces, or technical advisory groups.

SAMUEL NUNN

BIBLIOGRAPHY

Baker, K., S. Hinze, and N. Manzi, 1991. *Minnesota's Fiscal disparities Program.* Minneapolis: Research Department, Minnesota House of Representatives. July.
Bowman, J. H., S. MacManus, and J.L. Mikesell, 1992. "Mobilizing Resources for Public Services: Financing Urban Governments." *Journal of Urban Affairs,* vol. 14, no. 3–4:311–335.
City of Louisville, 1985. *Louisville–Jefferson County Compact.* Louisville, KY: City of Louisville, Department of Law.
Hackensack Meadowlands Development Commission (HMDC), 1972. *Intermunicipal Tax Sharing Theory and Operation.* Hackensack, NJ: HMDC, October.
Ladd, H. F., and J. Yinger, 1989. *America's Ailing Cities: Fiscal Health and the Design of Urban Policy.* Baltimore, MD: Johns Hopkins Press.
Lee, R. D., Jr., and R. W. Johnson, 1994. *Public Budgeting Systems.* 5th ed. Gaithersburg, MD: Aspen Publishers.
Pammer, W., and J. Dustin, 1993. "Fostering Economic Development Through County Tax Sharing." *State and Local Government Review.* (Winter): 57–71.
Wolman, H., R. Hanson, E. Hill, M. Howland, and L. Ledebur, 1992. "National Urban Economic Development Policy." *Journal of Urban Affairs,* vol. 14, no. 3–4:217–238.

FISCAL FEDERALISM.
A subfield of economic theory, concerned with the distribution of governmental responsibility between levels of government, and, more generally, an area of research and scholarship concerned with the financial aspects of intergovernmental relations in a federal system.

Important features of a federal system can be captured through legal and political analysis, but economic models of governmental activity are especially useful for understanding intergovernmental relationships and for exploring the effects that these relationships have on public policies. Through economic analysis of grants-in-aid and other exchanges of economic resources among governments, it is possible to test carefully specified models of the intergovernmental system.

Investigators who approach federalism from a "fiscal federalism" perspective suggest that the decentralization that characterizes federal systems is at least in part an economically rational effort to improve resource allocation in the public sector by recognizing variations in local taste. Many of the exchanges in which students of federalism are interested exist to compensate for externalities ("spillover" effects) of programs produced by constituent states. Goods and services that states produce serve not only the population of the individual states but also some living in other states as well, people who are not paying taxes to receive those benefits. In such circumstances, then, grants-in-aid are appropriate to compensate for spillovers.

Negative spillovers may also call for grants, as when cities find it cheaper to dispose of raw sewerage into a stream rather than to treat it first. Fiscal federalism advocates would suggest that grants for sewage treatment plants (or for downstream communities' water treatment plants) would be appropriate.

Students of fiscal federalism have focused attention sharply upon the effect that various types of intergovernmental fiscal exchanges have upon the economic behavior of governmental decisionmakers. Lump sum grants, categorical matching grants, and general revenue sharing have been examined. In addition to grants-in-aid, other types of subsidy can flow from one level to another, such as provisions of the tax code allowing deductibility of state and local taxes and interest on federal income tax returns. Most recently, attention has turned to the imposition of costs on constituent units of the federal system through the regulatory process, the imposition of unfunded mandates with which constituent units must comply at their own expense.

In the period since World War II, there are few more important developments in the United States political system than the many changes in fiscal federalism that have led to its emergence in its present form. In 1955, federal grants-in-aid accounted for only 10.2 percent of total state and local outlays and only 0.8 percent of gross domestic product (GDP). Even though grants-in-aid, as they are known, had been in use for over 40 years and had been of increasing importance since the Great Depression years, state and local governments were not, for the most part, looking to Washington for financial assistance.

That was soon to change. Beginning in the late 1950s—particularly with the advent of the interstate highway program—and continuing in the 1960s with federal aid programs associated with President Lyndon Johnson's Great Society initiative, the scope of aid sharply expanded. Many of these new grants were targeted as never before to urban areas. By 1980, state and local governments relied on federal grants-in-aid for 25.8 percent of state and local outlays (and these expenditures amounted to 3.5 percent of gross domestic product [GDP])–figures that declined somewhat in succeeding years but climbed again so that, by 1993, they stood at 21.9 percent and 3.1 percent, respectively.

F. TED HEBERT

BIBLIOGRAPHY

Rosen, Harvey, ed., 1988. *Fiscal Federalism: Quantitative Studies.* Chicago: University of Chicago Press.
Swartz, Thomas R., and John E. Peck, eds., 1990. *The Changing Face of Fiscal Federalism.* Armonk, NY: M. E. Sharpe.
U.S. Advisory Commission on Intergovernmental Relations, annual. *Significant Features of Fiscal Federalism.* Washington, DC: U.S. Advisory Commission on Intergovernmental Relations.

FISCAL POLICY.

A policy that uses government expenditures and taxes to stimulate the level of economic activity, as typically measured by gross domestic product (GDP). Fiscal policy advocates postulate that GDP responds to changes in the aggregate demand for goods and services. Aggregate demand includes consumption, investment, government and net export demand (exports minus imports). The government can influence aggregate demand by manipulating government expenditures and taxes. Government expenditures directly influence government demand; tax policy influences both consumption and investment demand.

Fiscal policy proponents recommend countercyclical fiscal policy to minimize macroeconomic fluctuations during business cycles. In essence, countercyclical fiscal policy offsets fluctuations in aggregate demand with changes in the federal budget deficit. The federal budget deficit is defined as net tax revenues minus government expenditures. During the business cycle's contractionary phase, the federal government stimulates aggregate demand and the economy by increasing government expenditures or reducing taxes. This action helps counterbalance the business cycle's contractionary phase but increases the federal budget deficit (or reduces the surplus). Conversely, contractionary fiscal policy reduces government expenditures or increases taxes; this reduces the federal budget deficit (or increases the budget surplus) and helps counterbalance an overheated economy during the business cycle's expansionary phase.

In the context of fiscal policy, government expenditures, on one hand, include the goods and services purchased by the federal government. National defense, highway construction and maintenance, education, and federal research and development projects are all examples of government expenditures. Government expenditures may vary from year to year, but they are not typically sensitive to changes in the GDP during the year. On the other hand, taxes include both programs to generate federal revenues (e.g., income taxes, corporate profits taxes, and social security taxes) and social programs that transfer income across individuals (e.g., Aid to Families with Dependent Children [AFDC], Social Security benefits). Net taxes are defined as tax revenues minus transfer payments. Net taxes fluctuate with the GDP.

Fiscal policy provides an alternative to monetary policy and supply-side economics. Monetary policy is also a demand-side policy. It influences aggregate demand indirectly by changing the money supply. Increasing the money supply directly increases consumption demand and decreases interest rates. Lower interest rates stimulate investment and consumption demand (see **monetary policy**). Supply-side economics hypothesizes that economic expansion must be supported by growth in productive capacity or it will increase prices rather than the GDP. Supply-side economics proposes reducing marginal tax rates to increase the labor supply and capital investment. Presumably, this increases economic capacity to accommodate growth while reducing prices (see **supply-side economics**).

Classical Economics and Fiscal Policy

Classical economics, the prevailing economic theory in the United States prior to the Great Depression, hypothesizes that market economies are inherently stable. In particular, the actual GDP automatically adjusts to the economy's productive capacity, called potential GDP. Economic capacity is determined by the quantity and quality of resources available (e.g., labor, capital, and natural resources). If resource prices are flexible, they will adjust until resources are fully employed and the economy is operating at economic capacity. If resources are underemployed, their prices will fall. Production becomes more profitable as resource prices fall, encouraging firms to expand output. The GDP expands until underemployment is eliminated. Conversely, prices will increase for overemployed resources, reducing profits, decreasing production, and eliminating overemployment.

With sufficient resource price flexibility, the economy will adjust to full employment relatively quickly. In this case, countercyclical fiscal policy is unnecessary in the short run and counterproductive in the long run. If resource price flexibility stabilizes the economy relatively quickly, fiscal policy is unnecessary in the short run. Furthermore, the economy cannot accommodate the increased aggregate demand after returning to full employment, assuming that the potential GDP is unaffected by expansionary fiscal policy.

Thus, expansionary fiscal policy increases prices, rather than the GDP, in the long run. As a result, classical economists believe that the federal government should maintain a balanced budget; flexible resource prices stabilize the economy at full employment.

Keynesian Economics and Fiscal Policy

John Maynard Keynes formalized a theory linking fiscal policy and economic performance in his 1936 book *General Theory of Employment, Interest, and Money.* He believed that classical economic theory was inconsistent with the Great Depression that the United States and world economies experienced in the 1930s. Even though the U.S. unemployment rate reached 25 percent in 1933, flexible resource prices failed to restore full employment.

Keynes offered two explanations for the Great Depression: sticky prices and pessimistic expectations. He hypothesized that resource and product prices are sticky rather than flexible, particularly with respect to price decreases. Sticky prices are slow to decrease as unemployment increases. Furthermore, if producers and consumers have pessimistic expectations, price decreases might not stimulate increased production. Lower resource prices will only increase output if producers expect to sell the extra output. If consumers are pessimistic about future economic conditions, they will not consume more as prices fall; accordingly, business will not increase output. Thus falling prices might not stimulate business investment and production.

Keynes believed that prices were sticky and expectations were pessimistic during the Great Depression. Under these conditions, the economy can experience prolonged high-unemployment rates. Keynes advocated countercyclical fiscal policy to supplement private spending and stabilize the economy. He felt that the potentially prolonged unemployment during an economic contraction imposes unacceptable social and personal costs. He supported countercyclical fiscal policy to minimize these short-run costs.

Keynes was among the first to advocate that federal budget deficits are appropriate in the short run when the economy is operating below full employment. This sentiment was embodied in the Employment Act of 1946, which stipulated that the federal government had a responsibility to promote full employment. The appropriate government stabilization role has been a continuing matter of debate ever since. Proponents tried to better define this role in the Full Employment and Balanced Growth (Humphrey-Hawkins) Act of 1978. Among other things, this act defined 4 percent unemployment as the full employment target for stabilization policy purposes. (For policy purposes, full employment means eliminating the unemployment associated with business cycle contractions, but not the "natural unemployment" associated with

a dynamic economy. Natural unemployment involves people voluntarily seeking better jobs and people transitioning out of declining industries. Currently, 5 percent to 6 percent unemployment is considered full employment.)

It should be emphasized that the major difference between the classical and Keynesian economists concerns the short run. Keynes appreciated the power of competitive markets to allocate efficiently society's scarce resources. He believed that the competitive market should be unencumbered by government intervention in the long run, after reaching full employment. He agreed with the classical position that expansionary fiscal policies are inflationary when the economy is at full employment. He certainly did not advocate a welfare state, as is frequently attributed to Keynesian economists. The problem he addressed was potential short-run instability. Countercyclical fiscal policy has its greatest impact in the short run, before prices have adjusted to their full employment levels. Keynes felt that prolonged short-run unemployment imposed a greater social cost than long-run inflation. As Keynes stated, "In the long run, we are all dead."

Discretionary Fiscal Policy and Automatic Stabilizers

Countercyclical fiscal policy can be implemented both passively, through automatic stabilizers, and actively, through discretionary fiscal policy. Automatic stabilizers are nondiscretionary adjustments in fiscal policy, primarily net tax revenues, that occur automatically as the GDP changes. Discretionary fiscal policy influences the GDP by intentionally changing government expenditure programs or tax rates.

Most taxes and many transfer payments depend on income, or on the GDP. As the GDP falls, tax receipts decrease and transfer payments increase. Both responses automatically reduce net tax revenues, which stimulates the GDP. As the GDP grows, tax receipts increase and transfer payments decrease, automatically increasing net tax revenues and retarding further the GDP growth. The stronger the relationship between income and both tax receipts and transfer payments, the stronger the stabilization effect. For example, a progressive income tax scheme would have stronger stabilization effects than a proportional income tax scheme. With proportional income taxes, tax liabilities are a constant percentage of income, for all income levels. As income increases, tax payments increase at a constant rate. With progressive income taxes, the marginal tax rate increases with income. Thus the tax liability increases with income at an increasing rate. Tax liabilities grow faster than income, providing a stronger stabilization effect.

Discretionary fiscal policy can stimulate the economy by increasing government expenditure programs or by reducing tax rates (expansionary fiscal policy); discretionary fiscal policy can retard the GDP by decreasing government expenditure programs or by raising tax rates (contractionary fiscal policy). As the economy falls into a recession, the government can manipulate federal expenditure programs and tax rates actively to increase the budget deficit. Conversely, as the economy expands, the government can consciously manipulate federal expenditure programs and tax rates actively to decrease the budget deficit. Thus, discretionary countercyclical fiscal policy can also reduce economic fluctuations during the business cycle.

Both discretionary fiscal policy and automatic stabilizers affect the federal budget deficit; thus, it is hard to distinguish between these two policy tools by simply observing changes in the federal budget deficit. For example, both expansionary fiscal policy and a declining GDP will increase the budget deficit. Distinguishing between these policies requires measuring the federal budget deficit at a constant GDP level. If the federal budget deficit would change even if the GDP level remained constant, the government has conducted discretionary fiscal policy. The resulting budget deficit is called an active deficit because it involves an intentional change in government expenditures or tax revenues. If the budget deficit changes only if the GDP changes, the government has not conducted discretionary fiscal policy. Any change in the actual budget deficit results from the automatic stabilizers. This is called a passive deficit.

Policy Implementation Lags and Sticky Prices

The major differences between Keynesian and classical economists concern the degree to which prices are sticky and the time period before fiscal policy affects the GDP. Classical economists believe that prices adjust quickly, compared to the lags in implementing discretionary stabilization policy. Thus, as previously described, fiscal policy is ineffectual in the short run and counterproductive in the long run. Conversely, Keynesians believe that stabilization policies can be implemented more quickly than prices can adjust. Thus there is justification for short-run federal stabilization policies. Understanding this debate requires understanding policy implementation lags and sticky prices.

Discretionary fiscal policy requires conscious actions by policymakers. Policymakers must identify whether the economy is expanding or contracting, agree on the appropriate countercyclical fiscal policy, and implement the policy. Lags are an implicit part of this process. There are lags in identifying changes in economic conditions, lags in determining and implementing the policy response, and lags before the policy affects economic conditions (referred to

as recognition lags, administrative lags, and impact lags, respectively). As a result, two or three years may elapse before fiscal policy affects unemployment, price levels, and the GDP.

Automatic stabilizers have a more immediate impact because they do not require conscious actions. Automatic stabilizers are inherent in the federal tax and transfer payment system. They work automatically because many taxes and transfer payments are tied to income (GDP). With automatic stabilizers, there are no recognition or administrative lags, only impact lags. The effect is more immediate, but not instantaneous. If prices adjust quickly, the economy will return to full employment before automatic stabilizers have an impact.

Much recent work by Keynesian economists has focused on explaining why prices are sticky. There are several possible explanations, including long-term labor contracts, menu costs, and efficiency wages. If nominal wage rates are established in long-term labor contracts, wage rates cannot adjust until the contracts expire. Long-term labor contracts are one of the earliest explanations for sticky wages. Unfortunately, this explanation has been criticized for several reasons. For example, if long-term nominal wage contracts are inefficient, why do employers and employees use them? Optimal contract theory suggests that other labor contracts provide mutual gains. Furthermore, sticky prices due to long-term nominal wage contracts would imply a countercyclical relationship between economic activity and real wages. Empirical data indicates the relationship may actually be a bit procyclical. These and other shortcomings led economists to find new explanations for sticky wages.

"Menu costs" are one alternative explanation. Menu costs are the costs involved with changing prices. These costs include the firm's internal costs of determining the new prices, the cost of implementing the price change (i.e., bringing new menus or price lists, distributing new catalogs, etc.), and potential customer annoyance. Imperfect competition and small menu costs can generate sticky prices that correspond to the empirical data.

Another alternative involves "efficiency wages." The efficiency wage hypothesis recognizes that higher wages may increase productivity by reducing turnover, improving the average quality of the firm's workforce, and reducing the employees' predilection to shirking (to avoid being laid off from their relatively high-paying job). If higher wages increase productivity and lower wages reduce productivity, firms may not reduce wages during an economic downturn.

Classical and Keynesian economists have different views regarding the length of the price adjustment and countercyclical fiscal policy implementation lags. Unfortunately, empirical data concerning these lags are generally ambiguous and open to interpretation. It is impossible to conduct controlled scientific experiments to settle the issue.

Thus the debate is likely to continue into the foreseeable future.

Fiscal Versus Monetary Policy

Keynes and the early Keynesian economists believed that countercyclical fiscal policy was more effective than monetary policy for stabilizing the economy. This belief considers the mechanisms through which monetary policy affects macroeconomic performance and experience during the Great Depression. Specifically, an increase in the money supply stimulates the economy both directly and indirectly (see **monetary policy**). As the money supply increases and supply exceeds demand, individuals will reduce their money holdings by increasing both consumption and savings. Increases in consumption increase aggregate demand. Increases in savings reduce interest rates. As interest rates fall, investment demand increases and consumption demand increases further (as savings rates fall). Thus, expansionary monetary policy stimulates the GDP in the short run through a direct increase in consumption demand and, indirectly, through a decrease in interest rates. As with expansionary fiscal policy, expansionary monetary policy is inflationary in the long run, after prices adjust to restore full employment.

Keynesians believed that pessimistic expectations during a recession would negate the short-run effects of expansionary monetary policy. In particular, as the money supply increases, pessimistic individuals will not use the excess money supply to increase consumption. Thus there is no direct effect on the GDP. Furthermore, investment and consumption demand will not increase as interest rates fall. Pessimistic individuals will not increase consumption as interest rates fall, and pessimistic firms will not invest. Thus there is no indirect effect on the GDP. Pessimism renders monetary policy ineffective in the Keynesian model. Keynes referred to this situation as a "liquidity trap." Therefore, early Keynesians relied on countercyclical fiscal policy to stabilize the GDP.

Most modern Keynesian economists recognize that monetary policy has a short-run impact on the GDP. Furthermore, the policy implementation lags are significantly shorter for monetary policy than they are for discretionary fiscal policy. Discretionary fiscal policy requires congressional approval; monetary policy can be implemented by the Federal Reserve (see **Federal Reserve System**). Thus, Keynesians increasingly support automatic fiscal stabilizers and monetary policy; discretionary fiscal policy plays a smaller role.

Fiscal Policy Versus Supply-Side Economics

Both traditional fiscal policy and supply-side economists suggest tax cuts to stimulate the GDP. Fiscal policy emphasizes the short-run effects of tax cuts on aggregate demand. Supply-side economics emphasizes the long-run effects of tax cuts on economic capacity. In the supply-side model, economic capacity is largely determined by the quantity of available resources. Reducing marginal tax rates can increase the supply of resources and expand productive capacity (e.g., by reducing taxes on personal income, corporate profits, capital gains, savings, and capital investment).

This introduces an apparent contradiction: The same policy is recommended to support two different goals. In actuality, both viewpoints may be correct. Fiscal policy focuses on fiscal policy's short-run effects. In the short run, lower taxes can increase household consumption and business investment; this increases the GDP. Supply-side economics does not address short-run economic fluctuations. It takes time to translate changes in marginal tax rates into increases in productive capacity. Supply-side economics focuses on the long-run impacts of tax rate changes.

Indirect Effects

Traditional fiscal policy, as envisioned by Keynesian economists, focuses on fiscal policy's direct short-run effects. However, fiscal policy also has many indirect short- and long-run impacts. Many of these indirect impacts reduce fiscal policy's effectiveness and have been used to argue against fiscal policy as a stabilization tool. Indirect effects involve the impacts on interest rates, prices, and the government budget deficit. Each are discussed in turn.

Expansionary fiscal policy increases interest rates because the federal government must borrow to finance the increased deficit. (The federal government cannot print money to finance a deficit. Only the independent Federal Reserve can print money. [see **Federal Reserve System**]. The federal government can only raise revenues through taxes or borrowing.) As the interest rate increases, private investment decreases. This is called "crowding-out." (See **crowd-out**.) Crowding-out has both short- and long-run effects. In the short run, it decreases private investment demand, a component of aggregate demand; this lowers the GDP. In the classical model, where prices and interest rates instantaneously adjust to their full-employment levels, every dollar of the federal budget deficit crowds out a dollar of private investment; debt financed expansionary fiscal policy is ineffective. In the Keynesian model, with sticky prices and interest rates, crowding-out is limited. In the long run, decreases in private investment can reduce GDP growth rates. If private investment contributes more than government expenditures to future human resource and capital stocks, current federal deficits reduce future potential GDP.

An increase in the federal budget deficit can also reduce current consumption. The new classical economists subscribe to the "rational expectations" doctrine. This doctrine maintains that decisionmakers consider all available information about current and future economic policies. Applied to fiscal policy, this doctrine implies that consumers realize that current budget deficits must be paid back with higher future taxes. In other words, if expansionary fiscal policy increases the federal budget deficit, rational consumers will expect offsetting future tax increases. To cover these future tax increases, they will reduce current consumption and increase savings. According to this reasoning, expansionary fiscal policy is met by an equal decrease in consumption demand, leaving aggregate demand and the GDP unaffected in the short run. Keynesians argue that expansionary fiscal policy has at least some stimulative effect because savings do not increase by the full increase in the budget deficit. Consumers will spend some of the increased government expenditures or tax savings.

Expansionary fiscal policy also affects inflation, in both the short and long run. The traditional Keynesian model maintained that fiscal policy could stimulate the GDP in the short run without increasing the price level, as long as unemployed resources were available. At full employment, expansionary fiscal policy would increase prices rather than the GDP. Drawing on the "Phillips Curve," which shows the relationship between unemployment and wage rates, economists currently believe that fiscal policy will have a short-run inflationary impact even when the economy is below full employment. In the long run, resource prices adjust to their full employment levels and the economy returns to potential GDP. Any attempt to sustain output above this level will translate into inflation. Over time, the inflation rate will accelerate as individuals anticipate continued inflation and take precautionary measures (e.g., building expected inflation into future wage and price agreements and interest rates). This creates an accelerating inflation spiral (called the "acceleration principle").

Inflation has an indirect effect on U.S. international competitiveness. As U.S. prices increase, U.S. products become more expensive relative to foreign products. This increased expense reduces the demand for U.S. exports and increases U.S. imports. Net export demand is one component of aggregate demand, so this contracts the GDP and partially offsets the expansionary fiscal policy. The degree to which this offsets expansionary fiscal policy depends on the sensitivity of U.S. exports and imports to relative international prices.

Fiscal Policy and the Balanced Budget Amendment

A constitutional amendment requiring the federal government to maintain a balanced budget would affect the gov-

ernment's ability to conduct countercyclical fiscal policy. The precise implications depend on the structure of the balanced budget amendment. If the amendment required a balanced budget over the business cycle, the government could still use both countercyclical discretionary fiscal policy and automatic stabilizers. If the amendment required a balanced government budget when the economy operates at full employment, automatic stabilizers could still operate, but discretionary fiscal policy would require changing both taxes and government expenditures equally. Countercyclical "balanced budget policy" does have a small effect because government expenditures have a stronger impact on the GDP than do equal tax changes. (Many balanced budget policy proposals prohibit countercyclical balanced budget policy by placing a cap on either government expenditures or tax revenues.)

Finally, requiring the government to balance its annual budget would virtually preclude both countercyclical discretionary fiscal policy and automatic stabilizers. Fiscal policy would become procyclical; discretionary fiscal policy would be required to offset the effects of the automatic stabilizers. As the economy contracted and automatic stabilizers increased the federal deficit, the government would have to increase taxes or reduce federal expenditures (contractionary fiscal policy). As the economy expanded, the government would have to adopt an expansionary fiscal policy.

Positions in the balanced budget amendment debate reflect, in part, the participants' views concerning fiscal policy's effectiveness. Classical economists tend to favor the balanced budget amendment. They believe fiscal policy is ineffective in the short run and counterproductive in the long run. They view the economy as inherently stable, so they would prefer that the government maintain a balanced budget and allow market price adjustments to ensure full employment. Keynesians tend to oppose the balanced budget amendment. If prices are sticky, they believe the economy can experience long periods of unemployment. Furthermore, they feel that short-run unemployment has higher social and economic costs than long-run inflation. In their opinion, fiscal policy can be an effective short-run stabilization tool, particularly automatic stabilizers.

The debate over the appropriate role for fiscal policy and the balanced budget amendment has not been resolved. Few economists currently support massive doses of discretionary fiscal policy to "fine-tune" the economy because of forecasting problems, a persistent federal budget deficit, and policy implementation lags. However, many economists support using automatic stabilizers and monetary policy to "coarse-tune" the economy. This debate will continue until economists can agree on the relative length of the price adjustment and fiscal policy implementation lags and the magnitude of fiscal policy's indirect effects, including reductions in investment and long-run growth (crowding-out), increases in short-run savings (rational ex-

pectations), increases in domestic prices (Phillips Curve), and the effect on net export demand (international price competition). Theoretical models can be constructed to support the spectrum of beliefs, from Keynesian to classical. Empirical analysis has not developed to the point where the correct model specification can be unambiguously identified.

WILLIAM R. GATES

BIBLIOGRAPHY

Baumol, William J., and Alan S. Blinder, 1994. *Macroeconomics: Principles and Policy.* 6th ed. Fort Worth, TX: Dryden Press.

Biven, W. Carl, 1989. *Who Killed John Maynard Keynes?* Homewood, IL: Dow Jones–Irwin.

Gwartney, James D., and Richard L. Stroup, 1995. *Macroeconomics: Private and Public Choice.* 7th ed. Fort Worth, TX: Dryden Press.

Keynes, John Maynard, 1936. *The General Theory of Employment, Interest, and Money.* London: Macmillan.

Mankiw, N. Gregory, 1990. "A Quick Refresher Course in Macroeconomics." *Journal of Economic Literature* 27 (December 1990): 1645–1660.

Samuelson, Paul A., and William D. Nordhaus, 1992. *Macroeconomics.* 14th ed. New York: McGraw-Hill.

FISCAL STRESS. A situation that occurs when government revenues are inadequate to meet the demands placed upon government for services. Fiscal stress can occur at any level of government. Several factors contribute to fiscal stress. Most taxpayers believe government is wasteful and therefore are reluctant to pay increased taxes to meet service needs. At times sentiment builds that taxes should be cut. Yet few citizens and public employees alter their expectations about government services and benefits, expecting both to continue. Often, public officials must make decisions in a complex environment that further contributes to stress. The institutional structure of the public sector is one of laws, procedures, and regulations, such as merit systems, line-item budgets, and rules of authorities and commissions. Slowdowns in economic growth also contribute to fiscal stress.

Signs of fiscal stress may vary by level of government. At the federal level, where deficit spending is possible, growing federal deficits and mounting federal debt are clear signs of fiscal stress. At the state and local level, declining revenues and an increase in the proportion of revenues declared to be collectible are signs of strain in achieving balanced budgets. Local signs of longer-term decline may also include an aging housing stock, an increase in multifamily dwellings, an increasing household occupancy rate, a decline in property values, a decrease in conventional mortgage financing and an increase in federally guaranteed mortgages, and a decline in employment and personal income and an increase in Aid to Families with Dependent Children (AFDC) recipients.

Fiscal stress is particularly likely within a metropolitan area when local government is very fragmented, allowing wealthy and middle-class people to politically separate and isolate themselves from the more needy and poorer citizens that tend to live in larger cities. In these Standard Metropolitan Statistical Areas (SMSAs), the greatest potential for revenue resides in the suburbs or in new parallel "edge cities" that are close to the older central cities, but the greatest social needs, and therefore potential expenditures and costs, are in the latter.

Once stress is recognized, officials may pursue several strategies. Government activities may be reviewed to determine which are mandated, so that policymakers know which are "musts" and which are activities that are performed mostly from habit or custom. The public may also be polled to determine which activities have low support. Revenue sources may also be scrutinized to see if additional revenues can be generated. Possibilities for generating revenue include imposing user charges and fees, collecting uncollected taxes, selling services to other government units, and obtaining grants from other governments or private sources. In some instances, services can be assigned to other service providers. Some shifting may result from contracting services out at lower cost, sharing costs and services with other governments or the private sector, or increasing client participation in service costs. Labor costs may also be examined for potential savings. Sometimes positions can be reclassified and downgraded. Tasks may be simplified, so that others with less training may perform them. In some situations, one-time capital investments may be substituted for ongoing labor expenses. Information systems may be improved to provide a better basis from which government officials can make financial and allocative decisions. Citizen demand may be held down through education as to costs and consequences, and some service rationing may reduce squandering of public services.

Each of these strategies falls into one of two basic approaches for dealing with fiscal stress: increasing government revenues or decreasing expenditures to bring the two more closely in alignment. The latter, especially, came to be known as "cutback management" during the 1980s when concern over fiscal stress peaked as a reform movement.

Proponents of cutback management contended that government officials and politicians should anticipate fiscal stress and decline and develop tactics first to resist the decline and then to smooth the decline. Proponents developed inventories of strategies, which included the following: To alleviate external political pressure, officials were exhorted to diversify programs, clients and constituents; improve their legislative liaisons; educate the public about the agency's mission; mobilize dependent clients; become "captured" by a powerful interest group or legislator; threaten to cut vital or popular programs; and cut a visible and widespread service a little to demonstrate client dependency. Combating economic entropy required finding a wider and richer revenue base, including metropolitan reorganization at the local level; developing incentives to prevent private sector disinvestment; seeking foundation support; luring new public and private sector investment; and adopting user charges whenever possible. To counter internal political pressures and political vulnerability, officials were to issue symbolic responses, such as forming study commissions and task forces, "circling the wagons" by developing the esprit de corp of a siege mentality; and strengthening expertise. Economic and technical pressure from internal sources, or organizational atrophy, was to be combated by improving hierarchical control, improving productivity, experimenting with less-costly service delivery systems, automating, and stockpiling and rationing resources.

Once government agencies and jurisdictions had embarked upon a trajectory of decline, proponents of cutback management advocated different tactics to smooth the process. These included making peace with competing agencies, cutting low-prestige programs, cutting programs to politically weak clients, selling and lending expertise to other agencies, and sharing problems with fellow agencies. Other tactics included improving targeting on problems, planning with preservation as an objective, cutting losses by distinguishing between capital investments and sunk costs, and yielding concessions to taxpayers and employers to retain them. Government officials were also exhorted to change leadership at each stage in the decline process, to reorganize at each stage, to cut programs run by weak subunits, to get temporary exemptions from personnel and budgetary regulations that limit discretion, to renegotiate long-term contracts to regain flexibility, and to install rational choice techniques such as zero-based budgeting. The public sector cutback manager would also mortgage the future by deferring maintenance and downscaling personnel quality, asking employees to make voluntary sacrifices—such as taking early retirements and deferring raises, improving forecasting capacity to anticipate further cuts, reassigning surplus facilities to other users, selling surplus property to lease back when needed, and exploiting the exploitable.

Plainly, the previous recommendations from those who heralded fiscal stress and advised government officials to engage in cutback management were a "kitchen sink" inventory of strategies and tactics. This cutback management reform movement began in the 1970s when the national economy appeared to be floundering. At that time, the U.S. economy was reeling from the inflationary consequences of the 1960s when President Lyndon Johnson attempted to fight simultaneously a foreign war in Vietnam and a domestic war against poverty without a tax increase

to fund either. In 1969, under President Richard Nixon, a temporary federal income tax surcharge was adopted to combat rising inflation, but it appeared to be too little too late. Inflation drove up costs of government operations, including labor and product costs. The Oil Petroleum Exporting Countries (OPEC) embargo on oil products exported to the United States contributed to rising inflation and unemployment, plummeting the country into stagflation. Cutback management reforms were the response.

Concern over government fiscal stress was also prompted by demographic changes at the local level, especially in large metropolitan areas. Suburbanization, begun in the 1950s, continued at a rapid pace during the 1960s, with the consequence that in many major metropolitan areas the stable middle class moved out to the suburbs, diminishing the tax base of large urban governments. Racial politics contributed to this demographic shift. At least initially, whites fled the cities, although in subsequent decades the black middle class began to leave also. The pace of suburbanization and "white flight" was exacerbated by the race riots of 1967 and 1968 that occurred in many major cities, including Newark, New Jersey, Detroit, Michigan, Washington, D.C., and Los Angeles, California. The loss of the middle-class tax base not only reduced revenues but also left large urban governments with a disproportionate share of the poor that needed services and support, further increasing expenditures.

Large cities especially experienced fiscal stress. By 1975, New York City was in financial default. Major New York City banks refused to purchase or underwrite any more city notes or bonds, driving the city to the verge of bankruptcy. Eventually, a holding corporation, representing the major interests (e.g. the banks, city officials, and state officials) was established to address the crisis. The corporation adopted many of the cutback management tactics suggested by proponents of this approach, including negotiating concessions with the unions, cutting back on services, searching for additional revenue sources, and offering incentives to prevent disinvestment. Eventually, the city was nursed back to greater financial health, although, like most large cities, fiscal stress continues to the present.

Concern with fiscal stress and its corresponding cutback management techniques is related to two other reform movements of recent decades: the "reinventing government" and "public productivity" movements. These reform movements share several key characteristics, although each sometimes uses slightly different language and stresses somewhat different aspects of the same general perspective. In the commonly posed trade-off between efficiency and equity, they emphasize efficiency as a primary government goal. Cutback management emphasizes the need to achieve greater efficiencies in order to lower expenditures to alleviate fiscal stress. Reinventing government stresses efficiency and alternative service delivery mechanisms to improve service to the customer. The public

productivity reform movement stresses efficiency to increase government productivity.

These efficiency-oriented reform movements embrace the notion of downsizing government as doable and desirable. Downsizing reduces government expenditures to ameliorate fiscal stress on government and the burden on the taxpayer (cutback management), to make government more flexible and adaptable to customer concerns (reinventing government), and to improve the input-output ratio of government programs (public productivity). The solution each espouses in some fashion is to cut back government, for different reasons: financial stress and excessive expenditures relative to revenues (the fiscal stress movement); lack of customer responsiveness (the reinventing government movement); and governmental inefficiency (the public productivity movement).

These reform movements strive to make public sector management more like private sector management, in many instances. They advocate that government officials use techniques that are used in the private sector, including using cost centers, making customers aware of benefits as well as costs of government services through public relations (advertising), developing marketing strategies to monitor customer satisfaction and preferences, encouraging the search for innovative revenue sources, incorporating competition into purchasing and wherever else possible, and holding the line on expenditure.

The efficiency-based reform movements, including cutback management, encourage privatization and dispersing services when doing so takes advantage of competition to lower costs and increase productivity and efficiency. These movements share a view that the private sector is more efficient than the public sector when the private sector fosters competition, and sometimes even when competition is absent, because the private sector labors under fewer bureaucratic rules and procedures than the public sector. These movements also share a view that government regulation frequently produces red tape and advocate reducing the number and complexity of government regulations.

The history of reform movements is one of cycles or "waves." Each reform goes through several clearly identifiable stages. First, a legitimate problem reaches public consciousness, such as the fiscal stress of cities in the 1970s and growing federal deficits. Second, reform consultants and advisers recognize the problem and develop an inventory or procedures and responses to deal with the problem. In some reform movements, such as the zero-based budgeting movement, the solutions are a specific procedure to be followed in all situations, in a uniform approach.

In other reform movements, including the efficiency reform movements of fiscal stress and cutback management, reinventing government, and public productivity, the reforms are an inventory of possible strategies, some of which may be adopted in any setting. More discretion is allowed the policymaker who must pick and choose among suggested solutions.

Third, given the rigidity of institutional arrangements within the public sector, the consultants who advocate the reform oversell its benefits to achieve some adoptions. Fourth, the reform recedes in importance and public consciousness as economic conditions change, disillusionment over the degree of success sets in, and other issues rise in importance on the public sector. The problems that fostered the reform movement initially, however, have likely not been permanently fixed. Fifth, the concepts of the previous reform movement, reworked and shrouded in different rhetoric, reappear in the next wave of reform that holds the same underlying precepts. Thus, the fiscal stress and cutback management movement of the 1970s anticipated and laid the foundation for the reinventing government movement and also incorporated ideas from the productivity movement. The problem of fiscal stress, especially for large cities whose financial exigencies fostered cutback management reform movement, still remains.

MARCIA LYNN WHICKER

BIBLIOGRAPHY

Levine, Charles H., 1980. *Managing Fiscal Stress: The Crisis in the Public Sector.* Chatham, NJ: Chatham House.
Rubin, Irene S., 1990. *The Politics of Public Budgeting.* Chatham, NJ: Chatham House.
Smith, Wade S., 1979. *The Appraisal of Municipal Credit Risk.* New York: Moody's Investors Service.
Whicker, Marcia Lynn, and Raymond A. Moore. 1988. *Making America Competitive: Policies for a Global Future.* New York: Praeger.

FLEXTIME. One of a number of alternate work schedules (AWS) used by governments and by the private sector, designed to allow more flexibility to the employee in setting his or her hours of work during the workday. Flextime still requires the 40 hour workweek; however, it allows employees some choice in the hour they arrive at work and the hour they depart work in a typical working day.

The world's governments have never arrived at a universally accepted workday schedule because the start time and ending time of workdays are influenced strongly by national cultural norms. The fast-paced workday of industrialized nations is still contrasted with the more leisurely paced workday of other countries, sometimes filled with the lunch-to-midafternoon break and later quitting hours.

As the composition of today's workforce changes, new and innovative ideas are required to deal with the changing demands of today's workers. Alternate work schedules allow workers more freedom and hold the promise to employers of greater workforce productivity. There are several variations of work hours in the alternative work schedules, including job sharing, part-time work, compressed work weeks, and flextime. Probably the most popular of these is flextime.

Flextime, dating from the 1960s, has been a constantly increasing trend for American workers. The federal workforce was introduced to flextime on a large-scale basis by the Federal Employees Flexible and Compressed Work Schedule Act of 1978. Although flextime can be implemented with some variations, there are usually some consistent features. First, the "band width" of the workday–the time between the beginning of the workday–and the end of the workday–will usually increase for the organization. The typical hours of operation may change from 8:00 A.M. until 5:00 P.M. (with an hour for lunch) to 6:00 A.M. until 7:00 P.M. Some employees will come to work earlier and leave earlier–for instance 6:00 A.M to 3:00 P.M. Some employees will choose to come to work later, around 10:00 A.M., and stay later, to about 7:00 P.M. There are some other slight variations possible, such as 7:00 A.M. to 4:00 P.M., and half hour variations if 30 minutes rather than an hour is allowed for lunch.

Second, there is commonly a period of time during each workday, called "core time," when all employees under this flextime system are expected to be at work. This allows supervisors time for needed coordination of tasks, time for meetings, and time for general tending to the details of work. The typical core time would be 10:00 A.M. until 3:00 P.M.

Two other features of flextime systems are common. There should be someone designated as the overall coordinator who will be responsible as a contact person and as a problem-solver. Finally, some decisions must be made regarding how often employees are allowed to change their selection of flexible hours. Can this be done daily, weekly, monthly, or yearly?

Studies indicate that flextime has much to offer both the employee and the organization. Improved employees' morale, decreased tardiness, more "family friendliness," decreased absenteeism, less traffic congestion, and decreased employee turnover are commonly cited benefits.

Flextime does have some drawbacks. Some managers complain about the increasing difficulty in coordinating group activities, work scheduling, and the unavailability of employees at certain times. Some managers also perceive a decreased level of productivity among employees during hours when supervisors are not present at work. Finally, increased paperwork problems arise when keeping track of employee work hours.

Despite these problems, flextime appears to be an option that will be a permanent fixture of workplaces for decades to come. Given the increase in working women, dual-career couples, and the advantages to organizations of better accommodating workers' family needs, flextime appears to offer great potential in the workplace of today and the future.

ROBERT H. ELLIOTT

BIBLIOGRAPHY

McGuire, Jean B., and Joseph R. Liro, 1986. "Flexible Work Schedules, Work Attitudes, and Perceptions of Productivity." *Public Personnel Management,* vol. 15 (Spring): 65–72.
Rubin, Richard S., 1979. "Flextime Implementation in the Public Sector." *Public Administration Review,* vol. 39 (May): 277–282.

FOG OF WAR.

The condition of administrative confusion experienced in battle, arising from the conflicting information and unplanned developments intrinsic to the conduct of war. Although originally a military concept, it now has much wider application.

As the early-nineteenth-century military philosopher, Carl von Clausewitz wrote, "Information . . . is the foundation of all our ideas and actions." For those given command and leadership in war, Clausewitz (1962) believed that the problem was "a greater part of the information obtained in War is contradictory, a still great part is false, and by far the greatest part is of a doubtful character" (p. 75). Accordingly, instead of operating in a clear-cut situation in which all salient information was observable and known, military commanders would normally expect to find themselves in a permanent fog of uncertainty, and would have to accommodate themselves to that unavoidable fact.

Even though some of the responsibility for this uncertainty can be directly found in deficiencies in the collection, transmission, processing, and exploitation of information, Clausewitz believed that much derives from the nature of war itself. War is the province of danger, fear, fatigue, exertion, and privation; in such circumstances, it was considered natural for those involved to make mistakes, and in particular, human timidity being what it is, to exaggerate the extent of the surrounding dangers. As such, information problems play a major part in creating that friction, which means that "everything is very simple in War, but the simplest thing is difficult" (Clausewitz 1962, p. 77).

The experience of the Royal Navy in its conduct of the Battle of Jutland on 31 May 1916 illustrates Clausewitz's point exactly. During that battle, the British fleet under Admiral John Jellicoe had a significant advantage in quantitative terms, comprised excellent equipment and first-rate personnel, and for some hours was barely 10 miles from its German adversary. Sometimes, in fact, it was *between* the German fleet and the base to which Admiral Rheinhard Scheer, its commander in chief, wanted quite desperately to return.

Nonetheless, Admiral Jellicoe's capacity to inflict a decisive defeat on the Germans was ruined, first, by inaccurate or inadequate reporting from the British ships of the situation they saw, and, second, by the fact that poor climatic conditions and the smoke of battle made it difficult for all concerned to make out friend from foe. Enemy forces and their activities could not be seen properly, nor, all too often, could the signals of friendly ships. "I wish," remarked Jellicoe in exasperation at one stage of the battle, "someone would tell me who is firing, and what they are firing at" (Marder, 1966 p. 85). With hindsight, the result seems inevitable: The German fleet escaped from the trap with far fewer losses than they might objectively have expected and, indeed, with rather fewer losses than the significantly more powerful British. It seemed that on that day, largely because of the fog of war, things had simply not gone the Royal Navy's way.

Clausewitz would not have been surprised by this. In his view, reality rarely conformed to expectation. War in practice was nearly always fundamentally different from war in theory. Nor could this be ascribed simply to the deficiencies of the commanders on both sides; instead, it was a consequence of the perilous and confusing nature of war itself.

Of course, military personnel have evolved ways of dealing with, or at least managing, this unavoidable aspect of their profession. Moreover, both their experiences in the fog and the manner in which they have sought to cope with uncertainty have relevance to the general field of public administration, just as do the concepts of "tactics" and "strategy." Most obviously, they have sought to improve the extent to which information is properly collected, processed, transmitted, and exploited in order that the best use can be made of the information that is available. This method requires investment in information technology, and in the training required to exploit its potential to the full.

The availability of satellite systems, microprocessors, and data links have transformed command and control for the modern military, increasing the quality and quantity of data available for the decisionmaker, making it far easier for commanders to see the overall picture and for those at home to supervise and control their activities.

But modern communications bring new vulnerabilities, too. They may create dangerous dependencies, which may be revealed all too clearly if the system crashes, is subject to attack, is penetrated by espionage, or has not been properly adapted to the particular scenario. Moreover, such communications are also available to adversaries, allowing them to make better-informed decisions, to respond faster, and very possibly to seek to uncover the enemy's secrets.

In a competitive situation of inherent uncertainty, significant effort and resources need to be expended to capture, exploit, and defend information. In Clausewitz's view, few things have higher priority. The deliberate attempt by one side to deceive and mislead the adversary in order to increase the opaqueness of the fog in which their enemies are enveloped has been an aspect of strategy long before the term "disinformation" was invented. In 1944, it applied to activities as various as the camouflaging of ships so that they looked like something else, the mechanical simulation of invasion convoys in the Pas de Calais (Strait of Dover) and the staging of elaborate ruses, involving dead bodies and false maps, in order to conceal the true landing sites for the invasion of Normandy. In many circumstances, such disinformation strategies have clear analogies in the field of public administration.

Finally, Clausewitz was particularly interested in the implications of the fog of war for leadership, especially in view of the fact that uncertainty bred fear and a tendency to exaggerate surrounding dangers. Commanders must be calm and resolute: "The rock against which the sea breaks its fury in vain" (Clausewitz 1962, p. 76). Leaders will be sustained in their role by some knowledge of the laws of probability, of what usually happens in such uncertain unknowable situations. They may well evolve and disseminate standard operating procedures (such as automatically marching toward the sound of gunfire) that usually work in situations of confusion. Again, there are obvious analogies in the more general field of public administration, in which in particular situations, stress, confusion, and uncertainty may dominate events unless key leaders prevent it.

GEOFFREY TILL

BIBLIOGRAPHY

Clausewitz, Carl von, 1962. *On War.* Translated by J. J. Graham. London: Routledge and Kegan Paul.
———, 1989. *On War.* Edited and translated by Michael Howard and Peter Paret. Princeton, NJ: Princeton University Press.
Marder, Arthur J., 1966. *From the Dreadnought to Scapa Flow.* Vol. 3. London: Oxford University Press.

FOLLETT, MARY PARKER (1868–1933). The early social psychologist who anticipated, in the 1920s, many of the conclusions of the Hawthorne experiments of the 1930s and the post–World War II behavioral movement. During the course of her career, she consistently wrote about individuals and groups in society, and how democratic governance helps the individual and the group develop full potential. The themes of groups, leadership, authority, power, conflict, and integration are as instructive today as when she wrote at the turn of the century. Much of the management discourse of the 1990s surrounding the titles of excellence, quality, reinvention, reengineering, culture, and chaos theory were introduced by Follett in *The New State* (1923), *The Creative Experience* (1924), and in a series of four lectures given in 1925. A similar observation could be made of the invasion of behavioral science into management thought in the 1960s and of systems theory in the 1970s. Mary Parker Follett, with her keen mind, anticipated the majority of the management themes of the last four decades of the twentieth century.

Early Life

Mary Parker Follett was born in Quincy, Massachusetts, on 3 September 1868. Her father was a blue-collar worker and her mother was the daughter of a prosperous banker. Follett was highly influenced by her history teacher, Anna Thompson, an idealist scholar who instilled in her the desire to work for the common good and correct social ills. Mary Parker Follett graduated from Thayer College (high school) at the age of 15. A year later her father died, and she spent the first four years after graduation caring for her invalid mother.

University Years

Through an inheritance from her father and maternal grandfather, she was able to attend a university in 1888. She chose to enter the Society for Collegiate Instruction of Women by Professors and Other Instructors of Harvard College. Known as the Annex, it was later called Radcliffe College. There she studied English, political science, political economy, and history.

In 1890 Follett traveled to England to continue her studies at Newnham College, Cambridge University. While there, she presented a paper on the U.S. House of Representatives. This paper later formed the nucleus of her first book, *The Speaker of the House of Representatives* ([1902] 1974). Before Follett could stand for examinations, however, she was called home to care for her still-ailing mother. As a result, she attended Radcliffe intermittently until she graduated summa cum laude in 1899.

Political Activist and Philosopher

After her university studies, Follett began working as a social worker. The idealism of her high school history teacher, combined with her experiences studying in England, convinced her that she could and should help the community. She focused on creating evening programs and vocational guidance programs for both youths and disenfranchised adults.

Follett was very active in establishing and sitting on numerous community boards, and she founded the Roxburg Debating Club for Boys (1900), the Highland Union (1902), and the Roxburg Industrial League for Boys (1902), which came to be knows as the Roxburg League. The League represented a pioneering attempt to use public school buildings after hours as sites for recreation, discussion groups, and the study of topics of special interest to the community.

As the leader of the newly founded Women's Municipal League of Boston from 1908–1920, she conducted trial projects in half a dozen public schools in eastern Boston to establish evening centers. To continue the effort, she later helped finance the Boston Placement Bureau–which later became Boston's Department of Vocation Guidance Advisory Committee. While a member of the board, she studied the philosophy of business management and the interaction of citizens and government. She served on many wage boards and began to develop a growing interest in industrial management and its effect on human relations.

Her work on community centers and vocational guidance projects, as well as her experiences while sitting on wage boards, led her to question the legitimacy and value of existing American political and social institutions. These concerns received a voice in her second book, *The New State* (1923), wherein she studied political parties, group interaction, institutions, and other topics of democracy. She wrote of a need for an organic form of democracy, and recommended abandoning political parties in favor of neighborhood groups.

Follett's study on groups was influenced greatly by Johann Fichte (1762–1814), a German philosopher who espoused a nationalism in which the freedom of the individual had to be subordinated to the group. Fichte did not believe that individuals had free will, but that they were bound up in an interpersonal network to which all people were committed.

Follett rephrased the views of Fichte in *The New State*. She wrote that the individual realizes his or her true freedom and potentialities only through the group. Her theories on group interaction and integration were formative at this stage, but would later be developed extensively in her third book. *The New State* went through several editions and received acclaim in both the United States and Europe.

Student of Group Interaction and Conflict Resolution

Her third book, *The Creative Experience* (1924), focused more extensively on the group experience. She sought to explain her theory of the psychological and social effects of effective interaction. The "law of situation" and coordination, coupled with cooperation, would lead to group unity and integration. Follett listed four ways to resolve conflict: (1) voluntary submission, (2) achieving domination by winning, (3) compromise, and (4) integration. Integration was, for Follett, the most positive; it involved finding a solution that did not require winning or losing or compromise, and it improved the lot of both parties.

The accepted theories of democracy, she claimed, did not afford individuals the opportunity to truly integrate themselves into society. The conflict of interest groups, the theory of majority rule, and reliance on experts placed the individual citizen on the sidelines as a passive spectator. The pluralist model, in contrast, overemphasized the individual at the expense of the whole. Both of these avenues were detrimental to the individual and society because the individual can only find his or her true individualism through group interaction. Follett's solution was a behavioral science approach to the study of social interaction, favoring participant, or in her terms, citizen involvement, and participative management. Follett had spent too much time as a social activist to conclude that integration was easy or inevitable, but she did conclude that it was possible in more cases than was assumed.

Management Philosopher

Follett's management philosophy grew from her early work on conflict and integration in *The Creative Experience* (1924), and she moved from a focus on political philosophy to an interest in business leaders. She was invited to give four lectures in New York City to the Bureau of Personnel Administration in 1925. These lectures brought together key ideas from her previous books and additional insight from her exceptional life and helped her to make a transition from political to business philosophy. She provided one of the earliest broad and eclectic definitions of the social philosophy of administration based on theories from political science, public administration, industrial and scientific management, and individual and group psychology, along with her extensive work experience. Many of her more influential lectures are published in three books edited by Henry Metcalf: *Scientific Foundations of Business Administration* (1926), *Business Management as a Profession* (1927), and *Psychological Foundations of Management* (1927), as well as in Lyndall Urwick's *Freedom and Co-ordination* ([1949] 1987). Urwick also honored Follett in 1941 with the publication of *Dynamic Administration: Collected Papers of Mary Parker Follett.*

Her lectures were based on three major themes, which composed her management philosophy: (1) integration, (2) authority and power, and (3) leadership. For her, integration comprised constructive conflict and integration of management and labor for a common purpose and included a larger view of the firm with all the various stakeholders (she even anticipated the concept of "stakeholder"). Her explorations on conflict resolution and integration led to an analysis of the way in which authority and power were conceptualized. On one hand, Follett wrote of "power with" rather than "power over," and "co-action" rather than "coercion." "Integration" leads to "power with." On the other hand, authority relationships lead to barriers that prevent accomplishing a commonality of interest and purpose. She listed three rules to help overcome barriers in authority relationships: (1) find the law

of the situation (consideration of the facts) to depersonalize orders, (2) teach workers techniques of the job in order to lessen the need for orders, and (3) give reasons for orders. Focus should be placed on standards rather than orders, and workers should be involved in the development of the standards. These would lead to an integrated unity of purpose.

The third theme of Follett's management philosophy, leadership, was essential to the accomplishment of the first two—reducing conflict through the integration of interests and obeying the law of the situation in power relationships. A grasp of the total situation and the ability to organize the group is essential to accomplish common purposes. She wrote about control and coordination in her paper "The Process of Control," published in the well-known *Papers on the Science of Administration* (edited by Luther Gulick and Lyndall Urwick in 1937). Her control was "fact control" rather than "man control"—control based on correlation rather than superimposed. Leadership was not based on power or authority but rather on the interaction of the leader and follower in the situation. Leaders provided the purpose, the common purpose. They also provided the coordination and control to the ends.

In 1928 she moved to London and lived with Dame Furse, a Red Cross leader, whom she had met and befriended earlier in her life. While in London, she studied the labor conditions in that country and became interested in the workings of the United Nations and the International Labor Organization (ILO). She often traveled to Geneva to observe the UN, and on occasion lectured at the ILO. During this time she was also a member of the Taylor Society and served as vice president of the Community Center Association. She gave her final lectures at the London School of Economics in the first months of 1933. She died of cancer in December 1933, in Boston, the city where she had pioneered community centers and vocational programs.

NORMAN DALE WRIGHT

BIBLIOGRAPHY

Books by Mary Parker Follett

[1902] 1974. *The Speaker of the House of Representatives.* New York: Longmans, Green. Reprint. New York: B. Franklin Reprints.
1923. *The New State: Group Organization, the Solution of Popular Government.* New York: Longmans, Green and Co.
1924. *The Creative Experience.* New York: Longmans, Green and Co.

Lectures and Papers by Mary Parker Follett

1941. *Dynamic Administration; The Collected Papers of Mary Parker Follett.* Lyndall F. Urwick, and Elliot M. Fox, eds. London: Pitman.

[1949] 1987. *Freedom and Co-ordination: Lectures in Business Administration.* Lyndall F. Urwick, ed., London: Management Publications Trust. Reprint. New York: Garland.

Works on Mary Parker Follett

Chambers, Peter, 1975. "The Woman Who Introduced Behavioral Science to Management." *International Management,* (November) 51–52.

Graham, Pauline, ed., 1995. *Mary Parker Follett—Prophet of Management: A Celebration of Writings from the 1920s.* Boston: Harvard Business School Press.

Gulick, Luther, and Lyndall Urwick, eds., 1937. *Papers on the Science of Public Administration.* New York: Institute of Public Administration, Columbia University.

Metcalf, Henry C., ed., 1926. *Scientific Foundations of Business Administration.* Chicago: A.W. Shaw.

———, ed., 1927. *Business Management as a Profession.* Chicago: A.W. Shaw.

———, ed., 1927. *Psychological Foundations of Management.* Chicago: A.W. Shaw.

FORD FOUNDATION.

The largest foundation in the world (as of 1 July 1995), with assets of US$6.9 billion. Henry Ford, Sr. (1863–1947), founder of Ford Motor Company, and his son Edsel (1893–1943) established the foundation on 15 January 1936, to receive and expend funds for charitable purposes and for the public welfare. In wills drawn up in 1936, they had each bequeathed to the newly established foundation their shares of Ford Motor Company's nonvoting stock. Subsequently, between 1937 and 1954, the Ford family donated a total of $387 million in cash and Ford Motor stock to the Ford foundation. Since its inception the foundation has disbursed more than $7 billion in grants.

Henry Ford did not believe that wealthy families or individuals had an obligation to distribute their wealth to benefit others but that people should be taught self-reliance and that charity is harmful. Nevertheless, he ultimately donated millions of dollars to the Ford Foundation, primarily motivated by a desire to protect his wealth from federal taxes. When Congress passed the 1935 wealth tax, it became clear that the tax rate on Ford's estate would force his heirs to sell Ford Motor Company stock to pay the inheritance taxes. By creating and donating a bloc of nonvoting stock to a foundation the Ford family was able simultaneously to maintain control of the company and to reduce significantly its estate tax liability.

Evolution to a National Foundation

In its early years, the Ford Foundation's grants were distributed mostly in the Detroit, Michigan, area, although a few projects in other parts of the country were funded. (By 1950, however, the foundation began to turn its attention to becoming a national and international presence in the philanthropic sector.) The foundation anticipated sizable infusions of Ford Motor Company stock as a result of the estate settlement of Henry Ford, Sr., and his son Edsel. In November 1948 Ford Foundation trustees commissioned a study to examine how it should use these significantly increased resources. Henry Ford II, who was then chairman of the board, appointed H. Rowan Gaither, Jr., to investigate "how [the] Foundation can most effectively and intelligently put its resources to work for human welfare" (Ford Foundation 1948, p. 10).

The resulting *Report of the Study for the Ford Foundation on Policy and Program* (Ford Foundation 1948) began by declaring that "the aim of The Ford Foundation is to advance human welfare." (p. 17), and it delineated five elements essential to this welfare: (1) freedom from preoccupation with survival and physical well being; (2) human dignity and the inherent worth of each person; (3) personal freedom and rights; (4) political freedom and rights; and (5) responsible exercise of power (political, social, and economic) and service to the broader welfare of society.

The authors of the 1948 *Report* then used these criteria to identity the greatest human needs and to suggest programs that would effectively respond to such needs. They recommended that the Ford Foundation support programs to establish world peace, to encourage democracies, and to strengthen the domestic and world economy. The foundation was also urged to fund programs to strengthen educational systems and to study human behavior to better understand how people function and how they can live productively and peacefully. Given the impossibility of meeting all of these needs, the Ford Foundation was urged to fund only areas with the greatest likelihood of success. Ideally, the support of one solution would contribute to the solution of other problems.

The *Report* also examined the Ford Foundation's role in public policy decisions. The authors recommended against a direct role in supporting or opposing particular political or social issues; instead, they suggested that the foundation should support research to illuminate public policy issues. The authors noted that foundations can influence public policy by providing consultants to public agencies, disseminating research results, convening special commissions, and helping public agencies to develop expertise. They believed that this approach would shield the foundation from political attacks if it supported controversial issues (*Ford Foundation* 1948, p. 114).

Governance of the Ford Foundation is provided by an autonomous board of directors. The board has the authority to determine how to maintain the foundation and how to disburse funds in accord with state and federal laws. The board also selects board officers and appoints staff to implement policies and programs. A staff of approximately 600 provides administrative support for the foundation's programs.

Areas of Interest and Funding Priorities

Several factors determine the foundation's funding priorities, including broad social and economic trends and the interests and values of top foundation officers. The foundation's interest in education, public affairs, and international affairs has persisted. It does not support projects for which there is significant government support, religious or sectarian activities, undergraduate scholarships, or construction or routine operating expenses (Foundation Center 1994, pp. 902–908). Funds are distributed on an international basis in the United States, Europe, Africa, the Middle East, Asia, Latin America, and the Caribbean.

Program Priorities

The Ford Foundation's early projects targeted education, economic development, public affairs, civil liberties, and international affairs. Its funding strategy was to establish and fund intermediary organizations, which, in turn, selected specific projects to support. For example, the foundation created the Fund for the Advancement of Education and the Fund for Adult Education to further its interest in education. The foundation's interest in the study of human behavior led to the creation of the Center for Advanced Study in the Behavioral Sciences in Palo Alto, California. The foundation established the Fund for the Republic in 1953 to focus on civil liberties in the United States. (The Fund for the Republic had a special interest in civil liberties for African Americans at a time when racial segregation and discrimination were legal and socially accepted.) In the international arena, the Ford Foundation created Resources for the Future to further economic development, with a special emphasis on India. Each of these organizations had its own board and functioned autonomously.

In 1956, five years after its transformation to a national foundation, the Ford Foundation convened a study committee to reassess its funding priorities. Its broad areas of interest were identified as promoting international understanding and strengthening democratic institutions, economic well-being, and education. Improving education was considered the foundation's most critical task. Funded programs were directed toward enhancing the attractiveness of the teaching profession by encouraging schools to increase teacher salaries. Other educational programs were developed to improve medical education, to use television as an educational tool, and to strengthen libraries through the Council of Library Resources. Graduate education in foreign area studies and international relations was supported through fellowships as well.

By the end of its first decade as a national foundation, Ford had awarded $744 million in grants. In 1961, the board of trustees undertook a comprehensive evaluation of its programs and policies. The result was a plan in which the board reaffirmed the foundation's commitment to "take affirmative action toward the elimination of the basic causes of war, the advancement of democracy on a broad front and the strengthening of its institutions and processes" (Ford Foundation 1962, p. 2).

While the basic commitments of the Ford Foundation remained unchanged, the board acknowledged its responsibility to adjust the foundation's programs in response to societal change. New leadership in 1966 was a catalyst for a more activist program and a change in the direction of the foundation. McGeorge Bundy, National Security Adviser to President Lyndon Johnson, assumed the presidency of the Ford Foundation on 1 March 1966, and began to move it in a different direction.

By 1969, the United States had experienced a decade of social unrest and significant change. The civil rights movement, the antiwar movement, and the assassinations of President John F. Kennedy, Martin Luther King, Jr., and Robert Kennedy posed challenges to established institutions. Bundy believed that the foundation had to respond to the political and social upheavals of the country by asserting responsibility for addressing poverty, racial conflict, and other social problems, such as crime. He argued that the Ford Foundation could not ignore the crises confronting society. The "privilege of freedom" obligates those who enjoy it to direct their attention to the greatest needs (Ford Foundation Report, 1969, p. xxii).

When Bundy initiated the National Affairs Program, the program's premise was that the greatest challenges in the United States were racial discrimination and poverty. Earlier, in the 1960s, the nation had begun to solve some of the problems of racism, discrimination, and poverty. Those who were just above the poverty line and those who were nonminorities, however, experienced a sense that society had ignored their needs and aspirations. Their frustration contributed to decreased political support for federal antipoverty programs. Thus, Bundy saw a need for national reconciliation, along with the resolving of urgent social programs. The National Affairs Program was designed to serve both ends.

The National Affairs Program goals were to support antipoverty programs, to strengthen the capacity of state and local government to deal with social problems, and to protect the environment. The Ford Foundation awarded funds to programs to support minorities and low-income people advocating for improved housing, employment, and education. The Center for Community Change, for example, was founded in Washington, D.C., to enable the poor to have a voice in shaping their own destiny. The foundation also awarded grants to established civil rights groups, such as the National Organization for the Advancement of Colored People (NAACP) and the Urban League.

Decreased political support for federal intervention in poverty and race-related issues was, in part, reflected in the election of Richard M. Nixon as president of the United States in 1968. Nixon called for a New Federalism, whereby state and local governments would assume a more active role in dealing with social and economic problems.

The Ford Foundation's leadership thus continued to support programs designed to enhance state and local government's capacity. Funded programs included those involved in the dissemination of information for modernizing state legislatures, those that encouraged internships to train minority professionals and young people for public service, and conferences sponsored for local government officials by the National Institute of Public Affairs.

The foundation's leadership believed that new strategies for solving social problems had to be developed, in light of the changed political climate. They were committed to continue supporting public policy research and graduate training, which they believed would generate new approaches. In 1972, the Ford Foundation created the Program of Public Policy and Social Organization. Support for graduate training went to ten relatively new public policy programs rather than to traditional public administration programs. The foundation had an interest in the application of social sciences to analyze and manage complex public policy problems. Examples of funded research included programs investigating the overall effects of government policy, the functions of state and local government, and the effect of income tax, social security, and child support policies on women.

The Ford Foundation, by virtue of its size and the scope of its work, has been a leader among foundations. As such, its programs and funding decisions, even if noncontroversial, attract attention. It is not surprising, therefore, that Ford Foundation support for antipoverty programs and race-related programs attracted attention and aroused criticism. The foundation's funding of voter registration drives, for example, was criticized as an intrusion into politics. Further, critics of all ideological persuasions questioned whether a legitimate public interest was served by exempting foundation assets from taxation in light of the pressing needs of the country. Congressional hearings, held in part in response to the types of programs the Ford Foundation supported, resulted in the Tax Reform Act of 1969, which stipulated more clearly the responsibilities of foundations if they were to continue their tax-exempt status.

In 1981 the Ford Foundation reorganized its programs around six themes: urban poverty, rural poverty, human rights and social justice, governance and public policy, education and culture, and international affairs. These themes provide a framework for targeting grant recipients and for evaluating the effectiveness of program decisions. In 1986, the foundation commissioned a panel of experts to review funding and program decisions made under the rubric of the six program themes. These six themes continue to serve as the framework for the foundation's grants into the 1990s.

Perspectives on the Role of Foundation in Public Policy

The Ford Foundation's evolution illuminates the way in which foundations are simultaneously creations and creators of public policy. Foundations themselves are made possible because of tax policy decisions to impose an income tax and an estate tax (in 1913 and 1917, respectively). The federal tax code exempts from federal taxes those funds used to establish private trusts for social, educational, charitable, religious, or other activities deemed to serve the common welfare. Foundations' importance in public policy can be attributed to the source of their funds and the influence their grant making has on how policy issues are addressed.

Foundations compose an important segment of the independent sector, which includes organizations, such as the Ford Foundation, that play a significant role in shaping public policy and in providing public goods and services. Foundations in the United States are the repository of $189.2 billion in privately held funds (Foundation Center 1995). As a consequence of the tax shelter provided by foundation status, the availability of public funds for public purposes is diminished. Thus, the public has an interest in the programs that foundations support.

A long-standing debate among foundation observers is whether foundations such as Ford significantly enhance the quality of life or whether they drain valuable resources from the public arena that could be used more effectively if distributed with broader input. Challenges to the continued existence of foundations and the indirect public subsidy of their continued existence surface periodically.

As early as 1915, the United States Industrial Relations Commission, headed by Frank P. Walsh, examined questions about the social and economic role of foundations in a democratic system (Coon 1938, p. 306). The Ford Foundation was investigated in the early 1950s as a Communist-front organization. In the late 1960s, Ford Foundation grants to community-based groups that targeted poverty, welfare rights, and voting rights of minorities drew attention from congressional critics, such as Representative Wright Patman of Texas (Nielsen 1972, p. 357).

Foundations Represent a Public Good

Proponents of a public policy role for foundations point to the positive contributions foundations make. The Ford Foundation's 1993 annual report, for example, articulates the positive role foundations play. According to the report, foundations can respond quickly to changing conditions in society and can support ventures that government and business might view as too risky. Unlike public policy makers, foundations are autonomous enough to allow for the failures that accompany experimentation. Furthermore, foundations are not pressed to find quick solutions to problems that require time. Finally, foundations provide an alternative resource given that government cannot respond to the societal problems.

Foundations Serve No Public Interest

Critics respond by saying that although foundations can potentially respond quickly to changing conditions, they have failed to do so. Furthermore, foundations spend the majority of their funds on noncontroversial causes. Most foundations have ignored the needs of the poor and the disaffected. Other arguments against the continued existence of foundations are that they perpetuate an elite that dominates the major centers of power in the society and that the interlocking directorates of the corporate sector and foundations lead to a concentration of power in a few hands. This concentration of power poses a danger to a democratic society. Critics also believe that foundations set the policy agenda for major universities, educational institutions, health institutions, and other social institutions by directing financial resources. They are accountable only to themselves and are not adequately monitored to ensure that they are acting in the best interest of the public.

The debate over the role of foundations in public policy is unlikely to subside. As we approach the end of the twentieth century, the appropriate role of government in providing public goods and services is being debated in the United States. Advocates of a diminished role for government argue for an increased activity by the private sector in meeting societal needs. Inevitably, foundations will be called upon to replace government initiatives and funds in responding to educational, social, and economic needs. The Ford Foundation will play an important leadership role in determining how foundations will respond to the new challenges of the twenty-first century.

DENISE E. STRONG

BIBLIOGRAPHY

Andrews, F. Emerson, 1956. *Philanthropic Foundations.* New York: Russell Sage Foundation.
Coon, Horace, 1938. *Money to Burn: What the Great American Philanthropic Foundations Do with Their Money.* London: Longmans, Green and Co.
Ford Foundation, 1948. *Report of the Study for the Ford Foundation on Policy and Program.* Detroit: Ford Foundation.
———, 1956. *The Ford Foundation Annual Report, 1956.* New York: Ford Foundation.
———, 1960. *To Advance Human Welfare.* New York: Ford Foundation.
———, 1962. *The Ford Foundation in the 1960s: Statement of the Board of Trustees on Policies, Programs, and Operations.* New York: Ford Foundation.
———, 1969. *The Ford Foundation Annual Report, 1969.* New York: Ford Foundation.
———, 1972. *Program in Public Policy and Social Organization.* New York: Ford Foundation.
———, 1994. *Current Interests of the Ford Foundation.* New York: Ford Foundation.
———, 1995. *1994 Ford Foundation Annual Report.* New York: Ford Foundation.
Foundation Center, 1994. *The Foundation 1000, 1994.* New York: Foundation Center.
———, 1995. *Foundation Giving.* 5th ed. New York: Foundation Center.
McDonald, Dwight, 1956. *The Ford Foundation: The Men and the Millions.* New York: Reynal and Company.
Nevins, Allan, and Frank Ernest Hill, 1962. *Ford: Decline and Rebirth 1933–1962.* New York: Charles Scribner's Sons.
Nielsen, Waldemar A., 1972. *The Big Foundations.* New York: Columbia University Press.
——— 1985. *The Golden Donors.* New York: E. P. Dutton (Truman Talley Books).
Richman, Harry et al., 1987. *The Ford Foundation: Leadership in Affecting Poverty.* New York: Ford Foundation.

FOREIGN AID. The provision of a range of economic assistance measures by the wealthier countries of the industrialized world to poorer states, primarily in the Third World. Support for foreign aid and assistance has waxed and waned in the industrialized world over a period of decades. Debates have addressed the purposes and consequences of aid. From the early 1990s, most industrialized countries embarked on a general reduction of aid provided to the Third World. The ending of the Cold War had a great deal to do with that set of decisions.

Wealthy nations have always given assistance to those less well-off, when such action squared with the richer state's overall objectives. Very few examples exist historically of selfless enlightened actions of this type. The U.S. government's decision to offer lend-lease aid–described by Winston Churchill as "the least unsordid act in history"– to Britain before the attack on Pearl Harbor, Hawaii, might be so regarded. More typically, the Marshall Plan's provision of aid to the economically beleaguered and politically traumatized states of western Europe after 1945 had at least as much to do with containment of the Soviet Union as with any idealistic commitment to international compassion for sister democracies temporarily disadvantaged by the economic consequences of waging total war. Most examples show a similar mixture of enlightened self-interest.

There are two broad but opposing views about foreign aid. The first is the widely accepted argument, stemming from the 1960s, that the provision of resources by the rich world to help those who, for whatever reason, have not been so fortunate is progressive and therefore desirable. This view corresponded conveniently with any residual European guilt over imperialism and chimed well with the need to demonstrate to the Third World that the ideological blandishments of the Soviet Union, coupled with its military assistance, were no substitute for hard cash from the West. The high point of this argument came with the publication of the Brandt Commission (1983) report in the early 1980s. The commission argued that it was in the interests of the industrialized Northern countries to provide the Third World with aid, on the straightforward grounds that *not* to do so would fail to develop export markets for the future. To be ungenerous would preclude subsequent profits.

The opposite argument developed as part of the 1990s critique of postwar economic paternalism by the "New Right." The case was made that aid had two deleterious consequences. The first was that it pandered to the disastrous ambitions of Asian, South American, and African leaders, encouraging them to develop showy projects that gratified their egos but impoverished their countries. The second was that, even where this did not occur, a climate of dependency was created and sustained that could only militate against self-sufficiency and economic self-respect in the medium and longer run. Rightly or wrongly, many Third World countries came to believe that this line of argument had outweighed the 1960s consensus and was most obviously to be seen in the policies of the UN financial agencies, the World Bank, and the International Monetary Fund. The conditions for finance offered by these institutions seemed to confirm to the poorer parts of the world that their conditions were of less importance than the maintenance of a stable international financial and trading environment.

Ironically, the West found considerable difficulty in responding to the demands for economic aid by the noncommunist successor states that formerly composed the Soviet Union. Having "won" the Cold War, the victors were now asked to bankroll the economic recovery of the East. No Western government was prepared to throw money at the problem; the lessons of irresponsible recipients who failed to develop sustainable infrastructure had been fully absorbed. The cruel jibe that the USSR was never more than "Upper Volta with missiles" became part and parcel of how the West reacted to the new strategic conditions.

The European Bank for Reconstruction and Development was created precisely to address these matters. Sadly, for the poorer states in the less-developed world, the perceived need to grant Russia and its neighbors a special place during the 1990s concentrated aid moneys within the Northern industrial region. Little was available to trickle down to the less-industrialized world. The general economic malaise of the global economy in the first half of the 1990s persuaded those responsible for statecraft that the long-run needs of the Third World could be safely, if with regret, delayed for consideration in due course.

PETER FOOT

BIBLIOGRAPHY

Bauer, P. T., 1985. *Reality and Rhetoric: Studies in Economic Development*. London: Weidenfeld.

Brandt Commission, 1983. *Common Crisis North-South: Cooperation for World Recovery*. London: Pan Books.
Thomas, Caroline, 1987. *In Search of Security: The Third World in International Relations*. London: Harvester/Riennes.
Todaro, P. T., 1989. *Economic Development in the Third World*. London: Longmans.

FORMAL MODELS OF BUREAUCRACY.

Theoretical constructs that are a simplification and an approximation of complex, observable bureaucratic events. The goal of this process is to strip away characteristics that are not fundamental or essential to some specific research question while retaining and simplifying those that are central to the query. This filtering allows researchers to quantify and manipulate a finite number of key variables. Exploration and study is accomplished by establishing situational relationships that correspond to actual scenarios. In public administration, the formal modeling approach is often applied to the analysis of bureaucratic behavior. The core idea is that complex organizations and their outputs can be analyzed as sums of discrete, rational subunits that are modeled with formalistic language and structures. In their most basic structure, formal models of bureaucracy establish and defend a finite set of assumptions that presumably underlie the relationship between actors in a specified system. Typically, these are defined in easily quantifiable terms. Hypotheses are tested deductively by applying different levels to the independent variables of interest and studying the ensuing changes in the dependent variables. Since each of the model aspects is controlled by the researcher, this process resembles experimentation rather than empirical research.

To be successful, a formal model of bureaucracy must highlight some previously untested relationship between variables and simultaneously produce an outcome that closely resembles empirical observation. In addition, formal models of bureaucracy face a fundamental trade-off with regard to generality. The greater the number and complexity of assumptions, the closer the model is to some observable phenomenon but the less generalizable it is to a broad class of situations. Therefore, the quality of a specific model is judged by how well these competing criteria are balanced against each other. The determination of model variables and the assumptions about the behavior of these variables is the fundamental process of model building.

In public administration, formal models can easily be divided into two general categories: models with a budgetary focus and models with a nonbudgetary focus. The literature on the budgetary relationship between an executive branch agency and a funding legislature is well developed and relatively mature. This class of models begins with William Niskanen, *Bureaucracy and Representative Government* (1971). Niskanen used simple microeconomic theory to model the funding process for a specific agency. This agency seeks ever-increasing budgets and can exploit perfect information about the legislature's preferences. The legislature has a standard demand function for the output of the agency: The lower the price, the higher the quantity desired. However, the legislature does not know the unit cost of the output from the agency. These assumptions allow the agency to submit an "all or nothing" ultimatum to the legislature, where the "all" is the maximum the legislature is willing to pay for an agency selected point along its demand function. Niskanen concluded that this agency always overproduces past the legislature's preferred level and past the socially optimal level. He further generalized that this situation produces a government that is always too large. Although this model serves as foundation for a body of literature, it has serious limitations. Niskanen clearly condensed a complex, iterative, and political process down to a small number of modeling assumptions. In doing so he left out critical aspects, such as the delineation between funding for agencies versus funding for programs, the role of the Office of Management and Budget (OMB), the existence of multiple principles for any agency action, and the role of agenda control within the legislature.

Niskanen's contribution serves primarily as a straw man architecture, which other scholars have used as a starting point. The ensuing work developed on this platform by incremental improvements in specific attributes: the addition of more complex budget options provided by Robert Mackay and Carolyn Weaver (1981), the inclusion of agency deception and legislative oversight from Jonathan Bendor, Serge Taylor, and Roland Van Gaalen (1985), and the provision of a dynamic, reiterative focus by Jonathan Bendor and Terry Moe (1985). There is also a current trend toward greater scope in formal models of bureaucracy beyond simply analyzing the budgetary dimension alone. For example, John Ferejohn and Charles Shipan (1990) concentrated on the policy output dimension but added judicial review and presidential veto to the model.

Another rich dimension of formal models of bureaucracy lies in the intersection of public administration and organizational theory. This class of models relies heavily on social choice theory, specifically, the principle of individual rationality: Individuals within a bureaucracy analyze alternatives and make decisions that maximize their own utility. The core idea is that organizational structure affects the aggregate behavior of the bureaucracy because the mechanisms for aggregating preferences are biased by individual preferences that are often expressed through informal, undocumented processes. Graham Allison (1971) has called these "action channels." Action channels have particular attributes: differing levels of individual power, definable jurisdictions, and specific historical precedents. Thomas Hammond (1986) applied this perspective to bureaucratic restructuring. Hammond asserted that organizational structures within bureaucracies behave like agenda-setting structures within legislatures, and he constructed a simple model of hierarchy to demonstrate that agency heads can manipulate the final choice-set of the bureaucracy in order to maximize their individual utility. In the simplified version of the model there are field managers with specified jurisdictions who evaluate two policy alternatives and propose their own individual preferences to a middle manager. The middle manager takes the proposals from each of his or her subordinate field managers and submits a preferred alternative to the director. Hammond showed that the director can get a preferred choice-set simply by rearranging lines of reporting between the field managers and the middle managers. This situation infers that bureaucratic output is not necessarily an aggregation of participant preferences and leads to what Hammond calls the "structure = agenda" metaphor.

Formal models of bureaucracy provide a unique perspective to students of public administration. This approach, borrowing tools from economics, statistics, and formal logic, enables one to look at public institutions in a simplified manner. These models ask the question, What central underlying features exist across a broad range of institutional settings? This approach also contributes to the public administration literature by providing an abstract theoretical framework that is flexible enough to address a wide range of administrative relationships. However, the quality of these models and their conclusions is primarily a function of the quality of the stated assumptions. Critics of formal modeling commonly focus on the oversimplification of some model assumptions. Since this criticism has justly focused on the reliance upon the rational choice assumptions of individual utility maximization and perfect information, recent models have employed progressively more realistic and sophisticated specifications.

JEFF GILL

BIBLIOGRAPHY

Allison, Graham, 1971. *Essence of Decision*. Boston: Little, Brown.

Bendor, Jonathan, Serge Taylor, and Roland Van Gaalen, 1985. "Bureaucratic Expertise Versus Legislative Authority: A Model of Deception and Monitoring in Budgeting." *American Political Science Review* 79 (December): 1051–1060

Bendor, Jonathan, and Terry Moe, 1985. "An Adaptive Model of Bureaucratic Politics." *American Political Science Review* 79 (September): 755–774.

Ferejohn, John A., and Charles R. Shipan, 1990. "Congressional Influence on Bureaucracy." *Journal of Law, Economics, and Organization* 6 (special issue): 1–44.

Hammond, Thomas, 1986. "Agenda Control, Organizational Structure and Bureaucratic Politics." *American Journal of Political Science* 30 (May): 379–420.

Mackay, Robert J., and Carolyn L. Weaver, 1981. "Agenda Control by Budget Maximizers in a Multi-Bureau Setting." *Public Choice*, vol. 36, no. 3: 447–472.

Niskanen, William, 1971. *Bureaucracy and Representative Government*. Chicago: Aldine-Atherton.

FORMAL ORGANIZATION.

A rational, legitimate, institutionalized relationship of people managed or coordinated from one center in order to accomplish certain common predetermined goals, objectives, or purposes.

This term collectively refers to any form of legitimate business, association, or government, or their subdivision. The related term "administrative organization" emphasizes relationships between line, staff, and auxiliary agencies or subdivisions through which the management and control of operations and personnel is accomplished (Banki 1981).

Basic elements of formal or administrative organization are specialization, authority, hierarchy, division of labor, communication, standard procedures of operations, and management. The combination of these elements, and the relationships among them, defines the structures of the organization, or organizational structure.

Organizational theory, which is an academic field of studies dealing with all types of organizations, describes various models of organization, emphasizes their common features, and at the same time makes distinctions among these types.

There are several approaches according to which one can classify different types of organizations. One approach is based on the underlying conceptual models. In essence, classification is according to the internal technologies of the organizations (i.e., what do they produce and how), which in turn is related to the environments in which the organizations operate (i.e., are they stable or uncertain). There are three basic types of such organization models: closed, behavioral, and open (Chandler and Plano 1988; Coll 1994).

Closed Model

The *closed* (administrative, bureaucratic, mechanistic) *model* is used to describe organizations in which organizational interests dominate the interests of individuals. These organizations are concerned with efficiency and effectiveness, specialization, and obedience to authority.

The closed model of organizations is often described through such terms as bureaucracy, hierarchy, pyramidal, vertical, formal, rational, and mechanistic. This type of organizational model is also widely known as the bureaucratic model. The basic prototype of such a model in government was described by German sociologist and political scientist Max Weber as an "ideal-type" bureaucracy. Concepts of bureaucracy were further developed by students of scientific management and classical organizational theory; they reached a pinnacle in the POSDCORB approach to managerial functions. (POSDCORB is the acronym for Planning, Organizing, Staffing, Directing, Coordinating, Reporting, and Budgeting.)

The popular understanding of the term bureaucracy is associated with unresponsiveness, red tape, and bungling inefficiency. But there have always been, still are, and will be organizations built on the closed model. In that sense, the bureaucratic or closed model has not lost its importance and positive meaning.

In a well-run bureaucracy, of which the best military divisions and agencies are the most appropriate examples, operations are managed in such a way that often the best compliment is that they "run like clockwork." Indeed, although people feel oppressed by the organization, its internal rules, legislation, fear of punishment, and so on, they still obey orders. The classic organizational model is often perceived as the most efficient model (at least in the short run) in terms of logic, cost, speed, control, and operational stability.

Basic features of this model are politically predetermined and clearly stated goals, centralized authority, a strict chain of command, and a prescribed set of impersonal and interconnected regulations for all aspects of the organization's activities (management and employees' rights and duties, punishments and benefits, operating and managerial procedures, etc.).

Goals for bureaucracies are determined either by the political establishment (for governmental public organizations) or by owners (for corporate bureaucracies). The core element of the structure of every bureaucracy is strict hierarchy, with a single chief executive at the top. Each position is under the direct administrative control of the supervisor one level above. Functions, rights, and duties are assigned to the positions and not to persons. Each member of the organization has limited, clearly defined rights, duties, powers, and expertise, fixed in written instructions. Vacancies are filled and promotions are accomplished due to formal technical qualifications (certificates, degrees), seniority or achievement.

Another characteristic feature of a closed model of formal organization is separation of ownership and management. This is why bureaucracies inside the public sector are stronger and more stable than in the private sector. Government cannot delegate full authority of public ownership to any level of management because the right to protect public interests is assigned by society to the government as a whole, not to the agencies or particular public officials.

Recently, the closed model has experienced a decline. Because of inflexibility, organizations following this model lacked the ability to respond quickly to problems or adapt to environmental changes. Employees who are most creative, and therefore most important for any organization facing complex tasks in a constantly changing and uncertain environment, are likely to be bored by dull, repetitive, routine work. More and more, organizations that remain competitive are organizations with a high degree of innovation, not only in technological fields but also in the fields of management and organizational design. Nonetheless, the closed model can be effectively used in situations in which technology is minimal or relatively standard and the environment is stable (Woodward 1965).

Behavioral Model

The *behavioral* (human resources) *model* emphasizes the importance of human relations and personal goals. If the closed model is primarily concerned with a technical system of organization–a system that produces products or services, or maintains operations–the behavioral model recognizes the equal importance of the social system–a system composed of the employees who operate the technical system. This approach is a modification of the closed model that brings to management's attention the social and psychological sides of organization.

The majority of organizations in modern society follow this model. Managers understand that, first of all, they deal with people; that is why they are concerned about the emotional and psychological status of employees. Both private and public organizations have recently adopted a variety of employee-oriented programs (in-house training, care for children and elderly members of the family, health education, part-time employment, etc.). Any technical system can fail, and often does, when the social and psychological needs of the people operating this system are neglected.

The behavioral model also stresses the responsiveness of organization to internal conditions and to the external environment. It emphasizes the need for more decentralization and less hierarchy, a weaker chain of command, and more freedom for lower-level managers in the decisionmaking process. Lower-level employees, as well as managers, are expected to participate in the decisionmaking process. They are encouraged to work in problem-solving teams, which are led by people who do not necessarily occupy high positions in the hierarchy but who are recognized (due to their personal accomplishments and ability) as being able to build successful relationships. Constant training of, and learning by, both employees and administrators is supposed to be one of the major concerns of the management.

Open Model

The behavioral model is a transition from a closed model to an open model of organization. The *open* (organic, systemic) *model* is a concept describing organizations in which authority and expertise are shared, hierarchy is less important and horizontal lines of communications dominate, and immediate response to environmental change is one of the basic managerial strategies. Although some routinization and standardization are essential components of effectiveness in the open model, as in any formal organization, the open model gives priority to creativity and innovativeness.

Even the behavioral model does not afford sufficient flexibility to organizations providing nonstandard goods and services and operating under conditions of high risk and uncertainty. In the open model, an organization's decisionmaking process is totally decentralized and is by consensus rather then by individual judgment of the formal (or even informal) leader; formal rules and instructions are almost eliminated; broad cross-disciplinary skills are of great importance; and the number of managerial levels is held to the minimum.

Peter M. Blau and Richard W. Scott (1962) identified four types of organizations, based on determination of the prime beneficiary: mutual-benefit, business, service, and commonweal. They have argued that all four types face dilemmas: coordination versus communication; discipline versus professionalism, and planning versus initiative. The varying importance of clients and subordinates in different organizations affects both the informal and formal organizations' abilities to deal with such dysfunctions.

These dilemmas are approached differently in formal organizations in the public and private sectors. In the public sector, formal organizations have some specific features, which bring additional complications: First, public organizations have goals that are predetermined by the government. Government never gives complete authority for government policy to any organization. As a result, public organizations cannot usually decide the level of their own budgets (with the exception of public authorities with a dedicated revenue stream), nor can they define (without special permission or at least consultations with some other governmental administrative bodies) changes in their organizational structure, number of employees, basic operations, managerial practices, and so forth. They are accountable to executive and legislative and judicial branches of government–through executive orders, budgets, and a body of administrative law.

Second, public organizations can be assigned to exercise functions or operations that are economically inefficient or too capital consuming, with insignificant if any rates of returns; that is why businesses are not eager to provide such services. And although providing such "uneconomic" services is supposed to be one of the major goals of the public sector, their provision also produces unjustified criticism that public organizations cannot compete with their private sector counterparts.

Government lacks a unified measure of performance, such as profit is for businesses. Without outputs (services or more rarely products) directly measurable in dollars, decisions concerning allocation of resources in public organizations are often based on quasi-objective procedures, formulas and calculations of various intangible benefits, or on subjective political considerations.

Third, public organizations usually receive funding from budgetary sources, not from their direct clients, so their priority is to satisfy those who provide the greatest portion of financial resources. As a result, some public organizations treat additional clients not as an opportunity, but as an additional strain on resources.

Fourth, organizations in the public sector are subjected to much greater pressure from nonmarket forces then are business institutions, although they often operate in virtually the same environment.

Taking into consideration these differences, it is becoming clearer why organizations formally designed in the same or similar ways may operate differently.

The way formal organizations operate or should operate is described at length in the management classics (Shafritz and Ott 1992). Some of the most widely quoted in the management literature are the American Management Association's (AMA) *Ten Commandments of Good Organization* (Rorty 1941) and Lyndall Urwick's (1952) "Ten Principles."

The ten commandments were formulated by AMA's president, M. C. Rorty, in 1934 and issued in commemorative form in 1941:

1. Definite and clear-cut responsibilities should be assigned to each executive, manager, supervisor, and foreman.
2. Responsibility should always be coupled with corresponding authority.
3. No change should be made in the scope or responsibility of a position without a definite understanding to that effect on the part of all persons concerned.
4. No executive or employee, occupying a single position in the organization, should be subject to definite orders from more than one source.
5. Orders should never be given to subordinates over the head of a responsible executive. Rather than do this, the officer in question should be supplanted.
6. Criticism of subordinates should be made privately. In no case should a subordinate be criticized in the presence of executives or employees of equal or lower rank.
7. No dispute or difference between executives or employees as to authority or responsibility should be considered too trivial for prompt and careful adjudication.
8. Promotions, wage changes, and disciplinary action should always be approved by the executive immediately superior to the one directly responsible.
9. No executive or employee should be assistant to, and at the same time a critic of, the person he or she is assistant to.
10. Any executive whose work is subjected to regular inspection should, whenever practicable, be given the assistance and facilities necessary to enable him or her to maintain an independent check of the quality of his work.

The AMA's ten commandments represent basic principles of managerial relationships inside formal administrative organizations built after the bureaucratic model. In a complementary sense, Lyndall Urwick's "Ten Principles" describe guidelines for organizational design that should be used in building up any formal organization:

1. *Principle of the Objective.* Every organization and every part of every organization must be an expression of the purpose of the undertaking concerned, or it is meaningless and therefore redundant. You cannot organize in a vacuum; you must organize for something.
2. *Principle of Specialization.* The activities of every member of an organized group should be confined, as far as possible, to the performance of a single function.
3. *Principle of Coordination.* The purpose of organizing, per se, as distinguished from the purpose of the undertaking, is to facilitate coordination, unity of effort.
4. *Principle of Authority.* In every organized group the supreme authority must rest somewhere. There should be a clear line of authority from supreme authority to every individual in the group.
5. *Principle of Responsibility.* The responsibility of the superior for the acts of his or her subordinate is absolute.
6. *Principle of Definition.* The content of each position, the duties involved, the authority and the responsibility contemplated, and the relationships with other positions should be clearly defined in writing and published for all concerned.
7. *Principle of Correspondence.* In every position the responsibility and the authority should correspond.
8. *The Span of Control.* No person should supervise more than five, or at most six, direct subordinates whose work interlocks.
9. *Principle of Balance.* It is essential that the various units of an organization should be kept in balance
10. *Principle of Continuity.* Reorganization is a continuous process; in every undertaking specific provision should be made for it.

The tenth principle is very important for understanding recent developments in the evolution of formal organizations and the management approach to innovation. Continuous improvement is becoming vitally significant for the survival of organizations in a fast-changing environment. Modern society faces a rapid shift from a closed to an open model of organization. All organizations are influenced by the same technological, economic, and demographic trends that affect the society overall. The most important impact of the modern changes to formal organizations is in the decline of traditional forms, especially those following the closed bureaucratic model.

The major driving force of these changes is transformation of the society into an information society. The power of organizations is increasingly coming from information. Proportionally, the value of such important factors as labor, capital, and material resources is decreasing. These factors will still be valuable, but they are increasingly expensive and are in growing shortage. The creative use of labor, capital, and raw materials will be aimed at lowering their costs and "stretching" their supplies (Hampton 1994).

Traditional forms of permanent employment will, more and more, be replaced by skilled contractors and part-time workers. Independent contractors will be increasingly used by organizations to solve particular problems and to provide components and services. People will receive their fees (but not wages) for the accomplishment of tasks, not for spending time inside the premises of formal organizations.

Overall, then, (1) such important functions of formal organization as controls will be less and less significant as skilled and highly professional people in the majority of cases will be able to manage themselves, and they will operate on an independent, contractual basis; (2) as a result of that, and of growing use of computers for automation of reporting, investigating, coordinating, and controlling tasks, middle management, as one of the key parts of formal organization, will be in less and less demand.

Organizations will still need to evaluate performance, but this function will be shifting more and more toward results and away from activities.

The decline of the entire bureaucratic model is another important trend affecting formal organizations. Even large organizations will no longer be able to follow this model. They will be shifting more and more toward the open model described previously, encouraging small teams with the highest level of both motivation and productivity, as well as cross-disciplinary skills; autonomous units (such as internal profit centers) will have both responsibility and authority to handle different problems. Formal organizations will also be challenged to recognize openly the importance and role of informal organizational systems. All this means a flattening of hierarchical structure, or an elimination of it completely. In other words, it means the decline of formal organization itself.

These projections are not just bold speculations. Big corporations, which are symbols of formal organizations, already feel this pressure. In one recent study of career preferences, just 1 percent of the 1,000 adult respondents said they would readily choose to be corporate managers. More and more often, top business school graduates prefer to start businesses of their own rather than to join big corporations. Typically, their arguments are that the best bureaucrats, not the best performers, are more likely to get ahead; it is too easy to get pigeonholed or stuck in a dead-end job with no way out; it takes too long to get enough responsibility, authority, and rewards; there is not enough flexibility about where and when you work; top

managers say they want risk takers, but they do not. Increasing numbers of students at top business schools want a career that involves a high level of social responsibility, such as running a successful small business and doing good works part-time, such as teaching in a school for the blind (Labich 1995).

This trend represents new opportunities for organizations inside the public sector. It is unrealistic to project that government will abandon the closed model. But it is quite possible that recent innovations in government—less bureaucracy and more responsibility, more customer orientation and less administrative control over operations of public sector organizations—will clear the way for the people who come not just to earn their living but to serve public needs, and will bring a new paradigm to the development of public sector organizations.

PAVEL MAKEYENKO, MARC HOLZER, AND
VATCHE GABRIELIAN

BIBLIOGRAPHY

Banki, Ivan S., 1981. *Dictionary of Administration and Management*. Los Angeles: Systems Research Institute.
Blau, Peter M., and W. Richard Scott, 1962. *Formal Organizations: A Comparative Approach*. San Francisco: Chandler.
Chandler, Ralph C., and Jack S. Plano, 1988. *The Public Administration Dictionary*. 2d ed. Santa Barbara, CA: ABC-Clio.
Coll, Joan H., 1994. "Organizational Models and Structures." In John J. Hampton, ed., *AMA Management Handbook*. 3d ed. New York: AMACOM.
Hampton, John J., 1994. "The Organization of the Future." In John J. Hampton, ed., *AMA Management Handbook*. 3d ed. New York: AMACOM.
Labich, Kenneth, 1995. "Kissing of Corporate America." *Fortune*, vol. 131, no. 3 (20 February): 44–55.
Robbins, Stephen P., 1990. *Organization Theory*. Englewood Cliffs, NJ: Prentice-Hall.
Rorty, M. C., 1941. *Ten Commandments of Good Organization*. New York: American Management Association (AMA).
Scott, W. Richard, 1992. *Organization*. Englewood Cliffs, NJ: Prentice-Hall.
Shafritz, Jay M., and J. Steven Ott, eds., 1992. *Classics of Organization Theory*. Pacific Grove, CA: Brooks-Cole.
Urwick, Lyndall F., 1952. *Notes on the Theory of Organization*. New York: AMA.
Woodward, J., 1965. *Industrial Organization: Theory and Practice*. New York: Oxford University Press.

FOUNDATION CENTER. An independent nonprofit organization that produces and disseminates to the public information about private and community foundations and corporate giving programs. It maintains comprehensive databases, produces directories, and analyzes trends in foundations' grant making, finances, and creation rates. Information is provided to the public on-line, in reports and directories, and in person at five Foundation Center libraries and through approximately 200 cooperating collections throughout the United States and in selected other countries.

Founded in 1956 as the Foundation Library Center, the Foundation Center was the brainchild of James Perkins and John Gardner of the Carnegie Corporation of New York, a private foundation that provided it with initial funding. Its mission was to improve foundations' accountability and accessibility to the public. The Foundation Center's first president was F. Emerson Andrews, an executive at the Russell Sage Foundation who was an author and observer of foundations. In 1958, Marianna Olmstead Lewis complied by hand the first *Foundation Directory,* which was published in 1960. The *Foundation Directory* is now the classic reference work that provides basic information on large grant-making foundations.

In addition to the *Foundation Directory,* which provides a brief factual and financial description of each of the largest U.S. foundations, the Foundation Center publishes approximately 50 reports and directories. *The Foundation Grants Index* is a compilation of grants awarded by the largest U.S. foundations and others, classified by the National Taxonomy of Exempt Entities. *Foundation Giving: A Yearbook of Facts and Figures on Private, Corporate, and Community Foundations* is an indispensable guide to current statistics on philanthropic foundations. *The Foundation 1000* provides in-depth analysis of the largest 1,000 foundations. *National Data Book of Foundations* lists all U.S. foundations. *Foundation Fundamentals* explains how to conduct research to identify potential sources of grant support among private grantors. *The Literature of the Nonprofit Sector: A Bibliography with Abstracts* reports annually on research and articles concerning philanthropy and nonprofit organizations.

The Foundation Center supplies its foundation directories and other publications to cooperating facilities in public, university, government, and foundation libraries in all 50 states, Puerto Rico, the U.S. Virgin Islands, Australia, Canada, England, Japan, and Mexico. Materials are available free of charge at these facilities. Through orientation programs and educational seminars the center instructs the grant-seeking public about private funding sources.

The public can also access the Internal Revenues Service disclosure forms (Forms 990–PF), required of each private foundation, at the Foundation Center libraries. These forms are public documents that report financial information, including expenses and assets, as well as grants awarded. In addition to the Forms 990–PF, the center's staffed libraries (New York, Washington, D.C., Atlanta, Cleveland, and San Francisco) include reference books, foundation annual reports, newsletters, clippings, application guidelines, and historical and other research materials. Each year approximately 250,000 people are served directly or indirectly by the center.

The Foundation Center is governed by a board of directors and supported by grants from more than 500 foundations and corporations, as well as by fees for services.

ELIZABETH T. BORIS

BIBLIOGRAPHY

Freeman, David, and the Council on Foundations, 1991. *The Handbook on Private Foundations.* Rev. ed. New York: Foundation Center.
Williams, Roger M., 1985. "The Readiest Reference: Foundation Center Every Grantseeker's Personal Library," *Foundation News,* vol. 25, no. 6 (November-December): 26–32.

FOUNDATIONS.

Nonprofit, nongovernmental organizations that promote charitable giving and other public purposes usually by giving grants of money to nonprofit organizations, qualified individuals, and other entities. Under United States law, philanthropic foundations must serve the public by being organized and operated exclusively for religious, charitable, scientific, testing for public safety, literary, or educational purposes. In addition to providing grants, foundations may provide services, make loans, conduct research, hold conferences, publish reports, and undertake other related activities.

Foundations are formed by individuals, families, and business corporations, which usually donate money, property, or other financial assets. These assets form an endowment or principal fund from which interest is derived and used to support expenses and grant making. Some foundations are not endowed, but receive periodic gifts from their donors.

Public Versus Private Foundations

There are two major types of philanthropic foundations: private foundations (independent, company-sponsored, and operating foundations) and public foundations (community foundations, women's funds, and others). The term "foundation," however, is often used by organizations that are not philanthropic grantors, and private foundations may use a variety of terms to describe themselves. In addition to "foundations," they are called "funds" (the Rockefeller Brothers Fund), "corporations" (the Carnegie Corporation of New York), "trusts," (the Lucille P. Markey Charitable Trust), and "endowments," (the Lilly Endowment).

Foundations may be organized in perpetuity or only for a specified time period. When a foundation is terminated, all of its assets must be used for charitable purposes.

In 1992 there were 35,765 foundations, according to the **Foundation Center**, a nonprofit organization that compiles and publishes information about foundations. The foundation field is highly concentrated. The largest foundations, those with US$50 million or more, are responsible for 66.2 percent of assets and 48 percent of grants. Most foundations are small and do not employ staff. Only about 9,600 have assets of one million dollars or more.

Foundations held assets of approximately $177 billion and made grants of more than $10 billion in 1992. Though significant in impact, this grant making is a modest 8 percent of total charitable giving, estimated to be $124 billion in 1992 by the AAFRC Trust for Philanthropy, an organization that compiles annual estimates of philanthropic giving. Foundations also provide only a small proportion of overall revenues received by nonprofit organizations in the United States, which was estimated at $408 billion in 1989 by the Independent Sector, a national nonprofit membership organization.

Private Foundations

Private foundations are created by individual or family donors (or by their representatives, if created by a will after death) or by business corporations. Donors select the boards of directors (or trustees), which determine how the foundations' money will be donated or used for charitable purposes. Private foundations provide donors with a maximum of control over the selection of charitable recipients but a more limited charitable income tax deduction than is available for gifts to public charities. Individuals may deduct from their taxable income cash gifts of up to 30 percent of income. All private foundations are regulated by the "private foundation" rules of the U.S. tax code. These rules are designed to ensure that foundations use their resources only for public benefit.

Public Foundations

Public foundations include community foundations, which are "public charities," the charitable designation that applies to most nonprofit organizations under U.S. law. Public charities are required to have broad public participation both in donations and in governance, and therefore provide less individual control of the assets and grants than private foundations. Public foundations are subject to the less-stringent regulations and more-favorable tax deductibility levels that govern public charities in the United States. For income tax purposes, donors may deduct the value of cash gifts up to 50 percent of their adjusted income.

Public charities are required to demonstrate their public support by raising a certain specified percentage of their revenues each year from the general public, a requirement called the public support test. No one donor may provide a majority of financial support.

Characteristics of Philanthropic Foundations

Private and public foundations in the United States have the following characteristics:

- They are governed by boards of directors or trustees which are responsible for their financial integrity and the fulfillment of their charitable missions.
- They make grants or operate programs or institutions that promote charitable purposes.
- They may employ a staff or use volunteers or consultants to conduct their charitable work.
- They receive gifts of money, property, or financial securities that are deductible from the donors' income tax up to certain limits specified by law (if the donor is alive) or gifts that are deductible from estate taxes if the gift is given through a bequest at the donor's death.
- Financial assets (for those that have endowments) are invested in financial securities (stocks, bonds, etc.), and the interest and dividends earned (and sometimes additional gifts from their donors) provide the money to make grants or operate programs to benefit society. Unless prohibited by their by-laws or trust instruments, foundations may also make grants from the principal fund.
- They are independent of government.
- They do not distribute a profit (nonprofit status).
- They are classified as tax exempt organizations under United States law (501 [c] [3] organizations) and therefore are not subject to taxes on their revenues (except that private foundations must pay an excise tax of one or two percent on their investment income).

Private Foundations

There are three types of private foundations, distinguishable by the source of their assets and the type of work they do.

Independent Foundations

Independent foundations are created by gifts from an individual, a family, or a group of individuals to provide funding for charitable activities, primarily by making grants. Many prominent American entrepreneurs and their families created foundations: the **Ford Foundation**, William and Flora Hewlett Foundation, Rockefeller Foundation, David and Lucile Packard Foundation, Charles Stewart Mott Foundation, W. K. Kellogg Foundation, and many others.

Foundations may be operated by the donors or their families, by staff hired for that purpose, or by banks or other entities designated by the donors to act in their behalf. Policy and grant decisions are made by the board of directors or trustees, which usually includes the donors and their families (if they are alive), trusted associates, and other civic, business, and academic leaders who can contribute to the work of the foundations. Many independent foundations, like the Ford Foundation, no longer have family members involved in the foundation. The board of directors is legally responsible for overseeing the finances and operations of the foundation; it also elects new directors.

When an independent foundation is primarily governed and operated by the donor and family members, it is often called a "family foundation." Donors and family members form the board of directors and often operate the foundation without employing a staff. In some family foundations, the family lawyer, trusted friends, and business associates may also be asked to serve on the board. (The Meadows Foundation in Texas is an example of a family foundation that includes family members as staff and board members, although it also employs nonfamily members as staff.)

Recently, some independent foundations were formed as a result of the sale of nonprofit hospitals (or similar charitable entities) to for-profit businesses. Several such sales resulted in the creation of new foundations with hundreds of millions of dollars in assets. Although the foundations are legally independent from the resulting for-profit companies, the foundations usually focus on health or issues related to the original charitable purpose of the former nonprofit organization.

Operating Foundations

Private foundations may also be organized as operating foundations to conduct research or provide a direct service; for example, they may operate an art museum or a home for the aged. The interest generated by the endowment pays for staffing and administering the program or organization. Operating foundations must use at least 85 percent of their investment income to operate programs. They are permitted to make grants, but only up to 15 percent of their income. (The Kettering Foundation of Ohio is a well-known operating foundation that publishes papers and organizes public issues forums throughout the United States. The Getty Trust operates the Getty Museum in California.)

Community Foundations

Community foundations are classified as public charities and are formed by a group of individuals to benefit their community or region. An endowment is created from the gifts of many donors, which are pooled, and the interest is used to make grants to nonprofit organizations, individuals, and governments to enhance the quality of life, primarily in their geographical area. Community foundations may have separate funds that are donated by different persons or families or businesses. A donor may name the fund and indicate the types of grants that the fund should make. The community foundation board oversees the foundation, and its staff conducts the grant-making program.

Boards of directors of community foundations (also called trustees or distribution committees) are selected to represent the community. Some members are chosen by certain designated public officials (for example, a judge or civic leader).

Other Public Foundations

There are several other types of public foundations that receive tax-deductible contributions from individual donors and use the money or the interest generated to make grants for specific types of activities. In the 1980s, groups of women in many cities created women's foundations to raise money and make grants to help meet women's and girls' needs that they felt were being neglected by both philanthropy and governments. There are now more than 60 women's foundations in the United States that raise money to benefit women and girls in their communities. Donors usually contribute to public foundations on a yearly basis, although some, like the Ms. Foundation for Women, has raised an endowment. There are women's funds in Chicago, New York, Colorado, San Francisco, and many other areas.

Members of minority groups have created public foundations to raise money and make grants to meet the needs of their groups. The Seventh Generation Fund was created in 1977 to benefit American Indian tribes in the United States and Canada. Public foundations are at present a small part of United States philanthropy, but their numbers are increasing rapidly.

Many public foundations make grants to promote social change. Often called alternative funds, they employ nonhierarchical decisionmaking structures and invite community members or grantees to participate on the grant making boards or distribution committees. (The Haymarket People's Fund in Boston is a well-known alternative fund.)

Government Foundations

The National Endowment for the Humanities, the National Endowment for the Arts, the National Science Foundation, and the National Endowment for Democracy are examples of foundations established by the U.S. government. Government-initiated foundations are usually supported by public money. They have independent boards of directors, but their programs often become part of the political debate during the budgeting process. In western European countries, government-supported foundations are often larger and more prominent than privately funded ones.

History of Philanthropic Foundations

Private foundations were popularized shortly after the turn of the twentieth century when Margaret Olivia Sage (1907), Andrew Carnegie (1911), John D. Rockefeller (1913), formed their foundations. These new organizations were created as corporations, like the businesses then responsible for generating the private fortunes that would be turned to charitable uses. Unlike the traditional charitable trusts handed down in common law from Elizabethan times, the new corporations were flexible and could more easily change with the times. They were governed by self-perpetuating boards of directors that had the power to make program and investment decisions and the legal responsibility for financial oversight.

At about the same time, Frederick H. Goff developed the concept of a community trust in Cleveland, Ohio. The community trust was designed to avoid the "dead hand" of the donor whose charitable purposes became outmoded after his or her death. By creating a charitable fund in a community trust, a donor permitted a distribution committee representative of the community to ensure that his or her gift always fulfilled a relevant charitable purpose. The idea caught on, and in 1914 the Cleveland Community Trust was formed. Numerous community trusts, later called community foundations, were formed in the following years.

Although the foundation as an institution was an innovation, it evolved from long-standing traditions of secular and religious giving as well as popular reform movements. Andrew Carnegie's *Gospel of Wealth* [1889] (1990) provides the classic rationale for the proper stewardship of wealth. He called upon men of wealth to regard surplus revenues as trust funds that they are duty bound to administer for the benefit of the community.

Philanthropic foundations flourished during the 1920s, when immense fortunes were made and there was unbridled optimism in the ability of reason and science to solve society's problems. Foundations were to be instruments of scientific charity, controlled by those of superior achievement and designed to support efforts to get at the root causes of poverty, hunger, and disease. Education and research were the favored methods.

The early foundations were formed before the adoption of a national income tax, although foundations were among the charitable organizations exempted from paying income taxes in the Revenue Act of 1913. By 1917 Congress enacted a charitable tax deduction for donors, and in 1919 deductions were permitted for charitable gifts made from estates after the death of the donor.

Despite the tax incentives, the number of foundations grew slowly, until the 1940s, when high rates of taxation (marginal rates up to 90%) and postwar prosperity combined to encourage the creation of a large number of new private foundations. This trend accelerated in the 1950s, slowed somewhat in the 1960s, and declined in the 1970s following the enactment of the Tax Reform Act of 1969, which contained many regulatory provisions that affected foundations. In the mid-1980s the creation of new large foundations reached an all-time high, following the revi-sion of some of the most restrictive provisions of the 1969 law and the creation of huge personal fortunes.

Achievements

In less than a century, philanthropic foundations have produced a long list of achievements. Major foundations that view their assets as social risk capital have financed breakthroughs in scientific research, the arts, and the humanities, and have built and sustained major nonprofit institutions both in the United States and in other countries. The majority of foundations, with modest resources and ambitions, have quietly contributed to local colleges, hospitals, and service organizations, providing needed resources and helping to improve the quality of life in their communities.

Foundations supported the research that led to the new grains that produced the Green Revolution in Asia; helped to create public television and its best-known show, *Sesame Street;* funded the Flexner Report that caused major reforms in medical education; funded the experiments that led to white lines on the right side of all of U.S. roads, championed population research before it was politically possible for the government to do so, and much more.

Criticisms

From the beginning foundations received mixed reactions. Even though some welcomed the dedication of surplus wealth to philanthropic purposes, many feared that the concentration of resources in foundations would subvert the public agenda and place too much power in the hands of those who already controlled business and politics. Foundations are faulted for their lack of public accountability, for their elitism, for their arrogance, and for their potential to benefit those who form and run them, rather than the public purposes they are ostensibly designed to serve. Periodic scandals reinforce these fears, although the growth of government, business, and the nonprofit sector over the course of the century has limited the negative impacts that early critics feared.

American culture celebrates individual initiative and daring that leads to financial success, but part of the negative reaction to foundations is a distrust of the donor's motives. In a study reported by John Edie (1987) in *America's Wealthy and the Future of Foundations,* donors' reasons for creating foundations were found to vary significantly. Some had a deeply felt religious background or a tradition of family social responsibility and concern for the poor, and others had political or ideological beliefs they wished to advance. Some donors desired to create a memorial to themselves or their families. Other donors felt a commitment to a community or pressure from their peers to be philanthropic. Relatively few formed foundations because of tax incentives, although the existence of tax incentives often influenced the size of the contribution to the foundation.

Recently, foundations were faulted for being both too political and too timid. Critics of the left challenge foundations for supporting the status quo and neglecting the needs of the poor, of girls and women, of racial and ethnic minorities, and of the disabled. Critics from the right accuse foundations of encouraging the growth of government programs and undermining the free enterprise system. The failure of many foundations to communicate fully with the public about their work inhibits informed assessments of their impacts. Only a minority of foundations issue annual reports or publications that describe their programs.

Government Regulation

The Internal Revenue Service oversees the activities of philanthropic foundations and other nonprofit organizations because the national laws governing foundations are in the tax code. The 1969 Tax Reform Act and its subsequent revisions provide the national regulatory framework for U.S. foundations. Foundations must pay fines for violating the law, and a foundation may lose its status as a tax-exempt entity for a serious offense.

Foundations may not control a business, provide monetary benefits to any donors or directors (except for reasonable compensation for services provided), make risky investments with their endowment funds, or accumulate assets without paying a reasonable amount for charitable activities. Private (nonoperating) foundations must make grants and operate programs that, with administrative expenses, amount to at least 5 percent of their assets each year.

Foundations may not try to influence the legislative process directly, except in their own defense, and they may not influence elections, except by providing independent research and analysis to inform the political debate.

At the state level, the attorney general or charities officer reviews a foundation's state information forms (if they are required) and oversees compliance with state charitable regulations. At the federal level, a foundation is required by law to complete a detailed disclosure form (Form 990–PF) every year. These documents include information on a foundation's revenues, expenses, investments, loans, salaries, gifts received, income-producing activities, and other financial and program information. Private foundations are also required to list all of the grants they make each year and to provide information about how to apply for a grant. These information forms (Form 990–PF for private, corporate, and operating foundations, and Form 990 for community foundations) are public documents. Foundations must make these forms available to the public. The Foundation Center (1994a) facilitates access to the disclosure forms by making them available in library collections around the country.

Regulatory History of Foundations

Foundations and other charitable organizations operated with little regulation or oversight for most of this century—although Congress has periodically turned its attention to philanthropic foundations to respond to abuses, both real and perceived. In 1916, after two years of hearings, the Walsh Commission prepared a report critical of philanthropic foundations as devices that permitted a small group of wealthy families to control social services and educational entities in addition to their control of whole industries. The reforms recommended by the commission were not implemented. The first limitation on charitable activities occurred in the Revenue Act of 1934, which prohibited charitable organizations from lobbying or carrying out propaganda.

Although foundations had not been identified as separate types of charitable organizations under the law, the distinction began to be made in 1943. In an attempt to determine if further regulations were necessary, the government enacted a requirement that charitable organizations had to file an annual report listing income, disbursements, and receipts. The rule exempted most types of charitable organizations, except foundations. The Revenue Act of 1950 required "arms-length" dealings between an organization and its donors and donors' relatives and denial of tax exemptions for organizations that unreasonably accumulated income. These provisions also exempted most organizations, except private foundations.

Foundations were investigated as part of the anticommunist fervor in the early 1950s. The House of Representatives in 1952 created the Select Committee to Investigate Tax-Exempt Foundations and Comparable Organizations, chaired by Representative E. E. Cox of Georgia, to determine if private foundations and similar organizations were engaged in "un-American" activities. The committee's report was fairly complimentary to foundations and did not implicate them in pro-communist activities.

A member of the Cox Committee, Representative Carroll Reece, recommended a more comprehensive study of foundations. It was authorized by the House of Representatives in 1953. The report of the Special Committee to Investigate Tax-Exempt Foundations and Comparable Organizations was issued in 1954 and was much more negative in tone. It asserted that foundations were exercising control over social science research, were promoting "moral relativity," and had been created to receive tax benefits rather than to reflect altruism.

In the reorganization of the tax code in 1954 a further distinction between foundations and other charitable organizations was introduced. The maximum income tax deduction for charitable gifts was raised from 20 percent of adjusted gross income to 30 percent—if the extra 10 percent were given to religious, educational, or hospital organizations. In 1964 Congress expanded this list to include almost

all charitable organizations except private foundations. In effect, Congress increased the tax incentive for donors to make direct gifts to charities, rather than through a foundation, reflecting the more negative views of foundations that were emerging. Subsequent regulations maintained the disparity, but raised the tax deduction to 50 percent for public charities and 30 percent for private foundations.

The watershed investigation of private foundations occurred under Representative Wright Patman of Texas. He began to investigate foundations in 1961 and spent ten years at his task. The impact of his decade-long attack, delivered with flamboyant style, populist passion, and media attention, reverberated through the foundation field for 20 years. His allegations—of financial concentration, control of businesses, abuse of tax deductions, and ineffective IRS oversight—resulted in a request for the Treasury Department to conduct a thorough investigation.

The *Treasury Department Report on Private Foundations* (U.S. Congress 1965) was based on extensive research. It summarized the contributions of foundations in U.S. society and made recommendations for regulations to deal with the identified problems: delay of benefits to society, ownership of businesses, control of property, questionable financial investments, self-dealing, and donor control. Abuses were identified, but not in the quantity that might have been expected from the allegations of the Patman hearings.

The Tax Reform Act of 1969 included many Treasury Department recommendations and began an era of close regulation and oversight of private foundations, which were defined for the first time under the act.

The immediate reaction of the foundation world was defensive, but it could produce little research on the status of foundations, on their impacts, or on their operations. The Council on Foundations emerged from its predecessor organization to become the voice of foundations. The Commission on Foundations and Private Philanthropy (1970), the Peterson Commission, was formed by John D. Rockefeller III, to investigate the allegations of abuse. Peter G. Peterson, chairman of Bell and Howell Corporation, was its chair. Its report, presented in 1970, found little evidence of the abuses alleged by Representative Patman.

The Commission on Private Philanthropy and Public Needs (1975) (the **Filer Commission**) was also initiated by John D. Rockefeller III, in 1973, with John H. Filer, chairman of Aetna Life & Casualty, as its chair. It conducted a series of studies that became the first systematic and comprehensive investigation of the nonprofit sector, philanthropic foundations, giving, and volunteering. Some of the commission's findings were reflected in subsequent revisions of the Tax Reform Act of 1969.

In the years following 1969, the regulations have been refined and amended and excesses corrected. The resulting legal framework has resulted in heightened public trust and congressional acceptance of foundations. The foundation field is now well organized, with regional associations and a national organization, the Council on Foundations, that looks after its interest in Washington, D.C., conducts research and training programs, promotes a code of ethics, and emphasizes disclosure and self-regulation. Most observers agree that the Tax Reform Act of 1969 achieved its goals; it corrected existing abuses and strengthened organized philanthropy in the process.

Foundation Governance

Foundations are governed by boards of directors or by trustees (in foundations that are set up as charitable trusts). Directors and trustees are responsible for the proper management of the foundation's assets and for implementing its grant making and other program goals. The foundation's goals may be spelled out in great detail by the donor, or, as in most large U.S. foundations, the goals may be quite general—to improve the lives of people—which leaves to the discretion of the board the definition and implementation of the foundation's program.

Private foundation boards are self-perpetuating. New members are identified and elected by the existing board. In addition to donors and family members, boards usually include business, professional, educational and community leaders. The majority of foundation board members are white males; approximately 29 percent of board members are women, and 4 percent are members of racial or ethnic minority groups.

Foundation governance may vary from complete donor control to almost complete staff control. There are four main types of foundation governance that capture the continuum: donor, administrator, director, and presidential. These models are somewhat related to the size and longevity of the foundations. Smaller foundations are more likely to be informally run by the donor and family. Larger ones are usually more professionalized, older, and more likely to be run by staffs than by the families that founded them.

The donor model is prevalent in many family foundations in which the donor and family members operate the foundation without a staff and make all of the decisions themselves. The process is informal and the donor's wishes are paramount.

In the administrator model, the foundation employs an administrative staff person who processes the paperwork, but the policy and program decisions are initiated and decided by the board members. In the director model, the foundation employs an executive director and relies on that person to process the requests and provide information and recommendations for the foundation's policy and grant decisions.

The presidential model gives wide discretion to the foundation's chief executive officer (CEO). This model is usually found in the few large foundations that make hundreds of grants and give away many millions of dollars each year. In these foundations, the board of directors employs an experienced national leader to whom it delegates operating and grant-making authority. The board sets fiscal and program priorities and monitors the foundation's finances and programs. It may also make decisions on very large grants.

Corporate Governance

In corporate foundations, the boards of directors usually comprise the chief executive officer of the corporation and other high-level managers. Infrequently, directors from outside the company may be asked to serve on the corporate foundation board. The decisionmaking process varies by company. In some companies all grant recommendations are brought before the board for final decisions, but in other companies staffs have greater discretion and can make many small grants on their own authority. With the trend toward decentralization in U.S. business, corporations are increasingly delegating grant-making authority to local managers.

Grant Making

Foundations make grants primarily to qualified public charities, although they may make grants to almost any type of organization or individual, as long as the purpose of the grant is "charitable" and the grantor monitors the use of the funds. Grants can be made to nonprofit organizations, individuals, corporations, and governments, both nationally and internationally. The majority of foundation grants are made to nonprofit organizations, often colleges and universities, that qualify as tax-exempt charitable organizations under section 501(c)(3) of the U.S. tax code.

Grant-making patterns do not change greatly from year to year. The Foundation Center reports that in 1993, 24 percent of foundation grant dollars supported educational projects; 18 percent funded health-related projects; 15 percent were for human services; 15 percent for arts and humanities; 11 percent for public or society benefit; 5 percent for the environment and animals; 4 percent for science and technology; 4 percent for international affairs; 3 percent for social science; and 2 percent for religion.

In addition to making grants, foundations may undertake a wide range of activities. They often bring people together in conferences or informally to discuss new research, ideas, or problems. They help other organizations do their jobs better by providing them with management assistance or training. Some provide space for service-providing organizations, and others conduct or publish research. Foundations may also make loans and invest in projects that have a charitable purpose.

Staffing

Most foundations in the United States do not employ staffs. They have limited assets and are operated by the donor(s) or by the board of directors. Some unstaffed foundations employ consultants or other part-time staffs for specific tasks, such as accounting, audits, and legal matters. Corporate foundations are often administered by employees of the sponsoring company.

In the largest 2,500 foundations, program, administrative, and clerical staffs are employed to operate foundations, under the guidance of boards of directors. Fewer than 13,000 men and women work for philanthropic foundations. The staff of a typical foundation may include an executive director who heads the foundation, a program officer who investigates grant requests, and a secretary who does the clerical work. A few very large foundations, like the Ford, Kellogg, and Rockefeller foundations, have a large number of employees and a complex organizational structure.

Foundations Worldwide

Philanthropic trusts and religious funds are traditionally found in many cultures. Recently, increasing numbers of foundation-like institutions of all recognized types are being created throughout the world. Regulations, sources of support, and grant-making patterns vary, but in most cases, foundations are playing important roles in building and maintaining civil societies. As in the United States, foundations often take the name of the individual donor or family. Prominent international foundations include: Soros, Tatas, Calouste Gulbenkian, Aga Khan, Eugenio Mendoza, Bernard van Leer, Sassakawa, and Nuffield foundations. Organizations like community foundations are also evident in many countries and are becoming more common. These include the Asian Community Trust, the Foundation de France, the Puerto Rico Community Foundation, and many others. Company-sponsored foundations are also increasing in number; for example, the Toyota Foundation, Suntory Foundation, and the Prasetya Mulya Foundation.

Government-initiated or -supported foundations are prominent in many countries. The Volkswagen Foundation in Germany, the Japan Foundation, and the Bank of Sweden Tercentenary Foundation are examples. These types of foundations fulfill charitable or educational purposes and may be permitted to receive donations.

The European Foundation Center was formed in the 1980s to provide services and advocate on behalf of the growing number of European foundations. That organization now compiles a directory of European foundations. Similar country-specific directories also exist in Germany, the United Kingdom, and elsewhere.

Foundations are proliferating around the world as wealth is created and societal needs become more pressing.

Sources of foundation funding vary, but the basic goals are the same: to use private resources and ingenuity to serve the public and to support alternative solutions to pressing social problems.

Elizabeth T. Boris

BIBLIOGRAPHY

Boris, Elizabeth, 1989. "Working in Foundations." In Richard Magat, ed., *Philanthropic Giving: Studies in Varieties and Goals.* New York: Oxford University Press.

———, 1992. *Philanthropic Foundations in the United States: An Introduction.* Washington, DC: Council on Foundations.

Carnegie, Andrew, [1889] 1990. "The Gospel of Wealth." In David L. Geis, J. Steven Ott, and Jay M. Shafritz, eds., *The Nonprofit Organization: Essential Readings.* Pacific Grove, CA: Brooks-Cole.

Commission on Foundations and Private Philanthropy, 1970. *Foundations, Private Giving and Public Policy.* Chicago: University of Chicago Press.

Commission on Private Philanthropy and Public Needs, Department of the Treasury, 1975. *Giving in America.* Washington, DC: GPO.

———, 1977. Department of the Treasury, *Research Papers.* Washington, DC: GPO.

Council on Foundations, 1993. *Foundation Management Report.* Washington, DC: Council on Foundations.

Cuninggim, Merrimon. 1972. *Private Money and Public Service: The Role of Foundations in American Society.* New York: McGraw-Hill.

Edie, John, A., 1987. "Congress and Foundations: Historical Summary." In Teresa Odendahl, ed., *America's Wealthy and the Future of Foundations.* New York: Foundation Center.

Foundation Center, 1994a. *The Foundation Directory.* New York: Foundation Center.

———, 1994b. *The Foundation Grants Index.* New York: Foundation Center.

Freeman, D., and the Council on Foundations, 1991. *The Handbook of Private Foundations.* New York: Foundation Center.

Hall, Peter Dobkin, 1989. "The Community Foundation in America." In Richard Magat, ed., *Philanthropic Giving: Studies in Varieties and Goals.* New York: Oxford University Press.

Heimann, Fritz. F., ed., 1973. *The Future of Foundations.* Englewood Cliffs, NJ: Prentice-Hall.

Kaplan, Anne, ed., 1994. *Giving USA 1994: The Annual Report on Philanthropy for the Year 1993.* New York: American Association of Fund-raising Counsel.

Karl, Barry D., and Stanley N. Katz, 1981. "The American Private Philanthropic Foundation and the Public Sphere, 1890–1930." *Minerva,* vol. 19: 236–70.

———, 1987. "Foundations and Ruling Class Elites." *Daedalus* 116 (Winter): 1–40.

Lagemann, Ellen Condliffe, 1989. *The Politics of Knowledge: The Carnegie Corporation, Philanthropy, and Public Policy.* Middletown, CT: Wesleyan University Press.

Nielsen, Waldemar A., 1972., *The Big Foundations.* New York: Columbia University Press.

———, 1985. *The Golden Donors: A New Anatomy of the Great Foundations.* New York: Dutton.

Odendahl, Teresa, ed., 1987. *America's Wealthy and the Future of Foundations.* New York: Foundation Center.

———, 1990. *Charity Begins at Home: Generosity and Self-Interest Among the Philanthropic Elite.* New York: Basic Books.

Odendahl, Teresa J., and Elizabeth Boris, 1983. "The Grantmaking Process." *Foundation News* 24 (September-October).

Odendahl, Teresa J., Elizabeth Boris, and Arlene K. Daniels, 1985. *Working in Foundations: Career Patterns of Women and Men.* New York: Foundation Center.

Renz, Loren, and Steven Lawrence, 1994. *Foundation Giving: Yearbook of Facts and Figures on Private, Corporate, and Community Foundations.* New York: Foundation Center.

Salamon, Lester, 1991. *Foundation Investment and Payout Performance: An Update.* Washington, DC: Council on Foundations.

U.S. Congress, 1965. *Treasury Department Report on Private Foundations.* 89th Cong. 1st sess., 2 February.

FRAGMENTATION.

The division of governmental authority among jurisdictions, agencies, and programs, with the degree of fragmentation determined by (1) the number of jurisdictions that share authority or compete, (2) the number of programs serving essentially the same purpose, (3) the number of agencies with overlapping or competing authority.

Fragmentation of political authority and programmatic effort can take many forms. It begins with the federal design of the American system, continues with the proliferation of general- and special-purpose local governments, and ends with the multiplication of programs, largely serving the same ends and administered by multiple agencies. It affects the ability of government to address complex problems, deliver coherent services, innovate and experiment with policy initiatives, and respond to the varying needs and preferences of geographically dispersed and socially differentiated populations.

Sources of Fragmentation

Fragmentation of authority and responsibility is often a design characteristic of modern democracies. Founders of the political systems of nations such as the United States, Canada, Germany, and Korea created federal systems of government that divide responsibility between national and regional units of government. Such designs are specifically intended to foster democracy by providing multiple points of access, by inhibiting the excesses of democracy by checking power with power, and by enhancing responsiveness to localized preferences; they are based on the notion that there are some things better handled for the nation as a whole and other things better handled at some level below the nation.

Authority and responsibility are further fragmented by the system of checks and balances that exists in the United States and other presidential systems of governments. Provisions that allow the executive, legislature, and judiciary to involve themselves in each other's activities are designed to dilute power and diminish the possibility of tyranny. Some conclude that these provisions also prevent effective action to address major public problems by so diluting authority that no one is able to act in a coherent manner. As compared to parliamentary systems, presidential systems fragment authority by separating control of the executive from control of the legislature.

Federalism fragments authority between a national and regional governments, and the United States exhibits extreme fragmentation of political jurisdictions through a multiplicity of local government jurisdictions. In all, there are more then 86,000 local governments in the United States. Some of these are general-purpose governments, such as cities and counties, which have responsibilities for diverse governmental functions, such as law enforcement, transportation, sanitation, fire protection, land use, public health, and recreation. In many cases, however, specific functions are handled by special-purpose governments. Depending on the state and locality, special-purpose governments may be responsible for such functions as education, water, sewage, public transportation, or cultural facilities, among others. Special-purpose governments may have geographical jurisdictions that are smaller than, contiguous with, or larger than general-purpose local governments.

Municipalities and counties themselves are quite diverse in size and scope of responsibility. They often divide control of a metropolitan area. Suburban jurisdictions have multiplied on the boundaries of most central cities. Metropolitan St. Louis, for example, spans 11 counties in 2 states (Missouri, and East St. Louis, Illinois) and encompasses 219 municipalities, 92 townships, 112 school districts, and 274 special districts. In all, it has 708 local governments. A much smaller metropolitan area, Louisville, Kentucky, covers 7 counties in 2 states with 263 local governments. The central city, Louisville, is in Jefferson County, which itself includes 95 municipalities, 2 school districts, and 33 special districts.

The creation of multiple programs serving generally common purposes further fragments authority and responsibility in the U.S. system. The national government, for example, sponsors 75 public assistance programs, most of which are carried out in cooperation with state and local governments. The federal government funds 163 employment and training programs that provide about US$20 billion in federal assistance. A report in 1986 identified 79 different literacy and literacy-related programs. In fact, the Congressional Research Service has identified 76 programs with funding levels of $100 million or more serving the needs of families and children. In addition to these intergovernmental programs, there are countless others sponsored by state and local governments without federal funding.

These multiple programs are overseen and administered by a complex array of congressional committees, federal agencies, and state and local governments. The 163 employment and training programs, for example, are funded through 10 federal departments and 4 independent agencies. The 76 major federal programs for families and children are the product of 19 congressional committees, 10 departments, and one independent agency. They involve 60 agencies and congressional subcommittees in all, according to the Institute for Educational Leadership. Most of these federal programs involve state and local governments and their multiple agencies as well.

As has been mentioned, much of the fragmentation of governmental authority and responsibility is deliberately designed into governmental systems as a way of dispersing and limiting power. That design encourages further fragmentation as problems are approached in a disjointed, incremental manner.

Cities and counties serve important governance and service-delivery functions in the U.S. system. These units have been fragmented as local communities sought autonomy in order to control taxes, services levels and quality, and land use. Quite typically in the United States, the spatial distribution of the population divides the population by race, ethnicity, and income. This division occurs as social groups seek to establish their own exclusive areas and screen out those who are different. This differentiation of the population into distinct geographic enclaves is facilitated by incorporation laws, which make it possible for very small areas to seek political independence, and annexation laws, which make it difficult to build more-encompassing political jurisdictions. Although reformers often issue calls to consolidate government in metropolitan areas, they seldom are able to overcome either the resistance of central city dwellers or, more particularly, the opposition of suburbanites. Thus, the quest for autonomy, control, exclusion, and responsiveness sparks much of the fragmentation of government in the metropolitan United States.

The fragmentation of municipal government in metropolitan areas fosters additional fragmentation as ways are sought to deliver services effectively and efficiently or to spread the cost of areawide functions throughout the region. Special districts are created to realize economies of scale that cannot be obtained by small municipalities or to rationalize the provision of some services on an areawide basis. Political leaders call for the creation of special districts to capture the externalities associated with some problems. Water pollution, for example, cannot be successfully addressed by small jurisdictions because they do not control the relevant catch basin.

Characteristics of the policymaking system lead to programmatic fragmentation. First, problems are seldom addressed in a comprehensive, integrated manner in the United States because of the difficulties of building a sufficient coalition of support to move such plans through the fragmented decisionmaking system. The dispersion of power provides access to many actors, contains multiple veto points, and makes it difficult to pursue large-scale change. Thus the system behaves in a way consistent with the intentions of its founders. Second, problems emerge in a stream over time, with varying definitions each time they emerge. When a problem appears in the problem stream, policy entrepreneurs attempt to attach their own solutions as a way of expanding activities that they believe will serve their policy visions, constituents, or interests. Each time a problem comes up in the same or a slightly new form, there is a tendency to create new programs to address it. Third, each legislative committee and each agency believes that it has something to offer to the solution to pressing national, state, and local needs. They define the problem from their own perspective and recommend solutions consistent with their own mission, culture, and constituency interests. The process of coalition building often involves making concessions to each committee and agency to buy its support for the legislative or administrative package. Finally, there are strong political pressures to create programs targeted at special groups. In addition to 75 employment and training programs serving the general public, there are 88 such programs targeted at special populations: youth, veterans, dislocated workers, Native Americans, the economically disadvantaged, women and minorities, migrants, the homeless, older workers, and refugees.

Consequences of Fragmentation

Fragmentation has multiple consequences to go with its multiple causes. Depending on one's interpretation of those consequences, fragmentation can be either beneficial or detrimental to public well-being. From one perspective, fragmentation undermines program efficiency and effectiveness; promotes social injustice; makes it impossible to deal effectively with areawide problems; allows the middle class and wealthy to evade their responsibility for the disadvantaged; saddles central cities with concentrated social problems; leads to wasteful duplication and overlap; fosters communities that are too small to deal with their problems; spurs unhealthy competition for industry, amenities, and desirable population groups; and diffuses authority in a way that makes it impossible for citizens to assign accountability to responsible parties. From another perspective, fragmentation promotes economic efficiency among governments through competition; stimulates innovation in laboratories of democracy; fosters responsiveness; allows jurisdictions to be tailored to the size of problems; and promotes freedom, choice, and self-responsibility.

Urban reformers have long lamented some of the perceived consequences of governmental fragmentation in urban areas. They believe that small municipal governments lack the capacity to develop highly professional public services, that fragmentation leads to higher governmental costs, and that the multiple points of policymaking and administration in urban areas undermine responsibility by making it difficult or impossible for voters to know whom to hold accountable. Fragmented local governments can find it difficult or impossible to address area-

wide concerns since no one is in a position to impose solutions. Barriers to collective action are widespread in the fragmented metropolis. In a different vein, advocates of the poor and minorities argue that governmental fragmentation concentrates social problems in central cities, providing an escape for the middle and upper classes to avoid addressing the problems or paying for solutions. Those concerned about racial segregation maintain that suburban communities employ exclusionary practices that effectively bar the poor and minorities from their jurisdictions.

Public choice advocates argue that a number of benefits accrue from the fragmentation of metropolitan governance. Citizens have greater freedom of choice to choose a package of taxes and services consistent with their preferences. Many services can be offered more economically by smaller units of government, and economies of scale quickly disappear as governments become too large. Competition among governments, it is argued, helps reduce costs and improve service quality. It also fosters innovation as policymakers search for and try out alternative solution to problems. Smaller units of government allow higher levels of participation and greater control by citizens. Fragmentation through special districts allows jurisdictions to be tailored to the size of a need or problem. It also puts the burden of paying for a service on those who benefit from the service.

Many of these same arguments apply in the relationship between the states and the national government. The intergovernmental system provides multiple points of access, numerous veto points, and considerable potential for innovation. It fosters responsiveness to multiple constituencies and promotes competition among governments. This competition can be good, as when it leads to innovative solutions to common problems. It can also be bad, as when it leads to tax breaks that encourage job shifting among states without fostering net economic growth.

Many policymakers, analysts, and reformers believe that program fragmentation has a variety of deleterious consequences. Duplication and overlap lead to wasted resources and excessive administrative overhead. Administrators multiply to manage and oversee competing programs. Those who need a service often find it difficult to identify the particular programs that will address their problems and are frustrated by the web of intersecting agencies and activities. It is difficult to put together the package of services that will address a family or a child's needs in a comprehensive manner. Plans for addressing common resource problems are difficult to develop and put in place. Complicated administrative routines and excessive red tape are introduced by the conflicting requirements of similar programs.

Program proponents are quick to point out that one-size-fits-all programs do not work because they fail to respond to the special needs of particular populations and leave some groups at risk of not receiving services. Programs can be tailored for different locales, groups, and circumstances. Competition among programs can have the same salutary effects that it has in market places. It leaves those in need with more than one place to find a solution, increasing the likelihood that their problem can be addressed. Redundancy helps fill in the cracks in the system of public services.

Solutions to Fragmentation

When fragmentation is a problem, a variety of solutions are available. The most commonly promoted solution, but most difficult to adopt and implement, is consolidation. If fragmentation promotes inequity, inefficiency and governmental ineffectiveness in a metropolitan area, metropolitan government can be a solution. If program and agency fragmentation make it difficult for people to find the service they need and fosters administrative waste, programs and agencies can be consolidated. The problem with this solution, which looks so clean and simple on the surface, is that it is extraordinarily difficult to accomplish. Every program has its advocate, every agency has its protectors, and every government has its officeholders who want to retain control. So many values and interests are affected by consolidation proposals that they seldom succeed.

There are solutions short of jurisdictional or functional consolidation. In metropolitan areas it is sometimes possible to consolidate selected services, even when integration of general government is not possible. Thus, special districts, which contribute to fragmentation in one sense, are a solution to it in another sense. When agencies and programs overlap and duplicate, administrators and policymakers can find partial solutions through a variety of coordination mechanisms. Coordinating bodies can be created or appointed to provide a forum for discussion of service linkages, information sharing, and resource allocation. Agencies can agree to divide functional roles in accordance with their strengths. Joint planning offers a way of reducing conflict and waste.

Abundant examples of coordination can be found in the social service, welfare, and employment and training arenas. National legislation often requires the creation of state- and local-level coordinating entities. Thus, the Job Training Partnership Act calls for state job training coordinating committees to advise the governor on employment and training policy and to coordinate the activities of diverse agencies and programs. That same legislation provides for private industry councils, composed of business and government leaders, to guide and coordinate program efforts at the local level. These coordinating bodies use their authority to sign off on various programs as one way of encouraging coordination. They engage in joint planning, share information, and provide a forum for discussion among policymakers and administrators of different programs and agencies. They try to make services more accessible and comprehensible to clients by creating one-stop service centers that bring together the services of multiple programs and agencies at one site. Successful efforts include attempts to create consolidated application forms that serve the needs of more than one agency or program. Of course, since coordinating councils have limited resources, authority, jurisdiction, and staffs, they are limited in what they can accomplish. Their success often depends on their ability to help agencies see how cooperation and coordination are in their interest and will serve their ends.

Coordination also can be accomplished through mutual adjustment. Agencies can adjust their own activities to take into account the activities of other organizations and service providers. In the San Francisco (California) Bay area, for example, multiple transportation authorities have created a reasonable level of coordination through mutual adjustment.

Conclusion

The most difficult aspect of fragmentation is to determine whether it is a problem or a solution. This is partly a matter of analysis but largely a product of the values and orientations one brings to the issue. Interest, values, and perceptions of what is critical substantially shape interpretations of fragmentation.

There are moves under way in the current U.S. Congress to decentralize domestic policy to the states and significantly consolidate a broad range of programs. If successful, these moves would signal a new era of public policy, one in which fragmentation might be much less of a concern on one level (program), but increasingly problematic at another level (interstate). It is also highly likely that the forces of fragmentation would quickly begin to undo what reform had wrought.

EDWARD T. JENNINGS, JR.

BIBLIOGRAPHY

Agranoff, Robert. 1991. "Human Services Integration: Past and Present Challenges in Public Administration." *Public Administration Review* 51 (November-December): 533–542.

Bish, Robert L., and Vincent Ostrom, 1973. *Understanding Urban Government: Metropolitan Reform Reconsidered.* Washington, DC: American Enterprise Institute.

Chisholm, Donald, 1989. *Coordination Without Hierarchy: Informal Structures in Multiorganizational Systems.* Berkeley: University of California Press.

Danielson, Michael, 1976. *The Politics of Exclusion.* New York: Columbia University Press.

Dye, Thomas D., 1990. *American Federalism.* Lexington, MA: Lexington Books.

Harrigan, John J., 1993. *Political Change in the Metropolis.* 5th ed. New York: HarperCollins.

Hayes, Michael T., 1992. *Incrementalism and Public Policy.* New York: Longman.

Jennings, Edward T., Jr., 1994. "Building Bridges in the Intergovernmental Arena: Coordinating Employment and

Training Programs in the American States." *Public Administration Review*, 54 (January-February): 52–60.

——,1993. *Welfare System Reform: Coordinating Federal, State, and Local Public Assistance Programs*. Westport, CT: Greenwood Press.

Jones, Bryan D., 1983. *Governing Urban American: A Policy Focus*. Boston: Little, Brown.

Landau, Martin, 1969. "Redundancy, Rationality, and the Problem of Duplication and Overlap." *Public Administration Review*, 29 (July-August): 346–358.

Lindblom, Charles, 1979. "Still Muddling, Not Yet Through." *Public Administration Review*, 49 (November-December): 517–526.

Lyons, William E., David Lowery, and Ruth Hoogland DeHoog, 1992. *The Politics of Dissatisfaction: Citizens, Services, and Urban Institutions*. Armonk, NY: M. E. Sharpe.

National Commission to Prevent Infant Mortality, 1991. *One-Stop Shopping: The Road to Healthy Mothers and Children*. Washington, DC: GPO.

Ostrom, Vincent, Charles Tiebout, and Robert Warren, 1961. "The Organization of Government in Metropolitan Areas." *American Political Science Review*, 55 (December): 831–842.

Seidman, Harold, and Robert Gilmour, 1986. *Politics, Position, and Power: From the Positive to the Regulatory State*. 4th ed. New York: Oxford University Press.

Wright, Deil, 1988. *Understanding Intergovernmental Relations*. 3d ed. Pacific Grove, CA: Brooks-Cole.

FRAUD, WASTE, AND ABUSE. Terms that are frequently grouped together to describe public policy inefficiencies, failures, maladministration, and general government ineffectiveness. Max Weber (1864–1920) was the first sociologist to analyze the weaknesses and strengths of public bureaucracies, likening them to "iron cages." Public bureaucracies have, over time, grown more powerful and more costly than Weber could have ever imagined, and issues relating to fraud, waste, and abuse have proliferated. Whether citizens condemn or condone fraud, waste, and abuse in the public sector is dictated by parochial customs, norms, and cultural mores. Susan Rose Ackerman (1978) has argued that corruption cannot be adequately understood without also knowing the governing theory of that society (pp. 10–11). As an example, the U.S. Congress passed the Foreign Corrupt Practices Act in 1977, which outlawed certain practices of U.S. multinational firms. These same practices are considered legal and normative in the foreign countries where these firms operate.

Public debate about fraud, waste, and abuse usually takes one of two perspectives. Jerome B. McKinney (1986) has delineated these positions as either moralist or functionalist. The moralists push for reductions in fraud, waste, and abuse, thus supporting the transfiguring of governmental institutions. The functionalists argue that fraud, waste, and abuse "level the playing field" between the advantaged and disadvantaged in society.

Of the three terms fraud is easiest to define because laws identify included offenses and proscribe specific sanctions.

However, many argue that separating fraud, waste, and abuse is almost impossible because, frequently, waste and abuse provide opportunities for fraud to be committed.

Fraud

Fraud is defined as actions or omissions that cheat, deceive, distort, or intentionally and willfully swindle or dupe. McKinney (1986) has noted that fraud encompasses a broad spectrum of crimes, including theft; embezzlement; counterfeiting; kickback schemes; collusive bidding; conspiracies; misuse of electronic, computer, and mail systems; and the making of false statements.

Even though the total amount of fraud that occurs in governments is not known, the costs of fraud are enormous. These expenditures account for financial and material damages (e.g., monetary losses), physical harm (e.g., diseases, disabilities, and deaths), as well as less-tangible losses, such as erosion of public confidence in government and its institutional forms and the compromising of governmental integrity. In addition, the net effects of fraud are especially difficult to quantify, describe, and identify for purposes of providing compensation, because victims may not recognize their losses immediately. Fraud crimes are frequently committed against unwitting victims, as in the recent U.S. savings and loan institutions scandal in which personal bank account deposits were used by these institutions to fund fraudulent and high-risk loans. At the height of the scandal (1989 to 1992), the U.S. Department of Justice convicted 102 thrift officers, as well as 166 thrift officials serving on boards of directors. The complexity of many fraud offenses makes particular groups or individuals in a society vulnerable to fraud because they are meek, economically powerless, or ignorant of their rights.

Fraud is expensive and time-consuming to detect, investigate, and prosecute. It is frequently characterized by sophisticated schemes utilizing accounting, auditing, and legal techniques that circumvent normal monitoring and regulatory checks. Investigation is particularly labor-intensive, requiring months and sometimes years to review records, conduct financial analyses, and gather legal evidence. The complexity of these offenses also thwarts easy presentation of evidence to juries, administrative law agencies, or other forums for dispute resolution.

Waste

Waste is defined as the maladministration of public resources. There is controversy, however, as to whether waste is merely a descriptor for citizens' contempt of government programs and entities or, more objectively, is a label given to unneeded government spending and management deficiencies. According to William Hamm (1986), under the former assumption, waste becomes a rallying point for political issues and agendas, and under the latter contention, waste becomes an important component of public policy analysis and debate. Calling attention to waste of public resources is either a method to label and propagandize or is a tool for ascertaining what succeeds and what fails in government operations.

Costs due to waste in the public sector are substantial. Waste obviously drains precious resources, reduces credibility of government agencies and program delivery, and provides opportunities for fraudulent schemes. Waste prevails when (1) internal controls (checks and balances) are weak, (2) regulations are vague, (3) budgetary systems are antiquated or ineffective, (4) management directives are distorted, (5) intergovernmental fiscal relationships are not clear-cut, and (6) when citizens are apathetic about strict accountability. Some public policy scholars argue that the number of layers of bureaucracy that can be politically influenced has an impact on the occurrence of waste in government. Another consideration raised by analysts is that both excessive regulation *and* underregulation create vulnerabilities that can lead to poor administration of public resources.

As with fraud, waste is detectable in the goods, services, financial payments, and entitlements that governments provide, as well as in licensure, permit grants, certifications, compliance agreements, and other processes and procedures whereby powers and rights are delegated to individuals or groups outside formal governing structure.

In the United States, oversight responsibilities for federal spending are split among different venues. The Office of Management and Budget (OMB) is tasked with part of this function, as are individual executive branch agencies through their Offices of Inspectors General. In addition, U.S. Congress has an appropriations oversight role. Committees and subcommittees of the U.S. House of Representatives and U.S. Senate hold hearings, subpoena witnesses, and report on expenditures and uses of public funds through an investigative arm known as the U.S. General Accounting Office (GAO).

Several incoming U.S. presidents have historically appointed special commissions composed of both private and public sector representatives to examine waste and methods for streamlining government spending; for example, the Hoover Commissions (Truman and Eisenhower administrations), the Grace commission (Ronald Reagan administration), and the National Performance Review (William Clinton administration).

When federal, state, or local governments have failed aggressively and effectively to self-monitor expenditures of public resources, nonprofit watchdog groups have assumed this role. Common Cause, Citizens Against Government Waste, and the Center for Ethics are grass-roots organizations, which point out spending problems, propose management reforms, and make cost-cutting recommendations. The 1995 agenda for Citizens Against Government Waste, for example, was to eliminate US$1.5 trillion in wasteful federal expenditures over five years by having the legislative and executive branches of government enact 622 specific recommendations.

Abuse

Abuse involves improper use of responsibility, duty, or fiduciary powers, but the determination of impropriety must be an official one. Compared with fraud and waste, abuse is the vaguest and slipperiest to define. Abuse falls in the realm of morals, ethics, and values. In an analysis, Michael Johnston (1986) has argued that multiple standards are used to judge whether governmental practices are abusive, including public opinion, determination of the public interest, and formal sanctioning criteria. Abuse may involve willful intent or it may result from negligence. It describes both good and bad decisionmaking, dependent upon the harm that results or the desired outcome that is achieved.

Fraud, waste, and abuse crimes are frequently classified as "white collar crimes"—a term originated by sociologist Edwin H. Sutherland (1883–1950)—because they can be committed by individuals or groups who hold power, status, and influence in the community.

Andrea G. Lange and Robert A. Bowers (1979) concluded in their study of 15 federally supported U.S. government benefit programs, however, that economic stratification accounted for only a portion of the crimes committed. Instead, four broad categories of individuals are potential offenders: (1) recipients of government benefits; (2) third-party providers of benefits, who are frequently reimbursed for their services; (3) government administrators charged with management and delivery of benefits; and (4) auxiliary providers who offer services integral to third-party providers (e.g., insurance carriers and fiscal intermediaries). Some recipient crimes are misrepresenting eligibility for benefits, creating "ghost" recipients, stealing specific entitlements, or improperly manipulating benefits. Third-party provider offenses include: misrepresenting eligibility or capability to deliver benefits; creating "ghost" recipients; receiving excess benefits; overcharging for services provided, or withholding services but claiming reimbursement just the same; providing unnecessary services or benefits to enhance claims payments; paying or receiving kickbacks and bribes; and tampering with files, records, and data.

For example, the United States health care entitlement systems, Medicare, Medicaid, and Champus operate on the principle of reimbursing costs to third-party service providers such as doctors, hospitals, pharmacists, ambulance services, home health care providers, and nursing homes. Since the inception of these programs, thousands of health care fraud, waste, and abuse schemes and wasted resources have been identified by government investigators, auditors, and insurance specialists.

Fraud, waste, and abuse offenses committed by administrative personnel in programs include: employee misrepresentation of recipient eligibility; overpayments or underpayments to recipients, third parties, or auxiliary providers; and withholding services and benefits to beneficiaries.

Examples of crimes perpetrated by auxiliary providers are collusive bidding, inferior delivery of services, and malicious destruction of records.

In addition, fraud, waste, and abuse are sometimes committed by organized criminal groups intent on shifting the balance of political power or wealth, creating "black markets."

Finally, some schemes are committed by street criminals who use government checks, food stamps, and so on for personal gain.

In some entitlement programs, the benefits themselves are counterfeited, altered, or manipulated, either manually or by technical means, thus compromising program objectives and derailing delivery networks. To reduce opportunities for fraud, waste, and abuse of checks, food stamps, coupons, or tokens in these programs, new electronic delivery systems are being installed that utilize computer debit "smart" cards. The risk-assessment premise is that by decreasing the number of benefit transfer points in the delivery process, program vulnerabilities can be reduced.

Fraud, waste, and abuse are particularly extensive in procurement. When public bureaucracies acquire and distribute large quantities of goods and services, the integrity of the process can be jeopardized by fraud, waste, and abuse. In the early 1990s, for example, over half of the U.S. Department of Defense budget was devoted to procurement. In one of the largest procurement prosecutions, dubbed "Ill Wind," dozens of defense contractors and Pentagon current and former employees were convicted for accepting kickbacks and paying bribes to obtain contract work illegally.

Typically, fraud, waste, and abuse occur in procurement systems in which there are excessive regulations and in those that lack competitive bidding processes or that require multiple layers of negotiations using intermediaries. Ineffective and inadequate internal checks and audits also create opportunities for malfeasance.

The number of civil and criminal prosecutions at both federal and state levels has increased dramatically over the past 20 years. In the federal court system, sentencing guidelines for white-collar offenses specify sanctions for fraud in government assistance programs and government procurement. Other prosecutorial techniques that have been used effectively include: the use of multijurisdictional task forces, targeting of prosecutions, and in very serious cases,

invocation of the independent counsel statute whereby a special prosecutor pursues the investigation. Prosecutorial and investigative techniques, such as the use of financial document search warrants to seize records, files, accounting ledgers, and computer hardware and software, have proved helpful for combating fraud. The initiation of undercover investigations, storefront or sting operations, and increased use of visual and telephonic interceptions have also aided investigations and prosecutions in certain cases.

Responses to fraud, waste, and abuse have also come from the administrative adjudication process. Administrative suspensions and debarments, for example, are being used with more frequency in benefit abuse and procurement cases now than in the past.

ANDREA G. LANGE

BIBLIOGRAPHY

Ackerman, Susan Rose, 1978. *Corruption: A Study of Political Economy*. New York: Academic Press.

Anthony, Robert N., and Regina E. Herzlinger, 1975. *Management Control in Nonprofit Organizations*. Homewood, IL: Richard D. Irwin.

Citizens Against Government Waste, 1995. "Prime Cuts, 1995 Menu to Cure the "Waste Tax." Washington, DC: GPO.

Coleman, James W., 1985. *The Criminal Elite: The Sociology of White-Collar Crime*. New York: St. Martin's Press.

Geis, Gilbert, and Ezra Stotland, eds., 1980. *White-Collar Crime: Theory and Research*. Beverly Hills, CA: Sage.

Hamm, William, 1986. "What Do We Mean by Waste in Government?" In Jerome B. McKinney and Michael Johnston, eds., *Fraud, Waste, and Abuse in Government*. Philadelphia: ISHI Publications.

Johnston, Michael, 1986. "Systemic Origins of Fraud, Waste, and Abuse." In Jerome B. McKinney and Michael Johnston, eds., *Fraud, Waste, and Abuse in Government*. Philadelphia: ISHI Publications.

Lange, Andrea G., 1994 "An Exploratory Study of Organizational Deviance and Insider White-Collar Crimes in the Savings and Loan Industry Using an Organizational Ecology Paradigm." Ph. D. diss., The American University, Washington, DC.

Lange, Andrea G., and Robert A. Bowers, 1979. *Fraud and Abuse in Government Benefit Programs*. Washington, DC: GPO.

McKinney, Jerome B., 1986. "Concepts and Definitions." In Jerome B. McKinney and Michael Johnston, eds., *Fraud, Waste, and Abuse in Government*. Philadelphia: ISHI Publications.

Pilzer, Paul Zane, and Robert Deitz, 1989. *Other People's Money*. New York: Simon & Schuster.

Sutherland, Edwin H., 1961. *White Collar Crime*. New York: Holt, Rinehart and Winston.

Weber, Max, 1947. *The Theory of Social and Economic Organization*. Trans. A. Henderson and Talcott Parsons, New York: Free Press.

FREEDOM OF INFORMATION (FOI).

Laws that provide members of the community with a legally enforceable right of access to information in the possession of government. The right so conferred is not absolute but is qualified by a number of important exemptions from disclosure. When a person's request for information is met by a claim of exemption, FOI laws provide for judicial or administrative review of the decision to withhold the documents requested.

FOI laws were first introduced in Sweden in 1766, but it was not until 200 years later that such legislation made its appearance in other Scandinavian, European, and North American countries. Traditionally, administrative argument had favored secrecy in government. Secrecy provided members of government with an assurance that the contrast between their private views and their public support for governmental decisions would not be revealed. Consequently, it assisted governments in maintaining their power. It also delivered significant administrative benefits. Secrecy enabled the executive branch to better manage and control the policy agenda; it provided that branch with the weapon of surprise; it insulated the administration from criticism and it concealed its mistakes. The more secrecy spread, however, the more it was subject to abuse.

The counterattack against secrecy began in international law following World War II. Shocked by the misuse and manipulation of information in Nazi Germany, the General Assembly of the United Nations resolved in 1946 that "freedom of information is a fundamental human right and is the touchstone for all the freedoms to which the United Nations is consecrated." Later, in the 1948 Universal Declaration on Human Rights, the General Assembly stated that "everyone has the right to freedom of opinion and expression; this right includes freedom to hold opinions without interference and to seek, retrieve, and impart information through any means regardless of frontiers." This theme was progressively adopted in other international instruments and recommendations and was later transformed by European and North American countries into access to information legislation.

The major arguments for FOI laws have been the following: With greater access to information about government, citizens are better placed to hold the government accountable for its actions. Similarly, the accountability of the executive branch to the legislature is enhanced if members of the legislature have more information about the way in which government operates. When members of the community are better informed, it is more likely that they will participate in public and political affairs. Greater participation ensures that government is conducted more democratically. Procedural fairness requires that individuals affected by administrative actions be given an opportunity to state their case. FOI laws enhance their capacity to do so by making available the criteria and information that form the basis for the exercise of administrative discretion. With the advent of new information technologies, the government's ability to collect and match personal information

has expanded exponentially to the detriment of individual privacy. By providing citizens with a right to access personal information, FOI laws act as a check on data collection practices and provide the individual with the means to correct information that is inaccurate, prejudicial, or misleading. FOI laws redress the disequilibrium between the state, with the vast sources of information at its disposal, and the individual or private organization, from whom increasing amounts of information are required and who, without a right conferred by legislation, find it difficult to extract the information that has been collected.

The effect of FOI legislation is to reverse the traditional presumption governing the disclosure of official information. Previously all information in the possession of government was presumed to be secret unless the administration exercised its discretion to disclose it. Now, in those countries having FOI laws, all information in the possession of government is presumed to be open unless the government can demonstrate that its disclosure would be contrary to the public interest.

Clearly, there is a strong public interest in the disclosure of official information. At the same time, however, it should be recognized that there are competing public interests that militate in favor of nondisclosure. If government is to be effective, a measure of both openness and secrecy is required. The question is not, therefore, whether as a community we prefer openness to secrecy but how the balance between them should best be struck in the public interest.

In recognition of the fact that there are cogent arguments against the routine disclosure of certain classes of official information, every country that has FOI laws has embraced a series of exemptions from access. The exemptions have been erected to ensure that government can operate properly and effectively. They protect essential public interests and the private and business affairs of people and organizations about whom information is collected. The content of these exemptions differs from jurisdiction to jurisdiction, but certain common threads are readily apparent. Exemptions apply most commonly to the following classes of information.

Cabinet Documents

Confidentiality attaches to the Cabinet's deliberations in order to permit Cabinet members to discuss matters of policy freely. It is in the nature of collective deliberation at the apex of government that competing views will be put, issues argued, compromises struck, minds changed, and individual submissions accepted or rejected. If confidentiality did not attach to such deliberations, the quality of debate in the Cabinet would suffer and so would the quality of decisions made by it.

Documents Concerned with Defense, Security, and International Relations

Each country is responsible for its own defense and internal security. Planning for defense and security cannot be conducted openly without prejudicing its effectiveness. Similarly, there is not as yet any general acceptance that international diplomacy can be conducted in full public view. Confidences between nations, therefore, need to be respected.

Law Enforcement Documents

Documents generated in the course of investigating and prosecuting crime will not usually be disclosed. To release investigative documents prematurely would clearly prejudice the ability of law enforcement agencies to complete their inquiries and obtain sufficient evidence to launch prosecutions successfully.

Documents Affecting the National Economy

Documents whose disclosure would adversely affect the government's capacity to manage the national economy will, necessarily, remain secret. The premature disclosure of documents that, for example, would reveal a government's intention to devalue its currency or introduce new taxation measures, might act to prejudice the government's capacity to pursue its economic agenda and serve to confer an unfair and private advantage on those to whom the information was released.

Deliberative Documents

Documents containing opinions, advice, or recommendations generated during the course of governmental deliberations on policy will not be disclosed when to do so will cause some tangible harm to the government's capacity to make and implement the policy decisions to which this information relates. Once such decisions are taken, however, the prior documentation will normally be accessible.

Documents Obtained in Confidence

Government is in constant receipt of information from individuals and organizations external to it who regard the information they provide as confidential. So, when information is confidential in nature, when it is communicated in confidence, and when there is an implicit or explicit understanding that its confidentiality will be maintained, it will not be disclosed.

Documents Affecting Individual Privacy

Individual privacy is recognized nationally and internationally as an important social value. It follows, therefore, that personal information collected by the government will not be made available to anyone other than the person to whom it relates.

Documents Relating to Commercial Organizations

Like individuals, commercial organizations provide information to the government to facilitate its economic or regulatory objectives. The routine disclosure of such information may prejudice the competitive position of the organizations providing it and so lead to the government being deprived of the information it requires. When competitive disadvantage is likely to follow from disclosure, documents containing commercial information will not be made available.

Documents Covered by Legal Professional Privilege

In all Western democracies, the importance of respecting the confidentiality of communications between clients and their legal advisers is recognized clearly. In the absence of such a recognition, the capacity of individuals and organizations to advance or defend their legal position would be prejudiced severely. Documents containing information subject to legal professional privilege will not, therefore, be accessible under FOI laws.

In each of the cases just described, clear reasons exist for the nondisclosure of documents. Whether such reasons will prevail in any individual instance will depend upon the balance of public interests that bear upon the resolution of the case. Most FOI laws recognize this by providing that documents will be withheld only when they fall within a class of documents that is defined as exempt *and* when their disclosure will be contrary to the public interest. To be exempt, therefore, a document must not only come within one of the categories described above but its disclosure must also be contrary to the public interest. Generally, it will be insufficient to demonstrate that a document falls within a class of documents said to be exempt. It must reasonably be expected that the harm likely to follow from disclosure will occur and that the public interest in that harm being prevented outweighs any competing public interest in permitting disclosure.

In all countries with FOI legislation, the task of determining whether documents should be disclosed or withheld falls to an independent reviewing authority. The power that such an authority has varies considerably between jurisdictions. This variation, in turn, reflects the degree to which governments have been willing to cede their authority to control the information in their possession. In some countries, most notably the United States, a tradition of independent judicial review of administrative action is well established. There, the courts straightforwardly determine disputes between parties in FOI litigation. In other countries, such as France, Canada, and New Zealand, governments have been more hesitant in engaging the courts and have chosen instead to adopt a form of administrative review, conducted, in the first instance, by an administrative tribunal or an information commissioner.

Similarly, the powers given to the independent reviewing authority also vary. Unsurprisingly, the more politically sensitive that information is, the less likely it is that final authority to disclose it will be vested in the authority concerned. In Australia, for example, a minister may issue a certificate with respect to the disclosure of certain classes of documents, for example, Cabinet documents. When a certificate is issued, the authority is limited to determining whether reasonable grounds exist for a claim that a document is one of the type described or for a claim that disclosure is contrary to the public interest. Then, even when no reasonable grounds for the claim are found to exist, the final decision about whether the documents should be disclosed is reposed in the minister, who is responsible to the Parliament for the decision that is taken.

Because FOI laws confer a legally enforceable right of access to governmental information, an onus is usually placed on the governmental agency concerned to demonstrate that disclosure of the information should not occur rather than on an applicant to demonstrate that it should.

In summary, FOI legislation has been introduced in many Western countries in order to reduce secrecy in and enhance the accountability of government, to redress inequalities in the power of government and citizens, to collect and disseminate information, and to recast the operation of government in a more democratic mold. Its success in achieving these ambitious objectives has varied. Its importance should not, however, be doubted.

SPENCER ZIFCAK

BIBLIOGRAPHY

Australia. Senate. Standing Committee on Constitutional and Legal Affairs, 1979. *Freedom of Information.* Canberra: Australian Government Publishing Service.
Birkinshaw, P., 1988. *Freedom of Information: The Law, the Practice, and the Ideal,* London: Weidenfeld and Nicolson.
Bok, S., 1982. *Secrets: On the Ethics of Concealment and Revelation.* Oxford: Oxford University Press.
Chapman, R. A., and M. Hunt, 1987. *Open Government.* London: Routledge.
Disclosure of Official Information: A Report on Overseas Practice, 1979. London: HMSO.
Kirby, Justice M., 1985. *The Right to Know.* London: Granada.
Marsh, N., ed., 1987. *Public Access to Government Information: A Comparative Symposium.* London: Stevens and Son.
Rowat, D. C., ed., 1978. *Administrative Secrecy in Developed Countries.* New York: Columbia University Press.
Towards Open Government: General Report I, 1980. Wellington: New Zealand Government Publishing Service.
U.S. Congress, House, Committee on Government Operations, 1972. *Administration of the Freedom of Information* Act. House of Representatives Report No. 92–1419. Washington, DC: GPO.

FREEDOM OF INFORMATION ACT (FOIA).

Legislation enacted in the United States in 1966 that sets forth the right of the public to obtain information from federal agencies, subject to certain exemptions having to do with national security and the invasion of personal privacy. Under the law, any member of the general public may make a written request for copies of federal agency documents. The agencies covered by the law include offices and departments of the executive branch (such as the Department of Energy), independent regulatory agencies (such as the Federal Communications Commission), and federal government-controlled corporations (such as the U.S. Postal Service). Congress, the federal courts, and units of the executive office that advise the President are not covered by the FOIA, and are not required to disclose information under the FOIA.

The FOIA provides access to "agency records," which the courts have generally held to include documents and other materials containing information (e.g., computer files and photographs). These agency records must have been (1) created or obtained by the agency in question, and (2) in that agency's possession at the time of the request. Materials that satisfy the above criteria cover virtually all of the areas that are affected by the federal government (for example, public health and environmental concerns, consumer product safety, government fiscal records, national defense, the economy, etc.). The FOIA stipulates that "any person" may seek to obtain information from federal agencies, which in practice means that U.S. citizens, permanent resident aliens, foreign nationals, and entities such as corporations, universities, and state and local governments may avail themselves of the FOIA.

In 1974, the FOIA was amended to require that agencies expedite the disclosure of personal information to individuals. The amendment also facilitated court access and gave judges the power to decide the propriety of information withheld by agencies under the FOIA. In this regard, the courts have held that a number of areas should remain "confidential," including national defense, and government financial information that may provide an unfair advantage to investors in the stock market.

Although the FOIA requires that federal agencies disclose documents to the public, the law contains exceptions to this requirement, known as "Exemptions." The exemptions are:

- *Exemption 1:* Classified documents that must be kept secret in the interests of foreign policy or national defense (for example, CIA surveillance records).
- *Exemption 2:* Documents that are related solely to an agency's internal personnel practices and rules.
- *Exemption 3:* Documents that are specifically excluded by a law other than the FOIA.
- *Exemption 4:* Documents obtained from a person, which contain trade secrets or financial or commercial information that is confidential or privileged.
- *Exemption 5:* Documents that are interagency or intra-agency memorandums or letters not available by law to a party other than a nonagency party in litigation with the agency. This includes common law discovery privileges, such as Executive Privilege (protecting advice, recommendations, and opinions that are part of the government deliberative process), attorney work-product privilege (documents that are prepared by an attorney, relating to a proceeding in which disclosure would reveal trial strategy), and attorney-client privilege (protecting the communications between a lawyer and his or her client).
- *Exemption 6:* Documents that are personnel and medical files and similar files that, if disclosed, would constitute an unwarranted invasion of personal privacy. This exemption requires the balancing of privacy interests with the public interest in a right to know.
- *Exemption 7:* Documents that are records compiled for the purposes of law enforcement. Such documents are exempt from disclosure *if* their production: (1) would interfere with a law enforcement proceeding, (2) would deprive an individual of a fair, impartial hearing or trial, (3) could constitute an unwarranted invasion of personal privacy, (4) could be expected to disclose a confidential source, (5) would lead to circumvention of the law by allowing the disclosure of law enforcement investigations or prosecutions, or (6) could reasonably be expected to endanger an individual's life or physical safety.
- *Exemption 8:* Documents that are contained in or related to reports prepared by, on behalf of, or for use of an agency responsible for supervision or regulation of financial institutions.
- *Exemption 9:* Documents that contain geological and geophysical information and data, including maps, concerning oil wells.

The last two exemptions are seldom asserted and seldom the subject of lawsuits.

The FOIA sets forth a detailed procedure that is to be followed once a member of the public makes a request for information from an agency. There are set times during which the agency is to respond and during which a member of the public may appeal a total or partial denial of FOIA request. Once internal appeal procedures are exhausted, an individual or entity still not satisfied with the result may file a lawsuit. Each agency has its own regulations relating to the FOIA requirements. These can be found in the *Code of Federal Regulations* (C.F.R.) under Information Availability.

ROBERT A. CROPF

BIBLIOGRAPHY

Adler, Allan Robert, 1990. *Using the Freedom of Information Act: A Step-by-Step Guide.* Washington, DC: American Civil Liberties Union Publications Department.
Chandler, Ralph C., and Jack C. Plano, 1982. "Freedom of Information Act." *The Public Administration Dictionary.* New York: John Wiley and Sons.

FRIEDMAN, MILTON (1912–).

The 1976 Nobel laureate in economics, acknowledged as America's most notable monetarist, who has persuasively argued the case about the efficacy of free markets for more than 60 years.

Background

Milton Friedman was born in 1912 to immigrant Jewish parents in Brooklyn, New York. At age 15 he won a scholarship to Rutgers University. He graduated from Rutgers in 1932, with a double major in mathematics and economics and then enrolled at the University of Chicago. He studied in the Economics Department under Frank Knight, whose tenets formed the central thinking of the "Chicago School."

The essence of the doctrine of the Chicago School was that since the dominant trait of humankind is avarice, it is useful to create an economic system that recognizes greed and harnesses it. This philosophy, called laissez-faire, has its intellectual origins in the teachings of Adam Smith, who posited the belief that self-seeking individuals must be allowed to pursue their own interests without interference from government.

Although lack of funds necessitated Friedman's leaving the University of Chicago within the year, the experience with laissez-faire economics left its mark upon him. Moving to Columbia University, Friedman began work on his doctorate, but he took time off while still a graduate student there to join the New Deal and, later, to work for the National Bureau of Economic Research.

He learned his simple and vigorous prose style at the bureau after being taken to task there for the poor quality of his writing. The new techniques helped his debating skills and helped him to win converts to his witty, terse style, sometimes called "Friedmanism" (Silk 1976, p. 55). Yet, the short, overly simplistic style has also come in for criticism.

In 1938 Friedman married fellow economist, Rose Director, who has remained a lifelong collaborator and from whom he has borrowed some measure of his libertarian zeal.

Friedman completed work on his doctorate in 1941, but was not granted his degree until five years later because of controversy from the medical community over the content of his thesis, which demonstrated that organized medicine had restricted entry into the field to protect the incomes of those in the medical profession (Rayack 1986). Some members of the National Bureau of Economic Research, where Freidman had been working during the years 1939 to 1940, also opposed the dissertation results. Because the growing controversy threatened his doctoral candidacy, Friedman was compelled to modify the harshness of his judgments about the medical profession and to bury his results deep within his lengthy study (Silk 1976).

During the 1950s and 1960s, Friedman returned to Chicago to become the intellectual godfather of the Chicago School. "With the sword of laissez-faire, he sought to cut knot after Gordian knot of economic problems" (Silk 1976, pp. 83–84).

In the international monetary field Friedman enthusiastically backed free-floating exchange rates, long before the rest of his fellow economists. Indeed, many of Friedman's ideas—such as, opposition to government subsidies and government regulation of industry—were at the time outside the pale of traditional economics, yet today in the late 1990s, as a result of his teachings and writings, the monetarist gospel is widely embraced by academics and policymakers (Rayack 1986).

The receipt of the Nobel Prize in 1976 guaranteed Milton Friedman a place in history, and it also situated him in the position of elder statesman, not only in the field of economics but also prominently in the field of public administration and its related disciplines. The 1980s brought Friedman even closer to national public administration when he was sought by the Ronald Reagan and the George Bush administrations as adviser on economic policy. In the 1990s Friedman still endures as the dean of a highly vocal group of libertarians, who perceive him less as a fanatical guru of laissez-faire and more of a defender of limited government.

The Friedman Legacy

In the first 20 years of his academic life, Friedman produced scholarly writings that established his reputation as an economic theorist. Among his accomplishments are the diagnoses of inflation, the theory of the iron triangle, and, of course, arguments for the efficacy of free markets and

opposition to larger government. He was influential in important developments of statistical methodology as well, such as sequential analysis and adaptive expectations (Jordan et al., 1993). He has also written widely in the area of business ethics.

Friedman, however, is best known for his work on monetarism, a doctrine that has two basic tenets: (1) that change in the money supply is the only systematic factor influencing the overall level of spending; and (2) that the only action required to ensure prosperity and price stability is for the central bank to stabilize the rate of growth of the money supply (Silk 1976).

Friedman's Impact on Public Administration

Even though Friedman is an economist by training and affiliation, his teaching goes well beyond economics into a milieu that encompasses all the related disciplines of public administration—political science, sociology, law, ethics, and others. Friedman believes that the paternalism inherent in public administration has had pernicious effects that impacts society in many ways—lawlessness, homelessness, collapse of families, deteriorating education, and the crisis of medical care, for example (Sheehan 1993). He maintains that reduction in government action would be effective in helping the poorest people in the United States. In his view, the whole welfare state can be replaced for those below a given income with a negative income tax and a cash grant equal to a fraction of the amount by which they are below that income.

Friedman has vigorously backed the proposals for the use of voucher systems for education. He is especially interested in the morality of public administration, which he believes is being marginalized in business and government with its concerns for profitability. Friedman teaches that this results in error and contradiction, an apolitical political base, altruistic agents of selfishness, and greed deriving from good.

For Friedman, economic freedom is a means toward political freedom. He sees public administration as a double-edged sword—as a protector of individual rights and (by its concentration of power in political hands) as a threat. Milton Friedman and his wife Rose have written about the efficacy of the free market system and have spoken in favor of personal liberties. They have backed their words with practical action. They are also among those who argued persuasively for the abolishment of the military draft in the United States.

In addition to their writings, the Friedmans produced a television series in 1979 modeled after their book *Free to Choose (1981)*. The book and the series detailed what the Friedmans call "the nuts and bolts" of the economic philosophy discussed in their earlier works. The series led to an additional series of videotaped lectures, which included question-and-answer sessions.

Criticisms of Milton Friedman

Friedman has detractors who decry his popular writings as ideological, simplistic, and cavalier of public administration and of social, political, and economic history. His work has been denounced as one-sided. Friedman is known for his short, dramatic statements, which he sometimes admits are partially wrong but have basic truths. His style of speaking makes him an inspiring debater and hard to pin down, and it infuriates his opponents. He was called a "paper tiger" by economist Joan Robinson. Paul Samuelson has said of him, "Now I don't think Milton is a charlatan. . . . He believes what he says at any time he says it" (quoted in Silk 1976, p. 52). Others have noted that despite his argument for freedom, the free market, and capitalism, Friedman has defended repressive regimes, such as that of the former apartheid government in South Africa and Augusto Pinochet's oppressive government in Chile, while attacking socialist planning in India, Sweden, and the United Kingdom. The irony is that many capitalist strongholds, such as Taiwan, South Korea, Argentina, Brazil, and Spain, whose systems of price indexing Friedman admires, are themselves restrictive governments, where civil liberties are daily infringed upon.

Summary

Friedman, now in his eighties, continues to teach, write, and influence public administration. Because he strongly inspired economic policy in the Reagan and Bush administrations, Friedman's views are fiercely harbored by many in the Republican Congress, who argue for the free market system and, like him, are against employer-paid medical care, Medicare, and Medicaid. Thus, one can see that this man, who has been called everything from a poet to an ideologue to a "brilliant economist" (Rayack, 1986, p. 8) continues to have a vital and enduring impact on public administration in the United States and, indeed, around the world.

BREENA E. COATES AND JEFFERY K. GUILER

BIBLIOGRAPHY

Friedman, Milton, 1962, *Capitalism and Freedom*. Chicago: University of Chicago Press.
Friedman, Milton, and Rose D. Friedman, 1981. *Free to Choose: A Personal Statement*. New York: Harcourt Brace Jovanovich.
Friedman, Milton, and Anna J. Schwartz, 1963. *A Monetary History of the United States, 1867–1960*. Princeton: Princeton University Press.
Interviews with Milton Friedman, *New York Times*, 14 December 1976, pp. 55, 59, and 2 December 1977, p. 16.

Jordan, Jerry, et al., 1993, "Milton, Money, and Mischief." *Economic Inquiry*, vol. 31, no. 2: 197–212.
Oi, Walter Y., "Milton Friedman, Starting His Ninth Decade." *Economic Inquiry*, vol. 31, no.2: 194–196.
Rayack, Elton, 1986. *Not So Free To Choose: The Political Economy of Milton Friedman and Ronald Reagan*. New York: Praeger.
Sheehan, Paul, 1993. "Friedman's Fundamentals." *Australian Business Monthly*, vol. 13, no. 12: 52–55.
Silk, Leonard, 1976. *The Economists*. New York: Basic Books.

FRIEDRICH, CARL JOACHIM (1901–1984).

Prominent German-American political theorist; professor of government at Harvard University for nearly 50 years. Although Friedrich's scholarly works ranged from an examination of the baroque period to the philosophy of law, he is best known in the field of American public administration for his debate with the British scholar Herman Finer concerning the issue of administrative responsibility.

Personal Background and Career

Carl Joachim Friedrich was born 5 June 1901, in Leipzig, Germany. The son of Paul Leopold Friedrich, a prominent physician, and Charlotte (Baroness von Buelow) Friedrich, he was one of the most influential political theorists of the United States. Friedrich received his formal education from the University of Marburg, the University of Frankfurt, the University of Vienna, and the University of Heidelberg–where he obtained a doctorate degree in 1925.

Friedrich first came to the United States as an exchange student in 1923. After completing his doctorate degree in Germany, he returned to the United States a year later to teach at Harvard as a lecturer in government at the Graduate School of Public Administration. Friedrich became a naturalized citizen of the United States in 1938.

A prolific scholar and demanding teacher, Friedrich rapidly progressed through the academic ranks. At the youthful age of 36, he attained the rank of full professor. In 1955, Friedrich became the Dorman B. Eaton professor of Science of Government, a position he held until retirement in 1971. He was a professor emeritus at Harvard (1971–1984) and at the University of Heidelberg (1966–1984). Friedrich received honorary degrees from the University of Heidelberg (Germany) (U.J.D.), Harvard University (A.M.), Grinnell College (Iowa) (LL.D.), Washington University, St. Louis University (LL.D.), Columbia University (L.H.D.), Colby College (Maine) (L.H.D.), University of Cologne (Germany) (Dr. rer. pol.), and the University of Padua (Italy) (Dr. rer. pol.). In 1967 Friedrich received the prestigious Knight Commander's Cross with Star, German Order of Merit award, given by the Federal Republic of Germany.

Although Friedrich spent his entire teaching career at Harvard, he did hold several prestigious appointments both inside and outside of academe. He held a joint appointment as professor of political science and law at the University of Heidelberg in Germany; was a visiting professor at Sorbonne, University of Paris; a Culver Lecturer at Brown University, and an Avalon Lecturer at Colby College. From 1946 to 1949, Friedrich served as an adviser to General Lucius D. Clay, the American military governor in Germany. During the 1950s, he served as an adviser on constitutional affairs to the government of Puerto Rico and was an adviser to the European Constituent Assembly. Friedrich was president of the American Society of Political and Legal Philosophy (1958) and the American Political Science Association (1962).

Friedrich's Scholarly Works

Friedrich wrote and edited nearly 50 books and numerous articles addressing a range of topics related to politics, government, and philosophy. His early writings were devoted to the study of constitutional government and the role of bureaucracy in constitutional regimes. Friedrich's first original work (coauthored with Taylor Cole), *Responsible Bureaucracy: A Study of the Swiss Civil Service*, was published in 1932. (In 1929 Friedrich edited and translated Alfred Weber's *Theory of the Location of Industry*.) *Responsible Bureaucracy* provided the foundation for many of Friedrich's ideas concerning the role of career civil servants in democratic government. He believed that responsible career civil servants were friends of democracy and instrumental in preserving constitutional regimes. Five years later (1937) Friedrich published *Constitutional Government and Politics: Nature and Development* (later revised and published in 1941 as *Constitutional Government and Democracy: Theory and Practice*).

During World Word II, Friedrich emerged as an influential spokesperson for a group known as the Council for Democracy. The council comprised academics, businesspeople, and civic-minded individuals concerned with promoting and preserving democratic values. As one of the council's central figures, Friedrich devoted a great deal of attention to the issue of government propaganda and public policy. He published several books dealing with this topic: *Controlling Broadcasting in Wartime: A Tentative Public Policy* (1940, with Jeanette Sayre), *The Development of the Control of Advertising on the Air* (1940), *Congress and the Control of Radiobroadcasting* (1944), and *The Poison in Our System* (1941).

Friedrich is perhaps best known in the field of U.S. public administration for his debate with Herman Finer, the British political scientist. This debate focused on the question of administrative responsibility and discretion. While serving as editor of *Public Policy* (a position he held from 1940 to 1953), Friedrich published an article in 1940 entitled "Public Policy and the Nature of Administrative Responsibility." In this article, he rejected the formal-legal

or hierarchical conception of administrative responsibility advocated by Herman Finer (1941) and others.

Finer's approach suggested that career civil servants are "responsible" when they strictly adhere to the orders and commands of democratically elected superiors. Friedrich argued that external political controls were insufficient when used as the sole means of ensuring bureaucratic responsibility. He maintained that despite the best efforts of political superiors, they could not devise or perfect external controls that totally eliminated irresponsible conduct by administrative officials. Friedrich viewed such efforts as an exercise in futility since a "considerable" amount of "irresponsible conduct" is inevitable in constitutional democracies. He suggested that, even though adherence to external political controls is desirable, administrative officials should also rely on *technical knowledge* and *popular sentiment* for guidance (1940, p. 232). According to Friedrich, "Any policy which violates either standard, or which fails to crystallize in spite of their imperative, renders the official responsible for it liable to charges of irresponsibility" (p. 232). Friedrich believed that technical knowledge provided a standard by which to guide and check the discretion of administrative officials. He contended that when such knowledge provided the basis for administrative action, career administrators were subject to "thorough scrutiny by their colleges in what is known as the 'fellowship of science'" (p. 233). With respect to public opinion, Friedrich argued that public administrators must also take into consideration the "existing preferences of the community" especially the "majority." In other words, administrative officials are responsive when their exercise of discretion is informed by the desires of the citizenry.

In addition to the spirited exchange with Finer, Friedrich is well known for his influential studies regarding the nature of totalitarianism. His classic work, *Totalitarian Dictatorship and Autocracy* (1956), coauthored with Zbigniew Brezinski (a former student, and President Jimmy Carter's National Security Adviser), is widely regarded as the first systematic attempt to articulate the distinguishing characteristics of totalitarianism (also see his *Totalitarianism*, 1954; and *An Introduction to Political Theory*, 1967).

Friedrich identified six characteristic traits that are readily apparent once the forces of totalitarianism take hold. These include: (1) total ideology, (2) a single mass party, (3) a terrorist secret police, (4) a monopoly of mass communication, (5) a monopoly of weapons, and (6) a centrally directed, planned economy.

In recent years, scholars have expressed a renewed interest in Friedrich's work on authority (see Terry 1995; Selznick 1992; Wamsley 1990; DeGeorge 1985; Cochran 1977). Although he devoted extensive attention to the concept of authority, public administration theorists in the United States have virtually ignored his treatment of the subject. Friedrich's writings on authority seem to have been overshadowed by Max Weber's (1947) influential work on charismatic authority. This is somewhat ironic, for Friedrich (1961) was extremely critical of his German counterpart's writings on authority.

Friedrich asserted that Weber's notion of charismatic authority was "unsound and should be discarded" for at least two reasons (see his 1961 article "Political Leadership and the Problem of the Charismatic Power"). First, Friedrich contended that Weber misplaced or inappropriately used the term "charisma" in his discussion of authority within the political sphere. The term "charisma," as originally used in the *New Testament* (Romans 12, and 1 Corinthians, 12), refers to "gift." Friedrich asserted that, although a numbers of gifts are listed, "the 'gift' of government or political leadership in not among them" (1961, p. 13). Second, Friedrich argued that Weber's authority typology (traditional, legal-rational, and charismatic), confuses authority with power and legitimacy.

Although Friedrich discussed the nature and use of authority in several works, he devoted considerable attention to the topic in two books. The first is an edited volume, *Authority: Nomos I* (1958), the inaugural annual publication of the American Society for Political and Legal philosophy. In addition to serving as editor, Friedrich contributed a chapter entitled "Authority, Reason, and Discretion."

His central thesis was that scholars who attempt to build a concept of authority solely on power have totally missed the mark. Why? Because authority based on power alone is weak and unlikely to endure over time. Friedrich strongly believed that authority must be grounded in *reason* and that any attempt to divorce the two concepts is profoundly misguided. Reminiscent of Chester Barnard (1938), Friedrich asserted that authority is contingent upon the capacity to issue communications or commands that have the "potentiality of reasoned elaboration" (1958, p. 35). If the potentiality of reasoned elaboration is present, then, the authoritative communications or commands are likely to be *accepted*. He believed that acceptance of a communication or command by the individual to whom it was directed is an indication that the person who gave the command possessed authority.

Friedrich further explored the notion of authority in *Tradition and Authority* (1972), one of three books published after his retirement from Harvard. This work reflects the culmination of Friedrich's lifelong thinking on the subject. As he had done earlier, Friedrich (1972) emphasized the essential link between reason and authority.

> The ancient connotation brings out the crucial role of reasoning in situations where men follow other men without being compelled to do so. When there are good reasons for doing or believing something, such actions or thought acquires quality that is otherwise lacking: it becomes "authoritative." What makes a particular course of action authoritative, that is to say, vested with

authority, is that convincing reasons may be offered in support of it (p. 48).

Friedrich continued:

> What we must ask is what enables a man to get his proposal accepted, that is to say, to gain another's assent. Our reply would be that when such ability to gain assent springs from his capacity for reasoned elaboration we have authority. It inheres in his communication! Only when what is commanded is asserted [and] can be reasoned upon and defined is real authority. . . . He who obeys authority does so because he who ordered him to obey appears to have a very sufficient reason to do so (p. 55).

In *Tradition and Authority*, Friedrich's concept of authority is more fully developed because he examined the role that tradition has in sustaining authority. He built a persuasive argument that "tradition"–the values, beliefs, habits, and customs of the political community–provides the basis for reasoned elaboration. Friedrich argued that "reasoning upon values [tradition]" is "in many ways the most important kind of reasoning there is" (1972, p. 115). According to Friedrich, such reasoning "demands authority" (p. 115). He criticized those who attacked tradition. Friedrich considered tradition "a fragile thing," for it is "quickly destroyed and hard to rebuild" (p. 114). He argued that attacks on tradition are, in a fundamental way, an assault on the political authority of the regime.

Conclusion

The British philosopher Anthony Savile (1982) noted that works of art pass time's test because of "survival of attention." That is, they hold our attention due to their high quality, excellence, and merit. Savile (1982) wrote that "great art is bound to be influential: such art leaves its mark on what follows" (p. 210). Savile's remarks are certainly relevant when applied to the works of Carl J. Friedrich. Friedrich left an indelible mark on the fields of American public administration and political science. His many works have withstood the test of time.

LARRY D. TERRY AND SHELLY PEFFER

BIBLIOGRAPHY

Barnard, Chester, 1938. *The Functions of the Executive.* Cambridge, MA: Harvard University Press.

Cochran, Clarke, 1977. "Authority and Community: The Contributions of Carl J. Friedrich, Yves R. Simon, and Michael Polanyi." *American Political Science Review,* vol. 71: 546–558.

DeGeorge, Richard, 1985. *The Nature and Limits of Authority.* Lawrence: University Press of Kansas.

Finer, Herman, 1941. "Administrative Responsibility in Democratic Government." *Public Administrative Review,* vol. 19: 277–289.

Friedrich, Carl J., 1940. "Public Policy and the Nature of Administrative Responsibility." In Carl J. Friedrich, ed., *Public Policy*, pp. 221–245. Cambridge, MA: Harvard University Press.

———1958. "Authority, Reason, and Discretion." In Carl J. Friedrich, ed., *Authority: Nomos I.* Cambridge, MA. Harvard University Press.

———1961. "Political Leadership and the Problem of Charismatic Power." *Journal of Politics*, vol. 23: 3–24.

———1972. *Tradition and Authority*. New York: Praeger.

Friedrich, Carl J., and Zbigniew Brezinski, 1956. *Totalitarian Dictatorship and Autocracy*. Cambridge, MA: Harvard University Press.

Levy, Margot, 1984. "Carl J. Friedrich." In Margot Levy, ed., *The Annual Obituary* 1984, pp. 473–475. Chicago/London: St. James Press.

New York Times, 1984 (22 September). "Carl J. Friedrich Dies at 83; Influential Harvard Professor," p. L1.

Savile, Anthony, 1982. *The Test of Time: An Essay in Philosophical Aesthetics*. Oxford: Clarendon Press.

Selznick, Philip, 1992. *The Moral Commonwealth: Social Theory and the Promise of Community*. Berkeley: University of California Press.

Terry, Larry D., 1995. *Leadership of Public Bureaucracies: The Administrator as Conservator*. Thousand Oaks, CA: Sage.

Weber, Max, 1947. *Theory of Social and Economic Organization*. Trans A. R. Henderson and Talcott Parsons. New York: Macmillan.

Wamsley, Gary L., 1990. "The Agency Perspective: Public Administrators as Agential Leaders." In Gary L. Wamsley, Robert Bacher, Charles T. Goodsell, Philip Kroneberg, John Rohr, Camilla Stivers, Orion White, and James Wolf, *Refounding Public Administration*, pp. 114–162. Newbury Park, CA: Sage.

FRINGE BENEFITS. A form of compensation, in addition to salary or wages, provided to all regular employees of an organization. Benefits include those which are required by national or state policy, such as social security, unemployment insurance, workers' compensation, and family leave, as well as those the employer may choose to offer, such as retirement pensions, health care coverage, or child and elder care services (see **family leave** and **retirement**). Many employers do not consider these benefits fringes but a necessary ingredient of the compensation system so that they can attract and retain their employees. In many countries (especially Europe and Canada), because of such programs as universal health care, employee benefits are a less-important part of the compensation picture.

Public sector pay in the United States, historically, has not been as high as most private sector compensation; therefore, benefit programs became generous partly as a means of attracting good employees and partly for political reasons. Particularly in local government, employees have exerted political influence so as to gain generous benefits. Because many benefits, especially retirement benefits, are not immediate cost items for the governmental jurisdiction, public officials have been willing to grant increases in

them to satisfy unionized employees and generally to maintain labor peace. The ambitious politician (mayor, for example) could persuade the city council to grant the benefits with the notion that the costs would be borne later. By the time the costs arose to pay for pensions, for instance, these public officials would have moved to another office and their successors would have to find the money to pay for the pensions. Financial crises resulting from these approaches have led to the greater use of prefunding benefits plans rather than the pay-as-you go systems popular in the past.

In recent years, health care coverage has become a major concern for employers. Because health care costs have risen sharply, employers have difficulty in funding the level of benefits employees have been used to in the past. In the public sector, it has not been uncommon to find full funding of health care benefits by the employer. The trend now is for employers to require employees to pay part of the cost of the coverage, as has been prevalent in the private sector. At the same time, the level of benefit coverage has been declining; thus, there may be greater limits on what will be paid for and how much will be paid.

Flexible, or cafeteria, benefits plans have achieved popularity among private sector employers and are spreading to the public sector. In this approach, the employee has a set amount of money set aside to use for benefits purchase. The employee may or must add money as well. This type of system allows individual employees to choose benefits most appropriate to their situations. Thus, if the employee has a spouse whose health care benefits package is better, the employee does not have to choose the health care benefit, and the money can be used to purchase more retirement benefits, legal services coverage, or dependent care. Most flexible benefit plans have some basic coverage imperatives. Thus, health care benefits usually must be carried by the employees through their employer or through their spouse's employer.

During the 1990s, domestic partnership benefits have emerged as controversial issues for public employers (see **domestic partnership benefits**). Domestic partnership policies regarding benefits, pushed especially by gay and lesbian groups, would make domestic partners eligible for benefits just as married partners are.

Because of increasing costs and decreasing revenues, most public jurisdictions are attempting to streamline benefit packages. By providing options to employees, it is possible that benefit costs can be controlled without a great deal of damage to the employee.

N. JOSEPH CAYER

BIBLIOGRAPHY

Employee Benefit Research Institute, 1985. *Fundamentals of Employee Benefit Programs*. 2d ed. Washington, DC: Employee Benefit Research Institute.

Hartmen, Robert W., 1988. *Pay and Pensions for Federal Workers.* Washington, DC: Brookings Institution.

McCaffery, Robert M., 1992. *Employee Benefit Programs: A Total Compensation Perspective,* 2d ed. Boston: PWS-KENT.

Moore, Perry, 1991. "Comparison of State and Local Employee Benefits and Private Employee Benefits." *Public Personnel Management* 20 (Winter): 429–439.

FULL FAITH AND CREDIT.   The clause provided by Article 4, Section 1, of the U.S. Constitution that obligates each state to honor the various statutes, civil actions (for example, a contract), and judicial decisions originating in another state. Full faith and credit has been used principally to extend to the final judgment of a court in a different state the same rights and powers accorded to those of a court within the same state.

In the above manner, the Supreme Court has held that the full faith and credit clause imposes the characteristics of a unified country with respect to the judgments of courts: "To make them (the states) integral parts of a single nation throughout which a remedy upon a just obligation might be demanded as of right, irrespective of the state of its origin" (*Milwaukee County v. M. E. White Co.,* 296 US 268, [1985]). The courts have held that the full faith and credit clause applies to all judgments, even though an appeal has been made in the state in which the judgment was originally rendered (for recent examples, see *Harbison-Fischer Mfg. Co. vs. Mohawk Data Sciences Corp., Tex App Fort Worth,* [1991]; *Brinker v. Superior Court,* 235 Cal App 3rd 1296, [1991]).

The full faith and credit clause is not absolute; in other words, states are not obligated to honor civil judgments of another state—particularly in the area of domestic relations (i.e., judgments involving divorce, alimony, and child custody). Failure to honor the judgments of a sister state has been the case traditionally in the area of child custody since this type of judgment is typically not final in that it can be altered to protect the best interests of the child at some future date. Moreover, a state will extend full faith and credit to the judgment of another state only if the original state had jurisdiction over the parties involved as well as the subject manner and had given all interested parties reasonable notice following the filing of a lawsuit in the second state. However, a judgment reached by a federal court of one state results in automatic enforceability in another state after it has been registered in a federal court of the other state. In the area of enforcement, the courts have ruled that the judgment of a state may be enforced by all other states in the manner they consider best.

The Supreme Court has not insisted on a too literal reading of the full faith and credit clause because this could produce the "absurd" result of a state's statutes being enforced in the courts of the others that could not be enforced in its own (*Alaska Packers Assn. v. Industrial Accident Commission.* 294 US 532, [1935]).

The principle of full faith and credit is similar to that of "comity" in international law. This doctrine holds that each nation is under obligation to respect and uphold the laws of other nations; however, the full faith and credit provision of the U.S. Constitution does not apply to the judgments of foreign nations.

ROBERT A. CROPF

BIBLIOGRAPHY

American Law Reports Digest. 3d ed., vol. 2., 1965. San Francisco: Bancroft Whitney. Annotation 1994–1995, pp. 1384–1388, supplement pp. 113–114.

Reese, Willis G. M., 1984. "Full Faith and Credit," pp. 320–321. In *The Guide to American Law.* St. Paul, MN: West.

———, 1994. "Full Faith and Credit Clause," p. 322. In *The Guide to American Law.* St. Paul, MN: West.

Warren, Kenneth F., 1997. *Administrative Law in the Political System.* Abridged Third Ed. Upper Saddle River, New Jersey: Prentice-Hall.

FULTON REPORT.   An important 1968 United Kingdom government-sponsored report of an investigation into the conduct of the British civil service and its potential for management reform.

Origins and Subsequent History

For most of the twentieth century the operating tenets of the United Kingdom civil service were the reforms introduced after the 1854 Northcote-Trevelyan Report. The Northcote-Trevelyan reforms had these basic premises: that the civil service should be divided between "superior" and "inferior" tasks, corresponding to intellectual and mechanical tasks; entry should be for young men to be "trained on the job"; recruitment should be on merit, based on independently administered examination; the entry examination should be based on the arts (rather than the sciences); all promotion should be on merit; and the civil service should become less fragmented and should allow individuals to move among government departments, and a unified pay structure should exist. The importance of these reforms were that they marked a departure from earlier systems of recruitment and promotion through patronage and personal favor.

After World War II the utility of the Northcote-Trevelyan approach to civil service organization and management in a modern industrial society was increasingly challenged in key respects. As J. Greenwood and D. Wilson (1989) have pointed out, the postwar civil service employed twenty times more staff than in 1854, government departments had become larger, workloads were greater and more complex, senior civil servants implemented and coordinated increasingly complex administrative schemes, and

TABLE I. IMPLEMENTATION OF ASPECTS OF THE FULTON REPORT

Findings	Recommendations	Implementation
Generalist philosophy	Preference for relevant degrees	Rejected
Generalist philosophy	Administrators should specialize	Little effect
Little management training	Civil Service College and management training	Implemented, but most training in departments
Staff management inadequate; career planning inadequate; promotion too dependent on seniority	Civil Service Department headed by prime minister	Established 1968 but abolished in 1981
Departmentalism and proliferation of grades	Unified grading and job evaluation	"Open structure" with little effect
Too inward	Two-way transfers with private sector	Pension rules modified with little effect

SOURCE: Adapted from Dowding 1992, p. 237.

the workings of government necessitated the employment of specialist personnel including economists, statisticians, and engineers (p. 102). What emerged from these concerns was the Fulton Report (1968)—the most significant inquiry into the civil service after Northcote-Trevelyan—which advocated a range of fundamental reforms.

The Fulton Report contained two major elements. The first was a critique of the organization and management of Northcote-Trevelyan reforms against the growing demands on the civil service. Here, the report pointed to deficiencies in the civil service arising from the "generalist" philosophy and the undervaluing of specialist skills, the lack of management skills and training, excessive departmentalism and proliferation of grades, too much secrecy and inward-looking orientation, and a system of "classes," which impeded the work of administration. The second was a series of recommendations including: a preference for "relevant" degrees and greater administrative specialization; the establishment of a civil service college and more management training; a unified Civil Service Department headed by the prime minister, unified grading and job evaluation; arrangements with the private sector to facilitate two-way transfer of personnel; and an inquiry into recruitment. The report was thus significant in its fundamental attack inter alia on the "generalist philosophy" that had characterized British public administration for over a century.

Implementation

As Greenwood and Wilson (1989) pointed out, the experiences of Fulton "reveal wider lessons about the problems of reforming bureaucracies" (p. 107). In 1968 the Fulton recommendations were officially accepted by the govern-

ment, with the exception of proposals that preference should be given to graduates with relevant degrees. However, as Table I illustrates, actual implementation was limited in scope and had far less impact than its advocates envisaged.

Commentators provide various explanations for the limited introduction of the Fulton recommendations. Peter Kellner and Lord Crowther-Hunt (1980), for example, have argued that implementation was hindered because the reform process was administered by senior civil servants, who in turn had considerable discretion over what to introduce and what to ignore. In a similar vein Greenwood and Wilson (1989) have pointed out that reform was undermined in part by the tension between department individualism and the "pull" of the center. Instead, more fundamental changes to British administrative institutions were to emerge later during the 1980s, under the initiatives adopted after the election of the Margaret Thatcher government in 1979—which were to include privatization, market testing, and new mechanisms for public sector management directed more proactively at "changing the culture" of Whitehall.

MATTHEW R. H. UTTLEY

BIBLIOGRAPHY

Dowding, K., 1992. "Managing the Civil Service." In R. Maidment, and G. Thompson, eds. *Managing the United Kingdom: An Introduction to Its Political Economy and Public Policy.* London: Sage.

Fulton Report, 1968. *The Civil Service,* Vol. 1. *Report of the Committee.* Cmnd. 3638. London: HMSO.

Greenwood, J., and D. Wilson, 1989. *Public Administration in Britain Today.* London: Unwin Hyman.

Kellner, P., and Lord Crowther-Hunt, 1980. *The Civil Servants: An Inquiry into Britain's Ruling* Class. London: MacDonald.

FUND-RAISING.

The century-old process by which nonprofit organizations formally secure the necessary capital or in-kind resources to pursue their missions. Fund-raising is often referred to as the process of development. Nevertheless, some in the nonprofit management field distinguish between fund raising and development and suggest that development is the primary task of fund-raisers (Harrah-Conforth and Borsos 1991). Despite this distinction, fund-raising executives are often referred to as development officers, without the distinction (see **development officer**).

Fund-raising, or development, is foremost a practitioner's field, guided by the public's demand for professional standards as incalculable numbers of tax free donations move from individuals to organizations domestically and internationally every day. It is a field that is maturing; one that has begun to rely on publications and accreditation procedures in recent years. It is a field wherein processes and techniques are explored and analyzed and information is disseminated among professional fund-raisers through a growing body of literature. (See the Bibliography for organizations and some titles of their various publications.)

Various methods for fund-raising have become commonplace. Prominent among these are establishing and maintaining an annual fund and its drive; employing computer programs to facilitate mass marketing efforts and direct mail solicitation and developing organizational-specific information campaigns about the mission, goals, achievements, and credibility of the organization seeking funds; and capital fund raising campaigns or drives for major projects. Fund-raising executives also engage in establishing and maintaining additional techniques to establish planned giving programs. Fund-raising professionalism and its trappings (specifically, certification and formalized ethical standards) result from the recognition among development personnel that the marketplace for funds is competitive and that organizational survival requires fund-raisers to be professional in their demeanor and communications as they pursue, court, and maintain major contributors.

Fund-raising professionals manage a diverse array of components, including the human resources within an organization and the organization's board of directors. In contrast, professional itinerant consultants are more often sought by small organizations unable to afford professional in-house development personnel but in need of guidance and fund-raising expertise.

Development officers rarely neglect the organization's board of trustees. This is traditionally a significant potential source of organizational sponsorship. The concept of the "power board" stems directly from the board members'

capacity to provide or bring sizable donations to the organization. Development officers, as noniniterant experts, must work to develop such boards in a way that often requires a combination of nurturing and aggressive bottom-line oriented behavior.

As implied, development officers must also manage technological resources. Computer databases can be relatively simple or extremely sophisticated. Most common are those that serve the fund-raiser as he or she seeks to develop and maintain records on prior and likely donors. The more sophisticated programs incorporate coding capacity for specific interests of prior donors, from the grass roots to the corporate level. Fund-raisers who use this capacity are able to compose "personal" letters by the thousands and post them to potential contributors. More advanced systems include coding schemes by which responses to those various solicitations can be analyzed; this analysis allows the development team to refine and further personalize the next wave of requests.

The concept of strategic management in the use of resources and in the development process is common to this growing professional fund-raising field. Strategic management includes the need for managers to place resources in boundary-spanning efforts, to assure that the organization will not be caught offguard when environmental uncertainty results in heavy demands upon the organization or in a necessary change in the direction of its mission.

Nonprofit organizations serve as a link between the private corporate world, with its bottom-line economic concerns, and the public sector's inability or disinclination to provide services in (for example) the social needs realm, the arts, education, and health care. Fund-raising executives, or in-house development officers, play an integral part by providing a guided outlet for philanthropy and human need. They serve as a linkage between what John Filer (head of the Commission on Private Philanthropy and Public Needs [1975]) called the "donor" and the "donee." (See **Filer Commission**.)

Fund-Raising and Philanthropy

Fund-raising is conceptually associated with philanthropic capacity and action. The philanthropist possesses the funds that he or she chooses to donate to various or specific causes, for a variety of reasons. Such giving may result from pure magnanimous desire, independent of or (in contrast to) a direct link to the desire for public recognition. The desire to share may be a quiet anonymous act of generosity. Or, giving may have little to do with charity or recognition but may be tied to concerns about the tax liability of the donor's estate. Individual giving tends to result from a combination of these and other personal factors. Without philanthropy, large and small, fund-raising as a practitioner's field would not likely have developed. It is the institutionalized techniques of the professional fund-raiser that guide beneficence, helping organizations to serve their clients and fulfill their missions, while providing feedback to fund-raising executives, guiding them and influencing research important to their field, both practical and theoretical.

As noted in *Giving in America* (Commission 1975), philanthropic services rarely pay for themselves. Central to an understanding of philanthropic activity is that donated funds encourage the extension of benefits (charitable, educational, cultural, or social activist) to individuals regardless of their ability to pay. And since most nonprofit activities do not lend themselves to economies of scale, nonprofit organizations experience what was referred to in *Giving in America* as a costly irony; with fees rarely covering the full cost of the social, educational, or artistic service; "the more successful philanthropic 'pioneering' has been in terms of reaching more people, the greater [its] operating deficit (Commission 1975, p. 85)." In effect, as fundraising succeeds, it is even more necessary.

The 1990s have witnessed a documented increase in fund-raising activities separate from philanthropy. Through the efforts of their in-house fund-raising personnel, organizations are seeking earned revenue through setting fees, creating for-profit subsidiaries (more than in years past), and developing unrelated business income ventures through product sales, as well as responding to a growing interest in the potential of the special event fund-raiser. In addition, competition is increasing among agencies seeking donations from all sources (Gronbjerg 1993). Some of this competition among organizations stems from the early 1980s government budget cuts to social programs, which were followed by the mid-1980s economic downturn. This resulted in increased service demand on the more limited sector capacity. The traditional source of funding during the twentieth century has been government. With government funding cuts, competition for funds among service providers has increased.

Environmental Uncertainty

To understand fund-raising, it is necessary to explore what Kirsten Gronbjerg (1993) calls a world of "multiple and disparate funding sources" as well as "diverse organizational environments" (p. xi). Fund-raising techniques, activities, and successes hinge on diverse organizational environments and missions. At the root of all fund-raising is environmental uncertainty and the reality of organizational dependence on external funding sources.

Environmental exigencies place greater demands on the services of nonprofits but at the same time threaten their capacity to provide the services. When corporate profits decline, or questionable ethical behaviors among

federated fund-raising executives are exposed (as they have been during the latter part of the twentieth century and ought to be if they occur), organizations dependent upon funding from these sources are confronted with a loss of funds. The result is organizational or program instability. This instability follows directly from public anger and uncertainty with the ethics of this mode of fund-raising.

The relationship between corporate donations through employee contributions and nonprofit organization viability is symbiotic, and the ramifications are broad. Even when nonprofit managers presume that they are independent of the corporate donors in a community, the result of corporate fiscal stress can have an indirect and powerful impact on the unwitting nonprofit manager. Frequently, when a corporate sponsor of a specific nonprofit organization faces bankruptcy, greater demands are placed on the sponsors that remain in the community. Organizations that have never directly benefited from the bankrupt organization's largess are affected. Donations suffer as the pool of philanthropic sources becomes smaller and competition for the more limited funds increases.

Professional nonprofit development officers must use creative techniques to deal with this type of environmental instability: What appears to be external to the nonprofit organization is often unanticipated by less-seasoned managers. One technique of dealing with this problem is to use managerial participation in boundary-spanning activities (Gronbjerg 1993) within the corporate or local community—activities that help organizations anticipate dramatic changes in resource availability. Such activities can serve to inform the nonprofit service provider of the probability of an increased demand for its services.

This type of corporate fiscal stress has a paradoxical quality. At the same time that philanthropic funds are ceasing to flow from the corporate sponsor to the nonprofit provider, employees of the corporation are losing their jobs, and nonprofit social service entities in the region are faced with an increased client load. This increased demand on the local nonprofit community comes from former corporate employees now seeking services, as well as from layoffs from other firms in the region, which are dependent on the corporate employees' business for their business's prior livelihood.

Development requires that fund-raisers also analyze the various demands of divergent funders. As Kirsten Gronbjerg (1993) has noted, demand complexity may be high

> if organizations receive funding from many streams of the same type. That is because nonprofit managers must give a minimum amount of attention to each discrete funding stream, to ensure that the exchange relationship meets the expectations of both participants. The larger the number of such relationships the organization main-

tains . . . the less likely the organization is to know the specific interests and concerns of individual funders. Therefore, the greater is the uncertainty it encounters (p. 58).

Funding Sources

Funding sources for nonprofits fall into three broad categories: (1) Public, or government funding; (2) mixed funding, which includes donations from individuals, corporation and foundation grants, federated funding sources, and special event revenues as well as sales revenues; and (3) fees or service charges. Boundarywise organization managers seek a variety of funding sources to avoid overexposure to capricious local economies.

Public Fund-Raising

Public fund-raising has both costs and benefits for nonprofit organizations, including (in exchange for the possibility of large government contracts) the need by organizational managers to keep abreast of the budget negotiation process, as well as the political and organizational ramifications inherent in shifting governmental priorities. With grants as well as purchases of service contracts, organizations must meet reporting requirements and be willing to adhere to legislative or agency-defined rules and regulations, which often dramatically limit managerial discretion. Gronbjerg (1993, p. 197) wrote about strategies nonprofits can employ to affect control on the vagaries of the public funding process, but successful strategic behavior tends to remain in the domain of only the largest of nonprofit organizations: those with skilled, politically astute managers who have the ability to remain informed of the various contingencies as they seek out new and stable revenue sources.

When nonprofit organizations seek public funding they are giving up some organizational autonomy, and often they do so because the funds are critical to the organization's ability to fulfill its ongoing mission within a particular program area. At times, the funds are necessary for the organization's virtual survival. Managers must accept whatever statutory or regulatory limits to funds are imposed and create organizational reserves to buffer them against the environmental uncertainty inherent in the capricious political funding environment.

Clients need to be protected. And, if not at the onset of funding, during a later funding cycle organizations often face a dramatic dilemma: to comply with new public funding guidelines that alter the organization's mission or to seek alternative, more limited, sources of revenue, with fewer strings but less to offer. One alternative is to engage in grant writing to foundations (identified later as a source of mixed-funding); this also entails complying with exter-

nal demands, but these demands tend to be less politically capricious and may allow the organization to remain true to its mission and its most needy clients. Foundations often have specific programmatic objectives, and an organization's external quest for funds may threaten the organization's mission. The difference between these two types of funding sources is that although foundations tend to have a political focus that may result in an organization or program director having to confront mission issues, foundations do not change their leadership every two, four, or six years, and their goals tend to be more stable in the long term. When they are seeking foundation support, professional fund-raisers must be aware of the limits and liabilities inherent in the funding requirements.

Mixed-Funding: Donations

Even though the nondistribution constraint prohibits the distribution of profits or dividends, organizations (as a fund-raising tool) may solicit, receive, and maintain capital resources in the form of donated stocks, bonds, or physical property. One fund-raising technique that is becoming more common as the World War II baby boom generation matures and receives inheritances from its elders is the request for bequests (to be remembered in one's will) or requests from savvy development officers to potential donors for contributions of inherited securities. Usually a long-term technique, appeals for donations of this sort come with a promise to the donor of lifelong income based on the securities' earnings. The intent is to safeguard, for the organization, ownership of the stocks or bonds when the donor eventually passes away. Real estate property, too, is often sought as a donation. Real estate may not cost the organization money in property taxes and can provide a consistent base of rental income. The Catholic Church has for generations owned and maintained this type of property, and now smaller religious and nonreligious nonprofit organizations are beginning to focus their development efforts in property acquisition.

When nonprofit fund-raising includes solicitation of stocks and securities—investment capital that can, over time, provide a secure source of revenue for the organization or one of its pet programs—the "donee" (see Commission 1975) will often apply normative criteria to the types of gifts to be accepted. Tobacco stock, for example, is not readily sought by health care providers, nor is utility stock eagerly sought by groups working on environmental issues (although such groups often hold a small number of shares in such corporations to allow them access to stockholders' meetings).

Mixed-Funding: Federated Fund-Raising

Federated fund-raising drives traditionally refer to the organized efforts of United Way agencies or community chests. In this type of drive, individuals are asked to make annual contributions to an organization that serves as a clearinghouse for a large number of "worthy" organizations within a community. Traditionally, Boys' and Girls' Clubs, Big Brother and Big Sister organizations, and various quasi-religious organizations—such as the YMCA, YWCA, Jewish Community Center Association, and the Salvation Army—that provide for needy individuals of all denominations benefit from federated fund drives. In the contemporary climate wherein family planning is often linked to abortion services, some organizations such as Planned Parenthood, which have benefited historically from federated-fund campaigns, have been dropped from the pool of recipient organizations. This action has forced them to join the large number of independent (nonfederated or creatively federated) nonprofit organizations that must seek revenues from other sources through fees, memberships, and annual, biannual, or multiannual campaigns.

One lucrative fund-raising method pioneered by federated campaigns, such as the United Way, is the workplace campaign. In this drive, employers are asked to contribute through payroll deductions. This procedure brings to the federated campaign extremely large overall contributions (small donations made by thousands of employees on a weekly or monthly basis) and carries with it a community legitimacy. Yet, it simultaneously thwarts myriad local, often very small, organizations not included on the federated-fund-raising recipient list. In the last decade of the twentieth century, complaints from smaller, independent nonprofits (those that are not federated with the community chests) have often resulted in a more inclusionary policy. Various local mechanisms have been established by the federated campaigns to include more organizations in the workplace solicitation and fund-distribution process, although the proportion of overall contributions afforded to the newer participants is significantly lower than that provided to the older, established federation recipient members. The process continues to undergo review within local communities that have active organizations seeking greater equity in fund-raising.

A new type of federated effort appeared in the early 1990s with the advent of electronic data processing methods and with the competition brought about by the breakup of the American Telephone and Telegraph monopoly. Credit card companies and telephone service providers have begun to offer various federated donation options. Customers can "join" a particular service, and when they use their credit card or phone system, they are ensured that a percentage of every dollar spent will be donated to one of a group of predetermined charities or organizations.

Environmental and social action groups from all political persuasions, often left out of the traditional federated campaigns, have found this federated route to be a lucrative supplement to their own fund-raising efforts. Unlike United Way affiliates—which distribute overall funds based on a formula defined by a local volunteer board and require that their member organizations (recipients) agree to limit their independent fund-raising efforts—these newer electronic federations each define their own system of fund distribution, often querying their contributors with annual questionnaires for philanthropic direction.

Fees and Memberships

Fees for service are a common method by which nonprofit organizations maintain their programming. Traditionally, tuition is charged at nonprofit colleges and private schools as the primary fund-raising tool. Yet, due to the nonprofit service mission of many educational institutions, such fees are often kept artificially low. This practice allows a broader range of students to enroll in the institution but requires a consistent fund-raising campaign to boost revenues to meet expenses. Schools often engage in sophisticated annual fund-raising campaigns to allow them to provide tuition or fee abatement. Sliding-scale fee reduction to needy families is also employed.

Colleges and universities with successful intercollegiate athletic departments are often able to raise large sums from alumnae seeking access to sporting events. The extent to which such fees are maintained for the benefit of the athletic program varies from institution to institution, but in recent years the needs of academic departments have seen the advent of formal demands from within the institution for a more-balanced proceeds distribution structure. Techniques for interinstitutional sharing vary but may include a required "contribution" to the university's general fund from those seeking preferred alumnae status in the purchase of season tickets to sports events, particularly when the tickets are costly and in high demand.

Membership fees to nonprofit organizations are also often provided on a sliding scale; this is common when professional organizations offer variable membership rates for students, retirees, and fully employed members. These rates are often based on a standard scale, but sometimes an additional categorical scale is defined in which members identify their level of household income and pay an annual membership fee based on this reported income status. When membership organizations do this, they often must rely on the good faith and honesty of their membership since the process necessary to confirm need is often inefficient and may offend potential members. Religious institutions frequently encounter this problem and the institution's board of directors may vote to establish a confidential procedure to confirm a parishioner or member's claim to indigence and need. In contrast, a simple procedure is sometimes employed, wherein to obtain a special membership rate or reduction based on income an individual must provide evidence of current status, enrollment, or otherwise.

Membership fees provide a stable base of income and are less capricious than funding secured from an annual special event. Yet as more and more organizations seek memberships, those with similar goals have begun to enter into a competitive marketplace to entice members. When this occurs, membership drives promise not only to provide the obvious service (such as quality programming on public radio or television, or a subscription to a professional journal or zoo magazine) but also offer to provide the member with an item of extrinsic value, such as a coffee mug, an umbrella, a calendar, or a tote bag. These items provide a dual service to the organization: The membership fee is viewed to be more competitive because a gift is included, and the gift often serves as an advertising tool. People carrying tote bags with the name of the museum act as advertising agents. Under federal law, the item received must be deducted from the tax-deductible membership fee to the organization, so such advertising is not publicly supported.

Another fund-raising technique used by nonprofit organizations with access to the airwaves is the use of the corporate challenge gift. This is the process whereby individuals or companies seek to leverage their support for a philanthropic cause or nonprofit organization during a public fund-raising campaign by requiring that a specific amount be raised from the general public prior to making a sizable donation (see **challenge gift**).

Special events such as bike-a-thons, marathons, golf tournaments, concerts, and auctions are common fund-raising methods employed by many organizations. School children are often involved; and recent research indicates that the demographic bump of post–World War II baby boomers, as a group, may give more readily when they can be physically involved in the process through some type of sporting event or physical competition organized to raise money for a cause.

Professional fund-raisers or development officers find that if their organization chooses to be involved in large-scale, ongoing campaigns of great significance (in health care, education, community development, or the arts, for example) they need to seek not only memberships and fees for services rendered but also additional revenues from granting agencies, corporations, or individuals, and sometimes government contracts. This desire, or the organizational need that comes from environmental uncertainty and fiscal stress, pressures the fund-raising personnel constantly and requires an ongoing attentiveness and professional focus, both intrinsic and extrinsic to the organization. Although fund-raisers may enter the field without professional training, once employed they find that other requisites of the profession (such as ethics and communication with others in the field through conferences and professional publications) are essential to their, and their organization's, success.

ERNA GELLES

BIBLIOGRAPHY

American Association of Fund-Raising Council (AAFRC), annual. *Giving USA.* New York: AAFRC.
———, quarterly. *Giving USA Update.* New York: AAFRC.
Burlingame, Dwight F., and Lamont J. Hulse, 1991. *Taking Fund Raising Seriously: Advancing the Profession and Practice of Raising Money.* San Francisco: Jossey-Bass Nonprofit Sector Series.
Chronicle of Philanthropy, biweekly (see various issues). Washington, D.C.
Clotfelter, Charles. 1985. *Federal Tax Policy and Charitable Giving.* Chicago: University of Chicago Press.
Commission on Private Philanthropy and Public Needs, 1975. *Giving in America.* Washington, DC: Commission.
Cutlip, Scott. 1965. *Fund Raising in the United States: Its Role in American Philanthropy.* New Brunswick, NJ: Rutgers University Press.
Filer Commission. See Commission on Private Philanthropy and Public Needs.
Fund Raising Management, monthly (see various issues). Garden City, NY: Hoke Communications.
Gronbjerg, Kirsten A., 1993. *Understanding Nonprofit Funding: Managing Revenues in Social Services and Community Development Organizations.* San Francisco: Jossey-Bass Nonprofit Sector Series.
Harrah-Conforth, Jeanne, and John Borsos, 1991. "The Evolution of Professional Fund Raising: 1890–1990," pp. 18–36. In Dwight F. Burlingame, and Lamont J. Hulse, *Taking Fund Raising Seriously: Advancing the Profession and Practice of Raising Money.* San Francisco: Jossey-Bass Nonprofit Sector Series.
National Charities Information Bureau (NCIB) (formerly National Information Bureau), quarterly publications include *Standards in Philanthropy* and *Wise Giving Guide.* New York.
National Council on Philanthropy (in 1980 merged with the Coalition of National Voluntary Organizations to create Independent Sector in Washington, D.C.). See its various publications.
National Society of Fund-Raising Executives (NSFRE) (formerly the National Society of Fund Raisers), quarterly *NSFRE Journal.* Alexandria, VA.
Seymour, H. J., 1966. *Designs for Fund-Raising.* Rockville, MD: Taft Group.

FUTURES ANALYSIS.

The methods used to establish, identify, and review alternative directions for public and private policy choices in the light of possible futures. When people think about the future, search for patterns in the past that predict new directions, or set out their expectations for tomorrow, they are engaged in "future analysis." Every culture depends for its growth and development on a capacity to analyze trends, patterns, hopes, expectations, and even dreams to establish "the possible."

Futures analysis incorporates a number of future studies techniques that enable futurists, futurologists, planners, and strategists methodically to review alternative directions for individuals, groups, communities, and societies. Futures analysis techniques facilitate critical thinking, encourage people to interpret and incorporate a wider range of facts, provide a rigorous, replicable approach to the establishment of decision criteria, help people assess possible positive or negative impacts on their future well-being and behavior, anticipate problems, and prepare to maximize options.

The most common techniques of futures analysis are the following:

1. trend analysis, which extends past and current experiences into future projections, including scientific methods, economic reviews, consumer segments, and sociotechnical extrapolations of historical patterns and attempts to forecast strategic gaps and required policy interventions;
2. foresight exploration, which establishes ideas and images of potential social, technological, economic, environmental, and political actions; including methods such as environmental scanning, sustainable growth modeling, competitive analyses, product lifecycle reviews, and the projection of critical success factors for proposed investments;
3. delphi studies, which bring together the experts' opinions on emerging issues and patterns of development—either through anonymous surveys or through structured forums, for discussion of potential pathways—and review results through nominal group techniques and lateral thinking;
4. cross-impact analyses, which develop statistical probabilities of desired, preferred, or projected futures and the potential impact of each of these events or incidents occurring if other incidents or events occur; which establish input-output relationships, and which set out chains of consequences;
5. simulations and models, which are based in computers, games, scenarios, and mathematical equations that enable the futures analyst to try hundreds, thousands, and even more experiments with input-intervention-output assumptions that represent either static or dynamic relationships;
6. futures studies, which incorporate activities that attempt to predict, imagine, design, extrapolate, formulate, confirm, and project longer term activities, events, or outcomes that increase freedom, choice, and power for clients and the analysts;
7. normative projections, which are based upon values and cultures that set constraints upon the range of responses that are preferred and desired in any community of interests. The "norms," or acceptable behav-

iors, can be analyzed to provide data, knowledge, information, understanding, perceptions, and insight that help people decide their future paths or actions and measure performance against benchmarks;
8. cost-benefit analysis, which calculates the relationship between the resources and effort required to maintain a current pattern of behavior against alternative policies, programs, or projects by comparing goals with outcomes to enable the conduct of a market opportunity analysis;
9. assumptive mapping, which records the underlying beliefs, assumptions, expectations, understandings, perceptions, and creative responses that determine values and directed actions. These maps show the branches, shifts, changes, and chaotic patterns that help people develop contingent responses or plans.
10. driving force analyses, which seek to represent the complex interrelationships among different forces, leading to change or resistance to change, that determine the rate of change in a system and increase replication of desired outcomes of environmental interventions.

These ten futures analysis techniques encompass many more futurist disciplines, research methods, and imaginative competencies of professional (and amateur) futurologists, futurists, futures research and other professional disciplines that contribute to considered approaches to the future. Futures analysis uses combinations of these techniques to assist public officials, educators, budget controllers, administrators, and technicians to identify alternative decisions, develop profiles of possible political options and select best or worst case scenarios. Profiles of the future incorporate a large number of explicit, rather than implicit or intuitive, variables to enable replication, scientific assessment, and methodological rigor.

Taken together, these analytical methods enable futures analysts to (1) *assist decisionmakers* to make effective choices, or at least comprehensible decisions, that can be evaluated after the event—comparing foresighting with hindsighting reviews—and generate insights into inherent instabilities and incompatibilities that underpin significant and *catastrophic changes;* (2) enable actuaries, investors, disaster planners, and defense authorities to *develop contingency plans* that identify potential risks and dangers of unconsidered consequences of decisions. Futures analysts, by consolidating the pattern of positive and negative consequences of each action step, *enable early warnings,* predisaster training, and risk management capabilities to be put in place or to be, at least, readily developed; (3) *encourage creative and innovative searches for new directions,* better options, and different alternatives that enable new and surprising futures and that introduce new ways of thinking and responding to the rapidly changing environments; (4) *help develop a range of different responses* to familiar patterns of reactions to current crises by establishing a variety of feasible responses that may provide solutions in the future. This form of analysis sets up *decision chains* with linked steps that together may help decision-makers attack a current problem and come up with a "something different" rather than a "more of the same" answer; (5) enable *cultural and parochial perceptions* and biases to be exposed to more global and contextual analyses. This ensures that the local and personal perspectives about *preferred and desired futures* are challenged by an examination of consequences and experiences formulated outside the immediate decisionmaking setting; and (6) these analytical methods allow future analysts to *facilitate a learning orientation* to educational processes by encouraging students to explore *second- and third-order consequences* of initial decisions and encourage a futures-oriented approach to research and development studies.

Futures analysis is not a scientific process, although it relies heavily on the products of scientific research. It is inherently normative (i.e., it is value based and attempts to influence perceptions and behaviors that have probable, possible, or preferable outcomes that accord with the political, professional, and personal goals of decision-makers. Skills, capabilities, and competencies for good futures analyses are therefore a matter of judgment, intuition, creativity, and enthusiasm as much as logic, thinking, rational decisionmaking, and precision. Effective futures analyses depends upon a combination of education, experience, and enterprise to establish a mix of practice, wisdom and professional expertise.

Clear and integrated thinking, cultural and social awareness, literacy and numeracy in futures research, environmental scanning, technological sophistication, and information-processing skills all constitute the baseline elements of the well-prepared mind. To improve the quality and practical value of futures analyses people seeking employment in the field engage in preparatory studies that include historical studies to establish a disciplined approach to documentation, research, and review processes; scientific method to consolidate the open-minded search for alternative and replicable observations; social and political science examinations of the human, and organizational impacts of different decisions and behavior patterns; sociological, anthropological, and psychological disciplines that generate perceptions and insights into underlying continuities and discontinuities in people's actions; economic and mathematical modeling capabilities that provide statistical and analytical frameworks for performance analyses; public administration, management, and political science conceptual techniques that review public policy and private market mechanisms for choice determination; and computer and cybernetic operational skills to enable the processing formulation, and reconstruction of information forecasts and associations between data sets and interpretive analyses.

Every decision involves an element of futures analysis. Items are examined from a set of choice options offering better or worse results. Each of those choices requires some review of the benefits and consequences of the choice in a future period of time. Selecting the best option relies on the quality of the information about preferred and desired future states. Futures analysis uses a range of different methodological approaches to evaluate the range of possible choices and reduce the risk associated with any one particular policy decision. The most effective sequence for futures analysis is determined by the nature of the decision to be made rather than the accuracy of the data available for analysis. Each option is examined for a range of descriptive, prescriptive, and intuitive elements that form the basis for a judgment of the chances that a subsequent event or pattern of events will emerge. The goals of the analyst are of critical concern and impact directly on the futures research method adopted to explore alternative futures.

Evaluation of futures analysis suggests that it has a limited value as a forecasting or predicting tool. Discontinuities, complexities, innovative responses, and personal creativity make "prescriptive" futures untenable. New variables, new learning, and the application of new and faster technological memories and processing capacities all combine to generate a continuing number of breakthroughs, innovations, and new factors that mitigate against the "crystal ball" approach to future reviews. The quality of the futures analysis is determined by the quality of the data, knowledge, and information that establishes the basis of choice and the understanding, perception, and insight that informs the judgment about potential future results of those choices.

Any application of futures analysis needs, accordingly, to go through filters of scrutiny, skepticism, simplicity, and sustainability. The greater the complexity, conflicting potentials, paradox, and problem-seeking capacity, the more chance exists for turbulence that unsettles the best extrapolations and anticipated responses. Surprises are the identifiable discontinuities that are the subject of analysis of the differences that emerge between expectations based on the projected past and the emerging future. Nevertheless, the disciplined use of futures analyses enables industry leaders to gain a competitive edge and strategists to develop a competitive advantage. People can develop their ability for control over choices that impact on their own lifestyles and that of others who are directly or indirectly impacted.

A richer more comprehensive insight into the drivers of change and choice, the values and vision that assist in organizational development, and the social construction of a better society all rely to some extent on competent disciplined and sensitive futures analysis.

COLIN BENJAMIN

BIBLIOGRAPHY

Cornish, Edward, 1977. *The Study of the Future: An Introduction to the Art and Science of Understanding and Shaping Tomorrow's World*. Washington, DC: World Futures Society.

Harman, Willis, 1988. *Global Mind Change: The Process of the Last Years of the Twentieth Century*. Indianapolis, IN: Knowledge Systems.

McHale, John, 1969. *The Future of the Future*. New York: George Braziller.

Naisbitt, John, and Patricia Aburdene, 1985. *Megatrends 2000: Ten New Directions for the 1990's*. New York: Avon.

Schaef, Anne Wilson, 1985. *Women's Reality: An Emerging Female System in a White Male Society*. New York: Harper & Row.

Schwarz, Brita Uno Svedin, and Bjorn Wittrock, 1982. *Methods in Futures Studies, Problems, and Applications*. Boulder: Westview Press.

Slaughter, Richard, 1988. *Recovering the Future*. Melbourne: Monash University.

Toffler, Alvin, 1980. *The Third Wave*. New York: Morrow.

Zey, Michael, 1994. *Seizing the Future*. New York: Simon & Schuster.

G

GENERAL AGREEMENT ON TARIFFS AND TRADE (GATT).
The main multilateral institution overseeing international trade since 1947.

Origins and Subsequent History

During World War II, the Western leaders identified the trade protectionism characterizing the 1930s as a major cause of hostilities. The result was a proposal to subject postwar international trade to systematic control under an international trading organization (ITO). Disagreement over the remit of the ITO precluded agreement, and what survived was the GATT—a compromise that included a procedural base and guiding principles for tariff negotiations. The GATT, concluded in 1947, was considered an interim arrangement, but when the ITO failed to emerge, it was further amplified and extended through a serious of negotiating rounds, becoming by default the world's trading organization.

Basic Principles and Exclusions

The GATT reflects the view that open trade allows countries to specialize according to their comparative advantage, thus promoting higher levels of international growth and economic well-being. To achieve these aims the GATT has operated on three basic principles. First, signatory states accept not to increase tariffs (duties levied against imports). Second, they agree not to impose quotas (quantative restrictions on imports). Finally, the Most-Favored Nation (MFN) principle, contained in Article 1 of the GATT agreement, holds that trade concessions realized by bilateral agreement among GATT parties are automatically extended to all signatories. Collectively, the rules are designed to restrain increases in trade restrictions and generalize any liberalization that may occur.

From the outset there were important exceptions to these principles, including special dispensations for agricultural products and trade in textiles from developing countries; nontariff measures; the permissibility of customs unions and free trade areas (e.g., the European Economic Community [EEC]); exemptions for developing countries from GATT obligations; and waiver arrangements for derogation from a GATT provision (Robertson 1992). Moreover, chapter 4 of the GATT enables signatories to accept and negotiate reductions in trade barriers without jeopardizing their domestic industrial objective.

Early Development (1947–1967)

In the two decades after its inception the GATT was successful in achieving a dramatic decline in tariff barriers and significant growth in world trade. Early negotiating rounds at Geneva (1947–1948), Annecy (1949), Torquay (1951), Geneva (1956, 1960–62, and 1964–1967) gradually reduced product-specific tariffs. The sixth meeting, the Kennedy round (1964–1967), produced agreement for a further average one third cut in tariff barriers. By 1967, the GATT had contributed to a growth in trade between industrialized countries at an average of 8 percent per annum.

The Rise of Protectionism

Since the late 1960s the GATT's achievements in liberalizing international trade have come under increasing attack from new protectionist policies. Protectionism has stemmed from a number of sources. First, the Oil Producing and Exporting Countries (OPEC) crisis and global stagflation of the 1970s resulted in slower growth and higher unemployment than in previous decades. As a result, governments have adopted discriminatory trade practices to protect jobs and domestic industries. Second, the growth in competition from Japan and the Newly Industrialized Countries (NICs), the shift to floating exchange rates, and the relative decline of U.S. manufacturing provided additional pressure for anticompetitive trade protection.

The "new protectionism," as it is commonly referred to, has not been based on tariffs but on devices that are much less visible and hence more difficult to detect. The success of the GATT in reducing tariff barriers led to widespread introduction of nontariff barriers (NTBs) to protect domestic economies (e.g., government procurement policies, national standards, and regulations). In addition, barter and export restraints agreements (exports or imports limited to an agreed number of units, or a percentage of the importing country's market share) have been adopted in direct conflict with the liberalization objectives of the GATT. Finally, states have adapted domestic industrial policies (e.g., subsidies and tax preferences) to protect indigenous industries from foreign competition.

The Tokyo and Uruguay Rounds

In response to new protectionism, the GATT negotiations entered a new phase in the Tokyo (1974–1979) and Uruguay (1986–1994) rounds. The outcome has been gradual extension of traditional tariff reductions coupled with new GATT codes to address the new challenges.

The Tokyo round's major achievements were further tariff cuts of 35 percent, "codes of good behavior" regarding NTBs, and clarification of international norms concerning government regulations and subsidies. In general, as Robert Gilpin (1987) has pointed out, the negotiations "sought to make more 'transparent' . . . those nontariff barriers and other national practices associated with what is called New Protectionism" (p. 197). However, agreement was not reached on proposals to reform GATT agriculture arrangements, provisions for dispute settlement, and "safeguards" allowing import restrictions for specific industrial sectors. Moreover, negotiations failed to codify trade in the service sector and constraints affecting Less-Developed Countries (LDCs).

The Uruguay round extended multilateral consensus in treating new forms of protectionism. Achievements included average tariff cuts of 38 percent in developed countries, improved market access for agricultural products, and the phasing out of textile quotas. Outline agreement was obtained on rules governing services, particularly finance and telecommunications, which account for some 20 percent of world trade. In addition, measures establishing stronger rules and procedures for dispute settlement emerged from the negotiations.

The final act of the Uruguay round created a new governing body, the World Trade Organization (WTO), to take over GATT functions. The WTO, which came into operation in 1995, is a permanent trade monitoring body with equal status to the International Monetary Fund (IMF) and World Bank, and headed by a ministerial conference meeting every two years. A number of recent developments are likely to have significant implications for the effectiveness of the WTO, however. First, domestic political factors have led the United States to include important unilateral withdrawal clauses: a panel to review WTO resolutions and options for Congress and the President to veto legislation. Second, the United States administration has agreed to a congressional vote on continued WTO involvement after five years of membership. And third, all member states retain the right to leave the WTO at six months' notice.

Future Issues for the GATT

Though the incrementalist approach embodied in the GATT has removed significant barriers to economic market liberalization, further issues confront multilateral trade policy: (1) *industrial policy and investment*–An implication of successive GATT negotiations has been a growth in trade and, hence, an increase in interdependence between national economies. A consequence has been that domestic national industrial policies and investment patterns have replaced tariffs as barriers to market access. A prominent issue for future trade negotiations concerns precisely how these barriers can be removed; (2) *agriculture and services*–Although the Uruguay round has created new rules in these highly protected areas of world trade, their scope is limited. The importance of services in the global economy is highlighted by the fact that they account for two-thirds U.S. gross national product (GNP) (Spero 1993). Further gains in terms of trade liberalization are likely to be a major preoccupation of future international trade management; and (3) *new membership*–Signatories of the GATT have risen from 23 states in 1947 to some 123 states in

1994. A major issue confronting free trade concerns the mechanisms by which new states, particularly China and the countries of the former Soviet Union, are incorporated into future trade negotiations.

In conclusion, as Vincent Cable has pointed out, "The GATT's main priority is to translate its strengthened mandate [since the Uruguay round] into an effective World Trade Organization which can command sufficient confidence in its impartiality and efficiency that it can uphold multilateral rules in the face of powerful protectionist groups and national governments" (Cable 1994, pp. 26–28).

MATTHEW R. H. UTTLEY

BIBLIOGRAPHY

Bhagwati, J., 1991. *The World Trading System at Risk*. London: Harvester Wheatsheaf.
Cable, Vincent, 1994. "GATT and After," *The World Today* (February): 26–28.
Gilpin, Robert, 1987. *The Political Economy of International Relations*. Oxford Princeton University Press.
Robertson, David, 1992. *GATT Rules for Emergency Protectionism*. London: Harvester Wheatsheaf.
Spero, Joan E., 1993. *The Politics of International Economic Relations*. London: Routledge.

GENDER POLICY. Policy machinery to ensure that women receive equal benefit from government activity as a whole, as well as specific programs to advance the status of women. The concept of the need for specialized government machinery for this purpose first received widespread acceptance as a result of the International Women's Year (1975) and the ensuing United Nations (UN) Decade for Women. The World Plan of Action adopted for the UN decade placed special emphasis on such government machinery, and more than two-thirds of UN member nations adopted some form of it during this period–it might be a ministry of women's affairs (self-standing or otherwise), women's bureaus within the bureaucracy, advisory bodies, or independent commissions. By the end of the decade there had been a general shift from reliance on advisory bodies to the creation of government units among 137 reporting countries (BAW 1987).

Women's ministries or bureaus took responsibility for special programs to advance the status of women. More importantly, they institutionalized the feminist insight that no government activity is likely to be gender neutral, given the different location of women and men in the workforce and in the family. In order to ensure women received equal benefit from government policy, women's bureaus were to ensure that all government policy was monitored and all government activity was audited for gender-specific effects.

To take a relatively simple example: A proposal might be made to effect savings in public transport by cutting back on services other than the peak commuter routes. The relevant women's unit would draw attention to the disparate impact of such a proposal on women, who characteristically have less access to private transport than men and are more likely to need public transport for purposes other than the journey to work. Similarly, a proposal to introduce time-charging for local telephone calls could readily be shown to have disproportionate impact on women, who make fewer purely instrumental calls and spend more time on the telephone as part of their invisible welfare work in sustaining kinship and other networks.

In developing countries a particular focus has been the gender-specific effects of economic restructuring and of cutbacks in social expenditure. Unfortunately, women's policy machinery is often underresourced and located away from central policymaking areas. A UN expert group recommended that "national machinery . . . be strengthened by enabling it to monitor the incorporation of women's concerns in all government ministries, including their budgets, and be provided with adequate resources to carry out theirs tasks" (DAW 1989).

Women's policy machinery should not be confused with agencies promoting equal employment opportunity, whether in the public or private sector. Although women's policy bodies may have carriage of employment equity legislation, this is subsequently administered by quite distinct bodies.

The United States is one of the few countries that has not developed women's policy machinery, despite its pioneering role in the establishment of equal employment opportunity agencies and the long history of the Women's Bureau in the Department of Labor (created in 1920). The fact that the United States has not ratified the UN Convention on the Elimination of All Forms of Discrimination against Women or other relevant international instruments means that it does not participate in international standard setting. By contrast, in the countries discussed later there has been a symbiotic relationship between status-of-women activities at the international and domestic levels.

Case Studies of Women's Policy Machinery

To illustrate different types of national machinery to advance the status of women one might take Australia, Canada, and New Zealand as benchmarks. Australia has been a leader in terms of the influence of feminist bureaucrats or "femocrats"—a neologism for which Australia was responsible (see Eisenstein 1995). Canada was a pioneer of women's policy machinery in the 1970s, both at home and in multilateral forums, and continues to be particularly active in the latter. New Zealand did not develop its machinery until a decade later, but tried something very distinc-

tive (see Curtin and Sawer 1995). In all three countries program responsibilities have been eschewed in favor of policy functions.

In the 1970s, Australian feminists decided against a self-standing bureau or ministry on the grounds that it would become a waste-paper basket for women's problems. They wanted a unit in the chief policy coordination agency of government so that there would be more clout and automatic access to all Cabinet submissions (see Sawer and Groves 1994). In the 1980s, the Office of the Status of Women in the Department of Prime Minister and Cabinet served as the hub of a network of women's policy units in line departments and other agencies, giving it the capacity to coordinate exercises such as the annual women's budget statement. Portfolios were required to disaggregate their expenditures for a budget document, showing to what extent women benefited.

In Canada the Coordinator for the Status of Women was also initially located in the chief policy coordination body—the Privy Council Office (PCO). However, from 1976, the Office of the Coordinator became a free-standing department, with ministerial responsibility being rotated among ministers of varying seniority and with varying portfolios. Despite its brief to monitor all federal policy, Status of Women Canada suffered in terms of access to Cabinet submissions and lost policy influence, particularly during the decade of conservative government from 1984.

Nonetheless, Status of Women Canada took a lead role in the UN Commission on the Status of Women, in the Organization for Economic Cooperation and Development (OECD), and the British Commonwealth, supported by a strong women's policy presence (integrative mechanisms) in External Affairs and in the Canadian International Development Agency. Canada remained the foremost advocate of inclusion of gender equality indicators in overseas aid programs and of the integration of adequate gender audits into the forward planning of multilateral bodies.

In New Zealand, women's policy machinery was delayed until the election of a Labour government in 1984. Labour women had pressed for a separate Ministry of Women's Affairs, which would enable the modeling of feminist structures and processes as well as the direct representation of feminist perspectives in Cabinet. The ministry engaged in extensive community consultation outside and collective decisionmaking inside, as well as trying to ensure other ministries built adequate consultation with women into their policy development.

Radical reforms to the public sector initiated by the Labour government in 1988 replaced the feminist collectivism of the ministry with more managerialist and hierarchical decisionmaking. There was, however, an attempt to strengthen the policy advice function, and under a conservative government (elected in 1990) a formal consultation obligation was finally imposed on other departments. New

Zealand participates in the regular intergovernmental meetings of Australian women's advisers as well as working with Australia and Canada on status-of-women initiatives at the UN.

Marian Sawer

BIBLIOGRAPHY

Branch for the Advancement of the Status of Women (BAW), 1987. *The Development of National Machinery for the Advancement of Women and Their Characteristics in 1985*. Vienna: UN.

Curtin, Jennifer, and Marian Sawer, 1995. "Gender Equity and the Shrinking State: Women and the Great Experiment." In Francis G. Castles *et al.*, eds. *The Great Experiment: Labour Parties and Public Policy Transformations in Australia and New Zealand*. Sydney: Allen and Unwin.

Division for the Advancement of Women (DAW), 1989. *Information on the Preliminary Results of the Review and Appraisal of the Implementation of the Nairobi Forward-Looking Strategies*. Vienna: UN.

Eisenstein, Hester, 1995. *Inside Agitators: Australian Femocrats and the State*. Philadelphia: Temple University Press.

Findlay, Sue, and Melanie Randall, eds., 1988. *Feminist Perspectives on the Canadian State*. Toronto: RFR/RDF.

Sawer, Marian, and Abigail Groves, 1994. *Working from Inside: Twenty Years of the Office of the Status of Women*. Canberra: Australian Government Publishing Service.

Stetson, Dorothy M., and Amy Mazur, eds., 1995. *Comparative State Feminism*. Newbury Park, CA: Sage.

GENDERED ORGANIZATION.

The argument that organizational structures, processes, symbols, and cultures are not gender neutral; instead, gender is deeply embedded in conceptualizations of organizational phenomenon (e.g., leadership) as well as substantive organizational practices (from interpersonal interaction and dress codes to division of labor and job evaluation).

The argument that organization is "gendered" is one result of an evolution in feminist theorizing that has affected not only organization theory (cf. Acker 1990) but also history (cf. Scott 1986), political philosophy (cf. Okin 1979), psychology (cf. Gilligan 1982), and public policy analysis (cf. Sapiro 1986). As Sandra Harding has documented (1993), feminist scholarship has moved from efforts to correct "biases against women" to projects designed to make women's experiences visible and, finally, to analyses that question and try to reformulate the fundamental theories and concepts of the existing knowledge base.

What this most recent feminist research has shown is that supposedly "neutral" or "universal" categories or theories are actually "male" in a variety of ways. First and most obvious, because of unequal access to education, the knowledge base has been constructed largely by men. Second, as often as not, women and "women's topics" have not been the subject of study. For example, until the 1970s, much psychological research was conducted predomi-

nantly with male subjects (Frieze *et al.*, 1991, p. 375). Third and most important, in their thinking about the world, researchers and scholars have taken male bodies and experiences as the standard, with the consequence that women are either ignored or defined as substandard, as "a problem" as in the question "What do women want?" Taken together, the effect is what Sandra Bem (1993) has termed "androcentrism," a male-centered view of the world.

Challenges to androcentric knowledge have occurred across the disciplines. Within political philosophy Susan Okin (1979) has shown the ways in which the public-private dichotomy underlying liberal political theory depends on a gendered division of labor. Zillah Eisenstein (1988) has demonstrated the gendered nature of the law, arguing, for example, that the conception of self-defense enshrined in common law assumes episodic violence between two men, thereby excluding battered women's experiences. Virginia Sapiro (1986) has argued that the standard version of American social policy is told in gender-neutral terms, masking the thoroughly gendered history of social policies that promoted independence for men and dependence for women.

What these examples show is that feminist scholarship has moved beyond the conception of gender as just one more variable for examination ("add women and stir") to an ontological commitment to gender as an analytical category. As an analytical category gender is multifaceted, encompassing not only physical bodies but also psychological identities, interaction patterns among and between men and women, and the ways in which conceptual foundations are constituted through the absence (or particular portrayals) of women. The argument is that "all of social life is gendered, reflecting the differences between and among women and men in activities undertaken, opportunities available, outcomes experienced, and values held and assigned to them" (Nelson 1989, p. 4). As important, to focus simply on the physical sex of individuals misleads more than it enlightens, neglecting differences among women (and among men) as well as the dynamic ways in which cultural and institutional factors construct and are constructed by gender.

Organization theory is ripe for this richer gender analysis. First, it is clear that most organization theory has been written by men, studying the men who occupy (especially the highest) organizational positions. Second, male scholars' neglect of women and gender has been persistent. Though it is perhaps not surprising that men trained in the Weberian and Tayloresque traditions neglected gender, this neglect was replicated with each new intellectual approach: Organizational psychologists whose focus was on the individual had little to say about workers' gender; the literature on workplace democracy failed to analyze the inequality of women; and even in intellectual approaches that are antiorganizational and antipositivist, women were still neglected as subjects. For example, Jeff Hearn and P. Wendy

Parkin (1983) observed that "it is men's rather than women's accounts of organizational reality that dominate most interpretive analyses" (p. 224). (See also, Acker 1990, p. 141.) In these basic senses, then, the knowledge base in organization theory is androcentric, though this male-centeredness is changing as more and more women enter organizations, including research universities (Katzenstein 1990). More troubling is the third possibility that the very concepts that scholars use to construct and test organization theory are androcentric—which, as described previously, is the general contention of much recent feminist scholarship.

This entry develops this contention, relying heavily on the work of sociologist Joan Acker, whose 1990 essay, "Hierarchies, Jobs, Bodies: A Theory of Gendered Organization" is the basis for this encyclopedia definition. First, Acker's framework is explained and then it is used to examine the existing literature on gender and organization within the fields of public administration and sociology. Then a few studies are reviewed in some depth in order to show how scholars are using the concept of gender to rethink organization theory.

Acker's Framework

Acker has built her framework on her insight that two of the classic works on women and organization (Kanter 1977; Ferguson 1984) do not make gender analytically central. Rosebeth Moss Kanter focused on the consequences of numerical superiority and inferiority within organizations (i.e., the treatment of "tokens," with women used as a case study), and Kathy Ferguson analyzed the ways in which hierarchical power "feminizes" subordinates regardless of their biological sex. Given this critique, Acker's framework has emerged from her commitment to make gender a central, yet multifaceted, analytical category.

Acker has identified five interacting processes that "gender" organizational phenomena: (1) the construction of gendered divisions of labor and other material tasks; (2) the construction of symbols and images that explain and justify these material divisions; (3) the interpersonal interactions between and among women and men that reflect and yet also contribute to the material divisions; (4) the ways in which the gendered division of labor and supporting symbols—as well as the interaction patterns among men and women—produce gender identities. Finally, Acker (1990) has argued that (5) "gender is implicated in the fundamental, ongoing processes of creating and conceptualizing social structures. . . . Gender is a constitutive element in organizational logic, or in the underlying assumptions and practices that construct most contemporary work organizations" (p. 147). This final process, then, points to the androcentric knowledge base within organizational theory in the academy and among the managers who have the

wherewithal to construct new organizations and reformulate existing ones.

The five processes laid out in Acker's framework vary in the extent to which their gendered nature is visible or obvious. The construction of gendered divisions of labor (Acker's first process) is a highly visible aspect of the labor market as a whole and within organizations as well. Not surprisingly, then, this aspect of organizational reality has generated a substantial literature. (For a recent study on occupational segregation in the United States, see Steuernagel and Yantek 1993. For an overview of the literature on English Canadian occupational segregation, see Armstrong and Armstrong 1990). The construction of gendered symbols and images (Acker's second process) takes analysis beyond the correlation between sexed bodies and task allocation to a deeper level—the ways in which inequalities are justified by recourse to cultural constructions of masculinity and femininity. Within public administration, this type of analysis is just beginning.

The analysis of interpersonal relations between and among women and men (the third process presented by Acker) takes analysis back to sexed bodies, but the emphasis on the interactions calls for a more complex and dynamic analysis than a simple "sex differences" perspective. Still, the connection to sexed bodies has meant that considerable research has been generated, particularly in the management field (for a review, see Morrison and Von Glinow 1990). The analysis of gender identity (Acker's fourth process) has been the province of social psychologists (cf. Bem 1993), and the connections to organizational behavior and theory are only now being made (cf. Peregrine Schwartz-Shea, *et al.* 1993). What this research does is to problematize the relationship between sexed bodies and behavior, by revealing the variability of gender identity within the sexes. Finally, analysis of gender as a "constitutive element in organizational logic" (Acker's final process) is similar to the analysis of symbols and images in that the connection to sexed bodies is less important than the influence of androcentrism on the history of ideas and social institutions. This type of analysis is just beginning within organization theory (particularly within public administration) precisely because so many ideas and institutions are accepted as neutral, or natural.

Given the substantive and disciplinary differences across these five research areas, the promise of Acker's framework is that it could provide a systematic means for examining the interactions among these processes—thus contributing to development of a more complete, and perhaps, cumulative knowledge base on gender and organization. Such a systematic effort is necessary because, despite the veritable explosion of feminist organization theory over the past decade, its impact on organization theory has been uneven at best. Judging by Donald Kettl's (1993) overview of the field, the impact within public administration has been minimal.

Two explanations for this state of affairs are possible. First, across the five areas of the Acker framework, there is considerable variability in the strength of the arguments and evidence presented by researchers. This variability is, in part, a function of the newness of gender scholarship; in some areas (e.g., number 1–gendered material divisions) considerable empirical work has been done but theoretical development has lagged; in other areas (e.g., number 5–reformulation) theoretical exploration has not yet been supported by an empirical base. Second, and more controversially, feminist scholars have noted that organization researchers have implicitly (and at times explicitly) collaborated with management (Mills and Tancred 1992, pp. 1–3). As Acker (1992) put it, "Researchers and theorists are part of the relations of ruling" (p. 249).

Based on this latter perspective, Acker's framework could be thought of as a prediction about which kinds of gender research are most likely to be "acceptable" to contemporary managers and their academic consultants. Analyses of the gendered division of labor (number 1) and interactions between and among men and women (number 3) are likely to be accepted because they are tied to existing organizational issues based on physical bodies. It has been argued, for example, that the relative success of Kanter's work has been due, in part, to its compatibility with "male-stream organization" theory, including its managerial focus (Mills and Tancred 1992, p. 12). In contrast, research on gender identity (number 4) or the gendered nature of organizational symbols (number 2) is likely to seem more esoteric. On one hand, as feminist researchers have shown (Bem 1993; West and Zimmerman 1987), any analysis that problematizes gender identity makes men and women uncomfortable. On the other hand, the increasing legal prominence of sexual harassment is likely to make organizational theorists and managers more receptive to analyses of the cultural scripts for male and female behavior.

Finally, because analyses of the gendered nature of basic concepts (number 5) is so threatening, so subversive of standard ways of knowing and doing, and because the façade of gender neutrality is so strong, managers are very likely to resist (or perhaps to dismiss as "silly," "utopian," or "irrelevant") the argument that the basic concepts with which they think are gendered. Most provocatively, in her most recent ruminations, Acker (1992) contends that "gender neutrality, the suppression of knowledge about gender, is embedded in organizational control processes" (p. 256). To allow readers to assess these possibilities on their own, three works are reviewed in more depth.

Three Studies in Gendered Organization

Camilla Stivers' (1993) book *Gender Images in Public Administration* falls squarely in category number 2 of Acker's framework. Stivers has analyzed the academic arguments used to justify the existence of the administrative state. She has argued that the three typical justifications—the expertise, leadership, and virtue of public administrators—are inadequate because they do not provide gender-neutral images but are, instead, culturally masculine, to the detriment of contemporary women both inside and outside public agencies.

Stivers' evidence is both analytical and historical. Using the considerable feminist analysis of Western political theory (from Plato through the founders) as well as her own feminist analysis of contemporary public administration theorists, she has shown the ways in which contemporary justifications are shaped by the androcentric history of key concepts. Expertise, for example, seems gender-neutral, but it is tied to the notion of professional autonomy and independence. Of course, it has been men who have historically had the independence to be autonomous decisionmakers, whereas women have had their autonomy restricted to the private sphere. Thus, the social expectations of a professional are in direct contrast with the social expectations of a woman. As important, an image of the administrator as expert also has implications for the image of those who find themselves dependent on the state. Dependence is a characteristically feminine quality, and by this reasoning, the image of expertise "feminizes" (i.e., devalues) clients' and citizens' ideas about what constitutes the public interest.

Stivers' greatest contribution to the public administration literature is her analysis of the mixed images contained in the notion of virtue. She has shown that when scholars use this image to justify the administrative state, they employ its male associations: The virtuous administrator is a guardian (i.e., a father figure) who protects, chastises, or tames the people (dependent "others," represented as feminine). Or the virtuous administrator is a hero, an image associated with physical prowess, honor, and autonomy. A female hero like Joan of Arc must "put on armor" (i.e., masculinity) in order to qualify. The concept of virtue, however, also has feminine connotations—service, obedience—which do fit the particular position of the public administrator who is to obey legislators and serve the public. Stivers' analysis has shown that the feminine qualities associated with virtue are employed less often as defenses of the administrative state, a reflection of the societal devaluation of feminine characteristics. She has bolstered her analytical dissection of virtue with an examination of the role of women in the progressive movement, showing that as the social welfare function of middle-class white women's charitable organizations were transferred from the private to the public sector, the feminine connotations of virtue were stripped away in favor of the masculine ones. She concluded that "when subjected to an analysis on the basis of gender, the image of the public servant remains paradoxical—claimed for its high moral tone, yet resisted due to its silent femininity" (1993, p. 72).

Stivers has not claimed that it is impossible for women to be professional experts or organizational leaders, but only that the gendered nature of these images makes it more difficult for women to be accepted and to be evaluated positively. "While many men may also feel some distance between their sense of themselves and what the role of professional expert requires, they never have to choose between being experts and being seen as masculine" (Stivers 1993, p. 54). Thus, her analysis of the images of public administration clearly suggests how these images reflect but also contribute to the contemporary gendered divisions of labor within the public sector (Acker's process number 2).

Whereas Stiver's analysis exemplifies Acker's second process, she also clearly contributes to process number 5, analysis of the androcentric nature of basic organizational concepts. Her contributions in this area are most evident in her thinking about how some of these concepts might be reformulated. She has argued, for example, that the administrative expert could be thought of as a midwife—"a skilled and caring person who facilitates the emergence of new possibilities by means of embodied and embodying action" (Stivers 1993, p. 132). Similarly, she has offered Sara Ruddick's (1989) analysis of motherhood as a means of uniting private and public images of virtue: The virtuous public administrator, like a mother, must "foster growth under conditions of complexity" (p. 136).

Stivers' analysis, impressive though it is, is still an analysis of scholars' ideas about public administration. Though she does an excellent job of demonstrating the impact of these ideas on contemporary organizations, her analysis is still at least one step removed from the practice of the people who themselves inhabit organizations. In contrast, Acker's primary accomplishment is to subject apparently neutral technical concepts used in the field to a gender analysis (Acker's process number 5). As an example of what such analysis involves, one can review Acker's evolving views on the concept of job evaluation.

Acker's initial assessment of the concept of job evaluation is based on her experience as a member of the Oregon State Task Force on Compensation and Classification Equity (1989). As an avowed feminist member of that task force, she participated in efforts to modify an existing job evaluation system (the Hay system) to decrease its gender bias. She further observed the Hay consultants' training of, as well as their work with, the job evaluation teams who reevaluated public jobs throughout the state of Oregon. According to her analysis, the effect of the reevaluation was muted in part because the Hay consultants used their technical expertise to keep change within a politically acceptable range. But the most important factor restricting change was the actors' implicit acceptance of organizational hierarchy. Job evaluation was used to rationalize the organizational hierarchy; participants accepted as legitimate the principle that the complexity and responsibility

of the job should be commensurate with hierarchical position and pay.

In her 1990 analysis, Acker stressed the abstract nature of job evaluation—the fact that, as the experts agree, one evaluates jobs, not the people who fill them. When conceived of at this abstract level, it follows that the "best" employee, the one who comes closest to the ideal is "the male worker whose life centers on his full-time, life-long job, while his wife or another woman takes care of his personal needs and his children" (Acker 1990, p. 149). Thus, the concept of a job assumes a particular gendered division of labor in the private sphere. Within this "organizational logic" it is men who "naturally" deserve the highest positions because their loyalties are not divided. Those with divided loyalties (primarily women) end up clustered in the lower positions, and job evaluation is used to justify the tasks they do as less complex and less worthwhile.

Finally, by 1992 Acker had emphasized the ways in which seemingly neutral technical tools and concepts (such as job evaluation or computer technologies) play a key role in the continued acceptance of ostensibly gender-neutral theory, hiding and obfuscating the gendered nature of concepts as well as their gendered effects. Given this perspective, it is not surprising that Acker's views on the possibilities for reforming organizations are more pessimistic than those of Stivers. For Acker, job evaluation is part and parcel of an organizational system (or, as she has put it, "organizational logic")—so that reformulating this concept in isolation from other organizational components (e.g., hierarchy) seems nigh impossible. A key part of this organizational logic is acceptance of the supposed neutrality of organizational structures, processes, and concepts: gender, body, emotion, and reproduction are "contaminants," the purging of which will set things right. Challenges to this perspective are ignored or even suppressed. Thus a critical place in which reform must begin is within organization theory itself. A theory of gendered organization must be developed in order to counteract androcentrism within the academy and within organizational management.

A final study supports Acker's reform strategy. Anne Statham (1987) illustrated the ways in which women's exclusion from academic research has produced androcentric knowledge about a single, but significant, topic within public administration—leadership. Statham (1987) began by criticizing the Kanterian assumption that "women's work orientations and behaviors are essentially the result of the structure of their labor force position, that men in similar situations act and feel the same about their job" (pp. 409–410). Statham cited Veronica Nieva's and Barbara Gutek's (1981) review of the literature, which found that no sex differences have been uncovered by researchers focusing on behavior. But Statham wanted to consider the possibility that this lack of behavioral differences may be a function of researchers using concepts and categorizing schemes originated by male researchers studying predominantly men. Thus, rather than going into an organization and testing under what conditions men and women fit Fred Fielder's (1967) or Rensis Likert's (1967) theories of leadership, she decided to use a grounded methodology: allowing women and men to tell her about their work in order to avoid "an imposition of preconceived categories that may be unlikely to tap the full range of their behaviors" (Statham 1987, p. 413).

On the basis of this approach, Statham produced a new typology that did reveal gender differences. She found that most women were primarily people and task oriented, whereas most men were primarily power and autonomy oriented. She did not evaluate whether one leadership style was better than another, but she noted that differing expectations of leadership among men and women made it difficult for them to work together, and, given that women were largely evaluated by men, women's different style was not appreciated—even though it may have been as or more effective.

Although Statham's results may deserve further scrutiny, her study is particularly instructive because it highlights the ways in which an androcentric academic knowledge base reinforces an androcentric managerial approach in the business and government sphere. To begin to break that connection requires a willingness to fundamentally question accepted approaches to (in this case) leadership in order to explore alternative conceptualizations. The three studies reviewed previously evince such a willingness and, in the process, provide provocative (and at times convincing) evidence of the gendered nature of some of the conceptual building blocks of organization theory. Whether the resistance to gender scholarship is due to its uneven and incomplete character or to the self-interest of those who benefit from the status quo, the study of "gendered organization" is here to stay, and it offers some of the most exciting research in contemporary public administration and organization theory.

PEREGRINE SCHWARTZ-SHEA

BIBLIOGRAPHY

Acker, Joan, 1989. *Doing Comparable Worth: Gender, Class, and Pay Equity.* Philadelphia: Temple University Press.
———, 1990. "Hierarchies, Jobs, Bodies: A Theory of Gendered Organizations." *Gender & Society,* vol. 4, no. 2: 139–158.
———, 1992. "Gendering Organizational Theory," pp. 248–260. In Albert J. Mills and Peta Tancred, eds., *Gendering Organizational Analysis.* Newbury Park, CA: Sage.
Armstrong, Pat, and Hugh Armstrong, 1990. *Theorizing Women's Work.* Toronto: Garamond.
Bem, Sandra L., 1993. *The Lenses of Gender: Transforming the Debate on Sexual Inequality.* New Haven and London: Yale University Press.
Eisenstein, Zillah R., 1988. *The Female Body and the Law.* Berkeley: University of California Press.

Ferguson, Kathy E., 1984. *The Feminist Case Against Bureaucracy.* Philadelphia: Temple University Press.
Fiedler, Fred E., 1967. *A Theory of Leadership Effectiveness.* New York: McGraw-Hill.
Frieze, Irene H., Esther Sales, and Christine Smith, 1991. "Considering the Social Context in Gender Research: The Impact of College Students' Life Stage." *Psychology of Women Quarterly,* vol. 15: 371–392.
Gilligan, Carol, 1982. *In a Different Voice: Psychological Theory and Women's Development.* Cambridge, MA: Harvard University Press.
Harding, Sandra, 1993. "Rethinking Standpoint Epistemology: What Is 'Strong Objectivity'?" In Linda Alcoff and Elizabeth Potter, eds., *Feminist Epistemologies.* New York: Routledge.
Hearn, Jeff, and P. Wendy Parkin, 1983. "Gender and Organizations: A Selective Review and a Critique of a Neglected Area." *Organization Studies,* vol. 4, no. 3: 219–242.
Kanter, Rosebeth Moss, 1977. *Men and Women of the Corporation.* New York: Basic Books.
Katzenstein, Mary F., 1990. "Feminism Within American Institutions: Unobtrusive Mobilization in the 1980s" *Signs,* vol. 16, no. 1: 27–54.
Kettl, Donald F., 1993. "Public Administration: The State of the Field," pp. 407–428. In Ada W. Finifter, ed., *Political Science: The State of the Discipline II.* Washington, DC: American Political Science Association.
Likert, Rensis, 1967. *Human Organizations: Its Management and Value.* New York: McGraw-Hill.
Mills, Albert L., and Peta Tancred, eds., 1992. *Gendering Organizational Analysis,* Oxford and New York: Pergamon Press.
Morrison, Ann M., and Mary Ann Von Glinow, 1990. "Women and Minorities in Management." *American Psychologist* (February): 200–208.
Nieva, Veronica F., and Barbara A. Gutek, 1981. *Women and Work: A Psychological Perspective.* New York: Praeger.
Nelson, Barbara J., 1989. "Women and Knowledge in Political Science: Texts, Histories, and Epistemologies." *Women & Politics,* vol. 9, no. 2: 1–25.
Okin, Susan Moller, 1979. *Women in Western Political Thought.* Princeton, NJ: Princeton University Press.
Ruddick, Sara, 1989. *Maternal Thinking: Toward a Politics of Peace.* Boston: Beacon Press.
Sapiro, Virginia, 1986. "The Gender Basis of American Social Policy." *Political Science Quarterly,* vol. 101, no. 2: 221–238.
Schwartz-Shea, Peregrine, Roberta Q. Herzberg, and Randy T. Simmons. 1993. "Understanding Gender Inequality: The Relative Influence of Institutional Power and Gender Consciousness." Paper presented at the Annual Meeting of the American Political Science Association, Washington, D.C.
Scott, Joan, 1986. "Gender: A Useful Category of Historical Analysis." *American Historical Review,* vol. 91: 1053–1075.
Statham, Anne, 1987. "The Gender Model Revisited: Differences in the Management Styles of Men and Women." *Sex Roles,* vol. 16, nos. 7–8: 409–429.
Steuernagel, Gertrude A., and Thomas A. Yantek, 1993. "More Than Pink and Blue: Gender, Occupational Stratification, and Political Attitudes," pp. 79–94. In Lois Lovelace Duke, ed., *Women in Politics: Outsiders or Insiders?* Englewood Cliffs, NJ: Prentice-Hall.
Stivers, Camilla, 1993. *Gender Images in Public Administration: Legitimacy and the Administrative State.* Newbury Park CA: Sage.
West, Candace, and Don H. Zimmerman, 1987. "Doing Gender." *Gender and Society,* vol. 1, no. 2: 125–151.

GENERAL ACCOUNTING OFFICE (GAO).

An organization formally established by the U.S. Congress in the Budget and Accounting Act of 1921. This new law gave responsibility for auditing executive branch financial actions to the GAO, an organization independent of the executive departments.

The early colonies in the United States developed a legislative system based on that of England, wherein the money bills should originate in the lower house and there should be no taxation without representation. After the American Revolution, the states insisted on legislative authority over finances and tried to adopt a system of control and audit. however, this new nation's financial weakness led to the establishment of a centralized federal structure of government.

The First Congress passed the Treasury Act of 1789, which created the Treasury Department, with a register, a treasurer, an auditor, a secretary, and a comptroller—a position that became the modern comptroller general. Over the next 100-plus years, many changes in personnel were adopted.

The national debt, incurred largely as a result of U.S. involvement in World War I, paved the way for the Budget and Accounting Act of 1921. Congress had debated whether accounting and auditing functions should remain in the executive branch. It eventually decided to establish an independent office—the General Accounting Office. The office of comptroller of the treasury was abolished and the comptroller general was to serve a semijudicial and independent function. The Comptroller general and assistant comptroller general, appointed by the President with the advice and consent of the Senate, would serve single 15-year terms, with mandatory retirement at age 70. This new law gave responsibility for auditing executive branch financial actions to an organization independent of the executive departments.

Early Days

The first comptroller general, nominated by President Warren G. Harding in 1921, was John R. McCarl, a lawyer. Although McCarl was clearly a political appointee, in time, he did establish his own independence and that of his office. Accounting personnel were scattered all over Washington, D.C., and McCarl endeavored to consolidate all GAO staff in one central location. Moving to a larger building in 1926 helped, yet ten years later the 4,000 GAO staff members were in a dozen buildings. Many worked under adverse conditions—cold, little ventilation, and so poorly lighted that flashlights were hand held for desk work.

One of the original divisions within the GAO, the Division of Law, in 1928 became the Office of General Council (OGC). The OGC was responsible for ascertaining whether an expenditure or collection was legal. This function included reviewing GAO settlements at the request of disbursing offices, claimants, or agency heads; helping the Justice Department prepare cases against debtors or claims disallowed by GAO; and preparing reports to the Department of Justice on claims filed against the United States.

Accounting work continued to be active. The GAO prescribed systems, forms, and procedures for administration and fund accounting in executive agencies. Some departments disputed the GAO's authority to prescribe accounting systems for the government. No enforcement power was accorded by law.

The GAO began to branch out into field offices with the onset of President Franklin D. Roosevelt's nationwide public works and relief programs. Comptroller General McCarl was concerned about lax systems of controls on government disbursing agents. This function was eventually transferred to a division of disbursement in the Treasury Department. The new division could delegate to local agents or establish local offices, but disbursement was made only after the authorized agency that incurred the debt for the government had certified the transaction.

McCarl also advocated the preaudit of government spending. In 1930, over 700,000 vouchers were preaudited, and 97 percent proved to be correct. McCarl dealt strictly in accordance with the letter of the law. He clashed with President Roosevelt without hesitation, and his actions strongly reflected objections to the New Deal program, which he felt was a threat to representative government.

Various executive agencies were skeptical of GAO power and were frequently in conflict. Some governmental departments, for example, Treasury and Attorney General, insisted on their own regulations, causing some agencies to choose either between the GAO and the department in question or to set up systems using both agencies. Various attempts were proposed through congressional committees to change the GAO; however, legislation was never enacted.

Upon McCarl's retirement, Assistant Comptroller General, Richard N. Elliott became acting comptroller general. Elliott served for three years, until President Roosevelt appointed Fred Herbert Brown as comptroller general in 1939. There were few changes in the GAO under Elliott's leadership. Brown resigned because of ill health after 15 months, having no real impact on the organization.

The War Years

In 1940, Lindsay Carter Warren, a career government official, became the comptroller general. Having served eight terms in the U.S. House of Representatives, he entered into office with the belief that the GAO should expand its relationship with Congress.

World War II determined the GAO's work priorities, however. The vast expenditures during this conflict meant a much larger volume of payments to audit and new forms and procedures for war agencies to be prescribed and approved. As a result, the War Contract Project Audit Section was created. Auditors were sent directly to war plants and military sites. Millions of documents were audited each year. By the end of World War II, to handle a severe backlog, several Army and Navy audit branches were established. At its wartime peak, the GAO had a staff of nearly 15,000.

After the war, final contract settlements and transportation payments had to be audited. A separate transportation division was established to handle these audits.

Due to the proliferation of government corporations (over 100 such corporations by 1945), legislation was enacted that authorized the GAO to conduct on-site audits. A corporate audits division of the GAO was created, and its in-depth audits paved the way for the "Comprehensive audit" program, begun in 1949.

About this same time the Joint Program for Improving Accounting in the federal government was begun; this was a cooperative effort among the GAO, the secretary of treasury, and the director of the Bureau of the Budget (BOB). The Accounting Systems Division of GAO was established to help lead and develop the joint program. It would provide standards guidance and expert assistance, and would review and approve installed agency systems. Agencies would develop their own accounting systems, thus moving the GAO away from keeping financial records for government agencies. A later reorganization of the GAO led to a decline in the work of the Joint Accounting Program, which adopted a new name, Joint financial Management Improvement Program.

The comprehensive audit program begun in 1949 was headed by the Corporation Audits Division. The Cold War and the Korean conflict influenced much of the GAO's work during this time, especially relating to defense and foreign policy issues.

In the early 1950s, a GAO reorganization was initiated. All audit divisions were merged into the Division of Audits, except for transportation and claims. Various individual audit groups were abolished during the merger, and others, such as the Field Audits Section, were elevated within the Audit Division. Six overseas offices were initially set up, and 23 regional offices were established. At the same time, the new GAO building was built in Washington, D.C., at 4th NW and G Street, thus enhancing the morale of the previously scattered employees.

After Lindsay Warren's retirement, congressional leadership could not agree on a candidate for comptroller general, so President Dwight Eisenhower appointed Joseph Campbell in November 1954 during a congressional re-

cess. Campbell was the first comptroller general appointee who was not a lawyer. His appointment was eventually confirmed, but not without much controversy.

Another conflict developed with the release of a GAO report on the purchase of defense materials during the Korean War and the possible conflict of interest of an agency's administrator. There were factual discrepancies in the GAO report, which temporarily weakened the reputation of the GAO and forced the resignation of one of its division chiefs. This conflict brought about another congressional study, which recommended yet another major reorganization of the GAO.

The Accounting System Division and the Division of Audits were abolished and the Defense Accounting and Auditing Division and the Civil Accounting and Auditing Divisions were created. The Office of Investigations was abolished, also, and its investigative functions were integrated into other parts of the GAO. The Field Operations Division was established, as was the International Division.

Comptroller General Campbell encouraged the professional development of the staff. The GAO began to hire college graduates with degrees in Accounting without the requirement of an exam and at higher entry pay levels. It also began a summer internship program for college juniors, as well as a college faculty residency program. The results were extremely successful, and professionalism of the GAO staff was extensive within a few years.

The number of defense contract audits increased during this time. There were critical reports of invalid contractors, and Department of Defense (DOD) practices and names of persons allegedly involved in fraud or malpractice were included in the reports. Congress took an interest, and lengthy hearings were conducted, many critical of the GAO. Before the conclusion of the hearings, Campbell asked for and received early retirement, thus beginning a new era, when Elmer Staats took over as comptroller general in 1966.

The Staats Era

Elmer Staats was well-known in Congress, having served in the BOB for several years, and he was well prepared for the challenges that lay ahead. He immediately dealt with the issue of defense contract audits, placing emphasis on implementing the Truth in Negotiations Act. He also stressed the importance of internal audit work of the Defense Contract Audit Agency, thus freeing the GAO from the detailed audits of defense contracts.

Following a joint study with the GAO, the DOD, and the BOB as to the feasibility of applying uniform cost accounting standards to negotiated defense contracts over US$100,000, Congress approved the creation of the Cost Accounting Standards Board (CASB), which was mandated for ten years. The board developed standards aimed at achieving uniformity and consistency in cost accounting principles for defense contracts and subcontracts over US$100,000.

The GAO began to evaluate government programs, specifically the poverty programs administered by the Office of Economic Opportunity (OEO) (i.e., Job Corps, Head Start, Volunteers in Service to America, Migrant and Seasonal Farm Workers Program, etc.).

Staats began participating in the International Organization of Supreme Audit Institutions (INTOSAI) and established the GAO's International Auditor Fellowship Program to provide extended training at the GAO for auditors from INTOSAI member nations.

Staats, at first, reorganized the GAO into the Defense Division and the Civil Division. The Accounting and Auditing Policy Staff became the Office of Policy and Special Studies, and the Program Planning Staff was created. He established the Office of Policy and Program Planning and the Financial and General Management Studies Division. Six new functional divisions replaced the old Civil and Defense Divisions, making a total of ten divisions. Three new assistant comptroller general positions were set up to head this newly structured organization.

Over time, and with emphasis on particular specialized work, various offices were established, some evolving to full divisional status. At the end of Staats' term, the GAO and 11 divisions and numerous staff offices, 15 regional offices, and 3 overseas offices.

Legislation affected the GAO's work and organization. The GAO Act of 1974 provided that the audit of transportation vouchers be transferred to the General Services Administration (GSA). Also, the annual audit of government corporations was changed to every three years, and the GAO was given authority to audit nonappropriated funds.

The GAO Act of 1980 provided for the establishment of a commission, made up of designated congressional leaders, for the purpose of submitting at least three names for comptroller general to the President for possible nomination. The President was encouraged, but not required, to choose from the list.

In line with the climate of the times, human resource problems within the GAO, such as equal employment opportunities for women and minorities and affirmative action, arose and were resolved. Also in the mid-1960s, the buildup in Vietnam began. For several years the GAO had an office in Saigon and did audit work in the field throughout Vietnam.

Two new laws also tempered GAO work in the early 1970s—the Presidential Election Campaign Fund Act, which provided a tax form checkoff of US$1 to a political party for presidential campaign expenses, and the Federal Election Campaign Act, which required the GAO to issue regulations on spending limits for use of communications media. Candidate expenses and campaign contribution accounts were to be audited and fund payments of the candidates certified. Eventually, when the new Federal Elections Commission was established by Congress, the role of the supervisory officer and administration of the Presidential Election Campaign Fund was transferred from the comptroller general.

New work areas in the 1970s included reviews of major weapons system acquisitions, environmental issues based on the Clean Air Act, investigative studies of the Federal Bureau of Investigation, reports on the Internal Revenue Service, and audits of International Organizations in which the United States participates such as the United Nations and World Bank. During Staat's last five years, GAO testified an average of 156 times per year before congressional committees.

The Bowsher Era

Responding to the GAO Act of 1980, President Ronald Reagan selected Charles Bowsher, one of eight candidates submitted by the nonpartisan congressional commission, to replace Staats at the completion of his 15-year term in 1981. Bowsher had a background in public accounting rather than government service. Like his predecessors, Bowsher reorganized the GAO staff. In 1982 three new assistant comptroller general positions were established–Human Resources, Planning and Reporting, and Operations. The Field Operations Division was abolished, and several divisions were merged. The National Security and International Affairs Division was created, as was the Information Management and Technology Division. Each of the six GAO divisions was supported by a unit of the Office of the General Counsel as a source of legal advice and assistance.

Working at increasingly sophisticated levels, the GAO staff needs were considered. A fitness facility and a day care center were established in the GAO building. Computers were made available to each staff member and recruiting and training programs were improved. A new training institute was established in 1988 in response to a government requirement that GAO evaluators earn 80 hours of continuing professional education credits every two years. Bowsher adopted a performance appraisal system and a pay-for-performance program for most employees, which made possible annual bonuses and base salary increases for meritorious performances. There was also significant progress in the human resources field during Bowsher's leadership.

Top management meetings, usually weekly, enhanced the quality control of the GAO's reports. Annual management meetings were initiated in 1983 at Leesburg, Virginia, as were annual technical conferences a few years later. The GAO also played a role in establishing the government Accounting Standards Board in 1984, an authority for setting accounting and financial reporting standards for state and local governments.

Recent Issues

Bowsher was very interested in the financial management aspects of the GAO's work and played a major role in the passage of the Chief Financial Officers Act of 1990. This law established a chief financial officer in the Office of Management and Budget (OMB), the executive departments, and major agencies. The comptroller general and the inspector general are to audit the financial statements of departments, agencies and government corporations. In 1990, the Federal Accounting Standards Advisory Board was established with the prior comptroller general (Staats) as chair.

Bowsher was also very active in INTOSAI, hosting the Fourteenth International Congress of Supreme Audit Institutions in Washington, D.C., in 1992.

The GAO was very concerned about the federal budget problems and its growing deficit. As a result of the Gramm-Rudman-Hollings Act of 1985 (otherwise known as the Balanced Budget and Emergency Deficit Control Act of 1985), the GAO was asked to do an analysis of the OMB and Congressional Budget Office annual reports, and report the needed deficit reductions to Congress and the President. The comptroller general's role in the act was challenged by several Congressional representatives. The Supreme Court decided that because the comptroller general was part of the legislative branch he could not direct the President to make budget cuts.

During the late 1980s, the GAO spent a significant amount of time and resources assisting Congress in investigating all aspects of the Iran-Contra affair. The GAO also was involved in reports concerning domestic and foreign policy and military spending. (A GAO report in 1985 warned that the Federal Savings and Loan Insurance Corporation insurance fund was inadequate.) The GAO reports and testimonies have contributed to legislation and, in many cases, to significant dollar savings in federal programs.

Over the years the GAO has shown than it can evolve to meet the needs of the nation and Congress. It has changed since its inception and will continue to change in the future in response to legislative inquiries and current affairs.

JESSE W. HUGHES

BIBLIOGRAPHY

Bowsher v. Synar, 106 S. Ct. 3181 (1986).
Freeman, Robert J., and Craig D. Shoulders, 1993. *Governmental and Nonprofit Accounting: Theory and Practice.* 4th ed. Englewood Cliffs, NJ: Prentice-Hall.
Hay, Leon E., and Earl R. Wilson, 1995. *Accounting for Governmental and Nonprofit Entities.* 10th ed. Chicago: Irwin.
Trask, Roger R., 1991. *GAO History 1921–1991.* Washington, DC: GAO.

GENERALISTS. In public bureaucracies, officials who carry out higher levels of policy advising or administration, wherein they use their general intellectual skills and abilities, often enhanced by nonspecialist academic training.

History

The origins of the notion of "generalist" may be traced to the eighteenth century. V. M. Subramaniam (1968, p. 332) noted the influential views of John Locke on the importance of the generally educated gentlemen who avoided pedantry as well as manual labor, which counteracted a natural tendency to promote scientific education at the expense of the humanities. Subramaniam explained the rise of the generalist tradition in two stages: (1) In the eighteenth century, the consolidation of a lay tradition and a decentralization of power to the local landed gentry; and (2) in the mid-eighteenth century, with an expansion of government functions, and the rise of organized political parties, ministers turned for advice with burdensome details to generalists from the same social and educational mold as themselves.

Subsequently, the generalists within the English Civil Service were recruited to its highest echelon–the administrative class from university graduates, mainly from Oxford and Cambridge, having good honors degrees in subjects such as history, modern languages, or classics, which were unlikely to have any direct connection with their future work. To the generalist was assigned the responsibility of advising ministers, the formulation of administrative policy, and of great importance, financial control.

United Kingdom

In the United Kingdom, generalists of the old administrative class (unlike lawyers or accountants requiring specialist qualifications before employment in the civil service) were intelligent all rounders, expected to learn the job quickly through experience and emulate their colleagues, rather than learning by way of formal instruction.

An argument in favor of generalist administrators was that their role was to take and understand the advice of experts in the different disciplines on any particular problem, to analyze and assess that advice, and, therefore, to reach a balanced view on the merits, or otherwise, of different possible courses of action. However, there are those in the United Kingdom who reject the view that only generalists can understand the intricacies of government and advise on policy. For them, the work of policy formulation and its subsequent management and implementation to achieve defined objectives depends on the successful integration of the skills and work of both specialists and generalists.

This latter viewpoint was supported by the conclusions of the 1968 Fulton Committee established by Prime Minister Harold Wilson to inquire whether the Civil Service was equal to the tasks expected of it in a technically advanced and complex society. The committee's report concluded that there was a pervading and dominant philosophy of the amateur (generalist), that insufficient scope was given to specialists, and that too few civil servants were trained in management—the task of ensuring that a number of diverse activities are performed in such a way that a defined objective is achieved. (Hughes 1992, p. 287). The Fulton Committee also recommended more training for specialists in management.

Despite the Fulton Committee proposals, the dominance of the generalist in the civil service hierarchy in the UK did not change materially for a number of years. Policymaking was still the preserve of the generalist administrator. Since the election of the first Thatcher government, however, the generalist administrator has been compelled to learn new managerial and budgeting skills (Drewry and Butcher 1991, p. 221). In particular, with the adoption of the "Financial Management Initiative" (FMI) in 1982 and the "Next Steps" in 1988, there has been a shift from policy to management, with the focus primarily on efficiency and costs of service delivery, leading to an emphasis on quantifiable methods of performance, investment appraisal, and efficiency criteria (Greer 1994, p. 8).

United States

In the United States the notion of a generalist had application in the creation under the Civil Service Reform Act 1978 (CSRA) of a senior executive service (SES) working in managerial, supervisory, and policymaking positions immediately below the President and his top policy appointees. Patty Renfrow (1989) has suggested that the model for this corps of versatile generalist managers was the British Higher Civil Service, although the U.S. model is based on program experts and specialists who have stayed in the one agency for most of their careers.

Mark Huddleston (1991, p. 182ff) refers to "separate service" and "separate track" plans, aimed to address what are seen to be the unique problems of scientists and engineers, as well as other specialists in the SES. Both plans share the assumption that technical specialists have needs that are distinct from and sometimes at odds with general managers.

The "separate service" proposals would aim to break scientists away from SES and create a separate, technically oriented senior personnel service or services. Unlike the separate service proposals, which would require legislative action by Congress to alter the structure of the SES, the separate track proposals would retain the general legal structure of the SES, while instituting distinct career ladders or tracks within the service for technical personnel.

Although these proposals for separating specialists and generalists have considerable surface appeal, a number of major issues would need to be resolved. These include such issues as the relative merits of a separate service as opposed a separate track system, the number of tracks that would be required, the level of government at which tracking would take place, and the relations between tracks.

Australia

In Australia, the concept was given credence in the establishment of the senior executive service in October 1984, in order to provide for a group of senior officers who (1) could undertake higher-level policy advice and managerial and professional duties in agencies and; (2) might be redeployed by agency heads within agencies or departments so as to promote the efficiency of the Australian Public Service. It was senior staff that Australian government ministers were closest to and the role that they played in policy advising that was regarded as most important. The governments of several Australian states have also each created a Senior Executive Service within their bureaucracies, wherein generalist appointees carry out the more-important higher-level policy advising functions or manage major functions of government and are interchangeable between these functions or policy advising.

No longer does the concept of the generalist as it originated in the UK Civil Service have application in major bureaucracies throughout the world. Instead, with the gradual evolution of managerialism in many countries and its emphasis on outcomes and accountability for results, senior bureaucrats must have not only policy advising skills but also management skills and experience of a high order so as to effectively promote and execute their missions.

ALEX. M. OWEN

BIBLIOGRAPHY

Drewry, Gavin, and Tony Butcher, 1991. *The Civil Service Today.* 2d ed. Oxford: Basil Blackwood.

Greer, Patricia. 1994. *Transforming Central Government—The Next Steps Initiative.* Buckingham, UK: Open University Press.

Huddleston, Mark. W., 1991. "The Senior Executive Service: Problems and Prospects for Reform." In Carolyn Ban and Norma M. Ricucci, *Public Personnel Management—Current Concerns and Future Challenges.* New York: Longman.

Hughes, Owen, 1992. "Public Management or Public Administration?" *Australian Journal of Public Administration,* vol. 51, no. 3 (September): 286–296.

Oxer, Rosemary, 1990. *The Senior Executive Service 1984–1989.* Public Service Commission. Senior Executive Staffing Unit. Occasional Papers no. 7 (January). Canberra: Australian Government Publishing Service.

Renfrow, Patty 1989. "The Senior Executive Service—An Assessment of the American Experience." *Canberra Bulletin of Public Administration* 9 (August): 64–68.

Ridley, F. F., 1968. *Specialists and Generalists.* London: George Allen and Unwin.

Subramaniam, V., 1968. "The Relative Status of Specialists and Generalists: An Attempt at a Comparative Historical Explanation." *Public Administration,* vol. 46 (Autumn) 331–340.

GERMAN ADMINISTRATIVE TRADITION.

The governmental organizational culture and management practices of Germany.

To the foreign observer, the German administration presents itself as a mighty authority, often copied by other countries. Its inner structure certainly seems difficult to overlook. The civil service, employing 6.49 million persons in 1993, thereof 1.13 million part-timers, 1.94 million officials, 2.91 million employees, 1.41 million workers and 231,000 professional or temporary soldiers, is by far the largest employer in the Federal Republic of Germany (FRG). The share of public services in the gross national product has meanwhile risen past the 50 percent mark on an average, and about 40 percent of the public budget must be spend on staff costs and pension payments. The FRG only ranges in the center with these characteristic quantities, and its civil service appears neither remarkably big nor particularly small when compared internationally.

Two problems, that is, the question of the size of the government and the possibilities of improvement, are closely linked-up with the German governmental and administrative structure, which is substantially influenced by specific traditions. Tradition means "passing on knowledge and skills, the cultural assets and the moral approach to the succeeding generations by verbal or written tradition" (*Brockhaus Lexikon* 1973). Accordingly, the term "administrative tradition" paraphrases the passing on of administrative structures, processes, and values—in short: the art of administration—from former times to the present. The question arises whether a specific German administrative tradition exists.

Looking beyond Germany's borders, most European nations give the impression of being distinguished by specific administrative cultures and traditions. The French administration, for example, virtually stands as a symbol for a centralized system, and the structures of the Italian and the Spanish administrations resemble it; in all three cases with more or less marked tendencies toward decentralization (Miller 1986) and regionalization. In Great Britain, however, the public administration is commonly regarded as negotiation-oriented and has for some time been the object of extensive privatization actions. The administrations in the Scandinavian countries are often investigated in connection with the development of the social welfare state. Regarding the Eastern European countries, the administration often is reduced to the aspect of transformation alone.

Such simplifications certainly are problematic. Characterizing the German administration in a similar way, the image of a hard-to-overlook conglomerate of different administrative bodies in a confusing network of legal and administrative relations is certainly not out of place. In addition to the federal government, there are a total of 16 federal states (Länder), of which three, Berlin, Bremen, and Hamburg, are called city-states. Bremen is the smallest federal state with respect to area and population, being constituted from the cities of Bremen and Bremerhaven. The city-states are federal states and communes at the same time.

The territory of the Federal Republic of Germany comprises 324 counties and 112 county-independent towns in 1994, which, as do the smaller towns and communes, hold the right of self-government—a right that has historically grown from and is guaranteed by the basic law (Grundgesetz). In the federal states of Baden-Württemberg, Bavaria, Hesse, Lower-Saxony, North Rhine–Westphalia, Saxony and Saxony-Anhalt, an additional administrative level has been established between the counties and the central administration, which is taken by the 32 district governments (Regierungspräsidien or Bezirksregierungen). In Thuringia, the "Landesverwaltungsamt" is a comparable authority as regards function, with a state-global responsibility. These bodies represent the government of the federal state in the respective district and are in no way subject to a democratic cooperation of the citizens, such as, for example, the regions in France, with their regional parliaments.

These numerous regional and local authorities are responsible for the so-called general administration, but there are approximately 20,000 institutions of indirect administration. These are to some extent autonomous from the regional and local authorities and have been established for specific purposes. They include, for example, the chambers of Industry and Commerce, the Federal Authority for Work with Subordinate Institutions, or other foundations under public law. Also, there are numerous public enterprises that are owned by the federal government, the federal states, or the communes.

It seems to be a difficult task to determine a common administrative tradition for all of these authorities and institutions, considering that the individual administrative branches show substantial regional differences and have, from a historical viewpoint, partly developed quite differently. Therefore, only up to a point can one speak of *the* German administration pure and simple. Also, contrary to France or Great Britain, the German national state can only be called such since the foundation of the German Reich in 1871. The German administration, if existing, therefore had much less time to develop its own administrative tradition.

Considering the history of ideas, in Germany the first statements on the implementation of law were made by Immanuel Kant (1724–1804) and Georg Wilhelm Friedrich Hegel (1770–1831). Hegel denied the separation of the constitutional powers in favor of a comprehensive governmental power, but this implicitly confirmed the existence of a differentiated executive power. Karl Marx (1818–1883), in his dispute with Hegel classified the efficiency of the bureaucracy as negative, but ultimately confirmed this as a governmental function, too. The Marxist approach that considers the administration as bureaucracy mainly results from the *Kritik des Hegelschen Staatsrechts* (Criticism of the Constitutional Law According to Hegel) (Marx 1843). This publication presents Marx's scathing criticism of the *Grundlinien der Philosophie des Rechts* (Main Outlines of the Philosophy of Law) (Hegel 1821) in which Hegel assumed that the state is the carrier of the interests of the general public, not the carrier of the special interests of the civil society. Consequently, it was the task of the executive to translate the monarch's decisions into actions. All mechanisms that insured for Hegel the unity of government and society to Marx represented nothing but evidence for the conflict between the two cases.

Considering the history of structure and tasks (Jeserich et al. 1983–1987), it cannot be denied that, particularly at the time of the late absolutism, the target of a strengthening of the governmental base of power was the cause for building up the administration. At the time of the absolutism the administration was mainly the instrument for collecting taxes, administering the property of the sovereign, and performing specific tasks in the fields police and commerce. In the first third of the nineteenth century the so-called "Stein-Hardenbergschen Reforms" resulted in a central buildup of the administration, with the five governmental departments called "classic" today—the Department of the Interior, the Foreign Department, and the Departments of Finance, Justice and War. This time also experienced the beginning independence of the administration, manifested in the beginnings of the civil service law and a local constitution.

The observation of more recent German history reveals that the public administration has outlasted several system changes. In this respect, it can be described as very stable: The administration endured the transition from the empire into the Weimar Republic rather undamaged. Also, the perversion of the administration in the Third Reich cost only relatively few civil servants, who were prosecuted for political and racial reasons, their offices and sometimes also their lives. Still, after the end of World War II, in Western Germany the majority of public servants stayed in office.

Only in East Germany did rather radical purges take place. Here, the system of a classically European administration, gave way to the socialistic cadre administration, in which it was not primarily the expertise but the political conviction that provided the decisive criteria for affiliation and for the chances of making a career in the administration. After the collapse of the German Democratic Republic (GDR), the public administration had to undergo another transformation, for the first time in world history from a socialistic or Stalinist system into a system of a free and democratic state under the rule of law (König 1992). The major part of the administrative employees survived even this turning point. At large, it was only the executives that were replaced.

Consequently, are the executives the carriers of the administrative tradition? The change taking place in the five new federal states supports that assumption; it is mainly characterized by the fact that civil servants from the Western federal states, most of them in executive positions, are adapting the administrative structures and administrative sequences to the practice in the former Federal Republic of Germany. There are signs in this connection that suggest that the value orientation of East German executives differs from the one maintained in the West: In the East the hierarchic thinking is substantially more marked than in the West, where over the past few years, to an increasing extent, the civil servants (who are commonly considered as rather conservative in their thinking) have started to orient themselves on postmaterial values (Reichard and Schröter 1993).

Regardless of all of the differences and also the very different development in more than 40 years of socialism or Stalinism in the East and a social economy in the West, the all-German heritage of Prussian administrative traditions is obvious. The organization and value orientation of the Prussian administration presents itself as a common clamp for the eleven "old" and the five "new" federal states. The essential part of this Prussian tradition is the strictly hierarchical administrative structure linked with an orientation of the civil servants on the principles of incorruptibility, the public welfare, and professionalism. Necessary as a precondition for this was and still is a system of written rules of laws that, following the German law positivism, safeguard the laws and the position of the citizens against the powers. The great German universal scholar Max Weber (1864–1920) described this system as the "bureaucracy," a term certainly understood to be positive at this time when the bureaucracy presented itself mainly as a rational system and as a contrast to the feudal arbitrary regime.

With regard to idea history for the development of public administration as a science, in addition to Weber, Robert von Mohl (1799–1875), Rudolf von Gneist (1816–1895), and Lorenz von Stein (1815–1890) should be mentioned. Mohl and Gneist are, on one hand, still considered as representatives of the so-called "Policey-Wissenschaft," that is, they are concerned with identifying the reasons for the existence of the state under the rule of law. On the other hand, Mohl and Gneist deal with a separation between constitutional law and administrative law, whereas von Stein still holds the theory of a comprehensive government and administrative science. His construction of the state still follows Hegel, but differentiates for function and organization. The impulse for the development of a new administration theory, however, mainly came from Max Weber.

In administrative law science and nearly simultaneous with Max Weber, according to Otto Mayer (1846–1924) (cf. Mayer 1895), the final separation of administrative function from the other governmental functions took place. This was only achieved by Hans Peters (1896–1966), whose interests centered around the division of the governmental functions, the governmental targets, and the pertinent realization, as well as the application, of law.

Finally, Werner Thieme is worth mentioning. In his standard work *Verwaltungslehre* (Administration Theory), he pretends to solve the "dogmatically open question," whether the government is part of the object of the administrative science in that he describes the functions "politics," "governing," and "planning." The more recent German science of administration scholars recognized problems with mixing governmental and administrative functions. Beginning with Fritz Morstein Marx and Niklas Luhmann, they start, on one hand, to adapt to American Public Administration Theory and, on the other hand, mainly influenced by Thomas Ellwein (1977), devote themselves to a political-scientific-historical approach to public administration.

An important factor for ensuring the continuity of the bureaucratic system was and has been the training of the junior administration staff. In the civil service of the Federal Republic of Germany, both in the federal administration and in the administrations of the federal states, cities, and communes, there are three groups of persons that must be differentiated: civil servants, employees, and workers. The basic difference between civil servants and employees is that civil servants are engaged for a specific career (Laufbahn) and shall be universally usable, whereas employees are engaged for a specific activity and must each apply or qualify for a different or higher ranking position. However, in comparable positions, the payment of civil servants and the remuneration of employees is practically identical.

Continuing with the group of civil servants, traditionally, the jurists represent the majority of civil servants in the senior service. Their share should range around 60 percent. Particularly in the larger cities, the positions of the senior service are, however, to an increasing extent staffed with promoted civil servants from the clerical service (Aufstiegsbeamte) that only graduated from a college. In the federal government administration, however, as well as in

the federal state administration, the permeability among individual career levels must be rated as very limited. In the senior service, the requirement for the study of law with a "Second State Examination" (Zweite Staatsprüfung), following a two- or three-year preparatory service (Referendariat), guarantees standardized working method throughout the Federal Republic and the socialization of this professional group. As jurists may generally be regarded as supporters of the state and not inclined to change, this kind of professionalization and standardization of the public service has been maintained since approximately the middle of the past century. To an increasing extent, however, criticism is heard that jurists are not sufficiently prepared for economic administrative acting, but, naturally, are there mainly to ensure the lawfulness of the administration. Additionally, it is criticized that the study of law prepares for an activity in the public administration only in a very restricted way, as it is the general basis for the profession of judge, state attorney, freelancing lawyer, and industrial lawyers.

Special preparations for activity in the public administration has, on the other hand, been provided by training the clerical general administration service in the administration colleges that were established in the 1970s. Beyond the borders of the federal states, comparable curricula ensure a largely uniform administrative training, distinguished especially by strict organization and a permanent change of theory and practice. Accordingly, the graduates of these institutions are generally esteemed in the administrations of the federal government, the federal states, the cities, and the communes—they are the backbone of the administration. Because starting salaries are typically very low not only in the clerical but also in the senior service as compared to those earned in private companies, the administration colleges have, especially in times of economic boom, some problems recruiting a sufficient number of qualified students. Payments in the public service increases every two years depending on the age, but not on the performance. New employees in the civil service are therefore worse off compared to the salary level received by new employee in private companies. A German secretary just reaches the salary level of a manager of a medium-size company.

Despite the common Prussian clamp, despite the structure of administration on principle divided into three stages throughout Germany, despite a rather uniform training regime for the administration service, and despite a rather uniform public service and budget law, naturally differences in the development of the eleven Western (and now five Eastern) federal states cannot be kept out. Though there are excellent presentations on the law and on the administration of individual federal states (Ipsen 1955, Rebe 1986), a systematic comparison of the different administrative traditions is still missing. On one hand, this fact is certainly due to the expected difficulties involved in possible empirical investigations. On the other hand, the political significance of the states seems to have decreased in the course of the German and the European unification process, so that no requirement is seen for providing a comparing analysis.

Still, within the scope of administrative aid for the new federal states, the different administrative traditions of individual states have become evident. Looking at today's structures and sequences in Saxony, Baden-Württemberg, and Bavaria traditions can be recognized that even extend to the adoption of a major part of the federal legislation. This applies analogously to the states of Thuringia, Saxony-Anhalt, Brandenburg, and Mecklenburg-Pomerania. During the building up of the administration in Thuringia, mainly the states of Hesse and Rhineland-Pallantinum stood sponsor, Saxony-Anhalt was coached by Lower Saxony, Brandenburg by North Rhine–Westphalia, and Mecklenburg-Pomerania mainly by Schleswig-Holstein. A change is in so far noticeable that the new states of Saxony and Thuringia were faced with South German administrative traditions, whereas Mecklenburg-Pomerania and Saxony-Anhalt have continued the North German traditions. A special course has been followed by Brandenburg, where in fact the essential laws were adopted from North Rhine–Westphalia, but the administrative buildup differs in decisive points from the one in North Rhine–Westphalia.

As indicated previously, it is quite difficult to describe the different administrative traditions in detail. Therefore, at best different traditions can be concluded from the differences in their legal provisions. In the new federal states, for example, the organization of the police or the design of the communal constitution follows (apart from some particularities, mainly in Brandenburg), very closely the structures of the respective partner states. Also the value approach of the civil servants seems to be very different, such that civil servants in the north seem to orient themselves more strictly on the ideal type of the bureaucrat and Prussian civil servants, whereas in the south, quite early, the helpful functions of pragmatism and networks were discovered, which sometimes cannot be unaffected by nepotism. Particularly in Barden-Württemberg, different historical documents point to an early beginning and a non-Prussian system of negotiation (Boelcke 1992).

A striking feature of the GDR was, in personnel respect, the substantial lacking of special training for the administrative service. Also, the jurists played a much minor part than in Western Germany. Government was less oriented by law, but rather by the politically-ideological reliability of civil servants. This resulted in a substantially lower demand in jurists. Moreover, in colloquial usage, the term "administration" was mainly replaced by the term "executive-instructing activity" (vollziehend-verfügende Tätigkeit) in order to deny any resemblance with the capi-

talist system. Largely, a finely differentiated administrative and law protection system was avoided for ideological reasons. Decisive for the evaluation of administrative tradition is, however, that one could not speak of the administration in the GDR as also masked as "executive-instructing activity." Instead of the principle of the separation of powers, the principle of the unity of powers applied. Legislation, jurisdiction, and administration merely represented different units of a common and centrally controlled governmental apparatus, which included also the towns and communes.

It might be interesting to notice that from an administratively-technical viewpoint the control span, that is, the proportion of the subordinate administrative units to be governed and controlled by a head unit, was much bigger in the governmental apparatus of the GDR than in the Federal Republic of today. The GDR was divided into 14 districts, 27 city districts, and 191 counties; 209 cities comprised over 10,000 inhabitants, 6,578 communes had less than 2,000 inhabitants, and 761 communes had between 2,000 and 10,000 inhabitants (*Statistical Yearbook* 1989). In addition, there was the capital Berlin (East). On an average, each district had 16 city districts and counties, each county, in turn, comprising 39 county-dependent towns and communes. Compared to this, in the West of the Federal Republic of today, the control span was drastically reduced in the course of the 1970s by rather rigid district and communal territorial reforms—such that number of counties decreased from 425 to 237, and the number of county-independent towns dropped from 135 to 87. At the time of the entry of the GDR in the scope of application of the basic law, one county in the West comprised 35 communes on an average. This considerable reduction of the control span as compared to before and the involved enlargement of the administrative units served the target of establishing a more effective administration that should better meet the increased scope of tasks and the increased requirements of the citizens the administration. However, the reduction did not result in cost savings, and these had not been intended.

A comparison of the communal structure of the GDR with the former FRG reveals that the "old" Federal Republic comprised 4,646 communes with less than 2,000 inhabitants, 2,713 communes with a population ranging between 2,000 and 10,000 inhabitants, and 1,078 cities and communes with more than 10,000 inhabitants. It should be noted that the population of the old Federal Republic was more than three times as much as the population of the GDR. Consequently the districts of the GDR were considerably smaller as compared to the states of the FRG and had substantially fewer city districts and counties to supervise. However, the substantially smaller counties of the GDR as compared to the FRG comprised approximately the same number communes. These, however, were much smaller. It is quite evident that such strong and, above all, independent units like the West German states were incompatible with the political system of the GDR. This is why in 1952 the states previously included in the territory of the former GDR were dissolved and replaced by the substantially weaker and thus easier to control districts.

It is by far more difficult to determine which traditions from the past of the GDR have outlasted than it is to identify the structural changes. Certainly, administrative cadres socialized in the GDR system could not and did not want to conclude their past by the stroke of a pen. Administratively technical innovations, which would have been worth saving over into the Federal Republic, seem not to have existed. The models applying in the GDR would not have brought about a lot of positive changes in the politically administrative scenery of the Federal Republic of Germany. At best, some few tasks, of the state and the administration, the right to work, the guarantee of social security, and others might have endured into the new Germany.

The phrase by the jurist Otto Mayer "Constitutional law passes, whereas administrative law will endure" is well-known in Germany. This interpretation has more and more given way to the interpretation of administrative law as "Concretised constitutional law" (Werner Weber). It was just as well that this did happen, as the administration, if it does not want to withdraw from its democratic legitimation, must receive its basic orientation from the Constitution. In the Federal Republic of Germany the basic law provides that the "executive force," that is, the governments and the administrations, are bound to law and right (Art. 20 sec. 3). This is called the principle of the state under the rule of law (Rechtsstaatsprinzip). In the states, the constitutional order must conform with the principles of the republican, democratic, and social state under the rule of law (Art. 28 sec. 1).

As we know, these principles did not apply to all parts of the country and not all times, so that, in this respect, we cannot speak of a uniform administrative tradition. Especially in the Third Reich, but also in the transitional phase from the empire into the Weimar Republic, the administration was often reproached as being at the beck and call of the respective rulers. This criticism can be explained by the proverbially neutral and unpolitical part of the German civil servants. This has today given way to a far-reaching politicization of the administration business, especially on the communal level and in the ministerial administrations of the states. The influence of the parties extends today as far as to the factual and personnel decisions of relatively minor significance. The criteria for the selection of civil servants, qualification, performance, and aptitude, have frequently in an impermissible way been put into the background against the qualification feature of the membership in a certain party. The incorruptibility of civil ser-

vants has been more and more called into question. This is why in Germany a break has taken place with the Prussian administrative tradition that is rooted in all regions of Germany.

From an organizational viewpoint, with the growth of its tasks, the administration has differentiated (Becker 1989) more and more, both in horizontal and in vertical direction. The public administration was in the tradition of the "liberal watchman state" until 1871, but the administration took over more and more tasks, parallel to the technical progress establishing corresponding authorities, as in the examples of the patent administration or the railway and post administration on central empire level toward the end of the past century prove. To the traditional governmental tasks of sovereign action, more and more tasks of the performance administration or the granting administrations were added; in particular, the social administration or the promotion and supervision of private enterprises.

With respect to reforms, naturally, apart from the tasks and the sequences, the outer and inner structures of public administration are being disputed—especially, an exchange of the hierarchically bureaucratic structure for a more flexible and more effective organizational forms is demanded. The hope for improvement is justified throughout: The federal system and the guarantee of the local self-administration insure a minimum of decentralization. The obligation of the administration as provided by the legislature is to act, not only legally but also economically; it does not exclude a stronger economic modernization, at least not a priori. In this connection a permanent point of controversy was and still is the part of the intermediate authorities, that is, mainly the governmental districts established in some states between the central administration and the administration of counties and communes. This organizational structure follows the former Prussian governmental organization, which comprised ten provinces, comparable with the states today. These were subdivided into 25 districts in total, which were administered by the heads of the district governments as representatives of the government on a regional level. Like today, the head of a district government (Regierungspräsident) fulfilled mainly supervisory functions and, at least at the beginning, relatively modest first-instance tasks which, however, were then extended.

The justification of an intermediate body, e.g., like the head of the district government, mainly results from the tasks and competencies allocated to him. At times of growing governmental tasks and of a growing differentiation of the governmental organization he certainly was entrusted with undoubtedly necessary functions. On one hand, he was the authority for bundling the special administrations; on the other hand, he was the opposition authority in preliminary proceedings of the administrative courts. In our times that are conceivably under the banner of a "lean administration," the part of the district government seems to be increasingly questionable. In addition, the administrative expertise of the county and communal administrations has increased as a result of the improved training of the civil servants, which coincides with the establishment of larger administrative units in the course of regional reforms. Considering, finally, also the modern technical possibilities of data transmission within seconds, the district government becomes more and more an anachronistic fossil from the Stone Ages of the administration.

The growth of the tasks of the public administration seems to have come to a halt since the public administration in the Federal Republic of Germany has been faced with a massive pressure to save money. For this reason, in nearly all federal states, more or less marked administrative reforms are implemented. These range from traditional reform actions in the organizational field to the introduction of a new public management. Certainly, these administrative reforms are not new. From the beginning, they have more or less accompanied the development of the public administration. Here, the civil service law and the public budget have proved to be particularly stable. As both differ in a decisive way from the labor law and from commercial accounting, once again the function of the law for the administration becomes evident. If the elimination of this decisive difference between public administrations and private companies fails, a stronger economic modernization of the public administration will not be possible in the foreseeable future (see Miller 1994).

MANFRED MILLER

BIBLIOGRAPHY

Becker, Bernd, 1989. *Öffentliche Verwaltung. Lehrbuch fur Wissenschaft und Praxis.* Percha: R. S. Schulz.
Boelcke, Willi A., 1992. *Glück für das Land. Die Erfolgsgeschichte der Wirtschaftsförderung von Steinbeis bis heute.* Stuttgart: Deutsche Verlags-Anstalt. *Brockhaus Lexikon,* 1973. Stuttgart: Verlag Das Beste.
Ellwein, Thomas, 1977. *Das Regierungssystem der Bundesrepublik Deutschland.* 4th ed., Opladen: Westdeutscher Verlag. Latest edition, Hesse, Jens Joachim/Ellwein, Thomas, 1992. *Das Regierungssystem der Bundesrepublik Deutschland.* 7th ed., Opladen: Westdeutscher Verlag.
Hegel, Georg Wilhelm Friedrich, 1821. *Grundlinien der Philosophie des Rechts oder Naturrecht und Staatswissenschaft im grundriß;* latest edition: 1981 Berlin: Akademie-Verlag.
Ipsen, Hans P., 1955. *Hamburgs Verfassungs–und Verwaltungsrecht.* Hamburg: Appel.
Jeserich, Kurt G. A., Guenter Pohl, Georg Christian von Unruh, eds., 1983–1987. *Deutsche Verwaltungsgeschichte,* vol. 1–5. Stuttgart: Deutsche Verlagsanstalt.
König, Klaus, 1992. "Zur Transformation einer real-sozialistichen Verwaltung in eine klassisch-europäische Verwaltung." *Ver waltungsarchiv,* vol. 83: 229–245.
Marx, Karl, 1843. *Kritik des Hegelschen Staatsrechts.* This work was first published as late as in 1927. Latest edition, 1973. Stuttgart: Reclam.
Mayer, Otto, 1895. *Deutsches Verwaltungsrecht.* Leipzig: Duncker & Humblot.
Miller, Manfred, 1986. "Politikverflechtung als Organizationsprinzip. Die Bundesrepublik Deutschland und Frankreich auf dem Weg zum 'dezentralisierten Einheitsstaat'?" *Die öffentliche Verwaltung,* 4: 140–148.
Miller, Manfred, 1994. Anmerkungen zur betriebswirtschaftlichen Modernisierung der Verwaltung. *Deutsche Verwaltungspraxis,* 278–289.
Rebe, Bernd *et al.,* 1986. *Verfassung und Verwaltung des Landes Niedersachsen.* Göttingen: Schwartz.
Reichard, Christoph, and Eckhard Schröter, 1993. "Berliner Verwaltungseliten. Rollenverhalten und Einstellungen von Führungskräften in der (Ost- und West-) Berliner Verwaltung." In Wolfgang Seibel, Arthur Benz, Heinrich Mäding, eds., *Verwaltungsreform und Verwaltungspolitik im Prozeß der deutschen Einigung.* Baden-Baden: Nomos, 207–217.
Staatliche Zentralverwaltung für Statistik, 1989. *Statistisches Jahrbuch 1989,* Berlin: Staatsverlag der DDR.

GIFTS.

Money or property transferred irrevocably to a nonprofit organization without compensation. The *Glossary of Fund-Raising Terms,* published by the National Society of Fund Raising Executives Institute, defines a gift as "a voluntary, irrevocable transfer of something of value without consideration at the time of transfer or at any future time. If the individual making the gift entertains any ideas of reclaiming it, the transfer is not a gift."

Effectively, gifts become gifts when the donor gives up control of the asset constituting the gift in favor of the recipient organization. Thus, usually, gifts of cash or securities become effective when mailed, with all instructions and conveyances signed and executed.

Gifts may come in many forms. Examples of common gifts to charity are cash or checks; securities; trusts, annuities, and life estates established irrevocably in favor of nonprofit organizations; real estate; gifts in-kind, such as computers, equipment, and so on; works of art; bargain sales (donor receives something that is of a lesser value than the property transferred to the nonprofit); gifts of income—the donor relinquishes the right to income from property in favor of the nonprofit, as in a lead trust; planned gift—a transfer legally provided for during the donor's lifetime but whose principal benefits do not accrue to the organization until some future time, generally at the death of the donor or the income beneficiary; unrestricted gifts—gifts not directed as to use; and, finally, restricted gifts—gifts whose use is directed by donor stipulation or binding agreement of acceptance.

ROBERT W. BUCHANAN AND
WILLIAM BERGOSH

GILBRETH, FRANK BUNKER (1868–1924) AND LILLIAN EVELYN MOLLER GILBRETH

(1878–1972). Industrial engineers who were among the first in the scientific management field and the first to conduct time-and-motion studies. They were contemporaries of Henry L. Gantt and Frederick Taylor. The Gilbreths' most significant contribution to the field of scientific management was the development of time-and-motion studies, by which they devised methods to identify wasteful and unproductive movements. As early pioneers of time-and-motion studies they shared the common goal of simplifying operations or making them physically easier. Operations were eliminated, fatigue was lessened, and the combination of these factors reduced the amount of time required to accomplish a task.

The Gilbreths incorporated the use of the motion picture camera to record and analyze human motions. Frank Gilbreth coined the term "therblig" (Gilbreth spelled backward) to classify an element of human movement. From this work grew the laws of motion economy and the techniques of projecting performance times. Time studies provided a factual method for recording the time elapsed when performing various industrial functions. Repetitive readings of different operators, shifts, and work methods enabled the Gilbreths to analyze variables that adversely affected work efficiency and to make recommendations for increased productivity. The use of the motion picture camera allowed the Gilbreths repeatedly to study individual movements with relatively little effort. The factual information obtained from the time-and-motion studies allowed for an evaluation of what actually happened, in contrast to what was planned and assumed to have happened.

Lillian and Frank Gilbreths' passion for efficiency and economy of motion carried over to their personal lives. As the parents of twelve children, they were immortalized in the 1948 classic *Cheaper by the Dozen*. The book was written by two of their twelve children and was made into a movie in 1950; it chronicled the adventures of the familial application of scientific management techniques.

Frank Bunker Gilbreth

Frank Gilbreth, an American engineer and building contractor, attained national and international recognition as a scientific management expert. He was among the first to conduct experiments in motion study. His practical experience as a bricklayer and building contractor prompted his interest and experiments in time-and-motion studies. As a young mason he discovered that bricklaying was considered an art rather than a science. Each bricklayer possessed his own style. For the most part, they were unproductive because they lacked a systematic approach to their craft. Gilbreth recognized the necessary skills for bricklaying, but believed that the craft was more a science than an art.

In his books *Field System* (1908) and *Concrete System* (1908), Gilbreth described the lines of authority and responsibility of the different jobs within his own business. His emphasis was on human effort, and Gilbreth believed that there existed one correct way to perform specific functions—one best way to do the work–provided that certain external factors were similar. Gilbreth studied the movement of bricklayers to identify wasteful and unproductive actions. He simplified the motions used in bricklaying, reducing their number from 18 to 5, and increasing the number of bricks laid per hour from 175 to 350. One of his recommendations, the use of scaffolding to hold the bricks and mortar at arm's reach, eliminated wasteful and tiring movements. Prior to his suggestion, bricklayers constantly bent over to pick up bricks and mortar.

The resulting gains in productivity that Gilbreth identified through the study of human motions complemented productivity improvements gained through modifications of the external environment, as identified by Frederick Taylor. Although Taylor focused on external factors, such as lighting and tools, Gilbreth emphasized the human capacity of the individual worker. Frank Gilbreth studied individual workers from a social science perspective, identifying ways individuals could broaden their ability and increase their capacity to be productive. His particular contribution was to develop management as a social science, with the human as the center, around which research and experiment revolved. With his wife, Frank Gilbreth coauthored numerous papers on motion study and scientific management.

Lillian Evelyn Moller Gilbreth

Lillian Gilbreth was a psychologist, industrial engineer, and teacher, and was an active collaborator with her husband in his work and writings. In 1916, with her husband, Lillian Gilbreth developed and presented a significant paper to the American Academy of Political and Social Science, on their "Three Position Plan of Promotion." Far ahead of their time, they outlined a procedure for developing personnel through a "man in charge of promotion," who utilized a "master promotion chart" and "individual promotion charts." This procedure called for regular meetings between the individual in charge of promotions and the worker to discuss the employee's progress, career goals, and potential for promotion.

Lillian Gilbreth was an extraordinary woman, achieving worldwide recognition in a male-dominated field at a time when women, for the most part, were relegated to the home. According to a 1944 article in *California Monthly*,

> Lillian Moller Gilbreth is a genius in the art of living. Known throughout the world as an outstanding woman engineer who successfully combined her unique engineering career with a delightful home life centering about

a beloved husband and twelve well assorted children, Dr. Gilbreth amazes one with the breadth of her interests, the sheer quantity of her activities, the dynamic quality of her daily living and her own unassuming simplicity. One feels conclusively that here is a woman whose history bears inspection. (*California Monthly* 1944, p. 20)

As a psychologist and industrial engineer she applied scientific rational principles for handling workers, equipment, and supplies and incorporated psychological methods for motivating the individual. In this way, her efforts were twofold, concerned with (1) identifying how to increase productivity by minimizing wasteful and unproductive movements and (2) determining how to motivate workers to take advantage of new methods and techniques. For example, in 1920, department store managers encountered difficulty in handling saleswomen and customers on the sales floor. These managers discovered that authoritarian approaches were ineffective and called upon Lillian Gilbreth to help them devise nonauthoritarian management approaches. Gilbreth recommended a creative combination of tactics such as motion study, rearrangement of workspace, rationalized schedules for work breaks, worker suggestion boxes, marketing research, demonstrations and other forms of physical and psychological intervention (Graham 1994).

After the death of her husband in 1924, Lillian Gilbreth continued their work for nearly half a century. She served as president of Gilbreth, Inc., specializing in physical working methods and the science of motion study. She became widely known as an international teacher and lecturer. Lillian Gilbreth advised many businesses, industries, and institutions in the United States and abroad. She served on numerous federal, state, and local government committees. In her later years, she focused much of her writing and lectures on increasing the efficiency of physically handicapped women as homemakers. Gilbreth earned thirteen master and doctoral degrees over a period of twenty-five years and was perhaps the foremost U.S. woman industrial engineer.

Gilbreth Principles of Motion Economy

The twenty-two Principles of Motion Economy, developed by the Gilbreths (Heyel 1982, p. 359), form a basis for improving efficiency and reducing fatigue in manual work.

Use of the Human Body
1. The two hands should begin as well as complete their therbligs at the same instant. (A "therblig" is Frank Gilbreth's elementary subdivision of a cycle of motions thought to be common to all work.)
2. The two hands should not be idle at the same instant except during periods of rest.
3. Motions of the arms should be in opposite and symmetrical directions, instead of in the same direction, and should be made simultaneously.
4. Hand motions should be confined to the lowest classification with which it is possible to perform the work satisfactorily.
5. Momentum should be employed to assist the worker wherever possible, and it should be reduced to a minimum if it must be overcome by muscular effort.
6. Continuous curved motions are preferable to straight-line motions involving sudden and sharp changes in direction.
7. Ballistic (rhythmic) movements are faster, easier, and more accurate than restricted (fixation) or controlled movements.
8. Rhythm is essential to the smooth and automatic performance of an operation, and the work should be arranged to permit easy and natural rhythm wherever possible.

Arrangement of the Workplace
9. Definite and fixed stations should be provided for all tools and materials.
10. Tools, materials, and controls should be located around the work place and as close to the point of assembly or use as possible.
11. Gravity feed bins and containers should be used to deliver the materials as close to the point of assembly or use as possible.
12. Drop deliveries should be used wherever possible.
13. Materials and tools should be located to permit the best sequence of therbligs.
14. Provisions should be made for adequate conditions for seeing. Good illumination is the first requirement for satisfactory visual perception.
15. The height of the workplace and the chair should preferably be so arranged that alternate sitting and standing at work are easily possible.
16. A chair of the type and height to permit good posture should be provided for every worker.

Design of Tools and Equipment
17. The hands should be relieved of all work that can be performed more advantageously by the feet or other parts of the body.
18. Two or more tools should be combined wherever possible.
19. Tools and materials should be prepositioned wherever possible.
20. Where each finger performs some specific movement, such as in typewriting, the load should be distributed in accordance with the inherent capacities of the fingers.

21. Handles such as those used on cranks and large screwdrivers should be designed to permit as much of the surface of the hand to come in contact with the handle as possible. This is particularly true when considerable force is exerted to use the handle. For light assembly work, the screwdriver handle should be so shaped that it is smaller at the bottom than at the top.

22. Levers, crossbars, and handwheels should be located in such positions that the operator can manipulate them with the least change in body position and with the greatest mechanical advantage.

KATHE CALLAHAN

BIBLIOGRAPHY

Works by the Gilbreths

Gilbreth. Frank B., 1908. *Concrete System*. New York: Engineering News Publishing.
———, 1908. *Field System*. New York: Myron C. Clark.
———, 1908. *Concrete System*. New York: Engineering News Publishing Co.
———, 1909. *Brick Laying System*. New York: Myron C. Clark.
———, 1911. *Motion Study*. New York: D. Van Nostrand.
Gilbreth, Frank B., and Lillian E. M. Gilbreth, 1912. *Primer of Scientific Management*. New York: D. Van Nostrand.
———, 1916. *Fatigue Study*. New York: Sturgis and Walton.
———, 1917. *Applied Motion Study*. New York: Sturgis and Walton.
———, 1920. *Motion Study for the Handicapped*. New York: Macmillan.
Gilbreth, Lillian E. M., 1912. *Psychology of Management*. New York: Macmillan.
Gilbreth, Lillian E. M., and Edna Yost, 1928. *Living with Our Children*. New York: Norton.
Gilbreth, Lillian E. M., and Alice Rice Cook, 1947. *The Foreman and Manpower Management*. New York: McGraw-Hill.
Gilbreth, Lillian E. M., O. M. Thomas, and Eleanor C. Clymer, 1954. *Management in the Home*. New York: Dodd.

Works About Lillian Gilbreth

California Monthly, 1994. "Lillian Moller Gilbreth: A Profile." (June): 20–21.
Graham, Laurel D., 1994. "Critical Biography Without Subjects and Objects: An Encounter with Dr. Lillian Moller Gilbreth." *Sociological Quarterly*, vol. 35, no. 4: 621–643.

Other Related Works

Heyel, Carl, ed., 1982. *The Encyclopedia of Management*. New York: Van Nostrand Reinhold.

GLASS CEILING. A term used to describe subtle (almost invisible) barriers that women and minorities face as they try to move up the career ladder in organizations. The term was popularized in the 1980s and applied to women. Later, it was acknowledged that minorities also may face elusive barriers in advancement as well. Often it is said that a glass ceiling exists when women and minorities can see the top of a career ladder, but bump their heads against an invisible obstacle when they try to climb it.

Overt discrimination in employment against women and minorities has been unlawful in the United States since the passage of the Civil Rights Act of 1964, and in the past three decades women and minorities have made significant strides in gaining employment in both the private and public sectors (see **discrimination, gender** and **discrimination, racial**). However, these gains have largely been in entry-level positions and nonminority men continue to hold the vast majority of top level jobs. For example, in its report on the Glass Ceiling Initiative released in 1991, the Department of Labor (DOL) noted that in 94 Fortune 1,000–sized companies it reviewed, women held 37 percent and minorities held nearly 16 percent of jobs. However, in these same companies, less than 7 percent of executives were women and less than 3 percent were minorities. In the federal civil service, 47 percent of jobs are held by woman and 27 percent by minorities. But less than 12 percent of senior executives are women and less than 8 percent are minorities. Similar patterns can be found in most state and local governments, where nonminority men are nearly two-thirds of "officials and administrators."

It is the combination of these two factors—the elimination of most forms of overt discrimination and the increased representation of women and minorities in lower-level jobs—that has focused attention on the glass ceiling. If most overt discrimination has been eliminated, but women and minorities do not enjoy the same opportunities for advancement as equally qualified nonminority men, the assumption is that there are more subtle barriers that are standing in their way. These barriers may not take the form of discriminatory practices that can be addressed through litigation, but are a powerful force nonetheless.

Identifying the Barriers

Because, by definition, the glass ceiling is invisible, it is not always easy to identify. However, research has been able to identify some aspects of organizational culture, attitudes, and stereotypes that have the effect of deterring the vertical progress of women and minorities.

For example, in its analysis of the glass ceiling as it affects women in federal employment, the U.S. Merit Systems Protection Board (MSPB) found that there is a common expectation in government agencies that those who are committed to their careers and serious about advancement must be willing and able to work long hours. This informal criteria for advancement works against women in two ways. First, as women still bear primary responsibility for child rearing, those who have children are often unable to work late into the evening. Even those women who are able to work late are presumed to need to leave at a specific time, and so they are often passed over for significant career-enhancing assignments and promotions. Even though women express the same level of commitment to their jobs as men and receive, on average, higher performance appraisals than men, their potential for advancement is frequently underestimated by managers using these traditional kinds of criteria to evaluate advancement potential. This is an example of what comprises a glass ceiling–a promotion requirement that seems to be gender-neutral, but has an adverse impact on women.

Similarly, women and minorities often confront stereotypes that cast doubt on their competence. For example, a task force studying the glass ceiling in the Canadian public service noted that there is a basic belief that women are better suited to support positions than supervisory or management positions. Another common belief is that women work only because they want to and not because they need to support their families. Women are, therefore, not given the same opportunities for developmental assignments that enhance their promotability. DOL found in its private sector review that minorities are also often steered into staff positions such as human resources, research, or administration, where they do not gain the experience necessary to make them competitive for executive positions.

Women and minorities are also disadvantaged by their "token" status in organizations. As Rosabeth Moss Kanter noted in her now classic work *Men and Women of the Corporation* (1977) when women and minorities are proportionally scarce in an organization or at a particular level, they become highly visible and are much more likely to be stereotyped. Any mistakes they make are immediately noticed, and these mistakes often serve as representatives of their category. For example, once a minority does not meet the expectations for a particular job, it is sometimes assumed that no minority will be suitable for that particular job.

Related Structural Metaphors

These are examples of the kinds of dynamics that operate in very subtle ways to thwart the advancement of women and minorities in organizations. Recently, other metaphors have joined the glass ceiling in describing barriers to the full participation of women and minorities in the workplace. "Glass walls" have come to describe occupational segregation, which results in the propensity for women and

minorities to be more heavily concentrated in particular kinds of jobs, usually ones that enjoy little power or prestige. The fact that women are often stuck in jobs that are at such a low level that they cannot imagine even bumping into a glass ceiling (e.g., para-professional, administrative support, or service and maintenance jobs), has been called a "sticky floor."

KATHERINE C. NAFF

BIBLIOGRAPHY

Kanter, Rosabeth Moss, 1977. *Men and Women of the Corporation.* New York: Basic Books.
Task Force on Barriers to Women in the Public Service, 1990. *Beneath the Veneer: The Report of the Task Force on Barriers to Women in the Public Service.* Ottawa: Canadian Government Publishing Centre.
U.S. Department of Labor, 1991. *A Report on the Glass Ceiling Initiative.* Washington, DC: U.S. Department of Labor.
U.S. Merit Systems Protection Board, 1992. *A Question of Equity: Women and the Glass Ceiling in the Federal Government.* Washington, DC: U.S. Merit Systems Protection Board.

GLASSCO COMMISSION. The Royal Commission on Government Organisation appointed by the Canadian government in 1960. It reported in 1962 and 1963.

The Commission's chairman, J. Grant Glassco, was a leading member of the Canadian business establishment, and many of the commission's recommendations were seen as private sector answers to public sector problems. They were summed up by the press and academic commentators in the slogan "Let the managers manage."

The problems that led to the commission's appointment was a perceived inefficiency in the conduct of public business. The Canadian civil service had been, since 1919, one of the world's outstanding examples of a service in which positions were minutely classified according to scientific management principles. Lack of flexibility and inability to adapt promptly to changing needs were widely alleged against the Ottawa bureaucracy and its guardian, the Civil Service Commission (CSC).

A principal aim of the Glassco Commission's recommendations was to transfer major parts of the personnel management function out of the hands of the Civil Service Commission and into those of the heads of departments (called deputy ministers in Canada, at that time). Other CSC powers, notably the setting of civil servants' pay and the classification of their positions, were to be transferred to the Treasury Board, an administrative unit that had already become the leading power center of the bureaucracy and that, if Glassco's aims were to be achieved, would become the supreme central coordinating agency.

Having been appointed by the John G. Diefenbaker (Progressive Conservative) government, the commissioners and their extensive staffs had to face the not-uncommon fate of such bodies in that they report to a quite different government, in this case the Lester B. Pearson (Liberal) government, elected in 1962. Some of their recommendations, particularly those concerned with personnel issues and industrial relations in the public sector, were overtaken by events because, on the eve of the 1962 election, both major parties were induced by the public service unions to adopt a policy of collective bargaining for civil servants. A further series of inquiries led to the adoption of legislation enacting a collective bargaining regime in 1967, contrary to the advice contained in the Glassco Commission's report.

The Civil Service Commission also staged a moderately successful counterattack against recommendations that would have trimmed its powers. It persuaded the government that rather than having its control over selection and promotion transferred to the heads of departments, these functions should remain legally vested in the CSC but should be delegated to departments under guidelines set by the CSC. But delegation implies the possibility that it may be revoked; the CSC (by this time renamed the Public Service Commission to reflect a broader jurisdiction covering statutory authorities and government agencies other than departments) thus retained a vital role as a central personnel agency and guardian of the merit principle.

If the Glassco Commission missed one of its main targets, it had more success in hitting others. For example, it opened a long-suppressed debate over the future role of the French language in Canadian government operations. English had been the language of official business, its dominance defended on the grounds that to use more than one language would be costly and inefficient. The Glassco Commission, however, challenged the linking of efficiency with unilingualism. It held that "valid arguments have been advanced that the public service should be representative of the country as a whole." It therefore recommended that the federal government recruit, retain, and promote to senior positions more French Canadians and that the bilingual capacity of the public service should be developed. It was left to a later body, the Royal Commission on Bilingualism and Biculturalism, and to the Official Languages Act of 1969, which embodied some of its recommendations, to make headway toward bilingualism in Canadian public sector management.

Another qualified success of the Glassco Commission was the promotion of program budgeting. The early forms of this technique were too complex, leading to much frustration and to the abandonment of the more formal aspects of the process. However, to the Glassco Commission must go some of the credit for the Canadian federal government's perseverance with program-related financial and managerial reforms, including forward estimates; planning and budgeting for outputs and outcomes, not inputs alone; and, more generally, corporate planning and management by objectives.

Finally, partly due to the Glassco Commission's support of its mission and approach, the Treasury Board Secretariat, now detached from the Department of Finance and established as a separate agency, did become, or was confirmed as, the pivot of federal government administration. Only later, in the Pierre Trudeau years, was its power to be rivaled, or occasionally surpassed, by that of the Privy Council Office. By then the political agenda had changed, and efficiency in public sector management had been supplanted by constitutional, economic, and other issues. The next two inquiries into public service matters, the Lambert Commission and the D'Avignon Committee of 1979, focused on accountability in financial management and personnel management and the merit principle, respectively. Both paid tribute to the Glassco Commission, but by that time its influence had diminished. Nevertheless, its report remains a great landmark in Canadian public administration.

DAVID C. CORBETT

BIBLIOGRAPHY

Canada. Royal Commission on Government Organisation, 1962. *Report.* (The Glassco Commission, report in 5 vols.) Ottawa: Canadian Government Printer.
———, Royal Commission on Financial Management and Accountability, 1979. *Final Report.* (The Lambert Commission.) Ottawa: Canadian Government Publishing Centre.
———, Special Committee on the Review of Personnel Management and the Merit Principle, 1979. *Report.* (The D'Avignon Committee.) Ottawa: Canadian Government Publishing Centre.
Hodgetts, J. E., W. McCloskey, R. Whitaker, and V. S. Wilson, 1972. *The Biography of an Institution: The Civil Service Commission of Canada, 1908–1967.* Montreal: McGill-Queen's University Press.
Hodgetts, J. E., 1973. *The Canadian Public Service.* Toronto: University of Toronto Press.
———, 1963. "The Grand Inquest on the Canadian Public Service." *Public Administration* (Australia), vol. 22, no. 3: 226–241.
McLeod, T. H., 1963. "Glassco Commission Report." Reprinted in *Canadian Public Administration: The Twentieth Anniversary Issue.* 1978: 92–108.

GLOBAL INTERDEPENDENCE.

The existence of direct and indirect interconnections that link all of the states of the modern world, to one degree or another, economically, politically, and environmentally; as a result, new local, national, and international policies and managerial strategies are needed to improve the quality of life and achieve sustainable economic growth. In the past several decades, public policy makers and administrators have faced an increasingly globalized, interconnected environment. Global, regional, and local interdependencies have greatly increased and are connecting the political and economic fortunes of city, county, state, provincial, and national governments more closely than ever before. As a result, the major challenge facing those in public service—elected officials, public administrators, executives in state-owned enterprises, and nonprofit executives—is how to define successfully and pursue the public interest in a globally interdependent world.

The shrinking world, tied closer and closer together by global interdependencies—between the economy, the polity, and the biosphere—is one of the most important macotrends of the late twentieth century. Economic interdependence was the first to be noticed; global economic interconnections, however, have now become intertwined with, connected to, and influenced by environmental, social, and political interdependencies.

Interdependence and Interconnectedness

Since the 1970s, global interdependencies have been generally defined as interactions characterized by reciprocal effects among policy actors—nation-states, institutions, or individuals. It is essentially a situation of "mutual dependence" where actions of one actor both impacts and is constrained by actions of another (Keohane and Nye 1977; Rosenau 1980; Scott 1982). These interactions can be further distinguished: *interdependencies* are high-cost, tightly linked, very important mutual dependencies; whereas loosely linked, low-cost, relatively unimportant mutual dependencies are considered *interconnections*. Metaphorically, interdependence can be characterized as overlapping, tightly connected webs where one's actions impact others and as well are constrained by others. Interconnectedness is a looser net, less tightly bound and reciprocally constraining, but a web nonetheless.

These interconnections and interdependencies did not develop slowly, in a linear fashion, one step at a time. Instead, their emergence is similar to the process of crystallization, of instantaneous networks forming to link historically separate and autonomous nation-states and institutions (Rosenau 1980). Evolutionary biologists call such quick shifts in a species' environment, like that witnessed in the past two decades with global interdependence, an "anagenesis"—a rather sudden, qualitative shift in evolutionary development. As a result, the historical nature of public policy and administration has changed fundamentally at the local, state, national, and global levels, leaving little resemblance to the context for self-governance that has existed during recent history.

The Shrinking World

The evidence of increasing global interdependence is widespread. Intricate network's of interdependencies, first noted in the economy after World War II, have spread to a wide variety of other public policy areas, such as immigration, air transportation, energy conservation, natural resources consumption, environmental degradation, law enforcement (e.g., international drug traffic), and public health (for example, infectious diseases). Four fundamental changes have created a web of overlapping interconnections, reduced separateness, and decreased political autonomy: (1) global communications and information technology; (2) worldwide economic integration; (3) environmental interdependencies in the biosphere; and (4) increased political pluralism.

Countries are now inextricably linked together in such an interlocking web that actions in another country can have both immediate and delayed effects on a nation, it's regions (provinces and states) and, its communities.

Rapid, Worldwide Communications

Significant advances in communications and information technology since the 1970s have bound the world's countries and communities more closely together than ever before in human history. Improvements in transportation technology which followed World War II, and the steady decline in costs of transporting people and goods, were instrumental in reducing geographical distance. However, it was the exponential rate of the development in information technology (satellite and fiber-optic communication networks, fax technology, and reliable computer information highways) that significantly accelerated cross-border and transnational interactions, reducing political and social distances and dramatically shrinking international space.

Distance has been rendered less relevant as the new information infrastructure—the "infostructure"—makes it possible to reach anywhere electronically almost instantaneously and is the new central infrastructure tying together the globe. The combination of electronic telecommunications and computer technologies facilitates the nearly instantaneous transport of complex data and its processing into usable information.

Increasing Global Economic Integration

The most significant impact of the new global infostructure is that it has reduced the effective economic distances among nations, integrating the once-insulated national economies into *one global interdependent market* (Bryant 1994). Over the last several hundred years, the world economies progressed from local to regional markets, from regional to national, and then to international. National economies are no longer insulated; they exist in a global interdependent economy that erodes national economic independence and forces public administrators and private sector executives to think in global terms. The markets for everything important are now global, significantly influencing governmental economic development policy strategies.

Since World War II, industrialized nations have experienced a gradual but steady escalation of economic and resource interdependencies. Successive rounds of the international negotiations through the General Agreement on Tariffs and Trade (GATT) over the last two decades has *reduced at-the-border trade restrictions and barriers* on major commodities and products between most national governments. Lower trade barriers, combined with recent reductions in barriers of capital flow between nations, has increased significantly cross-border economic integration.

The information technology breakthroughs since the 1970s, however, have created an even more tightly knit economic interdependence much beyond the historical existence of cross-border trade dependence. Where once trade of manufactured goods dominated the global economy, now the driving force is financial capital and information. Modern communication technologies now allow for the cost-efficient and rapid movement of complex financial information and data that *accelerates foreign financial investments and capital movement* across national boundaries and fosters the expansion of multinational corporations that globally link branch offices through electronic networks. Financial capital, a form of information, flows across borders and flows globally much faster and more freely than the slower-moving world of production and trading of commodities. Billions of dollars can be moved from one country to another at the touch of a computer key. Business and economic development in a globally interdependent economy is best described as a world market—or a "worldeconomy"—driven by increasingly mobile capital and information, less by slower-moving goods and commodities. The global infostructure has blurred the economic borders of nations, and the boundaries of economic markets now coincide less and less with national governmental jurisdictions (Bryant 1994).

Interdependencies in the Biosphere: Resource Constraints, Environmental Spillovers, and the Global Commons

Resource interdependencies among nations and regions of the globe have been commonplace during the twentieth century. The communication, energy, and transportation technologies facilitated faster economic growth and complex industrialization that stimulated faster extraction and consumption of natural resources. The result is that every government—local, regional, or national—now functions in a situation of *resource scarcity* in one resource or another. Trade between nations is thus heightened due to the export and import of natural resources considered

critical to a country's economic growth. None has enough natural resources to be totally self-sufficient; in a globally interdependent world, self-sufficiency is truly an impossibility.

In addition to the interdependence of the production and consumption of natural resources, there is increasing recognition that there exists an *intricate web of connections among the natural resources* themselves. Two key concepts best capture these environmental interdependencies: The world's "biosphere," the planet's natural life-support systems, is intricately connected in overlapping "ecosystems," and disturbances in one ecosystem affect other related aspects of the biosphere. In fact, there are direct interrelationships between environmental issues and almost every major area of international public policy—food, energy, trade, population, and defense (Caldwell 1990). These interconnections have caused increased political and scientific attention on three broad classes of environmental interdependencies: environmental spillovers, natural resources within a country that have values for a larger international community, and the global commons.

Cross-Border Spillovers

Causing considerable tension are environmental activities in one country that spill across borders and impact other countries. During the 1990s, important environmental issues essentially became international issues because of their significant ecological and biological ripple effects. These regional problems arise when neighboring countries share a common natural resource and one country's actions spill over borders and affect others, such as transboundary pollution and management of international rivers or regional seas. Acid rain is a tangible example, where industrial emission of sulfur dioxide mix in the atmosphere creates toxic rain. At least 50 percent of the acid rain falling in Canada originates in the United States, creating a transborder environmental and economic problem. Acid rain in Europe is linked to the acidification of lakes in Scandinavia and the death of forests in central Europe (World Bank 1992).

This is a common type of policy problem facing public administrators that emerges from global interdependence. First, what may be assumed to be an "internal" or "domestic" issue (e.g., industrial pollution) now becomes a global issue of foreign affairs. Second, nations must engage in cooperative action that often is typified by bargaining and negotiation. By 1991, for example, the United States was a party to 30 multilateral negotiated environmental agreements (GAO 1991) to manage cooperatively such transborder environmental problems. Similarly, individual border states in the United States have developed a wide variety of international agreements and related transborder environmental legislative initiatives.

In-Country Resources with Considerable International Values

There are also resources that clearly belong to one country and yet have significant value to the international community. The clearest example are tropical rainforests and their impact on Earth's oxygen supply. The rainforests of Africa, South America, and Southeast Asia, for example, through large-scale photosynthesis perform a crucial function in removing carbon dioxide from the atmosphere and converting it to oxygen. In addition, the rainforests provide irreplaceable habitats for an estimated 80 percent of the world's species of plants and animals (Tobin 1990).

The Global Commons

The "global commons" are natural and physical resources shared by all countries and people, resources that are potentially used by all, but owned or controlled by none: the oceans, the atmosphere and resulting climate, outer space, and Antarctica. Actions of one country that affect such global commons, have an impact on other countries, even if only small in some instances.

Commons dilemmas occurs when there is an overuse, deterioration, or erosion of the "common-pool" resource's ability to sustain its value use. The depletion of these four global commons resources thus affects all countries to one degree or another and have been the subject of considerable global negotiations to preserve the commons.

The Law of the Sea Treaty was completed in the 1980s, and establishes the deep oceans and their seabeds as the "common heritage of mankind," while simultaneously reserving for individual national control "exclusive economic zones," ocean space extending out 200 miles from the country's shorelines. (Except for a provision regulating the use of seabed minerals, which prevented the U.S. President from signing the treaty, it is regarded as customary international law by federal and state officials.)

Antarctica was established as a global commons in 1959 with the signing of the Antarctic Treaty and was reconfirmed by the original signers in 1991. This treaty restricts scientific exploration and research for nonmilitary purposes and bans commercial minerals exploration for 50 years on this icy continent. The Outer Space Treaty similarly established space as a "common province."

Attempts to manage collaboratively global climate change have been more difficult. The Environmental Modification Treaty of 1977 was established to prevent "hostile" modification of the earth's atmosphere; and the 1987 Montreal Protocol was negotiated and signed by 31 nations to protect the earth's stratospheric ozone layer by collectively reducing the emissions of chlorofluorocarbons (CFCs) by 50 percent by the end of the twentieth century. Global warming, which involves both environmental spillovers and a global commons, continues to be discussed and negotiated by countries and nongovernmental

stakeholders. The "greenhouse effect"–a global "heat trap" caused by the emissions of carbon dioxide, fossil fuel combustion, and deforestation–is forcing national and local governments to assess the validity of global warming and to analyze its potential impacts on their jurisdictions. Nongovernmental interests are increasingly concerned about possible global warming, including, for example, the insurance industry, which has the highest risk potential due to changes in weather patterns, hurricanes, and flooding that result in large insurance losses. Gaining governmental and nongovernmental agreement on effective policies to protect the atmosphere may be the biggest challenge emerging from global interdependence as the twentieth century comes to a close.

Increasing Political Pluralism

Although the world's national economies have become more tightly integrated, the number of nation-states has tripled during the same post World War II era. During this same recent period, there has been an explosion of nongovernmental actors engaging in economic, environmental, and political activities across borders. As a result, this global interdependence has diffused political power broadly among an expanding number of governmental and nongovernmental actors, dramatically increasing political pluralism in world politics. The relative role of the nation-state in international affairs declines as global interdependence increases.

Leakage of Economic Power

The reduction of historical "separation fences" at nations' borders are accelerating a leakage of economic power away from national governments. Economic influence is diffused to international regulators and regional cooperation systems, such as the European Community (EC) and the North American Free Trade Agreement (NAFTA), to international nongovernments (e.g., multinational enterprises and international trade associations) and to subnational authorities and states, for example the Red River Trade Corridor, which joins the U.S. states of North Dakota, Minnesota, and the Canadian province of Manitoba. Where once the world economy was dominated by only a few nations, the globally interdependent economy is characterized by more widely shared economic power and influence among governmental and nongovernmental institutions, which has eroded political sovereignty and diminished the power of the nation-state to control its economy directly (Bryant 1994).

Internationalization of "Domestic Affairs"

Governments and citizens could historically easily distinguish internal "domestic" issues from international or "foreign issues." The erosion of national boundaries due to the economic integration and cross-border environmental spillovers has blurred the boundaries between domestic and international issues. Global interdependence has thus expanded the openness of internal domestic affairs to global events, *increasing the vulnerability to outside forces* that cannot be necessarily anticipated or even seen. International markets, for example, set the price for a nation's or region's staple commodities (grains, energy) and can have drastic effects on local economies around the world.

One poignant case is the city of Troutdale, Oregon, a small northwestern U.S. town whose local economy was seriously weakened when the Soviet Union dissolved. Russia flooded the aluminum market with many of its raw materials, particularly aluminum, in order to generate additional sources of cash income to bolster its new, non-Communist economy. Driven by its aluminum plants, the northwestern town's economy was inextricably tied to global market forces nearly invisible to the town's residents. The aluminum market in the United States responded to the Russian policy strategy by drastically lowering its prices for the raw material and sharply curtailing production, resulting in several aluminum companies closing plants and the lay-off of thousands of workers. This situation had a dramatic local economic impact; several of the region's two aluminum plants closed due to the ripple effects of the break-up of the old Soviet Union, ending its decades-old dependence on the aluminum industry for local family-wage jobs.

Other examples further illustrate the trend of increasing vulnerability. The cross-border movements of people—seasonal labor movement, permanent immigration, as well as international refugees—change the ethnic mix of a nation, and its communities and thus influence the nature of their "domestic politics." Drug trafficking and other forms of international crime can similarly reach deeply into "local" communities and drive local policy priorities and budget allocations.

With global interdependence, *domestic policies are increasingly exposed to international scrutiny,* particularly when the activities of one country had consequences that spill across borders and affect other nations. For example, when one nation pollutes the water or air that other nations drink or breathe, it becomes an environmental matter for international scrutiny. An economic example, is when country A permits manufacturers to emit air and water pollutants but country B does not; companies that use pollution-generating methods of production will find it cheaper to produce in country A. Manufacturers in country B that are required to use more costly pollution-reduction technologies and compete worldwide with the polluting manufacturers in country A are likely to complain and stimulate negotiation to remove the competitive inequities. Nations then either propose that other nations adjust their policies to reduce competitive disadvantages or they press for international pollution standards which "level the playing field" (Bryant 1994). International

scrutiny is thus driven by diversity in nations' policies, which are perceived as politically sensitive or as presenting unacceptable externalities.

In some cases, a nation's internal policies or problems may be significant enough for the international community to constrain the exercise of an individual nation's sovereignties through stronger intervention than merely bargaining and negotiation. International law may be converging on five general principles to guide one nation's actions inside another nation's and may be used to justify stronger interventions by one country or several countries acting together: (1) when genocide and other gross violations of human rights are involved; (2) when a country's central authority loses control or breaks down; (3) when nations need to suppress terrorists, rescue hostages, or pursue drug traffickers; (4) when helping refugees with their repatriation or resettlement; and (5) when coping with catastrophe, whether natural (hurricanes) or due to human error, such as the Chernobyl disaster (Cleveland 1993).

Transnational Politics Replaces "Geopolitics"

The notion of "geopolitics"–that a nation's strength and power depended on its geography, its defensible borders, plentiful natural resources, and its seaports–historically guided actions between nation-states. The influence of countries was often based on the natural resources they had discovered or colonized and developed within their borders. The advances in global telecommunication technologies have reduced the relevance of geographic regionalism. *Geography has been rendered less relevant* as the new information technologies make it possible to reach anywhere electronically almost instantaneously, reducing political and social distances and dramatically shrinking international space. And as the world economy becomes increasingly driven by information and applied knowledge rather than the extraction and development of natural resources, the very nature of "comparative advantage" shifts away from the availability and price of physical resources.

In addition, the *proliferation of nongovernmental actors* and stakeholders engaging in activities across national borders has further diminished the power and influence of "nation-states," thus changing the focus from "international" behavior–behavior among nations–to transnational politics–political behavior between and among nongovernmental actors as well as national governments. Global economic interdependence, for example, heightens the attention public officials must give to private sector constituents. Advocacy groups, professional associations, and business lobbyists alike, once stationed at national capitals, have become more active and sophisticated in communicating their concerns and are turning their attention and energy to international arenas. They, too, are increasing in size and influence, due to the expanding availability of information once guarded by public officials and the increasing capacity to analyze data independently with the use of inexpensive computers. National and international news media are increasingly responsive to them as they become more skillful at working with the media to pursue their causes.

Understanding and Responding to Boundaryless Problems

No human society so interconnected has previously existed; there are no precedents for public administrators to follow. The critical policy problems confronting communities, regions, states, and nations–for example, jobs, environmental quality, and public health–have become so globally interdependent that public administrators need a broadened perspective, a worldview with widened concepts of governance.

Boundaryless Problems

Global interdependence creates a new class of problems. The types of issues facing governments today are global in the scope of their cause and nearly boundaryless in the reach of their effects. Pollution, for example, has no boundaries; wastes and toxic substances can be easily carried far beyond their original sources and across boundaries by air and water currents. Most critical policy problems facing public administrators, particularly those involving economic growth and quality of life, cannot be contained geographically within a particular jurisdiction.

Historical distinctions between what is "global" and what is "local" have blurred, with a considerable number on international issues now crossing national, state, and local government boundaries. The crystallization of global interconnections requires public administrators to *look outward more and inward less*. Actions taken in one part of the state, region, or globe have consequences for other geographical areas. This requires the capability to *assess potential ripple effects* from global events and to *react quickly and flexibly* in light of that analysis. Global interdependence also requires not only foresight but also responsibility. Public administrators now have the responsibility to assess the probability (not necessarily the certainty) of policy choices causing difficulties or damage to other jurisdictions in the "intersocietal web."

In the past, information on impacts may have been inadequate; and complete understanding of the causes and effects of public problems in the interconnected context is limited. Nevertheless, advances in computer technology and mathematical modeling can now provide reliable forecasts on alternative scenarios and interventions, greatly expanding the ability of public administrators to ask "what if" questions, and then to develop effective responses.

Multicultural Learning

The global interdependency demands *heightened understanding of cultures, markets, and languages of other countries*. Public administrators must learn for example, how to discuss exports, deal with foreign officials, and develop understanding of capital markets. *Cross-national comparisons* are increasingly used to evaluate the success of public programs. The United States compares itself to Western European countries in such diverse issue areas as teenage pregnancy, unemployment rates, airborne particulate matter, and literacy rates. The state of Oregon has a policy goal and specific benchmark indicators, for example, to have the best-educated and -trained workforce in the world by the year 2010. Understanding why another country is more effective in reaching certain policy outcomes requires considerable understanding of the country's unique culture, economy, and governance structure.

Not only is a broadened international perspective required, but also increased skills in international communications and foreign languages enable public administrators to observe, think, and act in an interdependent world. In general, we must learn as much from other cultures as they do from us.

Collaborative Approaches

Global interdependencies, by their very nature, require multilateral cooperation and collaborative initiatives across traditional boundaries and jurisdictions. Partnerships, alliances, and various forms of interorganizational strategies are fundamental. Bargaining and negotiation based on common values or common goals can fashion cooperative agreements. With increasing interdependence, however, comes increased potential for conflict and confrontation. Incentives for cooperation and effective conflict management strategies need to be designed that nurture shared stakes in solving particular global issues. Public administrators must also gain the personal skills to further stimulate, nurture, and maintain adequate levels of cooperation beyond one's institutional boundaries.

JEFFREY S. LUKE

BIBLIOGRAPHY

Bryant, R. C., 1994. "Global Change: Increasing Economic Integration and Eroding Political Sovereignty." *The Brookings Review* (Fall).
Caldwell, L. K., 1990. "International Environmental Politics." In Norman Vig and Michael Kraft, eds., *Environmental Policy in the 1990's*. Washington, DC: Congressional Quarterly Press.
Cleveland, H., 1993. *Birth of a New World.* San Francisco and Oxford: Jossey Bass.
Keohane, R., and J. S. Nye, 1977. *Power and Interdependence.* Boston: Little, Brown.
Luke, J. S., 1991. "Managing Interconnectedness: The Challenge of Shared Power." In John Bryson and Robert Einsweiler, eds., *Shared Power,* Lanham, MD: University Press of America.

The International Encyclopedia of Public Policy and Administration

Luke, J. S., and Gerald Caiden, 1989. "Coping With Global Interdependence." In James Perry, ed., *Handbook of Public Administration*. San Francisco and Oxford: Jossey-Bass.

Peach, J. D., 1991. "The International Dimensions of Domestic Programs." *G.A.O. Journal*, Summer/Fall 1991, p. 43–52.

Rosenau, J., 1980. *The Study of Global Interdependencies: Essays in the Transnationalization of World Affairs*. New York: Nicholas.

Scott, A., 1982. *The Dynamics of Interdependence*. Chapel Hill: University of North Carolina Press.

Tobin, R. J., 1990. "Environment, Population, and Development in the Third World." In Vig and Kraft eds., *Environmental Policy in the 1990's*. Washington, DC: Congressional Quarterly Press.

World Bank., 1992. *World Development Report 1992: Development and the Environment*. New York: Oxford University Press.

GOALS AND QUOTAS. In the context of equal opportunity policies, these terms are used to refer to numerical targets established for the employment and other placement of minorities and women. When combined with timetables or schedules for their accomplishment, goals or quotas make up a common and often controversial approach to affirmative action, since their use means that selection procedures have been developed to be racially, ethnically, and gender conscious (see **affirmative action; equal employment opportunity**).

It is often the case that much effort is made to draw a distinction between goals and quotas, and conceptually the two are different. On one hand, goals are usually thought of as objectives an organization seeks to achieve within the context of merit. For example, an organization may plan to hire a specified number of minority applicants provided that sufficiently qualified individuals can be found. Quotas, on the other hand, suggest that employment is restricted to minorities or women or that a specified number of minority group members or women are to be employed, without regard to merit principles.

This conceptual distinction, however, does not necessarily mean that there are dual approaches to numerically based affirmative action in practice. Numerical targets for minority and female employment have been included in affirmative action programs for more that two decades in the United States, but no court or other government organization has required employers to hire or promote individuals regardless of qualifications. Certainly, courts and legislatures have mandated that numerical strategies and preferences for minorities and women be part of the affirmative action process, and many organizations have voluntarily adopted such policies. There may also be sanctions for failure to comply with a court order or failing to meet statutory requirements. The burden on employers, however, is always limited by the availability of qualified applicants. In that sense, quotas have not been applied. Numerical approaches to affirmative action are actually goals.

Nevertheless, the debate over goals and quotas has continued. In general, those who oppose race-, ethnic-, or gender-conscious affirmative action prefer the term "quotas" to describe numerical strategies for the selection of women and minorities. The argument made by those with this point of view is that affirmative action distributes jobs and other valued positions solely on the basis of race, ethnicity, or gender. Proponents of compensatory affirmative action argue that numerical employment targets are more accurately viewed as objectives that an organization attempts to achieve within the context of merit principles. Numerical targets for the selection of minorities or women are set after an organization develops a projection of the number of vacancies or other opportunities expected to be available and estimates the number of minorities or women with the requisite qualifications in the relevant labor pools. The policies serve a remedial purpose of correcting the effects of past or current patterns of discrimination against minorities and women.

J. EDWARD KELLOUGH

BIBLIOGRAPHY

Glazer, Nathan, 1978. *Affirmative Discrimination: Ethnic Inequality and Public Policy*. New York: Basic Books.

Livingston, John C., 1979. *Fair Game? Inequality and Affirmative Action*. San Francisco: W. H. Freeman and Company.

Taylor, Bron Raymond, 1991. *Affirmative Action at Work: Law, Politics, and Ethics*. Pittsburgh: University of Pittsburgh Press.

GOBBLEDYGOOK AND OFFICIALESE. Obscure, verbose, bureaucratic language characterized by circumlocution and jargon. Gobbledygook usually refers to the meaningless officialese turned out by government agencies (Hendrickson 1987).

This style of writing is universal. The Apostle Paul, the American founding father Benjamin Franklin, the British poet Percy Bysshe Shelley, and U.S. President Franklin Roosevelt fought against it. Few government agencies in any country or historical era can claim to escape it.

The Concept Is Complex

Because gobbledygook is so popular, a precise definition does not communicate its many qualities and diverse forms. Scholars identify many characteristics. Stuart Chase (1971, pp. 63–65) states that it "means using two, three, or ten words in the place of one, or using a five-syllable word where a single syllable would suffice" and is "the squandering of words, packing a message with excess baggage and so introducing semantic 'noise'." Eric Partridge (1952) mentions long sentences of awkward construction and uncommon words. Other descriptions are "legalistic, wordy style ... often characteristic of government announcements" (Mager and Mager 1982, p. 40), "inflated, involved and obscure verbiage characteristic of the pronouncements of officialdom" (Morris and Morris 1962, p. 156) and "that form of nonmetrical composition ... which can be invariably interpreted as meaning and/or not meaning more and/or less than, rather than what, it seems to mean" (Partridge 1952, pp. 16–17). Jargon in the sense of officialese is clumsy, pompous, long-winded, and unnecessary in any context. Webster's *New Collegiate Dictionary* defines it as wordy and generally unintelligible jargon.

The number of synonyms for gobbledygook prove its popularity and rich complexity. These include bureaucratese, federalese, federal prose, federal jargon, official jargon, government jargon, governmentspeak, managerese, and bureauquack. Varieties of jargon include officialese, commercialese, expertese, bureaucrap, or gobbledegoop. In Britain, Whitehallese is the language of government in Westminster, London. Pentagonese, or militarese, is the language of the U.S. Department of Defense.

Characteristics of Gobbledygook and Officialese

Partridge (1952) has provided a comprehensive list of the qualities of officialese: using long words for short, abstract for concrete, unfamiliar for familiar, and Latin (occasionally Greek) for English; using phrases instead of single words; padding with unnecessary words; vagueness and woolliness; and caution and euphemism. Less frequently it will involve the use of technicalities with a sense not easily clear from the everyday meaning of the word. Don Miller (1981, p. 205) gives examples of the special properties of this language of government agencies. These are the use of polysyllabic and Latinate words whenever possible (utilization for use, implementation for doing); the use of special government terms (Title IX, Section 302, deinstitutionalization); and the rampant use of abbreviations and acronyms (HUD, CETA, UDAG, LEAA). Other traits are convolution, and ambiguity. Frank D'Angelo (1989, pp. 128–129) has added the preference for abstract nouns ending in -tion, -ity, -ment as in utilization, pertinacity, and apportionment; the use of stock phrases such as "in the final analysis," "other things being equal," and "within the framework of"; the overabundant use of clichés, such as "null and void," "lock, stock and barrel," and "all to the good"; and the extensive use of the passive voice, rather than the more direct active voice.

Origin and History

The term, "gobbledygook" is usually credited to Texas Congressman Maury Maverick, who as chair of the Smaller War Plant Committee in U.S. Congress was supposed to

have coined it in 1944. He had attended a meeting at which phrases such as "cause an investigation to be made with a view to ascertaining" were rife. He wrote a memo condemning such officialese and labeled it gobbledygook, explaining that he was thinking of the gobbling of turkeys while they strutted pompously (Hendrickson 1987, p. 223). Morris and Morris (1962), however, found evidence that "Clarence Denslinger" claimed to have first heard this word earlier as a schoolboy in northwestern Pennsylvania. They also cite a source that reports that it was coined at Camp Sheridan in Alabama in 1917 (pp. 156–157).

In the *New Testament* the apostle Paul thundered against gobbledygook in classical Greek when he wrote, "Except ye utter by the tongue words easy to understand, how shall it be known whereof ye speak? For ye shall speak into the air." When friends of Benjamin Franklin opposed property ownership as a qualification for the right to vote, they wrote, "To hold, for instance, that this natural right can be limited externally by making its exercise dependent on a ... condition of ownership of property ... ," Franklin saw that this style would not persuade ordinary folk and wrote, "To require property of voters leads us to this dilemma; I own a jackass; I can vote; the jackass dies; I cannot vote, Therefore, the vote represented not me but the jackass" (O'Hayre, 1966, pp. 45–46). The English poet Shelley likened this style to a cloud of winged snakes. Frances Perkins, U.S. President Franklin D. Roosevelt's secretary of labor, drafted a speech for the president with the words "We are endeavoring to construct a more inclusive society." Roosevelt rewrote it as "We are going to make a country in which no one is left out." John O'Hayre and the U.S. Bureau of Land Management (BLM) (1966) prepared a book entitled *Gobbledygook Has Gotta Go*.

Good and Bad Uses of Technical Jargon

A distinction must be made between legitimate and justified uses of technical language and the use of gobbledygook to mystify, awe, and befuddle. Specialists need technical languages for two good reasons. As a form of shorthand, professional and technical language speeds up discussion among specialists. This language also is a safeguard against their analyses being misinterpreted because some of their words might be understood with more than one meaning. This is especially necessary in the language of social science, which must be cleansed of the ambiguities of subjective interpretations because many everyday terms take on special meanings.

Carefully written technical language can be accurate and economical when used between experts in identical technical areas. But there is a risk of misinterpretation when it is used to communicate with technicians in other fields or with the general public. Militarese can be excused in wartime because lives may depend on what is, or is not, exactly revealed. The police, like those in many professions, have evolved a language to meet special needs, including the need for a shorthand to get work done quickly and efficiently. Also, they need to keep communication understandable to only friendly ears and to promote the feeling of belonging by knowing the "code of the lodge." In contrast, gobbledygook piles on words to impress and confuse.

Reasons to Use Gobbledygook and Officialese

Just as scholars differ widely in their identification of characteristics, they suggest a great variety of reasons for gobbledygook. Partridge (1952) has identified the need for a degree of impersonality, the laudable desire to remain dispassionate, and the less laudable but more natural desire to impress others. The need for dignity may lead to pomposity. Another reason is the dread of committing oneself. Frank D'Angelo (1989) states that officialese is sometimes used by public officials to cover up the clumsy mishandling of public affairs.

Some writers use jargon to obscure the truth, to sound impressive, or to give the user status. It helps to conceal a lack of ideas or to give authority to weak ideas. Gobbledygook demonstrates that one is intellectually and socially up-to-date (Hudson 1977). The use of this language is a way of keeping those who do not belong "out of the club."

A Story Illustrates the Problems of Gobbledygook

Stuart Chase (1971) has provided a story illustrating the importance of removing the gobble from gobbledygook. A plumber wrote to the U.S. Bureau of Standards that he had found hydrochloric acid fine for cleaning drains and asked whether it was harmless. The bureau replied, "The efficacy of hydrochloric acid is undisputable, but the chlorine residue is incompatible with metallic permanence." The plumber wrote back that he was very glad that the bureau had agreed with him. The bureau replied with a note of alarm, "We cannot assume responsibility for the production of toxic and noxious residues with hydrochloric acid and suggest that you use an alternate procedure." The plumber responded that he was happy to learn that the bureau still agreed with him. Whereupon the bureau exploded, "Don't use hydrochloric acid; it eats the (heck) out of the pipes" (Chase 1971, p. 72).

BLM Addresses the Problem of Gobbledygook

In *Gobbledygook Has Gotta Go*, according to O'Hayre (1966) and the U.S. Bureau of Land Management (1966), the "flossy, pompous, abstract, complex, jargonistic gobbledygook that passes for communication in government 'has gotta go'" (p. 6). O'Hayre has identified reasons for this style and has given solutions to the problem. He has pointed out that big words are not necessarily bad, unless the writer is obsessed with them, they are used for their own sake, or they are used to the exclusion of plain words. He believes that writers in the BLM often use unnecessarily complex sentences, put modifiers in wrong places, use wrong words, thread together too many related objects, and group together logically unrelated subjects and warns that every BLM employee, regardless of rank or position, must use a simple and direct writing style. He insists that gobbledygook cannot continue to clog communication lines. If the agency is to succeed in a time of new technologies, new demands, and new attitudes, agency communications must improve radically. Writers must abandon soggy formality and incoherence in favor of modern personal communications. Unnecessary complexity, stiffness, and pomposity must be avoided. Writing must be simple, natural, accurate, warm, friendly, personal, and easily understood.

O'Hayre (1966) contrasts ideas written in gobbledygook with the same ideas in simple English, as follows: "In numerous instances, the BLM has demonstrated the feasibility of judiciously harvesting timber on municipal watersheds and in drainage tributary to irrigation reservoirs." Translated, this means that the BLM "proves every day it can harvest timber without hurting municipal watershed or irrigation drainages" (p. 40).

Causes of Gobbledygook

O'Hayre has asked why those in the BLM are so complex and pompous in their writing and has answered himself by explaining that gobbledygook is used because of a fascination with the traditions of officialese, an in-grown compulsion to be impressively ornate rather than simply direct and to be proper rather than personal. False notions about writing are common because of the failure to review one's own writing through the eyes of potential readers.

"Imitation scientific language," loaded with pseudoscientific terms, is often combined with technical jargon. Employees attempt to imitate the language of science because it is popular and seems irrefutable in the public mind. Technical jargon compensates for a feeling of inferiority. It is used to impress, not to express, bearing complexity as the badge of wisdom.

Simple, straightforward English cannot be produced without much effort. Writers automatically fall back on technical jargon because it is where they feel safest and because it is easy to produce. Poor training in college, bad thinking habits, slavish imitation of other bad writing, wrong ideas about readers, lack of hard work, a confusion between dignity and pomposity, and a failure to understand that wisdom goes arm-in-arm with simplicity leads to poor writing.

O'Hayre has identified four fears that lead to abstract writing: (1) the fear of leaving something important out—abstractions can be interpreted to include everything important and unimportant; (2) the fear of making a clear-cut recommendation—abstract recommendations are simultaneously reversible and irreversible; (3) the fear of not writing one's share to keep the paper flowing, even when there is really nothing to write about; and (4) the fear of not sounding like everyone else, who are viewed to be important.

Remedies for Gobbledygook

O'Hayre gives advice to BLM employees that is useful for any organization. Because vague words can be misleading, misread, and misinterpreted, he urges staff members to make the extra effort to write clearly. Written expression must be simple and down-to-earth. Employees must spell out their ideas cleanly and clearly. They should use shorter sentences. They need to shrink and pare down their writing and use words the reader can handle. They need to be clear, exact, and precise. They should use specific and concrete words wherever they can and general and abstract terms only when necessary. Specific and concrete words must carry general abstract ideas.

J. WALTON BLACKBURN

BIBLIOGRAPHY

Alciere, Rose Mary, 1993. "Avoiding Government Speak." *Technical Communication*. 2d quarter: 262–264.

Chase, Stuart, 1971. "Gobbledygook," pp. 62–73. In Joseph A. DeVito, ed., *Communication—Concepts and Processes*. Englewood Cliffs, NJ: Prentice-Hall.

D'Angelo, Frank J., 1989. "Fiddle-Faddle, Flapdoodle, and Balderdash: Some Thoughts on Jargon," pp. 120–131. In William Lutz, ed., *Beyond Nineteen Eighty-Four: Doublespeak in a Post-Orwellian Age*, Urbana, IL: National Council of Teachers of English.

Garnett, James L., 1992. *Communicating for Results in Government*. San Francisco: Jossey-Bass.

Grolier Incorporated, 1994. *The Encyclopedia Americana—International Edition*. Danbury, CT: Grolier Incorporated.

Hendrickson, Robert, 1987, *Facts on File Encyclopedia of Word and Phrase Origins*. New York: Facts on File Publications.

Hudson, Kenneth, 1977. *The Dictionary of Diseased English*. London: Macmillan.

Mager, N. H, and S. K. Mager, compilers and eds., 1982. *The Morrow Book of New Words: 8,500 Terms Not Yet in Standard Dictionaries*. New York: William Morrow & Co.

Miller, Don Ethan, 1981. *The Book of Jargon: An Essential Guide to the Inside Languages of Today*. New York: Macmillan.

Morris, William, and Mary Morris, 1962. *Dictionary of Word and Phrase Origins*. New York: Harper & Row.

O'Hayre, John, and U.S. Bureau of Land Management, 1966. *Gobbledygook Has Gotta Go*. Washington, DC: GPO.

Partridge, Eric, 1952. *Chamber of Horrors; A Glossary of Official Jargon, both English and American*. New York: British Book Center.

Shipley, Joseph T., 1977. *In Praise of English: The Growth and Use of Language*. New York: New York Times Book Company.

GOVERNANCE OF NONPROFIT ORGANIZATIONS.

The term "governance" is defined to mean the strategic leadership of nonprofit organizations. It is therefore important to understand how this use of the term differs from the way it is used in the context of traditional public administration. In the latter context governance usually refers to the process of government policy making, which is intimately related to the political activities of elected officials.

Outside the realm of government, the concept of governance refers to an aspect of the management of a given organization. Indeed, in most dictionaries, the synonyms of governance are words such as management and administration. In current parlance, the term has taken on a more specific meaning as a process for making certain types of management decisions. These are commonly referred to as strategic decisions, which have to do with such matters as setting the organization's mission, establishing the values it wishes to embody, deciding the broad strategy for achieving the mission, and evaluating its effectiveness in meeting its goals.

This concept of governance is rooted in the positivist tradition of social science, which assumes that individuals can rationally choose among alternative actions based on information that is consciously gathered and assessed. These decisions are believed to then determine actual behavior, and the outcomes of such behavior, are thought to modify the subsequent decisions (Burrell and Morgan 1979). As we shall see, so-called postmodern critical theory takes issue with this concept of governance as an intendedly rational process, preferring instead to see the behavior of organizational members emerging from a much more complex, less-deterministic process.

This brief explication of the governance of nonprofit organizations focuses on problematic issues in the process of making governance decisions and their relationship to organizational effectiveness.

Problematic Issues in Nonprofit Governance

Considering governance as a decisionmaking process, there are two dominant issues of concern to scholars. One issue is who plays, or should play, which roles in the process, or, in practical terms, who is in charge of the organization and to whom is it accountable? The other issue is *how* governance decisions are, or should be, made.

Who Governs?

The literature on the question of roles in governance decisionmaking tends to be of two distinct types: normative and analytic.

The Normative Approach. The normative literature takes the position that the final authority on governance decisions ought to be the nonprofit organization's board of directors, governors, or trustees (e.g., Carver 1990; Houle 1989). It is the body to whom the rest of the organization is accountable and that, in turn, is accountable for the organization to the community, for which it acts as "trustee." It follows that the board must be both legally and morally responsible for establishing the organization's mission and ensuring that it is carried out.

The most common theme in this literature is to suggest that there are too many organizations in which the boards fail to govern properly. They are perceived as committing one of two cardinal sins. On one hand are those boards that allow the organization's paid top executives to make the governance decisions, which they then "rubber-stamp." On the other hand are those that do not have a clear understanding of how governance issues differ from detailed operational issues and, hence, get too involved in the day-to-day micromanagement of the organization, leaving no one to focus on the big picture of setting the strategic direction.

At this point, the normative literature launches into prescriptive recommendations on how the nonprofit board should be reformed so as to ensure that it effectively plays its governance role (and *only* this role). A brief summary of some of the most common recommendations is as follows:

- Since the role of the board is to act as trustee for the "owners" of the organization, it therefore ought to represent such owners and be fully aware of what the owners want from the organization. The problem, unfortunately, is that, except for nonprofit organizations created only to serve members who pay a membership fee, it is rarely clear who a nonprofit's owners actually are. The same dilemma arises when the term "community" is used in place of owners. This point is discussed further.

- The board must be the primary body to define the organization's mission and to articulate the values for which it stands.

- The board must obtain *independent* information on the threats and opportunities facing the organization and the organization's internal strengths and weaknesses in confronting its changing environment. To have this information selected and interpreted solely by the top management is to run the risk of becoming a rubber-stamp board.

- Board members must be carefully selected and thoroughly trained in how to make governance decisions, otherwise they can be lured into becoming either "rubber-stampers" or meddling micromanagers. Furthermore, this selection and training should not be the

responsibility of the paid chief executive officer but of the organization's "owners" and the board itself.

Many other general recommendations are also offered on how to create better boards, involving such matters as optimal size, number and type of committees, meeting leadership techniques, and so forth. These are not discussed here, however, since they do not explicitly relate to the governance function per se. (see **Board of Directors**).

In sum, the normative position on the governance of nonprofit organizations is quite clear and remarkably homogenous across a large number of writers on the subject: It ought to be the sole purview of the board of directors, and it ought to follow the classic principles of rational strategic planning.

The Analytic Approach. The alternative approach to nonprofit governance is to be found in the rather small body of literature that is concerned primarily with describing how governance decisions are actually made and with trying to discover why they emerge as they do. A subset of this literature takes on an implicitly normative cast in that it looks for what connections exist between the processes followed in making strategic decisions and the effectiveness of the organization. (See, for example, Herman and Heimovics 1990; Middleton 1987; Bradshaw, Murray, and Wolpin 1992, for surveys of this literature).

One of the primary concerns of the analytic approach to governance is who actually plays what role in governance decisionmaking. To address this question, a taxonomy of roles must be identified and the concept of the stakeholder must be evoked. As Jay Galbraith (1983), among others, has pointed out, there are three distinct roles in administrative decisionmaking. There are those who *make* the decisions de facto; there are those that *influence* those decisionmakers by providing information or recommendation; and there are those that *ratify* decisions. The latter role involves having little involvement in the choice of a preferred course of action but, in the last stage, having the authority to accept it or veto it. For example, in many nonprofit organizations, the chief executive officers (CEOs) are the primary decisionmakers, but some of their decisions are put to the board for ratification. The great majority of the time, the board routinely approves these motions, though occasionally one may be vetoed and returned to the CEO to be reconsidered.

The concept of stakeholder refers to any party that sees its interests being affected by the actions of a given organization. The potential stakeholders involved in governance decision for most nonprofits include some combination of the board as a whole, individual board members, board committees, the chief executive officer, other senior management staff, other paid staff and volunteers, users of the organization's services, members, funders, and government regulators.

Empirical studies of actual governance decisions in nonprofit organizations reveal several patterns to be quite common (e.g., Middleton-Stone 1991; Herman and Heimovics 1990; Bradshaw, Murray, and Wolpin 1992). The most common design in larger, more-established nonprofits is the "CEO-dominant" pattern, in which the CEO gathers information and advice from many stakeholders, formulates a decision, and has it ratified (rubber-stamped) by the board as a whole.

The next most common pattern is the "board-dominant pattern," often found in smaller, younger, more volunteer-driven nonprofit organizations, in which a small core group in the board plays a very influential role in recommending a course of action on governance issues. These are then debated and decided upon by the whole board. The CEO role in this situation is primarily one of several providers of information and advice.

Another common pattern is that of the "staff-dominant" situation, often found in "professional bureaucracies" such as universities and hospitals. As described by Henry Mintzberg (1979), these are organizations in which a core of senior professional staff (such as doctors or faculty members) have the power to make strategic decisions, which both the CEO and the board usually feel constrained to ratify.

Finally, there is the "collective governance" pattern, which operates according to an ideology of consensus among all key stakeholder groups. This design often turns out to be an active coalition of board members, staff of all levels, volunteers, and service users. Every effort is made to avoid giving any one of them more power than another. This pattern is commonly found in nonprofits with strong self-help or advocacy missions.

The Relationship Between Patterns of Governance and Outcomes. When one looks at the very limited research attempting to examine the link between governance decisionmaking processes and the actual performance of the nonprofit organization in achieving its mission, the picture is indistinct at best. There is very little of such research to begin with and, of what there is, most of it suffers from serious methodological problems arising out of the difficulties of measuring organizational effectiveness and the virtual impossibility of controlling other critical variables affecting it (e.g., see Bradshaw, Murray, and Wolpin 1992; Herman and Heimovics 1991; Knauft, Berger, and Gray 1991; Middleton 1987).

Given these limitations, the available evidence suggests that, contrary to the assertions of the writers of the normative literature on nonprofit governance, there is no one pattern of decisionmaking that is more effective than the others. Thus, even though it may be legally and morally

desirable for the board of directors to play the dominant role in setting the strategic direction and assessing the effectiveness of the organization, there is no guarantee that, if they do so, the organization will be better off than one dominated by its CEO or a group of professional staff or an all-stakeholder collective. It would seem that the decision pattern for governance issues that is most effective depends on the unique configuration of history, organization culture, key personalities, and contextual conditions in which the organization finds itself at any given point in time.

How Governance Decisions Are Made

As noted, nonprofit governance refers to the strategic leadership of the organization. The two most important aspects of this leadership are setting the strategic direction for the organization and assessing its past performance. Like the question of who governs, the literature on how these decisions are made divides into normative and analytic schools.

The Normative Approach to Strategic Planning

There is a vast body of literature on how organizational strategies ought to be arrived at (e.g., Bryson 1988; Nutt and Backoff 1992; Byers 1984). Although it is not possible to go into any detail here, it is fair to say that all processes for deriving these strategies share certain common characteristics. For example,

- It is a rational process, which involves setting clear objectives and priorities based on careful analysis of the organization's present, and likely future, its environment, and its internal strengths and weaknesses.
- It is based on the fullest and best possible information gathered and synthesized specifically for strategy-setting purposes. This information not only considers present conditions but also attempts to forecast likely futures.
- The process culminates in a planning document (the strategic plan), which is to be used as the basis for all subsequent policy decisions for a given period of time (though most suggest that the plan be reviewed at least annually and changed as needed if the environmental conditions have changed significantly).

The Normative Approach to Evaluating Effectiveness. The process of assessing how well an organization is performing in its efforts to reach its goals is similarly viewed as a rational process (e.g., Wholey et al., 1994; Love 1991; Murray and Tassie 1994). Though normative writers admit that it is difficult to reach in practice, most have in mind an ideal evaluation process to which evaluators should at least aspire. It involves (1) having clear objectives and criteria to be applied in judging the degree of success in attaining them; and (2) devising objective measures of progress that yield results that can be compared to the criteria, thereby producing an accurate evaluation.

The Analytic Approach to Strategic Planning. Perhaps the best, and most recent, work summarizing the empirical literature on what actually goes on when organizations develop strategies is that of Henry Mintzberg (1994). Several key points are made in this work and in others.

- Most documents that emerge labeled "strategic plan" have little influence on the strategic (board direction-setting) decisions actually made after the planning document is created.

- Organizations could be said to have "strategies" in the form of general guiding ideas that influence how problems are perceived and solved, but they "emerge" rather than appear as formal plans from a special planning group or process. Various stakeholders have varying amounts and kinds of power, and those with the greatest influence shape a strategy from a number of specific decisions.

- Major changes in strategy can and do occur but do so at disjointed intervals rather than evolving gradually over time; that is, the organization adheres to a given strategic position without changing it until eventually a "revolution" occurs that brings about a new strategy, which similarly lasts unchanged for a period, until the next revolution (Miller and Friesen 1984).

- The activity of engaging in a formal strategic planning process may, however, prove to be beneficial for reasons other than the limited value of the planning document it creates. It is valuable insofar as the process involves consulting with various external and internal stakeholders who do not have a regular influence on decisionmaking and requires gathering information on the organization's environment. Such activity can have the effect of improving the support of the external groups consulted, enhancing staff commitment to the mission, and resolving intraorganizational conflicts (Bradshaw, Murray, and Wolpin 1992).

The Analytic Approach to Evaluating Effectiveness. Despite the vociferous rhetoric from all sides calling for more and better evaluation of organizational performance, rigorous evaluation is not common in the nonprofit sector. Furthermore, what is done deviates substantially from the "ideal" model (Osborne, 1992; Murray and Tassie 1994). Other key points from the empirical literature are as follows:

- Evaluation tends to be carried out primarily at the program level, rather than at the organizational level. This means that comparisons of the relative costs and benefits of the range of programs are rare.

- The focus of evaluations tends to be on processes and inputs rather than on outcomes. Process-based evaluation checks the policies, practices, and procedures followed by organizations, under the assumption that certain actions will lead to certain outcomes; for example, that "participative decisionmaking" will eventually result in a reduction in substance abuse by low-income youth in an agency set up for that purpose; or that an increase in donations (inputs) will produce a corresponding increase improving the environment in an environmental protection agency.

- The "ideal" methods of evaluation are rarely followed because goals are unclear, criteria are not defined or prioritized, and measurement instruments yield ambiguous results. In addition, behind the formal evaluation procedures there are often nonformal methods at work. These methods may involve making judgments of effectiveness based on the organization's unofficial reputation in the eyes of key stakeholders (called "isomorphism" by Di Maggio and Powell 1983). Judgments are also based on the degree to which those in the organization being evaluated appear to hold values and beliefs that are congruent with unspoken values and beliefs held by the evaluator (Tassie and Murray 1995).

- When all is said and done, many evaluations only marginally affect major policy decisions, such as funding allocations or downsizing plans; this is because of the strength of other variables such as pressures from other, more powerful, stakeholders.

Conclusion

The study of the process of nonprofit governance is of great importance but suffers at present from the wishful thinking of normative writers and the general lack of knowledge about what really goes on. The possibility of improving governance depends on acquiring a better understanding of the actual processes and the factors that influence them. Until that time, the field will remain dominated by successive fads offering "the answer" to the problems of governance.

VIC MURRAY

BIBLIOGRAPHY

Bradshaw, Pat, Vic Murray, and Jacob Wolpin, 1992. "Do Nonprofit Boards Make a Difference?" *Nonprofit and Voluntary Sector Quarterly,* vol., 21, no. 3 (Fall): 227–250.
Bryson, John, 1988. *Strategic Planning for Public and Nonprofit Organizations.* San Francisco: Jossey-Bass.
Burrell, Gibson, and Gareth Morgan, 1979. *Sociological Paradigms of Organizational Analysis.* London: Heinemann.

Byers, Lloyd, 1984. *Strategic Management*. New York: Harper & Row.

Carver, John, 1990. *Boards That Make a Difference*. San Francisco: Jossey-Bass.

Di Maggio, P. J., and W. W. Powell, 1983. "The Iron Cage Revisited: Institutional Isomorphism and Collective Rationality in Organizational Fields," *American Sociological Review* 48: 147–160.

Galbraith, Jay, 1983. *Designing Complex Organizations*. Reading, MA: Addison-Wesley.

Hardy, Cynthia, ed., 1994. *Managing Strategic Action*. London: Sage.

Herman, R. D., and R. D. Heimovics, 1990. "An Investigation of Leadership Skills in Chief Executives of Nonprofit Organizations," *American Review of Public Administration*, vol. 20, no. 2: 107–124.

————,1991. *Executive Leadership in Nonprofit Organizations*. San Francisco: Jossey-Bass.

Houle, Cyril, 1989. *Governing Boards*. San Francisco: Jossey-Bass.

Knauft, E. B., R. A. Berger, and S. T. Gray, 1991. *Profiles of Excellence: Achieving Success in the Nonprofit Sector*. San Francisco: Jossey-Bass.

Love, Arnold, 1991. Internal Evaluation: *Building Organizations from Within*. Newbury Park, CA: Sage.

Middleton, M., 1987. "Nonprofit Boards of Directors: Beyond the Governance Function." In W. W. Powell, ed., *The Nonprofit Sector: A Research Handbook*. New Haven, CT: Yale University Press.

Middleton-Stone, M. 1991. "The Propensity of Governing Boards to Plan," *Nonprofit Management and Leadership*, vol. 1, no. 3 (Spring): 203–216.

Miller, D., and P. H. Friesen, 1984. *Organizations: A Quantum View*. Englewood Cliffs, NJ: Prentice-Hall.

Mintzberg, Henry, 1979. *The Structuring of Organizations*. Englewood Cliffs, NJ: Prentice-Hall.

————, 1994. *The Rise and Fall of Strategic Planning*. New York: Free Press.

Murray, Vic, and Bill Tassie, 1994. "Evaluating the Effectiveness of Nonprofit Organizations." In R. D. Herman, ed., *The Jossey-Bass Handbook of Nonprofit Leadership and Management*, San Fransisco: Jossey-Bass.

Nutt, Paul, and Robert Backoff, 1992. *Strategic Management of Public and Third Sector Organizations*. San Francisco: Jossey-Bass.

Osborne, David, 1992. *Reinventing Government*. Reading, MA: Addison-Wesley.

Tassie, William, and Vic Murray, forthcoming. "Rationality and Politics: What Really Goes on When Funders Evaluate the Performance of Fundees." *Nonprofit and Voluntary Sector Quarterly*.

Wholely, Joseph, H. P. Hatry, and K. E. Newcomer, eds., 1994. *Handbook of Practical Program Evaluation*. San Francisco: Jossey-Bass.

GOVERNING INSTRUMENT. The means through which the goals of public policy are realized. Public policy involves the pursuit of particular goals or sets of goals. But policy also involves the selection of particular means used to realize the goals. Such selection is referred to as "the choice of governing instrument" or "policy instrument." The successful implementation of a policy depends to a large extent on the careful and prudent selection of a governing instrument.

Governing instruments are distinguished on the basis of the degree of state intervention and legitimate coercion used in pursuing a policy goal. These range from self-regulation and exhortation at the lower end of the intervention-coercion scale to expenditure, regulation, and public ownership at the higher end.

First, there is the governing instrument of self-regulation. The level of state involvement and coercion here is minimal. Policymakers choose not to intervene directly in controlling private behavior, preferring instead to allow individuals, groups, or organizations to regulate their own behavior. Professional associations, such as those of doctors, for example, may themselves be allowed to regulate the professional conduct of their members. Similarly, families may be allowed to deal with matters relating to domestic conflict and violence themselves, the police being instructed not to get involved (the traditional policy). The second instrument is exhortation, where intervention is slightly stronger. Here, state authorities intervene only through encouraging certain kinds of desirable behavior. The emphasis is on persuasion and coaxing rather than on legal sanctions. Governments, for example, may encourage unions not to make excessive wage demands, but they will not enact legislation or regulations. If laws or regulations are created, they will be for symbolic purposes only, with little intention of enforcement, as is the case with many of the early antismoking laws. More common are official statements or government advertisements such as "keep fit" or "be nice—clean your ice."

The next three instruments involve increasing degrees of state involvement and coercion. Expenditure is a third instrument by which authorities of the state choose to intervene through a significant level of public spending. Forms of spending range from direct payments to individuals (e.g., old-age pensions) and transfer payments from one level of government to another to less-visible forms, such as subsidies, grants, loans, tax deductions, and tax credits. In most developed countries, the highest spending areas are public education, health care, and social welfare. A fourth instrument is government regulation, involving more legal coercion. Here, authorities of the state institute codes of formal rules to control private behavior, largely economic behavior, backed up by legal sanctions. These rules may be administered either by regular government departments or by specialized regulatory agencies. Their main purpose is to remedy failures of market forces or to realize goals that cannot be realized through market forces.

Finally, public ownership is a governing instrument wherein coercion and state involvement are at a maximum. Policymakers exert control not simply through spending or regulating but through the direct provision of goods and services, carried out by public enterprises. This is done mainly for purposes of nation-building, providing economic or financial infrastructure for a country, or carrying out risky ventures in the public interest, which private enterprises cannot or will not do.

The selection of governing instruments is guided by several considerations. One is public acceptability. For example, the legal regulation of discrimination was not generally acceptable in Western countries before World War II. Given the common view that discrimination was best met through education and goodwill, policymakers were left only with the options of self-regulation or exhortation. But after the war, with public demand for legislation, policymakers could and did choose the instrument of regulation.

Another consideration is the level of public expectations of the state. For example, before World War II, there was little expectation of the state to provide for social welfare. But after the war, with a shift to the belief that it was the responsibility of the state to ensure a basic level of social welfare, policymakers were under pressure to select the instrument of large-scale expenditure for social programs.

Finally, another factor is government revenue. In the relatively affluent postwar period, policymakers could and did choose the instrument of expenditure. But since the 1970s, in a period of declining revenues and middle-class tax resistance, regulation (and deregulation) has become a much more attractive instrument than expenditure or public ownership. It is more cost effective—in areas where it can be done—to control behavior through enacting regulations than through spending or operating public enterprises.

R. Brian Howe

BIBLIOGRAPHY

Doern, G. Bruce, and Richard W. Phidd, 1992. *Canadian Public Policy: Ideas, Structure, Process.* 2d ed. Toronto: Nelson Canada.
Lowi, Theodore J., 1972. "Four Systems of Policy, Politics, and Choice." *Public Administration Review* 33 (July–August): 298–310.
Spitzer, Robert, 1987. "Promoting Policy Theory: Revising the Arenas of Power." *Policy Studies Journal* 15 (June): 675–689.

GOVERNMENT ACCOUNTING.

The financial and managerial accounting performed by governmental units to ascertain the level of efficiency and effectiveness in their activities. Audited financial reports on these activities provide accountability to the general populace on the actions of government officials to maintain a balance between taxing and spending policies.

Origin and Subsequent History

Even though tax collectors were recognized in biblical writings, government accounting as a separate discipline is a relatively recent development, with extensive activity beginning early in the twentieth century. This activity has been driven by the desire for public budgets and the need for greater accountability by elected officials. Initially, government accounting developed at the local level, where taxpayers are closest to their elected representatives, then spread to the state and national levels. At present, extensive effort is being exerted in the international arena due to the increasing emphasis on globalization.

The major objectives of governmental accounting are to account for funds raised and to allocate public resources. The actual results of operations are compared with budgeted targets or goals in the financial statements where the efficiency and effectiveness of the governmental unit can be assessed.

The differences in the focus of accounting between governmental units (the public sector) and private enterprise (the private sector) are numerous. In the public sector, there is no private ownership. That is, power belongs to the people through their elected representatives. Further, there is no profit motive in the public sector, and revenues (i.e., taxes) received from individual taxpayers have no relationship to the services or benefits delivered to these same taxpayers.

State and Local

During the first decade of the twentieth century, considerable interest in government accounting was exhibited. In 1901 and 1902, financial statements were issued by the cities of Newton, Massachusetts; Baltimore, Maryland; and Chicago, Illinois. A *Handbook of Municipal Accounting* was issued by the City of New York in 1910 to standardize accounting practices in the city.

Interest dropped off, however, until the National Committee on Municipal Accounting was organized in 1934, under the auspices of the Municipal Finance Officers Association (MFOA). This committee published numerous position papers during its developing years. In 1951, these publications were formally issued in a book titled *Municipal Accounting and Auditing*. This book was revised in 1968, retitled *Governmental Accounting, Auditing, and Financial Reporting*, and continues to be revised periodically by the Government Finance Officers Association (GFOA)—the successor organization to the MFOA.

The National *Committee* on Municipal Accounting was replaced by the National *Council* on Governmental Accounting (NCGA) in 1974. It attempted to address many accounting issues among governmental units during a turbulent period of financial crises and bank defaults. The

NCGA was not fully effective, however, due to the use of volunteers with limited time and limited staff support.

The Governmental Accounting Standards Board (GASB) replaced the NCGA in 1984 as an independent standard setting body with jurisdiction over state and local governments. GASB is financed by the Financial Accounting Foundation (the same organization that oversees the Financial Accounting Standards Board). GASB is responsible for establishing accounting standards for activities and transactions of state and local governments. To provide a foundation on which to build their accounting standards, GASB issued a conceptual statement that identified the following qualitative characteristics as most desirable: understandability, reliability, relevance, timeliness, consistency, and comparability.

Federal

The Constitution of the United States mandates that federal expenditures are subject to legal appropriations. Further, it requires that a periodic accounting be provided for the receipts and expenditures of all public monies.

The first federal budget was published in 1921. However, early attempts to publish official financial statements (other than Statements of Revenue and Expenditures or Statements of Public Debt) were not successful. To provide a foundation on which to build these statements, an attempt has been made to define a conceptual framework for the federal government. The U.S. General Accounting Office (GAO) had originally prepared a conceptual framework in the early 1980s. From this effort, the GAO issued guidance suggesting that the full accrual method of accounting be used by the federal government. The General Accounting Office is an arm of the legislative body, however, and the administrative body, was not receptive to adopting GAO's recommendations.

To provide better financial management in the federal government, the Chief Financial Officers Act was passed by Congress in 1990, requiring chief financial officers in each of its 23 major federal agencies. In addition, financial statements of their activities were to be prepared. To insure consistency in these statements, federal financial governmental leaders (the secretary of the Treasury, the director of the Office of Management and Budget, and the comptroller general) agreed jointly in October 1990 to sponsor a new Federal Accounting Standards Advisory Board (FASAB). The purpose of the new board is to recommend accounting standards and principles for the federal government and to assist its sponsors in the fulfillment of their responsibilities for federal accounting and financial reporting. During the initial meetings of the FASAB in spring 1991, it became evident that the conceptual framework for governmental accounting needed to be reexamined. Much effort continues to be exerted in this endeavor while accounting standards for assets and liabilities are being established.

International

The International Accounting Standards Committee (IASC) was created in 1973 to establish international accounting standards. The committee was an outgrowth of the International Accounting Congress in 1972. In 1989, the IASC issued a pronouncement titled "Framework for the Preparation and Presentation of Financial Statements." Subsequently, the International Federation of Accountants (IFAC) was established to address international accounting issues.

Initially, IFAC's work concentrated on the private sector, with little effort exerted on the public sector. To fill this void, the Public Sector Committee of IFAC was established in 1990 with an objective to develop programs aimed at improving public sector financial management and accountability. Studies are undertaken by the committee to provide information that contributes to public sector financial reporting, accounting, or auditing knowledge. In March 1991, the committee issued its first study *(Financial Reporting by National Governments),* and it continues to build on that foundation with proposed standards for recognizing assets and liabilities.

Underlying Theoretical Framework

In the private sector, accounting standards are based on the "capital maintenance" concept. That is, attempts are made (through the measurement of income) to determine if the firm or individual is "as well off" after a period of operation as it was at the beginning of that period. This concept is not easily applied in the public sector since the capital (owner's contribution) to be maintained is difficult to define.

In the development of governmental accounting standards, it is more feasible to use a "standard of living maintenance" concept rather than the traditional "capital maintenance" concept. A system of national income accounting was developed in the early 1930s for governments to determine if the national standard of living had been maintained (versus maintaining capital). The per capita gross national product (GNP) is one measure that is used to identify the degree of change in this standard of living, and per capita gross domestic product (GDP) is another.

A conceptual framework is used to prescribe the nature, function, and limits of financial accounting and reporting in order to permit the issuance of consistent accounting standards. For the private sector in the United States, an attempt has been made by the Financial Accounting Standards Board to set forth the major issues to be addressed in establishing a conceptual framework. Subsequently, the FASB has issued five Statements of Financial Accounting Concepts (SFAC) that relate to financial reporting for business enterprises.

A void existed in the conceptual framework for governmental financial accounting and reporting, however, since decision-useful information in the private sector is not necessarily the same needed in the public sector. That is, the matching principle does not apply since expenses (e.g., education) cannot be matched against the revenue that is generated. Consequently, a profit or loss figure from operations cannot be computed. Instead, in the public sector, expenditures are matched against the period that benefits, under the concept of intergenerational equity.

Further, since there is no bottom line (i.e., profit or loss) in government by which to measure its efficiency or effectiveness, many governments compare their key financial indicators with governments that have similar characteristics (e.g., population, wealth). This has led to the development of a concept referred to as "selective comparability."

Current Practice in the United States

In the United States, the method of accounting in use depends on the level of government. State and local governments use the same bases of accounting, but the federal government uses a different basis.

Accounting Bases

In government, three bases of accounting are in common use: cash, accrual, and modified accrual. In some instances, generally accepted accounting principles (GAAP) may specify one method of accounting but legal provisions require another. The accounting system must be designed to meet the requirements of both GAAP and the legal provisions.

Cash Accounting. Many governments, especially smaller units, still use cash basis accounting. This is *not* a desirable practice, since cash basis financial statements are subject to manipulation. That is, the results of operations can be affected by speeding up or slowing down cash collections and payments near the end of the period. Further, these statements permit distortions due to shifts in the timing of cash receipts and disbursements relative to underlying economic events near the end of a fiscal period.

Cash basis accounting recognizes transactions only when cash changes hands, which does not permit recognition of assets and liabilities not arising from cash transactions. Cash basis financial statements could be in conformity with GAAP if accounts receivable, accounts payable, and other accrued items are nonexistent or immaterial. For governmental units, this limited activity might exist with some funds and, in such an activity, cash basis accounting

could be considered in conformance with GAAP. For simplicity, many smaller governmental units will maintain their records on a cash basis during the fiscal period and convert to the accrual or modified accrual basis (as appropriate) at the end of the period for financial reporting purposes.

Accrual Accounting. Accrual-based accounting recognizes transactions when they occur, regardless of the timing of the cash flows. Under this method, revenues are recognized in the accounting period in which they are earned and can be accurately determined. For example, if a governmental unit provides an electrical service to its customers, the revenue is earned when the electricity is used. The revenue is measurable when the electric meters are read, and the revenue would be considered earned regardless of when the customer paid the bill.

For expense recognition, the "matching principle" is applied and expenses that are incurred to generate the revenue are recognized in the period incurred. In the example of the electrical service, the costs incurred to produce the electricity for its customers are recognized when the personnel services are performed or the items purchased are received and used.

Modified Accrual Accounting. The accrual basis of accounting, as applied in the private sector, is modified for governmental units to recognize revenue in the accounting period when it is susceptible to accrual. The "susceptibility to accrual" criteria requires judgment, materiality and practicality considerations, and consistency in application. Further, since the present measurement focus of governmental fund accounting is on net financial resources, decreases in those resources are referred to as expenditures. These expenditures are recorded when the liability is incurred or, in the absence of a liability, when the cash disbursement is made.

State and Local

State and local governmental units in the United States account for their activities in three different fund types: governmental, proprietary, and fiduciary. Each fund is a separate accounting entity with a set of self-balancing accounts.

Governmental Funds. The general, special revenue, capital projects, and debt services funds are accounted for as governmental funds. The special revenue funds account for special designations, such as highway taxes for road construction or sales taxes for education. Capital project funds account for major construction (generally from bond proceeds), such as schools, court houses, or city halls. Debt service funds account for the payment of principal and interest on bonds when due. The general fund is used to account for all other governmental transactions not covered in the other three governmental funds. All governmental funds use the modified accrual basis of accounting. Since the governmental funds have a financial resources focus, long-term debt is reported in the General Long-Term Debt Account Group and fixed assets are reported in the General Fixed Asset Account Group.

Proprietary Funds. Enterprise and internal services funds are accounted for as proprietary funds. Internal services funds are used to account for services, such as data processing, provided internally to the governmental unit. Enterprise funds account for services provided by the governmental unit to individuals outside the governmental unit. Examples include water purification plants or electric utilities run by the governmental unit. All proprietary funds use the accrual basis of accounting.

Fiduciary Funds. Agency and trust funds are accounted for as fiduciary funds. Agency funds are used when the governmental unit serves as an agent for another. Only assets and liabilities are recorded since there is no equity interest. Trust funds are designated as expendable or nonexpendable, depending upon the intent when the trust was established. If the intent was to maintain the principal of the trust, it would be designated as nonexpendable; otherwise, it would be an expendable trust fund. Nonexpendable trust and agency funds are accounted for on the full accrual basis of accounting, but the expendable trust funds are accounted for on the modified accrual basis.

Financial Reports. Due to the complexity in the accounting structure, pyramidal reports are prepared. At the bottom of the pyramid are the myriad accounting transactions. These are summarized into the financial reports for each separate fund. Balance sheets, income statements, and statements of cash flows are prepared for all proprietary funds, agency funds, and nonexpendable trust funds to reflect the results of governmental activities for the period. Financial statements for all governmental funds and expendable trust funds are prepared with a financial flow focus. That is, only current assets and current liabilities are reported on the balance sheet, and the operating statements focus on changes in the financial position (i.e., fund balance) and not on net income.

At the next level of the pyramid, the financial reports for each separate fund are compiled by fund type (i.e., general, special revenue, debt service, capital project, enterprise, internal service, trust, and agency) into the *Combining* Balance Sheet and the *Combining* Statement of Revenues, Expenditures, and Fund Balance. At the next level, these combining statements are then compiled in (1) the combined balance sheet for all fund types and account groups, (2) the combined statement of revenues, expenditures, and changes in fund balance for all governmental fund types and expendable trust funds, and (3) the combined statement of changes in financial position and the combined statement of cash flows for all proprietary funds and nonexpendable trust funds. These combining and combined reports are referred to as the Comprehensive Annual Financial Report.

At the top of the pyramid are the "popular" reports. Basically, these reports are very general and show where the resources came from (primarily taxes) and where they went (primarily for education, social programs, public safety, and public works). There is no attempt to illuminate interfund transactions or to prepare consolidated statements.

GASB has issued an exposure draft on measurement focus and basis of accounting. This proposed standard would move state and local governments toward a full accrual basis of accounting. However, it has met with considerable resistance since there would be more liabilities recognized in the balance sheet, which would result in a reduction in the fund balance. GASB is working on a financial reporting project that will (if adopted) permit recognition of the liabilities and move the state and local governments more toward the full accrual basis.

Federal

Accounting at the U.S. federal level is provided via a dual-track (budgetary and proprietary) system for the 23 federal agencies and the federal government as a whole. The budgetary system is a system of control through the use of apportionments, allotments, commitments, and obligations. The objectives of the proprietary system are to provide useful information to allocate resources and to assess management's performance and stewardship. Four basic year-end financial statements are presently prescribed: a balance sheet, an operating statement, a statement of cash flows, and a statement of reconciliation between budgetary and proprietary amounts.

Typically, governmental accounting at the federal level is performed on a cash basis. Attempts have been made to move toward a full accrual basis, but these efforts have been met with considerable resistance. At the present time, FASAB has issued an exposure draft that would require liabilities to be recognized in the financial statements on the full accrual basis of accounting.

Variation of Practices in Other Countries

Much effort is being exerted in other countries to define a conceptual framework for the public sector. The Public Sector Committee of IFAC issued a pronouncement concerned with the conceptual framework of governmental accounting and reporting. This document recognizes that financial reporting is key to both accountability and decisionmaking. It develops a logical progression from users and user needs to the objectives of governmental financial reporting. Rather than recommending a single, preferred financial reporting model, the study describes the spectrum of possible bases of accounting and different reporting models, as well as the strengths and weaknesses of each in meeting the objectives of financial reporting. The study also recognizes the system of national accounts that was developed as a basis for economic analysis of income and expenditure flows in an economy. Further, it recognizes the difficulty of integrating this system with a country's accounting system. The study concludes that more complete and better information will meet the user needs through summary financial reports that account for total economic resources.

In addition, the Public Sector Committee of IFAC has issued exposure drafts on the recognition of assets and liabilities, as well as measuring the performance of international governmental units. Much work remains before these proposed standards will be accepted by the participating countries to assure consistency in the application of accounting standards.

New Zealand

New Zealand is at the leading edge of international development, with the presentation of accrual-based financial statements since 1992. The benefits it hopes to reap from these statements are as follows: show more clearly the economic impact of government activity; provide better information for Parliament and the electorate to assess the management of public resources; provide reports of revenue, expenses, and operating balance in an operating statement and reports of the Crown assets, liabilities, and net worth in a balance sheet; and establish a basis from which the Crown's financial operations and trends in its financial position can be monitored in the future.

Other Countries

Both Canada and Germany plan to switch to the accrual basis and to prepare consolidated financial statements. The timing for the switch has not yet been determined, however. The financial statements for Italy and Spain are similar and present revenues and expenditures classified by source and activity. Japan provides summaries of revenues and expenditures for different accounts, such as the general account, special accounts, tax collection, and debts. The Chinese financial statements are on the cash basis and emphasize centralized control, not information or accountability.

JESSE W. HUGHES

BIBLIOGRAPHY

Financial Accounting Standards Board (FASB), 1976. *Conceptual Framework for Financial Accounting and Reporting: Elements of Financial Statements and Their Measurement.* Stamford, CT: FASB.
———, 1980. *Concept No. 1, Objectives of Financial Reporting by Business Enterprises,* Stamford, CT: FASB.
———, 1980. *Concept No. 2, Qualitative Characteristics of Accounting Information.* Stamford, CT: FASB.
———, 1984. *Concept No. 5, Recognition and Measurement in Financial Statements of Business Enterprises,* Stamford, CT: FASB.
———, 1985. *Concept No. 6, Elements of Financial Statements,* Stamford, CT: FASB.
Freeman, Robert J., and Craig D. Shoulders, 1993. *Governmental and Nonprofit Accounting Theory and Practice.* 4th ed. Englewood Cliffs, NJ: Prentice-Hall.
General Accounting Office (GAO), 1980 (19 February). *Objectives of Accounting and Financial Reporting in the Federal Government.* Washington, DC: GPO.
———, 1980 (12 August). *Elements of Accounting and Financial Reporting in the Federal Government.* Washington, DC: GPO.
———, 1980 (31 October). *Federal Government Financial Accounting and Reporting Entities.* Washington, DC: GPO.
———, 1980 (11 November). *Measurement Concepts of Accounting and Financial Reporting in the Federal Government.* Washington, DC: GPO.
———, 1984 (31 October). *Title 2, GAO Policy and Procedures Manual for Guidance of Federal Agencies.* Washington, DC: GPO.
Governmental Accounting Standards Board (GASB), 1987 (May). *Concepts Statement 1: Objectives of Financial Reporting.* Stamford, CT: GASB.
Hay, Leon E., and Earl W. Wilson, 1995. *Accounting for Governmental and Nonprofit Entities.* 10th ed. Chicago: Richard D. Irwin.
Hughes, Jesse W., 1994 "International Governmental Accounting," pp. 15C1–15C25. In Mortimer A. Dittenhofer, contrib. ed. *Applying Government Accounting Principles.* New York: Matthew Bender.
Public Sector Committee, International Federation of Accountants, 1991 (March). *Study 1: Financial Reporting by National Governments.* New York: International Federation of Accountants.

GOVERNMENT CORPORATION.

An organization owned by the government, but independently managed and financed like a private business. Most government corporations are governed by a board of directors, administered by a professional executive, and financed through the issuance of tax-exempt bonds and the marketing of a service.

Government corporations exist at every level of U.S. government, but are perhaps most prominent at the federal and state levels. Other names for such organizations include public authority, public corporation, special purpose government, public enterprise, and public benefit corporation.

History

Quasi-public organizations have long been a part of U.S. government. In the 1800s and early 1990s, most corporations were considered to be performing functions of a public character. Consider, for example, the Erie Canal Commission, established in 1816 to manage New York's canal system; the Panama Railroad Company, purchased by

Congress in 1903 to assist in building the Panama Canal; and the Emergency Fleet Corporation, formed in 1917 to supply vehicles during World War I. These early government corporations were designed to be free of the uniform guidelines applied to other traditional government departments so that they could act efficiently in building public works or in financing projects. They were not exactly what is thought of as a government corporation today because each was largely funded by legislative appropriations.

The Port Authority of New York and New Jersey was the first modern-day government corporation. Created in 1921 to reflect the Progressive Era values of businesslike efficiency and public interest representation, the Port Authority was to coordinate port activities in the New York and New Jersey region. Under the clause in the Constitution permitting compacts between states, the authority's jurisdiction was called the "Port District," a 17-county bistate region within a 25-mile radius of the Statue of Liberty. The Port Authority's mandate was, and continues to be, to promote and protect the commerce of the bistate port and to undertake port and regional improvements not likely to be invested in by private enterprise nor to be attempted by either state alone. Governed by an appointed board of commissioners, the Port Authority does not use tax revenues to fund itself, but it is allowed to charge for the use of terminals and other facilities, and most important, to borrow money and secure the same by bonds.

The Port Authority's first major project was the construction of the George Washington Bridge over the Hudson River. The bridge, completed in 1931, was noteworthy because it symbolized the ability of a government corporation to transcend state and local political interests, to build a public conveyance ahead of schedule and under budget, and to do all this without the use of public funds. And most important, the bridge was built while Franklin D. Roosevelt was governor of New York. Through the bridge, Roosevelt came to see in the Port Authority a model for public administration, something to be replicated in New York, in the federal government, and throughout the nation.

When Roosevelt became president in 1933, he created several new agencies in his administration's first 100 days, including dozens of government corporations, such as the Federal Deposit Insurance Corporation (FDIC); the Commodity Credit Corporation (CCC), and the Federal Housing Administration (FHA).

The most prominent corporation established during the New Deal period was the Tennessee Valley Authority (TVA). Patterned after New York's government corporations, Roosevelt described the TVA in his State of the Union message of 1933 as "clothed with the power of government but possessed of the flexibility and initiative of private enterprise." Its mission was to improve regional conditions along the Tennessee River by developing river navigation, controlling frequent flooding, and producing

electricity. Soon after it was formed, the TVA designed and built high-voltage lines that carried the first electricity to homes, schools, and factories in the region. The prominent leader of the TVA during its formative years was David Lilienthal.

In 1934, the federal government distributed to the 48 states a sample of model legislation for the creation of what was termed "municipal improvement authorities" and "nonprofit public benefit corporations." Roosevelt followed this with a personal letter to the governors of each state, encouraging them to endorse this legislation and to modify their debt laws. By the time of Roosevelt's death in 1945, government corporations were operating throughout the federal government and within most states and localities.

After World War II, government corporations were created to develop housing, roads, bridges, airports, and parks. At the time, President Dwight D. Eisenhower was not especially in favor of government corporations; he referred to them as "creeping socialism." Nonetheless, many public officials were more than willing to use such agencies. Two notable individuals in this regard were Robert Moses and Austin Tobin.

Moses contributed to the overall development of government corporations in several ways. First, through his management of the New York State Triborough Bridge and Tunnel Authority (TBTA), New York Power Authority, and other state-level government corporations, he showed that it was possible to enlarge the mission of such agencies from single purposes to multipurposes. He transformed the TBTA, for instance, from an agency that built bridges to one that designed entire roadway systems. Second, Moses demonstrated that private investors could be drawn to government corporation projects by pledging that the revenues of existing projects would be used to pay off the bonds of new ones. And third, he gave government corporations a distinct identity, one that clearly distinguished them from traditional government agencies. The TBTA, for example, had its own logo, police force, and distinctive license plates.

Another person who transformed government corporations was Austin Tobin, the executive director of the Port Authority of New York and New Jersey from 1942 to 1971. With private financing and the use of proceeds from one project to finance another, Tobin greatly expanded the mission of the Port Authority. During his tenure, the Port Authority built two tunnels under the Hudson River; took control of LaGuardia, Idlewild (now Kennedy), and Newark airports; constructed a large bus terminal in Manhattan, began operating truck terminals in New Jersey and New York; and built the World Trade Center in lower Manhattan. Tobin's strategy, like Moses', was to develop strong relationships with the investment community, to enhance the Port Authority's independence through consolidated bonds, and to emphasize credit and bond marketability as the dominant criteria for evaluating the Port Authority's performance.

Beginning in the 1960s and extending into the 1990s, several additional uses were found for government corporations. Consider the following examples. In 1964, the Texas Legislature sought to ensure that hazardous wastes were disposed of safely and efficiently and so it established the self-financing Gulf Coast Waste Disposal Authority. In 1965, the North Carolina Education Assistance Authority was created to provide financial aid to postsecondary educational institutions. In 1968, the state of New York created the Urban Development Corporation to finance the construction of housing in blighted areas. In 1971, Congress formed a quasi-autonomous enterprise to deliver the mail—the U.S. Postal Service. In 1975, the Delaware General Assembly created the Delaware Solid Waste Authority to manage and control the disposal of solid waste in the state. In 1981, the New Hampshire Housing Finance Authority was authorized to provide low-interest mortgages for the purchasing of new homes by eligible residents. And, in 1985, the Maryland Stadium Authority was formed to construct a baseball stadium in Baltimore.

Theoretical Framework

The invention of government corporations has been the responsibility of chief executives (the President, governors, and mayors) and legislators (members of Congress, state representatives, and county or city commissioners). Public officials have used government corporations not only to resolve pressing public problems but also to further their own personal careers.

Information about the mission, governance, management, and financing of a government corporation can be found in its authorizing statute. There is no such thing as a model statute, so there is much variation among government corporations with regard to such things as the size of governing boards and the terms of office of board members. For example, the size of a board may range anywhere from three to 49 members and terms of office may extend from two to nine years.

In the political process, four public arguments have been made for government corporations. First, it is asserted that government corporations have a superior governance and management structure. Ideally, each is governed by a board of "average" citizens who serve part-time and without compensation. As a policymaking body concerned with the overall public interest, a board's job is to oversee matters broadly and to select a highly educated, experienced individual to actually manage the organization. The corporate manager, relieved of the rigid requirements that typically constrain traditional government agencies (civil service rules, pay scales, etc.), is supposed to carry out existing tasks with competence, but also with an entrepre-

neurial eye toward new strategies and new projects that will add to the organization's overall strength—in financial terms and in relation to broad social needs. The end result is an organization that maintains its linkage to the public interest through board governance and achieves its goals through professional management.

Second, government corporations are believed to have unique financial advantages. Government corporations are expected to generate from their own initiatives all, or almost all, of the moneys they require for development and operation. They are not subject to constitutional or statutory debt limitations, and as government entities, they can raise needed funds in the tax-exempt bond market. Government corporations are usually monopolies, so they do not have to be concerned with either private competition or making a profit. This, in turn, allows them to provide services at a lower cost than private firms. If government corporations do get in financial trouble, their parent governments can always provide them with subsidies.

Third, it is argued that government corporations are independent and nonpolitical. They are designed to be free of the politics surrounding the appointment of department heads, the claims of organized interest groups, and the pressures of elections. Governing boards, for instance, are appointed for fixed, overlapping terms so newly elected chief executives can not sweep out old boards and bring in new people, except over a period of several years. Many government corporations are even removed from jurisdictional politics because they are designed to deliver services or finance projects that cross city and county lines, state borders, or international boundaries. It is assumed that the employees of government corporations, distanced from politics, can dispassionately focus on the efficient achievement of public purposes.

Fourth, it is thought that government corporations get things done. It is easy to find bridges, highways, baseball stadiums, power plants, housing projects, canals, parks, and a host of other public works developed by government corporations. The facilities of government corporations usually appear well maintained. Government corporations appear to act as traditional public agencies vacillate and when private companies hesitate to risk their own capital.

Current Issues

The exact number of government corporations in the United States is difficult to determine because of differences in how they are defined. There are at least 47 government corporations operating at the national level. Examples include the Bonneville Power Administration, Saint Lawrence Seaway Development Corporation, and the Resolution Trust Corporation. Government-sponsored enterprises, such as the Student Loan Marketing Association, are not included because they are privately owned.

There are approximately 3,000 government corporations at the state level. This includes many state-level government corporations that operate with localities, such as New York's Metropolitan Transportation Authority in New York City and the Southeastern Pennsylvania Transportation Authority in Philadelphia. Subsidiaries of government corporations are counted separately, such as the Chicago Transit Authority, which is part of the Northeastern Illinois Regional Transportation Authority. Special districts are excluded because they have elected governing boards and the power to impose taxes or special assessments.

The central issue for government corporations is whether they are living up to expectations. Although most officials of government corporations see themselves as doing a good job, many Americans think otherwise. Government corporations are thought to be poorly managed, increasingly dependent on tax subsidies, politically biased toward economic elites, and generally unable to deal with pressing and complex problems of housing, education, health, economic development, transportation, and the environment. Anecdotal evidence of the problems with government corporations include such things as:

- The Port Authority of New York and New Jersey built a luggage tunnel at Kennedy Airport for US$21 million in 1990 even though the airlines said they would not use it.
- Of 17 nuclear power plants built by the Tennessee Valley Authority since the mid-1970s, 8 were canceled after $4 billion had been spent, one closed after a fire, and 4 others had their operations suspended for safety reasons.
- Between 1954 and 1973, the Delaware River Port Authority's board chairman benefited as the owner or principal in several construction companies that received $3 million in authority construction contracts.
- The Louisiana Public Facilities Authority issued $41 million in tax-exempt bonds in 1984 and then retired them in 1987, for a housing project that was never developed.
- The secretary-treasurer of the Kentucky Infrastructure Authority and his father made over $7,000 by buying bonds they knew could be resold to the authority at higher prices.

There is also evidence that indicates that government corporations are not controlling their debt issuance. In Illinois, for example, the state's per capita off-budget debt nearly doubled in a decade, from $5.1 billion in 1981 to $9.9 billion in 1990. Similarly, in New York, the debt of state corporations has risen three times faster than direct obligations of the state. The outstanding debt of New York's Energy Research and Development Authority, for

instance, rose almost tenfold from 1982 to 1990, from $327 million to $3.7 billion.

Even though it is difficult to generalize from specific cases, the perception and reality of problems has led to various reform initiatives. One approach has been to give elected officials greater control over the operations of government corporations. Beginning in the late 1980s, New York state required its corporations to adopt and publish comprehensive guidelines covering the whole spectrum of personal service contracts, such as how subcontractors were selected and the methods used to measure vendor performance. Similarly, at the federal level, the 1954 Government Corporations Act was strengthened in 1990 to require standardize financial recording-keeping among government corporations. Chief executives (the President and governors) have also been given the power to install their department heads as ex officio members of governing boards. For example, New Jersey's Commissioner of Transportation—a cabinet-level official—is now a member of the governing boards of several state transportation corporations.

A second approach has been to advocate the privatization of some or all of the functions of government corporations. To those who support privatization, it does not matter whether it is the Department of Education or the TVA, the public sector is necessarily inefficient, unresponsive to citizen needs, and a drain on taxpayers. For these reasons, arguments have been made to turn over New Jersey's Sports and Exposition Authority to a private company, to contract-out most of the functions of the Massachusetts Turnpike Authority, to transfer the facilities of the Tennessee Valley Authority to private utilities, and to sell-off the airports run by the Port Authority of New York and New Jersey. Although such proposals have received much attention, no major privatization has yet occurred, primarily because of the difficulty in transferring the tax-exempt debt of government corporations to private firms.

Comparisons to Other Nations

U.S. government corporations are strikingly similar to so-called public enterprises in other nations. Public enterprises also have boards of directors, professional managers, political independence, and separate systems of financing. In fact, the Port of London Authority was the model used for the creation of the Port Authority of New York and New Jersey.

One difference between the United States and other countries is that many public enterprises—such as those found in Europe, Africa, and Asia—are nationalized industries financed largely with tax receipts. Another distinction is that there is often a cabinet-level department responsible for the oversight of government corporations in parliamentary systems, but not in the United States.

Since the 1980s, there has been a committed effort to privatize nationalized industries in several nations, including Great Britain, Ireland, India, and much of Eastern Europe. Interestingly enough, even as the United States has been quick to champion the cause of private competition throughout the world, it has been slow to privatize its own government corporations. There appears to be an unwillingness among Americans to equate their government corporations with the public enterprises found in other nations, even though there are as many similarities as differences.

JERRY MITCHELL

BIBLIOGRAPHY

Axelrod, Donald, 1992. *Shadow Government: The Hidden World of Public Authorities—And How They Control over $1 Trillion of Your Money.* New York: John Wiley.
Caro, Robert, 1974. *The Power Broker: Robert Moses and the Fall of New York.* New York: Vintage Books.
Cohen, Julius Henry, 1946. *They Builded Better Than They Knew.* New York: Julian Messner.
Dimock, Marshall E., 1934. *Government-Operated Enterprises in the Panama Canal Zone.* Chicago: University of Chicago Press.
Doig, Jameson W., 1983. "'If I See A Murderous Fellow Sharpening a Knife Cleverly' . . . The Wilson Dichotomy and the Public Authority Tradition." *Public Administration Review* 43 (July/August): 292–304.
Henriques, Diana, 1986. *The Machinery of Greed: Public Authority Abuse and What to Do About It.* Lexington, MA: Lexington Books.
Mitchell, Jerry, 1993. "Accountability and the Management of Public Authorities in the United States," *International Review of Administrative Sciences* 59 (September): 477–492.
———, ed., 1992. *Public Authorities and Public Policy: The Business of Government.* New York: Greenwood Press.
National Academy of Public Administration, (NAPC) 1981. *Report on Government Corporations.* Washington, DC: NAPC.
Seidman, Harold, 1954. "The Government Corporation: Organization and Controls." *Public Administration Review* 14 (Summer): 183–192.
Selznick, Philip, 1966. *TVA and the Grassroots: A Study in the Sociology of Formal Organizations.* New York: Harper & Row.
Thurston, John, 1937. *Government Proprietary Corporations in the English-Speaking Countries.* Cambridge, MA: Harvard University Press.
Van Dorn, Harold A., 1926. *Government Owned Corporations.* New York: Knopf.
Walsh, Annmarie Hauck, 1978. *The Public's Business: The Politics and Practices of Government Corporations.* Cambridge, MA: MIT Press.
Wettenhall, Roger, 1978. "Public Enterprise in Eight Countries: A Comparative Survey." *Australian Journal of Public Administration* 37 (December): 398–403.

GOVERNMENT FAILURE.
A segment of economic theory that explains the conditions under which governmental provision of public goods and services is inefficient. Charles Wolf, Jr. (1979) described a variety of circumstances under which government intervention in the private economy to correct market failures may produce new inefficiencies and conditions under which government may over- or underproduce public services or provide them at too high of a cost.

Government failure is an important component in the theory of private nonprofit organizations. In particular, this body of theory has been used to explain why private nonprofit organizations arise to provide public goods and services on a voluntary basis, even in the presence of governmental provision. Government failure theory applied to nonprofit organizations focuses on the limitations of government and how private nonprofit organizations may fill in the niches left unserved by governmental action (Hansmann 1987).

James Douglas (1983, 1987) identified five sources of constraint on governmental action that create unsatisfied demands for public service to which private nonprofits may respond:

1. The "categorical constraint" results from the necessity of governments to provide goods and services on a uniform and universal basis. This constraint implies that the demands of individuals whose preferences for public services differ from the norm will go unsatisfied. This situation creates niches for nonprofit organizations to provide additional public services on a voluntary basis. Moreover, since government must provide its services universally to all its citizens, it is limited in its ability to experiment on a small scale with new programs, which creates another niche for private nonprofit organizations.
2. The "majoratarian constraint" of government reflects the fact that in a diverse population there may be multiple conception of the public good and what government should be doing. If government responds to the majority, it leaves niches for private nonprofit organizations to respond to minority issues and demands.
3. The "time horizon" constraint of government reflects the relatively short tenures of government officeholders and their consequent incentive to focus on short term-issues and results. This constraint leaves another area of action for private nonprofit organizations—the addressing of long-term societal issues and concerns.
4. The "knowledge constraint" connotes that government bureaucracies are organized in a relatively monolithic, hierarchical way and, hence, cannot be expected to generate all of the relevant information, ideas, and research needed for intelligent decisionmaking on public issues. This, too, creates a niche for private nonprofit advocacy groups, research centers, and other institutions.
5. The "size constraint" reflects the view that government bureaucracy is typically large and intimidating, thus, it is difficult for ordinary citizens to engage government. This situation creates a niche for nonprofit organizations to serve as "mediating institutions"

between government and the citizenry (see Berger and Neuhaus 1977).

Burton Weisbrod's (1975) seminal economic theory of nonprofit organizations focuses essentially on James Douglas's categorical constraint. Weisbrod considers the implications of government as a provider of a particular public service to constituents with diverse preferences (demands) within a given political jurisdiction. The service is assumed to be a classical "pure public good," which is simultaneously consumed in the same quantity by all constituents once it is provided, and from which no one can be excluded. The government finances this good by imposing the same "tax-price" per unit of output on all citizens, no matter how much or little each values the good. Moreover, the government is assumed to use a voting mechanism to decide how much of the good to provide. For example, the use of majority voting would lead the government to provide an amount of the good that would correspond to the preferences of the "median voter," that is, the voter whose preferences fell in the middle of the distribution of voter preferences for this good.

The particular voting mechanism utilized is beside the point. The essential result is that one particular level of public goods provision will be selected and consumed by all voters, no matter what their individual preferences. Some voters may thus find the marginal value of the good less than the imposed tax-price and, hence, would prefer less of the good, and others may find the marginal value more than the tax-price and would prefer the government to provide more. Only those voters whose preferences resembled that of the median voter would be relatively satisfied. Thus, government is seen to be potentially inefficient in its provision of the good because it provides too much of it to some citizens and too little of it to others.

Weisbrod (1975) has considered various mechanisms available to correct such inefficiency. For example, he noted that people can move to different jurisdictions, where their preferences more closely match those of their neighbors (Tiebout 1956). He has also pointed out that private goods can be purchases as partial substitutes when citizens desire more than government provides. For example, people can buy watchdogs and install burglar alarms to make up for a lower-than-desired level of police services. Finally, Weisbrod pointed out that when mobility and private consumption fail to fill the gap, nonprofit organizations can arise to provide public goods on a private, voluntary basis. For example, neighborhood watch organizations may arise to supplement governmental police services.

One of the important predictions of the Weisbrod theory of government failure is that it suggests that the nonprofit sector will be most active where citizen populations are most diverse, and that nonprofit organizations are important for satisfying the service needs of political minorities. Thus, the theory gives us insights into the important role of nonprofit organizations in a democracy in accommodating the needs of diverse groups and averting conflicts over government service policy (Douglas 1987). It also helps to explain, at the international level, why some countries more than others rely on the nonprofit sector to provide public services. Estelle James (1987), for example, noted that the cultural diversity of such countries as Holland and Belgium helps to explain why these countries, have more significant nonprofit sectors than more homogeneous countries such as Sweden.

Other evidence of the utility of government failure to understand the role of private nonprofit organizations derives from examination of the sources of funding of these organizations (Weisbrod 1988). In particular, Weisbrod presumes that if the function of the nonprofit sector is to provide public goods on a voluntary basis then a substantial fraction of their financing should derive from charitable contributions, gifts, or grants, rather than revenues from sales or membership fees. He thus created a "collectiveness index" from the ratio of contributions, gifts, and grants to that of the total revenues of nonprofit organizations in a variety of fields. The ratio was found to vary widely among industries in which nonprofit organizations participate, but substantial evidence was found to support the notion that nonprofit organizations classified as charitable (501 (c) 3) by the Internal Revenue Service enjoyed relatively high collectiveness indices (typically in the range of 20% to 40%) and hence were indeed providing collective goods on a voluntary basis.

DENNIS R. YOUNG

BIBLIOGRAPHY

Berger, Peter L., and Richard J. Neuhaus, 1977. *To Empower People*. Washington, D.C.: American Enterprise Institute.

Douglas, James, 1983. *Why Charity?* Beverly Hills, CA: Sage.

———, 1987. "Political Theories of Nonprofit Organization," chap. 3, pp. 43–54. In Walter W. Powell, ed., *The Nonprofit Sector: A Research Handbook*. New Haven: Yale University Press.

Hansmann, Henry, 1987. "Economic Theories of Nonprofit Organization," chap. 2, in pp. 27–42. In Walter W. Powell, ed., *The Nonprofit Sector: A Research Handbook*. New Haven: Yale University Press.

James, Estelle, 1987. "The Nonprofit Sector in Comparative Perspective," chap. 22, pp. 397–415. In Walter W. Powell, ed., *The Nonprofit Sector: A Research Handbook*. New Haven: Yale University Press.

Tiebout, Charles, 1956. "A Pure Theory of Local Government Expenditure." *Journal of Political Economy* (October): 414–424.

Weisbrod, Burton A., 1975. "Toward a Theory of the Voluntary Non-Profit Sector in a Three-Sector Economy." In Edmund S. Phelps, ed., *Altruism, Morality, and Economic Theory*. New York: Russell Sage Foundation.

———, 1988. *The Nonprofit Economy*. Cambridge: Harvard University Press.

Wolf, Charles, Jr., 1979. "A Theory of Nonmarket Failure: Framework for Implementation Analysis." *Journal of Law and Economics.* (April): 107–139.

GOVERNOR.

The chief elected officer and head of the executive branch of government in each of the fifty states in the United States. In other countries, the governor is elected or appointed to serve as the principal administrative and political leader of a provincial or state government. Such appointed governors are found predominantly in countries where no formal democratic principles and institutions exist. In contrast, the Queen of England is represented by a nonelected ceremonial *governor-general* with limited political and administrative powers, as in some of its former colonies that are currently members of the Commonwealth of Nations (for instance, Canada, Australia, etc.), or she is represented by a powerful appointed governor-general, as in territories still under direct British rule, such as Hong Kong (until 1997).

Role of Governor

In the U.S. federal system, the governor is the state's chief executive and key political figure. In this capacity, the governor performs many duties, notably: formulation and execution of policy, development of legislative strategy, performance of ceremonial duties, administration of the government, and representation of the state on national matters, such as at political conventions. The governor is constitutionally given the mandate to ensure that the laws of the state are faithfully executed. Because the governor is the most powerful political figure in the state, his or her policies are among the key issues of deliberation by the state legislature and are the main focus of the state-level media.

Evolution of Gubernatorial Roles

Governors historically had limited roles to play in state affairs; however, by the turn of the nineteenth century governors progressively assumed greater political, administrative, and legislative responsibilities as states amended their constitutions in response to rapid urbanization and public demand for more services. As Larry Sabato (1983) observed,

> Governors have gained major new powers that have increased their influence in national as well as state councils. Once maligned foes of the national and local governments, governors have become skilled negotiators and, importantly, often crucial coordinators at both levels. Once ill prepared to govern and less prepared to lead, governors have welcomed a new breed of vigorous, incisive, and thorough leaders in their ranks (p. 2).

Over the past 200 years, the job of the governor has become more demanding and complex. The modern governor deals with a wide array of issues and challenges, most noticeably, crime, the budget, public welfare, education, the environment, intergovernmental relations, infrastructure and economic development, attracting new businesses, and creating jobs. Finding solutions to such problems and resolving conflicting public demands, expectations, and concerns have made the governor's job more demanding and often difficult. As one writer noted, "The modern governor is caught in a crossfire between growing demands for services and protests against rising taxes, between the problems of cities and legislatures that are often dominated by rural and suburban representatives" (Williams 1972, p. 1).

Managerial Leadership

As the principal *policymaker* and *administrator* of the state, the governor is in charge of the formulation and the implementation of public policy, the preparation and execution of the budget, and the appointment of personnel to key administrative positions, as well as the oversight of the administrative machinery of various departments, boards, and commissions within the state government. In recent years, governors orchestrated constitutional revisions and reorganizations, consolidated and fortified their control of administration, and strengthened their management and planning tools (Sabato 1983).

In executing public policy and carrying out administrative responsibilities, the governor depends to a great extent on the support of his or her personal staff. A governor, upon assuming office, begins by appointing personnel to key policy positions, such as department heads, commission or board members, and senior administrative posts. Major gubernatorial appointments of state officials usually include individuals who worked for and provided support during the governor's election campaign and people who hold similar political views and support the governor's political platform. A governor also makes minor appointments, especially of lower-level administrators, as part of his or her routine administrative decisions. Governors rely extensively on their senior and close advisers when making minor appointments to avoid bad postings. The repercussions of designating "wrong" individuals to key positions often include the potential of creating an unfavorable public relations quandary for the governor (Ransone 1982).

Legislative Role

The modern governor is the *chief legislator* in the state. The success or failure of a governor's administration often depends on his or her relationship with the legislature. As the *legislative leader,* the governor usually develops strategies to safeguard the passage of pieces of legislation that favors his or her agenda and to prevent bills contrary to his or her legislative programs. Legislatures in recent years, however, have garnered sufficient independence and motivation to challenge gubernatorial power in such areas as policymaking and passage of the budget (Rosenthal 1990). The ability of governors to get their agendas or specific proposals passed by legislatures often indicates the strength of their own political power.

The governor's authority is sometimes put to the test when he or she is forced to exercise a *veto power*. All the states in the United States, except North Carolina, have constitutionally given their governors a veto power, or the power to reject bills passed by the legislature. As a leadership instrument, governors use the veto to shape their legislative agendas, especially in areas pertaining to budgetary matters.

A state legislature can still override a governor's veto and pass a particular bill, provided that it can garner the votes of more than a majority of the state's House and the Senate. Thirty-eight of the 50 states require a two-thirds majority to overturn a gubernatorial veto; 6 states require three-fifths majority vote, and the remaining 6 states require just a simple majority vote to override the veto and pass the bill (Sabato 1983). Moreover, 43 of the 50 governors have a *line-item* veto power (a power that the president of the United States lacked until 1996). A line-item veto enables a governor to veto a specific item in the budget or an appropriation without rejecting the entire bill. Thus, the line-item veto can strengthen the governor's power in controlling spending decisions. A gubernatorial veto or a line-item veto can be overridden by the legislature in many states by a vote of at least two-thirds of the legislature.

Recent studies indicate variation in the frequency and effectiveness of gubernatorial vetoes among states. Generally, however, the number of vetoes are higher when the legislature is controlled by a party different from that of the sitting governor (Dressang and Gosling 1989). Other factors also play a part in determining the success of legislative approval of the governor's program, most notably, his or her personal popularity among voters and legislators and his or her persuasive abilities in maintaining a less-partisan governing coalition and minimizing a confrontational approach to governance.

In their capacity as legislative leaders, governors in all of the 50 states in the United States have power to call *special sessions* of their state's legislatures during emergency situations. When a governor convenes a special legislative session, the subject matter addressed is usually spelled out in a proclamation, as required by state constitutions. Some states, however, allow the governor to include subject matter in the special sessions that is usually discussed during regular legislative sessions.

Ceremonial Leader

A traditional but important role of a modern governor is performing ceremonial duties. As the state's *ceremonial leader*, the governor is often involved in various formal activities, such as welcoming and hosting foreign dignitaries, presiding over solemn occasions, dedicating or opening public projects, attending charity events, delivering speeches at graduation ceremonies, and so on.

Commander in Chief

The governor is the *commander in chief* of the national guard in each state, in addition to being the most important player in preparing and organizing the state for "civil defense or protection of the civilian population in the event of armed attack" (Snider and Gove 1965, p. 255). As the commander in chief of the state militia, the governor can use his or her military authority to mobilize the national guard to suppress insurrection, repel invasions, preserve property, and protect life in the event of natural disasters—such as floods, earthquakes, hurricanes, or civil disturbances (riots, etc.).

National Figure and Party Leader

The governor plays a key role as a *national figure* in his or her capacity as the leader of the state political party. Through the annual *National Governor's Conference*, the governors of the 50 U.S. states and those of Guam, the Virgin Islands, American Samoa, and the Commonwealths of Puerto Rico and the Northern Mariana Islands jointly influence the development and implementation of a national policy by working closely with Congress and the President on state-federal policy issues (National Governors' Association 1978). Although governors play certain limited roles at the national level, they are not directly involved in foreign policy matters, a domain reserved exclusively to the executive branch of the federal government. After serving the gubernatorial term(s) of office, governors often run for national office, especially for Congress or the presidency.

As the leader of his or her state's political party, "The governor is to play a role in determining who fills party leadership positions, raising funds, formulating and articulating positions, selecting candidates, and participating in national party affairs" (National Governors' Association Center for Policy Research 1978, p. 3).

Governor's Tenure and Power

The *term of office* of the modern governor ranges from two to four years in the United States. Many states historically, restricted their governors to only one term without letting them contest for reelection. By 1987, however, 47 of the 50 states allowed governors to serve for four years, with 20 of the states having no limits on the number of times governors may be reelected; 21 states allow one chance of reelection, and 6 states do not allow reelection (Dressang and Gosling 1989).

The range of gubernatorial powers is largely determined by constitutional provisions and tenure in office; some states still restrict the powers of their governors, but many have expanded the roles of their governors. On this basis, a governor is often perceived as "strong" or "weak." (A weak governor rarely stands a chance of reelection to a second term of office.) Specifically, a "weak-governor" state is one characterized by fragmented executive structures coupled with constitutional restrictions on the governor's term of office, limited control over the governor's personnel appointments and firings, limited formal powers, restricted power to veto bills passed by the legislature, and constitutional prohibition to succeed him- or herself in office.

In addition to constitutional and statutory provisions, gubernatorial power is a function of competence, ability, and personality (Sabato 1983). Moreover, in a democratic system the most important source of political power is the people. The ability of a governor to persuade the populace ultimately determines whether he or she succeeds or fails to exercise the powers conferred to him or her under the law.

ALEX SEKWAT

BIBLIOGRAPHY

Dressang, Dennis L., and James J. Gosling, 1989. *Politics, Policy, and Management in the American States.* New York: Longman.
National Governors' Association Center for Policy Research, 1978. *Governing the American States: A Handbook for New Governors.* Washington, DC: National Governors' Association.
Ransone, Coleman B., Jr., 1982. *The American Governorship.* Westport, CT: Greenwood Press.
Rosenthal, Alan, 1990. *Governors and Legislatures: Contending Powers.* Washington, DC: Congressional Quarterly Press.
Sabato, Larry, 1983. *Goodbye to Good-Time Charlie: The American Governorship Transformed.* Washington, DC: Congressional Quarterly Press.
Snider, Clyde F., and Samuel K. Gove, 1965. *American State and Local Government.* New York: Meredith.
Williams, J. Oliver, 1972. "Changing Perspectives on the American Governor." *The American Governor in Behavorial Perspective,* eds. J. Oliver Williams and Thad L. Boyle. New York: Harper and Row.

GRANT-IN-AID.

Assistance from a central to a regional government, usually taking the form of fiscal assistance, but including distribution of commodities as well.

Governments that rely upon both central and regional authorities must provide for a structure of financial relationships among those units. This is an especially critical concern in federal systems, such as the United States, Australia, and Canada, in which governments at the various levels each impose taxes, generating significant revenue for their own operations. Despite the financial independence this can give governments at various levels, each of these federal systems provides for money grants through which central governments assist the regional and local ones.

In the United States, modern federal grants-in-aid (those from the federal government to governments at other levels) date from passage of the Weeks Act in 1911, which provided for grants to assist states in protecting against forest fires. The act required states that would receive the money to first secure federal government approval of a state plan. It also specified the nature of federal government scrutiny of state programs operated with the money received.

Although the program the Weeks Act created was a small one, Congress soon used grants-in-aid for larger assistance efforts. The Smith-Lever Act established the Agricultural Extension Service, making millions of dollars available to states to provide assistance to farmers and rural families. The Federal-Aid Highway Act initiated highway construction grants to the states in 1916—focusing first on surfacing rural postal roads—and established the precedent of setting organizational and construction standards that states had to meet to receive aid. Additionally, the act provided that grants had to be matched on a dollar-for-dollar basis by recipients. Highway construction grants quickly became the largest aid program of the early twentieth century.

These grant-in-aid programs established the pattern Congress followed in succeeding decades, but they were not the first aid programs, nor even the first money grants from the federal government to the states. They were presaged by over a century of land grants that had supported elementary and secondary schools, transportation (roads, canals, railroads), and higher education. Even more immediate, the Hatch Act of 1881 had provided for annual money grants to each state of US$15,000 to create Agricultural Experiment Stations, although it did not include the type of controls and matching requirements that became associated with later grant-in-aid programs.

As grant-in-aid availability expanded in the twentieth century, there were two periods of dramatic growth—the 1930s and the 1960s. Among the more prominent of the programs adopted during the first of these grant explosions were those included in the Social Security Act of 1935—old-age assistance, aid to the blind, aid to dependent children (added in 1939). Additionally, temporary emergency relief measures were adopted to help state and local governments cope with the immediate problems of the depression years.

During and immediately after World War II, expansion of the number of grants was much slower, but in the 1950s the amount of money expended through grants-in-aid grew. A particularly significant addition was initiation of grants for construction of the Interstate Highway system, begun in 1956.

The 1960s produced sweeping change. This change was characterized by the U.S. Advisory Commission on Intergovernmental Relations as "grant proliferation," with 109 programs added in 1965 alone and the total number of programs available growing from 160 in 1962 to 330 in 1966. Major programs added in this period include those in the Economic Opportunity Act (Headstart, the Job Corps, VISTA, Work Study) and those funded through the Urban Mass Transit Act, the Elementary and Secondary Education Act, and the Higher Education Act. Of especially large financial importance was the Medicaid program, an extension of the Social Security Act.

In addition to expanding the number of programs, the 1960s brought important innovations to grants-in-aid. The new programs carried a wider variety of matching ratios, some were available to private organizations as well as to governments, and the flow of federal funds shifted toward metropolitan areas.

Table I displays trends of grant-in-aid expenditures. The dramatic expansion between 1960 and 1980 in both nominal and constant dollars is evident. The effect this had on state and local governments is suggested by the expansion of grants from 14.5 percent of state-local outlays in 1960 to 25.8 percent in 1980. As a proportion of federal spending, too, grants-in-aid grew, even as the United States was also financing a substantial defense commitment.

Types of Grants-in-Aid

This expanded use of the grant-in-aid mechanism created strains in the U.S. federal system, not only because states and localities increasingly depended on grants as a revenue source but also because of the complexity of many individual grant programs. The pervasive form of grant in the 1960s (and the type that has retained its predominance 30 years later, despite the introduction of alternatives) was the categorical grant, directed at a single, narrowly defined purpose. These moneys are distributed as either formula grants or project grants. In the former case, either the statute that created the grant program or the administrative rules specify the basis for determining the amount that each eligible recipient government or other entity will receive. Some formula grants provide for "open-end reimbursement," under which the federal government matches all approved expenditures by the state or local governments.

Project grants require specific applications from the government or other agency that seeks funding, and the administrator of the federal grant program has discretion over which projects to fund. Depending on the specific type of program, obtaining a project grant can be more or less competitive. Some programs combine features of formula and project grants by distributing funds first to states or areas by formula and then requiring project applications in a competition for individual grant awards.

One of the often-cited difficulties that state and local government officials have noted about the grant-in-aid process is excessive paperwork and administrative com-

TABLE I. Trends in U.S. Federal Grants-in-Aid to State and Local Governments

	Federal Grants-in-Aid			
Fiscal Year[a]	Amount in US$ (billions)	Amount in 1987 Constant US$ (billions)	State-Local Outlays (%)	Federal Outlays (%)
1955	3.2	15.3	10.2	4.7
1960	7.0	29.1	14.5	7.6
1965	10.9	41.8	15.1	9.2
1970	24.1	73.6	19.0	12.3
1975	49.8	105.4	22.6	15.0
1980	91.5	127.6	25.8	15.5
1985	105.9	113.0	20.9	11.2
1986	112.4	115.9	19.9	11.3
1987	108.4	108.4	18.0	10.8
1988	115.3	110.8	17.7	10.8
1989	122.0	112.2	17.3	10.7
1990	135.4	119.7	19.4	10.8
1991	154.6	130.9	20.5	11.7
1992	178.1	146.9	21.5	12.9
1993	193.7	155.2	21.9	13.8
1994[b]	217.3	169.6	–	14.6

[a]For 1955–1975, fiscal years ended June 30; later years ended September 30.
[b]Office of Management and Budget estimate.

Source: U.S. Advisory Commission on Intergovernmental Relations, *Significant Features of Fiscal Federalism, 1994. Vol. 2., Revenues and Expenditures.*

plexity; another is the excessive number of "strings" attached to categorical grants, requiring recipients to follow strict federal procedures (sometimes these are referred to as "mandates" and may become confused with "unfunded mandates"); still another problem is the wide variety of formulas used to allocate grant money, a diversity that suggests failure to establish consistent national policy. The formulas used to allocate grants differ from one another in such fundamental matters as whether they assist states and communities with fewer resources or help those that are better equipped to finance their own programs.

Some critics of the grant-in-aid system have argued that categorical grants-in-aid take policymaking out of the hands of state and local officials and transfer it to national decisionmakers, since recipient governments' resources must be used to meet matching requirements in order to obtain lucrative grants. This criticism, though, like many of the objections, flows directly from one of the primary purposes of grants-in-aid. They are designed at least in part to achieve national objectives, not merely to fund state programs—a point the 1955 Kestnbaum Commission made in the first comprehensive study of the grant system, but a feature that particularly characterized the growing number of categorical grants adopted in the 1960s.

Congress, responding to some of these criticisms of categorical grants-in-aid, in 1966 passed the first of a new grant type, the block grant, when it adopted the Partnership for Health Act, consolidating 16 categorical grants into two broad programs. A second block grant, the Safe Streets Act, soon followed, providing broad law enforcement funding for state and local governments, without consolidating previously existing categorical grant programs. Characteristics of these and other block grants that followed (there were 15 in 1993) are that each is a formula grant and covers a broad functional area. Within these areas, recipient governments have wide discretion on how to use the funds.

An effort to further simplify grants-in-aid came in 1972, with passage of General Revenue Sharing. This type of formula grant was available until 1981 for state governments and until 1986 for local governments. It differed significantly from all other grant-in-aid programs in that, under it, the federal government imposed virtually no functional restrictions on the uses recipients could make of the funds. Its adoption was strongly advocated by associations representing states, cities, and counties nationwide, and its passage was a mark of their political power. At its peak in 1976, General Revenue Sharing accounted for almost 10 percent of all federal grants-in-aid.

The various types of grants can be compared by considering approximately where they fall along two dimensions—the discretion federal administrators have in distributing funds and the discretion recipients have in expending them. Figure I suggests approximate placement of the major grant-in-aid types.

The Effects of Grants-in-Aid

Advocates of grants-in-aid offer economic and political justifications for their extensive use in the United States, including the argument that they are critical to overcoming the effect of spillovers in a federal system. Spillovers occur

FIGURE I. RANGE OF FEDERAL ADMINISTRATOR'S VERSUS RECIPIENT'S DISCRETIONARY USES OF VARIOUS TYPES OF GRANTS.

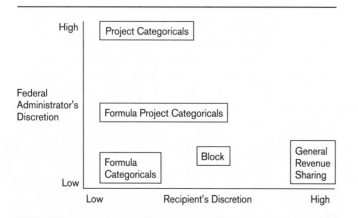

when not all of the costs and benefits of programs undertaken by a state or local unit of government remain within that unit's geographical boundaries. It is argued that grants should be used to lower the price for the local unit providing the service, particularly when some of the benefits the unit provides may flow to other areas of the country. One example is the provision of education to residents, many of whom will move away, taking the benefits of their education elsewhere. Therefore, some portion of education cost should be covered by a system of grants-in-aid, with costs shared by other regions.

A second economic justification of grants concerns income distribution. Local and state governments are restricted in their abilities to use progressive taxation to achieve income redistribution, since higher-income groups could move outside jurisdictional boundaries. A progressive national tax system, coupled with a system of grants, can achieve an equalization of programs across communities differing in income levels.

Third, grants can be used as a form of economic stimulation, as a means of encouraging state and local governments to spend and thereby to encourage employment during periods of economic recession. This was a particularly critical argument during the grant explosion of the 1930s.

In addition to economic factors, political factors have encouraged the use of grants-in-aid. Interest groups have an incentive to nationalize issues, to focus on Washington in their efforts to secure funding for their causes. With such a strategy, victory may be possible at one point rather than in 50 state capitals. Such interest groups may not even be organized in the states that ultimately are affected by the grants. In addition, state and local governments themselves—sometimes their individual agencies, and often the associations representing them as units of government—have participated in the political process supporting new or continued funding of grants. In the face of these political forces, the federal government simultaneously acts through grants to maintain control over revenue resources and spending, directing spending toward particular national purposes but accomplishing those purposes through the grant-in-aid process.

In assessing the effects of grants, political scientists and economists have examined both the distribution of grants and the effects they have on recipients' spending. Studies of some programs (or combinations of them) have shown that cities or states with political power (as measured by membership on key congressional committees, for example) receive significantly greater amounts of grants-in-aid than do other state and local governments. Michael J. Rich, writing in the *American Political Science Review* (1989), reviewed a number of these studies and examined determinants of grant allocations in six programs. He found that the political effect does not hold for all programs and that it may be particularly important for project

grants (over which federal administrators have greater discretion and, perhaps, over which members of Congress, through those administrators, have more influence). The political effect tends to be especially important during the initial stages of program development.

"Grantsmanship" also has received scholars' attention, including the effectiveness of such efforts as hiring staffs to represent cities or states in Washington in the pursuit of grants, and the general administrative capacity of recipient governments and their prior experience with federal programs. Even though grantsmanship can be particularly important for obtaining project grants, it contributes as well to a recipient government's abilities to manage formula grants, since under many of them it is possible for recipients to apply for waivers of regulations and thereby to increase the freedom from limitations the grant imposes.

Regarding the effect of grants on government spending, each grant type is expected to induce particular behavior by the receiving governments; this is the purpose of each type when it was passed. Most notably, governments that receive grants are usually expected to increase their spending for the aided programs. Many grants incorporate "maintenance of effort" provisions, in an attempt to keep recipients from substituting grant money for resources they otherwise would have provided themselves—to help ensure that recipients do not simply shift funds to other programs or reduce their own taxes.

But do grants, in the aggregate, stimulate recipient government spending? Or do recipients replace own-source revenues with grant money? Does the outcome depend upon the type of grant employed?

Many investigators have sought to answer these questions. In an excellent summary, Edward Gramlich (1977) reviewed conclusions of more than 25 of these studies. Most of them found that grants do stimulate spending as intended, and even more than economic theory would suggest. This was particularly true of fixed-amount categorical grants, but also true of open-end categoricals and unconditional lump-sum grants. The fact that grants do not typically result in tax cuts by recipient governments came to be known as the "flypaper effect," recognizing that money sticks with the recipient government rather than being passed to taxpayers, as theory suggested. This may be so because local voters believe that the public goods provided are less expensive than they actually are (since the taxes to pay for them are collected by a different level of government), or because local bureaucrats seek to maximize their budgets and power by maintaining control over money received from grants.

An aspect of the question about grant effects that goes beyond their effect on aggregate state or local spending is whether they lead to accomplishment of particular objectives. There could be, of course, as many answers as there are grant programs, each subject to evaluation. Despite the negative comments of state and local officials about grants—concerning the lack of flexibility and discretion, the complexity of paperwork required, the uncertainty of fund availability, and the problems caused by crosscutting regulations that apply to multiple grant programs—an important investigation by the Brookings Institution that examined how federal grant-in-aid programs work in practice produced rather positive results. A distinction between developmental grants (ones that focus on improving the economic positions of recipient governments) and grants that are redistributive (ones that focus on benefiting low-income persons or groups that are otherwise needy) is central is its analysis. The former (such as developmental grants for hospital construction, highway construction, aid to schools in federally impacted areas, and vocational education aid) conform closely to the traditional goals of state and local governments. The latter (such redistributive grants as those for special education, compensatory education, rent subsidy, and health maintenance) fund activities that traditionally are not carried out by state and local governments.

The Brookings Institution examination of programs in these two categories found a high level of federal permissiveness and intergovernmental cooperation in the administration of developmental grants. These programs were not tightly regulated by the federal government and were generally well received by grant recipients.

The analysis of redistributive grants was more complex. In general, it revealed a pattern of programs that were difficult to manage, especially during their early stages. As enacted by Congress, these programs incorporated new national objectives to be implemented through the grant-in-aid system. Doing so required the federal government to implement systems of oversight and to establish specific regulations for recipients to follow regarding the allocation of funds. Despite complicated and often difficult beginnings, and frequent criticism from politicians and administrators alike, most of these programs survived and thrived. Significantly, in later stages, administration of them became highly cooperative, and many were deeply integrated into state and local government activities.

Grants-in-Aid Today

Historical and constitutional traditions of the United States have encouraged and continue to encourage the use of categorical grants-in-aid. Although the federal government has increased the application of other mechanisms to institute national programs in the context of a federal system (most notably preemption of state and local prerogatives by federal actions and the imposition of federal mandates for state and local actions), grants-in-aid remain particularly appealing. This is so because, unlike their alternatives, the grant-in-aid process preserves a tradition of decentralized decision-making, since acceptance of the grants is not mandatory. Although grants are widely accepted, in principle at least, state and local governments are free to turn them down and, hence, are able to avoid the restrictions that come with the money.

As to types of grants, categorical grants remain dominant, and their strength has been clearly demonstrated by the short life of General Revenue Sharing and the infrequent use of block grants. For both political and administrative reasons, Congress has been inclined to maintain a rather close link between revenue and spending decisions. Some members emphasize the failures of state and local governments to administer programs adequately in the absence of close federal monitoring, and others point accusing fingers at states and localities for not responding to particular constituents (for example, urban ones). By attaching "strings" to categorical grants, Congress can retain the degree of control it needs to ensure that funds are, from its perspective, both well administered and properly targeted.

This control, though, incorporated into the laws that authorize grants and the agency rules that are used to administer them creates a complex web of procedures that governments at all levels must follow to participate in the grant process. To simplify the grant-in-aid system is a daunting task, one requiring changes in grant programs that have been approved over many decades and involving separate agencies—each with its own constellation of interest groups that lend support to their particular causes—and including a large number of crosscutting requirements that apply to all federal grants. Further consolidating of categorical grants into block grants, providing recipients greater flexibility to determine the uses to which the funds will be put, is often suggested as an appropriate reform. (Despite strong support in the past from both Presidents Richard Nixon and Ronald Reagan, consolidations have been difficult to achieve.)

Grants-in-Aid in Other Systems

Both in the United States (between the states and their local governments) and in other national systems, grants-in-aid are used in ways that vary in detail from their application in the U.S. federal system previously presented. Among the U.S. states, "tax sharing" is a common practice, one in which the state collects revenue from a particular tax (for example a motor fuel tax charged on each gallon of gasoline sold) but allocates a portion of it to local governments. Similarly, a portion of the general sales tax, usually collected at the retail level, may be distributed to local entities, based on the locations in which the tax was collected (point of origin) or according to a formula recognizing population, financial resources, or programmatic need of the local government.

In addition to shared revenues, states provide both project and formula categorical grants-in-aid to local gov-

ernments. Local school districts have particularly benefited from these programs, as states have developed sophisticated and complex formulas for educational aid distribution. Aid to education accounts for more than 60 percent of all state intergovernmental aid to local governments.

International comparisons of grants-in-aid reveal similar wide variety. Tax-sharing and general purpose grants are used much more extensively elsewhere than in the United States. In Canada, the federal government, through a system of tax collection agreements with the provinces, collects the income tax. Participating provinces use the federal tax base and rate structure, applying a single rate "tax on tax." Units at the two levels share in taxes collected, each according to its own rate of tax, with the central government administering the collection. The income tax system in Germany provides for division of the federal income tax with the states and cities. Schemes such as these are tax-sharing systems, in various forms.

General purpose grants are used to a much greater extent in Canada and Australia than they are in the United States—a type of grant employed by the United States as General Revenue Sharing from 1972 to 1986. Unlike categorical grants, which are common in the United States, such general purpose grants expand the capacity of regional governments without giving the central government specific, narrow control over spending decisions.

Nations with federal systems of government are not the only ones that have found grants-in-aid useful policy tools. The United Kingdom, Italy, and France, among other systems with unitary governments, also provide grants to subnational units.

F. TED HEBERT

BIBLIOGRAPHY

Anton, Thomas J., 1989. *American Federalism and Public Policy: How the System Works.* New York: Random House.

Gramlich, Edward M., 1977. "Intergovernmental Grants: A Review of the Empirical Literature," pp. 219–229. In Wallace E. Oates, ed., *The Political Economy of Fiscal Federalism.* Lexington, MA: Lexington Books.

Peterson, Paul E., Barry G. Rabe, and Kenneth K. Wong., 1986. *When Federalism Works.* Washington, DC: Brookings Institution.

Rich, Michael J., 1989. "Distributive Politics and the Allocation of Federal Grants." *American Political Science Review* 83 (March): 193–213.

Schwallie, Daniel P., 1989. *The Impact of Intergovernmental Grants on the Aggregate Public Sector.* New York: Quorum Books.

U.S. Advisory Commission on Intergovernmental Relations, 1978. *Categorical Grants: Their Role and Design.* Washington, DC: U.S. Advisory commission on Intergovernmental relations.

Wright, Deil S. 1988. *Understanding Intergovernmental Relations.* 3d ed. Pacific Grove, CA: Brooks-Cole.

GREAT SOCIETY, THE.

GREAT SOCIETY, THE. The domestic policies and programs generated by the administration of U.S. President Lyndon Baines Johnson (1963–1969), which were premised on the belief that social and economic problems could be solved by new federal programs (Shafritz 1992). Most of the current programs that are characterized as the safety net for the poor and elderly populations were Great Society programs that responded to Johnson's initiative, the War on Poverty.

The team the "Great Society" has been found to exist in political and sociological literature: "William Blackstone (1723–1780), in his commentaries on the Laws of England (1765–69), wrote how it was 'impossible for the whole race of mankind to be united in one great society.' Graham Wallace (1858–1932) wrote of the utopian aims of an industrial society in his 1914 *The Great Society*. Even Harold Laski (1893–1950) in his 1931 *Introduction to Politics*, wrote of the 'place of the state in the great society'" (Shafritz 1992, p. 265).

Democrats since the New Deal campaigned on the platform of New Deal-Great Society programs. Republicans never ran against these policies but were pushing to "tighten-up" the administration and budgeting of Great Society programs. During his presidency, Richard Nixon realized that the Democratic Congress would not allow the dismantling of entitlements, so he developed an "administrative presidency," which sought to use the bureaucracy to change the regulations rather than to stop the entitlements. The Ronald Reagan administration capitalized on the split that was developing in the Democratic Party as a result of the tension between the need to have Great Society programs and the ability to pay for them. President Reagan rode this wave into the White House, and the Great Society was further unraveled. Now, in the late 1990s, the attitude of the country is to further reduce the size of the federal government, and is most likely that the growth that is causing the most public angst occurred during the Great Society.

Arguably, the Great Society was the opening of a window to allow further development of the policy sciences in that much of the social legislation generated mandated evaluation. From a public administration perspective, however, the growth of government during this period rivaled the New Deal as the epitome of bureaucratization.

There is debate about whether the Great Society would have occurred at all, considering that the person behind it, President Johnson, the thirty-sixth president of the United States, had become president by virtue of an assassin's bullet. There are others who question the breadth that the Great Society could have encompassed if Johnson had sought reelection in 1968.

Although these debates ebb and flow, many of the Great Society programs remain. Some programs are obscure and mundane, providing little staying power. Others have made an impact on the very fiber of U.S. democracy, and those programs will endure despite political initiatives to the country.

The historian, Doris Kerns Goodwin, in her book *Lyndon Johnson and the America Dream* (1976), quotes a new president who was not only saddled with responsibility but was also struggling with his identity: "I took the oath, I became President. But for millions of Americans I was still illegitimate, a naked man with no presidential covering, a pretender to the throne, an illegal usurper. . . . The whole thing was almost unbearable". This was not the man who was the Senate power broker, the mythic personality, the politically astute genius, the 87-vote wonder (referring to Johnson's margin of victory in the 1948 Senate race) that changed history.

Those who have been close to President Johnson have said that they felt the presence of power when he was in the room. Certainly, there were many bills that were passed because Johnson was president. The Civil Rights Act of 1964 might not have ever made it through Congress had John F. Kennedy still been president at the time. The Great Society was to be Johnson's legacy and the designation of his presidency.

The accomplishments of the Great Society are even more compelling when they are reviewed in the context of the issues that faced the presidency in the 1960s, any one of which could have defined a presidential administration: the Vietnam War and the foreign and domestic turmoil it embodied, Civil Rights issues, riots, and the struggle for justice, the Panamanian crisis, the dominican Republic crisis, India's food crisis, the race in space, the Arab-Israeli Six-Day War, and the capture of the U.S. Navy ship *Pueblo* by North Korea. Despite these issues, the Great Society was an initiative and a body of work so extensive that many of the other defining issues of that time are today merely vague memories.

Four months after Johnson became president he spoke at the University of Michigan, and it was here that he referred to the Great Society in a substantial way. As Johnson addressed the crowd, he told them that, in the United States, we would begin to build the Great Society in the cities, the countryside, and the classrooms.

The Great Society has become almost synonymous with the War on Poverty. Even though the War on Poverty bill was a significant part of the Great Society, it tends to overshadow other programs that had far-reaching benefits; and, for some of these more obscure programs, the United States may just be realizing their benefit 30 years later. (Some examples of Great Society programs that are often overlooked are the acquisition of federal land, the creation of national parks, and the Public Broadcasting Act.)

In order to provide a thorough overview of Great Society programs, the following offers a year-by-year illustration of some significant Great Society programs and laws. In 1963, the Great Society had not been officially inaugurated. It was a time of establishing boundaries and shoring up the congressional support that was becoming more politically allied with the President. In that year programs involved with the following were initiated: college facilities, clean air, vocational education, Indian vocational training, and manpower training. In 1964, programs were established for federal airport aid; urban mass transit; and recreational revenues, including programs for forests, rivers, parks, and waterways. There were farm programs and new pesticide controls, federal highway programs, and new acts and policies concerning taxes, housing, criminal justice, and securities.

Significant legislation of 1964 proved to be the social programs, however. The first full year of the Great Society began the War on Poverty, an initiative called for in President Johnson's State of the Union address. The War on Poverty began with a food stamp program and aid to the Appalachian region. As the War on Poverty was launched, the Civil Rights Act of 1964 was passed, which strengthened voting rights and desegregation in public accommodation and facilities, increased the power of the Civil Rights Commission, and established the Equal Employment Opportunity Commission. Furthermore, the Economic Opportunity Act established such programs as the Job Corps, VISTA, Work Study, and Community Action.

President Johnson's 1965 State of the Union Address, as well as his inaugural speech, detailed more Great Society proposals, which ranged from a voting rights bill and aid to schools to the development of the Department of Housing and Urban Development. On July 30, 1965, Johnson signed the Medicare Act as part of the Social Security law. (The Medicare Act, which provides national health care to the elderly and disabled population, remains a significant part of the national budget.) Also in 1965, the Housing and Urban Development Act was passed, which provided rent subsidies for low-income families, and as a present to his wife, Lady Bird, President Johnson signed the Highway Beautification Act. Other 1965 programs include the new Voting Rights Act, the Water Quality Act, the establishment of the National Crime Commission, new environmental and pollution controls, more aid to small businesses, a fair immigration law, and many other programs concerned with education, law enforcement, health, and the arts.

In 1966, President Johnson's Great Society programs continued to be developed. There were traffic safety and mine safety projects, programs for better child nutrition, truth-in-packaging for consumers, and model cities and low-income rent supplement programs. Also in 1966, the Teachers Corps was established, and there were more programs and acts passed regarding water, fish, and wildlife protection. There was an anti-inflation program, civil procedure reform, and legislation on the freedom of information. During the year over a thousand bills were passed. Johnson also made more than 66,000 appointments.

Moreover, he signed the Urban Mass Transportation Act and a bill creating the Department of Transportation.

Legislation passed and programs implemented in 1967 involved education, more pollution control, age discrimination, more aid to small businesses, and increases in Social Security and pay of civilian postal workers. Treaties were passed that concerned space and the sea. The Consumer Product Safety Commission, summer youth programs, and urban fellowships were established. Johnson's administration saw changes in Vietnam veterans' benefits, in the selective service, and in the government of the District of Columbia.

Great Society programs continued in 1968. Examples are the Fair Housing Act, Food for Peace, breakfasts for school children, fire safety, pipeline safety, vocational education, wilderness establishment, the Guaranteed Student Loan program, the FHA-VA interest rate programs, river reclamation, and increases in veterans' pensions.

On March 31, 1968, President Johnson decided not to run for reelection. He claimed that his reason for not seeking reelection was to save the integrity of the presidency. Five days after Johnson's address, Dr. Martin Luther King, Jr., was assassinated. Riots broke out in over 125 cities. Two months later, Attorney General Robert F. Kennedy was assassinated, following his victory in the California Democratic Primary election. But the Great Society continued. Johnson signed a bill establishing the Federal School Lunch Program, and the assassinations of King and Kennedy brought about stricter gun control. He signed the Conservation and Beautification bill, marking the fiftieth bill in the area of conservation and preservation of federal land.

President Lyndon Johnson made his final farewell to the nation in his 1969 State of the Union Address. He asked the new administration to carry on the goals of the Great Society. His final words to the country again exposed a personality that still expressed doubt, despite the many accomplishments he had made in the face of extreme national and international conflict: "I hope it may be said a hundred years from now that by working together we helped to make our country more just—that's what I hope. But I believe that at least it will be said that we tried."

The focus of the Great Society, which is that the federal government became the provider of environmental, educational, and social programs that guaranteed a better life for all Americans, has blurred, and the continued funding of some of these programs has become a central issue. Notwithstanding shifts in the agenda of liberal and conservative elected officials, the Great Society persists as basic American social policy.

NICHOLAS A. GIANNATASIO AND
ROBERT R. KLEIN

BIBLIOGRAPHY

Caro, Robert A., 1982. *The Years of Lyndon Johnson: The Path to Power.* New York: Alfred A. Knopf.

———, 1990. *The Years of Lyndon Johnson: Means of Ascent.* New York: Alfred A. Knopf.

Furer, Howard B., ed., 1971. *Lyndon B. Johnson, 1908: Chronology-Documents-Bibliographical Aids.* Dobbs Ferry, NY: Oceana Publications.

Goodwin, Doris Kerns, 1976. *Lyndon Johnson and the American Dream.* New York: Harper & Row.

Johnson, Lyndon Baines, 1971. *The Vantage Point: Perspectives of the Presidency, 1963–1969.* New York: Holt, Rinehart and Winston.

Shafritz, Jay M., 1992. *The HarperCollins Dictionary of American Government and Politics.* New York: HarperCollins.

GREEN POLITICS.

The agenda of minority, single-issue parties proposing that industrialization's despoliation of the global environment ultimately threatens human survival. The intellectual underpinning for this largely European political movement of the 1980s was provided by American author Rachel Carson's *Silent Spring* (1962). She made the case that inadvertent but irresponsible environmental engineering through the use of such things as pesticides carried catastrophic consequences for all life on this planet. The argument is summed up in Albert Schweitzer's observation, cited by Carson in her book's dedication to him: "Man has lost the capacity to foresee and to forestall. He will end by destroying the earth."

Green politics have tended toward a predominantly left-wing bias. This fact stems naturally from conclusions derived from Carson's work that unfettered activity by large-scale industries in search of short-term profits produces human-made, self-destructive pollution on a global scale. Nature may be adaptable to change but, the argument goes, human enterprise is imposing change at such a rate that nature has insufficient time to make adjustments to sustain the climatic, chemical, and biological status quo. The consequence is the breakdown of natural life and, by extension, the end of civilization. From a left-wing perspective, this situation seems to embody the point that capitalism is not only pernicious socially and economically but also, in a secular sense, evil. E. F. Schumacher's hugely successful book, *Small Is Beautiful,* published in 1973, developed the point further. It showed that large-scale industries are dehumanizing, economically unsustainable, and environmentally dangerous; the solution can only be the commitment to sustainability and human survival through the conscious reduction of consumer expectations and the application of smaller-scale enterprises to every area of economic activity.

These generalized impulses were given a significant political dimension by being adopted by elements of the European antinuclear protest movement of the early 1980s. These groups recognized, however, that in France,

West Germany, the Netherlands, the United Kingdom, and elsewhere the electoral likelihood of success with an antinuclear manifesto was slim. So-called "green issues," therefore, provided a context for the opposition groups protesting about deploying nuclear weapons and building nuclear reactors. As the U.S. motion picture *The China Syndrome* seemed to show, the threat represented by poorly managed nuclear reactors for power generation purposes epitomized the potentially destructive relationship between high-tech industries and human survival.

By the mid-1980s, most Western European countries had seen the establishment of a green party. The most notable electoral achievement was that of the Green Party in the Federal German Republic, which achieved sufficient support to be represented in the *Bundestag,* offering at least the possibility in a multiparty assembly of holding the balance of power. However, the ending of the Cold War introduced a different agenda, and the German Greens faded politically. (Given that the newly liberated states of the Warsaw Pact and the constituent parts of the former Soviet Union were some of the worst polluted areas of the industrialized world, and Germany professed a willingness to help, this was nothing if not ironic.)

Arguably, the high point of the Green movement came in June 1992, with the UN-sponsored Earth Summit in Rio de Janeiro, Brazil. Here, after a long campaign by Canadian Maurice Strong, the secretary-general of the Summit, the world's powers addressed the Green agenda set out by academics some two decades previously.

Despite media hype that the Rio Summit represented the last chance to save the world, very little was achieved, for three reasons: First, governments in Western Europe and elsewhere had acknowledged public concern by uniting areas of public activity—urban and rural planning, conservation, and the like—thereby creating new ministries with titles such as Department of the Environment. There was a public perception that such matters were being addressed, however imperfectly. (The widespread practice of recycling household glass, cans, and paper indicates the level of individual awareness.) Second, in the United States, the George Bush administration made it abundantly clear before and after the Summit that, as the world's largest consumer of energy, for example, it would do nothing to implement policies that would impact U.S. consumers. Other Western governments were thereby strengthened in their resolve to resist change. Third, the campaign against industrial pollution had surprisingly become, by the early 1990s, an attack on Third World countries like India, who claimed that the Green movement was an attack on its legitimate aspirations to economic progress and growth.

It was easy for center and center-left opposition parties in the 1980s to attack greed and wealth creation by capitalists; it was quite another thing to be accused of discriminating against poor people in the Third World by insisting that their aspirations to physical comfort and economic achievement be curtailed while the industrialized countries made only marginal adjustments, if that, to their lifestyles.

Despite the political failure of the Green movement in the 1980s and early 1990s, the issues of poverty, consumption patterns, technology, population, health, human settlement, waste, and trade have not gone away. Politicians are aware of this but find it virtually impossible to offer to a national electorate a range of solutions that cannot be other than at the cost of the electorate itself. To that extent, green politics peaked at a time when Western European voters were insufficiently aware of the significance of the Green agenda. It may well be that supranational arrangements—whether European Union, United Nations, or some other regional or global grouping—will in due course be the setting for a more careful consideration of that agenda.

PETER FOOT

BIBLIOGRAPHY

Carson, Rachel, 1962. *Silent Spring.* New York: Houghton Mifflin.
Schumacher, E. F., 1973. *Small Is Beautiful: A Study of Economics as if People Mattered.* London: Sphere.

GRIEVANCE MACHINERY.

The method or system established to resolve problems and conflicts arising in applying and interpreting the terms and conditions of the collective bargaining contract. Although virtually any serious employee complaint may be considered a grievance, it does not achieve formal status until it becomes part of the procedure established by law, employment contract, or collective bargaining contract to resolve such complaints.

The complaint, which may be registered by an individual or by a union, may concern any aspect of the employment relationship as it applies to an individual or to some or all members of the bargaining unit. However, to be taken into the formal grievance machinery, the complaint must normally concern the application and interpretation of the language, terms, and conditions of the contract (e.g., alleged failure of the union or management to fulfill the terms of the contract or as the result of disciplinary actions by the employer). Grievance procedures are the heart of contract administration and day-to-day labor-management relationships. They are specified in nearly all public and private sector contracts. Grievance procedures are found in many nonunionized settings as well.

Grievance procedures are defined and explained procedurally in terms of the type and number of steps involved, official labor and management representatives, time limits, and other considerations.

They are usually designed so that those individuals closest to the dispute have the initial opportunity to settle it peacefully, fairly, and expeditiously. Employer and union representatives investigate the circumstances and facts of the complaint and attempt to resolve it to the satisfaction of both parties.

The typical grievance machinery has four steps. The initial step involves the grievant and his or her immediate supervisor discussing the complaint. If a settlement is not reached within five days, the grievance is placed in writing for consideration by the department head or agency head. At this second step the union steward or business agent becomes involved. In step three, the grievance is taken to the level of the personnel manager or director of labor relations for the employer, and to the local, state, or national union representative by the union. The final step entails final and binding arbitration, which in most jurisdictions is enforceable in court. It is estimated that 80 percent of public sector contracts have formal grievance machinery. Under the Civil Service Reform Act of 1978, all federal contracts with bargaining unit representatives have grievance procedures. Nearly all contractual grievance procedures contain an arbitration clause.

A key issue concerns the determination of whether a particular complaint may be taken to arbitration. Certain topics are prohibited from grievance arbitration by law or management rights clauses. Examples include agency mission, employment levels, workload assignments, and governmentwide rules and regulations. However, the *procedures* for implementing such topics may fall within the scope of arbitration.

Several standards are used by arbitrators in interpreting the contract language that often underlies the grievance. Mutual intent of the parties when they negotiated the contract is of primary importance. If two different interpretations are evident, the arbitrator interprets the language in light of the overall contract, relevant law and public policy, and common sense. Specific language takes precedence over general language.

In public jurisdictions there is sometimes a choice of grievance procedures, depending on the nature of the complaint. For example, affirmative action complaints may be taken to the Equal Employment Opportunity Commission at the national level or to its state counterpart. Sexual harassment cases may be heard in a special proceeding. At the federal level, the U.S. Merit Systems Protection Board hears certain types of grievances directly. Multiple avenues for grievances usually cannot be pursued simultaneously.

The costs of grievances are generally shared equally by the employer and the union. In 1992, US$5000 per grievance was estimated to be the average cost. Employees and union representatives are usually compensated for time spent in grievance proceedings. Full-time union representatives often enjoy superseniority, which protects them from management layoffs in response to what management might consider to be overzealous prosecution of grievances.

Grievance machinery is valuable to employer-employee relationships. Its availability helps management identify workplace problems before they balloon into insurmountable crises. It also helps defuse stress and contain it, while channeling the energies of workers and their unions. Yet grievance procedures are widely criticized for for being slow (it may take months for arbitration to settle a grievance), expensive (money spent on grievance processing is money taken from the accounts of the union and the operating budget of the employer), and a great consumer of time. Moreover, the grievance process has become characterized by extreme formality in many jurisdictions, with the presence of lawyers, stenographers, transcripts, and the other trappings of American jurisprudence. It is said that the focus is now primarily on the "rights" of the parties rather than on solving the problem that originally spawned the grievance.

As a result of dissatisfaction with traditional grievance machinery, alternative techniques for resolving disputes have developed. Alternative dispute resolution methods include expedited arbitration, which speeds up the process by seeking arbitration decisions within 48 hours (among other changes), and mediation, in which a neutral third party seeks to determine the real issues behind the grievance and devise a solution.

It is generally believed that an effective grievance procedure resolves the great majority of complaints at the lowest possible level, and especially before arbitration is necessary. A very high rate of grievances carried to arbitration may indicate a poisonous labor relations climate in which the union is encouraging, provoking, and filing grievances in order to antagonize management.

RICHARD C. KEARNEY

BIBLIOGRAPHY

Bohlander, G. W., 1992. "Public Sector Grievance Arbitration: Structure and Administration." *Journal of Collective Negotiations* 21 (4).

Kriesky, Jill, 1994. "Workers' Rights and Contract Grievance Dispute Resolution," pp. 233–251. In Jack Rabin, *et al.*, *Handbook of Public Sector Labor Relations*. New York: Marcel Dekker.

McPherson, Donald S., 1983. *Resolving Grievances*. Reston, VA: Reston Publishing Co.

GROUP DYNAMICS.

Group refers to "a number of individuals assembled together or having some unifying relationship" (*Webster's Ninth New Collegiate Dictionary*, 1985, p. 539). This definition is in line with an academic definition offered by Cartwright and Zander (1968, p. 46) which states that "a group is a collection of individuals who have relations to one another that make them interdependent to some significant degree." "Group dynamics" came into use as a social science term after World War II to refer to the study of the nature, development, and interrelationship of groups.

Groups are an inescapable part of our society. There is not a day that goes by in which we do not hear on the radio, see on television, or read in newspapers or magazines something about groups—ranging from the Supreme Court to street gangs. Groups are not a product of contemporary society but of early human existence. Although there is some disagreement among social scientists as to why people desire groups, two theories are frequently cited: The first states that the need for affiliation is a learned behavior from infancy and childhood, and the second theory contends that instinctive drives draw humans to one another. Essentially, our biological ancestors relied on groups for survival. Specifically, groups offered tremendous advantages in securing food, defense, nurturance, and reproduction (Harvey and Greene 1981). Continuing to use groups as a means for improving human survival has resulted in the establishment of a genetic code that encourages participation in groups (Forsyth 1990).

This entry considers what purpose groups serve today—including the variety of groups that form. First, a brief history of the group literature will be reviewed. Then, the following sections will discuss why individuals join groups, type of groups, group composition and size, group structure, stage of group development, practical implications for managers, and research on groups.

Brief History

The literature is replete with information about groups. After World War II, the term "group dynamics" was used for the branch of science that pertained to groups. Essentially, the field of group dynamics focuses on the nature of groups, the precepts of their development, and their interrelations with individuals, other groups, and organizations. Kurt Lewin is the social scientist who is designated as the father of the field of group dynamics (Cartwright and Zander 1968; Forsyth 1990; Luft 1984). He was also the first to establish an organization devoted to its study (Cartwright and Zander 1968). Because of the laboratory experiments conducted by Lewin and his associates, this approach is frequently used to study group dynamics.

Why People Join Groups

There are many reasons why individuals join groups. Membership may be based on needs, proximity, attraction, group goals, and rewards.

Satisfying Needs

For some people, group affiliation satisfies their needs for security, socializing, and esteem (Maslow 1943). The need for security, for example, can be addressed when an individual leans on group members for support when a problem arises. In this case, the individual will discuss his or her problem with other members in order to vent feelings or obtain advice. One benefit from this sharing process is that the individual may learn that others have encountered the same or a similar problem. This shared experience provides tremendous psychological relief and comfort because it indicates to the individual that he or she is not alone in his or her perceptions or feelings and can, moreover, gain confidence in the knowledge that there are viable solutions that may resolve the problem. This validation of perceptions and knowledge of possible solutions fortifies the individual to confront the challenges within the environment. Without group support, the individual will experience loneliness, which ultimately leads to some form of insecurity or anomie (social disconnection).

Human beings have a need to socialize. One forum that fulfills this drive is group membership. Although the need to socialize varies among people, individuals with a high need for socializing will frequently participate in groups. This activity will provide numerous opportunities for communication and interaction with others. Hopefully, these exchanges are functional so that the individual experiences comfort and satisfaction.

Finally, some individuals join groups in order to satisfy esteem needs. Basically, esteem is an individual's perceptions about him- or herself in such areas as capability, significance, success, and worth. According to a study by Arthur Bedeian, Kevin Mossholder and Achilles Armenakis (1983), individuals with both low and high self-esteem benefit from group participation. People with low self-esteem, however, appear to benefit more from the support they receive from other members. It seems that people with low self-esteem require exceedingly more peer-group validation of their capability and worth, whereas people with high self-esteem rely more on their own judgment about their worth.

Thus, people join groups to fulfill one or more needs. Whether an individual remains with a group is a question of perceived—and expected—need satisfaction.

Proximity and Attraction

The proximity of individuals, the physical distance between one individual and another, and their attraction to one another can result in group formation. It appears that people who live or work near one another tend to become friends. This finding has been tested in numerous studies and indicates that humans tend to like stimuli that they are exposed to repeatedly. Another explanation is that nearness provides numerous opportunities for ex-

changes, thereby uncovering the similarities among the individuals. Assuming the interactions are enjoyable and coupled with the closeness, individuals will experience "groupness" or unity. These feelings will foster the need for group affiliation.

Group Goals

Individuals may join a group because of its goal. For example, individuals who want to overcome their fear of public speaking commonly join the Toastmaster's Club. Since the goal of the group is to help members improve their public speaking, an individual will receive instruction as well as have opportunities for practice if she or he joins this club. Furthermore, the individual will also satisfy his or her security, social, and self-esteem needs. Groups also form when several individuals realize a collective effort will accomplish a common goal more successfully and efficiently (Zander 1985). One such example is Alcoholics Anonymous, a voluntary organization formed to help alcoholics stop drinking.

Reward of Groups

People join groups because they perceive sufficient rewards and minimal costs from the affiliation. Benefits from group membership can range from psychological (intrinsic) rewards to economic (extrinsic) rewards. One example of a group where members join primarily for economic reasons is a union. Employees join because they believe the union (as a body) can exert more pressure on management to improve wages and benefits than can any one employee (Fisher, Schoenfeldt and Shaw, 1993). Specifically, the union negotiates for job security, higher wages, greater benefits, and better occupational safety and health protection for its members (Fossum 1992). Regardless of the goal of the group, individuals join or form groups in order to acquire some type of reward.

Types of Groups

Within organizations, people are assigned to groups or join groups for various reasons. Formal groups are created by the organization in order to accomplish specific goals. Informal groups are formed by individuals who wish to interact with one another because of common interests and friendships.

Formal Groups

There are two types of formal groups: the command group and the task group. The command group is all the individuals listed on the organizational chart as part of management. Naturally, these individuals are also a part of another group that is comprised of themselves and their subordinates.

A task group consists of all the employees who are working on the same project or assignment. Since these employees must interact with one another in order to complete their work, a need develops to create a group. The formulation of the group therefore justifies the frequent communication exchanges among the employees. In addition, these employees will experience other psychological benefits from their group affiliation.

Informal Groups

Informal groups are created because of a mutual interest among individuals, and members can be based in any department or location within an organization. Furthermore, the goal of the interest group may or may not be related to organizational goals. Some examples of informal interest groups found in organizations include technical, technology, statistics, chess, bowling, golf, swimming, literature, and so on. When interest groups form in order to attain organizational goals, it generally signifies that the formal (command) groups have not provided the proper structure, information, or resources to accomplish the work. As a result, employees must join interest groups if they wish to meet established goals. In some organizations, it is the informal groups that govern the day-to-day functioning of the organization. In the event that the group was established for nonwork-related interests, members may also interact after normal working hours.

The basic difference between the formal (command and task) groups and informal groups is that the former groups are sanctioned by the organization while the latter groups are generally not planned. In addition, formal groups are designed to achieve an organizational goal, but informal groups may be formed solely to satisfy psychological needs.

Group Composition and Size

Groups may vary in composition and size and on many dimensions. Group members can consist of the same or different gender, age, educational level, and so on. It is the goal of the group, however, that largely drives the variation among members. When a group's goal yields a small membership, the difference among the members may be negligible, but when the group's goal results in a large membership, the difference among the members may be significant. For example, when the group's goal is to do a large project of interdisciplinary research, the many members of the group will differ tremendously.

Group size varies considerably, but according to Donelson Forsyth (1990), the average group size is two to seven members. Based on the task the group wishes to accomplish, group effectiveness is affected by the size. Philip Yetton and Preston Bottger (1983) indicate that for quality decisions the best size is five members. It also appears that odd-numbered groups (such as three, five, or seven members) are ideal for resolving majority-rules issues. Other researchers report that as the size of the group increases there

is a tendency for some members to loaf (Kidwell and Bennett 1993). This behavior occurs because it is difficult for a large group to influence and monitor all of its members. Finally, as the size of the group increases, a few members tend to make decisions for the whole group (Cartwright and Zander 1968).

Group Structure

All groups develop a pattern of relationships among members as it becomes apparent that some members can contribute more than others to the group's goals. As this realization occurs, roles unfold. (A role is the expected behavior when performing a specific task for the group.) Two roles commonly observed in groups are task roles and maintenance roles. A task role enables the group to define, clarify, and accomplish the work. Whether this role is formalized within the group, the individual filling this position is looked to for advice, instructions, and decisionmaking. Furthermore, this individual is generally allocated an elevated status in the group. A maintenance role, in contrast, involves fostering supportive and constructive interpersonal relationships. In sum, task roles are concerned about the work and maintenance roles are concerned about the psychological well-being of the membership.

Stages of Group Development

There is some disagreement among social scientists as to the number of stages of group development, but most models appear to overlap with Bruce Tuckman's five stages of group development: forming, the orientation stage; storming, the conflict stage; norming, the cohesion stage; performing, the task-performance phase; and adjourning, the dissolution stage (Tuckman 1965; Tuckman and Jensen 1977).

Forming: The Orientation Stage

During this ice-breaking period, group members are generally feeling uncomfortable and anxious. Naturally, all members are on guard so as to avoid any embarrassing situations. Therefore, members evade discussing their personal views or values with the other members, who are viewed as strangers. Such precautions appear to be justified since newly formed groups have not established specific norms of interaction or assigned roles to members. According to Mark Cook (1977) and to Mark Leary (1983), the tension can be so intense that some avoid joining groups because these individuals believe they are unable to cope with the situation.

After some time has elapsed, members begin to feel at ease with each other. During this period, members start sharing information about themselves, thereby allowing others to see their less-guarded self. Members will also experience increasing feelings of interdependence and trust.

Storming: The Conflict Stage

Groups reach this point when politeness ceases and conflict arises, because individuals are testing the policies, assumptions, and power structure of the group (Finley 1992). As a result, subgroups develop and conflict erupts in a variety of forms. There can be conflict because of misunderstanding or situational factors, for example, when a member is habitually late for meetings due to the location or time of the meeting. This minor conflict can be easily resolved by changing the meeting site or time.

In contrast, escalating conflict occurs when a minor concern causes one or two members to disclose an avalanche of suppressed issues and emotions. In the event that the exchange is nonconstructive, which is often the case, the conflict is intensified several fold. Since negative feedback has been shared, the remaining members will seize the opportunity to express their disagreements.

Even though the discussion of conflict appears to be negative, it is a natural part of every group. As members within a group evolve, they experience stress, tension, and conflict. The energy generated through this process can either stall the group or propel it into another stage in its development. In the event the group stalls, it can remain in this state until it disbands, which means the group has thwarted its development. If the group mobilizes its energy toward discovering solutions for resolving the conflict, it can learn and grow. Consequently, the group will move to the next stage of its development. Whatever the outcome, conflict is a powerful force for energizing groups into action.

Norming: The Cohesion Stage

At this stage in the process, the group has resolved most, if not all, of its conflict. As a result, the group experiences cohesion. This means that there is a strong desire to retain members and remain as a group. These feelings also signify that there are renewed feelings of team spirit, stability, and unity. When members feel unity, the relationship among them is extremely positive. They provide more positive feedback to one another, and negative feedback decreases. One by-product of this experience is that members show pride about being a part of the group. As a result, they will defend the group against any criticism from outsiders. This constellation of emotions appears to culminate in group feelings of satisfaction, enjoyment (Hare 1976; Stokes 1983), and positive self-esteem (Myers 1962).

Performing: The Task-Performance Phase

During the early stages of development, groups are rarely productive. When they reach the performing stage and are extremely cohesive, there is a tendency for groups to be productive. Cohesiveness does not automatically translate into productivity, however.

Productive groups, also known as high-performing groups or teams, are invaluable assets to organizations because they meet or exceed performance standards and expectations. In addition to contributing to organizational goals, these groups improve the daily functioning of the organization by being role models for the rest of the organization. Specifically, members of high-performing groups exhibit trust and respect to one another, show commitment to the organization and to each other, and they share leadership, followership, and accountability for their work (King 1988; Katzenbach and Smith 1993). These groups also illustrate a sense of humor and have more fun than other groups (Katzenbach and Smith 1993). Another way high-performing teams improve the functioning of the organization is through management processes such as planning, budgeting, and evaluating (Katzenbach and Smith 1993).

Adjourning: The Dissolution Stage

The adjourning stage can be either planned or spontaneous. When it is planned, it signifies that the group has achieved its goal. One example is a sports team that has played the last game of the season. After the game, the members resume their normal lives until the next season. This annual departure of members is generally stress free. Spontaneous adjourning, in contrast, is unanticipated and stressful for members. It occurs when a problem arises that makes interaction dreadful or impossible. After repeated failed attempts to resolve the problem, members eventually conclude that it is not advantageous to remain in the group. When this decision is reached, the dissolution results in negative or distressed feelings. Eventually, all the members mourn for the group. And some members may suffer significantly from the loss of support they experience from the group.

Practical Implications for Managers

Based on the foregoing discussion, it should be clear that group membership can gratify several needs for its members. Satisfaction of needs can range from psychological to monetary rewards. This entry has minimally discussed the implications of groups for managers, so the next section will examine a few of these.

Regarding transformation programs, groups can be a vital means for fostering change. Basically, the change agent or manager can design the program so that employees can remain together in the same group. The continuity of groups will enable employees to support one another—thus minimizing the stress, tension, and fear associated with change. Essentially, the transition from the old state to the new will be easier for the organization.

When managers assemble cross-functional teams, autonomous groups, or quality teams, remembering that group size can impact performance is vital. Therefore, when possible, managers should form small groups. If this is not possible, they should bear in mind that there is a tendency for large groups to have loafers. To discourage this threat, managers can delegate work assignments that require everyone to participate in various roles and hold all members accountable for their participation (Kidwell and Bennett 1993).

When managers are leaders in a group, they need to vary their leadership styles based on the developmental stage of the group. Essentially, in the early stages of group life (e.g., forming, storming) managers may need to use a more directive and structured leadership style (Bushe and Johnson 1989). Continuing to use this leadership style, however, may lead to a negative impact on group cohesion and the quality of work. Therefore, as the group matures, the leadership style should change to be supportive, democratic, and participative in order to increase productivity and satisfaction among group members (Bushe and Johnson 1989).

Research on Groups

Regarding the specific problems associated with group research within public organizations, four concerns are evident. The first issue relates to finding research in this domain of interest. This author was surprised that conducting a library search using the keywords "group dynamics" with "public administration," "public sector," "public organizations," and "government" yielded articles almost exclusively on decisionmaking. Broadening the search, however, to include keywords such as "organizational development (OD)," "team development," and "diversity" with "public administration," "public sector," "public organizations," and "government" resulted in numerous articles and books. Those seeking information about group dynamics in the public sector, therefore, will need to use the latter keywords, and others, in order to generate the wealth of information in this area.

The second concern is that researchers must be prepared to present information to a number of people throughout a project. On the surface, this requirement does not present a problem because most researchers do expect to present interim status reports. However, a difficulty arises when researchers must present information to multiple decisionmakers with different interests (Golembiewski 1985). The consequence of this unique situation is that research projects can be delayed or thwarted.

The third issue relates to top appointees who are voted out of office. When this occurs, the goals of the agency may change, which then may result in the termination of research projects. This practice of changing goals is due to the political nature of government, or as Paul Appleby (1992, p. 147) states, "Other institutions are not free from politics, but government *is* politics."

A fourth problem is that public employees may be less open or more evasive than private sector employees.

Essentially, to protect U.S. national security, public employees may be hesitant to disclose certain information. As a result, researchers may not obtain the information they seek. In sum, the unique circumstances of public organizations may add some special instabilities and uncertainties that are generally not experienced in private organizations.

Conclusion

Groups are an integral part of our lives. With human cognitive limitations, we desperately need groups more than ever before, but differently from our biological beginnings. Essentially, when people confront the many challenges of our complex and interconnected environment, we need groups for information, support, solutions, creativity, and productivity. If managers and employees pool their efforts and use the information presented here, more individuals will experience satisfaction on the job–and in their personal lives–from participating in one or more groups.

INES KILMANN

BIBLIOGRAPHY

Appleby, Paul H., 1945 and renewed 1973, "Government Is Different." In Jay M. Shafritz, and Albert C. Hyde, eds. 1992. *Classics of Public Administration*. 3d ed. Pacific Grove, CA: Brooks/Cole.

Bedeian, Arthur G., Kevin W. Mossholder and Achilles A. Armenakis. "Role Perception-Outcome Relationships: Moderating Effects of Situational Variables." Human-Relations. v. 36 (Feb. '83) p.167–187.

Bushe, Gervase R., and A. Lea Johnson, 1989. "Contextual and Internal Variables Affecting Task Group Outcomes in Organizations." *Group and Organization Studies* (December): 462–482.

Cartwright, Dorwin, and Alvin Zander, eds., 1968. *Group Dynamics*. 3d ed. New York: Harper & Row.

Cook, Mark, 1977. "The Social Skill Model and Interpersonal Attraction." In Steve Duck, ed., *Theory and Practice in Interpersonal Attraction*. New York: Academic Press.

Finely, Michael, 1992. "Belling the Bully." *HR Magazine*, vol. 37, no. 3 (March): 82–86.

Fisher, Cynthia D., Lyle F. Schoenfeldt, and James B. Shaw, 1993. *Human Resource Management*. 2d ed. Boston: Houghton Mifflin.

Forsyth, Donelson R., 1990. *Group Dynamics*. 2d ed. Pacific Grove, CA: Brooks/Cole.

Fossum, John A., 1992. *Labor Relations: Development, Structure, and Process*. Homewood, IL: Irwin.

Golembiewski, Robert T., 1985. *Humanizing Public Organizations: Perspectives on Doing Better-Than-Average When Average Ain't At All Bad*. Mt. Airy, MD: Lomond Publications.

Hare, A. Paul, 1976. *Handbook of Small Group Research*. 2d ed. New York: Free Press.

Harvey, Paul H., and Penelope J. Greene, 1981. "Group Composition: An Evolutionary Perspective." In H. Kellerman, ed., *Group Cohesion*. New York: Grune & Stratton.

Katzenbach, Jon R., and Douglas K. Smith, 1993. *The Wisdom of Teams: Creating the High-Performance Organization*. Boston: Harvard Business School Press.

Kidwell, Roland E., and Nathan Bennett, 1993. "Employee Propensity to Withhold Effort: A Conceptual Model to Intersect Three Avenues of Research." *Academy of Management Review*, vol. 3, no. 13 (July): 429–456.

King, Dennis, 1988. "Team Excellence." *Management Solutions*, vol. 33, no. 10 (October): 25–28.

Leary, Mark R., 1983. *Understanding Social Anxiety.* Newbury Park, CA: Sage.

Luft, Joseph, 1984. *Group Processes: An Introduction to Group Dynamics.* 3d ed. Palto Alto, CA: Mayfield.

Maslow, Abraham H., 1943. "A Theory in Human Motivation." *Psychological Review*, vol. 50: 370–96.

Myers, Albert E., 1962. "Team Competition, Success, and the Adjustment of Group Members." *Journal of Abnormal and Social Psychology*, vol. 65: 325–332.

Stokes, Joseph P., 1983. "Components of Group Cohesion: Intermember Attraction, Instrumental Value, and Risk Taking." *Small Group Behavior*, vol. 14: 163–173.

Tuckman, Bruce W., 1965. "Developmental Sequences in Small Groups." *Psychological Bulletin*, vol. 63: 384–399.

Tuckman, Bruce W., and MaryAnn C. Jensen, 1977. "Stages of Small Group Development Revisited." *Group and Organizational Studies*, vol. 2: 419–427.

Yetton, Philip, and Preston Bottger, 1983. "The Relationships Among Group Size, Member Ability, Social Decision Schemes, and Performance." *Organizational Behavior and Human Performance* (October): 145–159.

Zander, Alvin F., 1985. *The Purpose of Groups and Organizations.* San Francisco: Jossey-Bass.

GROUPTHINK. The psychological drive for consensus, which tends to suppress both dissent and the appraisal of alternatives in small decisionmaking groups. Groupthink tends to occur when individuals value membership in the group and identify strongly with their colleagues. It may also occur because the group leader does not encourage dissent or because of stressful situations that make the group more cohesive. The essence of it though, is that the members suppress doubts and criticisms about proposed courses of action, with the result that the group chooses riskier and more ill-advised policies than would otherwise have been the case. Groupthink, because it refers to a deterioration of mental efficiency and moral judgment due to in-group pressures, has an invidious connotation. The term derives from Irvin L. Janis, *Victims of Groupthink: A Psychological Study of Foreign-Policy Decisions and Fiascoes* (1972).

Social commentary in Western settings has long been full of references to the negative features of groups or other human collectivities. The autonomous individual has reigned in many circles as the ideal, and human aggregates often have been portrayed as a major cause of the fast fall from inherent grace of people when they are part of some human aggregate. Thus many early commentators were impressed by the power of people in collectivities, and this basic perception often got translated as a fear of "the mob" or the "the group mind" that could

arouse normally docile and God-fearing folk to do things they otherwise would not even contemplate (e.g., Golembiewski 1962, esp. pp. 8–26).

Freud's theoretical interpretation is as elegant as anyone's, and as extreme. He proposed directly that "In a group an individual is brought under conditions which allow him [or her] to throw off the repressions of . . . unconscious instincts." That constituted a fateful unshackling for Freud, no doubt about that. For the "unconscious" is nothing less than the mental databank "in which *all that is evil* in the human mind is contained as a predisposition" (quoted in Strachey 1955, p. 74, emphasis added).

Put a person in a group context, then, and (at least for Freud) a troubling array of "apparently new characteristics" will appear. Those characteristics are not really new, however, but activations of potentialities for evil already in the person, and suddenly released by a "group condition."

Among the latest variants in this tradition about human collectivities as generally troublesome, if not absolutely evil, is the concept of "groupthink" elaborated so brilliantly by Janis (1972). In turn, the two sections below detail Janis's views, and then emphasize several elaborations of his basic model.

Janis on "Groupthink"

There is not much doubt about where Janis came down concerning the consequences of the "groupthink." That evaluation is clearly implied in the subtitle of his seminal book: *A Psychological Study of Foreign-Policy Decisions and Fiascoes.* Janis grounded his analysis in a number of case studies chosen to illustrate why and how decisions became fiascoes, given common features of groups. The cases include the abortive and aborted invasion of Cuba at the Bay of Pigs; the United States war with North Korea; and a revisit to the tragedy of Pearl Harbor, among other detailed illustrations-in-action.

What is "groupthink," then? Janis detailed eight generalizations about the symptoms of the "groupthink syndrome," as well as three hypotheses concerning the probability that the condition will develop (1972, pp. 197–198). Here, consider only a thumbnail summary. The key for Janis is *high cohesiveness*, by which he means a high degree of "amiability and esprit de corps among the members." As cohesiveness grows, so increases the insulation from "outsiders," or individuals or groups that might challenge the decisions or processes of the insiders. In part, this insulation reflects the optimism among group members, and even their sense of invulnerability, which are reasonably associated with high cohesiveness. Relatedly, the insulation also can result from the group members' happy sense of self, which can encourage the undervaluing of outsiders, when they are not seen as overt enemies of the in-group. The tendencies toward groupthink get a big push when the group's leader promotes his or her own point of view.

Now, nowhere has Janis said that all groups generate "groupthink." Indeed, he took pains to emphasize that he isolated necessary but *not* sufficient conditions (e.g., Janis 1972, pp. 198–201), and that he focused on tendencies rather than inevitabilities.

Many of Janis's critics have seen him as less-subtle on this crucial point and, on occasion, Janis often invited just this kind of criticism. For example, he too-sharply distinguishes "independent critical thinking," ostensibly only by individuals, from what too often (for him) occurs in groups. Indeed, at times, Janis comes close to allowing this view to creep into the minds of readers —that the only human aggregate really safe from groupthink are those sorry cohorts having a low degree of "amiability and esprit de corps."

Some Elaborations of "Groupthink"

Two elaborations of Janis's basic conceptual scheme may help in the sense of discouraging groupthink about groupthink. First, Janis's basic position is at least too broad, if not flat wrong. Ample evidence establishes that increasing cohesiveness *tends to be* associated with positive outcomes like productivity, creative ideas, and low absenteeism, *and strongly so.* Indeed, the association between high cohesiveness and favorable outcomes seems to occur in eight or nine of every ten cases, more or less. Groups seem to help more than they harm, in short. This conclusion was obvious some time ago (e.g., Golembiewski 1962, pp. 149–170), and remains so (e.g., Zander 1994; 1982, pp. 4–10). Janis implies that it is the other way around.

Second, Janis might well distinguish several types or kinds of groupthink. Strategic possibilities include at least three kinds of "crises of agreement," which could be included under the rubric "groupthink":

- the crisis of agreement among the "best and the brightest," based on a cohesiveness resting on high self-esteem as well as mutual regard, and with a confidence about future employment or life-chances. This seems to characterize most of those involved in Kennedy's Cuban missile crisis (e.g., Halberstam 1969).
- the crisis of agreement resting on an authoritarian cohesiveness based on seeing outsiders as "enemies" in a state of "war," with low self-esteem and fear dominating among members—fear not only concerning "enemies" but perhaps especially fear of losing their jobs, reinforced by low confidence about similar placements should that happen. This seems to have been the dominant case among Watergate Nixonians (e.g., Raven 1974).

- the crisis of agreement existing among persons having strong affective ties that are expected to continue, as in a family or a "close" work unit (e.g., Harvey 1988).

These three types differ in important ways. Thus, fear of exclusion because of expressing deviant opinions exists in all three cases, but is clearly apparent in the second. Moreover, conformity will exist in all cases, but the temptation will be strongest in the second type. Relatedly, different interventions seem appropriate for each of the three types of crises of agreement.

ROBERT T. GOLEMBIEWSKI

BIBLIOGRAPHY

Golembiewski, Robert T., 1962. *The Small Group.* Chicago: University of Chicago Press.
Halberstam, David, 1969. *The Best and the Brightest.* New York: Random House.
Harvey, Jerry B., 1988. "The Abilene Paradox: The Management of Agreement." *Organizational Dynamics,* vol. 17 (Summer): 17–34.
Janis, Irving L., 1972. *Victims of Groupthink: A Psychological Study of Foreign-Policy Decisions and Fiascoes.* Boston: Houghton Mifflin.
Raven, Bertram, 1974. "The Nixon Group." *Journal of Social Issues,* vol. 30, no 2: 297–330.
Strachey, James, ed., 1955. *The Standard Edition of the Complete Psychological Works of Sigmund Freud.* London: Hogarth.
Zander, Alvin, 1994, 1982. *Making Groups Effective.* San Francisco: Jossey-Bass.

GRUNDGESETZ (GG) (BASIC LAW). The Constitution of the Federal Republic of Germany. Originally only applicable to West Germany, since the reunification of East and West Germany on 3 October 1990, it has become the normative basic order for government and society throughout Germany.

The Grundgesetz should be seen as an example of Western type constitutions. Accordingly, it presents the components and features of a modern constitution: It safeguards the freedom of the citizens by basic rights, determines the basic structure of both governmental and social order, regulates the governmental organization, and creates the different governmental organs—providing each of these with special competences. As a constitutional law its provisions have priority over other laws, that is, it enjoys the "supremacy of constitution."

The Grundgesetz asserts itself against the standards of ordinary law and has a radiating effect on the interpretation of ordinary law sentences, thus serving the vertical integration of law. For the special protection and the enforcement of the Constitution, it has its own Constitutional Court, which also holds the right of judicially reviewing laws for their conformance with the Constitution.

Contents

The Grundgesetz includes the common regulations of a liberal constitution, but beyond that features some particularities.

The German Constitution commences with the basic rights. This is a remarkable feature: Usually constitutions first deal with the nation, the state, and its organization. The precedence the basic rights are given throughout the Grundgesetz is of symptomatic significance. In particular, it is bound to protect the individual and his or her rights. This accentuation of the basic rights implies a deliberate disassociation from the time of National Socialism.

The first provision of the Grundgesetz declares the dignity of humans as inviolable and obliges all governmental power to respect this dignity. Resulting from this protection of human dignity, the other basic rights are guaranteed. These are directly applicable laws, and bind the legislature, the executive, and the judicial branches of government. The different rights of freedom and equality are standardized in detail, as they are common in the relevant catalogs of other constitutions; the Virginia Bill of Rights of 1776 and the French Declaration of Human Rights of 1789 being examples. These rights include freedom of religion, freedom of opinion, freedom of the press, freedom of information, free practice of arts and science, freedom of meeting and association, protection of the secrecy of letter and telecommunication, the inviolability of housing, freedom of choice of profession, and guarantee of property. In addition, there is the obligation to treat all humans equally before the law, supplemented by the prohibition of discrimination for gender, race, or other special features (Art. 3 GG). This provision was added by the liability to assess the factual equality of the status of men and women.

Article 4, Section 3 GG should be emphasized because it provides the right of refusing war service for reasons of conscience. Remarkable in international comparison is also the right of asylum, which Article 16a GG grants to all who are politically persecuted. On the authority of this right, every year several hundred thousand people come as legal immigrants to the Federal Republic of Germany, and this is why the right was limited in 1993. Since then, persons who are safe from being prosecuted in a different country, where the application of the convention on the legal status of refugees and the convention for the protection of human rights and basic rights is insured, have not been entitled to the right of asylum.

The second section of the German Constitution defines and details the federal structure of the governmental organization. The federal structure, which can be seen from the name "Federal Republic of Germany," represents an identity-determining principle of the Grundgesetz and is embodied as such in Article 20, Section 1 GG. This means, first of all, that beside the level of the Bund (the federation of the German states) there are in addition the levels of the Länder (federal states). The Länder themselves have the quality of states; they are not merely administrative units. If the Grundgesetz does not provide a different regulation, the Länder will be responsible for exercising the governmental authorities, and not the Bund.

As in every national confederation, regulations must be established for the distribution of competences between Bund and Länder, for the possibilities of the Bund to influence the constituent states and, the reverse, the influence of the constituent states on the Bund. Also, provisions must be found for the common performance of tasks. The Grundgesetz provides a distribution of competences between Bund and Länder in a way that means that basically the Länder are responsible. According to the legal construction, the Bund will only be responsible in exceptional cases (i.e., when the Grundgesetz assigns tasks to the Bund). If the Grundgesetz does not state who is responsible, the Länder will automatically be responsible (Art. 30 GG).

With regard to the field of legislation, the relevant regulation is detailed in Article 70ff. Of course, the majority of important legislative states were transferred from the Grundgesetz to the Bund so that the rule-exception ratio for the competence of the Länder and the Bund is in fact reversed in the field of legislation: Here, the Bund clearly dominates. On the whole, the Länder are only responsible for legislation in the field of police administration (but there are factual coordinations between the Länder here), the sector of communal law, and the whole sector or education and culture, as well as regards the right of broadcasting and television.

Alternatively, in the field of administration, the Länder dominate again. The Länder hold the executive competence for their own laws anyway, but as a rule, for the federal laws, too (Art. 83 GG). Here, the Bund has only supervisory rights and limited possibilities of exercising influence. The jurisdiction is divided up between Bund and Länder. Although the courts are assigned to the Länder, the Supreme Courts for the different legal fields are courts of the Bund (Art. 92ff. GG). Thus the uniformity of jurisdiction is insured all over Germany. Also contributing to this uniformity is that the court procedural law is the business of the Bund, as well as the civil law and the economic law (civil law and public law).

Finally, the part of the Grundgesetz that is dedicated to finances (Art. 104aff. GG) defines that the Bund and the Länder are separated regarding their budgetary management. Each of them bears the costs that are involved in exercising those tasks for which they are responsible. The distribution of taxes is performed in a complicated system between Bund and Länder. Besides, Länder that are substantially behind others in their economic and financial power can be supported by other (richer) Länder.

In the form of the Bundesrat (Upper House of the German Federal Parliament), the Länder have their own organ to exercise influence on the Bund (Art. 50 GG). The Bundesrat plays a codetermining part in legislation and in the influence of the Bund on the Länder in the field of administration. The Bund holds the beforementioned supervisory rights over the Länder where these implement federal laws. Additionally, the Bund will insure that the Länder and the federal constitutions are within the scope of the essential principles of the Grundgesetz (Art. 28, Sections 1 and 3 GG) and that the Länder fulfill their liabilities in accordance with the federal law. Here, the Bund has enforcement possibilities, but these have never had to be applied, so far. Also the rule included in Article 31 GG, the supremacy of the federal law: "Federal law breaks Länder law," serves for legal clearness and uniformity.

Common activities of Bund and Länder are not provided in the Grundgesetz; it is actually quite the opposite: for reasons of the clear distribution of responsibilities either the Länder or the Bund shall be responsible. Only for a restricted field of tasks that exceed the financial possibilities of the countries the so-called collective tasks are standardized (Art. 91a and b GG).

In the history of the Federal Republic, so far the coexistence of Bund and Länder has proved to be satisfactory for the major part. Of course interest conflicts between Bund and Länder have always existed, same as party-political conflicts between Bund and Länder governed by different political directions, but, finally, compromises tolerable by both sides would be found or the conflict would be settled by appeal to the Federal Constitutional Court. Nevertheless, a long-term shifting of weight from the Länder to the Bund can be observed. Only recently the Länder achieved a situation whereby a constitutionally legal change may strengthen their position toward the Bund.

In a democracy, legal regulations are required for free and open political communication, the same as for the institutionalized input structures that give citizens the chance of feeding their interests and opinion into the political system. Political communication among the citizens is protected by the basic rights, especially by the freedom of opinion, meeting, and association. A special feature of the Grundgesetz that it at first only shared with the Italian Constitution and later also with some other constitutions, is its display of the political parties.

Article 21 GG, on one hand recognizes the part the political parties play in the political process, guaranteeing the free foundation of parties, their free practice, and the equality of chances. On the other hand, it binds the parties to organize their internal structure following democratic principles and render account of their finances in public.

As a reaction to the takeover by the National Socialists, the Federal Republic of Germany has developed the political philosophy of a "defensive democracy." All citizens are granted political freedom, but this freedom must not be used to abolish the freedom of the political order itself—to use a slogan: "No freedom for the enemies of freedom." Accordingly, parties that aim at abolishing the liberally democratic basic order can be prohibited by the Federal Constitutional Court (and only by this!). Also, a provision has been established for an individual abuse of the basic laws to fight the liberally democratic basic order. According to Article 18 GG, for such cases the forfeiture of the political substantial basic rights can be declared by the Federal Constitutional Court.

The democratic central organ is the Parliament, the Bundestag (Lower House of the German Federal Parliament), which is dealt with in Article 38ff. GG. In this provision, first of all, the principles of general, direct, free equal, and secret elections are embodied. It also determines the freedom of the delegates toward orders and directions. Details of the electoral procedure are not defined in the Constitution, however. These need to be defined by a simple law. The other parliamentarily legal regulations correspond to the parliamentary tradition as it is also found in other parliamentary governmental systems.

The delegates are granted protection against prosecution in the form of indemnity and immunity; Parliament debates in public; the details of its internal procedures are defined in its own standing order. Important for the function of the Parliament as a control organ is the instrument of the fact-finding committees (Art. 44 GG). These committees are entitled to provide evidence themselves, that is, inspect files and interrogate witnesses.

The logic of the parliamentary split between the majority bearing the government on one hand and the opposition minority on the other hand implies the grant of this control right to a minority. The Grundgesetz presupposes a quarter of parliamentarians for instituting such a fact-finding committee. In practice, a parliamentary inquiry organ represents an important means for the opposition, which has repeatedly led to political consequences in the history of the Federal Republic of Germany.

As regards the other governmental organs, the Bundesrat (Upper House of the German Federal Parliament) (Art. 50ff. GG) has been mentioned before as the organ by which the Länder exercise influence on the Bund.

The Bundesrat

The Bundesrat consists of members of the Länder governments, however, not of Länder representatives directly elected by the people. Thus the Bundesrat does not represent a senate in the sense of a second representation of the people originating in the population of the individual Länder.

Its most important competence is cooperation in the legislative procedure. As a rule, laws that concern the own interests of the Länder can only be passed by the consent of the Bundesrat. Thus the political power of the Bundesrat is not insignificant. This will especially play a part if the majority in the Bundesrat is politically oriented differently from the government-bearing majority in the Bundestag.

As a result, there is structural pressure that the major political powers communicate with each other and find compromises. This is why, in certain parts, the democracy in the Federal Republic of Germany shows concordance-democratic features.

The Bundespräsident

The Bundespräsident (Federal President) (Art. 54ff. GG) is sovereign of the government and represents the Federal Republic to the world. This office involves only little political power and has mainly representative functions. Only in the times of parliamentary crises when the government cannot assemble a majority in Parliament, the Bundespräsident will hold substantial competences. In particular, he or she can determine whether new elections will be held or whether a solution to the crisis will be tried with the present Parliament. The Bundespräsident has no authority in emergency cases.

The Bundesregierung

The political leading organ is the Bundesregierung (Federal Government) (Art. 62 GG). It is designed strictly parliamentary, that is, its existence depends on the confidence of Parliament. This dependence concentrates in the Bundeskanzler (Federal Chancellor), who is elected by the Bundestag. The Bundeskanzler is free to select the other members of the Federal Government and also to determine political guidelines. Corresponding to this function as a confidential person of Parliament, the government is also supported in that it is the Bundestag that declares the no-confidence vote to the Bundeskanzler. A special feature of the Grundgesetz that has grown from the experience of the preceding Constitution, the Constitution of the Weimar Republic, is that the Bundeskanzler can only declare the vote of no-confidence, if, with the majority of the votes of Parliament, a new Bundeskanzler is elected. This means that a government can only be overthrown if an alternatives is available that forms a majority—a condition that substantially strengthens the position of the government. This is one of the points wherein the Grundgesetz, as a reaction to the failure of democracy before 1933, has chosen regulations different from the Constitution of that time.

In the Grundgesetz are provisions for the legislature (Art. 70ff. GG) and administration on a federal level (Art. 83ff. GG); mainly, the responsibilities of the Bund are demarcated from the responsibilities of the Länder, and the cooperation authorities of the Bundesrat are determined in detail. Important for the administration in Germany is also Article 33, which, apart from the equality of chances for access to the Public Service, also determines that the "supreme authorities" must be performed by members of the Public Service, which are in a relationship of service and faith under public law. Thus, on a constitutional level, the civil servant relationship is prescribed as the basic structure for the work relationship of governmental officials.

The judicial arm (Art. 92ff. GG) is provided with the guarantee of independence and is bound to the principles of a fair trial (so-called justice basic rights, Art. 101ff. GG), such as guarantee of a legal hearing, the prohibition of multiple punishment, and the *nulla poena sine lege* sentence.

The Bundesverfassungsgericht

An outstanding position is taken by the Bundesverfassungsgericht (Federal Constitutional Court). Its major competencies are centered around conflicts between governmental organs, (in other words, the classic field of governmental jurisdiction), and between further conflicts between Bund and Länder or between different Länder, as well as the decision whether statutes or other laws, conform with the Constitution. A special instrument for the protection of the basic rights of citizens has been created in the form of the constitutional complaint by which the individual citizen can appeal to the constitutional court him- or herself, if he or she maintains being violated by the public power in a basic law.

The Federal Constitutional Court and the performance of its competences play a great part in Germany. This institution enjoys great esteem by the population, an esteem that has grown from its jurisdictional activity, which has rendered the observance of the Constitution and, in particular, the effectiveness of the basic rights. Not least due to the basic-right-friendly jurisdiction, the basic rights play an important part in the legal as well as in the political culture of the Federal Republic. The strong position accrued to the Federal Constitutional Court in reality also has an aspect to be considered critically: this involves the danger of an excessive political jurisdictional behavior. However, the view that the fundamentals of politics should be determined by parliament and not by the Constitutional Court seems to have been effective over the past few years in Federal Constitutional Law, meaning that a certain judicial self-restraint can be observed.

The Grundgesetz opens wide for international cooperation and can, therefore, be characterized as an open Constitution, friendly to international law. It overcomes the seclusion of the conventional national state. This is shown by the fact that the general rules of international law are by that fact alone part of German law and are beyond that given priority over the laws. Actions that shall interfere with the peaceful coexistence of nations and, in particular, the performance of an offensive war are prohibited as unconstitutional and must be punished. The Constitution itself limits the production and distribution of war arms (Art. 26 GG). Above all, however, the Grundgesetz allows the transfer of the sovereignty to intergovernmental institutions (Art. 24 GG).

The Constitution of the Federal Republic of Germany provides for the limitation of German sovereignty in favor of international organizations. A constitutional change performed only recently refers to the process of European unification (Art. 23 GG). The Constitution enables and welcomes it, but also presupposes that the substantial leading principles of democracy, the rule of law, and social welfare are guaranteed and the federal structure remains protected.

These are exactly the principles that determine the identity of the Grundgesetz. They are written down in Articles 20 and 28. The rule of law, the rule of social welfare, the federal structure, and the republican character of the governmental system must be added to the democracy. A constitutional change that touches these principles is impermissible by authority of a constitutional declaration (Art. 79, subsection 3 GG). One therefore must speak of an "eternity guarantee." Of course, this eternity guarantee can only insure what can be guaranteed by legal means. Other parts of the Constitution can be changed, for example, by a law that has a two-thirds majority both in Parliament and in the Bundesrat (Art. 79, Sections 1 and 2 GG).

History

The Grundgesetz dates from 1949 and founded the former Bundesrepublik as a state within the territory of the occupation zone managed previously by the three Western Allies, and it originated on their initiative. This impulse for the establishment of a constitution was received from the German side with hesitation, as it feared that a constitution for West Germany would deepen the separation between West and East Germany and that this would be long-lasting—a fear that would become absolutely true. Without the Constitution an alternative may have appeared.

The designation as "Grundgesetz" goes back in German history as far as to the old Reich before 1805, where basic provisions were designated as "leges fundamentale," that is, basic laws. From the German side, however, the term "Constitution" was not chosen deliberately. It did not want to give the separate West German creation the seal of approval. Only gradually did it grow into a fully valid Constitution because of the appreciation it met.

The Grundgesetz has incorporated different influences. It mainly follows the Atlantic constitutional tradition, which includes human rights measures as well as provisions for the operation of governmental organs. A detailed analysis shows that the Grundgesetz can be retraced

to the tradition of different European Constitutions of the past and also to the impact of the United States, not least of which is the superiority of the U.S. Constitution and the Supreme Court, which controls the observance of the Constitution by the legislature.

Naturally, the German tradition has exercised a strong influence. Different constitutional documents of the past have left their marks. Also important is the Constitution of the revolution year 1848, with its liberal basic law declaration, a Constitution that was never put into practice. The last preceding constitution, the Constitution of Weimar (1919), serves as an example in some provisions, in others, however, the Grundgesetz deliberately chose a different regulation in consideration of the failure of the Weimar Republic. In these parts, the Grundgesetz may be understood as a counterconstitution to Weimar: For example, in the weak position of the governmental leader, who is also no longer elected by the people, in the concept of the defensive democracy, and in the limitation of a constructive no-confidence vote. The federal structure corresponds to German history, which contrary to that of the European central states, was featured by a splitting up of individual states.

The Allies' 1948 specifications for the establishment of the Grundgesetz were a relatively weak central government and strong Länder, which were both in accordance with German tradition.

The Grundgesetz was amended and supplemented relatively frequently, 42 times until autumn 1994. These amendments partly concerned inferior matters, reflecting important elements of Germany's postwar history, such as the restoration of the armed forces. The latter was linked with a Grundgesetz amendment just as was the achievement of the sovereignty of the Federal Republic, the provisions for emergencies from within and without Germany and provisions for the case of war. Finally, the reunification of the two German states in 1990 also involved several amendments to the Constitution.

In a legal-technical respect, the reunification of Germany on 3 October 1990, was performed by the entry of the German Democratic Republic (GDR) into the scope of application of the Grundgesetz. In 1949 the basic laws had provided the possibility of such an entry in Article 23 GG, with Germany hoping for a reunification with the Soviet-occupied zone in the not-so-distant future, a possibility which was only much later made use of under absolutely different conditions. Thus the Grundgesetz was of decisive significance in historical events twice. The West German state was founded by the involved (West German) Länder, by working out and taking over the Grundgesetz. In the reunification of the German states it acted as the technical instrument of unification.

Differing from what the Grundgesetz had originally provided (Art. 146 GG), no new constitution was established after the reunification of Germany. The Grundgesetz was merely amended in some (not central) parts. Article 23 GG, for example, included a provision for the unification of Europe. This amendment resulted from the fact that the common policy, on a European level, involves a loss of influence for Parliament and that the Europeanization had led to an increasing dominance of the Bund at the cost of the Länder. Both developments will be counteracted by cooperation rights of the Bundestag and the Bundesrat in matters of the European Union. Further, the increasing dominance of the Bund at the cost of the Länder will be stopped by changes in the area of competence assignments.

Finally, the current political tendencies were accounted for in that the legal assimilation of the status of men and women was amended by the liability of the state to promote the factual implementation of equal rights for women (Art. 3–II, Sect. 2 GG), and by including the liability of the state to protect the natural bases of life (Art. 20a GG).

Significance

The Grundgesetz represented a substantial basis for the success of the democracy in Germany after World War II. It effectively disciplined and controlled political power, insured political, economic, and private freedom, and enabled stable governments.

A substantial functional prerequisite of a successful constitution is its acceptance by the population. Constitutions cannot be obtruded against the will of the citizens. The Grundgesetz is also in this sense a successful constitution. Also, forces that strived for a basic reform of the Grundgesetz did not assert themselves after German reunification. In different sectors, one may perceive that there exist constitutional possibilities to better tackle the tasks and challenges of the present and the near term. Through political process, a rather conservative tendency could assert itself that will change the well-proved Grundgesetz (apart from the beforementioned amendments for the equality of women and men, for the environmental protection, and for European unification).

The success of the Grundgesetz has caught attention abroad. In the same way as Germany could fall back on an accumulated treasure of the constitutional states for its own Constitution, other states also oriented on the Grundgesetz in some points when working out their new constitutions. This situation mainly applies to the southern European states that overcame a dictatorship and consulted the German experience (Greece, Spain, and Portugal). Also, after the collapse of the Communist rulership in Eastern Europe, the German experience with the basic law is being studied there in ongoing discussions.

MARTIN MORLOK AND
MANFRED MILLER

BIBLIOGRAPHY

Benda, Ernst, Werner and Maihofer, Hans-Jochen Vogel, eds., 1994. *Handbuch des Verfassungsrechts der Bundesrepublik Deutschland.* 2d ed. Berlin and New York: De Gruyter.
Hesse, Konrad, 1993. *Grundzüge des Verfassungsrechts der Bundesrepublik Deutschland.* 19th ed. Heidelberg: C. F. Müller.
Isensee, Josef, and Paul Kirchhof, eds., 1977–1994. *Handbuch des Staatsrechts der Bundesrepublik Deutschland* (7 volumes so far). Heidelberg: C. F. Müller.
Stern, Klaus, 1980-1994. *Das Staatsrecht der Bundesrepublik Deutschland* (4 volumes so far). München: Beck.

GUBERNATORIAL BUDGETING. A budget system granting the chief executive the authority to receive and analyze agency requests, to estimate revenues, to prepare a unified budget proposal for submission to the legislature, and to veto all or part of legislatively enacted appropriations bills.

American executives lack the powers of their counterparts in strong two-party parliamentary systems who serve simultaneously as head of the government and leader of the majority party. The separation of powers system in the United States makes budget adoption a cooperative endeavor, involving an executive and legislature elected independently of each other. Although final spending approval rests with the legislature, the extent of executive and legislative leverage over budget outcomes varies across the United States. Arron Wildavsky (1992) has pointed out that allocation of budget decisionmaking power between the legislative and executive branch affects "who gets what." An executive-dominated budget system appeals to supporters of majority democracy since a person selected by the entire electorate allocates resources. A legislatively dominated budget system attracts supporters of a pluralist democracy. Legislators represent diverse districts and bring an array of divergent views into play. Budget outcomes reflect bargains and accommodations among the multiple participants in the budget process.

Until the twentieth century, U.S. legislatures dominated budget approval. Agencies bypassed executives and submitted spending requests directly to appropriations committees. Explanations of budget requests came from agencies unfiltered by executives. Once the legislature authorized spending, agencies carried out their budgets with little oversight.

By the early twentieth century, except for small local governments, size and complexity made diffused legislative-centered budgeting dysfunctional. Since no standardized format existed, agency requests lacked uniformity and were difficult to compare. Legislators found it harder to keep spending within available revenues. Accountability proved difficult since no procedures existed to guarantee that spending conformed to appropriations. As Allen Schick (1971) has pointed out, legislatures increased gubernatorial budget authority in exchange for greater spending accountability and efficiency. The President and most governors were mandated to prepare an executive budget.

With an executive budget, agency budget proposals conform to a standardized format. Executives analyze agency requests, consider their relationship to the requests of other submitters, and make revisions. The executive branch concurrently estimates revenues. Executives compile the revised agency requests and revenue estimates into one unified budget proposal and submit it to the legislature. Standardized formats also allow cross-agency comparisons by the legislature and help executive monitoring of spending.

Executive influence over budget outcomes stems from the ability to set the budget consideration agenda for the legislature. Strong agenda-setting powers result in budget outcomes that closely mirror executive recommendations. At the federal level and in 42 states the executive branch possesses exclusive responsibility for preparing the unified budget proposal. Many executives prepare budget guidelines that shape the dollar value and program content of agency requests. Some budget preparation instructions also require performance indicators (e.g., average cost of clients served) to assess program efficiency and outcome measures (e.g., percentage increase in test scores) to judge program effectiveness. Executives sometimes use quantitative indicators to bolster their budget proposals.

The veto power gives governors an important tool to influence budget outcomes. All governors, except in North Carolina, possess the veto. Governors in 43 states operate with an item veto that permits them to void part of an appropriations bill. (Until 1996, the President lacked the line-item veto.) With the exception of four states, successful veto overrides require an extraordinary majority. Glen Abney and Thomas Lauth (1985) have demonstrated that governors use line-item vetoes for partisan and policy reasons rather than to restrain spending.

The scope of a veto impacts its usefulness as a gubernatorial policy-shaping tool. The Illinois governor may amend or rewrite legislation as part of the veto process. The Wisconsin governor may change wording as long as the law remains workable and the changes do not alter the purpose of the law.

Legislatures may structure appropriations bills to negate the governor's item veto power. Money appropriated by program gives the governor the opportunity to cut unwanted endeavors. Money appropriated to agencies in one lump sum makes it impossible for the governor to eliminate part of the appropriation bill. Money appropriated to a limited number of object classifications, such as personnel, equipment, and so forth, creates a situation in which a line-item veto would cripple the agency and thus have the same impact as a veto of the entire appropriations bill.

Governors may impact budget policy if budget cuts take place during the spending year because revenues fall short of projections. The federal government may run a deficit. Consequently, federal spending remains untouched if revenues fail to materialize. Governors may cut budgets during the spending year without legislative permission in 40 states. Gubernatorial action is limited to across-the-board cuts in seven of these states. In the others, governors may selectively reduce spending, although seven limit the percentage that budgets may be decreased without legislative involvement.

The separation of powers system keeps governors from completely eclipsing the legislature. In the twentieth century, many governors gained leverage over budget outcomes at the expense of the legislature. Edward Clynch and Thomas Lauth (1991) have argued that during the past 20 years, however, some legislatures with limited involvement have expanded their authority. In Kentucky the legislature assumed the task of writing budget instructions. Clynch and Lauth classified patterns of executive influence, based on information concerning 13 states. Executive-dominant states like California, Illinois, and Ohio have systems that resemble the federal budget process. Governors prepare the unified budget to serve as the legislative budget agenda, deny the legislature access to original agency requests, and possess strong vetoes. Governors in Connecticut, Georgia, Idaho, and Minnesota possess the same budget powers as their counterparts in executive-dominant states, except for maintaining the confidentiality of agency requests. Consequently, legislators hold information to challenge executive assumptions. Executives in Florida, Mississippi, Texas, and Utah exert more limited influence over budget outcomes since legislative leaders or key committees develop the unified budget that serves as the legislature's budget agenda.

Even though executive budget proposals exist, these proposals play marginal roles during the legislative process. In Texas and Mississippi both the governor and legislative leaders formally submit a budget proposal. In Florida and Utah governors submit budget proposals, but arms of the legislature receive agency requests and informally assemble a second document for legislative review. In South Carolina the structure limits the governor's impact. The Budget Control Board, which is composed of the governor, two other statewide elected officials, and two legislative leaders, assembles the budget proposal for legislative consideration.

EDWARD J. CLYNCH

BIBLIOGRAPHY

Abney, Glen, and Thomas P. Lauth, 1985. "The Line-Item Veto in the States: An Instrument for Fiscal Restraint or an Instrument of Partisanship." *Public Administration Review* 45 (May-June): 372–377.
——— 1989. "The Executive Budget in the States: Normative Idea and Empirical Observation." *Policy Studies Journal* 17 (Summer): 829–840.

Beyle, Thad, 1991. "Governors," pp. 53–61. In *The Book of the States*, vol. 28. Lexington, KY: Council of State Governments.

Clynch, Edward J., and Thomas P. Lauth. eds., 1991. *Governors, Legislatures, and Budgets: Diversity Across the American States.* New York: Greenwood Press.

Lee, Robert D., Jr., 1991. "Developments in State Budgeting: Trends of Two Decades." *Public Administration Review* 51 (May-June): 254–261.

Polivka, Larry, and Jack B. Osterholt, 1985. "The Governor as Manager: Agency Autonomy and Accountability." *Public Budgeting and Finance* 5 (Winter): 91–104.

Schick, Allen, 1971. *Budget Innovation in the States.* Washington, DC: Brookings Institution.

Wildavsky, Aaron, 1992. "'Political Implications of Budget Reform': A Retrospective." *Public Administration Review* 52 (November-December): 594–599.

GULF COOPERATION COUNCIL (GCC).

Also known as Cooperation Council for the Arab States of the Gulf (CCASG). A cooperative body comprising Gulf-region Arab states whose objectives are to strengthen cooperation, coordination, integration, and interconnection among member states in political, economic, and social arenas.

The GCC was established on 25 May 1981 by the leaders of the United Arab Emirates (UAE), Bahrain, Saudi Arabia, Oman, Qatar and Kuwait. It is located in Riyadh, Saudi Arabia. The basic objectives of the GCC are to effect coordination, integration, and interconnection between member states in all fields in order to achieve unity between them; to deepen and strengthen relations, links, and areas of cooperation now prevailing between their peoples in various fields; to formulate similar regulations in various fields including the following: (1) economics and financial affairs; (2) commerce, customers, and communication; (3) education and culture; (4) social and health affairs; (5) information and tourism; and (6) legislative and administrative affairs. The GCC is also to stimulate scientific and technological progress in the fields of industry, mining, agriculture, water and animal resources, to establish scientific research, to establish joint ventures, and to encourage cooperation by the private sector for the good of their peoples.

The Gulf Cooperation Council is headed by the Supreme Council, which is the executive authority representing the member states. The council is formed of heads of member states and meets annually. The commission for settlement of disputes is attached to the council.

Every three months the Ministerial Council of the GCC, formed by the foreign ministers of the member states, meets to propose policies and to prepare recommendations, studies, and projects aimed at developing cooperation and coordination between the member states in various fields and to adopt the resolutions required.

The Secretariat General of the GCC is composed of a secretary-general, who is helped by an assistant. The Supreme Council appoints the secretary-general for a period of three years, which may be renewed only once. The secretary-general represents the GCC with other parties, within the limits of his authority. The Secretariat General has a budget to which the member states must contribute in equal amounts.

The Gulf Cooperation Council is composed of various departments, as follows: (1) the Department of Political Affairs, comprising security, international relations, and Arab relations; (2) the Department of Economic Affairs, comprising transportation and communications, agriculture and hydroponics, trade and industry, energy, and fiscal affairs; (3) the Department of Environmental and Human Resources, comprising cultural affairs, social affairs, human resources, health, and education; (4) the Department of Legal Affairs, comprising treaties, precedents, and cases, legislation and research, and legislative institutions; (5) the Department of Mass Media, comprising information center documents and library and the computer databank; and (6) the Department of Financial and Administrative Affairs, comprising personnel accounts and support services.

MUSAED A. FURAYYAN

GULICK, LUTHER HALSEY (1892–1993).

A pioneer in the study of American public administration, with interests ranging from the "managerial executive" to the staff functions of budgeting, personnel, and planning at all levels of government. Although an advocate of the universality of management, he maintained his intellectual and practical base in government administration.

Early Life

Luther Gulick was born in 1892 to missionary parents in Japan. In 1904 the Gulicks left Japan for California, where Luther attended school for a year. They then moved to Germany, where his father lectured at various universities. After his return to the United States, he attended school in Oakland, California, where his high marks earned him a scholarship to the prestigious Hotchkiss School in Connecticut. There, his studies concentrated on math, Greek, and Latin. He applied for early admission to Oberlin College (Oberlin, Ohio); based on his examination scores, he was admitted.

University Years

Luther Gulick graduated in political science from Oberlin with high honors in 1914. He met his future wife, Helen

Swift, while at Oberlin, and they married during his junior year. Luther Gulick spent the next academic year at Oberlin Theological Seminary, but then decided to pursue his own path and not follow his father's career. He felt he could help humankind more by working for governmental and political reform.

While at Oberlin, he made the acquaintance of Charles Beard, then director of Columbia University's Graduate School of Political Science. At Beard's encouragement he applied to Columbia University and was granted a fellowship. He also became a staff member at the Bureau of Municipal Research, where he worked on a project with the Commission of Budgetary Reform of the Commonwealth of Massachusetts. He later became secretary of the commission, and in 1920 published his dissertation, *Evolution of the Budget in Massachusetts.*

In addition to his mentor Charles Beard, Gulick met Walter Lippmann, James Robinson, and Ida Tarbell. While working for the commission, he befriended Frederick Taylor, Mary Parker Follett, Henry Dennison, Henry Bruere, Frederick Cleveland, and other influential voices in the public sector.

World War I

In 1917 Gulick applied to the Army Air Corps, but because of poor eyesight was not commissioned. After registering for the draft, he eventually landed in the Statistical Branch. Through an odd turn of events, the entire branch was commissioned in the General Staff Corps even though they had not attended West Point Academy. Gulick left military service at the conclusion of the war as a captain.

National Institute of Public Administration

Upon his return to civilian life, Gulick succeeded Charles Beard as director of the Bureau of Municipal Research, later renamed the National Institute of Public Administration (IPA). The institute became Gulick's base for the rest of his professional life.

During this time, Gulick was involved in studies of state and local government. Most of his work was done in public finance, especially budgeting, state and local revenue, and taxation.

Gulick gradually became involved in the design and reorganization of government, the area in which he made his most noted conceptual contribution. He also involved himself in local government reform while working for the bureau prior to World War I, and continued this work through the next two decades. Local government during the nineteenth century was fragmented and disorganized, but from attempts at reform at the turn of the century there grew what came to be called the "integrationist

model" of classical management. This model involved a strong centralized executive management, functionally organized, with well-developed staff functions.

Gulick, although not the originator, became one of the greatest articulators and promoters of the concept of the "managerial executive," for he approached this work with an earlier learned missionary zeal. His promotion of the executive was not limited to theory building, but was, more importantly, an attempt to equip government executives with the ability to carry out their significant duties. With the publication of "Politics, Administration and the New Deal" in the *The Annals of the American Academy of Political and Social Science* in 1933, Gulick gained national exposure.

The emphasis on the managerial executive led to accusations that Gulick was a political-administration dichotomist. These accusations were unfair, he clearly understood the relationship between politics, policy, and executive work. He also understood the strategic usefulness of the dichotomy in reforming local government. (A short time before his death in 1968, John Pfiffner, founder of the School of Public Administration at the University of Southern California, lectured in a doctoral seminar at the School of Public Administration at the University of Southern California on the importance of the clear distinction between policy and administration. The distinction provided a useful strategy in the attempt to reform local government. A value-free, administrative, engineering way to pave a road—that is not Democratic or Republican—does exist. The "dichotomy" was a method of breaking down entrenched political regimes during the course of reform.)

Luther Gulick began actively publishing in 1920. Following his dissertation, his next major effort, *Modern Government in a Colonial City* (1932), explored governmental procedures and structure. He followed this book with the summary volume of a decade's worth of work on planning and personnel in government, *Better Government Personnel* (1935). This volume stresses the importance of a competent civil service and explains the process by which it can be achieved.

The most acclaimed of Gulick's works was the result of the President's Committee for Administrative Management, often referred to as the Brownlow Committee. Gulick received a call from President Franklin D. Roosevelt in 1936, requesting that he join the committee to study the national administration. This committee changed the role of the presidency into that of a managerial executive, a theme Gulick had been working on since 1919. His "Notes on a Theory of Organization," published in 1937, was the opening chapter in the famous *Papers on the Science of Administration.* This book was compiled for the President's Committee's research staff and then published in 1937. *Papers* shows the close relationship between theory and practice that characterized Gulick's professional career.

Luther Gulick joined Lyndall Urwick to edit *Papers*. The volume included contributions by James D. Mooney, Henry S. Dennison, L. J. Henderson, T. N. Whitehead, Elton Mayo, Mary P. Follett, V. A. Graicunas, Henri Fayol, and the editors themselves. *Papers* was so widely cited, and Gulick's and Urwick's names so closely tied to it, that later students of public administration mistakenly thought Gulick and Urwick always worked together.

The significance of *Papers* to administration is difficult to overestimate. Paul Van Riper has written that Gulick's "Notes on a Theory of Organization" became the first text focused on the universality of administration. In it Gulick elaborated on the administrative requisites for developing a powerful and effective executive. It also provides one of the clearest descriptions of classical management.

In "Notes" Gulick sets forth the famous acronym, POSDCORB—his view of a manager's functions. The acronym represents the following activities:

- Planning: working out in broad outline the things that need to be done and the methods for doing them to accomplish the purpose set for the enterprise;
- Organizing: the establishment of the formal structure of authority through which work subdivisions are arranged, defined, and coordinated for the defined objective;
- Staffing: the whole personnel function of bringing in and training the staff and maintaining favorable conditions of work;
- Directing: the continuous task of making decisions and embodying them in specific and general orders and instructions and serving as the leader of the enterprise;
- Coordinating: the all-important duty of interrelating the various parts of the work;
- Reporting: keeping those to whom the executive is responsible informed as to what is going on, which thus includes keeping him- or herself and his or her subordinates informed through records, research, and inspection;
- Budgeting: all that goes with budgeting in the form of fiscal planning, accounting and control.

Luther Gulick also developed a theory of departmentalization. He postulated that the primary purpose of organization was coordination. His "principle of homogeneity" required the grouping of similar activities under one head. Gulick listed four primary means for grouping activities: (1) *purpose*, or function performed, such as providing roads, fighting fires, or conducting education; (2) the *process* used to carry out the activity, such as engineering, accounting, or teaching; (3) *persons* or *things* served, such as students, Indians, or the elderly; and (4) *place* where the activity or service is carried out. He believed these basic groupings were the foundations of departmentalization and could be used in ways that served the basic purposes of the organization.

World War II

When Gulick received a call from President F. D. Roosevelt in 1937, he was working on a three-year study for the New York State Board of Regents, investigating education policy and finance. The report to the regents, given in 1939, was hailed as the most important contribution to education in the 1930s. This report precipitated numerous calls to Gulick, offering him the presidency position of various universities. Instead, he went to Washington, D.C., to help with the mounting war effort.

Gulick performed a variety of tasks in Washington from 1939 to 1946. He acted as a consultant for the Treasury Department and the secretary of war. He coordinated postwar programs for the National Resources Planning Board, helped develop the War Production Board's organizational structure, headed the Office of Organizational Planning, and attended the Potsdam Conference in 1945 and the meeting of Foreign Ministers in 1946. In addition to these duties and activities, he found time to prepare memoranda, proposals, and official reports covering a wide range of issues.

Gulick authored two works during this period. The first, *The United States at War* (1947), is the U.S. Bureau of the Budget's war history summary. He worked as the editor of this volume and contributed the final chapter, which focused on administrative efficiency. He analyzed the efficiency of the German and Japanese autocracies and compared them to the U.S. democracy under wartime conditions. He assaulted the cliché that democracies are less efficient than authoritarian governments during war and other situations that require quick, effective action.

The second work, *Administrative Reflections from World War II* (1948), was originally a collection of lectures on wartime administration. This work reflected a "unified field theory" on large-scale organizations and included a review of wartime administrations. Gulick discussed the guidelines for effective administrative action, concentrating on the managerial requirements.

Return to the Institute of Public Administration

Luther Gulick's return to the IPA marked the end of his writing on wartime administration. He turned his attention to metropolitan problems, particularly those in New York City. He directed the Mayor's Committee on Management Survey, the most extensive and costly study ever done by a government or its agencies. During the two-and-a half year study, Gulick examined the operation and structure of New York's administration. The study's report, entitled *Modern Management for the City of New York* (1953), included the recommendation for the creation of a city administrator position. Gulick himself assumed this new position in 1953, and for two years occupied and magnified this office by initiating reforms and establishing a precedent for citizen and administrative coordination and cooperation. Although he was able to make many reforms, the politics of the situation hindered many improvements.

The delays motivated Gulick to resign in 1954 and to return to the IPA. There, he initiated studies of metropolitan problems he encountered during his time as city administrator. In 1961 he published his insights and conclusions in *Metropolitan Problems and American Ideas*. Originally a collection of lectures, the book reflected Gulick's experience and expertise in understanding and solving complex issues. He also authored a second volume on these subjects, *Program Planning for National Goals* (1968).

Gulick the Consultant

In 1961 Gulick retired as president of the IPA and began accepting many consulting assignments that took him overseas. The Ford Foundation invited him to Egypt to help review the Egyptian government's planning and organizational problems. His report to the Egyptian government in 1962 covered topics including civil service systems, executive organization, decisionmaking, fiscal and administrative control, and the role of free enterprise in socialist societies. Iran and Peru also requested his assistance to study their governments and administrations. He subsequently went to India to help with water supply problems.

Conclusion

Luther Halsey Gulick left a legacy of administrative theory developed from practical application. During his life, he formulated cogent ideas on many issues of government and public administration that would guide theorists and practitioners in the years to follow.

These ideas include:

- Government's role is to serve the common good. Citizen-government cooperation should always be sought, with emphasis on planning.
- The executive should be the decisionmaker in government. The legislature should only approve or reject executive proposals.
- The executive should be strengthened through implementation of the managerial executive policies.
- The policy-politics dichotomy is rejected. However, scientific methods should still be employed to analyze

and solve problems. Efficiency and effectiveness can also be improved using the general principles revealed through the scientific method.

- The executive branch must be hierarchal, with the executive coordinating activities and instilling a sense of purpose and mission throughout the organization.

Luther Gulick authored more than 20 books, including: *Evolution of the Budget in Massachusetts* (1920); *Modern Government in a Colonial City* (1932); *Better Government Personnel* (1935); *The U.S. at War* (1947); *Administrative Reflections from World War II* (1948); *American Forest Policy* (1951); *The Coming Age of Cities* (1956); *Changing Problems and Lines of Attack* (1957); *The Metropolitan Problem and American Ideas* (1961); and *Program Planning for National Goals* (1968). Gulick also published more than 160 articles. He wrote official memoranda and a large number of proposals and other official communications, presently stored at the National Archives in Washington, D.C. He also produced more than 200 pages of personal history and insights on government, administrative practices, and structure.

Positions he held and awards he received are as follows:

- Director of Bureau of Municipal Research 1920–1960
- Eaton Professor of Municipal Science and Administration, Columbia University, 1931–1942
- Trustee of Oberlin College 1940–1948
- President of American Political Science Association 1953
- President of Institute of Public Administration 1954–1956
- Man of the Year 1954
- Director of American Society of Public Administration
- Gruenberg Award, Governmental Research Association 1978
- Canadian Institute of Public Administration (lifetime membership)
- Phi Beta Kappa
- Phi Kappa Phi

NORMAN DALE WRIGHT

BIBLIOGRAPHY

Blumberg, Stephen K., 1981. "Seven Decades of Public Administration: A Tribute to Luther Gulick." *Public Administration Review* 41 (March-April): 245–249.
Fitch, Lyle C., 1990. "Luther Gulick." *Public Administration Review* 50 (November-December): 604–608.
Fry, Brian, 1989. *Mastering Public Administration: From Max Weber to Dwight Waldo.* Chatham, New Jersey: Chatham House Publishers.

Gulick, Luther, 1933. "Politics, Administration, and the New Deal." *The Annals of the American Academy of Political and Social Science* 169 (September): 55–56.

———, 1937. "Notes on the Theory of Organization," pp. 1–46. In Luther Gulick and L. Urwick, eds., *Papers on the Science of Public Administration.* New York: Institute of Public Administration, Columbia University.

Gulick, Luther, and L. Urwick, eds., 1937. *Papers on the Science of Public Administration.* New York: Institute of Public Administration, Columbia University.

Van Riper, Paul P., 1990. "Literary Gulick: A Bibliographical Appreciation." *Public Administration Review* 50 (November-December): 609–614.

H

HALO AND HORNS EFFECTS.

A halo effect, as used in personnel assessment or evaluation, describes the tendency to minimize someone's faults or weaknesses. The horns effect is the tendency to evaluate someone negatively because of their inappropriate behavior.

The halo effect is seeing a person's good points and minimizing or ignoring any bad points. Halo effect also refers to the bias whereby someone is perceived positively by another but for reasons that are unrelated or irrelevant to the standard that should be used in evaluating them, such as friendship, appearance, or personality. Because the positive evaluation is usually based upon attributes unrelated to the evaluation criterion, this phenomenon is also called the "halo error." When discussing the halo effect or error, the implication is quite clear that the evaluator has based his or her assessment upon inappropriate characteristics or behaviors or inaccurate data. An example of the halo effect would be a supervisor who rates an employee as superior or excellent on 20 different traits during a quarterly review. In reality, the employee may deserve a high rating on only 5 of the 20 items, but because the employee did an outstanding job in a presentation before the budget committee only weeks before his or her review, the evaluator "carries over" these positive feelings toward the employee and rates him or her higher than his or her actual performance in other areas unrelated to those wherein the employee actually performed in an excellent or superior manner.

The tendency to ascribe positive characteristics to someone because of irrelevant attributes or behaviors is very old. In the classical work *Brutus or Remarks on Eminent Orators,* the writer says of Caius Piso, his son-in-law, that "it is scarcely possible to mention anyone who was blessed with a finer capacity." He acknowledges that the reader and he may be inclined to conclude that this praise may be influenced by his bias, saying, "I am rather fearful, indeed, that I should be thought to have been prompted by my affection for him to have given his a greater character than he deserved." However, he assures the reader that the praise was deserved because of Caius' abilities and not because of his affection for his son-in-law.

Equally as old is the opposite of the halo effect, commonly called the "horns effect." The horns effect is the tendency to err in the opposite direction by evaluating someone negatively due to irrelevant or inappropriate characteristics or behaviors. Julius Caesar (Shakespeare, *Julius Caesar,* Act 1, scene 2), for example, expressed his dislike of Cassius as a statesman because Cassius was too lean. Caesar tells Marcus Antonius, "Let me have men about me that are fat; sleek-headed men." It was Cassius's personal appearance and not his abilities that influenced Caesar's opinion of Cassius as a politician.

This error in personnel assessment is also known as a "dualistic fallacy" referring to the false assumption by the supervisor that there are two distinct types of employees; good performers and bad performers. It neglects the possibility that an individual employee may have some characteristics of each.

Origin

The term "halo effect" has its origins in science. In astronomy and physics, "halo" refers to the phenomenon of light refraction caused by ice crystals in the atmosphere, which causes a circle of colored light to surround the sun or moon.

Artists have historically used a circle of light or halo around the head of a person to represent "holy" persons, saints, or other venerated persons in works of art. This practice by artists is very prevalent in religious artwork. The artist, by placing a visible halo above the person's head, identifies the good character of the person. Angels, for example, are frequently depicted with such halos. Similarly, artists frequently have depicted the devil as having horns upon his head. Thus, the rendering of a person in such a manner has become a symbol of someone who is evil or bad.

The use of the terms "halo effect" and "horns effect" in personnel assessment does not refer to a spiritual evaluation of the person but to the initial perception by the supervisor that the employee is either a good performer or a poor performer.

Halo effect (and horns effect) is also common to psychology, wherein it refers to the global tendency by one person to think of another person as *good.* The person's motives and behaviors are viewed in the best light. Again, the term implies that the evaluation is biased or based upon irrelevant factors. A person may perceive positive attributes that are not present or may exaggerate the good that does exist. Spouses, family members, and friends may be erroneously evaluated because of the feelings the evaluator has for these people. For example, spouses, lovers, and parents have a strong tendency not to see the "bad" in their partner or child, although their negative attributes or behaviors may be readily apparent to others. Psychologists emphasize that this erroneous perception may lead to inappropriate responses and behavior.

Halo Effect and Personnel Evaluation

Accurate performance appraisal of employees by supervisors is important to the operation of the company or agency and because of the legal consequences for inaccurate performance appraisals. In personnel evaluation, "halo effect" describes the process by which an evaluator ascribes positive attributes and behaviors to employees whom he or she evaluates based upon inappropriate or irrelevant traits or inaccurate information. The horns effect or error is the process by which the evaluator ascribes negative attributes and behaviors to employees. Both halo effect and horns effect are errors committed in personnel evaluation due to bias or inaccurate information, and both errors have serious organizational and legal consequences.

Reasons for the Halo Effect

Experts agree that accurate judgment of personnel performance is difficult even when there is the best of intentions. To achieve fair and accurate performance appraisals many organizations mandate the use of an objective and standardized evaluation process. Even with the use of such methods, as George Odiorne (1984, p. 253) has claimed, it is impossible to distinguish differences in personnel performance if the rate of difference in performance is less than 15 percent. Thus, evaluations performed without such a system are likely to be biased.

Performance appraisal is complicated by the fact that the work environment may not be conducive to producing the most accurate appraisal of personnel performance. The reason for this is that although "right-sizing" has resulted in the elimination of layers of supervisors, sometimes it has also resulted in reducing contact between the supervisor and those he or she evaluates. Today, many employees are expected to operate independently and make decisions without supervisor approval. Because of changes in the workplace, the "empowered" employee operates in a less-supervised environment. As a result, supervisors may be expected to evaluate employees whom they have not observed frequently. Supervisors may not be familiar with the job their employees perform and, thus, may not know what behaviors and attributes are characteristic of good job performance.

Under such conditions, it is not surprising that biases can be introduced into the performance appraisal. Rather than an accurate evaluation of performance, supervisors may be likely to make judgments based upon indirect information, insufficient observation, unconscious bias, or inappropriate emphasis upon a characteristic or behavior or accomplishment. For example, evaluations may be made upon personal characteristics such as appearance rather than performance. In the classical work *Rhetoric* (1372, p. 20), Aristotle asserted that appearance influences judgment and cited the example that "a weakling is unlikely to be charged with violent assault, or a poor and ugly man with adultery." Besides appearance, supervisors may be improperly influenced by other personal characteristics of the employee that are unrelated to job performance. The supervisor may be rating the employee on conformity to social and group norms rather than on competence.

Perhaps the most common reason a supervisor commits the halo or horns error in evaluating an employee is that there is a strong tendency for recent success or failure to influence personnel evaluations. A stunning success near the end of the evaluation period may overshadow a record of mediocre performance. Similarly, the quarterly evaluation of an employee who has committed a significant error or lapse in judgment near the end of the evaluation period may completely wipe out a whole quarter of excellent performance.

Erroneous evaluations of the employee's performance may be made by the supervisor because of factors beyond the control of the employee, such as being transferred to a new work group. Frequently, the supervisor's perception of the employee's performance is influenced by the reputation of the work group to which the employee belongs. Thus, an outstanding employee who is transferred from a high-performing work group to a lower-performing work group may be mistakenly evaluated by the supervisor as a mediocre employee.

Supervisors who do not maintain adequate contact with their employees may be unfairly critical. The American Jewish Committee conducted a poll in 1992 of about 1,500 Americans who were asked to rank the social standing of 58 ethnic groups. One of the ethnic groups that ranked low in social standing was the "Wisians." The Wisians were a fictional ethnic group inserted into the survey for control purposes. When asked to justify their ranking of the fictional group, respondents replied that they rated Wisians low in social standing because they were not familiar with them and had little contact with Wisians. Apparently, frequency of contact influences one's opinion of a group or person.

Other irrelevant attributes can include compatibility, personality traits, similarity of the employee's personality and abilities to the evaluators' personality and abilities, or job-related conflicts. Even when the employee is correct in pressing an issue contrary to his or her supervisor's viewpoint, the supervisor may consciously or unconsciously give the employee a low performance rating.

Harms

The problems associated with the halo effect and horns effect can be serious. If the error is widespread the cumulative effect of the halo effect and horns effect is to distort the company's or agency's assessment of their human resource talents and skills. Such a distortion can cause the agency to either be overconfident about its abilities to achieve goals or to underestimate its ability to achieve goals.

Furthermore, the halo and horns error can impact upon the potential of the agency and its employees. An employee cannot achieve his or her maximum potential without proper feedback as to their current performance. Biased performance appraisals may reduce productivity. Good evaluations for poor performance disguise the need for improvement, and poor evaluations for good performance stifle motivation.

Finally, inaccurate performance appraisal because of the halo or horns error may expose the company or agency to legal sanctions. Legislation and case law has mandated that certain standards be observed in performance appraisals, especially in decisions affecting hiring and promotion. State and federal legislation provides remedies to certain protected groups against job discrimination. It is illegal (and can be costly) to let decisions be influenced by gender, race, religion, or other legislatively projected criteria. For example, any performance evaluation based upon a characteristic that could be attributed to ethnic identity, such as accent, skin color, or place of birth, could be held to be illegal.

Appraisals of job performance must be grounded in standards related to job performance (*Griggs v. Duke Power*) and cannot be based upon subjective ratings by supervisors on qualities such as attitude toward people, appearance and grooming, leadership, alertness, loyalty, and so on (*Wade v. Mississippi Cooperative Services*). If a test of performance is used in evaluation, the test must be an objective test of performance administered and scored under controlled and standardized conditions.

Remedies for the Halo and Horns Error

The consequences of the halo or horns effect can be quite damaging, but, fortunately, there is a ready remedy. The remedy embraces sound management techniques and also legal and ethical considerations. The use of a performance management system or standard personnel evaluation system can increase the objectivity and enhance the validity of personnel decisions (Beer and Ruh 1990, p. 232). Michael Beer and Robert Ruh's research with Corning Glass Works found that managers tended to rate employees' performance rather unidimensionally. Supervisors tended to rate employees either positively or negatively on all traits. Depending upon the initial perception that the supervisor had of the employee, the performance appraisal ratings tended to commit the dualistic fallacy and rate employees as either a good performer or a poor performer (p. 226). Supervisors were not able to distinguish the qualities of the good performer that needed improvement nor the good qualities of the poor performer. These errors in personnel assessment were brought to the attention of the supervisor by use of a profile of the employee using an objective performance profile instrument developed by Beer and Ruh. They concluded that "a performance management system can increase the objectivity and enhance the validity of personnel decisions" (Beer

and Ruh 1990, p. 232). There is general agreement among experts that the use of objective, standardized performance appraisal instruments, training and retraining of supervisors who evaluate employees, clearly defined performance based standards, and review of performance ratings by a third party are measures that suppress the tendency for the halo or horns error to occur.

JAMES A. FAGIN

BIBLIOGRAPHY

Beer, Michael, and Robert Ruh, 1990. "Employee Growth Through Performance Management." pp. 217–232. In Harvard Business Review, *Manage People, Not Personnel: Motivation and Performance Appraisal.* Boston: Harvard Business School Press.
Griggs v. Duke Power 420 Federal 2nd 1225.
Odiorne, George S., 1984. *Strategic Management of Human Resources.* San Francisco: Jossey-Bass.
Wade v. Mississippi Cooperative Services 615 Federal Supplement 1574.

HAMILTONIAN PUBLIC ADMINISTRATION THEORY.

The concepts on American governance espoused by Alexander Hamilton (1755–1804). Born a bastard child in Nevis Island, British West Indies, he was quickly recognized as having genius and noble ambitions. Provisions were made for his travel to the American colonies for a formal education. Hamilton conducted most of his studies on an independent, accelerated basis at Kings College (now Columbia University) in New York. He then prepared for the legal profession, to which he contributed mightily in terms of public and constitutional law.

During his studies, Hamilton became a dedicated member of the independence movement. He subsequently joined an artillery company in the New York militia during the Revolutionary War. There, Hamilton impressed General George Washington so much that he became Washington's aide-de-camp. His experience during the war instilled in him an intense desire to reform the governing system operating under the Articles of Confederation.

Alexander Hamilton, with James Madison's collaboration, used the poorly attended Annapolis, Maryland, trade convention of 1786 as a forum to call for a constitutional convention in Philadelphia, Pennsylvania, in 1787. He is best known today for his coauthorship, with James Madison and John Jay (all under the pseudonym "Publius"), of *The Federalist Papers* essays, advocating ratification by the states of the constitution adopted at that convention. The 85 essays remain the most brilliant and authoritative commentary on the United States Constitution.

Less commonly known today are Hamilton's vital contributions to the formation of United States legal, financial, and economic systems and to an American constitutional theory of public administration. His contemporaries, friends and foes alike, regarded him as the administrative genius of the period. Historians and biographers concur in that judgment. He was unique among the founders for giving even more attention to administering the Constitution than to its design. In his splendid biography of Hamilton, Forrest McDonald (1979) noted that Hamilton's chief advantage lay in his belief that "how things are done governs what can and will be done: the rules determine the nature and outcome of the game" (p. 123).

Many of Hamilton's contributions emerged from his tenure as the first secretary of the treasury (1789–1795). In this post he could reach virtually every aspect of national organization and policy. He organized the greater part of the new national administration; articulated an administratively oriented doctrine of constitutional interpretation, commonly referred to as broad or liberal construction; and designed and implemented plans for a stable financial and economic system.

His financial system included (1) assumption of state debts incurred during the Revolutionary War with Britain, thereby gaining favor among state leaders and restoring confidence in notes and securities; (2) creation of a sinking fund with which to retire national debt gradually and inspire public confidence in national-level management of public finances; (3) establishment of a national bank with which to provide a stable source of credit for private economic development and to lead sound banking standards and practices; (4) creation of a national currency to facilitate market exchanges and more uniform valuations across the new nation; and (5) enunciation of taxation principles and practices for spurring economic development and funding national policies.

These measures succeeded in putting the new American nation on a firm financial footing. Many aspects of his policies have been used repeatedly throughout United States history. For example, as Bray Hammond (1957) has indicated in *Banks and Politics in America*, Hamilton's charter for the national bank (Bank of the United States) still serves as a model not only for many banks within the United States but also for the entire Canadian banking system (pp. 128–131). Hamilton's insights on taxation policy have also endured, especially those concerning tariffs, which dominated government finance until the early twentieth century; and his astute management of public debt, especially as a device for gaining public confidence in government, has been parroted by a host of American politicians, especially Franklin D. Roosevelt in the New Deal years.

Hamilton's economic vision involved bringing the United States from its Third World, colonial status to a great industrial and agricultural empire. His *Report on Manufactures* (1791) is justly famous for its industrial development policy as a stimulus and balance to agricultural development. He premised the plan on a unique and sophisticated blend of European mercantilist practices and defended it

cogently against contending physiocratic and free enterprise philosophies of the day. His refutation of these philosophies remains one of the most powerful, yet largely forgotten, insights in United States economic thought.

Though Hamilton's plan failed in Congress, it later formed the basis for the "American System," advocated in the nineteenth century by such luminaries as Henry Clay, Matthew Carey, Henry Carey, and Frederick List. List exported it to Europe, especially to his native country, Germany. The relevance of Hamilton's plan—with its balance of protective, regulatory, and stimulative practices—persists, especially in light of current neomercantilist practices in Europe and Asia. Many of these practices bear striking resemblance to Hamilton's vision and strategy.

In legal matters, Hamilton not only secured flexible administrative powers for government through liberal construction and the implied powers doctrine but he also set extremely important precedents for the protection of individual rights. For example, his arguments in *Croswell v. New York* (1803) led to important statutory changes in American libel law, giving freedom of the press real meaning in state as well as federal law. On both fronts, Hamilton's legal cases and arguments inspired a whole generation of lawyers, such as Chief Justice John Marshall, Joseph Story, and James Kent, who integrated Hamiltonian legal principles into nineteenth- and twentieth-century American law.

Hamilton's Theory of Public Administration

Hamilton believed that the administrative form or structure of a government must be tailored to the political character of its people. The American people would have none other than a republican form of government, and so he focused his attention on sound republican administration.

Hamilton defined public administration in *The Federalist* essay number 72. The definition entails two important and related meanings (Rossiter 1961).

> The administration of government, in its largest sense, comprehends all the operations of the body politic, whether legislative, executive, or judiciary; but in its most usual and perhaps in its most precise signification, it is limited to executive details, and falls peculiarly [or, especially] within the province of the executive department. The actual conduct of foreign negotiations, the preparatory plans of finance, the application and disbursement of public moneys in conformity to the general appropriations of the legislature, the arrangement of the army and navy, the direction of the operations of war—these, and other matters of a like nature, constitute what seems to be most properly understood by the administration of government (pp. 435–436).

The first meaning treats all public officials and institutions as administrative, regardless of differences in level, power, and function. The second meaning remains as the more common understanding of public administrative activity. Hamilton retained both senses in his theory of public administration because they are both necessary and appropriate to the United States constitutional scheme of partially separated powers. Subordinate agencies cannot ignore the three superintending branches in the administration of public affairs. When conflict ensues among the branches, agencies must choose which master(s) they will follow.

Hamilton understood that this constitutional scheme necessarily conferred substantial autonomy as well as great responsibility upon the subordinate administration. He aspired to run the Treasury in part because of its highly ambiguous status. The combination of constitutional and organic (agency-creating) statutory provisions required him to report directly to both Congress and the President. He had substantial access and, therefore, influence with both branches. He played one off against the other when needed, but also had to assuage the concerns of both.

Hamilton's administrative theory, then, proceeds from the level of general governance—where the three partially separated branches superintend with their distinctive competencies—to levels of "executive detail"—where the three powers run entirely together, but are limited through statutory focus. To Hamilton, executive power represented the focal point of interbranch governance. All powers eventually percolate through executive operations. The presence of quasi-legislative (rulemaking) and quasi-adjudicative powers in virtually all public agencies provides ample evidence for this.

Hamilton treated this constitutional scheme as vital to what he called "high-toned" government. This is government that can act wisely as well as expeditiously in the public interest. It requires institutional stability, wisdom, and firmness. The three branches would contribute to these qualities in distinctive ways, working toward the controlled improvement of executive administration. This, he hoped, would be achieved through "partial agency," and "energy" in the executive.

Partial Agency

Partial agency refers to constitutional sharing of powers among the branches of United States government. Each branch shares in some of the powers of the other branches as a check and balance. For example, the President enjoys a veto power over all legislative bills for the purposes of resisting inappropriate encroachments on his powers and bringing executive insight to the laws. On one hand, veto power is legislative power residing in the executive. On the other hand, the Senate enjoys some executive power through the "advice and consent" clauses on presidential appointments and treaties. The Senate was viewed by many founders as an important executive advisory body as well as lawmaker. It also exercises judicial power when it tries impeachments.

For Hamilton, partial agency served four important functions in the public administration. First, it would check powers so that each branch could stave off attempts by other branches to usurp all powers. Such an usurpation amounted to uncontrollable power, or "tyranny," and should be avoided at all costs. Second, partial agency would encourage some specialization of competencies among the branches. Judges could work mainly at improving the art of adjudication and legal interpretation. Legislators could focus much of their energy upon enactment of wise laws, and the executive could work mainly on well-formed policies and astute implementation. Third, it would induce substantial long-term cooperation among the branches because each is partly dependent upon the powers held by the others. (Such cooperation has dominated United States government in a vast majority of decisions, despite popular impressions to the contrary.) Fourth, partial agency allows for integration of all three powers within subordinate agencies for specific statutory purposes. Although this integration of powers within agencies occasionally sparks controversy, it has survived judicial scrutiny and remains vital to the effective functioning of United States government. Both Madison and Hamilton emphasized its necessity to the governance process.

Energy in the Executive

Hamilton believed energy in the executive resulted from a combination of unity, duration, adequate provision for support, and competent powers.

Unity meant that executive authority and responsibility should generally be focused and centralized through single heads, as in a single President (some founders advocated an executive board instead) and single department and program heads. Hamilton deemed this wiser not only for the sake of accountability but also for encouraging "decision, activity, secrecy, and dispatch." The broader constitutional system would bring deliberation and wise judgment to bear upon execution, but the executive branch itself must at times also act quickly, secretively, and decisively.

Duration meant at least the hope of serving a long tenure in executive office in order to see one's plans through their implementation. The expectation of a short tenure would encourage corruption and raise private agendas over public agendas. Long tenure would give the public more time to assess an official's policies and would give officials more time to improve their administrative knowledge and skills. Though Hamilton would have preferred a much longer term for the president, reeligibility and four-year terms presented a workable compromise, partly because he expected much longer terms for presidential appointees and their subordinates.

Adequate provision for support refers more specifically to the protection afforded the President from legislative manipulation of his salary. Hamilton believed that those who controlled a person's support controlled his will. If his support is protected, the public official will act more vigorously and objectively. Civil service protection today rests upon the same premise.

Competent powers refers to the basic administrative principle of granting authority commensurate with responsibility. To Hamilton, the executive should enjoy great powers within the context of constitutional checks and balances. He should be the leader among the constitutional equals. With a relatively unified hierarchy of officials below him, the executive is most capable of presiding over systematic and multifaceted policies. This did not mean that the President should "manage" all executive affairs himself. As the title implies, he should "preside" over a wide array of very significant "executive details" that would in large part be governed by subordinates.

Hamilton's theory and practice encouraged independence among executive subordinates rather than servile and partisan complicity. This stemmed in part from the fact that all federal officials swore an oath to uphold the constitutional system rather than to follow one branch or another exclusively. It also stemmed from the belief that substantial powers in these offices would interest the occupants' nobler passions for honor and fame in the eyes of posterity. In Hamilton's day, many regarded an honorable reputation and the high regard of subsequent generations as vital to a meaningful and successful life. Hamilton's theory, therefore, combined a balance of carefully arranged institutional inducements and internal motivations in an attempt to bring out the best in public officials. Without such an attempt no powers could be safely entrusted to the government for long. Hamilton refused to accept that cynical conclusion as inevitable.

Energy in the executive completed Hamilton's plan for a stable and competent government—one that could inspire public confidence. Under George Washington's aegis, his measures helped the new national government win unparalleled public confidence. Without that success it is unlikely that the new American constitutional system would have survived at all.

Many fragments of Hamilton's administrative theory survive to the current day in United States, Canadian, and European administrative practice. It is interesting that such English reformers as Jeremy Bentham borrowed heavily from Hamilton's theory (especially regarding executive energy) in the early nineteenth century, while American politicians largely abandoned it. Ironically, American progressive reformers would subsequently borrow from the English reforms.

Hamilton's theory, as a coherent whole, has been largely forgotten in the twentieth century. Though vestiges survive in practice, those who practice them are usually unaware of their origins.

Twentieth-century American administrative theory has grown principally from two other sources: the management and behavioral sciences and the theory of overhead democ-

racy. Both were given strong impetus in the Progressive Reform era. Progressive reformers, such as Woodrow Wilson and Frank Goodnow, employed the idea of a neutral, technically trained cadre of administrative experts responding to the will of the people through elected politicians as a persuasive alternative to the corrupt party patronage system that had arisen during the nineteenth century.

The idea of neutrally responsive bureaucrats has taken root in administrative practice ever since, despite some glaring problems. One such problem lies in the fact that administrative expertise quickly becomes a formidable political power in its own right. Neutral responsiveness invokes the image of experts working according to the dictates of scientific knowledge employed for democratic purposes. This can easily pervert, on one hand, into a self-serving professional-technical agenda because many experts in fact enjoy tremendous discretion and, therefore, political power.

On the other hand, it can also lead some experts to obey mindlessly the dictates of elected politicians whose agendas may run contrary to law and public interest. Blind professional obedience constitutes tremendous and dangerously unaccountable power as well. Experience has shown that both problems persist today. In short, neutral competence and democratic responsiveness have provided an insecure foundation for the subordinate public administration. The public administration's status continually troubles citizens of the United States.

In this light, Hamilton's theory deserves renewed attention (as do other founders' administrative theories) because it provides a constitutionally sensible and accountable role for the subordinate public administration. The public administration should buttress and represent the competencies of all three superior branches in the administration of public affairs. In this capacity, it must be autonomous, even though it is subordinate and jealously checked. The responsibilities of the public administration are therefore highly political, though not usually partisan in character. Instead, at times party agendas may be thwarted in favor of broader public interests. When public administration is managed accordingly, it emulates the highest standards set by Hamilton two hundred years ago and raises the possibility of a restored public confidence in government.

RICHARD T. GREEN

BIBLIOGRAPHY

Works on Hamilton. Many fine works on Hamilton exist. The following heavily influenced this entry and are recommended for further reading:

Caldwell, Lynton K., 1964. *The Administrative Theories of Hamilton and Jefferson: Their Contribution to Thought on Public Administration.* New York: Russell & Russell.

Flaumenhaft, Harvey, 1976. "Hamilton and the Foundation of Good Government." *The Political Science Reviewer* 6 (Fall): 143–214.

Green, Richard T., 1987. "Oracle at Weehawken: Alexander Hamilton and Development of the Administrative State." Ph.D. diss., Center for Public Administration and Policy, *Virginia Polytechnic Institute and State University.* Blacksburg, Virginia.

Hammond, Bray, 1957. *Banks and Politics in America.* Princeton: Princeton University Press.

McDonald, Forrest, 1979. *Alexander Hamilton: A Biography.* New York: W. W. Norton and Company.

Miller, John C., 1959. *Alexander Hamilton: Portrait in Paradox.* New York: Harper & Row.

Mitchell, Broadus, 1957. *Alexander Hamilton, 2 vols., Youth to Maturity, 1755–1788, and The National Adventure.* New York: Macmillan.

Rossiter, Clinton L., 1961. *The Federalist Papers; Alexander Hamilton, James Madison, John Jay.* New York: New American Library.

———, 1964. *Alexander Hamilton and the Constitution.* New York: Harcourt, Brace and World.

Stourzh, Gerald. 1970. *Alexander Hamilton and the Idea of Republican Government.* Stanford: Stanford University Press.

Works by Alexander Hamilton. Hamilton's complete works are now compiled and splendidly edited and annotated in the following:

Goebel, Julius, and Joseph H. Smith, 1980. *The Law Practice of Alexander Hamilton: Documents and Commentary,* 4 vols. New York: Columbia University Press.

Syrett, Harold C., and Jacob E. Cooke, 1969–1979. *The Papers of Alexander Hamilton,* 26 vols. New York: Columbia University Press.

HAWTHORNE STUDIES.

The best known and most widely influential series of worker productivity experiments yet undertaken. The Hawthorne studies were conducted under the charge of the National Academy of Sciences Research Council at the Hawthorne, Illinois, plant of Western Electric Company beginning in 1924. The major purpose of these studies was to research ways to increase productivity by manipulating conditions of the plant's physical environment. In order to understand the outcomes and conceptual implications of these studies, this entry presents the following: (1) a limited historical perspective and description of the core question at hand, that is, motivation of organizational members; (2) an overview of the Hawthorne studies; (3) a brief description of how the outcomes of the studies have affected motivational theory in current literature; and (4) a summary and conclusion.

Historical Perspective: Motivation

One of the most frequently asked management questions over the past few centuries has been how to motivate or inspire organizational members to perform at higher levels,

thus achieving optimal output. This question has been of great importance to management teams as well as to researchers and students of organizational behavior. If organizational members could be motivated to produce at somewhat higher levels, the gain for organizations and the larger society would be extensive (Ott 1996). A great need exists for motivation in organizational spheres; however, there is no consensus about how organizational managers should proceed to encourage motivation.

Many studies have been conducted relative to motivating organizational members. In some studies, researchers have made the assumption that organizational members act in a rational and logical manner. For example, organizational managers need only to offer rewards and punishment in a rational and logical manner in order for organizational motivation to increase. Other researchers believe that reward and punishment manipulation stifles and hinders employee creativity, thus negatively affecting overall organizational motivation. As a result, organizational managers are left with many frameworks but few concrete answers to the motivation question.

Prior to the industrial revolution, goods were produced by independent craftspeople and agrarians, thus individuals were not accustomed to working within the time frame or strict rules that accompany life in a factory (Wren 1972). In 1760 (the early stages of the industrial revolution), the discipline and motivation of the mass factory worker was of great concern and importance. How could the factory foreman maintain discipline and increase overall production? The basic rule followed to accomplish this task was the essential and critical use, by the foreman, of negative sanctions. If a factory worker was not producing at the desired levels, strict sanctions or punishments were used as tools to increase output.

A few early industrialists tried to offer congenial organizational environments for factory members. For example, occasional feasts were given to build factory loyalty and motivation, help lower absenteeism, and keep the factory member working at optimal levels of production. During this period, the compensation strategy employed was the incentive piece-rate system, that is, factory workers were not paid by the hour but were paid for production output (Ott 1996). The notion of pay-for-production carried into twentieth-century management philosophy. Frederick Winslow Taylor, Henry Gantt, and Lillian and Frank Gilbreth were all disciples of the piece-rate form of management (Shafritz and Ott 1996).

In 1911, Taylor wrote *The Principles of Scientific Management.* The basic premise was that if individuals worked for money, a tie between production and compensation should exist. In fact, the best way to increase efficiency was through scientific management. Taylor assumed that there was a great loss in efficiency levels in the workplace, thus, a systematic management approach, or a true science of management, was needed to remedy this condition. Scientific management sought to increase output by discovering the fastest, most efficient, and least fatiguing production methods. Taylor's notion made use of systematic analysis and data, rather than individual experience and opinion, to solve problems and dictate working practices. Within the system of individual "incentive and initiative," Taylor postulated that efficiency would be limited because the employee was responsible for thinking and doing. In scientific management, the employee is relieved of thinking and planning and is expected only to complete and carry out management directions.

Under ideal circumstances, according to Taylor, there is a division of duties between management and employees. Management is responsible for planning tasks to be completed and employees are responsible for carrying out those instructions.

Description of the Hawthorne Studies

In 1924, a team of researchers from the National Research Council began a study of how to improve productivity; specifically, what motivates workers to increase individual production levels? The study was conducted at the Western Electric Company's Hawthorne plant, located outside Chicago, to determine whether or not manipulation of the environment could influence higher levels of output. The research team worked from the perspective of scientific management, believing that individual organization members reacted to rewards and punishments and that a human was an economic person who acted in a rational and logical manner. Specifically, the team was interested in and charged with studying which environmental changes in a factory were related to an increase or decrease of productivity.

The studies used standard scientific methods, including experimental as well as control groups. The primary experiments focused on temperature, illumination level, and humidity. The intent was to determine if environmental variables affected production levels with the control groups or the experimental groups. Illumination was added to the studies because of the findings of Taylor (1911) 15 years earlier. Taylor had postulated that illumination was an easily controlled variable for influencing higher production levels.

In an attempt to explain the overall outcome of these studies, a few specific experiments are discussed to add clarification to what actually occurred at the plant. The information offered in this section is from *Management and Morale* (Roethlisberger 1941).

In one of the original experiments, employees at the Hawthorne plant were divided into two groups. The test group was to labor in one room under various illumination intensities. The control group was to labor in another room under a constant illumination intensity. During this experiment, the test group experienced three different in-

tensities of illumination. The intensity increased in strength from 24 to 46 to 70 foot-candles. The outcome of this experiment was that the productivity levels were about the same for both groups (Roethlisberger 1941).

In a separate experiment, plant employees were led to believe that the illumination was being increased, but there was no actual change made to the illumination intensity. The employees commented on how much more they liked the increased level of illumination, but no measurable increase in output was detected. In a third experiment, employees were led to believe that the illumination intensity was decreasing, when in fact no change had occurred. This time employees commented unfavorably about the decrease, but no measurable decrease in output occurred (Roethlisberger 1941). In yet another experiment, the illumination intensity was decreased to a .06 foot-candle, which is equivalent to moonlight. Not until the illumination had decreased to this level did productivity actually decrease (Roethlisberger 1941).

The original studies at the Hawthorne plant caused a great deal of confusion because when the illumination decreased overall productivity remained high. The same result was true for humidity as well as temperature. The original research produced such tangled results that the team almost quit in 1927, after three years of research. Instead, however, team members began to question what had been learned from these experiments. The researchers were confused as to the outcomes. The results were negative relative to illumination and to the increase or decrease of productivity. Therefore, they decided that more experiments needed to be designed in which other variables that might affect employee output could be better controlled (Roethlisberger 1941).

For the next few years, many experiments were conducted relative to the physical environment. These experiments had moved beyond the original measurements of temperature, humidity, and illumination, however. They had been augmented with other physical variables such as food eaten for breakfast, hours slept, and break patterns in the workday. The researchers were still looking at how the physical environment affected productivity levels. When employees received little sleep, productivity remained high; when employees received no breaks or very short breaks, productivity remained high; when employees were placed on a 48-hour-a-week work schedule, without breaks or lunch hours, productivity levels remained high (Roethlisberger 1941).

A few of the researchers had suspected that aspects of human motivation were playing a large role and that the employees were only acting the way in which they believed they should behave. Regardless of the physical or environmental changes taking place, the researchers had also behaved in a manner that supported the concept of the original experiment, manipulation of the physical environment to increase productivity (Roethlisberger 1941).

Because of the confusion and pending termination of the studies, George Pennock, the superintendent of inspection for the Western Electric Company's Hawthorne plant, invited Elton Mayo, a professor of industrial research at Harvard University's Graduate School of Business Administration, to the Hawthorne plant. Mayo accepted the invitation and eventually assembled a team of researchers, consisting most notably of Fritz Roethlisberger, George Homans, and T. N. Whitehead.

The new researchers did not get their big breakthrough until they were able to change their theoretical perspectives relative to how they viewed humans. Specifically, the teams had to drop the assumptions that a human was inherently economic and always acted in a rational and logical manner. The teams also had to drop their notions regarding scientific management. With this theoretical perspective shift, the researchers were able to understand what had actually been happening over the past years of research, relative to environmental changes such as temperature, humidity, and illumination.

The researchers discovered that the time-honored assumption of industrial and organizational psychology were being challenged on all fronts. The wheels were put in motion that would change how managers, as well as researchers, viewed humans. Specifically, scientific management would become an outdated theory relative to motivation of organizational members.

Post-Hawthorne Perspective

During the Hawthorne studies, a vast amount of data had been gathered regarding motivation, specifically addressing how a highly motivated workforce can increase organizational productivity. Many researchers have used the conceptual notions that originated at the Hawthorne plant as a springboard for their own studies on motivation.

In his article "A Theory of Human Motivation," Abraham Maslow (1943) drew upon themes developed at the Hawthorne plant. Specifically, Maslow developed a motivational framework that utilized a "hierarchy of needs." Maslow's theory has become a building block for other theories of motivation, and his assumptions about human motivation have become major cornerstones in the humanism literature.

According to Maslow, the theories of organizational humanism extend beyond the conventional view that leaders are only responsible for the organizational members' physiological and safety needs. He contends that these theories encompass higher needs, including social, ego, and self-fulfillment needs. These needs are categorized in a "hierarchy of importance" (McGregor 1957).

The physiological needs consist of food, rest, and shelter. These needs are generally satisfied by organizational management and are not motivating factors for most organizational members. Safety needs include protection against danger, threat of criminals, murder, assault, and the extremes of temperature. These lower-level needs tend to follow the basic beliefs of the scientific approach developed by Frederick Taylor. In other words, management is responsible for providing a safe environment.

According to Maslow's theory, higher needs also must be addressed relative to increasing motivation. Organizational members' social fulfillment is essential as a motivator. Organizational members need to feel a sense of belonging and tend to form friendships with other members in and out of the organization. The ego need deals with an organizational member's image and self-confidence and is directly correlated with an individual's reputation, need for appreciation, and respect of one's coworkers. Self-actualization is the highest, most abstract need in the hierarchy. Satisfying this need helps organizational members to realize their potential and to foster their ambition to become more of what "one is," that is, to become everything one is capable of becoming (Maslow 1943).

Over the years, Maslow's theory on the hierarchy of needs of individuals has been attacked for its oversimplification of how humans are motivated. Few empirical studies have been conducted that have supported the hierarchy's validity or reliability. However, even with criticism, it is generally agreed that the notions developed by Maslow using the Hawthorne studies as a building block have influenced how research and organizational managers view and study motivation (Ott 1996).

Another important writer who drew upon both the Hawthorne studies and Maslow's work, is Douglas McGregor (1957). He believed that there are two extremes to organizational management: The first is Theory X, the hard and strong style, which involves coercion and threat to the organizational member; the second is Theory Y, the soft or weak method, which involves satisfying demands to achieve harmony. McGregor, even though disdaining characterizations such as "hard" or "soft" styles, favored the Theory Y method.

McGregor acknowledged, however, that both theories have drawbacks. Theory X can produce antagonism and then sabotage management goals. Through Theory Y, however, organizational members may take advantage of management and continue to expect more from the organization. According to McGregor, "Man is a wanting animal"; that is, people are never satisfied. As soon as one need is fulfilled, another comes into importance. Nevertheless, McGregor believed that organizations will remain ineffective unless they begin shifting their emphasis to the higher needs of organizational members, such as ego and self-fulfillment (1957).

Organizational members who feel a part of the decisionmaking process in conjunction with the leadership will have increased satisfaction, as demonstrated by the Hawthorne studies. With this increased individual satisfaction, productivity and goal attainment will rise (Lawler 1986). This conceptual notion of subordinate involvement with organizational leadership was defined by E. E. Lawler (1986) as "participative management."

In one study that grew out of the Hawthorne studies and subsequent research, a form of participative decision-making and inclusion of employees was introduced into a hospital subsystem. Over the 18-month period of the study, attitudes improved, absenteeism declined, and productivity increased. Absence and productivity rates in the comparison groups did not change during the study period. Performance differences between the experimental and comparison groups were significant practically as well as statistically. Productivity during the 18-month period increased 42 percent (Bragg and Andrews 1973).

In another study, questionnaire responses were collected from 400 managers in the six divisions of a manufacturing organization, along with company data on division performance. Analysis of data collected from the six divisions indicated a relationship among leadership behavior, satisfaction, and performance. Specifically, the study showed that democratic-participative leadership behavior and daily inclusion of the employee are related to individual organizational member satisfaction and to overall organizational performance and motivation (Roberts, Miles, and Blankenship 1968).

In 1986, K. I. Miller and P. R. Monge developed a meta-analysis literature review that tested cognitive, affective, and contingency models of the effects of participation in decisionmaking on employee's satisfaction and productivity. Results from field studies provided some support for cognitive models, but strong support was provided for affective models, linking a participative climate with worker satisfaction. The meta-analysis also showed that incorporating organizational members into organizational decisionmaking had a positive effect on the overall performance of the organization (Miller and Monge 1986).

The two studies and the meta-analysis just discussed exhibit evidence that if a leader incorporates subordinates in the decisionmaking process and includes them in the daily operation, organizational performance will increase. Thus, the early conceptual notions of Maslow (1943) and McGregor (1957), derived from the Hawthorne studies, have guided many researchers to look deeper into the issue of human phenomena. Hundreds of studies in motivational literature are still trying to answer earlier notions developed at the Hawthorne plant.

Conclusion

F. J. Roethlisberger (1941) wrote that the Hawthorne studies seemed to be a beginning on the road back to sanity as far as employee relations are concerned. The Hawthorne studies offered a working hypothesis that produced a few simple and clear ideas for further research in understanding the motivations of people in the workplace. If a business is to understand what motivates a worker, it must treat the worker as a human. Roethlisberger also believed that all issues or problems do not have complex solutions. For example, a human problem of how to increase productivity requires a human solution; it does not require a set of complex solutions about to how to manipulate the physical environment. It simply requires that humans be understood and that human needs be fulfilled.

The Hawthorne studies initiated a combination of researchers' intellectual and emotional strength to form the embryonic stages of the study of organizational behavior (Ott 1996). The Hawthorne experiments provided the first empirical challenge to the scientific management notions of Taylor (1911). These studies also significantly changed how researchers, as well as organizational managers, view behavior in organizations with regard to the motivations of the individual worker. The Hawthorne experiments demonstrated that there are many complex, interactional, and interconnected variables that can help to develop a highly motivated workforce, thus improving overall output and productivity. Variables such as listening to the individual worker, allowing discussion of topics on how best to improve specific technology, paying attention to the workers, granting autonomy to individuals during the workday, developing creativity, and allowing the employee to take charge of his or her employment destiny have all become a greater part of organizational management because of the Hawthorne studies.

DOUGLAS L. CHRISTIANSEN

BIBLIOGRAPHY

Bragg, J. E., and I. R. Andrews, 1973. "Participative Decision Making: An Experimental Study in a Hospital." *Journal of Applied Behavioral Sciences,* vol. 9: 727–735.
Lawler, E. E. III., 1986. *High Involvement Management.* San Francisco: Jossey-Bass.
Maslow, Abraham H., 1943. "A Theory of Human Motivation." *Psychological Review,* vol. 50: 370–396.
Mayo, Elton, 1933. *The Human Problems of Industrial Civilization.* New York: Macmillan.
McGregor, Douglas M., 1957. "The Human Side of Enterprise." *Management Review* (November): 278–301.
Miller, K. I., and P. R. Monge, 1986. "Participation, Satisfaction, and Productivity: A Meta-Analytic Review." *Academy of Management Journal,* vol. 29: 727–753.
Ott, J. Steven, ed. 1996. *Classic Readings in Organizational Behavior.* 2d ed. Belmont, CA: Wadsworth.
Roberts, K., R. Miles, and V. L. Blankenship, 1968. "Organizational Leadership, Satisfaction, and Productivity: A Comparative Analysis." *Academy of Management Journal,* vol. 11: 401–414.
Roethlisberger, F. J., 1941. *Management and Morale.* Cambridge, MA: Harvard University Press.
Roethlisberger, F. J., and W. J. Dickson, 1939. *Management and the Worker.* Cambridge, MA: Harvard University Press.
Shafritz, J. M., and Albert C. Hyde, eds. 1992. *Classics of Public Administration.* 3d ed. Pacific Grove, CA: Brooks-Cole.

Shafritz, J. M., and J. S. Ott, eds. 1996. *Classics of Organizational Theory*. 4th ed. Belmont, CA: Wadsworth.

Taylor, F. W., 1911. *The Principles of Scientific Management*. New York: Harper & Row.

Wren, D. A., 1972. *The Evolution of Management Thought*. New York: Ronald Press.

HEALTH INSURANCE POLICY.

Policy concerned with health insurance, or the pooling, across a defined population, of losses arising from ill health and its consequences. A more common (and considerably narrower) definition confines the term to the pooling of the costs of medical care.

Health and Health Insurance

Ill health, with its connotations of pain, disability, and premature death, has always been one of humankind's most central concerns. As far as individuals are concerned, the potential severity of its consequences is matched by the uncertainty of its incidence. Although genetic inheritance, aging, and life experiences have predictable impacts on the chances of future ill-health, much of the variability of individual outcomes is due to unknown factors.

Against this background, the relatively recent appearance of health insurance as a major social issue requires some explanation. The answer lies in the huge improvements in population health status and medical care in developed countries, where the chances of individuals living long and productive lives have been greatly increased. However, this progress has been achieved at ever-increasing economic cost: whereas 50 years ago few countries would have spent more than 3 percent of their gross domestic product (GDP) on health services, developed countries now typically spend between 8 and 10 percent of their very much larger GDPs on them. This means that, although their inhabitants are on average far healthier than their forebearers, those who do experience illness and injury incur much larger *financial* losses from health care costs and reduced earning capacity.

The combination of rising incomes and more effective but more costly medical care has generated a growing demand for health insurance as a means of reducing the direct and consequential impacts of ill health on individuals and families. At the same time, the social valuation placed on good health is such that there is general acceptance of the principle that no person should be denied necessary medical care on the grounds of inability to pay. These two factors have been variously reflected in different arrangements for pooling health costs.

The extent to which competitive insurance markets can meet the demand of individuals, groups, and society as a whole for reduced risk in relation to health care is a keenly debated issue. In a seminal article written in 1963, Nobel laureate Kenneth Arrow depicted many anticompetitive features of health care systems as responses to the pervasive existence of risk, including nonfinancial risks, such as the risks of experiencing illness and of ineffective medical treatment. As demands for risk reduction have grown stronger, nonmarket responses have increasingly taken the form of government intervention, which has now progressed, in all developed countries, well beyond the level that could be justified by "market failure" as defined in formal welfare economics. More than ever in the past, health care financing has become a prominent component of public policy.

A Historical View of Health Insurance

Massive inequalities between the health services available to the wealthy few and the majority of the population persisted well into the second half of the nineteenth century, but since most of what was available was useless or hazardous, this was of little social consequence. The first organized response to the financial toll of ill health took the form of mutual self-help organizations, such as lodges, sickness funds, and friendly societies. Most of these organizations had other functions, and for a long time benefits to cover loss of earnings and funeral expenses far outweighed the costs of medical care. This was partly due to the fact that much care received by low-income and indigent patients (and the nonworking poor) was provided without cost by charitable hospitals.

These self-help funds became the basis for social insurance programs implemented by most European governments between 1883 and the outbreak of World War I in 1914. Many countries, including Great Britain in 1911, followed Bismarck's German model, based on compulsory membership of lower paid employees of statutorily recognized sickness funds, largely financed by employer levies. Other countries, such as Sweden and France, took the path of subsidizing voluntary membership of mutual societies. Medical coverage under these schemes was part of a broader benefit package, including payments to make up income loss due to illness, accident, and disability. In the aftermath of the two world wars and the Depression of the 1930s, coverage of these programs was extended by widening compulsory coverage and extending eligibility to dependents and other nonemployees. By the 1950s, the health insurance arrangements of most Western European countries had become part of comprehensive social security systems funded by taxes and compulsory contributions. The only exemptions from compulsory coverage (in some countries) were the people in the highest income brackets: in other words, the poor had (and have) the same entitlements as the great bulk of middle-income earners.

The English-speaking countries of the New World (the United States, Canada, and Australia) have a very different history, in the sense that public health insurance at the national level was notably absent from their social security legislation until the mid-1950s or later. A mixture of charity, self-help societies, and public subventions from lower levels of government provided support for those who could not meet the costs of their care, until the 1930s, when the demands of middle-income earners for financial protection against the rising costs of hospital care led to the growth of private hospital insurance—first at the individual hospital level and then from statewide and provincewide Blue Cross organizations. The parallels among the three countries cannot be carried too far, especially in the sense that the role of government was consistently greater in the two British dominions than in the United States, first in the funding of public hospitals, and later, over the period from 1945 to 1975, in the progressive implementation of fully fledged national health insurance programs providing universal coverage of hospital and medical costs.

The tortuous history of health insurance in the United States is described in Paul Starr's (1982) Pulitzer Prize–winning book *The Social Transformation of American Medicine*. Between 1932 and 1935 a battle was fought within the Franklin D. Roosevelt administration over the inclusion of health insurance in the new social security program: In the end, in the face of vigorous opposition from organized medicine, health insurance was deleted from the legislation in order to secure its passage through Congress. In 1948 President Harry S Truman promised to introduce national health insurance, but the combination of an opposition campaign and the outbreak of the Korean War led to its abandonment. Subsequent attempts by presidents Richard Nixon, Jimmy Carter, and Bill Clinton to secure electoral and congressional support for national health insurance have been no more successful.

The only big steps that have been taken at the federal level in the direction of social insurance have been the enactment in the United States of the Medicare and Medicaid programs in mid-1960s. Medicare essentially provided national health insurance coverage, within the Social Security program, to the over-65s, the largest group left out of coverage under private health insurance. Medicaid implemented conditional grants to state governments, which set up programs to provide free care to recipients of federal welfare programs, who constituted the other major group of uninsured people. However, among developed countries, the United States remains more than ever the odd man out in the field of health insurance.

Health Insurance in Theory and Practice

Much public debate about health insurance policy is confused by differences in what is meant by "health insurance." As the initial definition indicates, pooling of health care costs is a much more inclusive concept than that of "insurance" as it is ordinarily understood.

Insurance and Subsidy

In the broad sense of the term, "health insurance" included three components:

1. "pure insurance": pooling of random deviations from the expected costs incurred by people in various risk groups, the average expected costs of which can be calculated from known factors such as age and previous health status
2. transfers between risk groups: pooling across risk groups (e.g., through group insurance), under which people with higher expected costs pay more than actuarially fair premiums, and those with lower expected costs pay less
3. transfers between income groups: people on low incomes cannot afford actuarially fair premiums; if they are to be covered, their premiums must be paid for in part or in whole by others

The key issue for policy is that relatively little of the cross-subsidies in 2 and 3 will be achieved by competitive markets: Attempts to achieve them by manipulating premiums will create opportunities for other insurers to attract better risks by offering lower premiums. Two types of government action have been used in all countries to effect the cross-subsidization between risk and income groups: (1) *regulation or subsidization of the health insurance industry* to secure desired cross-subsidies within the premium structure and to minimize "cream skimming" (nonprice strategies favoring selection of good-risk subscribers); and (2) *risk pooling outside the insurance model*. Publicly administered national health and national social insurance programs, financed by taxation and by earmarked levies, are now the predominant sources of finance for mainstream health services in most countries. Such programs are substitutes for marketed insurance as a means of pooling individual health risks. In some countries, the national systems are so comprehensive as to leave little or no scope for private health insurance. In others, private insurance plays an important role in pooling the costs of people or services not covered by public programs.

Health Insurance and Market Behavior

All third-party financing of health care, whether in the form of insurance or not, reduces out-of-pocket prices paid by patients and thereby alters the financial incentives applying to both consumers and providers of health services. In general, the greater the price reduction, the greater will be the increase in demand. All health services are not equally affected, however. Demand for services that are occasioned by serious injury or illness, such as acute hospital care, are less sensitive than others to price changes. The impact of health insurance on demand for various health services has been definitively assessed by the RAND Health Insurance Experiment, which has enabled governments to make more informed decisions on health insurance program design.

Other things being equal, stronger demand for health services can be expected to result in higher prices and increased production. Major extensions of national health insurance programs in most countries in the 1960s and 1970s were followed by rising levels of health care use, prices, and provider incomes. The budgetary consequences were relatively easily sustained until the slowdown in world economic growth in the mid-1970s. Since then, containment of expenditures on health care has become a major objective of health policy: Having intervened on the demand side, governments have been inevitably drawn into intervention on the supply side to redress the imbalance. The importance of health insurance in public policy does not arise only from its function in pooling health care costs: it also reflects the fact that the performance of a complex industry of great economic and social significance is heavily influenced by the way in which health insurance is organized.

Health Insurance Policy Options

The public policy implications of health insurance largely arise from the fact that its existence increases the demand for health care, hence, the volumes and prices of health services. There are two ways in which the *economic* consequences of health insurance have been viewed and analyzed: First, the extent to which the welfare gains from the reduction in risk are offset by welfare losses caused by distortion of price relativities between health services and other goods and services, and second, the extent to which the additional services make a progressively diminishing contribution to the health status of the population (commonly described as more "flat-of-the-curve" medicine).

These consequences would have few implications for public policy if "health," and consequently health services, were not generally held to be "special" in the sense that people should not be precluded from access to necessary health services by reason of inability to pay for them. The social rationale for government intervention in health care markets is basically that health–like justice–is a basic right that justifies the normal allocative system of the market being at least partly set aside. Any position one takes on this issue rests totally on moral and philosophical valuations. The relevance for public policy is that the view of health as being special is very widely held in all societies and that any action to implement it has profound economic and political consequences.

Policy Alternatives

There is a range of possible policy countermeasures to the cost-inflating and efficiency-sapping effects of widespread health insurance. Governments in all developed countries have implemented all of them, to a greater or lesser degree.

- *Conservative/market-oriented:* Restore balance in the market by passing more of the risks back to consumers of health services, by reducing health insurance benefits (e.g., higher coinsurance) and tightening eligibility and benefits under public programs. This option has much wider acceptance in the United States than elsewhere.

- *Regulatory cost containment:* Contain costs by the imposition of price controls or global budget caps. Price controls, such as freezes on hospital fees and health insurance premiums and all-payer hospital limits, have proved relatively ineffective. Global budget ceilings are certainly effective in containing costs, but are likely to result in overt rationing of services and do not necessarily increase efficiency.

- *National health insurance:* A single public insurer is in a better position to contain its payments by bargaining on prices and controlling the conditions under which services are provided. In addition, it also lowers reserve requirements and administrative costs.

- *Public provision of health services*: National health systems based on public provision have even greater capacity for cost containment and administrative savings than national health insurance programs. The British NHS is the quintessential example of such a model. The capacity to contain expenditures in integrated public systems comes at a cost, however, both in terms of operational efficiency and consumer choice.

What Influences National Differences?

Given the near-uniformity of the underlying morbidity patterns and medical technology, developed countries exhibit a remarkable diversity in the way health service delivery and financing are organized. The patterns in individual countries are partly explained by the fact that cultural attitudes and historical inheritances set limits to institutional change, so that present health insurance systems incorporate features of, and accommodation with, social institutions inherited from previous periods. The factors that shape health insurance policies at the national level include:

- *ideology,* in the sense of value systems that are held by the majority of the population and that set the limits for political action. These are not confined to the collectivist-individualist spectrum. Among developed countries, only Britain and the Scandinavian countries developed socialist traditions strong enough for transitions to national health systems that emphasized public provision of services;

- *self-interest,* on the part of vested interests (notably associations of health providers and insurance companies), whose income and market opportunities could be threatened by changes in health insurance arrangements.

- *government structure,* notably the extent to which governments face constitutional and other limitations on their power to legislate. To formal restraints, such as federalism, bicameralism, and separation of executive and legislative powers, must be added the electoral systems and social divisions that determine political party structures.

Although ideological and self-serving factors can be identified as factors responsible for the failure of various attempts to implement national health insurance in the United States, institutional obstacles to legislation have been decisive on at least two occasions.

Health Insurance in the United States

The absence of a structured national health insurance program covering the whole population has resulted in unique features of the health financing arrangements of the United States, with corresponding singularities in the health policy agenda. The unique features include: 16.1 percent of the population uninsured in 1993 (up from 14.3 percent in 1989); 43.6 percent of 1992 health expenditures publicly funded, compared with a range of 62 to 95 percent in other Organization for Economic Cooperation and Development (OECD) countries (excluding Turkey), per capita health spending ($3,094 in 1992)–50 percent higher than any other country and more than double the OECD average and, over the previous ten years, growing more rapidly than in any of the other countries; and much greater diversity in the standards and levels of care available to different people in different income groups. As a result, in health policy debates in the United States, the unresolved questions of how to extend coverage and provide services to the uninsured compete for attention with the cost-containment issues common to all developed countries. Some underlying trends are illustrated by four-year statistics to 1993.

The percentage of United States population covered by private insurance in 1989 was 74.2 percent; in 1991, 71.7 percent; and in 1993 it was 69.3 percent. Of those covered by public insurance, the statistics are in 1989, 22.4 percent, but 24.6 percent and 25.6 percent, respectively, in 1991 and 1993. Of those with no insurance, in 1989 the total was 14.3 percent; in 1991, 14.7 percent; and 16.1 percent by 1993.

Of the percent of United States expenditures met by the federal government, for 1989 the figure was 28.0 percent; for 1991, 29.7 percent; and 31.7 percent in 1993. The following represent the percentage provided by state and local government: in 1989, 12.5 percent, in 1991, 13.0 percent, and in 1993, 12.1 percent. Patients' out-of-pocket expenditures were 20.5 percent, 19.0 percent, and 17.8 percent in 1989, 1991, and 1993, respectively. Other private sources (including private insurance) met 38.9 percent of expenditures in 1989, 38.3 percent in 1991, and 38.3 percent of expenditures in 1993. Total health expenditures (as a percentage of the GDP) were 11.9 percent in 1989, 13.2 percent in 1991, and 13.9 percent of the GDP by 1993.

Private Health Insurance

More than 83 percent of privately insured Americans were covered through their employers in 1993. Insurance coverage written for employer groups is much less costly than individual policies because individual risks are spread within the groups and administrative costs are lower. The advantage is extended by the exemption of employer contributions from company or personal income tax, which constitutes a substantial public subsidy. Finally, the scale of employer contributions makes employer-based group insurance appear much less costly to its beneficiaries than it really is, since employees generally underestimate the extent to which these contributions are a substitute for higher wages.

As compared with coverage under universal programs, employer group insurance has several disadvantages. First, job changes may involve loss of coverage. Second, trends to more flexible employment contracts and a higher proportion of the workforce self-employed or working for small employers have been factors in the observed decline in private insurance coverage. Third, the system has a poor record of cost control since, until recently, neither employers nor insurers have striven very hard to contain health care prices or service use. However, this is changing, with tighter links being forged between insurance and service delivery.

The major structural change in the health industry–the rapid expansion of prepaid care organizations (Health Maintenance Organization [HMO]) involving greater control over service costs and utilization–was facilitated by the United States federal HMO Act of 1973. Since then, the HMOs and a bewildering array of more loosely structured "managed care" organizations, such as independent practice associations (IPAs), preferred provider organizations (PPOs), and point-of-service (POS) plans have expanded their membership from about 12 million in 1980 to an estimated 96 million–about 54 percent of all privately insured people–in 1992.

Medicare and Medicaid

The passage of Medicare and Medicaid legislation in 1965 represented the largest-ever extension of American government activity in health insurance and financing: As a result, the public sector share of personal health care expenditures has more than doubled its 21.4 percent share in 1960.

Medicare is a federally administered social insurance program covering acute care costs incurred by virtually all people aged 65 and over, and certain categories of non-aged disabled. Benefits are of two kinds: Part A (covering hospital care) and funded out of payroll taxes placed on employers and employees, and Part B (covering physicians' and some other ambulatory services) funded out of voluntary premiums. Medicare incorporates substantial deductibles and coinsurance and allows physician extra-billing, so that its benefits cover only about half of its beneficiaries' health costs. The majority of beneficiaries have additional private "Medigap" insurance.

The enactment of Medicare involved many compromises with opponents, so that cost reimbursement and fee-for-service were accepted as the basis of paying hospitals and physicians. As a result, program costs rapidly escalated, and, since 1980, cost containment has been a major focus of government policy. In 1983 the Medicare prospective payment system (PPS) replaced cost reimbursement for hospital inpatient care with payments for each patient treated (adjusted for case mix), and 1992 saw the phasing-in of payment for physicians' services in accordance with a new Medicare fee schedule, in place of the previous base of "reasonable and customary" charges.

Medicaid is essentially a grant-in-aid program to the states, which administer their own programs within federal guidelines limiting eligibility for benefits, the scope of services covered, and levels of payment to providers. The proportion of Medicaid costs met by federal grants varies between states, depending on average personal incomes: The range is from 50 to about 80 percent. Federal eligibility criteria for Medicaid confine benefits to those who are not only poor but also aged, disabled, or parents of dependent children, and most state programs fall short of covering all those who meet federal criteria. It is estimated that about 60 percent of people below the federal poverty line are excluded from Medicaid eligibility. The range of services covered by Medicaid is wider than that of Medicare, and many poor, aged and disabled receive benefits under both programs. Mothers and dependent children compose more than two-thirds of the beneficiaries, but nearly half of all Medicaid costs are incurred by aged inmates of nursing homes and other nonacute facilities.

Until 1988 Medicaid costs tended to grow at about the same rate as those of Medicare, but over the past few years they have accelerated, largely because of increased beneficiary numbers, which rose from 22.9 to 28.1 million between 1988 and 1992. About half of the increase resulted from federal legislation mandating coverage of pregnant women and children in poor families, and the remainder from rising numbers of families in poverty and from state initiatives. Since 1980 states have endeavored to contain costs by moving to prospective payment for hospital care, on the Medicare PPS model, by paying physician fees at rates that are mostly well below those paid by Medicare and private insurers, and by contracting for care with PPOs' other managed care organizations. However, litigation based on the 1980 Boren Amendment requiring states to pay providers at "reasonable and adequate" rates threatens the states' capacity to contain costs by holding down prices.

State Programs

As in other federal countries, state and local authorities have major responsibilities in the provision, financing, and regulation of health services. In 1991 these authorities undertook about 28 percent of total public expenditures on health services, of which 15 percent was on Medicaid programs, and 8 percent on non-Medicaid hospital services. State and local authorities have traditionally filled gaps not covered by private and federal health insurance through cross-subsidization of charitable and uncompensated care in public and community hospitals. In recent times, under the stimulus of matching federal grants, this function has increasingly been undertaken through state Medicaid programs.

Since 1988, many states have sought to reduce the impact of rising Medicaid costs on their general budgets by using donations and taxes raised from providers as a funding source, and by attracting additional federal grants by increasing their grants to disproportionate share hospitals (DSHs). Faced by sharp growth in its share of Medicaid costs, the federal government passed legislation in 1991 to limit the extent to which states could attract future federal grants by these means.

Although many states have set Medicaid eligibility levels well below those permitted by federal legislation, others have been inhibited by federal laws from implementing programs that would extend health insurance coverage. In particular, the Employment Retirement Income Security Act (ERISA) of 1974 prohibits states from imposing employer mandates to provide health benefits, and antitrust laws prevent collaboration by purchasers and third parties to reduce prices. Hawaii is the only state to have enacted a universal employer mandate before the passage of ERISA, but more recently several states—including Minnesota, Oregon, and Washington—have proposed relatively ambitious plans for universal or near-universal coverage. Limited funding sources and lack of access to the types of cost-control measures available in countries with national health insurance programs have required vary cautious phasing-in schedules, however. The extent to which the gaps in health insurance can be filled by action at the state level remains unresolved.

The Future of Health Insurance in the United States

The defeat of President Clinton's proposals has once again demonstrated the impediments to integrated action at the national level to extend coverage and control total health care costs. Unfortunately, the basic problems that such programs are designed to address will not go away. The proportion of non-aged Americans without health insurance is rising, and the gap between American health case costs and those in other comparable countries has steadily widened since the mid-1980s.

As an indication of the momentum built into existing financing and delivery arrangements, official projections of the consequences of existing policies show the percentage of total health expenditures to GDP rising from the current level of 14 percent to 18 percent in 2000 and 32 percent in 2030. Of course, it is impossible for these figures to be realized. The question is what will slow them down? And what will be the consequences for health outcomes or equity of access to health services?

Health Insurance Worldwide

Despite striking differences among the structures of health care systems, the similarities of demographic and disease patterns and medical technologies and cost pressures mean that there is a large substrate of shared problems among developed countries. These basic influences toward greater uniformity have been reinforced by the globalization of information and the widening acceptance of market-based philosophies. The result has been a stronger emphasis on countries raising efficiency in their health care financing and delivery systems. What this means in individual countries depends very much on where they are coming from: It is possible to discern three distinct strands in policy development.

The first of these relates to global budgetary ceilings on health expenditures, the capacity for which depends largely on the extent of government control over funding sources. For the past twenty years, the trend in most countries has been to tighten budgetary constraints. The United States is the notable exception, but there are many American advocates of global ceilings on health outlays, especially among supporters of national health insurance.

The second strand has been toward devolution of more detailed resource allocation decisions from central governments to smaller (public and private) agencies, closer to the point at which services are provided. This trend in part reflects the increased complexity of services and variety of providers. Within the public sphere, budgets and spending authority have been devolved to regional and area agencies, and there has also been a tendency for

greater involvement with the private sector. In many cases, devolution to private agencies has been accompanied by changes in payment formulas, incorporating incentives to improved efficiency.

The third policy strand, which is of most direct relevance to health insurance, has been a trend toward integration of financing and service delivery. The traditional forms of health insurance—especially those based on indemnification or reimbursement of expenses incurred by patients—reflected a separation between these functions, which was deliberately designed to strengthen the professional autonomy and financial independence of individual practitioners. The cost and efficiency outcomes of open access arrangements have become increasingly insupportable, more so in the United States than in countries with national health insurance and comprehensive global budgets. It is an ironic consequence that United States "managed care" organizations intrude on clinical decisionmaking in a more direct and intrusive manner than the national health insurance agencies in most other countries. However, there is a general trend toward payment arrangements that involve output-related payment of providers and contractual conditions that constrain treatment and billing options.

The archetypal examples of integration of insurance and service delivery are the British national health scheme and the staff model HMO, as exemplified by the Kaiser-Permanente organization. The achievements of the HMO model have stimulated proposals to generalize its principles as the basis for reform (and, in the United States, introduction) of national health insurance. The most vigorous proponent of "managed competition," based on coverage of defined populations by competing "health plans'" contracting with selected providers for comprehensive care of their enrollees, has been Alain Enthoven, of Stanford University. The concept of managed competition has been profoundly influential not only in the United States but also in significant reforms of national programs in many other countries, including Britain, the Netherlands, Sweden, Israel, New Zealand, and Russia.

Many of these reforms are in their early stages of implementation, and it would be easy to overstate the similarities between what is happening in these highly diverse contexts. The last decade has seen an unprecedented degree of international cross-fertilization in health insurance policy, however. Although the achievements of European countries and Canada have enlivened United States interest in its national health systems, the Europeans have been stimulated by U.S.-initiated concepts such as diagnostic related groups' (DRG-based) prospective payment for hospital care and managed competition. The result is a discernible shift toward convergence in the concepts and language of health insurance policy. The longer trend may be toward programs in which national governments retain responsibility for overall funding and budgetary control, but in which the management of care is delegated to risk-bearing "health plans" or "budget holders." These agencies, which could be public or private, would integrate the insurance function with other aspects of risk pooling and risk management functions, across a broad spectrum of health services.

RICHARD B. SCOTTON

BIBLIOGRAPHY

Arrow, Kenneth J., 1963. "The Welfare Economics of Medical Care." *American Economic Review*, vol. 53: 941–973.

Burner, S. T., D. R. Waldo, and D. R. McKusick, 1992. "National Health Expenditure Projection Through 2030." *Health Care Financing Review*, vol. 14: 1–30.

Employer Benefit Research Institute, 1994. "Effectiveness of Health Care Management Strategies: A Review of the Evidence." EBRI Issue Brief No. 154, Washington, DC.

———, 1995. "Sources of Health Insurance and Characteristics of the Uninsured: Analysis of the March 1994 Current Population Survey." EBRI Special Report SR–28 and Issue Brief No. 158, Washington, DC.

Enthoven, A. C., 1993a. "The History and Principles of Managed Competition." *Health Affairs*, vol. 12, supplement: 24–48.

———, 1993b. "Why Managed Care Has Failed to Contain Health Costs." *Health Affairs*, vol. 12, no. 3 (Fall): 27–43.

Frech, H. E., ed., *Health Care in America: The Political Economy of Hospitals and Health Insurance*. San Francisco: Pacific Research Institute for Public Policy.

Luft, H. S., and E. M. Morrison, 1991. "Alternative Delivery Systems." In E. Ginsberg, ed., *Health Services Research: Key to Health Policy*. Cambridge, MA: Harvard University Press.

Newhouse, J. P., and the Insurance Experiment Group, 1994. *Free for All? Lessons from the RAND Health Insurance Experiment*. Cambridge, MA: Harvard University Press.

Organization for Economic Cooperation and Development, 1992. *The Reform of Health Care: A Comparative Analysis of Seven OECD Countries*. Paris: OECD.

Phelps, Charles E., 1992. *Health Economics*. New York: HarperCollins. (Especially chapters 3 and 10–13.)

Starr, Paul, 1982. *The Social Transformation of American Medicine*. New York: Basic Books.

White, J., 1995. *Competing Solutions: American Health Care Proposals and International Experience*. Washington, DC: Brookings Institution.

Up-to-date information and analysis of major issues is contained in the following journals, of which the content consist wholly or principally of commissioned articles written by expert authors:

Health Affairs, vol. 12, no. 2 (1993). Special section: state models. (Contains articles on reform programs in Florida, Hawaii, Maryland, Minnesota, New Jersey, Oregon, Vermont, and Washington.)

Health Affairs, vol. 12, Supplement (1993). "Managed Competition: Health Reform American Style?"

Health Affairs, vol. 13, no. 1 (1994). Special issue: "The Clinton Plan: Pro and Con."

Health Affairs, vol. 13, no. 2 (1994). Special issues: "Mandates: The Road to Reform?"

Health Care Financing Review, 1989 Annual Supplement. "International Comparison of Health Care Financing and Delivery: Data and Perspectives."

Health Care Financing Review, 1991 Annual Supplement. "Cost-Containment Issues, Methods, and Experiences."

Health Care Financing Review, 1992 Annual Supplement. "Medicare and Medicaid Statistical Supplement."

Social Science and Medicine, vol. 39, no. 10, (1994). "Forming and Reforming the Market for Third-Party Purchasing of Health Care."

HEALTH POLICY.

In the United States, a patchwork of programs, financing, health benefits, and medical care offered by the federal government, private insurers, managed care providers, hospitals, outpatient clinics, and physicians. Health policy has been developed in a decentralized manner by both congressional legislation and market forces. The absence of many normal market constraints, however, has led to escalating health care expenditures.

During the post–World War II period, health care in the United States grew into a multibillion-dollar industry, consuming, by the early 1990s, 14 percent of the gross domestic product (GDP). These expenditures represent a mosaic of programs and funding streams. Yet, despite the large proportion of GDP spent in this policy area, considerable disgruntlement exists among reformers, leading them to charge that the system itself is unhealthy.

The health care system was and is bewilderingly complex, consisting of public and private programs and delivery mechanisms. Health policy appears to have been developed in a somewhat chaotic incremental approach in response to various crises and situations rather than in a rational, comprehensive manner. Health care costs rose dramatically toward the end of the twentieth century, rising from 4.4 percent of GDP in 1950 to double-digit levels by the 1990s, and many quality and access issues remained unresolved.

Rising Health Care Costs

Several factors have contributed to the increase of United States health care costs. The first factor is the shift in the United States from a focus on sometimes quickly cured and prevented infectious diseases to more costly chronic diseases. About 40 percent of all deaths in 1900 were caused by eleven major infectious diseases (typhoid, smallpox, scarlet fever, measles, whooping cough, diphtheria, influenza, tuberculosis, pneumonia, disease of the digestive system, and poliomyelitis). Only 16 percent of deaths then were caused by three major chronic conditions (heart disease, cancer, and stroke); 4 percent were caused by accidents, leaving 37 percent for a mixture of other causes.

With the development and widespread distribution of antibiotics, as well as vaccines for specific diseases, the incidence of infectious diseases began to decline. By 1973, only 6 percent of all deaths were caused by infectious diseases.

As antibiotics began to be overused and cases of infectious diseases previously thought to be conquered reappeared, some feared that the decline of morbidity from this source was a temporary phenomenon. The discovery and spread of acquired immunodeficiency syndrome (AIDS) contributed to this fear. But with the decline of infectious diseases that marked the last decades of the twentieth century, there was an accompanying shift to greater concern with chronic diseases—particularly heart disease and cancer. In 1977, two in five deaths resulted from heart disease, one in five from cancer, and one in ten from accidents.

Until the advent of AIDS and antibiotic-resistant strains of other communicable diseases, most infectious diseases in the United States were easily treated or cured, or both. Health care costs associated with these activities were modest in comparison to those connected with chronic diseases. With chronic diseases, no easy cure was available, nor was prevention as simple as inoculation with a vaccine. The medical goal for chronic diseases was a more costly one—maintenance to prevent further deterioration of the patient's quality of life. People with chronic diseases often undergo treatment for the rest of their lives. Thus, the shift from predominant concern with infectious disease that preoccupied the medical profession at the opening of the twentieth century to the refocus on maintenance strategies in response to chronic diseases at its close contributed to escalating health care costs.

A second factor pushing health care costs upward is a rise in the use of complex and expensive medical technologies, sometimes called "halfway technologies" because they may fail to cure, and sometimes even to arrest, chronic diseases. Among these technologies are organ transplants, heart bypass surgery, chemotherapy and radiation therapy for cancer, and kidney dialysis. Expensive technologies are also used with increasing frequency for diagnostic purposes.

Traditional payment schemes also contributed to cost escalation. Traditional health insurance involved a third-party payer, the insurance company, that assumed most or all of the costs of treatment. In some programs, the third-party payer was the government rather than a health insurance company. In either instance, consumers had little incentive to consider costs when making health services choices. The demand for health care is also said to be relatively inelastic, or price insensitive, further contributing to rising costs.

Under traditional payment schemes, physicians were paid on a piece-good or fee-for-service-rendered basis. This method provided a direct incentive to physicians to increase the volume of services rendered in order to increase total personal income. The more services they provided, the greater were the physicians' incomes. Critics charged that such payment schemes induced physicians to perform

questionable and even unnecessary procedures, driving up total health care costs. The number of surgeries performed in metropolitan areas for example, has been found to be most closely correlated with the number of surgeons in the region rather than with any other more-objective indicator of need, such as various morbidity and mortality rates.

As the health care system has become more complex, it has also became more impersonal. With the growth of medical specialties, generalists, such as family doctors, have diminished as a proportion of the total number of physicians, in part because many medical subspecialties produce considerably higher average incomes than does family medicine.

The growth of the detachment of the average consumer from the physician supplier, coupled with the growing litigiousness in the United States, has contributed to increased malpractice suits against physicians. Rising numbers of malpractice suits have driven medical costs up further in three ways. First, premiums themselves have contributed to rising costs, as well as to physician operating expenses. Annual premiums on some specialties in large cities exceeded six figures by the close of the 1980s. Second, many physicians have started practicing defensive medicine, ordering more tests and laboratory procedures than they otherwise would have to deflect charges in court of negligence and inadequate diagnoses.

Excessive tests and laboratory procedures have also increased the nation's health care bill. Additionally, many physicians in high-risk specialties, especially obstetrics and gynecology, have simply quit practicing, limiting the physician supply in those areas and increasing subspecialty fees.

Patchwork Incremental Development of Health Policy

Health care policy, not unlike other national policies, has developed incrementally in response to crises and specific problems. At times, it resembled a patchwork, with some patches missing, especially when health care coverage was the indicator. National policy encompassed several areas, including research, planning and regulation, service, consumer demand, and health care supply, especially through education and training. Much of the federal legislation in the period around World War II and thereafter consisted of amendments and refinements to two major acts: the Social Security Act of 1935 and the Public Health Service Act of 1944 (PHS Act).

Early federal interest in health care policy focused on controlling the spread of infectious diseases caused by infected sailors moving from seaport to seaport. The Merchant Marine Services Act of 1798 provided health services to United States seamen. The Marine Hospitals Services Act of 1870 revitalized and extended services to United States merchant seamen.

By the early 1900s, health policy had expanded to include women and children. The Maternity and Infancy Act of 1921, also called the Sheppard-Towner Act, provided grants to states to develop maternal and child health services. Title V of the Social Security Act of 1935 provided grants to states for maternal and child health and child welfare services, including services for crippled children.

In the same period, health services were extended to veterans. The Veterans Act of 1924, with its various amendments, extended medical care to former members of the armed services, not only for treatment of disabilities associated with military service but also for other conditions requiring hospitalization. This led to the development of a Veterans Administration health care system that is available to retired, disabled, and otherwise deserving veterans of military service. This system has traditionally been hospital and long-term care oriented, unlike the system for active duty personnel, which operates some 170 hospitals and 200 outpatient services for over one million citizens in uniforms.

The close of World War II saw the expansion of health policy to concerns of the general population, mostly through attempts to increase the supply of health services. The Public Health Service Act of 1944 further expanded health policy to include a public health service core. This act provided grants to states for the treatment of venereal diseases and tuberculosis and for the establishment and maintenance of health departments. It continued support for maintaining marine hospitals and provided services to penal and correctional institutions. The Hill-Burton Amendments of the PHS Act, also called the Hospital Survey and Construction Act of 1946, provided grants for hospital construction. Subsequent amendments provided additional moneys for medically related nonhospital institutions and for modernization of hospitals.

By the 1950s, health policy had expanded to include mental health. The Health Amendments Act of 1956 (amendments to the PHS Act) added special project grants to deal with problems of state mental hospitals. The focus on expanding the health services supply shifted from hospital construction to training health workers. The Health Amendments of 1956 also authorized traineeships for public health personnel and for the advanced training of nurses.

The 1960s saw the passage of several key pieces of legislation that expanded coverage to previously excluded disadvantaged groups. Anticipating Medicare and Medicaid, the Social Security Amendments of 1960, called the Kerr-Mills Act, established a program of medical assistance for the aged, which gave payments to states for medical care for indigent persons 65 and over. State participation, however, was optional, and only 25 percent of states chose to participate. The Health Services Act of 1962 for Agricultural and Migratory Workers established a program of grants for family clinics and other health services for mi-

gratory workers, who, like seamen, by their mobility could spread infectious diseases to a much broader population. Amendments to Title V of the Social Security Act in 1963 and 1964 added special project grants for maternity and infant care for low-income mothers and infants and comprehensive services for low-income children and youth. Neighborhood health centers in poor neighborhoods were established in the Economic Opportunity Act of 1964 as part of the antipoverty program.

Along with an expansion to disadvantaged and previously excluded groups, such as low-income mothers and infants, the 1960s saw a renewed emphasis on mental health problems. The Mental Retardation Facilities and Community Mental Health Centers Construction Act of 1963 added mental retardation services into previous grants and facilities construction programs. Amendments passed in 1965 provided personnel grants to staff community mental health centers; 1968 amendments added grants to construction and staff alcohol and narcotics addiction services and included drug abuse and drug dependence services as well as child mental health services; 1970 and 1965 amendments included programs for those with developmental disabilities and other neurologically handicapping conditions.

The two most significant pieces of health legislation in the 1960s were those that created Medicare for the elderly and Medicaid for the poor. Medicare was passed as the Health Insurance for the Aged Act of 1965. This act added Title XVIII to the Social Security Act. It established a program of national health insurance for the elderly. Part A provides basic protection against the costs of hospital and selected post-hospital services. Part B is a voluntary program financed by premium payments from enrollees, with matching federal revenues, and provides supplemental medical insurance benefits. Amendments were subsequently added for people who receive cash payments under the disability provisions of the Social Security Act and, later, for people who require hemodialysis or renal transplants.

Medicaid was passed as the Grants to the States for Medical Assistance Programs of 1965. This act added Title XIX to the Social Security Act. It created a federal-state matching program, with voluntary state participation to partially replace the Kerr-Mills program. Participating states had to provide five basic services: those for inpatients and outpatients, services for other laboratory tests and X rays, and physician and skilled nursing home services. States could included a number of other optional services, which were changed and expanded with subsequent amendments. Federal categorical welfare recipients were made eligible for Medicaid. By option, states could also include medically needy persons with incomes too high for cash federal welfare payments.

The late 1960s through the early 1980s saw an expansion of federal involvement in health, primarily through block grants and encouragement of nontraditional payment schemes. The Partnership for Health Act (the 1966 comprehensive Health Planning and Public Health Service Amendments to the PHS Act) provided block grants to state health departments for discretionary purposes. The Health Maintenance Organization Act of 1973, along with amendments in 1976, 1978, and 1981, provided grants and contracts to determine the feasibility of Health Maintenance Organizations (HMOs). HMOs consist of an alternative delivery system to that of the traditional fee-for-service-rendered systems. Pools of physicians are paid a standard, preset fee to deliver health services to subscribers. The 1973 legislation provided grant contracts and loan guarantees for initial operating costs for HMOs; amendments provided loans for the acquisition of facilities and equipment and for the training of administrators and directors.

The trend toward block grants continued in the Omnibus Budget Reconciliation Act of 1981. This act created block grants in the areas of prevention, primary care, and maternal and child health. However, in accordance with the Ronald Reagan administration's philosophy, it also reduced federal health services funding by 25 percent in the process of replacing categorical grants with block grants. The Omnibus Reconciliation Act replaced all mental health, alcohol, and drug abuse programs, including those under the 1963 Community Mental Health Centers Act, with a single block grant and a concomitant 25 percent reduction in mental health funding. It eliminated new funding for planning and start-up of HMOs; closed or transferred to state or local authority Public Health Service hospitals and clinics; eliminated some Medicare services, including alcohol detoxification and occupational therapy to qualify for home health services; and gave states discretion as to whether to cover 18- to 20-year-olds under Medicaid. It also indirectly reduced the number of people eligible for Medicaid by tightening requirements for Aid to Families with Dependent Children (AFDC), cut federal funds for Medicaid, added adolescent pregnancy services, and allowed states to waive Medicaid consumer freedom of choice about physicians.

Retrenchment of the federal role and cost curbing continued with the Tax Equity and Fiscal Responsibility Act of 1982. This legislation included changes in both Medicare and Medicaid. For Medicaid, it allowed enrollment fees, costsharing, and similar charges for some categories of recipients and services. For Medicare, it added payments for some portions of hospice care, made extensive changes in reimbursement methodologies for hospital-related services under Medicare, and began a shift to a case mix (diagnostic related groups, or DRGs) for reimbursements for most acute care hospitals. Other Medicare curtailments included the elimination of nursing salary cost differentials and private room subsidies, the elimination of the lesser of cost or charge provisions, changes in reimbursements for HMOs, and an increase of recipient-paid premiums to 25 percent of Part B costs.

As a consequence of DRGs for Medicare, the growth in hospital costs was contained for a few years, but it then began to rise again. The DRG system did shift more patient care from hospital-based clinics to outpatient clinics. Physician costs under the Prospective Payment System continued to rise, however. In 1992, a new physician reimbursement system was proposed that uses a resource-based relative value scale (RBRVS). The new system utilizes studies that examined how long it took physicians to perform various tasks and that assigned those tasks a relative weight based on three geographically adjusted values for work, practice costs, and malpractice premiums. Physicians were opposed to the implementation of RBRVS, even though the Health Care Financing Administration (HCFA) did revise Medicare financing rules somewhat, after negotiations with various groups from organized medicine. The consequence was to decrease fees for specialists while increasing fees for family practice physicians.

Access to Health Care Services and Quality of Care

A persistent criticism of United States health care policy is that it does not provide universal access to care. Although many other industrialized nations provide comprehensive health care to their citizens, the United States does not. Controversy remains about issues of equity and whether access to health care is a basic right. These issues remain unresolved, and the poor continue to differ from the non-poor in the amount of health care received, as well as in the source of that care. The poor are less likely to have regular care and health insurance and are more likely to be less healthy. Those with limited access to regular health care are more likely to end up in hospitals, where they are unable to pay for their health care, causing policymakers to dub them the "uncompensated care group." The proportion of children in this group may be as high as one-third.

Not all hospitals share equally in the burden of providing uncompensated medical care for the indigent. The proportion of caseload that is devoted to uncompensated care is higher in public, general, and teaching hospitals. In these hospitals in 1983, uncompensated care was almost 12 percent of all costs, compared to about 5 percent of hospital costs on average.

The number of medically uninsured has been growing. In 1992, estimates of the numbers of those without some form of insurance ranged from a low of 22 million to a high of 37 million. Included in this group are the homeless, the socially dislocated, the unemployed, part-time workers without benefits, and increasingly, full-time workers without benefits.

Lack of access affects both quality of care and health outcomes. One study found that the nonpoor in fair or poor health had 37 percent more ambulatory hospital visits than the poor. When those without insurance are admitted to hospitals, they are more likely to have deteriorated further in health status, are less likely to get specialized services, and are more likely to die. Rates for the uninsured for in-death hospitals were 1.2 to 3.4 times higher than for insured patients, even after taking account statistically of the poorer health status of the uninsured when they gain hospital admission.

Early quality control efforts in health care occurred at the state level when states adopted a regulatory stance by certifying medical facilities, especially hospitals, and licensing physicians. Yet regulation of unethical and incompetent behavior of health care providers has largely been subject to self-regulation, a practice critics contend is ineffective. One study in 1995, for example, found that one out of five illnesses afflicting hospital inpatients were contracted while they were hospitalized. The distribution of inappropriate medicines to patients occurred with some frequency. Yet findings against health care providers, especially physicians, by state boards created to hear grievances were infrequent and sanctions against them were often weak.

In 1972, the federal government became involved in a quality control effort by establishing Professional Standards Review Organizations (PSROs). These organizations consisted of committees of practicing physicians who were to provide effective oversight of medical services paid for through Medicare and Medicaid by revising records and making recommendations. PSROs, however, had limited options for either punishment or changing behavior. In 1982, legislation was passed to create PROs (Peer Review Organizations), to be administered by the Health Care Financing Organization. PROs are, typically, groups of contracted physicians who operate statewide and are charged with reviewing the professional activities of physicians, other practitioners, and institutional providers of service to Medicare beneficiaries. The work of PROs remains controversial in the 1990s.

Since its creation in 1944, the Public Health Service (PHS) has been devoted to research to improve the health status of the United States population and the quality of health care. Within the PHS are the Centers for Disease Control (CDC). Various CDC units include those focused on programs for venereal disease control, immunizations, infectious diseases, chronic diseases, and work-related diseases. In the 1980s, the CDC became involved in tracking and documenting the spread of AIDS. Another PHS division is the Food and Drug Administration (FDA), which has four basic program areas: food, drugs and medical devices, radiological products, and the National Center for Toxicological Research. The National Institutes of Health

(NIH) are also organizationally within the PHS and are devoted to research to improve the health status and quality of care in the United States. NIH is organized predominantly on a disease basis and includes 11 major institutes: Cancer; Heart, Lung, and Blood; Dental Research; Arthritis, Diabetes, Digestive and Kidney Diseases; Neurological and Communicative Disorders and Stroke; Allergy and Infectious Diseases; General Medical Sciences; Child Health and Human Development; Eye; Environmental Sciences; and Aging. Another major division in PHS, the Alcohol Drug Abuse and Mental Health Administration, includes the National Institute of Mental Health, the National Institute on Drug Abuse, and the National Institute on Alcohol Abuse and Alcoholism.

Some critics concerned with quality of care contend that United States health care policy has historically been focused too much on acute care and that insufficient attention has been devoted to prevention and other factors. The health status of individuals is affected not only by access to acute care but also by human biology, including genetic components, safety concerns, and lifestyle, including diet and exercise and the environment. Broadly defined, then, environmental regulation and health education programs have become integral parts of quality health care. Various U.S. statutes have attempted to improve health by creating a safe and clean environment. The Federal Water Pollution Control Act of 1965 switched enforcement responsibilities for water control from the U.S. Department of Interior to the Department of Health, Education, and Welfare, and amendments set and strengthened standards to prevent illness induced by water pollution. The Water Quality Improvement Act of 1970 increased restrictions on thermal pollution from nuclear power plants. The Clean Air Act Amendments of 1970 and 1977 established ambient air quality standards, strengthened automobile pollution standards, and set emission standards for high-pollution plants.

The Occupational Safety and Health Act (OSHA) of 1970 and its various amendments established strong standard-setting authority in the secretary of labor to set a minimum level of protection for workers against specified hazards, and it attempted to prevent occupational and work-related diseases. Required registration of pesticides was introduced by the Environmental Pesticide Control Act of 1972, which also gave the Environmental Protection Agency (EPA) the authority to ban use of hazardous pesticides. Standards for allowable levels of pollutants and chemicals in public drinking water systems were set in the Safe Drinking Water Act of 1974. The Toxic Substances Control Act of 1976 regulates chemical substances impacting on health and the environment; it also provides grants to the states and bans manufacture and use of polychlorinated biphenyls (PCBs). Management plans for the safe disposal of discarded materials and regulation of hazardous waste management was covered by the Resource Conservation Recovery Act of 1976. Title IV of the Health Services and Centers Amendments of 1978 requires the secretary of the Department of Health and Human Services to submit a national disease prevention profile to Congress every three years, and the Comprehensive Environmental Response, Compensation, and Liability Act of 1980 established a controversial federal superfund to clean up chemical dumps and toxic wastes.

Health Care Reform

In 1992, William Jefferson Clinton was elected United States president, and he made health care reform the major issue of the first year of his administration. The administration effort to reform U.S. health care generated widespread discussion and input but was largely unsuccessful. Clinton administration officials cited many problems with the health care system, including rising insecurity, growing complexity, rising costs, decreasing quality, declining choices, and growing irresponsibility. Of the 37 million Americans who lacked insurance at that time, 85 percent were in families that included an employed adult, reflecting a trend toward reduced or no employer-provided health care benefits for employed workers. Of the dollars paid in health care premiums, one out of two went to administrative costs. The large number of insurance providers increased costs. Health care costs were rising. State spending on health care outstripped spending on education. The United States spent more on health care than its competitors, including Canada, Denmark, France, Germany, Greece, Japan, and the United Kingdom, but a lower proportion of Americans had health security, and the indicators of health status for United States citizens, including infant mortality and morbidity rates, were less favorable. Traditional delivery systems have not produced the information most valuable to doctors, nurses, or consumers. As employers reduced health care benefits, fewer choices were available. The growth in medical malpractice fostered irresponsible behavior.

The Clinton administration proposed a Health Security Act that emphasized five principles: security (guaranteeing comprehensive benefits to all Americans), simplicity (simplifying the system and cutting red tape), savings (controlling health care costs), quality (making the world's best care better), choice (preserving and increasing the options for consumers), and responsibility (making everyone responsible for health care). The Clinton plan emphasized expanded mandatory employer provision of health care benefits, with increased copayments and cost sharing by consumers and workers. Elaborate hearings around the nation, led by Hillary Clinton and Ira Magaziner, were held. Eventually, a coalition of insurance companies and health care providers opposed the plan, running numerous television ads to reach the public with its message. The opposi-

tion prevailed, and many of the issues that the National Health Security Act sought to remedy remain unresolved.

MARCIA LYNN WHICKER

BIBLIOGRAPHY

Judis, John B., 1995. "Abandoned Surgery: Business and the Failure of Health Care Reform." *American Prospect,* no. 21 (Spring): 65–73.
Kendall, David, and Will Marshall, 1995. "Health Reform, Meet Tax Reform." *American Prospect,* no. 21 (Spring): 74–79.
Kronenfeld, Jennie Jacobs, 1993. *Controversial Issues in Health Care Policy.* Newbury Park, CA: Sage.
Kronenfeld, Jennie Jacobs, and Marcia Lynn Whicker, 1984. *U.S. National Health Policy.* New York: Praeger.
White House Domestic Policy Council, 1993. *The President's Report to the American People.* New York: Touchstone.

HEALTH PROMOTION. According to the World Health Organization (WHO), health promotion enables people to gain control over their health, but a slightly narrower definition is any combination of educational, organizational, economic, and environmental support for actions leading to health. Health promotion represents a growing area of public administration.

Health promotion is a comparatively new field, coming into existence as a field of public policy in the early 1970s with the 1974 Lalonde report in Canada and given wide currency with the 1976 Healthy People 2000 project in the United States. It had its genesis in a growing realization that medical services by themselves did not cover the majority of the most important determinants of population health.

During the twentieth century, Western nations have undergone an epidemiological transition—from high rates of death and disease because of infections such as tuberculosis and cholera to the situation in which the main causes of death are cancers and heart disease, diseases that are closely woven into the fabric of the western culture. The medical model of intervention that had worked well to reduce mortality and morbidity from infectious diseases was found to be inadequate for people unable to cope with threats to their health stemming from patterns of lifestyle, pervasive pollution, poverty, or discrimination.

Health promotion thus developed as an intersectoral enterprise, involving the professions of public health, medicine, health education, epidemiology, sociology, and social work, among others. Its mandate is to improve the health of the population in the widest sense of the word "health," a state of physical, mental, and social well-being.

Health promotion is a form of empowerment, and it involves the community at every stage of the process, whether that is working through the community's particular aspirations for health, consulting it throughout the implementation of any project, or enlisting it in the evaluation of that project.

Within this collaborative process, properly coordinated health promotion campaigns, first, *identify the target population* or populations, taking care to include disadvantaged groups, such as minority ethnic groups, women, people living with a disability, and people with low socioeconomic status. These campaigns use epidemiology to determine a community's health status and health needs. Researching the health status of each population group allows one to address the particular prevention needs of each group from before birth to old age, ensuring that social, economic, and structural conditions are built into the strategy from the beginning.

Second, a health promotion program should *identify the risk factors* that threaten the achievement of these needs—risk factors associated with noncommunicable diseases, such as illness caused by smoking, using alcohol and other drugs, or by maintaining a poor diet, with little exercise; risk factors for communicable diseases, such as those caused by incomplete immunization coverage and sexual risk-taking; risk factors for injuring mental health, such as substance abuse, and living and working under stressful conditions; and risk factors for disturbing environmental health, such as food contamination and pollution.

Modern health promotion models tackle all of these areas with an integrated program, since risk factors do not operate in isolation. Psychosocial factors, such as mental health status, lead to behaviors that affect noncommunicable and communicable disease risk factors, and environmental health conditions have a structural impact on communicable disease risk factors and mental health status.

A third health promotion campaign device is to *identify relevant settings* or organizations that can develop healthy and supportive environments, such as health promoting hospitals, schools, workplaces, and towns, and to match these to population groups. Organizations should provide for the occupational health and safety of their members or employees. They should be supportive of health in the people that they deal with, and they should be healthy themselves, that is, they should provide a supportive, rewarding, and fulfilling environment for those who work there.

Fourth, health promotion campaigns should *identify methods to support people* who are combating health problems in these settings. These methods can include social marketing (including mass media advertising and sponsorship of sports and arts by health agencies), community development projects to build capacity at the local level, and legislative and fiscal activities, such as the banning of cigarette advertising or the implementation of an increased tax on cigarettes.

Health promotion establishes epidemiological baselines for mortality, morbidity, and behavior patterns, enabling health outcomes to be plotted and compared with predicted effects. Outcome evaluations, however, have to take account of the fact that the timelines for health promotion are much longer than those for crisis care. If a cancer is surgically removed, one knows within a day whether the patient will live; if a young girl is dissuaded from beginning to smoke, it will be 30 years before she shows up in the statistics as a fraction of a death avoided. The reduction in male lung cancer rates since the antismoking campaigns began, however, and the fall in cardiovascular deaths following the move to lower-fat diets, show that when behavioral change can be embedded in the culture it can be very effective indeed.

Health promotion is also highly cost effective; in one Australian study, antismoking activities alone returned Aus$212 million for an outlay of $19 million. Some progressive governments around the world have followed the lead of the Australian state of Victoria and the Victorian Health Promotion Foundation. The foundation is funded by an increased tax on cigarettes, as life-threatening items of consumption, and it invests the extra money thus gained in specialized health-promotion agencies.

As the World Bank has made clear, investment in health promotion and disease prevention strategies represent the most efficient way to improve the health of the world's people, yet in many countries funds for health promotion are still hard to find. Victoria's model is a way of taxing one of the most harmful disease-creating products to promote wellness. The tax is possible electorally because of its association with health, so the government is able to raise the price of cigarettes much higher, which in turn acts as a disincentive to smokers (especially younger smokers). Health promotion areas unrelated to tobacco—promotion of a healthy diet and exercise, campaigns for safe drinking, anti–skin cancer campaigns, encouragement of Pap smears for women, and the promotion of mental health, safety, and safer sex—all benefit because the agency is able to support these programs from the tobacco tax.

RHONDA GALBALLY

BIBLIOGRAPHY

Green, Lawrence, and Marshall Kreuter, 1991. *Health Promotion Planning: An education and environmental approach.* Mountain View, CA: Mayfield Publishing Company.
Downie, Robert, Carol Fyfe, and Andrew Tannahill, 1991. *Health Promotion: Models and Values.* Oxford and New York: Oxford University Press.

HEARSAY. Evidence offered at an adjudicative hearing regarding a statement made outside the hearing when offered to prove the truth of matters asserted in the statement; a secondhand account of an event offered into evidence to prove that the event occurred.

Whether particular evidence constitutes hearsay depends upon the purpose for which the evidence is offered. If offered to prove the truth of matters asserted in the statement, the evidence is hearsay. If offered for some other purpose, the evidence is not hearsay.

The most widely recognized form of hearsay is testimony by a witness regarding what some other person said about a matter in issue, if such testimony is offered to prove the truth of such a matter. For example, at a hearing investigating the cause of an industrial plant explosion, a worker at the plant who saw a leaking valve the day before the explosion may testify from personal knowledge as to what he or she saw. It would be hearsay, however, if a government investigator testified as to what the worker told him or her about the valve if the investigator's testimony is offered to prove that the valve was leaking. If, however, the fact that the valve was leaking had been established by other evidence and the investigator's testimony is offered only to prove that the company knew about the leaking valve before the explosion, the investigator's testimony as to what the plant worker told him or her would not be hearsay.

Documentary evidence may also constitute hearsay, depending on the purpose for which it is offered. In the previous example, a written report, describing the leaking valve, that was prepared by the plant worker before the explosion would be hearsay if offered into evidence to prove that the valve had been leaking. If offered to prove that the company knew about the leaking valve before the explosion, it would not be hearsay.

Courts have traditionally regarded hearsay as unreliable evidence because it depends on the credibility and competency of a person who has not taken the witness stand and who is not subject to cross-examination. The "hearsay rule" is a common law doctrine developed by the courts proscribing the admission of hearsay evidence unless it fits one of several narrowly drawn exceptions recognized by the courts or created by legislative enactment. The hearsay rule has been criticized as having little justification in administrative agency hearings, and the modern trend has been to allow administrative agencies to use and rely upon hearsay evidence.

The disfavor with which courts have regarded hearsay evidence arises out of a concern that juries of laypersons, which hear and decide many types of court cases, might be confused or misled by hearsay. In judge-tried court cases, the hearsay rule has been considerably relaxed; however, even in judge-tried court cases, the judgment of the court will not stand if it is based on hearsay evidence only.

Unlike the courts, administrative agencies do not use juries to hear and decide issues. Furthermore, administrative agencies are staffed by professionals who bring special knowledge, skill, and expertise to the adjudicative process. For these reasons, most courts have allowed administrative agencies more leeway to use and rely on hearsay evidence than has been permitted in court cases. Nonetheless, judicial acceptance of hearsay in administrative proceedings

has come slowly, and there are still exceptions to the now-prevalent rule allowing administrative agencies to use and rely on hearsay evidence.

Administrative agencies face two important legal issues when confronted with hearsay. First, should the hearsay be received into evidence by the hearing officer who conducts the hearing? Second, if the hearsay is received into evidence, may the agency rely on such evidence to support its administrative decisionmaking?

Admissibility

As early as 1903, the United States Supreme Court ruled that administrative agency hearings "should not be too narrowly constrained by technical rules as to admissibility of proof," and declined to apply to administrative hearings "those narrow rules which prevail in trials at common law" (*Interstate Commerce Commission vs. Baird*, 194 U.S. 25, 44, 24 S. Ct. 563, 568 [1903]). This broad view of the admissibility of evidence in administrative proceedings has been affirmed by subsequent rulings of the Supreme Court and applied to hearsay evidence.

The rationale for not applying the technical rules of evidence to administrative agency hearings is that administrative agency hearings are more similar to judge-tried court cases than to jury-tried court cases. According to this view, if an agency is capable of accurately ruling on the admissibility of evidence, it is also capable of sifting through the evidence once received to determine whether the evidence is competent to support the agency's findings.

In 1946, Congress adopted the Administrative Procedure Act, which establishes procedures for the conduct of hearings by federal administrative agencies. The hearing procedures established by the Administrative Procedure Act apply to any agency hearings not otherwise subject to a specific statute establishing hearing procedures for that agency.

Section 7 of the Administrative Procedure Act (5 U.S.C. §556[d]) provides that

> any oral or documentary evidence may be received, but the agency as a matter of policy shall provide for the exclusion of irrelevant, immaterial, or unduly repetitious evidence. A sanction may not be imposed or rule or order issued except on consideration of the whole record or those parts thereof cited by a party and supported by and in accordance with the reliable, probative, and substantial evidence.

This section has been interpreted by the federal courts to allow administrative agencies covered by the act to receive and consider hearsay evidence in making adjudicative findings.

Other federal statutes governing the conduct of administrative hearings not covered by the Administrative Procedure Act also have been interpreted by the courts to allow the agencies to receive and consider hearsay. At the state level, many legislatures have enacted statutes allowing state administrative agencies to receive and consider hearsay. Thus, at both the federal and state level, administrative agencies are authorized to receive and consider hearsay evidence at administrative hearings.

There remains, however, the issue of whether hearsay, standing alone, constitutes substantial evidence to support an administrative decision or rule. In other words, if the only evidence supporting an administrative determination is hearsay, can the agency decision be overturned on judicial review on the grounds that it is not supported by competent and convincing evidence?

Residuum Rule

Early in this century, the New York Court of Appeals (*Carroll vs. Knickerbocker*, 218 N.Y. 435, 173 N.E. 507 [1916]) ruled that hearsay, although admissible in an administrative hearing, will not support an agency adjudication in the absence of other nonhearsay evidence in the record to support the decision. In other words, hearsay evidence, standing alone, is not substantial evidence. This rule, known as the "residuum rule," quickly gained wide acceptance in both state and federal courts across the country.

In 1971, the Supreme Court handed down a decision that cast considerable doubt on the continued viability of the residuum rule in the federal courts, although the Court did not reject the rule outright. In *Richardson versus Perales* (402 U.S. 389, 91 S. Ct 1420 [1971]), the Supreme Court ruled that the Social Security Administration did not err in relying on written medical records to deny an applicant's claim for disability benefits. The reports had been prepared by physicians who had examined the applicant but who did not appear and testify at the hearing on the applicant's claim for benefits.

The applicant appealed the agency's denial of benefits on the grounds that the hearsay medical reports, although admissible into evidence at the disability hearing, were not competent evidence to support the agency's decision and were insufficient to overcome the testimony of the applicant's treating physician, who appeared and testified at the hearing, that the applicant was permanently disabled. The Supreme Court rejected the applicant's argument and affirmed the decision of the Social Security Administration, holding that hearsay medical reports can support an administrative decision when the physicians who prepared the reports are subject to being subpoenaed and cross-examined regarding their findings.

When the Court included in its decision the caveat that the physicians could have been subpoenaed to testify, it left the door open to future applications of the residuum rule in cases when the underlying statement is not subject to cross-examination. On one hand, nonetheless, most federal courts that have considered the issue since *Perales* have treated the residuum rule as having been abandoned and have upheld administrative decisions based solely on hearsay evidence. On the other hand, most state courts still consider the residuum rule to be a viable doctrine, though few have used it in recent years to reverse administrative adjudications. Hearsay is still regularly received into evidence at agency hearings and is used to support administrative decisions at both the state and federal levels.

PAUL M. BROWN

BIBLIOGRAPHY

Davis, Kenneth Culp, 1980. *Administrative Law Treatise.* 2d ed. San Diego, CA: K. C. Davis.

Stein, Jacob A., Glenn A. Mitchell, and Basil J. Mezines, 1994. *Administrative Law.* New York: Matthew Bender.

Strong, John William, ed., 1992. *McCormick on Evidence.* vol. 2 4th ed. St. Paul, MN: West.

Warren, Kenneth F., 1994. "Adjudication." In David H. Rosenbloom and Richard D. Schwartz, eds., *Handbook of Regulation and Administrative Law,* pp. 225–286. New York: Marcel Dekker.

HIERARCHY. A group of persons arranged in order of rank, grade, class, and so on. In the context of organizational theory; a formal structure denoting a chain of command whereby authority and power are vested at the top. Hierarchy provides the framework for the relationships of roles within organizations. Often hierarchy has been charted as a tall vertical structure such as a triangle, pyramid, or ladder, but more recently, horizontal or "flattened" hierarchical forms are shown.

Hierarchy has a long tradition as a means of political, social, and religious organization. Evidence of hierarchy spans thousands of years. In 1491 B.C.E., during the exodus from Egypt, Jethro, the father-in-law of Moses, urged Moses to delegate authority over the tribes of Israel along hierarchical lines (Shafritz and Ott 1996, p. 30). The ancient Romans organized along hierarchical lines, with the affluent and aristocratic males occupying the top positions (patricians) and the poor (plebeians) at the bottom. An often-used example of a hierarchically arranged organization is the Roman Catholic Church. The pope occupies the top position, followed in descending order by the cardinals, bishops, priests, deacons, and so on. In a hierarchy, the authority vested in the top echelon grants it the power to organize and command those below. This authority, in theory, remains unquestioned, therefore orders are obeyed as given, which facilitates coordinated action since there is no deliberation about the orders nor consensus to be reached.

Hierarchical stratification can take various forms, including social and class distinctions related to birthright or privilege (as in England's aristocracy or India's historical caste system) and occupational stratification, in which the status and position ascribed to an individual are defined by the roles and relationships to others within an organization. Overlaps of position in an organizational setting and relative ranking in society as a whole can occur. For example, Chie Nakane has explained that in Japan most Japanese, whatever their status or occupation, are involved in *oyabun-kobun* (boss-subordinate) relationships. According to Nakane, "The oyabun-kobun relationship comes into being through one's occupational training and activities and carries social and personal implications, appearing symbolically at the critical moments in a man's life" (1988, p. 11).

The prevalence of hierarchy is not confined to discussions of social, political, and organizational stratification, however. Hierarchy has been used as a model for the simplification of ideas, such as psychologist Abraham Maslow's use of the form to explain his theory of motivation as a "hierarchy of needs" (Maslow 1954).

Organizational Hierarchy

In the United States, hierarchy has been the dominant form of organization since the 1800s. There are a number of reasons for this. In the late 1800s and early 1900s, economic factors changed the United States from largely a trade and agricultural society to a mechanized industrial one. This change resulted in large population shifts, from rural areas to the cities. Along with the increasing levels of immigration and urbanization, the number and size of organizations and the number of industrial laborers increased. Divisions of rank occurred between laborers and supervisors within organizations, structured upon supervisor-subordinate lines, which can be understood as a hierarchy.

Along with industrialization came a preoccupation with efficiency. Utilizing methods new at the time, such as scientific management (Taylor 1911), organizations attempted to increase productivity through structural means. Scientific management concentrated on discovering "one best way" for work to be carried out, and its methods placed control and decisionmaking firmly in the hands of the superior (manager). Although this system increased the manager's influence and power, it was alienating for the worker, who was simply an extension of the machinery and performed his or her job without providing input to the

manager. Methods such as scientific management lend themselves to reinforcing the manager as the decision-maker and the subordinate as order taker. The legitimacy of this relationship (for one person to control or dictate the actions of another) is questioned in a number of antihierarchy arguments, but this opposition has remained largely ignored.

Robert Denhardt (1993) outlined how students of public administration in the 1930s looked toward business management for advice on increasing efficiency and production. Especially important at the time were writings on organizational structure. The problem that occupied many writers was how large and complex organizations might best be designed to permit efficient operations. Not surprisingly, the hierarchical model of the military and the Catholic Church was adopted.

In organizational theory and in practice, a hierarchy is often enacted as a bureaucracy (Weber 1954). This form, even with its faults, is probably the most influential organizational form of the twentieth century. Bureaucracy combines the framework of a hierarchy with the compatible notions of a centralized chain of command, top-down communication, and formal rules and regulations that remove individual discretion. The terms "hierarchy" and "bureaucracy" are used almost interchangeably in much organizational literature, and it becomes difficult to differentiate them in some respects, but hierarchy, as such, provides the form of structure that underlies Weber's description of bureaucracy rather than incorporates all of his notions. Bureaucracy, along with scientific management, stresses efficiency, accountability, and control.

Two former General Motors executives, James Mooney and Alan C. Reiley (1939) offered four abstract principles by which organizations should be structured, including: coordination through a hierarchical chain of command, a "scalar principle," a functional principle (referring to horizontal divisions of labor), and a relationship between line and staff. Organizational principles such as these helped legitimate and advocate the use of a hierarchy in organizations and establish and institutionalize the form in United States workplaces, both public and private. Furthermore, all of these principles have been closely aligned with powerful theoretical perspectives for organizational management, further cementing their acceptance.

Advantages of Hierarchy

Elliott Jaques (1990) has asserted that "managerial hierarchy is the most efficient, the hardiest, and in fact the most natural structure ever devised for large organizations. Properly structured, hierarchy can release energy and creativity, rationalized productivity, and actually improve morale"

(p. 127). This view in some ways seeks to advocate the position that there are natural leaders who will rise to the top and effectively lead others. Jaques admits that hierarchical structure has "been the source of a great deal of trouble and inefficiency" but attributes these problems to managerial design and organizational fads and gimmicks. The solution to correcting problems often attributed to hierarchy (alienation, illegitimate authority, etc.) according to Jaques is not to "redesign" the hierarchy but rather to place the emphasis on accountability for getting work done. Jaques's analysis suggests that the problems attributed to hierarchy are actually problems that may be caused by the hiring and retention of poorly performing individuals and an improper distribution of work assignments. These situations result in the managers' inability to enforce the notion of accountability in the individual worker, thus removing managers' ability to be accountable for the work done. Again, the essential focus, according to Jaques, is to concentrate on insuring accountability within a hierarchy rather than changing from a hierarchy to another form.

Disadvantages of Hierarchy

According to Frederick Thayer, hierarchy is the single cause of alienation. "Quite literally, hierarchy has separated us from others and ourselves, by externalizing authority from out inner selves" (Thayer 1981, p. A10). "Any superior-subordinate relationship makes sense only if the designated superior knows what subordinates should do. Similarly, the action of a subordinate can be described only as a response to knowledge external to him or her" (Thayer 1981 p. A14).

Even though hierarchy may be considered an efficient process in some respects, it is also inefficient, since orders are given by those who are removed from the work processes themselves, thus, the methods may not be effective. Also, there are negative effects that impact workers, which may outweigh the benefits gained by using the structure (Hummel 1994).

In terms of advancement, the way to the top of an organization has been through promotion into managerial ranks. Persons who do not desire a managerial role are usually destined to remain at the bottom of the hierarchy, with no outlet for advancement. Thus, the hierarchy acts as both a machine for advancement and as a potential trap. Promotions through the hierarchy also can be discriminatory, and ideas may stagnate. Studies have shown that people who are promoted tend to replicate the characteristics of those who are already at the top of the hierarchy—usually white males. "Followers must assimilate the characteristics of leaders if they wish to get ahead" (Thayer 1981, p. A3).

Ulla Ressner (1987) explains that in Sweden a dual hierarchy exists that allows ascent to men but keeps women on the bottom rungs of the organization. Ressner has said that

in connection with women's arrival at executive levels, two gender-related, internal executive labour markets appear to develop within one and the same organisation/authority. From a single point of departure, with the woman occupying the same formal position in the hierarchy of the government authority as her male colleague, two distinct career paths develop . . . one for female executives in a staff function carrying less influence and status, and one for male executives in the line organisation leading to the top of the organisation and the centre of power (1987, p. 58).

She further observed that the structure of career and development opportunities in organizations has been found to do a great deal to influence people's expectations, ambitions, and vision concerning their futures. This is also reflected by their behavior and attitudes. At lower levels in the government service organization (office worker–level), the effects of the authoritarian hierarchical structure appear to be the biggest obstacle to developmental opportunities at work. Some of the workers' dysfunctional responses to a hierarchical system included little involvement and participation in work-related activities, less self-confidence, critical toward and unable to identity with people at higher levels, little disposed to protest actively or to try to change things. Instead, people channeled their dissatisfaction into passive resistance and anti-cultures, creating peer groups for security and protection (Ressner, 1987 p. 59).

Several studies discussed in Rosabeth Moss Kanter's (1977) *Men and Women of the Corporation* confirmed the development and apparent need for peer support groups in organizations where upward mobility is an institutionalized characteristic of a social system. Sociologist Robert K. Merton (as cited in Kanter 1977) argued in a classic analysis that when people face favorable advancement opportunities, they compare themselves upward in rank, with one foot already out of the current peer group, in the process of what he calls "anticipatory socialization." But, unfavorable advancement prospects lend themselves to comparison with peers and concern with peer solidarity (Kanter 1977, p. 148). Arthur Cohen (as cited in Kanter 1977) in a laboratory study about the relationship between the structure of opportunity situations and the development of work opportunities, concluded that those who foresee mobility opportunities in a hierarchical structure were less critical of upper groups, were more oriented toward the high-power groups than to members of their own peer group, were careful about criticism, stayed more with tasks, and tended to be less attracted to members of their own group than to high-power people. The nonmobiles centered their affection and attention on members of their own group, were more likely to feel that their "social validity" was received from their own rather than from the upper groups, and were more openly critical of the upper group (Kanter 1977, p. 148).

These countersystems within hierarchical organizations can be dysfunctional for a number of reasons. It is apparent that those who feel they cannot advance will lose commitment and very probably their motivation to excel. As workers who move upward break their ties and common concerns with peers, the resentment that develops may lead to foot dragging, antagonism, and low self-esteem and aspirations by the nonmobiles. The authority granted to occupants of the top of the hierarchy may be seen by those at the bottom as an illegitimate grant of power. Perhaps as important, the loss of association with and concerns about people who are lower in the hierarchy may lead to poor decisionmaking and the inability to motivate people or to anticipate or recognize problems developing in the workplace.

For women, hierarchical systems can be a curse. Kanter (1977) has demonstrated the manner in which hierarchical organizations discriminate against women. Her studies indicated that even when women are promoted, there are detrimental consequences. Kanter's research has revealed that females experience many impediments and disadvantages in a hierarchical organization. A general lack of mobility, coupled with the shortage of female mentors in the higher echelon, creates a dilemma not experienced by men. Moving up means cutting oneself off socially. "It was easier for the women to support a culture devaluating hierarchical success because of tradition, [which advantages males] and because they had few women upward in the hierarchy with whom to identify. Men did not face this problem because there were men at every level of the system, whereas women tend to occupy lower positions" (Kanter 1977, p. 151). These studies have created a desire by feminists and others to create more equal opportunities by dismantling hierarchical structures.

The Future of Hierarchy

The question remains whether hierarchy is a natural and inevitable form that will continue to exist in our societies and workplaces or if it is something unnatural and oppressive that time, economic factors, and different structural forms will eventually replace. Although the definition of hierarchy may seem to indicate a straightforward structural form, it has been criticized extensively, especially regarding its legitimacy and efficacy in the modern workplace.

In recent decades, other organizational forms have been tried that flatten or reduce the number of levels structured in the hierarchy. As the world becomes even more in-

volved in what has been termed the "information age," the hierarchical form will continue to be perceived as woefully slow and inadequate. The main reason is that "The hierarchical structure of organizations in particular discourages open and free upward disclosure of information. Because of authority relationships and reward systems, subordinates are likely to distort or omit information that will reflect adversely on themselves, [that will] lead to decisions they do not favor, or that their bosses do not want to hear" (Gortner, Mahler, and Nicholson 1987, p. 163). Since information is seen as power and the means by which competitive advantages are reached, blocks, or deliberate sabotage of communications, are unhealthy for an organization.

Also, there is a growing acceptance of the tenets of Total Quality Management (TQM) (Deming 1986), including the reduction of fear as a goal in the workplace, the use of small groups, and the empowering of employees, in which a strict hierarchy is rejected. Hierarchy creates disunity in organizations; it fosters fear, and information becomes distorted. Computer networks reduce a subordinate's reliance on upper management for information, which may have the effect of reducing the perceived "superiority" of one level of employee over others. According to Thayer, "the thrust of the organizational revolution is toward the transformation of superior-subordinate relationships into non-hierarchical small group processes in which no single individual can impose his style upon others" (Thayer 1981, p. 4).

In addition, increasing professionalism challenges the staying power of a hierarchical form. Loyalties to a profession outweigh loyalties to an organization, thus the attractiveness of mobility through a hierarchy become less of a motivating force than other factors. The career path of professionals tends to be a series of lateral moves between organizations rather than a vertical climb within just one organization.

Economic factors and planned attempts at change threaten hierarchy. Charles Handy (1989) has explained that organizations have already changed in response to economic realities that have altered the composition of the workforce. Having likened the new organizational form to a "shamrock" rather than to a ladder or pyramid, Handy related that contracting-out work and a tendency toward a part-time labor force have changed the nature of commitment. Thus, hierarchy has become less relevant. Peregrine Schwartz-Shea and Debra D. Burrington (1990) discussed an experiment that was organized in part in opposition to standard organizational forms. These forms included the hierarchical structure, which may in part "coerce and degrade subordinates and followers" (Schwartz-Shea and Burrington 1990, p. 7).

Although all of these challenges may reduce reliance on tall hierarchical ladders, it remains unclear how long it may take to do so or how successful the transformation will be.

Major problems confront those who would attempt to restructure organizations. Kanter has described a case in which the director of one function, (company division) experimented with flattening the hierarchy. He tried to collapse three levels of managers into one, giving them all the same titles and having them report directly to him. He hoped thereby to improve communication. He was soon moved to South America, however, and after his departure, the new director reinstated the titles. In any case, responsibilities had not changed, and everyone knew that levels one, two, and three of the new management positions corresponded to the old hierarchical grades (Kanter 1989).

Kanter has illustrated both the attack on hierarchy and its resilience. For those who consider hierarchy an evil, it is reassuring to know that it may not remain a permanent fixture. Yet, hierarchy is deeply entrenched not only as a traditional structural form but also in the culture of organizations and the memories of workers. Long-held values hamper restructuring. An attack on the legitimacy of a hierarchy may conflict with the core arrangement of a number of religious views, family traditions, Western society's assumptions, and patriotic feelings. Not only is it difficult to change long-held views, but attacks on the legitimacy of one to command another are also, in some respects, attacks on the moral base of reference for large numbers of people and on the ways in which they organize their personal relationships and societies.

Individual self-interest also impedes a movement against a hierarchy. Those who have benefited from or believe they will benefit from hierarchical organizational structures will continue to be advocates for them. If, for example, seniority leads to a higher position in a hierarchy (and includes better pay, status, etc.), a self-interested individual would not be likely to lobby for the demise of that hierarchy. Although the move in much of the United States business and government sector has involved an increase in the use of group decisionmaking and more participative management, the final decisions and the direction of the organization are often commandeered by those who control the resources or who are direct financial investors. Until there are equal resources involved in the start-up and maintenance costs of organizations (not compatible with a capitalistic society), it remains unlikely that a genuine sharing of power and control over them would result.

Accountably in a partnership arrangement, (in contrast with a hierarchical manager-subordinate arrangement) is intriguing because questions remain about who hires and fires and by what criteria people are retained or dismissed. What are the measures of success or failure? If goals or projects are not deemed successful, does expulsion of the entire group occur, or do nonproductive or unsuccessful groups continue? Hierarchical organizations simplify the problems of employee separations and judgments of success, judgmental as it may be.

Finally, concerns with efficiency, accountability, and semblance of order will tend to bolster the use of some form of hierarchy in organizations, especially in times of war and in militarily constructed institutions—at least until a truly alternate form of organization has been proven to "work better" or is accepted as effective. Tradition and a belief that hierarchy is the "best way" to structure an organization will hinder the use of alternate forms.

Given the changes in many contemporary organizations in terms of the nature of duties and responsibilities expected from employees (which has widened) and the distinction between the relationships of roles among workers (which has narrowed), it is unlikely that the tall vertical structures of the modern age will ever be as popular again.

LISA A. DICKE

BIBLIOGRAPHY

Deming, W. Edwards, 1986. *Out of the Crisis.* Cambridge, MA: MIT Center for Advanced Engineering Study.

Denhardt, Robert B., 1993. *Theories of Public Organization.* 2d ed. Belmont, CA: Wadsworth.

Gortner, Harold F., Julianne Mahler, and Jeanne Bell Nicholson, 1987. *Organization Theory: A Public Perspective.* Chicago: Dorsey Press.

Hall, Richard H., 1991. *Organizations: Structures, Processes, and Outcomes.* 5th ed. Englewood Cliffs, NJ: Prentice-Hall.

Handy, Charles, 1989. *The Age of Unreason.* Boston: Harvard Business School Press.

Hummel, Ralph P., 1994. *The Bureaucratic Experience.* New York: St. Martin's Press.

Jaques, Elliott, 1990. "In Praise of Hierarchy." *Harvard Business Review* (January-February): 127–133.

Kanter, Rosabeth Moss, 1977. *Men and Women of the Corporation.* New York: Basic Books.

———, 1989. *When Giants Learn to Dance.* New York: Simon and Schuster.

Maslow, Abraham, 1954. *Motivation and Personality.* New York: Harper & Row.

Mooney, James D. and Alan C. Reiley, 1939. *The Principles of Organization.* New York: Harper & Brothers.

Nakane, Chie, 1988. "Hierarchy in Japanese Society." In Daniel I. Okimoto and Thomas P. Rohlen, eds., *Inside the Japanese System: Readings on Contemporary Society and Political Economy.* Stanford, CA: Stanford University Press.

Ressner, Ulla, 1987. *The Hidden Hierarchy: Democracy and Equal Opportunities.* Avebury, England: Gower.

Schwartz-Shea, Peregrine, and Debra Burrington, 1990. "Free Riding, Alternative Organization and Cultural Feminism: The Case of Seneca Women's Peace Camp." *Women and Politics,* vol. 10, no. 3.

Shafritz, Jay M., and J. Steven Ott, eds. 1996. *Classics of Organization Theory.* 4th ed. Belmont, CA: Wadsworth.

Taylor, Frederick, 1911. *Scientific Management.* New York: Harper & Row.

Thayer, Frederick C., 1981. *An End to Hierarchy and Competition: Administration in the Post-Affluent World.* 2d ed. New York: New Viewpoints.

Weber, Max, 1954. *On Law in Economy and Society.* Ed. Max Rheinstein. Cambridge, MA: Harvard University Press.

THE HIGHER COMMITTEE FOR ADMINISTRATIVE REFORM (HCAR).

A Saudi Arabian agency, under the direct leadership of the king, that supervises administrative reform efforts for the government of the kingdom.

In the late 1950s, the government of the Kingdom of Saudi Arabia realized that its agencies were lacking efficiency and effectiveness and that there was a deficiency of qualified and skillful nationals to run the government. That state of affairs provoked the need for external help. In due course, the government sought assistance from the International Bank for Reconstruction and Development, the Technical Assistance Committee of the United Nations, and the Ford Foundation. These organizations conducted various studies on government agencies and provided several recommendations to the government of Saudi Arabia.

The **Ford Foundation** arrived in the Kingdom of Saudi Arabia in 1963 and continued to conduct its studies on government agencies until 1969. The studies resulted in major recommendations, that were adopted by the government of Saudi Arabia, one of which was the creation of the Higher Committee for Administrative Reform. The HCAR was established by Council of Ministers Resolution No. 520 on 21 November 1963, with the aim of supervising administrative reform programs and speeding up the process of reorganizing government agencies and developing administrative performance. Since its establishment, several modifications were made to its membership. The most recent modification was brought about by Council of Ministers Resolution No. 99 in 1991. The resolution reformulated the committee to be composed of the king as president, the minister of finance and national economy as vice president, and four ministers as members.

The HCAR's responsibilities include: (1) setting and approving the general plan for government administrative organization and issuing necessary resolutions and instructions to execute that plan; (2) reviewing and approving results and recommendations of reports presented by the Preparatory Administrative Committee; (3) reviewing drafts of new bylaws, or amendments of current ones, in order to present them to concerned parties, who will issue them following the necessary formal procedures as required by Resolution No. 570 of the Council of Ministers; (4) consulting with the Council of Ministers concerning the committee's resolutions, if the committee believes it is necessary to do so, either to obtain the council's views or merely to inform the council; (5) notifying ministries and government agencies through their presidents of resolutions and instructions that should be executed; (6) inviting executives from any ministry or government agency to obtain the committee's opinion regarding reports and recommendations presented to it; (7) reviewing and approving the general plan for controlling and supervising the execu-

tion of the committee's resolutions, which are conveyed to government organizations; and (8) taking all measures that either directly or indirectly insure the reform of government administrative practices and that facilitate the achievement of such reform.

To carry out its responsibilities, the Higher Committee for Administrative Reform is assisted by the Preparatory Administrative Committee for Administrative Reform, which consists of the director general of the Institute of Public Administration (IPA) as president, vice president of the General Civil Service Bureau for Service Development as a member, and director general of the Central Department of Organization and Management as a member. The Preparatory Administrative Committee for Administrative Reform supervises and oversees the work of the HCAR's general secretariat, which conducts research and studies through its experts at the IPA. Since it was established in 1963, the HCAR has played a very significant role in reorganizing the government agencies in Saudi Arabia. From 1963 until 1993, the general secretariat of the HCAR and the Preparatory Administrative Committee for Administrative Reform prepared 350 studies for the Saudi Arabian government agencies, of which 225 were accepted by both the Preparatory Administrative Committee for Administrative Reform and the Higher Committee for Administrative Reform.

ABDULRAHMAN ABDULLAH AL-SHAKAWY

HOMELESSNESS.

A condition of being without a residence, dwelling, or regular and adequate shelter.

Being without at home or adequate shelter is a condition that has been and is part of virtually all societies. Homelessness is a worldwide phenomenon that has occurred throughout history, although it takes varying forms and meanings in different cultures and periods of history. In the United States, homelessness has been a feature of society since colonial days, but, except for the years of the Great Depression, has not been considered a major national problem until recent times. During the 1980s and 1990s, however, homelessness became a highly visible social issue in the United States.

The emergence of homelessness as a visible and disturbing social problem was a result of changes in both the size and composition of the homeless population. The earlier homeless were primarily older men, most of whom lived in skid rows, or districts of inexpensive flophouses and hotels. In comparison, the "new homeless" are younger and include more women and families and more ethnic minorities. A large number of the new homeless live on the streets and are more visible than those in earlier periods. The fact that more people are visibly homeless and that a broader band of people are part of this population has created an advocacy movement that in turn has elevated the homeless problem on the social policy agenda.

This entry begins with a discussion of the definitions of homelessness and then briefly summarizes information about the number and composition of the homeless population, a discussion of factors thought to contribute to homelessness, and, finally, a summary of the response to the homeless problem.

Defining Homelessness

The current use of the term "homeless" usually refers to the absence of regular and adequate housing. Perhaps indicative of the more severe deprivation of shelter among the "new homeless," an earlier definition of the term referred not to the absence of physical housing so much as to *detachment from social and family relationships*. The detachment orientation is used in the 1968 entry on homelessness in the *International Encyclopedia of the Social Sciences*: "Homelessness is a condition of detachment from society characterized by the absence or attenuation of the affiliative bonds that link settled persons to a network of interconnected social structures" (Caplow *et al.* 1968, p. 494).

The definition used in most of the current discussion about the problem focuses on the *absence of adequate housing*. Although both definitions are sometimes used in contemporary United States, the absence of dependable housing is the dominant meaning of homelessness, with social detachment sometimes used as a partial explanation of the housing loss. In many cases, it is the severing of the last ties with friends and family that immediately precedes housing loss.

There is a lack of consensus, however, about how operationally to define the absence of adequate housing. The most narrow definition restricts homelessness to conditions of living on the street or in emergency shelters, what has been termed "literally homeless." A broader definition includes conditions of being "precariously housed," including those living by necessity with family or friends in "doubled-up" situations or otherwise living under conditions below accepted standards. The definition used has political and policy ramifications; the broader the definition, the larger the number in the homeless count, and consequently, the more serious the problem and the more deserving it is of public resources.

Literal homelessness is essentially the definition used in the Stewart B. McKinney Act, the principal federal legislation in the United States regarding homelessness. According to the act a homeless person is (1) an individual who lacks a fixed, regular, and adequate nighttime residence; and (2) an individual who has a primary nighttime residency that is, first, a supervised publicly or privately operated shelter designed to provide temporary living accommodations (including welfare hotels, congregate shelters, and transitional housing for the mentally ill); second, an institution that provides a temporary residence for individuals intended to be institutionalized; or, third, a public or private place not designed for, or ordinarily used as, a regular sleeping accommodation for human beings; and (3) this term does not include any individual imprisoned or otherwise detained under an act of Congress or a state law.

From a global perspective, far more variations of homelessness emerge. For example, in many developing countries, those living in squatter villages may or may not be considered homeless, and doubling-up may be normal and expected. In addition, terms used to describe homeless vary widely. What is considered "inadequate shelter" in one country may not be meaningful in another country. In fact, some who are homeless in one country may be living better than those in another country who have a "regular place of residence." Homelessness, like poverty, is in part a culturally relative concept. The United Nations has tried to bridge these differences by using two broad categories in its studies of homelessness—people who live outdoors or in emergency shelters and people whose housing does not meet basic standards of protection from the elements, access to safe water, and other criteria.

The Number and Composition of the Homeless Population

Determining the number of persons in the United States and elsewhere who are homeless has been a significant focus of attention among advocates, analysts, and policymakers. Methodological difficulties abound in counting people who lack a stable residence, in large part because residency and an address are the primary components of the traditional census. Further, a person may be on the streets one night, staying with an acquaintance another, or in a shelter or a voucher motel a third. The task of counting individuals living on the streets and in the shelters is plagued by all these problems; if a count attempts to include those who are precariously housed, additional sources of ambiguity are confronted.

A critical distinction in estimating the number of homeless is between a point-in-time estimate—a "snapshot"—that includes only those who are homeless on a specific day (or other short period) as opposed to an estimate over time that seeks to count all who have experienced homelessness at least once during an interval of time, perhaps a year or five years. A point-in-time (usually single night) count produces a smaller number than does a "period" count that attempts to determine how many are homeless at some time during a longer period.

According to *Priority: Home!* published in 1994 by the United States Department of Housing and Urban Development (pp. 17–20), point-in-time estimates suggest that up to 600,000 may be homeless on a given night in the United States, and between four and eight million are estimated to have had at least one episode of homelessness during the latter half of the 1980s.

Unattached individuals make up the largest segment of the homeless population, approximately 70 percent. Most of the unattached homeless are men, but the number of homeless single women appears to have increased. Families have been a growing part of the homeless population during the 1980s and 1990s in the United States, and now represent 20 to 30 percent of the homeless population. Most homeless families are headed by a single mother with one or more children. Minorities, especially African Americans, are disproportionately represented in the homeless population. Estimates indicate that approximately one-half of the adult homeless population now have or at one time had a substance abuse problem, that as many as one-third of the homeless have some level of mental illness, and that other health problems, such as tuberculosis and HIV or AIDS, have a higher incidence in the homeless than in the general population.

Worldwide estimates and descriptions of homelessness are more difficult to obtain because standards and definitions vary. United Nations studies that included those living outdoors or in emergency shelters and those whose housing did not meet UN standards have estimated that one billion people are either literally homeless or have inadequate shelter. Although homeless counts in individual countries are not comparable in a strict sense, they do indicate that homelessness and other forms of inadequate shelter are worldwide problems. India, for example, counts the "houseless," using a point-in-time approach, as part of its census. Its homeless count for 1981 was well over 2 million in a total population of 683 million. In Finland, the definition on which the count is based is much broader, including the literal homeless as well as those who are doubled-up and those who are separated from their families. Finland's 1990 estimate of the homeless population was 18,000 to 20,000 singles and 1,000 to 2,000 families, out of a population of just under 5 million.

Factors Contributing to Homelessness

A variety of explanations have been offered to explain why the sudden increase in homelessness occurred during the 1980s. These accounts include growth of a service economy with low-paying jobs; reduction in social welfare benefits relative to the cost of living; demographics, especially the baby boom generation reaching the age most vulnerable to homelessness; deinstitutionalization of the mentally ill without providing comparable community services; reduction in low-cost housing availability, especially as related to income; increase in drug use, especially crack (co-

caine); a decline in the casual labor market and the demand for unskilled labor.

Although research has not isolated any single explanation, it does suggest that homelessness has a complex etiology. It is not simply the result of housing costs, or the labor market, or individuals being unable or unwilling to work, or the deinstitutionalization of the mentally ill, or changes in federal housing policy, or alcohol and drug abuse, or any other single cause. The factors contributing to homelessness are multiple and often overlapping. Individual and structural explanations compete in the effort to explain homelessness. Individual explanations place emphasis on the characteristics of individuals and their behavior; structural explanations focus on macro conditions: the economy, culture, and public policy.

Both structural and individual factors are plausible contributors to the loss of housing. Strong structural conditions—that is a healthier economy, an increase in the availability of jobs, better income opportunities, and more housing available at a low cost—make it less likely that personal factors will push people to the point of losing their housing. As these structural conditions become weaker, it is even more likely that the personal factors will precipitate homelessness. Likewise, the stronger the individual conditions, the less likely are the structural weaknesses to result in housing loss.

There may be important international distinctions in the causes of homelessness. For example, Third World homelessness appears to be due in part to rapid urban growth, whereas United States and European homelessness appears to have been fostered by other economic and political causes. International comparative research could offer insight into the role structural conditions play in contributing to homelessness, but such research has been limited to date.

Responding to Homelessness

The early response in the United States during the late 1970s and early 1980s to homelessness as a visible and pressing problem was initiated at the local level, with non-profit and religious organizations taking the lead. The emphasis was on developing an emergency response, with a focus on shelters and soup kitchens. During this period, local, state, and national advocacy groups were developed, most commonly in the form of "coalitions for the homeless." As the problem continued, many local governments became involved, some more actively than others.

Until the passage of the Stewart B. McKinney Homeless Assistance Act in 1987, the federal government took only a minor role, largely through assistance provided by the Federal Emergency Management Agency. With the United States Department of Housing and Urban Development (HUD) designated as the lead agency, the McKinney legislation authorizes funds for several federal agencies to provide grants to states and localities to increase subsidized housing and shelter support for the homeless and to provide services to the homeless and those vulnerable to becoming homeless.

States have generally played a lesser role than localities and the federal government in addressing homelessness. A number of states have initiated eviction-prevention programs, provided matching funds for federal programs, and undertaken coordinating efforts.

The policy and programmatic response to homelessness has evolved over the years from, essentially, short-term emergency efforts to recognition that resolving the homeless problem requires a more sustained and broad-based effort. Recent initiatives include providing priority to homeless families for permanent housing subsidy; supporting transitional housing programs, which provide six-month to two-year housing, along with job training and other services; linking services with permanent housing; and other efforts. Many localities are working to develop coordinated systems of services for homeless individuals and families. some are developing centralized intake services, even though much of the emergency support is provided by a diverse collection of nonprofit and governmental organizations.

Homelessness as a problem has an uncertain future. Although the policy response has begun to recognize the serious and enduring nature of the problem, there are few indications that certain solutions have been found. Indeed, one fear is that large-scale homelessness will become accepted; some would say that it has already been accepted as a normal part of society. Others believe that a foundation has been laid for genuine, sustained progress in eliminating the problem.

RALPH S. HAMBRICK, JR., AND DEBRA J. ROG

BIBLIOGRAPHY

Baum, Alice S., and Donald W. Burnes, 1993. *A Nation in Denial: The Truth About Homelessness.* Boulder, CO: Westview Press.

Blau, Joel, 1992. *The Visible Poor: Homelessness in the United States.* New York: Oxford University Press.

Burt, Martha R., 1992. *Over the Edge: The Growth of Homelessness in the 1980s.* New York: Russell Sage Foundation.

Burt, Martha R., and Barbara E. Cohen, 1989. *America's Homeless: Numbers, Characteristics, and Programs That Serve Them.* Washington, DC: Urban Institute Press.

Caplow, Theodore, Howard M. Bahr, and David Sternberg, 1968. "Homelessness." In David L. Sills, ed., *International Encyclopedia of the Social Sciences.* pp. 494–499. New York: Macmillan and the Free Press.

Fallis, George, and Alex Murray, eds., 1990. *Housing the Homeless and Poor.* Toronto: University of Toronto Press.

Glasser, Irene, 1994. *Homelessness in Global Perspective.* New York: G. K. Hall.

Jencks, Christopher, 1994. *The Homeless.* Cambridge, MA: Harvard University Press.

Rossi, Peter H., 1989. *Down and Out in America: The Origins of Homelessness.* Chicago: University of Chicago Press.

Schutt, Russell K., 1992. *Responding to the Homeless: Policy and Practice.* New York: Plenum Press.

Seltser, Barry Jay, and Donald E. Miller, 1993. *Homeless Families: The Struggle for Dignity.* Urbana: University of Illinois Press.

U.S. Department of Housing and Urban Development, 1994. *Priority: Home!: The Federal Plan to Break the Cycle of Homelessness.* Washington, DC: GPO.

Wright, James D., 1989. *Address Unknown: The Homeless in America.* New York: Walter deGruyter.

HOOVER COMMISSIONS. Two comprehensive studies established by congressional statute in 1947 and again in 1953 and undertaken in the years 1947–1949 and 1953–1955 that focused on the executive branch of government in United States. The two commissions examined the organization and functions of public administration and the need to curtail government growth.

Although the formal designation of each of these study commissions was "A Commission on Organization of the Executive Branch of Government," the Hoover Commission derived its title from its popular chair, President Herbert Hoover. Indeed, the studies themselves were infused with his personality and philosophy, derived first from his international business background and then from his experience as a public administrator and President (Moe 1982).

The studies of the Hoover Commission were significant because they were inspired and commissioned by Congress and because they enjoyed the cooperation of both Congress and President in a unique joint effort to limit the size of government and to curtail the growth of the executive branch. The studies were broad and comprehensive in their coverage of these goals and bipartisan in their underlying assumptions concerning the role that public administration should play in the life of the nation. Over the years, numerous bills have been introduced in Congress to establish major study commissions patterned after the two Hoover Commissions.

The First Hoover Commission: 1947–1949

The first Hoover Commission was established by statute (*Statute* 61 [1947]: 246) and was a milestone in public administration. As the first major national inquiry after World War II, it impacted United States public administration and initiated similar studies in other Western democracies.

The first Hoover Commission's charge was to examine the machinery of government. Its calling was supposed to be to reduce the number of government agencies created during World War II, but it did not do this. Instead, if focused its efforts on strengthening the executive branch of government by reorganizing executive branch agencies to achieve a coherent purpose for each department via the integration and elimination of overlapping services. Instead of simply calling for a reduction of government agencies, the commission made a vigorous call for increased managerial capacity in the Executive Office of the President (EOP) through: (1) allowing unlimited discretion over presidential organization and staff, (2) establishing a strengthened Bureau of the Budget (BOB), (3) creating an office of personnel located in the EOP, and (4) establishing the position of a staff secretary to provide liaison between the President and his subordinates. In addition, the commission recommended that executive branch agencies be reorganized to permit an integrated purpose for the departments and that the President be given greater control over these agencies. Seventy-two percent of the first Hoover Commission's recommendations (196 out of 273) were adopted, including passage of the Reorganization Act of 1949 and the establishment of the Department of Health, Education, and Welfare in 1953.

The Second Hoover Commission: 1953–1955

The second Hoover Commission was also established by congressional statute (*Statute* 67 [1953]: 184) and was also chaired by President Herbert Hoover. The second commission was unique; there has been no other example in the history of public administration of such an important commission being virtually reconvened to continue its work after four years had passed. It even retained many of the same commission members and staff. The second commission also had a specific machinery of government focus, being required to promote efficiency in public business, to define and limit executive functions, and to curtail and abolish government functions that competed with private enterprise.

The commission had three ostensible purposes: (1) the promoting of economy, efficiency, and improved service in the transaction of the public business; (2) the defining and limiting of executive functions; and (3) the curtailment and abolition of government functions and activities competitive with private enterprise. A major recommendation was the elimination of nonessential government services and activities competitive with private enterprise, based on the assumptions that the federal government had grown beyond appropriate limits and that such growth should be reversed. In contrast to the earlier commission, the second commission's recommendations accomplished little. Congress accepted few of its recommendations.

It is interesting to note, however, that the Second Hoover Commission rigorously argued that a whole host of government activities should be turned over to the private sector. Nevertheless, there was not a strong political will to do this in the mid-1950s. This issue would not surface again until the Ronald Reagan administration.

Influence Upon Future Administrations

By the mid-1960s, the constituency that had called for smaller government was becoming less strident, and at the same time the dominant academic position was in favor of greater government involvement in all aspects of public life. There was also the growing interest in using public- and private-sponsored enterprises to perform public services. Yet concerns about government growth remained.

Presidents John Kennedy and Lyndon Johnson appointed many low-visibility task forces to study governmental reorganization. Two task forces were appointed that had broader mandates than the others–the Task Force on Government Reorganization, and the Task Force on Government Organization. Both suffered the fate of not having their recommendations widely used, but their indirect influence on the day-to-day public administration of the time was said to have been substantial. President Richard Nixon appointed the President's Advisory Council on Executive Organization, which submitted thirteen memorandums on reorganization. The council's recommendations were rejected by Congress, however. Under the administration of President Jimmy Carter, 30 studies were undertaken, but none of their suggestions were adopted (Moe 1982). President Ronald Reagan decried government as inefficient and wasteful and advocated moving many services it provided to the private sector.

The rhetoric against big government gained momentum, and the call to privatize parts of government as earlier voiced by the Hoover Commissions was again raised. The term "privatization" took hold during the Reagan administration. Numerous experiments in contracting-out to the private sector were undertaken, along with joint government–private sector ventures. These reforms to reduce government were continued in the administration of Reagan's successor, President George Bush. President William Jefferson Clinton also ran on a reformist platform, as well; although his means to accomplish the reduction of government differed from his Republican predecessors. This difference was evidenced in real terms by the budget impasses and government shutdowns in 1995 and 1996.

Despite the numerous studies undertaken by various administrations, United States public administration officials have not heeded the cautions raised by the Hoover Commissions concerning the exponential expansion of public administration. In the late 1990s, one still finds a plethora of public agencies that have been born with little regard for duplication, which has led to competition, overlap, and administrative problems between the legislative and executive branches of government. For example, there is the Congressional Budget Office and its counterpart on the executive side, the office of Management and Budget. The average American citizen has become uncomfortably conscious of the size of government, and many citizens would agree that the best government is one that governs least (McNeil and Metz 1956).

Summary

The two Hoover Commissions were not the first efforts to review the structure and functions of the executive branch of government, but they were significant in that they were joint cooperative ventures between the legislative and executive branches of government and in that they were bipartisan in their underlying assumptions about the appropriate function that public administration must play in the nation. In light of the great interest today about reducing the size of federal government and curtailing its role, it is interesting to see that there is still a connection between the present political climate and that existing at the time of the Hoover Commissions. There was a conviction then, as there is now, that government should exercise restraint in the functions it provides and a belief (even though radical reform was not undertaken then) that the basic strength of the political system lies in a healthy private sector (Moe 1982).

Of the five orders given to the Hoover Commission in July 1947, all remain relevant for public administration in the 1990s—the need to (1) limit expenditures to the lowest amount, consistent with efficient performance of essential services; (2) eliminate duplication and overlapping of services; (3) consolidate services and functions of a similar nature; (4) abolish services no longer necessary; and (5) define and limit executive functions, services, and activities (Hoover 1949, p. xiii).

Of the eight defects of government subsequently put forth in the reports of the task forces of the two Hoover Commissions, several are again pertinent to discussions going on in government today: (1) improved accountability of administrators; (2) the development of administrative capability; and (3) decentralization of routine administrative services (Nash and Lynde 1950, p. 21).

The enduring legacies of this work by Hoover and his associates is that (1) it maintained that government is for the benefit of the all people and not for special interests; (2) it supported civil control of the government; (3) it reaffirmed the rule of the law; (4) it suggested that some services that government provides could be handled more effectively by the private sector; (5) it served the cause of states' rights by asserting that the federal government should not do what state and local government can do equally well by themselves; and, (6) it maintained that if democracy is to survive, action must be taken to bring about a coordinated, competent, and responsive public administration (Nash and Lynde 1950).

The Hoover Commissions' reports serve to remind people that the cost of the huge United States public enterprise must be met in tax dollars paid for by the work of its citizenry, who, consequently, have the right to demand limits on governmental power and growth. The two reports bring into even sharper focus that government, in one form or another, throws its long, ever-present shadow over the United States citizen in all aspects of his or her existence. In this connection, then as now, many believe that the public has less rights and are more of a cog in the huge machinery of government than ever before (MacNeil and Metz 1956).

BREENA E. COATES AND JEFFERY K. GUILER

BIBLIOGRAPHY

Arnold, Peri E., 1976. "The First Hoover Commission and the Managerial Presidency." *Journal of Politics*, vol. 38 (February).
Hoover, Herbert, 1949. *The Hoover Commission Report.* New York: McGraw-Hill.
McNeil, Neil, and Harold W. Metz, 1956. *The Hoover Report 1953–1955: What It Means to You as a Citizen and Taxpayer.* New York: Macmillan.
Moe, Ronald C., 1982. *The Hoover Commissions Revisited.* Boulder, CO: Westview Press.
Nash, Bradley D., and Cornelius Lynde, 1950. *A Hook in Leviathan: A Critical Interpretation of the Hoover Commission Report.* New York: Macmillan.
Waldo, Dwight, 1948. *The Administrative State: A Study in the Political Theory of American Public Administration.* New York: Ronald Press.
Wilson, James Q., 1989. *Bureaucracy.* New York: Basic Books.

HOOVER, J. EDGAR (1895–1972).

The director of the Federal Bureau of Investigation (FBI), from 1924 until 1972, who established a reputation as one of the most powerful career civil servants in the federal government. He served as FBI director under eight presidents, from Calvin Coolidge to Richard Nixon and transformed the bureau into one of the most professionally run law enforcement agencies in the world. Hoover was accused in later years of abusing the powers of the FBI, and his tenure became synonymous in many circles with unchecked executive rule. He acquired a power base so strong that he could resist the United States attorneys general and presidents to whom he was officially accountable.

John Edgar Hoover was born in Washington, D.C., on January 1, 1895, the last of four children. His father, a clerk with the United States Coast and Geodetic Survey, was a frail man who was institutionalized for depression and forced to resign his government post without a pension.

After graduating from Central High School, J. Edgar took a job as a file clerk at the Library of Congress in order to support himself as a nighttime law student at George Washington University. He received his bachelor of laws degree in 1916 and a master of law in 1917. (At that time, law was an undergraduate program of study.)

In July 1917 he secured a position with the United States Department of Justice, where he was assigned to work with military intelligence agencies preparing evidence for the deportation of anarchists. In 1919 Hoover became special assistant to Attorney General A. Mitchell Palmer, a position from which he and Palmer launched a wide-ranging antiradical campaign. In 1921, after the national Red Scare died down, Hoover took over the day-to-day management of the FBI, as its head assistant director.

The Federal Bureau of Investigation was created by executive order in 1908, ostensibly to allow the United States Department of Justice to manage its growing caseload of antitrust and interstate commerce cases. The corps of investigators quickly became involved in controversial issues, prosecuting the leaders of radical labor unions and burglarizing the offices of members of Congress. The scandals heightened fears that a federal corps of investigators whose leaders owed their appointment to the incumbent administration would inevitably become a secret police force and a threat to democracy.

To head off criticism as he entered his 1924 election campaign, President Calvin Coolidge replaced the incumbent attorney general with the highly respected Harlan Stone. In turn, Stone sought a professional lawyer-administrator with high moral standards to clean house at the FBI. At the age of 29, Hoover became director of the FBI, a position he did not relinquish until his death 48 years later.

Hoover set out to change the organizational culture of the bureau. Stone ordered that the FBI confine its investigations to violations of federal law and cease its political activities. Hoover in turn insisted that the bureau be divorced from outside political interference and that all internal appointments be based on merit. He instituted strict rules of behavior, which, among other standards, forbid the use of intoxicating beverages, established a uniform dress code, prohibited the acceptance of gratuities, and discouraged divorce. Personal evaluations of all agents were conducted every six months. All important communiques and policy decisions went through the director.

During the Great Depression, Hoover took center stage in a widely publicized national crusade against crime. The crusade resulted in the apprehension or death of a number of famous criminals, including John Dillinger, Pretty Boy Floyd, "Ma" Barker, and Clyde Barrow. Although a number of law enforcement agencies were involved, Hoover became the leading symbol of the effort, an image reinforced by a series of popular films and books

that mythologized the work of FBI special agents (called G-men). In order to protect the FBI's public image, Hoover established a system of central review for all news stories emanating from the bureau.

As the United States prepared for World War II, President Franklin D. Roosevelt provided Hoover and the FBI with broad discretionary authority to combat domestic espionage. Hoover used this authority to step up the surveillance of leftists and trade union leaders, whose activities had obsessed him since his early years. By the end of the war, the bureau dominated domestic intelligence activities. Building on this position, Hoover and the FBI mounted an extensive postwar effort to control radical movements in the United States.

Liberals accused Hoover and the FBI of a variety of questionable tactics, including break-ins, wiretaps, and the infiltration of organizations that Hoover thought subversive. The FBI conducted extensive wiretaps in an effort to discredit civil rights leader Martin Luther King, Jr., for example, with whom Hoover had a running public feud. Hoover kept an extensive file on the activities of President John F. Kennedy, and personally confronted the president in an effort to discourage a liaison with Judith Campbell, who was also carrying on a relationship with a leading figure in organized crime. During the administration of President Richard Nixon, the FBI placed wiretaps on the phones of White House aides and other high government officials in an effort to stem national security leaks.

Many believed that Hoover's extensive political files, along with his support among congressional conservatives, discouraged prospective efforts to remove him from office. In fact, many politicians viewed Hoover as an asset whose capabilities provided them with much desired information. As Hoover approached the mandatory retirement age of 70, President Lyndon Johnson issued an executive order allowing Hoover to stay on indefinitely. Hoover died at his home in Washington, D.C., on May 1, 1972, ending his tenure at the Federal Bureau of Investigation.

HOWARD E. MCCURDY

BIBLIOGRAPHY

Gentry, Curt, 1991. *J. Edgar Hoover: The Man and the Secrets.* New York: Norton.

Keller, William W., 1989. *The Liberals and J. Edgar Hoover: The Rise and Fall of a Domestic Intelligence State.* Princeton: Princeton University Press.

Summers, Anthony, 1993. *Official and Confidential: The Secret Life of J. Edgar Hoover.* New York: Putnam & Sons.

Theoharis, Athan G., and John Stuart Cox, 1988. *The Boss.* Philadelphia: Temple University Press.

HUMAN CAPITAL. The stock of knowledge, skills, abilities, and similar attributes embodied in human beings that can be used productively to yield future income for individuals and for the economy. These productive human capabilities can be formed or acquired by combining individuals' inherent abilities with investment in human beings in the form of education, training, migration, and health care and nutrition.

The concepts of human capital and human capital investment were derived from human capital theory, developed mainly by American economists Theodore Schultz, Gary Becker, and Jacob Mincer in early 1960s, based on works of early economists in previous centuries. Human capital theory holds that individuals undertake human capital investments to increase their future earning capabilities and that individuals' earnings are positively correlated with the amount of human capital embodied in them. Human capital theory regards all accumulated investments in such activities as education, job training, and migration as part of society's wealth and, therefore, society's total wealth is a combination of both human capital and nonhuman capital.

The theory has had enormous impact on modern labor economics and human resources management both at the macro and micro levels, and has provided major explanations for a wide spectrum of labor market phenomena such as individuals' wage differentials, uneven rates of unemployment across jobs and occupations, and individuals' decision to engage in education, training, and other human capital investment behaviors. The theory has also contributed greatly to policy decisions on the allocation of resources to education, training, and medical care, vis-à-vis other claims on resources.

The term "capital" usually refers to produced goods that are to be used for further production. The process of creating capital is called investment. Investment, by definition, requires initial cost that is then recouped over some period of time. A common criterion for deciding if a particular investment makes economic sense is to look at whether the benefits to be derived from the investment are worth the initial cost of making the investment. These basic economic principles are equally applicable to human capital investment. Human capital theory holds that individuals, as economic agents, can increase their capabilities by investing in themselves and that governments can increase national income by allocating resources in human capital investment. The underlying argument is that investments in human beings to increase human capital can yield returns in the form of higher productivity and higher salary in the labor market and that the enhanced productivity will justify the initial investment costs. Thus, expenditures on schooling, training, and medical care are all human capital investments, which can lead to increased productivity, enhanced earnings ability, and prolonged life expectancy; this will in turn benefit the national economy and increase national income.

Forms of Human Capital Investment

Human capital can take on various forms. In general, any acquired skills or knowledge or even information that will help individuals to be more productive and thus to command a higher salary can be considered a form of human capital. Any investment made in human beings to enable them to be more productive economic agents can be considered human capital investment. Typical types of human capital investment include the following activities:

1. *Schooling.* Schooling can range from acquiring a formal college education or advanced degrees to attending evening classes to improve computer skills or to participating in a one-day crash course on defensive driving. Schooling in its various forms constitutes the primary activity of human capital investment, because it usually requires considerable time commitment and substantial costs.
2. *Training.* Training can be vocational training, by which a trainee acquires the knowledge and skill for a particular occupation, or special training, by which a special type of skill is acquired. It can also be on-the-job training, such as an apprenticeship, or off-the-job training, such as classroom or conference training. Training is further classified as general (to acquire reading skills, math skills, and to raise the general literacy level) or specific (to acquire skills useful only to one particular organization or to one particular job). Training in its various formats also constitutes a major portion of human capital investment.
3. *Migration and job search.* Migration is viewed as human capital investment because moving from an area with low earnings to an area with enhanced earnings potential involves not only a gain for the individual in the form of higher salary but also a gain for the economy in the sense that the individual's skills are better utilized. The moving itself clearly involves costs, which are a type of human capital investment cost. Further, if earnings are viewed as proxy of productivity, the increased earnings due to migration signifies an increase in productivity. Job search is human capital investment in that spending considerable effort gathering labor market information and looking for a better job also involves laying out costs while expecting future benefits.
4. *Health care and nutrition.* Various kinds of health and nutrition services represent another form of human capital investment, since they increase labor supply by reducing illness, mortality, disability, and debility and help keep individuals in good health so

that their productivity can be increased and their productive life can be prolonged.

In addition to the previous activities, human capital investment, viewed in a broad sense, includes day care, family care, family education, and so on. These activities all have the common characteristic of incurring some costs in the present for promised benefits in the future.

Origin and Development of the Human Capital Concept

Although the human capital theory was mainly developed in the early 1960s, the idea of treating human beings as capital is by no means new. B. F. Kiker (1971) reviewed the origin and development of the human capital concept and summarized the various reasons in history for treating human beings as capital as the following: (1) to demonstrate the power of a nation; (2) to determine the economic effects of education, health investment, and migration; (3) to awaken the public to the need for life and health conservation; (4) to determine the total cost of war; and (5) to aid courts in making fair decisions in cases dealing with compensation for injury and death.

One of the first serious applications of the concept of human capital was made in 1676 by Sir William Petty's comparison of the loss of armaments and other instruments of warfare with the loss of human life. He recognized the monetary value of human life lost in war and considered loss of human life to be a monetary loss to England. A century later, Adam Smith and other classical economists also recognized the capital nature of human beings. Adam Smith pointed out in his 1776 classic treatise *The Wealth of Nations* that a crucial part of a nation's wealth lies in the number of workers in an economy and the level of their skills. Adam Smith's work demonstrated the positive relationship between labor market skills and personal incomes. About another century later, Alfred Marshall stressed the long-term nature of human capital investments and the role of the individuals in undertaking them. In short, throughout the history of economic thought, various economists have suggested the human capital concept in demonstrating the magnitude and economic importance of the stock of human resources and have foreshadowed treating human capital in the same scientific manner as conventional physical capital.

The impetus for the modern resurgence of human capital research can be precisely attributed to Theodore Schultz's presidential address at the 1960 meeting of the American Economic Association. This speech ushered in a period of active research in human capital theory during the early 1960s, mainly represented by the writings of American economists Gary Becker, Theodore Schultz, and Jacob Mincer. These economists explicitly introduced the notion of human capital: individuals making investments in themselves to increase their stock of human capital for greater future earnings. They emphasized the analogy between investment in physical capital (physical capital is associated with such things as manufacturing facilities, machines, etc., that are acquired for production purposes) and investment in human capital as both involving forgoing current consumption to increase expected future earnings possibilities and future consumption possibilities. Human capital theory has since had substantial impact on labor economics, manpower analysis, and national labor policies.

Distinctions from Physical Capital

To understand fully the concept of human capital, it is helpful to draw some distinctions between physical capital and human capital. Although parallel with physical capital in some aspects, especially in terms of incurring present costs for future benefits, human capital does have unique features that distinguish it from physical capital.

Unlike physical capital, human capital is nontransferable. Physical capital can be bought and sold, but human capital is inextricably tied to the person who possesses it. Ownership of human capital in a free society is restricted to the person in whom it resides. Although a person may "rent" out this capital to employers for a wage, he or she may not sell it in the way a firm may sell a machine. A person cannot, even voluntarily, sell a legally binding claim on future earning power in the absence of slavery. Because of this feature, human capital can depreciate in a rather unusual way. It depreciates drastically if the owner of the human capital should become ill. Furthermore, it is totally lost upon the death of the owner. This makes human capital investment riskier than physical capital investment.

The nontransferability feature also introduces a volitional quality to human capital. Because of tastes, values, or preferences, individuals can choose to make varying degrees of productive use of the human capital embodied in them. The congeniality of the work, location, or environment will play an important role in individuals' decisions of how much of their human capital they would like to exert. Likewise, initiation, motivation, and various personality traits can also play an important role in the utilization of human capital. Consequently, the human capital embodied in a particular individual may not be put to its highest use, as would normally be true of nonhuman capital. Therefore, the productivity of a given quantity of human capital (if it is measurable) can vary significantly according to individuals' propensity to use their human capital. In fact, there may be a big difference between the stock of human capital in the population and the amount actually in use in the labor market.

The inseparability of human capital from its owner also makes the financing of human capital investment difficult. For example, arrangements for loan collateral are impossible as a form of human capital financing, because individuals as human beings cannot be held in bondage as guarantee of the loan. There are no private capital credit markets to finance human capital investment on credit. There is not even a guarantee that the skills and knowledge, once acquired, will ever be used productively at all. The investment can be totally lost as the person passes away. This further underscores the risky nature of human capital investment.

The cost of human capital investment is very difficult, if not impossible, to assess. Unlike physical capital, the costs of which are basically direct, human capital involves important indirect costs in the form of forgone earnings. How to value these forgone earnings, and hence calculate the real costs of human capital investment, is a serious empirical problem. Similarly, the exact quantity of human capital is also difficult to assess, if not impossible.

Another major characteristic of human capital is that a portion of human capital investment, that is, the cost to engage in activities to acquire human capital, is sometimes inseparable from consumption. Although nonhuman capital investment is usually for profit only, investment in human capital can be partially for consumption. Its cost, therefore, cannot be considered exclusively investment. In other words, human capital investment can sometimes be valued in and of itself rather than being valued because of its promised future benefit. For example, most individuals who engage in educational activities are not doing so solely for the purpose of increasing productivity (consider college students majoring in art history, fine arts, and literature). Instead, the process of getting an education itself is enjoyable in its own right, either because it is fulfilling or satisfying as it occurs or because it may serve to enhance the quality of life, irrespective of increases in productivity or earnings in the labor market. This confounds the calculation of the cost and return of human capital investment. To the extent that part of the cost is for consumption, the cost of human capital investment could be overestimated, and its return underestimated.

The Cost and Return of Human Capital Investment

The costs of investment in human capital generally take three forms. First, there can be out-of-pocket, or direct, costs, including tuition, fees, and books for education and training; transportation and gasoline costs for migration and job search; and all other tangible incidental expenses. Second are the opportunity costs in the form of forgone earnings. People forsake their jobs and associated earnings fully or partially in order to attend schools or to engage in other forms of human capital creation activity.

Even if one takes evening classes and keeps his or her regular full-time job, the person is incurring opportunity costs in the sense that the person could be spending his or her time and energy on some other productive endeavor. The third form of costs for the investment in human capital are often psychic costs, for example, taking classes incurs difficulty, stress, anxiety, boredom, and fatigue; migration means saying good-bye to friends and relatives, giving up friendships and familiar surroundings, and so forth. All of these are considered psychic costs of human capital investment.

Rates of return on human capital investment can provide a convenient and complete summary of the economic effects of human capital investment. One difficulty in calculating the exact rate of return of human capital is that there is greater variability in the productive capacity of a given amount and a given kind of human capital investment than there is in the case of physical capital. But, overall, the standard investment criteria in calculating the rate of return of physical capital still apply.

The key question is to find out whether investment in human capital is economically worthwhile. Investment expenditures, here, consist of all direct and indirect costs and returns that are restricted to the incremental monetary earnings from human capital investment. Numerous empirical studies have found that the rate of return in human capital investment is comparable to that of physical capital investment, although different types of human capital investment may yield different rates of return. For example, for males in the United States, the rate of return to elementary schooling is higher than to that of a high school education; and, in turn, the rate of return to a high school education is higher than to that of a college education; and the lowest of these rates of return has been about 12 percent annually. Gary Becker (1975) found that there were many investments that individuals could make in themselves that would yield returns substantially in excess of the prevailing rate of return on other investments.

Applications of Human Capital Theory

One of the basic neoclassical economic assumptions is that each human being is a labor unit, and all labor units are homogeneous and interchangeable. This assumption neglects any qualitative differences in human beings and in individuals' added value acquired from investments in productive capacities. With this assumption, neoclassical economic theory fails to explain a number of phenomena in the labor market, such as wage differences, uneven unemployment rate across occupations, and individuals' differences in propensity to undertake additional schooling. Human capital theory, however, can provide a much more satisfactory framework for explaining these and other seemingly unrelated phenomena.

Human capital theory provides one of the main explanations for wage and salary differentials by skills, age, and occupation. For example, the skilled enjoy a higher rate of pay because they possess a greater amount of productive capacities, in other words, human capital. The steeper age-income profiles of the skilled than of the unskilled—that is, the greater rise in income with increasing age—also reflects the payoffs to the greater human capital investments that skilled workers have made in themselves.

By the same token, human capital theory explains the uneven incidence of unemployment by knowledge, skill, and occupations. The relatively lower unemployment rates of highly skilled individuals or highly skilled occupations than that of the less skilled individuals or occupations reflect the fact that the former have been the beneficiaries of having greater amount of human capital.

Human capital theory also has useful applications to the study of job search and migration activities. The greater tendency of young than of older workers to change jobs or to migrate reflects the fact that, other things being equal, the benefits of mobility are greater for younger workers because the payoff period for them is longer. For the same reason, young people generally have greater propensity than older people to take additional schooling and training.

Human capital theory also offers good framework for analyzing the implications of private and social decisions on the allocation of resources to such things as education, health, and nutrition, training programs, family education, and family planning, vis-à-vis other claims on resources.

Human Capital and Economic Development

One important implication of human capital theory is that the growth of human capital is one of the major reasons for economic development since human capital makes up a major portion of a society's wealth. Research indicates that great social and economic benefits arise from investment in education, training, health and nutrition, and other human capital investment activities. Therefore, investment in human capital is an absolute imperative for any national economy, especially for developing economies.

Major industrial nations developed their economies by heavily relying on human capital, together with financial and physical capital. The outstanding economic records of Japan, Taiwan, South Korea, and of other Asian economies in recent decades dramatically illustrate the importance of human capital to economic growth. The so-called Asian economic tigers grew rapidly by relying on a well-educated, well-trained, hard-working, and conscientious labor force. The United States economy has no doubt benefited from absorbing talented people from all around the world by its fairly liberal immigration policies.

Like any capital investment market, the human capital investment market has various imperfections. The imperfections of the human capital investment market can be outlined as follows: (1) the free mobility of labor makes it irrational for employers to invest as much as they might think desirable; and (2) serious information gaps exist in the human capital market—for example, individuals, especially young people, are often not in a good position to understand the value of education and therefore may underinvest in human capital or invest unwisely; and (3) significant portions of the population lack the economic means to invest extensively in human capital.

Because of the various imperfections in the human capital investment market, it is unlikely that reliance on market mechanisms alone will produce the optimal level of human capital investment for an economy. Therefore, government involvement in human capital investment becomes vitally important. Governments need to study the various types of human capital investment and the costs and benefits associated with them, and then allocate the optimal level of resources accordingly for human capital investment.

Controversies on Human Capital Theory

A number of controversies on human capital theory currently exist at both the theoretical and the empirical levels. One important issue is that although human capital theory offers better perspectives for some aspects of labor market analysis than the neoclassical economic theory, it also inherently relies on the neoclassical economic assumption of "perfect" information: It assumes that perfect information exists about human capital investment alternatives both at a given point in time and in future periods. The theory assumes that individuals have a good estimate of the investment costs and expected returns in terms of future earnings. This assumption does not allow the numerous economic or even political factors that may influence the earning ability of certain skills and occupations.

A second issue is related to the empirical importance of human capital theory. Some studies found that human capital investment, such as education, account for only a small part of variations in actual earnings among individuals. Failure to consider factors such as family background and motivation may produce upward bias about the returns of human capital investment.

A third issue is whether human capital investments, particularly in education or in training, actually increase productivity. An alternative explanation was offered by Michael Spence (1973) who argued that education does not enhance individuals' productivity; it merely reveals their inherent capabilities and signals their potential productivity to potential employers.

WILLIAM Y. JIANG

BIBLIOGRAPHY

Becker, Gary S., 1975. *Human Capital: A Theoretical and Empirical Analysis, with Special Reference to Education.* 2d ed. New York: Columbia University Press.

Berg, Ivar, 1969. *Education and Jobs: The Great Training Robbery.* New York: Praeger.

Hornbeck, David W., and Lester M. Salamon, eds., 1991. *Human Capital and America's Future.* Baltimore, MD: Johns Hopkins University Press.

Kiker, B. F., 1971. *Investment in Human Capital.* Columbia: University of South Carolina Press.

Mincer, Jacob, 1974. *Schooling, Experience and Earnings.* New York: National Bureau of Economic Research.

"Investment in Human Beings," 1962. *Journal of Political Economy.* Supplement (October).

Parnes, Herbert S., 1984. *People Power: Elements of Human Resource Policy.* Beverly Hills, CA: Sage.

Schultz, Theodore W., 1961. "Investment in Human Capital." *American Economic Review* 51: 1–17; reprinted in Kiker 1971, pp. 3–21.

———, 1963. *The Economic Value of Education.* New York: Columbia University Press.

———, 1971. *Investment in Human Capital: The Role of Education and Research,* New York: Free Press.

———, 1981. *Investing in People: The Economics of Population Quality.* Berkeley, CA: University of California Press.

Smith, Adam, (1776) 1936. *The Wealth of Nations.* New York: Modern Library.

Spence, Michael, 1973. "Job Market Signaling." *Quarterly Journal of Economics* 87: 344–74.

HUMAN RELATIONS.

The study of problems that may arise from people's organizational and interpersonal relations; or a program designed to develop better interpersonal adjustments. The human relations model is an organizational model that offers an alternative paradigm to the traditional scientific management model. It employs five key behavioral domains to explain an organization's human system: (1) the social system and informal organization; (2) team or group behavior; (3) participatory management; (4) the behavioral effects of organization structure; and (5) the organization's values, norms, and beliefs.

The Organization's Social System

The early human relationists viewed organizations as complex social systems characterized by group interrelations, group pressure, and group cooperation. Mary Parker Follett (1924) first wrote about an organization's social system, and her model of "integrative solutions" to individual and group conflict is considered the initial construct that formed the basis for examining the role of individuals and their identity within a group.

F. J. Roethlisberger and William J. Dickson (1939) took Follet's concept of group further in their study (1924–1939) of work groups in the Western Electric labs in Cicero, Illinois. This series of studies, known as the Hawthorne experiments, documented an organization's social and informal structure. In describing an organization's social system, they illustrated how a group's norms and values evolved. Their research illustrated how these norms and values affected the behavior and performance of individual team members. The Hawthorne experiments provided scientific documentation on the social system and informal structure of an organization. Perhaps most important, these experiments recognized the existence of an informal social structure within organizations (peer groups and supervisor-employee relationships). An organization's social structure evolves into its own set of norms and values. It impacts the behavior of individual group members.

In contrast to the early human relationists, Chester Barnard (1938) and Herbert Simon [1947] adopted a neohumanist position. Barnard and Simon recognized the importance of the individual-to-group interface and its relationship to administration and the decisionmaking process within organizations. For example, Simon [1947] approached cooperation in relation to the administrator's role to achieve conformity between the individual and the organization in the decisionmaking process: "The basic task of administration [is to] . . . provide . . . each operative employee with an environment of decision . . . which is rational from the standpoint of the group values" (p. 243). Simon believed that through cooperation and consensus, the administrator had much to gain and little to loose.

The laboratory experiments conducted by Eric Triste (1985) and Wilfred R. Bion during World War II continued the behavioral science research initiated by the early human relationists and neohumanists. In their experiments, Triste and Bion examined the relationship of "frontline" cooperation to officer success. Their research attempted to question Frederick Taylor's scientific management (1911) and, at the same time, give Taylor's values a new lease on life (i.e., labor-management cooperation).

In many respects, the work of Bion and Triste had far-reaching consequences for the field of administrative science. In the short term, their work inspired the T-group practitioners of the 1950s. In the long term, their work established the foundation for writings concerning teamwork and participative management.

From T-Groups to Participatory Management

Beginning in the 1950s, the human relationists conducted laboratory (T-group) experiments based on the early work of Triste and Bion. These behavioral scientists often concluded that well-functioning teams would lead to collaborative problem solving within organizations. Kenneth Benne sought to fuse democratic and scientific values and to translate these into principles for guiding group team effectiveness (Benne 1943; Benne *et al.* 1975). Herb Shepard's article (1958) produced what could have been the first attempt at developing a theory of group interaction. His theory suggests that a group, or team, evolves through an ascending order of phased maturity and growth.

By the late 1950s the T-group became synonymous with participatory management. In many respects, it offered to managers and practitioners alike an alternative to bureaucracy and authoritarianism. In his early work, Douglas McGregor explained the application of T-group skills to solving complex organizational problems. By 1960, McGregor emerged as the most noted writer and practitioner in the human relations field. With Richard Beckard, McGregor coined the term "organization development" to describe how the T-group evolved into an innovative bottom-up change effort at General Mills Foods.

With publication of McGregor's *The Human Side of the Enterprise* (1960), participatory management emerged into a recognized paradigm (Theory Y). Theory Y clearly evolved from the decades of human relations research: To build a constructive group, a manager need to employ Theory Y's assumptions on employee participation. To this day, the principles of teamwork and participatory management remain central to the field of administrative science. For example, the language of the human relationists ("cooperation," "teams," "groups," and "participation") permeates David Osborne and Ted Gaebler's (1992) *Reinventing Government*. They state that today's entrepreneurial managers (in the public sector) must "use participatory management to decentralize decision making; they encourage teamwork, to overcome the rigid barriers that separate people in hierarchial institutions; they create institutional 'champions'" (1992, p. 254).

Contemporary Human Relations Theory

Since the 1960s, the human relationists Warren Bennis and Chris Argyris have shifted the emphasis from group or team participation to the changing nature of bureaucracies and centralized hierarchies. Many of the management techniques of the 1980s and 1990s (see Peters and Waterman 1982) address the challenges of bureaucracy and culture initially examined by Bennis and Argyris.

Bennis (1993) maintained that the bureaucratic organization is at an important crossroad. According to Bennis, the new postbureaucratic world will comprise democratic organizations that are dynamic and didactic. According to Bennis, these organizations need to be more readily adaptable to environmental pressures.

Osborne and Gaebler identify with Bennis' vision of a new postbureaucratic world: "In today's world, public institutions also need the flexibility to respond to complex and rapidly changing conditions. . . . Bureaucratic governments can do none of these things easily. . . . In effect, they are captive of sole source, monopoly suppliers: their own employees" (Osborne and Gaebler 1992, p. 34).

Argyris seeks to replace the human relations principles of motivation and growth with new values and beliefs. Argyris believes that T-groups and organization development lacked precision as to how to improve the quality of life within organizations. Beginning with his 1973 article, "Some Limits of Rational Man Organizational Theory," Argyris sought to describe a problem-solving and decision-making process in organizations that could move organizations "from X to Y."

Argyris (1982) took his theory of change further. The central premise of his *Reasoning, Learning and Action* is that the organization's human potential is best achieved by breaking an institution's bureaucratic barriers. Eliminating such barriers will increase the organization's decisionmaking and problem-solving capacities.

According to Argyris, the culture of bureaucratic organizations is "entropic," a single-loop mentality. Argyris advocates an opposite outlook, which he calls "double-loop learning." Through self-examination of behavior against assumptions, this type of learning allows the individual to enhance his or her capacity to solve problems. Argyris sees double-loop learning as empowering both manager and employee to break away from stifling barriers brought on by the nature of a bureaucracy. In his 1993 publications Argyris described the double-loop model as critical to moving organizations forward in the 1990s.

Argyris's learning paradigm has influenced other writers, who echo his learning and action formula (see Senge 1990 and 1994; and Oakley and Krug 1993). These writers see the need for today's organization to function as "learning systems," as they undergo structural change. Like Argyris, they believe that higher-level thinking will allow an organization to adapt and grow, ad infinitum. Like Argyris, these authors attempt to build upon the rich tradition of human relations: that today's organization can renew itself via the human system's growth and development.

PHILIP NUFRIO

BIBLIOGRAPHY

Argyris, Chris, 1973. "Some Limits of Rational Man Organizational Theory." *Public Administration Review*, vol. 33: 253–267.
———, 1982. *Reasoning, Learning and Action.* San Francisco: Jossey-Bass.
———, 1993a. *Knowledge for Action: A Guide to Overcoming Barriers to Organizational Change.* San Francisco: Jossey-Bass.

———, 1993b. *On Organizational Learning.* Reading, MA: Addison-Wesley.

Barnard, Chester I., 1938. *Functions of the Executive.* Cambridge, MA: Harvard University Press.

Benne, Kenneth, 1943. *The Discipline of Practical Judgement in a Democratic Society.* Chicago: University of Chicago Press.

Benne, Kenneth, Leland P. Bradford, Jack R. Gibb, and Ronald O. Lippitt, eds., 1975. *The Laboratory Method of Changing and Learning: Theory and Application.* Palo Alto, CA: Science and Behavior Books.

Bennis, Warren, 1993. *Beyond Bureaucracy, Essays on the Development and Evolution of Human Organization.* New York: Jossey-Bass.

Follett, Mary Parker, 1924. *Creative Experience and Dynamic Administration.* New York: David McKay.

McGregor, Douglas, 1960. *The Human Side of the Enterprise.* New York: McGraw-Hill.

Oakley, Ed, and Doug Krug, 1993. *Enlightened Leadership: Getting to the Heart of Change.* New York: Simon and Schuster.

Osborne, David, and Ted Gaebler, 1992. *Reinventing Government: How the Entrepreneurial Spirit Is Transforming the Public Sector.* Reading, MA: Addison-Wesley.

Peters, Tom, and Robert Waterman, 1982. *In Search of Excellence: Lesson from America's Best-Run Companies.* New York: Harper & Row.

Roethlisberger, F. J., and William J. Dickson, 1939. *Management and the Worker.* Cambridge, MA: Harvard University Press.

Senge, Peter, 1990. *The Fifth Discipline: The Art and Practice of the Learning Organization.* New York: Doubleday.

———, 1994. *The Fifth Discipline Fieldbook.* New York: Doubleday.

Shepard, Herb A., 1958. "Changing Personal and Intergroup Relationships in Organizations." In J. March, ed., *Handbook of Organizations.* Chicago: Rand-McNally.

Simon, Herbert A., [1947]. Revised, 1957, 1976. *Administrative Behavior: A Study of Decision Making Process in Administrative Organizations.* New York: Free Press.

Taylor, Frederick, 1911. *Scientific Management.* New York: Harper & Row.

Triste, Eric L., 1985. "Working with Bion in the 1940's: The Group Decade." In M. Pines, ed., *Bion and Group Psychotherapy.* London: Routledge and Kegan Paul.

HUMAN RESOURCE MANAGEMENT (HRM).

That part of an organization concerned primarily with the "people" aspects of management. This involvement encompasses a very broad spectrum of activities designed to maximize the contributions that people make to an organization through acquisition of human resources, development of those resources, and motivation and maintenance processes.

A part of this spectrum of activities includes the development of processes designed to acquire the best candidates for employment in an organization. This development involves the traditional staffing processes of recruitment and selection, which focus heavily on bringing into the organization a representative group of qualified candidates and using valid testing devices to determine

their appropriate roles. Once selected, HRM is committed to the development of employees. Competent employees do not remain competent forever, and as jobs change, organizations must provide additional training or education programs tied to the employees' and the organization's changing needs.

Also, assuring a constant flow of managers for the future requires some attention to career development. Good job performance is a function not only of a person's competence but also of his or her motivation and desire. To contribute their maximum, employees must have well-defined and well-designed jobs, well-educated supervisors, opportunities to participate in decisions, challenging work, and appropriate evaluation, recognition, and reward systems.

To retain competent employees, HRM professionals must maintain equitable systems of compensation management and provide attractive benefit packages. This entire retention system must include some opportunities for meaningful labor-management relations.

Finally, all of these activities must be based on a sound research base. Public personnel administration, the precursor of human resource management, evolved simultaneously with scientific management, and many of the processes of the personnel field have always been quantitative. Job analysis, written testing, performance appraisal, and job evaluation are just a few of the personnel processes that are quantitatively based. The evolving HRM function must also have a firm quantitative base. Managers' constant attention to research and their commitment to demonstrating the utility of the processes of research is an essential ingredient in modern organizations.

What was historically known as "personnel management" has evolved into what is now regarded as human resource management. This evolution has affirmed a gradual expansion of traditional personnel management from an all-consuming concern for customary processes, such as job analysis, recruitment, selection, and labor-management relations, to a more all-encompassing, people-focused definition of the field.

Today, in the late 1990s, with elected officials constantly exhorting those in the management field to become more flexible, efficient, and less centralized, public sector human resource managers are being called on constantly to "reinvent" HRM. Accelerated processes and a more "consumer-oriented" attitude are being called for as a part of the move toward **Total Quality Management**. Detailed rules and regulations, once a prominent feature of governmental HRM, are now becoming a thing of the past. Human resource managers are now being asked to change from referees and umpires *vis-à-vis* line managers, to the facilitating and educating roles of advisers, innovators, and supporters.

ROBERT H. ELLIOTT

BIBLIOGRAPHY

DeCenzo, David A., and Stephen P. Robbins, 1988.
Personnel/Human Resource Management. Englewood Cliffs,
NJ: Prentice-Hall.
Hyde, Albert C., 1995. "Total Quality Management: A Personnel Perspective." In Steven W. Hays and Richard C. Kearney, *Public Personnel Management: Problems and Prospects,*
pp. 306–318. Englewood Cliffs, NJ: Prentice-Hall.
Klingner, Donald E., 1995. "Strategic Human Resource Management." In Jack Rabin, *et al., Handbook of Public Personnel Administration,* pp. 633–659. New York: Marcel Dekker.

HUMAN RESOURCE PLANNING.

One element of an overall human resource management system that is designed to insure that the organization acquires the necessary human resources from its external environment at the proper time to allow the organization to accomplish its objectives. It may also be designed to allow an organization to cutback on its human resources in an orderly systematic way. A good human resource planning system will take the organization's objectives and translate them into the proper number and quality of people needed to attain those objectives.

Planning has historically been a luxury in government service. It was considered something desirable, but little long-term planning was done because day-to-day demands forced attention to immediate concerns. Long-term planning in government was made difficult, given the constant changeover of political administrations, with short-term rather than long-term achievements receiving highest priority. Political decisionmaking yardsticks often demanded that attention be paid to the immediate consequences, with the long-term consequences being left for later administrations.

In recent decades, because of decreasing revenues and increasing public demands, strategic planning has become more important in government service. Strategic planning requires organizations and their subunits to establish missions, goals, and objectives. They are required to establish priorities among those goals, and determine the positive and negative factors in their external environments relevant to achieving these goals. The availability of human resources is a critical component necessary for achieving organizational goals, and human resource planning is therefore a vital part of the overall strategic planning process.

Given the financial constraints governmental systems are facing worldwide, reductions-in-force (RIFs), or cutbacks in human resources, have become more common in governmental service. Departments of human resource management have been called upon to develop strategic plans, with layoff options available for decisionmakers.

One tool commonly used in human resource planning is a profile of the current status of people-skills within the organization—a skills inventory. Human Resource Information Systems (HRIS) are computerized programs designed to allow easy storage and easy access to skills inventories. Once this information is available, links must be made between current employee skills and promotional expectations and the current and expected future status of position vacancies and potential skills shortages within the organization. Other tools necessary for meaningful human resource planning include job analysis and career planning systems. Job analysis information can help provide links between employee skills and job knowledge, skills, and abilities. Career planning systems can begin to make links between the expectations and desires of individual employees and the future needs anticipated by the organization.

Thus, what in the past was a very low priority, informal process has now become a more formalized, complex process that is important in helping citizens and elected officials answer complicated questions about the role of government. More and more, as these questions are answered in the direction of less government, planning for cutback management and RIFs have become common.

ROBERT H. ELLIOTT

BIBLIOGRAPHY

Cayer, N. Joseph, 1995. *Public Personnel Administration in the
United States.* 3d. ed. New York: St. Martin's Press.
DeCenzo, David A., and Stephen P. Robbins, 1988.
Personnel/Human Resource Management. Englewood Cliffs,
NJ: Prentice-Hall.
Johnston, William, 1988. *Civil Service 2000.* Washington, DC:
GPO, Hudson Institute.
Shafritz, Jay, Norma M. Riccucci, David H. Rosenbloom, and
Albert C. Hyde, 1992. *Personnel Management in Government.*
4th ed. New York: Marcel Dekker.

HUMAN RIGHTS COMMISSION.

An official body established for the purpose of protecting and providing for the enforcement of human rights as defined in human rights law.

Human rights commissions exist at international, national, and subnational levels. At the international level, the relevant law is found in international treaties, covenants, or conventions; at the national level, in national human rights acts; and at the subnational level, in special state or provincial human rights legislation. It was only after World War II that commissions came into existence, reflecting a determined global effort to raise standards on human rights not present before or during the war.

At the international level, a leading body is the United Nations Commission on Human Rights. Established in 1946 by the UN Economic and Social Council, its general role is to make reports and recommendations to the council in matters of international law on human rights, the protection of minorities, the prevention of discrimination, and situations of human rights abuse. In carrying out this role, the commission has assisted in the preparation of the leading international human rights agreements and covenants—for example, the Universal Declaration of Human Rights, the International Covenant on Economic, Social, and Cultural Rights, the International Covenant on Civil and Political Rights, and so forth. The commission also has engaged in the organization of fact-finding missions, investigating special issues or situations of alleged violations of human rights. To deal with alleged violations, the commission documents the situation, invites a response from the government in question, and refers the matter to a special expert working group. If a pattern of violations is detected by the working group, the commission makes a report to the council, recommending whatever action it thinks necessary. The primary approach is one of persuasion and negotiation.

The UN Commission on Human Rights is not to be confused with the UN Human Rights Committee. The latter was established with the implementation of the International Covenant on Civil and Political Rights in 1976. Under the covenant, state parties agree to uphold civil and political rights within their jurisdictions, to insure effective remedies if rights are violated, and to insure effective enforcement of remedies. State parties also agree to submit reports to the UN Secretary-General for assessment by the Human Rights Committee. The reports are to contain a description of the measures taken to secure civil and political rights and of progress made. The general function of the committee is to examine the reports, make comments, and send these to the state parties and to the UN Economic and Social Council. The work of the committee also involves responding to complaints of violations of the covenant. Complaints may be made by state parties against other state parties or they may be made by private individuals. In the case of state parties, the committee itself may try to settle the complaint immediately or appoint a special conciliation commission to effect a settlement agreeable to both state parties. In the case of complaints from individuals, the committee checks to insure that the complaint is admissible, relays information to the state party in question, considers information from both the individual and the state party, gives its conclusions to both, and gives a report to the Economic and Social Council.

Human rights commissions also operate on a regional basis. Leading ones are the European Commission on Human Rights, set up by the Council of Europe in 1955, the Inter-American Commission on Human Rights, established by the Organization of American States in 1959, and the African Commission on Human and Peoples'

Rights, established by the Organization of African Unity in 1987. These commissions are responsible for insuring compliance of state parties with respect to the European Convention on Human Rights, the American Convention of Human Rights, and the African Charter on Human Rights and Peoples' Rights. Although they operate somewhat differently, they share a similar complaint procedure for dealing with alleged violations of rights. They can receive a complaint from one state party against another, providing that the parties have previously declared that they recognize the authority of the commission to do this. Similarly, provided that state parties have previously agreed, the commission can receive petitions from individuals and organizations against a state party violating rights. The commission investigates the complaint, attempts to achieve a settlement, and, if a settlement is achieved, makes a report. If a settlement cannot be achieved, the commission may make a report and refer the matter to a higher political authority (e.g., the Committee of Ministers in the European System) or to a relevant court (e.g., the European Court of Human Rights).

At the national level, human rights commissions operate to protect the civil and political rights of citizens under national human rights acts and to protect citizens against discrimination. Examples include the Australian Human Rights Commission, the American Civil Rights Commission, and the Canadian Human Rights Commission. Their general functions include the review of government policy and legislation to insure conformity with national human rights law, the administration of special programs such as public education, and the handling of complaints.

In responding to complaints, the commission typically attempts to achieve a settlement through conciliation. If conciliation does not work, the commission may refer the matter to a relevant government authority (e.g., the attorney general in Australia) or to the courts for legal action. In some jurisdictions (e.g., Canada), the commission may refer the matter to a special human rights tribunal independent of the commission for adjudication.

Commissions also operate at the subnational level, especially in political systems that are federal. Examples are the United States and Canada, where the control of discrimination is largely the responsibility of states and provinces. As at the national level, state and provincial commissions perform a complaint-handling role, as well as functions of public education and legislative review. When state or provincial commissions handle complaints of discrimination, their main focus again is on conciliation, but provision is usually also made for adjudication by special human rights tribunals or boards of inquiry. Common problems of commissions are the perceived lack of commission independence from government (members are usually selected by the government or by the executive) and lack of adequate funding to effectively enforce the legislation.

R. BRIAN HOWE

BIBLIOGRAPHY

Alston, Philip, 1992. *The United Nations and Human Rights: A Critical Appraisal.* Oxford: Clarendon Press.

Donnelly, Jack, 1993. *International Human Rights.* Boulder, CO: Westview Press.

Henkin, Louis, 1990. *The Age of Rights.* New York: Columbia University Press.

Lustgarten, Laurence, 1980. *Legal Control of Racial Discrimination.* London: Macmillan.

Robertson, A. H., 1992. *Human Rights in the World.* Manchester: Manchester University Press.

Tarnopolsky, Walter, and William Pentney, 1985. *Discrimination and the Law in Canada.* Toronto: Richard De Boo.

IBN TAIMIAH, AHMAD ABDULHALEEM
(1263–1329). An Islamic teacher, writer, and reformer, who sought to improve government and its leaders, and thereby rid society of immorality and corruption.

Ahmad Abdulhaleem Ibn Taimiah, was born in Harran, Syria. In 1268 he moved with his father to Damascus, Syria, where he got his education and became a very influential teacher and propagator of Islam. Ibn Taimiah is best known as a reformer because all of his writings and teachings were aimed at reforming the government and its leaders. He was raised in a religious family, where he learned the Qura'an and the teachings of the Prophet Mohammed.

Ibn Taimiah was led by his belief that a society cannot be reformed unless the government and the leader are reformed first, because a corrupt government will result in a corrupt society. He was heavily influenced by the spread of nepotism, immorality, bribery, and all types of corruption during the second Abbasyah Caliphate, which led to the collapse of the Islamic state.

In Ibn Taimiah's reforming efforts, he wrote two major and influential books: *Al-Syasah Al-Shara'yah fe Islah Al-Ra'ai wa Al-Ra'ayah* (Islamic Policies for Reforming the Leader and the Followers); and *Al-Hesbah wa Masa'oliat Al-Hukumat Al-Islamiah*) Control and the Responsibility of the Islamic Government). In the first book, Ibn Taimiah talked in great detail about the selection and recruitment of government employees. His main criteria is that the person be qualified. For Ibn Taimiah, no other criteria should be considered if the goal is to have a government that functions well. He attributed the Islamic government's failure to protect its territories to the spread of corruption, which he believed is caused by the absence of a merit system. (Employees are appointed to government positions based on factors that have nothing to do with the job being performed and they are promoted on the basis of the same factors.)

In his second book, Ibn Taimiah detailed the responsibilities of the Islamic government and its employees from an Islamic perspective. He also provided the principles of government reform. According to him, reforming the government requires adherence to four major principles: (1) forbidding monopoly, (2) controlling prices, (3) providing services, and (4) fixing wages. Governments must adopt these principles, according to Ibn Taimiah, and they must also undertake their responsibilities efficiently, be accountable to the people, and must be governed by the principles of Islam, not by the desires of its leaders.

Ibn Taimiah's ideas of reform and views of the Islamic rulers agitated the caliphs. As a result, he was put in prison, where he died in 1329. His teachings continued to be influential after his death, however.

ABDULLAH M. AL-KHALAF

IMPASSE PROCEDURES.
Methods developed to help end deadlocks in collective bargaining negotiations over the terms and conditions of employment and over grievances that arise from interpretations of the language and meaning of the contract. Impasse procedures are intended to provide alternatives to the strike, which is the most extreme form of impasse resolution. The most commonly used methods to end deadlocks other than the strike are mediation, fact-finding, and various forms of arbitration.

In rights disputes (those concerning interpretation of an existing contract), grievance machinery comes into play (see **grievance machinery**). Grievances not resolved during the first stages of the grievance process go to binding arbitration for final resolution. Arbitration helps avoid strikes during the term of a contract.

Interest disputes are those that develop during negotiations over the terms and conditions of a collective bargaining contract, including such issues as wage or benefit increases or reductions, reductions in force, and changes in staffing patterns or work rules. Ideally, the parties should work out their differences through collective bargaining. When such efforts have been exhausted short of an agreement, impasse resolution techniques are applied.

Dispute resolution techniques vary across labor-relations systems. In some nations and in many public jurisdictions in the United States, strikes are outlawed and impasse procedures are mandatory. In most European countries, rights disputes are submitted to labor courts or to general courts for resolution.

In the United States private sector, unions are guaranteed the right to strike by the National Labor Relations Act of 1935. As a result, third-party procedures such as mediation, fact-finding, and arbitration are used much less frequently than in the public sector. However, the Federal Mediation and Conciliation Service, an independent federal agency, is available for mediation or fact-finding services on a voluntary basis.

Compulsory impasse procedures must be followed by the disputing parties in most federal, state, and local jurisdictions in the United States when bargaining impasses are reached. The specific type of procedures may be mandated by law or by a labor board, or they may be negotiated by the parties. In some jurisdictions, the state labor board may unilaterally declare an impasse and intervene. There is much variation in the steps and types of impasse resolution techniques utilized. In some jurisdictions, dispute resolution begins with mediation, followed by fact-finding, and finally by binding arbitration. In other jurisdictions, mediation is followed immediately by arbitration.

Mediation is the most common impasse procedure. The mediator, or neutral, has the task of helping the parties settle the dispute themselves through his or her use of facilitating techniques. Mediators may be appointed from certified lists by agreement of the parties or by the state public employee relations board. Federal Mediation and Conciliation Service mediators are also available where no state or local assistance is provided.

The success of a mediator depends largely on the confidence and trust he or she commands from the parties. The mediation process is informal, private, and highly individualistic. Written records are not kept. The third-party neutral usually begins by calling a joint meeting to establish the issues needing resolution and to set ground rules for the mediation efforts. The positions of the parties on unsettled issues are noted. Next, individual meetings with the parties in dispute may be held by the mediator to explore negotiating room on the issues. The mediator attempts to keep the process dynamic and moving progressively toward an acceptable settlement.

The specific strategies of the mediator vary with individual circumstances. Kenneth Kressel has identified three basic strategies: reflexive, nondirective, and directive. Reflexive strategies involve the mediator gaining an understanding of the nature of the dispute and the points of power and influence among members of the negotiating teams. The mediator also seeks to cement a relationship of perceived trust with the parties. Nondirective strategies are intended to produce a climate conducive to settlement and to help the parties move toward the goal of settlement. Among the details the mediator must attend to are the times and places of negotiations, the order in which individual issues are considered, and the privacy of negotiations. The mediator tries to help the parties explore potential paths of accommodation by launching trial balloons and assisting the parties in preparing offers and counterproposals.

Directive strategies are used in an effort to bring the parties to a resolution of their differences through suggesting specific points for settlement and, when appropriate, applying pressure on the parties.

Effective mediators are in great demand but short supply. The qualities associated with successful mediators include patience, intelligence, creativity, and stamina. Formal training programs are available for mediators, but much of one's success or failure is attributable to personal characteristics that cannot be transmitted in a classroom.

Mediation, as noted previously, is by far the most frequently used impasse procedure, and its achievements are notable. Its flexibility and informality helps the parties to work productively toward settlement. It is also relatively inexpensive. The fact that mediated settlements are attained voluntarily by the parties supports the institution of collective bargaining and promotes a positive relationship between labor and management. However, there is no requisite finality to mediation. Sometimes it works, but at other times it fails because the neutral cannot force a resolution. The odds of successful mediation are much improved by the presence of an experienced, highly skilled neutral.

Fact-finding, like mediation, may usually be initiated by either party, or in some cases invoked by a labor board. It may involve an individual fact finder or a panel of three or more individuals. In some cases mediators act as fact finders. Fact-finding, which is a much more formal proceeding than mediation, consists of a quasi-judicial hearing of the parties' positions and evidence, a written record, and, in most cases, written (but nonbinding) findings.

The key task of the fact finder is to determine, based on the evidence, which set of "facts"—those of the union or those of management—are most convincing. But mediation plays an important secondary role in the fact finder's work. The fact finder, by investigating and probing the points of opposition and possible accommodation between the parties, can make each side's expectations and bottom line apparent to the other. Voluntary agreement may be the result. In some instances, the parties perceive the fact finder as an ally in a struggle against the legislative body or public opinion. The expectation is that the "facts" as disclosed will promote the welfare of both parties in the long run (such as by providing evidence in favor of increased compensation, for example). Fact-finding may also give representatives of one party a scapegoat to blame for an impasse resolution that the membership of the union or citizens of the jurisdiction are likely to criticize. Usually the fact finder's recommendations are released to the media. This in itself may encourage settlement by publicizing a party's untenable position.

Fact-finding has some positive features. It provides a cooling-off period for the parties after heated negotiations and an opportunity for them to reassess their positions. The report can serve as a point of departure for further negotiations. But there are negative features as well. Like mediation, fact-finding lacks finality, and its record for producing settlements is modest. It is expensive, and may be used excessively but to little avail by parties with sour bargaining relationships. Several states have discontinued use of fact-finding as an impasse resolution technique.

Arbitration involves submitting a dispute to a neutral third party for a final binding settlement. An exception is advisory arbitration, in which a nonbinding determination is made of the issues at impasse. In many public jurisdictions, arbitration is compulsory when an impasse is not resolved through mediation or fact-finding. In others, the parties themselves declare an impasse and request arbitration of the dispute. Arbitration is a formal quasi-judicial procedure involving the presentation of evidence before a single arbitrator or a board, usually made up of three members: one member selected by each of the parties and the third selected by the two newly designated arbitrators. In the case of three-member panels, the "neutrals" selected by the union and management actually represent the interest of and make arguments for the party that appointed them. Arbitrators may be appointed by a state agency or by an independent arbitration agency, or a list of eligible names may be obtained from an organization such as the American Arbitration Association. The parties carefully screen candidates for indications of bias, based on examinations of past decisions and on reputation. Law firms or other businesses may screen arbitrator candidates as well.

In rendering their decisions, arbitrators follow statutory criteria and professional judgment. Some states have broad criteria that include terms such as the "public interest." Others are more specific, with requirements for the arbitrator to consider factors such as the jurisdiction's ability to pay and comparable wages and benefits in neighboring jurisdictions. Comparative data are especially important in guiding arbitrators' deliberations.

Arbitration was first used in the United States in the eighteenth century to settle disputes in Connecticut copper mines. It was later used in the shoe industry and coal mines, and in World Wars I and II by the National War Labor Board to prevent interruptions in the supply of war goods. It was first applied in state and local government during the 1960s, and in the federal sector in the 1970s for postal workers.

Arbitration may be conventional or final offer. Conventional arbitration is practiced in a majority of jurisdictions. Here, the arbitrator has the authority to accept one party's offer in its entirety or to split the difference between the parties' final positions. Final-offer arbitration requires the arbitrator to select either the union's or the management's final proposal; there is no freedom to design a compromise settlement. Final-offer arbitration may require the arbitrator to accept one or the other party's final position on all items at impasse, or permit him or her to select positions issue by issue. In some cases, an arbitrator may impose a fact finder's recommendations instead of what the parties seek.

Once it has been determined, the arbitrator's decision is placed in writing, along with its justifications. Grounds for appeal are very restricted and are usually limited to awards involving fraud, corruption, or bias, or to cases in which an arbitrator exceeds his or her legal authority or issues a ruling that violates public policy.

Arbitrators, when rendering awards, usually focus narrowly on the bargaining context at hand, grounding their rulings on the previous collective bargaining contract. They often split the difference between final positions when conventional arbitration is used, or select the most moderate of final offers when that is the impasse resolution technique. The extensive use of comparative data and the tendency to make awards that only change contract terms incrementally makes arbitration a fairly predictable activity in terms of outcomes.

Arbitrators must be concerned with the fairness and acceptability of their awards. Many arbitrators encourage the parties to continue with collective bargaining activities during arbitration in order to move them closer to a voluntary settlement. One specific device, known as mediation-arbitration, explicitly promotes settlement before the arbitrator has to issue a decision. With this method, the arbitrator engages in mediation strategies during the stages of arbitration, by, for example, giving the parties clues as to what the final arbitration award might look like.

The major advantage of arbitration is its finality. In addition, it is a balanced means of settling impasses, short of a strike, with the interests of the union and management receiving equal consideration. Arbitration has undeniably been successful in resolving bargaining and grievance impasses. However, it remains a controversial technique.

It is claimed that arbitration constitutes an illegal delegation of government authority to individuals who are in no way democratically accountable. Arbitrators make critical decisions regarding the public payroll and public policy, for example, yet elected and appointed officials in government are shut out of the process until it is essentially concluded. Indeed, early court decisions declared arbitration illegal, and it remains so today in several states (Colorado, Maryland, and South Dakota). Arbitration has been upheld by courts in at least 15 other states. And some measure of democratic accountability can be retained by restricting the arbitrator's scope of authority through statute, requiring arbitrators' rulings to be made public, and insuring that the appropriate legislative body takes seriously its power to override arbitrators' decisions.

It is sometimes claimed by management that arbitration favors the union position, instead of balancing the positions of the two parties. Unions are typically strong proponents of mandatory arbitration, and management tends to oppose it. The principal arguments of management are that arbitration results in financial windfalls for union members and drives up compensation costs and that it leads to decisions that dilute management rights. Although the results of empirical research are mixed, it does appear that unions benefit from arbitration, not so much because they win more often or win overly generous settlements but because the availability of the process exercises a positive influence on salaries and benefits throughout the entire jurisdiction. Using arbitration appears to be less important to union success than the potential to use it.

A third criticism of arbitration is that it "chills" collective bargaining. When there is no credible strike threat to drive the parties toward settlement, unions may perceive that they have little or nothing to lose and potentially much to gain from taking an interest dispute all the way to arbitration. Thus, bargaining activity becomes somewhat of a sham, with the union, and perhaps a recalcitrant management as well, biding their time until binding arbitration becomes operational. There is some indication of a related "narcotic effect," with arbitration becoming a crutch for a weak union, which may regularly move impasses into arbitration rather than take its chances with a strong bargaining opponent at the table. Empirical evidence of the chilling and narcotic effects has been found in several scholarly studies, but other studies have not detected them. It does appear that final-offer arbitration exercises less of a chilling and narcotic effect than conventional arbitration; this is attributed to the higher level of uncertainty involved in selection of a last best offer from one party or the other—essentially, a winner-take-all situation.

As noted, mediation-arbitration is a technique for resolving impasses in which the mediator, if he or she cannot broker a voluntary settlement, is transformed into an arbitrator with the power to impose a solution. This technique, although promising, has not been widely adopted in the United States.

Another alternative impasse resolution technique is to let the voters of the jurisdiction decide the outcome of the dispute through a referendum. This type of ballot-box arbitration is used to a limited extent in Colorado and Texas. There are problems with it, however, including the timeliness and expense of organizing and holding a referendum, the difficulty in reducing complex labor-management disagreements to simple language, the tendency of voters not to educate themselves on the issues or show interest in the referendum, and potential bias against the union from the activities of antitax groups.

RICHARD C. KEARNEY

BIBLIOGRAPHY

Kearney, Richard C., 1992. *Labor Relations in the Public Sector.* New York: Marcel Dekker.

Lester, Richard A., 1984. *Labor Arbitration in State and Local Government: An Examination of the Experience in Eight States and New York City.* Princeton, NJ: Princeton University, Industrial Relations Section.

Simkin, William E., 1971. *Mediation and the Dynamics of Collective Bargaining.* Washington, DC: BNA Books.

Word, William R., 1972. "Fact-finding in Public Employee Negotiations," *Monthly Labor Review* 95 (February): 60–64.

Zack, Arnold, 1985. *Public Sector Mediation.* Washington, DC: Bureau of National Affairs.

IMPEACHMENT.

The process by which the legislature may remove civil officials, including judges, from office for offenses that demonstrate the officeholder's unsuitability for public service. In addition to removing a public official from office, impeachment may include disqualifying the impeached officeholder from ever holding public office in the future.

In the United States, impeachment does not include fines or imprisonment for wrongdoing; however, an impeached officeholder may be subject to prosecution in separate criminal proceedings. In Great Britain, Parliament's power to punish an impeached officeholder is not only limited to removal and disqualification from office but also includes the power to impose other types of sanctions.

Impeachment is intended as a check on excesses by members of the executive and judicial branches of government. It originated in Great Britain as a limitation on royal prerogative and as a means for controlling abuses by ministers and justices of the Crown. Thus, impeachment may be brought against a public official for offenses not rising to the level of criminal conduct.

In Great Britain, Parliament has sometimes used its power of impeachment to remove public officials for no reason other than disagreement with the official's policy judgments. In the United States, impeachment has been restricted to cases of official wrongdoing.

The United States Constitution specifies the following grounds for impeachment: treason, bribery, or other high crimes or misdemeanors. Although this language suggests a criminal standard for impeachment, it is apparent from the debates of the Constitutional Convention that the framers, on one hand, intended that impeachment be allowed for a much broader range of offenses than purely criminal behavior. On the other hand, it is equally clear that the framers of the United States Constitution did not intend that congressional disagreement with the policies of a public official constitute grounds for impeachment. In 1974, while studying the issue of impeachment during the tumultuous presidency of Richard M. Nixon, Congress released a report describing its power of impeachment as being "directed to constitutional wrongs that subvert the structure of government or undermine the integrity of the office and even the Constitution itself" (U.S. Congress 1974).

In the United States, Congress has the power to impeach any civil officer of the United States, including the President, vice president, and federal judges. The several states of the United States have separate provisions in their state constitutions for impeachment of state officials and judges. For the most part, the state provisions for impeachment parallel the federal model.

Constitutional scholars have debated whether Congress has the power to impeach one of its own members. Judicial and congressional precedent now support the view that Congress's power of impeachment does not extend to impeachment of one of its own members. Other constitutional provisions give Congress the power to expel one of its members for misconduct; however, the power of expulsion does not include the power to bar an expelled member from again seeking public office, whether the office from which he or she was expelled or another office. In Great Britain, Parliament has used impeachment against its own members as well as against members of the executive and judicial branches.

In both the United States and Great Britain, impeachment is a two-step legislative process: the first step involving the lower house, the House of Commons in Great

Britain and the House of Representatives in the United States, and the second step involving the upper house, the House of Lords in Great Britain and the Senate in the United States. Impeachment is initiated by the lower house, which conducts an investigation and votes articles of impeachment detailing the alleged offenses. The second step is a trial in the upper chamber, which decides the truth or falsity of the charges contained in the articles of impeachment.

In both the United States and Great Britain, articles of impeachment must be approved by the lower house by a simple majority vote of those present. Since a quorum in the United States House of Representatives is 50 percent of the membership, impeachment may be approved by a vote of one-fourth of the total membership of the House plus one. Although not required by the Constitution, the United States House has always used one of its committees to investigate charges that a public official has committed an impeachable offense. This has usually involved fact-finding hearings by the committee.

Once articles of impeachment have been voted by the lower house, the upper house conducts a trial and then votes on each article of impeachment to determine whether the charge contained in that article is true. A finding that a charge is true is known as a "conviction." In the United States, a conviction must be approved by a two-thirds majority of the senators present. In Great Britain, the house of Lords may convict by a simple majority. No conviction may be based on offenses not included in the articles of impeachment voted by the lower house.

In the United States, the vice president presides over all impeachment trials in the senate, except those involving the president. In cases involving impeachment of the president, the trial in the Senate is presided over by the chief justice of the Supreme Court. This latter provision was included because it would be unfair for the vice president to preside over a trial in which conviction of the charged party would result in the judge being elevated to the presidency.

The House selects managers from their own membership to serve as prosecutors in the Senate. The senators serve as jurors in deciding the truth or falsity of the charges. The charged official may be represented by counsel and has the right to appear in person. Each side may call witnesses and introduce documentary evidence. The presiding officer rules on questions of admissibility of evidence, but may be reversed by a majority vote of the senators present. There is no provision in the United States Constitution for disqualifying a senator from voting in an impeachment trial because of bias, prejudice, or interest.

Impeachment results in an immediate judgment of conviction and an order of removal from office by the presiding judge or officer of the trial. In addition, the Senate may vote to disqualify the convicted official from ever again holding public office in the United States. The United States Supreme Court has ruled that impeachment is not subject to judicial review.

PAUL M. BROWN

BIBLIOGRAPHY

Berger, Raoul, 1973. *Impeachment: The Constitutional Problems.* Cambridge, MA: Harvard University Press.
Black, Jr., Charles L. 1974. *Impeachment: A Handbook.* New Haven and London: Yale University Press.
Schaapper, M. B., ed., 1974. *Presidential Impeachment: A Documentary Overview,* Washington, DC: Public Affairs Press.
U.S. Congress. House of Representatives, Committee on the Judiciary, 1974. *Constitutional Grounds for Impeachment: Report by the Staff of the Impeachment Inquiry,* House of Representatives, Committee on the Judiciary. Ninety-third Congress, Second Session, February 1974: Washington, DC: GPO.

IMPERIALISM. The exertion of political dominance by one nation-state over the people of another nation-state or territory. As shall be seen, the precise source and nature of that domination varies considerably according to the nation-states and historical context concerned in specific cases. Indeed, the historical diversity of imperial systems makes it difficult to assert generalized principles that apply in all cases. Perhaps the only valid generalization is that imperialism is always based upon an uneven power relationship in which the imperializing nation is ultimately able to exert its will over the imperialized. This statement conjures up images of military coercion, but some systems of imperial control have endured without resort to such methods, and in some cases without the capacity for such aggressive measures. Economic sanctions can prove even more effective (and cheaper) than military assault.

Inevitably, generalized statements about imperialism have emerged from specific studies of particular imperial systems, and therefore the best way to address the subject is to examine some of the most important historical and sociological theories of imperialism. To this end, this entry is divided into three subsections. The first considers theories seeking to explain the motives and causes of imperial expansion. The second explores the varying natures of imperial systems, focusing upon the wide variety of ways in which imperial rule is maintained in different circumstances. The final section is concerned with the debate over the consequences of imperialism, whether harmful, indifferent, or beneficial.

Before proceeding, it is worth noting that imperialism appears to have been a constant in history. It was a feature of most stages of historical development in most ethnic and cultural communities. In Europe, imperialism was a characteristic of ancient Greece and Rome. China and the Muslim world also saw the development of empires. From the sixteenth century, the emergent modern European societies exerted control over Africa, Asia, and the Americas, creating a European hegemony by the nineteenth century. In the process, the earlier decaying empires of Turkey and China were ruthlessly swept away. So varied has been the experience of empire that an attempt to define imperialism requires a careful survey of the evolution of the concept.

The Motives and Causes of Imperialism

Studies of imperialism have identified several different motives for imperial expansion that have been evident in various examples of imperialism. These include economic motives, demographic pressures, resolution of domestic political divisions, ideas of religious, racial, and cultural supremacy, atavistic psychological drives, and strategic or defensive expediency. It is important to note that these motives are not mutually exclusive; indeed, in most cases of imperial expansion a range of these motives is evident. These motives and the people who identified them are considered later, with some illustrative examples.

The various economic motives for imperialism include the pursuit of markets for trade and supplies of essential resources, such as food and raw materials, and the protection of overseas assets arising from overseas investment. The acquisition of colonies by European powers in the seventeenth and eighteenth centuries are probably the best examples of trade as a motive for imperial expansion. According to the tenets of mercantilist economic theory as espoused by such writers as Thomas Mun ([1664] 1964), colonies were acquired to protect trade between the imperial power and its subservient territories. In the mercantilist view, the world's wealth was finite, and the only way to insure a share of it was by imperial acquisition of markets and resources. Though the high rate of economic growth associated with industrial capitalism dispelled mercantilist assumptions about the limits of wealth, competition for overseas markets remained a potent motive for imperialism. The quest to find markets for industrial produce and raw materials to maintain growth in output were evident in the analyses of Karl Marx, John A. Hobson, and V. I. Lenin. Recently, historians such as John Gallagher and Ronald Robinson have stressed the importance of Britain as an industrial exporting nation as a reason for its growing international and imperial clout. For them, foreign dependence upon British-manufactured imports and British markets to consume their own produce led to a growing assertion of Britain's authority, even in regions technically outside the formal British Empire.

Britain's foreign investment in the latter half of the nineteenth century was also identified by John A. Hobson ([1902] 1988), the English liberal journalist, as a key motivation behind the acquisition of colonies in Africa and elsewhere. For Hobson, imperialism was a consequence of a dysfunctional capitalist system in Britain, where social inequality and poverty forced capital to seek profitable opportunities abroad, while a class of wealthy financiers used

their political influence to insure that these foreign investments would be protected by acquisition of territory.

Whereas Hobson saw these developments as an abberation from the normal peaceful course of capitalist development, which could be rectified by social reform, Marxists have always regarded imperialism as an inevitable and unavoidable consequence of capitalist development. Territorial expansion by the leading industrial capitalist powers to secure markets, resources and outlets for investment were identified by Lenin ([1916] 1978) as the product of a particular phase of capitalist development in which large capitalist organizations competed for the world's resources; using their political control of nation-states to assert imperial control in defense of their economic interests. Conflict and global war were the inevitable results, according to Lenin.

More recently, Peter Cain's and Anthony Hopkins's (1993) study of British imperialism identifies the financial interests of the City of London ("Gentlemanly capitalists") as the dominant social group in Britain and the main instigators of imperial expansion. This is in contrast to the heavy emphasis upon industry as the prime imperial driving force in Marxist theories.

This wide variety of economic explanations of imperialism, and the ideological differences that underly them, has inevitably generated lengthy debate, which continues.

Some of the other motives for imperial expansion are also closely linked to economic concerns. Edward Wakefield (1834), writing in the 1830s argued for the systematic colonization of parts of the world in order that surplus capital and population could find an outlet. Shortage of land and other resources in Britain led Wakefield to believe that emigration was essential if social revolution at home was to be avoided. This emigrant population in the colonies would also provide an expanding market for industrial exports and supplies of food and raw materials for Britain. In this respect, imperialism was seen as a solution for domestic social and economic difficulties.

Domestic considerations have also been identified as the principal motives for expansion by Imperial Germany in the late nineteenth century. Hans Wehler (1985) has argued that imperial expansion under Otto von Bismarck and William II was motivated partly by a desire to preserve domestic political unity by making imperialism a common national cause, through which rival social groups such as the industrialists and the aristocratic landowners (the Junkers) could be reconciled. In particular, the acquisition of markets and raw materials for the industrialists was seen as a way of compensating them for their continuing exclusion from political power.

Imperial rule and expansion have also required cultural and religious justification, and it is possible to identify the resulting ideologies as motivating factors in themselves. Soviet imperialism after 1917 was justified in terms of the prevailing communist beliefs, and although geopolitical concerns were often the main reasons for expansion, an ideological hostility toward capitalism was undoubtedly an important factor. In Britain's case, ideological justifications for imperialism were steeped in the assumptions about the racial and religious superiority of the white race, in general, and the British, specifically. Assertions that the British Empire was a civilizing agent, spreading the virtues of Britain's Christianity, social customs, and political structures, are to be found in the work of many literary and religious figures of the nineteenth century. Edward Said's (1993) study of culture and imperialism identified these features in the work of numerous Victorian writers, including Rudyard Kipling and Joseph Conrad.

Nowhere is this notion of imperialism as a necessary result of white supremacy stronger than in the writing of the Social Darwinists, who saw human history as a continuing struggle between nations and races. In this view, imperialism was both an inevitable consequence of white superiority and a necessity for national survival. The exponents and intellectual roots of this movement were fully discussed by G. R. Searle (1971).

Others have also seen the causes of imperialism lying in human nature and traditional social forms, but without accompanying assumptions about racial or national superiority. For Joseph Schumpeter (1919), the causes of imperialism lay in the continuing strength of premodern feudal political institutions and attitudes. These were depicted by Schumpeter as militaristic and expansionist, emerging as they did in agrarian societies where scarcity of food and the importance of land as the main means of producing wealth made the acquisition of territory highly advantageous. This depiction of imperialism as being an atavistic remnant of feudalism was also echoed by Hobson ([1902] 1988) as one of a variety of factors promoting expansion.

Historians since the 1950s have shifted the attention away from developments within the societies of imperialist nations, focusing instead upon events at the imperial frontier, in those territories being absorbed into an empire. This new emphasis upon the periphery was first broached by Gallagher and Robinson (1953, 1953a). The need to defend essential trade routes and other strategically important objectives at the edge of an empire were identified as the main motive for acquiring new territory. For example, the annexation of Egypt by Britain in 1882 is explained as a strategic move to protect the trade route to India through the Suez Canal.

This theme has been expanded upon by others, most notably D. K. Fieldhouse (1973). Fieldhouse has argued that much of Britain's expansion in India and Southeast Asia in the nineteenth century was a response to perceived strategic threats at the periphery from either indigenous polities or rival European imperial powers. Gallagher, Robinson, and Fieldhouse are deeply skeptical of "metropolitan" theories of expansion, which focused on developments within the imperial power itself, preferring

the notion of imperialism as an unplanned response to events at the periphery. Great emphasis was placed on the role of "the man on the spot," the colonial administrators at the edge of an empire, who exercised great power in an age of slow communications and dependence upon the judgment of those with immediate knowledge of colonial problems.

Other historians have stressed the destabilizing effect of economic links with expanding European economies upon indigenous societies subsequently triggering imperial annexation of those territories by Europeans seeking to protect their economic interests by "restoring order." For example, Khoo Kay Kim (1972) has described how indigenous states in the Malay Peninsula were brought close to political collapse by the effects of trade with the British, thereby prompting annexation in the early 1870s.

It is important to recognize that there is fierce debate among historians about the relative merits of these postulated motives for imperial expansion, both as generalized explanations of imperialism and as causes in specific cases.

The Nature of Imperial Rule

Before the 1950s, definitions of imperial rule stressed the existence of formal political control over the territory concerned. Sometimes this resulted from migration of people to sparsely populated regions without a clear and separate political identity (e.g., Australia, Canada), and sometimes from the conquest of existing states (e.g., India), but the common feature was the existence of formal structures of political rule, whereby ultimate authority and power was vested in the agents of the metropolitan society. This concept of imperialism as a formal political arrangement permeated the theories of Marx, Hobson, Lenin, and Schumpeter. Of course, the precise details of imperial rule varied from empire to empire, and from colony to colony within the same empire. This variety was always recognized as a product of socioeconomic differences between colonial societies. For example, in the British Empire the "White Dominions" enjoyed far greater local control in the later nineteenth century than did India. This advantage resulted partly from assumptions about the inability of Indians to govern themselves and a growing recognition that overcentralized direct rule over Canada and Australia would aggravate aspirations for independence. Thus the nature of "formal empire" in the sense of formalized structures of imperial political control was always complex and varied, given its many different manifestations.

Gallagher and Robinson (1953) redefined the concept of imperial control in a radical way. They argued that control could be exerted by imperial economic powers over territories not subject to formal political rule. This "informal empire" was possible through the economic dependence of less-developed countries upon the more-advanced industrial or imperial powers. This economic dependence took various forms; dependence upon the imperial countries as profitable markets for raw material exports, for capital to modernize and improve the indigenous economy, or for the supply of modern industrial manufactures. This economic dependence was compounded by the expanding military strength of the European imperialist powers, who could transform an informal empire into a formal empire as a last resort. In simple terms, where possible, informal rule was to be preferred over formal empire. It was ultimately less expensive to use quiet diplomacy to persuade weaker states to follow instructions that it was to conquer and subdue them.

Even though the concept of informal empire was used initially by Gallagher and Robinson to explain an alleged continuity in Britain's imperial expansion throughout the nineteenth century, it has come to be recognized as a general feature of all imperial systems. Thus, imperialism is no longer regarded as synonomous with direct colonial rule, it is also seen as the true character of the relationships between states that appear to be sovereign and without formal political connections but that, in reality, are based upon the deliberate economic and political exploitation of the weaker state by the stronger.

This wider definition of imperialism has become particularly important in explaining the durability of imperialism in an age of formal decolonization. Thus, although the major European colonial empires were dismantled during the 1950s and 1960s, Western imperial control over large parts of Africa and Asia was sustained by the dependence of these newly independent states upon the major Western industrial powers for capital investment, markets, loans, and aid. The uneven economic relations between the developed and less-developed countries resulted in indebtedness of the poorer countries on a scale that insured their subservience to financial interests and governments in the industrialized capitalist world. According to this neocolonialist view, which emerged from revisionist Marxists such as J. O'Connor (1970), European formal imperialism was replaced by an informal imperialism, which was largely based on United States economic power.

Imperial rule is thus no longer defined solely as formal colonization but includes a wide range of economic and political relationships in which one power is able to exert deliberate control over political and economic decisions made by another.

The Consequences of Imperialism

Since the decolonization of the European empires during the 1960s and 1970s, there have been attempts to evaluate the long-term consequences of imperialism for both metropolis and periphery. These evaluations have focused primarily upon the economic and social effects of imperialism on the former European colonies and secondarily upon certain European imperial powers themselves, particularly Britain. Much of this debate revolves around predictions by Marx that imperialism by the more-advanced capitalist powers (particularly Britain) would pave the way for the industrialization and modernization of the less-developed world. Capitalist imperialism would sweep away precapitalist social orders and integrate the economies of the less-developed world into an emergent world system of capitalist trade and production. Markets in the advanced capitalist world would facilitate the growth of export-oriented capitalism in the colonies, and industrial technologies imported from Europe would trigger industrialization on the European model. European industrialism provided preindustrial societies with an image of their own future development; thus, capitalist development would prepare the way for proletarian revolution on a world scale.

Marxist writers of the "New Left" during the 1950s and 1960s drew very different conclusions. For example, Andre Gunder Frank (1969) identified colonial rule as economically debilitating because it drained the colonies of wealth and natural resources in order to fuel metropolitan economic development. Frank's work focused primarily upon the experience of Latin America under Portuguese and Spanish rule but also considered the effects of informal imperialism by the United States in the twentieth century. Frank has argued that imperialism was characterized by "the development of underdevelopment," a process by which the colonial and informally ruled territories were depleted of their natural resources and their indigenous entrepreneurial classes were subdued for the benefit of the capitalist imperial economies. Indigenous political and economic elites (such as the great landowners involved in plantation agriculture producing for export) were engaged as collaborators and enjoyed considerable benefits, but the overall effect was to curtail any prospects of modernization or industrialization of the local economy. Though Frank's work on Latin America has been criticized, the wider notion of imperialism as a factor retarding economic development has attracted quite widespread support.

Finally, the effect of imperialism upon the metropolitan society has also come under scrutiny. Hobson, for example, was deeply concerned that imperial expansion encouraged the export of capital overseas, effectively denying domestic industrialists the finance they required for modernization. The outcome would be not only the deindustrialization of Britain but also its social and political domination by rentier interests with little commitment to the domestic economy. This view contrasted sharply with contemporary celebrations of empire by such groups as the Tariff Reform League in Britain and with the assumptions of most Marxist writers of the benefits of imperialism for its perpetrators. The debate is still continuing, and as the long-term consequences of decolonization unfold, the future priorities of historians and social scientists may lie in this area.

Anthony Webster

BIBLIOGRAPHY

Cain, Peter, and Anthony Hopkins, 1993. *British Imperialism*, 2 vols. New York: Longman.

Fieldhouse, David K., 1973. *Economics and Empire*. London: Weidenfeld and Nicolson.

Frank, Andre Gunder, 1969. *Capitalism and Underdevelopment in Latin America*. New York: Monthly Review Press.

Gallagher, John, and Ronald Robinson, 1953a. "The Imperialism of Free Trade." *Economic History Review* (2d series), vol. 6: 1–13.

———, 1953b. *Africa and the Victorians: The Official Mind of Imperialism*. London: Macmillan.

Hobson, John A., [1902] 1988. *Imperialism: A Study*. 3d ed. London: Unwin Hyman.

Khoo Kay Kim, 1972. *The Western Malay States 1850–73: The Effects of Commercial Development on Malay Politics*. Kuala Lumpur, Maylaya : Oxford University Press.

Lenin, Vladimir Ilyich, [1916] 1978. *Imperialism: The Highest Stage of Capitalism*. Reprint. Moscow: Progress Publishers.

Mun, Thomas, [1664] 1964. *England's Treasure from Foreign Trade*. Reprinted in Oxford: Blackwell.

O'Connor, J., 1970. "The Meaning of Economic Imperialism." In Robert I. Rhodes, ed., *Imperialism and Underdevelopment: A Reader*. New York: Monthly Review Press.

Said, Edward, 1993. *Culture and Imperialism* London: Chatto and Windus.

Schumpeter, Joseph, 1919. "The Sociology of Imperialisms." Reprinted in Joseph Schumpeter, 1951. *Imperialism and Social Classes* pp. 3–130. New York: Augustus M. Kelley.

Searle, G. R., 1971. *The Quest for National Efficiency*. Oxford: Blackwell.

Wakefield, Edward G., 1834. *England and America*. New York: Harper.

Wehler, Hans Ulrich, 1985. *The German Empire 1871–1918*. Leamington Spa: Berg.

IMPERIALISM, ECONOMIC.

Economic domination of one state by another; a general description of several theories that explain imperial expansion as an economically motivated phenomenon. Historians and social scientists tend to identify the term with the work of three analysts of imperialism: Hobson, Marx, and Lenin, but others have also subsequently contributed to this body of work, and some of their ideas have been summarized elsewhere. The preceding entry (see **imperialism**) has provided background knowledge of the wider issues of imperialism. This entry focuses on the work of Karl Marx, V. I. Lenin, and John A. Hobson. (Note that some of the main criticisms of their work and later contributions to their views are outlined in the imperialism entry.)

Marx and Lenin

Although Karl Marx ([1887] 1974) himself did not develop a specific theory of economic imperialism, his theory about the nature of capitalism did provide the basis for others to construct a model. It is therefore necessary to summarize Marx's ideas before outlining how V. I. Lenin derived his explanation of the emerging struggle between the imperialist powers in the early twentieth century.

Marx argued that the way in which wealth was produced was the determining factor in human social and historical development. Political and social power throughout history were held by the social groups (classes) that owned the means of producing wealth. Thus, in the preindustrial feudal societies of Europe, it was the landed aristocracy (personified by the monarch) who were the dominant social group. Their command over the means of producing wealth (agriculture) provided the wealth needed to maintain the military prowess required to sustain their authority. From this economic basis of power sprang social and religious institutions and a value system that legitimized aristocratic domination.

In the long run, growing agricultural surpluses, increasing purchasing power, and expanding trade promoted the emergence of new forms of wealth production. The growth of commerce (both international and domestic) increased the wealth of merchants and encouraged them to develop new technologies of production, a cumulative process that propelled, first, Britain and, then, the world economy into industrial capitalist development. The owners of this new means of producing wealth (the bourgeoisie) were ultimately able to challenge and supplant the aristocratic elite, ushering in a new epoch in which the bourgeoisie established itself as the dominant class, over a new class of urbanized industrial labor (the proletariat).

For Marx, the ultimate source of capitalist profit lay in the intense exploitation of the proletariat. The capitalist owned the means of production and the proletarian was forced by necessity to sell his labor on disadvantageous terms. Marx believed that the ultimate source of value of commodities was the quantity of labor it took to bring them into existence, and the capitalist secured his profit by effectively paying his workers less than the full value of their labor. Profit was thus surplus value extracted by the capitalist.

Early industrial capitalism was characterized by small-scale enterprises, with limited capital resources, engaged in cutthroat competition with each other. This fierce competition compelled capitalists constantly to seek ways of reducing costs of production (and therefore prices of their finished output) and improving the quality and desirability of the finished product. Competition was thus a prime motivator of an unprecedented degree of technological innovation designed to gain advantage in the market. Marx argued that this high rate of technological development—especially in the techniques of production—would lead in the long run to a falling profit rate. This result was possible because the costs of technological innovation would grow and would have to be incurred more frequently as scientific advancement accelerated. Although the amount of surplus value (profit) might increase in absolute terms, the high costs of new technologies would mean larger amounts of wealth being tied up in machinery and other fixed capital. Marx believed that eventually the rate of growth of fixed capital would exceed the rate of growth of profit, meaning that higher levels of investment would be needed to generate profits. In simple terms, the return per unit of investment would tend to fall in the long run, resulting in a squeeze on profits and threatening many capitalists with extinction.

One obvious response to this situation was to intensify exploitation of the proletariat by cutting wages to subsistence level, but Marx also noted that the profit rate could be bolstered by opening new sources of labor and raw materials in the less-developed parts of the world, where these factors of production were even cheaper. Herein lay the principal cause of imperial expansion—an attempt to curtail the fall in the profit rate by acquiring and exploiting tracts of virgin territory in the less-developed world.

V. I. Lenin's ([1916] 1978) refinement of this theory was written during World War I and was largely an attempt to explain the causes of that war, as well as to expand upon Marx's analysis. According to Lenin, the logical outcome of the ferocious competition of early capitalism described by Marx was the emergence of a relatively small number of large capitalist organizations, which would dominate the economies and societies of the industrialized countries. Drawing upon the work of Hobson and the Austrian economist Hilferding, Lenin argued that important characteristics of this later stage of capitalist development included a merging of bank and industrial capital, with the leading financial institutions taking an active part in the ownership and control of industry. The large firms were able to exert considerable control over their markets because there were so few of them, and they were able effectively to fix prices by agreement between them. Indeed, Lenin described this phase as "monopoly capitalism" because of the high concentration of control and market share in the hands of these large firms.

According to Lenin, monopoly capitalism emerged at the end of the nineteenth century in the leading industrial nations, particularly Britain, the United States, and Germany. In each of these countries, monopoly capitalism resulted in the political dominance of a small but extremely wealthy elite, able to insure that the state would act to protect its interests. As Marx had predicted, later capitalism had entailed progressive exploitation and impoverishment of the proletariat in order to resist the consequences of a falling profit rate. Deepening poverty and social inequality in the domestic market resulted in "underconsumption" (an idea taken from Hobson's work). Specifically, this was a problem stemming from the inability of the domestic

market to either provide an adequate market for the rapidly expanding productive capacity of industry or to furnish financial institutions and investors with sufficiently rewarding investment opportunities. Consequently, a feature of monopoly capitalism was the search overseas for new markets and new outlets for investment, with the power of the state being utilized by each nation's capitalist class to secure and protect new opportunities overseas.

Herein lay the cause not only of late-nineteenth-century European imperialism but also of the world conflict that erupted in 1914. This latter consequence resulted from the uneven pace of capitalist development between the advanced industrial powers. As the first industrial power, Britain had been able to construct a world order in which it not only governed a large portion of the less-developed world but also exercised control over the international financial system and world trade. These were advantages to be jealously defended, and which were inevitably challenged by newcomers such as Germany. It was from this rivalry that conflict, and, eventually, war were to arise. Thus, for Lenin, imperialism and war were inevitable consequences of the historical development of capitalism.

Hobson

J. A. Hobson, the English liberal journalist writing at the beginning of this century is best remembered for *Imperialism: A Study* ([1902] 1988), but Hobson's views on imperialism are also scattered through a wider body of literature in a series of articles published between the 1890s and 1910. Although he was aware of some theoretical studies of non-British imperialism, he was primarily concerned with the peculiarities of British expansionism, and this emphasis dominated his work.

Like Marx and Lenin, Hobson detected a distinctly economic facet of British imperialism, but whereas the Marxists saw imperialism as an inevitable product of capitalism, for Hobson it was a distortion of capitalist development that could be rectified without dispensing with capitalist free enterprise. Hobson located this economic "taproot" of imperialism in the emergent financial sector of Britain's economy, which in Hobson's view had amassed to itself a disproportionate degree of wealth and political influence. Hobson consciously distinguished industry from finance, emphasizing the modest scale and profits of British industrial firms and their location in the Celtic and northern fringes of Britain, away from the metropolitan center of power. Finance, in contrast, generated vast wealth and was well placed socially and geographically to influence government decisionmaking. Coupled with this hegemony of financiers, British society was also characterized by a gross maldistribution of wealth, with a small elite enjoying a growing share of national wealth in the face of an impoverished majority.

Here lay the economic origins of imperialism. Hobson noted that the expansion of productivity and productive capacity generated by industrialization necessitated the simultaneous growth of markets to absorb the increased production. The impoverished state of the mass of Britain's population prevented the domestic market from providing that expanding outlet, thereby forcing industrialists to seek overseas markets. This problem of domestic underconsumption also deprived the financiers of sufficiently profitable investment opportunities in domestic industry and compelled them to seek higher returns overseas, especially in the developing world, where raw materials and the demand for improvements to the economic infrastructure attracted investment.

From 1870, to protect these overseas investments, the financial interests increasingly used their strong political influence over the British state to secure the absorption of such territories into the British Empire. Hobson stressed that other groups, notably administrators, military officers, arms traders and missionaries also benefited from, and lobbied for, such expansion; but it was the financiers, who were so well placed politically, who were the main force behind imperial expansion. Thus, for Hobson, imperialism was largely a product of Britain's peculiar form of finance capitalism.

Hobson was fearful of the economic and social consequences of the continued export of capital and overseas imperial expansion. The unwillingness of financiers to invest in domestic industry threatened to undermine its competitiveness by denying it the latest innovations in technology and organization. Ultimately, this would lead to deindustrialization as foreign competitors drove British industry out of business, with terminal decline in Britain's position as an international power. The financiers and rentier capitalists who earned their incomes from foreign investment would be the only beneficiaries in this sorry scenario of national decay.

There are undoubtedly similarities between the work of Hobson and Lenin. This is unsurprising, given that Lenin drew heavily upon Hobson's work, especially with regard to concepts such as underconsumption. Some debate has ensued about the extent to which the two theories can be regarded as being effectively the same, and that controversy continues. Perhaps the most important point of departure between the two theories concerns the question of remedy. For Lenin, on one hand, imperialism was an inevitable and unavoidable consequence of capitalism, and no measure of reform could divert monopoly capitalism from its expansionist destiny. Hobson, on the other hand, saw the redistribution of wealth by social reform as a way of turning British capitalism away from imperialism. By increasing the incomes of the poorer section of the population, the problem of domestic underconsumption would be overcome, thereby boosting industry and financial investment in the domestic economy. The drive for overseas

colonies as outlets for capital export would diminish; and British capitalism would emerge strengthened and without the need for imperial expansion. It is here, on this question of the alleged dependence of the capitalist system upon imperialism, that the two theories diverge.

ANTHONY WEBSTER

BIBLIOGRAPHY

Barratt Brown, Michael, 1974. *The Economics of Imperialism.* Harmondsworth: Penguin.

Bukharin, Nikolai, [1917] 1972. *Imperialism and the World Economy.* Reprint. London: Merlin Press.

Hobson, John A., [1902] 1988. *Imperialism: A Study.* 3d. ed. London: Unwin Hyman.

Hodgart, Alan, 1977. *The Economics of European Imperialism.* London: Edward Arnold.

Lenin, Vladimir Ilyich, [1916] 1978. *Imperialism: The Highest Stage of Capitalism.* Reprint. Moscow: Progress Publishers.

Marx, Karl, [1887] 1974. *Capital.* Reprint. London: Lawrence and Wishart.

Porter, Andrew, 1994. *European Imperialism 1860–1914.* London: Macmillan.

IMPLEMENTATION.

IMPLEMENTATION. Activities that carry out authoritative public policy directives or mandates (e.g., statutes, executive orders, judicial orders); the stage in the policy process that follows the formal adoption of a policy and precedes the evaluation or assessment of a policy's impact on society. Implementation typically involves a wide range of actors with diverse interests and competing goals, including formal policymakers, bureaucratic officials from all levels of government (i.e., local, state, national), private sector organizations, nonprofit organizations, clientele groups, and other interested citizen groups. Typical activities include procuring resources (e.g., personnel, equipment, space, money), interpreting policy directives, planning, communicating and negotiating among implementing organizations and clientele groups, and the delivery of a service. Academic research on policy implementation can be classified into three phases or generations, each of which is discussed later.

First-Generation Implementation Studies

In the early 1970s, scholarly attention turned to the issues of policy implementation. Prior to this time, implementation generally was treated as automatic, as informed by a classical model of administration. Early implementation research was descriptive and relied on a case-study approach that provided few generalizations across cases. These studies focusing on the barriers to effective implementation did little more than identify a list of what could go wrong.

Jeffrey Pressman and Aaron Wildavsky's ([1973] 1984) classic study highlights the problems of policy implementation and is representative of this early research. They studied a United States Economic Development Administration effort to create 3,000 jobs for the unemployed inner-city residents of Oakland, California. A large number of interested groups, with varying interests and objectives, were to be involved in a wide range of administrative decisions during planning. Pressman and Wildavsky identified the "complexity of joint action" inherent in this program as sufficient to hamper implementation efforts. They subtitled the third edition of this classic work: *How Great Expectations in Washington Are Dashed in Oakland; or Why It's Amazing That Federal Programs Work At All.*

A pessimistic conclusion regarding the effectiveness of government programs emerged from this collection of case studies (e.g., Derthick 1972; Murphy 1973; Pressman and Wildavsky [1973]1984; Bardach 1977). The observation that an inevitable gap exists between the goals articulated in legislation and the outcomes of the programs as delivered, led to the inescapable conclusion that government programs indeed were generally ineffective. The implicit assumption was that major failures in policy are generally the result of failures in implementation. This conclusion is represented by the following quote from Eugene Bardach (1977), "Even the most robust policy—one that is well designed to survive the implementation process—will tend to go awry. The classic symptoms of underperformance, delay, and escalating costs are bound to appear" (p. 5).

Second-Generation Implementation Studies

By the early 1980s, a second generation of implementation research emerged that is characterized by an effort to develop a broader theoretical understanding of the policy implementation process. Scholars sought to develop conceptual frameworks to explain implementation success (or failure) or modifications to policy that occur during service delivery. Two distinct approaches have been utilized in this effort to build a framework of implementation: top-down and bottom-up.

Top-Down Approach

Consistent with earlier research, scholars associated with the top-down approach (e.g., Van Meter and Van Horn 1975; Edwards 1980; Sabatier and Mazmanian 1980; O'Toole and Montjoy 1984) assume a rational, hierarchical view of the public policy process that is based on a traditional notion of political accountability. Elected officials are seen as the legitimate policymakers as they can be directly held accountable to citizens through the electoral process. It is the responsibility of these officials to formulate policy and to hand it down to bureaucrats for action. Instructions are formulated at the top of these bureaucratic

organizations and passed down to street-level bureaucrats to be carried out without discretion. It is assumed that key bureaucratic officials possess the ability to control the organizations under their direction.

Thus, in the hands of bureaucrats, implementation is merely a technical matter. Implementation aims to deliver policies that are true to the policymakers' intent as initially written. Policy is a stable product of policy formulation activities and marks the beginning of the implementation stage. Successful implementation occurs when the intent of policy, the stated objectives, is met. Any deviation from these formal objectives is undesirable. Unfortunately, something typically interferes with the implementation of policy as formally articulated.

The focus of top-down research is on the gap between legislative intent and bureaucratic action. If the reasons for this inevitable gap can be understood, policy can be designed and implementation processes can be structured to achieve bureaucratic action true to the intentions of legitimate policymakers. Hence, a primary objective is the development of empirical theory that accurately predicts implementation success or failure. Top-down research typically relies upon positivist assumptions and related methodological tools.

The first top-down model was developed by Donald Van Meter and Carl Van Horn (1975). This model identified six variables that shape the links between policy and performance: policy standards and objectives; policy resources; interorganizational communication and enforcement activities; characteristics of the implementing agencies; economic, social, and political conditions; and the disposition of implementors. They hypothesize that implementation will be most successful where only marginal change is required and goal consensus is high. In general, successful implementation requires that bureaucrats in implementing agencies know what they are suppose to do, are willing to do it, and possess sufficient organizational capacity to do it.

The most comprehensive list of factors affecting implementation was offered by Paul Sabatier and Daniel Mazmanian (1980), who identify seventeen variables that affect the achievement of statutory objectives throughout the implementation process. In this framework, variables are grouped in the following three categories: tractability of the problem, ability of statute to structure implementation, and nonstatutory variables affecting implementation. They concluded that successful implementation is likely to occur under the following conditions. First, formal policy objectives are stated in a clear and consistent manner. Second, the policy is based on sound theory regarding the nature of the problem and impact of relevant solutions. Third, sufficient authority is granted to implementing officials to structure implementation and affect target group behavior. Fourth, leaders of implementing agencies possess the necessary political and managerial skills and are committed to official policy goals. Fifth, the program receives sufficient political support by constituent groups and key legislators. Sixth, the relative priority of the policy's goals are not diminished over time.

Top-down scholars view the implementation process from the perspective of the formal policymaker and accept that it typically occurs within an interorganizational context. The likelihood of successful implementation is increased if the policy is based on sound theory regarding the causes of the behaviors targeted for change. Additionally, this approach has identified legal and political variables that can be manipulated by policymakers to constrain the behavior of street-level bureaucrats and target groups. Although complete control as assumed in a hierarchical model is impossible, such behavior can be kept within acceptable bounds to increase the likelihood of implementation success. Laurence O'Toole, Jr., (1986) has identified principles that serve as the conventional wisdom of the top-down perspective: (1) design policies to keep the degree of required behavioral change low, (2) simplify the structure of implementation and minimize the number of actors, (3) seek more consideration of the problems of implementation during policy formation, and (4) leave the responsibilities of implementation among units sympathetic to the policy.

The centralized, hierarchical, rational view of the policy process held by top-down scholars has been challenged as an inaccurate description of reality. First, it is argued that policies are often vague due to the necessity of compromise in political decision making. Often, objectives are not clearly articulated to provide a guide for formulating bureaucratic actions or a baseline against which implementation efforts can be judged. Second, the top-down approach presents policy as static. The formulation stage is assumed to end once policy is officially adopted. Instead, policies often are unstable; they change during implementation in response to modifications in political support and the changing nature of public problems. Third, there is little room for bureaucratic discretion in the top-down approach. The role of street-level bureaucrats is devalued as impediments to successful implementation. However, the vagueness of official policy statements and the need for expertise of bureaucratic officials provides much room for the influence of bureaucrats on the shape of public policy. Fourth, the top-down approach ignores those policy initiatives that are generated by street-level bureaucrats, the private sector, and sources other than formal policymakers.

Bottom-Up Approach

In contrast to the top-down perspective, the bottom-up or "backward mapping" approach (e.g., Lipsky 1971; Elmore 1979; Hjern 1982) to policy implementation views policy as dynamic and the result of a decentralized process. Given the vague nature of official policy statements and the need for expertise, bureaucrats possess a substantial amount of discretion. Given that implementation generally involves several organizations or sets of actors, numerous opportunities are presented for the continual shaping of public policy. Official policymakers cannot anticipate the difficulties of program delivery, so policies are modified by street-level bureaucrats to insure that the needs of affected clientele are properly addressed. Formulation and implementation activities blur together, for policy is constantly being redefined by bureaucrats and affected clientele. Street-level bureaucrats are crucial actors in the implementation process. An accurate description of the policy process must incorporate the actions and attitudes of street-level bureaucrats and their clientele.

Bottom-up scholars view policy implementation as an adaptive process. Implementation involves bargaining and accommodating policy goals and strategies between bureaucrats delivering services and the clients of government programs. Numerous interests engage in a struggle to effect the outcome of policy. Implementation involves continuous problem solving during service delivery. In this view, policy implementation is an extension of the pluralistic process of legislative institutions and is quite democratic.

Under this approach, successful implementation cannot be objectively examined and thus is not easily defined. In the top-down approach, modifications of policy during implementation (i.e., a gap between legislative intent and program output) are a sign of failure; for bottom-up scholars goal modification is unavoidable and even desirable. Multiple meanings occur in the language of any formally adopted policy. Policy intentions are a matter of perceptions, and implementation helps to unfold perceptions of intentions inherent in policy language. Implementation success cannot easily be measured against objective goals. The success of a policy can be judged in relation to nearly anything that is relevant to the policy issue.

Bottom-up research studies the effect that different perspectives (i.e., interpretations and meanings) have on implementation efforts. Implementation is not the simple enactment of stated objectives, but involves persuading others to see one's interpretation of the policy. Policy intentions cannot be understood outside the context of implementation. The top-down researcher begins with formally articulated policy goals, and the bottom-up researcher starts by identifying the network of actors involved in service delivery in a policy area. The focus is on identifying the interactions of these actors by understanding "their goals, strategies, activities, and contacts" pertaining to a policy problem (Lester *et al.* 1987, p. 204). As Sabatier has written, "[Bottom-uppers] are not primarily concerned with the implementation (carrying out) of a policy per se but rather with understanding actor interaction in a specific policy sector" (1986, p. 36). In contrast to the top-down focus on predictive theory, bottom-up research is concerned with developing an explanatory theory.

Consequently, scholars conclude that bottom-up policies generally are more successful than indicated by the narrow definition of program success employed by the top-down approach, because the bottom-up approach permits examining the full range of policies that impact a particular policy problem. Evaluating a single program on its own ignores the complexity that results from interrelated programs addressing the same social condition. The bottom-up approach also focuses on policy over a longer period of time, allowing for the gradual impact of policy on a public problem. Because bottom-up scholars do not focus on a particular formal objective, they are able to see a wide range of policy consequences, some of which are unintended (Sabatier 1986).

The methodological tools built on positivist assumptions have limited utility for bottom-up scholars. For instance, Charles Fox (1990) has identified the need to transcend positivism to understand bottom-up implementation. He has argued that an interpretive approach accepts the existence of multiple policy interpretations and seeks to foster an understanding of these different perspectives among relevant actors.

The primary critique of the bottom-up approach to implementation is that it weakens the importance of political accountability inherent in the American political system. It is one thing to state that street-level bureaucrats possess expertise about conditions for policy implementation, but the resulting discretion must be exercised within some bounds established by a centralized political authority. A related concern is that the bottom-up approach defines what policies should be pursued by what policies can be effectively carried out by bureaucratic organizations. Again, this implication is troubling, as it reduces the authority and significance of formal policymakers.

Third-Generation Implementation Studies

Although much has been learned about policy implementation from the top-down and bottom-up approaches, second-generation research is characterized by several shortcomings. It is characterized by theoretical pluralism (no adequate overarching theory to explain and predict) and is noncumulative. This research also is based on a restricted view of the nature of policy implementation in that it emphasizes a short time frame, case studies, single measures of implementation success, and either a top-down or a bottom-up approach. In response to these and other shortcomings of second-generation scholarship, the third-generation implementation research presents an effort to synthesize parts of both approaches to develop a more

complete theory of policy implementation (e.g., Elmore 1985; Sabatier 1986; Lester et al. 1987; Goggin et al. 1990).

Richard Elmore's (1985) "forward and backward mapping" combines a focus on the motivations of street-level bureaucrats and target groups (backward mapping) with a consideration of the policy instruments and resources available to policymakers to constrain behavior of these actors (forward mapping). Implementation demands both. His framework is geared primarily to aiding policy practitioners.

Paul Sabatier (1986) emphasizes theory-building. Drawing from the bottom-up approach (i.e., its unit of analysis), he has examined the strategies employed by relevant actors as they attempt to deal with the policy issue as it relates to their own objectives. This method is combined with the top-down concern with the legal and socioeconomic factors that structure (or restrict) the behavior or bureaucrats and target groups, and the validity of the causal assumptions underlying policies and their programs. Attention is shifted from policy implementation to policy change as a longer time frame (e.g., 10 to 20 years) is adopted.

Similarly, Malcolm Goggin et al. (1990) have integrated top-down and bottom-up variables in their model of intergovernmental policy implementation. State implementation of policy is a function of the inducements and constraints provided by other components in the federal system and the state's likelihood and ability to act to achieve its own objectives. This model represents the dynamic nature of the implementation process by focusing on policy evolution across decades.

In general, third-generation research is set apart from earlier studies by the following characteristics. First, it addresses the dynamic nature of policy implementation by focusing on policy over a long time. Hence, it is concerned with policy learning or evolution. Second, it synthesizes components of both top-down and bottom-up approaches in an effort to develop a more complete theoretical framework of the implementation process. Third, these scholars contend that it moves beyond the second-generation concern with theory-building and will enable them to engage in more rigorous quantitative hypothesis testing. Fourth, it encourages a comparative emphasis to go beyond case studies and compare implementation efforts across jurisdictions and types of policies. Fifth, third-generation research embraces a multimethod or "mixed-method" approach (e.g., regression techniques, time series analysis, dynamic modeling, network analysis, elite interviewing, content analysis).

Although third-generation research holds promise for developing a fuller understanding of the implementation process, it has yet to be fully applied. Thus far, less effort has gone into empirically applying and testing these theories. To accomplish this task, scholars must overcome the following obstacles: define precisely what constitutes implementation activities, identify the crucial variables for implementation, adopt designs that are comparative and longitudinal, and develop measures of policy changes over time.

Conclusion

Implementation is defined as activities that carry out authoritative public policy directives or mandates. Pressman and Wildavsky's ([1973] 1984) classic study stimulated early research on policy implementation. Prior to this time, implementation generally was treated as an automatic process in line with the tenets of the classical model of administration.

Three generations of research characterize the academic literature on implementation. First-generation studies relied on case studies to identify common barriers to effective implementation, providing a pessimistic conclusion regarding the effectiveness of government programs. Second-generation research sought to develop theoretical frameworks to explain or understand the implementation process by utilizing either a top-down or bottom-up perspective. Top-down scholars focus on the gap between the policymakers' intent and bureaucratic action. In contrast, bottom-up research views policy implementation as bargaining or adaptation. The latter approach is consistent with contemporary management theory, which is moving away from centralized bureaucracy toward devolving responsibility to the lowest level of the organization (i.e., empowering the worker). Third-generation research synthesizes components of the top-down and bottom-up approaches in an effort to develop a more complete theoretical framework of policy implementation. Although its proponents see much potential in third-generation research, its contributions have yet to be fully demonstrated.

DAVID J. HOUSTON

BIBLIOGRAPHY

Bardach, Eugene, 1977. *The Implementation Game: What Happens After a Bill Becomes a Law.* Cambridge, MA: MIT Press.
Derthick, Martha, 1972. *New Towns in Town.* Washington, DC: Urban Institute.
Edwards, George C., III, 1980. *Implementing Public Policy.* Washington, DC: Congressional Quarterly Press.
Elmore, Richard F., 1979. "Backward Mapping." *Political Science Quarterly* 94: 601–616.
———, 1985. "Forward and Backward Mapping: Reversible Logic in the Analysis of Public Policy." In K. Hanf and T.A.J. Toonen, eds., *Policy Implementation in Federal and Unitary Systems.* Dordrecht: Martinus Nijhoff.
Fox, Charles J., 1990. "Implementation Research: Why and How to Transcend Positivist Methodologies." In Dennis J. Palumbo and Donald J. Calista, eds., *Implementation and the Policy Process: Opening Up the Black Box.* New York: Greenwood Press.

Goggin, Malcolm L., Ann O'M. Bowman, James P. Lester, and Laurence J. O'Toole, Jr., 1990. *Implementation Theory and Practice: Toward a Third Generation.* Glenview, IL: Scott, Foresman/Little, Brown.
Hjern, Benny, 1982. "Implementation Research: The Link Gone Missing." *Journal of Public Policy,* 2: 301–308.
Lester, James P., Ann O'M. Bowman, Malcolm L. Goggin, and Laurence J. O'Toole, Jr., 1987. "Public Policy Implementation: Evolution of the Field and Agenda for Future Research." *Policy Studies Review* 7: 200–216.
Lipsky, Michael, 1971. "Street Level Bureaucracy and the Analysis of Urban Reform." *Urban Affairs Quarterly* 6: 391–409.
Murphy, Jerome T., 1973. "The Education Bureaucracies Implement Novel Policy: The Politics of Title I of ESEA." In Allan P. Sindelar, ed., *Policy and Politics in America.* Boston: Little, Brown.
O'Toole, Laurence J., Jr., 1986. "Policy Recommendations for Multi-Actor Implementation: An Assessment of the Field." *Journal of Public Policy* 6: 181–210.
O'Toole, Laurence, J., Jr., and Robert S. Montjoy, 1984. "Interorganizational Policy Implementation: A Theoretical Perspective." *Public Administration Review* 49: 491–503.
Pressman, Jeffrey, and Aaron Wildavsky, [1973] 1984. *Implementation.* 3d ed. Berkeley, CA: University of California Press.
Sabatier, Paul A., 1986. "Top-Down and Bottom-Up Approaches to Implementation Research: A Critical Analysis and Suggested Synthesis." *Journal of Public Policy* 6: 21–48.
Sabatier, Paul, and Daniel Mazmanian, 1980. "The Implementation of Public Policy: A Framework of Analysis." *Policy Studies Journal* 8: 538–560.
Van Meter, Donald S., and Carl E. Van Horn, 1975. "The Policy Implementation Process: A Conceptual Framework." *Administration and Society* 6: 445–488.

IMPLIED POWERS. Prerogatives that, although not specifically enumerated in a constitution, may be inferred from powers expressly granted. For example, the power to institute a draft is a power that is implied from the United States Constitution's enumerated power to raise armies and navies. The doctrine of implied powers under the United States Constitution was most clearly articulated by Chief Justice John Marshall and the United States Supreme Court in the landmark case of *McCulloch v. Maryland* (1819). Their broad interpretation of implied powers was extremely important in the development of the national government and administration of the United States since it limited state encroachments on federal power and allowed government to expand into policy areas not expressly defined by the Constitution. Implied powers have made it possible to retain the United States Constitution largely intact (only 26 amendments), though it was written for a far different, simpler era.

The doctrine of implied powers expanded upon the powers of the national government suggested in essay number 45 of *The Federalist Papers* (see Rossiter 1961), wherein James Madison wrote, "The powers delegated by the proposed Constitution . . . are few and defined. Those which are to remain in the State Governments are numerous and indefinite." In 1804, in the case of *U.S. v. Fisher*, the Supreme Court seemed to suggest that implied powers were highly restricted: "Under a constitution conferring specific powers, the power contended for must be granted, or it cannot be exercised." However, rapid changes in American society led to a number of new problems and situations, which resulted in a more expansive view of powers not enumerated in the Constitution.

The *McCulloch* case arose over the controversial National Bank, first approved in the 1790s. Although it was popular with the Federalists, the bank was despised by Democrats and many of the states. In 1818, the state of Maryland levied a tax of US$15,000 on the Baltimore branch of the National Bank. The officers of the bank refused to pay, and James McCulloch, the bank's cashier, was sued for payment. The state court upheld the tax, but the case was appealed to the United States Supreme Court. Daniel Webster represented the National Bank and, in oral arguments before the Court, made an eloquent defense of a broad interpretation of the powers of the national government. Chief Justice Marshall and the Court, sympathetic to Webster's arguments, ruled against the Maryland tax of the National Bank with a sweeping interpretation of the scope of implied powers.

The Court held that Congress had the authority to create a National Bank because of Article I, section 8 of the Constitution, which allowed the national government to take actions "necessary and proper" to carry out powers explicitly granted. The Court ruled that neither Maryland nor any other state had the authority to tax a creation of the federal government since it reflected the sovereign will of all of the people. Noting that "the power to tax is the power to destroy," the Court, in establishing broad implied powers (see Gunther 1969), established the supremacy of federal policy over state policy. Marshall's expansive views of implied powers expressed in 1819 is one of the most famous passages in United States history: "Let the end be legitimate, let it be within the scope of the Constitution, and all means which are appropriate, which are plainly adapted to that end, which are not prohibited, but consistent with the letter and spirit of the Constitution, are constitutional."

Implied powers of the United States government have been of critical importance in a number of policies and regulatory areas. One of the more wide-ranging interpretations concerns the power vested in Congress to regulate interstate commerce. As the economy industrialized in the last half of the nineteenth century, the enumerated power to regulate interstate commerce formed the basis of the implied power of the government to create bureaucracies and regulations to carry out this power. In 1887, Congress created the Interstate Commerce Commission (ICC), the nation's first regulatory agency. The broad sweep of implied powers in relation to the commerce clause was demonstrated by the 1964 Civil Rights Act, which used that power to provide a constitutional means of guaranteeing open accommodation in hotels and restaurants in the South.

A related category of constitutional powers are the implied powers of each of the three branches of the United States government. Often referred to as inherent powers, they are related to the authority necessary to each branch's ability to carry out its enumerated responsibilities. Inherent powers of Congress, for example, include the power to hold hearing, conduct investigations, and subpoena witnesses. The power of executive privilege has been recognized by the Supreme Court as sometimes necessary for the president to carry out the functions of office. Alexander Hamilton first discussed the principle of inherent executive powers in essay number 74 of *The Federalist Papers* (Rossiter 1961).

By the courts taking an expansive view of implied powers under the United States Constitution, they paved the way for the expansion of national government, its supremacy over the states, and its ability to adapt to a wide range of policy issues—from environmental protection to affirmative action—never envisioned by the Founders. Implied powers have diminished the need to amend the Constitution or to rewrite it every generation, as Thomas Jefferson and others envisioned. Some critics believe that the courts have gone too far in expanding the scope of implied powers, particularly with regard to state prerogatives. In discussing the implied powers under the commerce clause in a 1981 case, Justice William H. Rehnquist noted that "one of the greatest 'fictions' of our federal system is that the Congress exercises only those powers delegated to it, while the remainder are reserved to the States of to the people" (*Hodel v. Virginia Surface Mining*, 1981).

LANCE T. LELOUP

BIBLIOGRAPHY

Gunther, Gerald, ed., 1969. *John Marshall's Defense of McCulloch v. Maryland.* Stanford: Stanford University Press.
Peltason, J. W., 1973. *Understanding the Constitution.* Hinsdale, IL: Dryden Press.
Rossiter, Clinton L., 1961. *The Federalist Papers; Alexander Hamilton, James Madison, John Jay.* (espec. nos. 45, 74.) New York: New American Library.

IMPOUNDMENT. Any executive branch action to withhold or delay spending funds appropriated by a legislative body. There are two general categories or impoundments: deferrals and rescissions.

The budgeting process consists of four main phases. These are: (1) the executive branch budget formulation and the transmittal of the chief executive's budget recommendations to the legislative branch; (2) legislative action, including the hearing and appropriations process; (3) budget execution and control; and (4) budget assessment and evaluation by the appropriate body.

The term "impoundment" of funds refers to actions by the executive branch during the budget execution phase to limit the expenditure of funds appropriated by a legislative body during phase three of the budgetary process. Conceptually, an impoundment can be considered a "control action" of the executive branch, undertaken for financial or policy reasons. Such actions may consist of a "deferral" or delay of expenditure or a "rescission," which reduces expenditures for programs and agencies by simply not allowing agencies to spend appropriated sums (*Congressional Digest* 1993).

Impoundments have been used most frequently by the federal government. Such actions are the only fiscal tools available for the President to attempt to constrain the expenditure of funds once the budget has been passed by Congress (Wlezien 1994). By contrast, most of the states allow governors the use of a line-item veto as a means of intervention in the postappropriation process. Therefore, the use of impoundments has generally been limited at the state level.

Key policy issues regarding impoundment actions involve the duration or the intention of such actions: whether the President's intent is permanent cancellation of the expenditures in question (rescission) or merely a temporary delay in availability (deferral). Rescissions have led to the greatest executive-legislative branch confrontations due to legislative body concerns regarding the thwarting of legislative intent by such executive branch actions. By contrast, deferrals have been less contentious, as it has been recognized that such actions might be natural outcomes of efforts to accomplish greater efficiency of government operations.

The importance of executive branch "intent" in determining the level of legislative-executive disagreement regarding impoundments can be visualized by comparing impoundment actions of the Lyndon Johnson and Richard Nixon presidencies. During his term, President Johnson actively impounded funds by deferring appropriated funds for the Vietnam War effort as a strategy of reducing the economic and, especially, the inflationary impact of the war on the United States economy. Although such actions were the result of policy considerations, the intent of the President was to delay expenditures temporarily rather than to reduce expenditures permanently after Congress had appropriated the funds for defense procurement. Such temporary expenditure delays created limited conflict with legislative intent. And President Johnson's consultation with Congress regarding the purpose of his actions limited the confrontation between the executive and legislative branches regarding those impoundments (*Congressional Digest* 1993).

President Nixon also used impoundments for a policy purpose. In contrast to President Johnson's policy goal of "temporarily" delaying defense procurements for economic reasons, President Nixon's policy purpose was to reduce permanently the expenditures for certain federal programs (such as subsidized housing, community development, disaster assistance, farm programs, and for implementation of the Clean Water Act). Such actions, made with the public purpose of reducing congressional appropriations, led to serious conflict and confrontation between the administration and Congress, which was concerned about the usurpation of the expenditure authorization authority of Congress (*Congressional Digest* 1993).

These confrontations over impoundment led to the passage of the Congressional Budget Reform and Impoundment Control Act of 1974 and various efforts to restore programs subjected to Nixon's rescission actions. The act, among other provisions, made a distinction between "rescissions," whose "intent" was to cancel or permanently reduce program expenditures, and "deferrals," whose "intent" was to delay temporarily the expenditure of appropriated funds by the executive branch for efficiency or other reasons. Other provisions of the 1974 Act included requirements that the executive branch inform Congress of both rescissions and deferrals, along with specified information regarding such actions. In addition, the act gave the comptroller general the responsibility to inform Congress of unreported impoundment actions or the misreporting of such actions (*Congressional Digest* 1993).

The 1974 reform, though providing formal means of executive-legislative branch communications regarding impoundment, did not end all impoundment controversies. An original provision of the act, which permitted the executive branch to continue deferrals within the fiscal year, unless disapproved by one house of Congress (an action known as a one-house veto), was found unconstitutional by the Supreme Court in *I.N.S. v. Chadha* in 1983. Even though the decision initially had little impact on impoundment policy, the President, in his 1987 budget proposal, identified a lengthy list of deferrals, which brought objections from private interests and members of Congress, who challenged the President's deferral authority in court. In a 1986 federal district court ruling, eventually upheld on appeal in 1987, it was determined that the president no longer held deferral authority (as prescribed by the Act) because such authority could not be separated from the one-house veto aspect of the law, which was dismissed in the 1983 case. The series of court actions that followed the 1974 Reform were codified in the 1987 Balanced Budget Reaffirmation Act (Section 206). Specifically, the 1987 act eliminated policy deferrals and constrained the use of deferrals to contingency situations, for efficiency reasons, or for conditions specifically permitted by law (*Congressional Digest* 1993).

Given the original 1974 legislation and clarifying court actions, appropriations targeted for rescission by a president must be approved by both houses of Congress within 45 days of "continuous session" or they will be available for obligation. As a matter of practice, the continuous session requirement translates into approximately 60 to 75 calendar days. Thus, rescissions remain a presidential fiscal policy option even though proposed rescissions must now be formally authorized by congressional action (*Congressional Digest* 1993).

As indicated, the impoundment of appropriated funds (both rescissions and deferrals) have been used by presidents in budget and expenditure battles because they are the only fiscal policy tools available to the president to affect spending after the appropriation process is complete. Such actions may be initiated either for policy or for efficiency reasons.

Recent congressional actions severely restricted the use of rescissions, but deferrals are permitted under specific conditions. By contrast, the use of impoundments by governors has been limited. Quite possibly, the urge to utilize the impoundment option as a fiscal policy management tool at the state level has been limited because most governors have the opportunity to use the line-item veto to attempt to eliminate appropriations that they disagree with for either policy or efficiency reasons. The line-item veto has only recently (1996) emerged as a formal option for the president, but the issue of impoundments will likely continue as an issue of controversy between the president and Congress.

MERL HACKBART

BIBLIOGRAPHY

"Impoundment and the Item Veto," 1993. *Congressional Digest* (February): 34–39.
Wlezien, Christopher, 1994. "The Politics of Impoundments." *Political Research Quarterly* (March): 59–84.

INCENTIVE PAY. The use of extrinsic monetary and intrinsic psychological rewards to motivate increased or enhanced employee effort and performance (see **pay-for-performance and performance appraisal**).

Strategic pay requires that all decisions relative to compensation and benefits be designed to attract, retain, or motivate employees. As such, the entire organization's reward structure is designed to serve its mission or purpose fully. In reality, most organization's limit incentive pay to only a portion of the compensation package (see **compensation policy and fringe benefits**). All employees who perform satisfactorily are guaranteed a set base pay and benefits package. Even so, this guarantee serves to calm fears with regard to financial security and, hence, helps attract and retain individuals.

Extrinsic Rewards

Extrinsic incentives are, primarily, the use of monetary rewards as a motivating factor (see **pay-for-performance** for

a more detailed discussion of extrinsic monetary rewards). Career development and training opportunities (see **training and development**) that can lead to promotion or to interesting, fulfilling assignments (which also provide intrinsic motivation through their recognition of merit) are another source of extrinsic motivation in the sense that, in addition to higher compensation levels, they pay individuals in terms of power and responsibility.

Intrinsic Rewards

The formal focus on the existence of intrinsic incentives as a part of incentive pay began with the development of industrial psychology following World War I. Scholars and practitioners who applied Frederick W. Taylor's (1856–1915) principles of scientific management noticed serious discrepancies with respect to its motivational aspects. Scientific management had heretofore dealt with employee motivation as a simple extrinsic function; for the most part, it was a simple task of relating salary to work. Totally ignored was the human dimension inherent in work. In the era's art deco culture, this human dimension was seen as harkening back to medieval craft notions instead of serving as a harbinger of modernity.

Because employers' experienced difficulties in their early efforts at using scientific management, due to employee resistance and a lack of motivation, they turned to psychologists (who had already begun to develop the tests used in selecting workers) for motivational answers on how to deal with these "sick" workers. For example, the Hawthorne experiments (1924–1932) at Western Electric Company's Hawthorne, Illinois, plant, conducted by Elton Mayo (1889–1949) and Fritz Roethlisberger (1898–1974), highlighted this problem for management and contributed to the study of organizational productivity (see **Hawthorne studies**). Following this type of study came scholars from the human relations school, who focused on the intrinsic human aspects of motivation as a part of incentives. The popular contemporary motivational theories, Abraham Maslow's (1908–1970) "needs hierarchy," Frederick Herzberg's (1923–) "Two-Factor Motivation Hygiene-Motivator Theory," and David McCelland's (1917–) "achievement, affiliation, and power needs" theory, helped to establish intrinsic motivation as an important dimension (see **Maslow, Abraham**).

Maslow posited that human beings possessed preexisting, innate needs for sociability, recognition, and self-actualization (more recently, C. P. Alderfer condensed or simplified these to "relatedness and growth needs"). All of these are inherently psychological concepts intrinsic to the individual. Yet, because they are innate needs, these intrinsic factors serve to motivate individuals (by fulfilling physiological and safety needs) just as do extrinsic rewards.

For the public sector, intrinsic rewards are doubly appealing. First, intrinsic motivation programs are relatively less expensive than extrinsic schemes. The employee values the intrinsic rewards for their recognized symbolic or trophy qualities. Second, the public sector, with its inherent pursuit of the public interest and general welfare, is in a far better and easier position to emphasize and convince people of the symbolic importance or worth of its activities.

Practice in the United States varies quite widely (as it does for pay-for-performance schemes). The use of employee recognition awards, however, is quite widespread.

Certificates and plaques along with newsletters highlight outstanding employees with recognition. Flextime, vacation scheduling priorities, or extra time off might all serve as recognition awards. Special equipment (or being among the first to obtain additions) for the employee's office can also serve as a recognition award.

More "substantial" intrinsic rewards can also be offered, such as dinners, trips to seminars, or even merchandise (often donated by private sector organizations and individuals). A physical recognition award, whether it is a certificate of merit or a television, has added value because it is a trophy; it is also an object that constantly serves to remind individuals of their accomplishments and the organization's appreciation.

Variations in intrinsic reward practices do occur. The extent to which local society favorably views public employment may determine how cooperative external actors are (whether the reward involves donations or space in a local newspaper for employee recognition). State laws and local ordinances may also limit the extent to which even small financial expenditures are allowed.

Of course, the manner in which political leaders and administrative managers approach the intrinsic reward process is also highly important. Substantial rewards lose their trophy value (and engender negative memories) if they are awarded begrudgingly. If rewards are undeserved or universal (everyone a winner), their value is eroded. A truly friendly smile and heartfelt thank you can be more meaningful than the formal award itself.

Regimes based on monarchical governments enjoy the opportunity to include prominent civil servants on their "honors lists," conferring various knighthoods and, in exceptional cases, peerages and life peerages. Because of their ties to a country's historical traditions and ceremonies, for example, these types of rewards are highly valued as symbols that recognize career accomplishments. Military-based systems, of course, use the full array of medals and ribbons associated with the armed forces as intrinsic awards in addition to other forms of incentive pay.

DENNIS M. DALEY

BIBLIOGRAPHY

Greiner, John M., Harry P. Hatry, Margo P. Koss, Annie P. Millar, and Jane P. Woodward, 1981. *Productivity and Motiva-tion: A Review of State and Local Government Initiatives.* Washington, DC: Urban Institute.

Lawler, Edward E., III, 1990. *Strategic Pay: Aligning Organizational Strategies and Pay Systems.* San Francisco: Jossey-Bass.

Milkovich, George T., and Alexandra K. Wigdor, eds., with Ranae F. Broderick and Anne S. Mavor, 1991. *Pay for Performance: Evaluating Performance Appraisal and Merit Pay.* Washington, DC: National Academy Press.

INCOME TAXES.

Taxes levied on the income accrued during a specific period by an individual or other unit. Income is defined as the money or other gain received over a period of time by an individual, corporation, or other entity from labor or service rendered; from sales of products, services, or property; from earnings on property, natural resources, or investments; or from other sources. Income taxes vary in structure and impact by the type of unit to which they are applied (individuals, partnerships, corporations, etc.) and by the government that is applying the tax (federal or state). Discussions about the yield response, collectability, equity, and economic effects of income taxes, then, must be specific to the type of income tax being levied and to the taxing jurisdiction.

The Federal Individual Income Tax

The United States adopted an income tax in 1913. Doing so required an amendment to the United States Constitution, as the government had prohibited any direct taxes that were not apportioned among the states according to population. Such apportionment would have limited any direct taxation to a "head" tax not linked to the income of the state. Prior to 1913, the predominant sources of government revenues had been derived from customs taxes and other trade related fees. With the expansion of the federal government that occurred in the early 1900s and the potential involvement in World War I, the need for new sources of revenue became more apparent. The Sixteenth Amendment to the Constitution was passed to create the income tax as that source. It provided that "Congress shall have the power to lay and collect taxes on income, from whatever source derived, without apportionment among the several States."

Initially, the levels of income effected by the federal income tax were high, and only a small proportion of comparatively high-income people were subjected to the tax. Across time, the generous exemptions that were included in earlier versions of the tax were lowered, as was the minimum taxable income, so that most of the income-earning population is now covered. Critics of the expansion questioned whether a wide-based income tax could be administered effectively and efficiently. By using a withholding system on wages and salaries, however, and by pushing initial collection costs off onto employers rather than government agents, the administration costs of the tax have been held to 0.5 percent of total revenues collected. Problems remain with tax avoidance, especially on unearned income and activities in the underground economy, but the feasibility of a broad-based income tax has become widely accepted.

Calculation of the federal individual income tax is based on the concepts of taxable income and adjusted gross income (AGI). Adjusted gross income is similar to total individual income but not identical to it. Traditionally, only money income was considered, so that in-kind benefits received from employers and the government were excluded in AGI. In recent years, certain kinds of in-kind employer-provided benefits have been added to AGI, such as employer-paid insurance premiums and club memberships. Some sources of money income have been excluded from AGI, including interest on state and local government bonds; certain transfer payments, such as Social Security benefits for most workers, welfare payments, food stamps, and veterans' benefits; some types of fringe benefits paid by the employer, such as health and pension benefits; and income on savings from life insurance. Automatically excluded because they have not yet been converted to income are unrealized capital gains.

Taxable income (TI) is typically smaller than AGI, and is the income to which appropriate federal income tax rates are applied. Two sets of deductions are subtracted from AGI to get TI: personal income-related deductions and the personal exemption. The first set, personal income-related deductions, includes charitable contributions, interest paid on home mortgages, state and local income and property taxes, medical and dental expenses above 7.5 percent of AGI, losses from casualty or theft above 10 percent of AGI, employee business expenses, expenses related to production of investment income, and other miscellaneous expenses above 2 percent of AGI. If taxpayers do not have any of these items, or if their value is sufficiently low, they may take a standard deduction, which is frequently adjusted for inflation. Blind and elderly are allowed an additional, smaller standard deduction. First adopted in 1944 during World War II, the standard deduction at that time was taken by 80 percent of all tax filers. By 1990, only 30 percent of tax filers used the standard deduction, as rising incomes allowed more taxpayers to adopt expenditure patterns that made itemized deductions more attractive. The second set of deductions subtracted from AGI to get TI are personal exemptions. Parents get personal exemptions not only for themselves but also for dependent children under the age of 18.

Income tax rates have varied across the history of the tax. Typically, the range of income is divided into brackets, and different tax rates are applied to income falling in the different brackets. The income tax has historically been progressive, so that higher-income brackets have higher tax rates applied to income in those brackets than do lower-income brackets. The Tax Reform Act of 1986, adopted during the Ronald Reagan administration, significantly lowered the number of income brackets, from 14 to two. The brackets that remained after the act were the 15 percent tax bracket and the 28 percent tax bracket. The advantages of the lower first-bracket rate and personal exemptions were phased out for high-income taxpayers, so that, in the phase out range, an effective third bracket of 33 percent created a higher taxed bulge. Above the bulge, the rate returned to 28 percent, effectively creating four brackets. The Revenue Reconciliation Act of 1993 expanded the brackets to five, with marginal tax rates of 15 percent, 28 percent, 31 percent, 36 percent, and 36.9 percent. Marginal tax rates are the rates placed on the additional income in the higher bracket, not applied overall to the taxpayer's total taxable income. The average tax rate for each individual taxpayer is the average of all the appropriate marginal tax rates and thus is considerably lower than the highest marginal tax rate applied.

The basic tax rates apply to married taxpayers filing separate returns. For married taxpayers filing jointly, income splitting is used, so that the tax rates are applied to half of the taxable income of the couple and the result is multiplied by two, a procedure that doubles the width of the rate brackets for the married couple. Single individuals and single heads of households have special rates, so that four rate schedules are used. Especially with the growing income inequality that characterized the 1980s, the largest number of taxpayers are clustered in the lower rates. After the 1986 reduction in numbers of brackets, two-thirds of all taxable income was subjected to the 15 percent rate.

An alternative minimum tax (AMT) is imposed on taxpayers whose tax preferences would allow them to pay little or no tax, despite substantial incomes. The AMT tax base is calculated by adding select tax preferences to the AGI and subtracting certain itemized deductions. Tax preferences subjected to the AMT are accelerated depreciation; percentage depletion for oil and gas and intangible drilling and development expenses in excess of the costs for oil and gas drilling and mining; untaxed appreciation on charitable contributions of appreciated property, tax-exempt interest on certain private activity bonds; net losses from passive investments and farming; and other minor items. The itemized deductions allowed for AMT calculations include the deductions for casualty losses and medical expenses above 10 percent of income, charitable contributions, interest on home mortgages, and other interest up to the amount of the property income reported in the return. The tax rate for the AMT is 21 percent.

Between 1913 and 1942, federal income taxes were paid in quarterly installments each year, after the income being taxed was accrued. With the expansion to middle- and lower-income persons in World War II, policymakers revised the system, realizing that lower- and middle-income tax payers tended to spend their incomes as soon as they earned it. Further, their future incomes were uncertain. The timing of taxation was revised to make taxes due when income was accrued, and a system of employer withholding on wages and salaries was installed. Self-employed individuals pay estimated taxes in quarterly installments. Withholding applies to all employees except farm laborers, domestic servants, and casual workers.

Most income tax revenues collected are generated through the withholding system. By 1984, for example, total tax liability was US$312 billion, of which US$282 billion was collected through withholding. Critics contend the absence of a withholding system on unearned income has led to an underreporting of income from those sources, and to tax avoidance. An attempt to combat the deficit by imposing withholding in 1982 on interest earned on savings accounts was defeated by a massive public campaign by the banking and savings and loan industries, who implied the withholding was a new tax. No subsequent efforts to expand withholding have been attempted.

Economists have been concerned with three economic effects of the individual income tax: its role as a stabilizer of consumption expenditures, its impact on work incentives, and its influence on savings. Concerning the first issue, the income tax has a stabilizing impact on individual consumption expenditures and on the overall economy. This stabilizing impact results from the higher marginal tax rates that are embodied in the progressive rate structure of the tax. As an individual's income rises, he or she is pushed into a higher tax bracket, which extracts a greater proportion of tax from the additional income than was extracted from the initial lower income. Thus, disposable income and, presumably, consumption expenditures do not rise proportionate to the rise in gross income.

At the macroeconomic level, the same impact occurs. The stabilizing impact of the income tax was reduced when the number of income brackets was decreased after 1986, when marginal tax rates and the number of income tax brackets were both lowered, although it is still present in a weaker form. Indexing tax brackets to account for inflation further reduces the stabilizing impact of the income tax. Economists contend that this stabilizing effect helps to counter inflationary pressures automatically.

Economists do not agree how the individual income tax affects work incentives. If a substitution effect dominates, the tax causes taxpayers to substitute leisure for work, because the rewards of work are reduced by the tax. If an income effect dominates, the tax may actually cause taxpayers to increase their work efforts, because the tax reduces their income and they must continue working to attain a desired after-tax income level. Some economists contend that these two effects likely balance each other, so the overall impact of the income tax on work incentives is negligible. Measurement of this is complicated by the fact that other factors, including age, job opportunities, pensions, the inflation rate, and demographic shifts, also effect work incentives, and workers have little flexibility in a modern postindustrial economy to vary their work in response to tax rates.

The effect of the income tax on savings is also difficult to ascertain. Again, substitution and income effects compete with each other to make the impact of the tax ambiguous.

The tax incidence impact of the federal income tax varies throughout the income range and is only slightly progressive overall, in large part due to tax expenditures. Despite the attempt of the 1986 legislation to reduce tax expenditures (income exempted from normal income tax due to special circumstances of the taxpayer), many remain. The federal income tax is modestly progressive at the lower end of the income range, virtually flat or proportional throughout much of the middle of the income range, and regressive at the upper end of the income scale.

Tax expenditures also reduce revenues available to the government that would, in theory, lower the deficit. Tax expenditures include three types of itemized personal deductions that allow one taxpayer to pay a tax below that of others with similar income. The first group of deductions is for extraordinary expenditures outside the control of the households, such as excessive medical and dental expenditures and losses from casualty and theft. The second is expenditures for purposes the federal government wishes to encourage, such as charitable deductions and interest on home mortgages. The third is to assure that the income tax applies to net income and not to gross receipts, and includes the expenses of moving to a new job and some job-related expenses. Estimates of gains from eliminating major tax expenditures in the United States in 1988 were $91.3 billion, including $15.1 billion for the elimination of state and local tax deductions, $25.7 billion for eliminating mortgage interest deductions, and $30.9 billion for imposing a floor for itemized deductions of 20 percent of AGI.

One of the largest exclusions from the income base are transfer payments and wage supplements. This practice originated in the 1930s when social insurance and relief programs were passed to alleviate hardship, so taxing them seemed counterproductive. With the expansion of the tax base to include most citizens and with increases since World War II in the average amounts of transfers paid as well as the expansion of such programs to include the nonpoor, the consequence of such exclusions today is that some transfer recipients are better off than the working poor, who cannot exclude any portion of their income from taxation.

Military personnel and veterans receive untaxable benefits, as do many employees. These types of benefits may include scholarships for children of university professors, free parking for company cars, other employee privileges, and pension and health benefits. Beginning in 1984, one-half of Social Security payments for individuals with incomes over $25,000, or for couples with incomes over $32,000, were made taxable. Resistance has persisted, however, to treat the remainder of Social Security and other transfer payments as ordinary taxable income.

The Federal Corporate Income Tax

The federal corporate income predates the federal individual income tax. First enacted in 1904, it is a tax that is applied to net earnings of a corporation. Prior to the United States entry into World War II in 1941, the corporate income tax raised more revenue than the individual income tax in 17 of those 28 years. Between 1941 and 1967, the corporate income tax was the second largest source of federal revenue, behind the income tax. After 1968, it was surpassed by the payroll taxes used to finance Social Security and has been declining in importance ever since.

The peak rate reached by the corporate income tax was 52 percent during the years of 1952 to 1963. The rate dropped afterwards to 35 percent for companies with corporate income over $10 million in 1993. As a concession to small businesses, there are three corporate income tax rates: 15 percent, 25 percent, and 34 percent, with a 5 percent surtax on income between $100,000 and $335,000, but most income is taxed at the highest rate. Unlike the personal income tax, there are no personal exemptions or personal deductions allowed for corporations. The corporate income tax does allow, however, deductions for charitable contributions and for operating costs. The tax is applied to total profits, including both earnings retained by the firm and dividends paid to stockholders. Since these dividends, in turn, are taxed again, with individual income tax applied to the stockholders, critics have contended that dividends are subjected to double taxation. Others counter that the corporation is a separate legal entity with separate income streams and expenditures from individual stockholders, and the income of each is fairly subjected to tax.

The corporate income tax is complicated because it must be applied to a large number of organizations doing business in a wide variety of industries. The tax has several key characteristics. As with individuals, corporate capital gains are taxed when they are realized. Between 1921 and 1986, these gains were taxed at lower rates than for ordinary income, but this preference was removed in 1987. Corporations are allowed to offset capital losses only against capital gains, not against all income. Net operating losses may be carried back and offset against the operating income of the three preceding years. The cost of capital can generously be written off against taxable income, with

plant and equipment being depreciated over a specified number of years. Outlays for research and development may be deducted in full in the year in which they are made. Dividends paid by one corporation to another are subject to an additional tax at a low rate.

Corporations must pay United States tax on foreign as well as domestic income, but credit against foreign tax is allowed for foreign income taxes and withholding taxes paid on earnings and dividends received from abroad. Corporations with no more than 35 shareholders may choose to be treated as a partnership for tax purposes. Financial institutions—including commercial banks, savings and loan associations, mutual savings banks, and insurance companies—are taxed, but are allowed to accumulate tax-free reserves and also are allowed some special deductions.

Religious, educational, and charitable organizations, trade associations, labor unions, and fraternal organizations are exempt from the corporate income tax as applied to operations concerning their primary purpose. These organizations, however, must pay corporate income tax on "unrelated business income." Private foundations must pay a special excise tax of 1 percent on their investment incomes.

Who actually pays the corporate income tax—shareholders, consumers, or workers and employees—is unclear. In part, who pays depends on whether the tax is shifted from its point of application (stockholders and workers) to consumers. If demand is elastic, shifting is less likely to occur than if it is inelastic.

Economic globalization has contributed to declining corporate tax revenues, as large companies can more easily hide income from United States tax collectors. United States collections on foreign firms doing business in the United States become more important as well. Critical for taxing international businesses is the price a foreign owner charges its United States branches for supplies, services, or inventory. If the price is excessively high, the profit of the United States subsidiaries is understated and United States tax liability is lowered artificially. Multinational firms have frequently been charged with setting internal prices in a way to minimize taxes due. Transfer-pricing rules are critical in establishing corporate tax liabilities that are realistic and reflect actual business activity.

State and Local Income Taxes

States relied heavily upon sales taxes from the Great Depression through the 1950s, but increasingly, under pressures of fiscal stress and expanded citizen demands, began to adopt income taxes. By 1993, 41 states and the District of Columbia had individual income taxes. The exceptions were Alaska, Florida, Nevada, New Hampshire, South Dakota, Tennessee, Texas, Washington, and Wyoming. New Hampshire and Tennessee allowed a more-limited tax on dividends and interest in lieu of a comprehensive income tax.

Individual income taxes have become an important source of revenue for most states that have adopted them, receiving more revenue from this source than any other. The combined tax collections for the states from individual income taxes, however, remain significantly smaller than those collected by the federal government from this source, predominantly because the tax rates applied by states are typically much lower. The structure of many state income taxes parallels and mirrors that of the federal income tax. Many states allow taxpayers to copy information directly from federal returns when computing state income tax liability. About 3,500 cities also levy individual income taxes, but in most cases, they limit coverage to payroll income, not income derived from all sources. Many of these cities are in Pennsylvania; about 900 cities are outside of Pennsylvania.

Forty-four states and the District of Columbia use a corporate income tax. Exceptions are Nevada, South Dakota, Texas, Washington, and Wyoming. Michigan applies a single business tax, which is a modified value-added tax. Complicating the application of state corporate income taxes is the operation of many corporations in more than one state, and sometimes more than one country. Though some income can be identified as originating in a particular state and therefore legitimately subject to its corporate income tax, the origin of other income is sometimes more difficult to determine. To facilitate the calculation of corporate income tax due it, each state with a corporate income tax has adopted its own income apportionment formula, to determine how much of the total profit earned by the multistate corporation it will tax. The most common approach is the single-weighted three-factor formula, with state shares of total corporate property, payroll, and sales used as approximations of corporate activity in the state. Some states do not use the formula, however, and may weight the factors differently. Most states lack sufficient auditors to verify corporate tax returns and must accept the calculations done by corporations. Consequently, state corporate income tax avoidance is a common problem, and a local corporate income tax is totally infeasible.

MARCIA LYNN WHICKER

BIBLIOGRAPHY

Conlan, Timothy J., Margaret T. Wrightson, and David R. Beam. 1990. *Taxing Choices: The Politics of Tax Reform.* Washington, DC: Brookings Institution.

Mikesell, John L. 1991. *Fiscal Administration.* Belmont, CA: Wadsworth.

Pechman, Joseph A. 1987. *Federal Tax Policy.* 5th ed. Washington, DC: Brookings Institution.

Pechman, Joseph A., ed. 1988. *World Tax Reform: A Progress Report.* Washington, DC: Brookings Institution.

Samuelson, Paul A., and William D. Nordhaus. 1989. *Economics.* 13th ed. New York: McGraw-Hill.

Stein, Herbert, ed., 1988. *Tax Policy in the Twenty-First Century.* New York: John Wiley and Sons.

Stiglitz, Joseph E. 1986. *Economics of the Public Sector.* New York: W. W. Norton and Co.

INCREMENTAL BUDGETING.

The routines of budgeting that are marked by predictability and stability. Incremental budgeting is a description of both the outcomes of year-to-year changes in budgets and the method used to make the budget decisions. Year-to-year decisions, interpreted as outcomes of a budget process, are measured as percentage changes from the previous year. Therefore, the increment is the budget in year t minus the budget in year $t-1$, divided by the budget in year $t-1$. This provides the percentage change from one year to the next; the percentage change, when displayed graphically over several years, will show a pattern of stable growth. Increments are expected to be modest from year to year. The modest changes reflect new activities, new programs, and increases to existing programs.

These statistical properties of budgets that demonstrate incrementalism as an outcome were summarized over three decades ago by Aaron Wildavsky as follows, "The largest determining factor of the size and content of this year's budget is last year's budget" (Wildavsky 1984, p. 13).

The specification of incremental budgeting as modest percentage changes from last year's budget is less obvious than it seems at first. One of the first questions to ask about increments is: What percentage increase qualifies as an increment? Is a 5 percent increase an increment? What about a 10 percent increase? Could a decrease in a budget from one year to the next be called an increment? Scholars debated this very point without reaching consensus because there is simply no objective way to define what constitutes a "modest" percentage increase over last year's budget.

Perhaps the best answer to these questions is that the size of the budgetary increment is not the important issue. Instead, it is the *stability* of the year-to-year changes that defines an incremental budget process. Using this definition, year-to-year changes in the one percent to three percent range may be incremental; so may year-to-year changes falling into a 5-to-9 percent range. Notice that it is not the size of the increment that is important but the *predictability* of the changes that defines a budget process as incremental.

The statistical description of incrementalism described previously has additional ambiguity. Stable budgetary patterns at one level of organization may mask considerable budgetary variation at a different level of organization. For example, a department with four bureaus may show budgetary stability when the budget for the entire department is examined over a given time period. However, there may be considerable year-to-year variation among the bureaus. Similarly, if one examines the programs within a bureau, one may also find much year-to-year variation. A further disaggregated look at line-item detail may also show less budgetary stability than the aggregated departmental level budget may display. For example, a budget may show significant variation among personnel and nonpersonnel objects of expenditure even when the aggregate level of spending is stable.

These illustrations point out that incremental budgetary patterns are sensitive to the organizational level of aggregation and disaggregation that frames the focus of investigation.

Incremental Processes

Incrementalism can also be interpreted as a decision *process*. Here, the emphasis shifts from statistical properties to modes of behavior. For example, one can observe the ways in which the principal budgetary actors–the agency, the budget office, and the legislative body make decisions. As a theoretical interpretation of behavior it is necessary to make some core assumptions. First, we must assume that there is some level of *consensus* among the actors. This consensus is reflected through general agreement about prior year budgetary commitments, which can be labeled the *base*. Base-level (or prior-year) decisions are rarely fully reviewed by the principal actors. Instead, budgetary decisions focus on the marginal adjustments to the base. These are the year-to-year changes that are stimulated by agency requests. Budget review and subsequent negotiations between the executive and legislature focus on the marginal changes rather than on the agency's total budget. This focus can be called incremental since only a small portion of the entire budget is actually subjected to detailed scrutiny.

Why would budgeting adopt this decisionmaking behavior? Incrementalism presumes that individuals develop ways to reduce the information that they must process in complex decisions. Individuals in the process have neither the time nor the capacity to (1) absorb *all* of the information relevant to a decision and (2) evaluate in a comprehensive way *all* of the alternatives.

Herbert Simon (1976) introduced his famous notion of "satisficing," in which the decisionmaker chooses the first satisfactory alternative. This means that, in the abstract, there will often be a superior choice; however, the decisionmaker, because of the pressure of time and the complexity of information processing, chooses a satisfactory alternative. Timing, in other words, is crucial to satisficing behavior.

Incrementalism is a "close cousin" to satisficing behavior. Aaron Wildavsky observed that in budgetary processes

decisionmakers find ways to reduce the informational burdens that are embedded in budgets. For example, *history* accounts for much of the stability (or, incremental character) of budgets. History explains why agencies and programs exist, in the first place, and why they have the budgetary characteristics that they display. History also explains the constituency base and political support for programs and agencies. Participants are able to shape current choices they face by having an appreciation of the historical dimension of the programs and agencies under consideration.

Wildavsky also noted that budgeting is *experiential*. This means that participants base their budgetary decisions on the cumulative learning that takes place in the process. The learning includes knowing how the participants in the process are likely to act when faced with budgetary decisions. In other words, experience improves predictability. So does *repetition*, another characteristic of incremental budgeting, which allows participants to learn their roles and simplify an otherwise complex process.

Budgeting has the quality of a political game. The players are known and their behaviors are also predictable. Moreover, the strategies used by them are also well understood. Budget claimants want more financial resources, the controllers (such as the central budget office) try to dampen the spending proclivities of the operating agencies, and legislators try to use the budget to advance their chances of reelection. These roles are well documented and the strategies employed by the budgetary actors revolve around the addition to the agencies' budgetary base.

Incrementalism and Fiscal Stress

The portrait of incrementalism described previously came under serious strain by the beginning of the 1980s. The major source of strain for the past 20 years has been fiscal stress. Essentially, claims outstrip resources, which breaks down budgetary consensus and thereby undermines the bases of incrementalism. In his preface to *The New Politics of the Budgetary Process*, Aaron Wildavsky (1992) wrote that "when there was (mostly) agreement on the base, the old *Politics* stressed conflict over the increments. The new *Politics* stressed the base because it is often disagreed. Conflict is now about the fundamentals" (p. xiv).

In an intriguing essay, Allen Schick identified four levels of fiscal scarcity and the corresponding impact of the level on budgetary conflict. Schick pointed out that, although budgeting is inherently about resource allocation (which, by definition, concerns scarcity), the level of scarcity influences the ways budget decisions are made. When governments can fund the budgetary base and take on new activities incrementalism can flourish. There is no incentive to scrutinize the budgetary base, nor are there likely to be sharp disagreements about how to allocate scarce resources. Unfortunately, what Schick called "relaxed scarcity" is extremely rare in practice.

Chronic scarcity, by contrast, requires budget controllers to dampen the demand for greatly expanded resources, though modest enhancements can be funded. This level of scarcity protects the base and small incremental increases in spending. Conflict is contained and controllers look for management improvements to defray the costs of programmatic expansion. The incremental process is clearly intact.

When increments are no longer available the budget has reached acute scarcity. The main attribute is an increase in political conflict since techniques to control spending, such as hiring freezes, midyear budget reductions, and spending restrictions, heighten tension between spenders and controllers. Though the emphasis is on short term "quick fixes," the relative harmony of incrementalism is shattered because of the eroding fiscal condition.

The fourth level of fiscal scarcity is total scarcity. In this situation, there are not enough resources to fund the base of public programs. When forced to make very difficult choices decisionmakers are inclined to first avoid the budgetary reality that confronts them. Schick has observed various budgetary "pathological" behaviors, such as resorting to gimmicks to artificially balance the budget. Political conflict is likely to increase as political claimants challenge the legitimacy of one another. The implicit rules that undergird incrementalism collapse.

Increasingly, governments find themselves in the environment of either acute or total scarcity. This means that budgetary conflict is exacerbated and the stability associated with incrementalism is less useful.

The past 25 years have witnessed a gradual shift in budgeting in the United States, particularly at the national level. To explain, it is useful to distinguish between the "bottom-up" and the "top-down" features of budgeting. The bottom-up features have already been identified. They are the essential features of incrementalism that pertain to agency strategies, the negotiation between spenders and controllers, and the containment of conflict. With increasing fiscal scarcity, however, the budget process at the federal level in the United States shifted emphasis toward top-down budgeting. Top-down budgeting includes the determination of major policy tradeoffs (such as the amount of defense spending versus the amount of domestic discretionary spending), tax and spending targets, the size of the deficit, and the share of government spending of the gross domestic product (GDP). When fiscal scarcity worsens, top-down features of budgeting become more salient since they can be incorporated into broad budget control strategies. In the United States, top-down elements of the federal budget process have expanded since the passage of the Impoundment Control Act of 1974. Congress has experimented with efforts to set deficit reduction targets and, more recently, pay-as-you-go requirements to finance new spending from budget cuts or revenue increases. The main point to emphasize is that the last quarter of the twentieth century in the United States has been characterized by continual efforts to control spending.

Incrementalism has suffered as the preferred mode of making budget decisions because of increasing fiscal scarcity. But it has also suffered because of the political tendency to make multiyear commitments that constrain choices. In the United States, entitlement spending for programs for the poor and the elderly, for veterans, and for myriad other entitled groups place multiyear demands on the public fisc. Entitlements are rights that cannot be altered without a change in the particular statute under question. Spending is therefore open-ended and not subject to the same negotiation that takes place for discretionary programs.

Political assessments about rights cannot easily be translated into marginal adjustments (which are the hallmark of incrementalism). In particular, choices that reflect value conflicts surrounding the appropriate scope of government activity, particularly programs that provide cash and in-kind benefits to target populations, strain incremental decision processes. Since choices that have this characteristic are not likely to be marginal adjustments, one would be hard-pressed to call them incremental.

In addition, public programs that are premised on the belief that a target population has "rights" to government benefits—entitlements are the common, though not exclusive, example—necessarily conflict with a fiscal orientation to public spending primarily aimed at budget control. Rights are political claims for either a benefit or a procedural guarantee. Benefits may be cash (such as Social Security payments) or in-kind—such as medical treatment. Some are means-tested (such as public assistance), some are not (such as Medicare). The continual federal budget deficit—and rule-based methods to cope with it—bring such programs and their associated value conflicts to the political surface.

A budget process can be partly incremental. The distinction turns on the separation of decisions that are routine from those that are nonroutine. In a provocative essay, Bernard Pitsvada and Frank Draper (1984), argued that incrementalism still pertains to much of federal budgeting. They pointed out that budgeting for inflation through indexing, multiyear budgeting, continuing resolutions, and budget displays in federal budget documents reinforce incremental processes. These methods encourage routines and promote stability by doing what incrementalism has always done—focus decisionmakers' attention on marginal adjustments.

For example, one can say that in any given fiscal year the size of the defense budget versus domestic spending—the proverbial "guns versus butter" tradeoff—is routine. To say that this is routine is not to diminish its importance or even its contentiousness. Instead, it merely highlights the fact that there is a predictable character to the issue, regularity, which is the heart of incrementalism.

The "gaming" nature, for example, of the interactions between agencies and the budget office is what predictability is all about. Incrementalism as a description of how the typical budget process normally works was never intended to be a comprehensive theory. It captured instead the essential features of a rather complex process that gave rise to predictability and stability. If one takes away stability and predictability, one diminishes incrementalism as a useful conceptual and analytical construct.

Can incrementalism be alive and well and, at the same time, analytically and empirically suspect? It depends on one's focus. Surely, stability, regularity, and predictability–the hallmarks of incrementalism–apply to *some* parts and some features of public budgetary processes. Budgets still have a natural rhythm guided by the routines of the *cycle*. Similarly, formula-driven features, such as automatic compensation adjustments, inflation factors, and, perhaps most important, "base budget" starting points, all reinforce incrementalism. Even the measures that are adopted to manage fiscal stringency have a certain cyclical predictability: Banning out-of-state travel, hiring freezes, and across-the-board reductions made during the execution of the budget to respond to revenue shortfalls all share the incremental trademark of predictability. Even state and local government "rainy day" funds could be interpreted as a mechanism to reduce uncertainty–and therefore could be incremental at their conceptual core.

As Pitsvada and Draper pointed out, the concept still has a great deal of empirical value–despite the criticisms received for more than twenty years. What has incrementalism, as a dominant budgetary concept, done *least* well to explain? The answer is straightforward: Incrementalism takes the budgetary world as it finds it and provides a conceptual edifice to explain role patterns and norms of behavior. It is less useful in interpreting significant alternations in that world, especially changes that percolate through the political agenda.

Entitlements and the Loss of Budgetary Discretion

The politics of entitlements–a subject that necessarily combines empirical and normative dimensions–is not well understood. Even though there are case studies of the genesis of specific entitlement programs, middle-range theories that attempt to explain bureaucratic, legislative, or electoral behavior are not persuasive as *comprehensive* explanations of entitlement growth. Wildavsky's (1984) formal break with his own classic portrait of incrementalism was interesting on this score. He showed that entitlements fundamentally changed the *process* of budgeting because they removed most of the discretion from budget decisions. Their political and economic significance can hardly

be exaggerated. Why did the "politics of addition" develop so easily?

A study by R. Kent Weaver (1985) tries to answer this question by explaining why politicians are willing to give up budgetary discretion for various programs. Using indexation as his focus, Weaver offered three broad explanations for the motivations of elected officials. One possibility is that indexation is adopted because the legislator believes that it is good policy. Second, the adoption of indexing may be influenced by the opportunities to "take credit" for the decision. And third, politicians want to "avoid blame" and may find indexing a handy vehicle to achieve that objective.

According to Weaver, the specific explanation varies with the program and the clientele. For example, indexing a popular entitlement program such as Social Security is a blame-avoidance strategy since it provides the elected official with a vehicle to reconcile the incompatible objectives of budget control and support for a politically sensitive beneficiary group. In contrast, where beneficiaries are *not* well organized, or where they lack political influence, indexing is less likely. Weaver's argument can be used to interpret the different political treatment afforded Social Security and Medicare compared with Aid to Families with Dependent Children (AFDC), which is continually subjected to intense political and budgetary scrutiny.

Since the heart of budgeting is tradeoffs across competing purposes, entitlements are anathema to the budgeteer who relishes flexibility. Rights claimants, in contrast, prefer less budgetary flexibility so that entitlements are not easily altered. Whereas the budgeteer thinks of options, the rights advocate wants an unalterable decision. To the budgeteer, rights mortgage the future; for the rights advocate, this is precisely the point. The uncontrollable character of federal entitlement spending has received so much attention because it highlights the erosion of budgetary discretion.

Every budget process watcher can recite V. O. Key's famous 1940 question: "On what basis shall it be decided to allocate x dollars to activity A instead of activity B?" (Key as quoted in Hyde 1992). Recall that Key's emphasis was that welfare economics, circa 1940, was not an especially good guide for answering his question. By the end of the essay he lamented that "the most advantageous utilization of public funds resolves itself into a matter of value preferences between ends lacking a common denominator. As such, the question is a problem political philosophy" (Key 1992, p. 24).

Who, even today, could argue with Key for–at broad levels, budgeting is the reflection of policy preferences. But, surely, most budgetary routines are still done the old-fashioned, incremental way, as Draper and Pitsvada argued. Rights-based budgeting falls somewhere between Key's "big picture" image of budgeting and the routines so easily accommodated to incremental processes.

Rights-Based Budgeting and Top-Down Fiscal Management

The shift toward a greater emphasis on top-down budgeting has the effect of reducing some of the major features of incrementalism: strategy and negotiation and the predictability of well-established roles and decisions at the budgetary margins. Given the chronic feature of the federal deficit, top-down budgeting has become a larger and larger part of the budgetary landscape.

How does top-down fiscal management accommodate rights-based budgeting? Not very easily. Having rights means spending *more* not less—even when the right is a procedural guarantee and does not mandate additional expenditures. Rights are anathema to budget control because they invariably mortgage the future. It is not surprising then, that top-down budgeting encourages close scrutiny of new entitlements. More broadly, rights-based budgeting requires an expanded vision of budget management.

One feature of the expansion is the *management of rights via the management of the budget*. A change in Social Security toward a means-tested benefit—admittedly a politically volatile idea—would reflect a changed perspective toward rights and their budgetary ramifications.

Homelessness, in the absence of court-ordered, procedural due process guarantees, has other budgetary options. For example, intergovernmental grant formulas that cap the federal or state share could be used to manage spending. An entitlement alternative that restricts benefits to a subset of the homeless population (such as children) is a second way—though probably a less-effective one—of controlling costs. The point, nevertheless, is that it may make a big difference whether rights drive budget decisions or whether budgets define rights. Budgeteers prefer it the second way.

Finally, rights-based budgeting muddies the budgetary waters. Consider the courts once again. Even though judges do not *make* budget decisions (a small number of judges have actually required that specific spending be made or taxes be raised), they can help to shape options. As silent partners in the budget process, the courts subtly undermine what was once a neat and tidy budget process. The simple reason for this is that they are not bound by fiscal constraints. As a result, the old hallmark of budgeting, incrementalism, with its emphasis on stability and predictability, does not apply when the courts enter the budgetary game. The discipline of the game is therefore shattered.

Top-down budgeting can be interpreted as a structural response to the loss of this discipline. But top-down budgeting, though appropriate for shaping broad budget policy, is less suited for managing rights-based programs. The reason, at root, is that rights-based political claims are unconcerned with matters fiscal; they push for *more* spending, not less. More than two decades ago, in the late 1950s, Paul Appleby summarized the budget function as one that was "preponderantly negative" (Appleby as quoted in Schick 1987). His point was that the budget examiner had an uncompromising role to play because there was no shortage of budgetary claimants. The budget norm that Appleby referred to was built on the conceptual and behavioral structure of incrementalism. Rights-based claims within severely constrained fiscal climates have eroded the value of incrementalism as the best way to make budget decisions and the most plausible explanation for how budgeting works.

JEFFREY D. STRAUSSMAN

BIBLIOGRAPHY

Appleby, Paul, 1987. "The Role of the Budget Division." In Allen Schick, ed., *Perspectives on Budgeting*, pp. 119–123. 2d ed. Washington, DC: American Society for Public Administration.

Key, V. O., Jr., 1992. "The Lack of a Budget Theory." In Albert C. Hyde, ed., *Government Budgeting*, pp. 22–26. 2d ed. Pacific Grove, CA: Brooks-Cole.

Pitsvada, Bernard T., and Frank D. Draper, 1984. "Making Sense of the Federal Budget the Old Fashioned Way—Incrementally." *Public Administration Review* 44 (September-October): 401–407.

Schick, Allen, 1980. "Budgetary Adaptations to Resource Scarcity." In Charles H. Levine and Irene Rubin, eds. *Fiscal Stress and Public Policy*, pp. 113–134. Beverly Hills, CA: Sage.

Simon, Herbert A., 1976. *Administrative Behavior*. 3d ed. New York: Free Press.

Weaver, R. Kent, 1985. "Controlling Entitlements." In John E. Chubb and Paul E. Peterson, eds. *The New Direction in American Politics*. pp. 307–341. Washington, DC: Brookings Institution.

Wildavsky, Aaron, 1984. *The Politics of the Budgetary Process*. 4th ed. Boston: Little, Brown.

———, 1992. *The New Politics of the Budgetary Process*. 2d ed. New York: HarperCollins.

INDEPENDENT SECTOR.

A nonprofit coalition of more than 800 corporate, foundation, and voluntary organization members, based in Washington, D.C., with national interest in and impact on philanthropy and voluntary action. The coalition's mission is to establish a national forum that is able to encourage giving, volunteering, and not-for-profit initiatives, which helps all Americans to better serve people, communities, and causes. The mission and organization of the Independent Sector derives from the members' shared values, which relate to the establishment and maintenance of a free society. Forty percent of the Independent Sector's membership is made up of corporations, and the balance is voluntary organizations. It is a 501(c)(3) coalition and qualifies as a public charity.

Six Program Goals

The goals, objectives, and activities central to the pursuit of the mission of the Independent Sector are concentrated in the following six program areas:

1. *Public Information and Education:* to achieve increased public awareness of this sector and of giving and volunteering, while promoting active citizenship and community service.
2. *Government Relations:* to develop and maintain effective relationships with government, based on mutual respect and support for each other's roles, coupled with a commitment to realistic independence from one another. This relationship includes protection of the freedoms that allow new causes to be created and a reversal in the trend toward greater government restrictions on nonprofit initiatives.
3. *Research:* to develop an identifiable and growing research effort that produces the body of knowledge necessary to define, chart, and understand this sector and the ways it can be of greatest service to society.
4. *Give Five:* to increase support for the pubic services of voluntary organizations by helping Americans understand and move toward the national standard of giving—5 percent of income and 5 hours per week to the causes of their choice.
5. *Leadership and Management, Including Values and Ethics:* to enhance the capacity of the not-for-profit sector; to achieve excellence in leadership and management of philanthropic and voluntary organizations.
6. *The Meeting Ground:* to create and maintain a significant sense of community among the organizations of the nonprofit sector; to provide a "meeting ground" for cooperation and learning.

The Independent Sector has available special publications, research surveys, public statements, information on government relations, and periodicals that are a source of information about philanthropic and voluntary activity. Its dues structure seeks to achieve a balance between encouraging participation of the maximum number of qualifying groups and providing the essential core support for the organization.

Since its founding in 1980, the Independent Sector has established itself as a significant vehicle for strengthening voluntary initiatives. It has taken special measures to strengthen university educational programs in nonprofit management by assisting educators to integrate both nonprofit management issues and the philanthropic experience into the curriculum. It has sponsored major research conferences to gather and disseminate major findings about the sector. The Independent Sector coalition has addressed major legislative and regulatory challenges to its mission and has placed substantial emphasis on accountability and performance standards for nonprofit organiza-

tions. It has worked with Congress and the media, educating both about the sector and its important role in society. It has placed special emphasis on and has created programs and materials directed at recruiting, developing, and retaining talented staff and trustees in the nonprofit world. Through its mission and members, the Independent Sector intends to preserve independence for voluntarism and philanthropy so that people can have greater influence on their own destinies and communities.

RICHARD D. HEIMOVICS

BIBLIOGRAPHY

Independent Sector, 1994. *Annual Report of the Independent Sector.* Washington, DC: Independent Sector.

INDEXING. The process whereby governmental programs and revenues are adjusted for changes in a selected social or economic indicator–quite often a consumer price index (CPI).

As with so many social science concepts, indexing possesses numerous connotations that can be quite broad or rather specific. Indexing and indexation, in their broadest sense, refer to the process or the end product by which index numbers and composite indexes are created to describe a phenomenon and the possible changes in that phenomenon across time and space. Many of the leading economic indications found in financial newspapers are primary examples of indexes constructed to measure certain types of economic activity and to gauge the changes in the economic activity from one designated point in time to another. Standard and Poor's 500, the Dow Jones Composite, and Lehman brothers Long-Term Treasury Bond Index are three of many.

An index may be as simple as the use of a murder rate to signify the degree of serious crime or as complex as a composite index of various indicators to describe the level of urban decay (poverty rate, age of housing and infrastructure, etc.). Indexes are quantitative; however, many are rather subjective, based on different opinions as to what constitutes serious crime or urban decay, for example.

The primary purpose of indexing is descriptive. In terms of indexes' purported objectivity, however, they serve to inform private and public choices when it comes to investment decisions, collective bargaining, federal urban assistance, and so on. For government, indexing serves as a basis for calculating what benefit increases individual citizens may receive in a given year. The most famous type of governmental indexation is found in the efforts of governments to index their programs for inflation. This specific connotation of indexing has received the most attention of political scientists and policy analysts. It serves as the basis of R. Kent Weaver's (1988) definitive study of the politics of indexation and the assorted purposes behind applied indexation in the public sector.

Applied, as opposed to descriptive, indexing involves constructing an index and linking it to some private or public sector program, thereby producing a cause-and-effect relationship whereby the index's application results in a change in the program's costs or payments. Adjustable-rate mortgages and Social Security increases are primary examples.

Applied indexing is central to many business and financial decisions, social support levels, and eligibility determination procedures. It is used to stimulate local governmental revenue efforts, to limit governmental spending, and even to integrate and maintain public housing. Applied indexing may be formal and explicit, as in federal indexing for inflation, or it may be implicit, as in the effects of the externalities of formal and explicit indexing or of informal indexing, in which policymakers pretend as if something is indexed.

Indexing as Good Public Policy

The question of whether governmental indexing constitutes good public policy involves taking into account not only the economic, political, and social equity implications of indexing in general but also the wisdom of indexing a particular public sector program or revenue source at a particular point in time. Assessing the value of indexing requires specifying whether it is a solution to a policy problem or a policy problem in need of a policy solution.

Constructing Good Public Policy Indexes

The benefits of indexing as good public policy necessitate selecting appropriate index numbers, constructing good composite indexes, and being able to measure a particular social phenomenon over time and space.

The United States Bureau of Labor Statistics has developed many indexes to describe the state of the American economy for governments, businesses, and unions (for example, producer price index, employee cost index, and an international price index, among others). Its most famous and most used indexes are its consumer price indexes. The use of the bureau's CPIs are central to many collective bargaining agreements and to the federal government's efforts to index for inflation the benefits of Social Security and other entitlements. The problems that the Bureau of Labor Statistics has had in constructing a "good" CPI over time help to illustrate some of the methodological problems that policymakers may have in developing indexes that are acceptable to all interested parties.

The indexing of Social Security and other programs for inflation has its critics as well as its supporters. The desirability of such indexing depends, to a large degree, on the capability of the bureau's (or anyone else's) CPI to measure accurately the true rate of inflation. Problems have been caused by poor or incomplete data, by the right to keep some data secret in order to acquire them in the first place, and, most of all, problems have been caused by the inherent difficulty in sampling consumers and in weighting their purchases and the sites of their purchases. In its efforts to measure the rate of inflation, the bureau has had to face problems as to the internal and external validity of the CPIs.

Some indexes fail to measure what, in theory, they are designed to measure, hence, creating a problem of internal validity. The Bureau of Labor Statistics' two most-comprehensive CPIs are composite indexes of the price of certain goods and services, of which the major item is shelter. Before 1985, the bureau had problems in separating consumption from investment when it came to calculating the true price changes for shelter. During the late 1970s, a period of high inflation for the United States, President Jimmy Carter criticized the bureau for overstating the nation's inflation rate thanks to its inclusion of the price of borrowing money to purchase a house as a consumption cost associated with the price of shelter.

In one regard, the internal validity of a CPI depends on all costs associated with consumption being clearly separated from those that are not. The bureau worked over ten years to produce a satisfactory solution to isolate consumption from investment in the case of shelter. Nevertheless, the bureau, being faithful to the idea of a consumer price index, has long separated out those taxes that are not consumer related (income and Social Security taxes) from those that are (sales).

Until 1945, the Bureau of Labor Statistics formally referred to its index for measuring consumer prices as a cost-of-living index. Faced with arguments that its index was in fact a consumer price index, the bureau agreed with its critics by recognizing the external validity problem it had created by labeling its consumer price index a cost-of-living index.

A CPI is an example of a fixed index, or one that reflects only the changes in prices in regard to a specific market basket chosen as the standard for measuring all future price changes. A true cost-of-living index measures the changing costs for a consumer purchasing an ever-changing standard of living.

Sampling problems account for many of the more significant external validity problems associated with consumer price and other indexes. The Bureau of Labor Statistics encounters problems continually in adapting its indexes to reflect changing consumption patterns, alterations in places where consumption takes place (department and other stores, such as discounters), and the degree to which the sampled consumption purchases truly constitute the purchases of the consumer population sampled by the bureau. In the latter regard, labor leaders have charged, from time to time, that some of the goods in the bureau's market basket are not all that reflective of the purchases of moderate- or low-income workers. This perceived problem is seen to be a result of the bureau's weighting consumption purchases in terms of the amount of its overall purchase vis-à-vis other items in the market basket. Since wealthier consumers consume more goods and a wider variety of products, it is their purchases and the level of their purchases that receive added emphasis in the bureau's CPIs. (The bureau's CPIs have been criticized for their possible "plutocratic" look.)

The Bureau of Labor Statistics updates its market baskets to reflect changes in consumer tastes as well as to account for the different new and old items that can and cannot be purchased at a certain point in time. These periodic updates create new market baskets, which are supposed to reflect the original market basket. The inability of the bureau to choose good substitutes for the items being replaced in the original market basket or the addition of new items creates noncomparable market baskets or CPIs that do not completely resemble the old ones. Consequently, the old and new CPIs have a break in continuity.

One may question the external validity of the inflation rate. Variations between different market baskets, and, hence, different CPIs, may be small, but when aggregated and then applied—as in the case of Social Security—they may have significant impacts when it comes to the size of the federal budget outlays.

Not all methodological debates and problems involving an index or how best to construct one can always be solved. Accounting for the methodological problems that may inhibit the creation of a good index, and adapting that index to changes over time, improves the quality of indexing as the basis of good policy. Critical evaluation of any particular index used to help determine the outcomes of a public policy is necessary for insuring that policymakers become aware of the possible unintended ramifications of using that index when accepting the methodological and policy assumptions on which it is based.

Purposes and Ramifications of Indexing as Public Policy

Indexing, in its broadest sense, serves informational purposes—as in the Bureau of Labor Statistics' efforts and as in economic indexes created by financial newspapers, organizations, and advisory services. Financial and economic indexes are only informative when the stocks, bonds, and so forth that compose them accurately reflect the overall changes in the stock and bond markets. To use these indexes to develop desired information as to what course of action to follow often requires the insight of a person who has thoroughly familiarized him- or herself with the meanings of the numbers in an index and how that index's numbers are related with still other indexes. For example, only some investors know that a movement in the composite numbers of a bond index informs them as to whether to sell or buy utility stocks. Indexes inform, but they always require interpretation.

When one is indexing for inflation, or using the narrowest of the connotations of indexing, one may discern that there are many purposes—economic, political, and social equity—behind the current indexing of some wages and government programs. The indexing of private governmental bonds (as in England) or wages for inflation helps economically to remove some of the uncertainties of doing business, especially in relatively high inflationary times. Such indexing may, as R. Kent Weaver has argued, serve the political self-interests of politicians in their efforts to claim credit as well as to avoid being blamed by others for certain political and social problems. In terms of public interest concerns, indexing for inflation may give politicians less temptation to raise benefits during election times, or it may even give them more time to tackle more important and pressing legislation rather than deciding between a 2-or-3 percent cost-of-living adjustment. And, in terms of social equity, indexing may provide the fairness that allows the more socially and economically dependent citizens to receive a measure of protection against inflation.

Indexing for inflation may be good for many people or for just a few. There are many ramifications to a decision to help protect the purchasing power of senior citizens. Such indexing helps to stimulate the economy. At the same time, it creates in one less of a willingness to save for one's retirement. As more people retire, indexing for inflation helps to create the prospect of a bankrupt trust fund, the likelihood of new payroll taxes, and more budgetary and fiscal constraints for the federal budget as overall tax burdens rise.

For economists, indexing for inflation symbolizes the government's lack of willpower to fight inflation. Indexing for inflation stimulates even more inflation, which adversely affects wages and salaries not protected by cost-of-living adjustments. Indexing, by creating winners and losers, creates social and economic inequalities for some people while alleviating inequalities for others. For Social Security, indexing for inflation has raised the problem of intergenerational inequities, where the younger generations will possibly have to pay more payroll taxes to support the older retired generations. However, if there were no indexing of Social Security benefits there would still be efforts made to protect the recipients against their loss of purchasing power. Hence, indexing is but one policy option for policymakers and politicians. (For reasons of electoral or political stability concerns, politicians find ad hoc ways of substituting for indexing.)

The benefits and costs of indexing for inflation can be seen in the Republican's desire in the early 1970s to index

Social Security for inflation. The Richard Nixon administration desired to depoliticize Social Security rate hikes by indexing the benefits for inflation. A bidding war between Republicans and Democrats followed, whereby Social Security benefits were doubly indexed. Recipients received a cost-of-living adjustment and a standard-of-living adjustment (benefits indexed to a rise in wages of current workers). The recipients enjoyed both adjustments for some 6 years, thus, they were overcompensated for inflation, compared to all other Americans.

The politicians' acceptance of indexing, in this case and others, indicates that added benefits were provided so that these politicians would perhaps receive support from those that would be affected by indexing in the future. In theory, however, indexing could be used to avoid possible higher expenditures through ad hoc or yearly efforts to compensate those same programs and beneficiaries for inflation. Republican desire in the early 1980s to index Medicaid for inflation is an example. The costs of Medicaid in the 1980s and 1990s exceeded the general rate of inflation.

Not Indexing as Public Policy

The government's decision to index Social Security and other governmental benefits for inflation illustrates only one aspect of the politics of indexation. Its decision not to index and to remove indexation from existing indexed programs discloses two other policy options that define the "new" politics of indexation in regard to inflation and other index numbers.

The policy goals behind indexing and who proposed indexing tell a lot about why indexing is perceived to be a good or bad policy. Democrats and Republicans have their own policy interests in indexing, given their different constituencies.

American economists have proposed that the United States do more to stimulate investment in order to be more competitive at the international level. The lowering of the capital gains tax rate is one suggestion. Another is to index the tax for inflation. Republicans have called for indexation of capital gains since the capital gains rate was increased as part of the Tax Reform Act of 1986. Many Democrats have resisted.

Indexing of capital gains for inflation has been proposed based on the assumption that the owners of capital pay an exceedingly high tax rate. Inflation drives up the prices of their investments, but the investments are taxed at current, not constant, value when they are sold. Inflation increases tax burdens, but it also increases the government's tax revenues. For many economists and owners of capital, the "high" taxation of capital gains provides disincentives to invest as well as to sell their investments. Indexing of capital gains for inflation would, it is suggested, be fairer to the owners and would likely stimulate the economy through in-

creasing the propensity to buy and sell investment opportunities. However, for Democrats and those worried about large governmental deficits and sufficient revenue for social support programs, the potential loss of revenue from indexing is the reason not to index capital gains.

Indexing capital gains (as well as the estate tax and depreciation) for inflation is a policy option that as of 1995 had not been adopted by Congress. As of this writing, given Republican control of the One Hundred Fourth Congress, there may be a window of opportunity for passing legislation indexing capital gains, estate taxes, and so on, for inflation. Pre-1986 efforts to "rectify" the perceived tax burden associated with capital gains were undertaken informally, through substitutes for actual indexing of capital gains. For example, the ability to exclude some capital gains and to allow for more rapid depreciation of assets were two favored ways for compensating some people for the inflation penalty in capital gains taxation. These pre-1986 substitutes for formal indexation of capital gains again illustrate how policymakers can devise informal substitutes for formal indexation.

Not all indexing of a political nature is done by governments. Some inhabitants of public housing argue that racial balance is the key to the overall quality of public housing, and racial balancing is practiced in some cases. This practice represents an informal example of people indexing because of their desire to avoid "tipping" or having a public housing unit become preponderantly one race. Concerning the public housing units of Sterrett City (Brooklyn, New York), the Ronald Reagan administration sought to outlaw this informal type of indexing to prevent racial quotas. The residents (African Americans, Puerto Ricans and whites), however, desired to preserve their informal indexing or balancing policy.

The decision not to index capital gains and not to allow public housing inhabitants to engage in their own informal indexing policy put the Reagan administration on both sides of the issue of indexing. All decisions to index or not to index require contextual explanations and policy justifications.

Removing Indexing as Public Policy

The Reagan administration in 1985 helped pass legislation to index the federal income tax. The stated purpose was to prevent "bracket creep," in which individual taxpayers were pushed into higher tax brackets because of inflation. Although indexing of the federal income tax was popular among taxpayers, it ended the revenue windfall that the federal government enjoyed thanks to inflation, and it eliminated the built-in fiscal stabilizers that helped counterbalance inflationary pressures in the first place. Most of all, indexing the federal income tax helped give rise to larger federal deficits by preventing the growth of inflation to increase federal tax revenue while indexing of some federal expenditures were greatly increasing governmental budgetary outlays. Collectively, the two types of indexing are public policies that greatly contribute to federal budget deficits.

Removing indexing has been proposed as a possible public policy option for limiting the increase in expenditure outlays. It is a bargaining chip for those worried about federal deficits. What has *not* been proposed is the removal of indexing from revenue sources. And, when it comes to Social Security and other popular social support programs, there is also little political support to remove indexing. To do so for Social Security, if it is to occur, one must await the added pressure on the trust fund and the full effect of demographic changes brought on by the future retirement of those born in the immediate post–World War II years.

There are a few examples of efforts to remove or to partially or momentarily remove indexing from federal programs. Original efforts to index the minimum wage in terms of one-half of the average manufacturing wage have been stopped. Recent presidents have chosen not to index or only partially to index federal workers' wages, when they have been given the discretion to index federal wages in terms of an increase in the wages of private sector workers. On occasion, there has been a delay in phasing-in cost-of-living payments or skipped payments to Social Security and other governmental recipients. These latter two incremental solutions constitute the preferred policy options when it comes to politically popular programs.

Both private and public sector workers in the 1980s experienced overall decline in cost-of-living adjustment protection. Such protection has become ad hoc and has been left more to collective bargaining negotiations. There have been increased efforts by local governmental officials to eliminate indexation of the wages of local police, fire, and sanitation workers, especially when it concerns increases in their wages and their indexation in terms of comparable wages in other localities. Removing the index, in this case, ends wage parity. The ability of local governments to get voter support for a change in a city charter is often required, just as legislation needs to be approved to make comparable wages (or worth) an empirical example of indexation.

Recent fiscal pressures and budgetary constraints have helped put elimination of indexes on many political agendas, and as a possible public policy it is even more visible than new discussions of the need to index new federal programs. The budget deficit, more than inflation, is considered the greater of the two problems, thanks to low inflation rates in the 1980s and early 1990s. Any success in removing indexes will most likely be explained contextually in light of macro budget problems and the possible viability of other policy options, such as policy and program termination, new taxes, or lower benefits.

Indexing Governmental Spending or Indexing as a Deficit Reducing Solution

Indexing need not always be a source of possible greater governmental deficits and budgetary problems. Indexing of governmental spending in terms of yearly changes in the gross national product (or other economic and demographic indicators) is a policy option open to policymakers who are interested in achieving balanced budgets and executive line-item vetoes for the purposes of limiting governmental spending and deficits. In the context of macro budgeting, indexing may be a solution to some people's worries about the size and rate of governmental spending.

In theory, governmental policymakers could index both expenditures and revenues after a designated trigger number has been exceeded. For example, Canada uses 3 percent inflation as the trigger to begin to index both expenditures and revenues; indexing is only selectively used to compensate citizens for high rates of inflation. Any attempt to use the Canadian model in the United States would be seen as eliminating indexes and might require strong public support.

At local and state levels there have been successful efforts to limit state and local spending by indexing governmental spending in terms of population growth, personal income, and assessed valuation of property. These are substitutes for or additions to indexing governmental spending for inflation. The tendency has been to limit the growth of governmental spending below the general inflation rate and well below the yearly inflation rate for government itself.

Aaron Wildavsky (1980) has suggested cutting growth in governmental spending by limiting any increase in terms of the percentage of increase in the gross national product. The economic productivity of the American economy would determine the degree to which the federal government's spending could grow in a given year. Wildavsky would doubly index federal spending by reducing it more once inflation exceeded 3 percent. For Wildavsky, the government, then, would not be able to use inflationary pressure to drive up the size of the increase in the gross national product so as to benefit governmental spending.

Indexing government in terms of economic productivity is one of many alternatives designed to limit the growth in governmental spending. A more direct approach to cutting governmental spending is through developing a mandate for cuts in federal spending (such as in 1981 and 1995, in the case of limiting spending). This more-direct approach may or may not be politically viable, depending on politicians' lack of political willpower and election-year self-interests. For those who would limit governmental spending, the possibility of a constitutional amendment indexing governmental spending in terms of economic productivity may also be all the more attractive, given the problematical political viability of a true antispending political coalition over time.

Indexing as Good Public Policy

There are not any easy answers to whether indexing constitutes good public policy. Public policy makers have illustrated a wide range of choices when it comes to indexing. Indexing expenditures, as opposed to revenues, presents a clear example of how policymakers, even of the same ideological persuasion, can be for and against indexing for inflation. Policymakers, in terms of their options, need to be aware of the many positive and negative externalities involved in any decision to index for inflation or otherwise. Explicit indexing of Social Security benefits, for instance, affects not only the fiscal soundness of the trust fund but also saving and replacement rates. Only by accounting for the more implicit and informal dimensions of indexing can a policy analyst fully comprehend the wisdom of indexing a program or a revenue source for inflation. The value of indexing is not easily separated from the value attached to a particular public or social policy, or to government itself.

GEORGE FREDERICK GOERL

BIBLIOGRAPHY

Derthick, Martha, 1979. *Policymaking for Social Security.* Washington, DC: The Brookings Institution.
Munnell, Alicia, 1977. *The Future of Social Security.* Washington, DC: Brookings Institution.
Savoie, Donald, 1990. *The Politics of Public Spending in Canada.* Toronto: University of Toronto Press.
Steurele, C. Eugene, 1985. *Taxes, Loans and Inflation.* Washington, DC: Brookings Institution.
————, *The Tax Decade.* Washington, DC: Urban Institute.
United States Department of Labor, 1992. *Bureau of Labor Statistics Handbook of Methods.* Washington, DC: GPO.
Weaver, R. Kent, 1988. *Automatic Government.* Washington, DC: Brookings Institution.
Wildavsky, Aaron, 1980. *How to Limit Governmental Spending.* Berkeley: University of California Press.
————, 1992. *The New Politics of the Budgetary Process.* 2d. ed. New York: HarperCollins.

INDIAN ADMINISTRATIVE TRADITION.

The management practices and organizational culture of the civil service in India.

The Heritage

In 1853 the British Parliament passed the act directing that recruitment to the Indian Civil Service (ICS) be made by open competitive examination (Drewry and Butcher 1988). That the ICS was then the torch bearer of the British tradition in civil service is amply borne out by the fact that it was not until 1870 that the civil service commissioners in London gained control over graduate recruitment for higher posts in the home civil service through open competitive examination. By 1913, there were as many as 30 Indians in the combined Bengal-Bombay-Madras establishment of nearly 800 officers administering the subcontinent from Burma to Baluchistan. Even in 1947, the permanent secretary in Whitehall drew almost the same salary as his ICS counterpart in New Delhi, and the total cadre strength of the ICS was still in three figures.

The uniquely unified civil service structure of the ICS provided talent not only for the top levels of the country's executive bureaucracy but also for the top levels of the country's judiciary and diplomatic posts. There is today a powerful school of thought that considers this heritage a handicap rather than an advantage, providing a rigid hidebound framework suitable for colonial administration that made subsequent restructuring and modernization almost an impossible task. The fact that inclusive of the perquisite of a large bungalow and exclusive chauffeur-driven car, a permanent secretary of the Indian government at New Delhi in 1995 drew less than one-tenth of the salary of his or her counterparts in London–who often share the common background of an Oxbridge education–is only one aspect of this difference, if not deterioration. Indeed, the counterparts at Islamabad, Pakistan, and Dacca, Bangladesh, are even worse off. Equally, the fact that Britain itself is fighting to modernize the bureaucracy is another aspect of the similar realization dawning in India.

The sentiment expressed by India's first prime minister from 1947 to 1964, Pandit Jawaharlal Nehru (1937), that "no new order can be built up in India so long as the spirit of the ICS pervades our administration and our public services" is, in a sense, still relevant today nearly two decades after the extinction of the last ICS officer from Indian bureaucracy (the last of the Indian civil servants recruited by the British Raj in 1943 retired in the years 1979 to 1980).

Ironically, the ICS tradition of high talent, integrity, and independence has also been replaced with mediocrity, corruption, and sycophancy in the post–ICS structure. And yet, there is some lingering similarity between the two structures–which makes comparative analysis of the failures in India with those in United Kingdom particularly instructive. Although the degree of failure varies, there are interesting lessons to be learned from each case. The apprehension often heard in England is that a growing civil service can be a harbinger of collectivism, even of socialist revolution, and the attempts have been made by democratically elected governments, like those in the UK and India, to reduce its size. The civil service in both of these countries, however, not only survived but grew greatly in size, and also, by and large, in stature, as an essential instrument in the establishment of a welfare state and a managed economy.

Size of The Indian Bureaucracy

Has the size of India's "ever proliferating bureaucracy" (*Economist* 1991) become unduly large? In absolute terms, the growth of India's bureaucracy has been phenomenal. If, however, one compares the bureaucracy in developed countries to that of India and consider India's size, the statistical results do not entirely confirm this. The estimated current employment of about 20 million in India's central, state, and local governments, and its general government and public enterprises works out to less than 2.5 percent of the population. In a recent study conducted on the size of bureaucracy in developed and developing countries (Rowat 1990), the findings confirm that public employees, as a percentage of the population, range from 16 percent in Sweden and Denmark to 13 percent in the UK, and 8 percent in the United States and Canada. The size of other countries bureaucracies ranged from about 6 percent in Argentina to less than 2 percent in Guatemala, and in the developing countries, like India, Korea, Kenya, Philippines, and Tanzania, ranged at 2 to 3 percent. The analysis also shows that the cost of the civil service in many of the developing countries also remained at levels comparatively lower than those in the developed countries. In India, it is over Rs15,000 crores, or US$1 billion, for the federal government alone. (India, Ministry of Finance 1995.)

Personal and Administrative Reforms in India, 1947–1994

The administrative reorganization of modern India after the country attained independence in 1947 can logically be studied under two broad headings, personnel reforms and administrative reforms.

The personnel reforms in India can be analyzed under the following: (1) civil service recruitment and selection, (2) vertical hierarchy of government, (3) pay and remuneration, including pension, (4) training succession and appraisal, and (5) issues of political neutrality, permanency, and corruption.

Civil Service Structure and Hierarchy

After 1947, the unified interchangeable top cadre structure of the ICS was replaced by a set of nearly fifty Group A civil services, divided horizontally into administrative, foreign, police, finance and accounts, revenue, railways, post and telegraphs, ordnance factories, forest, medical, and engineering services (excluding the judicial cadres at subdivision, district, state high courts, and Supreme Court). All of these cadres have a broadly similar pay structure, but have some marginal variations in their promotion prospects, de-

pending on whether their cadre reviews had been taken up from time to time.

Though many of these Grade A services were also inherited, they were, in the preindependence era, the noncovenanted cadres supervised by members of the unified superior service, the "covenanted cadre" of the ICS. The purpose of the foreign ruler having a plethora of noncovenanted cadres underpinning the ICS was to divide the ranks to provide conflict between them. By the ICS merely adding several new cadres to this list–such as the Indian Administrative Service, Indian Foreign Service, and other services for accounts, finance, revenue, customs, defence, railways, etc. the structure of the civil service in India in the post-1947 era continued to suffer from this conflict syndrome. Members of different services were encouraged to protect their boundaries by a strong vested interest of power, privilege, and promotion in reserved posts within their cadre, often with low salaries and poor fringe benefits. Instead, if the services had been unified and if competition had been built into the structure for promotion on merit, the overall effectiveness of the services would undoubtedly have improved. Even more unfortunate, the elaborate vertical hierarchy only made the impact of the horizontal hierarchy of multiplicity of services even more disastrous. Between the permanent secretary and the section officer in a federal government ministry at New Delhi there are today nearly twelve levels in the hierarchy: namely, special secretary, director general, additional secretary, joint secretary, adviser, director, joint adviser, deputy secretary, deputy adviser, joint director, undersecretary and deputy director, causing enormous delay in decisionmaking as well as avoidable dilution of responsibility centers. Also, the system of written competitive examination now being conducted in 14 regional languages is causing its own difficulties in merit rating, although the objectivity of the civil service commissions (despite its–according to some–poor and inadequate manning with not-so-talented commissioners) both at the federal and state level continues to be an important hallmark of impartial selection.

Although this rather fragmented civil service structure remained more or less unchanged over the decades, the decision to organize two new "high-talent fast-track" cadres in 1957 in the federal government (by the setting up the Industrial Management Pool and the Central Administrative Pool) broke refreshingly new ground. This action followed the recommendation of the second Appleby report, as well as of reports of several parliamentary committees, which foresaw and emphasized the need for professional managerial cadres within the public services distinct from the various administrative cadres already in existence.

An abortive attempt was also made in the years 1986–1987 to organize a senior management pool. This would integrate the concept of the two earlier pools in the federal government as a select group of high-talent fast-track managers, civil servants to fill top management posts in the central secretariat and the public sector, at the level of joint secretary and above.

Salary, Pensions, and Other Fringe Benefits

Four federal pay commissions in the past 40 years have succeeded in progressively revising and substantially improving the salary structure in the civil services in India. In purchasing power parity, civil servants of India draw a living wage, despite its comparatively low value in foreign exchange. (The Fifth Pay Commission appointed in 1994 recently undertook another review.)

The basic pay of a permanent secretary at New Delhi, which was reduced overnight from Rs4,000 per month (applicable to ICS officers on 14 August 1947) to Rs3,000 per month (applicable to non-ICS officers on 15 August 1947), was increased to Rs8,000 per month in 1985 on the recommendations of the Fourth Pay Commission. In addition, an index-linked cost-of-living allowance scheme was also introduced for all levels of civil servants up to the level of permanent secretary, who in the mid-1990s drew nearly Rs5,000 in cost-of-living allowances. Similarly, the entry pay into Group A civil services, which was reduced to Rs350 per month in 1947 from Rs450 per month in the ICS, has now been revised to Rs2200 per month, with an index-linked cost-of-living allowance of an equivalent amount.

Other major reforms in 1985 on the basis of the Fourth Central Pay Commission were:

- the introduction of elongated pay scales with efficiency bars, to eliminate the problem of stagnation;
- rationalization of pay scales from the minimum Rs750 per month to the maximum Rs8,000 per month, and the consequent reduction in the number of scales from 153 to 36;
- other fringe benefits, including provision of government accommodation as well as use of exclusive or sharing chauffeur-driven cars for senior officers at the level of joint secretary and above;
- introduction of five-day week (Monday through Friday), abolishing the half-day work on Saturdays; and, finally,
- it was recognized that the pension structure is as important as the pay structure to attract talent in the government services (India, Ministry of Finance, 1982).

Training, Succession, and Appraisal

A comprehensive training strategy was evolved in the mid-1980s, which sought to make training compulsory and to cover all the civil servants at all levels—including the introduction of compulsory training programs for senior officers. These programs were structured to meet the needs of

officers with 6 to 9 years' of service—10 to 16 years in regard to program implementation, management concepts and decisionmaking techniques, and 17 to 20 years for policy planning and analysis—with emphasis on decentralized administration and training in project formulation, implementation, monitoring, and evaluation.

A new thrust was also given to management education for civil servants by the launching of the intensive 15-month National Management Programme, specially designed for a mix of young officers from government and managers of public and private sector organizations. The program is held with the academic cooperation of all of the four Indian Institutes of Management at Calcutta, Ahmedabad, Bangalore, and Lucknow.

The system of reporting on the performance of civil servants has been streamlined to make performance appraisal a tool for human resources development. The Annual Confidential Report has been revised so as to provide an objective appraisal—in the form of a joint exercise between the officer reported upon and the reporting officer who would evaluate the performance of the officer during the prescribed period, in terms of the achievement against preset quantitative performance targets, wherever quantification is feasible.

Permanency, Political Maturity, and Corruption

One of the main attractions of a civil service career is security of service guaranteed under the Constitution. Unlike the permanent civil servant in a government department, managers of public enterprise do not enjoy this security since they are hired on contracts with a termination clause of 3 months' notice on either side.

The permanency of civil services is also considered to be one of the main preconditions for insuring political neutrality of civil servants in a democratic government. In the interest of reaping the benefits of competition through opening up of the cadres as well as ensuring loyalty and commitment of individual civil servants, particularly at the top level of the government, both of these concepts of permanency and political neutrality are being questioned. The issue of corruption is also linked to this, because it is extremely difficult to dislodge a civil servant on the grounds of corruption unless the charges are framed and established after going through an elaborate procedure, which involves years of trial and litigation. (However, it is an open secret that there is an unwritten schedule of dowry levels for officers of different Group A services in the marriage market.)

A three-pronged strategy of prevention, surveillance and detection, and deterrent punitive action, has been adopted by the government to fight the malaise of corruption. The Action Plan on anticorruption measures includes identification of corruption-prone areas, simplification of rules and procedures, strengthening of departmental vigilance machinery, expeditious finalization of vigilance cases, regular review of performance of the government employees who attain the age of 50 to 55 years, or those completing 30 years of service, with a view to weeding out corrupt and inefficient elements (under Fundamental rules Section 56[J]).

The existing anticorruption laws were also strengthened with the enactment of the 1988 Prevention of Corruption Bill.

Organizational Reforms in the 1970s and 1980s

The Secretariat Reorganisation Committee in 1947 was followed by a review of the workings of the ICS machinery of federal government undertaken towards the end of 1949. In July 1951, A. D. Gorwala, an eminent planner and an ICS officer, was asked to assess whether the existing administrative machinery and methods were adequate to meet the requirements of planned development. Two subsequent reports that had a significant impact on administrative reforms were Paul Appleby's first report, "Public Administration in India: Report of a Survey, 1953," followed by his second report "Reexamination of India's Administrative System with Special reference to Administration of Government's Industrial and Commercial Enterprises, 1956."

Following a review in the mid-1960s of administrative deficiencies responsible for slowing down economic growth in the third plan, a Department of Administrative Reforms (DAR) was set up in March 1964. In 1965, a new Bureau of Public Enterprises (BPE) was also formed within the government of India to provide a management consultancy service to economic ministries controlling public enterprises in the federal government. This was followed by similar organizations in the State Governments of the Indian Union.

The Administrative Reforms Commission (ARC) was formed in January 1966 to cover the entire gamut of India's public administration, at the center as well as in the states.

The decade of 1970–1980 witnessed enormous changes as a result of the implementation of the ARC's recommendations. Management studies thereafter occupied an important place in the scheme of administrative reforms, carried out by the DAR and BPE, covering organizational structure and relationship; methods and procedures; financial administration; information systems; records management; use of modern office machines and equipment; and citizen satisfaction. The full-fledged Ministry of Personnel, Public Grievances, and Pensions was set up in March 1985, under the overall charge of the prime minister.

Another important landmark of the 1980s reforms was the creation of the new Ministry of Programme Implementation (MPI), which has been the charge of successive prime ministers (Rajiv Gandhi, V. P. Singh, Chandrasekhar, and P. V. Narsimha Rao) in improving the overall economic management of the country through better coordination of poverty-alleviation programs, enforcement of accountability of individual ministries or departments, on-line monitoring of infrastructure sector performance as well as of major projects, and greater delegation of powers.

Long-Term Impact of Personnel and Organizational Reforms:

The overall impact of personnel reforms was as diffused and unsatisfactory as the impact of the organizational reforms discussed. The civil service structure–horizontally fragmented into a multiplicity of services, providing little scope for healthy competition due to their closed career patterns–has become out of date. The vertical structure of the hierarchy is also unsuitable for speedy decisionmaking and empowerment down the line, for encouraging bright, young talent to make decisions and be accountable for them.

Despite the quantitative efforts of imparting training to civil servants in India, the qualitative content and impact of training efforts remained inadequate in the absence of any rigorous system of training needs survey and managerial succession plans. These can be conducted far more rationally where personnel and position classification exercises have been used and updated on a regular basis, still a far cry from the Indian scene.

The significant innovation of organizing two fast-track cadres for highly talented administrative and managerial personnel into the Central Administrative Pool (consisting of secretaries, additional secretaries, joint secretaries, and deputy secretaries in the federal government) and the Industrial Management Pool (consisting of chairman, CEOs, and potential top management talent for the public enterprise)–with interchangeability within these two pools–was not followed through after they were initially set up in 1957. This was due to the bargaining power of people of the various Group A services, who rightly viewed these pools as threats to their promotion prospects. Unless these Group A services are unified and opened up, providing competition between them, the feasibility of organizing pools of high-talent fast-track cadres, which involves "selection within selection," from the existing cadres may prove difficult.

The proposal for the Senior Management Pool mooted in the late 1980s under the leadership of Rajiv Gandhi as prime minister also could not be implemented owing to the absence of these preconditions. And yet, no civil service can be modernized unless it is opened up, unified, and replenished with new talent at all levels, which can provide competition to those inside the cadre.

It is also necessary to mention the still-unfinished democratic decentralization efforts in the past five decades. The administrative structure of the Indian federation today consists of (1) the central government at New Delhi; (2) 32 state governments, including union territories; (3) 430 districts; (4) and 5,092 blocks, consisting of (5) 500,000 villages.

Prior to 1947, the district was the focal point of colonial administration, with all emphasis on law and order and governance of the country. It is ironical that even after 40 years of independence, the district continues to be the focal point of administration in democratic India, where one has yet to take the bureaucracy down to the masses and serve them effectively. Even the archaic designations of district collector and deputy commissioner, introduced by the Raj in the latter part of the nineteenth century, have been retained, although it is not clear today what these district officers (as they are appropriately called in Malaya) collect or how they share their commission! (Several committees, like Balwantrai Mehta Committee of 1959, GVK Rao Committee in the 1970s, and the Advisory Council of Programme Implementation in the late 1980s went over this.)

Neither has the district planning procedure been streamlined nor has it been effectively introduced, except in some states like Karnataka (where the new institution of district chief secretaries is interesting and needs special mention), Maharashtra, Gujerat, Andhra Pradesh, West Bengal, and Kerala. The Panchayati Raj institutions thus fell into a state of suspended animation in most parts of the country. And yet, the block development officer is entrusted with executing poverty alleviation programs amounting to nearly Rs2 million per block, on an average. This underscores the need for strengthening administration at this level.

It is time that the blocks were broken into smaller formations, such as the Mandal, as was done in the state of Andhra Pradesh. These consist of 30 or so villages, and they have had a beneficial impact on the implementation of the various social sector programs. There is wide recognition that to derive full benefit from the enormous amount of money allocated, as well as to improve management of public action programs in health, education, housing, and drinking water, will require not only that these programs are packaged approximately but also that their efficient implementation and delivery will be possible only if the grass-roots bureaucracy is strengthened by the people power of democratically elected panchayats (Basu 1991).

The paradoxical absence of any long-term impact of the administrative reforms from 1947 onward on modernizing India's bureaucracy can only be explained by India's preoccupation with forms, facades, intentions, and rituals rather than with providing any real long-term solutions to the issues that can truly restructure an out-of-date framework. To illustrate, though, on one hand, powers were delegated for improved management of the government, the Appointments Committee of the Cabinet continues to retain its power to approve all appointments at the relatively junior level of deputy secretaries and their equivalent. Similarly, the purpose of encouraging speedy inter-ministry decisions through problem-solving initiatives is often defeated by the temptation of administrative ministries not to take decisions even when such decisions clearly lie within their jurisdiction. Whenever decisions involve replacing any old system with the new, inertia continues to operate strongly against such change. This has been the fate of committees and commissions and task forces appointed from time to time, many of whose reports are either not read or not considered for years. (Thus, the October 1987 recommendations of an important committee set up by prime minister's order in 1986, under the chairmanship of Ratan Tata, to look into the causes of delay in major projects are still awaiting consideration of the government.

As the years passed, the various attempts made to institutionalize ministerial accountability that were launched with great enthusiasm have become routine. These attempts included the system of Annual Active Plans, which would help articulate the different corporate objectives of departments and ministries who have been encouraged by the MPI to identify their "mission" as well as "key result areas."

The experiment with Public Enterprise Memoranda of Understanding (MOUs) also seemed to meet the same fate. It was seen as a mere procedural imposition from the government, and was not seized as a management opportunity either to empower public enterprise boards with responsibilities discharged earlier by the administrative ministry or even to install a modern effective system of "Performance Evaluation for Performance Improvement" (Basu 1991a).

Unless administrative reforms encourage microlevel improvement of performance and microlevel self-evaluation, with a view to providing a managerial feedback loop for bringing about further improvement in performance, any elaborate machinery for external evaluation can only degenerate into evaluation for evaluation's sake. In fact, performance itself often becomes a casualty. It also helps to "pass the buck" upwards and reduce accountability from those who should perform to those who supervise. The organizational reforms in India have thus, on the whole, tended to become mainly in form rather than in real substance, leaving little impact on the efficiency of the system. One cannot have effective administration without a close fit between policy objectives, organizational design, operational procedure, and personnel motivation. What has been lacking in India's administrative reforms in the past five decades is a congruence between strategy, structure, and substance (Basu 1992).

To conclude, the first of two phases of progress have been achieved by India's bureaucracy in its transition from governance to administration in the past 50 years. Today, it stands poised at the threshold of a new breakthrough in its transition from administration to management.

P. K. BASU

BIBLIOGRAPHY

Basu, P. K., 1991a. *Institutional and Methodological Aspects of Managing and Monitoring Poverty Alleviation Programmes: The Indian Case.* Cambridge University, Management Studies Research Paper 6/91.
——, 1991b. *Performance Evaluation for Performance Improvement, An Essay–Strategic Management of Public Enterprises in India.* London: Allied Publishers.
——, 1992. *Strategic Issues in Administrative Reorganisation: A Developing Country's Perspective.* Cambridge University, Management Studies Research Paper No 4/92.
Drewry, G., and T. Butcher, 1988. *The Civil Service Today.* Oxford: Blackwell.
The Economist, (London) "A Survey of India," 4th May 1991.
India. Ministry of Finance, 1982. *Report of Fourth Central Pay Commission,* vols. 1 and 2. New Delhi: Government of India Printing Office.
——, 1995. *Expenditure Budget* 1995–96, (vol. 1, p. 87) New Delhi: Government of India Printing Office.
Nehru, Jawaharlal, 1937. *Autobiography of Jawaharlal Nehru.* London: Allen and Unwin.
Rowat, D. C., 1990, "Comparing Bureaucracies in Developing and Developed Countries." *International Review of Administration Science.*

INDIGENOUS PEOPLES, HABITAT.

The special immediate relationships that link small-scale traditional societies with their habitats and their uses of natural resources, which form the basis for native title- and land-rights policies in a number of settler countries.

The term, indigenous people, is rightly applied to any who have established a particular country as their home and who were born there. It has, however, been given a more specific political meaning; that is, that part of a country's population that has been there beyond the memory of humans; who are members (and/or their descendants) of small-scale, low-energy societies that live, or once lived, by hunting and gathering, horticulture, or pastoralism, and whose present cultural meanings and values are directly oriented toward that tradition.

These modes of subsistence connect peoples to their respective habitats with obvious immediacy. The technologies of foragers and low-energy farmers do not enable them to manipulate the productivity of their habitats to any great extent, contrasted with, for instance, high-energy farmers who use irrigation, mechanical tillage and cultivation, and radical change in the genetics of crops and livestock. Instead, those termed "indigenous" peoples developed profound knowledge of the patterns of nature and its effects on the productivity of the local flora and fauna. They used their mobility, low population densities, and generalized, rather than specialized, technology to enable them to follow opportunistic strategies of utilizing the resources until the resources' abundance passed, when they were able to change to other strategies.

The connection between indigenous peoples and their habitats should not be seen in the simplistic terms of Marxian economic determinism. Their knowledge of, and their strategies for exploiting, resources developed and was maintained in the contexts of belief systems and forms of social organization that led to a much more intimate connection, in which land and natural resources were accorded meanings that far transcended bare utilitarian values. The connection between the habitats and their resources, and the purpose and ways of life of indigenous peoples is complex and closely knit. Disruption of any part of that intricate web has consequences far more damaging than merely changing the way in which women and men get their daily bread.

Although not isolated, these societies were politically autonomous, or nearly so, with their own economies and cultures, including languages. Overtaken by the sequence of colonial conquest of their homelands, followed by the local development of the nation-state, they are now dispossessed, disadvantaged ethnic minorities, sometimes derided for what is perceived as their primitive technology (often rationalized–quite falsely–as indicative of moral and mental backwardness) by the dominant society of which they have involuntarily become part.

Modern nation-states must necessarily participate and integrate themselves in the world market economy, which entails a view and use of natural resources that is consonant with that of Western industrialized economies. The need for profit is inherent in economic endeavor in the market economy. Continuing profit requires improving efficiency and productivity, usually only feasible at a limited number of critical junctures in the operations. To this end, industrialized economies increasingly develop and use technology to enable them to move away from labor-intensive operations toward greater use of capital in the form of impersonal equipment and information. A consequence has been a steady decrement in the perceived significance of social relationships in economic operations. The former are now seen as no more than peripherals to the economy. This is demonstrated by the extreme difficulty and small success that sociologists and economists have had in meaningfully relating their respective concepts and data to each other's frames of reference, and in sensibly integrating each other's data. The dislocation of the economic from the social is further illustrated by the lack of success in applying ethical principles to the applications of technology and other economic operations. There is also no clear vision of how to reconcile conservation imperatives with the demands of economic and technological development. Pollution and loss of space and species are costs of which no meaningful evaluation can presently be made and are, therefore, usually left out of the fantasy accounting of economic rationalism.

In allocating natural resources, a society bestows on its constituent groups individuals rights in which their interests in and the value that they place on, the land and its resources are recognized and protected. In Europe, and the many nation-states that were former colonies of European powers, rights to land are derived from the model of the Roman legal system and have developed to serve, with greater or lesser convenience and efficiency, the capitalist, industrialized orientation of the economies of those countries. Rights range from private ownership through gradations of individual and group tenancy to rights of way and access and other concepts of amenity. In many, if not all of these countries, private ownership is seen as the ideal, the "right" relationship between land and individual. Land and natural resources are commodities to be acquired, used, and disposed of for the benefit of the owner. In the vulgar view, private ownership is seen as allowing owners to do as they please with their land, including disposing of it as they choose. However, statutory restrictions, obligations to other members of society, and considerations of what is decreed to be proper management diminish the complete range of rights and freedom to do with their land what they will. Fiduciary encumbrances oblige owners to preserve the estate and the rights to it in a prescribed state for the benefit of future owners. Legal processes, such as bankruptcy and divorce, may result in the courts' disposing of the land in ways that are quite contrary to the owner's wishes. These restrictions are widely regarded as impediments to economic gain, however, to be overcome or circumvented, rather than as rightful duties and obligations. Although ownership may, in fact, amount to rather less than is commonly supposed, it nevertheless influences public notions of the use of land and its assets and conflicts with the simply and reluctantly perceived necessity for maintaining the present and future utility that the land and its resource have for the rest of present and future society.

It is characteristic of economic and technological development that an ever-greater fraction of existing energy and materials is made available and is exploited. Population growth and its concomitant demand for economic development have precipitated the erstwhile foragers and farmers into competition with the dominant society for these resources, including living space. Disadvantaged by their small numbers, material poverty, and their political impotence, indigenous peoples have slender chance of success. Failure and consequent loss of resources clearly imperil their economies. Because of the closely integrated, specialized nature of their cultures and forms of social organization, these peoples give natural resources a signifi-cance that extends beyond their pragmatic economic value and embraces the moral, social, and psychological aspects of their lives. In the systems of belief and value of small-scale societies, natural resources are an essential component of the affirmation and expression of self and society. To the extent that the people are denied their traditional rights of use of resources, the logic of the meanings that these resources have for them is negated, vitiating both the structures within which they, their fellows, and their very lives have value and purpose and the processes by which they affirm and express them.

One cannot here make a detailed survey of the resource requirements of indigenous peoples. Each case entails comprehensive statements of, first, the entire spectrum of the people's patterns of use, the social and cultural systems by which such use is ordered, and the epistemology of their conceptualization of use in order to understand its social and psychological significance to them. It also involves an exhaustive statement of the ecology of their habitat, including the short- and long-term effects of the people's activities and accurate assessment of the consequences of any changes. Instead, a few illustrative case studies will indicate the complexity and difficulties of competition between the dominant population of a nation-state and its indigenous peoples.

In the view of Australia's Western Desert peoples, such as the Pitjantjatjara and Pintupi Aborigines, people are an integral part of the environment, as are streams and mountains, plants and animals (see Myers 1986; Silberbauer 1994; Stanner 1966). Human beings (here, specifically Western Desert peoples themselves) have an essential and reciprocal role in the maintenance of the orderly operation of natural processes. It is only through the proper performance of rituals and conduct of personal lives that these processes can continue and their benefit be conferred on all and on everything that lives in the country. Neglect will not only disrupt natural order, threatening natural resources, thus endangering health and well-being, but people will wither away in the ensuing lack of spiritual nutrition.

In the geomorphology of Western Desert Aborigines, landforms and prominent features of the countryside are the results of acts of heroes in the mythical epoch, *Tjukurpa*, the Dreamtime. They moved around the land, raising mountain ranges, cleaving valleys, or petrifying other Beings, or themselves becoming petrified into masses of rock. Each act is an episode in the myth of each particular hero, and the route traveled by her or him is marked and closely identified with the character. Land is, therefore, not anonymous, impersonal topography but is variously imbued with the personality of each Being—here powerfully charged by Malu (red kangaroo), elsewhere by Ili (fig), Kuninka (native cat), or Milpali (perentie lizard). Routes twist and turn and extend into neighboring countries, crossing language boundaries without changing identity, here going underground to emerge somewhere else, potentially covering the entire continent. The route of Malu, for instance, stretches from the Indian Ocean to the northeast Pacific coast.

A special, totemic relationship between individuals and mythical heroes is acquired by birth and descent and, less intimately, by marriage. Descent and marriage are socially structured. Totemic relationships, thus, reflect that structure and are criteria for membership of certain groups. Although a totemic group is not corporate in that it is conceived of as a legal identity that holds rights to property, its members severally share particular rights and obligations in respect of the land that is associated with the hero's route. This common characteristic requires them to periodically take joint action that relates to the land, for example, initiating and conducting appropriate ceremonies and rituals.

Totemic relationships are pervasive. They give and mark each person's place in society and in the environment that is an inextricable blend of the physical and the spiritual. An individual derives and expresses personal identity by social interaction, including appropriate observance and participation in ceremonies. Relationships of state, cause and effect between heroes, land, flora and fauna, totemic, and other social groups, and individuals are expressed in coded form in song cycles. (The latter were explained to me during my work in Central Australia.) There is an intimate triadic link of hero with land, hero with individual, and social group with land and all that is in it. Self is defined, sensed, and expressed in the context of that triad. To exist in an identity, to have Self, requires meaningful behavior that expresses that identity (see Bain 1992). Any discontinuity within the triad will diminish the whole—land, hero, Self, and one's social group. To Western Desert peoples, as to other Australian Aborigines, their land is more than the sum of its natural resources; to be in it, to behave appropriately when there, and periodically to give to and draw strength from the heroes are as necessary to personal and community well-being as are the natural resources.

In the late 1960s Pitjantjatjara people of Ernabella in Central Australia (Silberbauer 1972) bought nearly all their food from the local general store. From the perspective of white Australian economics, they were low-income shoppers. From an empirical nutritional point of view, the additional and frequent forays that they made into the bush to hunt and gather merely served to add garnishes and delicacies to their store-bought diet. But in their own eyes, the hunting and gathering met the strong need they felt to affirm their existence as social identities. Use of traditional foodstuffs and of artifacts made from local raw materials in exchanges and the sharing of traditional knowledge had deeper social and psychological meaning than those of store-bought commodities. The time and energy they spent on foraging, rather than on the wage-earning activi-

ties available to them, would appear to be economically irrational if Pitjantjatjara reality were to be ignored. Within that reality, however, it is completely rational to invest time and energy in maintaining oneself in a state of being. Without that, nothing—including wage-earning—would have any purpose.

Pitjantjatjara reasoning, in contrast with that of many academics and intellectuals, holds knowledge and competence to be synonymous: To know is to do, and without the doing of it, it is not knowledge. Knowledge is respected and is, indeed, an essential element of senior, responsible status. Only those women and men who have been initiated into successive levels of the mysteries of mythology and ritual may take certain essential roles in the performance of ceremonies. Here, also, the tight connection between the land and its resources, social structure, and individual identity and Self is demonstrated. Western Desert peoples, then, have an interest in their environment that includes, but goes far beyond their subsistence and economy.

Indirectly or directly we are all dependent on the land for our sustenance—our food and potable wear. All forms of life utilize the resources found in their habitats to resist the environmental pressures of hunger, thirst, cold, heat, disease, enemies, and other threats. The human strategy of evolution and survival has long been to extend our meager physical prowess by the extrasomatic means of weapons, tools, and other artifacts. Instead of adapting to cold by genetic change to grow thermal insulation in the form of hair, wool, or fur, or to accumulate deposits of blubber, humans wove plant fibers into protective coverings and robbed other animals of their coats. Much later we developed synthetic substitutes for both types of fiber. Instead of developing a faster gait and growing more powerful claws and teeth to catch and kill prey animals, our ancestors threw things at them. Although the last 100,000 years of human history have seen relatively little anatomical change, our forebears progressed from sticks and stones to sharpened projectiles of greater aerodynamic sophistication and powers of penetration, propelled by bows and spear-throwers. Eventually, they added poison to the points, using biochemical means to reduce the amount of physical force needed to kill. Those ancestors learned which plants could be eaten and used for medicines. They devised ways of taming fire to warm themselves and cook their foods, greatly increasing the range of species that, because they were not nourishing or poisonous when raw, were useful additions to their diet when cooked, and so on, through the history of human technological development. These adaptations enabled our species to resist environmental species so successfully that, with our rat symbionts, we are now one of the most numerous and widely distributed mammals.

The human strategy was invented and, therefore, had to be learned by its practitioners. Teaching, and learning a syllabus of this complexity, could only occur in a context of stable and altruistic relationships. Those involved must be confident in their expectations of others' behavior toward them, and toward one another, and of others' responses to their own behavior. This relationship entails flexible, dynamic, and versatile forms of organization that are capable of retaining coherence despite the changes of personnel that birth, death, and migration bring and those occasioned by the ever-fluctuating seasonal and annual circumstances of life in small-scale societies. Without these, people would not be motivated to invest their teaching in others who can be expected eventually to reciprocate and reward the efforts of the former, and pupils would not be in the company of their mentors long enough to learn. Cooperative and complementary effort would be improbable without faith in promises of eventual return of goods and services rendered. Adequate and effective forms of social organization are, in their way, as necessary to human survival as are the resources and the technology by which they are utilized. If the fabric of a society is torn, its members' deprivation will be as great as if bereft of their physical resources.

The anthropologist, Marshall Sahlins (1965), gave a useful definition of a society's economy as the means whereby it provisions itself. This entails the society's devising systems through which natural and human resources are identified and utilized as such and are allocated among the members of the society, who manage them and who distribute and reward goods and services. The definition embraces the society's inventory of tools and other artifacts, knowledge of their use and application, and the ways in which this knowledge is developed, propagated, and controlled. It is clear from Sahlins's definition that the integrity of a people's social organization becomes as vitally important to them as is their subsistence base.

The Ik of northern Uganda and Kenya, previously hunted and gathered in what was for them, with their technology and skills, a fruitful territory (Turnbull 1972). The productive portion of their country was declared a game reserve and they were barred from entering and using it. Having been forced into the barren mountains, they survived on the meager crops they could raise and sporadic success in finding small prey, neither of which was traditional currency of economic and social exchanges. The crafts by which women and men had gained pride and prestige could no longer be plied. The exchanges by which they formed, expressed, affirmed, or modified social relationships became impossible. In the absence of any meaningful way of maintaining relationships, they lost their previous confidence in one anothers' behavior, and responses to behavior, and their social order fell apart. With that, their values and moral orientation lost their meanings. In describing their lot, Colin Turnbull depicted a dog-eat-dog existence, in which friendship, loyalty, and love—and even what we regard as common humanity—have no part. As

well as miserable material poverty and hunger, the Ik were left to suffer the dreadful deprivations of social and psychological starvation.

Before the late 1960s the interplay of economics, populations, and politics was such that the Central Kalahari Desert, in what was then the Bechuanaland Protectorate (now Botswana), was regarded as a wasteland for which nobody had any use. Until then the G/wi Bushmen lived there in autonomous, self-regulating bands of about 60 men, women, and children (Silberbauer 1981). Each occupied its own territory, within which it controlled the disposition of the members and the use of the resources. In G/wi belief, the deity N!adima had created the universe and owned everything in it. Humans, in the G/wi view, were merely one species of N!adima's creatures, neither superior nor inferior to the others. As with each species, humans were created with characteristic capabilities and needs, and it was up to them to use the former to devise a modus vivendi to meet the latter. How they did these things was their affair, and N!adima would not intervene in their lives unless they did something to offend him, or for his own unfathomable, capricious reasons. He would be angered by anyone's disregard for his creation: The people could beg for the burning sun and drought to pass and relieve the burden of heat and thirst, but they should not be cursed. The G/wi could hunt the animals that they managed to kill, eat the plants that they discovered to be foods, and use other resources, provided proper respect was always shown (e.g., in not being "greedy" and taking no more than was required to meet one's immediate needs). There were no acts of worship by which N!adima might be influenced to benefit people or individuals. Without the comfort or authority of a higher power, the G/wi were alone in their struggle to survive in an environment in which, in favorable years, plenty is known only between December—the onset of the three-month wet season—and the first frosts that come to blight plants and the food they bear some time between May and late June. After that come the drought and bitter cold of winter (lows of −13°C), followed by strong winds and intense heat (highs in the shade of 48°C) in early summer. They saw their social and cultural adaptations as of their own creation, a way of life that they had devised, agreed upon among themselves, and could maintain only by working always to foster the harmony that such consensus depends upon. They viewed humans as essentially reasonable beings, but subject to error and shortcomings, from which would come inevitable misunderstanding and conflict. These they sought to reduce by organizing their society so as to give all a fair share of what they needed and to maximize the opportunities and rewards for interaction and communication. Among their adaptations were numerous ingenious and, generally, effective means of resolving conflict.

As sufferance tenants in N!adima's world, the G/wi agreed among themselves how to allocate territories to bands. During the wet season, and before winter, each band lived together in a series of shared camps, moving approximately every six weeks to a new site and fresh supplies of plant foods. In the hard, lean seasons of winter and early summer, when food became too sparse for a whole band to live together, the members dispersed in separate households. By agreement, each was allocated a winter range that would meet its needs as well as was feasible in that year. There they remained alone, relying on the family's knowledge, skills, strength, and mutual support to find sufficient means to survive until the fickle rains came again, bringing relative affluence and the inestimable comfort of the company of the rest of the band, in another series of shared camps. Also by agreement, bands would visit, staying for four or six weeks and sharing their host's camp and food. These were occasions for gossip, for a wider social circle in which prospective marriage partners might find each other and get to know one another better, and occasions for the pleasure of different company.

It was also the time for exchanges of imported commodities like tobacco, soft iron for tools and hunting weapons, and trade beads. These were sold by trading outside the central desert and by traveling across it through a series of visits between bands. The vagaries of this haphazard import system, and those of the uncertain endeavor of foraging, would lead to irregularities of supply and, in an entrepreneurial economy with a demand criterion of values like ours, to wide price fluctuations. In the G/wi view, economics exchange, whether of goods or of services, is perceived as a social activity in which gifts are given or favors are performed and received. The value of either is assessed by, first, the need of the recipient. If you were to do something for me or give me something that I badly wanted, it would be accorded high value. The second criterion of value is a discounting factor proportional to the giver's ability to do the favor or give the gift. Thus, if you had plenty of that which you gave me, or could easily spare it, its value would be reduced. Similarly, if you were adept at performing some activity, or had nothing else to do, its value would diminish. Also, if you were a renowned expert at doing that which you did for me, I am seen as having conferred on you an opportunity for demonstrating your expertise, and the value would be lessened. In this way, the gradient in the flow of goods and services between the haves and have-nots is prevented from becoming too steep, and any differential in the distribution of wealth is reduced. G/wi ethics insist on reciprocation. Bookkeeping, however, does not go back beyond the last entry. That is to say, when A gives something to B, the latter must make a return presentation, but, having done so, B becomes A's creditor, and exchanges are, at least nationally, self-perpetuating (in the same way as are our cycles of dinner invitations, or "shouts" in a drinking circle). Any desired good or service is acceptable in reciprocation for any gift or favor received, so exchanges are not cut off because a commod-

ity is unobtainable. (Clearly, the system can only be expected to work among people who, although experts, are not specialists and each of whom is essentially self-reliant and capable of finding, making, or doing whatever she or he needs.)

The G/wi have a universalistic kinship system in which kin of kin are kin, and thus extends to all persons with whom one can discover some shared relative—potentially the whole G/wi population and beyond. It gives fairly detailed precepts for the attitudes and behavior of those close relatives (e.g., parents and children or siblings) who are expected to spend much of their lives in each others' close proximity. For others including kin of kin, there are broad categories of relationship and generalized patterns of appropriate behavior. Within that generalized framework, interpersonal relationships are demarcated more precisely, intensified and expressed by exchange of goods and services. These include utilitarian transactions, but even these express the kinds of relationship that exists between the participants.

Meat of hunted game is the most commonly exchanged commodity during the period that the band is in a shared camp. Artifacts made from local materials, including leather, make up nearly all of the remainder of traded commodities, with imported items constituting a small fraction. Thus, there is interdependence between the consensual social order on which the people depend to lead their lives in harmony and regular, predictable access to those resources for all, without ruinous competition for them.

In the 1980s this interdependence was demonstrated when, in response to political pressure from international conservationists, the Botswana government removed Bushmen hunters and gatherers from their customary territories in the Central Kalahari Game Reserve and placed them elsewhere in large camps.

Consensus is the outcome of a series of judgments made by people who all have access to a common pool of information. That includes the matter to be decided, the propositions relating to that matter (e.g., the proposed course of action), and the criteria by which the merits of the propositions are to be judged (factors relevant to the problem, objectives of the proposals, the values and their different weights, and a shared knowledge of the causal or logical relationships believed to exist among these items of information). In the company of unprecedented numbers of kin, friends, and complete strangers, G/wi consensus was an impossibly unwieldly way of conducting their affairs; the G/wi and others could not maintain the stability of their customary social order. The G/wi were forced into a sedentary existence, in numbers too large for the sparse local resources of flora and fauna to support, and the traditional exchange networks faltered. Community decision-making and conflict resolution came to a halt (see Kent 1989 and Silberbauer 1996).

These are volatile, passionate people, and without their usual vectors of appropriate expression of strong feelings, they soon found themselves in a deeply distressing mess of escalating confusion, which turned into aggression. They saw that consensus could not work here. To persist with it would precipitate the further evil of destructive and futile formation of factions and internal schisms as they fought among themselves over whose aspirations and notions of right and wrong should prevail. Instead, they followed the example of those Bushmen who, for over a century, had placed themselves in servitude to the dominant Tswana and Kgalagadi cattle-herders (see Silberbauer and Kuper 1996), and turned to Tswana and Kgalagadi men who worked in the camps as their decisionmakers. Flattered by the ascription of political power, the latter accepted the burden of responsibility. It was not altogether satisfactory, but the Bushmen had previously arrived at a tolerable measure of consensus to abide by the decisions of outside authority, and they have managed to dodge the unhappy fate of the Ik.

Although nation-states involved in the capitalist world economy and indigenous peoples both depend on natural resources, they do not always use them in the same ways or require the same range of resources. As low-energy opportunists who extract from their habitats no more than a small amount of the total energy and materials, hunters and gatherers generally have low population densities; G/wi Bushmen bands, for instance, varied from 0.046 to 0.097 persons per square kilometer in their territories (i.e., between 10 and 22 sq km per capita).

Their requirements necessarily catered for the worst case, in other words, in the worst-experienced drought, space was required that contained sufficient essential resources to sustain enough survivors to rebuild the population once conditions improved. The habitat requirements of the flora and fauna on which they depend must be integrated in the total. The G/wi hunt animals that are migratory and sensitive to disturbance; the total human requirements therefore include the extent and integrity of the routes and seasonal ranges of the relevant species, far beyond their band territories and the Central Kalahari. The per capita area cannot be accurately calculated, but would amount to more than 100 square kilometers. This was tolerable 30 years ago, when the central and northeastern parts of Botswana, through which the antelope migrated, were thinly populated, when the cattle industry was rudimentary; and when the migrating herds were large enough to provide everybody with meat. Now, with a human population too large to share the hunting and a sophisticated cattle industry, the migratory antelope would consume valuable pasture and present a significant threat of communicable disease.

These changes do not necessarily prevent hunting and gathering by Bushmen. If some means could be devised of obviating migration and stabilizing antelope herds within the Central Kalahari Game Reserve—perhaps by providing permanent waterholes—hunting could conceivably continue at lower rates.

But the world regards hunting and gathering, and other low-density, low-energy forms of subsistence, as a failure to exploit valuable resources. In fairness, it is reasonable to question the morality of devoting large tracts of land and its resources to the exclusive use of a small number of a nation's population when others suffer in poverty as a result. This must be weighed against the ethical obligation that the nation can be held to have toward its people to allow them to maintain their traditions, particularly when these traditions furnish those people's meanings of life and framework of order and are the rationale for action. To negate tradition of this significance is profound, pervasive dispossession.

Very few contemporary indigenous peoples maintain their traditions intact. No tradition is *sub specie aeternitatis*, and "intact" does not imply customs forever frozen in the immutable in the grip of the past. Culture is dynamic and ever-changing and, in an ordered society, change is coherent and is perceived as being under the control of the society. Nor was any indigenous culture wholly the product of only its practitioners. If ever the case, it is a very long time since any society lived in hermetic isolation. With contact, however indirect, came new ideas, objects, and materials.

In an autonomous society, the people gave their own place and meaning in their culture, values, and practices to the imports and, by this manner of incorporation, made them their own. Man Friday and Robinson Crusoe, although physically isolated, each brought to the island his own knowledge, skills, and ideas, and the currents brought to its shore other imports. The two men synthesized an amalgam of all this to create their own culture and controlled its applications according to their needs and abilities. With a people's loss of their autonomy goes too their power to accord meaning to alien imports and to control their use and application, their culture is no longer intact, their choices of action are prescribed by the dominant society, with corresponding loss of power to determine their own fates. However, their tradition persists as a palimpsest from which they continue to derive their meanings and identity.

Gause's Principle of Competitive Exclusion is implacable; unless there is superabundance of environmental resources, including food, no two species with identical ecological requirements can exist together in the same habitat. The relationship between indigenous people and a dominant society has usually been construed as one in which they are competing for identical ecological requirements and, when the pressures of increased population and technological development reach a critical level, the resources are no longer abundant and exclusion is the consequence of the ensuing competition. This construction of the relationship is an unnecessary illusion; as previously mentioned, small-scale societies and industrialized ones do not use resources in the same way, nor do they both use the same range of resources. If the obligation to allow a people choice and control of their way of life is accepted as valid, then there may be negotiation of the relationship, to change it from adversarial competition to one of cooperative complementarity.

Negotiation, like consensus, requires that the participants have access to a common pool of information. Each must be enabled to know and understand the other's position and aspirations, and their reasons. It is also necessary that they proceed on a basis of mutual respect; at least to the extent of each recognizing the sincerity and validity of the other's position and aspirations. This is not a panacea. Factors like racism and the prevailing political and economic climate may not be conducive to conceding equality to indigenous peoples, and a history of oppression is a substantial obstacle to fostering their respect and trust of the dominant society. Nevertheless, the feasibility of the improbable was demonstrated by the granting of land rights to Australian Aborigines and the relinquishing of political power by white nationalists in South Africa. Negotiation, and the redefinition of the status and role of an indigenous people in the nation does hold the possibility of their gaining a measure of self-determination within the vernacular construction of reality.

GEORGE SILBERBAUER

BIBLIOGRAPHY

Bain, Margaret, 1992. *The Aboriginal-White Encounter: Towards Better Communication.* Australian Aborigines and Islander Branch, Summer Institute of Linguistics Occasional Papers, Darwin, Australia.

Kent, Susan, 1989. "And Justice for All: The Development of Political Centralization Among Newly Sedentary Foragers." *American Anthropologist* 91:703–712.

Myers, Fred R., 1986. *Pintupi Country, Pintupi Self: Sentiment, Place, and Politics Among Western Desert Aborigines.* Canberra: Australian Institute of Aboriginal Studies.

Sahlins, Marshall, 1965. "On the Sociology of Primitive Exchange." In *The Relevance of Models for Social Anthropology.* ASA Monographs 1. London: Tavistock.

Silberbauer, George, 1972. "Ecology of the Ernabella Aboriginal Community." *Anthropological Forum* 3: 21–36.

———, 1981. *Hunter and Habitant in the Central Kalahari Desert.* Cambridge: Cambridge University Press.

———, 1994. "A Sense of Place." In E. S. Burch and L. J. Ellana, eds., *Key Issues in Hunter-Gatherer Research.* Oxford: Berg.

———, 1996. "Neither Are Your Ways My Ways." In Susan Kent, ed., *Cultural Diversity Among African Foragers.* Cambridge: Cambridge University Press.

Silberbauer, George, and Adam Kuper, 1966. "Kgalagari Master and Bushmen Serfs." *African Studies,* vol. 24, no. 4: 171–179.

Stanner, W. E. H., 1966. *On Aboriginal Religion, Oceania.* Monograph No.11. Sydney: Sydney University Press.

Turnbull, Colin M., 1972. *The Mountain People.* New York: Simon and Schuster.

INDIGENOUS PEOPLES, POLICY.

Refers to government policies affecting indigenous, or native, people. Most countries in the world have indigenous minorities, people with prior histories of independence from national of imperial state control. One recent estimate suggests that there are 250 million native people, with 12,000 different cultures and social organizations. They include the better-known Maori of Aotearoa/New Zealand, Native Americans and Canadians, Australian Aborigines, the Arctic peoples of Russia, North America, and Scandinavia, and the Indian people of Central and South America. They also include other populations, such as the various hill tribes of Southeast Asia and the Negritos of the Central Malay Peninsula and the Philippines. The concept is now often extended to other national minorities with long-term historical or territorial ties, such as the Basques, the Palestinians, and the Kurds.

This entry focuses on the broad trajectories of government policies toward indigenous people within former settler colonies of the Western world. Though recognizing the partial nature and Eurocentric bias of such an approach, this writer considers that indigenous aspirations and historic wrongs these native peoples endured are starkly portrayed against the backdrop of Western democratic institutions.

The incorporation of the New World (along with the other parts of the post-Renaissance colonial world) into "Old World" historical processes is relatively recent. These places enter "history" as outposts, as places of plunder and expansion de novo. For the New World, this expansion is at once economic, political, military, demographic, and culture (Wolf 1982). The colonies that were established became the settler societies of the New World (Denoon 1983).

Claims to sovereignty and self-government are being voiced by indigenous peoples throughout the world. The claims of the indigenous peoples of the New World are modest when compared to the independence claims of other colonized people; in recent decades, they have been concerned with three issues: (1) retaining or, more often regaining, community rights, particularly to land and cultural processes; (2) obtaining civil and welfare equity within the wider society; and (3) achieving forms of communal political autonomy. The historical bases for these claims are prior occupancy of the territory; social and political sovereignty within that territory, which is separate from and independent of the political claims of the native people's colonizers; and the absence of cultural or political continuity between aboriginal ways of life, including sovereignty, and those of the colonizing state.

Definitions

Indigenous people (also first people or aboriginal people), in contemporary political discourses, are identified as people (and their descendants) who occupied territories that, during the course of post-1500 European expansion, were the object of European colonization. These territories became settler colonies and, later, independent states ruled by the descendants of the European colonists.

Settler societies are sovereign states whose present political institutions are products or processes that started with European colonial conquest, which was accompanied by extensive (now majority) European settlement.

Sovereignty, following Hobbes, originally referred to state power that has a single locus and that is both absolute and autonomous. The locus may be a ruler or other supreme authority. There is considerable political argument for the idea of shared sovereignty within nation-states. James Tully has identified three necessary modifiers to this approach in the contemporary world: popular sovereignty, which imbeds the necessity of consent; interdependency, which acknowledges the international obligations of contemporary states; and divisions of power among a number of levels, as in the federal systems of government in Australia, Canada, and the United States (Tully 1995, pp. 193–196). Sovereignty surfaces in debates on the rights of indigenous people where indigenous people argue for the recognition of their territorial, cultural, and political claims alongside those of the state.

Assimilation refers to a range of policies designed to incorporate indigenous people into the mainstream of the society. It is premised on a largely unitary cultural view of and by the host society. On the positive side, it is the policy aimed at establishing equality of civil and political rights; on the negative side, these policies have variously attacked (or undermined) specific cultural differences, governmental and land rights, other forms of group protection, and treaty arrangements.

Domestic dependent nation was a concept defined by Chief Justice John Marshall of the United States Supreme Court, in a number of judgments handed down between 1823 and 1832, wherein he, inter alia, enunciated the constitutional position of tribes having treaties with the United States. This included the sovereign rights of tribes, their position as dependants of the United States (and not the individual states), and the duty of care toward the tribes and their interests, which rests with the United States.

Land rights refers to the claims of indigenous people to the ownership and control of specific territories with which they have cultural and historical ties. The claims are based on their having prior and continuing associations with such territories and are necessitated by the loss of control to governments or other nonindigenous interests.

Mabo is the shorthand name for a landmark Australian legal case that was settled by the High Court in June 1992. The judgment overturned the doctrine of Terra Nullius as applying to Australia and gave limited recognition to claims of prior rights in land to the Merriam Island people of the Torres Straits. It provided the impetus for the initiation of National Native Title legislation, which was enacted at the end of 1993.

Self-determination, self-government and *self-management* are concepts that form the centerpieces of present-day policies toward indigenous people. Their meaning varies. At the minimum, there is a commitment to indigenous representation and input in matters that concern natives and cultural differences (in a similar way that multiculturalism, a policy recognizing and supporting ethnic cultural diversity, has formal support in Canada and Australia). The devolution of administrative responsibilities and forms of political control are part of the negotiating agenda.

Terra nullius refers to a government's claim to sovereignty over new territory, where that territory is regarded as not being occupied by any civilized society. There is, therefore, no recognizable authority governing the territory. It is thus land belonging to no one. The British Crown asserted sovereignty over the continent of Australia, in 1788, on these grounds. Terra nullius does not mean that the land was uninhabited.

A Historical Overview

Today, the indigenous people of North America and the South Pacific live in societies where liberal democratic ideals temper predominantly capitalist and bureaucratic forms of organization. These societies have complex divisions of labor and cultures, and relatively entrenched patterns of inequality. Here, indigenous people remain a small, dependent group in this wider society. An essential difference between the preconquest indigenous societies and the position of indigenous people today is their loss of independence and encapsulation in a vastly more powerful, and, for them, oppressive, society. Political and economic control have their locus outside of any specific indigenous domain. Indigenous people's lives are heavily constrained by significant structures and processes within the dominant society.

Early relations between colonial powers and indigenous people were largely dependent on the relative strength of the native groups and the degree of competition between different European powers. Treaties between sovereign nations formed the early background of political developments in North America. The changing power relations resulting from the ascendancy of Britain and then the establishment of the United States saw the status of the indigenous groups decline to that of domestic dependent nations by the 1830s.

The Treaty of Waitangi, signed in 1840, established a relation similar to that of domestic dependent nation for the Maori with the New Zealand government. The treaty is the basis for Maori Pakeha (New Zealanders of European descent) relations.

The circumstances for Australia's indigenous people were markedly different. Not only were no treaties made but also the political and territorial interests of the indigenous people went unrecognized. The concept of terra nullius has been applied to this situation. Britain merely occupied the continent of Australia. The legal fiction was that Australian Aboriginal people lacked possessory title so were not conquered and did not cede their land.

Before the Depression of the 1930s, policies differed widely among the countries in question, and indeed even within each. The nineteenth century and the early twentieth century were major periods of territorial expansion, and therefore government and colonial focus was on expropriation of land and removal of the indigenous population.

Indigenous people, on the whole, played a minor role in the labor markets of the developing capitalist economies of the settler societies. Government actions vary, but the result was the containment of much of the rapidly declining indigenous populations on reserves (or reservations) and the dispersal of others on the fringes of colonial settlements. Policies varied within a spectrum of elimination to containment, physical and cultural oppression, and the application of basic welfare and education measures to provide minimal support for the remaining indigenous populations. In some places, for example the United States during the Franklin D. Roosevelt administration, there was qualified support for tribal government and indigenous culture. But more widespread was the view that indigenous populations were dying out, and the phrase used in much of the literature was the humane role of government was to smooth the "dying pillow."

The policies of the settler societies have converged over the past 60 years. The continued existence and the revitalization of indigenous people perhaps forced many changes, and, certainly, the rapidly changing domestic and international political climate during World War II and after hastened change in the area of policy toward native people. Throughout the period, a paternalistic welfare regime has been a significant part of government policy formulations. This approach treats indigenous people as dependants in need of care and concentrates on issues of social security, health, housing, education, and training. However, from at least the 1960s, this view has competed with arguments for rights-based approaches, which give some regard to justice and autonomy claims by indigenous people.

The period immediately before and after World War II saw a major change in policy toward indigenous people in North America and Australasia. The impetus was the desire of the democratic governments to create unified nations and, in the process, eliminate the oppressed and underprivileged minorities by making them equal citizens. This was the policy of *assimilation.*

In its full form, which was roughly the period from the end of World War II to the late 1960s, this was an interventionist policy. It was characterized by government attempts to remove some forms of discriminatory legislation and practices, whether there were positive or negative discriminations, and incorporate indigenous people culturally, socially, and politically into the national society. On the positive side, full citizenship rights were gradually extended to all. Education, health, and welfare were prime concerns, but these were largely governed by the ideals of the mainstream, resulting in suppression of aspects on indigenous culture and language. The removal of children from their families was a widespread government practice, especially in Australia, in the pursuit of assimilation goals.

The same approach applied at the political level. The unsuccessful termination policies, under the Harry Truman and Dwight Eisenhower presidencies, in the United States, which aimed to remove the special status of Indian lands, and the Canadian White Paper of 1969, which aimed at the eventual elimination of privileges for the aboriginal peoples of Canada, are examples of this monocultural approach (Fleras and Elliott 1992).

Movement away from the imposed monoculturalism of assimilation developed, hesitantly at first, during the late 1950s and 1960s, and had significant impacts on policy in the 1970s. In New Zealand and Australia, for example, new policies are first labeled as integration, to emphasize the idea of partnership. But, again, these policies gave priority to integration into the mainstream. To quote a Maori saying, "'Let's integrate!' the shark said to the kahawai, and opened its mouth to swallow the small fish for breakfast." (Fleras and Elliott 1992, p. 182)

Significant changes are associated with the resurgence of a more public indigenous politics, often marked by demonstrations and other forms of direct political action. The 1972 Aboriginal Tent Embassy in Australia's capital, Canberra, and the occupation of Wounded Knee in South Dakota in 1973 are two such significant events. The claims are various and complex, but they focus, as a minimum, on cultural autonomy, political consultation, and the recognition and rectification of past and present injustices.

Current Policies

Current policies employ a rhetoric of self-management or self-determination for the desired outcomes of the administration of indigenous people. This rhetoric focuses attention on the internal regulation of everyday living conditions (including actions to improve these). It may also include some devolution of the formulation of policy and fiscal control. Self-management is premised on a model that sees local communities as the principal conduit of ad-

ministration. These local communities are often dependent on higher levels of government for policy, funding,
and fiscal accountability, and therefore they have extremely limited autonomy.

Major contemporary public affairs, such as land rights,
health, education, and rights to decide priorities and determine their implementation, are matters for negotiated
settlement between indigenous people's representatives
and governments. On the whole, management of these affairs is in the hands of state-territory-province and national
governments. Arenas of extensive, extralocal indigenous
control have also been built or strengthened since the
1970s. The direct political action of that period has largely
been replaced by political negotiation and use of the
courts. Indigenous land rights again became a central feature of relations with governments and a vehicle for the
pursuit of greater political autonomy by indigenous people. The establishment of the Waitangi Tribunal in New
Zealand in 1975, and the Northern Territory Land Rights
Commission in Australia in 1973, were significant developments on this path. In Australia, the *Mabo* decision in
1992 and the subsequent Native Title Act of 1993, have
placed the Australian Aboriginal and Torres Strait Islander
people in a position closer to that enjoyed by the indigenous people of Canada, New Zealand, and the United
States in the negotiation of land claims.

Self-determination focuses attention on empowering
indigenous people. Sovereignty, albeit limited, is implied
in native people's acceptance that the setting of agendas,
development of policies, and control of their implementation are the right of indigenous people. Issues of self-
government are today central to relations between governments and the indigenous people in their jurisdictions.

JOHN BERN

BIBLIOGRAPHY

Bennet, Scott, 1989. *Aborigines and Political Power.* Sydney: Allen
and Unwin.
Deloria, Vine, 1985. *American Indian Policy in the Twentieth Cen-
tury.* Norman, OK: University of Oklahoma Press.
Denoon, Donald, 1983. *Settler Capitalism: The Dynamics of Depen-
dent Development in the Southern Hemisphere.* Oxford: Oxford
University Press.
Fleras, Augie, and Jean Leonard Elliott, 1992. *The Nations
Within: Aboriginal-State Relations in Canada, the United States,
and New Zealand.* Toronto: Oxford University Press.
Sharp, Andrew, 1990. *Justice and the Maori: Maori Claims in New
Zealand Political Argument in the 1980s.* Auckland: Oxford
University Press.
Tully, James, 1995. *Strange Multiplicity: Constitutionalism in an Age
of Diversity.* Cambridge: Cambridge University Press.
Wolf, E. R., 1982. *Europe and the People Without History.* Berkeley:
University of California Press.

INDONESIAN ADMINISTRATIVE TRADITION.
A complex and comprehensive body of customs, values,
attitudes, beliefs, and thoughts that reflects influences
from indigenous Indonesian (especially Javanese) cultures,
from colonial legacies, and from the political and
administrative needs of the present "New Order"
government.

The Cultural and Political Tradition

Four major factors shape the perception of the role and
working mechanisms of the adminstrative system:

1. The Indonesian public administration is influenced by
traditional Javanese concepts of power and conflict solution like *"rukum"* (the harmonious state of the society), *"musyawarah"* (discussion aimed at reaching a
consensus), *"mufakaat"* (social consensus based on
mutual concessions), and *"gotong royong"* (mutual assistance). Consensus, harmony, cooperation, social
equilibrium, respect for the hierarchy and for the superiors who have to provide leadership and who mo-
nopolize the decision-making authority feature prominently in the working culture of the administration,
and influence their internal working mechanisms.

The concept of centralization of power is one of
the dominant characteristics, and supports a highly
centralized and paternalistic bureaucracy with a preference for a top-down decision-making system
(MacAndrews, 1986). Centralization of power can be
seen in an administrative line of command running
from the president, as chief executive, to the lowest
level of state administration. The governors and mayors act in their regions as direct representatives of the
president.

2. Patrimonial attitudes of the administration have been
strengthened by the "indirect rule" pattern of the
Dutch colonial administration, which neglected local
initiative and local decision-making and stressed centralization (Devas, 1989). By relying on the indigenous
power elite, the *"priyayi,"* the Dutch colonial administration perpetuated the position of the *"priyayi"* as the
most influential indigenous group of the society,
which remained in command of the administrative
system.

3. Indonesia is characterized by a huge diversity of ethnic
groups, languages and cultures, distribution of population and of natural resources, religions, and geographical and ecological conditions. This diversity is
reflected in the official state motto *"Bhineka Tunggal
Ika"* (meaning "Unity in Diversity"). One of the most
important objectives in the struggle for independence
(1945–1949) and the first two decades of the republic

was to secure national unity and territorial integrity, and to put down separatist movements in a number of provinces (like Aceh, Sumatra, and the Moluccas). The experience of such centrifugal forces again supported a tendency for a centralized administrative system, where the government in the capital determines the activities of the bureaucracy down to the lowest level, and leaves little autonomy to the regional authorities.

4. With the beginning of the "New Order" government under President Suharto in 1996–67, the state assumed a leading role in determining the process of economic and social development. A burgeoning public enterprise sector, high rates of public investment, and the regulation of private economic and social activities by the state gave the public administration a wide area of intervention and jurisdiction. Jointly with the military as the strongest pillar of the "New Order" government, the administrative system assumed the most influential role in the policy-making process.

Various political concepts constitute the ideological framework of the Indonesian administrative system. The most important one is *Pancasila* (literally, "five principles"): "Belief in one supreme god," "Just and civilized humanity," "Unity of the Indonesian nation," "Democracy in the form of deliberations of representatives," and "Social justice." *Pancasila* utilizes indigenous concepts that stress the togetherness of the members of social organizations. The nation becomes one huge family in which conflicting interests of different groups and different sections of the society will be solved in the common interest of the whole. Under the "New Order" government, *Pancasila* became an all-embracing concept for every aspect of life. The political system of the country was labeled *"Pancasila* democracy" to distinguish it from the previous phases of "Liberal democracy" (1949–1955) and "Guided democracy" (1955–1965). The economy is supposed to function as *"Pancasila"* economy, without antagonistic interests of employers and employees. Since 1985 *Pancasila* is by law the official ideological platform of all mass organizations, including the political parties and religious groups.

Relationship with the Society

By making *Pancasila* the compulsory ideological platform for all mass organizations, the "New Order" government limited the scope of political discussion in the society. The administration relied on officially recognized and registered bodies and organizations, which acted as channels of communication between the society and the administration, while the direct access of the citizen to the administration was rather limited.

However, a greater openness for public debate, the introduction of a system of administrative law which allows

individual citizens to sue the administration, and a greater emphasis on the quality of services provided by the administration are examples of a change of the relationship.

Outlook

Since 1983, there has been a paradigm shift concerning the public administration and its role in the society. Deregulation of the economy, decentralization of the administration, and debureaucratization have been necessitated by several factors: declining government revenues from the oil and gas sector, which require greater use of and reliance on private sector funds for investment and development; an increasing demand for more and better public services, which cannot be met anymore by a rigid and centralized administrative system; and a politically more mature society, which demands greater political transparency and greater participation in the policy-making process. The principle policy direction now is to shift from direct government involvement to a more indirect mode of administrative operation, in which the government will define the overall rules for private sector activities but will refrain from direct intervention. Functions of the government and their administrative implementation will be decentralized to the autonomous regions (provincial and local administration) while the central government will focus on general policy-making. Professionalism of the civil service will be increased by a stronger emphasis on the so-called "functional positions" *(jabatan fungsional),* with emphasis on specific professional and technical skills (Salamoen, 1993).

RAINER ROHDEWOLD

BIBLIOGRAPHY

Devas, Nick, ed., 1989. *Financing Local Government in Indonesia.* Ohio University Centre for International Studies Monographs in International Studies, Southeast Asia Series Number 84. Athens: Ohio University Press.
Government of Indonesia (GOI), 1989. *The 1945 Constitution of the Republic of Indonesia.* Jakarta.
———, 1993. *The 1993 Guidelines of State Policy.* Jakarta.
MacAndrews, Colin, ed., *Central Government and Local Development in Indonesia.* Singapore: Oxford University Press.
Salamoen, Soeharyo, 1993. *Changes and Trends in Public Administration in Indonesia.* Paper for the 15th Eastern Asia Research Organization on Public Administration (EROPA) Assembly and Conference, Tehran, October 31–November 8, 1993.

INDUSTRIAL RELATIONS POLICY.

Efforts to influence employee-employer interactions at the national level by government and at the organizational level by management and labor.

Students of industrial relations have long been apprised of the importance of governmental attitudes to the conduct of relationships between managements and labor within, and in certain respects beyond, their frontiers. Until recently, however, the world "policy" has rarely passed the lips of those more directly concerned with the day-to-day *practice* of industrial relations. When used, the context of its use has usually been governmental. It has seldom been related to businesses or undertakings. The latter have been apt to regard all policies as a luxury that, unlike governments, they could not afford.

It has never been easy logically to defend such attitudes. The absence of policy is in itself a policy. More to the point, though both governments and companies can make some decisions "on the fly," it has always been unconvincing to suppose that any company can act entirely from immediate impulse or simply at random. Although policies can be explicitly *declared*, they can also be *inferred* from actions that have already been taken, the pattern of which is due to either continuity or deliberate change. Some dictionary definitions of "policy" accept such a proposition without question by defining the word as a *course of action adopted or pursued*. Others suppose that some *principle* ought logically to predate action. Evidently, both approaches to policymaking are possible, and both are formally correct.

Some companies, of course, have always been willing to admit to labor "policies" under one heading or another. Today, their explicit existence, in whatever form, is more openly accepted than it once was, though the word "strategy" may be preferred. The question of definition—in the West at any rate—has moved elsewhere, to the meaning of "industrial relations."

At one time, practitioners, whether economists, historians, lawyers, sociologists, or personnel specialists were usually content to regard industrial relations as a generic term that subsumed all their different approaches. This is no longer so. Each specialty has tended to go its own way—economists concentrating on labor markets and human capital and lawyers on employment law; sociologists, have moved from human relations to organizational behavior; personnel specialists have moved into human resource management.

Industrial relations now refers, as some academics always thought it did, to "union-management relations." The change has been associated with a change in attitude to trade unions. A former tendency to regard unions almost automatically as an essential adjunct to the application of democratic values has given way to a growing belief in the necessity to regard them with caution, as likely inhibitors or economic efficiency and good government—as expressed in political determination to secure economic control, particularly over inflation and the stimulation of enterprise.

Such attitudes, of course, are not new; nor are they uniformly held country by country or consistently applied.

Employers have always, expressly or when it has suited their immediate purpose, adhered to the doctrine of "managerial rights" or "managerial functions." To some executives, and to some politicians also, management has appeared to be inhibited to such an extent by the presence of trade unions as to make the proper exercise of such functions impossible; others have been prepared to compromise or to act tactically to contain unions whenever they could; yet others have seen positive virtues in pluralism and welcomed unions as partners in industrial endeavor.

And there have undoubtedly been changes in the attitudes of some, if not all, governments in the developed world from policies in favor of collective bargaining and trade union representation to those implacably or more cautiously opposed. Oddly, these same views have not been extended to their policy preferences for developing countries subject, or potentially subject, to central dictatorships. Here, the existence of strong trade unions often appears as an indication of and reinforcement to their democratic credentials, but the discouragement, suppression, or incorporation of unions into the government is seen as a reason for exclusion from international recognition.

Elements and Instruments of Policy

At governmental level, the fundamentals of industrial relations systems were explored and plotted by John Dunlop (1958) almost four decades ago. In every context the same items for regulation appear—pay, conditions of work, training, hiring and firing—and in every context there is a continuing need for procedures to deal with issues on which disputes are likely to arise—individual and collective grievances, the whole being conveniently regarded as a subsystem of each context's social system and its stability, dependent on a minimum level of "shared understandings" between the actors in the system (hierarchies of managers and their representatives, of workers and their spokespeople, and of government and its specialized agencies).

The instruments of regulation, law, collective agreements, custom, and practice, can be generalized from one context to another; the mix of regulative instruments cannot. The notion that the logic of industrialization would lead to the convergence of industrial relations systems has proved to be illusory. The balance of technology, manpower, political conviction, and convenience make it inevitable that systems are always in movement, constrained by certain rigidities in most developed economies but in more fundamental situations of change in others.

Dunlop's original formulation now appears to have been uncomfortably normative or even static. It also appears to espouse a structure of value preferences, which might be assumed to govern policy preferences within each system.

Traditionally high among these preferences at governmental level has been the commitment of Western states to certain value judgments—(1) that joint control involving managers and workers' representatives is to be preferred to unilateral control by managers only, (2) that the role of the state is to set high standards in the provision that it will treat its own employees well and that it will promulgate these standards generally, and (3) that it is a function of government to act as an impartial conciliator and arbiter when management and workers are in dispute.

This situation supposes policies that are at once committed, benign, conciliatory, and unconcerned with outcomes arising outside the system itself. Such a proposition has never been universally accepted. It was for many decades almost universally taken for granted in Britain, but this was less true in the United States.

Today, there are few economies in which the credibility of the doctrine of the "neutrality" of the state survives, either because governments are seen as favoring one party or another or because they may have their own agenda, which may conflict with the logic of the system itself, for example, between a governmental objective to stabilize prices and the traditional acceptance of free collective bargaining. Value free governmental industrial relations policies are now as rare as the legendary free lunch.

Industrial Relations Policies in Practice

At governmental level, industrial relations policies in the late 1990s can be divided into two types, those that can be regarded as historically conditioned but not necessarily accepted and those that are in a more indeterminate state of flux, derived either from the breakdown of an imposed system or from the difficulties of creating a system where no presently acceptable system has existed before. Broadly speaking the former, as might be expected, are characteristic of developed economies and the latter of developing economies.

Developed Economies

Though subject to many pressures, traditional systems of industrial relations tend to be exceedingly tough and resistant to fundamental change. In the United States and Britain, for example, many traditional structures and practices have survived Reganite and Thatcherite deregulation; in France, the so-called Auroux Reform of workplace relations have been regarded as not wholly successful; and, above all, in Germany, where devotion to the notion of social partnership expressed in Works Council and Codetermination legislation has remained substantially untouched since it was redeveloped and expanded with great rapidity after World War II. This may mean little more than that continuity is important. But it may also mean that governmental attempts to secure change are likely to produce only temporary results or are likely to "squeeze" a system

into a slightly different shape without altering its fundamentals because these have come to embody values that the parties are reluctant to abandon. In Britain, for example, it is by no means certain to what extent Thatcherite legislation to restrain trade union influence has fundamentally changed the attitudes of more traditional managements to workplace representation. Change is disruptive, or potentially so, and may be regarded with caution.

In part, this uncertainty may be associated with the degree of resolution required to pursue and maintain industrial relations policies at company levels. For all the publicity given to the notion of human resource management (HRM), it remains questionable whether, in a free market economy, employers are likely to be able to so influence their hierarchies of managers so as to adopt consistent attitudes and practices for substantial change. In part, the problem is that few HRM practices appear to be so sound so as to stand the test of time. The problem lies partly in the market itself.

Companies traditionally quoted as success stories in applying internal industrial relations policies are usually those that have been dominated by particular personalities or cushioned by monopoly or near-monopoly conditions. Rapid market or technological change may call for policies of such flexibility that they can only be defined in terms of their absence. In any positive sense, they may have become, as employers have customarily claimed, too difficult to afford. For how long can such a situation be allowed to develop without a decay of labor standards of such magnitude that the state will be compelled to reassume its role as their policies curator? In the European Union (EU) this pressure may well become allied to other imperatives to be found within the EU itself.

Of particular interest in this context is pressure for industrial relations policy convergence within the 15 member states, the logic of which is twofold. First, but by no means most important in practice, is the political consideration that the European Union ought to be seen to have benign and progressive social as well as economic consequences; that citizens ought to experience enhancement in their working lives as well as, hopefully, in their living standards. Second, it is evident that in the absence of convergence, some member states will perceive that the playing field is far from level. Those with less-favorable working conditions, and those with the least-generous and well-regulated social provision and industrial systems will, if only on financial grounds, have unjustifiable advantages over the others. The acceptance of such a situation does not, at present, extend to the British government, for ideological reasons, though other member states appear to have less difficulty in accepting its validity.

Developing Economies

In developing economies, governmental regimes appear to show no consistent pattern in any parallel development of industrial relations policies. Former colonies or politically dependent territories either build on or reject inherited systems as soon as they are free to do so; most continue to be influenced by them. The choice is usually far from easy. Inheriting a repressive system is likely to produce an initial consensus on policy between government and trade union elements built on resistance to a common enemy. Sustaining such an alliance in changed political circumstances may be difficult when government is required to act in matters that unions perceive as against their interests. Inheriting a nonrepressive system may have the effect of depriving government of an institutionalized labor response.

In either event, adjustment, especially in unfavorable economic circumstances, is likely to cause problems exacerbated by local labor behavior, the inexperience of local management, the presence of multinationals, and the impact of industrialization strategies. "Shared understandings" in any system take time to develop, and relationships easily become sour. Moreover, most developing countries are likely, initially at least, to base their economic futures upon the existence of cheap labor and low costs. Some find it difficult to proceed beyond such a stage and find themselves pursuing policies of cost containment, which are, or appear to be, repressive. Alternatively, as in some Southeast Asian economies, low-cost developments are followed by high-technology based on foreign investment, which demand policies based on skill development, training, and education and consequent higher levels of remuneration, which may not be matched in other sectors of the economy.

There has been all to little study of industrial relations policies in developed countries; the developing world has been subject to practically no study at all.

A. I. Marsh

Bibliography

Deyo, Frederick, 1989. *Beneath the Labour Miracle: Labour Subordination in East-Asian Development.* Berkeley: University of California Press.

Dunlop, John T., 1958. *Industrial Relations Systems.* New York: Holt.

Ferner, Anthony, and Richard Hyman, 1992. *Industrial Relations in the New Europe.* Oxford: Blackwell.

Kerr, Clark, John T. Dunlop, Frederick Harbison, and Charles A. Myers, 1964. *Industrialism and Industrial Man.* New York: Oxford University Press.

Purcell, John, 1991. "The Rediscovery of the Management Prerogative: The Management of Industrial Relations in the 1980s," Vol. 17, no. 1: 41.

Sharma, Basu, 1985. *Aspects of Industrial Relations in ASEAN.* Institute for Asian Studies.

Southall, Roger, ed. 1988. *Labour and Unions in Asia and Africa.* Hong Kong: Macmillan.

Storey, John, ed. 1992. *Developments in the Management of Human Resources: An Analytical Review.* Oxford: Blackwell.

Strauss, George, 1994. "Reclaiming Industrial Relations Academic Jurisdiction." In Paula B. Voos, ed., *Industrial Relations Research Association Series, Proceedings of the 46th Annual Meeting.* January 3–5, 1994, Boston, pp. 1–11.

Taylor, Robert, 1993. *The Trade Union Question in British Politics.* Oxford: Blackwell.

INFLATION.

A generalized rise in prices, when the prices of most, if not all, goods and services increase simultaneously. This can be contrasted to a relative price increase, in which the price of a particular product, such as oil, or a particular service, such as health care, rises relative to other goods and services. Since goods and services are priced in terms of money, inflation lowers the value, or purchasing power, of money.

There are a number of standard indexes that are used to track inflation. One of the most commonly used is the consumer price index, which measures changes in the prices of a fixed basket of consumer goods and services. This basket varies across countries and over time. For instance, United States consumers have different spending patterns than Japanese consumers, and these differences are reflected in the composition and weights in each country's consumer price index. Also, the index is periodically updated to take account of new consumer products and services, such as VCRs, as well as changing spending patterns, such as more dining out than in earlier periods.

Two other standard indexes are the producer price index and the wholesale price index. These indexes, in general, measure changes in the prices of industrial and agricultural goods before they get to the retail level; they exclude services.

A broader measure of inflation, the gross national product or gross domestic product deflator, captures price increases for all goods and services produced in an economy. The deflator is the most comprehensive measure of inflation because it captures price changes in all the goods and services the economy produces.

Inflation indexes for most countries can be found, with varying lags, in the *International Financial Statistics,* published monthly by the International Monetary Fund (IMF). The IMF obtains these indexes primarily from reported national indexes.

Postwar Inflation: A Departure

For nearly 150 years, the United States economy was characterized by alternating periods of inflation and deflation (a generalized decline in prices). Although there was a high level of price volatility (See Figure I), over this long period there was no noticeable upward or downward trend in prices. Recognizing that there are difficulties in accurately capturing price changes over such a long period of time, the United States consumer price index in 1943 stood at approximately the same level as in 1800! The United Kingdom, over this same time, experienced a roughly similar pattern of volatile but trendless prices. The most notable periods of inflation are connected to

FIGURE I. U.S. Consumer Prices

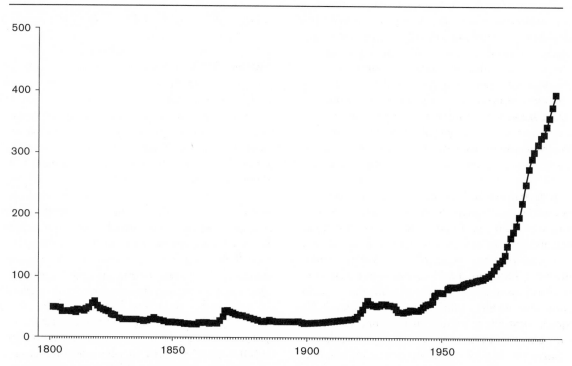

Sources: *Historical Statistics of the United States,* U.S. Department of Commerce, Bureau of the Census, September 1975; *International Financial Statistics Yearbook,* 1994, International Monetary Fund.

wars. The most recent period of deflation was the worldwide Depression of the 1930s.

In contrast to the price experience from 1800 to 1943, the period since World War II has been characterized by continually rising prices, but far less volatility. This quite different pattern reflects, in part, changed perceptions of the role of government. Prior to 1945, governments, in general, were not expected to intervene to moderate the business cycle. Economic booms were often accompanied by sharply rising prices. These booms were followed by recessions or depressions, which were accompanied by falling prices.

After 1945, citizens of the industrial countries viewed governments as having a role in stabilizing the economy. Governments intervened to "prime the pump" during recessions and to slow the economy when booms threatened. This more activist role for governments had implications for inflation as well as growth: Prices rose more moderately during good economic times and slowed down, but rarely declined, in bad economic times. In fact, 1955 was the last year in which consumer prices declined in the United States, by 0.2 percent. The last year consumer prices declined (−0.3 percent) for the industrial countries as a whole was in 1950.

Prices not only rose steadily but also accelerated decade by decade in the 1950s, 1960s, and 1970s. For the industrial economies as a whole, consumer prices in-

creased an average of 2.4 percent a year in the 1950s, 2.9 percent a year in the 1960s, and 8.1 percent a year in the 1970s. With most governments implementing anti-inflationary policies as inflation neared or reached double-digit levels, consumer price increases slowed in the 1980s, to an average of 6.1 percent a year.

Developing countries have also experienced continuous inflation in the postwar period. A number of developing countries experienced periods of triple-digit inflation. A few have even experienced hyperinflation, commonly characterized as rapidly accelerating price increases, with yearly price increases in five digits.

Origins of Inflation

Numerous causes have been cited to explain the origins of inflation. Demand-pull inflation occurs when excessive growth in aggregate demand triggers general price increases. The excess demand created in the United States by the Vietnam War in the late 1960s is an example of demand-pull inflation.

Cost-push inflation refers to generalized price increases originating on the supply side, with rising prices for raw materials, intermediate products, or wages pushing up costs, which then inflate general price levels. The two oil shocks in the 1970s, with substantial increases in real oil prices, touched off cost-push inflation worldwide.

A. W. Phillips, in a 1958 article, identified a relationship between wage increases (later translated to inflation) and unemployment. Higher wages, he argued, were associated with lower unemployment levels and lower wages with higher unemployment. This relationship was dubbed the Phillips Curve. His article led to a widespread belief in the 1960s and 1970s that there was a tradeoff between unemployment and inflation. If a country were willing to tolerate a higher level of inflation, it could enjoy lower unemployment. The concept of a tradeoff between inflation and employment lost favor among economists in the 1970s when rising prices were accompanied by rising unemployment levels.

Once triggered, inflation can also become persistent because of a wage-price spiral. In this case, rising wages can lead to a rise in general prices, which, in turn fuel demands for still-higher wages. This phenomenon characterized the United States and much of the industrial world in the 1970s.

Milton Friedman, America's well-known monetarist, has said that "inflation is always and everywhere a monetary phenomenon" (Friedman 1987, p. 377). According to him and other monetarists, prices in general can only rise if the money supply accommodates such increases. Almost all economists agree that excessively rapid money supply growth will fuel general price increases. But nonmonetarists are interested in the nonmonetary origins of inflation as well as the monetary causes.

The industrial economies in the 1970s also experienced what came to be called stagflation, an economic situation characterized by both stagnant growth and rising prices.

Policies to Combat Inflation

Restrictive fiscal and monetary policies are the traditional tools governments use to dampen inflation. Restrictive fiscal policies include cuts in government spending and/or tax increases. Tight monetary policies curb inflation by restraining demand, particularly in interest-sensitive industries, such as housing and consumer durables, and private-sector investment. Such policies can produce unwanted side effects as tighter fiscal and monetary policies often tip the economy into recession. The United States imposed a tight monetary policy in late 1979 to curb the double-digit inflation triggered by the twin oil price shocks of the 1970s. Though they eventually subdued inflation, these policies resulted in a United States recession and contributed to the worldwide recession in 1982. Tight United States monetary policy, with record-high interest rates, was also an important factor in the 1982 Third World debt crisis because most commercial bank debt was at floating rates that rose when United States interest rates rose.

Anti-inflationary policies can take longer to work if the population has high inflationary expectations. If people expect rapid price increases, their behavior in trying to protect themselves from its consequences can, in turn, fuel inflation. For instance, if workers expect prices to rise

rapidly, they will increase wage demands to protect their real incomes, thereby fueling inflation.

Less-traditional policy tools to combat inflation include wage and price controls, social compacts, and incomes policies. Price controls have traditionally been used by nations during wartime, but they have also been used during peacetime. The United States imposed voluntary wage and price controls in 1971 to curb inflation. These controls were successful in slowing inflation, but their success was, at least in part, because they were short-lived and were imposed on a populace that did not have high inflationary expectations. Mainstream economists generally believe wage and price controls are not an effective tool for slowing inflation, but only a temporary palliative at best. Social compacts seek agreement between government, business, and labor to act in unison to restrain inflation. Mexico's social pact worked effectively from 1988 to 1994, but the consensus broke down in the wake of the late-1994 devaluation and then float of the peso. Incomes policies entail a government setting norms or guidelines for wage increases.

Supply-side economists look at decreasing regulatory restrictions as policies to reduce costs, and, therefore, prices. Friedman and other monetarists denounce discretionary fiscal and monetary policies. They recommend a monetary rule, say 4 percent-a-year growth in the United States money supply, as the best policy to promote economic growth and stable prices.

Indexation is another policy tool governments have adopted to limit the harmful effects of inflation. Financial instruments, contracts, wages, and so on, can be indexed to an inflation rate to protect parties from inflation. The United States and many other countries have used cost-of-living adjustments (COLAs) in wage contracts. The UK, Finland, Brazil, and Israel, to name just a few, have at various times indexed some or all financial instruments. Brazil's indexing was viewed as a success by Milton Friedman and others. But Brazil began experiencing rapidly accelerating inflation in the late 1980s, which undermined indexing's claim to success.

Appropriate Level of Inflation

There is no general consensus on what is an appropriate level of inflation. Although some economists support zero inflation, many find a moderate level of inflation acceptable on the grounds that it facilitates relative price adjustments. A moderate level of inflation, although not defined precisely, is a level that is low enough that the decisions of economic actors are not affected by inflation. It would be a rare economist that would find hyperinflation acceptable.

Countries also differ considerably in their tolerance for inflation. Germany, because of its experience with hyperinflation during the 1920s, is less tolerant of inflation, as measured by its actual inflation performance, than many other industrial countries, which have accepted

FIGURE II. PERCENTAGE OF INCREASE IN CONSUMER PRICES

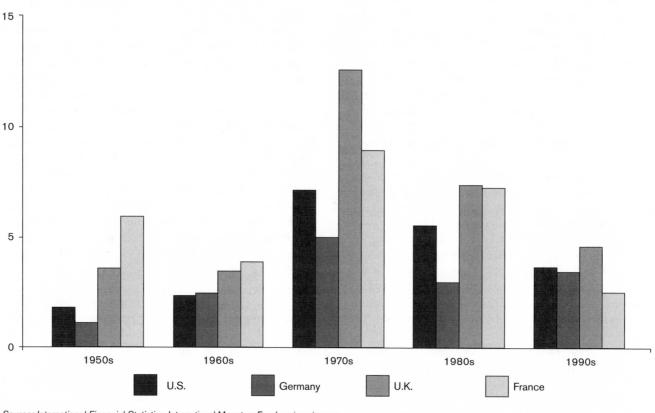

Source: *International Financial Statistics*, International Monetary Fund, various issues.

higher average levels of inflation. Argentina, which experienced near-hyperinflation in 1989 and 1990, is much less tolerant of inflation today.

In the United States, as well as many other industrial countries, tolerance for inflation increased in the first three decades of the postwar period. United States consumer prices rose an average of 1.8 percent per annum in the 1950s, 2.3 percent in the 1960s, and 7.1 percent in the 1970s. The rapid inflation in the 1970s, triggered by the two oil shocks, led to a greater commitment to controlling inflation in the United States and other industrial countries. United States consumer price increases slowed to 5.5 percent in the 1980s and then 3.6 percent in the first half of the 1990s. Figure II graphs the inflation experience of the United States and three other major industrial economies in the postwar period.

SANDRA D. WILLIAMSON

BIBLIOGRAPHY

Friedman, Milton, 1987. "Notes on the Quantity Theory of Money." In Kurt R. Leube, ed. *The Essence of Friedman.* Stanford, CA.: Hoover Institution Press.
Parkin, Michael, 1994. *Economics,* 2d ed., Reading, MA: Addison-Wesley.
Phillips, A. W., 1958. "The Relation Between Unemployment and the Rate of Change of Money Wages in the United Kingdom, 1861–1957." *Economica* (November).
Samuelson, Paul A., and William D. Nordhaus, 1992. *Economics,* 14 ed. New York: McGraw Hill.

INFORMAL ORGANIZATION SYSTEMS.

The totality of uninstitutionalized, multidimensional, and nebulous networks of relationships between individuals or groups within an organization.

Another name for these types of organizational systems are collateral, parallel, reflective, or shadow structures (Huczinski 1987). D. E. Zaud (1981) defined this type of entity "as supplemental organization co-existing with the usual, formal organization." These organizations usually emerge spontaneously, but they may also be created purposefully to deal with "ill-structured" problems. Formal organizations often place demands on individuals that are inconsistent with their needs for activity, independence, flexibility, and superordination. Informal organizations arise to fulfill these needs (Argyris 1957).

The term *informal organization* was introduced to the management literature by Chester I. Barnard (1938). The first documented study of the phenomenon by management specialists is known as the Hawthorne experiments. In their experiments in Western Electric's Hawthorne, Illinois, plant, Elton Mayo (1945), Fritz Roethlisberger (1941 and Roethlisberger and Dickson 1939) revealed that the primary working group (or, the arrangement of everyday, routine working relations in the group) was as important for productivity as were physical facilities and monetary remuneration. Barnard (1938) noted that the informal organization was fulfilling necessary functions for the organization (which, in Barnard's definition, is a cooperative endeavor), namely: communicating, maintaining cohesiveness in a formal organization, and supporting the feelings of self-respect and integrity of the employees. Barnard also argued that as formal organizations create informal ones, informal organizations in turn give rise to some form of formal organization, which makes explicit relationships and attitudes that have developed informally.

An informal organization system is usually considered to fulfill the following functions:

1. to augment, interpret, speed up, or alter the formal communication system (or lack of it);
2. to regulate the flow, extent, manner, and enforcement of formal authority;
3. to "humanize" the formal organization by helping to maintain a feeling of individuality of the members, while providing some security, unity, and integrity; and
4. to meet related psychological and social needs to such an extant as to give the impression of being the organization (Banki 1981).

Informal organizations can soothe frictions that arise in formal organizations. Although as a function of inertia they may resist change, sometimes informal organizations are agents of change. As such, an informal organization may be considered as a modified and advanced form of task force and team-building activities. It deals with those urgent problems or opportunities that affect the organization as a whole and that involve more than one unit of organization. Usually, these are problems focused on the future; they are new to an organization and extremely complex. In informal organizations, hierarchy-based relationships and attitudes are set aside to facilitate creative problem solving (although unintended outcomes may be dysfunctional). They are typically led by individuals without positions of direct authority—leaders whose power and authority over a group are derived from acceptance by the group, rather then from office, position, status, or rank in the chain of command in the formal organization. Sometimes leadership is provided by a facilitator who gives process consultation, leads data-gathering, and fulfills feedback procedures.

In such an interpretation, the informal organization uses task-oriented, team-building activities that involve a change agent, data gathering, feedback, and process consultation. Some researchers argue that there are considerable distinctions between team-building activities and informal organizations. Though in both cases attention is focused on ill-structured (i.e., "messy") problems, team-building activities commonly concern just one unit or several closely related units of an organization and do not really address systemwide problems. Informal organizations can identify and solve systemic problems that have not been solved by the formal organization, thus creatively complementing it. Both organizations contain the same people. The output of the informal organization represents an input to the formal one. The success of the former is linked to that of the latter (Huczynski 1987; Zaud 1981).

There are other important features of informal organizations that distinguish them from both task force (or team-building) activities and from formal organizations. Informal organizations develop their own different norm system from that of the formal organization. These norms encourage constant questioning of both traditional and newly introduced goals, methods, and alternatives. All communication channels within informal organization are open, to ensure rapid and complete exchange of information. When it is necessary to solve problems, managers or leaders within the informal organization can address not only their subordinates or members of their group but also any member of the organization.

Team-building, intergroup activities, and task forces are always created purposefully with the high involvement of the organization's management. Informal organizations often emerge first as a result of the unauthorized efforts of an organization's members to deal with problems that are not currently addressed or even recognized by the management of the formal organization. Such informal organization may be a threat to a formal one to the extent the two are in conflict as to goals, objectives, and priorities. Formal organizations should and can handle destructive structures if they are willing to negotiate to change formal rules, directive leadership, and management controls.

One of the important features of modern, flexible management is to be able to use informal organizational systems to improve the creativity and performance of formal organizations. If management is sensitive to the ideas and aspirations of the organization's members, the informal organization may provide a structural solution to the problem of gaining the benefits of de facto parity in decisionmaking, while preserving the official hierarchy that itself connotes the inequality of power and authority in an organization. Thus, it preserves one facet of the status quo while creating an alternative to it.

Today in the late 1990s, formal organizations are more inclined to change in order to adapt to existing informal organizational systems, that is, reduce the differences between the formal and informal organization. This means flattening the hierarchical structure, or eliminating it completely. People in large organizations already know that the informal structures of alliances, cooperative arrangements, and partnerships make the place run (Hampton 1994). Management can purposefully use the advantages of informal organizational systems by identifying a work unit within the organization or creating a synthetic group consisting of the representatives of other groups, and then authorizing that group to function independently of the "old" culture. This group then develops problem-solving techniques that are not hampered by the traditions, practices, or values of the past.

The concept that use of informal structures can lead to better performance is not new. In 1951, researchers at the Tavistock Institute in England studied the adjustment problems of informal work organizations when the ownership and technology of the coal mines changed (Trist 1963). This five-year study illustrated how sizable informal work groups in several mines, when allowed to be self-regulating, were more capable of adapting to changes in the technology of work.

A "merger" of formal and informal organizations is, in fact, one of the core ideas of the modern managerial revolution. The transition from a closed to open organizational model to a Theory Z type of organization means that more and more emphasis is given to informal relationships rather than to the formal organizational structure characterized by hierarchy, a chain of command, rigid job descriptions, and formal managerial procedures.

Modern managerial concepts present these ideas under a variety of labels; authors of "fourth generation management," "internal entrepreneurship" (or "intrapreneurship"), "the learning organization," and so forth, suggest different approaches and techniques for taking advantage of emerging informal organizations and building them up in order to produce organizational changes necessary for survival in turbulent and uncertain environments.

The role and performance of informal organizations inside governments and public sector organizations have also attracted the recent attention of both scholars and practitioners. According to Senge (1994), governments can benefit from using these approaches. But there are and always will be some limitations for recognition of informal structures in governmental institutions. They are strongly dependent on political considerations, and their managerial structures are designed in a way which is most suitable for preserving administrative-control procedures. As government is based primarily on formal structural arrangements derived form the political power of the state, informal structures will always be treated with suspicion and curiosity.

PAVEL MAKEYENKO, MARC HOLZER, AND
VATCHE GABRIELIAN

BIBLIOGRAPHY

Argyris, Chris, 1957. *Personality and Organization.* New York: Harper and Brothers.

Banki, Ivan S., 1981. *Dictionary of Administration and Management.* Los Angeles: Systems Research Institute.

Barnard, Chester I., 1938. *The Functions of the Executive.* Cambridge, MA: Harvard University Press.

Hampton, John J., 1994. "The Organization of the Future." In John J. Hampton, ed., *AMA Management Handbook,* 3d ed. New York: AMACOM.

Huczynski, Andrzey, 1987. *Encyclopedia of Organizational Change Methods.* Aldershot, England and Brookfield, VT: Gower.

Mayo, Elton, 1945. *The Social Problems of Industrial Civilization.* Cambridge, MA: Harvard University Press.

Roethlisberger, Fritz J., 1941. *Management and Morale.* Cambridge, MA: Harvard University Press, 1941.

Roethlisberger, Fritz J., and W. J. Dickson, 1939. *Management and the Worker.* Cambridge, MA: Harvard University Press.

Senge, Peter M., 1994. *The Fifth Discipline Fieldbook.* New York: Doubleday.

Trist, E. L., 1963. *Organizational Choice.* London: Tavistock.

Zaud, D. E., 1981. *Information, Organization and Power.* New York McGraw Hill.

INFORMATION RESOURCES MANAGEMENT (IRM).

A phrase used to describe the strategic perspective on information as a major resource in organizations and government. IRM is a managerial framework for the planning, organizing, and control of data and information to achieve the purposes of the organization. IRM is not dissimilar to human, financial, and capital resource management. IRM views data and information as strategic organizational resources with both value and cost. It addresses problems in information production, distribution, and utilization within the organization and the external environment of the organization.

IRM was building on the newfound belief first demonstrated by Fritz Machlup (1962) in his classic book outlining and establishing the contribution of information and knowledge to the traditional model of economic production as a function of land, labor, and capital. Later Marc Porat (1977) completed a nine-volume work for the Department of Commerce, presented as a final summary to the Federal Paperwork Commission, that linked the economic domains of the production of goods and services to the production and use of information and knowledge. Productivity growth was and now continues to be understood as a function of information and knowledge in economic systems. This work placed new emphasis on organizations developing strategies for creating, obtaining, distributing, and using information and knowledge. Public and private organizations alike adopted this strategic perspective on information resources management.

IRM was popularized in the mid-to-late 1970s as a new way to manage an organization's information resources, including but not limited to computers and information

Infrastructure

technologies (Horton 1985). IRM is the organizational response to the trend of seeing information as a strategic resource. It required managers to develop information plans, make organizational design changes based on information flows, and evaluate the effectiveness of information technologies as applied to organizational problems. Forest W. Horton and Donald A. Marchand (1982) edited a book in which contributors explained the value of thinking of information as a strategic organizational resource for the public organization.

In the federal government, the Paperwork Reduction Act of 1980 mandated that information resource management be adopted in all departments and agencies. Later, Office of Management and Budget Circular A-130 spelled out the relationship between IRM and other federal information policies such as privacy, freedom of information, access, security, and secrecy. Sharon Caudle (1988) evaluated the impact of IRM on the federal government, finding that, although some emphasis had been placed on developing information management plans, increases and decreases in budgets and agency performance was not directly tied to information resource management.

IRM is an idea that will continue to influence government and public agencies, even though it has failed to produce specific managerial methods or policy prescriptions or to demonstrate its utility. As with many such ideas in information technology, the pace of change is very rapid, and many concepts, regardless of how innovative they may be, have a very short half-life. Most governments today are examining their place on the information superhighway as part of their information resources management. The information highway is seen as the interacting set of information and telecommunications technologies, private industries and markets, and public policies. Federal, state, and local governments are all involved in the process of making policy and regulating the growing information highway often with substantial conflict. An IRM perspective directly links the development of the information highway to economic development of the state, region, or locality.

E. SAMUEL OVERMAN

BIBLIOGRAPHY

Caudle, Sharon, 1988. "Federal Information Resources Management After the Paperwork Reduction Act." *Public Administration Review.* (July-August.), vol. 48, 790–799.
Horton, Forest, 1985. *Information Resources Management.* Englewood Cliffs, NJ: Prentice-Hall.
Horton, Forest, and Donald A. Marchand, eds., 1982. *Information Management in Public Administration.* Arlington, VA: Information Resources Press.
Machlup, Fritz, 1962. *The Production and Distribution of Knowledge in the United States.* Princeton, NJ: Princeton University Press.
Porat, Marc, 1977. *The Information Economy.* Washington, D.C.: U.S. GPO.

INFRASTRUCTURE. The vast and vital network of public works facilities and resources necessary to produce and deliver public services–including highways, streets, and bridges; mass transit; rail; airports; sewers and water systems; schools; and prisons.

The public facilities, resources, and services known as infrastructure are vital to the production and distribution of private economic output in the United States, in addition to its citizens' overall quality of life. The construction, maintenance, and operation of such infrastructure is costly: During the 1980s, approximately 2.7 percent of the nation's gross domestic product (GDP) was spent annually for those purposes. By 1991, total public spending for infrastructure was US$158 billion. In 1989, the net stock of physical infrastructure amounted to $1 trillion; another $1.1 trillion was in the infrastructure stocks of utilities. Each year, roughly $50 billion more is added to the public infrastructure stock by all levels of U.S. government.

Origins

The term "infrastructure" came into prominent use in the early 1980s. Alarming articles in the popular press aroused public concern. Studies done by professional and municipal associations, research institutions, consulting firms, and government documented the problems resulting from the deterioration of existing facilities and difficulties of new development. A 1983 Congressional Budget Office (CBO) study highlighted three problems related to declining investments in infrastructure: deterioration, technological obsolescence, and insufficient capacity to serve future growth. The report also suggested the adverse effects of declining investment: (1) higher costs borne by users of inadequate or deteriorated facilities; (2) higher life-style construction costs for facilities that are not properly maintained; and (3) potentially significant constraints on economic development.

Most of what was said and written about the nation's infrastructure after the alarming reports of the early 1980s related to finance, with "big bucks" solutions in vogue until the budget woes of the national government became more evident. In the early 1980s the estimated price for dealing with the problems of the nation's infrastructure was unclear, ranging from US$470 billion to $3 trillion dollars within a 20-year period, with most studies at the high end of the range. Increased capital spending to compensate for the "disinvestment" of America's public infrastructure was widely advocated.

The early analyses of trends were somewhat misleading. Later studies suggested that revenue shortfalls were not as serious as previously presumed and that the average individual infrastructure project costs were not so high as to cause a doomsayer attitude. Similarly, dealing with the basic infrastructures may be accomplished in relatively piecemeal fashion–community by community and state

1139

by state—rather than in a truly comprehensive national approach.

Cost estimates depend on how infrastructure is defined. Basic public infrastructure refers to highways, transit, water facilities, and so forth. Human services public infrastructure includes at least educational, medical, and correctional facilities. Quasi-public development infrastructure refers to civic centers, parks, and hotels, among other projects. Housing and prisons are also significant infrastructure issues.

If cost estimates are disaggregated among infrastructure types, reasonable approaches may be planned for dealing with problems for which institutional, legal, and financial responsibility is highly dispersed among separate government entities. Also, demographic shifts and the use of better pricing mechanisms (which reduce demand), such as user fees, and changes in service delivery (e.g., privatization), decrease the demand for public provision of some infrastructure.

Thus, although maintaining infrastructure is a national problem that affects every region, there are vast differences in both degree and kind. How to finance the repair of deteriorating facilities is one problem; another is to build facilities for the first time, for example, water systems, in many rural areas. Congestion or deteriorated roads are problems in many places, but not evidence of a crisis in the nation's highway system. Similarly, bridge deficiencies are sometimes glaring, but 40 percent of all such deficiencies occur in just six states.

The tendency to look for single-approach options to deal with what are really pervasive problems makes success unlikely. The considerable variation across types of infrastructure and within types, across facilities owned and maintained by different government agencies and other entities, complicates coherent political action. The diversity of problems and needs has led to the necessity for local solutions.

Infrastructure is often invisible, leading to lack of public awareness, political support, and necessary fiscal resources. When financial resources dwindle, local governments traditionally cut back on operating budget allocations for maintenance and repair of existing infrastructure and limit capital investments for expansion and rehabilitation.

The recent shifting of more responsibilities to the state and local levels for decisionmaking, funding, and implementation may, in the long run, have positive effects in motivating local decisionmakers to exert the political will necessary to deal with problems. State laws and practices that inhibit local governments' abilities to solve their infrastructure problems are receiving increased attention. This attention includes statutes that place legal restraints and controls on local revenue-raising and spending capacity and laws that prevent local governments from creating capital reserves to finance future capital expenditures.

The capacity of some communities to plan and implement infrastructure has become a key concern of the United States Environmental Protection Agency and the various states. Revolving loan funds have been developed, along with more flexible mandates, and greater technical assistance is offered to less managerially and financially capable local governments. Infrastructure issues are linked more broadly to economic development.

Current Practice

Public infrastructure outlays have risen in real (inflation-adjusted) terms throughout most of the period from 1956 to 1991, according to a 1995 CBO report prepared for the United States House of Representatives, Committee on Transportation and Infrastructure.

In 1994, total federal spending for infrastructure was US$45.3 billion in nominal terms (not adjusting for inflation), with the mix between capital and noncapital outlays at 70 and 30 percent, respectively. The national government's capital spending, inflation-adjusted, for most categories of infrastructure, has decreased, however. For example, such spending for drinking water and wastewater infrastructure peaked in the late 1970s and has gradually decreased since then, with the downward trend expected to continue through the end of the 1990s. Similarly, national spending on water supply and wastewater treatment infrastructure peaked at $7.9 billion in 1977, but by 1988 that figure had dropped to $3.1 billion.

The vast majority of the federal spending goes into wastewater efforts, such as the United States Environmental Protection Agency's funding for municipal wastewater treatment plants. Water supply funds include loans to rural water systems.

The CBO lists the sum of all public infrastructure spending in the United States—reflecting national, state, and local government outlays—for each year from 1956 through 1991. The CBO report also provides annual data for eight infrastructure categories—highways, mass transit, rail, aviation, water transportation, water resources, water supply, and wastewater treatment. Compared to levels in the mid-1990s, national infrastructure spending is expected to decline approximately 11.6 percent from 1995 to 2000. Water supply and wastewater treatment will experience the greatest percentage decrease in funding, although other categories may experience a greater dollar amount loss.

The local and state government share of infrastructure spending has increased in recent years, a trend that is predicted to continue. By the end of the 1980s, state and local governments had contributed approximately 75 percent of the United States infrastructure outlays. Thus, the relative contributions of national, state, and local governments have varied widely in recent years. From 1956 to 1976, national spending was approximately 40 percent of state and local government infrastructure spending and approximately 30 percent of total public spending. After peaking in 1977 at 39.4 percent, the national share has continued to decline as a percentage of the total.

Capital outlays have fluctuated more than noncapital outlays since the mid-1950s. Noncapital outlays tend to grow each year; capital outlays have had a pattern of rising and falling during the same period, although capital investment has increased each year since 1982. Though national infrastructure spending has always been dominated by highway spending, the focus in the 1970s was relatively more toward wastewater treatment, transit, and water supply. In the 1980s and 1990s, the national funding shift has been back to highways and to aviation. Compared to national spending, state and local infrastructure spending has changed little since the 1970s in most categories of infrastructure, although there were some increases in mass transit, aviation, and water resources. The projected national budget as the next decade approaches would cut surface and air transportation funding and have most national spending for highways, transit, rail, and aviation come from a single unified account. This would give state and local governments more decisionmaking control over investments.

BEVERLY A. CIGLER

BIBLIOGRAPHY

Cigler, Beverly A., 1988a. "Political and Organizational Considerations in Infrastructure Investment Decision-Making." In Thomas G. Johnson, Brady J. Deaton, and Eduardo Segarra, eds., *Local Infrastructure Investment in Rural America*, pp. 201–213. Boulder, CO: Westview Press.
———, 1988b. "Rural Infrastructure Research Needs." In Thomas G. Johnson, Brady J. Deaton, and Eduardo Segarra, eds., *Local Infrastructure Investment in Rural America*, pp. 233–244. Boulder, CO: Westview Press.
Congressional Budget Office, 1995. *Public Infrastructure Spending and an Analysis of The President's Proposals for Infrastructure Spending from 1996–2000*. Washington, D.C.: Congressional Budget Office (June).
National Science Foundation, 1993. *Public Infrastructure Research: A Public Infrastructure Research Agenda for the Social, Behavioral and Economic Sciences*. Washington, DC: National Science Foundation (April).

INITIATIVE AND REFERENDUM.

Two types of political processes that empower citizens to take direct control of lawmaking. Collectively, initiative and referendum are basic forms of direct democracy that provide the means for voters to either override an act of the legislature or to bypass the legislature altogether. An initiative allows voters to introduce a law for approval at the polls; a referendum allows voters to approve a law proposed by the legislature. In the United States, initiative and referendum apply only to state and local governments, as no provision exists for direct citizen lawmaking at the national level. Direct democracy at the national level is more common in European countries. France, Ireland, Italy, and Sweden, for example, allow referenda to decide major policy issues.

American voters have used the initiative and referendum at the state level to decide upon an increasing number of important and often controversial policy issues. Early in this century, several western states approved women's suffrage through the initiative, and Nebraska voters used the citizen initiative in 1934 to establish the only unicameral state legislature. In recent years, citizens have voted whether to impose the death penalty, restrict the use of nuclear power, limit school busing, allow gays to teach in public schools, decriminalize marijuana, and decide how much government can tax its citizens. More and more, tough policy questions are being decided in the polling booth instead of the legislative chamber.

The Initiative

In cities, states, or counties that use the initiative, anyone may draw up a proposed law. For the law to be voted on, a predetermined number of voters must sign a petition favoring it, usually about 10 percent of the eligible voters. Once the petition is approved, the proposed law goes to the public vote, in the case of the direct initiative, or, in the case of the indirect initiative, voters petition the legislature to enact a measure that otherwise will be placed on the ballot if the legislature fails to approve it.

Laws providing for the initiative vary greatly from state to state, and no two states have identical initiative systems. Of the 24 states allowing the initiative, the number of signatures required for a successful petition ranges from a low of 2 percent of voting-age population in North Dakota, to 15 percent in Wyoming. Five states (Maine, Massachusetts, Michigan, Nevada, and Wyoming) require the legislature to consider an initiative before it can be placed on the ballot. Six states (Alaska, Idaho, Maine, Utah, Washington, and Wyoming) allow only statutory initiatives. Florida allows only constitutional initiatives.

The Referendum

Most city charters and state constitutions provide for a referendum to allow a proposed law to be placed on the ballot at the next general or special election. All states except Alabama hold constitutional referenda on proposed amendments. Twenty-five states allow for a statutory referendum giving citizens the power to approve or override laws passed by the legislature or proposed by initiative.

The use of the referendum continues at a high rate. In recent years, hundreds of state constitutional amendments and thousands of local issues have been subjected to voter referenda. Referenda calling for voter approval on state legislation have been less frequent and usually fall into two categories: referenda dealing with changes to government organization and those that concern financial matters. Legislators, who are often reluctant to vote for higher taxes or additional government programs, submit unpopular fiscal proposals for direct public vote.

History

Although the initiative is a relatively recent political phenomenon, the referendum has been used for hundreds of years. Forms of referenda trace to ancient Greece, and two states of Switzerland have allowed referenda since the 1500s. The Massachusetts Constitution of 1780 provided for statewide constitutional referenda for the adoption of amendments, and Texas provided the legislative referendum in the mid-1800s. However, the widespread movement for United States state legislatures to submit laws to the voters did not develop until the turn of the century.

The Progressive movement, lasting from about 1880 to 1920, crusaded for political reform and an end to the corrupt spoils system that began in 1828 with the election of Andrew Jackson as president and peaked during the Ulysses Grant administration (1869–1877). The Progressives, like the Populists a few years before, viewed lawmakers as politically and financially corrupt and controlled by the large trusts of railroads, banks, and mining interests. Beginning in 1885, reform leaders such as South Dakota priest Robert Haire and New Jersey newspaper publisher Benjamin Urner proposed direct citizen legislation as one solution to break the control of large corporations and improve democracy. New York labor activist James Sullivan founded the People's Power League (1892), a group advocating the initiative and referendum options on party platforms. Sullivan had traveled to Switzerland to study the use of initiative and referendum in that country and many early reform proposals were modeled after the Swiss. To Haire, Urner, Sullivan, and other reformers, initiative and referenda would give citizens the power to pass laws directly and bypass corrupt, incompetent, and unresponsive legislators. They joined with other Progressive movements fighting for women's suffrage, direct election of senators, and civil service reform to form a strong national coalition. With the support of President Theodore Roosevelt, and with reforms having been popularized by a muckraking press, the Progressives successfully introduced an unprecedented number of social and political reforms at all levels of government. Of those reforms, the initiative and referendum processes were two cornerstones of direct citizen democracy that remain today as major legacies of the Progressive era.

In 1898, South Dakota became the first state to adopt the initiative, followed by Utah (1900), Oregon (1902), and several others. Most of the states adopting the initiative and referendum were primarily from west of the Mississippi River. Midwestern and western states were the bedrock of the reform movements where both Populism and Progressivism had strong support. Many western states only recently had attained statehood and were more likely to adopt reforms than eastern states. The initiative was never successful in most northeast and southern states. Some of the reasons for the relative failure of direct democracy in those regions include stronger control by urban party machines and anti-immigration feelings in the Northeast, and a weaker populist base and labor movement in the South.

By the end of World War I, Progressivism began to decline and the movement for direct democracy lost popularity. Massachusetts (1918) was the last state of that era to adopt the initiative. Since World War II, Alaska (1957), Florida (1968), Wyoming (1968), Illinois (1970), and Mississippi (1993) have adopted the initiative. Once adopted, no state has abandoned either the initiative or the referendum.

Although neither the initiative nor the referendum exist at the national level, they have been proposed as constitutional amendments on several occasions. During the Progressive era, Samuel Gompers and the American Federation of Labor endorsed both a national initiative and a referendum during its 1902 convention. Several unsuccessful constitutional amendments were proposed during World War I that would require a national referendum on whether the nation should go to war. A similar "war referendum" introduced in 1937 failed in the House of Representatives by only 21 votes. Support for a national initiative increased during the 1970s, and endorsements for its adoption ranged from conservative congressman Jack Kemp to consumer advocate Ralph Nader. Although the Senate held hearings on a national initiative in 1977, the proposal failed to gain serious political support.

The Direct Democracy Debate

The use of the initiative and referendum is not without controversy. As early as 1787 delegates to the Constitutional Convention debated the question of direct democracy versus representative democracy. Two distinct ideologies emerged: the Jeffersonians advocated a laissez-faire, citizen-based government, while the Hamiltonians argued for strong representational government. The basic question then was whether the people could be trusted to vote intelligently on complex issues, as the Jeffersonians argued. In the case of direct democracy, the debate continues today.

Recent critics of the initiative and referendum argue that they are contrary to the general concept of United States government that is based on representative rather than direct democracy. Many fear that direct democracy can lead to rule by an oppressive majority, at the expense of minority rights. Opponents argue that it may be unwise to have the electorate vote directly on complicated legislation that cannot be understood fully. Direct democracy dilutes the power and effectiveness of the legislature.

Numerous initiatives and referenda clutter the ballot with technical issues that even the informed voter cannot comprehend. Often, initiatives are poorly written and even unconstitutional. Critics contend that bypassing the normal legislative process lessens the ability to compromise on difficult issues. Instead, citizens are given only a yes-or-no choice on an often complicated ballot initiative.

Opponents criticize the initiative as a tool of special interests. It allows minority groups to seek their own narrow agenda, especially when supported by well-financed special interest lobbies. The side that spends the most money usually wins. Critics argue that the Progressive vision of grassroots democracy has not been realized. Instead, professional petition circulators use sophisticated signature-gathering techniques to insure that their clients' issues are placed on the ballot. Direct democracy, critics argue, is only a myth.

Alternately, proponents for the initiative and referendum argue that they are needed in cases where lawmakers refuse to enact, or even to consider, a law the people want. The initiative and referendum serve as a stimulus for legislative action, provide a necessary check on corrupt and incompetent governments, and ensure responsive and accountable public officials. These devices are nonviolent means of political participation that guarantee a citizen's right to petition the government. Both offer a counterbalance to the trend toward centralization and growth of government.

Proponents also argue that the initiative and referendum produce a more open and focused debate on critical issues and increase voter interest and participation. A better-informed citizenry tends to participate in government if it believes its involvement makes a difference. Initiative and referendum provide means for putting new ideas on the political agenda when legislators are reluctant to address the tough issues.

Both opponents and proponents generally agree that the initiative and referendum are no replacement for the traditional legislative process and representative democracy. To most, they complement the system and provide an important safety valve to the legislative process. Most also agree that in years to come the initiative and referendum will continue to be powerful influences in the politics of many states.

Recent Events

Since the early 1980s, the number of initiatives appearing on statewide ballots has been rising. Voter dissatisfaction with the legislative process, coupled with increased involvement of lobby and special interest groups, has led to a more turbulent state political scene and a return to grass-root politics. From 1900 to 1939, a total of 253 initiatives were brought before state voters. From 1940 to 1980, there were 248 initiatives, and from 1981 to 1992 the total in-

creased to 346. In 1992, voters in 19 states decided on 69 initiatives at the polls, the most since 1932. Generally, initiatives have been divided equally between conservative and liberal causes.

The bellwether of citizen dissatisfaction with the legislative process took place in June 1978 when Californians voted on Proposition 13, an initiative cutting property taxes in half. The proposal received nationwide attention, and more citizens voted on Proposition 13 than on the gubernatorial primary held on the same day. Beginning in the 1980s, taxpayer revolts similar to Proposition 13 spread to other states and became symbolic of the public's rising antigovernment sentiment. Between 1978 and 1984, citizens in 19 states voted on tax-cut initiatives. Of those, California, Idaho (1978), and Massachusetts (1980) voters approved major tax cuts.

Besides efforts to control taxation, other major policy issues have been decided by the public ballot in recent years. In the mid-1970s, opponents of nuclear power were successful in placing antinuclear initiatives on the ballots of several western states. Despite overwhelming campaign contributions from the pro-nuclear lobby, Montana (1978) and Oregon (1980) voters approved restrictions on nuclear power plant construction. Other major policy initiatives brought before the public vote have been efforts to restrict the discharge of toxic chemicals, to allow gambling and state lotteries, to restrict homosexual rights, and to declare English as the official state language.

The profound effect initiatives and referenda are making on the political process is demonstrated by recent efforts to limit the terms of congressional and state legislators. In 1992, term-limit supporters were successful in presenting ballot initiatives in fourteen states, and three state legislatures (Florida, Mississippi, and Rhode Island) put term limits on the referendum ballot. All of the term-limit initiatives and referenda passed, most by overwhelming margins. In 1994, voters in six more states passed congressional term limitations. The ballot initiative greatly facilitates term-limit supporters, who bypass state legislators reluctant to limit their own tenure and take the issue directly to the people. Of the 22 states enacting term limits, 21 began the process with the ballot initiative. In states without the initiative, term limits can become law only if their legislatures and governors approve the measure. Only the Utah legislature (1994) has taken the unusual step to limit its own term of office.

Without the ballot initiative, the term limit movement would have made little progress against entrenched legislators. In the future, the movement may slow its progress, as Illinois is the only ballot-initiative state yet to enact term limits. If additional states adopt the ballot initiative, they, too, can be expected to limit the terms of their legislators.

RICHARD D. WHITE, JR.

BIBLIOGRAPHY

Butler, David, and Austin Ranney, eds., 1978. *Referendums: A Comparative Study of Practice and Theory.* Washington, DC: American Enterprise Institute for Public Policy Research.

Cronin, Thomas E., 1989. *Direct Democracy: The Politics of Initiative, Referendum, and Recall.* Cambridge, MA: Harvard University Press.

Kehler, David, and Robert M. Stern, 1994. "Initiatives in the 1980s and 1990s." *The Book of the States 1994–95.* Lexington, KY: Council of State Governments.

Magelby, David B., 1984. *Direct Legislation: Voting on Ballot Propositions in the United States.* Baltimore: Johns Hopkins Press.

McGuigan, Patrick B., 1985. *The Politics of Direct Democracy in the 1980s: Case Studies in Political Decision Making.* Washington, DC: Free Congress Research and Education Foundation.

Schmidt, David D., 1989. *Citizen Lawmakers: The Ballot Initiative Revolution.* Philadelphia: Temple University Press.

Zisk, Betty H., 1987. *Money, Media and The Grass Roots: State Ballot Issues and the Electoral Process.* Newbury Park, CA: Sage Publications.

INJUNCTION. A court order requiring a person to refrain from a particular act or course of conduct or, in more limited circumstances, requiring a person to perform a particular act or series of acts.

This remedy grew out of the English Chancery proceedings, and is a primary remedy for courts exercising equitable powers in the American system. An injunction can be issued, generally speaking, to prevent an injurious course of conduct, particularly if the person who would be injured would not have an adequate remedy at common law in the form of money damages.

The purpose of an injunction is to preserve matters in status quo and to restrain actual or threatened acts that could cause irreparable harm. Because an injunction is a preventive remedy, the injunction is not intended to compensate or to punish a party for actions that have already occurred.

An injunction may be classified according to the type of command contained within the injunctive order, commonly referred to as prohibitory or mandatory injunctions.

Prohibitory injunctions, which are the most common, order a party to abstain from performing a certain act or series of actions. Such injunctions are designed to maintain the status quo and may be utilized to disrupt or avoid an ongoing wrong or to prevent a contemplated or threatened action from occurring. The person seeking an injunction must show that the other party's action threaten a legal right and that the threatened damage to this right would be irreparable and that no legal remedy exists to make up for the injury in the form of money damages.

A mandatory injunction requires a party to perform a positive act that would alter existing circumstances. In most cases, mandatory injunctions are utilized to eliminate wrongful existing conditions that are likely to continue. Courts have demonstrated an aversion toward mandatory injunctions, largely because injunctions are designed to prevent future wrongs rather than to remedy wrongs that have already occurred. Courts are also reluctant to issue orders that require ongoing judicial supervision, which would be the case with most forms of mandatory injunctions. Accordingly, the standard for granting a mandatory injunction is higher than that required for issuing a prohibitory injunction.

Injunctions also are categorized according to their duration, either as temporary or permanent. A temporary injunction, also called a preliminary injunction, is issued before trial on the merits on the controversy. The purpose of a temporary injunction is to maintain the status quo and to preserve the subject matter in controversy until the merits of the case are decided. In emergency situations, a court can grant a temporary restraining order, without a hearing, to avoid immediate, irreparable harm. Courts have broad discretionary power to decide, in accordance with principles of equity and justice, whether a temporary or preliminary injunction should be granted. However, courts do inquire into several issues—the relative convenience or inconvenience a temporary injunction would place on each party, the existence and adequacy of a complete remedy of common law, and the nature, extent, and irreparable character of the injury that is sought to be remedied. Moreover, persons seeking a temporary or preliminary injunction must show that they will probably prevail on the merits of the case.

If the person seeking a temporary injunction later fails to succeed in the trial of the merits of the case, the temporary or preliminary injunction will be dissolved. In situations in which the person succeeds in the merits of the case, the terms of the preliminary or temporary injunction may be incorporated into a court order granting a permanent injunction.

A permanent injunction is granted or denied after a full adjudication on the merits of the suit.

In public policy context, injunctive relief is sought if a litigant challenges the validity of statute, rule or ordinance. For example, in *Weaver v. Reagen,* 886 F. 2d 194 (8th Cir. 1989), the plaintiff, an AIDS patient, challenged a state medical assistance (Medicaid) rule denying AIDS patients the drug AZT. They found that the state rule was contrary to federal law and granted an injunction requiring that the drug be provided to AIDS patients.

Although it is common to have a preliminary or temporary injunction precede a permanent injunction, a permanent injunction may be granted regardless of whether or not a preliminary injunction was granted, denied, or not sought.

Injunctions are enforceable by contempt of court proceedings. These proceedings allow the court the power to enforce its orders. A person found to be violating an injunctive order may be subjected to imprisonment, fines, or other financial penalties.

MICHAEL A. WOLFF

BIBLIOGRAPHY

42 *American Jurisprudence* 2d, §§ 1–41.
43 *Corpus Juris Secundum*, §§ 1–31.
Rule 65, Federal Rules of Civil Procedure.

INNOVATION. Any creative and risk-taking process by which new ideas, values, standards, methods, procedures, technologies, or products are conceived, developed, introduced, and/or followed up for the purpose of meeting existing or future objectives or needs.

The most widely used such term is "technological innovation," which refers to the ideas and processes in the "new technologies" area. In the past, it was a field of activity mainly occupied by inventors, engineers, and scientific researchers. The industrial society, and especially the postindustrial era of the twentieth century, have dramatically changed this situation. The complexity of new manufacturing and other modern technologies based on advances in science and engineering, as well as new ideas emanating from the social sciences, required new methods and techniques of management. These technologically driven changes in the society necessarily defined new approaches for talking both private and public sector problems; thus, the process of innovation generated new responses by businesses and governments to the challenges of societal transformation.

Innovative ability is conceptual and creative, rather than technical and scientific. It is the ability to look at the organization's activities as a system and to provide missing elements that will convert the already existing elements into a new and more productive whole. The major task is the determination of what can change needs, values, and satisfactions of a customer, a client, or a user of the organization's outputs.

From the general society's point of view, innovations are predominantly economically driven. Economic growth requires purposeful, responsible, risk-taking actions of entrepreneurs and managers, actions that are innovative. The immediate generator of economic growth is investment—in new products, new processes, new resources, new services—which often arises from new ideas, new knowledge, and new developments in science and technology. By emphasizing research, and by systematizing innovation, industry and government now make regular provision for the occurrence of new, innovative developments.

The roles of government and business in the innovation process are substantially different. Government is a basic promoter of technological innovations. Governments spends a great deal of money to support research and development in certain industries and areas of basic research. Private industries usually do not invest sufficiently in those areas considered vital to the nation's well being, such as education and health care; such investments are considered very risky to business, as the returns are unclear and rather distinct. This is particularly true of modern

complex technologies, where the costs of research and development are very high and the payoffs are uncertain.

Government is the only institution that could fund large-scale space programs, the initial stages of computer and communication technology development such as the creation of first generation computers in the 1940s and 1950s, or the promotion of electronic networks in the 1970s and 1980s. The private sector did not fund such projects because they were too expensive and their immediate profit-making potential was not apparent. However, modern governments worldwide fund projects whose benefits are believed to contribute to society as a whole. This type of public policy is usually implemented through sets of public institutions. In the United States, these are both major departments, such as Defense, and special governmental agencies, such as NASA, the National Science Foundation, the National Institute of Health, and some others. However, among policy-level officials (both elected and appointed), the willingness and ability to free up discretionary funds to make such collective investments may be declining.

One of the basic mechanisms through which the economy and society have benefited from governmentally funded research and development is known as the "spin-off" effect. New processes and materials that were created under governmental programs aimed at the development of military and aerospace technologies have been licensed to commercial and nonprofit firms and have become available for civilian purposes. Businesses use them to design and market innovative products and services for both industrial and consumer needs. Governmental agencies frequently support special programs for technology transfer (i.e., disseminating spin-off technologies), thus providing preferable conditions for their use in private sector innovations. In the United States, there is legislation institutionalizing technology transfer in several agencies. On the federal level, there are at least two dozen such programs and at least five laws since 1979 have promoted technology transfer, particularly to small businesses and nonprofit corporations.

Another important function of the government in promoting technological innovations in the society is the implementation of public policy that sets up special incentives for businesses to adapt new technologies and develop new products. Examples of such mechanisms are tax credits and rates of depreciation. Companies that expand or modernize, investing in new plants and equipment, are given a tax credit. Special depreciation schedules allow businesses to write off their production facilities over a shortened period of time, thereby reducing their tax bills to the government and ultimately making more capital available to invest in new technologies.

A predominant role for the private sector is dissemination of technological innovations in the society. Through commercialization, innovations enter industrial and consumer markets and become part of everyday life. But this is not the only role of business in promotion of innovations. Businesses also generate innovations. In order to handle technological innovations and dynamic social innovations, business companies also develop innovations: They change their managerial practices, labor-management relations, the ways they interact with the government, and so forth.

The private sector has a reputation as the major innovator in management. Classic studies of scientific management based their findings on the experiences gained inside privately owned production plants. Major types of organizational structure, such as divisional or network, emerged inside private businesses. But the private sector is not the only innovator. For example, an important managerial innovation—matrix structure—was developed under post–World War II, governmentally funded research and development projects. What is clear is that businesses tend to be faster in adoption of new managerial techniques. For them, backwardness is a real threat to survival, whereas governmental organizations enjoy more stability as their existence is dependent on governmental decisions, but not on profits or revenues from business operations.

On the organizational level, as in the society as a whole, innovations occur in both technical and social arenas, both of which are important to the other. Results of the explosive development of technological progress and change cannot be productive unless this process is accompanied by major innovations in the social area. Of equal importance are real advances in methods, tools, and measurements for conducting managerial jobs, as well as improvements in the management and organization of knowledge workers.

In terms of innovation, social-technical-managerial goals for both private and public organizations should include

- new products, services, or practices needed to attain marketing and/or operational objectives;
- new products, services, and practices, or improvements of existing ones, needed to meet technological competition and/or offset technical and other forms of obsolescence;
- new resources, materials, equipment, and processes needed to keep pace with technology;
- social innovations and improvements in all major areas of an organization's activities;
- managerial innovations and improvements needed to implement technical and social innovations in order to meet the challenges of rapidly changing environments.

There are two basic types of innovation in every organization: (1) innovations in products services, or operations and (2) innovations in skills and activities needed to

support them. Since the innovation process extends across all functions and activities of an organization, every managerial level should have clear responsibility and definite goals for innovation. Innovative performance should be built into the job and into the spirit of organization and should be made an important criterion for personal progress in the organization.

Why is it so important to be innovative? What are the basic changes in technology and society that make innovative performance a prerequisite of success both in business and the public sector? Why should managerial practices and organizational structures be subjected to constant changes?

Change is necessary in an extraordinarily dynamic type of postindustrial society. Burns and Stalker (1961) were among the first to question traditional administrative theory. They suggested that dynamic conditions might make traditional hierarchy obsolete. As they and Woodward (1965) found, organizations built on a bureaucratic closed model offer some advantages and might be appropriate in stable conditions, but dynamic and uncertain conditions require more open forms of organization with much greater flexibility for managers. Since then, many researchers, management theorists and practitioners have paid a great deal of attention to such issues as innovative management and management of innovation, management in turbulent times, management under uncertainty and risk, and so forth. Speed of adaptation and responsiveness to emerging new technologies and other innovations are now considered critical measures of success for any organization.

The most influential part of contemporary technological progress, which greatly affects the innovation process, is the information revolution. In a way, it produced an overall label for the present phase of development—the information society. Information technology has had a tremendous impact on today's organizations. It subjects technical and social systems to dramatic changes and induces new managerial methods and techniques.

As early as 1958, Leavitt and Whisler forecast the following basic changes in organizations for the 1980s:

1. The role and scope of middle managers will change and decline. Many middle-management jobs will become more structured and more downward oriented in status and compensation. Flattening of organizations will occur due to the decrease in the number of middle managers. Remaining mid-management positions will be more technical and specialized rather than supervisory. Instead, new middle-level positions will emerge, with titles such as analyst.
2. Top management will almost entirely switch to innovating, planning, and creating. The rate of obsolescence and change will quicken, and top management will have to continually focus on the horizon.

3. Large organizations will recentralize. New information technologies will give managers more information. This will extend top management's control over critical decisions of subordinates. Top executives will choose to decentralize because they will be unable to keep up with the changing size and complexity of their organizations. Given the chance, however, they will use information technology to take more control and recentralize.

Public organizations are now enmeshed in a turbulent environment–perhaps beginning in the United States with the passage of California's Proposition Thirteen in 1978–and continuing worldwide in the present rush to reduce government and privatize the remaining public services. On a process level, public managers have had to become conversant with concepts such as total quality management, continuous improvement, fourth generation management, the learning organization, internal entrepreneurship, benchmarking, cross-cultural management, environmental management, and the like. Summarizing these ideas and practices, for an organization to be innovative in order to survive in the present turbulent environment it is important to

- give much grater attention to quality;
- search for and implement organization innovations purposefully (benchmarking), learning constantly from best practices both inside the outside of the immediate field of activity;
- make constant improvement a way of life of the entire organization;
- shift from the traditional administrative bureaucratic organization model to a model of an open, flexible, flat, knowledge-based organization in which frontline workers have both responsibility and decisionmaking power for their own performance and in which key persons are specialists, not managers merely exercising authority due to their positions in a hierarchy;
- make customer satisfaction the first priority and important criteria of an organization's performance;
- recognize that the most valuable skill of the new organization's managers and employees is a combination of internal entrepreneurship and the ability to communicate both horizontally across intraorganizational boundaries and with outside counterparts: customers, consumers, suppliers, and so forth.

"Total Quality Management" may be the most significant such innovation to reach the public sector. The goal of the quality movement in organizations is to achieve continuous improvement using a specific set of approaches, methods, and techniques. By 1992, there were more than 200 county and city "quality initiatives" in the United States. In 1988, the federal government initiated a total quality management program, and the United States Office of Management and Budget has provided leadership for a joint public and private sector quality improvement. The Office of Personnel Management and the Federal Quality Institute (now defunct) also provided leadership, support, and technical assistance to the "federal quality movement." For several years, special Presidential Quality Improvement Prototype awards have been given out to a public sector organization recognized as the most successful in development and implementation of innovation by raising productivity, efficiency, and effectiveness. This prize is a public sector equivalent to the Baldridge Award, which contributed much to spreading quality management practices throughout the private sector.

Osborne and Gaebler's *Reinventing Government: How the Entrepreneurial Spirit Is Transforming the Public Sector,* published in 1992, was a related initiative. It provided the Clinton administration with both a model and an inspiration for the start of reforms in the federal government system. "Reinventing government" aimed to create "a government that works better and costs less." The basic broad goals of the National Performance Review, headed by Vice President Al Gore, are cutting red tape, putting the customer first, encouraging employees to get results, and cutting back to basics. As evidence that government is indeed being reinvented there are a series of annual awards. At the federal level, the National Performance Review makes "Hammer" Awards. At the state and local level, there are also annual award programs, such as the Innovations in Government awards, which are presented by the Ford Foundation and the Kennedy School of Government at Harvard University, and the Exemplary State and Local Government Awards, which are presented by the National Center for Public Productivity at Rutgers University's campus at Newark.

An important part of these innovation initiatives, on the federal, state, and local levels, is establishing standards for measuring progress and institutional performance of governmental organizations. One such powerful technique widely used in private sector is benchmarking, which recently attracted the attention of governmental organizations. The state of Oregon, for instance, has introduced 270 benchmarks to measure performance of public institutions in order to evaluate their progress toward agreed outcomes.

Within many of these efforts, there are emphases on "internal markets" and "internal entrepreneurship"–ideas long advocated for their application to debureaucratization of large corporations by management scientists such as Russell Ackoff (1994). But innovations derived from the private sector may not be applicable in a public setting. For instance, the slogan that "government should operate like business" overstates and simplifies government's roles. Private sector managers work under threat of bankruptcy; government, by contrast, can increase taxes to balance budgets. Public sector managers must follow multiple rules and regulations. For example, the merit compensation systems currently used in the public sector often suppress innovation by discouraging constructive competition, creating fear, and inhibiting motivation among employees. Employees are not rewarded on quality of services provided because the criteria for assessing productivity, performance, and merit often emphasize processes and activities, rather than results. Line-item budgeting systems used by governments also act as a disincentive to innovation to the extent they highlight cost reduction rather than investment. The new management systems may inhibit innovation to the extent that they are mutually contradictory. Downsizing supposes that workers are expendable and that quality management is an invaluable resource. The core idea of reengineering is to rip up the organization and to start from scratch. Total quality management's basic assumption is continuous incremental improvement.

Nevertheless, many attempts to apply management theory and innovative managerial techniques have proven successful. Breaking huge bureaucratic organizations into manageable units, introduction of performance measures and accountability, creating a customer consciousness—all these and other renovations have helped to improve the public sector. It is probably innovating, that is adapting to environmental pressures, as rapidly as ever and can maintain that accelerated rate of innovation indefinitely.

PAVEL MAKEYENKO, MARC HOLZER, AND
VATCHE GABRIELIAN

BIBLIOGRAPHY

Ackoff, Russell L., 1994. *The Democratic Corporation: A Radical Prescription for Recreating Corporate America and Rediscovering Success.* New York: Oxford University Press.

Banki, Ivan S., 1981. *Dictionary of Administration and Management.* Los Angeles, CA: Systems Research Institute.

Bogan, Christopher E., 1994. *Benchmarking for Best Practices: Winning through Innovative Adaptation.* New York: McGraw-Hill.

Burns, Tom, and George M. Stalker, 1961. *The Management of Innovation.* London: Tavistock Publications.

Gore, Al, 1994. *Creating a Government That Works Better and Costs Less. Status Report of the National Performance Review.* Washington, DC: U.S. Government Printing Office.

Harris, Philip R., 1993. *Managing Cultural Differences,* 3d ed. Houston, TX: Gulf.

Joiner, Brian L., 1994. *Fourth Generation Management: The New Business Consciousness.* New York: McGraw-Hill.

Leavitt, Harold J., and Thomas L. Whisler, 1958. "Management in the 1980's." *Harvard Business Review* (November–December) 41–48.

Oregon Benchmarks: Standards for Measuring Statewide Progress and Institutional Performance. Report to the 1995 Legislature, 1994. Salem: Oregon Progress Board.

Osborne, David, and Ted Gaebler, 1992. *Reinventing Government: How the Entrepreneurial Spirit Is Transforming the Public Sector.* Reading, MA: Addison-Wesley.

Peters, Thomas J., 1992. *Liberation Management: Necessary Disorganization for Nanosecond Nineties.* New York: A. A. Knopf.

Senge, Peter M., 1990. *The Fifth Discipline: The Art and Practice of the Learning Organization.* New York: Doubleday.

Woodward, J., 1965. *Industrial Organization: Theory and Practice.* New York: Oxford University Press.

INSPECTOR GENERAL.

A government official responsible for preventing and detecting fraud, waste, and abuse in government programs through a consolidated audit and investigation function.

Congress passed the Inspector General Act of 1978 in response to concerns regarding fraud, waste, and abuse in the federal government. The act established offices of inspectors general in 12 federal establishments (including 6 cabinet-level departments and 6 other agencies and administrations) to oversee and conduct audits and investigations of the establishments' operations and programs. The inspectors general were given broad authority and independence to carry out their function. In subsequent legislation, including the 1988 amendments to the act, statutory offices of inspectors general were created in numerous other federal establishments, bringing the total number of federal inspectors general to more than 60.

History

Prior to the passage of the 1978 act, offices of inspectors general had been established in several federal departments. One of the earliest inspector general positions was established by statute in 1961 in the Office of Foreign Assistance in the State Department. However, the office of the inspector general that was created in the Department of Agriculture in 1962 usually is cited as the earliest example of an inspector general position that was similar to the statutory positions created in 1978.

The office of the inspector general in the Department of Agriculture was created largely in response to congressional hearings related to the fraudulent undertakings of a Texas multimillionaire named Billie Sol Estes. Although several different investigative units had addressed activities related to the Estes case over a period of years, the investigations were not coordinated and did not result in timely corrective action. In attempts to prevent a similar occurrence, the secretary of Agriculture created an office of inspector general to consolidate and oversee the agency's audit and investigation functions. However, the office was eliminated by the secretary of Agriculture in 1974. The office was reestablished in 1977 and, in 1978, became one of the 12 statutory offices established by the Inspector General Act.

Another nonstatutory office of inspector general was established in the Department of Housing and Urban Development (HUD) in 1972. This office was created in response to problems involving collusion of construction firms and builders in HUD housing projects. The creation of the office was proposed by the Assistant Secretary of

HUD, Lester Condon, who previously had been the first inspector general at the Department of Agriculture. The HUD office of inspector general became a statutory office as a result of the 1978 Inspector General Act.

One of the first inspector general offices to be initiated by federal statute was established in the Department of Health, Education and Welfare (HEW) in 1976. (HEW was the predecessor to the Department of Education and the Department of Health and Human Services.) In response to reports of widespread cheating in the medicare and guaranteed student loan programs, Congress undertook a review of the procedures and resources within HEW to prevent and detect fraud and abuse. The review found that the basic data needed to prevent and detect fraud and abuse were not available; the department had an insufficient number of investigators; existing investigators lacked independence and coordination; and deficiencies disclosed in reports were often not given serious attention or addressed in a prompt manner. To address these problems, Congress passed the HEW Inspector General Act.

Two other offices of inspectors general preceded the passage of the Inspector General Act of 1978. The office of inspector general for the Energy Department was created when the department was established in 1977. A nonstatutory office of inspector general was established in early 1978 in the Veterans Administration, which was later replaced by a statutory office created by the Inspector General Act of 1978.

A bill to expand the inspector general concept to other federal agencies was introduced in 1977 by Representative Jack Brooks (D.–Tex.) and Representative L. H. Fountain (D.–N.C.) of the House Governmental Operations Committee. The hearings on this bill addressed concerns regarding the inability of the federal government to identify, correct, and prevent problems associated with fraud, waste, and abuse in federal programs. The hearings disclosed that many federal auditors or investigators lacked sufficient independence to conduct their work. For example, it was not uncommon for auditors or investigators to report to the people who were responsible for the programs that were being audited or investigated. There also was a problem with understaffing of audit and investigation units, even though testimony indicated that auditor and investigator positions usually more than pay for themselves through their findings and the associated corrective action. Other concerns also were expressed, such as the existence of multiple audit or investigative units without effective coordination and leadership, insufficient programs to identify the possibility of fraud or abuse, and potential fraud cases that had not been referred to the Department of Justice for prosecution.

The bill proposed the establishment of offices of inspectors general, which would consolidate the audit and investigative units of an agency. The office would be headed by an inspector general, who would be appointed by the president subject to Senate confirmation. The inspector general would report to the number one or two person in the agency and would have broad authority and independence. The inspector general would be required to file reports with the agency head and Congress, documenting the findings and results of the audits and investigations.

At the congressional hearings on the bill, officials from the departments that would be affected by the legislation voiced their opposition. They were concerned that the office of inspector general would be politicized as a result of the inspector general being a presidential appointee. They also felt that there might be tension between the agency head and the inspector general since the latter would make reports directly to Congress. In addition, agency officials noted that the reporting requirements would be burdensome. However, the secretary and inspector general from the Department of Health, Education, and Welfare testified that they had not experienced significant problems related to these concerns.

The United States attorney general also raised concerns that several provisions of the bill might violate the doctrine of separation of powers between the executive and legislative branches. For example, he questioned the provisions that directed the inspector general to report directly to Congress and that imposed limitations on the president's power to appoint and remove the inspectors general.

In spite of these concerns, the bill had widespread support. After several revisions by the conference committee, the act passed the House and Senate and was signed by President Carter on October 12, 1978. The Inspector General Act of 1978 was enacted establishing offices of inspectors general in 12 federal agencies.

Functions of the Inspector General

The stated goal of the Inspector General Act is to increase the economy and efficiency in the federal executive branch. The main mechanism for doing this was by consolidating the audit and investigation units in each of the affected federal establishments into an office of inspector general. This office is responsible for providing leadership in this area and keeping Congress and the agency head informed. The inspectors general have been referred to as the "watchdogs" of the federal government.

The audits conducted by the inspector general's office address issues such as internal controls, accountability, efficiency, and effectiveness. The audits can be initiated by the inspector general's offices directly or by a request from agency officials or members of Congress. The auditors usually produce a written report summarizing their major findings and conclusions, along with recommendations for improvement. The reports are then provided to the officials responsible for overseeing the program that was audited.

Investigations undertaken by the office of inspector general usually involve an allegation of wrongdoing associated with agency officials, operations, or programs that may be criminal in nature. The investigators conduct a study and present their information to government prosecutors who decide whether to pursue criminal or civil legal action.

The office of inspector general is responsible for providing leadership and coordination and recommending policies to promote economy, efficiency, and effectiveness, and to prevent and detect fraud and abuse. In this capacity, the office of inspector general reviews and makes recommendations on existing and proposed legislation and regulations. The office of inspector general also coordinates the relationships among its agency and other federal entities, state and local governments, and nongovernmental organizations on related matters.

The inspector general has the authority to receive and investigate complaints from agency employees concerning problems with operations or programs. The inspector general is to refrain from disclosing the identity of the employee without the consent of the employee. The act also protects the employee against possible reprisals. Most of the offices of the inspector general operate a hot line in which agency employees, businesses, or private citizens can call to report fraud, waste, or abuse. These calls can result in follow-up audits or investigations.

Independence of the Inspectors General

Congress created the offices of inspector general with the intent that they would be independent and free from undue influence or constraints from within or outside the department or agency. Legislative provisions to try to ensure this independence include presidential appointment of the inspectors general, the ability of the inspectors general to select and employ their own staff, and the authority for the inspectors general to obtain materials that are necessary for their audits and investigations.

The offices of inspectors general created by the 1978 Act are each directed by an inspector general who is appointed by the president with the advice and consent of the Senate. The inspectors general are to be selected solely on the basis of integrity and competency in accounting, auditing, financial analysis, law, management analysis, public administration, or investigations without regard to political affiliation. The inspector generals can only be removed from office by the president, who must inform Congress regarding the reason for dismissal. (Many of the inspectors general in the smaller federal agencies that were established by the 1988 amendments to the act are appointed by the head of the respective agency rather than the president.)

Each inspector general reports directly to the head of the organization or the next in rank and is authorized to have direct and prompt access to the agency head in matters related to the inspector general's function. However, the act prohibits the agency head or next in rank from preventing or interfering with the inspector general's audits, investigations, or issuance of a subpoena.

The inspector general has the authority to select and employ staff that are necessary for carrying out the responsibilities of the office. The statute specifically states that the inspector general shall employ an assistant inspector general for auditing and an assistant inspector general for investigations. The inspector general also has the authority to enter into contracts for services related to the office's functions.

The statute authorizes the inspector general to have access to all information, documents, reports, and other materials necessary to carry out an audit or investigation. This includes the authority to subpoena materials that are necessary for the performance of the functions assigned to the inspector general. The inspector general also has the authority to request information or assistance from any federal, state, or local governmental agency.

Reporting Requirements

Another major goal of the Inspector General Act was to establish a means to keep the head of the agency and Congress informed about matters related to fraud, waste, and abuse. As a result, the act includes detailed reporting requirements.

The inspector general is required to prepare and submit semiannual reports to Congress. These reports are to summarize the activities of the office of the inspector general for the prior six-month period. The reports are submitted to the head of the department by April 30 and October 31 of each year. The head of the agency must then submit the report without any changes, along with a report containing any comments the agency head wants to make in response to the report, to the appropriate congressional committees or subcommittees within 30 days. The semiannual report is to be made available to the public within 60 days of when Congress receives the report.

The semiannual reports must include a listing of each audit report issued during the reporting period, a description of significant problems disclosed by the audits and investigations during the reporting period, recommendations for corrective action made by the office of the inspector general, an overview of cases referred to prosecutive authorities, and any resulting prosecutions and convictions. The report also must identify signification recommendations from previous reports in which corrective action has not been completed and any instance in which information or assistance related to the inspector general's undertakings was unreasonably refused or not provided.

The inspector general also is required to report immediately to the agency head any serious or flagrant problems related to program abuse or deficiencies. Within seven days, the agency head is required to submit the report, along with a report by the agency head if desired, to the appropriate committees or subcommittees of Congress.

Coordination with Other Federal Agencies

The Inspector General Act requires the inspectors general to coordinate, cooperate, and avoid duplication with the comptroller general, the head of the General Accounting Office. The inspectors general must comply with audit standards established by he comptroller general for audits of federal programs and ensure that any work performed for the inspector general by non–inspector general auditors also comply with the standards.

When the office of inspector general has reasonable grounds to believe that federal criminal laws have been violated, the inspector general is required to make a report to the attorney general. The inspectors general are allowed to approach the Department of Justice directly without going through the agency's own general counsel's office.

To facilitate coordination and information sharing among the inspectors general in different agencies, the President's Council on Integrity and Efficiency (PCIE) was established by President Reagan in 1981 through presidential executive order. All of the statutory inspectors general created in the original act, as well as in subsequent legislation, who are appointed by the president are members of the council. The Executive Council on Integrity and Efficiency (ECIE), which was created by a later presidential executive order, consists of the remaining inspectors general who are not appointed by the president. Non–inspector general members of each of the councils include representatives from the Office of Management and Budget, the Federal Bureau of Investigation, the Office of Government Ethics, and the Office of Special Counsel. The deputy director for management of the Office Management and Budget is the chair of both councils. The vice chair of each of the councils has a position on the other entity's council.

The members of the PCIE and the ECIE work on an interagency basis to promote economy and efficiency. They undertake joint projects and work on audit and investigation issues that cut across more than one agency.

State and Local Government Offices of Inspectors General

One of the first statewide offices of the inspector general in the country was established in Massachusetts in 1981. Like its federal counterparts, the goal of this office is to prevent and detect fraud, waste, and abuse in government. The office employs a staff consisting of investigators, lawyers, management analysts, and an engineer. The office has the authority to subpoena records and people and to investigate criminal and noncriminal violations of laws.

Various other states also have a statewide office of inspector general or an inspector general that addresses specific functions or programs. Local governments also can have an office that functions similarly to that of an inspector general even through the office may have a different title.

BEVERLY S. BUNCH

BIBLIOGRAPHY

Fountain, L. H., 1979. "What Congress Expects from the New Inspectors General." *Government Accountants Journal,* vol. 28 (Spring) 8–12.

Inspector General Act of 1978, 1978. Public Law 95-452, 95th Congress, October 12.

Light, Paul C., 1993. *Monitoring Government: Inspectors General and the Search for Accountability.* Washington, DC: Brookings Institution and Governance Institute.

Moore, Mark H., and Margaret Jane Gates, 1986. *Inspectors-General: Junkyard Dogs or Man's Best Friend?* New York: Russell Sage Foundation.

INSTITUTE OF PUBLIC ADMINISTRATION (IPA) OF SAUDI ARABIA.

An autonomous corporate body, established by Royal Decree on April 9, 1961, to promote and improve the efficiency and effectiveness of government agencies and to provide qualified human resources to contribute to the performance of government.

In the late 1950s, the government of the Kingdom of Saudi Arabia realized that while its agencies were lacking efficiency and effectiveness, there was a major deficiency in qualified, skillful, and trained nationals that could run the government. To overcome the problem, the government sought external help from the International Bank for Reconstruction and Development, the Technical Assistance Committee of the United Nations, and the Ford Foundation. The foreign experts conducted several studies that resulted in major recommendations, one of which was establishing the Institute of Public Administration. On April 9, 1961, the IPA was established by Royal Decree No. 93 as an autonomous corporate body with the aim of promoting and improving the efficiency and effectiveness of government agencies, and preparing and providing qualified and skillful human resources that could contribute to the performance of government.

To accomplish its general goal, the IPA has been working on four dimensions: training, research, consultations, and documentation. These four dimensions are served through the following activities:

- preparing and performing instructional and training programs to the various echelons of employees; conducting and supervising academic administrative research at the institute, in collaboration with the key officials concerned in the ministries, government organizations and branches thereof, whenever the research is of the field type in any one of them;
- collecting, tabulating, and classifying the administrative documents of the Kingdom of Saudi Arabia;
- holding conferences on administrative development addressed to the top management levels of government personnel;
- hosting Arab, regional, and international conferences on matters related to public administration in the kingdom and participating in similar conferences held abroad;
- publishing research and administrative information and exchanging such publications with relevant organizations in the kingdom, the Arab world, and other countries;
- encouraging academic research in administrative affairs and allocating study grants and royalties to achieve this purpose;
- offering the IPA's staff academic and training scholarships in various administrative sciences in order to enhance their administrative efficiency;
- offering training grants to some of the personnel of brotherly Arab countries.

Undertaking these activities have resulted in the preparation of over 1,000 consultations to different government agencies in the kingdom and some Arab countries through the department of consultation. The IPA also submitted, through the general secretariat of the Higher and the Preparatory Administrative Committee for Administrative Reform, over 350 studies on government agencies to the Preparatory Administrative Committee for Administrative Reform. In the area of research, the IPA has published over 250 books in addition to its quarterly journal in public administration. Finally, in the area of training, over 11,500 students have graduated from the preservice training programs, and over 100,000 public employees have attended the over 120 different in-service training programs the IPA offers. In addition to the pre and in-service training programs, the IPA provides workshops to top public officials and special training programs designed based on a specific need of government agencies. From these various training programs and workshops, over 130 government agencies have benefited over the years since the IPA was established.

All these activities have been performed by the IPA staff, which consists of 513 faculty members, 230 administrators, 106 technicians, and 223 workers. They work at the headquarters in Riyadh and in two other branches located in Dammam (Eastern Province) and Jeddah (Western Province), as well as a women's branch in Riyadh.

MOHAMMED ABDULRAHMAN AL-TAWAIL

INTELLIGENCE AGENCY.

A formally organized collection of individuals charged with and paid for collecting information, including secret information, to assist the agency's superiors in making decisions. There are several different types of agency, each with its specialist functions. Private detective agencies undertake a variety of operations such as labor espionage, industrial espionage, and divorce work. Military intelligence agencies keep a watch on potential foreign enemies in order to secure their nation against attack. Other agencies specialize in criminal detection, international drugs intelligence, counterespionage, and antiterrorist data. Finally, there are omnibus intelligence agencies that are required to perform a wide range of tasks ranging from collection and analysis to covert propaganda and assassination. Such organizations are sometimes referred to as "full-service intelligence agencies" to distinguish them from those engaged in "pure" (collection/analysis) intelligence.

Professionalization is a hallmark of the intelligence agency. Intelligence agents are vetted, trained, and paid. They are expected to comply with a code of conduct—designed to satisfy not so much ethical standards as the requirements of their employers. In particular, intelligence agencies seek to demonstrate that in spite of being secretly funded, they are in firm control of properly organized budgets. They stress their professional attributes and deride and exclude would-be competitors on the ground that they do not meet their own proclaimed standards.

Espionage is often referred to as the "second oldest profession" and is certainly of some antiquity. Its early practitioners included the ancient Egyptians and Moses. In the Middle Ages, the Venetians used their ambassadors as spies. In modern times, Grotius accepted espionage while Kant and Tolstoy condemned it. In Russia in 1565, Ivan the Terrible set up the Oprichnina as his political police. In foreign intelligence, England showed early signs of preeminence. Sir Francis Walsingham organized a spy network on behalf of Elizabeth I—he claimed successes in codebreaking and in contributing to the defeat of the Spanish Armada (1588). Napoleon's spy network answered to the notorious Fouché, and by the middle of the nineteenth century, every major European power had a foreign espionage capability in peacetime as well as in war, typically organized through a system of military and naval attachés located in foreign embassies.

Nineteenth-century intelligence arrangements were increasingly bureaucratic in character, and the intelligence agency took on its contemporary form. In 1865, at the last cabinet meeting before his assassination, Abraham Lincoln established the United States Secret Service. Great Britain created the Intelligence Branch of the War Office in 1873 with its permanent secretariat. Scotland Yard (the London police force) in 1878 set up its Criminal Investigation Department. In 1880, Nicholas II established the Okhrana, the tsarist ancestor of the Soviet Union's Cheka (1917) and Komitet Gosudarstvennoy Bezopasnosti (KGB, 1954). Other nations followed suit.

In the twentieth century, the intelligence agency grew to become a notable feature of what is sometimes referred to as the "national security state." There have been several reasons for this growth: sophisticated new weapon systems and encoding procedures made bigger demands on spies and intelligence analysts; the invention of the typewriter, carbon paper, modern filing systems, satellite reconnaissance, high-definition photography, telemetry, and the computer made possible larger-scale operations. Competition between increasingly centralized, bureaucratic, and rich societies encouraged the process. In dictatorships like Hitler's Germany, Soviet Russia, and Communist China, the leader's fear of their own people led to the construction of major internal surveillance systems, with millions of informers serving the national intelligence agencies. In democracies whose leaders feared the moral opprobrium of the masses, intelligence agencies were entrusted with the covert enactment of operations that would otherwise have proved too controversial. In theory, at least, the ostensibly expensive intelligence agency was supposed to save money by helping the leaders entrusted with a nation's security to spend money wisely and economically.

Those who have sought to establish a theoretical framework for the understanding of intelligence have addressed two distinct themes: organization (dealt with here) and practice (see **intelligence policy**). One distinction that has to be made in the organizational sphere is that between the holistic model and the split model. According to the holistic arrangement, an intelligence agency knows no international boundaries. Nazi Germany's Gestapo and the Soviet Union's KGB operated externally as well as internally. The unfettered nature of their domestic atrocities has been attributed to an excess of power. According to this theory, citizens' liberties are better safeguarded by a system that divides internal and external responsibilities. Great Britain assigns domestic security matters to its MI5 and foreign intelligence to MI6. Similarly, in the United States, the Federal Bureau of Investigation (FBI) takes care of domestic matters, whereas the Central Intelligence Agency (CIA) looks after foreign affairs. However, according to the American philosopher and intelligence theorist Wilmoore Kendall (*World Politics,* vol. I, 1948–1949), the split arrangement gave rise to the problem of the "three-mile limit": analysts forbidden from looking at both sides of the international territorial limit could not produce "joint estimates," in other words answer the question, what are the potential capabilities of an enemy when measured against our own?

Other problems in organizational intelligence theory are just as vexatious. Because Western societies are open, the agents of foreign powers can move relatively freely within them, and counterintelligence becomes a major problem—as the cases of Kim Philby and Richard Ames so notoriously demonstrated in 1950s England and 1990s America, respectively. Vertical compartmentalization is a theoretical solution to the problem. Secret information is funnelled to the top of an agency and may not be imparted horizontally: You may communicate your findings to the head of your branch, but not to the man in the room next to you in the same agency building. Thus, if one part of the organization is compromised, the others still retain their integrity. The great fault in this arrangement is, though, that lower-level coordination becomes cumbersome and sometimes impossible. On the ground level, members of the same organization have been known to stalk each other. A related theoretical problem is that of centralization. It is argued that some of history's intelligence disasters—the Pearl Harbor surprise attack is the classic case—have stemmed not from a lack of raw intelligence data but from the lack of a central mechanism to coordinate the data and analyze them, to sort out the real "signals" from the background "noise."

Intelligence agencies abound in the present-day United States. Thousands of private detective agencies undertake intelligence work, amongst them such industrial giants as the Pinkerton and Burns agencies. The police force in every major city has its detectives. On the federal level, most major government departments have an intelligence capability and, in addition to the CIA and FBI, there are several agencies exclusively concerned with intelligence. The National Security Agency deals with message interception and codebreaking; the Defense Intelligence Agency coordinates military intelligence; the Drug Enforcement Agency fights an intelligence war against international suppliers; the Bureau of Intelligence and Research (known as the INR) serves the intelligence needs of the Department of State. In theory, the head of the CIA is the coordinating overlord of the entire federal intelligence effort; in practice, the directors of the individual intelligence agencies jealously guard their fiefdoms and sometimes withhold cooperation. Nevertheless, in terms of size, budget, and expertise, the United States has developed a massive intelligence superiority over other nations.

Intelligence arrangements in countries other than the United States have been influenced by the Cold War. The CIA has trained intelligence officers in countries supportive of American foreign policy goals, and in these countries methods of organization have tended to reflect those in the mentor nation: for example, in the cases of the Korean CIA and the Australian Secret Intelligence Organization. Such agencies are sometimes accused of subordinating their goals, as well as their methods of organization, to the United States Imperial. Even more heavily influenced by a foreign power, in fact to the point of being directed by it, have been the intelligence agencies in communist countries under the influence of the Soviet Union. For example, the KGB dominated Bulgaria's Darjavna Sugurnost and used it as a Soviet surrogate.

The ending of the Cold War has changed the picture. The Russian Intelligence Service has inherited some of the goals and methods of the KGB but is no longer so vigorously involved in crimes against its own citizens and in imperialism abroad. Communist China's Central External Liaison Department is efficient but is not treated as a serious threat to the West. Even in the Cold War, some intelligence agencies—for example, Britain's MI6, Israel's MOSSAD, the Canadian Security Intelligence Service, and smaller-scale organizations in nonaligned countries—had striven to maintain their independence from the American and Soviet superpowers. The demise of superpower rivalry removed the compulsion to take sides. But it raised fears of unchallenged United States intelligence dominance. In 1991, the United Nations General Assembly unanimously adopted a Fact-Finding Declaration mandating the secretary-general to "monitor the state of international peace and security regularly and systematically in order to provide early warning of disputes or situations which might threaten international peace and security." This reflected an international desire that the world's decisionmakers should be informed impartially about impending and current crises.

RHODRI JEFFREYS-JONES

BIBLIOGRAPHY

Andrew, Christopher, 1985. *Secret Service: The Making of the British Intelligence Community*. London: Heinemann.
Andrew, Christopher, and Oleg Gordievsky, 1990. *KGB: The Inside Story of Its Foreign Operations from Lenin to Gorbachev*. London: Hodder & Stoughton.
Dvornick, Francis, 1974. *Origins of Intelligence Services*. New Brunswick, N.J: Rutgers University Press.
Fergusson, Thomas G., 1984. *British Military Intelligence, 1870–1914: The Development of a Modern Intelligence Organization*. London: Arms and Armour Press.
Jeffreys-Jones, Rhodri, 1977. *American Espionage: From Secret Service to CIA*. New York: Free Press.
Kirkpatrick, Lyman B., 1975. *The U.S. Intelligence Community: Foreign Policy and Domestic Activities*. New York: Hill & Wang.
Laqueur, Walter, 1988. *A World of Secrets: The Uses and Limits of Intelligence*. New York: Basic Books.
Rowan, Richard Wilmer, 1938. *The Story of Secret Service*. London: John Miles.
Whitnah, Donald R., ed., 1983. *Government Agencies*. Westport, CT: Greenwood Press. Essays on the CIA, FBI, and U.S. Secret Service.

INTELLIGENCE POLICY. The direction of activities designed to obtain information, by secret as well as overt means, that will help the intelligence tasker to make wise decisions; the philosophy behind the shaping of an intelligence community's bureaucratic structure; and a government's formal response to problems arising from intelligence activities, including the problems of civil liberties, open government, and legislative oversight.

The origins of intelligence policy stretch back to the beginnings of the human species. When hunters learned the value of scouting and adopted the practice as a matter of policy, they appreciated the equation between information and power, beginning with the power to survive. Successful monarchs exploited the same equation and had a policy of seeking information, often by clandestine means, on their internal and external foes, and about their intended victims. The generals in charge of their armies sought strategic intelligence that would help them win wars and tactical intelligence that would assist them in particular battles.

Exploration is an aspect of intelligence policy that also has a long history. China, for example under the emperor Wu Ti (140–86 B.C.E.), undertook exploration in pursuit of empire and trade; the China sought out the peoples of the Asian interior long before Marco Polo left Venice in 1271 to "discover" Asia and China, and even longer before the Genoan Christopher Columbus set foot in the New World (1492) believing it to be the "Indies." Nevertheless, particular peoples' ignorance of other parts of the globe persisted and with it the urge to explore. In 1803, for example, President Thomas Jefferson dispatched the Lewis and Clark expedition to the area that is now the northwestern United States, accumulating data that helped to make the USA a continental nation. Ameringer (1990) is a historian who treats this expedition and the establishment of the Army Corps of Topographical Engineers in 1838 as a part of United States intelligence history.

Exploration might not at first sight seem to be an aspect of intelligence policy in that it is often openly conducted and proclaimed. But the word "intelligence" denoted publicly available information in the eighteenth century, and it is still an axiom of good intelligence policy that open as well as secret sources should be used. Furthermore, the sponsors of exploration, for example, the monarchs who financed Spain's search for gold in the sixteenth century and the United States government, which launched the "Discoverer" satellites to spy on the Soviet Union, have not always rushed to share their findings with the world at large. The appropriation of exploration as an aspect of intelligence policy is in part an attempt to confer respectability on a despised profession, yet it is also fairly logical.

In spite of the tendency of Americans to perceive themselves as pragmatic and even anti-intellectual, theories on intelligence have abounded in the United States—more so than in other nations, where espionage and intelligence policy only slowly emerged from the closet and could not therefore attract open debate and scholarly discussion. At first, most American theories stemmed from the ease with which Japan surprised United States forces at Pearl Harbor in 1941. With Pearl Harbor in mind, there was a determined effort to theorize about the nature of surprise attack and about countermeasures such as the analysis of naval radio traffic as distinct from content.

However, theoreticians of intelligence practice later criticized the surprise attack agenda for being too narrow and for having an undue influence on intelligence procedures. They broadened the discussion to include such matters as the necessity of maintaining functional distinctions between intelligence consumers, intelligence producers, and the government policymakers who are the intelligence taskers; the divorce of intelligence analysts and operators in the interest of objectivity; the need for "circuit-breaking" committees to take the heat instead of the policymakers should "plausibly denied" operations come unstuck; and the avoidance of mirror-imaging—the phenomenon of an analyst assuming that an enemy's action will be the mirror image of what one's own would be in similar circumstances. This later problem has encouraged the policy of developing technical and therefore supposedly more objective means of espionage and intelligence analysis and has contributed to the relative subordination of HUMINT (human intelligence). But in the 1970s, the new TECHINT (technical intelligence) emphasis ran into opposition on the ground that the people who ran the computers were subjective, fallible, and relatively ignorant of international affairs.

Another body of intelligence theory is about counterinsurgency. Thinking on this subject is not so heavily dominated by the Americans, for imperial European powers have had long experience of putting down various forms of colonial resistance. The United States adapted some European practices and theories in suppressing or attempting to suppress left-wing insurrections in several nations during the cold war era. On the theoretical level, emphasis was placed on indigeneity and on native spontaneity, and on winning the "hearts and minds" of the people in the nation affected by strife.

In the United States especially, there has been some theoretical speculation about legislative oversight of the intelligence community. Harry H. Ransom (1984) perceives an inverse relationship between the intensity of the Cold War and congressional attempts to institute oversight—the most determined attempts at oversight occurred in the mid-1970s, in a period of détente. Frank J. Smist (1990) argues that in the case of the relationship between Congress and the intelligence community, the theoretical distinction between temporary investigative committees and permanent select committees is an important one—in the long term, permanent committees tend to become part of the institutionalized consensual framework.

Executive, civilian control over intelligence matters is current policy in the United States. It is the president's duty to "task" the intelligence community and to tell it whom to "target." Since the National Security Act of 1947 (which also set up the CIA), a National Security Council (NSC) has assisted him in the performance of this duty, and his adviser on national security affairs, the senior official of the NSC, has been especially influential. The president directs the large intelligence community, as well as agencies like the National Aeronautics and Space Administration whose activities need to be coordinated with it. A director of central intelligence, who is always the head of the CIA, is expected to coordinate the overall intelligence effort. Within the CIA are housed the facilities and secretariat for coordination, facilities for independent intelligence-gathering, and a covert action division.

As a general rule, it has always been United States intelligence policy to target a main enemy. After the surrender of Germany and Japan in World War II, this main enemy was the Soviet Union. However, the intelligence community was tasked to perform other duties, too. For example, it had to inform the executive of disputes between America's allies, such as those between Israel and some of its neighbors and between Britain and Argentina, and was expected to help in the international war against drugs.

With the collapse of the Soviet empire and communism within Russia, the main enemy disappeared and intelligence policy came under review. Some called for a cut-and-save policy. Others took advantage of reduced international tension to call for wholesale reform—the abolition of the CIA, or at least the separation of analytical intelligence and covert action programs into separate agencies. The CIA fought back, arguing that Russia was still a problem if in different ways. The Federal Bureau of Investigation and other agencies joined the effort to contain the export of Russian gangsterism and to regulate the export from former components of the Soviet Union of fissionable materials and dangerous weapons.

The intelligence community looked for new enemies elsewhere, too. These included Muslim fundamentalists, especially those who tried to control the world's supply of oil. Terrorists of various types and international drug barons fell under surveillance. So did foreign governments and businesses in commercial competition with the United States: Industrial espionage had always been a widespread activity in the private sphere; at the end of the Cold War, the White House made it a major government priority.

Current policy on intelligence oversight stems from the controversies of the 1970s, when Congress investigated the intelligence community after revelations of serious abuses. In the course of congressional investigations, it became clear that the CIA was not, as some critics had charged, a "rogue elephant" that abused the privilege of secrecy to rampage "out of control." On the contrary, executive control of intelligence policy had rarely wavered. This meant that the executive had abused its powers, indeed had used the CIA to bypass Congress's constitutionally vested powers. Congress therefore established two select committees, one in the House and the other in the Senate, to oversee the activities of the intelligence agencies as directed by the White House. The House Committee had, under the provisions of the United States Constitution, the power of the purse string; the Senate Committee had the powers of advice and consent; neither committee, however, directed intelligence policy, even if both had some control over its shape. The intelligence agencies remained under executive control, but they and, through them, the president had to submit to congressional scrutiny.

Since the 1970s, the oversight mechanisms have remained essentially unchanged, but a lively debate continues over several aspects of intelligence policy, ranging, from open government at home to the particular merits of overseas operations such as the Iran-Contra affair, a clandestine attempt to sell weapons illegally to Iran's fundamentalist government and to divert the profits from the Middle East to Central America with the object of overthrowing, without congressional approval, the left-wing government of Nicaragua. In response to the furor over Iran-Contra, the Reagan and Bush administrations began to bypass the CIA and to use the NSC to direct intelligence as a means of avoiding what they judged was overintrusive congressional oversight.

Intelligence policy in countries around the world is executive driven, as it is in the United States. Apart from exceptional cases like Nigeria's State Security Service, which answers to a military dictatorship, the instruments of intelligence policy are civilian dominated. The British Joint Intelligence Committee consists of the intelligence chiefs of the three services or their deputies. It was chaired by a Foreign Office official until 1983 and thereafter by a civilian appointed by the prime minister. In the Soviet Union the GRU (Glavnoye Razvedyvatelnoye Upravlenic/Soviet military intelligence agency) was an influential agency but firmly subordinate to the civilian authorities, and there has been no change of emphasis in present-day Russia. As in the case of the CIA, covert action and analysis in nations other than the United States tend to be combined within the same organizations. The Australian Secret Intelligence Organization is one case in point. Wartime Britain had a separate covert action agency, the Special Operations Executive, but in 1946 its operations were taken over by the Secret Intelligence Service (SIS or MI6). In the Soviet Union, the KGB undertook covert operations as well as intelligence work, though intelligence analysis tended to be left to its political masters, in contrast to American practice, whereby the DCI (director of Central Intelligence) supplies the president with intelligence "estimates."

In most countries, it has been intelligence policy to identify a "main enemy." For the KGB and GRU, it was the United States. For MI6 (foreign Intelligence) and MI5 (counterintelligence) in Cold War Britain, it was the Soviet Union. For several Middle Eastern nations, it is Israel. But for Israel's MOSSAD, there are several enemies to watch, and for China's intelligence community, there are threats from Russia as well as from the United States, Japan, and Britain. This diversification of target is becoming more widespread because of the end of the Cold War. For example, as relations with Russia improved, MI5 went in search of a new enemy. It took over responsibility for countering the threat posed by the Irish Republican Army, then upon the IRA cease-fire in 1994 sought to become responsible for the war against drugs.

The United States is by no means unique in having a policy on legislative oversight of the intelligence community. The Australians, Canadians, and Scandinavians all have provisions of that kind. But this is one area in which several countries, Russia and Britain included, lag behind. In Russia, totalitarianism's lingering traces are to be discerned. In Britain, the lack of oversight is excused on the ground that the chief executive in charge of intelligence, the prime minister, is a member of parliament and already accountable to it.

RHODRI JEFFREYS-JONES

BIBLIOGRAPHY

Ameringer, Charles D., 1990. *U.S. Foreign Intelligence: The Secret Side of American History*. Lexington, MA: Lexington Books.

Andrew, Christopher, 1985. *Secret Service: The Making of the British Intelligence Community*. London: Heinemann.

Andrew, Christopher, and Oleg Gordievsky, 1990. *KGB: The Inside Story of Its Foreign Operations from Lenin to Gorbachev*. London: Hodder & Stoughton.

Blaufarb, Douglas S., 1977. *The Counterinsurgency Era: U.S. Doctrine and Performance, 1950 to the Present*. New York: Free Press.

Eftimiades, Nicholas, 1994. *Chinese Intelligence Operations*. Annapolis, MD: Naval Institute Press.

Granatstein. J. L., and David Stafford, 1990. *Spy Wars: Espionage and Canada from Gouzenko to Glasnost*. Toronto: McClelland and Stewart.

Jeffreys-Jones, Rhodri, 1989. *The CIA and American Democracy*. New Haven: Yale University Press.

Ransom, Harry H., 1984. "Secret Intelligence in the United States, 1947–1982: The CIA's Search for Legitimacy." In Christopher M. Andrew and David Dilks, eds., *The Missing Dimension: Governments and Intelligence Communities in the Twentieth Century*. London: Macmillan, 199–226.

Richelson, Jeffrey T., 1985. *The Ties That Bind: Intelligence Cooperation Between the UKUSA Countries—the United Kingdom, the United States of America, Canada, Australia, and New Zealand*. Boston: Allen & Unwin.

Smist, Frank J., 1990. *Congress Oversees the United States Intelligence Community, 1947–1989*. Knoxville: University of Tennessee Press.

INTERCULTURAL COMMUNICATION.

The exchange of information among people from groups that, for historical and cultural reasons, perceive the world differently.

Culture can be defined as a pattern of learned, group-related perceptions—including both verbal and nonverbal language, attitudes, values, belief systems, disbelief systems, and behaviors—that are accepted and expected by members of any group. There was a time when cultural anthropologists used to argue that only whole societies could be said to have their own culture; other differences within societies were called "subcultural." Indeed, it was presumed that it was only those primitive peoples living on remote islands in the Pacific or in the rain forests of Brazil and Africa that had distinct cultures. Now it is generally agreed that every group has a culture of its own. Even separate organizations in the same field (to say nothing of organizations in different fields) have been recognized as having their own ways of doing things, their own perceptions, attitudes, values, beliefs, identities, and language—in sum, their own cultures.

It is perhaps one of the most basic laws of human behavior that people act or react to stimuli from the external world, not on the basis of any objective "reality," but on the basis of their perceptions of those stimuli and of that reality. And, though there are both physical and environmental differences that assure that no two humans can perceive those stimuli with 100 percent similarity, cultural differences are even more determining of how we perceive the world. Will we salivate or regurgitate at the thought of eating the flesh of a cow, a pig, a snail, or a dog? It all depends upon the values of the groups into which we have been socialized.

All of us grow up associating with many different groups. To the degree that we accept membership, each of those groups socializes us into accepting its definitions of right or wrong, beautiful or ugly, good or bad. The group's attitudes, values, and beliefs soon become our attitudes, values, and beliefs. Yes, presumably, we are free to reject attitudes and values we do not like, but the fact is that most of us do not. Overwhelmingly, people accept, if not always on a conscious level, much of the cultural baggage that goes along with being part of their particular groups. We learn to perceive the world as we have been taught by our groups to perceive it, and it is very difficult for us to escape that.

Since all of us have grown up being part of certain groups—but not of others—virtually all communication among people is, to some degree, intercultural. The more similar the group perceptions, attitudes, and values are that we share, the less intercultural the communication is likely to be. The less similar the cultures of the individuals involved, the more intercultural—and the more difficult—the communication is likely to be.

The Dutch sociologist Geert Hofstede has described culture as the "software of the mind," and that is a very apt analogy. Culture does for our minds what software packages do for our computer hardware. We could not function without it. Just as software determines how we process data, culture determines how we use all of the sensory data that come into our brains from the world around us. Our very identities—who we believe we are—depends on the groups that have molded us most.

While we do hold many identities simultaneously, we rank order each of those identities differently in different contexts. Thus, one can be a father to one's children, a husband to one's wife, a son to one's parents, a boss to one's subordinates and a subordinate to one's boss, a liberal in one's politics, an American in one's nationality, a Presbyterian in one's religion, an Anglo-Saxon in one's ethnicity, upper-middle-class in one's social status, a college graduate in one's education level, and an opera lover in one's musical taste all at the same time. We communicate and behave differently with each set of people. But we also rank order those identities, so that they do not come into conflict, if we can help it.

How we rank those groups is, of course, an individual, subconscious decision. But if we are not at some point socialized into a particular group—and there are thousands of groups into which we are not socialized—there is no way one of those groups could become part of our identity. Needless to say, our identity may also depend on how others perceive us. We may think we are a part of a particular group, but if the majority of that group rejects us, it would be difficult to maintain that identity. For example, many German Jews thought, and behaved, as though they were Germans until 1932. When the Nazis came to power they deprived the Jews not only of their German identity but also of their very lives.

Each of our identity groups come into much sharper focus when juxtaposed against any of "them." Most of us surround ourselves with people who are more or less like us. This makes our lives easier in the sense that we do not have to make everything explicit. People in other groups to which we belong often share so many common cultural languages with us that we can speak with them in a kind of shorthand and still expect to be understood. But once we step out of that comfortable cocoon of familiarity, we are instantly struck by how different "they" are from us. We do not always have to go abroad to find that unfamiliarity. Just walk into the "wrong" neighborhood, and one instantly is aware of having stepped over an important cultural boundary. It is just more difficult to operate there. Everything has to be made explicit. We cannot take for granted that we will be understood as we wanted to be. Indeed, that is one of the things that makes day-to-day living so much more difficult for people who constitute a minority in the population. Many minority people spend most of their working day in an environment in which they are forced to be very explicit, at least with their bosses, if not with their peers. Women or African American managers in the workplace may constantly be reminded of the fact that they are different, every time they go to work.

Hofstede's data show that for many North American and Japanese men, their jobs come first, naturally. Then comes time with their families. For a Latin American or Scandinavian man, that would be, just as naturally, reversed. Interestingly, North American women tend to be more family- and relationship-oriented than men when they are younger, but in their forties and fifties frequently become more career oriented, while their husbands begin to get more relationship oriented.

Culture affects even our attitudes toward space and time. North Americans like to stand approximately two feet away from someone when they talk to them on impersonal subjects. Latins and Arabs are more comfortable talking to someone who is no more than a foot or a foot and a half way. Thus, the Latin keeps moving closer, making the North American feel that his/her personal space is being violated, while the North American backs away, making the Latin feel rejected. Similarly, with time. North Americans and many Northern and Western Europeans are extremely punctual when it comes to time, Southern Europeans, Latins, Arabs, South and Southeast Asians, and most Africans place much less emphasis on precise timekeeping. For them, to wait an hour or two for an appointment is not at all unusual or insulting. The North American and Western European would take such a wait as an extreme insult. Indeed, unless the person they were waiting to see was very important, they probably would not wait.

Other things being equal, the greater the degree of similarity of perception that exists among a number of individuals, the easier communication among them is likely to be and the more communication is likely to take place. That is why small organizations and groups tend to function so well. People within the group are constantly calibrating their mutual perceptions and reinforcing each other's values. Conversely, where there is little or no communication among people, there tends to be a decrease in similarity of perception, which in turn makes further communication that much more difficult. And so it goes, spiraling with increasing lack of communication, until all communication becomes very difficult, indeed.

All of this is extremely important to people who make policy and people who manage it, because most frequently the people for whom one is making and/or managing policy are from a different cultural group, who simply perceive things differently. In the United States in the 1960s, it was predominately men from white, middle-class cultures who decided to build high rise apartment projects to house predominantly black, lower-class women and children. By the 1980s and 1990s, many of those projects had to be torn down because they proved to be unsafe.

In international work, the situation can become even more difficult because the people with whom we work may be even more different than the people we work with in our own country. (This is not always the case, however. Sometimes the people with whom we work internationally are far more similar to us in educational and class background then are the people with whom we work domestically, and sharing class and educational cultures with people may make communication with them that much easier and more accurate.) For example, English-speaking people prefer to think about getting from point A to point B in the most direct manner possible. Our thinking is linear. In other cultures, however, the thinking may be analogy driven or even circular. Similarly, most North Americans like to start working on a project by looking at empirical data first, and then they derive the theory, inductively. Many Europeans, by contrast (particularly the French and Italians), prefer to start with the theory or concept and then look for the data, deductively.

In an international environment, work can also be difficult because there are different cultural expectations about how a manager should manage. In some countries, the boss is expected to have all of the information and make all of the decisions. Workers look for the superior to be decisive and authoritarian in (usually his) decisionmaking. In other countries, the boss is expected to motivate and empower the workers to make decisions on their own. Needless to say, one who is familiar with working in an environment where one gets to make many decisions would find it very difficult to work in an environment where the boss had to countersign every letter sent out. Yet, that is precisely the case in many organizations in a country like Germany.

On another dimension of cultural differences, in some countries one is taught to make individual decisions and to get individual rewards and punishments for those decisions. That is true in most of the English-speaking countries. In much of Latin America and many Asian countries, exactly the opposite is expected. People are taught to work in teams—not infrequently in family teams—and to make team decisions. One does not want to stand out. Even physical space in an office may be divided to reflect this. A manager in North America is more likely to have an office with a view; and the higher the position, the larger the private office is likely to be. In Japan, the higher the position, the more likely the manager will work in the center of a vast office surrounded by many people.

What does all of this mean for effective intercultural communication? It means that if it is important for us to work with them—whoever they are—then we must try to learn as much about their culture (i.e., perceptions, attitudes, values, and beliefs) as we can—and as quickly as we can. We need not only speak their spoken language but also their cultural language. That takes time and effort, it is true, but without that the likelihood of intercultural conflict and failure to communicate is enormous. And learning about them does not mean simply learning about them when we go abroad. It means learning about them—whoever they may be—even in our own countries.

MARSHALL R SINGER

BIBLIOGRAPHY

Hofstede, Geert, 1991. *Cultures and Organizations: Software of the Mind.* London: McGraw-Hill.

Kaplan, Robert B., 1966. "Cultural Thought Patterns in Intercultural Education." *Language Learning,* vol. 16, nos. 1 and 2.

Rhinesmith, Stephen H., 1996. *A Manager's Guide to Globalization: Six Keys to Success in a Changing World.* Second Editon Alexandria, VA: American Society for Training and Development; and Homewood, IL: Business One Irwin.

Samovar, Larry, A., and Richard E. Porter, eds., 1994. *Intercultural Communication: A Reader,* 7th ed. Belmont, CA: Wadsworth.

Singer, Marshall R, 1987. *Intercultural Communication: A Perceptual Approach.* Englewood Cliffs, NJ: Prentice-Hall. (Rev. abr. ed., 1997. Yarmouth, ME: Intercultural Press.)

INTEREST GROUPS.

Associations of individuals who share common objectives and seek, through coordinated effort, to make direct contacts with public officials in order to influence administrative and legislative decisions of government. Interest groups are organized and composed of individuals affected directly by the operations of government agencies or private companies and have tangible stakes in their programmatic output and impact.

Background

Individuals band together in organized groups because they believe they can promote their interests more effectively as opposed to working individually. Moreover, interest groups continuously monitor the activities of government and big business so that they can institute change or maintain the status quo when their interests are at stake.

Unlike the general public, interest groups have easy access and contacts with administrators and legislators. Because of their expertise, desire, money, and commitment, interest groups have the ability to keep abreast with the activities of both public and private organizations. Interest groups continually monitor legislative and administrative activities of government to ensure that "no decision affecting their clientele goes unchallenged" (Levine, Peters, and Thompson 1990, p. 201). Interest groups have the ability to influence how executives direct, manage, and control government operations, as well as influence the process of policy development and implementation. Walter F. Scheffer (1981) in his essay *The Clienteles of Executive Branch Agencies* noted the impact of interest groups on public agencies as follows: "Interest groups have carved out their niche in the bureaucracy; and since their support is crucial to many agency programs, their priorities come first" (p. 129).

In the international scene, the existence and influence of interest groups is more pervasive in the United States than in any country. A comparative study by Gabriel Almond and Sidney Verba (1963, p. 246) of political culture in the United States, Britain, West Germany, Italy, and Mexico revealed that the formation of voluntary associations seemed to be more prevalent in the United States than in the other four countries. Almond and Verba's study further indicated that American citizens seemed more inclined to use "formal" and "informal groups" to influence public policy than citizens in the other four countries. Moreover, the French philosopher and aristocrat Alexis de Tocqueville ([1835] 1964) in his book *Democracy in America* also observed that the use of associations is more successful in American than elsewhere. According to Tocqueville

> Americans of all ages, all conditions, and all dispositions, constantly form associations. They have not only commercial and manufacturing companies, in which all take part, but associations of a thousand other kinds, religious, moral, serious, futile, general or restricted, enormous or diminutive. The Americans make associations to give entertainment, to found seminaries, to build inns, to construct churches, to diffuse books, to send missionaries to the antipodes, and in this manner they found hospitals, prisons, and schools (p. 31).

The exact number of interest groups in individual countries worldwide is difficult to know. In the United States, the estimated number is around 20,000 at the national level. No reliable estimates exist at the state and local levels. The number of individuals representing the various voluntary associations or interest groups operating in Washington, D.C., stood at 50,000 in 1980 with one or two associations added to that number weekly thereafter (Hrebrenar and Ruth 1990). Most of the associations based in Washington, D.C., are represented by several agents with each specializing in a particular policy area of interest to the groups.

Distinction Between Interest Groups, Political Parties, and Social Movements

Interest groups differ from political parties and social movements in a number of ways even though at the outset they appear to share similar social and political goals. Interest groups seek to influence government decisions, whereas the primary goal of political parties is to capture and gain control of the major institutions of government. Interest groups and political parties develop a working relationship based on reciprocity, where each has some political commodity from which the other can benefit. The greatest strength of interest groups is their voting power and their ability to raise money to support elections; political parties thus need their support in order to gain control of the machinery of government. In return, interest groups expect political parties to support their agenda and deliver the programs that they desire.

Interest groups also differ from social movements. Social movements usually arise as a result of dissatisfaction of a group or groups in society triggered by unequal treatment or social and political repression. In the United States, several social movements emerged during the tumultuous decade of the 1960s. The most notable examples include the civil rights movement, the feminist, or women's, liberation movement, abortion rights, and the consumer movement. These movements surfaced as a result of dissatisfaction of their members with the manner in which they are treated in society. Social movements usually decline and disappear when they fail to attain their preselected objectives or, alternatively, evolve into several interest groups that will continue to safeguard and expand their hard-won rights.

Classification of Interest Groups

Interest groups can be classified into four broad categories, namely, economic groups, public interest groups, solidarity groups, and special interest groups. Economic interest groups are formed and organized around the occupation of their members and strive to advance both their economic and financial interests. Groups falling under this category include professional associations, farmers associations, business associations, and labor unions. In the United States, groups that operate in the professional sector are prominent in the fields of medicine, education, and law. The American Medical Association (AMA), the American Federation of Teachers, and the American Association of University Professors (AAUP) are examples of groups that serve and represent professional interests. The members of these groups are generally highly educated and earn on average high salaries. The most prominent business associations are the National Association of Manufacturers (NAM), the Business Roundtable, Chamber of Commerce of the United States, the National Federation of Independent Businesses, and the Business Council. Business associations perform a number of functions that foster the interests of their members, such as information gathering, assessment of political climate, lobbying on their members' behalf, and coordinating the strategies of companies that have similar concerns. Similarly, the American Bar Association (ABA) strives to advance the interests of their members in the legal profession and society.

Labor interests are represented by various groups with the majority of them federated under the American Federation of Labor and Congress of Industrial Organizations (AFL-CLO). Powerful labor groups in the United States include the United Auto Workers of America (UAWA) and the American Mine Workers of America. Representatives

of labor groups generally seek to preserve and advance the interests of their members through collective bargaining procedures, especially regarding concerns about wages, hours, fringe benefits, union security, and other conditions of employment. While the number, extent of influence, and power of labor groups has declined in the United States during the last three decades, in Europe they still represent a formidable force. European governments and unions generally operate on a mutually supportive basis or under "social contracts" where instituting changes or reforms is very difficult.

The interests of farmers in the United States are represented by two major groups: the American Farm Bureau Federation and the National Farmers Union (NFU). The majority of agricultural interests seek and lobby for financial aid from the federal government, price supports, marketing, credit, insurance, and international trade among others.

Public interest groups, also known as "cause groups," are formed and organized around specific causes and issues of concern to the public; members of public interest groups are generally unified by an image of what is "wrong with society or what society should be" (Sinclair 1976, p. 2). Public interest groups claim to speak for the public and seek to promote the noneconomic interests of society or pursue remedies to problems that have potential benefits to all groups in society. Unlike "other" interest groups that attempt to convert government to support their causes, public interest groups seek to convert the public to challenge government policies that are detrimental to society and the self-centered interests of private groups. Their typical areas of concern and activity include environmental protection, consumer protection, equal opportunity, and political reform. In the United States, examples of groups that claim to speak for the public are Public Citizen Inc., Common Cause, and the American Civil Liberties Union (ACLU).

Public Citizen Inc., headed by the reknowned consumer advocate Ralph Nader, centers its activities on policy matters that affect the common consumer. Public Citizen Inc. seek to protect consumer interests from unfair business practices by lobbying for legislation and regulations that safeguard consumer interests. Common Cause, by contrast, seeks reforms in the political process and changes in the ways government conducts business. Public interest groups strive to foster accountability, responsiveness, and responsibility among public officials. As a public interest group, the primary goal of the ACLU is to defend individuals whose constitutional rights are violated regardless of their group affiliations and to challenge laws that infringe on individual liberties.

Rozene A. Buchholz (1992) in his book *Business Environment and Public Policy* defines solidarity interest groups as "groups that draw on feelings of common identity based on shared characteristics such as race, age, or sexual orientation" (p. 131). The major objective of solidarity groups is to promote and maintain their identity; they may also pursue economic interests such as equal pay, which still remains an important goal of women's rights groups. Maintaining and promoting the identity of their group members is the major objective of solidarity groups.

Special interest groups pursue narrowly defined objectives and are concerned and motivated by single policy issues. In recent years, special interest groups have increased their activism especially in the area of policy development and implementation. They provide the impetus for government action in specialized areas such as the environment, consumerism, and industry. Their power and influence on administrative and legislative processes is probably more effective than that of most groups. The National Rifle Association of America (NRA), which supports the constitutional rights of American citizens to own guns, claimed victory in defeating the reelection of congressmen who supported regulation of gun ownership in the past general elections. As the most highly motivated and organized pressure groups in Washington, D.C., special interest groups are perceived by the general public to have too much influence on government.

Interest Group Tactics

Interest groups use several tactics to draw public attention to their concerns or to influence public officials. Lobbying, public demonstrations, litigation, use of the media, coalition building, and terrorism are among the tactics frequently used. Lobbying is used by interest groups to persuade or pressure public officials to either defeat legislation or secure its passage. Typically, lobbyists strive to promote passage of legislation that is in the interest of their members and defeat legislation that is not in their interests. The tactic of lobbying can involve direct face-to-face contacts with public officials or indirect contacts through letter-writing campaigns, electronic mail, phone calls, and the like. In addition to increasing their impact on public policy, interest groups use the process of lobbying to secure access to public officials, to establish links with regulatory agencies, to monitor legislative and agency activities, and to influence outcome of legislation or bureaucratic decisions.

Interest groups also use the media to advance their interests in society by attempting to influence both public opinion and government officials. Placing advertisements in newspapers or magazines, buying radio and television time, sending direct campaign letters to public officials, and using electronic media are some of the techniques employed by interest groups. For instance, the use of graphic television images is a very effective media technique that interest groups often use to garner public support or gain government attention to involve them in stopping hunger, deforestation, torture, and so forth. Human rights groups

such as Amnesty International and environmental groups such as Greenpeace rely on the media to influence public opinion or effect change in government policy. Organized groups also utilize the media to expose improper bureaucratic behavior and activities.

Interest groups use litigation as a tactic to effect changes in laws that they believe affect their interests. The legal system often becomes the last resort for interest groups to challenge the constitutionality of a measure, to compel the government to enforce the law, or to stop the implementation of a policy measure detrimental to their interest. They may sue a government agency or a private party directly or bring *amicus curiae,* or "friend of the court," briefs to court, especially when constitutional issues are involved.

Terrorism is another tactic used by some interest groups. While not extensively practiced in the United States, terrorism is used by some groups around the world to pressure governments into taking certain action demanded by such groups. The objective of groups using terrorism is to disrupt the normal functioning of government or society by engaging in hostage taking, hijacking, property destruction, and bombings.

To draw public attention to a specific issue of concern, interest groups sometimes hold public demonstrations in support or opposition of particular public policy action or inaction. Demonstrations staged by these groups may begin peacefully and often turn violent, especially when the government decides to suppress demonstrators by employing organized forces such as the police and the national guard. For instance, groups seeking racial equality in the United States as well as an end to apartheid in South Africa used public demonstrations as one of their tactics and often met brutal suppression by government forces.

Interest groups build coalitions when they share certain concerns and believe that working together can enhance their ability to influence public policy. Coalitions are usually formed around issues. Environmental groups, for example, relied on coalitions to counter the government's efforts to relax regulations on businesses during Ronald Reagan's presidency in the 1980s (Buchholz 1992).

ALEX SEKWAT

BIBLIOGRAPHY

Almond, Gabriel, and Sidney Verba, 1963. *Civic Culture.* Boston: Little, Brown.

Buchholz, Rogene A., 1992. *Business Environment and Public Policy: Implications for Management and Strategy.* Englewood Cliffs, NJ: Prentice-Hall.

Levine, Charles, B. Guy Peters, and Frank J. Thompson, 1990. *Public Administration Challenges, Choices, Consequences.* Glenview, IL: Scott, Foresman.

Hrebenar, Ronald J., and Ruth K. Scott, 1990. *Interest Group Politics in America.* Englewood Cliffs, NJ: Prentice-Hall.

Murphy, Thomas P., 1973. *Pressures upon Congress: Legislation by Lobby.* Woodbury, NY: Barron's Educational Series.

Scheffer, Walter F., 1981. "The Clienteles of Executive Branch Agencies." In Thomas Vocino and Jack Rabin, eds., *Contemporary Public Administration*. New York: Harcourt Brace Jovanovich, 31.

Sinclair, John E., 1976. *Interest Groups in America*. Morristown, NJ: General Learning Press.

Tocqueville, Alexis de, [1835] 1964. *Democracy in America: Selections Number 13*. Chicago, IL: Great Books Foundation, 31.

INTERGOVERNMENTAL MANAGEMENT (IGM).

The process of solving intergovernmental problems under conditions of high uncertainty and complexity through the creation and use of governmental and nongovernmental networks.

Intergovernmental management (IGM) has neither a fixed nor a consensual definition. It is a term of recent vintage, specialized usage, limited visibility, and uncertain maturity. IGM was first employed in the early 1970s but assumed a new meaning and significance in the 1980s and 1990s. The sections that follow discuss the meaning, origins, evolution, and relative maturity of IGM. The concept is explored generally and then specifically with comments aimed at highlighting the connection(s) among IGM, intergovernmental relations (IGR), and federalism (FED).

The Meaning of IGM

In the absence of a fixed definition of IGM, there is an advantage to examining the concept from an exclusionary approach. A grasp of IGM accrues by clarifying what it is not. One important contributor to the concept's development and clarification identified several features that were placed at the margins of the domain of IGM (Agranoff, 1986). These marginal or peripheral elements were cataloged in the context of the delivery of human service programs among multiple local and urban-metropolitan governments.

The elements placed at the fringes of IGM were

1. fundamental change in social structure(s), basic power relationships, or fiscal responsibilities;
2. realignment(s) in national-state-local relationships;
3. major intergovernmental shifts in program or functional activities;
4. significant policy revisions or redirection in the scope of service level(s) of existing programs; and
5. structural change in metropolitan governance (pp. 1–2).

IGM, in other words, takes systems, structures, policies, and programs largely as givens.

IGM concentrates more on incremental adjustments in managerial activities that enhance effective service delivery. It focuses less (or not at all) on major change(s) that alter significant political, economic, and social equilib-

rium. This does not imply that politics, policies, systems, and structures are irrelevant to IGM. It means only that these factors or features lack centrality in day-to-day conduct (management) of interjurisdictional relationships. In sum, IGM is embedded in political systems and structures, but the dominant nature of IGM activities assumes that those larger systems and structures are stable and not subject to short-run change.

There is an alternate exclusionary approach to clarifying IGM. Simply put, IGM is not federalism (FED) nor is it intergovernmental relations (IGR). The differences among the three concepts have been discussed by Wright (1990a) and include (1) leading actors/participants, (2) jurisdictional involvement, (3) value scope, (4) means of conflict resolution, (5) authority relationships, and (6) political quotient. The distinguishing features of IGM on each of these characteristics will emerge below.

What might be highlighted historically and commented on conceptually as the distinctive features of IGM? The conceptual elements are discussed first and the historical patterns later. It is important initially to clarify a significant contextual-conceptual point, namely, that IGM practice(s) existed before the term/concept was invented and used. Although this essay traces IGM origins to the 1970s, a case can be made that the practices, policies, problems, and relationships currently encompassed by IGM probably existed as early as the 1940s or 1950s. In short, IGM was present before it was given a name (in the 1970s).

The common components first identified with IGM were (1) problem solving, (2) networks and networking, and (3) coping/managing under uncertainty (Mandell 1979; Agranoff and Lindsay 1983; Wright 1983, 1987; Agranoff 1986, 1989, 1990a, 1990b; Gage and Mandell 1990). Marando and Florestano (1990) subsequently clarified and added noteworthy features in moving "toward a theory of IGM" (p. 299). They grounded their assessment of IGM within (1) the blending (continuum) of politics and administration and (2) linkage to FED and IGR historically, descriptively, and analytically. They observe, for example, that "neither politics nor management can be minimized by researchers in their effort to understand governmental performance and capacity" (p. 294) but also note that "the distinguishing feature of IGM is that it *emphasizes* the management process" (p. 299).

Marando and Florestano offer a summary judgment: "IGM is a bold step toward recasting the politics/administration issue within the context of contemporary assessment of the American federal system" (p. 299). This statement frames their substantial (eight-item) comparison of IGM with IGR as well as questions aimed at clarifying how IGM helps enhance an understanding of human and organizational behavior. Their questions are worth restating: "Must all involved parties have a visible stake in the outcome for IGM to be successful? How much inequality in the authority, status, and resources among intergovernmental actors can be assumed in the IGM process? To what extent do different problem areas require variations in IGM approaches?" (p. 299)

The central features of IGM can be summarized through a series of questions and responses.

1. *Who are the leading actors or prime participants in IGM?* They are the program/policy professionals first, followed closely by administrative generalists, such as city managers and county administrators. Some generalist managers may be former program managers who received their original training in a specialized profession, such as engineering, mental health, or social work. These administrative professionals possess the technical expertise to manage the specialized personnel who populate the "street-level" bureaucracies that deliver goods and services to citizen-recipients (Lipsky 1980). Thus, the central players on the IGM "stage" are "technocrats" (Beer 1978) or "policy professionals" (Peterson, Rabe, and Wong, 1986).

2. *What jurisdictional entities are the featured participants in IGM?* All governmental entities–national, state, and local–are the structures within which IGM functions. In this respect, IGM operates on similar institutional bases as FED and IGR. As noted earlier, however, IGM encompasses more than units of government (Agranoff 1983, 1986, 1989). It includes (1) a significant degree of policymaking in administration/management (the policy-in-administration continuum) and (2) the prominent presence of private and/or nonprofit sectors in service delivery process(es). The latter element has been referred to as the public-private sector mix, or the "array of public and private actors" with "membership in several implementation structures" (Mandell 1990, p. 35). Agranoff (1990a) notes, "Indeed, public-private sector interaction has been the key component in the operation . . . to mount local attacks on social concerns" (p. 22).

3. *What goals or values tend to dominate IGM?* With so many different agencies, enterprises, jurisdictions, and organizations intertwined in IGM, it is no surprise that a multiplicity of ambiguous and competing goals and values motivate the various actors. Lipsky (1980; pp. 40–48) identified the basis of four conflicting goals within human service programs: (1) agency managers, (2) program specialists, (3) clients, and (4) elected officials and general public. The chief task confronting IGM actors is overcoming the goal conflicts among the various participants. Skillful public management entails building consensus upon which positive program results can be achieved (Agranoff 1990a; Wright 1990a).

4. *What are the main means of conflict resolution in IGM?* In contrast to elections, courts, and legislation for FED, and apart from coalitions, games, and markets for

IGR, conflicts are resolved in the IGM arena through bargaining, negotiation, dispute resolution, informal personal linkage, and "trust-building" (Jennings and Krane 1994). When or where conflicts cannot be resolved, the differences are endured, tolerated, accommodated, or "coped with" (Agranoff 1986, 1989; Mandell 1990). The coping strategies may include referral of issues or problems to the political arena for change or conflict resolution.

5. *What is the distinctive character of authority relationship in IGM?* In contrast to national supremacy (contingent hierarchy) for FED, and different from the often-perceived hierarchy (asymmetric influence) for IGR, nonhierarchical networks or loosely coupled patterns of influence characterize IGM (Mandell, 1990). The interactions among IGM actors tend to occur on relatively level playing fields. It is important to note, however, that the interactions can assume many different forms–sequential, reciprocal, or collective (Alter and Hage 1993), and mediated or unmediated (Mandell 1990).

6. *What is the level of partisan politics in IGM?* The level is muted or modest, if not minimal. Effective program implementation and problem solving strategies in service delivery are the primary or focal issues (Agranoff 1989, 1990b). Rather than above-board partisan politics (i.e., Democrats versus Republicans), one is more likely to find political struggles in IGM cast as organizational or professional "turf" wars, such as nurses versus hospital managers or police versus social workers.

What IGM is as well as what it is not has been discussed. Based on these conceptual clarifications, distinctions, and meanings, it is useful to trace IGM across two decades of its origins and evolution.

The Origin and Emergence of IGM (the 1970s)

No single or specific date has been or can be confirmed for the origination of IGM. As noted earlier, the practice(s) of IGM undoubtedly predated its denomination. The approximate time of the concept's gestations and birth, however, can be reasonably fixed as the early 1970s. Two special issues of *Public Administration Review (PAR)* presented substantial manifestations of the problems, issues, and questions connected with a "management" approach to interjurisdictional relations (Groesnick 1973; Clayton, Conklin, and Shapek 1975). Limited space prohibits an attempt to summarize or synthesize the dozen articles in "The Administration of the New Federalism" (1973) or the twenty-one essays in "Policy Management Assistance" (1975).

It is sufficient to note, however, the "top-down," or national-based, springboard from which IGM was launched. A joint OMB-NSF management initiative culminated in the 1975 *PAR* issue. The initiative was called SCOPMA: Study Committee on Policy Management Assistance. Its report, *Strengthening Public Management in the Intergovernmental System* (Executive Office 1975), came in several parts in addition to the special issue of *PAR*. These included an OMB document, an NSF volume of 1,200 pages containing 40 background papers, and a 40-minute color video cassette. In a curious and ironic twist, the NSF director of this project became *persona non grata* among national administrative agencies for his role in unleashing (through the various SCOPMA activities) a torrent of state-local criticisms of "the feds."

Apart from personalities, career conflicts, and bureaucratic byplays, a central point remains. The origin of IGM in the 1970s was largely nationally initiated, Washington-based, and hierarchical in tone and temperament. Subsequent activities during the remainder of the 1970s appeared to confirm what James Stever (1992) later called "the hierarchical approach to intergovernmental management dominant during the 1970s" (p. 347). A list of developments included the following:

1. U. S. Advisory Commission on Intergovernmental Relations (ACIR), *Improving Federal Grants Management* (Washington, DC: A-53, February 1977).
2. American Society for Public Administration (ASPA), *Strengthening Intergovernmental Management: An Agenda for Reform* (Washington, DC: April 1979).
3. Executive Office of the President, Office of Management and Budget, *Managing Federal Assistance in the 1980s,* Report to the Congress pursuant to P. L. 95-224 (Washington, DC: March 1980).
4. Creation of SIAM (Section on Intergovernmental Administration and Management) within ASPA in 1978.
5. Creation of NAMA (National Assistance Management Association) in 1979. (In 1991, this organization changed its name to the National Grants Management Association.)

As national actions and activities expanded, ranging from preemption statutes and unfunded mandates to conditions of aid and project grants, IGM became more and more prominent. Furthermore, the difficulty of implementing intergovernmental programs pushed IGM to the forefront (Pressman and Wildavsky 1973). The emphasis on top-down management was reflected in two ways: (1) by the array of multiple management circulars (15 in all) that were operational in the 1970s and (2) in *Managing Federalism* (Shapek 1981), which discussed both the numerous circulars as well as the many complications associated with the evolution of the federal grant-in-aid "system."

Gordon (1980) appeared to capture the tenor of the time(s) at the close of the decade. In an article on IGM that was part of a symposium entitled "The State of American Federalism in 1979," he noted:

What is new is the distinctive management orientation of current assessments and the simple fact that many national government agencies are now equipped to undertake their own staff research on intergovernmental relations. One result is that many of these [reform] efforts reflect the tacit and often undiscriminating acceptance of *national* policy as a proper framework for most public policy issues. This, in turn, has led to a confining view of intergovernmental relations as merely an instrument of national policy formulation and implementation. In this view, state and local governments are seen primarily as lobbyists for and implementors of national assistance programs (p. 138).

This perspective changed significantly during the 1980s.

IGM Evolution in the 1980s: From Top-Down to Bottom-Up

The foregoing recitation of events, activities, and publications provides potential overkill by way of emphasis on the top-down orientation(s) of IGM in the 1970s. The 1980s reflected a secular if not a sea-change shift in outlook and approach to IGM. The multiple forces at work might be provisionally classified in two categories: (1) practical/political and (2) intellectual/ideological. The first includes the significant intergovernmental policy redirection that accompanied the Reagan administration's "New Federalism" (Farber 1983; Williamson 1983; Conlan 1987, 1988; Yoo and Wright 1994). In the second category are the sharp academic attacks on the concept of IGM. These took to task the hierarchical, technocratic, prefectorial, and nonconstitutional dimensions of the term (Gordon 1980; Elazar 1981; Schechter 1981). It is curious but not coincidental that these three referenced critiques of IGM all appeared in *Publius: The Journal of Federalism.*

It may be taken as given but unproved that the double-barreled attack of practical politics and academic argument undercut the hierarchical foundations on which IGM was constructed in the 1970s. Two possibilities emerged from those circumstances. One was that the concept might atrophy and disappear as a consequence of having few real-world, empirical referents. The second option was to fill the seemingly vacant conceptual space with new and different real-world operating experiences. The second option was the path pursued, whether purposefully or providentially. IGM, in short, lost its national-based, hierarchic connotation. Those elements were replaced by state-local and especially interlocal practice(s), research, and reconceptualization.

This locally based, community-focused, bottom-up approach to IGM in the 1980s remains relatively unexamined. A modicum of evidence makes the thesis plausible. The following references reflect the bottom-up approach to understanding IGM in the 1980s: Agranoff and Lindsay 1983; Rosenthal 1984; Peterson, Rabe, and Wong 1986; Johnson and Heilman 1987; Agranoff 1986, 1989, 1990a, 1990b; Gage and Mandell 1990. Evidence is also available to extend the IGM thesis for human service and other programs into the 1990s and to state-local service delivery (Jennings and Krane 1994; Nathan 1993). This shift in focus also coincided with "state-centered federalism" in the larger political-institutional context. The local, interlocal, and state-local focus and emphasis further coincided with a dramatic decline in the national government's institutional capacities to assess/analyze and manage national-state-local relationships (Kincaid and Stever 1992). The reductions affected OMB, GAO, ACIR, as well as other national administrative agencies.

Gage and Mandell (1990) provided a timely and significant synthesis of IGM. Stever's review (1992) of the Gage and Mandell work captures not only a major theme of their volume but also the two-decade reversal thesis in the understanding and use of IGM. He notes, "These authors attempt to stimulate the metamorphosis of a new paradigm for intergovernmental management, one that does not depend on central coordination by the federal government" (p. 347). Stever extracts another relevant assessment from the volume: "The policy arenas and intergovernmental networks the authors propose are consensually created from the bottom up in incremental fashion by actors in diverse institutional settings" (p. 350). If Stever is correct, and there is no basis for doubting him, the IGM constitutes an important "hidden dimension" of interjurisdictional and interorganizational activity that is extensive, significant, and largely unrecognized within public administration/management literature and practice(s).

IGM: Adolescence or Maturity?

Has IGM reached maturity or is it still in a state of adolescence? The maturity referenced here involves concept meaning and usage. IGM, as a concept, would be labeled mature if it had a stable, standardized, or consensus meaning and a common or generalized usage.

Of course, there are no neat aging calibrations with which to measure the life stages of a concept and the real-world practices for which it stands. It is possible, however, to compare IGM with IGR in terms of development and usage. It has been argued elsewhere (Wright 1983, 1990b) that IGR, from its origins in the 1930s, required more than a quarter-century (until the 1960s) to reach maturity.

Using IGR as a comparative base, a reasonable case can be made that IGM falls short of the mature stage. IGM is more likely in the late adolescent period where uncertainties as to further development(s) and direction(s) still abound. Changing contextual factors could, for example, alter the role and significance of IGM in the near- or long-term future.

One is a prospective major alteration of the partisan political scene. If the 1994 election constituted a prelude rather than an interlude of Republican domination of national and state-level political control(s), then partisan politics may overshadow and significantly displace management as a dominant dimension affecting American interjurisdictional relationships. If politics and partisanship dominate the public agenda then federalism, and the debate over its coercive and/or preemptive character, will likely frame the dominant discourses of the day (Kincaid 1990, 1993, 1994; Walker 1995; Zimmerman 1991, 1992). Depending on the degree and extent of resurgent partisanship, interlocal relations may or may not remain predominantly within the domain of management.

A second factor intruding on and perhaps overriding IGM is globalization. This single word stands for a constellation of international and transgovernmental forces that have altered the cultural, demographic, economic, fiscal, and social character of countries and communities. Terms such as "intermestic," "perforated sovereignties," "beer wars," and "the internationalization of local government" have emerged to express the penetration of international influences at the microcommunity level (Beaumont 1994; Duchacek, Latouche, and Stevenson 1988; Jones 1994; Kline 1994; Patton 1992). One possible consequence of these developments is that cultural, economic, and other issues will overwhelm management problems and processes as objects worthy of prominent attention on the public agenda.

Several other factors could be mentioned as forces affecting the content and direction of IGM. Changing technology, especially the information/communications revolution(s), could significantly reshape or refocus IGM. Likewise, TQM (Total Quality Management) and its variants might reorient the social technologies of organizational operations in ways that could change IGM. Last but not least, major societal value shifts such as voluntarism and communitarianism could reconfigure IGM.

IGM: Closing Observations

Where does all this leave IGM? Quite simply, it leaves the concept's future in some doubt as to direction and significance. It suggests that IGM has yet to mature and that this discussion of IGM is, of necessity, open-ended. It is a concept with elements of uncertainty at its core and with no small amount of ambiguity at its fringes. A few friendly critics, particularly practitioners, were even bold and candid enough to contend that IGM is so ambiguous and hidden that it does not really exist!

This analysis of IGM has been more exploratory and expository than empirical and explanatory. Few firm conclusions are forthcoming but selective closing observations provide a useful summary. For brevity and focus they are listed on page 1166.

1. *For two decades IGM has been the subject of articulation, clarification, controversy, and metamorphosis.* It has evolved, however, into a viable and selectively useful concept for practical, analytic, and theoretic purposes.

2. *Public administration (and public administrators) cannot be separated from politics and policy processes.* Public administration cannot be removed or isolated from the multidimensional features of FED, IGR, and IGM either. Marando and Florestano (1990) note: "We wonder if much of public administration is not now intergovernmental" (p. 309). The gist of this essay is that virtually all of public administration is inseparable from changing blends or balances among and between IGM, IGR, and FED.

3. *"Good" decisionmaking, constructive conflict resolution, and effective service delivery hinge on a strategic balance between actor roles and institutional responsibilities.* One way to understand institutional responsibilities (activities/duties) is through the conceptual framework of IGM. Actor roles can be usefully understood in the three-category scheme of elected generalists, administrative generalists, and program professionals. These three types of officials each occupy more significant roles, relatively and respectively, in FED, IGR, and IGM.

4. *It is not surprising that IGM originated and emerged so prominently in the 1970s.* The concept of management received endorsement and strong support from the highest office in the land–the Presidency. Richard M. Nixon was one president who took the concept of management most seriously. Witness one initiative (among many) in changing the name of the old Bureau of the Budget to the Office of Management and Budget. In spite of controversy, change, and evolution, IGM has emerged as management has become a more pervasive and critical process in society generally and in the public sector in particular.

We turn to a historian for a recent and expansive expression of management's significance. Samuel Hays (1991) discussed three decades of environmental policy in "The Politics of Environmental Management." His language as well as his focus on regulatory policy provide an extended exclamation point to this essay's emphasis on the prominence and pervasiveness of management.

As environmental politics evolved, its context shifted from broader public debate to management. Increasingly one spoke of air quality management, water quality management, forest management, range management, the Bureau of Land Management, Coastal Zone Management, risk management, river management, and wilderness management. Hardly an environmental problem could be dealt with outside the terminology and conceptual focus of management, and, in turn, management played a powerful role in shaping the world of environmental choice. The influence of management grew because of its power and its authority to coordinate discordant elements in the "system" on its own terms, and even more because it constituted the persistent institution of government, with ongoing day-to-day capabilities of communication and action. Institutional power was the stuff of political power; it arose from a continuous presence requiring that others reckon with it day in and day out; it set the bounds of choice if not the actual agenda. While the larger ideological debates in environmental affairs came and went, management shaped the world of day-to-day political affairs (p. 49).

Since the 1960s, the ad hoc proliferation of national programs, even in a single policy area such as environmental protection, compounded the difficulties of effective public action within America's highly fragmented governmental structure. Program performance became the "shared responsibility" of a network of government agencies, nonprofit organizations, and for-profit enterprises (Williams 1980; Mosher 1980). The task of public administration became much more than the smooth operation of a traditional government agency. It became the coordination and orchestration of the discordant organizations that made up a program's implementation network (Mandell 1990). Achieving public objectives within today's complex networks depends less on hierarchical controls and rests more on negotiation of joint courses of action.

This discussion has been almost exclusively at the conceptual level. It may therefore be instructive to conclude with one illustration based on recent efforts to implement reforms in public welfare programs.

Numerous demonstration projects in different states have attempted to shift welfare recipients into the workforce. This has required integrating the activities of several different public agencies as well as volunteer and private organizations. In one of these pilot projects the manager of a regional office of a state social service department took the initiative to contact managers in the state department of labor, the president of the local community college, the director of the regional private industry council (which operated a job-training program), the director of a child care resource agency serving the largest city in the region, and the director of the United Way. The regional social service manager also contacted several business leaders. The manager's motivation for building these linkages with the other organizations was the effective provision of necessary services to welfare recipients (e.g., education, job training, child care, transportation). Without increased connection and coordination among the different service providers in and out of the public sector, effective service delivery would have failed.

The major obstacle to effective service delivery was the absence of a shared philosophy of joint action for the benefit of the recipients. Each agency and organization had its own goals, procedures, services, and timeframes. In the words of the regional social service manager, a "whole new way of thinking was required" to being the different agencies and organizations into unified action. Once acceptance of joint action was achieved, more formal mechanisms of articulation were established. These included shared progress reports, regular joint meetings, memoranda of agreement, and contracts which specified services to be provided to the welfare recipients.

This example highlights one of the most typical forms of intergovernmental management—the integration of services provided by several separate organizations. Ensuring that different entities work together means overcoming the natural tendency of organizations to protect their turf. This requires the development of joint action and shared responsibility, not just at the local service delivery level but also at higher management levels.

The "M" in IGM gives both symbolic and operational significance to management (and administration) in the larger arenas of politics, policymaking, and governance in its broadest sense. It expresses in a different manner what one United States senator posed as a question to the American Municipal Congress in the early days of the shift toward shared responsibility. "How do we make sure that the powers of government [will] continue to be diffused while at the same time the chores of government are effectively performed?" (Muskie 1961). The "M" also captures the larger political and social significance of a phenomenon that Carl Friedrich (1950), an intellectual leader of political science, identified several decades ago. "Bureaucracy," which to Friedrich included administration and management, "is the core of modern government" (p. 37).

DEIL S. WRIGHT AND DALE KRANE

BIBLIOGRAPHY

Advisory Commission on Intergovernmental Relations, 1977. *Improving Federal Grants Management.* Washington, DC: Government Printing Office.

Agranoff, Robert J., 1986. *Intergovernmental Management: Human Services Problem Solving in Six Metropolitan Areas.* Albany: State University of New York Press.

———, 1989. "Managing Intergovernmental Processes." In James L. Perry, ed., *Handbook of Public Administration.* San Francisco: Jossey-Bass; 131–147.

———, 1990a. "Managing Federalism through Metropolitan Human Services Intergovernmental Bodies." *Publius: The Journal of Federalism,* vol. 20: 1–22.

———, 1990b. "Responding to Human Crises: Intergovernmental Policy Networks." In Robert W. Gage and Myrna P. Mandell, eds., *Strategies for Managing Intergovernmental Policies and Networks.* New York: Praeger, 57–80.

Agranoff, Robert, and Valerie A. Lindsay, 1983. "Intergovernmental Management: Perspectives from Human Services Problem Solving at the Local Level." *Public Administration Review,* vol. 43: 227–237.

Alter, Catherine, and Jerald Hage, 1993. *Organizations Working Together.* Newbury Park, CA: Sage Publications.

American Society for Public Administration, 1979. *Strengthening Intergovernmental Management: An Agenda for Reform.* Washington, DC: American Society for Public Administration.

Beaumont, Enid F., 1994. "Domestic Consequences of Internationalization: Emerging Conflicts." *The Annals,* vol. 509 (May) 9–152. Paper presented at a conference on centralization and decentralization in Japan and the United States. Sponsored by the National Institute for Research Advancement (Tokyo) and the National Academy of Public Administration (Washington), Georgetown University, Washington, DC.

Beer, Samuel H., 1978. "Federalism, Nationalism, and Democracy in America." *American Political Science Review,* vol. 72: 9–21.

Clayton, Ross, Patrick Conklin, and Raymond Shapek, eds., 1975. "Policy Management Assistance: A Developing Dialog." Special issue of *Public Administration Review,* vol. 35.

Conlan, Timothy J., 1987. "Federalism and Competing Values in the Reagan Administration." *Publius: The Journal of Federalism,* vol. 16: 29–48.

———, 1988. *New Federalism: Intergovernmental Reform from Nixon to Reagan.* Washington, DC: Brookings Institution.

Duchacek, Ivo D., Daniel Latouche, and Garth Stevenson, eds., 1988. *Perforated Sovereignties and International Relations: Trans-Sovereign Contacts of Subnational Governments.* New York: Greenwood.

Elazar, Daniel J., 1981. "Is Federalism Compatible with Prefectorial Administration?" *Publius: The Journal of Federalism,* vol. 11: 3–22.

Executive Office of the President, 1975. *Strengthening Public Management in the Intergovernmental System.* Report prepared for Office of Management and Budget by the Study Committee on Policy Management Assistance. Washington, DC: Government Printing Office.

Executive Office of the President, Office of Management and Budget, 1980. *Managing Federal Assistance in the 1980's.* Washington, DC: Government Printing Office.

Farber, Stephen B., 1983. "The 1982 New Federalism Negotiations: A View from the States." *Publius: The Journal of Federalism,* vol. 13: 33–38.

Friedrich, Carl J., 1950. *Constitutional Government and Democracy.* New York: Ginn.

Gage, Robert W., and Myrna P. Mandell, eds., 1990. *Strategies for Managing Intergovernmental Policies and Networks.* New York: Praeger.

Gordon, George J., 1980. "Managing Leviathan: The Intergovernmental Management Agenda for 1980." *Publius: The Journal of Federalism,* vol. 10: 137–144.

Grosenick, Leigh E., ed., 1973. *The Administration of the New Federalism: Objectives and Issues.* Washington, DC: American Society of Public Administration.

Hays, Samuel P., 1991. "Three Decades of Environmental Politics: The Historical Context." In Michael J. Lacey, ed., *Government and Environmental Politics: Essays on Historical Developments Since World War Two.* Baltimore, MD: Johns Hopkins University Press.

Jennings, Edward T., Jr., and Dale Krane, 1994. "Coordination and Welfare Reform: The Quest for the Philosopher's Stone." *Public Administration Review,* vol. 54: 341–348.

Johnson, Gerald W., and John G. Heilman, 1987. "Metapolicy Transition and Policy Implementation: New Federalism and Privatization." *Public Administration Review,* vol. 47: 468–478.

Jones, Ben, 1994. "Free Trade and State Sovereignty." *Spectrum: The Journal of State Government,* vol. 67: 37–43.

Kincaid, John, 1990. "From Cooperative to Coercive Federalism." *The Annals,* vol. 509 (May) 139–152.

————, 1993. "From Cooperation to Coercion in American Federalism: Housing, Fragmentation, and Preemption, 1780–1992." *Journal of Law and Politics,* vol. 9: 333–430.

————, 1994. "From Dual to Coercive Federalism in American Intergovernmental Relations." Paper presented at a conference on centralization and decentralization in Japan and the United States. Sponsored by the National Institute for Research Advancement (Tokyo) and the National Academy of Public Administration (Washington), Georgetown University, Washington, DC.

Kincaid, John, and James A. Stever, 1992. "The Rise and Decline of the Federal Government's Intergovernmental Analysis Capacity and the Reorientation of Federal Policy from Places to Persons." Paper presented at the annual meeting of the American Political Science Association, September, Chicago, IL.

Kline, John M., 1994. "State and Local Boundary-Spanning Strategies: Political, Economic, and Cultural Transgovernmental Interactions." Paper presented at a conference on centralization and decentralization in Japan and the United States. Sponsored by the National Institute for Research Advancement (Tokyo) and the National Academy of Public Administration (Washington), Georgetown University, Washington, DC.

Lipsky, Michael, 1980. *Street-Level Bureaucracy: Dilemmas of the Individual in Public Services.* New York: Russell Sage Foundation.

Mandell, Myrna p., 1979. "Letters to the Editor: Intergovernmental Management." *Public Administration Times,* vol. 2: 2, 6.

————, 1990. "Network Management: Strategic Behavior in the Public Sector." In Robert W. Gage and Myrna P. Mandell, eds., *Strategies for Managing Intergovernmental Policies and Networks.* New York: Praeger, 29–53.

Marando, Vincent L., and Patricia S. Florestano, 1990. "Intergovernmental Management: The State of the Discipline." In Naomi B. Lynn and Aaron Wildavsky, eds., *Public Administration: The State of the Discipline.* Chatham, NJ: Chatham House Publishers, 287–317.

Mosher, Frederick, 1980. "The Changing Responsibilities and Tactics of the Federal Government." *Public Administration Review,* vol. 40: 541–547.

Muskie, Edward S., 1970. Speech to the American Municipal Congress, 1961. Quoted in Richard Leach, *American Federalism.* New York: W. W. Norton, 48.

Nathan, Richard P., 1993. *Turning Promises into Performance: The Management Challenge of Implementing Workfare.* New York: Columbia University Press.

Patton, H. Milton, 1992. "The Internationalization of Local Government." *SIAM Newsletter,* vol. 15: 2–3.

Peterson, Paul E., Barry G. Rabe, and Kenneth K. Wong, 1986. *When Federalism Works.* Washington, DC: Brooking Institution.

Pressman, Jeffrey L. and Aaron B. Wildavsky, 1973. *Implementation: How Great Expectations in Washington Are Dashed in Oakland.* Berkeley, CA: University of California Press.

Rosenthal, Stephen R., 1984. "New Directions for Evaluating Intergovernmental Programs." *Public Administration Review,* vol. 44: 491–503.

Schechter, Stephen L., 1981. "On the Compatibility of Federalism and Intergovernmental Manager." *Publius: The Journal of Federalism,* vol. 11: 127–141.

Shapek, Raymond A., 1981. *Managing Federalism.* Charlottesville, VA: Community Collaborators.

Stever, James A., 1992. "Intergovernmental Management in a Revolutionary Era." *Journal of Public Administration Research and Theory,* vol. 2: 347–350.

Walker, David B., 1995. *The Rebirth of Federalism: Slouching toward Washington.* Chatham, NJ: Chatham House Publishers.

Williams, Walter, 1980. *The Implementation Perspective: A Guide for Managing Social Service Delivery Programs.* Berkeley: University of California Press.

Williamson, Richard S., 1983. "The 1982 New Federalism Negotiations." *Publius: The Journal of Federalism,* vol. 13: 11–32.

Wright, Deil S., 1983. "Managing the Intergovernmental Scene: The Changing Dramas of Federalism, Intergovernmental Relations, and Intergovernmental Management." In William B. Eddy, ed., *Handbook of Organizational Management.* New York: Marcel Dekker, 417–454.

————, 1987. "A Century of the Intergovernmental Administrative State: Wilson's Federalism, New Deal Intergovernmental Relations, and Contemporary Intergovernmental Management." In Ralph C. Chandler ed., *A Centennial History of the American Administrative State.* New York: Macmillian, 219–260.

————, 1990a. "Federalism, Intergovernmental Relations, and Intergovernmental Management: Historical Reflections and Conceptual Comparisons." *Public Administration Review,* vol. 50: 168–178.

————, 1990b. "Policy Shifts in the Politics and Administration of Intergovernmental Relations, 1930s–1990s." *The Annals,* vol. 509: 60–72.

Yoo, Jae-Won, and Deil S. Wright, 1993. "Public Policy and Intergovernmental Relations: Measuring Perceived Change(s) in National Influence–The Effects of the Federalism Decade." *Policy Studies Journal,* vol. 21: 687–699.

Zimmerman, Joseph F., 1991. *Federal Preemption: The Silent Revolution.* Ames: Iowa State University Press.

————, 1992. *Contemporary American Federalism: The Growth of National Power.* New York: Praeger.

INTERGOVERNMENTAL RELATIONS.

The various combinations of interdependencies and influences among public officials–elected and administrative–in all types and levels of governmental units, with particular emphasis on financial, policy, and political issues.

Intergovernmental relations (IGR) as a term originated in the United States of America in the 1930s. It was a new way of describing significant changes in relationships among levels of government and among the officials who held important policymaking posts. Many of these changes and interactions resulted from efforts to ameliorate the effects of the Great Depression, but some even antedated that major economic and social upheaval. The United States national government inaugurated many new activities and programs that altered the relatively separated spheres of national and state government functions, commonly referred to as "dual federalism" (see **federalism**). These progressive adaptations, consisting mainly of national policy initiatives, created new and complex working arrangements that could not be easily described using the constitutional-legal language typical of federalism issues. Because of its origins, IGR is viewed as a dynamic concept, which "pictures the intergovernmental relationship as one of constant change in response to social and economic forces as well as to changes in such significant political factors as the party and electoral systems" (Reagan, 1972, p. 3).

Origin and Historical Development

William Anderson (1960), who is often credited with originating the term, defined IGR as

> an important body of activities or interactions occurring between [or among] governmental units of all types and levels within the US federal system.... Underlying the concept . . . is the fact that the nation as a whole, each one of the [fifty] states, and every county, town, city, school district and other special district or local unit is a territorial and corporate or quasi-corporate entity that has a legal existence, rights, functions, powers, and duties within its territory [that are] distinct from those of every other such unit (p. 3).

Notice that this approach to the relationships among and between all manner of public units and jurisdictions "goes far beyond such formal matters as structure and legal powers" and pragmatically emphasizes that "few if any basic problems of local, state, or national government can be successfully resolved without reference to their intergovernmental aspects or implications" (Casella, 1995, p. 43).

For some scholars, IGR transcends the traditional denotations of federalism. For example, Gordon (1992) observes that "IGR involves virtually all governments and public officials, though, largely out of public view; it is highly informal and very dependent on human interactions; and it involves the private sector" (p. 111). Denhardt (1991) explains that a "key to understanding intergovernmental relations . . . is understanding the changing patterns used to fund public programs. Although intergovernmental relations involves more than money, financial questions are inevitably at the core of the process" (p. 69). Glendening and Reeves (1977) expand the meaning of IGR to include "all public officials—administrators as well as elected executive, legislative, and judicial officers—and it encompasses political, economic, and administrative interactions as well as legal ones" (p. 9). Glendening and Reeves include not only the behavior of officials but also their attitudes and perceptions. This shift toward behavioral and attitudinal features as distinctive aspects of IGR moves the concept further away from formal, legal, and structural characteristics. In this sense, there are no relationships among governments; rather, there are arrays, of complex cooperative and conflictual relationships among officials who govern.

Some scholars have gone so far as to declare "Federalism—old style—is dead. Yet, federalism—new style—is alive and well and living in the United States. Its name is *intergovernmental relations*" (Reagan 1972, p. 3). Other scholars are not yet willing to entomb federalism as a dead concept. Elazar (1987) distinguishes IGR from federalism by saying,

"Federalism is the generic term for what may be referred to as a self-rule/shared-rule relationships; 'intergovernmental relations' has to do with particular ways and means of operationalizing a system of government" (p. 16). He goes on to point out that IGR, because of its American origins, is a highly "culture-bound" term that does not easily comport with the European theories of the state. Hamilton and Wells (1990, pp. 9–12) reject IGR because it is a term limited by its "how-to-control" perspective, and they prefer federalism because, for them, federalism includes ideas about political economy that more correctly reflect the reality of interactions among governmental units. Subsuming IGR under federalism, Zimmerman (1992; p. 201) recently called for a general theory of [American] federalism that combined elements of classic federalism with more contemporary matters such as regulatory controls, the political maneuvering of subnational jurisdictions, and efforts to coordinate changes in national-stage relations.

Because Zimmerman's prescription is a large order, most scholars differentiate between the two terms. Cochran et al. (1993) succinctly note:

> The term *intergovernmental relations* is sometimes used interchangeably with federalism, but the two do not really mean the same thing. Federalism refers to the formal, legal structure of the political system, whereas intergovernmental relations refers to all the interactions of governmental units within the political system. Therefore, although not provided for specifically in the formal document establishing the political system, some intergovernmental activities occur anyway (p. 138).

Because IGR activities happen with or without formal constitutional status, the term has been accepted in comparative studies of unitary governments as well as of federal governments (for example, Rhodes 1980; Muramatsu 1982; Samuels 1983). Thus, despite the lack of agreement among scholars, the term IGR increasingly serves as the conceptual basis for the analysis of interactions among units of governments and officials, even in nations without the formal features of federalism.

Conceptual Approaches

Descriptive analyses of the features and practices of intergovernmental relations in a given country represent one prominent approach to this topic. Wright (1988, pp. 14–26) sets out a list of items that is commonly used to guide studies of IGR. Five distinctive features are identified: (1) number and types of governmental units, their legal status, and changes over time; (2) the number and types of public officials by jurisdiction and unit, their backgrounds and training, the attitudes and perceptions of their roles and responsibilities, and the actions they normally pursue; (3) the patterns of interaction among and between officials representing various jurisdictions and governmental units;

(4) the range of involvement by all public officials—elected and appointed, national and local, executive, legislative, and judicial—especially in the formulation of policies and programs that have impact on more than one unit; and (5) the policies and programs implemented through intergovernmental arrangements, with particular concerns about administrative discretion by official and by unit, control over and flow of fiscal resources, and differential effects of policies and programs delivered via different intergovernmental routes. Typically, descriptive studies of IGR focus on one or more of the above features.

In contrast to the focus on structure common to descriptive studies of IGR, a second analytic strategy, which in the United States of America is one of the most characteristic styles of analyzing IGR, classifies changes and trends in the relations among governments by historical eras or phases. Analysis proceeds by describing the main problems, the most commonly used mechanisms of public action, and the attitudinal and behavioral shifts that typify a given time period. Some analysts use presidential terms (e.g., Nixon's New Federalism, Reagan's New-New Federalism) to demarcate changes in IGR (Conlan 1988). Other analysts utilize metaphors to portray the distinctive features of a given phase; for example, one finds references to "layer-cakes" and "marble-cakes," even "fruit-cakes" as well as references to "picket-fences," "whiplashes," and "fending-for-yourself" (Grodzins 1966; Stewart 1984). While highly informative about the details of change from one time period to the next, this historical or metaphorical approach to IGR is atheoretical and offers no framework for theory-building.

European scholars have adopted a focus on decentralization issues as an analytic approach to IGR within the context of a unitary government (Smith 1985). This approach moves away from the historical-legal tradition in political research to one that measures changes in the degree of decentralization, the extent of devolution, and the creation of autonomous jurisdiction. A somewhat similar approach to IGR found on both sides of the Atlantic is an emphasis on political power, especially as exercised by local government officials. Who makes which decisions and to what extent local decisionmakers may act without constraint by the central government are common questions in this "community power" approach to IGR.

Several attempts to transcend the atheoretical nature of IGR analyses grounded in structural relationships have been made in the last decade (Krane 1993a, pp. 188–189). The first of these nonhierarchical approaches derives from the recognition that the policy process is intertwined with the basic features of a country's IGR. Thus, the focus shifts to policy arenas and issue types, policy professionals and implementation networks, agenda-setting and coalition-building (Treadway 1985; Peterson, Rabe, and Wong 1986; Anton 1989; Robertson and Judd 1989). The advantage of this policy strategy approach to IGR is to facilitate a linkage between the behavior of IGR players (e.g., elected officials, interest groups, program administrators) and the impacts (benefits and costs) of policy choices on citizens.

Fiscal federalism and public choice theory constitute a second significant effort to go beyond simple descriptive studies of IGR. Using the theory of markets, fiscal federalism and public choice analyses strive (1) to model IGR by formal or quantitative means and (2) to prescribe an optimal division of functions among levels of government. Much of the impetus for this market-based analysis comes from an argument that competition among jurisdictions is widespread, desirable, and yields efficient results (Ostrom, Tiebout, and Warren 1961; Peterson 1981; Schneider 1989; Dye 1990; Kenyon and Kincaid 1991).

A third attempt to develop a theory of IGR relies on concepts commonly used in the analysis of interorganizational relations. In the 1970s, European scholars applied organizational sociology and the emerging public policy models to the study of center-local relationships and argued that complex dependencies within matrixlike networks typified intergovernmental policy implementation (Hanf and Scharpf 1978; Rhodes 1980; Smith, 1985). Similar developments in the USA produced a growing body of studies based on the problems of IGR implementation, network management, and interjurisdictional and interorganizational coordination (Pressman 1975; Van Horn and Van Meter 1976; Hjern and Porter 1981; Mandell and Gage 1988; Goggin et al. 1990; Jennings and Krane 1994). Interorganizational concepts permit the development of IGR models that capture the complexities and dependencies that determine the courses of action that are possible among and between governmental jurisdictions.

Over 20 years have passed since Edner (1976) declared that a "virtual wasteland" in the development of a theory of IGR existed. Recent efforts to model IGR have not yet produced consistent results, but these proposed conceptual frameworks do hold the promise of ameliorating the long-standing "conceptual crisis" in IGR studies (Lovell 1979).

Current Practices

In today's modern governments, public officials utilize numerous types of public authorities and jurisdictions to satisfy citizen demand for a wide array of public goods and services. Administrative, programmatic, and territorial differentiation produces complex and diverse patterns of activity among units that vary by authority, resources, and tasks. This organizational complexity and functional fragmentation across tiers of government result in intricately intertwined relationships that do not form a coherent system. At the same time, these fragmented and pluralistic politico-administrative units must be integrated, at least partially, in order to deliver public services with reasonable efficiency and effectiveness. Not all of this policy activity can be directed by a central government or by a single government. Some aspects of public service(s) provision emerge from choices made autonomously by, or at the discretion of, subnational units. Consequently, IGR is generally characterized by reciprocal activity and interdependent choices among multiple governmental units and political interests.

The various combinations of interdependencies, even in one country, can be bewildering. For example, in the United States one finds, in addition to the national government and the 50 states, nearly 83,000 units of local government. Each of these jurisdictions is represented by one or more elected officials who exercise varying degrees of authority over the policies, finances, and administration of the governmental unit. Similarly, many of the major administrative organizations of the national government (e.g., the 14 cabinet rank departments and several independent executive agencies) are replicated at the state and local government level (so-called counterpart organizations). Policy, financial, and political networks link the national government through state governments to local governments and create differing structures of program implementation. It is within these networks that public officials engage in the intergovernmental pursuits of their preferences. The behavior of public officials and the features of the linkages among and between governmental units shape the particular character of IGR in each country.

Because there are so many possible combinations of action and influence, it is impossible to catalogue them all in a brief discussion. The following subsections offer some selective illustrations of the principal forms of IGR in the United States and in other nations.

Financial Issues

One of the principal dynamics in IGR is the struggle over the allocation and distribution of funds by jurisdiction and by function. Mismatches between the needs or problems found in local communities and their ability to raise revenues and to develop sufficient capacity to solve local problems drive many local officials to seek additional resources from superior levels of government. In particular, a "vertical fiscal imbalance" or "fiscal mismatch" exists because (1) it is relatively easier to raise revenues at higher levels of government, which can tap the resources of a wider geo-economic area, (2) most problems affecting the quality of life require action by local authorities, and (3) variations in the wealth of local communities can lead to inequities in service accessibility and quality (Break 1980, pp. 76–87; Reagan 1972, pp. 31–36). The result of this "fiscal mismatch" is that local governments in almost all nations exhibit a higher degree of fiscal dependence on the central or national government than in the past (Bahl and Linn 1994, p. 6).

Different countries devise different mechanisms for distributing funds to subnational units. One can simplify these intergovernmental fiscal transfers into three basic forms: (1) shared revenues, (2) grants-in-aid, and (3) loans. Shared revenues are funds collected by a higher level of government, some proportion of which is returned to subordinate (receiving) governments. The amount returned can be a guaranteed (constitutional or statutory) percentage of the monies collected or may be the amount collected less an administrative fee. Typically, the receiving governments have no direct control over the determination of the rate, base, and proportion of revenues distributed. To alter the amount "shared" usually requires political action at the higher level of government (Bahl and Linn 1992). Taxes levied on motor vehicle fuels is one of the most common shared taxes. The 50 American state governments impose a tax on the sale of gasoline, and these monies are divided by formula for state highways, county roads, and municipal streets. The national government also levies a motor fuel tax, which pays for the federal highway system. Similar arrangements for sharing motor fuel taxes are found in countries around the world. In some countries as much as 90 percent of local government expenditures have their source in fiscal transfers from the national government (Bahl and Linn 1994).

Grants-in-aid, which are monies raised by a higher level of government and distributed to lower levels of government, come in different forms—the three most common are (1) formula grants, (2) reimbursements, and (3) discretionary grants. Formula grants are funds distributed to lower tiers of government according to a formula composed of demographic, economic, political, and/or social factors. Formulas may be fixed (in a constitution or statute) or may change annually; whatever the case, the factors included in the formula become the focus for political maneuvering by various interests seeking to write the formula to their benefit. Once the formula is set, the administrative agency responsible for allocations can calculate the monies to be received by each jurisdiction or recipient.

Reimbursement grants are payments by a higher government for all or a portion of the costs incurred by a local government for some specified purpose (e.g., education or police). Reimbursements differ from formula grants in that reimbursements normally take into account the actual costs of the approved activity. Formula grants may fall short of actual costs. The key features of a reimbursement are the items eligible for cost recovery and the percentage of the item's cost to be reimbursed.

Discretionary grants are fiscal transfers completely controlled by the donor government. That is, the amount of money appropriated, the criteria by which funds are to be awarded, the conditions and obligations imposed on the recipients, and the selection of the recipients are all at the discretion or choice of the donor government. Unlike formula and reimbursement grants, a system of discretionary grants typically does not guarantee or provide funds to every lower level jurisdiction or even very eligible recipient. Rather, the funds available in any one budget cycle are distributed by the officials in the national (or provincial) agency to local governments. Sometimes a competition is established among the eligible jurisdictions, who must submit an application for the funds (Break 1980, pp. 123–186; Bahl and Linn 1992, pp. 432–450).

Loans of money from superior governments to lower units form a third type of intergovernmental fiscal transfer. Critical to any loan are the terms of the contract—the amount of the principal, the interest due, the time allowed to repay the principal and interest, and the purpose(s) of the loan. In addition to loans, higher level governments may act to guarantee (to the lender) loans taken by lower units of government (Kettl 1988, pp. 97–119; Lund 1989, pp. 125–166).

Each form of intergovernmental fiscal transfer embodies one or more choices about its features that structure the way in which the specific transfer mechanism can be used to attain policy goals. Examples of the choices officials make in designing a mechanism for transferring money between governments include amount, duration, eligibility, function or purpose, intended impacts and outcomes, recipient discretion and obligations, and targeting to places or to people. These design choices are also intensely political and open to innumerable "games" of strategy for increasing one's share of the transferred funds (see Wright 1988, Appendix B).

It is important to remember that IGR encompasses horizontal as well as vertical movements of authority and money. Consequently, interactions among jurisdictions located on the same plane of government constitute an important source of IGR. Three of the most common horizontal mechanisms are (1) contracts and agreements, (2) the transfer of functions, and (3) the use of interjurisdictional agencies (Berman 1993). A common motive for interjurisdictional cooperation is cost savings. Two or more jurisdictions may purchase or support a service (e.g., an emergency response system) that would be too costly for each jurisdiction to buy individually. Other reasons for interjurisdictional collaboration include more effective action (e.g., law enforcement), complementary planning (e.g., roadways), and reducing negative externalities (e.g., pollution control). The horizontal dimensions of IGR add to the complexity of possible arrangements and greatly increase the points of access by which public officials and citizens may influence policy choices.

Policy Issues

Questions about intergovernmental fiscal transfers invariably provoke important policy issues. Decisions about where to allocate funds (from central to local government) and how to transfer funds (shared taxes, grants, or loans) are joined to decisions about the goals and objectives to be achieved and which officials will be in control of monies for given parts of a specific program. The growth in United States national government aid to state and local governments from 1960 to the early 1980s was so expansive and rapid (Walker 1995, p. 206) that many officials and many

observers of IGR developed a "fiscal fixation," which led them to see IGR as mostly moving money among jurisdictions. In addition to fiscal transfer decisions, intergovernmental policy choices include the imposition of legal penalties, the use of regulatory authority, and the nature of implementation structures. Intergovernmental policy issues go beyond the fiscal instruments of public action to encompass choices that affect the outcomes in all types of policy areas—distributive, regulatory, redistributive, and boundary-spanning.

From a policy perspective, IGR involves the effort by one or more public officials to impose some degree of control over their interaction with officials in another public jurisdiction or unit. Put another way, there is much more to IGR than moving money. Higher level governments may "donate" or transfer money and authority to lower level governments in order to achieve specific national (or provincial) purposes. At the same time, officials in recipient governments seek to obtain additional resources, but they also strive to retain autonomy and discretion in the use of the transferred resources. Officials in donor governments, to achieve their ends, must obtain the compliance of local officials. The trade-offs that result from the interaction among officials of national and local levels directly determine the character of the policy or program established (Pressman 1975). How the particular program is designed (e.g., the grant formula) and how it is to be administered (e.g., by local governments) go a long way in determining the distribution of benefits and costs among the intended as well as actual targets (jurisdictions and/or citizens) of the public program.

Intergovernmental regulatory issues can conveniently illustrate the policy aspects of IGR. Donor governments usually impose some rules on the use of transferred funds, even if only to prohibit the misappropriation of funds. The number and variety of conditions and rules that may be attached to intergovernmental fiscal transfers is extensive and nearly defies enumeration. In the United States, for example, state and local government officials who accept grants-in-aid from the national government must comply with regulations on (1) general administrative and procedural standards, (2) access to government information and decision processes, (3) standards for public employees, (4) health, safety, and welfare, (5) labor and procurement standards, (6) nondiscrimination, (7) protection of the environment, (8) advancement of the economy, (9) the utilization of nonprofit organizations, and (10) state and local government-related administrative and fiscal requirements (Walker 1981, pp. 180–183).

The policy issues embodied in rulewriting vary from mundane operational matters about which there is little disagreement to fundamental and politically charged questions about the balance of authority between national and subnational governments (ACIR 1984; ACIR 1993). For example, few would disagree that donor governments should impose rules that make local officials liable for the embezzlement or theft of grant monies or that require local officials to create drug-free workplaces. By contrast, rules attached to grants from the national government that require local officials to use crumb rubber from recycled tires in future street projects or that require local officials to house juvenile offenders outside of the local jail provoke intense opposition from local officials who see their authority and autonomy severely reduced, if not eliminated. Recently, this battle over intergovernmental regulatory policy in the United States has been exacerbated by the national government's decision to impose unfunded mandates—that is, new rules governing the actions of state and local officials without any new money for the implementation of the rule. American state governments, it must be noted, have long imposed unfunded mandates on their respective local governments.

Although the examples of regulatory IGR have been drawn from the United States national experience, these same types of policy issues can be found in the relationships between the levels of government in other countries. As pointed out above, donor governments want to achieve their objectives, so they seek to control the actions of recipient governments through regulation. However, provincial and local officials want more discretion to pursue their own preferences. Because both parties need each other to achieve their own ends, continuous political jockeying characterizes IGR.

Political Issues

The constitutions of federal countries, by giving significant autonomy to officials of regional and local governments, create a framework of multiple structures and interests, which cannot be easily controlled by national government officials. In the United States of America, national government officials rely substantially on state governments to implement national government programs; at the same time, state government officials depend on the national government for additional resources. Furthermore, the United States constitution, like other federal constitutions, gives state and local areas direct input into the making of national policy. Although there is an asymmetry of authority and resources, state and local officials possess sufficient autonomy and freedom to force national officials to bargain over the formulation and implementation of public policy. As a consequence, national, state, and local officials adopt various strategies by which to influence each other's actions (Pressman 1975, pp. 10–16; Krane and Shaffer 1992, pp. 250–251). It should be noted that even in unitary nations, with their formal "top-down" legal relationships, many of these same intergovernmental dynamics prevail (Graham 1982).

Studies of IGR often analyze these political battles by classifying them according to the type of government officials involved. It is commonplace to find descriptions of

national-state, national-local, or interstate and interlocal conflicts. Officials from one tier of government (e.g., municipalities) often advocate for the interest of their tier to officials representing other, usually superior, tiers of government. Using levels of government as the unit of analysis may have the merit of simplicity. It can, however, divert attention from more important underlying dynamics, such as the policy or program area in which the official is seeking advantage, the constituency base of the official, the official's professional background and training, or the organizations in which the official participates. Asymmetry of influence based in the formal, legal structures may be altered by other informal networks of association and organization.

If there is any statement bordering on a generalization about the politics of IGR, it is this last idea—that informal networks emerge within the formal legal structures of government and make it possible for officials representing different interests to exercise varying degrees of influence over policy. One of the most venerable metaphors of American IGR—"picket-fence" federalism—illustrates this informal exercise of influence across levels of government. Because the administration of most national programs depends on the "shared responsibility" (see **intergovernmental management**) of national, state, and often local governments, the vertical implementation network creates a program-based access for the program managers and beneficiaries at all levels of government (e.g., child development, mental health). These "vertical functional autocracies" enhance the influence of the program specialists vis-à-vis the elected, generalist officials (e.g., governors or mayors). Second, the vertical network also creates "an alliance of like-minded program specialists or professionals, regardless of the level of government in which they serve" (Wright 1988, p. 83). Program specialists at all levels become allies in defending and enlarging their particular program, whether or not this course is desired by the elected, generalist officials of a given level. Program administrators have even constructed national associations, for instance, the National Community Development Association, for the purpose of lobbying elected officials. Consequently, political tension between generalist and specialist officials prevails.

Generalist officials at the state and local level are not without their own resources in the politics of IGR. First, governors and mayors, by the nature of their office, possess advantages in the articulation of local citizen preferences to national officials (Krane 1993b). Second, governors and mayors, because of national rules, also possess significant leverage (via the "sign-off" authority) with specialist officials over the use of grants-in-aid within their jurisdiction. Third, these generalist officials have organized their own national associations for the purpose of representing to the United States president and to Congress their collective policy positions. The "Big Seven" public interest groups, termed by Beer (1977) the "intergovernmental lobby," include (1) the National Governors' Association (NGA), (2) the National Conference of State Legislatures (NCSL), (3) the National League of Cities (NLC), (4) the US Conference of Mayors (USCM), (5) the National Association of Counties (NaCO), (6) the Council of State Governments (CSG), and (7) the International City/County Management Association [ICMA] (Wright 1988, pp. 281–283).

The presence of overtly political alliances and associations of public officials—elected and administrative—within the matrix of the United States federal arrangements contributes to several important features of American IGR. First, the political actions of these officials are important variables influencing outcomes. Second, the degree of influences exercised by a given type of official or organization varies significantly; that is, some officials and organizations are more influential than others. Third, proposals for "program shifts and policy redirections [will] take substantial amounts of time to take effect and to be observable throughout the IGR system" (Wright 1988, pp. 283–284). And fourth, while a tendency toward equilibrium exists, because all parties are organized and active, no output is final (Leach 1970, p. 64). The politics of IGR result in a never-ending struggle to influence the shape of public policy at each and every level of government. It is this continuous dynamic action that distinguishes IGR from federalism, in which some structural features must remain relatively permanent.

Future Issues and Trends

The open-ended nature of IGR makes any discussion of the future problematic, but it is worthwhile to convey some sense of what we and others believe to be important issues and trends. Robert W. Gage (1990), after surveying a group of persons knowledgeable about IGR and a group of state and local officials, identified three key intergovernmental issues that the respondents suggested will affect the future course of IGR in the United States: first, and it comes as no surprise, that the budget difficulties of the United States national government are perceived to be a powerful force driving actions and outcomes in the intergovernmental system; second, the rising role of state governments, with their enhanced executive and administrative capabilities, has resulted in an impressive array of innovations since 1980 and shows no signs of stopping (e.g., reforms of education finance, health care, and public welfare); third, the continuing expansion of funded and unfunded mandates imposed by the national government on states and localities heightens the political conflict between national and subnational officials. We concur with Gage's issues assessment, and we have no reason to doubt the importance of these three issues for the future of American IGR.

We also believe that several distinct trends driven by specific political controversies will dominate the IGR

agenda in the decade ahead. Pressure to hold the line on taxes with little or no reduction in the demand for public services will continue to strain public budgets at all levels of government. The ongoing structural realignments in national economies will exacerbate both the resistance to enhanced public revenues and the demand for public services. Thus, fiscal-economic trends suggest that the intergovernmental burden sharing and cooperation of the recent past may well be replaced by burden shifting and interjurisdictional competition.

A related trend derives from the effort to economize by using improved public management techniques. Emerging as an important concern in the 1970s and gaining momentum in the 1980s and 1990s, the various efforts to redesign, reengineer, reform, and reinvent the institutions and procedures of government put a premium on the management dimensions of IGR (Cigler 1995, pp. 1–2). In a time of tight agency budgets, overcoming turf wars, and fostering joint action toward program goals become critical to policy success and to cost control (Stone 1992). The coordination and orchestration of the many different organizations (public, nonprofit, and for-profit) necessary to the implementation of public programs has now become the primary task of public managers (see **intergovernmental management**).

Ideological battles over social issues are forcing government officials to confront choices that are not easily reduced to fiscal problem. The effort by various jurisdictions or levels of government to shift the fiscal burden for particular services has been joined by efforts to completely pass the buck for the responsibility. This avoidance of service provision and payment is most likely to occur in the social services area. Rather than relying on economic evidence (there are not enough funds available), the push to avoid program responsibility is justified on moral grounds; that is, the recipients of the services are not "worthy" or do not "merit" aid.

Underlying the growing appeal to ideological or moral reasoning are social trends influencing the shape of IGR. Few nations are homogeneous and most are becoming more heterogenous in ethnic, racial, and religious groupings. This increasing sociodemographic diversity coupled with the longstanding movement to expand civil and political rights to all persons fuel conflicts among various social groups. The movement to the suburbs in the United States, for example, has resulted in a new and fastest growing form of government, the residential community association (ACIR 1989). "A major reason people move out to suburbs is simply to be able to buy their own government. These people resent it when politicians take their money and use it to solve other people's problems." (Schneider 1992, p. 37). With income disparity related directly to demographic diversity in many places, the resulting polarization reinforces the fiscal-economic and political-ideological trends to reduce spending for services (provided to other persons) and to leave problems to the mercy of the marketplace.

The quickening pace of global economic competition impels subnational governments to act as entrepreneurs for their region's population. Not only are nation-states engaged in economic trade, so also are cities, metropolitan areas, provinces, and states (Fry 1990; Rose 1991). International activity by local and regional governments heightens the effort on their part to be granted more autonomy and to exercise more discretion. At the same time, the global involvement of subnational governments can easily run counter to central government plans (Brown and Fry 1993; Hobbs 1994).

Another important IGR trend is the emergence of intermestic issues (Manning 1977). These are issues that result from the increased interconnection(s) between international and domestic problems—hence, intermestic. These issues are noteworthy for their novelty, intensity of conflict, and the degree to which the issue "comes as a surprise" to individuals and jurisdictions. Examples include the taxation of foreign corporations by subnational governments, the promotion of direct foreign investment, the enforcement of international treaties protecting the environment and wildlife, and actions in support of United Nations sponsored agreement (e.g., on the rights of children). Intermestic issues constitute a new source of likely IGR tension because the catalyst causing the conflict can be any one or a combination of different planes of government—international, national, state, local—often located in another country. Global agreements, for example, to reduce the use of toxic chemicals, can create an unexpected source of mandates or regulations that local authorities must enforce, whether the local industries or populace wishes it.

The decade ahead will see these several trends work to intensify the fundamental conflicts associated with IGR in all nations. The problems of fiscal mismatch and interjurisdictional disparities are not likely to be resolved in this era of constrained resources. Similarly, the tensions caused by the struggle of local governments to gain more autonomy will grow as economic and social problems force local officials to maintain their local political support. Whether these twin tensions—finances and authority—result in more centralization or decentralization will depend on the political alignments within given countries. What can be said for sure is that the basic struggle among public officials at all levels of government to pursue their own and their jurisdiction's preferences will drive the politics of IGR.

DALE KRANE AND DEIL S. WRIGHT

BIBLIOGRAPHY

Advisory Commission on Intergovernmental Relations (ACIR), 1984. *Regulatory Federalism: Policy, Process, Impact, and Reform.* Washington, DC: February, no. A-95.

———, 1989. *Residential Community Associations: Private Governments in the Intergovernmental System?* Washington, DC: A-112.

———, 1993. *Federal Regulation of State and Local Governments: The Mixed Record of the 1980s.* Washington, DC: A-126.

Anderson, William, 1960. *Intergovernmental Relations in Review.* Minneapolis: University of Minnesota Press.

Anton, Thomas J., 1989. *American Federalism and Public Policy: How the System Works.* New York: Random House.

Bahl, Roy, and Johannes Linn, 1992. *Urban Public Finance in Developing Countries.* London: Oxford University Press, published for the World Bank.

———, 1994. "Fiscal Decentralization and Intergovernmental Transfers in Less Developed Countries" *Publius: The Journal of Federalism,* vol. 24, no. 1: 1–19.

Beer, Samuel H., 1977. "Political Overload and Federalism." *Polity,* vol. 10 (Fall): 5–17.

Berman, David R., 1993. "Relating to Other Governments." Chapter 7 in Charldean Newell, ed., *The Effective Local Government Manager,* 2nd ed. Washington, DC: International City/County Management Association.

Break, George, 1980. *Financing Government in a Federal System.* Washington DC: Brookings Institution.

Brown, Douglas M., and Earl H. Fry, eds., 1993. *States and Provinces in the International Economy.* Berkeley: Institute of Governmental Studies Press, University of California.

Casella, Jr., William N., 1995. "The National Civic League and Intergovernmental Relations." *National Civic Review,* (Winter) 42–47.

Cigler, Beverly, 1995. "Governance in the Re–Ing Decade of the 1990s." *SIAM Intergovernmental News,* vol. 18, no. 2 (Spring). Section on intergovernmental administration and management, the American Society for Public Administration.

Cochran, Clark E. et. al., 1993. *American Public Policy: An Introduction,* 4th ed. New York: St. Martin's .

Conlan, Timothy, 1988. New Federalism: Intergovernmental Reform from Nixon to Reagan. Washington, DC: Brookings Institution.

Denhardt, Robert B., 1991. *Public Administration: An Action Orientation.* Pacific Grove, CA: Brooks/Cole.

Dye, Thomas R., 1990. *American Federalism: Competition Among Governments.* Lexington, MA: D. C. Heath.

Edner, Sheldon, 1976. "Intergovernmental Policy Development: The Importance of Problem Definition." In Charles O. Jones and Robert D. Thomas, eds., *Public Policy Making in a Federal System.* Beverly Hills, CA: Sage.

Elazar, Daniel J., 1987. *Exploring Federalism.* Tuscaloosa: University of Alabama Press.

Fry, Earl H., 1990. "State And Local Governments in the International Arena." *The Annals of the American Academy of Political and Social Science,* vol. 509 (May) 118–127.

Gage, Robert W., 1990. "Key Intergovernmental Issues and Strategies: An Assessment and Prognosis." In Robert W. Gage and Myrna P. Mandell, eds., *Strategies for Managing Intergovernmental Policies and Networks.* New York: Praeger.

Glendening, Parris N., and Mavis Mann Reeves, 1977. *Pragmatic Federalism: An Intergovernmental View of American Government.* Pacific Palisades, CA: Palisades.

Goggin, Malcolm et al., 1990. *Implementation Theory and Practice: Toward a Third Generation.* New York: HarperCollins.

Gordon, George J., 1992. *Public Administration in America,* 4th ed. New York: St. Martin's.

Graham, Lawrence S., 1982. "Intergovernmental Relations in Comparative Perspective: Results from a Five-Country Study." Paper delivered at the annual meeting of the American Society of Public Administration, Honolulu, Hawaii.

Grodzins, Morton, 1966. *The American System: A New View of Government in the United States.* Chicago: Rand McNally.

Hamilton, Christopher, and Donald T. Wells, 1990. *Federalism, Power, and Political Economy: A New Theory of Federalism's Impact on American Life.* Englewood Cliffs, NJ: Prentice-Hall.

Hanf, Kenneth, and Fritz W. Scharpf, eds., 1978. *Interorganizational Policy Making: Limits to Coordination and Central Control.* London: Sage.

Hjern, B., and David O. Porter, 1981. "Implementation Structures: A New Unit of Administrative Analysis." *Organization Studies,* vol. 2, no. 3: 211–227.

Hobbs, Heidi H., 1994. *City Hall Goes Abroad: The Foreign Policy of Local Politics.* Thousand Oaks, CA: Sage.

Jennings, Jr., Edward T., and Dale Krane, 1994. "Coordination and Welfare Reform: The Quest for the Philosopher's Stone." *Public Administration Review,* vol. 54, no. 4: 341–348.

Kenyon, Daphne, and John Kincaid, eds., 1991. *Competition Among States and Local Government: Efficiency and Equity in American Federalism.* Washington, DC: Urban Institute Press.

Kettl, Donald F., 1988. *Government by Proxy: (Mis?)Managing Federal Programs.* Washington, DC: CQ Press.

Krane, Dale, 1993a. "American Federalism, State Governments, and Public Policy: Weaving Together Loose Theoretical Threads." *PS: Political Science & Politics,* vol. 26, no. 2 (June) 186–190.

———, 1993b. "State Efforts to Influence Federal Policy." In Edward T. Jennings, Jr. and Neal S. Zank, eds., *Welfare System Reform: Coordinating Federal, State, and Local Public Assistance Programs.* Westport, CT: Greenwood.

Krane, Dale, and Stephen D. Shaffer, 1992. *Mississippi Government and Politics: Modernizers Versus Traditionalists.* Lincoln: University of Nebraska Press.

Leach, Richard H., 1970. *American Federalism.* New York: W. W. Norton.

Lovell, Catherine, 1979. "Where We Are in Intergovernmental Relations and Some of the Implications." *Southern Review of Public Administration,* vol. 3: 6–20.

Lund, Michael, 1989. "Between Welfare and the Market: Loan Guarantees as a Policy Tool." In Lester M. Salamon, ed., *Beyond Privatization: The Tools of Government Action.* Washington, DC: Urban Institute Press.

Mandell, Myrna P. and Robert W. Gage, eds., 1988. "Management in the Intergovernmental System: Networks and Strategies." *International Journal of Public Administration,* vol. 11, no. 4 (Special Symposium).

Manning, Bayard, 1977. "The Congress, the Executive, and Intermestic Affairs." *Foreign Affairs,* vol. 55: 306–324.

Muramatsu, Michio, 1982. *A Lateral Competition Model for Japanese Central-Local Relations.* Kyoto, Japan: Kyoto University.

Ostrom, Vincent, Charles Tiebout, and Robert Warren, 1961. "The Organization of Government in Metropolitan Areas: A Theoretical Inquiry." *American Political Science Review,* vol. 55, no. 4 (December) 831–842.

Peterson, Paul E., 1981. *City Limits.* Chicago: University of Chicago Press.

Peterson, Paul E., Barry G. Rabe, and Kenneth K. Wong, 1986. *When Federalism Works.* Washington, DC: Brookings Institution.

Pressman, Jeffrey L., 1975. *Federal Programs and City Politics: The Dynamics of the Aid Process in Oakland.* Berkeley: University of California Press.

Reagan, Michael, 1972. *The New Federalism.* New York: Oxford University.

Rhodes, R.A.W., 1980. "Analysing Intergovernmental Relations." *European Journal of Political Research,* vol. 8: 289–322.

Robertson, David B., and Dennis R. Judd, 1989. *The Development of American Public Policy: The Structure of Policy Restraint.* Glenview, IL: Scott, Foresman.

Rose, John Eck, 1991. "Foreign Relations at the State Level." *Journal of State Government,* vol. 64, no. 4 (Oct. Dec.) 1–8.

Samuels, Richard J., 1983. *The Politics of Regional Policy in Japan: Localities Incorporated?* Princeton, NJ: Princeton University Press.

Schneider, Mark, 1989. *The Competitive City: The Political Economy of Suburbia.* Pittsburgh, PA: University of Pittsburgh Press.

Schneider, William, 1992. "The Suburban Century Begins." *The Atlantic Monthly* (July) 33–44.

Smith, B. C., 1985. *Decentralization: The Territorial Dimension of the State.* London: George Allen & Unwin.

Stewart, William H., 1984. *Concepts of Federalism.* Lanham, MD: University Press of America.

Stone, Donald C., 1992. *Improving Local Services through Intergovernmental and Intersectoral Cooperation.* Pittsburgh, PA: Carnegie Mellon University, Coalition to Improve Management in State and Local Government.

Treadway, Jack M., 1985. *Public Policy-Making in the American States.* New York: Praeger.

Van Horn, Carl E., and Donald S. Van Meter, 1976. "The Implementation of Intergovernmental Policy." In Charles O. Jones and Robert D. Thomas, eds., *Public Policy Making in a Federal System.* Beverly Hills, CA: Sage.

Walker, David B., 1981. *Toward a Functioning Federalism.* Cambridge, MA: Winthrop.

———, 1995. *The Rebirth of Federalism: Slouching Toward Washington.* Chatham, NJ: Chatham House.

Wright, Deil S., 1988. *Understanding Intergovernmental Relations,* 3d ed. Pacific Grove, CA: Brooks/Cole.

Zimmerman, Joseph F., 1992. *Contemporary American Federalism: The Growth of National Power.* New York: Praeger.

INTERNAL SECURITY. Guarding against threats and dangers to the stability of the state. The term is linked to the wider concept of national security, namely, the preservation of the state from all threats from wherever they come. Internal security can be regarded as one important component of national security, implying as it does the safeguarding of state and society from threats arising from, or manifesting in, the domestic political, economic, and social environment.

Beyond this relatively straightforward understanding of internal security, it is difficult to pin down the term with precision because it depends on how one approaches the concept. In its most fundamental form, internal security can refer simply to the maintenance of civil order through legal systems, which detail prohibited acts. Civil police forces and the criminal courts are, in this respect, responsible for upholding internal security through the prevention, detection, and punishment of crime.

Most people, however, probably do not relate the notion of internal security directly to the criminal justice system. More commonly, the term is associated with shadowy and indistinct threats that are believed to represent a danger to the fabric of society or risk compromising the independence and integrity of the state. These threats may be of either domestic origin or sponsored by foreign powers. The nature of the danger might vary from a terrorist conspiracy, or espionage conducted by hostile foreign powers, to serious forms of organized crime.

Many countries have special agencies, distinct from civil police forces, tasked with maintaining internal security. In the United Kingdom, the organization known as MI5 has responsibility for counterespionage and in recent years has taken on the role of countering terrorist activities in Britain. The equivalent organization in the United States is the Federal Bureau of Investigation (FBI). In addition to dealing with spying activities and counterintelligence work, the FBI also functions as a federal police force, enforcing federal criminal law across the United States of America. The example of the FBI emphasizes that, in the end, it is impossible to separate clearly internal security from law enforcement.

Another problem is how to quantify threats to the internal security of a state. The answer will vary widely and, to a large extent, depends on the nature of government and civil society. An authoritarian state may, in extreme cases, regard all forms of political dissent as a threat to internal stability and repress any views that conflict with those of the ruling regime. For example, the government of the former Soviet Union, though its Committee for State Security, the Komitet Gosudarstvennoy Bezopasnosti, or KGB as it was more commonly known in the West, would spy on its own people and routinely imprison or even execute critics of the government. More liberal democratic societies permit freedom of expression and association and confine threats to internal security usually to the illegal procurement of classified government information or conspiracies against the state using, or threatening to use, violence. Even this statement needs to be qualified, however. Democratic states sometimes feel the need to protect themselves from particular view or political ideologies deemed to be subversive. In the United States, the House Un-American Activities Committee (HUAC) was set up in 1938 as a special committee of the House of Representatives to investigate profascist and communist groupings. Later in 1950, at the height of the cold war and the fear of communism, HUAC supported the creation of the Internal Security Act, also known as the McCarran Act after its sponsor, Senator Patrick McCarran (1876–1954) of Nevada. The act required all communist organizations within the United States and their members to register as foreign agents. Communists were prohibited from government employment and denied United States passports. In retrospect, the anticommunist purge sanctioned by HUAC and the Internal Security Act was seen to contradict democratic values by persecuting individuals with minimal involvement in communist or subversive activities. The Internal Security Act fell into disuse by the early

1970s. HUAC was renamed the Internal Security Committee in 1969 but was itself abolished in 1975.

The experience in the United States illustrates the difficulty of trying to generalize about approaches to internal security, except to demonstrate that the concept is premised on the belief that there are particular acts and viewpoints that pose a risk to society and need to be countered by the state.

M.L.R. SMITH

BIBLIOGRAPHY

Kessler, Ronald, 1995. *FBI: Inside the World's Most Powerful Law Enforcement Agency.* London: Corgi.
Knight, Amy W., 1988. *KGB: Police and Politics Inside the Soviet Union.* Boston, MA: Unwin Hyman.
Lustgarten, L., and I. Leigh, 1994. *In from the Cold: National Security and Parliamentary Democracy.* Oxford: Clarendon.
West, Nigel, 1982. *Matter of Trust.* London: Weidenfeld and Nicolson.

INTERNATIONAL ASSOCIATION OF SCHOOLS AND INSTITUTES OF ADMINISTRATION (IASIA).

An entity that promotes cooperation among a worldwide association of educational organizations that focus on public administration and its management so as to strengthen and enhance their capacity to serve the government agencies and enterprises with which they are associated.

Origins

For more than three decades, public administration researchers, teachers, and trainers have been coming together yearly to learn from each others' experiences and to develop materials and methodologies relevant to their work. The opportunity to do this has been provided by the International Association of Schools and Institutes of Administration, popularly known as IASIA.

IASIA in its present form dates from 1971. It grew from seeds planted ten years earlier when participants in a roundtable of the International Institute of Administrative Sciences (IIAS) recognized the need to pay more attention to what we now refer to as institutional development. Three months spent visiting training centers in 11 countries in Europe and Africa had shown Donald Stone, Dean, Graduate School of Public and International Affairs, University of Pittsburgh that a great deal of innovation was taking place. He was persuaded that information on developments should be shared among schools and institutes. The rapidly increasing number of such centers at the time gave a certain urgency to his drive to create a channel for achieving this. On July 14, 1961, Dean Stone wrote to heads of schools and institutes of public administration inviting them to attend special meetings on "matters of common concern" being organized in association with the IIAS roundtable in Lisbon, Portugal, in the following September.

The response to the invitation showed clearly that the initiative struck a chord in many countries. Almost 200 persons attended one or more of the special meetings in Lisbon. More than a third of those who attended the special meetings came from schools and institutes. The remainder included university professors engaged in preparing personnel for public administration responsibilities and civil service and training officials concerned with improvement of capacity of government personnel. Many of them were attending an IIAS event for the first time. They were there because of the focus on the specific needs of their, in many cases fledgling, organizations. They felt acutely the need to have an opportunity to learn of and from the experience of those in similar situations, a feeling intensified by the fact that many of them had no point of comparison in their own countries; generally, each country had only one institute or school of public administration.

Arising from these meetings in Lisbon, a working group was established within the framework of IIAS and provided opportunities for special meetings ten times in the following decade—often in association with meetings of IIAS. During that period, the interest in the activities of the working group spread to virtually all regions of the world and attracted the attention of a number of agencies supporting creation of capacity in the public services in the newly independent states of Africa and Asia.

In 1971, on the occasion of the IIAS congress in Rome, the working group of schools and institutes was transformed into an autonomous organization entitled the International Association of Schools and Institutes of Administration (IASIA). It remained and remains a constituent organ of the International Institute.

What is IASIA?

Today, IASIA is a worldwide association of organizations and individuals whose activities and interests focus on public administration and management. Its membership includes over 180 national institutes in 70 countries as well as several international organizations. Members are grouped in seven geographical regions—Africa, Asia, Australia and South Pacific, Europe, Latin America and the Caribbean, Middle East, and North America. The activities in which its member organizations engage include education and training of administrators and managers, and related research, consulting, and publications. It is a not-for-profit association supported by membership fees, income from services, the voluntary services of its members and contributions from funding organizations. Its small secretariat is located at the headquarters of the IIAS in Brussels, Belgium.

What Does IIAS Do?

Aims

IASIA aims to promote and support cooperation among participating organizations and individuals in order to enhance their capacity to strengthen the administrative and management capabilities of government organizations, agencies, and enterprises they serve.

In pursuit of this aim, the association seeks

1. to provide an opportunity for personnel of member organizations and individual members to exchange information, ideas, experiences, and materials on issues and developments of common interest;
2. to study public sector management issues and developments of current and future concern;
3. to advance their professional knowledge, expertise, and development; and
4. to foster international and regional support for and interest in public service education/training, management development, and increased management capacity in the public sector.

Activities

With its minimal resource base, IASIA depends substantially on the readiness of its members to voluntarily undertake responsibility for many of its activities. What might have been a limitation has become an advantage. It means that the association must keep in close touch with the current concerns of these members.

Annual Conference

The annual conference—the core activity of the association—is hosted by a member organization or group of organizations in a different region each year. This practice allows regular participants to get detailed insights into the operations and methodologies of member institutions in different cultural, political, and economic environments. It also facilitates greater participation of individuals in the host region, which makes the association accessible to a wider range of staff of member organizations. This is an important consideration. The worldwide nature of the association means inevitably that, whatever the location of the conference, each year some regions have difficulty in attending. One of the intentions of the founders was that the value of the work done at meetings should be felt throughout the member organizations. Rotation of venue helps to achieve this. So also, of course, do publications including the reports on the annual conference.

Each year, the theme selected for the conference is a topic of major concern for public administration and management. The opening day of the meeting is devoted exclusively to consideration of this theme. The remainder of the conference is largely devoted to the working/research groups. The program is arranged in such a way that it is possible for each participant to take full part in the proceedings of at least two working groups. Provision is also made for a number of "breakaway sessions." These are used to complement the established plenary activities and working/research groups. They allow up-dating previously treated topics and introducing new subject areas that may lead to formation of working groups or once-off discussions.

Working/Research Groups

The major mechanism for study and development of specific topics and for the exchange of information and experiences among members is that of the working/research group. Each group is managed by a project director and chairperson and normally works on a three-year program. Groups concerned with a generic theme (e.g., programs and methods of training for public administration or public service reform) or with sectoral concerns (e.g., public enterprise management education and training) have programs comprising a number of projects and studies generally designed within a three-year cycle. The groups continue for several three-year periods. Other groups may be created to consider a single issue and cease to exist when they have completed their brief. An example of such a group is one that worked on improving the consulting capabilities of schools and institutes.

Input to the studies comes by way of papers prepared by group members and discussions on them in the working sessions. An important feature of an IASIA conference is that these papers are presented rather than read, a practice which allows time for more active contributions by all those attending. Arising from the discussions, contributors may be invited to further develop or edit their work for inclusion in the final publication. This approach has proved beneficial to all—but perhaps particularly to those new to the international scene—as a means of bringing high-level expertise to bear on work in progress.

The work of each group is geared toward a publication or series of publications. The end products include books, articles, reports, and case studies that are of use to teaching organizations and to others interested in human resource development throughout the public-sector and to public sector management itself.

Publications

IASIA's publications represent the product of the annual conferences and the working/research groups. The annual conference reports contain the discussions of the conference, including the reports of the individual working/research groups and help keep staff of member institutions abreast of progress on matters of interest to them. The activity aims to keep teachers, trainers, researchers, and students of public administration and management, as well as practitioners, abreast of new ideas and developments. They are produced either by IASIA itself or in association with a publishing house. In addition to formal publications,

IASIA sometimes makes papers available in the form of working documents as "gray" literature.

How Is IASIA Organized and Managed?

IASIA is governed by a board of management consisting of the president of IASIA–elected by the board of management–the immediate past president, the functional and regional vice presidents, and 25 members from member organizations nominated on a regional basis. The vice presidents are selected by the president and approved by the board of management. Members hold office for three years. The board meets on the occasion of the annual conference.

The annual general meeting, in which all members are entitled to participate, takes place on the occasion of the annual conference. Every three years, members of the board of management other than the vice presidents are elected at this meeting.

The program committee manages the annual conference and determines the organization and membership of the working groups. This committee, presided over by the vice president meets on the occasion of the annual conference and once in the interval between conferences.

The secretariat of the association assists the president and board in carrying out the association's functions and work program. The executive secretary operates from the headquarters of the international institute of administrative sciences in Brussels.

Who Can Become a Member?

Corporate membership of the International Association of Schools and Institutes of Administration is open to schools; institutes; colleges; universities; education, training, or research centers that share the aims of the association. National, regional, or international organizations engaged in the practice of public administration or in improving the management capacity of public agencies may become associate members. Individual membership is open to persons concerned with the aims of IASIA who are not staff of organizations eligible to be but are not currently corporate members. Members receive a copy of each issue of the *International Review of Administrative Sciences,* of the *Report of the Annual Conference,* and all IASIA publications free of charge. Staff of member organizations pay a reduced registration fee for attendance at IASIA conferences.

JOAN CORKERY

INTERNATIONAL CITY/COUNTY MANAGEMENT ASSOCIATION. Professional and educational association of city managers and other chief administrators in local government.

When the International City/County Management Association (ICMA) was organized in 1914, two major purposes were stated in its constitution: to promote the efficiency of City Managers and municipal work in general. Over the years, this wording has been changed to accommodate a more diversified membership, but the two purposes have stayed the same: (1) to foster the professional development of members and (2) to improve the management of all local government.

The ICMA value system has been remarkably stable since the association's founding: the high worth of local government; efficient, economical, and equitable provision of services; a unified governing body; an active and informed citizenry; council and manger teamwork in blending policy and administration; and the unique contribution of professional management to the betterment of local government.

ICMA was started in 1914 when 8 city managers (out of 32 in the United States and Canada) met in Springfield, Ohio, and established the City Managers' Association. In 1924, the word "International" was added to the name in recognition of substantial Canadian membership. In 1969, the word "Managers'" was changed to "Management" to recognize broadened membership eligibility for mayor-appointed and council-appointed administrators with overall management responsibility and directors of councils of governments (COGs). In 1991, ICMA changed its name again from "City" to "City/County" to recognize the rapid growth in counties with appointed managers and other chief administrators. By the mid-1990s, ICMA had about 8,000 members, one-half of whom are local government managers.

Although ICMA advocates the council-manager plan as the preferred form of local government, the association promotes professional management in all forms of local government. In addition, the association sustains and enforces the ICMA Code of Ethics. Adopted in 1924 as the City Managers' Code of Ethics, it has grown in influence and stature over the years into one of the most widely recognized governmental ethics codes in the United States. The code has been translated into several languages for use in the emerging democracies of central and eastern Europe.

The ongoing activities of ICMA include workshops and seminars geared toward management improvement; a monthly magazine and several newsletters covering local government developments; an annual conference; subscription services for management information and local government data; international municipal programs to strengthen local government management in developing countries; and a wide variety of publications, including the Municipal Management Series, local government training texts for general management, police, fire, public works, finance, and other subjects, and *The Municipal Year Book*, a comprehensive data and reference source on local government developments.

The ICMA University, established in 1994, provides members with unified access to programs, courses, and other professional development opportunities offered by universities, institutes of government, state and public official associations, and private consultants.

Council-Manager Plan

Although in 1908 the Staunton, Virginia, city council appointed the first "manager" to direct the day-to-day operations of the city government, the first city to adopt the council-manager plan was Sumter, South Carolina, in 1912. Dayton, Ohio, in 1914, was the first sizable city (population of 140,000 at that time) to adopt the plan.

The council-manager plan was a significant part of the municipal reform movement in the early part of the twentieth century. Other elements of the movement included civil service, the secret ballot, the short ballot, nonpartisan elections, elections at large, and the initiative, referendum, and recall.

Adoption of the council-manager plan has been the most significant change in American local government during the twentieth century. Except for the largest cities (the term city is used here to encompass cities, towns, townships, boroughs, villages, and counties), it is now the most widely used form of government in cities with population of over 10,000. One of the reasons for the plan's popularity is its simplicity. The city council, with the mayor serving as its presiding officer, appoints the city manager, who serves at the pleasure of the council. Unlike state and national governments in the United States, the plan rejects the separation of powers between the executive and legislative branches and places all powers in the elected legislative body with the appointed executive responsible to that body.

The council adopts ordinances and resolutions, reviews and adopts the budget, appoints citizen boards and commissions, signs off on major contracts and other legal actions, and maintains ongoing surveillance of the operations of the city government and the work of the city manager.

The city manager enforces laws and ordinances, appoints and supervises department heads and key staff, prepares the budget, supervises the ongoing work of city departments, recommends policies to the city council, and, above all, works with the city council to address policy issues, concerns of citizen groups, tax and revenue questions, citizen petitions and demonstrations, and almost all of the other hurly-burly that makes up the governmental process.

Some observers believe that the principal shortcoming of the council-manager plan has been the lack of political and policy leadership that can be provided by the elected mayors in mayor-council cities. However, in many council-manager cities, the leadership issue has been addressed by recognizing the mayor as the chief legislator and political leader of the city with an important role as the representative of the city in intergovernmental relations and as the city's advocate in promoting the city's interests with the private sector.

Approximately 3,000 places have been recognized by ICMA as meeting its criteria as "council-manager local governments," which place in the manager full managerial powers over appointment of employees and preparation of the budget. The council-manager plan's emphasis on professional city management has been extended, however, to another 1,400 places that are recognized by ICMA as "general management local governments." These include places where professional managers are appointed by the governing body or by the elected chief executive (mayor or county executive) but do not have the clear-cut authority associated with the manager in the council-manager plan.

The council-manager plan and professional local government management offer significant benefits to cities in addition to professional values and standards. They include executive budgeting, long-range policy planning, stronger financial management, and a stronger role for the city council that blends policy and administration to meet the dynamic needs of a changing society.

ICMA membership includes approximately 700 persons in Canada, Australia, and 23 other nations. Many of these persons serve as chief administrators in local governments or hold other significant management positions.

City Managers

During the first four decades of the council-manager plan, the managers were largely trained as engineers and brought an "operations manager" point of view to the city government that was well suited for the times. This began to change after World War II as managers became more professional, more cosmopolitan, and more externally oriented to their communities and to other governments. From the 1970s on, managers have moved to focusing on policy concerns and working directly with the city council.

These and other changes since the early 1900s can be summarized as follows: (1) Managers' working environments have broadened to include social, demographic, and economic issues that demand expertise in public policy formulation. (2) Educational backgrounds of managers have shifted sharply from engineering to public administration. (3) Educational levels have advanced from the bachelor's degree to the master's degree, usually in public administration. (4) The managers' responsibilities have grown to encompass community leadership and a policy role in a governance setting that includes the private and nonprofit sectors as well as the local government. "Today's city manager . . . spends substantially less time on administration in the conventional sense than did his or her predecessors" (Arnold and Plant 1994, p. 193).

In the complex urban world of the late twentieth century, local governments whether evaluated by day-to-day operations, community meetings, negotiations for a baseball stadium or revenue options to be considered by the city council demand the specialized knowledge and information provided by professional managers. Their work with city councils increases the effectiveness of both the political and administrative sides of local government.

DAVID S. ARNOLD

BIBLIOGRAPHY

The International City/County Management Association publishes manuals and guides on a continuing basis on the council-manager plan, the management profession, and the work of local government governing bodies. [ICMA, 777 North Capitol Street NE, #500, Washington DC 20002-4201.]

Arnold, David S., and Jeremy F. Plant, 1994. *Public Official Associations and State and Local Government: A Bridge Across One Hundred Years.* Fairfax, VA: George Mason University Press.
Frederickson, H. George, ed., 1989. *Ideal and Practice in Council-Manager Government.* Washington, DC: International City/County Management Association.
Green, Roy E., 1989. *The Profession of Local Government Management: Management Expertise and the American Community.* New York: Praeger.
Nalbandian, John, 1991. *Professionalism in Local Government: Transformations in the Roles, Responsibilities, and Values of City Managers.* San Francisco: Jossey-Bass.
National Civic League, 1989. *Handbook for Council Members in Council-Manager Cities,* 4th ed. Denver, CO.
———, 1989. *Model City Charter,* 7th ed.
———, 1990. *Model County Charter,* rev. ed.
Newell, Charldean, ed., 1993. *The Effective Local Government Manager,* 2d ed. Washington, DC: International City/County Management Association.
Stillman, Richard J., II., 1974. *The Rise of the City Manager: A Public Professional in Local Government.* Albuquerque: University of New Mexico Press.
Svara, James H., 1990. *Official Leadership in the City: Patterns of Conflict and Cooperation.* New York: Oxford University Press.
Svara, James H. and Associates, 1994. *Facilitative Leadership in Local Government.* San Francisco: Jossey-Bass.

INTERNATIONAL INSTITUTE OF ADMINISTRATIVE SCIENCES. A nongovernmental international organization, consisting of many states and organizations, set up to study and improve public administration around the globe.

The International Institute of Administrative Sciences is a nongovernmental organization that is competent in the study and improvement of public administration. It was established in 1930 and has its headquarters in Brussels. It works with about 100 countries and international organizations in all the regions of the world. It includes three fully integrated specialized or regional associations:

the International Association of Schools and Institutes of Administration, the International Association of Information and Documentation in Public Administration, and the European Group of Public Administration.

Historical Background

The institute goes back to 1910. That was the year when an international congress took place in Brussels, on the initiative of a simple committee. It was therefore a matter merely of a meeting and not of an institution. It was not the institution that organized the first congresses, but the first conferences that resulted in an institution. The date and the place are of interest in themselves: In 1910, we were on the eve of World War I at a time when the internationalization of activities of every kind was developing and when public administration started to play an increasingly important role in the life of nations. The place was a European capital, because it was in the countries of Europe that administration had reached its apogee of development at that time and the civil servants from those countries wished to meet and compare their experiences. No congress took place during World War I, naturally, but meetings resumed after peace returned. It was during one of those congresses held in Madrid in 1930 that the institute was founded.

Brussels was designated as the headquarters from that date onward, notably because of the interest Belgium had shown in this kind of activity by organizing the first congress and because of the proposal of the Belgian government to house the institute and to provide it with financial resources and, finally, because of the legal facilities written into a law of 1919 for the setting up of international associations. Permanent administrative services were set up and new congresses were organized. The institute's activities were interrupted by World War II and its assets were transferred to Berlin. Steps were taken to reestablish it immediately after the end of the war. An international congress was organized in Bern in 1947 and new headquarters, still in Brussels, were allocated to the organization. The institute developed well for 20 or so years, particularly under the chairmanship of René Cassin, winner of the Nobel Peace Prize and principal author of the Universal Declaration of Human Rights of 1948. In the 1970s, however, the institute underwent a period of crises: a crisis of identity, a financial crisis, and a political crisis. These crises were due both to circumstances to do with the inner life of the institute and also to difficulties resulting from world changes at that time, notably owing to the emergence of a very large number of newly independent countries and the appearance of numerous international organizations. That period was rapidly overcome and the International Institute has been in continuous expansion and development since about 1980.

In the meantime the International Institute had obtained advisory status with the United Nations Organization and UNESCO, and it had been admitted to the International Social Science Council attached to UNESCO.

In the course of the last decade its assignments were specified, its activities were widened and multiplied, its statutes were strengthened and finally membership was marked by a trend toward universalization.

Purpose

The purpose of the Institute is defined in Article 4 of the statutes as follows: "The purpose of the International Institute of Administrative Sciences shall be to promote the development of the administrative sciences, the better operation of public administrative agencies, the improvement of administrative methods and techniques, and the progress of international administration." It can be seen from this list that the aims of the institute are dual ones.

First, the development of the science—that is, knowledge of administration and from that point of view all disciplines (history, law, management, economics, sociology) must be represented and, in particular, a fundamental balance must be achieved between the legal disciplines and those that relate to management.

Second, a practical approach—that is, a pursuit of the means to improve the operation of public authorities and to improve their methods and their techniques. The field is therefore very broad, with objectives covering both knowledge and reform. Obviously, the two go together: It is not possible to have knowledge without wishing to reform, and it is not possible to reform without even being aware or knowledgeable. The discipline of history is important because, as Professor Wright, a general rapporteur at one of the institute's congresses, noted, in administrative matters, the main decision-maker is history.

With regard to science and research, one of the principal objectives of the institute is the development of comparative administration. It is particularly well placed to make comparison possible or to develop comparison between the different authorities of its member states and even of other states, irrespective of their region, their language, and system of government. Another major objective consists of what is referred to in the statutes as "the progress of international administration." In fact, since the start of the century, we have witnessed the development of international organizations, each of which has its own administration, bureaucracy, and problems relative to its structure or its regulations concerning civil servants, for example.

Our task is specified in Article 5a of the statutes. The institute, in order to achieve the purpose above, shall "study, taking into account the experience of the various countries, the means of action at the disposal of administrative authorities for performing their duties under the best conditions. Its field of interest shall include the teaching of the administrative sciences, the pre-entry and post-entry training of officials, the rationalisation of work, the mechanisation of offices, and the application of scientific discoveries to administration." It can be seen that looming behind these expressions are all the questions of innovation and of technological progress that have drastically unsettled public services for a certain number of years now, such as computerization, telecommunications, or information highways.

Another aim of the institute, formally expressed in the statutes, is the development of administrative cooperation between all countries and, in particular, the assistance that can be given to the developing countries or countries in transition—in practical terms, to the countries of the South as well as to the Eastern European countries. As far as the first group is concerned, cooperation started in the early 1960s at the time when many states were gaining independence and needed to be equipped with a modern, efficient administration, but whose means were minimal. For the Eastern European countries, which abandoned a system of complete socialization and have recently turned to a market economy and the law-based state, they have needed to reorganize their administration completely.

Another objective of the institute is to collect the necessary documents for carrying out the above tasks, and for replying for requests for information concerning the matters within its field of study.

To accomplish its tasks, the institute must bring together researchers, professors, and academics, on the one hand, but also practitioners, higher civil servants, and magistrates in public service, on the other. It must combine a theoretical approach and a practical approach, and it is in that combination that both its originality and the reason for its effectiveness can be found. There are not many places either at the national level and even more so at the international level, where theoreticians and practitioners can come together in this way to compare their views and their experiences. This initial balance between theory and practice is one of the conditions for the success of the institute, which is also very much committed to two other kinds of balance: between the North and the South, or between the developed and developing countries; and between the main disciplines, which are law and management, both of which also affect administration. It has always taken care not to have either a purely legal approach to the administrative phenomenon or to have an approach that excludes the law, which is an important pillar of public administration.

Activities

The institute's tasks are carried out through a certain number of activities, which should now be analyzed. The institute's activities can be classified in four main categories:

Meetings

As has been seen, the institute originated from a series of congresses. It has continued to organize such congresses and also other meetings of greater or lesser importance and frequency. Such meetings are both occasions for exchanges and discussions between representatives from different countries or from different international organizations and also tools for joint research on specific topics. In this respect, a distinction can be made between major meetings and restricted meetings. Major meetings are currently held at least once a year. They are international, even if their importance varies. The main category consists of congresses, which take place every three years. These are characterized both by the fact that they are open to all persons interested in the administrative sciences (no matter the reason) and that they are the occasion for statutory meetings during which the governing bodies of the institute are elected or appointed. They are thus large, universal administrative science forums and gatherings at which the executive bodies of the institute may meet.

These congresses are held in increasingly varied regions. At the beginning—during the interwar period and after World War II—they generally took place in countries of Western Europe. They are now held in all regions of the world. To take only recent examples, the 1992 congress took place in Vienna; in 1995, the congress was held in Dubai. Others were held in the Ivory Coast or in Mexico, for example. Between 600 and 1,000 people attend the congresses.

Two other annual meetings are held in the interval between two congresses. These are qualified as round tables or international conferences, or yet again symposiums or seminars. Here, too, the geographical diversity of the venues is characteristic. To take recent examples, the 1993 International Conference was held in Toluca (Mexico), the 1994 Round Table in Helsinki (Finland), and the conferences of 1996 and 1997 took place in Beijing and Quebec, respectively.

In the course of these meetings, more or less broad themes of interest to all the participants and directly relating to current events are examined. Recent examples would include the 1993 Toluca meeting devoted to "Redefining the State Profile for Social and Economic Development and Change." The Helsinki meeting in 1994 was concerned with "The State, the Market, and Development: Regulation or Deregulation." Finally, the conference held in Dubai in 1995 was devoted to "Administration and Society: The Administrative Response to Globalization and Sociocultural change." From these few examples, it may be seen that the institute devotes its major meetings to broad themes that do not concentrate solely on public administration in the narrow sense, but underline the relationship of public administration with developments in society and the world. These general themes provide an opportunity for broaching more precise subtopics, which, for example, concern regulation, decentralization, citizen participation in government, or the administrative management of major cities.

These meetings require serious scientific preparation carried out by the directorate general of the institute with the participation of a general rapporteur and particular rapporteurs. Papers are proposed and submitted to a selection procedure to ensure both the quality of their content and the homogeneity of discussions.

The more restricted meetings are of variable size. These are sometimes simple bilateral meetings between two member states of the institute or two national sections focusing on a particular subject. For example, in 1994 the French National Section held such meetings with the German National Section on the one hand and with the Chinese National Section on the other. There are sometimes regional meetings and amongst them it is, of course, necessary to mention the annual symposiums of the European Group of Public Administration, which are attended by 150 to 200 persons each time. Numerous still are the more restricted meetings of 5, 10, or 15 persons of the working groups and study groups set up by the institute on particular subjects. These groups are one of the essential pillars of the scientific policy of the institute, which organizes and supports them as well as ensures that they meet at regular intervals.

It thus becomes evident that the aim of these meetings is not simply a comparison of ideas and opinions. They result in the progress of the administrative sciences and are one of the instruments that promote the scientific activities of the institute.

Work, Research, and Publications

The Institute's scientific policy has developed considerably in the course of recent years. Research Committees are currently seven in number. Their chairs have a seat on the executive committee of the institute. These committees are concerned with the major themes of administrative sciences, such as law, civil service, history, international administration, or public finance. Each committee manages and promotes a certain number of research groups, which are frequently renewed as, in principle, their activity is limited to three years. These groups focus, for example, on human rights, government, public sector productivity, and the training of civil servants. Their work generally results in a report, which, when of sufficient quality, is published in the two working languages of the institute—French and English. Also with the passing of the years, the institute has set up a library of considerable specialization, which has, moreover, been supported or facilitated by the Institute. Many volumes have been published either by the Institute or by other publishers but always, in principle, with a reference to the role played by the institute in the preparation of their work. There are always 10 to 15 groups of this kind, which, depending on the period and subject, are more or less active and productive but whose work must be monitored by the chairs of the research committees; also the publication of their work has recently been placed under the control of the institute's director of publications.

These publications are not limited to the studies and reports of the working groups. The minutes of the major meetings (which always form the subject of a volume) must be added, as also the *International Review of Administrative Sciences*. This Review is a quarterly and is published simultaneously in the two working languages of the institute. It endeavors to reflect both the activities of the institute and the general trends of administrative research worldwide, notably by ensuring, like the institute, a balance between the industrial and the developing countries, and also between the problems of administrative law and those of public management. The Review is today considered to be one of the best periodicals of the administrative sciences and comparative administration, and the readers it attracts are growing in number. In addition to the original articles it publishes, it includes information columns and an important bibliography by which readers may be kept abreast of the main publications on administrative sciences worldwide.

Scientific activities are also carried out in the context of the institute's specialized organizations, for example, the International Association of Schools and Institutes of Public Administration directs about 10 research groups and the European Group of Public Administration about half that number. There are therefore about 30 groups operating at the same time. Steps have been taken to avoid overlapping and to harmonize the scientific policies of the three institutions. Joint groups comprising members of both the institute and the Association of Schools and Institutes also exist. These specialized organizations also carry out their scientific activity within the framework of their annual meetings, and they publish their proceedings. The projects of research groups are also published insofar as possible.

Library and Documentation

From the beginning, the founders of the institute intended to collect international documentation at its headquarters. This objective is expressed in Article 6c of its statutes, as follows: "The Institute shall: establish an information and documentation centre, a library and records, to be made available to members of the Institute, scholars, officials, persons interested in politics, students and interns under conditions determined by the Executive Committee." That library exists. It did, unfortunately, disappear during the war, but was reconstructed immediately afterward. Currently, it includes approximately 15,000 volumes and 200 reviews, which come from many countries in varied and numerous languages. It is without doubt the best collection worldwide of publications relative to the administrative sciences coming from different regions. It is therefore an incomparable working tool.

The library is not sufficiently used, unfortunately, partly because it is not well known and partly because the institute's resources restrain the development of this activity. It is certain, however, that it would be very useful to set up a documentary network around the library and to put in at the disposal of researchers and civil servants throughout the world. It must be added that the institute's documentation includes a large portion of "gray literature," notably a certain number of reports of conferences or of symposiums or administrative documents that have not been published, without being secret/confidential. This "gray literature" is now being more fully developed so that researchers can benefit from it.

Consultancy and Cooperation

This is a new activity the institute has been developing for some years. The institute can play the part of consultant to international organizations or to countries seeking to have their administration make progress. It can also take up a role of initiator of projects and studies, which includes assisting countries to equip themselves with modern administration by adopting the laws/legislation or methods necessary for that purpose. This activity may be carried out either directly by the institute or on behalf of international or regional organizations such as the European Community, for example, or yet again the World Bank. This activity may be more fully developed in the future, particularly in liaison with the major organizations such as the United Nations and UNESCO. The institute also has the task of promoting national or regional initiatives within its field.

These various activities are being carried out increasingly in partnership either with international, governmental organizations or with other associations of a regional nature acting within the same sector. Agreements or contracts are drawn up and concluded for this purpose.

Structures and Statutes

The structure of the institute is complex. Although, legally, it is a nongovernmental organization, it does include member states, which are voluntary members and which have a seat on the council of administration. But it also includes national sections, which are generally associations either set up specially for that purpose or which have other objectives in their country. These, for example, are institutes of public administration or other agencies of the same kind. When a national section has no purpose other than to be the representative of the International Institute within its country, it is generally set up as an independent association with a chairman, vice chairman, a board and members. Sometimes a country belongs to the institute both as a member state and having a national section. Corporate members are

also included; these are institutions that adhere directly to the institute. Individual members from countries where there is no national section are also admitted.

Member states and national sections have a seat on the council of administration, as do the international organization members of the institute. In fact, in 1980 the Institute, as a consequence of internationalization and the development of international organizations, allowed these latter to join it directly. It was, indeed, in this way that the European Community became a member of the institute, whereas other international institutions such as the World Bank or the OECD became corporate members. The institute is no longer based, as in the beginning, solely on the nation states that reigned in the interwar years. Now and in the future, international organizations of a regional or universal vocation are being added to those nation states that are still present and always in the majority within the institute.

In total, the institute counts among its members approximately 50 member states and 50 national sections. Certain countries, such as France, Germany, or Japan, have a dual status; in this case, it is the state that pays the largest contribution, with the national section paying only symbolic subscription fees. In other cases, only the country is a member state, or it has only a national section.

The member states, the national sections, and the member governmental international organizations each have a seat on the council of administration, which meets twice every three years; one of those meetings is held during a congress to elect the executive committee of the institute. The members of the executive committee include the president of the institute, the vice presidents (a vice president representing the host country and seven regional vice presidents for Western Europe, Eastern Europe, the Middle East, Africa, Latin America, North America, Asia, and the Pacific), seven members, the chairmen of the permanent research committees, which are also seven in number, the presidents of the specialized associations, such as the International Association of Schools and Institutes of Administration and the International Association of Information and Documentation in Public Administration, and also, but in an advisory capacity only, the president of the European Group of Public Administration.

The council of administration endeavors to ensure a certain balance, both geo-political and intellectual, within the executive committee. The members of the executive committee are chosen on the basis of their personality, competence, and renown in the framework of such balances. The members of the executive committee may be reelected to the same post only once and cannot carry out three terms of office for more than a total of nine years. In this respect, an attempt has been made to ensure regular renewal and infusion of young blood in the executive body of the institute. In addition, the president is elected, like the other members, for three years and may not be reelected immediately; the president simply remains on the executive committee for another three years as the retiring president.

The executive committee is responsible for the management and monitoring of the affairs of the institute. It prepares the budget, receives reports, and also ensures the liaison with the different national sections and member states. It has responsibility for management of the Review, publications, and documentation.

The president plays an important role in the formation of the institute's policy, the monitoring of it, and external relations. The president presides over the main statutory bodies such as the Council of Administration, the executive committee, and the research advisory council. The most recent presidents of the institute have come from Germany, Saudi Arabia, the United States, and France. The International Institute of Administrative Sciences also has permanent administrative services, which are set up in Brussels and placed under the authority of a director general. The present incumbent is a woman of African origin, Mrs. Turkia Ould Daddah. Such a choice, irrespective of her personal qualities, is doubly symbolic.

The director general, who must be both an excellent manager and an expert in administrative services, is assisted by a very small number of staff, a dozen or so in all, one half of whom are graduate management staff and the other half office personnel. The effectiveness of this small and exemplary nonbureaucratic team must be stressed. This extremely small team manages to operate the institute with all its major or restricted meetings, its documentation, publications, contracts, and cooperation activities. It is not possible to increase the number of staff significantly, even if the institute's finances permitted this at present, because, as in any nongovernmental organization, its finances are fragile. In fact, they are dependent on the goodwill of the member states and national sections. Indeed, if only one large contribution were to remain unpaid during the course of a year, this would suffice to unbalance the budget.

The Membership of the Institute

The most characteristic and important recent development concerns the geographical extension of the institute during the last ten years. In the beginning, the institute was essentially European; it then developed in certain American countries. Today, it is truly worldwide. It still includes European countries, which are generally member states having a national section; these include, in particular, Germany, Belgium, France, Italy, and Sweden. Beyond Europe, the United States have been an active member of the institute for a long time but, apparently for constitutional reasons, which prevent the United States government from belonging to any nongovernmental organization, they have only a national section, which is notably a federation of organizations or authorities interested in the activities of the institute. One major event was Canada's membership both as a member state and as a national section in 1980. Major new memberships have been recorded since then, in particular that of China in 1988, which thus joined a certain number of Asiatic countries, including Japan, which has been a long-time member of the institute. The institute is also widely represented in North Africa, in Black Africa, and in the Middle East. It is somewhat weaker today in Latin America, with the exception of Mexico, which remains very active, and in Eastern Europe, where some countries are starting to join the institute following their recent political transformation.

This internationalization of the institute is enhanced by the fact that major international organizations have been members of it for about 15 years, either as full members, such as the European Economic Commission, or as corporate members, such as the OECD and the World Bank. In addition, the institute's relations with UNESCO and the United Nations, which have always been active, have been greatly strengthened during recent years. The institute takes place in various UNESCO activities and, through funds allocated, UNESCO helps support the institute's activities. The same applies to the United Nations: relations have always been maintained and may be further developed within the framework of preparations for a future world conference on public administration.

The specialized associations widen still more the circle of people or countries connected with the institute. For example, the International Association of Schools and Institutes of Public Administration includes approximately 170 participating institutions belonging to 70 countries, and the European Group of Public Administration has about 300 individuals members.

Conclusions

The International Institute of Administrative Sciences, which was set up at the beginning of the twentieth century thus appears at the dawn of the twenty-first century to be an institute that is genuinely international; indeed, the only one in a position to study the broad scope of public administration problems on a planetary basis. Regional or thematic organizations do, of course, exist. They are generally in contact with the institute, but the institute remains the sole organization with a global vocation able and prepared to carry out comparative administration on a worldwide scale.

In a world in which administration is increasingly developing and becoming a greater factor in development, on the one hand, and in which states and peoples are becoming more numerous, on the other, it is important to have this tool at the disposal of the world community, notably to improve both the knowledge and practices of public administration.

GUY BRAIBANT

INTERNATIONAL INTELLIGENCE. National
government information gathering, analysis and covert
action to influence external developments and to deal with
such endeavors by foreigners targeted on one's own
country and its public and private organizations.

History

International intelligence is as old as the existence of politically organized groups with a defined territory whose interests are affected by developments outside their borders.
Types of activities involved have long included the collection and analysis of information and covert operations to
influence and disrupt foreigners. Since no country or
group has a monopoly on these instruments of statecraft,
pertinent activities also include counterintelligence to degrade the intelligence activities of others. International intelligence has long been the province of specialized organizations of the state and of interest to the highest political
authorities.

Historically, international intelligence was thought of
as a matter of spies and agents amateur and professional.
For the present and future, the technological element is at
least as important in two ways. First, heightened priority
goes to collecting information about the military and civil
technology of foreigners. Second, developments since
World War II have led to an age of transparency across and
within national borders. Of particular importance are technologies for (1) remote sensing from outside of national
territory of military and economic phenomena (e.g.,
nuclear weapons activity, food crop yields); (2) signals collection of communications, data flows, and electronic
signs of activity; and (3) computerized exploitation of large
masses of observations to determine their content and implications. Information collection and analysis have gone
high-tech for the industrially large and advanced nations,
and the means involved are diffusing rapidly to others.

Conceptual Framework

The priority states give to pertinent activities follows from
(1) the importance of external developments to national
interests military and economic; (2) the extent to which
other instruments of power are enhanced by information
about the current and prospective capabilities and intentions of others; (3) the presence of factors that make clandestine activity more attractive to governments and political leaders than openly acknowledged or readily attributed
courses of action; and (4) the perception that currently or
potentially hostile or competitive foreign entities (governments, movements, firms) are committed to vigorous intelligence programs.

As these factors suggest, international intelligence
matters as nations and groups affect one another's future.

Demand increases then as military conflicts are imminent
or under way, as international economic activity becomes
more important, and as groups with shared political aspirations are spread across national borders. The value of international intelligence increases whether the interdependence involved argues for conflict or cooperation.

Demand also increases as states and movements can
gain leverage and a power multiplier through information—when tangible assets alone are not enough to determine outcomes. As weapons or economic resources are effective because they are used in clever and timely ways,
states and their leaders are driven to securing the information international intelligence can provide about others
and to denying an "information edge" to others. Restraint
in the face of vigorous activity by others comes to seem unwarranted, naive, and irresponsible. Indeed, the importance of information about others only seems to increase
when a government has invested heavily in military assets
that depend on being used in a time-limited window of opportunity, or on economic and technological advantages
that can dissipate quickly. The chances of rapid change that
is hard to reverse magnifies the value of anticipatory information about what others can do, are inclined to do, and
the basis on which they will act in particular ways.

The tendency of states and their leaders to rely on secretive organizations and activities to become informed
about and to influence others largely follows from domestic politics. For their own polity, reliance flourishes
when political elites have difficulty mobilizing support
for open measures from nonintelligence organizations
and mass publics (e.g., the Iran-Contra controversy in the
United States). With respect to foreign targets, secretive
activity gains attractiveness against closed societies or
those likely to react in a hostile fashion to more visible
and less deniable means (for example, American CIA subsidies to one competing political party in allied countries,
or British efforts to pull the United States into World
Wars I and II).

Public Management Issues

The secretive aspect of relevant government organizations
and practices has long created serious issues of control and
accountability. These occur within intelligence organizations themselves, especially between operations and analysis units, and between independent intelligence organizations within a national government. They occur between
intelligence organizations and other parts of government
(executive and legislative). They occur between governments and the public. Attempts by political leaders to
maintain control through segmentation lead to turf battles
(e.g., between the United States CIA and FBI over counterintelligence as shown by the Ames affair), which can adversely affect performance. Lack of control can lead to a

state within a state with resulting erosion of the authority of political leaders. These problems are chronic and recurrent. The cult of secrecy in order to preserve methods and sources impedes performance evaluation–the same organization is defendant, judge, and jury. The consequences impede organizational learning and obstruct reasoned independent judgment about the merits of increased or reduced budgets or personnel for intelligence purposes (indeed, the current and historical budgets are themselves usually state secrets). "Clandestinity" also degrades independent assessments of the value of collection technology, human agents, and analytic work.

Regardless of how they are handled, several policy issues will repeatedly arise entangled with organizational conflicts of interest. Priority battles over overt versus covert information collection pit admitted foreign policy instruments of observation (e.g., diplomats and military attachés) against secret services. The emphasis on collection and analysis of open source information must be weighed relative to that for other sources (human and technological). The benefits of keeping foreigners in the dark about their transparency must be weighed against the benefits of sharing and thus using the information a government has collected about foreigners with its own bureaus, firms, and citizens. The benefits of internal secrecy to deny foreigners information about one's national situation must be weighed against the economic, social, and political costs of denying that information to one's own government units, firms, and citizens that could benefit from it. Modern technologies of information collection, analysis, and dissemination only worsen these dilemmas.

Ostensible international intelligence advantages can often be secured and maintained only at the price of barriers to the adaptive actions that motivated international intelligence and counterintelligence efforts in the first place.

DAVIS B. BOBROW

BIBLIOGRAPHY

Blackstock, Paul W., 1966. *Agents of Deceit: Frauds, Forgeries, and Political Intrigue Among Nations.* Chicago: Quadrangle Books.
Jones, R. V., 1978. *The Wizard War: British Scientific Intelligence, 1939–1945.* New York: Coward, McCann & Geoghean.
Kipling, Rudyard, 1912. *Kim.* Garden City, NY: Doubleday, Page.
Richelson, Jeffrey, 1988. *Foreign Intelligence Organizations.* Cambridge, MA: Ballinger.
Richelson, Jeffrey, 1989. *The U.S. Intelligence Community.* Cambridge, MA: Ballinger.
Wark, Wesley K., 1993. "The Intelligence Revolution and the Future." *Queen's Quarterly,* vol. 100 (Summer) 273–287.

INTERORGANIZATIONAL COLLABORATION.

A process in which organizations with a stake in a problem seek a mutually determined solution by which they seek to accomplish objectives they could not achieve working alone.

Interorganizational collaboration has grown out of the fields of organization theory and development, on the one hand, and operations research, on the other, into a vital, productive, frustrating, but increasingly popular form of problem solving. Its growing use–in the lexicon and practices of organizations–indicates the complex and intractable nature of problems that face society today and the responding realization by many organizations that they cannot solve them alone. A willingness to join in collaborative efforts suggests that organizations are overcoming their tendencies to seek independent solutions, which often lack the breadth and comprehensiveness of application and effect. Yet, a multitude of studies suggests that collaborative efforts often fail for reasons that range from difficulties in establishing, facilitating, and maintaining interorganizational relations to problems that relate to the nature of the problem or conflict that caused collaborative formation in the first place.

Theoretical Framework

Collaboration is an emergent interorganizational arrangement through which organizations collectively cope with the complex nature of the work around them. In her book *Collaborating,* Barbara Gray (1989) explains that collaboration is an emergent process rather than a prescribed state of organization. The collaboration process organizes a previously unconnected set of stakeholders to address common problems. In one of the few book-length treatments of the topic, Gray develops a theory of collaboration with roots in negotiated order theory. She contends that increasing environmental turbulence (Emery and Trist 1965) demands that organizations seek collectively devised strategies. In response to the growing complexity of their environments, organizations can collectively negotiate agreements to govern their interactions. Through collaboration, those organizations that have a stake in outcomes or solutions to their common problem are able to exchange information, plan to utilize that information in a strategically advantageous way, and apply mutually concocted approaches to the defined problem(s).

A need for creating a theory of interorganizational behavior suggests that individual organizational strategies may prove ineffective when confronted with rapid external change, complex interactions among organizations comprising the environment, and those among the organizational members and their individual representatives in a potential collaborative arrangement. Individual organizations lack the variety of responses necessary to match the increased number and complexity of the potential threats and opportunities that confront them.

Development and Application of Interorganizational Collaboration

Collaboration has been widely used in Europe and North America as an alternative means of confronting and solving complex problems. Likewise, collaboration as a strategy of resolving conflict or furthering shared vision has been employed on an international, national, regional, and small jurisdiction scale. It has been used in the private, public, and nonprofit sectors. Importantly, it has enjoyed success in bridging traditional boundaries and facilitating multisectoral approaches.

An important and sustained strain of research and writing on interorganizational collaboration is found in the United Kingdom. With roots in operational research and management theory, researchers/facilitators have developed or extended sophisticated models of computer-based group decision support systems. An example is strategic options development and analysis (SODA), which sees strategic management in terms of changing thinking and action rather than planning. Developed by Colin Eden and his associates at the University of Strathclyde, Scotland, SODA is built from theories and practice about small groups and uses aggregate cognitive mapping as a methodology to facilitate negotiation about values and goal systems and key issues as they relate to group decision making. An excellent introduction to the various strategies developed by Eden and his associates is *Tackling Strategic Problems,* a collection of articles edited by Eden and Jim Radford (1990).

This so-called softer side of operations research melds nicely with facilitative methodologies and action research born in the applied behavioral science movement of the researchers at the Tavistock Institute such as Eric Trist and leading theorists in the United States such as Kurt Lewin, Rensis Likert, and Chris Argyris. Extensive cross-fertilization between the United States and UK schools occurred in the 1950s and 1960s. The sharing of research that concentrates on both the process and content of collaboration continues today among practitioners and academicians on both sides of the Atlantic. Of concern as well are the obstacles that collaborative efforts face. Unilateral, competitive approaches as expressions of individualism and traditional organizational strategy appear to know no cultural boundaries.

In the broadest sense, collaboration is a strategy that can be applied to situations in which organizations are in conflict or in which they share a common vision. In the former case, a mediator helps the conflicting parties work out their differences and construct a mutually acceptable solution. A myriad of examples of conflict resolution exist at all levels and sectors of society. For example, negotiations over

environmental quality, land use, management and labor disagreements, and international boundaries and treaties are but a few. In the latter case, a third-party facilitator helps cooperating organizations establish a membership, an agenda, a definition of the problem or task, and the specific strategies to be undertaken by the collaborative. Each approach is important and deserving of explanation. The former however, is better depicted as conflict resolution or dispute management, a growing field of endeavor in itself. The latter, where organizations start out with and seek to advance a shared vision, has come to be thought of more universally as collaboration. The remainder of this entry will concentrate on this latter interpretation.

Distinguishing Collaboration from Other Change Strategies

In common usage, the word "collaboration" has been used interchangeably with coalition building and partnerships. These are generally accurate depictions, especially as the terms imply a formalized exchange of power. Of more concern is the interchangeable use of words such as networking, coordination, and cooperation. Arthur Himmelman (1992), in his provocative monograph entitled *Communities Working Collaboratively for a Change,* carefully distinguishes between these change strategies. He positions networking at the less complex end of a continuum and defines it as "exchanging information for mutual benefit" (p. 23). Networking is an interorganizational change strategy, albeit an informal one, which tends to work best where trust building and initial commitment among organizations is important. Coordination adds "altering activities" to exchanging information as group activities and implies this activity is designed so as to achieve a common purpose. Coordination requires more organization involvement. Moving toward the more complex end of the continuum, cooperation adds the "sharing of resources" to the list of activities related to networking and coordination. Finally, collaboration is defined as "exchanging information, altering activities, sharing resources, and enhancing the capacity of another for mutual benefit and to achieve a common purpose" (Himmelman 1992, p. 23). Hence, collaboration is distinguished from lesser forms of interorganizational relations as it involves the sharing of risks, responsibilities, and rewards.

It is useful, as well, to distinguish interorganizational collaboration from the widely researched and practiced change strategy called organization development (OD), or planned organizational change. Organization development is a change strategy designed to improve an organization's problem-solving and renewal processes. Since OD works within one organization, the change agent is confronted with well-established, overorganized systems with an identifiable culture. In contrast, facilitators of collaboration are dealing with underorganized systems. They begin from scratch and must work at increasing shared norms and values and establishing reliable, predictable structures, roles, and technologies (Brown 1980). This comparison is not meant to diminish the value of OD but to point out that collaborative formation must deal with a more complex set of political relations, power distribution, and potential conflicts of interest. Unless most of the stakeholders perceive benefit to be gained from being involved in a collaborative structure, they likely will not participate. Participating in a collaborative means giving up some power. Stakeholders individually weigh that cost against the benefits to be gained, at least as best they can predict them. The ultimate strength and success of the collaborative depends upon the collection of organizations acting together, yet the rewards actually accrue to the individual agencies. In situations in which some target population is the intended benefactor of the collaboration—for example, poor people, endangered animal species—the rewards may be extended. However, since predicting outcomes of collaborative formation is problematic, participating stakeholders forge on, often as an article of faith with hopes for positive outcomes. The growing realization that problems confronting society today often defy solution by organizations acting singly may somewhat reduce that risk or at least increase the likelihood that organizations in all sectors—public, private, and nonprofit—will seek collaborative partners.

Process and Substance Issues

By the decade of the 1990s, interorganizational collaboration had become a vital and permanent thread in both theoretical and practical organizational cloth. Collaboration represents the action extension of more static discussions of organization-sets, coalitional networks, and action-sets that marked research in earlier decades. In this mode, collaboration became a comfortable intellectual home for both organizational theorists and facilitators. An interesting combination of these two tracks is represented in the work of Chris Huxham and associates in Scotland. Huxham (1993) has advanced the concept of "collaborative advantage," which was designed to capture the idea that it is possible to achieve desirable outcomes through collaboration that could not be achieved by any single organization acting alone. If this realization is achieved, organizational stakeholders should become aware of two alterations in the way they approach accomplishing their missions. First, the goals and objectives of the collaborative are more highly organized beyond those of any one participant. Huxham terms these "meta-strategies," which can be accomplished only through collaborative advantage. Second, facilitators who help form collaboratives must realize that traditional methods of intervention, practiced on one organization, likely will not work in a multiorganizational setting.

Typical facilitation has focused on process issues, in which the facilitator helps members in a group consider how they work together as a team. A growing practice enlarges the facilitators role to a focus on substance as well. Here the facilitator helps stakeholders explore the nature of their objectives as well as how to achieve them. Shifting from a process to a substance focus challenges the traditional roles of the facilitator because it demands an awareness and familiarity with the metastrategy of the collaborative. Such knowledge suggests that one of the stakeholders, rather than an outside consultant, may be best suited to facilitate the formation and development of the collaborative. The task of this role is that a stakeholder with much to gain or lose from outcomes of collaborative action may exert undue power and influence on the behavior of the collaborative. Inherently, this may not be a disadvantage for the group, but member organizations should be aware of the altered dynamics. A comprehensive approach to facilitation may suggest a valuable link between the two foci of process and substance. Appropriate processes of collaborative development may be informed by a thorough airing of organizational thinking about metastrategy.

The Nature of the Collaborative Process

Various researchers/practitioners have prescribed processes of accomplishing collaborative advantage. Their work may be found in a volume entitled *The Search for Collaborative Advantage,* edited by Huxham (1995). A fairly standard checklist derives from their work, which emphasizes three general stages of action. First is the problem-setting stage in which stakeholders identify the problem, its causes, and the changes that need to occur. They then identify and recruit the stakeholders. Second, collaborative participants involve themselves in direction-setting in which they agree on a metastrategy, determine actions to be taken, and develop a collective will to act. Third, the collaborative structure itself monitors and evaluates its activities and attempts to sustain itself, where appropriate. Although these stages suggest a linear process, the inexact art and craft of collaborative formation most often requires repeating or redirecting several of these major process tasks. Evidence indicates that sustaining and adjusting a collaborative effort are difficult phases to accomplish.

The Nature of Collaborative Substance

The purposes for which collaboratives are formed are numerous, but may be grouped in a manageable typology so as to reflect their robustness. Seven types are social problem-solving, agenda-building, enabling, service-providing, advocative, empowerment, and betterment. The last two relate particularly to the redistribution of power and, as such, are not mutually exclusive of the others.

Social problem-solving frequently requires metastrategy in that addressing such broad, entangled issues requires multi-organizational approaches. Social problems are inherently difficult to solve due to their unbounded nature and resistance to quick fixes (McCann 1983). Agenda-setting is a purposive planned-change strategy in which collaborative attempts to provoke some external agency or government with its own power resources to act on their issues or set of issues. Enabling, like agenda-setting, seeks assistance from outside the collaborative, but imparts power, authority, and/or resources to those outside agents. Service-providing or functional collaboratives come together to integrate resources and expertise in order to improve a system of service delivery. Advocative or normative collaboratives are formed to promote norms and values through a joint lobbying or education effort.

Collaborative empowerment and collaborative betterment are intriguing methods of community change described by Himmelman (1992). Unlike some efforts, which are shaped after the collaborative is convened, these forms describe purposive approaches to power and ownership in the collaborative process. Betterment begins outside the community within various institutions and is brought into the community. Community involvement is invited into a process designed and controlled by larger institutions. This strategy can produce policy changes and improvements in program delivery and services but tends not to produce long-term ownership in communities or to increase significantly communities' control over their own destinies (Himmelman 1992). This approach, while a necessity in highly unorganized settings, might be termed doing collaboration to the target population.

Conversely, collaborative empowerment begins within the community and is brought to public, private, and nonprofit institutions. Community stakeholders are empowered because they have the capacity to set priorities and control resources that are essential for increasing community self-determination. The empowerment approach can produce policy changes and improvements in program delivery and services. It is also more likely to produce long-term ownership of the collaborative's purpose, processes, and products in communities and to enhance communities' capacity for self-determination (Himmelman 1992). Empowerment might be termed doing collaboration with the target community.

Obstacles to Successful Collaboration

Despite a growing advocacy of collaboration and a realization on the part of many organizations that such extraorganizational arrangements are the only means of dealing with metaproblems, obstacles remain. Nine are articulated here under three categories: cultural norms and values, institutional rigidities, and power issues.

Cultural Obstacles

The persistent normative inclination, found most notably in the United States, of individualism discourages community approaches to problem-solving. Second, the traditional or dominant paradigm that governs the behaviors of many organizations is founded on social Darwinism and stresses more of a competitive environment. Third, a resistance to change, based on uncertainty, insecurity, and love of the status quo, prevents breaking the traditional mold.

Institutional Rigidities

Certain intraorganizational characteristics mitigate against collaboration. Organizational purpose, derived from internal negotiation and planning, may prevent an organization from collaborating, even if it is a legitimate stakeholder. There can exist a great discrepancy between organizational representatives who work well and agree with the work of a collaborative and their institutional leaders who do not perceive collaborative participation in the best interests of the organization. Second, many organizations are structured so as to discourage risk taking. This appears to be particularly true among public, bureaucratic organizations. Third, limited resources ironically discourage reaching out for help. Whatever benefits may accrue for collaborative formation are outweighed by a perceived loss of autonomy.

Power Issues

Potential collaborative partners may have a long history of adversarial relations that are too great to overcome. Second, some stakeholders are concerned about retaining an institutional power base, especially when competitive entities are at the table. Finally, extreme power differentials between otherwise copacetic stakeholders may discourage participation by either party.

As has been argued by most students of interorganizational collaboration, facilitating this inventive and dynamic form of partnership requires persistence and perserverence. Process and substance skills are necessary. Overcoming the natural tendency to rely on traditional methods of operation, which favor single-organization action, is problematic but critical to a realistic tackling of the problems facing society.

DAVID W. SINK

BIBLIOGRAPHY

Brown, L. David, 1980. "Planned Change in Underorganized Systems." In T. G. Cummings, ed., *Systems Theory for Organizational Development.* New York: Wiley.

Cummings, T. G., 1984. "Transorganizational Development." In B. Staw and L. Cummings, eds., *Research in Organizational Behavior,* vol. 6. Greenwich, CT: JAI Press.

Eden, Colin, and Jim Radford., eds., 1990. *Tackling Strategic Problems: The Role of Group Decision Support.* London: Sage.

Emery, Fred E. and Eric L. Trist, 1965. "The Causal Texture of Organizational Environments." *Human Relations,* vol. 18: 21–32.

Gray, Barbara, 1985. "Conditions Facilitating Interorganizational Collaboration." *Human Relations,* vol. 38, no. 10: 911–936.

———, 1989. *Collaborating: Finding Common Ground for Multiparty Problems.* San Francisco: Jossey-Bass.

Himmelman, Arthur Turovh, 1992. *Communities Working Collaboratively for a Change.* Minneapolis: Himmelman Consulting Group.

Huxham, Chris, 1993. "Collaborative Capability: An Intra-organizational Perspective on Collaborative Advantage." *Public Money and Management,* vol. 12 (July/Sept) 21–28.

Huxham, Chris, ed., 1995. *The Search for Collaborative Advantage.* London: Sage.

McCann, Joseph E., 1983. "Design Guidelines for Social Problem-Solving Interventions." *Journal of Applied Behavioral Science,* vol. 19: 177–189.

INTERORGANIZATIONAL COLLABORATION IN THE NONPROFIT SECTOR.

The extent to which contemporary nonprofit organizations cooperate, coordinate, collaborate, and form partnerships with other organizations. Major funders wish to see greater rationalization of delivery systems; client groups want smoother integration between the various agencies they deal with; and managers see collaborative efforts as potential ways to achieve synergy for raising money or making more effective use of increasingly limited resources.

One of the problems with the dialogue surrounding this trend is that it is not always clear what the participants mean by the terms they use. This article will attempt to clarify the concept of collaboration by arguing that there is no one definition of the term but rather a typology of forms of collaboration. This typology is based on the model of interorganizational interaction in the nonprofit world created by Alter and Hage (1993). The typology is followed by a brief overview of the hypotheses provided in the literature on the variables affecting the probability that any type of collaborative effort will come to fruition and be sustained.

Though there is a considerable body of literature dealing with cooperative interorganizational relationships (see Ring and Van de Ven 1994, for a recent discussion of much of it), it is almost entirely focused on the world of business. Studies that concentrate on nonprofit organizations are comparatively few (e.g., Alter and Hage 1993; D'Aunno and Zuckerman 1987; Galaskiewicz and Shatin 1981; Gray 1985, 1986, 1989; Hord 1986; Mattessich and Monsey 1992). However, with the exception of the work of the Wilder Foundation (Mattessich and Monsey 1992), they tend not to attempt generalizations about the special problems of collaboration in the sector per se. And yet there is a good possibility that certain characteristics of the sector might well have a bearing on the nature and extent of interorganizational relations in it. Some of these will be noted in the following discussion.

A Taxonomy of Forms of Collaboration in the Nonprofit Sector

The simplest variable on which to commence building a typology for understanding the different forms of collaboration is that of the degree of interdependence between the parties. At one end of the continuum in interdependence is the simple one-time transaction in which organization A exchanges something with organization B. At the other end is the full legal merger of two organizations. For practical purposes, the following basic five types of collaboration can be identified.

1. *Collaboration that involves only the sharing of information or the coordination of services.* For example, all agencies providing services for seniors in a given community making sure that each knows what the others do and that clients get passed from one to another smoothly and appropriately.

2. *Joint efforts at community planning, advocacy, public education, or fund-raising.* For example, multiorganizational meetings to develop and plan "better beginnings" for children from deprived backgrounds; an antismoking campaign jointly sponsored by the heart and cancer organizations; a group of environmental organizations collaborating to raise money from the corporate sector. Such efforts do not usually require change in the core services of the organization.

3. *Joint delivery of programs using "new" money.* For example, a new program for language and life skills training for recent immigrants jointly provided by an educational and an immigrant aid organization using special money offered by a government department. In this situation, a joint venture occurs but no sacrifice of existing resources is required; in fact, new resources are acquired. However, core services may be affected.

4. *Rationalization of existing services.* This involves diverting funds from existing programs to newly created joint endeavors with other organizations or sharing resources such as space, equipment, or staff for greater efficiency. The rationale can be either to improve service quality and quantity or simply to cut costs. This, too, is a joint activity like type (3); however, to support it requires at least one of the organizations to divert resources from existing uses.

5. *Full partnerships and mergers.* This is the ultimate collaborative activity in which whole organizations legally come together, merging their respective identities into a new organization. Extensive reorganization and reallocation of resources is required.

Understanding the Phases of the Collaborative Process

To properly understand why various types of collaboration succeed or fail, it is necessary to realize that the activity of collaborating is a multiphase process (Ring and Van de Ven, 1994). Each phase must be passed through in order to achieve a sustainable collaboration. Failure at any stage will mark the end of that particular collaborative effort. Indeed, it can cast a large shadow over the likely outcome of subsequent efforts as well since a history of unsuccessful attempts at collaboration often sets up difficult barriers for subsequent efforts to overcome.

Although there is no agreement on the definition of the phases of the collaborative process (Alter and Hage 1993), the following categorization has heuristic value:

1. *The Precontact Phase.* Each of the parties to potential collaborative efforts must be internally "ready" to enter into the process. Readiness involves two elements: (1) a general openness to the kind of internal changes that many forms of collaboration require and (2) an awareness of the potential parties and a perception that these parties can be trusted (where trust is defined as "faith in the moral integrity or goodwill of the other," Ring and Van de Ven 1994). Internal readiness would be deemed low to the extent that there is found to be a wilful disregard of environmental pressures for collaboration or an excessively strong belief that "our ways are the best ways" or a belief that other parties will not cooperate, be unable to carry out their side of the bargain or will attempt to dominate the arrangement.
2. *The Preliminary Contact Phase.* This is the phase during which each of the parties "discover" each other. This discovery may proceed during exploratory meetings "to discuss mutual interests" and "share information." It is here that crucial impressions are formed about the personalities of key leaders and the overall culture of the other organization(s). Of these impressions, again the most critical is the extent to which one can "trust" the other. Of course, other crucial impressions are also formed in these early investigations and encounters. They have to do with perceptions of what the others hope to get from the collaborative venture and what they are prepared to "pay" for such benefits. Distorted perceptions at this stage due to inadequate information or negative past experiences can color the subsequent negotiations and sink them prematurely.
3. *The Negotiating Phase.* This is the phase during which the collaborative agreement is worked out through a series of focused meetings set up for this purpose.
4. *The Implementation Phase.* Once an agreement on a collaborative venture is reached, it must be carried out. In the early stages of implementation, a myriad of details must be worked out about who will do what with whom, when, and how. The process of deciding on specific allocations of time and money becomes critical here.
5. *Evaluation and Continuity.* The final phase in the collaborative process is that of assessing the value of the joint activity once it has been in place for a certain period and deciding whether it should continue or be terminated.

Factors Affecting the Outcomes of Collaborative Efforts

Drawing broadly from the literature on interorganizational relations, it is possible to identify four sets of factors that affect the probability of collaborative efforts being initiated, successfully concluded, and sustained for the duration planned for them. These are

1. factors associated with the type of collaboration sought;
2. factors associated with characteristics of the organizations entering into collaboration;
3. factors associated with the process of developing and implementing the collaborative activities;
4. environmental or contextual factors impinging on the organizations involved in a collaborative effort.

Type of Collaboratin

The typology of collaboration introduced at the beginning of this entry is based on the variable of level of interdependence. The five types identified differ in terms of the extent of the costs that would be incurred at each level. The hypothesis is that a collaborative effort will not be entered into, or sustained, so long as one of the parties believes that the costs incurred exceed the anticipated or actual benefits received (Galbraith 1973; Pfeffer and Salancik 1978). Among the more common costs indentified in the literature are perceived loss of autonomy or control—colloquially known as "turf"—(Gouldner 1959; Moxon *et al.* 1988) and perceived loss of resources such as money, information, status, legitimacy, time, and the like (Benson, 1975).

Type 1 forms of collaboration (the exchange of information or coordination of services) do not usually require significant changes in core activities or loss of autonomy. Costs mainly involve the investment of the time needed to reach agreement on the exchange and implement it.

Type 2 forms (joint efforts at planning, advocacy, public education, and fund-raising) require somewhat more time and effort to design and implement but still do not require any significant reduction in the organization's autonomy and control over their primary programs and services.

Type 3 forms of collaboration involve the creation of new joint ventures but funded with "new" resources and not requiring any diminishment in the resources supporting existing activities. These forms take on a significant new dimension in that existing services may nevertheless be affected (loss of status, loss of clients, etc.) and the new joint venture does require all parties to it to share in the control and management of it.

Type 4 forms are considerably more costly than any of the others, involving, as they do, joint ventures that are supported by resources that have to be taken away from existing activities. Thus, all possible kinds of costs are incurred.

Type 5 is the merger, which, by one definition, is no longer a form of collaboration in that whole organizations meld together to form, in effect, a new single entity. The creation of a merger is clearly the most costly of all interorganizational interactions.

An important dimension of collaborative ventures is their duration (the length of time for which a collaboration is intended to last). The addition of the duration variable adds another dimension to the cost-benefit calculus. Organizations may readily agree to give up autonomy or resources for a relatively short, fixed amount of time in the hope of gaining desired benefits; however, the longer the duration of the intended collaboration, the greater the costs may be perceived. As well, the cost-benefit calculus may change over time and this can threaten the sustainability of the collaboration.

Another aspect of the form of collaboration that can affect its success is the number of parties involved. The greater the number of parties involved, the greater the probability that the cost-benefit calculus of each will not be compatible. Issues of equity also grow larger as the number of parties increases. Not only do the parties need to believe that the benefits received outweigh the costs incurred; they also need to believe that the other parties are receiving benefits commensurate with the costs they incur. The perception that there are "free riders" who gain benefits far in excess of their investments can breed dissatisfaction with the venture. The larger the number of parties, the greater the likelihood that inequities will be perceived among some of them.

Organizational Factors

Three broad sets of organizational factors affect the outcome of collaboration, particularly during the preliminary contact and implementation phases. They are also more significant when higher levels of collaboration are attempted, which are more costly and longer term. The key sets of organizational factors are culture, leadership, and structure.

Organizational culture refers to beliefs, values, attitudes, and perceptions widely shared throughout an organization regarding what it stands for and how it should op-

erate (Schein 1985). Organizations may vary in terms of the number of these shared views how widely they are shared and how strongly they are held. From the limited point of view of the study of collaboration, a well-established organizational culture can significantly influence all phases of the process. It may contain shared attitudes about the other parties: how trustworthy they are and what they bring in the way of benefits to the potential partnership. Most important, culture can color the organization's perception of itself in terms of how open to change it is and how autonomous it believes it should be. Intense pride in the organization's reputation, traditions, and so on can breed an implicit belief in superiority, which may effectively block any compromises that must be made in developing a joint venture with others.

Although there remains considerable controversy over what shapes and changes organizational cultures, most would agree that its leaders are extremely influential. Students of organizational change have documented numerous instances in which leaders cause an organization to change (e.g., Jick 1993). The attitudes of leaders toward the need for entering into collaboration, how they perceive the other parties (their status, trustworthiness, etc.) and their skills in negotiation (see below) are key. They also influence the readiness of the rest of the organization to change through the nature and extent to which they consult and communicate with others. Failures on the part of leaders to prepare middle and lower levels of their organization for the changes required by joint ventures can result in failure at the implementation phase.

Studies of organizational structure, such as those of Mintzberg (1979) and Galbraith (1973) suggest that some structural forms are more likely than others to impede successful collaborative efforts among nonprofit organizations. "Professional bureaucracies" are organizations such as hospitals and universities in which power lies primarily with a large group of employees trained as professionals. During their training, professionals are socialized to believe that their work should not be changed by anyone other than their own professional bodies. This makes it difficult for them to enter into partnerships with those from other occupational groups, especially if they are from other organizations.

Conventional bureaucracies, by contrast, with their centralized control and high levels of formality cause problems for complex collaborations (types 3 to 5) in the implementation phase since subordinate staff who must undergo much of the change when entering into joint ventures may be unable to be flexible enough to make them work.

These organizational factors become even more significant when the cultures, leadership styles, and structures of the organizations entering into collaborative activities are incompatible. In spite of the benefits agreed to during the negotiating phase, the parties tend to experience great difficulties in working together during the implementation phase.

Process Factors

Many attempts at interorganizational collaboration fail because of lack of attention to the processes followed in developing the agreement. For example, if there is a very short, or nonexistent, preliminary contact phase in the process (during which low stake contacts allow the parties to get comfortable with one another before serious negotiations begin), faulty perceptions can develop, which make the negotiation phase much more difficult. Similarly, the process may be erroneously ended by the parties with the conclusion of the joint agreement on future collaborative activity. Unless equally careful attention is paid to the implementation phase, the misunderstandings that arise there can destroy the potential outcomes. Finally, a failure to consciously undertake an evaluation phase can cause "fixable" problems to be overlooked to the point at which the frustrations they cause become too great to be resolved easily.

However, it is at the negotiation phase that process factors are the most important. This is the phase during which the collaborative agreement is worked out. It is at this stage that the parties need their best negotiating skills, such as those so usefully explicated by Fisher, Ury, and Patton (1991). Other important variables at work during this stage (which cannot be explicated here due to space restrictions) are as follows:

- Having the "right" people at the table, that is, with sufficient knowledge about the issues and authority to reach agreement. In general, the more complex the proposed collaborative venture, the more important it is to have the organization's leader(s) at the table.
- Consulting with key internal and external stakeholders as the negotiations proceed. One of the chief determinants of failure at the implementation phase of a collaborative venture is that it is rejected by those affected by it because the agreement comes as a total shock to them. If they are kept informed, even consulted informally as the negotiations proceed, they are more likely to implement the outcome willingly.
- Timing: moving too fast, too slow, too soon, too late. Parties to the process who "come on too strong" can breed mistrust ("What's really in this for them?"). Parties who drag their heels, calling for more studies, more special committees, and so forth will eventually encourage others to look elsewhere for partners. Knowing just when the others are ready to make concessions in order to reap the benefits of the new joint activity, is a subtle aspect of the process.
- Achieving the right balance between formal, legal terms of agreement and "the psychological contract." As Ring and Van de Ven (1994) point out, too great a

concern with legal safeguards (contracts, dispute mechanisms, courts, etc.) can breed mistrust between the parties on the one hand. On the other hand, too great a reliance on "verbal agreements" or vaguely worded memoranda of agreement can, as conditions change during the implementation phase, lead to subsequent disagreement that can prove impossible to resolve. The greater the degree of complexity of the collaborative venture (for example as it moves from types 1 to 5 in the previously mentioned list), the more necessary it is to work out in advance formal understandings of the allocation of costs, benefits, and authority as well as how subsequent disagreements about such matters will be handled.

Environmental Factors

There is one additional set of variables that has not been discussed to this point but is critical in that it creates pressures on the parties that can either support their efforts or make them much more difficult. This is the environmental context of the collaborative process. Among the more important aspects of the external environment are the following:

Informal Networks. Institutional theory applied to nonprofit organizations (e.g., DiMaggio and Powell 1983) notes that organizations in the same field often form informal associations for exchanging information and interpreting events in their shared environment. It is common for such networks to influence the nature of the reputation of individual organizations in terms of its trustworthiness, status, and legitimacy. Networks can also form shared norms regarding the need for, and preferred type of, collaboration among network members. To the extent, therefore, that any given organization is embedded in an informal network, it will clearly be affected by the network's collaboration-relevant norms.

Third Party Influences. One of the more unique characteristics of the nonprofit sector is that the distribution of power among the stakeholders who determine the survival of an organization can be very different from that in the business sector. Specifically, it is common for there to be a small handful of funders (governments, United Ways, large foundations) on which many nonprofits are dependent for resources (Alter and Hage 1993). These powerful stakeholders can play two basic roles in the collaborative process. They can act as supporters of it or they can equally strongly discourage it.

For example, funders may be very interested in system rationalization—the desire to find the optimum set of organizations for the delivery of a given array of services. They can express this interest in two ways: as "cupids" or as "enforcers." As cupids, they offer incentives—both moral and financial—to encourage agencies to work together. As enforcers, they take a stronger role, in effect ordering rationalization with the threat of cuts in funding if it does not occur. In the case of governments, they may go so far as to dictate the form a collaboration should take, for instance, a series of mergers. The cupid role is usually very beneficial to the collaborative process in that it trusts the parties to reach their own agreements and provides positive reinforcements when they do so. The enforcer role usually breeds massive resentment and concerted efforts by those being coerced to attack the third party's position. The original potential for collaboration can be lost as a result.

Resource Scarcity. A strong motivation to enter collaborative ventures can be created by a moderate amount of anxiety over declining resources (Lawrence and Dyer 1983). Joint ventures can offer the prospect of synergy and leverage—more or better service for less money. Conversely, if cuts in resources appear too suddenly or are too large, they can create such stress and burnout that a "bunker mentality" sets in at the leadership level. This can quickly paralyze the willingness to innovate, including the effort needed to build collaborative ventures.

General Community and Social Values. Successful collaboration usually requires a basic trust in the other party and a willingness to trade off some of one's own interests to allow the others to gain some of theirs. In society at large, and in particular communities, there are general social values that address the willingness to trust others and compromise on one's interests. Various social commentators on the current state of North American society have pointed out that, in fact, these values are changing in a negative direction (e.g., Bethke-Elshtain 1995). Trust between people and organizations is breaking down and interests are more and more being defined as nonnegotiable rights. Such trends do not auger well for complex, large-scale collaborative efforts between voluntary sector organizations.

By way of conclusion, it is clear that the pressure for more collaboration in the nonprofit sector is great, but we need to know much more about what will get the actual process started and what determines its success. Consciousness of the various forms of collaborative effort and the factors affecting the process is an important beginning to the necessary research.

VIC MURRAY

BIBLIOGRAPHY

Alter, Catherine, and Jerald Hage, 1993. *Organizations Working Together.* Newbury Park, CA: Sage.
Benson, J., 1975. "The Interpersonal Network as a Political Economy." *Administrative Science Quarterly,* vol. 20, no. 2: 229–249.
Bethke-Elshtain, Jean, 1995. *Democracy on Trial.* New York: Basic Books.
D'Aunno, T. A., and H. S. Zuckerman, 1987. "A Life Cycle Model of Organizational Federations: The Case of Hospitals." *Academy of Management Review,* vol. 12: 534–545.
Di Maggio, P. J., and W. W. Powell, 1983. "The Iron Cage Revisited: Institutional Isomorphism and Collective Rationality in Organizational Fields." *American Sociological Review,* vol. 48: 147–160.
Fisher, Roger, William Ury, and Bruce Patton, 1991. *Getting to Yes.* New York: Penguin.
Galaskiewicz, J., and D. Shatin 1981. "Leadership and Networking among Neighborhood Human Service Organizations." *Administrative Science Quarterly,* vol. 26: 434–448.
Galbraith, Jay, 1973. *Designing Complex Organizations.* Reading, MA: Addison-Wesley.
Gouldner, Alvin, 1959. "Organizational Analysis." In R. K. Merton, L. Broom and L. J. Cottrell, eds., *Sociology Today.* New York: Basic Books.
Gray, Barbara, 1985. "Conditions Facilitating Interorganizational Collaboration." *Human Relations,* vol. 38: 911–936.
———, 1986. "Political Limits to Interorganizational Consensus and Change." *The Journal of Applied Behavioral Science,* vol. 22: 95–112.
———, 1989. *Collaborating: Finding Common Ground for Multiparty Problems.* San Francisco: Jossey-Bass.
Hord, S., 1986. "A Synthesis of Research on Organizational Collaboration." *Educational Leadership,* vol. 43: 22–26.
Jick, Todd, 1993. *Managing Change.* Boston: Irwin.
Lawrence, Paul, and Davis Dyer, 1983. *Renewing American Industry.* New York: Free Press.
Mattessich, Paul, and Barbara Monsey, 1992. *Collaboration: What Makes It Work?* St. Paul, MN: Amherst Wilder Foundation.
Mintzberg, Henry, 1979. *The Structuring of Organizations.* Englewood Cliffs, NJ: Prentice-Hall.
Moxon, R. *et al.,* 1988. "International Cooperative Ventures in the Aircraft Industry." In F. Constructor and P. Lorange, eds., *Cooperative Strategies in International Business.* Lexington, MA: Lexington Books 255–278.
Pfeffer, Jeffrey, and Gerald Salancik, 1978. *The External Control of Organizations.* New York: Harper and Row.
Ring, Peter Smith, and Andrew H. Van de Ven, 1994. "Developmental Processes of Cooperative Interorganizational Relationships." *Academy of Management Review,* vol. 19: 90–118.
Schein, Edgar, 1985. *Organizational Culture and Leadership.* San Francisco: Jossey-Bass.

INTERPERSONAL COMMUNICATION.

The exchange of messages from one person to another, not necessarily verbally.

One of the interesting things about communication is that it is impossible not to communicate. That is, for 24 hours of every day, as long as we are alive, we are simultaneously both sending and receiving communications. What we choose to wear, how we comb our hair, how we stand, what we prefer to eat or not eat; everything we do or don't do sends messages of some sort to others. They may not be the messages we would have liked to have communicated, or they may not be what we thought we were communicating, but as long as there is someone there to see us, or to hear us, we will have communicated something.

We are also receiving messages 24 hours of every day. Most of the messages we receive are nonhuman messages, frequently about the environment around us (the temperature, the light, odors in the place we are, etc.). We may not be conscious of them but that does not matter; we receive them anyway. When they are from people, they are interpersonal messages, even if they are not received—or sent—consciously. For example, just walking down a crowded street requires taking in and sending out a continuous stream of messages to people around us so as not to bump into any of them, and we do it all on "automatic pilot," never having to actually think about it.

In the context of public policy and administration, interpersonal communication means communicating messages to other people in ways that enable them to understand our messages the way we intend them to be understood. The less well we communicate, the more misunderstanding and confusion there is likely to be. That may sound simplistic, but it is one of the most difficult tasks all of us face. Whether in the public or private sectors, all of us have superiors, subordinates, clients and/or customers. How well we communicate with all of them determines, in a very real sense, how well we do our jobs.

Because no two humans in the world have been raised in exactly the same way, by the same people, sharing exactly the same group identities, attitudes, values, beliefs, and disbeliefs, not to mention the same language or dialect (all of which is sometimes called "group cultures"), no two people can share exactly the same perceptions. Therefore, every interpersonal communication is also, to some extent, an intercultural communication (see **intercultural communication**). The more similar the shared cultural backgrounds between two people, the easier it should be to communicate accurately. The more dissimilar the backgrounds of individuals, the more difficult communication among them is likely to be, and the more likely there are to be misperceptions and misunderstandings. The more different the individuals are, the harder they are likely to have to work to communicate effectively.

White, middle-class, college-educated, English-speaking, suburban, male, Catholic accountants in their thirties, with wives and kids, should have an easier time communicating accurately with each other than they would have if one or more of the adjectives used to describe them were left out or changed.

This is so because in the course of being socialized into the many cultures in which we have been raised, and with which we identify, we have learned a number of "codes" or languages, shared primarily by members of the same group. These codes make communication among us easier. We have learned the same codes, therefore we can "decode" the messages "one of us" may be sending more quickly and more accurately than a message "one of them" may be sending. For example, the word "bat" conjures up totally different images for a rural person than it does for a city person. Similarly, the word "conservative" is a very positive word and "liberal" is a bad word for some people, while the reverse tends to be true for others. Leaving every-

thing else aside, it is just easier to communicate when "they" speak "our" language.

In reality, however, everything else is not left aside. We do tend to trust "one of us" more than "one of them," and that is true regardless of who "they" are. In fact, "we" come into much sharper focus when juxtaposed against one of "them." We—whoever we are—tend to be honest, virtuous, just, trustworthy. They, by contrast, are the dishonest scoundrels who are unfair and simply cannot be trusted. Note that many groups divide the world into just two categories of people, us and them. For the ancient citizens of Athens, there were Athenians and non-Athenians, and the latter were called "barbarians." The Jews consider themselves "God's chosen people." What does that make everyone else? Unchosen? The Chinese used to call themselves the "Central Kingdom." Doesn't that make everyone else peripheral? In some tribes, the word for membership in the tribe is the same as the word for "human being." To be outside the tribe is to literally not be human. The Nazis claimed that the Germans were the master race, hence everyone else was inferior. One could go on. The point is that even the word "they" is mildly pejorative. Regardless of how sophisticated we may be, most of us tend to trust one of "us" more than we are likely to trust one of "them."

This is important in all human communication. No matter what may be said about opposites attracting, most people grow up sharing the same language, religion, politics, and general values as their parents (not always, to be sure, but frequently enough to be the norm rather than the exception). Further, we tend to know and trust people like us. That is why we speak to "our own kind" so much more than we do with "one of them." It is easier. The problem for policymakers and administrators is that a very great deal of their work involves communicating to "them." But if "we" policymakers and administrators are to be successful in our work, we have to be certain that our messages are understood the way we intended them to be. This is frequently a very difficult task.

This is particularly important because all human communication is interpersonal communication, at some level of analysis. Organizations, groups, nations do not communicate; people do—in the name of the entities they represent, perhaps, but real communication is always between people. People often play multiple roles, to be sure, but they usually do not confuse them. When a man is talking to his boss, he behaves and communicates differently than he would if he were talking to his subordinates, his mother, wife, girlfriend, or daughter. In each situation, he assumes a different role, and he knows how to behave and communicate within each.

Despite the difficulty of sustaining good interpersonal communications over long periods of time, many people do succeed. This may be because they spend so much of their working and social hours with people who are, at least to some degree, more or less like themselves. Take for example, Mr. A of the A Agency, who talks with Ms. B of the B Bureau and Mr. C of the C Corporation. While they all may come from different "corporate" cultures, there are probably a hundred other cultural groups that they have in common. Most are likely to come from more or less the same linguistic, national, educational, social, economic, and even religious backgrounds (broadly defined). This means that they will probably share a great many common perceptions and codes among themselves. Hence communication between them is likely to be relatively easy. In our work life it is very common for lawyers to talk to lawyers, accountants to accountants, computer people to computer people, and managers to managers. Outsiders may not be able to follow what they are saying, but that is not what is important. What is important is that the person with whom they are communicating can readily understand the meaning of what they are trying to communicate. However, anyone who is not one of the specialists mentioned will have difficulty understanding, unless the specialist translates the message for the nonspecialist. One of the cardinal rules of effective interpersonal communication is to put one's message into cultural language that can be readily understood by the receiver.

There is also a rule in communication theory that argues that the more steps any communication goes through, the more distortion is likely to occur. That rule is certainly correct. However, there are times when it makes sense to break that rule. Consider the case where someone from group A does not understand "how things are done" in group C—its culture. If it were important for a person in A to communicate with someone in C, it might be possible to do so, but it is not likely to be either as easy or as successful as it might be. That would especially be the case if A and C did not speak each other's cultural language. That is where a B—someone who was familiar with the cultures of both groups A and C—would come in handy. Understanding both groups A and C, presumably B would speak the cultural language of both A and C. That person would speak to A in A's language and to C in C's language. A and B, speaking A's language, are more likely to share common identities and perceptions and thus to trust each other more than would A and C. (That is important because there is no more effective communication than that which occurs between people who know and trust each other.) Similarly when B and C communicate (presumably in C's cultural language), they too will likely share more identities and perceptions and thus be more trusting; hence, communication between B and C should be more successful than it could have been between A and C if they had communicated directly.

This rule is very important for interpersonal communication, and it is particularly important for getting things done in a work environment, regardless of which society one is in. In every society, whom you know is important.

Yet, it is more important in some than in others. There is a concept that is popularly known as "six degrees of separation." In this concept, everyone within one country, like the United States, indirectly knows everyone else in the United States, going through people they know and trust. For instance, while you may not know anyone who knows the president of the United States personally, someone reading these pages may know someone, who knows someone, who knows someone, who knows the president personally. And since communication with people we know (and presumably trust) is so much more effective than communication between people who do not know and trust one another, it pays to add those extra steps to the communication process. But it is not just the president one needs to know. Every day, decisions are being made and implemented the way they are because someone knew and trusted the person who counselled them.

In sum, organizations do not communicate: people who work in them do. If we are to improve the effectiveness of those organizations, it is necessary to improve the interpersonal communication skills of the people who work in those organizations. That can be done simply by each person making the effort to put a message into language that the receiver can understand.

MARSHALL R SINGER

BIBLIOGRAPHY

Knapp, Mark L. and Gerald R. Miller, eds., 1985. *Handbook of Interpersonal Communication.* Beverly Hills, CA: Sage.
Littlejohn, Stephen W., 1989. *theories of Human Communication,* 3d ed. Belmont, CA: Wadsworth.
Reardon, Kathleen K., 1987. *Interpersonal Communication: Where Minds Meet.* Belmont, CA: Wadsworth.
Singer, Marshall R, 1987. *Intercultural Communication: A Perceptual Approach.* Englewood Cliffs, NJ: Prentice-Hall. (Rev., abr. ed., 1997. Yarmouth, ME: Intercultural Press.)
Verderber, Rudolph F. and S. Kathleen, 1995. *Inter-Act: Using Interpersonal Communication Skills,* 7th ed. Belmont, CA: Wadsworth.

INTERSTATE COMPACT. A binding legal agreement between two or more states entered into in order to deal with a difficulty or interest that spans state borders.

A compact differs from other statutes because it is also a contract between the participating states. As a contract, an interstate compact is binding on member states in the same manner as any other contract entered into by a person or organization. Because of its contractual nature, a compact takes precedence over prior law and over legislation that may later be enacted by member states. Compacts cannot be unilaterally altered or rescinded once they have been enacted. They are an obligation for all residents of the member states. A state or states may sue in state or federal court if another state breaches or does not respect the conditions of a compact. The language in the document and on the necessity for congressional approval determines which judicial level is used. If congressional consent is involved, the case would likely go to federal court.

According to historians, the interstate compact was used within the British North American colonies prior to the American Revolution. Nine intercolonial agreements pertaining to boundary issues were signed during the colonial period. The Articles of Confederation (Article VI) acknowledged the need for a way to resolve controversies while at the same time protecting the new government from the potentially harmful alliance of two or more states. Accordingly, the Articles allowed the use of compacts approved of by the Congress. Under the Articles, four compacts were signed: three dealing with boundary issues and one with regulation of navigation and fishing. The United States Constitution kept the compact provision of the Articles basically unaltered. Article 1, Section 10 reads: "No State shall, without the Consent of Congress . . . enter into any Agreement or Compact with another State, or with a foreign Power."

Congressional Consent

One of the most complicated facets of interstate compacts has been the constitutional requisite for the consent of Congress. The courts have given judgments on the purpose of congressional consent, the types of compacts needing consent, how consent is given, when it must be given, and other concerns. The United States Supreme Court has said that consent can be suggested as well as deliberately granted (*Virginia v. Tennessee,* 148 U.S. 503, 1893). The distinction is ambiguous between compacts that require consent and those that do not. The United States Court of Appeals found in 1962 that interstate compacts of a political character are ineffective unless sanctioned by Congress, but states do not need congressional consent to join nonpolitical compacts (*Tobin v. United States,* 306 F. 2nd 270 at 272-4, D.C. Cir., 1962). Congressional approval is generally needed for those that influence the political equilibrium among the states or those that modify a power entrusted to the federal government, such as state border adjustments, arrangements over water domain, and compacts with the potential for discrimination against nonparticipants. Congressional consent is not needed for those agreements that seek consistency in the law, or apply to areas where actions on the part of states is common, such as criminal law, education, or child welfare. The consent power of Congress is undisputed, and Congress determines if a compact is political and how and when consent will be granted. Once a compact receives congressional approval, it carries the power of federal law.

Literature Review

Research on interstate compacts, particularly legal research was abundant in the twentieth century up to the 1970s.

Noted scholars published books and articles during the decades of the 1930s and 1940s in which they appraised varieties of compacts, the reasons for their passage, and their benefits and problems. During the following decades, books about interstate compacts examined their arrangements, objectives, management, and political features. Up to the decade of the 1960s, texts on federalism and intergovernmental relations continued to pay some attention to interstate relations and interstate compacts, but during the 1970s and 1980s, scholarly focus on interstate compacts declined. A few exceptions to the trend were works by Paul T. Hardy (1982), Richard C. Kearney and John J. Stucker (1985), Parris N. Glendening and Mavis Mann Reeves (1984), David C. Nice (1987), and Joseph F. Zimmerman (1992).

Scope and Use

Although compacts have been used for many years, they were few in number until the twentieth century, with only 36 authorized by 1920. Between 1920 and 1970, the number of interstate compacts grew, especially during the 1950s and 1960s. Between 1950 and 1970 the rate of adoption accelerated to more than 4 compacts a year. The growth rate decreased after 1970. From 1920 to 1980, more than 140 new compacts were enacted, with the majority of those coming after World War II. The most compacts enacted were the 45 passed in the decade of 1960 to 1969 (4.5 per year) and 22 between 1955 and 1959 (5.5. per year).

The scope of interstate compacts has altered significantly since the founding the United States. Although compacts began as tools for settling problems between two adjoining states, the number of regional and national compacts has grown over the years while the number of bistate border compacts has declined. Most of the compacts did not institute commissions or agencies before the 1970s, but the majority of compacts enacted during the last two decades have initiated such entities. They come in varied shapes, from those that manage and operate complex facilities to those that are purely advisory in nature.

Since the colonial era, the functions of compacts have also been extremely diverse. Boundary compacts have decreased from over two-thirds of the initial acts to less than 1 percent of the newest. Likewise, the use of compacts for river water management, a significant portion of early enactments, has declined recently. About 10 percent of the total in most years have been industry and business-related compacts, while compacts for transportation and environmental concerns are more frequent in recent years.

Although compacts continue to be enacted, their growth has slowed. Nevertheless, state officials seem to judge the interstate compact as a workable tool of interstate activity. One of the key series of compacts in recent years stemmed from Congress's passage in 1980 of the Low-Level Radioactive Waste Policy Act. The targets of this legislation were the states, and the device was regional cooperation through interstate compacts. Authority was delegated to the states to deal with the problem of deciding where to dispose of low-level radioactive waste.

Participating States

What is the frequency of use of compacts among the states? State enactments vary from 11 to 34, while the average is 20. Thirty or more compacts have been enacted by six states: Pennsylvania, Virginia, Colorado, New Mexico, Kentucky, and Maryland. Seven states have enacted 15 or less: Hawaii, South Carolina, Michigan, Alaska, Wisconsin, North Dakota, and Iowa. It would be of interest to know if there are shared attributes among the states that enact numerous compacts. Thus far, there are no solid findings that differentiate the earmarks of state compact participation.

Conclusion

Since the founding of this nation, enactment of interstate compacts has varied greatly. Even though the use of compacts has not maintained a steady upward course, state officials across the country have persisted in advancing, considering, and passing national, regional, and bistate compacts. Interstate compacts today remain a plausible form of cooperation that holds out the potential for settlement of difficulties among and between states in the American federal system. It is apparent that states see the compact as an achievable way of resolving interstate problems that include environmental protection, transportation regulation, service provision, criminal justice activities, boundary problem resolution, and regulation of rivers and river resources. Additionally, regional trade corridors are growing in importance, and they involve compacts in the economic development arena. Moreover, ongoing growth in interstate metropolitan areas requires interstate accords, particularly in the regulation of the transportation function.

It is unlikely, however, that the states will be inventing new and innovative uses of compacts in the near future. Every state has enacted at least one, and the existing compacts encompass an assortment of subjects. Their titles are illustrative: the Connecticut River Atlantic Salmon Compact, the Interstate Extradition Compact, the Nonresident Violators Compact, the Southern Growth Policies Compact, an Interstate Compact on Adoption and Medical Assistance, and the South Dakota–Nebraska Boundary Compact. Current compacts will probably be amended and the numbers of signatories will increase. It is probable that the use of regional compacts will expand as the number of bistate compacts declines, while more compacts between the federal government and one or more states are apt to be enacted. Environmental and natural resource problems are certain to be a continuing but not the sole focus of compacts, and numerous other practical management issues will be dealt with by compacts in the future. Interstate compacts will continue to evolve as they are reviewed and revised to deal with persistent problems and issues.

PATRICIA S. FLORESTANO

BIBLIOGRAPHY

Barton, Weldon 1967. *Interstate Compacts in the Political Process.* Chapel Hill: University of North Carolina.
Glendening, Parris N., and Mavis Mann Reeves, 1984. *Pragmatic Federalism.* Pacific Palisades, CA: Palisades Publishers.
Hardy, Paul T., 1982. *Interstate Compacts: The Ties That Bind.* Athens: University of Georgia.
Interstate Compacts 1783–1977, 1977. Lexington: Council of State Governments.
Interstate Compacts and Agencies, 1983. Lexington: Council of State Governments.
Kearney, Richard C., and John J. Stucker, 1985. "Interstate Compacts and the Management of Low Level Radioactive Wastes," *Public Administrative Review* (January-February) 210–220.
Leach, Richard, and Redding Sugg, Jr., 1959. *The Administrative of Interstate Compacts.* Baton Rouge: Louisiana State University Press.
Nice, David. C., 1987. "State Participation in Interstate Compacts," *Publius,* vol. 17, no. 2:69–83.
Ridgeway, Marian 1971. *Interstate Compacts: A Question of Federalism.* Carbondale: Southern Illinois University.
Zimmermann, Frederick L., and Mitchell Wendell, 1951. *The Interstate Compact Since 1925.* Lexington: Council of State Governments.
———, 1976. *The Law and Use of Interstate Compacts.* Lexington: Council of State Governments.
Zimmerman, Joseph F., 1992. *Contemporary American Federalism.* New York: Praeger.

INTERVIEWING. Part of the overall employment selection process involving a face-to-face communication between at least two people designed to accomplish several objectives. For the employer, the interview is designed to get information from the candidate for the purpose of making an evaluation decision. A secondary purpose is to educate the candidate about the organization. For the job candidate, the purpose is to convince the interviewer of his/her suitability for a given position or to gather more information about the position with which to make a decision about his/her own suitability for the organization.

Historically, the selection interview is widely used in government service throughout the world. Although it may be the only element in the selection process, normally it is combined with other selection factors such as information from an application form and knowledge-based information drawn from a written test. The application form yields basic personal background information, level of educational attainment, and employment history. The selection test is normally used to measure achieved levels of job-related knowledge and abilities. The interview then is used primarily to double-check information, to evaluate the candidate's interpersonal skills, communication skills, and the degree to which the candidate will work well with others in the organizational unit—organizational fit. It is also used to present the candidate with a positive image of the organization.

Fear of litigation and the complexity of validating tests have led many organizations in the United States to rely more heavily on the interview as the primary selection method. This may not be a wise course of action since the interview is technically no different than a written test in terms of its legal job-relatedness requirements.

Research on the accuracy and validity of the oral interview as a part of the selection process is at best "mixed," and it clearly has some substantial problems with biased results. Employers should be very careful when relying heavily on the interview process due to demonstrated interviewer bias as a result of prior knowledge about the applicant; that is, prior knowledge of factors such as sex, physical attractiveness, and age will predispose an interview into certain stereotypical anticipations. Other problems with interviews include such factors as interviewers tending to favor applicants who share their attitudes, the order in which the interviews take place influencing the results (contrast effects), and poor interviewer recall of information serving as a source of bias.

Before organizations rely too heavily on the oral interview as a selection device they should be willing to take certain steps to minimize bias in the interviewing process. Steps that organizations can take to enhance the accuracy of interview information include the following:

1. use structured interviews and certify that the interviewer follows a set procedure;
2. affirm that the interviewers are properly educated regarding the potential interview bias factors and are trained regarding structure and procedure and note-taking for later accurate recall of information;
3. ensure that the interviewers are informed about the required knowledge, skills, and abilities of the jobs they are interviewing for;
4. guarantee that the questions asked are based on job-related factors and do not explore personal factors that might be considered discriminatory in nature.

ROBERT H. ELLIOTT

BIBLIOGRAPHY

Cascio, Wayne F., 1991. *Applied Psychology in Personnel Management*, 4th ed. Englewood Cliffs, NJ: Prentice-Hall.

DeCenzo, David A., and Stephen P. Robbins, 1988. *Personnel/Human Resource Management*, 3d ed., Englewood Cliffs, NJ: Prentice-Hall.
Rabin, Jack, Thomas Vocino, W. Bartley Hildreth and Gerald J. Miller, 1995. *Handbook of Public Personnel Administration*. New York: Marcel Dekker.

ISLAMIC ADMINISTRATIVE TRADITION.

The collective doctrine of administrative principles, based on the Holy Qura'an and the teachings of the prophet Mohammed that provide the guidelines for the practice of public administration in the Arab world.

The Islamic administrative tradition cannot be understood without understanding the Islamic principles that relate to the practice of public administration and its practice. Islam is a very comprehensive way of life. Its tenets cover all aspects of life including the principles of managing public affairs. In the Holy Qura'an and the sunnah (Prophet Mohammed-Peace Be upon Him-sayings and teachings), the guidelines for effective and ideal practice of public administration are explicitly stated. They form the doctrine of Islamic public administration. As derived from the Holy Qura'an and the Sunnah, the principles of and guidelines for Islamic public administration are consultation, ethical behavior and decision making, cooperation, justice and equity, equality and merit.

Consultation

Allah ordered his messenger, Prophet Mohammed (Peace Be upon Him—hereafter PBUH), to consult the people prior to making a decision; thus, it is a requirement in Islam for anyone in a leadership position to consult with those one leads and to take their opinion as a basis for the decision to be made. This fundamental Islamic principle is based on the following Qura'anic verses: "It is part of the mercy of Allah that thou dost deal gently with them, wert thou severe or harsh-hearted, they would have broken away from about thee: so pass over (their faults) and ask for (Allah's) forgiveness for them; and consult them in affairs (of moment). Then when thou hast taken a decision, put thy trust in Allah" (3:159) and "Those who respond to their Lord, and establish regular prayer; who (conduct) their affairs by mutual consultation . . ." (42:38). According to these two verses, it is a requirement for leaders to seek the opinion of their followers before any decision is made and it is the right of the people to demand that their input is taken into consideration. This is what is known as participative management in contemporary public administration with the exception that in Islam it is a right, not a privilege.

Ethical Behavior and Decisionmaking

In Islam, the reward for using righteousness, justice, honesty, and fulfilling a promise is paradise. Violating any of these principles, by contrast, leads a person to the hell-fire. Muslims are ordered by Allah to conduct their affairs according to these Islamic codes of ethics. They are the governing factors with which both the behavior and the practice must comply. A number of Qura'anic verses emphasize the importance of complying with these principles. With respect to justice, Allah says: "Oh, believers! stand out firmly for justice" (4:135). In another verse, Allah orders Muslims to command to what is right: "Hold to forgiveness; and command to what is right" (7:199); "and fulfill the covenant of Allah" (6:152). Allah also warns Muslims from falling in hypocrisy in a Qura'nic verse where He says, "when they fall in with those who believe, they say: We believe, but when they go apart to their devils they declare: Lo, we are with you; verily, we did but mock" (2:14). In addition to these Qura'anic verses that command Muslims to ethical behavior, the Prophet (PBUH) warns Muslims from unethical behavior in His teachings. He (PBUH) says, "Allah's curse is on the one who offers the bribe and on the one who accepts it" (ibn Hibban) and "Cursed is the one who offers the bribe, the one who receives it, and the one who arranges it" (Al-Hakin).

Cooperation

Both the practice of Prophet Mohammed (PBUH) and the Holy Qura'an encourage cooperation. Allah says, "Help ye one another in righteousness and piety, but help ye not one another in sin and rancour: Fear Allah: for Allah is strict in punishment" (5:2). The verse orders Muslims to cooperate with each other in righteousness and prohibits cooperation in unlawful matters. In public administration terminology, when the goal to be achieved is legitimate, cooperation is required; otherwise, cooperation is prohibited. In this regard, Prophet Mohammed (PBUH) says, "Help your brother, be he wrongdoer or wronged." Thereupon a man exclaimed, "O Apostle of God! I may help him if he is wronged; but how could I be expected to help a wrongdoer?" The Prophet (PBUH) answered, "You must prevent him from doing wrong: that will be your help to him" (Al-bukhari and Muslim). Accordingly, cooperation is a fundamental principle of Islamic public administration only when the goal to be achieved is a legitimate one.

Justice and Equity

In Islam, the practice of public administration must be guided by justice and equity. It is expressed in the Holy Qura'an and the teachings of Prophet Mohammed (PBUH) that the reward for just and equitable practice is directly from Allah and any deviation from just and fair practice is a sin that leads to the hell-fire in the hereafter. Allah says, "Allah doth command you to render back your trusts to those to whom they are due; and when ye judge between people that ye judge with justice: verily excellent is the teaching which He giveth you! For Allah is He who heareth and seeth all things" (4:58). Allah also says in another verse, "give measure and weight with (full) justice;– no burden do we place on any soul, but that which it can bear;–whenever ye speak, speak justly, even if a near relative is concerned; and fulfill the covenant of Allah: Thus doth he command you, that ye may remember" (6:152). The verses order Muslims to speak and act justly, even when that conflicts with personal interests. When the people involved are your enemies or the people you hate, a Muslim must not diverge from just and fair dealing. This is expressed in the Qura'an where Allah says, "O ye who believe! Stand out firmly for Allah, as witnesses to fair dealing, and let not the hatred of others to you make you swerve to wrong and depart from justice. Be just: that is next to piety: and fear Allah. For Allah is well-acquainted with all that ye do" (5:8). Accordingly, in Islam, the practice of public administration must be guided by justice and fair dealing and any violation of this principle is prohibited.

Equality and Merit

A fundamental principle of Islam is that all people are equal and should be treated equally despite their race, origin, social status, sex, age, and color. This principle is emphasized in the Holy Qura'an where Allah says, "Behold, the noblest of you before God is the most righteous of you" (49:13). It is also expressed in the Prophet's teachings where He (PBUH) says, "Hear and obey, even though your leader be an Abyssinian slave with crinkly hair" (Al-Bukhari and Muslim). Accordingly, it is prohibited to discriminate against people on the basis of their race, origin, social status, sex, age, or color. This principle prohibits the appointment of anyone to a certain position or promoting anyone on any basis other than qualification. The practice of public administration, in Islam, must comply with this principle and no deviation is justifiable. Allah says, "Truly the best of men for thee to employ is the (man) who is strong and trusty" (28:26). This verse is further supported by the teachings of Prophet Mohammed (PBUH), who says, "Whoever entrusts a man to a public office where in his society there is a better man than this trustee, he has betrayed the trust of Allah and his messenger and the Muslims" (Al-Bukhari and Muslim). He also says, "anyone who has been made responsible for some affairs of the Muslims and he had entrusted some responsible job to someone, influenced by his relatives, then Allah's curse on him. No virtue of justice from him will be accepted before Allah, so much that he will be thrown into Hell" (Al-Bukhari and Muslim).

These five Islamic principles form the framework of the ideal Islamic public administration. According to Islam, they must govern the practice of public administration, and any deviation from these principles is prohibited because compliance with them is explicitly commanded in the Holy Qura'an and the teachings of Prophet Mohammed (PBUH). They derive their power from the Islamic belief that Muslims will be held accountable for everything they do during their lifetime in the day of judgement. It is the Muslims' faith that determines the extent to which these principles govern their practice and behavior. Very faithful Muslims will be driven by an intrinsic power that forces them to comply with the principles of Islam including the principles of Islamic public administration. In an Islamic state that is run in accordance with the Holy Qura'an and the teachings of Prophet Mohammed (PBUH), the need for control and supervision to ensure compliance with these rules and principles is limited because the intrinsic force caused by the fear of Allah and the willingness to please Him drives faithful Muslims more than they are driven by the fear of the management that is incapable of detecting violation in all cases. While the management cannot always detect all violations of its rules, violation of any Islamic principles including the principles of Islamic public administration can always be detected by Allah, who says in the Holy Book, "If thou pronounce the word Aloud, (it is no matter): For verily He knoweth What is secret and what is yet more hidden" (20:7). He also says in another verse of the Holy Book, "And whether ye hide Your word or publish it, He certainly has (full) knowledge, Of the secrets of (all) hearts. Should He not know, He that created? And He is the One That understands the finest Mysteries (and) is Well-acquainted (with them)" (67:14). Based on these verses, faithful Muslims strongly believe that no matter what they do or plan to do is well known by Allah and they will be held accountable for it. This prevents them from violating the principles of the Islamic public administration, even in the absence of the management. Adherence to the Islamic rules is also enforced by the belief that a person might be able to hide unlawful actions and behaviors from other people, but they will never be able to hide them from Allah. This is expressed in the verse where Allah says, "They may hide (their crimes) from men, But they cannot hide (them) from God, seeing that He is in their midst When they plot by night, In words that He cannot Approve: and God Doth But He, the Living, the Self-Subsisting, Eternal. No slumber can seize Him Nor sleep" (2:355).

In theory, these principles should and must govern the practice as well as the behavior of public administrators. They must not be violated by anyone under any circumstances. Yet, the practice of public administration throughout the history of Islamic state, with the exception of the

Prophet (PBUH) and the wise caliphs period (611–661), has been strongly influenced by the politics more than it has been by the Islamic principles of public administration. Since the assassination of the fourth wise caliph (Ali ibn Abi Taleb) in 661, political interests, goals, and objectives have always been the determinant factor of how the Islamic state should be run. After the Prophet (PBUH) and the wise caliphs period, two Islamic states were established and then the Islamic state collapsed and divided into many small states. Each of these eras has its own characteristics and political environment that drove the practice of public administration.

The Holy Qura'an was revealed to Prophet Mohammed (PBUH) in 611 in Mecca. Due to the inacceptance of His (PBUH) prophethood by Quraish tribes and the conflicts that emerged thereafter, He (PBUH) and the believers migrate to Al-Madinah in 622 where He (PBUH) established the first Islamic state according to the principles of Islam. In Al-Madinah, the Prophet (PBUH) inscribed the constitution of the Islamic state, which included all aspects of life including the practice of public administration and how the Islamic state should be run. The rights, responsibilities, and obligations of all the citizens–Muslims, Jews, and Christians–were all explicitly prescribed in the constitution along with those of the leader.

In Al-Madinah, the principles of the Islamic public administration were not only espoused, but they were the principles in use. The actions and the behavior of Prophet Mohammed (PBUH) as a leader of the Islamic state and as a prophet were governed by these principles. He taught these principles to his followers by doing and applying them rather than by preaching them. When the Islamic state expanded and a judge position in Yemen was vacant, Prophet Mohammed (PBUH) called Muadh ibn Jabal to interview him and determine if he was the most qualified individual (merit principle) for the position. Prophet Mohammed (PBUH) asked Muadh, "How will you decide the cases that will be brought before you?" Muadh answered, "I shall decide them according to the Book of Allah."–"And if you find nothing related to the matter in the Book of Allah?"–"Then I shall decide according to the Sunnah of God's apostle."–"And if you find nothing about it in the Sunnah of God's Apostle?"–"Then I shall exercise my own judgment without the least hesitation." Thereupon the Prophet (PBUH) slapped his chest and said, "Thank God who has caused the messenger of God's messenger to please God and his messenger" (Aat Tirmidhi and abu Daud). This example demonstrates the Prophet's (PBUH) adherence to the principles of the Islamic public administration.

During this period, the Islamic state expanded from Al-Madinah to cover all of the Arabian Peninsula, which required an expansion in the government itself. The Prophet (PBUH) divided the Islamic state into eight provinces. For each province, the Prophet (PBUH) appointed a judge and a governor, who reported directly to Him (PBUH) as the leader of the state. He (PBUH) also established the first consultative council in Islam located in Islam located in Al-Madinah. Knowledgeable citizens and Islamic scholars were appointed by the Prophet (PBUH) for the council to provide consultations in civilian as well as religious matters.

After the Prophet's (PBUH) death in 632, Abu Baker was elected to be the first wise caliph (632–634). In his inauguration speech Abu Baker said, "Obey me only when I obey Allah and His Apostle, and if I disobey Allah or the Prophet (PBUH), disobey me." Abu Baker strictly followed the steps of Prophet Mohammed (PBUH) as he said in the speech. He kept the structure of the government as it was established by the Prophet (PBUH). The Islamic state did not expand beyond the Arabian Peninsula, which limited the need for modification or expansion of the government structure.

Omar ibn al-Khatab (581–644), the second wise caliph, was elected in 634 at 53. He started his ten-year administration by a speech that demonstrated his very well known administrative and leadership skills. In his brief speech, ibn al-Khatab emphasized that he did not choose the leadership that he would reward whoever did the right thing and punish who deviated from the right path, and he would delegate authority equivalent to the responsibilities to powerful and trustworthy governors of the Islamic provinces. During his reign, the Islamic state expanded well beyond the Arabian Peninsula. His army captured Syria, Palestine, Egypt, Iraq, and Persia. The expansion of the Islamic state required a more sophisticate administrative system that the one that existed during the Prophet's and Abu Baker's periods. Accordingly, ibn al-Khatab introduced major changes in the administrative, military, and judicial systems. Administratively, ibn al-Khatab established for the first time the concept of *diwan* (bureau). Four main bureaus were established in Al-Madinah (the capital of the Islamic state), known as the central bureaus: bureau of army (*Diwan al-Jund*), bureau of expenditure (*Diwan al-Atta*), bureau of postal services (*Diwan al-Bareed*), and bureau of revenue (*Diwan al-Jibayah*). The heads of these bureaus report directly to the caliph, Omar ibn al-Khatab, along with the heads of the other main departments such as the judicial branch, the departments of control, investigation, translation, grievance, clerks, statistics, education, and personnel. In the 12 provinces of the Islamic state, ibn al-Khatab established administrative systems identical to the one in Al-Madinah with the exception of the size and the official language. Ibn al-Khatab designated the native language of the province to be the official language. For example, after the conquest of Persia, Persian continued to be the official language. In each of the 12 provinces, Omar ibn -al-Khatab appointed a governor (*Wali*) and a judge, who report directly to the caliph. The judge and the gover-

nor were given the authority to employ their assistants and supporting staff. Omar's administrative system was the first decentralized system in Islam.

Concerning the military, Omar ibn al-Khatab modernized the Islamic army by the development and addition of new concepts and functions that were not known prior to his administration. He included, for the first time, a judge, a treasurer, physicians, surgeons, interpreters, and servants in every expedition. He also developed a report system that informs him as a commander-in-chief of the performance of the Islamic army in the battlefields, which enabled him to make changes as needed. The effective military system developed by Omar ibn al-Khatab resulted in a major expansion of the Islamic state during his reign.

Omar ibn al-Khatab was the first judge in Islam. His knowledge and experience in this area influenced him to establish a very effective judicial system. One of the principles that was developed and applied by Omar ibn al-Khatab and is still being used today in modern states is the separation between the judiciary and the executive. He separated the judiciary from the executive in the capital of the Islamic state and in every Islamic province. Additionally, to prevent corruption and bribes, judges were given relatively high salaries, and they were not permitted to engage in trade or in any other profession as long as they are in the government.

The principles of the Islamic public administration have never been applied to all the operations of government after the death of Prophet Mohammed (PBUH) as they were during Omar ibn al-Khatab's reign. He introduced new administrative traditions that are compatible with the Islamic principles. His assassination in 644 is a turning point in the history of the practice of the Islamic public administration. The conflict over who would be the Muslim's caliph elevated after the assassination of Omar ibn al-Khatab.

In 644, Othman ibn Affan became the third wise caliph (644–656), following ibn al-Khatab. During his reign, the focus shifted to the internal conflicts. The 11-year period was spent in defending his caliphate and the territories that were conquested by Omar ibn al-Khatab. No major changes in the Islamic administrative tradition were established during ibn al-Khatab's reign. The only change was his tendency to appoint his relatives (the Ummayahs) in important positions. This practice was strongly rejected by the majority of Muslims and generated a very strong opposition that was determined to terminate the practice. In 655, the rebellions blockaded ibn Affan in his house for 40 days and killed him.

Similar to the period of ibn Affan was the time of Ali ibn abi Taleb, the fourth wise caliph (656–661). When Ali was elected, Mua'wayah ibn Abi Suffyan (Wali Damascus) rejected Ali as the Muslims' caliph and declared war against Ali in Al-Kofa from Damascus. Mua'wayah's resistance to Ali's caliphate resulted in three major battles between the two armies. The three battles did not conclude the conflict between Ali and Mua'wayah. The rejection to Ali's caliphate by Mua'wayah and the battles between the two inaugurated a new tradition in the Islamic public administration. The use of force to maintain and stabilize the government became an Islamic administrative tradition during Ali's caliphate and has continued since then.

Another change in the Islamic administrative tradition during Ali ibn abi Taleb's reign was moving the capital from Al-Madinah to Al-Kofa in Iraq. This was an indication of a major shift in the administrative tradition. Since Ali's caliphate, the factor that determines the capital of the Islamic state has always been a military one. Each caliph chose the city in which he had the most support in order to defend his caliphate.

From the time Ali was elected as the Muslim's caliph until his assassination, he was in a state of war with Mua'wayah and other opposition parties. These internal conflicts prevented Ali from introducing any other major changes in the structure of the government. His focus was on defending his caliphate. In 661, Ali was assassinated by one of his opponents, marking the end of the wise caliphate, which had lasted 29 years, and inaugurating the Ummayah caliphate.

Despite the conflicts during the administration of the last two wise caliphs, the wise caliphs' period is known as the golden age of the Islamic public administration. During these 29 years, the wise caliphs, particularly Omar ibn al-Khatab, developed the structure of the government and introduced some of the principles that are still being used by modern government such as the separation between the executive and the judiciary branches of government.

After Ali's death, Mua'wayah ibn abi Suffyan assumed the caliphate with minimum resistance, marking the beginning of the Ummayah caliphate (661–750). During this period, major changes in the practice of public administration emerged. The first caliph of the Ummayah state set the stage for a new and totally different administrative tradition. The first step toward the new Islamic administrative tradition was moving the capital city from Al-Kofa in Iraq to Damascus in Syria. Moving the capital city to Damascus represented the Ummayahs' interest in showing that a new era in Islamic history was emerging. It was a sign that the new state was not a continuation of the wise caliphate.

The most notable change in the practice of public administration was changing from a consultative system to a monarch system. The monarch system was new but has since become an Islamic administrative tradition. With the monarch system, the Ummayah caliphs introduced a new administrative position—al-Hajib—that supported the new trend. The role of al-Hajib was to determine who can see and meet the caliph. During the wise caliphate, people did not need the permission of an agent to see or meet the caliph he could be met or seen at any time with no restriction, but from the caliphate of Mua'wayah onward, seeing

or meeting the caliph was limited to certain people at certain times. Al-Hajib in the Ummayah caliphate separated to a great extent the caliphs from the subjects. Most of the social and administrative matters were delegated to al-Hajib.

The major expansion of the Islamic state demanded other changes in the Islamic administrative tradition. Under the Ummayah caliphs, the boundaries of the Islamic state extended across North Africa and into Spain in the West. In the East, the Islamic army conquered Asia Minor, the Indus Valley, and Transoxiana. This resulted in the need for a decentralized administrative system. While the caliph during the wise caliphate handled most of the matters by himself, the Ummayah caliphate delegated all the power to the governors (Walis) in the Islamic provinces, including the decisions to organize expeditions and conquer new territories. The decentralized system with most of the authorities delegated to the governors encouraged some of them to fight for independence. To suppress the rebellions, the Ummayah caliphs shifted gradually to a very centralized government, but it was too late to maintain control over all the Islamic provinces. The emergence of major opposition parties such as the Shi'ites and the dissenters and very powerful governors who competed with the Ummayah caliphs and declared independence in some of the Islamic provinces significantly weakened the Ummayah caliphate.

These independence movements were accompanied by other factors that contributed to weakening the Ummayah caliphate and its control over the Islamic provinces. Chief among these was the dissatisfaction of the non-Arab Muslims, who were being treated as a second class by the Ummayah caliphs. While the non-Arab Muslims, who were being treated as a second class during the Ummayah caliphate, they were treated equally with the Arab-Muslims during the wise caliphate, and since they were the majority during the Ummayah caliphate, their dissatisfaction generated imbalance in the Islamic state.

These factors resulted in the collapse of the Ummayah caliphate, which introduced a new Islamic administrative tradition that had no similarities with the administrative tradition established by the Prophet (PBUH) and the wise caliphate except for the judiciary system, which was not changed by the Ummayah caliphs. In 750, the last of the Ummayah caliphs was killed, inaugurating the beginning of the Abbasyah caliphate (750–1258). For over five centuries, the Abbasyah caliphs ruled the Islamic state. The Abbasyah caliphate is divided into two caliphates: the Abbasyah caliphate I (750–847) and the Abbasyah caliphate II (847–1258). The first caliphate was very strong and efficient, whereas the second was inefficient and corrupted.

During these five centuries, new administrative traditions were introduced and some old ones were changed. The Abbasyah caliphs were strongly influenced by the Persians, who supported them in defeating the Ummayah caliphate and in developing a new administrative system that adopted most of the Persian administrative tradition. The concept of *Wazarah* (ministry) was borrowed from the Persians and adopted by the Abbasyah. To effectively run the government, they established two types of ministries. The first one known as the executive ministry (Wazart al-tafweeth) and the second one was the delegative ministry (Wazart al-Tanfeeth). In the first one, the minister executes the orders of the caliphs, whereas in the second one, the minister has the power to make orders and to execute them. In the delegative ministry, the minister appoints the governors and removes them without the need for the caliph's approval.

In the first Abbasyah caliphate, the administrative system was centralized to the extent that the *wali* (governor) had no power other than executing the orders of the caliphs. To maintain control over the Islamic provinces, the wali had to provide a report to the caliph by the end of the year, detailing the revenues and the expenditure of his province. Any mishandling would result in the wali removal and the confiscation of his fortune. The wali had also, upon the request of the caliph, to provide detailed description of his wealth and the means by which he made it. Any suspicion about the sources of the wealth would result in the removal of the wali and the confiscation of his wealth.

During the second Abbasyah caliphate, however, the government was run by the ministers and the governors in total absence of the caliphs. The caliphs surrounded themselves with servants and bondmaids. Their interest was in the caliphate and the luxury it provided more than it was in the affairs of the government. The separation between the caliph and his subjects reached its zenith during the second Abbasyah caliphate. The affairs of the citizens were left to the governors, who were corrupted and bribable. To be a wali (governor) depended in most cases on how much a person could pay.

The behavior and the practice of the caliphs of the second Abbasyah caliphate resulted in a gradual loss of the Arab control in most of the Islamic provinces. In the eleventh century, Spain and North Africa were ruled by Berbers, and the Ottoman Turcks ruled Persia, Iraq, and Asia Minor. By the twelfth century, the Islamic empire was divided into several independent Islamic states. Each of these states had its own characteristics and administrative practices.

The last Abbasyah caliph, Al-Musta'asim (1242–1258) failed to defend the last territory under the Abbasyah caliphate against the Mongols, who captured Baghdad in 1258 and put Al-Musta'asim and his family in jail, inaugurating the end of the Abbasyah caliphate. The end of the Abbasyah caliphate marked the end of a united Islamic state with common characteristics and administrative tradition. Since 1258, the Islamic territories and their Muslims have never again been ruled by one leader. There have always been more than one Islamic government and more than one Islamic leader.

ABDULLAH M. AL-KHALAF

J

JAPANESE ADMINISTRATIVE CULTURE.

A contemporary system of governance that has been shaped by history, traditional values, interdependence, consensus decisionmaking, personal responsibility, hard work, stability, and order, which taken together accomplish the goals of Japanese public organizations.

Cultural Influence

Throughout Japanese history, changes have come about slowly and have been brought about more by internal forces than external pressures; thus, the people have led a relatively undisturbed existence. Paradoxically, their culture has transformed itself many times: It was a primitive tribal society in the sixth century; it was a county governed by aristocratic bureaucrats from the seventh through the twelfth centuries; after that, it was a feudal society until the Meiji restoration in 1868; later, it went through World War II; and today Japan is a world economic superpower. Japanese history has not been merely a succession of disconnected events but rather a process of continuous development and collective growth that has left its impact on the culture and its socioeconomic and administrative institutions.

Today's administrative structures, however, have developed largely since the Meiji Restoration, when the country began to modernize its governmental structures. The essential nature of Japanese administration is seen in the way that administrative organizations govern and in the people's acceptance of organizational culture. The norms and beliefs of the past 300 years have contributed to the development of contemporary Japanese administration. One way of understanding how Japanese administration works is to critically examine the cultural factors that influence the behavioral and action orientations of administrators. Without understanding cultural phenomena, it is almost impossible to understand the inner workings of Japanese politics and administration (Reed 1993).

As in every society, Japanese administration is very much influenced by history and tradition. Traditional Japanese culture not only has shaped the behavior of people in administration but has also provided a context for the administrators' understanding of social reality as they interpret the symbolic meanings of shared norms, values, beliefs, ideologies, and languages. In order to understand society's influence on administrators' behaviors and actions, it is necessary to explore tacit elements of society rather than the obvious rules, procedures, tasks, functions, or symbolic activities. The efficient functioning of structures and roles is profoundly dependent on how adminis-

trators accept and internalize the meanings of organizational requirements. Accordingly, administrators commit themselves to institutional goals if they perceive that these goals will afford them the opportunity for growth.

The thrust of an administrative culture in the United States is, to a large extent, related to the policy and administrative philosophy of top executives, such as the president and cabinet secretaries in the federal government, the governor and department heads in the states, and the chief administrators in the municipal governments. By contrast, Japanese administrative culture, by and large, reflects prevailing societal values: It does not readily change because of the ideology of a new leader, such as a prime minister, a cabinet member, a provincial governor, or a mayor. In fact, leaders must respect the existing culture and cannot radically depart from it. The administrative processes and workers' activities are largely guided by shared norms regarding the appropriate behavior of the individual. Administrators realize that these norms are needed in order to accomplish the collective goals of the organization.

Administrative Culture

A number of cultural elements have influenced the patterns of administrative organizations. Several distinctive characteristics of administrative culture include (1) stability and order, (2) groupism and interdependence, (3) paternalism, (4) consensus building in decisionmaking, and (5) personal responsibility and hard work. All of these characteristics are discussed in this section.

First, Japanese administration has a stable and orderly system of governance that operates under strong national and subnational governments. The cultural aspects of public organizations, by and large, are not much different from the social norms and beliefs of the Japanese society. Japan is characterized as a vertical society (Nakane 1970) in which all human relationships are based on a person's hierarchical position, socioeconomic status, educational background, seniority, and gender. Vertical relationships are evident in all organizations, as seen in superior and subordinate, senior and junior, management and labor, the group and individual, and male-female relationships. These relationships existed in the samurai-dominated feudal society before the Meiji Restoration. The vertical relationship is also supported by the respect that people give to the functional relationship between superior and subordinate and to the seniority system, which also provides hierarchical order in a group setting. The seniority system, which is based on length of service and age, is also linked to the salary scale.

Vertical relationships have provided a high degree of stability and order in organizations. Stability is also influenced by the job security that employees in the public sector enjoy as compared with those in the private sector. During periods of economic recession, private sector employees fear unemployment while public employees retain their jobs and are still well respected by the public. Stability and order are maintained by organizational members as they realize the meaning of their loyalty to the government. Today, top administrators are not the main source of stability and order. Instead, stability and order are continuously constructed and reconstructed by public administrators as they see the value of organizational (group) cohesiveness and the responsibility of the organization to Japanese society.

Another important phenomenon in Japanese administration is "groupism," which promotes interdependence and harmony among organizational members. Japanese society attaches importance to group-oriented values, such as harmony, loyalty, and obligation to the organization. Under Tokugawa law during the Edo period (1615–1868), the individual as such did not exist. The family, rather, was the smallest unit recognized by society. The individual held validity only as a family member. The family unit's preservation and status was of concern at all levels of society. In Japanese society, this phenomenon is known as "familyism," which was built upon attitudes absorbed from the vertical culture.

The phenomenon of family orientation has had a major influence on groupism in private and public organizations today. The characteristics of groupism, loyalty, and harmony in public organizations are not as strong as in private organizations. Groupism and loyalty to the company are considered the major attributes of high productivity in Japanese corporations. Although public sector employees may have less organizational loyalty than private sector employees, they do share similar characteristics. First, public administrators give preference to organizational (or group) needs over individual needs. Because group pressure on the individual is high, the individual self is very much integrated into the public self: it is difficult to separate personal life from organizational life. Also, loyalty to one's immediate ministry or agency is an important concern for the individual. When an employee is sent off to do other duties at a different ministry or at an agency in the provincial government, the employee remains faithful to the home ministry or agency. The individual's loyalty to a home agency or ministry often creates difficulty in horizontal coordination between agencies or ministries (Muto 1991; Koike 1994).

Paternalism also contributes to a high degree of stability, harmony, and group cohesiveness. In the private sector, the philosophy of paternalism was based on the idea that the organization was a family: The employer was expected to take care of the welfare of employees; employees were expected to be loyal and grateful for the employer's largesse. This was an extension of the paternalism that prevailed prior to the Meiji Restoration. Public employees enjoy job security and good fringe benefits, such as bonuses, housing allowances, and transportation allowances, although the benefits are not as attractive as benefits provided by large corporations. Despite long work hours (many public employees work 12 hours every work day without receiving overtime pay), they are dedicated to their work and have a strong sense of identification with their agency.

One of the most important qualities of Japanese managers is the ability to lead a group and take care of the problems of subordinates. Because an agency's goal cannot be carried out without the commitment of employees, a manager should be able to hold a group together in vertical relationships (Jun and Muto 1995; Nakane 1970). One of the strategies for promoting a sense of belonging is to provide an extensive training program that lasts three to six months for newly recruited employees in each ministry. This program helps to ensure that the new recruits are "docile ones" with a strong sense of ministerial identification. During the training period, they are reminded to embrace the basic goals, norms, and functions and to feel a personal responsibility toward the organization. In large private corporations, new workers go through an average of six months training, basically learning about the missions and unique characteristics of the company.

Another important phenomenon is the process of decisionmaking in Japanese administration. Although Japanese bureaucracy seems very bureaucratic, hierarchical, and rule-bound, the process of making decisions is often horizontal, involving a series of informal dialogues and meetings among the people whose agencies will be affected by the decision. Because of the homogeneous nature of Japanese administration, consensual decisionmaking is promoted, which emphasizes communication among individuals and with competing agencies (Hempel 1982, p. 25). The lengthy process of negotiation and bargaining is known as *nemawashi*, which mean "the laying of the groundwork for an important decision" (Jun and Muto 1995, p. 131). *Nemawashi* is an important administrative skill that is practiced by executives and managers who negotiate with other government agencies, business organizations, and politicians at the *Diet* (Reed 1993, pp. 129–133).

Routine decisionmaking and proposals originating from low-ranking employees in an agency are made by circulating a written document known as a *ringi sho* ("policy proposal"). As a document moves from the bottom to a higher level, all administrators affix their seal if they agree with the recommended decision. When this *ringi* system (*ringi sei*) is applied to a nonroutine decision that involves the officials of different agencies, bureaus, and divisions, much time is needed for interactions to take place among the administrators of each section, department, bureau, and agency that is involved. Because *nemawashi* on a proposed policy is conducted separately at the different levels of the bureaucracy, the decision process takes a long time.

Because the *ringi* system is highly participatory and requires consensus among all the parties, decisionmaking on a difficult, controversial issue takes a long time and often results in a small incremental change. Although there are some drawbacks to this participatory decisionmaking, the *ringi* system can produce a satisfactory decision that every participating administrator can support. It is a procedure for involving lower-level employees in the decisionmaking process and a way of promoting relationships and loyalty.

Finally, it is widely known that Japanese management in both the public and private sectors has contributed significantly to Japan's economic development and modernization. For the first three decades after World War II, public administrators used their role in designing and implementing development policy to be the main force in bringing about social change. They are loyal and dedicated to their work and their organization. Many have developed a habit of working 12 hours a day without overtime pay. Why they work so hard is still a mystery to Westerners. Working long hours may not be efficient or productive. They, however, seem to believe that there is plenty of work to do. New recruits and newly transferred employees are especially unlikely to leave work while their seniors and supervisors are still working.

Japanese workers in the public and private organizations are expected to develop generalist skills by rotating their jobs every two to three years. For example, when a public administrator who belongs to a special career becomes a division head (*kacho*), that person is likely to accumulate at least ten different job experiences while working as a *kacho*. Every time individuals are assigned to a new position, they are likely to work late into the evening and sometimes socialize until late with their peers. Because the organization provides security and is concerned with employee welfare, workers are dedicated to their work. This dedication, however, does not necessarily spring from self-motivation or job satisfaction. Rather it is a manifestation of an individual's loyalty to the organization and a commitment to one's duty.

Implications

In summary, Japanese administrative culture has a major effect on the life and thinking of the administrator. When the people who work in public and private organizations interact with others, whether professionally or socially, they represent their company or agency. Unlike American organizations, Japanese organizations integrate the workers into the organization both physically and psychologically; the organization provides a major source of social identification and a sense of belonging for its employees. Japanese administration is effective in allaying a worker's sense of alienation and maintaining organizational efficiency.

Administrative culture does much to influence a worker's way of life. It is a truism that when an employee is taken out of the organization, the individual may not function well. Employees are socialized into the dominant administrative culture so that they act according to the expectations of their superiors as well as peers. Although a strong administrative culture provides the context for stability, loyalty, harmony, paternalism, and dedication to work, large Japanese private and public organizations have become stagnant. They lack the vitality needed to change old procedures and develop innovative ways of problem solving. The government's response to the Kobe earthquake symbolized the bureaucratic rigidity and the lack of decisionmaking at the local level. Because of a quirky bureaucratic procedure, the order to send a full-fledged contingent of the self-defense forces was not issued until nine hours after the quake occurred. The crisis management was slipshod, and the confusion regarding emergency operations, such as fire fighting, traffic congestion, food and water supplies, and international aid, shook citizens' trust in government.

The stability and group orientation of Japanese administration promotes interdependence and predictable relationships among organizational members, but it does not further the development of an individual's potential or career. Because Japanese administration emphasizes conformity and hard work above all else, administrators do not display individuality, creativity, or risk-taking behavior. Although constructive ideas are welcome, those who criticize or flout an existing norm are not appreciated: An old saying in Japan is, "The nail that sticks out must be hammered down." To a great extent, Japanese public employees act as others wish them to act. Although employees at the lower echelon often work on new projects that require creative thinking and information gathering, many perform repetitive activities. The middle manager (*kacho*) assigns tasks to employees and encourages group problem solving. Although workers enjoy job security, it is unlikely that they are motivated or satisfied with their work.

Japanese administrators have come to realize that large public organizations are too conservative and rule-bound to cope with challenges in the global environment. Global changes occurring today are creating new, complex, and decentralized systems of networks that are radically different from the old centralized system of governance. As Japanese administrators become more conscious of global influences, they will learn new values and ideas that will help them and other employees become more proactive. At the same time, rigid bureaucracies are gradually transforming themselves into democratic organizations that emphasize decentralization and citizen participation. Japanese administrators are aware that a strong traditional culture provides a context for organizational solidarity, but as they work with diverse cultural and ethnic values in the environment of global politics, they come to understand that some aspects of the traditional culture are a hindrance to the understanding of other cultures and ethnic groups.

JONG S. JUN

BIBLIOGRAPHY

Hempel, T. J., 1982. *Policy and Politics in Japan: Creative Conservatism.* Philadelphia: Temple University Press.

Jun, J. S., and H. Muto, 1995. "The Hidden Dimensions of Japanese Administration: Culture and Its Impact." *Public Administration Review,* vol. 55 (March/April) 125–134.

Koike, O., 1994. "Bureaucratic Policy-making in Japan: Role and Function of Deliberation Councils." In J. S. Jun, ed., *Development in the Asia Pacific: A Public Policy Perspective.* Berlin: Walter de Gruyter, 433–447.

Miyamoto, M., 1994. *Straitjacket Society.* Tokyo: Kodansha International.

Muto, H., 1991. "Institutional Reform for Improving Policy Coordination in Japanese Government." *International Review of Administrative Sciences,* vol. 55, no. 1: 85–94.

Nakane, C., 1970. *The Japanese Society.* Rutland, VT: Charles E. Tuttle.

Reed, S. R., 1993. *Making Common Sense of Japan.* Philadelphia: Temple University Press.

JOB ACTION.

The temporary stoppage of work or concerted activity by employees in order to express dissatisfaction with management practices (see **strike**). Although most often associated with the collective bargaining process, it can also occur when collective bargaining is not sanctioned and can involve nonunion employees (see **collective bargaining**). The strike is considered to be the ultimate form of job action.

With the emergence of union activity in the public sector, the debate over the right of government employees to withhold their services became an issue. One of the early strong arguments against allowing the public sector worker to collectively bargain was based on the right to strike. The labor relations model established in the National Labor Relations Act specifically gave private sector workers the right to strike as a way of balancing the power between management and unions. The withholding of labor is a strong economic weapon that can be used to bring closure to labor disputes. In the public sector, a far different environment exists.

The illegality of the strike in the public sector is based on the issues of governmental sovereignty, essentiality of services, and the monopolistic nature of public employers. The reality of striking in the public sector is that it becomes a political weapon, which often creates a backlash for the union and thus exacerbates the situation. A good example of this is the 1981 strike by the Professional Air Traffic Controllers (PATCO) that ended with the firing of many of the people who took part and the decertification of the union.

As a result of the illegality and sometimes ineffectiveness of public sector strikes, workers have developed more creative means to force management to come to terms. Job actions for government workers are tailored to their specific occupations. Police contract "blue flu"; medical personnel admit large numbers to hospitals while cutting down on discharges, thus overloading the system; firefighters refuse to do hazard inspections, thus jeopardizing federal monies; and teachers are overcome by strange illnesses on days when the substitute pool is depleted. Work slowdowns can also occur without employees losing any days of work. To accomplish this, government workers pay attention to every single rule, thus causing delays in the implementation of policy. Job actions can also be as innocuous as informational picketing or tying up an elected board's time with numerous speeches or points of order during meetings.

Job action strategies by workers have become more creative as they perceive a narrowing of options. Whether it is a concerted activity or strike, workers in both sectors use job actions to try to bring attention to workplace issues that they feel are not being addressed by management. In the private sector, this can be done using economic pressure by withholding labor. In the public sector, more creative means are used in order to bring political pressure on the decisionmakers.

SHERRY S. DICKERSON

BIBLIOGRAPHY

Kearney, Richard C., 1992. *Labor Relations in the Public Sector,* 2nd ed. New York: Marcel Dekker.

Piskulich, John P., 1991. *Collective Bargaining in State and Local Government.* New York: Prager.

Rabin, Jack et al., eds., 1994. *Handbook of Public Sector Labor Relations.* New York: Marcel Dekker.

Riccucci, Norma M., 1990. *Women, Minorities, and Unions in the Public Sector.* New York: Greenwood Press.

JOB ANALYSIS AND EVALUATION.

Techniques used to determine the worth, primarily in terms of salary, of a particular position to the organization. As such, job analysis and evaluation focuses on the position rather than the performance of the incumbent who performs actual job duties and responsibilities.

The concept of job evaluation, a term of relatively recent usage, first developed as the position classification movement in the early part of the twentieth century. Many writers now use the terms "position or job classification" and "job evaluation" interchangeably. Technically, "job analysis and classification," as used herein, refers to the first and second stages of the traditional job evaluation process. However, an examination of traditional job evaluation techniques finds these terms used synonymously.

As so often occurs with traditional approaches, in personnel theory and elsewhere, attacks on job evaluation methodologies have been leveled under the twin banners of innovation and reform. The 1993 Report of the National Performance Review, chaired by Vice President Al Gore, urged policymakers to "dramatically simplify the current classification system to give agencies greater flexibility in how they classify and pay their employees" (National Performance Review 1993, p. 4). Despite the vice president's plea for classification reform, probably no other area of personnel management has been so ignored. As Harold Suskin (1977) metaphorically stated, "(It) has remained as an island surrounded by the seas of change" (p. vii). Ironically, both advocates and critics of job evaluation studies would concur that the field is important, both to the merit principle and the civil service system.

Evaluating Positions, Not People

As Glen Stahl (1983) observed of traditional position classification, it is "the analyzing and organizing of jobs in an enterprise into categories or classes on the basis of their duties and responsibilities, and the knowledges and skills required to perform them" (p. 184). It is far more than "duties classification"; job classification quite simply puts jobs into categories according to their comparative value (rank) with all other jobs in an organization.

Appropriately, one might question the necessity of job classifications at all. Couldn't each worker's job description serve as the basis for developing a wage compensation system, employee performance appraisals, hiring and promotional qualifications and other personnel activities? Yes, in a totally abstract sense. Yet left alone, job descriptions are not organized or related to each other. In this situation, a personnel manager would be faced with formulating equitable wage and benefits separately for each worker's position—a herculean task for even the smallest governmental unit. Personnel specialists traditionally simplify this chore by classifying similar jobs or positions into categories based on information gathered from job analysis.

As an objective, job evaluation studies seek to include all job positions that are sufficiently similar in subject matter of work, level of difficulty, responsibility, and qualification requirements. A "series of classes" links all jobs in ascending level of difficulty within a specific type of work, for example, Clerk-Typist (I-II-III). At the federal level, jobs that are close in level of difficulty, responsibility, and qualification requirements may be placed together in a "grade." Larger jurisdictions utilize grade schedules to group positions by comparable levels of difficulty. Unlike classifications, grades such as the General Schedule (GS) system, covering many federal employees, are not based on related subject matter of work. For instance, a GS level within the federal personnel system might bring together, for purposes of comparison only, such disparate classifications as a Work Unit Conservationist, a Border Patrol Officer I, and an Account Auditor.

Traditionally, the position classification approach has been predicated upon a carefully detailed and written position (job) description. This document generally reflects job characteristics, regardless of the impact on the person (incumbent) who actually holds the job. Although formats vary, most position descriptions include the following items: an appropriate title, job duties and examples of tasks, employee responsibilities, and qualifications criteria when selecting new employees for the position. As the number of positions expands within an agency, there is generally a need for more specificity within position descriptions. Position descriptions in smaller organizations will frequently inject the caveat "and other duties as assigned" as a means for discretionary changes by management in stated duties and responsibilities—often to the chagrin of employees and their unions.

It is upon the building blocks of position descriptions that classification specifications (commonly used by state and local personnel specialists) or class standards (used by federal classification analysts) are constructed. Like the position descriptions, class "specs" in the position classification approach set duties and responsibilities criteria for an entire classification of jobs. In smaller agencies, position descriptions and class specs will be combined.

Job Evaluation: The Foundation Stone of Civil Service

The personnel reform movement in the United States, as embodied in the merit principle, sought to develop an objective and consensus statement of each public employee's duties and responsibilities. If workers were to be selected according to the merit system, duties and responsibilities of each job must be clearly understood and specifically defined. If public employees were to be given equal pay for comparable jobs, they should be grouped together so that an appropriate level of difficulty might be determined. This quest for merit and pay equity in the public workplace provided the genesis for position evaluation. The thrust occurred initially at the federal level and was later disseminated through state and local personnel systems.

Job evaluation efforts were given added legitimacy when they became essential information for line-item budgeting reforms (see **position classification** and **budget formats**). Financial control systems in the public sector dictated that positions rather than individual employee characteristics should be the basis of compensation systems. Interestingly, position classification in the private sector during the same era was implemented for different reasons. It was supported as a mechanism for increasing efficiency and productivity rather than as a personnel reform. Managerial efficiency instead of employee merit was the guiding light. Only later was the job evaluation function in the private sector expanded to include job enrichment aspects.

Perhaps the sine qua non of the job evaluation movement was achieved in the passage of the Classification Act of 1923, which one scholar calls "one of the great milestones in public personnel legislation," because it solidified position classification as a federal personnel technique (Stahl 1983, p. 186). It established a federal Personnel Classification Board charged with grouping positions into classes on the basis of job duties and responsibilities. And in a phrase anticipatory of the equal rights movement, the board was committed to enforcing "equal compensation for equal work, irrespective of sex."

Subsequent classification acts further defined and expanded the role of position classification in federal employment. For instance, the Classification Act of 1949 delegated the task of developing job evaluation standards to the Civil Service Commission. Each agency was assigned responsibility for classifying its own employee positions, with the commission retaining authority for reclassification whenever necessary. By the post–World War II era, position classification was entrenched at the federal and state levels, as well as in progressive local governments.

Undoubtedly, position classification is also subject to a certain amount of misuse and misunderstanding. Briefly, the position classification approach is not (1) a specific description of what employee X does, (2) shaped by other personnel functions, such as wage compensation hiring, promotion, or training, (3) designed to reflect automatically changes in a particular position's responsibilities, knowledge, or duties, (4) a classification of specific employees. Furthermore, any civil service system includes a mix of both classified and unclassified positions, with elected officials, legislative employees and department heads being excluded from the classified service.

Job evaluation as it is currently practiced by most personnel managers follows established principles and guidelines that focus on the position, not the employee. They have historically involved qualitative and quantitative methodologies.

The Job Evaluation Process

Depending on whether a complete or partial job evaluation study is needed, three possible stages may be required:

- *Job Analysis (Factfinding).* The gathering and documenting of a job's content.
- *Job Classification.* The grouping together of positions with similar duties and responsibilities, as well as setting job standards.
- *Monitoring.* The periodic reevaluation of position classifications for purposes of possible revision or reclassification.

It bears emphasizing that no two job evaluation studies are alike and each should be based on organizational needs (Candrilli and Armagast 1987). Only rarely will every phase of a complete job evaluation study be implemented. Reasons for carrying out a job evaluation study vary as greatly as the problems encountered. One study may simply seek a reassessment of qualification standards,

duties, or responsibilities. Other studies may focus on an occupation found only in one agency, or they may develop a standard for classifying a common function, such as executive management, among many agencies and for unrelated occupations. An evaluation study will even occasionally redefine an occupation/profession or define a new one; an evaluation study may also be the basis of job redesign so that an incumbent works "smarter" rather than harder (Reilly and DiAngels, 1988). Job evaluation studies can be undertaken as an outcome of labor-management negotiations, as standard operating procedure for reassessing vacant positions, or as requested by a supervisor or position incumbent.

The Job Analysis Stage

Job evaluation begins with a detailed job analysis phase that usually involves the following steps: collecting job information, organizing it by selecting the data most useful, and finally documenting all supporting data related to the job duties, responsibilities and qualification requirements. Most frequently, the job analysis process results in a "position description" document. Again, reliable and precise position descriptions are usually utilized in each facet of personnel management, that is, selection, training, promotion, adverse actions, and others. Perhaps the most direct application of position descriptions occurs in developing employment qualification standards used in selecting new employees. Once position descriptions have been prepared, all job qualifications–knowledge, skills, and abilities–can be compared for consistency with actual duties performed and thus may be useful in refuting unintentional discrimination charges (Cook 1992).

A number of factfinding tools are available to job analysts, but these techniques should be used only following a thorough and well-planned preliminary job analysis in order to collect critical information for designing an appropriate job analysis study.

Preliminary Analysis

Thoughtful preliminary research should precede any job analysis study of any depth. For instance, a position standards study at the federal level might involve perusing the following sources of information: (1) standards division files, (2) library materials, (3) other personnel offices, (4) other agencies, and (5) union and professional organizations.

Background information obtained from these sources can aid in deciding the types of jobs and specific agencies to be included in the factfinding or job analysis stage. This information can also identify problems to be explored as well as the kinds of information needed from employees, coworkers, and supervisors.

Accuracy of information is the most important facet of job evaluation. Inaccurate or omitted facts concerning an employee position can skew the entire job evaluation process. Personnel specialists must possess both a preliminary understanding of the types of information needed and an appreciation for thoroughness in data-gathering methodology.

The Content of Job Analysis

What to look for in factfinding depends partially on the job evaluation's objectives, even though certain types of data are always required. In order to ensure accuracy of information, several categories of information must be kept in mind; otherwise, a job's importance may be inflated or misunderstood. Not only must one analyze the nature of the work being performed but also its intended purpose within the agency's overall mission.

As a framework for data collection, the factfinder must remember that employee knowledge, skills, and abilities (KSAs) should mesh with position duties and responsibilities. Job analysts are particularly sensitive to kinds of decisions and specific decisionmaking situations within each position. These are often subject to fluctuation as jobs change.

Briefly, KSAs are reflected in those qualifications used as minimum standards for recruitment and selection of new employees to a position. Knowledge, skills, and abilities might be assumed by formal degrees, certificates, or license requirements. Or they might be attained through prior employment experience and training. Other KSAs, such as the ability to supervise or delegate tasks, might be observable to the job analyst.

As indicated, job qualifications are only half the focus for factfinding or job analysis. These must be related to duties and responsibilities in a particular job situation. Although qualifications in two positions might be identical; duties and responsibilities can differ remarkably. An Attorney-Investigator I position in the Department of Justice's Office of Civil Rights might require highly specific, narrowly focused duties and responsibilities, while the same position on a congressional committee staff might involve generally unstructured, discretionary responsibilities and duties. As a rule of thumb, the more diverse the jobs in an evaluation system, the more varied will be the qualifications against which all jobs and occupations in the system are to be evaluated.

The process for determining job-related KSA requirements for specific jobs usually involves the following five steps:

- *Step 1.* Develop a detailed listing of tasks performed by incumbents; tasks should be considered preliminary—neither complete nor confirmed as representing work that is actually performed, pending further verification;

- *Step 2.* Evaluate tasks; decide which tasks are important for job success and are "first day" priorities and thus can be used later for selection procedure development.

Tasks that are unimportant, rarely performed, not required upon job entry or are only executed with close supervision can be eliminated.

- *Step 3.* Generate KSA listing to define KSAs needed to perform tasks effectively. Some observers recommend that knowledge requirements be generated separately and prior to skill and ability components. Knowledge for each task should include all types of knowledge requirements, the level of knowledge, as well as different situations in which tasks are performed.

- *Step 4.* Evaluate and link KSAs that are required to perform various critical tasks and specifically if a particular KSA is essential for performing an identified task (see discussion regarding the ADA below).

- *Step 5.* Finally, review results (from steps 1–4) as surviving critical tasks, KSAs, and linkages so that job analysis produces meaningful product.

The determination of job related KSAs and critical tasks provide documentation as the appropriate basis for a new hire or promotional selection as required in the Uniform Guidelines on Employee Selection Procedures (1978) and the Americans with Disabilities Act (1991).

Techniques in Job Analysis

A combination of alternative techniques in factfinding is usually advisable. The first phase of factfinding, data collection, is dependent on verification of information from multiple sources. The following methodologies are generally employed by job analysts.

Questionnaires are particularly suited for obtaining basic information from employees. Questionnaires may be used as a source of data preceding an individual interview or as the sole information source together with spot-check interviews of randomly selected employees. In both instances, an employee's supervisor, together with the employee, should review each questionnaire for accuracy. A study by Veres, Green, and Boyles (1991) found that job analysis questionnaires may be subject to the racial bias of employees completing questionnaires. It was determined that a sample of African American and white incumbents tended to complete questionnaires differently, based on an incumbent's race.

Questionnaires vary considerably in purpose and format. A narrative-type questionnaire, with open-ended response items, asks the employee to write one or more paragraphs describing various job characteristics. Questionnaires allow employees to express their own perspectives but frequently suffer from lack of clarity and specificity in expression. Checklist questionnaires require the employee to check appropriate job characteristics and duties. The checklist trades flexibility in expression for a more rigid job focus. Checklist questionnaires are readily available for a range of occupations commonly found in the civil service, thus saving time in interpretation and analysis.

Individual interviews or desk audits are generally conducted on the job site. Usually, both employee and supervisor are interviewed. Interviews should provide a job analyst with divergent sources of information regarding key job characteristics. For instance, interview discrepancies might occur in such areas as the degree of supervision required or the nature of specific tasks. Interviewers have sufficient understanding of employee tasks when they can clearly articulate what the employee does, to whom or where the employee does it, what the output is, and what tools, equipment, processes, or work aids are used in accomplishing job tasks.

An alternative to the individual interview approach in factfinding is the group interview, a technique particularly helpful whenever a large number of jobs in a single occupation are under analysis. However, one should realize that group interviewing is more difficult, requiring the job analyst to function as a small group facilitator as well. Often two job analysts are needed to conduct a group session adequately.

Job analysts frequently utilize supplemental techniques along with individual or group interviews, including participant logs that may provide an alternative factfinding tool for jobs that are nonrepetitive and vary considerably in the degree to which KSAs are utilized on a daily basis. This may be simply a desk calendar on which an employee notes each time an activity changes. More comprehensive logs would include detailed notes by the employee on tasks throughout the day. Before embarking on a participant log project, job analysts usually conduct a pretest session with employees along with a postlog review.

Subject Matter Experts (SMEs) are individuals who are directly familiar with the job, but who may be other than the position incumbents or supervisors. They are persons who have a visionary construct of what job KSAs should be in an ideal environment, regardless of who actually fills the position. Subject Matter Experts can also be asked to generate, refine, and confirm tasks performed by job incumbents.

If conducted thoroughly and systematically, the job analysis, or factfinding phase, yields a wealth of job-related information. From these data, the job analyst can prepare an accurate statement or description of specific job duties, responsibilities, and employee abilities. The analyst now has a basis for evaluating the job's importance. The process of placing the job in an appropriate classification may begin; it is a task that requires of the evaluator an analytic precision and organizational perspective.

The Job Classification Stage

Following the job analysis phase, the stage is set for the job classification process. The job has been described and analyzed; it must also be evaluated. Actually, position classification, historically most utilized in the public sector, is only one approach to job evaluation, even though many observers use the terms interchangeably.

A number of issues should be decided before embarking on the job classification phase, regardless of jurisdiction size. First, the number of classes should be limited to the minimal number necessary to accomplish the study's objectives. Nuances among jobs do not deserve separate classifications. Second, concerns of methodology should be determined by the study's purposes, not vice versa. What is appropriate in one situation might not be so in another. Third, consistency as well as creativity in approach will reduce the seemingly inevitable conflict engendered by comprehensive classification studies. Finally, the decision of who should be involved in classification must be decided in advance; is it the role of a classification specialist or is it desirable to involve line managers in the process?

There are two fundamentally different approaches employed in job classification: Those that evaluate the job as a whole (qualitative) and those that break a job down into its component factors (quantitative). From these two orientations there have developed different evaluation systems, that is, classification, ranking, factor comparison, point factor, market pricing, and decision band systems. Although during the 1980s and 1990s quantitative approaches became more widely adopted in job evaluation, qualitative techniques still prevail among many state and local governments.

Qualitative Approaches

Qualitative, or whole-job, methods of job classification historically dominated job evaluation in the public sector. Usually, such techniques involve either ranking the whole job, or position, classification. Position classification connotes a procedure whereby jobs are compared and grouped into classes on the basis of their perceived similarities. Similar job duties and responsibilities allow job evaluators to devise standard specifications for the entire class, such as descriptive titles, rates of pay, or qualification requirements.

Position Classification. The basic elements of a position classification system include a class of positions, written specifications for each class of positions, and allocation of each position to an appropriate class as evaluated by set allocation criteria. Although the number of job allocation elements may vary among jurisdictions, the following are consistent in position classification studies:

- Subject matter, function, profession, or occupation. In larger bureaucracies, highly specialized studies determining the field of work may not pose a particular obstacle for the analyst. In smaller jurisdictions, where polyglot groupings of jobs into a single position often occur, determining the nature of work may be quite sensitive. In one particular classification study, building, plumbing, and electrical inspectors quite vigorously objected to being reclassified together as Construction Inspectors I and II. They considered the new classification title an affront to their professional craft identities.

- The difficulty and complexity of duties performed is always relative to other jobs, either those within closely related or substantially different occupational categories. Difficulty and complexity variables include how job assignments are made for employees, procedures to be followed, processes performed, plans and actions initiated, or decisions made by the employee. In addition, the variety and scope, as well as control of employee work as exercised by others, affect the job's difficulty and complexity.

  It should be noted that a greater variety of tasks in a job does not always reflect a more difficult or complex job. In fact, greater complexity or variation in tasks may be the basis of job-enrichment strategies because greater variety and complexity may actually increase worker satisfaction.

- Nonsupervisory responsibilities, although sometimes involving employee review of other employee work, more usually focus on employee authority to proceed with relative independence of action, that is, freedom from prescribed work activities. It includes development and implementation of programs and the degree of responsibility for final action.

- Supervisory and administrative responsibilities for which the work of others is administered, directed, or supervised in the job. The demarcation between supervisory and nonsupervisory responsibilities is whether an employee has authority to merely review or actually change the findings or activities of designated subordinate positions.

- Qualification standards, although essential for each classification, are usually formulated following, rather than as a part of, the position classification process. These basic allocation factors within a classification and among other classifications are highly interrelated. Position classifications are based on the logic that a range of difficulty and responsibility exists, both within a particular class and among classes. Most positions are readily categorized into specific classifications, provided that systematic and accurate job analysis has been carried out. As in many personnel activities, those positions that are borderline require considerable effort and sensitivity by the job analyst or position classifier.

Whole-Job Ranking. The other major qualitative approach that has been widely used by smaller governments is whole-job ranking. A committee usually ranks each job in terms of its value to the organization and in a hierarchy from highest to lowest in comparison to all other posi-

tions. The basis for ranking may even include such subjective factors as the organizational unit involved, importance of the job to the agency's mission, prestige of the incumbent or perceived pay inequity attributable to gender bias.

Quantitative Methods

Factor comparison and point-factor rating approaches exemplify efforts to quantify job evaluation studies. Both methodologies attempt to make the job evaluation process more precise and less arbitrary, although critics would argue that quantifiable rigidity diminishes managerial discretion to restructure jobs. Both techniques break jobs down into their component factors.

Point-Factor Rating. This procedure defines job factors, which are then broken down into levels or degrees and are subsequently assigned a specific point value by the classifier. The cumulative point total for all job factors determines a job's classification level. Jobs in a point-factor system are not compared with other jobs in the organization, as in factor comparison. Each job element is evaluated by various degrees in terms of typical tasks performed. For each degree, point values have been assigned. At each succeedingly higher degree, task difficulty and responsibility are supposedly greater. Each ascendant level should require different and more sophisticated judgment, knowledge, ability, and skill. Again, evaluation is based on typically performed tasks rather than an exceptional occurrence.

Supporters of the point-rating system argue that it provides a valuable tool in evaluating a uniform set of elements for each position and a consistent weighting of each job element. Variations of work difficulty as well as kinds of work performed, whether in large or small departments, can supposedly be objectively evaluated (Plachy 1987).

Despite these claims, it is also clear that considerable opportunity exists for subjectively assigning points to various factors and subfactors. Who is to say whether a particular job factor, such as "problem solving" or "accountability," should have a maximum of 80 rather than 40 points or that each subfactor should be in increments of 10 rather than 15 points? Under the factor of "supervision given," does it matter whether part-time employees supervised are work-study students, graduate assistants, or nonstudent clerks? Though controversial, the point factor rating approach has traditionally been the mainstay of efforts to quantify job classification.

One of the most commonly made criticisms of point factoring is that any change in a job duty or responsibility will automatically result in a change in the number of points assigned to the job. Gerald Barnett and Dennis Doverspike (1989) argue that many times, this is not the case. For example, the level of education required to perform most clerical jobs will not change as a result of minor alterations in job duties and responsibilities. They contend that point factoring includes a fair amount of flexibility in the system; changes in job duties, tasks, and responsibilities need not actually change the number of points assigned to the job.

Other observers disagree regarding point factoring's ability to adjust to rapidly changing jobs. The case of clerical support workers is a prime example. With the advent of user-friendly computer software, it has become acceptable for managers to plug away in front of a screen, a task formerly left to secretaries. Yet, point factoring may not keep up with these changes.

Factor Comparison. This method is similar to the point-factor approach in that both methodologies break a job down into its factors (elements). Jobs within an organization may then be compared according to particular factors as a means of job evaluation. Factor comparison may be directly linked to wage determination through a series of compensation factors, that is, aspects of the job that are worthy of compensation. Jobs generally include five compensable factors: mental requirements, physical requirements, skill, responsibility, and working conditions. For example, all secretary positions in an organization might include a responsibility factor. Instead of assigning points to each factor, a dollar amount would be awarded. One departmental secretary might receive US $4,000 annually for the responsibility factor, whereas another with lesser responsibilities would only be rated US $2,000 on the same factor.

In large organizations, both governmental and nongovernmental, only a few key jobs are selected for evaluation by factor comparison. These benchmark positions usually reflect all levels, departments, salary ranges, and tasks performed within the organization. Once the job-analysis phase is completed for benchmark jobs, position descriptions are prepared in a factor-analysis format. Benchmark jobs are ranked under each factor, and later other jobs are ranked in reference to these factors.

The Hay Method. One widely adopted version of factor comparison is the Hay Method, which is practiced by a consulting firm known as the Hay Group. It selects three primary factors common to all jobs: know-how, problem solving, and accountability; and it quantitatively measures the extent to which each of these three elements is required in each job. Although reliance on three job factors appears easy to comprehend, the Hay Method is linked very specifically to one organization and usually requires a classification committee comprised of employees to make definite comparable identification of assigned weights. The Hay Method not only assigns worth to jobs, it also converts jobs to monetary value.

The major disadvantage of the Hay system as a technique is its level of difficulty and complexity; it is somewhat difficult to explain to employees and may not be appropriate for an organization with many similar jobs. For example, an organization with numerous clerical positions may find that clerical positions do not vary significantly on the accountability factor. This situation may lead to possible "conflict of interest" among classification committee members who may subjectively apply non–job content factors to the classification process, that is, organizational status of the secretary's supervisor, incumbent skills, and so forth.

It is important to realize that quantitative point-factor, factor-comparison, and the Hay methodologies were developed by private sector personnel specialists and are the most common approach used by corporations (Sahl 1989). As with many other personnel reforms, its advocates believe that quantification or factor analysis will achieve greater rationality and pay equity into public sector job evaluation. Despite increasing usage of such techniques among state and local personnel managers, position classification and position-ranking methods are still widely employed. Surveys of state and local evaluation practices reveal that quantification or whole-job methods predominate (Craver 1977; Ganschinietz and McConomy 1983).

A comparison of Ganschinietz and McConomy's data (1983) with earlier studies suggests several important job evaluation trends among states and counties. First is the existence of a movement toward increased use of quantitative methodologies. A growing number of personnel specialists believe that quantitative approaches are more objective and technically superior. By 1985, point factor had become the most widely used technique in both the private and public sectors. Second, there is an increasing tendency to adopt methods and pay practices that are occupationally specific, for example, to apply different job evaluation methods and separate pay schedules for various occupational groups.

An important caveat to these developments in position classification must be borne in mind. Any quest for a single approach to job classification that is effective and satisfying to all parties is probably a dubious venture. A study by the National Academy of Public Administration (1991) suggests that a combination of various job-analysis and evaluation strategies is most workable for federal agencies. The potential for utilizing several job evaluation methodologies simultaneously is evident in the mixed approaches developed within the federal bureaucracy.

Traditional qualitative and quantitative approaches to job evaluation in the public sector are currently undergoing rethinking and experimentation, with a growing utilization of a variety of methods rather than a single technique for job evaluation. The array of techniques available to job evaluators/analysts is already quite diverse, yet legislative and bureaucratic restrictions severely limit the degree of reform that can occur. For example, the 1991 study by the National Academy of Public Administration called for sweeping changes in the federal classification structure wherein the fifteen grades would be replaced by occupational family bands.

The Position-Monitoring Stage

One must consider the plight of public sector job evaluation in the twenty-first century. There is substantial evidence that job evaluation, particularly position classification, is either widely abused or simply ignored. That the federal classification system is frequently misused was indicated by a study conducted by the former Civil Service Commission (CSC).

Specifically, the CSC study found that 10 percent of white-collar jobs in the General Schedule were overgraded, 2.9 percent undergraded, and 4.2 percent not properly classified by title or occupational series (May 1978). These findings translated into 176,000 jobs that were incorrectly graded, with overgrading costs of more than US $370 million per year. Percentagewise, grades GS-7, GS-8, GS-10, and GS-15 accounted for the highest error rates.

It is important to underscore the apparent causes of misgrading. Errors in judgment by position classifiers accounted for 27 percent of overgrading, while management considerations, that is, administrative allocations, management pressure, and so forth, were primarily responsible for the remaining percentage. A management study of the New York City merit system practices by Columbia University revealed that "broadcasting"—combining several job titles into one—and consolidation of job titles was the single most feasible and worthwhile reform supported by a wide range of civil service reformers.

Intense pressures, both personal and political, exist to reclassify (upward) many positions. Consider the case of New Mexico, whose personnel situation is typical of numerous state personnel systems. In a one-year span (1980–1981), the New Mexico State Personnel Department received 3,008 requests for reclassification. Of these, 2,672 were reclassified upward and 336 downward. Clearly, the personal and political pressures are to reclassify upward as a means of rewarding faithful employees.

Roger Plachy (1987) argues that a major contributor to reclassification abuse is the tendency of managers to manipulate a classification system that they view as inequitable, so managers protect their employees by juggling the system to their best advantage. The solution is to persuade managers "to play on the same team, to work for the same goals." In essence, Plachy believes managers should be trained and involved in the classification process (p. 32).

A major reclassification movement was initiated following passage of the Americans with Disabilities Act (ADA) in 1991, which necessitated that employers answer three fundamental questions: (1) What are the essential job functions of a position? (2) Are there accommodations that would allow the individual to perform its essential functions? (3) Would accommodations impose an "undue hardship" on the employer? (Boller and Massengill 1992).

Under ADA, a qualified individual with a disability is someone who meets legitimate skill, experience, education, or other requirements of an employment position that the person holds or seeks and who can perform the "essential functions" of the position with or without reasonable accommodation. Requiring the ability to perform "essential" functions assures that an individual will not be considered unqualified simply because of inability to perform marginal or incidental job functions. If the individual is qualified to perform essential job functions except for limitations caused by a disability, the employer must consider whether the individual could perform these functions with a reasonable accommodation.

In identifying an essential function through job evaluation, an employer must focus on the purpose of the function and the result to be accomplished rather than the manner in which it is usually performed. Essential functions are the fundamental job duties of the employment position and not the marginal functions of the position. In order to determine an essential function, an employer can assume a function is essential if the following criteria exist: (1) The position exists to perform the function; (2) there are a limited number of other employees available to perform the function or among whom the function can be distributed; and (3) a function is highly specialized, and the person in the position is hired for special expertise or ability to perform it.

The ADA interprets "reasonable accommodation" as any modification or adjustment to a job, an employment practice, or the work environment that makes it possible for an individual with a disability to enjoy an equal employment opportunity. Title I of ADA requires reasonable accommodation in all aspects of employment (Greenlaw and Kohl 1992). The result has been that, quite literally, massive numbers of job descriptions were rewritten in the 1990s as organizations conducted job reevaluation studies in order to separate essential from marginal job functions.

The Future of Job Evaluation

As the standard line goes, "There's some good news and some bad news." The good news is that job evaluation approaches are demonstrating a greater degree of innovation and job redesign experimentation than previously. The bad news is that no one may really care anymore. Take the case of secretaries: Evaluators have become very adept at classifying, comparing, rating, ranking, and evaluating secretarial positions. The Bureau of Labor Statistics projects that job openings in the secretarial field grow at nearly 300,000 new positions a year, the highest among the 299 job classifications that it surveys. One problem exists—a declining number of people want to be stereotypical "secretaries".

Evaluators may have devised more sophisticated techniques for classification only to miss the essence of job evaluation.

Job evaluation, in its philosophical sense, encompasses far more than methodologies for determining position KSAs, factor-comparison criteria, and point-rating scales. Yet, job evaluation often has concerned itself with these narrow methodological issues. It has failed to link job evaluation to valid performance appraisal, motivational concerns, rapidly changing job KSAs or to address pay equity/comparable-worth disparities.

The dilemma that job evaluation studies find is threefold. First, the role of employee performance in job evaluation studies is deliberately ignored; second, job evaluation assumptions are in apparent conflict with the prevailing winds of civil service reform; third, job evaluations often do not keep up with rapidly changing job KSAs.

Esther Lawton (1977) describes a rather typical manipulation of job classifications: "More often than not, an employee has been around a long time, was conscientious, and probably deserved some kind of recognition, preferably money" (p. 55). Frequently, managers see upward reclassification as the most appropriate means of rewarding the faithful worker. Reclassification is also justified whenever an employee no longer requires supervision, works independently, widens the job's scope, and performs more difficult tasks. In both instances, job evaluation, and particularly position classification, approaches are utilized as employee incentives. That this regularly happens is partially due to the compartmentalization of performance evaluation and job evaluation functions. Performance appraisal approaches have only occasionally been directly related to job elements, despite some encouraging efforts in this regard. Frequently, the classification plan is viewed as pure and inviolable, as if it were unrelated to the rest of personnel management and line managers should be kept out of the job classification process.

Nowhere is the ambivalence surrounding the purposes of job evaluation more exemplified than in the prevailing maxim, "It is the job, not the person, that is classified." Among quantitative methods, one supposedly rates or compares abstract job factors, not actual tasks performed by particular employees. Traditional evaluation studies also do not consider employees who bring additional skills to their job. These approaches, at least in theory, disregard the impact of an employee on job duties and responsibilities. Even so, an employee's performance impact on a job's nature may occur in two ways: (1) by changing the actual job itself or (2) by performing the job either more or less efficiently. Yet, job evaluation strategies may not directly acknowledge either aspect of employee impact.

Finally, job evaluation methodologies suffer an uncertain future because their theoretical assumptions run counter to civil service reform efforts. The debate between proponents of quantitative and qualitative approaches to job evaluation is secondary to a broader, more fundamental controversy in public-management circles: Should managers be delegated more discretion in human resources management? Should the civil service system, with its traditional emphasis on employee neutrality and protection, be restructured so that managers play a greater role in performance appraisal and job assignment? A growing number of human resource managers contend that managers should be more active participants in the job evaluation process: "Most managers who cheat the system do so because they do not know a better way to manage; they are stuck with an inequitable system, or they can protect their employees only by juggling the system to their best advantage" (Plachy 1987, p. 32).

Traditional position-classification and job-evaluation studies are believed by many observers to defeat productivity and managerial effectiveness. Others see such studies as a throwback to outmoded scientific management theories and maladapted to contemporary human-resources management (Shafritz and Hyde 1983). Position-classification studies are criticized as unreasonable constraints on top management, hurtful to employee morale, and little more than polite fictions in substance. They are viewed by some observers as the triumph of technique over substance (Lawler 1987).

An IPA study of personnel management and productivity in eight medium-sized cities revealed that many administrators were critical of the classification plan's irrelevance to actual work activities. There was little effort to keep classification systems current or to allow for managerial flexibility in job assignment or supervision. The results were "organizational anachronisms and rigidities that defeat the purposes of classification, impair the ability of managers to manage, and . . . raise productivity."

Job-evaluation studies and position-classification plans are caught in the vortex of the controversy. The inherently subjective nature of position evaluation is demonstrated in a study by Lewis and Stevens (1990), in which a job-evaluation committee's knowledge of a job holder's gender was found to significantly bias committee ratings. In effect, the same position was rated more highly when it was held by a male than when it was held by a female, regardless of whether the job evaluation committee was dominated by males or females. Classification plans are the bedrock of a merit system that is under extreme attack. If job-evaluation efforts are going to survive and even prosper, they must become a part of contemporary reform efforts. Rather than remaining a sanctified and untouchable bastion, classification plans must incorporate job evaluation methodologies that are flexible and responsive to managerial discretion. For instance, job responsibilities and duties need to reflect work as it is actually performed and should be susceptible to change and ongoing innovation by management. Just as certainly, job responsibilities and duties at an increased level of difficulty would ideally be rewarded through a fair wage compensation plan. Perhaps the cry "It's not in my job description" will be heard with less stridency.

T. ZANE REEVES

BIBLIOGRAPHY

Barnett, Gerald V. and Dennis Doverspike, 1989. "Another Defense of Point-Factor Job Evaluation." *Personnel* (March) 33–36.

Boller, Harvey, and Douglas Massengill, 1992. "Public Employers', Obligation to Reasonably Accommodate the Disabled under the Rehabilitation and Americans with Disabilities Acts." *Public Personnel Management* (Fall) 273–300.

Candrilli, Alfred J., and Ronald D. Armagast, 1987. "The Case for Effective Point-Factor Job Evaluation, Viewpoint 2." *Personnel* (April) 33–36.

Cook, John C., 1992. "Preparing for Statistical Battles under the Civil Rights Act." *HR Focus* (May) 12–13.

Craver, Gary, 1977. "Survey of Job Evaluation Practices in State and County Governments." *Public Personnel Management* (March-April) 121–130.

Ganschinietz, Bill, and Stephen McConomy, 1983. "Trends in Job Evaluation Practices of State Personnel Systems." *Public Personnel Management* (Spring) 1–12.

Green, Samuel B., John G. Veres and Wiley R. Boyles, 1991. "Racial Differences on Job Analysis Questionnaires: An Empirical Study." *Public Personnel Management*, vol. 20, no. 2 (Summer): 135–144.

Greenlaw, Paul S., and John Kohl, 1992. "The ADA: Public Personnel Management, Reasonable Accommodation and Undue Hardship." *Public Personnel Management* (Winter) 411–427.

Lawler, III, Edward E., 1987. "What's Wrong with Point-Factor Job Evaluation." *Personnel* (January).

Lawton, Esther C., 1977. "Job Evaluation Principles and Problems." In Harold Suskin, ed., *Job Evaluation and Pay Administration in the Public Sector.* Chicago: International Personnel Management Association, 25–63.

Lewis, Chad, and Cynthia Stevens, 1990. "An Analysis of Job Evaluation Committee and Job Holder Gender Effects on Job Evaluation." *Public Personnel Management* (Fall) 271–278.

National Academy of Public Administration, 1991. *Modernizing Federal Classification: An Opportunity for Excellence.* Washington, D.C. (July).

National Performance Review, 1993. *From Red Tape to Results: Creating a Government That Works Better and Costs Less.* Washington, D.C.: Government Printing Office.

Plachy, Roger, 1987. "The Case for Effective Point-Factor Job Evaluation, Viewpoint 1." *Personnel* (April) 30–32.

Reilly, Bernard J., and Joseph A. DiAngels, Jr., 1988. "From 'Hard Work' to 'Smart Work': A Look at Job Redesign." *Personnel* (February) 61–65.

Risher, Howard, and Charles Fay, 1991. "Federal Pay Reform: A Response to an Emerging Crisis." *Public Personnel Management* (Fall) 385–395.

Sahl, Robert J., 1989. "How to Install a Point Factor Job-Evaluation System." *Personnel* (March) 38–42.

Shafritz, Jay M., 1977. "Job Evaluations' Behavioral Facet." In Harold Suskin ed., *Job Evaluation and Pay Administration in the Public Sector.* Chicago: International Personnel Management Association, 561–567.

Shafritz, Jay M., and Albert Hyde, 1983. "Position Classification and Staffing." In Steven Hays and Richard Kearney, ed. *Public Personnel Administration: Problems and Prospects.* Englewood Cliffs, NJ: Prentice-Hall, 98–177.

Stahl, Glen, 1983. *Public Personnel Administration*, 8th ed. New York: Harper & Row.

JOB DESIGN. The organization of tasks, duties, and responsibilities assigned to a unit of work in order to achieve a certain objective. When designing a job, consideration is given to the content, the methods used, the effect on the person doing the job, and its relationship to other jobs within the organization. To state it in another way, it is the way in which the skills, knowledge, abilities, and relationships are arranged to accomplish organizational goals. The results of job design are expressed in the job description.

History of Job Design

Before the Industrial Revolution, job design was all but nonexistent. Work was viewed as a static process and was defined by the skill necessary to accomplish a specific task. A person who was able to demonstrate the skill would be hired. With the Industrial Revolution and developing technology, work became more complex. Job design in the early 1900s was focused on methods to make the tasks as simple as possible and to make the worker more efficient in accomplishing these tasks. This era was characterized by the "engineering approach" known as scientific management. Frederick W. Taylor, an industrial engineer, was the leading proponent (see **Taylor, Frederick W.**).

The middle decades of the twentieth century brought about a change in the way work was defined. The focus switched from the needs of the job to the needs of the person. Work relationships and work responsibilities became entwined. Instead of job simplification, the strategy of job design was one of job enrichment. This approach, known as the Human Relations School, combined knowledge, skills, and abilities with the personal desires and motivations of employees and organizational factors to create meaningful work experiences.

Along with organizational and employee needs, federal legislation now plays an important role. The 1935 Wagner Act is considered by some to be the first time legislation was used to regulate the workplace. Since then a number of laws have been enacted dealing with employee issues, which have had an impact on job design. A recent example is the 1991 Americans with Disabilities Act (ADA). The ADA, in conjunction with the Rehabilitation Act of 1973, addresses the issue of discrimination against qualified individuals with a disability. The act requires that employers not only make the physical accommodations necessary for those in this protected class but critically review the essential functions of each job to ensure compliance.

Job Design in the Public Sector

Job design in the public sector has its origins in the Scientific Management School. While building an efficient workforce certainly played a large part in job design, other overriding factors such as the protection of government employees from undue political influence, guarding against corruption, and neutrality must be included with those values used in the private sector. Job design is the basis for the classification processes known as civil service or merit systems. Civil service systems were designed to be efficient and effective while maintaining a neutral stance in implementing policy.

Job design in the public sector has remained entrenched in the scientific management approach. While it has been subject to some of the same changes that the private sector has, human resources have still focused on the technical aspects of managing positions. The issue of maintaining a neutral workforce has been used to preserve a civil service system, with some modifications mandated by legislation. Job design in the public sector, however, is currently under attack. These same systems that were thought to be efficient and effective are now seen as being over-regulated and obstacles to responsive government and a highly productive workforce. The issue of management flexibility, the move toward the downsizing of organizations, both public and private, along with the concomitant reinvention movement are forcing government to review its approach to job design. Not since the early days of civil service reform have governments been under such pressure to reevaluate the way in which government work is performed.

Job Design in the Future

Work and worker expectations are continually evolving and so is job design. The early 1900s brought about an industrial model that focused on work tasks. In the middle of the twentieth century, a second element, worker needs, was included as a determinant for structuring jobs. Now as the twenty-first century is fast approaching, a third element, technology, is becoming a major factor. The "information super highway" is the road on which all workers will have to travel regardless of the level of the position within the organization.

In today's workplace, all three elements must be present and all are constantly being redefined. A litigation explosion, especially in the area of employee rights, has created a number of policies. Legislation such as the Americans with Disabilities Act has forced a reevaluation of job tasks. Other laws and court decisions have struck down mandatory retirement, forced employers to provide

family leave, enforced or altered affirmative action plans, and mandated (in areas of public safety) or allowed drug testing, to name a few.

The changing composition of the workforce combined with the restructuring of organizations are forcing a reevaluation of not just jobs but of the workplace as well. By most accounts, the workforce in the next decade will be more diverse, mobile, better educated, and technologically savvy. Organizations designed to suit the baby boomers will not fit those from generation X. For those fed on a diet of quality of life issues and growing up in an age of fax machines, cellular telephones, electronic mail, and a global economy, flexibility within and among jobs will no longer be an expectation, but a demand.

SHERRY S. DICKERSON

BIBLIOGRAPHY

Ban, Carolyn, and Norma M. Riccucci, eds. 1991. *Public Personnel Management: Current Concerns, Future Challenges.* White Plains, NY: Longman.
Cayer, N. Joseph, 1986. *Public Personnel Administration in the United States,* 2nd ed. New York: St. Martins.
Hyde, Albert C. 1983. "Placing the Individual into the Organization." In Jack Rabin et al., eds., *Handbook of Public Personnel and Labor Relations.* New York: Marcel Dekker.
National Commission on the State and Local Public Service, 1993. *Hard Truths/Tough Choices: An Agenda for State and Local Reform.* Albany, NY: Rockefeller Institute of Government.
National Performance Review, 1993. *From Red Tape to Results: Creating a Government That Works Better and Costs Less.* Washington, D.C.: Government Printing Office.

JOB SATISFACTION. A personal evaluation of an aspect of the work situation such as liking or being satisfied with one's job.

Historical Overview

Since the advent of the Human Relations School of Management in the 1930s, the concept of job satisfaction has been the subject of great attention by academics, business managers, government personnel, and the media. In fact, many observers suggest that job satisfaction has received more attention from scholars in the organizational sciences than any other topic. By 1976, Edwin Locke (1976) estimated that approximately 3,350 manuscripts had been written on the topic. Certainly this number has increased substantially through the 1980s and 1990s.

One of the major themes in this vast literature on job satisfaction is that the morale of employees represents an important factor of organizational life, which is predictive of employee behavior and organizational outcomes. It is either explicitly stated or implicitly assumed that high levels of job satisfaction bring about high levels of individual productivity, lower rates of employee turnover, and promote organizational effectiveness. It is assumed that successful organizations will have satisfied employees.

Although job satisfaction has been of considerable interest to public administration scholars and governmental managers for some time, in recent years it has received increased attention due to the broadly held view that public-sector morale is in a very bad state (National Commission on the Public Service 1990). Due to extensive "bureaucrat bashing" (see **bureaucrat bashing**) by the media, politicians, spokespersons for business, and the general public (Farazmand 1989) and due to the continuing predominance of overly rigid and too highly centralized work environments in the public sector (Thayer 1981), many observers have concluded that there is a "crisis" in public employee job satisfaction.

The dangers argued to be associated with declining levels of public sector job satisfaction and morale are smaller pools of qualified recruits, higher turnover rates, lower levels of productivity and organizational commitment, and discouragement of young people from seeking a public service career. While the empirical evidence of declining public sector job satisfaction is mixed at best (see Steel and Warner 1990), the theme of a "crisis" in public service morale remains a common refrain among public administration scholars and public managers alike.

Underlying Theoretical Framework

According to Edwin Locke's (1976) comprehensive overview of job-satisfaction research, two theories are predominant in most job-satisfaction research—namely, Frederick Herzberg's Motivator-Hygiene Theory (1966) and Abraham Maslow's Need Hierarchy Theory (1970). Maslow's theory postulates a hierarchy of five basic categories of human needs, including physiological (eating, drinking), safety (physical, economic), belongingness, esteem, and self-actualization. As lower-order needs are satisfied, such as physiological needs, new needs become prevalent, such as the desire for safety. The implications of this theory for the workplace and job satisfaction have structured the thinking and actions of many public administration scholars and public service managers.

One of the most influential books on the modern American workplace influenced by a Maslowian perspective was Charles Reich's *The Greening of America*. Reich, along with other social and workforce critics such as Alvin Toffler and Judson Gooding, argued that a new generation of workers would become alienated working in the established industrial system. Central to the argument of these commentators was the notion that the socioeconomic status of Americans in general had increased drastically in the postwar period, producing what many contemporary observers have come to call a "postindustrial" or "self-actualized" workforce. This modern workforce knows more and

expects more from work than earlier generations of employees. They value quality of worklife, sense of purpose in one's work, and participation in decisionmaking more heavily than the material rewards of work. The problem arises when such postindustrial workers find employment in organizations that require uniformity of thought, strict rules and fixed procedures, and stark hierarchy—much of what continues to characterize the workplace settings in the public sector.

Herzberg's theory of motivation and hygiene factors in the workplace focuses on different causes of satisfaction and dissatisfaction in one's job. He argues that humans have a "dual nature," and therefore job satisfaction involves two sets of unrelated factors. Humans have physical needs at work (e.g., salary and working conditions) and psychological needs (e.g., creativity, individuality). Work satisfaction is the result of psychological factors (labeled "motivators") and dissatisfaction is the result of physical factors (termed elements of "hygiene"). Since the publication of Herzberg's work on job satisfaction, exhaustive research has been conducted on the relationship between motivators, hygiene, and public sector employee motivation (see Bruce and Blackburn 1992).

Empirical Research on Job Satisfaction

As discussed above, there are literally thousands of studies of job satisfaction in the literature. Most of these studies entail private sector employees (see Locke 1976) or limited case studies of public sector settings. Many national surveys have measured levels of job satisfaction obtaining among Americans—including the NORC series, Gallup polls, the National Longitudinal Surveys, and the Quality of American Life surveys. All of these national surveys show most Americans to be satisfied with their jobs. Unfortunately, there have been few national comparisons, however, of private and public sector job satisfaction.

One recent study using data from the National Longitudinal Survey's Youth Cohort—a national sample of early labor force participants—found that job satisfaction was higher among young public sector employees than among private sector employees (Steel and Warner 1990). Another study of federal executives by Turek-Brezina and Tanner (1991) found relatively high levels of job satisfaction. In addition, personal satisfaction with their jobs was the most important factor affecting their positive view of federal government employment. However, these same federal executives were reluctant to encourage young people to pursue a career in public service, sensing a worsening of opportunities for career advancement in the future.

While many researchers have produced evidence to support the hypothesis of a causal connection between job satisfaction and productive individual behavior and organizational outcomes, many studies have found little if any relationship between productivity, the work environment, the quality of work life, and job satisfaction (e.g., Bruce and Blackburn 1992; Locke 1976, p. 1343).

Although research on the level and likely correlates of job satisfaction has produced mixed findings, the belief that job satisfaction leads to positive employee behavior and organizational accomplishment remains strong. This is likely the case because common sense would seem to dictate that satisfied workers will be more productive, they will exhibit higher organizational commitment, and they will manifest longer job tenure.

Current Practice

Following the work of Maslow, Herzberg, and others, most applied approaches for enhancing or increasing job satisfaction have focused upon the following factors: physical and general working conditions, pay and benefits, participation, recognition, opportunities for advancement and personal growth, the character and quality of management, and communications. Three of the most popular contemporary management approaches intended to enhance job satisfaction include organizational development (OD), job enrichment, and Total Quality Management (TQM). All of these approaches involve the fashioning of a more "humane" work environment and the active encouragement of employee participation in organizational goal setting and problem solving.

Currently, one of the most popular methods for enhancing job commitment and promoting job satisfaction is TQM. This represents an organizational philosophy based upon a belief in the value of employee participation, pursuant customer satisfaction, and the building of teamwork to perfect service production processes to increase organizational effectiveness. TQM encourages a long-term commitment by the organization in its employees, and it has been adapted for public-sector settings ranging from local government to federal agencies.

OD focuses on organizational culture in an attempt to make lasting changes in how employees treat one another and collaborate in a democratic and trusting environment. By coming to a shared understanding of the complex values underlying the organization as a whole, the needs of individual employees in the organization, and the sociopolitical environment of the organization, members of an organization can achieve a vision of the workplace wherein the core values of mutual respect and celebration of human dignity will result in satisfied and highly motivated employees. The end result of successful OD intervention is greater job satisfaction, which leads to higher levels of motivation and thus responsiveness to the public.

A third approach to job satisfaction is job enrichment. This management technique focuses on the provision of intrinsic rewards for desired workplace behavior. Job satisfaction is seen as a cognitive state that is dependent on the performance of meaningful work. Job satisfaction is understood as resulting from an individual's perception of being appreciated for making contributions toward a valued end and experiencing personal growth in the process. Instead of assuming that job satisfaction will occasion worker productivity, job enrichment theory suggests that proper job design and supervision practices predetermine both job performance and job satisfaction. Organizations reflecting this approach to job satisfaction are typically "flat" as opposed to hierarchical, and emphasis is placed on training and employee development in preparation for taking on more complex tasks and more responsible duties.

BRENT S. STEEL

BIBLIOGRAPHY

Bruce, Willa, and J. Walton Blackburn, 1992. *Balancing Job Satisfaction and Performance.* Westport, CT: Quorum Books.
Farazmand, Ali, 1989. "Crisis in the U.S. Administrative State." *Administration and Society,* vol. 21 (August) 173–199.
Herzberg, Frederick, 1966. *Work and the Nature of Man.* Cleveland: World Publishing.
Locke, Edwin, 1976. "The Nature and Causes of Job Satisfaction." In Marvin Dunnette, ed., *Handbook of Industrial and Organizational Psychology.* Chicago, IL: Rand McNally, 1297–1349.
Maslow, Abraham, 1970. *Motivation and Personality,* 2d ed. New York: Harper & Row.
National Commission on the Public Service, 1990. *Leadership for America: The Report of the National Commission on the Public Service.* Lexington, MA: Lexington Books.
Steel, Brent S., and Rebecca L. Warner, 1990. "Job Satisfaction Among Early Labor Force Participants: Unexpected Outcomes in Public and Private Sector Comparisons." *Review of Public Personnel Administration,* vol. 10 (Summer) 4–22.
Thayer, Frederick, 1981. *An End to Hierarchy and Competition: Administration in the Post Affluent World,* 2d ed. New York: Franklin Watts.
Turek-Brezina, Joan and Lucretia Dewey Tanner, 1991. "Top Men and Women View Public Service." *The Bureaucrat,* vol. 20 (Fall) 29–32.

JOB SHARING. A method of scheduling in which two (or more) workers share a single full-time position. These arrangements are most often found among clerical positions, but increasing numbers of professional jobs are being structured in this manner (Mueller, 1992).

Two Models: With or Without Benefits?

Technically speaking, a formal job sharing program differs from part-time work in that the fringe benefits enjoyed by permanent staff are divided between the workers. In many settings, however, job sharing arrangements are instituted purely for their cost-saving features. Where this is the case, the participating workers are treated as if they are part-timers. In such instances, job sharing is essentially a system in which full-time positions are cannibalized to maximize the output from each personnel dollar.

Public organizations are most likely to institute job sharing as a means to trim their labor costs. The technique first emerged during the recessionary 1970s, when many communities were battling reductions-in-force and other forms of retrenchment. Some workers who were facing lay-offs were found to be willing to accept part-time employment as an alternative to termination. By dividing permanent positions among two or more workers, the number of layoffs could be reduced and the jurisdictions could derive an added bonus of lower personnel expenditures.

The cost savings from job sharing are primarily attributable to the fact that the participating workers can be treated as part-timers and therefore do not qualify for fringe benefits. Because medical, leave, and retirement benefits can add between US $0.30 and US $0.50 to each dollar spent on a public sector salary, the elimination of such costs can save a considerable amount of money. Relatedly, part-time workers usually earn substantially lower salaries than full-time employees. Thus, employing two part-time workers instead of one full-timer can potentially save up to 60 percent or more of a position's ordinary salary. During reductions-in-force and other types of fiscal crises, job sharing thereby offers an attractive way to maintain a given level of productivity at lower costs.

Although it arose to prominence in the public sector due primarily to its cost-saving features, all job sharing arrangements are not based on financial considerations. Many long-standing job sharing programs arose as a means to accommodate the needs of workers with family obligations. Due to childcare responsibilities, as well as the increasingly common need to care for elderly relatives, many potential members of the labor force are unable to work a traditional 40-hour schedule. Job sharing provides a convenient means for many such workers—especially women with small children—to reenter the labor force. Because job sharers generally enjoy great flexibility in setting their schedules (provided that both parties agree to the arrangement), the participants can decide to work different hours (mornings or afternoons, for example), different days, and even different weeks.

Where cost savings are not the primary catalyst for job sharing programs, organizations often elect to divide applicable job entitlements (fringe benefits, parking privileges, and other perquisites) between the participating workers. If, for example, the organization devotes 40 percent of a typical position's base salary to fringe benefits, the individuals sharing a single position would divide that amount of job entitlements between them on some pro-rated basis. If each person were to devote an equal amount of time to the position (20 hours per week), then the distribution would be 50/50. Alternatively, if one worker were to invest 30 hours per week in the job, then that worker would retain 75 percent of the benefits while the person working 10 hours per week would get only 25 percent of the benefit package. One obvious consideration in fash-

ioning such arrangements is that the two parties need to reach a mutually acceptable accommodation as to the distribution of work hours and benefits.

Research indicates that between 10 percent (Dessler 1993) and 25 percent (Austin 1994) of large private-sector corporations allow for formal job sharing programs in which job entitlements are retained by the participants. Because of the public sector's current financial difficulties, as well as the inflexibility of public personnel practices, such arrangements are exceedingly rare in government.

Other Advantages of Job Sharing

Like any scheduling innovation that increases worker choice, job sharing offers a variety of additional benefits. The technique potentially has great appeal to some older workers who are trying to ease their way into retirement. Flexible schedules are also credited with reducing worker tardiness, absenteeism, and turnover. Moreover, productivity is thought to improve because the workers' minds are less cluttered with off-the-job concerns (Messmer 1990). They can (theoretically) devote their full attention to the tasks at hand. Scheduling flexibility also enables the organization to provide continuous coverage of worker responsibilities during vacations and other absences.

Job sharing also appeals to some managers because of certain intuitive advantages that may accrue to the organization. If "two heads are better than one," then two employees for one salary may indeed be a good deal. Sharing unquestionably broadens the base of skills and experience that are brought to the position. The organization may thus gain an additional increment of creativity and insight. Moreover, under a typical job sharing schedule—one in which the workers divide the day between morning and afternoon "shifts"—the organization is rewarded with two "fresh" workers rather than a single exhausted one.

Possible Disadvantages

The chief practical impediments to job sharing are coordination costs and management's loss of control. When two workers share one job, difficulties may surface in maintaining the day-to-day continuity that many positions require. Either the workers must demonstrate initiative in coordinating their respective efforts—such as keeping a notebook summarizing the issues each one needs to be aware of—or management must assume that responsibility (Austin 1994). A related dilemma springs from the fact that sharing arrangements make many supervisors uncomfortable because of the difficulties inherent in monitoring and controlling performance. As one writer points out, "Much of the political context within which work is carried out is difficult to pass on or is forgotten . . . resulting in more fragmented working relationships with fellow workers and supervisors" (Mueller 1992, p. 319).

Other potential problems arise most particularly in job sharing programs that provide fringe benefits to the participants. Working out the specifics of a shared benefits package can be a daunting experience, especially within the rigidly controlled world of public personnel management. Likewise, job sharing will almost certainly increase the paperwork burden for supervising managers and personnel departments. Thus, some managers can be expected to resist the implementation of this and other forms of scheduling innovations.

Despite these limitations, job sharing offers managers a relatively inexpensive (if not money-saving) means of meeting the needs of the contemporary workforce. It helps the organization attract workers who might otherwise be shut out of the labor market and provides important job coverage and motivational advantages. For these reasons, its use is likely to accelerate in future years.

STEVEN W. HAYS

BIBLIOGRAPHY

Austin, Nancy, 1994. "How Managers Manage Flexibility." *Working Woman* (July) 19–20.
Dessler, Gary, 1993. *Human Resource Management.* Englewood Cliffs, N. J.: Prentice-Hall.
Messmer, Max, 1990. "Strategic Staffing for the '90s." *Personnel Journal* 69 (October) 90–99.
Mueller, Wally, 1992. "Alternative Work Schedules." In Jean Hartley and Geoffrey Stephenson, eds., *Employment Relations.* Oxford, England: Blackwell, 318–323.

JOB TENURE.
A legal term denoting that an employee has certain rights to the expectation of continued employment with the organization so long as performance remains satisfactory, and also conferring certain legal procedural protections for the employee in the event that adverse personnel actions are initiated by the organization.

Unlike American private-sector employment with its history of the "employment-at-will" doctrine governing the basic employment relationship, in public employment job tenure has long been a feature of the civil service concept. Hugh Heclo (1977) stated this philosophy in his book *A Government of Strangers* when he said, "Since jobs are to be filled by weighing the merits of applicants, those hired should have tenure regardless of political changes at the top of organizations ... [and] the price of job security should be a willing responsiveness to the legitimate political leaders of the day" (p. 20). In 1897, at the urging of the United States Civil Service Commission, President McKinley issued the first rules restricting the arbitrary removal of classified employees. These were further elaborated by President Theodore Roosevelt in 1902.

Although for a time the judicially applied "Doctrine of Privilege" seemed to give public employers certain rights to restrict the constitutional protections in the employment relationship of public employees in the United States, since the 1960s this doctrine has gradually given way to one that is more protective of their employment status.

In the 1972 case of *Roth v. Board of Regents,* the American Supreme Court abandoned the privilege doctrine and indicated that the expectation of continued employment creates a property interest in the job–an interest protected by the Fourteenth Amendment to the Constitution. This amendment states, "No state shall ... deprive any person of life, liberty, or property, without due process of law." Therefore, if an employee has a propertied right to a job, due process protections apply against the employer (the state) in trying to deny to an employee that property.

When can a public employee be said to have an expectation of continued employment and therefore a propertied interest in a job? On this the Court has been less clear, but it is quite probable that when a civil servant has passed through a probationary period as a part of the selection process and has been granted job tenure, this propertied interest is present. Cases subsequent to Roth, such as *Perry v. Sindermann* and *Bishop v. Wood,* have further delineated these basic property rights. These cases have dealt with employee rights to pre- and posttermination hearings and, in effect, try to flesh out what the term "due process" means in a day-to-day employment setting.

Although job tenure does not grant to public sector employees unlimited rights to permanent employment, this concept has been important throughout U.S. history. Given the volatile political environment within which public sector employees must operate, it has been recognized that some guarantees of job tenure be a part of a healthy merit system, and such tenure should not be removed arbitrarily, but carefully, following prescribed procedures giving employees notice of such actions and an opportunity to respond with reasons why such proposed actions should not be taken.

ROBERT H. ELLIOTT

BIBLIOGRAPHY

Bishop v. Wood, 1976. 426 U.S. 341.
Board of Regents v. Roth, 1972. 408 U.S. 564.
Heclo, Hugh, 1977. *A Government of Strangers.* Washington, DC: Brookings Institution.
Lee, Yong S., 1992. *Public Personnel Administration and Constitutional Values.* Westport, CT: Quorum Books.
Perry v. Sindermann, 1972. 408 U.S. 593.

JUDICIAL ACTIVISM/RESTRAINT.
Refers to an ongoing academic/legal debate that is as old as the U.S. Constitution. Simply put, judicial activism is when judges make law rather than interpret it. The philosophy of judicial restraint suggests that this practice should stop and that policymaking powers should return to the legislative

branch. In doing this, judges are neutral arbiters without interference from politics. This view offers up an image of a stripped-down judge. If a judge is without a political agenda, he or she can answer constitutional questions according to a strict construction of the Constitution far more easily. Underlying the philosophy of judicial restraint is an assumption that a single meaning can be found in the Constitution and that this meaning is fixed. This philosophy has also been referred to as legal formalism.

Judicial activism, by contrast, is a philosophy that grants judges broad powers. Instead of being stripped-down, a judge is cloaked with powers that are quasi-legislative and discretionary. Here the constitution is viewed as "a living document" rather than a fixed one, and judges are left to fill the Constitution with meaning as a way to achieve desirable social ends. One of the strongest justifications for judicial activism is that it is a viable form of policymaking. The amendment process does not provide an avenue for change because it is long, cumbersome, and offers proposed changes a limited probability for success. The passage of amendments requires supermajorities and the judicial process does not. The former is not structured to protect minority rights while the latter is. Defenders of judicial activism place more value on societal needs than they do on "original intent." Accordingly, there is no defense to a strict construction of the Constitution or the need to draw from "original intent" when such a philosophy stands in the way of progressive social change and does little to enhance the public interest. A philosophy of judicial activism demonstrates a greater willingness to infuse the Constitution with meaning. It is more suited to meet the realities of modern society and more able to eliminate social wrongs of the past and present. To ignore this feature makes the Constitution nothing more than a mechanical document.

Origins and Subsequent History

The search for the constitutional legitimacy of judicial review begins with its formal establishment in *Marbury v. Madison,* 1 Cranch 137 (1803). The second time a court struck down a federal statute was in the ignominious Dred Scott decision (*Scott v. Sanford,* 12 Howard 299 [1857]). Although this decision almost destroyed the legitimacy of the court, it sparked considerable debate over how the constitution should be interpreted. The most famous of these debates occurred between Abraham Lincoln and Stephen Douglas in 1858. Douglas cited the framers of the Constitution in his defense of the Supreme Court's decision to let the states decide whether there should be slavery or not. He insisted that the national government has no place imposing uniform laws on the states and used Article IV, Section 4 as his defense: "[T]he great men of that day made this government divided into free states and slave states

and left each state perfectly free to do as it pleased on the subject of slavery. Why can it not exist on the same principles on which our fathers made it?" Although Douglas accused Lincoln of disregarding the framers' intent, Lincoln also built an argument around his conception of the Constitution's original meaning. Lincoln responded, "I am fighting it upon these 'original principles,' fighting it in the Jeffersonian, Washingtonian, and Madisonian fashion." Lincoln goes on to say that a reading of the Constitution that defends slavery "is, in my judgement, penetrating the human soul and eradicating the light of reason and the love of liberty in this American people." Lincoln and Douglas both bandied the names of the founders as if they knew exactly what they intended. (Current, pp. 94–103).

Lincoln brought forth a line of argument that holds true today. Even though he argues according to "original intent," he raises the possibility for constitutional dissent. Suppose that the intentions of the founders offend current understandings of justice? This question lays groundwork for the Constitution as a "living document" rather than as a fixed one. The point to be made is that the content of the Lincoln/Douglas debates bears similarities to the contemporary dialogue on judicial activism and judicial restraint. The central question over how the Constitution should be read has been an ongoing one throughout U.S. history.

The Supreme Court struck down laws in the 1890s and 1900s that related to economic regulation. The court in the 1930s viewed pieces of Roosevelt's New Deal legislation as an encroachment on rights guaranteed in the Constitution. These interpretations were based on the Court's laissez-faire emphasis on private property rights and economic liberty. Here the Fourteenth and Fifteenth Amendments were construed broadly to give businesses due process protections as individuals. This presents an example of a conservative court actively interpreting particular rights over others. In doing so, many of Roosevelt's progressive reforms, designed to spread relief to Americans in the midst of the depression, were struck down. Here Roosevelt had a financial crisis and a strong justification to circumvent the Supreme Court's ruling.

Roosevelt's standoff with the Court marks the beginnings of the usage of judicial restraint as a form of American jurisprudence. Roosevelt later appointed Justice Felix Frankfurter, who is well known for his judicial restraint philosophy. The example of President Roosevelt's call for judicial restraint presents a common theme where there is some kind of emergency and an available remedy. The remedy is judicial restraint. Frankfurter served on the Court from 1939 to 1962. His judicial philosophy sometimes situated him with conservatives and lead to criticism from those who expected him to defend civil liberties. In private, he was a staunch supporter of civil liberties, but as a judge he refrained from deciding according to his political beliefs. Although characterized as two different people, Frankfurter made the distinction between being a legislator and being a judge. Throughout Frankfurter's tenure on the Court, it became clear that judicial restraint sometimes furthers liberal causes, and at other times it benefits those of conservatives. The Court practiced judicial restraint when it came to legislation regulating the economy but as more and more civil liberties cases came before the Court, Frankfurter's leadership on judicial restraint was limited.

There were great expectations that Frankfurter, as the founder of the American Civil Liberties Union (ACLU), would uphold individual civil liberties. *Minersville School District v. Gobbits*, 310 U.S. 586 (1940), posed a situation where Frankfurter's judicial philosophy was in conflict with his personal beliefs. Frankfurter wrote the majority opinion, upholding a state law requiring a pledge of allegiance in school. Even though a Jehovah's Witness said that this violated the right to practice religion without state interference, the Court deferred to the powers of lawmakers. Three years later, in *West Virginia State Board of Education v. Barnette*, 319 U.S. 624 (1943), the Gobbits precedent was overturned and Frankfurter wrote a dissenting opinion. Frankfurter did not see the Fourteenth Amendment as a way to make the Bill of Rights applicable to the states. This perspective is evident in Frankfurter's opinion in *Wolf v. Colorado*, 338 U.S. 25 (1949). He upheld the use of the exclusionary rule in federal cases but concluded that it was not applicable to the states. However, the *Wolf* precedent would be overturned in *Mapp v. Ohio*, 367 U.S. 643 (1961); Frankfurter wrote a dissenting opinion on the precedent set in *Mapp*, consistent with his judicial restraint philosophy.

By the 1940s, more and more cases relating to the Bill of Rights and their application were coming before the Courts. These cases proved to be quite different than those pertaining to the regulation of the economy. The presence of these cases is said to have changed the nature of the Court. The Court had begun to address legal questions relating to flag salutes, religion, and the prosecution of communists. The legal questions involved put the judicial restraint philosophy to the test. Did the Fourteenth Amendment incorporate the Bill of Rights? Could this amendment be used to force states to comply with rights guaranteed in the Constitution? Judicial activists on the Court answered yes to these questions. While Frankfurter remained true to his judicial restraint philosophy, others such as William O. Douglas and Hugo Black did not.

President Eisenhower's appointment of Earl Warren to the Court added another justice willing to expand the Bill of Rights. Eisenhower is well known for his saying that his appointment of Warren was "the biggest damned fool mistake I ever made" (in Janda, p. 520). Although Warren's tenure as chief justice marks the Court's most active period (1953–1969), his conservative background created expectations that he would make like decisions. During this time, the Supreme Court not only struck down laws on segregation and prayer in public schools but also created standards on obscenity, discarded the political question doctrine, and rewrote a mandatory code on rights of criminal defendants.

In *Baker v. Carr*, 369 U.S. 186 (1962), the court agreed to hear challenges to reapportionment by the states. As the Court entered "the political thicket," the political question doctrine gave way. The decision demonstrated that the Court was no longer reluctant to make decisions once deferred to legislative expertise.

In another series of cases, the Court made decisions on rules of evidence, court fees without regard to the income of a defendant, and procedures required of all law enforcement officers in the arrest and conviction of criminal defendants. These activist decisions reflected a need to make state and federal criminal procedures more uniform and to minimize the unequal treatment between the rich and the poor.

The justices appointed after 1957 (Potter Stewart, Byron White, Arthur Goldberg, Abe Fortas, and Thurgood Marshall) paved the way for old precedents to be overturned and new precedents to be set. Mapp overturned the Wolf precedent by making the exclusionary rule applicable to the states. *Gideon v. Wainwright*, 372 U.S. 335 (1963), established a new precedent that all defendants, rich or poor, had a constitutional right to counsel. *Miranda v. Arizona*, 384 U.S. 436 (1966), required police and prosecutors to inform all criminal defendants of their basic constitutional rights.

Many of these decisions are what led Richard M. Nixon to run for the presidency on a campaign platform of law and order. Nixon blamed the rising crime rate on the decisions made by the Warren Court and once president, he selected appointees who he thought would adhere to a strict construction of the Constitution. Nixon appointed Warren Earl Burger to serve as chief justice, Harry Blackman and Lewis Powell to serve on the high court. The hope here was not so much judicial self-restraint but that criminal defendant rights would be limited, namely, the Miranda Rule, an indigent's right to counsel, and strict application of the exclusionary rule in gathering evidence against a defendant. Burger served as chief justice from 1969 to 1986, and during this time there was some decline in judicial activism. The decline in judicial activism, however, should not be taken to mean that the precedents of the Warren Court were overturned. The Burger Court upheld the exclusionary rule with some limitations and did not strike down the death penalty. Despite expectations that this Court would hand down conservative decisions, it has been noted for advancing the equality of women and for striking down a state law limiting abortions in *Roe v. Wade*, 410 U.S. 113 (1973). The defense of legal abortions through the right to privacy remains one of the most controversial examples of judicial activism. In *Reed v. Reed*, 404 U.S. 71 (1970), Burger wrote the majority opinion striking down a state law that gave males preference over females in probate court. Both *Roe v. Wade* and *Reed v. Reed* indicate that the Burger Court was still willing to make activist decisions. The incorporation of the right to privacy as a guaranteed right adds to the list of protections not explicitly stated in the Constitution.

Despite some activism by the Burger Court, there are some noteworthy examples of judicial restraint. The Warren Court gave states and localities more discretion to make and interpret laws relating to pornography and obscenity. Another example is the Court's decision in *Regents of the University of California v. Bakke,* 438 U.S. 265 (1978). Here the Court did not strike down affirmative action. This case stirred the debate around judicial activism and restraint once more. It brought on criticism by the conservatives and praise from liberals.

Although the Burger Court loosely adhered to a philosophy of judicial restraint, President Ronald Reagan's appointments were designed to tighten this philosophy up. Others would argue that the goal was to create a conservative court and that judicial restraint was only a tool. William Rehnquist's appointment to the position of chief justice and the appointments of Sandra Day O' Conner, Antonin Scalia, and Anthony Kennedy paved the way for changes in the Court's philosophy. There is a general agreement that these appointments made the Court more conservative but views are mixed on whether or not the Court is exercising judicial restraint. While the Rehnquist Court has loosened requirements for valid confessions and the gathering of evidence, it has not overturned the criminal rights precedents established by the Warren Court. The Rehnquist Court's limitations on abortion rights in *Webster v. Reproductive Health Services,* 109 S.Ct. 3040 (1989), and strictures on affirmative action in both *Wygant v. Jackson Board of Education,* 476 U.S. 267 (1986), and in *Richmond v. J. A. Croson,* 109 S.Ct. 706 (1989), suggest that this conservative court is willing to abandon a philosophy of judicial restraint for the sake of its political beliefs. Judicial philosophy may begin to shift again. While George Bush's appointment of Clarence Thomas added one more conservative Supreme Court justice, Bill Clinton's appointments of Ruth Bader Ginsburg and Stephen Breyer represent the first two Democratic appointees in 25 years.

Just as FDR espoused this philosophy to put forth multiple social reforms, Richard Nixon espoused it in the name of law and order. Ronald Reagan took it to mean that the Supreme Court's work of the previous decades should be overturned. Although the call for judicial restraint assumes that there is a common vision of the Constitution, the phenomenon of liberal and conservative justifications for judicial self-restraint represents a profoundly conflicted ideological strategy.

Underlying Theoretical Framework

The history of judicial activism and judicial restraint represents two philosophical extremes. The two polar philosophies are oversimplifications that are often misinterpreted. They are misinterpreted because the call for judicial restraint is so often used as a political tool. In theory, a philosophy of judicial restraint is neither conservative nor liberal. Both philosophies come down to the basic question of when the Court should enter the field. Extreme forms of judicial restraint would have judges deferring to the powers of Congress, the president, and the growing administrative branch of government.

Judicial activism is based on a belief that the public interest needs to be defended. Judicial activist advocates would argue that judges are not only in the best position to represent the public interest but also the readiest branch to represent minority interests. Underlying this view is an inherent distrust of the other branches. Those favoring a judicial activist approach are critical of Congress and the president. Accordingly, the judiciary can respond to the public interest while the other branches tend to special interests. Judicial activism is defended because it offers one last opportunity for those who have often been left out of the system to be represented.

Despite public interest defenses of judicial activism, it is criticized because it represents a form of judicial policymaking. Here it is evident that both sides have strong arguments. The philosophy of judicial restraint gives deference to lawmakers because they are more representative than judges. To do otherwise assumes that the judges can do a better job than lawmakers, and this presumption brings on charges of judicial arrogance. In defense of activists, vague legislation provides an open invitation for judges to offer their guidance and interpretation. The philosophy of judicial restraint, however, defines the role of judges narrowly because the courts were never intended to be a major policymaking force. It considers Congress to be far more representative than the judiciary. Judges, therefore, should make decisions that reflect the law and not a policy choice, regardless of whether a particular law is a good one or a bad one.

The philosophy of judicial restraint is also advocated by some administrative law scholars. Since agencies deal with areas of technical expertise and judges do not, judges are not always in a position to settle disputes relating to some public policy programs. Administrators are in a position to make well-researched public-policy decisions because they are experts in a given field, have time to gather and analyze data on an ongoing basis, and can respond to issues that arise more quickly than the courts. The role of judges is to answer legal questions and in doing so, judges may never achieve a comprehensive understanding of the multiple and conflicting public-policy issues that are so often involved. Judges are further limited because judicial decisionmaking is done on a piecemeal basis without a structured follow up. A final structural shortcoming to judicial review is the fact that the judiciary does not have the power to monitor, implement, or enforce their decisions.

Extreme forms of judicial activism violate the separation-of-powers doctrine because they would intrusively encroach on all branches of government.

The debate between judicial activism and judicial restraint continues into the present. The battle over Judge Robert Bork represented this debate in heightened form. Judges are not only evaluated for their competence but also for their judicial philosophy. Although Bork had a résumé full of scholarship attacking judicial activism, his conservative ideology led his opponents to charge him with using the cloak of judicial restraint to further conservative causes. Bork's open responses to the Senate explain why other Supreme Court justice candidates do not answer questions about their legal philosophy. Justices Sandra Day O'Conner and Antonin Scalia have been noted for not even answering questions regarding the judicial review precedent established in *Marbury v. Madison* (1803). The confirmation of Clarence Thomas brought the issue up again, and this time the Supreme Court candidate refused to reveal his philosophy or discuss his opinions on particular cases.

Although the Rehnquist Court is not making the sweeping changes made by the Warren Court, it is making changes incrementally and making public policy from smoking restrictions in penitentiaries to decisions on the form congressional districts should take.

In areas of administrative law, the Court is moving in the direction of extreme deference. In *Chevron v. Natural Resources Defense Council, Inc.*, 467 U.S. 837 (1984), the Court has exercised restraint by not insisting on clearer guidelines for agency administration. This kind of judicial restraint has been criticized because extreme deference yields agencies considerable powers and possibly more powers than a system of checks and balances should allow.

The debate over judicial activism and judicial restraint is likely to continue, just as it has throughout the nation's history. Throughout history, we see that the debate between judicial activism sometimes comes up with the right to privacy and abortion, sometimes with the rights of criminals compared to society at large, sometimes with regard to liberalism, and other times the push for conservatism is in question. The debate is located in law schools, in courts, in politics, and in society at large. The crux of this debate is based upon the Constitution and its meaning.

K. KIM LOUTZENHISER

BIBLIOGRAPHY

Bronner, Ethan, 1989. *Battle for Justice: How the Bork Nomination Shook America.* New York: W. W. Norton.
Current, Richard. ed. 1967. *The Political Thought of Abraham Lincoln.* New York: Bobbs-Merrill.
Elliott, Stephen P., 1986. *A Reference Guide to the United States Supreme Court.* New York: Facts on File Publications.
Ferguson, Andrew, 1994. "Power Hungry High Court: Even Conservative Justices Succumb to Lure of Policy Making." *Los Angeles Daily Journal,* June 29, 6.
Janda, Kenneth, Jeffrey Berry, and Jerry Goldman, 1992. *The Challenge of Democracy: Government in America.* Boston: Houghton Mifflin.
Koch, Charles H., 1991. "An Issue-Driven Strategy for Review of Agency Decisions." *Administrative Law Review* (Fall) 511–558.
Lash, Joseph P., 1975. *From the Diaries of Felix Frankfurter.* New York: W. W. Norton.
Meier, Kenneth J., 1993. *Politics and the Bureaucracy: Policymaking in the Fourth Branch of Government,* 3d ed. Belmont, CA: Brooks/Cole.
Warren, Kenneth F., 1996. *Administrative Law in the Political System,* 3rd ed. Upper Saddle River, New Jersey: Prentice-Hall.
Wolfe, Christopher, 1991. *Judicial Activism: Bulwark or Precarious Security?* Belmont, CA: Brooks/Cole.

JUDICIAL ADMINISTRATION.

The study and practice of management theories and techniques directly relevant to enhancing the ability of courts and other quasi-judicial bodies to perform their duties with professionalism, expeditiousness, and fairness.

Judicial administration directs attention to a host of bureaucratic issues that can be conveniently encompassed under the topics of court organization and the management of litigation. Under the former topic, judicial administration involves such matters as the structure of courts and other quasi-judicial bodies; the selection, tenure, and training of members of the judiciary; personnel relations with respect to court staff; financial management with respect to all court operations; and the operational relationship between the courts, as democratic institutions, and the broader community inclusive of the media.

At its core, however, and as the second great topic of judicial administration, stands the processing of litigation and caseflow management. The ultimate purpose of courts is the dispensation of justice through the resolution of legal disputes and this, in turn, is contingent upon the expeditious management of cases. Caseflow management itself, then, addresses a number of issues respecting how best to organize courts to undertake their prime task. Attention is directed to such matters as the managerial roles of judges and court administrators, administrative rules of procedure, calendaring systems, and antidelay initiatives.

Although the practice of judicial administration can now be found throughout the courts and justice systems of the Western world, the elaboration and development of judicial administration is very much rooted in the American experience and American interest in management theory and public sector reform.

The origins of judicial administration in the United States can be traced to the early decades of the twentieth century. Through the nineteenth century the judicial system in America developed in an unsystematic manner. Not only was it complicated by American federalism, necessitating the establishment of separate hierarchies for federal and state courts, but within each hierarchy there was a distinct lack of managerial order and formalization. A hallmark of the American judicial system has been the independence of the judiciary, but it is to be noted that well into the twentieth century independence in practice pertained not only to adjudication but to management. Individual courts, individual judges were free to develop, or not to develop, their own methods of judicial administration. In certain instances effective administration followed, but in most instances decentralized administrative independence resulted in the ill-management of American courts.

By the first decade of the twentieth century, this state of affairs was increasingly subject to criticism from a host of court reformers—principally found in the national and state bar associations but including leading legal academics and some members of the federal judiciary. Amongst these were Roscoe Pound (dean of Harvard Law School, 1916–1936) and William Howard Taft (U.S. President, 1909–1912, and chief justice of the United States Supreme Court, 1921–1929), men who were intent on bringing the ideals and practices of scientific management, business administration, and nonpartisan centralized planning to the operation of the American courts. In 1913, and with the support of the American Bar Association, the American Judicature Society was established with the specific mandate to promote the improvement of the courts through a mixture of research, education, and active support of reform initiatives.

Such initiatives were first felt at the federal level of court organization. In 1922, the United States Congress authorized legislation providing the chief justice of the United States with wide personnel and managerial authority to assign federal district judges to areas where they were most needed and, far more significantly, the legislation inaugurated the Judicial Conference. This was an institutionalized annual convention, long advocated by then Chief Justice Taft, which would witness the bringing together of the senior federal circuit judges with the chief justice so as to enable this group to assess the administrative needs of the federal courts and promote professional managerial reform of these courts. The judicial administration movement had begun.

These steps toward the development of professional judicial administration in the American courts were strengthened in 1939 when Congress established a permanent secretariat for the conference. This body, working under the direction of the conference, was titled the Administrative Office of the United States Courts and was given responsibility for the administration of all federal courts. It has responsibility for the collection of all statis-

tics relevant to assessing the working of the courts, it engages in both personnel and financial management of the federal courts, and it has the mandate to promote and undertake training in the area of caseflow management. A crucially important financial initiative that was part of this 1939 reform package was the Congress's vesting and centralization of the federal judicial budget within the auspices of the Administrative Office. This had the result of transferring effective administrative control of the courts to the Administrative Office and its judicial leadership within the conference.

Currently the Judicial Conference of the United States consists of the chief justice of the United States, the chief judge of each federal judicial circuit, and a federal district judge elected from each circuit. This group of 26 persons has become the executive steering committee of the federal courts, promoting administrative reform within their courts and lobbying the legislative branch on such matters as additional funding, judgeships, and court reorganization.

The work of the Judicial Conference and the Administrative Office, in turn, is assisted through the efforts of the Federal Judicial Center. This body, established by the Congress in 1967, with a board of directors composed of the chief justice, three district judges and two judges from the courts of appeals, and the director of the Administrative Office, is specifically mandated the task of conducting research into judicial administration, of making recommendations on ways and means of reforming the federal judiciary, and of offering training programs on judicial administration for judges and court personnel. This center, with a staff numbering roughly 100, has become a key element in professionalization and modernization of court management within the federal courts. Indeed, such was the center's impact in this field that it served as an example for the states, which moved to create the National Center for State Courts in 1972.

Though the early initiatives respecting judicial administration were found at the federal level, many have asserted that the greatest need for reform has always been observed at the state level. Historically, judicial administration within the states has been extremely decentralized and nonprogrammatic. In most states, courts have been largely independent of one another both in terms of organization and management, with jurisdiction respecting judicial administration divided between judges and local court clerks. Furthermore, financial management of the courts was usually divided between state and local governments.

Given these dynamics, initiatives in the sixties and seventies respecting administrative reform at the state level concentrated as much on the issue of court unification as on managerial improvement. Advocates of broad court unification, such as the National Center for State Courts and the Institute for Court Management have argued in favor of centralized administrative control being exercised over all state courts by the state supreme court. Through the use of state judicial conferences and councils, the judicial elite in each state would be in a position to provide direct leadership over the state court hierarchy with respect to matters of financing, personnel relations and training, rules of procedure and caseflow management.

This approach to reform, of course, is highly influenced by the elaboration of judicial administration at the federal level. Although there have been some significant developments in centralization in certain states, such as Connecticut, Colorado, and New Jersey, the drive for such centralization can often elicit much critical commentary from a number of actors in the state judicial process fearful of the centralization of administrative power in the state supreme court leading to the emasculation of the executive power of individual courts and local officials. This tension between center and periphery has been a trademark of state politics generally from the very inception of the Union, with the sociopolitical dynamics giving rise to these tensions proving to be quite long lasting.

Regardless of the drive to centralize authority over state courts, all states have, to greater or lesser degrees, witnessed the modernization of their practices of judicial administration through the adoption of professional approaches to court management. In this respect, the leadership and demonstration role of the National Center for State Courts and the Institute for Court Management is not to be underestimated. These bodies have done much to promote model techniques of financial and personnel management as well as to enhance knowledge regarding ways and means to engage in effective caseflow management. Most states now possess an office of court administration, usually under the direction of the state supreme court. These offices will usually play a role similar to that of their federal counterpart, but the formal power they exercise over the various courts in their state varies. In certain instances, as with Connecticut, all court administration is highly centralized in the hands of the state office. In other states, such as Georgia, the Administrative Office of the Courts has limited educational responsibilities; it can promote enhanced judicial administration but executive power remains vested with individual courts and local authorities.

Leading Issues in Judicial Administration

A host of matters have dominated the field of judicial administration in recent years. The leading issues would include the following:

Caseflow Management

The just resolution of cases in a timely and economical manner has always stood as the prime *raison d'être* of courts. On the maxim that "justice delayed is justice de-

nied," many involved in judicial administration–from judges through court administrators to educators and researchers–have devoted great attention to the ways and means of expediting the flow of cases through the justice system. While there is a voluminous literature on caseflow management, major studies by Church, Goerdt, Solomon and Somerlot have suggested a number of key criteria for expeditious justice. As Solomon and Somerlot have argued, effective caseflow management requires judicial leadership and commitment to court management; judicial consultation and managerial involvement with the bar; the establishment of reasonable standards and goals respecting the flow of cases through the judicial process; the establishment of a rigorous caseflow monitoring and information system capable of providing court managers with the knowledge necessary to make informed managerial decisions; the scheduling of credible trial dates, which attorneys will recognize as creating firm deadlines for trial preparation; and, last but not least, the maintenance of rigorous court control over the granting of continuances.

It is interesting to note that through the leading work of authors such as Church and Goerdt, expeditious caseflow management is not contingent upon a court system modelled on an individual calendar system or a master calendar or hybrid calendar system. These systems refer to the form of judicial organization with respect to the ordering of cases through the courts. Under the former system, one judge has control of a case from the initiation of proceedings through disposition; in the latter forms, certain preliminary matters and motions are dealt with either by a specialized master judge or by a variable pool of judges. These alternative forms of organization were developed as representing more systematic and efficient ways by which to address cases, thereby promoting expeditiousness. As Church and Goerdt have argued, expeditiousness has less to do with the calendaring system used than with judicial and managerial adherence to the caseflow management principles listed above.

Implicit in this approach to caseflow management, which has been endorsed by the American Bar Association, is the leading role of court managers. Although judges need to be important figures in judicial administration because they ultimately control the working of their courts, judges need and benefit from the expert advice of managers professionally trained in the theories and practices of caseflow management. The development of judicial administration as a managerial practice has thus been co-equal to the development of court management as a subprofession within public administration.

Alternative Dispute Resolution (ADR)

The great increase in caseloads faced by the courts over the past two decades has led certain court analysts to suggest that an appropriate judicial and managerial response should be the development of alternative means of addressing many of these cases. Proposals extend from outright decriminalization of certain matters, such as the possession of "soft" drugs or prostitution, through to the use of nonjudicial arbitration of commercial disputes to the establishment of small claims courts for the resolution of minor civil and property disputes to the creation and sanctioning of private courts for commercial disputes.

Interest in ADR arises from its promise to divert certain high volume but arguably mundane matters or quite complex but arguably narrow matters of limited public interest from the already overburdened common courts. ADR is predicated on the principle that the path of justice is not unidimensional but rather that there can be an array of avenues taken to arrive at a just destination. Contemplation of such avenues, however, is highly contentious. Decriminalization itself marks a nonadjudicative means to address certain "problems" by asserting that the perceived criminal problem is, in fact, not a criminal problem at all. Reasonable persons can and will reasonably differ on the application of this logic to the issues of drug possession and prostitution. The other forms of ADR represent alternative administrative mechanisms for dealing with certain forms of cases. Here, one encounters a variety of critical responses. As Goldberg, Green, and Sander have argued, the use of mediation, although having its benefits, is also subject to the criticism that it exerts a not too subtle class bias in that it divides dispute settlement between that found in traditional courts to that found in nontraditional mediation and arbitration forums. And the latter could become the forums in which the less wealthy would be directed to bring their suits, with these forums having a predisposition to have "clients" mediate and compromise on their rights. A stigma of second-class justice could ensue, especially if systems of mediation and arbitration are not carefully regulated by the courts with respect to the maintenance of fidelity to law, due process, precedent, and judicial impartiality and independence. The potential use of private courts, in turn, sparks fears of the development of privatized law in which concern for the "public interest" could be wholly lost.

Judicial Selection

The manner in which American judgeships are filled is one that has always elicited both public and academic discussion within the United States as well as engendered attitudes ranging from fascination to bewilderment amongst many non-American observers of the judiciary. The American judicial system contains a vast array of judicial selection mechanisms within the states ranging from gubernatorial appointment, legislative election, partisan and nonpartisan election to what is known as the Missouri Plan—a complex system of ostensibly nonpartisan nominating commissions, gubernatorial appointment followed by merit retention elections after the appointee has served

a set number of years on the bench. At the federal level, all judicial positions are filled through presidential nomination requiring the assent of the Senate.

With respect to appointment to the United States Supreme Court, the process can become highly partisan and controversial, as with the Robert Bork nomination in 1987 and the Clarence Thomas nomination of 1991. Appointments to the federal circuit courts and courts of appeal have tended to attract less public scrutiny on account of their greater number, their more routine occurrence, and the public perception of their lesser importance.

Within the scope of judicial selection, two major issues predominate. At the state level, as Wold and Culver assert, there is concern over the success of the merit retention system. As evidenced in California with respect to the removal from office of Chief Justice Rose Bird in 1986, there is concern felt by a number of analysts that retention elections can simply degenerate into a popularity contest in which certain well organized interest groups with preconceived positions on justice issues can target particular judges as a means to advancing their own partisan agenda. The fear then becomes that judges, sensing this partisan reality, will tailor judgments to fit the prevailing political climate, notwithstanding their own assessments as to what is legal and just.

In a similar fashion, recent debates over the nature of Senate confirmation hearings for Supreme Court nominees has sparked complaints that the process has become far too partisan, combative, and personally intrusive, so much so that many good men and women will likely refuse to allow their names to stand for nomination simply on account of their fear of the nomination process turning into a witch-hunt. Although the confirmation process can be undertaken in a manner far more decorous and solemn, exposing nominees to hard and pointed questions regarding their professional and ideological beliefs nevertheless stands as a fundamental rationale for the ratification process. The attendant controversies with such an approach can then be observed as a necessary by-product of such an open and democratic procedure—a selection procedure far more open and democratic than that found in such countries as Britain, Canada, and Australia.

Judicial Education

Just as methods to select judges can be controversial, so too can be the process of ongoing judicial education once judges are on the bench. Given the diverse backgrounds and legal experiences, and often limited administrative knowledge that men and women may possess when they are chosen for judicial service, as Baum and Glick illustrate, most court systems in the United States have now developed some form of organized judicial education program. Such programs offer courses ranging from updates on caselaw and practice to materials dealing with caseflow management and delay reduction initiatives to courses addressing such matters as judicial ethics, personnel relations, organizational behavior, and the use of electronic mail and the internet as a means toward promoting enhanced communication within the court system and outward to the broader community. The organization and operation of these programs has become a significant part of the work of those court managers and justice system administrators concerned with judicial improvement. Much of the work of the National Judicial College in Reno, Nevada, and the Institute of Court Management in Denver, Colorado, is given over to these tasks, with these bodies developing an international reputation in such educational activities.

Gender Bias

As concern for judicial education has increased from the 1970s through the 1990s, much particular attention has been devoted to the issue of gender bias within the legal system and within the courts. Beginning with the pioneering work of certain feminist analysts associated with the National Organization of Women, such as Schafran and Carroll, and extending to include the work of particular judicial task forces, increasing attention has come to be directed to the discriminatory treatment of women within the judicial system. In the mid-1980s, for example, both the New Jersey and New York task forces on women and the courts found that women were subjected to harmful bias in the process and application of the law. Attention was drawn to hostile attitudes toward women with respect to such matters as domestic violence, rape, family law, and child custody disputes. Moreover, these studies also found that women working within the courts, either as attorneys or clerical staff, also reported numerous incidents of sexist behavior being directed against them by men in the system, inclusive of judges. In an effort to reduce and ultimately eliminate such discriminatory behavior, a number of jurisdictions launched task forces and factfinding initiatives and have included gender sensitivity and gender equality as subjects for review and discussion in judicial education and training sessions, as well as being elements for judicial codes of conduct. Although some will claim that these initiatives are illustrative of political correctness, the evidence of sexist discrimination in the courts is palpable, requiring reasonable corrective measures.

Budgeting and Personnel Policy

As with any organization, the ongoing viability of the institution is contingent upon its effective financial management and the ability of the organization to attract, train, and retain competent and dutiful employees. Thus the matters of budgetary and financial policy are of critical importance to the courts, particularly at the state level. As outlined earlier, given the substantive administrative centralization found in the federal courts, budgetary and

personnel matters are also subject to centralized authority exercised by the judicial conference and the Administrative Office of the Courts. At the state level, however, although the state supreme courts generally exercise centralized authority over such matters as the temporary assignment of judges and the creation of uniform rules of practice and procedure, their involvement in financial and personnel management has been limited. In fully half of the states, supreme courts exercise no review over local court budgets and expenditures, over capital equipment purchases, or over the supervision of personnel, employment standards, or professional training. Financial management and personnel policy thus stand as policy matters substantially vested in local courts with managerial authority divided between local judges and local administrative officials such as court clerks, finance officers, and secretaries to county governments. This division and fragmentation of administrative authority in turn is viewed as highlighting the unfinished business of the court reform movement of the 1960s and 1970s. Although much organizational and managerial improvement has been witnessed over this time period in the state courts, as Glick and Baum suggest, court reform and administrative professionalism remain live policy matters.

In this regard, it is fascinating to observe the current debate respecting court funding and the issue of inherent powers in the courts to demand sufficient funding to maintain the judiciary as a viable and independent third branch of government. American law has long recognized the doctrine of inherent powers in the American courts to undertake administrative and financial actions necessary to maintain their institutional integrity up to and including court orders mandating particular budgetary appropriations. This doctrine was pushed to the breaking point in 1991 when the chief judge of New York, Sol Wachtler, brought an inherent powers lawsuit against then Governor Mario Cuomo, contending that the state's judiciary budget of some US $890 million was inadequate to meet the needs of the state courts; Wachtler contended that the courts were in need of some US $968 million. The suit raised a host of legal and political difficulties. How could any New York judge hear such a case while maintaining a semblance of impartiality as to the outcome? Should the judiciary be granted preferential treatment in the political process of budgetary restraint? Yet, do the courts not have a duty to defend their institutional and adjudicative independence when these qualities may be threatened by budgetary cutbacks? In the end, *Wachtler v. Cuomo* was settled out of court in 1992 through mutual compromise, but the very existence of the case, not to mention its magnitude, highlights not only increasing budgetary tensions experienced within judicial systems but also the dramatic means which may be turned to as the judiciary struggles to assert its integrity in future years.

The International Perspective

Although the systematic study and practice of judicial administration has been spearheaded by concerned individuals and institutions within the United States, interest in judicial administration and court reform have extended far beyond American borders. In countries such as Britain, Canada, Australia, and Germany, for example, the 1970s and 1980s witnessed increasing interest amongst certain members of the judiciary, government officials, and academics respecting the need to modernize and streamline court organization and, most important, to professionalize the process of court administration and caseflow management. Over this time period, there have been major court reorganization and centralization initiatives undertaken in Britain and Canada, for example; and in Australia, Canada, France, Germany, and India, there have been concerted moves to systematize and rationalize the process of caseflow management.

Within these initiatives it is quite common to witness officials from these and other countries devoting close attention to judicial administration undertakings found in the United States via recourse to the burgeoning American literature on judicial administration to attendance at courses and conferences offered by the various American bodies, as listed above, specializing in judicial administration education and training. In this fashion we very much observe the thought and practice of American judicial administration coming to exert significant influence over judicial systems throughout the Western world. This does not mean that we witness these countries developing Americanized systems of judicial administration within their judicial systems but that concerned individuals can and will seek out the American experience of addressing similar issues and problems regarding judicial administration and will then work to fashion viable administrative and managerial solutions to these matters from within the given national political, judicial, and administrative culture.

DAVID A. JOHNSON

BIBLIOGRAPHY

Abraham, Henry J., 1993. *The Judicial Process: An Introductory Analysis of the Courts of the United States, England, and France*, 6th ed. New York: Oxford University Press.

Baum, Lawrence, 1986. *American Courts: Process and Policy.* Boston, MA: Houghton Mifflin.

Church, Thomas W., Jr. *et al.*, 1978. *Justice Delayed: The Pace of Litigation in Urban Trial Courts.* Williamsburg, VA: National Center for State Courts.

Church, Thomas W. and Milton Heuman, 1990. "The Limits of 'Crash' Programs." *Judicature,* vol. 74 (August-September) 73–76.

Friesen, Ernest C., 1971. *Managing the Courts.* Indianapolis, IN: Babbs-Merrill.

Glaser, Howard B., 1994. "*Wachtler v. Cuomo:* The Limits of Inherent Powers." *Judicature,* vol. 78 (July-August) 12–24.

Glick, Henry R., 1988. *Courts, Politics, and Justice,* 2nd ed. New York: McGraw-Hill.

Goerdt, John, 1987. *Examining Court Delay: The Pace of Litigation in 26 Urban Trial Courts, 1987.* Williamsburg, VA: National Center for State Courts.

Goldberg, Stephen B., Eric D. Green and Frank E. A. Sander, 1986. "ADR Problems and Prospects: Looking to the Future." *Judicature,* vol. 69 (February-March) 291–299.

Mahoney, Barry, 1988. *Caseflow Management and Delay Reduction in Urban Trial Courts.* Williamsburg, VA: National Center for State Courts.

Melone, Albert P., Alan R. Morris, and Marc-George Pufong, 1992. "Too Little Advice, Senatorial Responsibility, and Confirmation Politics." *Judicature,* vol. 75 (December-January) 187–191.

Millar, Perry S., and Carl Baar, 1981. *Judicial Administration in Canada.* Montreal: McGill-Queen's Press.

Schafran, Lynn H., 1987. "Documenting Gender Bias in the Courts: The Task Force Approach." *Judicature,* vol. 70 (February-March) 280–290.

Solomon, Maureen, and Douglas K. Somerlot, 1987. *Caseflow Management in the Trial Court: Now and for the Future.* Chicago, IL: American Bar Association.

Stumpf, Harry P., 1988. *American Judicial Politics.* San Diego, CA: Harcourt Brace Jovanovich.

Wasby, Stephen L., 1989. "Technology in Appellate Courts." *Judicature,* vol. 73 (August-September) 90–97.

Wheeler, Russell R., and Howard R. Whitcomb, eds., 1977. *Judicial Administration: Text and Readings.* Englewood Cliffs, NJ: Prentice-Hall.

Wold, John T., and John H. Culver, 1987. "The Defeat of the California Justices: The Campaign, the Electorate, and the Issue of Judicial Accountability." *Judicature,* vol. 70 (April-May) 348–355.

JUDICIAL REVIEW. The power of the judiciary to determine the constitutionality and validity of actions of the other branches of government. This power designates the courts as having the last word on all governmental action.

Origin and Subsequent History

The origin and subsequent history of judicial review indicate that this power has evolved into a legitimate and accepted practice. This "evolution" or historical precedent is contentious, namely because judicial review involves an institutional power not spelled out in the Constitution. Historical documentation from the Philadelphia Constitutional Convention in 1787, state ratification conventions, and the Federalist Papers reveal differences of opinion on how judicial review should work in practice. In fact, there is no solid evidence supporting judicial review in the way it is practiced today. At most, historical documents indicate that the founders envisioned some kind of judicial review. Article VI explicitly makes the Constitution "the Supreme

Law of the land" but does not designate the judiciary as the branch to enforce it. This matter remained unsettled until *Marbury v. Madison*, 1 Cranch 137 (1803). Chief Justice John Marshall wrote the opinion that formally established the practice of judicial review. Alexander Hamilton's *Federalist No. 78* represents the strongest constitutional endorsement of judicial review. Hamilton characterized the judiciary as guardians of the Constitution. As lifetime appointed public servants, judges are positioned to rise above popular passions of the day and serve as "bulwarks of a limited constitution against legislative encroachment" (Hamilton, p. 469). Hamilton's reference to the judiciary as "the least dangerous branch" (Hamilton, p. 465) represents his belief that legislative supremacy would prevail given that the judiciary lacks spending and enforcement powers.

Chief Justice Marshall's opinion in *Marbury* bears a remarkable similarity to the reasoning provided in *Federalist No. 78*, which states that interpretation of laws "is the proper and peculiar province of the courts" (Hamilton, p. 467). In declaring portions of the Judiciary Act of 1789 unconstitutional, the Supreme Court declared an act of Congress unconstitutional for the very first time. The rationale in *Marbury* establishes the judiciary as arbiters of the Constitution because "it is emphatically the province and duty of the judicial department to say what the law is." In 1816, Justice Joseph Story wrote an opinion in *Martin v. Hunter's Lessee*, 1 Wheaton 122 (1816), furthering the application of judicial review to state court judgments involving a constitutional question. The supremacy clause of Article VI provides the justification for the judicial review of state court decisions as well. This decision is significant because it imposes a hierarchy with the national government above state governments. In the 1960s, some state public servants invoked the doctrine of interposition, where they would literally stand in between civil rights mandates by the federal government and the resistance of the people in the state to the federal government's desegregation directives. This doctrine of interposition has been invoked by way of the Tenth Amendment. This amendment is known as the states rights amendment and is used to suggest that the Constitution does not impose a hierarchy implied by federal court decisions or federal law. However, the Court's usage of judicial review has tipped the balance of power in favor of the federal government.

Underlying Theoretical Framework

Although constitutional theory derives from the Constitution and its founding documents, the documentation supporting some form of judicial review does not offer full agreement on whether this power should lie with the judiciary branch alone. The primary basis for judicial review lies in the belief that the Constitution is superior to all other law and that the judiciary is the most appropriate body to act as interpreters on what the law means. While

the supremacy of the Constitution is explicitly stated, judicial review is not. Since there is no solid theory supporting judicial review, controversy over its practice lies in the question of whether a constitution can exist without the judiciary as the final interpreter. The designation of the Constitution as supreme law provides the strongest theoretical foundation for the judiciary to administer and interpret constitutional issues.

Although most have accepted the power of judicial review, Judge Gibson's ruling in *Eakin v. Raub*, 12 S.&R. 330 (1825), repudiated Marshall's claim that judges should have this power. Gibson questioned whether the judiciary was the proper authority to rule on conflicts between a constitution and a legislative act, namely because the legislature is more representative than the judiciary. Gibson argued against judicial review because its practice is countermajoritarian. In making this argument, he does not consider the democratic value of protecting minorities against the tyranny of the majority. Twenty years later, in *Norris v. Clymer* (Pa. 1845), Gibson supported the practice of judicial review.

The general recognition of judicial review has led to developing theories on the proper scope of review. Judge Learned Hand argues that judicial review should be practiced rarely on the grounds that neither the Constitution nor various founding documents fully support it. Others, such as Justice Felix Frankfurter and Professor Herbert Wechsler, suggest that judicial review is legitimate when it defends "neutral" constitutional principles. This limited notion of judicial review lays the foundation for a judicial philosophy known as "judicial restraint."

The counterpart of judicial restraint is a philosophy that has been referred to as "judicial activism." The opinion in *Cooper v. Arron*, 358 U.S. 1 (1958), espouses this philosophy because of its expansive view of judicial review. It goes beyond a traditional understanding of judicial power because it not only reinforced the principles of judicial review asserted in Marbury but supported a view that the judiciary's interpretation of constitutional issues is supreme and final: "The federal judiciary is supreme in the exposition of the law and the Constitution" (at § 18). In essence, this wording gives the judiciary the last word on all government actions.

Judicial Review in Practice

The history of the courts shows that the practice of judicial review has evolved from a traditional approach to the Constitution to a more modern approach. The Court began to depart from its traditional role in the beginning of the twentieth century. From 1900 to 1936, judicial review went through a transitional period, as did other government institutions, industry, and the population. This era is transitional because it is marked by growth and change. The modern era begins in 1937 with the Court's willingness to make decisions that support progressive government policy.

The traditional era is marked by limited usage of judicial review. The Court struck down a federal statute for the very first time in *Marbury* and did not act again until *Dred Scott v. Sanford,* 19 Howard 393 (1857). The Dred Scott decision ignited internecine controversy that lead to the Civil War. It is one of the few decisions reversed by a subsequent constitutional amendment. Up until the Dred Scott decision, the traditional era is marked by an absence of discussion on rules for interpreting the Constitution. Throughout this era, there was a general agreement on what the words in the Constitution mean and a tendency for judges to guide their interpretation according to historical circumstance, debates in the Constitutional Convention, and ratification debates. The Court's emphasis was on established constitutional doctrines, such as the separation of powers and delegation of authority.

The transitional era reflects the complex changes going on in society and an influx of cases involving legal questions that were no longer simple, narrow, or well defined. With the growth of administrative agencies during the 1930s, judicial agreement on the rules of interpretation began to dissipate and the restrictive use of judicial review loosened. The Court's growing emphasis on private property rights and economic liberties shaped the course of judicial review. As the Court struck down federal statutes on economic and labor regulation, controversy ensued, especially when President Franklin D. Roosevelt's New Deal legislation was struck down. *Louisville Joint Stock Land Bank v. Radford,* 295 U.S. 555 (1935), *Humphrey's Executor v. United States,* 295 U.S. 602 (1935), and *Schechter Poultry Corp. v. United States* (1935) invalidated the Frazier-Lemke Act, the National Industrial Recovery Act, and the discretionary actions of the National Recovery Administration. Roosevelt responded with a philosophy of judicial self-restraint and a strategy to reorganize the judiciary. This strategy is known as the "court-packing plan." Although Roosevelt's famous court-packing plan failed in the Senate Judiciary Committee, the Court began to reverse its position on New Deal legislation. In *NLRB v. Jones and Laughlin Steel Corp.,* 301 U.S. 1 (1937), the Supreme Court upheld the constitutionality of the National Labor Relations Act of 1935. That same year, the Court upheld the state minimum wage laws. The perspective that business activity and the freedom to contract was protected by due process gave way to a judicial philosophy that supported remedies to social problems.

The modern era paralleled a period of government growth and an emerging administrative state. In 1946, Congress responded with the Administrative Procedure Act (APA) as a check on bureaucratic power. This established uniform minimum procedures and provisions for judicial review of agency actions. The passage of the APA and the reversal of Schechter has allowed agencies and the

Supreme Court to peacefully coexist. Cases that relate to administrative law are significant because it has become a common type of law.

The Court's willingness to hear a broader variety of cases came with increased willingness to make decisions on both procedural and substantive grounds. Doctrines that had once limited judicial review include the requirement of standing, mootness, ripeness, and political question. In cases relating to agency actions, the following doctrines were invoked to avoid making a substantive decision: jurisdiction, standing to sue, exhaustion of administrative remedies, and the "substantive evidence rule."

The Court began making decisions in a variety of substantive areas. The court ruled against segregation in favor of racial equality in *Brown v. Topeka Board of Education,* 347 U.S. 483 (1954). The Court ordered reapportionment to achieve the principle of "one person, one vote" in *Baker v. Carr,* 369 U.S. 643 (1962). The Court revamped the criminal justice system through the expansion of criminal rights. *Mapp v. Ohio,* 367 U.S. 643 (1961), provided search-and-seizure protections. *Miranda v. Arizona,* 384 U.S. 436 (1966), imposed the requirement that suspects must be informed of their rights. In *Griswold v. Connecticut,* 381 U.S. 479 (1965), the court struck down a Connecticut state law regarding the use of contraceptives because it violated the penumbral right to privacy. *Roe v. Wade,* 410 U.S. 113 (1973), made the right to privacy extremely controversial because it struck down laws limiting abortions.

In sum, the Court's willingness to decide on substantive and procedural issues combined with changes in various doctrines meant that the judiciary had transformed itself into a body that is not only willing to deal with problems but also willing to implement a solution. The courts now have experience in school and prison administration, the management of election procedures, and the authority on expenditure decisions. The resurgence of arguments focusing on judicial review and its nonmajoritarian character came out of debates over the Court's increasing role in school desegregation, prison conditions, right to treatment in mental hospitals, housing desegregation, and police abuse cases. The courts have acted in these areas because other branches of government have not. Judicial review in the form of prescribed remedies has been challenged on grounds that judges have gone too far beyond their legal expertise. Judges now have a relationship with administrators that depends on the amount of discretion the courts choose to give them.

The active use of judicial review under the tenure of Chief Justice Earl Warren, who served on the Court from 1953 until 1969, is well documented. Once Warren Burger became chief justice in 1969, the Court decided on some administrative law cases that shaped the scope of review. Both *Vermont Yankee Power Corp. v. Natural Resources Defense Council Inc.,* 435 U.S. 519 (1978), and *Chevron v. Natural Resources Defense Council,* 467 U.S. 837 (1984), set precedents that severely limited the Supreme Court's scope of review. In *Vermont Yankee,* the Court ruled that an agency's decisions based on procedure should be given deference by the courts. The deference principle was also employed in *Chevron.* The *Chevron* decision has been criticized by administrative law scholars because it limits the scope of review to the point where there is no institution left to check on agency discretion. Although the courts are demonstrating a growing reluctance to decide on cases that require technical knowledge or expertise, the *Chevron* doctrine places extreme limits on judicial review. Critics question the wisdom of unreviewability or unreviewable discretion, namely because it runs against the long-standing principle of checks and balances. The *Chevron* decision is an important administrative law decision because of the Court's willingness to give deference to agency decisions. The Court's rationale for this degree of deference rests in the technical expertise of agency administrators. The question that follows is whether or not Congress intends to make agencies as powerful as the *Chevron* decision has made them. Since agencies exercise powers that are quasi-legislative and quasi-judicial, the possibility of judicial review serves as the last check to guarantee that agency decisions are not arbitrary or capricious. The *Chevron* doctrine severely limits this check. Given that Antonin Scalia described this as one of the most important decisions regarding administrative law, it appears that the Rehnquist Court will uphold the precedent set in *Chevron.* Thus regardless of criticism of recent administrative law decisions, the courts are retreating from activist positions and allowing agencies considerable deference. Where vague enabling legislation used to be interpreted by the courts, agencies are now empowered to do this.

A Comparative Perspective

The United States is one of 65 countries that has adopted some form of judicial review. Australia and Canada have a form of judicial review that is most comparable to the United States. Australia, Brazil, Burma, Canada, India, Japan, and Pakistan have a court system with judicial review powers. Japan is the only one of these governments that is not a federal system of government. Pakistan and Iran require an Islamic review of all laws. France is not listed here because its form of judicial review is not a power of the judiciary. Instead, special councils have been created to determine whether or not laws are constitutional.

Although the judiciary in the United States exercises policymaking powers that go beyond the judicial powers found in other countries, there are countries in which the judiciary is equally, if not more, powerful. The German Constitutional Court not only has the power to strike down laws but also has the power to rule on lawmakers'

failure to act. While the U.S. Supreme Court legalized abortions in 1973 through the right to privacy–a right read into the Constitution–the German Constitutional Court did the opposite. It ruled that the German government had the duty to protect the unborn.

Legislative supremacy is greater in both Great Britain and Switzerland. In Great Britain, no court has the power to strike down the laws passed by Parliament. In Switzerland, the people can determine the constitutionality of the laws passed by the national assembly through a constitutional initiative or a referendum. The Belgian constitution goes as far as to deny the practice of judicial review: "Authoritative interpretation of laws is solely the prerogative of the Legislative authority."

K. KIM LOUTZENHISER

BIBLIOGRAPHY

Ferguson, Andrew, 1994. "Power Hungry High Court: Even Conservative Justices Succumb to Lure of Policy Making." *Los Angeles Daily Journal,* June 29, 6.
Hamilton, Alexander, James Madison, and John Jay, 1961. Original pub. 1787. *The Federalist Papers.* New York: Mentor Books.
Janda, Kenneth, Jeffrey Berry, and Jerry Goldman, 1992. *The Challenge of Democracy: Government in America.* Boston: Houghton Mifflin.
Koch, Charles H., 1991. "An Issue-Driven Strategy for Review of Agency Decisions." *Administrative Law Review* (Fall) 511–558.
Meier, Kenneth, J., 1993. *Politics and the Bureaucracy: Policymaking in the Fourth Branch of Government,* 3d ed. Belmont, CA: Brooks/Cole.
Rehnquist, William H., 1987. *The Supreme Court: How It Was, How It Is.* New York: William Morrow.
Warren, Kenneth F., 1996. *Administrative Law in the Political System,* 3rd ed. Upper Saddle River, New Jersey: Prentice Hall.

JURISDICTION. The power that a court, or other entity such as an agency or legislative body, has over a person or thing. There are two types of jurisdiction: subject matter jurisdiction and personal jurisdiction. In everyday usage, jurisdiction also refers to a place, such as a country, a state, a city, a county, or other geographic entity.

Subject matter jurisdiction concerns a court's power over certain types of cases. This power is usually granted through a statute or constitutional provision. For example, a small claims court will be given jurisdiction only over civil cases and only those cases involving less than US $500. For another example, Article III of the United States Constitution gives subject matter jurisdiction to federal courts over cases involving federal statutes, federal treaties, and the U.S. Constitution, among other matters. Congress, by statute, has further limited the jurisdiction of the federal courts, for example, by requiring that there be more than US $50,000 at stake in cases between citizens of different states. Administrative agencies are given jurisdiction over matters specified by statute; for example, the National Labor Relations Board (NLRB) has jurisdiction to decide disputes between unions and employers in matters specified by the National Labor Relations Act, such as unfair labor practices.

Typically, statutes give jurisdiction to courts to review administrative adjudications, but sometimes Congress or state legislatures seek to by-pass courts and give the final decisionmaking power to the agency. The U.S. Supreme Court held that agencies can be given the final say over most factual issues but not those facts that are "jurisdictional" (*Crowell v. Benson*, 1932). Crowell stated that judicial review of jurisdictional issues must be *de novo*. The sources of the Crowell holding are Article III of the Constitution, which states that the judicial power is vested in the federal courts–not in administrative agencies–and the due process clause, which sometimes requires judicial, not administrative, process. Crowell also stated that courts must review decisions of agencies concerning matters of law. Although the specifics of Crowell are no longer followed, it is still true that certain important facts, typically constitutional facts or other determinations that affect a person's liberty, cannot be finally decided by agencies free from judicial review. And the Supreme Court has never permitted agencies to have the final say over matters of law.

The most important U.S. Supreme Court case, *Marbury v. Madison* (1803), involved a question of subject matter jurisdiction–whether Congress could give the Supreme Court original jurisdiction over cases involving high U.S. government officials. The Supreme Court held that the Constitution permitted the Court to take original jurisdiction only over those categories of cases specified in Article III, such as cases between two states; since cases involving U.S. officers were not so specified, Congress could not give original jurisdiction to the Court. That case established the proposition that the lack of subject matter jurisdiction in federal cases could be raised at any time, even by the Court itself when the parties did not raise the issue, as in *Marbury*. (Normally, issues not raised by the parties will be considered waived.)

Congress has the power to limit the jurisdiction of the U.S. Supreme Court and the lower federal courts. In *Ex parte McCardle* (1869), the Supreme Court permitted Congress to take away jurisdiction even while the case was on appeal to the Supreme Court. Several bills have been introduced in Congress to strip the federal courts of jurisdiction after the Supreme Court has issued a particularly controversial decision in such areas as obscenity, abortion, school bussing, school prayer, and reapportionment. None

of these bills has become law since that would have the effect of freezing into law the very decisions that bothered the sponsors of the bills and of having the meaning of the Constitution be determined in the future by 50 state courts, since the Supreme Court would not have jurisdiction to review the state court decisions.

Unless Congress excludes state courts from hearing certain subjects–such as bankruptcy, antitrust, and patents–the states have concurrent jurisdiction over federal law. Even if states do not want to hear federal matters, they must do so (*Testa v. Katt,* 1947) unless they have a valid excuse for not doing so. The framers of the Constitution envisioned state courts enforcing federal law, since Article III of the Constitution contemplated the possibility that there would be no lower federal courts, in which case states would be the only place where federal law matters would be heard in the first instance, except for the few types of original jurisdiction cases to be heard in the U.S. Supreme Court.

Personal jurisdiction means that the court can only render a valid judgment against a defendant if the defendant or the defendant's property is properly before the court. Personal jurisdiction requires some connection between the person or the person's activities and the place where the court is located–for example, the person is a resident of the state. In addition, the person must be given appropriate notice of the court proceeding–for example, the person is personally served by a sheriff with a summons and complaint to appear in court in one month. Without personal jurisdiction, a judgment rendered against the person is not valid and cannot be enforced.

There have been many cases that involve the question of what type of notice is required for obtaining personal jurisdiction. It used to be common in lawsuits involving real estate to post a notice in the courthouse and in local newspapers of the proceeding. These types of notices, called constructive notification, were held to be inadequate by courts because those notices were not likely to come to the attention of defendants and because sending a notice to the defendants at their home or business was more likely to give actual notice of the lawsuit.

The major types of personal jurisdiction are *in personam* jurisdiction, which subjects the person to a judgment in any amount; *in rem* jurisdiction, that is, jurisdiction over land or other tangible property that limits the judgment to the value of the property; and *quasi in rem* jurisdiction, that is, jurisdiction over something intangible, like a debt, limited to the value of the intangible.

The U.S. Supreme Court has developed the law of personal jurisdiction in a series of cases involving defendants from out of state–either persons or corporations–who claimed that their constitutional right to due process of law was violated by state courts taking jurisdiction over them. The test the court uses to determine if jurisdiction is appropriate is to determine if the defendant has "minimum contacts" with the state, that is, if there are sufficient activities carried out by the defendant within the state to make it fair for the court to hear the case and render judgment against the defendant (*International Shoe Co. v. State of Washington*, 1945).

ROGER L. GOLDMAN

BIBLIOGRAPHY

Crowell v. Benson, 285 U.S. 22 (1932).
Ex parte McCardle, 74 U.S. 506 (1869).
International Shoe Co. v. State of Washington, 326 U.S. 310 (1945).
Marbury v. Madison, 5 U.S. 137 (1803).
Testa v. Katt, 330 U.S. 386 (1947).

K

KAUFMAN, HERBERT (1922–). A significant figure in the field of public administration whose work helped chronicle how public organizations function. Kaufman's major contributions are in the areas of administrative management, organization theory and behavior, and state and local government. Yet, during his professional career, which has spanned five decades, Kaufman also has worked in numerous related areas such as comparative public administration (public administration in countries outside the United States).

A son of a lawyer, Kaufman studied political science at City College of New York in preparation for a career in law. However, he found the study of the legal system to be less engaging than the newly emerging field of public administration. He enrolled in Columbia University's Department of Public Law and Government and received a master's degree with a concentration in public administrative. After military service and an assignment as an administrative intern in the federal government's Bureau of the Budget, Kaufman returned to New York City and Columbia University to complete a Ph.D. These early experiences helped prepare the way for pursuing a broad line of inquiry about how public organizations work that would span more than 40 years and contribute significantly to the development of public administration as a field of study.

Kaufman helped advanced the understanding of public organizations through his analysis of two very different organizations; the U.S. Forest Service and the New York City government. His work was heavily influenced by the thinking of Herbert Simon as expressed in his classic book *Administrative Behavior* (1957). Following Simon, Kaufman focused on the decisionmaking processes of these organizations as a means to understand how they operated.

In the case of the Forest Service, Kaufman described how that highly respected and geographically decentralized agency was able to maintain uniformity and quality control over its large workforce through careful selection and socialization of personnel. He found the homogeneity of the managers in terms of background, education, values, and sense of mission to be striking. This resulted in a condition he called "voluntary conformity." Kaufman noted that while such an approach and organizational culture produced uniform results, it also could result in organizational rigidity and an inability to change. In fact, the 1980s and 1990s have seen the Forest Service come under fierce attack for its slowness in changing.

In studying the New York City government, Kaufman again focused on who made the decisions and how they were made. Influenced by an earlier study of Atlanta by Floyd Hunter, he tested the hypothesis that a small elite core controlled decisionmaking in New York City. This was not at all what he found. In fact, Kaufman painted a picture much the opposite; multiple parties with divergent values and interests working independently in many different policy spheres. This first comprehensive study of New York City concluded with a recommendation to retain the strong mayor form of city government and to reject calls for a change to a city manager format. Managing New York City's many diverse interests remains a major challenge today, and the strong mayor form of government remains.

Although different characteristics were observed in the Forest Service and in the New York City government, Kaufman argued that they both were vulnerable in a changing environment because they both lacked the capacity to change course effectively. The Forest Service was blocked by its uniformity and resulting rigidity while the New York City government was immobilized by its many fragmented parts. This finding helped turn Kaufman's work, and in part the field of organization theory, from an orientation of internal focus to one of an external orientation.

Kaufman's work continued with projects that examined the effects various influences had on organizations. For example, in one project he studied the impact of federal government bureau chiefs. In another he analyzed the "red tape" often associated with government organizations. These and other projects helped Kaufman better describe the significant limits to change that exist in public organizations.

Most recently, Kaufman has explored organizations through a conceptual lens of organizational ecology, which basically says that organizations are like living organisms in a physical environment. Concepts such as organizational survival, adaptation, death, and extinction are explored in their application to public organizations. Kaufman concludes that organizational survival is more a matter of luck than skill. This and other findings by Kaufman have been challenged by other organization theorists and behavior researchers.

Kaufman's efforts not only helped shape the intellectual landscape of public administration and organization theory but also established him as a key figure in the public administration community. Working with luminaries such as Wallace Sayre and Luther Gulick and associating with prominent institutions such as the Brookings Institution, the Russell Sage Foundation, and the Yale University Department of Political Science (from where he retired), Kaufman helped contribute both to the intellectual underpinning and institutional capacity that supported the growing field of public administration.

TERENCE J. TIPPLE

BIBLIOGRAPHY

Kaufman, Herbert, 1960. *The Forest Ranger: A Study in Administrative Behavior.* Baltimore: Johns Hopkins Press for Resources for the Future.

———, 1971. *The Limits of Organizational Change.* Montgomery: University of Alabama Press.

———, 1973. *Administrative Feedback.* Washington, D.C.: The Brookings Institution.

———, 1976. *Are Government Organizations Immortal?* Washington, D.C.: The Brookings Institution.

———, 1977. *Red Tape.* Washington, D.C.: The Brookings Institution.

———, 1981. *The Administrative Behavior of Federal Bureau Chiefs.* Washington, D.C.: Brookings Institution.

———, 1991. *Time, Chance, and Organizations: Natural Selection in a Perilous Environment,* 2d. ed. Chatham, NJ: Chatham House.

Sayre, Wallace S. and Herbert Kaufman, 1965. *Governing New York City.* New York: Norton.

Simon, Herbert, 1957. *Administrative Behavior, 2nd ed.* New York: Free Press.